The Norton Reader

SIXTH EDITION

The Norton Reader

An Anthology of Expository Prose

SIXTH EDITION

Arthur M. Eastman, *General Editor*
VIRGINIA POLYTECHNIC INSTITUTE AND STATE UNIVERSITY

Caesar R. Blake
UNIVERSITY OF TORONTO

Hubert M. English, Jr.
UNIVERSITY OF MICHIGAN

Joan E. Hartman
COLLEGE OF STATEN ISLAND,
CITY UNIVERSITY OF NEW YORK

Alan B. Howes
UNIVERSITY OF MICHIGAN

Robert T. Lenaghan
UNIVERSITY OF MICHIGAN

Leo F. McNamara
UNIVERSITY OF MICHIGAN

James Rosier
UNIVERSITY OF PENNSYLVANIA

W · W · NORTON & COMPANY · *New York · London*

Library of Congress Cataloging in Publication Data
Main entry under title:
The Norton Reader.
    Includes index.
    1. College readers.   I. Eastman, Arthur M.,
1918-
PE1122.N68   1984   808.88'8   83-13423
ISBN 0-393-95296-7

Published simultaneously in Canada by George J.
McLeod Limited, Toronto. Printed in the United
States of America.

The text of this book is composed in Electra, with display type set in
Bernhard Modern. Composition by Vance, Weaver Composition. Manufacturing by R. R. Donnelley. Book design by Antonina Krass.

Cover illustration: Edward Hopper *The Dories, Ogunquit.* Reprinted by
permission of The Whitney Museum.

W. W. Norton & Company, Inc. 500 Fifth Avenue,
New York, N.Y. 10110

Contents

PEOPLE, PLACES

MIND

EDUCATION

LANGUAGE AND COMMUNICATION

PROSE FORMS:
AN ALBUM OF STYLES

SIGNS OF THE TIMES

HUMAN NATURE

ETHICS

HISTORY

POLITICS, ECONOMY, GOVERNMENT

SCIENCE

LITERATURE AND THE ARTS

PHILOSOPHY AND RELIGION

An Index of Essays Illustrative of Rhetorical Modes and Devices

THESIS[1]

---

1. The section headings of this index represent one of many ways of dividing the same subject matter into manageable units. The rationale for this particular arrangement may be examined in the Notes on Composition, p. 1203, where each of these headings is treated more fully.

MEANS OF DEVELOPMENT

STYLE

Preface

Since its first edition in 1965, *The Norton Reader* has sought to provide for students and teachers a solid and exciting selection, both chronologically and stylistically, of a great art form: the essay. A vital culture is constantly in motion. The interests of readers change with the times. Essays which stood at the forefront of student concern only a few years ago, now seem dated, calling for us to address new issues and to reinforce old ones, always with one prime prerequisite—quality.

In size, quality, and value, the Sixth Edition of *The Norton Reader* maintains the standard set by its predecessors. Of its 218 selections (slightly more than in the Fifth Edition), 65 are new. The new essays figure prominently in Signs of the Times, inevitably; in Science, where they display the remarkable recent flowering of science writing for intelligent men and women; in Human Nature, a section new to the Fifth Edition, that we have reconstituted by half in the Sixth, including the extraordinary and moving piece by Paul West, "A Passion to Learn"; and finally in Education, where a very old favorite makes its first appearance in the *Reader*, James Thurber's "University Days."

Once again annotation has been slightly increased. Publication dates continue to appear at the ends of selections in the right margins with the date of composition, when significantly earlier, in the left. Although there are no new sections or deletions of old ones, the title of Politics and Government has been judiciously expanded to Politics, Economy, and Government, the change drawing attention to such essays as Kirkpatrick Sale's "The Myths of Bigness" and Robert Heilbroner's "Does Capitalism Have a Future?" (to which the answer is, "yes, but with a difference").

Additions come at the price of deletions, which, although made on advice from many teachers who have used the Fifth Edition, inevitably cause some regret; but 153 selections continue from the past, including from Personal Report a round dozen, and eleven out of fourteen in Philosophy and Religion. Thomas (Dylan and Lewis), Baker, Angelou, Dobbs, Didion, E. B. White, Thurber, Edwards, Tillich, Dillard, and Sartre, to name but a few, are still here, tested and proved, for users of former editions. And our basic principles of selection remain essentially unchanged. Contemporary essays are set beside earlier pieces, and easy and entertaining essays beside those that challenge and stretch the mind; the Prose Forms continue to provide seeds for student essays and suggestions for using prose in modes other than the full-scale essay. Women writers discuss a far wider range of topics than matters exclusively female. Huxtable, for example, writes on "Conquering Clutter," Mitford on the undertaking profession, Kübler-Ross "On the Fear of Death," and Carol Bly on trying out some of Bruno Bettelheim's ideas in Madison, Minnesota. Canadian writers, such as Laurence, Dobbs, Simpson, and Maynard, speak to issues far less national than broadly human, as do writers from such diversified homelands as the Barbados, Wales, the Isle of Man, Greece, Germany, England, Italy, France, Ireland, Austria, Czechoslovakia, Switzerland, Judea, and every section of the United States.

The essays in the Reader are gathered into sections titled according to major fields of human concern, some of them familiar ground to students —Personal Report, Mind, Education, Language and Communication —and others inviting ventures into more specialized kinds of knowledge, such as History, Science, Philosophy and Religion. These and others of the rubrics correspond to the divisions of the liberal arts curriculum. The ordering has been slightly changed—People and Places has been brought near to the beginning as belonging close to Personal Report; History, as appearing slightly less abstruse, now precedes Politics, Economy, and Government; and Literature and the Arts has been placed after Science and just before Philosophy and Religion, not from any claim of superiority but because experience has shown these matters, especially in their theoretical dimensions, to be more difficult for students.

Essays within a topical division can be read together for contrasts in point of view; teachers, moreover, on gaining familiarity with the text and perhaps with help from Craig B. Snow's fully revised A Guide to the Norton Reader, will discover thematic links among the different sections. E. B. White's "Once More to the Lake" in Personal Report ties in with the essays by Lewis Thomas, Kübler-Ross, and Fries in Human Nature and with Woolf's "The Death of the Moth" in Philosophy and Religion, all these being but a sampling of essays dealing with intimations of mortality and the emotions attaching thereto. Not all selections about ethical issues are to be found within the limits of the section called Ethics, nor are political, linguistic, or esthetic matters frozen within the boundaries of their titled sections. Instructors interested in exploring different manifestations of the same voice through differing subjects and tones will find a number of authors represented by two or more selections —Red Smith, Lewis Thomas, E. B. White, James Thurber, Benjamin

Franklin, Virginia Woolf, Jonathan Schell, George Orwell, Adrienne Rich, and many others.

Besides subject matter for class discussion and writing assignments, the Reader offers many models for rhetorical and stylistic emulation, both in An Album of Styles and elsewhere. Teachers who prefer to organize their courses rhetorically will, we hope, find useful the Index of Essays Illustrative of Rhetorical Modes and Devices. Other pedagogical aids include study questions on content and rhetoric for many of the essays, and at the end of the book the Notes on Composition—a précis of basic rhetorical principles and an explanation of basic terminology, with examples from the Reader. All of these aids have been fully revised to reflect the contents of the Sixth Edition, and in some cases new study questions have been provided for essays retained from the Fifth Edition. Asterisks found at the beginning and/or the end of an essay indicate that the piece has been excerpted from a larger work. Asterisks within an essay indicate a deletion.

It is a pleasure to acknowledge the help we received in bringing the Sixth Edition to completion, especially from the many dedicated teachers who, by drawing on their classroom experiences with The Norton Reader and by giving generously of their time to answer our questionnaires, have offered a wealth of ideas and suggestions for its improvement. These include: Guy Allen, University of Toronto; Anthony Amberg, Roosevelt University; Linda K. Barlow, University of North Carolina, Chapel Hill; Mackie JV Blanton, University of New Orleans; Joseph Boles, Rutgers University; B. W. Boothe, Kutztown State College, Pennsylvania; Roderic C. Botts, Marquette University; Norman P. Boyer, Saint Xavier College; John C. Brereton, Wayne State University; Dr. Patrice Caldwell, Eastern New Mexico University; Glenn O. Carey, Eastern Kentucky University; Elizabeth Cassell, University of Wisconsin, Milwaukee; Cynthia Caywood, Wake Forest University; Ralph B. Church, Juniata College; A. E. Claeyssens, George Washington University; Susan Cottle, University of Wisconsin, Milwaukee; Reed Dasenbrock, New Mexico State University; Patrick Day, University of Pennsylvania; Richard C. Day, Humboldt State University; Jay Delman, University of Texas, Arlington; James Denham, Miami University; Daniel Dervin, Mary Washington College; John A. R. Dick, University of Texas at El Paso; Gerald Duchovnay, Jacksonville University; Charles R. Duke, Murray State University; Laura J. Emer, University of Wisconsin, Milwaukee; David Ewick, Wichita State University; B. L. Fitzpatrick, Duke University; E. Jack Fulgham, Thomas Nelson Community College; Ideale Gambera, City College, San Francisco; Frederick Goldberg, Clayton Junior College; W. J. Gracie, Jr., Miami University of Ohio; James Griffith, Ohio State University; Scott K. Hammer, Virginia Commonwealth University; Thomas Hamel, St. Olaf College; John K.

Hanes, Duquesne University; Ruth M. Harrison, Arkansas Tech University; Janet D. Hertzbach, Gettysburg College; John M. Hill, University of Scranton; William Hofelt, Jr., Juniata College; Woodrow L. Holbein, Citadel Military College of South Carolina; Francis Hubbard, University of Wisconsin, Milwaukee; Craig Hudziak, University of Wisconsin, Milwaukee; John Huxhold, St. Louis Community College at Meramec; Ann Jones, Smith College; Stewart Justman, University of Montana; Lynn Kellermann, Livingston College, Rutgers University; Arpine Khatchadourian, University of Wisconsin, Milwaukee; Paul Klemp, Oklahoma State University; Raymond A. Klopsch, Pacific Lutheran University; Lucia Z. Knoles, Rutgers University; Catherine Lamb, Albion College; David M. Larson, Cleveland State University; Elizabeth Larsen, University of Wisconsin, Milwaukee; T. Lavelle, University of Wisconsin, Milwaukee; Douglas Novich Leonard, Washington and Lee University; Cynthia Lewis, Davidson College; Jeannie Lloyd, Ohio University; Judith A. Lockyer, University of Michigan, Ann Arbor; Richard J. Marciniak, University of Wisconsin, Milwaukee; Pramod Menon, University of Wisconsin, Milwaukee; R. J. Merrett, University of Alberta; Margaret J. Meyer, University of Cincinnati; Margaret Mika, University of Wisconsin, Milwaukee; Michael Mikolajezak, Marquette University; John R. Milton, University of South Dakota; Shirley Morahan, Northwest Missouri State University; Merritt Moseley, University of North Carolina, Asheville; David Ostrenga, University of Wisconsin, Milwaukee; John H. Ottenhoff, University of Wisconsin, Milwaukee; N. Parker-Jervis, University of Alberta; Linda Peterson, Yale University; James Plath, University of Wisconsin, Milwaukee; Kenneth Pobo, University of Wisconsin, Milwaukee; Leonard A. Podis, Oberlin College; Stephanie Richardson, Ohio State University; Grant C. Roti, Housatonic Community College; Frederic A. Roux, Shippensburg State College; Ronald R. Rutters, Duke University; T. J. Saben, Portland Community College; James C. Schaap, University of Wisconsin, Milwaukee; Carroll R. Schoenewolf, Stephen F. Austin State University; Sandra Schor, Queens College; H. E. Shaw, Cornell University; Dr. M. P. A. Sheaffer, Millersville State College; William R. Siebenschuh, Case Western Reserve University; Eleanor Honig Skuller, University of Wisconsin, Milwaukee; Malinda Snow, George State University; H. M. Solomon, Auburn University; Bruce Spiegelberg, Franklin and Marshall College; Marjorie Thompson, University of Wisconsin, Milwaukee; John Emerson Todd, Bernard Baruch College; Karen Toossaint, Towson State University; Steven C. Tracy, University of Cincinnati; Debra K. Vest, University of Wisconsin, Milwaukee; Ann A. Warren, Kansas State University; Bernice W. White, Southwestern at Memphis; Baird W. Whitlock, Midwestern State University; Debra Wilson, University of Wisconsin, Milwaukee; Carlson W. Yost, Texas A&M University; Mary Zinke, University of Wisconsin, Milwaukee.

Arthur M. Eastman

The Norton Reader

SIXTH EDITION

Personal Report

Dylan Thomas

MEMORIES OF CHRISTMAS

One Christmas was so much like another, in those years, around the sea-town corner now and out of all sound except the distant speaking of the voices I sometimes hear a moment before sleep, that I can never remember whether it snowed for six days and six nights when I was twelve or whether it snowed for twelve days and twelve nights when I was six; or whether the ice broke and the skating grocer vanished like a snowman through a white trap-door on that same Christmas Day that the mince-pies finished Uncle Arnold and we tobogganed down the seaward hill, all the afternoon, on the best tea-tray, and Mrs. Griffiths complained, and we threw a snowball at her niece, and my hands burned so, with the heat and the cold, when I held them in front of the fire, that I cried for twenty minutes and then had some jelly.

All the Christmases roll down the hill towards the Welsh-speaking sea, like a snowball growing whiter and bigger and rounder, like a cold and headlong moon bundling down the sky that was our street; and they stop at the rim of the ice-edged, fish-freezing waves, and I plunge my hands in the snow and bring out whatever I can find; holly or robins or pudding, squabbles and carols and oranges and tin whistles, and the fire in the front room, and bang go the crackers, and holy, holy, holy, ring the bells, and the glass bells shaking on the tree, and Mother Goose, and Struwelpeter[1] —oh! the baby-burning flames and the clacking scissorman!—Billy Bunter[2] and Black Beauty, Little Women and boys who have three helpings, Alice and Mrs. Potter's badgers,[3] penknives, teddy-bears

---

1. The title character of *Struwelpeter (Slovenly Peter)*, or *Merry Tales and Funny Pictures*, a children's book originally in German, by Dr. Heinrich Hoffmann, containing gaily grim admonitory narratives in verse about little Pauline, for example, who played with matches and got burned up; or the little boy who sucked his thumbs until the tall scissorman cut them off.

2. The humorous fat boy in Frank Richards' tales of English school life.

3. Beatrix Potter, creator of *Peter Rabbit* and other animal tales for children, among them *The Tale of Mr. Tod*, a badger.

—named after a Mr. Theodore Bear, their inventor, or father, who died recently in the United States—mouth-organs, tin-soldiers, and blanc-mange, and Auntie Bessie playing "Pop Goes the Weasel" and "Nuts in May" and "Oranges and Lemons" on the untuned piano in the parlor all through the thimble-hiding musical-chairing blind-man's-buffing party at the end of the never-to-be-forgotten day at the end of the un-remembered year.

In goes my hand into that wool-white bell-tongued ball of holidays resting at the margin of the carol-singing sea, and out come Mrs. Prothero and the firemen.

It was on the afternoon of the day of Christmas Eve, and I was in Mrs. Prothero's garden, waiting for cats, with her son Jim. It was snowing. It was always snowing at Christmas; December, in my memory, is white as Lapland, though there were no reindeers. But there were cats. Patient, cold, and callous, our hands wrapped in socks, we waited to snowball the cats. Sleek and long as jaguars and terrible-whiskered, spitting and snarling they would slink and sidle over the white back-garden walls, and the lynx-eyed hunters, Jim and I, fur-capped and moccasined trappers from Hudson's Bay off Eversley Road, would hurl our deadly snowballs at the green of their eyes. The wise cats never appeared. We were so still, Eskimo-footed arctic marksmen in the muffling silence of the eternal snows—eternal, ever since Wednesday—that we never heard Mrs. Prothero's first cry from her igloo at the bottom of the garden. Or, if we heard it at all, it was, to us, like the far-off challenge of our enemy and prey, the neighbor's Polar Cat. But soon the voice grew louder. "Fire!" cried Mrs. Prothero, and she beat the dinner-gong. And we ran down the garden, with the snowballs in our arms, towards the house, and smoke, indeed, was pouring out of the dining-room, and the gong was bombilat-ing, and Mrs. Prothero was announcing ruin like a town-crier in Pompeii. This was better than all the cats in Wales standing on the wall in a row. We bounded into the house, laden with snowballs, and stopped at the open door of the smoke-filled room. Something was burning all right; perhaps it was Mr. Prothero, who always slept there after midday dinner with a newspaper over his face; but he was standing in the middle of the room, saying "A fine Christmas!" and smacking at the smoke with a slipper.

"Call the fire-brigade," cried Mrs. Prothero as she beat the gong.

"They won't be there," said Mr. Prothero, "it's Christmas."

There was no fire to be seen, only clouds of smoke and Mr. Prothero standing in the middle of them, waving his slipper as though he were conducting.

"Do something," he said.

And we threw all our snowballs into the smoke—I think we missed Mr. Prothero—and ran out of the house to the telephone-box.

"Let's call the police as well," Jim said.

"And the ambulance."

"And Ernie Jenkins, he likes fires."

But we only called the fire-brigade, and soon the fire-engine came and three tall men in helmets brought a hose into the house and Mr. Prothero got out just in time before they turned it on. Nobody could have had a noisier Christmas Eve. And when the firemen turned off the hose and were standing in the wet and smoky room, Jim's aunt, Miss Prothero, came downstairs and peered in at them. Jim and I waited, very quietly, to hear what she would say to them. She said the right thing, always. She looked at the three tall firemen in their shining helmets, standing among the smoke and cinders and dissolving snowballs, and she said: "Would you like something to read?"

Now out of that bright white snowball of Christmas gone comes the stocking, the stocking of stockings, that hung at the foot of the bed with the arm of a golliwog dangling over the top and small bells ringing in the toes. There was a company, gallant and scarlet but never nice to taste though I always tried when very young, of belted and busbied and musketed lead soldiers so soon to lose their heads and legs in the wars on the kitchen table after the tea-things, the mince-pies, and the cakes that I helped to make by stoning the raisins and eating them, had been cleared away; and a bag of moist and many-colored jelly-babies and a folded flag and a false nose and a tram-conductor's cap and a machine that punched tickets and rang a bell; never a catapult; once, by a mistake that no one could explain, a little hatchet; and a rubber buffalo, or it may have been a horse, with a yellow head and haphazard legs; and a celluloid duck that made, when you pressed it, a most unducklike noise, a mewing moo that an ambitious cat might make who wishes to be a cow; and a painting-book in which I could make the grass, the trees, the sea, and the animals any color I pleased: and still the dazzling sky-blue sheep are grazing in the red field under a flight of rainbow-beaked and pea-green birds.

Christmas morning was always over before you could say Jack Frost. And look! suddenly the pudding was burning! Bang the gong and call the fire-brigade and the book-loving firemen! Someone found the silver three-penny-bit with a currant on it; and the someone was always Uncle Arnold. The motto in my cracker read:

> Let's all have fun this Christmas Day,
> Let's play and sing and shout hooray!

and the grown-ups turned their eyes towards the ceiling, and Auntie Bessie, who had already been frightened, twice, by a clockwork mouse, whimpered at the sideboard and had some elderberry wine. And some-one put a glass bowl full of nuts on the littered table, and my uncle said, as he said once every year: "I've got a shoe-nut here. Fetch me a shoehorn to open it, boy."

And dinner was ended.

And I remember that on the afternoon of Christmas Day, when the others sat around the fire and told each other that this was nothing, no, nothing, to the great snowbound and turkey-proud yule-log-crackling holly-berry-bedizined and kissing-under-the mistletoe Christmas when *they* were children, I would go out, school-capped and gloved and muffered, with my bright new boots squeaking, into the white world on to the seaward hill, to call on Jim and Dan and Jack and to walk with them through the silent snowscape of our town.

We went padding through the streets, leaving huge deep footprints in the snow, on the hidden pavements.

"I bet people'll think there's been hippoes."

"What would you do if you saw a hippo coming down Terrace Road?"

"I'd go like this, bang! I'd throw him over the railings and roll him down the hill and then I'd tickle him under the ear and he'd wag his tail . . ."

"What would you do if you saw *two* hippoes . . . ?"

Iron-flanked and bellowing he-hippoes clanked and blundered and battered through the scudding snow towards us as we passed by Mr. Daniel's house.

"Let's post Mr. Daniel a snowball through his letter box."

"Let's write things in the snow."

"Let's write 'Mr. Daniel looks like a spaniel' all over his lawn."

"Look," Jack said, "I'm eating snow-pie."

"What's it taste like?"

"Like snow-pie," Jack said.

Or we walked on the white shore.

"Can the fishes see it's snowing?"

"They think it's the sky falling down."

The silent one-clouded heavens drifted on to the sea.

"All the old dogs have gone."

Dogs of a hundred mingled makes yapped in the summer at the sea-rim and yelped at the trespassing mountains of the waves.

"I bet St. Bernards would like it now."

And we were snowblind travelers lost on the north hills, and the great dewlapped dogs, with brandy-flasks round their necks, ambled and shambled up to us, baying "Excelsior."[4]

We returned home through the desolate poor sea-facing streets where only a few children fumbled with bare red fingers in the thick wheel-rutted snow and catcalled after us, their voices fading away, as we

4. "Higher"—recalling Henry Wadsworth Longfellow's poem "Excelsior," in which a traveler who has adopted that word as his motto perishes while climbing a dangerous, snowy mountain trail, and is found by monks of Saint Bernard and their "faithful hound."

trudged uphill, into the cries of the dock-birds and the hooters of ships out in the white and whirling bay.

Bring out the tall tales now that we told by the fire as we roasted chestnuts and the gaslight bubbled low. Ghosts with their heads under their arms trailed their chains and said "whooo" like owls in the long nights when I dared not look over my shoulder; wild beasts lurked in the cubby-hole under the stairs where the gas-meter ticked. "Once upon a time," Jim said, "there were three boys, just like us, who got lost in the dark in the snow, near Bethesda Chapel, and this is what happened to them . . ." It was the most dreadful happening I had ever heard.

And I remember that we went singing carols once, a night or two before Christmas Eve, when there wasn't the shaving of a moon to light the secret, white-flying streets. At the end of a long road was a drive that led to a large house, and we stumbled up the darkness of the drive that night, each one of us afraid, each one holding a stone in his hand in case, and all of us too brave to say a word. The wind made through the drive-trees noises as of old and unpleasant and maybe web-footed men wheezing in caves. We reached the black bulk of the house.

"What shall we give them?" Dan whispered.

"'Hark the Herald'? 'Christmas comes but Once a Year'?"

"No," Jack said: "We'll sing 'Good King Wenceslas.' I'll count three."

One, two, three, and we began to sing, our voices high and seemingly distant in the snow-felted darkness round the house that was occupied by nobody we knew. We stood close together, near the dark door.

> Good King Wenceslas looked out
> On the Feast of Stephen.

And then a small, dry voice, like the voice of someone who has not spoken for a long time, suddenly joined our singing: a small, dry voice from the other side of the door: a small, dry voice through the keyhole. And when we stopped running we were outside our house; the front room was lovely and bright; the gramophone was playing; we saw the red and white balloons hanging from the gas-bracket; uncles and aunts sat by the fire; I thought I smelt our supper being fried in the kitchen. Everything was good again, and Christmas shone through all the familiar town.

"Perhaps it was a ghost," Jim said.

"Perhaps it was trolls," Dan said, who was always reading.

"Let's go in and see if there's any jelly left," Jack said. And we did that.

1945

Wallace Stegner

THE TOWN DUMP

The town dump of Whitemud, Saskatchewan, could only have been a few years old when I knew it, for the village was born in 1913 and I left there in 1919. But I remember the dump better than I remember most things in that town, better than I remember most of the people. I spent more time with it, for one thing; it has more poetry and excitement in it than people did.

It lay in the southeast corner of town, in a section that was always full of adventure for me. Just there the Whitemud River left the hills, bent a little south, and started its long traverse across the prairie and international boundary to join the Milk. For all I knew, it might have been on its way to join the Alph:[1] simply, before my eyes, it disappeared into strangeness and wonder.

Also, where it passed below the dumpground, it ran through willowed bottoms that were a favorite campsite for passing teamsters, gypsies, sometimes Indians. The very straw scattered around those camps, the ashes of those strangers' campfires, the manure of their teams and saddle horses, were hot with adventurous possibilities.

It was as an extension, a living suburb, as it were, of the dumpground that we most valued those camps. We scoured them for artifacts of their migrant tenants as if they had been archaeological sites full of the secrets of ancient civilizations. I remember toting around for weeks the broken cheek strap of a bridle. Somehow or other its buckle looked as if it had been fashioned in a far place, a place where they were accustomed to flatten the tongues of buckles for reasons that could only be exciting, and where they made a habit of plating the silver with some valuable alloy, probably silver. In places where the silver was worn away the buckle underneath shone dull yellow: probably gold.

It seemed that excitement liked that end of town better than our end. Once old Mrs. Gustafson, deeply religious and a little raddled in the head, went over there with a buckboard full of trash, and as she was driving home along the river she looked and saw a spent catfish, washed in from Cypress Lake or some other part of the watershed, floating on the yellow water. He was two feet long, his whiskers hung down, his fins and tail were limp. He was a kind of fish that no one had seen in the Whitemud in the three or four years of the town's life, and a kind that none of us children had ever seen anywhere. Mrs. Gustafson had never

1. The imaginary, mysterious river of Samuel Taylor Coleridge's poem "Kubla Khan."

seen one like him either; she perceived at once that he was the devil, and she whipped up the team and reported him at Hoffman's elevator.

We could hear her screeching as we legged it for the river to see for ourselves. Sure enough, there he was. He looked very tired, and he made no great effort to get away as we pushed out a half-sunken rowboat from below the flume, submerged it under him, and brought him ashore. When he died three days later we experimentally fed him to two half-wild cats, but they seemed to suffer no ill effects.

At that same end of town the irrigation flume crossed the river. It always seemed to me giddily high when I hung my chin over its plank edge and looked down, but it probably walked no more than twenty feet above the water on its spidery legs. Ordinarily in summer it carried about six or eight inches of smooth water, and under the glassy hurrying of the little boxed stream the planks were coated with deep sun-warmed moss as slick as frog's eggs. A boy could sit in the flume with the water walling up against his back, and grab a cross brace above him, and pull, shooting himself sledlike ahead until he could reach the next brace for another pull and another slide, and so on across the river in four scoots.

After ten minutes in the flume he would come out wearing a dozen or more limber black leeches, and could sit in the green shade where darning needles flashed blue, and dragonflies hummed and darted and stopped, and skaters dimpled slack and eddy with their delicate transitory footprints, and there stretch the leeches out one by one while their sucking ends clung and clung, until at last, stretched far out, they let go with a tiny wet *puk* and snapped together like rubber bands. The smell of the river and the flume and the clay cutbanks and the bars of that part of the river was the smell of wolf willow.

But nothing in that end of town was as good as the dumpground that scattered along a little runoff coulee dipping down toward the river from the south bench. Through a historical process that went back, probably, to the roots of community sanitation and distaste for eyesores, but that in law dated from the Unincorporated Towns Ordinance of the territorial government, passed in 1888, the dump was one of the very first community enterprises, almost our town's first institution.

More than that, it contained relics of every individual who had ever lived there, and of every phase of the town's history.

The bedsprings on which the town's first child was begotten might be there; the skeleton of a boy's pet colt; two or three volumes of Shakespeare bought in haste and error from a peddler, later loaned in carelessness, soaked with water and chemicals in a house fire, and finally thrown out to flap their stained eloquence in the prairie wind.

Broken dishes, rusty tinware, spoons that had been used to mix paint; once a box of percussion caps, sign and symbol of the carelessness that most of those people felt about all matters of personal or public safety.

We put them on the railroad tracks and were anonymously denounced in the *Enterprise*. There were also old iron, old brass, for which we hunted assiduously, by night conning junkmen's catalogues and the pages of the *Enterprise* to find how much wartime value there might be in the geared insides of clocks or in a pound of tea lead[2] carefully wrapped in a ball whose weight astonished and delighted us. Sometimes the unimaginable outside world reached in and laid a finger on us. I recall that, aged no more than seven, I wrote a St. Louis junk house asking if they preferred their tea lead and tinfoil wrapped in balls, or whether they would rather have it pressed flat in sheets, and I got back a typewritten letter in a window envelope instructing me that they would be happy to have it in any way that was convenient for me. They added that they valued my business and were mine very truly. Dazed, I carried that windowed grandeur around in my pocket until I wore it out, and for months I saved the letter as a souvenir of the wondering time when something strange and distinguished had singled me out.

We hunted old bottles in the dump, bottles caked with dirt and filth, half buried, full of cobwebs, and we washed them out at the horse trough by the elevator, putting in a handful of shot along with the water to knock the dirt loose; and when we had shaken them until our arms were tired, we hauled them off in somebody's coaster wagon and turned them in at Bill Anderson's pool hall, where the smell of lemon pop was so sweet on the dark pool-hall air that I am sometimes awakened by it in the night, even yet.

Smashed wheels of wagons and buggies, tangles of rusty barbed wire, the collapsed perambulator that the French wife of one of the town's doctors had once pushed proudly up the planked sidewalks and along the ditchbank paths. A welter of foul-smelling feathers and coyote-scattered carrion which was all that remained of somebody's dream of a chicken ranch. The chickens had all got some mysterious pip at the same time, and died as one, and the dream lay out there with the rest of the town's history to rustle to the empty sky on the border of the hills.

There was melted glass in curious forms, and the half-melted office safe left from the burning of Bill Day's Hotel. On very lucky days we might find a piece of the lead casing that had enclosed the wires of the town's first telephone system. The casing was just the right size for rings, and so soft that it could be whittled with a jackknife. It was a material that might have made artists of us. If we had been Indians of fifty years before, that bright soft metal would have enlisted our maximum patience and craft and come out as ring and metal and amulet inscribed with the symbols of our observed world. Perhaps there were too many ready-made alternatives in the local drug, hardware, and general stores; perhaps our feeble artistic response was a measure of the insufficiency of the challenge we

---

2. An alloy used for lining chests in which tea was stored and transported.

felt. In any case I do not remember that we did any more with the metal than to shape it into crude seal rings with our initials or pierced hearts carved in them; and these, though they served a purpose in juvenile courtship, stopped something short of art.

The dump held very little wood, for in that country anything burnable got burned. But it had plenty of old iron, furniture, papers, mattresses that were the delight of field mice, and jugs and demijohns that were sometimes their bane, for they crawled into the necks and drowned in the rain water or redeye that was inside.

If the history of our town was not exactly written, it was at least hinted, in the dump. I think I had a pretty sound notion even at eight or nine of how significant was that first institution of our forming Canadian civilization. For rummaging through its foul purlieus I had several times been surprised and shocked to find relics of my own life tossed out there to rot or blow away.

The volumes of Shakespeare belonged to a set that my father had bought before I was born. It had been carried through successive moves from town to town in the Dakotas, and from Dakota to Seattle, and from Seattle to Bellingham, and Bellingham to Redmond, and from Redmond back to Iowa, and from there to Saskatchewan. Then, stained in a stranger's house fire, these volumes had suffered from a house-cleaning impulse and been thrown away for me to stumble upon in the dump. One of the Cratchet girls had borrowed them, a hatchet-faced, thin, eager, transplanted Cockney girl with a frenzy, almost a hysteria, for reading. And yet somehow, through her hands, they found the dump, to become a symbol of how much was lost, how much thrown aside, how much carelessly or of necessity given up, in the making of a new country. We had so few books that I was familiar with them all, had handled them, looked at their pictures, perhaps even read them. They were the lares and penates, part of the skimpy impedimenta of household gods we had brought with us into Latium.[3] Finding those three thrown away was a little like finding my own name on a gravestone.

And yet not the blow that something else was, something that impressed me even more with the dump's close reflection of the town's intimate life. The colt whose picked skeleton lay out there was mine. He had been incurably crippled when dogs chased our mare, Daisy, the morning after she foaled. I had labored for months to make him well; had fed him by hand, curried him, exercised him, adjusted the iron braces that I had talked my father into having made. And I had not known that he would have to be destroyed. One weekend I turned him over to the foreman of one of the ranches, presumably so that he could be cared for.

3. The region of Italy settled by the Trojans after their defeat by the Greeks in the Trojan War. Later, in Roman families, the lares and penates were the ancestral household gods; they came to embody the continuity of the family.

A few days later I found his skinned body, with the braces still on his crippled front legs, lying on the dump.

Not even that, I think, cured me of going there, though our parents all forbade us on pain of cholera or worse to do so. The place fascinated us, as it should have. For this was the kitchen midden of all the civilization we knew; it gave us the most tantalizing glimpses into our lives as well as into those of the neighbors. It gave us an aesthetic distance from which to know ourselves.

The dump was our poetry and our history. We took it home with us by the wagonload, bringing back into town the things the town had used and thrown away. Some little part of what we gathered, mainly bottles, we managed to bring back to usefulness, but most of our gleanings we left lying around barn or attic or cellar until in some renewed fury of spring cleanup our families carted them off to the dump again, to be rescued and briefly treasured by some other boy with schemes for making them useful. Occasionally something we really valued with a passion was snatched from us in horror and returned at once. That happened to the mounted head of a white mountain goat, somebody's trophy from old times and the far Rocky Mountains, that I brought home one day in transports of delight. My mother took one look and discovered that his beard was full of moths.

I remember that goat; I regret him yet. Poetry is seldom useful, but always memorable. I think I learned more from the town dump than I learned from school: more about people, more about how life is lived, not elsewhere but here, not in other times but now. If I were a sociologist anxious to study in detail the life of any community, I would go very early to its refuse piles. For a community may be as well judged by what it throws away—what it has to throw away and what it chooses to—as by any other evidence. For whole civilizations we have sometimes no more of the poetry and little more of the history than this.

1959

QUESTIONS

1. *Stegner begins his reminiscence of the town dump by saying that it had "poetry and excitement" in it. In what ways does he seek to convey those qualities to the reader?*
2. *Is Stegner's description of the dump and its surroundings vivid? Where does his writing directly appeal to the senses, and which senses are called into play?*
3. *In his second paragraph Stegner speaks of the Alph, the "sacred river" of Coleridge's poem "Kubla Khan." Why? How does allusion to that poem help him convey the strangeness and wonder he then felt?*
4. *In paragraphs 5–8 Stegner departs, as he had departed to a lesser degree in the two preceding paragraphs, from his description of the*

dump. *Explain how that departure is justified and whether the writing there is appropriate to the essay as a whole.*
5. *Why does Stegner say (p. 9) that finding the three volumes of Shakespeare in the dump was "a little like finding my own name on a gravestone"? What is the purpose and effect of his allusion to Virgil's* Aeneid *in the sentence just before that?*
6. *Through what particular details does Stegner portray the dump as a record of his childhood? How is it shown to be also a record of the brief history of the town? In what respects does it reflect and suggest more widely yet, European and American history and culture and, ultimately, the ancient past, the foundations of civilization? Explain how and to what effect Stegner's focus on the dump enables these considerations to widen in scope but remain associated.*

Margaret Laurence
WHERE THE WORLD BEGAN

A strange place it was, that place where the world began. A place of incredible happenings, splendors and revelations, despairs like multitudinous pits of isolated hells. A place of shadow-spookiness, inhabited by the unknowable dead. A place of jubilation and of mourning, horrible and beautiful.

It was, in fact, a small prairie town.

Because that settlement and that land were my first and for many years my only real knowledge of this planet, in some profound way they remain my world, my way of viewing. My eyes were formed there. Towns like ours, set in a sea of land, have been described thousands of times as dull, bleak, flat, uninteresting. I have had it said to me that the railway trip across Canada is spectacular, except for the prairies, when it would be desirable to go to sleep for several days, until the ordeal is over. I am always unable to argue this point effectively. All I can say is—well, you really have to live there to know that country. The town of my childhood could be called bizarre, agonizingly repressive or cruel at times, and the land in which it grew could be called harsh in the violence of its seasonal changes. But never merely flat or uninteresting. Never dull.

In winter, we used to hitch rides on the back of the milk sleigh, our moccasins squeaking and slithering on the hard rutted snow of the roads, our hands in ice-bubbled mitts hanging onto the box edge of the sleigh for dear life, while Bert grinned at us through his great frosted mustache and shouted the horse into speed, daring us to stay put. Those mornings, rising, there would be the perpetual fascination of the frost feathers on

windows, the ferns and flowers and eerie faces traced there during the
night by unseen artists of the wind. Evenings, coming back from skating,
the sky would be black but not dark, for you could see a cold glitter of
stars from one side of the earth's rim to the other. And then the sometime
astonishment when you saw the Northern Lights flaring across the sky,
like the scrawled signature of God. After a blizzard, when the snowplow
hadn't yet got through, school would be closed for the day, the assumption being that the town's young could not possibly flounder through five
feet of snow in the pursuit of education. We would then gaily don
snowshoes and flounder for miles out into the white dazzling deserts, in
pursuit of a different kind of knowing. If you came back too close to night,
through the woods at the foot of the town hill, the thin black branches of
poplar and chokecherry now meringued with frost, sometimes you heard
coyotes. Or maybe the banshee wolf-voices were really only inside your
head.

Summers were scorching, and when no rain came and the wheat
became bleached and dried before it headed, the faces of farmers and
townsfolk would not smile much, and you took for granted, because it
never seemed to have been any different, the frequent knocking at the
back door and the young men standing there, mumbling or thrusting
defiantly their requests for a drink of water and a sandwich if you could
spare it. They were riding the freights, and you never knew where they
had come from, or where they might end up, if anywhere. The Drought
and Depression were like evil deities which had been there always. You
understood and did not understand.

Yet the outside world had its continuing marvels. The poplar bluffs
and the small river were filled and surrounded with a zillion different
grasses, stones, and weed flowers. The meadowlarks sang undaunted
from the twanging telephone wires along the gravel highway. Once we
found an old flat-bottomed scow, and launched her, poling along the
shallow brown waters, mending her with wodges of hastily chewed
Spearmint, grounding her among the tangles of yellow marsh marigolds
that grew succulently along the banks of the shrunken river, while the
sun made our skins smell dusty-warm.

My best friend lived in an apartment above some stores on Main Street
(its real name was Mountain Avenue, goodness knows why), an elegant
apartment with royal-blue velvet curtains. The back roof, scarcely slop-
ing at all, was corrugated tin, of a furnace-like warmth on a July afternoon, and we would sit there drinking lemonade and looking across the
back lane at the Fire Hall. Sometimes our vigil would be rewarded. Oh
joy! Somebody's house burning down! We had an almost-perfect callousness in some ways. Then the wooden tower's bronze bell would clonk
and toll like a thousand speeded funerals in a time of plague, and in a few
minutes the team of giant black horses would cannon forth, pulling the

fire wagon like some scarlet chariot of the Goths, while the firemen clung with one hand, adjusting their helmets as they went.

The oddities of the place were endless. An elderly lady used to serve, as her afternoon tea offering to other ladies, soda biscuits spread with peanut butter and topped with a whole marshmallow. Some considered this slightly eccentric, when compared with chopped egg sandwiches, and admittedly talked about her behind her back, but no one ever refused these delicacies or indicated to her that they thought she had slipped a cog. Another lady dyed her hair a bright and cherry orange, by strangers often mistaken at twenty paces for a feather hat. My own beloved stepmother wore a silver fox neckpiece, a whole pelt, with the embalmed (?) head still on. My Ontario Irish grandfather said, "sparrow grass," a more interesting term than asparagus. The town dump was known as "the nuisance grounds," a phrase fraught with weird connotations, as though the effluvia of our lives was beneath contempt but at the same time was subtly threatening to the determined and sometimes hysterical propriety of our ways.

Some oddities were, as idiom had it, "funny ha ha"; others were "funny peculiar." Some were not so very funny at all. An old man lived, deranged, in a shack in the valley. Perhaps he wasn't even all that old, but to us he seemed a wild Methuselah figure, shambling among the underbrush and the tall couchgrass, muttering indecipherable curses or blessings, a prophet who had forgotten his prophecies. Everyone in town knew him, but no one knew him. He lived among us as though only occasionally and momentarily visible. The kids called him Andy Gump,[1] and feared him. Some sought to prove their bravery by tormenting him. They were the medieval bear baiters, and he the lumbering bewildered bear, half blind, only rarely turning to snarl. Everything is to be found in a town like mine. Belsen,[2] writ small but with the same ink.

All of us cast stones in one shape or another. In grade school, among the vulnerable and violet girls we were, the feared and despised were those few older girls from what was charmingly termed "the wrong side of the tracks." Tough in talk and tougher in muscle, they were said to be whores already. And may have been, that being about the only profession readily available to them.

The dead lived in that place, too. Not only the grandparents who had, in local parlance, "passed on" and who gloomed, bearded or bonneted, from the sepia photographs in old albums, but also the uncles, forever eighteen or nineteen, whose names were carved on the granite family stones in the cemetery, but whose bones lay in France.[3] My own young mother lay in that graveyard, beside other dead of our kin, and when I

1. Chinless character in a comic strip popular in the 1920s and 1930s.
2. The Nazi concentration camp Bergen-Belsen.

3. That is, who had been killed in World War I. The Canadian war dead were buried in Canadian cemeteries in northeastern France and Belgium.

was ten, my father, too, only forty, left the living town for the dead dwelling on the hill.

When I was eighteen, I couldn't wait to get out of that town, away from the prairies. I did not know then that I would carry the land and town all my life within my skull, that they would form the mainspring and source of the writing I was to do, wherever and however far away I might live.

This was my territory in the time of my youth, and in a sense my life since then has been an attempt to look at it, to come to terms with it. Stultifying to the mind it certainly could be, and sometimes was, but not to the imagination. It was many things, but it was never dull.

The same, I now see, could be said for Canada in general. Why on earth did generations of Canadians pretend to believe this country dull? We knew perfectly well it wasn't. Yet for so long we did not proclaim what we knew. If our upsurge of so-called nationalism seems odd or irrelevant to outsiders, and even to some of our own people (*what's all the fuss about?*), they might try to understand that for many years we valued ourselves insufficiently, living as we did under the huge shadows of those two dominating figures, Uncle Sam and Britannia. We have only just begun to value ourselves, our land, our abilities. We have only just begun to recognize our legends and to give shape to our myths.

There are, God knows, enough aspects to deplore about this country. When I see the killing of our lakes and rivers with industrial wastes, I feel rage and despair. When I see our industries and natural resources increasingly taken over by America, I feel an overwhelming discouragement, especially as I cannot simply say "damn Yankees." It should never be forgotten that it is we ourselves who have sold such a large amount of our birthright for a mess of plastic Progress. When I saw the War Measures Act being invoked in 1970,[4] I lost forever the vestigial remains of the naïve wish-belief that repression could not happen here, or would not. And yet, of course, I had known all along in the deepest and often hidden caves of the heart that anything can happen anywhere, for the seeds of both man's freedom and his captivity are found everywhere, even in the microcosm of a prairie town. But in raging against our injustices, our stupidities, I do so as *family*, as I did, and still do in writing, about those aspects of my town which I hated and which are always in some ways aspects of myself.

The land still draws me more than other lands. I have lived in Africa and in England, but splendid as both can be, they do not have the power to move me in the same way as, for example, that part of southern

4. By Prime Minister Pierre Elliott Trudeau, citing an "apprehended insurrection" in the wake of terrorist kidnapings by the separatist FLQ (Front de Libération du Québec). Under the provisions of this act, the armed forces took over many police functions, and certain civil liberties—notably habeas corpus—were suspended so that suspected terrorists could be held in jail without being charged.

Ontario where I spent four months last summer in a cedar cabin beside a river. "Scratch a Canadian, and you find a phony pioneer," I used to say to myself in warning. But all the same it is true, I think, that we are not yet totally alienated from physical earth, and let us only pray we do not become so. I once thought that my lifelong fear and mistrust of cities made me a kind of old-fashioned freak; now I see it differently.

The cabin has a long window across its front western wall, and sitting at the oak table there in the mornings, I used to look out at the river and at the tall trees beyond, green-gold in the early light. The river was bronze; the sun caught it strangely, reflecting upon its surface the near-shore sand ripples underneath. Suddenly, the crescenting of a fish, gone before the eye could clearly give image to it. The old man next door said these leaping fish were carp. Himself, he preferred muskie, for he was a real fisherman and the muskie gave him a fight. The wind most often blew from the south, and the river flowed toward the south, so when the water was wind-riffled, and the current was strong, the river seemed to be flowing both ways. I liked this, and interpreted it as an omen, a natural symbol.

A few years ago, when I was back in Winnipeg, I gave a talk at my old college. It was open to the public, and afterward a very old man came up to me and asked me if my maiden name had been Wemyss. I said yes, thinking he might have known my father or my grandfather. But no. "When I was a young lad," he said, "I once worked for your great-grandfather, Robert Wemyss, when he had the sheep ranch at Raeburn." I think that was a moment when I realized all over again something of great importance to me. My long-ago families came from Scotland and Ireland, but in a sense that no longer mattered so much. My true roots were here.

I am not very patriotic, in the usual meaning of that word. I cannot say "My country right or wrong" in any political, social or literary context. But one thing is inalterable, for better or worse, for life.

This is where my world began. A world which includes the ancestors —both my own and other people's ancestors who become mine. A world which formed me, and continues to do so, even while I found it in some of its aspects, and continue to do so. A world which gave me my own lifework to do, because it was here that I learned the sight of my own particular eyes.

1970

Russell Baker

SUMMER BEYOND WISH

A long time ago I lived in a crossroads village of northern Virginia and during its summer enjoyed innocence and never knew boredom, although nothing of consequence happened there.

Seven houses of varying lack of distinction constituted the community. A dirt road meandered off toward the mountain where a bootleg still supplied whisky to the men of the countryside, and another dirt road ran down to the creek. My cousin Kenneth and I would sit on the bank and fish with earthworms. One day we killed a copperhead which was basking on a rock nearby. That was unusual.

The heat of summer was mellow and produced sweet scents which lay in the air so damp and rich you could almost taste them. Mornings smelled of purple wisteria, afternoons of the wild roses which tumbled over stone fences, and evenings of honeysuckle.

Even by standards of that time it was a primitive place. There was no electricity. Roads were unpaved. In our house there was no plumbing. The routine of summer days was shaped by these deficiencies. Lacking electric lights, one went early to bed and rose while the dew was still in the grass. Kerosene lamps were cleaned and polished in an early-morning hubbub of women, and children were sent to the spring for fresh water.

This afforded a chance to see whether the crayfish population had multiplied. Later, a trip to the outhouse would afford a chance to daydream in the Sears, Roebuck Catalogue, mostly about shotguns and bicycles.

With no electricity, radio was not available for pacifying the young. One or two people did have radios that operated on mail-order batteries about the size of a present-day car battery, but these were not for children, though occasionally you might be invited in to hear "Amos 'n' Andy."

All I remember about "Amos 'n' Andy" at that time is that it was strange hearing voices come out of furniture. Much later I was advised that listening to "Amos 'n' Andy" was racist and was grateful that I hadn't heard much.

In the summer no pleasures were to be had indoors. Everything of delight occurred in the world outside. In the flowers there were hummingbirds to be seen, tiny wings fluttering so fast that the birds seemed to have no wings at all.

In the heat of mid-afternoon the women would draw the blinds, spread blankets on the floor for coolness and nap, while in the fields the cattle herded together in the shade of spreading trees to escape the sun. Afternoons were absolutely still, yet filled with sounds.

Bees buzzed in the clover. Far away over the fields the chug of an ancient steam-powered threshing machine could be faintly heard. Birds rustled under the tin of the porch roof.

Rising dust along the road from the mountains signaled an approaching event. A car was coming. "Car's coming," someone would say. People emerged from houses. The approaching dust was studied. Guesses were hazarded about whom it might contain.

Then—a big moment in the day—the car would cruise past.

"Who was it?"

"I didn't get a good look."

"It looked like Packy Painter to me."

"Couldn't have been Packy. Wasn't his car."

The stillness resettled itself as gently as the dust, and you could wander past the henhouse and watch a hen settle herself to perform the mystery of laying an egg. For livelier adventure there was the field that contained the bull. There, one could test his courage by seeing how far he dared venture before running back through the fence.

The men drifted back with the falling sun, steaming with heat and fatigue, and washed in tin basins with water hauled in buckets from the spring. I knew a few of their secrets, such as who kept his whisky hidden in a mason jar behind the lime barrel, and what they were really doing when they excused themselves from the kitchen and stepped out into the orchard and stayed out there laughing too hard.

I also knew what the women felt about it, though not what they thought. Even then I could see that matters between women and men could become very difficult and, sometimes, so difficult that they spoiled the air of summer.

At sunset people sat on the porches. As dusk deepened, the lightning bugs came out to be caught and bottled. As twilight edged into night, a bat swooped across the road. I was not afraid of bats then, although I feared ghosts, which made the approach of bedtime in a room where even the kerosene lamp would quickly be doused seem terrifying.

I was even more afraid of toads and specifically of the toad which lived under the porch steps and which, everyone assured me, would, if touched, give me warts. One night I was allowed to stay up until the stars were in full command of the sky. A woman of great age was dying in the village and it was considered fit to let the children stay abroad into the night. As four of us sat there we saw a shooting star and someone said, "Make a wish."

I did not know what that meant. I didn't know anything to wish for.

1978

QUESTIONS

1. *Baker attempts to describe a boyhood summer of perfect contentment and fulfillment. Do you think he succeeds? If so, can you indicate those features of his manner, his style, as well as his choice of what to talk about, that are designed to convey that sense of perfect contentment?*
2. *The essay is written by a man looking back upon his boyhood. Are there any places in the essay where we seem to hear the boy himself —that is, where the writing expresses things just as the boy (not the older man) would experience them? Why does Baker choose to treat these particular things this way?*
3. *Near the beginning Baker says that "nothing of consequence happened there." Do you agree? Are any unusual happenings described? In what way might they be important—"of consequence"?*
4. *Do you find the conclusion of the essay effective? Why, or why not? What details substantiate the thought conveyed in the conclusion?*

Maya Angelou

GRADUATION

The children in Stamps[1] trembled visibly with anticipation. Some adults were excited too, but to be certain the whole young population had come down with graduation epidemic. Large classes were graduating from both the grammar school and the high school. Even those who were years removed from their own day of glorious release were anxious to help with preparations as a kind of dry run. The junior students who were moving into the vacating classes' chairs were tradition-bound to show their talents for leadership and management. They strutted through the school and around the campus exerting pressure on the lower grades. Their authority was so new that occasionally if they pressed a little too hard it had to be overlooked. After all, next term was coming, and it never hurt a sixth grader to have a play sister in the eighth grade, or a tenth-year student to be able to call a twelfth grader Bubba. So all was endured in a spirit of shared understanding. But the graduating classes themselves were the nobility. Like travelers with exotic destinations on their minds, the graduates were remarkably forgetful. They came to

---

1. A town in Arkansas.

school without their books, or tablets or even pencils. Volunteers fell over themselves to secure replacements for the missing equipment. When accepted, the willing workers might or might not be thanked, and it was of no importance to the pregraduation rites. Even teachers were respectful of the now quiet and aging seniors, and tended to speak to them, if not as equals, as beings only slightly lower than themselves. After tests were returned and grades given, the student body, which acted like an extended family, knew who did well, who excelled, and what piteous ones had failed.

Unlike the white high school, Lafayette County Training School distinguished itself by having neither lawn, nor hedges, nor tennis court, nor climbing ivy. Its two buildings (main classrooms, the grade school and home economics) were set on a dirt hill with no fence to limit either its boundaries or those of bordering farms. There was a large expanse to the left of the school which was used alternately as a baseball diamond or basketball court. Rusty hoops on swaying poles represented the permanent recreational equipment, although bats and balls could be borrowed from the P.E. teacher if the borrower was qualified and if the diamond wasn't occupied.

Over this rocky area relieved by a few shady tall persimmon trees the graduating class walked. The girls often held hands and no longer bothered to speak to the lower students. There was a sadness about them, as if this old world was not their home and they were bound for higher ground. The boys, on the other hand, had become more friendly, more outgoing. A decided change from the closed attitude they projected while studying for finals. Now they seemed not ready to give up the old school, the familiar paths and classrooms. Only a small percentage would be continuing on to college—one of the South's A & M (agricultural and mechanical) schools, which trained Negro youths to be carpenters, farmers, handymen, masons, maids, cooks and baby nurses. Their future rode heavily on their shoulders, and blinded them to the collective joy that had pervaded the lives of the boys and girls in the grammar school graduating class.

Parents who could afford it had ordered new shoes and readymade clothes for themselves from Sears and Roebuck or Montgomery Ward. They also engaged the best seamstresses to make the floating graduating dresses and to cut down secondhand pants which would be pressed to a military slickness for the important event.

Oh, it was important, all right. Whitefolks would attend the ceremony, and two or three would speak of God and home, and the Southern way of life, and Mrs. Parsons, the principal's wife, would play the graduation march while the lower-grade graduates paraded down the aisles and took their seats below the platform. The high school seniors would wait in empty classrooms to make their dramatic entrance.

In the Store I was the person of the moment. The birthday girl. The center. Bailey[2] had graduated the year before, although to do so he had had to forfeit all pleasures to make up for his time lost in Baton Rouge.

My class was wearing butter-yellow piqué dresses, and Momma launched out on mine. She smocked the yoke into tiny crisscrossing puckers, then shirred the rest of the bodice. Her dark fingers ducked in and out of the lemony cloth as she embroidered raised daisies around the hem. Before she considered herself finished she had added a crocheted cuff on the puff sleeves, and a pointy crocheted collar.

I was going to be lovely. A walking model of all the various styles of fine hand sewing and it didn't worry me that I was only twelve years old and merely graduating from the eighth grade. Besides, many teachers in Arkansas Negro schools had only that diploma and were licensed to impart wisdom.

The days had become longer and more noticeable. The faded beige of former times had been replaced with strong and sure colors. I began to see my classmates' clothes, their skin tones, and the dust that waved off pussy willows. Clouds that lazed across the sky were objects of great concern to me. Their shiftier shapes might have held a message that in my new happiness and with a little bit of time I'd soon decipher. During that period I looked at the arch of heaven so religiously my neck kept a steady ache. I had taken to smiling more often, and my jaws hurt from the unaccustomed activity. Between the two physical sore spots, I suppose I could have been uncomfortable, but that was not the case. As a member of the winning team (the graduating class of 1940) I had outdistanced unpleasant sensations by miles. I was headed for the freedom of open fields.

Youth and social approval allied themselves with me and we trammeled memories of slights and insults. The wind of our swift passage remodeled my features. Lost tears were pounded to mud and then to dust. Years of withdrawal were brushed aside and left behind, as hanging ropes of parasitic moss.

My work alone had awarded me a top place and I was going to be one of the first called in the graduating ceremonies. On the classroom blackboard, as well as on the bulletin board in the auditorium, there were blue stars and white stars and red stars. No absences, no tardinesses, and my academic work was among the best of the year. I could say the preamble to the Constitution even faster than Bailey. We timed ourselves often: "WethepeopleoftheUnitedStatesinordertoformamoreperfectunion . . ." I had memorized the Presidents of the United States from Washington to Roosevelt in chronological as well as alphabetical order.

My hair pleased me too. Gradually the black mass had lengthened and

2. The author's brother.

thickened, so that it kept at last to its braided pattern, and I didn't have to yank my scalp off when I tried to comb it.

Louise and I had rehearsed the exercises until we tired out ourselves. Henry Reed was class valedictorian. He was a small, very black boy with hooded eyes, a long, broad nose and an oddly shaped head. I had admired him for years because each term he and I vied for the best grades in our class. Most often he bested me, but instead of being disappointed I was pleased that we shared top places between us. Like many Southern Black children, he lived with his grandmother, who was as strict as Momma and as kind as she knew how to be. He was courteous, respectful and soft-spoken to elders, but on the playground he chose to play the roughest games. I admired him. Anyone, I reckoned, sufficiently afraid or sufficiently dull could be polite. But to be able to operate at a top level with both adults and children was admirable.

His valedictory speech was entitled "To Be or Not to Be." The rigid tenth-grade teacher had helped him write it. He'd been working on the dramatic stresses for months.

The weeks until graduation were filled with heady activities. A group of small children were to be presented in a play about buttercups and daisies and bunny rabbits. They could be heard throughout the building practicing their hops and their little songs that sounded like silver bells. The older girls (nongraduates, of course) were assigned the task of making refreshments for the night's festivities. A tangy scent of ginger, cinnamon, nutmeg and chocolate wafted around the home economics building as the budding cooks made samples for themselves and their teachers.

In every corner of the workshop, axes and saws split fresh timber as the woodshop boys made sets and stage scenery. Only the graduates were left out of the general bustle. We were free to sit in the library at the back of the building or look in quite detachedly, naturally, on the measures being taken for our event.

Even the minister preached on graduation the Sunday before. His subject was, "Let your light so shine that men will see your good works and praise your Father, Who is in Heaven." Although the sermon was purported to be addressed to us, he used the occasion to speak to back-sliders, gamblers and general ne'er-do-wells. But since he had called our names at the beginning of the service we were mollified.

Among Negroes the tradition was to give presents to children going only from one grade to another. How much more important this was when the person was graduating at the top of the class. Uncle Willie and Momma had sent away for a Mickey Mouse watch like Bailey's. Louise gave me four embroidered handkerchiefs. (I gave her crocheted doilies.) Mrs. Sneed, the minister's wife, made me an undershirt to wear for graduation, and nearly every customer gave me a nickel or maybe even a dime with the instruction "Keep on moving to higher ground," or some such encouragement.

Amazingly the great day finally dawned and I was out of bed before I knew it. I threw open the back door to see it more clearly, but Momma said, "Sister, come away from that door and put your robe on."

I hoped the memory of that morning would never leave me. Sunlight was itself young, and the day had none of the insistence maturity would bring it in a few hours. In my robe and barefoot in the backyard, under cover of going to see about my new beans, I gave myself up to the gentle warmth and thanked God that no matter what evil I had done in my life He had allowed me to live to see this day. Somewhere in my fatalism I had expected to die, accidentally, and never have the chance to walk up the stairs in the auditorium and gracefully receive my hard-earned diploma. Out of God's merciful bosom I had won reprieve.

Bailey came out in his robe and gave me a box wrapped in Christmas paper. He said he had saved his money for months to pay for it. It felt like a box of chocolates, but I knew Bailey wouldn't save money to buy candy when we had all we could want under our noses.

He was as proud of the gift as I. It was a soft-leather-bound copy of a collection of poems by Edgar Allan Poe, or, as Bailey and I called him, "Eap." I turned to "Annabel Lee" and we walked up and down the garden rows, the cool dirt between our toes, reciting the beautifully sad lines.

Momma made a Sunday breakfast although it was only Friday. After we finished the blessing, I opened my eyes to find the watch on my plate. It was a dream of a day. Everything went smoothly and to my credit. I didn't have to be reminded or scolded for anything. Near evening I was too jittery to attend to chores, so Bailey volunteered to do all before his bath.

Days before, we had made a sign for the Store, and as we turned out the lights Momma hung the cardboard over the doorknob. It read clearly: CLOSED. GRADUATION.

My dress fitted perfectly and everyone said that I looked like a sunbeam in it. On the hill, going toward the school, Bailey walked behind with Uncle Willie, who muttered, "Go on, Ju." He wanted him to walk ahead with us because it embarrassed him to have to walk so slowly. Bailey said he'd let the ladies walk together, and the men would bring up the rear. We all laughed, nicely.

Little children dashed by out of the dark like fireflies. Their crepe-paper dresses and butterfly wings were not made for running and we heard more than one rip, dryly, and the regretful "uh uh" that followed.

The school blazed without gaiety. The windows seemed cold and unfriendly from the lower hill. A sense of ill-fated timing crept over me, and if Momma hadn't reached for my hand I would have drifted back to

Bailey and Uncle Willie, and possibly beyond. She made a few slow jokes about my feet getting cold, and tugged me along to the now-strange building.

Around the front steps, assurance came back. There were my fellow "greats," the graduating class. Hair brushed back, legs oiled, new dresses and pressed pleats, fresh pocket handkerchiefs and little handbags, all homesewn. Oh, we were up to snuff, all right. I joined my comrades and didn't even see my family go in to find seats in the crowded auditorium.

The school band struck up a march and all classes filed in as had been rehearsed. We stood in front of our seats, as assigned, and on a signal from the choir director, we sat. No sooner had this been accomplished than the band started to play the national anthem. We rose again and sang the song, after which we recited the pledge of allegiance. We remained standing for a brief minute before the choir director and the principal signaled to us, rather desperately I thought, to take our seats. The command was so unusual that our carefully rehearsed and smooth-running machine was thrown off. For a full minute we fumbled for our chairs and bumped into each other awkwardly. Habits change or solidify under pressure, so in our state of nervous tension we had been ready to follow our usual assembly pattern: the American national anthem, then the pledge of allegiance, then the song every Black person I knew called the Negro National Anthem. All done in the same key, with the same passion and most often standing on the same foot.

Finding my seat at last, I was overcome with a presentiment of worse things to come. Something unrehearsed, unplanned, was going to happen, and we were going to be made to look bad. I distinctly remember being explicit in the choice of pronoun. It was "we," the graduating class, the unit, that concerned me then.

The principal welcomed "parents and friends" and asked the Baptist minister to lead us in prayer. His invocation was brief and punchy, and for a second I thought we were getting on the high road to right action. When the principal came back to the dais, however, his voice had changed. Sounds always affected me profoundly and the principal's voice was one of my favorites. During assembly it melted and lowed weakly into the audience. It had not been in my plan to listen to him, but my curiosity was piqued and I straightened up to give him my attention.

He was talking about Booker T. Washington, our "late great leader," who said we can be as close as the fingers on the hand, etc. . . . Then he said a few vague things about friendship and the friendship of kindly people to those less fortunate than themselves. With that his voice nearly faded, thin, away. Like a river diminishing to a stream and then to a trickle. But he cleared his throat and said, "Our speaker tonight, who is also our friend, came from Texarkana to deliver the commencement address, but due to the irregularity of the train schedule, he's going to, as they say, 'speak and run.'" He said that we understood and wanted the man to know that we were most grateful for the time he was able to give us and then something about how we were willing always to adjust to another's program, and without more ado—"I give you Mr. Edward Donleavy."

Not one but two white men came through the door off-stage. The shorter one walked to the speaker's platform, and the tall one moved to the center seat and sat down. But that was our principal's seat, and already occupied. The dislodged gentleman bounced around for a long breath or two before the Baptist minister gave him his chair, then with more dignity than the situation deserved, the minister walked off the stage.

Donleavy looked at the audience once (on reflection, I'm sure that he wanted only to reassure himself that we were really there), adjusted his glasses and began to read from a sheaf of papers.

He was glad "to be here and to see the work going on just as it was in the other schools."

At the first "Amen" from the audience I willed the offender to immediate death by choking on the word. But Amens and Yes, sir's began to fall around the room like rain through a ragged umbrella.

He told us of the wonderful changes we children in Stamps had in store. The Central School (naturally, the white school was Central) had already been granted improvements that would be in use in the fall. A well-known artist was coming from Little Rock to teach art to them. They were going to have the newest microscopes and chemistry equipment for their laboratory. Mr. Donleavy didn't leave us long in the dark over who made these improvements available to Central High. Nor were we to be ignored in the general betterment scheme he had in mind.

He said that he had pointed out to people at a very high level that one of the first-line football tacklers at Arkansas Agricultural and Mechanical College had graduated from good old Lafayette County Training School. Here fewer Amen's were heard. Those few that did break through lay dully in the air with the heaviness of habit.

He went on to praise us. He went on to say how he had bragged that "one of the best basketball players at Fisk sank his first ball right here at Lafayette County Training School."

The white kids were going to have a chance to become Galileos and Madame Curies and Edisons and Gauguins, and our boys (the girls weren't even in on it) would try to be Jesse Owenses and Joe Louises.

Owens and the Brown Bomber were great heroes in our world, but what school official in the white-goddom of Little Rock had the right to decide that those two men must be our only heroes? Who decided that for Henry Reed to become a scientist he had to work like George Washington Carver, as a bootblack, to buy a lousy microscope? Bailey was obviously always going to be too small to be an athlete, so which concrete angel glued to what country seat had decided that if my brother wanted to become a lawyer he had to first pay penance for his skin by picking cotton and hoeing corn and studying correspondence books at night for twenty years?

The man's dead words fell like bricks around the auditorium and too many settled in my belly. Constrained by hard-learned manners I couldn't look behind me, but to my left and right the proud graduating class of 1940 had dropped their heads. Every girl in my row had found something new to do with her handkerchief. Some folded the tiny squares into love knots, some into triangles, but most were wadding them, then pressing them flat on their yellow laps.

On the dais, the ancient tragedy was being replayed. Professor Parsons sat, a sculptor's reject, rigid. His large, heavy body seemed devoid of will or willingness, and his eyes said he was no longer with us. The other teachers examined the flag (which was draped stage right) or their notes, or the windows which opened on our now-famous playing diamond.

Graduation, the hush-hush magic time of frills and gifts and congratulations and diplomas, was finished for me before my name was called. The accomplishment was nothing. The meticulous maps, drawn in three colors of ink, learning and spelling decasyllabic words, memorizing the whole of *The Rape of Lucrece*[3]—it was for nothing. Donleavy had exposed us.

We were maids and farmers, handymen and washerwomen, and anything higher that we aspired to was farcical and presumptuous.

Then I wished that Gabriel Prosser and Nat Turner[4] had killed all whitefolks in their beds and that Abraham Lincoln had been assassinated before the signing of the Emancipation Proclamation, and that Harriet Tubman[5] had been killed by that blow on her head and Christopher Columbus had drowned in the *Santa Maria*.

It was awful to be a Negro and have no control over my life. It was brutal to be young and already trained to sit quietly and listen to charges brought against my color with no chance of defense. We should all be dead. I thought I should like to see us all dead, one on top of the other. A pyramid of flesh with the whitefolks on the bottom, as the broad base, then the Indians with their silly tomahawks and teepees and wigwams and treaties, the Negroes with their mops and recipes and cotton sacks and spirituals sticking out of their mouths. The Dutch children should all stumble in their wooden shoes and break their necks. The French should choke to death on the Louisiana Purchase (1803) while silkworms ate all the Chinese with their stupid pigtails. As a species, we were an abomination. All of us.

3. A narrative poem of 1,855 lines, by Shakespeare.
4. Leaders of Virginia slave rebellions in 1800 and 1831 respectively.
5. Nineteenth-century black abolitionist, a "conductor" on the Underground Railroad.

Donleavy was running for election, and assured our parents that if he won we could count on having the only colored paved playing field in that part of Arkansas. Also—he never looked up to acknowledge the grunts of acceptance—also, we were bound to get some new equipment for the home economics building and the workshop.

He finished, and since there was no need to give any more than the most perfunctory thank-you's, he nodded to the men on the stage, and the tall white man who was never introduced joined him at the door. They left with the attitude that now they were off to something really important. (The graduation ceremonies at Lafayette County Training School had been a mere preliminary.)

The ugliness they left was palpable. An uninvited guest who wouldn't leave. The choir was summoned and sang a modern arrangement of "Onward, Christian Soldiers," with new words pertaining to graduates seeking their place in the world. But it didn't work. Elouise, the daughter of the Baptist minister, recited "Invictus,"[6] and I could have cried at the impertinence of "I am the master of my fate, I am the captain of my soul."

My name had lost its ring of familiarity and I had to be nudged to go and receive my diploma. All my preparations had fled. I neither marched up to the stage like a conquering Amazon, nor did I look in the audience for Bailey's nod of approval. Marguerite Johnson, I heard the name again, my honors were read, there were noises in the audience of appreciation, and I took my place on the stage as rehearsed.

I thought about colors I hated: ecru, puce, lavender, beige and black.

There was shuffling and rustling around me, then Henry Reed was giving his valedictory address, "To Be or Not to Be." Hadn't he heard the whitefolks? We couldn't *be*, so the question was a waste of time. Henry's voice came out clear and strong. I feared to look at him. Hadn't he got the message? There was no "nobler in the mind" for Negroes because the world didn't think we had minds, and they let us know it. "Outrageous fortune"? Now, that was a joke. When the ceremony was over I had to tell Henry Reed some things. That is, if I still cared. Not "rub," Henry, "erase." "Ah, there's the erase." Us.

Henry had been a good student in elocution. His voice rose on tides of promise and fell on waves of warnings. The English teacher had helped him to create a sermon winging through Hamlet's soliloquy. To be a man, a doer, a builder, a leader, or to be a tool, an unfunny joke, a crusher of funky toadstools. I marveled that Henry could go through with the speech as if we had a choice.

I had been listening and silently rebutting each sentence with my eyes closed; then there was a hush, which in an audience warns that something unplanned is happening. I looked up and saw Henry Reed, the conserva-

---

6. An inspirational poem by the nineteenth-century poet William Ernest Henley, once very popular for occasions such as this one.

tive, the proper, the A student, turn his back to the audience and turn to us (the proud graduating class of 1940) and sing, nearly speaking,

> "Lift ev'ry voice and sing
> Till earth and heaven ring
> Ring with the harmonies of Liberty ..."

It was the poem written by James Weldon Johnson. It was the music composed by J. Rosamond Johnson. It was the Negro national anthem. Out of habit we were singing it.

Our mothers and fathers stood in the dark hall and joined the hymn of encouragement. A kindergarten teacher led the small children onto the stage and the buttercups and daisies and bunny rabbits marked time and tried to follow:

> "Stony the road we trod
> Bitter the chastening rod
> Felt in the days when hope, unborn, had died.
> Yet with a steady beat
> Have not our weary feet
> Come to the place for which our fathers sighed?"

Each child I knew had learned that song with his ABC's and along with "Jesus Loves Me This I Know." But I personally had never heard it before. Never heard the words, despite the thousands of times I had sung them. Never thought they had anything to do with me.

On the other hand, the words of Patrick Henry had made such an impression on me that I had been able to stretch myself tall and trembling and say, "I know not what course others may take, but as for me, give me liberty or give me death."

And now I heard, really for the first time:

> "We have come over a way that with tears
> has been watered,
> We have come, treading our path through
> the blood of the slaughtered."

While echoes of the song shivered in the air, Henry Reed bowed his head, said "Thank you," and returned to his place in the line. The tears that slipped down many faces were not wiped away in shame.

We were on top again. As always, again. We survived. The depths had been icy and dark, but now a bright sun spoke to our souls. I was no longer simply a member of the proud graduating class of 1940; I was a proud member of the wonderful, beautiful Negro race.

Oh, Black known and unknown poets, how often have your auctioned pains sustained us? Who will compute the lonely nights made less lonely by your songs, or the empty pots made less tragic by your tales?

If we were a people much given to revealing secrets, we might raise monuments and sacrifice to the memories of our poets, but slavery cured us of that weakness. It may be enough, however, to have it said that we survive in exact relationship to the dedication of our poets (include preachers, musicians and blues singers).

1969

Kildare Dobbs

RUNNING TO PARADISE

The sound of a train whistle at night—now reincarnate as a diesel klaxon—is the key experience of North Americans, so often written about that it may have become too familiar to mean much. Yet not to me, an immigrant when I first heard it. A lonely sound. I imagined the train rushing on into the dark, past sleeping farms and fields, through forests and by lakes and across the vast prairies to the west, running westward, running to the far mountains and beyond them to an ocean on the other side of the world. It spoke rather of voyages than journeys, seafaring overland, an ocean of loneliness scattered with villages and cities like lighthouses winking from shores of sleep. The Canadian sound, suggesting the vastness and emptiness of a country still in the future, it was hinting at a destination as yet unimagined. That is the place I am restlessly faring to, riding westward, running to Paradise.

"*Aida*," the train sang through its steel nostrils, running westward from Toronto, myself stretched snugly in a roomette. "*Aiii-da*."

Aida wasn't opera, but a mnemonic given me by the sales manager. For I was now one of the travelling fraternity, the boys on the road: the sample cases stuffed with books and bibles out there in the porter's care attested me a book salesman, a bible man. *Aida* was how to sell books, or boots or toothpaste or whatever. A, I, D, A. A for Attention. "The bookseller, he sees a lot of salesmen. He's heard it all before. You got to go in there and grab his attention, okay?" Okay. And I for Interest: once you had your man's attention, you had to hold his interest. Then you came to D for Desire. The next step was to awaken desire. . . . "Let's keep this discussion on a decent level, shall we? Desire here is for the product, which in your case is books. You got to make the customer want what you're selling." Which in my case was also bibles. (But I'm coming to that.) After desire—then A for Action! This was what you had joined for. Close the deal and make the sale. Nothing to do but write up the order and mail it.

Aida, Muse of Salesmanship, invoked with Attention, pursued with

Interest, wooed with Desire, possessed in Action—it was she who led me
into the cities of the West, into the châteaux of railway hotels with hot
and cold gracious living, the principality of bell captains and sample
rooms, territory of the taxi-meter and the expense claim. In some of those
hotels (the Paralyser of C——for instance), a whole floor was given over
to salesmen. The corridor was cluttered with what appeared to be big
black coffins. In these, I was told, the garment salesmen carried not
corpses but their wares. Theirs seemed a gruesome trade. Once I lay
awake half the night in the next room to a pair of garment salesmen who
had invited in two women. At first it sounded fairly genial: much laughter
and the clink of glasses. Later it changed. There was a drone of female
talk from one side of the room; on the other side the men had their heads
together. Not my idea of fun. Much later the women, frustrated perhaps,
began to scream abuse at the men, demanding at last that a taxi be called.

Drinking with old John Lush in his prairie city, I learned Aida's hidden
mysteries. He was, as they say, a valued customer, and the visits of book-
travellers were the most exciting events in his year. Unlike the girls who
work in candy factories, he enjoyed the product he dealt in: he would
dream over the *Memoirs* of Casanova of an evening before he went to
bed, and from the way he handled the samples you could see he liked a
good read.

John was a man who had in youth been visited by an experience much
like that of Saul of Tarsus on the road to Damascus. He had been training
for the Ministry. Zealous and devout in his studies, he believed he had
forsaken the world. And then one evening, on his way back to his
lodgings from a lecture on Predestination, he became conscious that a
woman was smiling at him from a doorway. "I saw the light!" From that
moment his life changed. "It was a red light." He drowned his theology
books in the river.

All this he imparted as we knocked back a bottle of Scotch in my hotel
room. I'm afraid I was a disappointment to him, though he gave me a
good fat order to keep my employer happy. He was accustomed to more
lively entertainment than I offered. "Do you know Charley Magnum?"
he said wistfully. "He used to travel for Green Press." I remembered
meeting him. A little black-haired goat of a man, ugly as sin. He was blind
drunk at the time, roaring out obscene songs.

"That's the fella." John seemed pleased. He shook his head, shocked
and delighted at the memory of Charley Magnum. He assumed a more
demotic turn of speech, coarsening his accent to signify that we were
boys together. "The times we had. Well, sir, they fired him. Yes, sir, after
fifteen years of his carryon they gave him his marching orders. I never
saw a fella like him." He began to cough and creak with laughter. I filled
his glass again. "Hey, whoa there! Oh well, okay. . . . I sure miss Charley.
First thing when he came to town he'd call me up and say, 'Come on over

the room, I got something for ya.' So I'd climb right in a cab and come over. Well, he'd pick up the phone and grin like a devil—homely little bugger he was too—and he'd say, 'Whaddya want John—a woman?' *Jeesus*—well, I've been married a good many years. I'm past all that. But —'Whatsa matter, John?' he'd say. 'Hell, give the cat a canary, it's on the house!'"

John was obviously pleased at these courtesies, though he felt (since his retirement to marriage) that he could not take advantage of them. "God, Charley could get away with murder! One time, on our way to his room in the hotel, the corridor was half blocked by a chambermaid. She was bending down with her back to us, fixing her vacuum-cleaner or something. And Charley, he just went right up to her and gave her a tremenjous smack on the ass. She let a squawk and shot up with her hand on it, mad as hell. A redhead, not bad either. I walked away pretty quick, but before she could say a word, Charley leaned over and said something to her. Don't know what it was, but would you believe it, the next thing I saw was that girl taking her vacuum-cleaner into Charley's room. . . ."

It was at about this point that John and I went through my book catalogue. (Action!) Later he told me that Charley had turned up once at his house with a woman—a terrible female. "Who was that dreadful creature?" John's wife wanted to know after they had left. "I think," said John, honest even in adversity, "it was a chambermaid from the Grand Prairie Hotel."

These things I learned from old John over a period of some hours, the Scotch giving way at last to a case of beer. In a thickening fog of booze and reminiscence we transacted our business. The names of eminent authors, some Canadian, were mentioned eruditely or brushed rudely but knowledgeably aside as beneath the notice of civilized bookmen. Hours after John had left, stepping high like a man walking through long grass, I was grimly writing out titles, prices, and (incorrect) totals.

Aida had not deserted me. A for Alcohol, she began in her new dispensation, I for Incofluence, D for Drunk. And lastly A for Alcohol again. In my end (as we reading-men like to say) is my beginning.

Aida worked all right for the books, once I had got through my head what she really stood for. It was the bibles that defeated me. *Biblical*, I discovered, was not the same as *bibliophile*, certainly had no connection, etymological or otherwise, with *bibulous*. The bible accounts were dry; not only dry but the cause of dryness in others. A for Alcohol was out. It would have to be A for Attention. But how to attract it? Bible-selling is a bitterly competitive game. Since all the texts are the same (with a few exceptions, latter-day freaks such as Revised Versions, modern translations, and texts "designed to be read as literature"—heretical no doubt), the Word as dedicated to King James I, what the bible man has to put across is their format. Paper, print, binding, zip-fasteners, yapped edges, not to mention more spiritual considerations such as price, discount, service, and shipping dates—these are the subjects that interest the bible-buyer.

How could I hope to talk convincingly of such matters? There were about three hundred bibles in my list, all with code numbers which to adepts revealed at a glance whether they were bound in Persian Morocco, Full Morocco, Pigskin, Goatskin, Rexine, Rhinoceros hide, or whatever; whether yapped, zipped, warped or wrapped (don't ask me, I'm a stranger myself); whether printed in Pearl, Onyx, Chasuble, Urim, Thummim or Bourgeois (this, one thing I knew, was pronounced "Boorjoys"); or whether equipped with indexes, cross-references, maps, concordances, introductions, translators' prefaces, baptismal certificates, confirmation documents, driving licences, charts, questions, answers, apocryphas, pseudepigrapha, illustrations, pop-ups or singing covers.

From a mine so thoroughly exploited, what jewel could an ignoramus like myself hope to extract and hold shining before the case-hardened buyer of a fundamentalist church-chandler? True, I had the advantage of having read the book, parts of it several times. There was the example of the Moderator of the Church of Scotland, that grim black figure, like a crow among peacocks, at the pomp and glamour of the Queen's coronation. "Here is Wisdom," he had said, moving, bible in hand, to the centre of my TV set. "This is the Royal Law. These are the lively Oracles of God." I knew enough about blurb-writing to recognize first-class work. But after all, the Moderator wasn't putting across merchandise. To introduce a note of that sort into the sales situation would have been an embarrassing reminder of those money-changers' tables in the Temple.

After a few kindly rebuffs, so cleverly administered that I was lucky to leave the various premises without having actually *bought* some of the competing merchandise, I decided to use physical violence. Bursting into a religious-goods store in the next prairie city on my itinerary, I seized my most expensive bible-sample in both hands, bent it double to show the beautiful suppleness of its fine leather and India paper, thrust it under the nose of the buyer.

"Smell that!"

Backed up against a bookcase, the poor woman capitulated on every point: A, I, D, A. She gave me a splendid order. It wasn't till later that I found out from my home office that her credit was shot. I wasn't supposed to have called on her at all.

Perhaps it was not my destiny to sell holy writ. I could *read* it with pleasure, a refuge from the duller non-fiction among my current samples. And I read:

Where shall wisdom be found?

But I was seeing Canada, a limitless territory rising from imagination

into fact, and now sunk down to memory. The prairies—before I set eyes
on the prairies I imagined them a region of unspeakable desolation, as
dreary and oppressive to the spirit as they appear on the back of a dollar
bill. Now that I had seen them—I knew them to be a region of unspeakable desolation, as dreary and oppressive to &c. &c. There is a sense in
which the paradox is true, that travel narrows the mind. Yet you could
see what it was about the region that had prairie people by the heart. It
was like the open sea, that wide flat land under the vast sky, a brown sea
now, though winter would soon cover it in greyish white, its loneliness
more than earthly, more than mortal. Like the loneliness of God (I told a
prairie poet in a fit of Aida-induced confidence) before he made the
universe. The poet nodded enthusiastically. "You're right, you're *right*
—that's just it!"

I had to go and spoil it for him. "The only trouble is, he couldn't stand
it. . . . He made the universe."

Between hotels—from the windows of trains or airliners—it was possible to catch a notion of the country. The hotels, like the cities, tend to
merge into each other in memory, so that the commercial places of
Winnipeg, Regina, Saskatoon, Edmonton, Calgary, now seem all one
hotel, and the cities themselves—for all their several peculiarities—one
city. Smaller cities are more distinct. Moose Jaw, with its heroic public
library; Medicine Hat, crouched in a sort of amphitheatre in a bend of its
river; Lethbridge, haunted by the sombre figures of Hutterites, black-
suited, black-bearded, accompanied by women like Victorian dolls in
their long skirts and headkerchiefs. But the land—as you went westward
it changed. At first flat in the continental doldrums, it began to take on a
long undulation, like the heavy groundswell of the Western Ocean.
Gradually over hundreds of miles it continued to work itself up by ever
shorter and steeper waves into a flurry of foothills till at last it broke over
the horizon in a storm of jagged mountains, the icy peaks of the Canadian
Rockies.

At the Paralyser Hotel, for me the climax of the foothills, I drank late
with my brother-traveller Ken Tupper. My room was by the freight yard
of the railroad; we could hardly hear ourselves speak above the metallic
clank and clash of shunting trains. At three a.m. Ken phoned the desk and
made his polite enquiry. "What time does the hotel leave for Vancouver?"

For we were impatient to get to the Coast—that by now almost
mythical destination. That first time I went by train, climbing slowly till
dark by the boulder-strewn Bow River and through the forested passes,
looking up with awe at bare crags of the terrible mountains—those
mountains that men from flat country fear and feel oppressed by, though
to me, brought up in view of Mount Leinster, nostalgic and exciting

—and staring, at night-fall, at the last of the sun touching faintly a distant white peak.

And I woke to a new light, the soft, changing light of British Columbia, its green grass and blue distances that drew me like a song. Running still westward to the sea, an Irish melancholy came over me, that pleasant sadness which was one of the seven deadly sins of the Middle Ages. Accidia now took Aida by the hand, enfolded her in a damp and mildewy embrace, stifling her voice so that in Vancouver's Stanley Park I almost forgot her in contemplation of captive king penguins. My employers, bookmen to the backbone, roused me with a telegram: SIT NOT UPON THE ORDERS OF YOUR TAKING BUT MAIL AT ONCE.

Still I was running westward. I took ship for Victoria, some hours away on Vancouver Island, and there checked in at the hotel which is like no other. I had the feeling that they did not care for salesmen, particularly bookmen and bible men.

The bellhop picked up my suitcase. I began to walk toward the main elevator. "No, sir!" he called to me. "Not that one. This way, sir." I turned. He was heading in the opposite direction. I followed him for some distance to a smaller, meaner elevator. We mounted one floor, emerged and walked about a thousand yards or so along a corridor. Then we came to a staircase and walked *down* two floors. From there we began a second long march—I don't know how far, but I would say at a guess at least a mile—along another corridor or tunnel. We might have been in a mine. I had that feeling of being at a great distance from the world.

The bellhop let me into my sample room. It was a vast chamber, carpeted in decaying green felt, and equipped all round with display counters. In a distant corner was the bed I hoped to sleep in. "Good-bye, sir," said the bellhop, pocketing his tip.

I shivered.

Some time later I decided to pick up my mail. Back I went along the tunnel, up those two flights of stairs, along that thousand yards of corridor and down one flight in the little elevator. Somewhat breathless, I asked the desk clerk for my mail.

"It will be delivered to your room, sir."

"But I want to pick it up now."

"I'm sorry, sir. It will be delivered to your room."

I could see that they didn't want fellows like me hanging round where the guests could see us. I turned away, and reluctant to face that descent into the earth again for a while, looked about me for something to do. A notice caught my eye. TO THE GLASS GARDEN. A hand pointed in the direction of a conservatory. I followed it.

There was a fountain like a sort of giantess's *bidet*, ornamented with encaustic tiles. Near it a door opened on a garden, pleasant with lawns and flowers. Another notice pointed into the garden. Out I went and along a path that led to some trees. To one of them was attached a third sign indicating the way to the Glass Garden (whatever it was). I followed. It led me to a blank wall—or wooden fence. I could see no way through it. And so, of the Glass Garden I may not speak properly, for I was not there.

Did I dream this? Was it a trap set for me by the hotel—as paranoia whispered at the time? Or was it a hint, perhaps, that that country I was running to, and still seek, was not to be found? Aida had led me to this, of that I was convinced, so that I realized at last that I was not her favourite. I gave up (or was given up) as a bible man and book salesman.

Months afterwards, on a journey of another sort, a journey made for pleasure, I drove by night farther to the west—to Point No Point on the Pacific Coast of Vancouver Island. As I got out of the car I could hear it, loud as guns in the darkness, the crash of surf from the main deep. I walked down to the shore, behind me the black forests—and behind them the whole of Canada and the world and my life, before me the gleam of the Pacific, the waves running over sand and pebbles to my feet, the heavy drum of the surf beating on my brain. I looked out to the open ocean.

And the sea saith, It is not with me.

1962

Leo Simpson

OF COWS AND MEN

"Cows," said my neighbor Burt, when I moved to the country ten years ago, "can't run downhill. Their front legs are shorter than their back legs, that's why. If you are ever chased by a cow, run down a hill. The same thing applies to bears."

Burt was a gaunt man in his seventies with leathery skin and coal-black hair. His face was as solemn as an undertaker's. My wife and I, being city folk, were grateful for all tips. I kept his information about cows in mind as a truth until one day some two months later, while out with the dog, I chanced to disturb a cow and her new calf. Fortunately I was on a hill. Down the slope I staggered, the cow in pursuit, my overweight mongrel out ahead and making for home at greyhound speed. Before long I was alarmed to hear the thump of hooves getting nearer. Sure enough, the 1,100-pound mother was overtaking me. As it happened, the cow—who could run downhill much faster than she could run uphill, of course

—simply lumbered past in a bored way and veered off to return to her calf.

This experience taught me a lesson. I learned to be skeptical of information from country people. Their sense of humor has elements of irresponsibility in it, as if no punishment can be too harsh for believing everything you hear. Notice that a bear was thrown into the misinformation. Picture the suicidal stupidity of trying to escape downhill from a bear, an animal that is speedier than a cow, much angrier when roused, and rarely bored by a chase. In fact, although I was acting on criminally humorous advice, my life was spared by virtues commonly displayed by cows—mainly economy of effort and mellowness of temperament.

It was Burt who gave me the dog, Andy, as a gift. A good cow dog is essential in cow country, Burt told me, which is true enough. A dog brings the cows home from far distances and keeps them out of your orchard in the fall and your garden in the spring. I had seen how a cow dog works in Burt's fields. His dog, Lassie, running and circling, could gather scattered cows into a cohesive drive with lovely efficiency. The cows always obeyed the dog.

Imagine my bewilderment, as the new owner of a cow dog, when I was awakened one summer morning by the bawling of cows. My garden was full of cows. They seemed as distressed about where they were as I was, as they milled around and trampled lettuce, radishes, corn and beans. I had no idea how to approach cows. I had never been so close to cows in my life, and the questions I asked myself were primitive, the kind early man probably asked himself upon encountering a strange new beast, an auroch, say—the ferocious distant ancestor that evolved into the cow. What is its power? What is its nature? Is it intelligent? I also asked myself this: How come my splendid cow dog, Andy, let these bloody animals in here?

Andy was on the verandah, half-hidden behind the rain barrel, watching the cows in naked fear. When I shouted at him he flinched, pulled himself together a little and charged, desperately, without style, straight at the cows. Most scattered to parts of the garden they hadn't trampled yet. Some spun on the axis of their legs, dipped their heads and attacked Andy. At this point I felt very insecure. Shooing a cow from one place to another is an operation that depends entirely on the cooperation of the cow. Any cow who sees the business as a contest of wills and decides to fight has a fantastic advantage in weight and muscle.

Andy flashed by me, making for the cover of the rain barrel, the whites of his eyes rolling in terror. Not wanting to retreat and leave my garden to be ravaged and certainly not willing to make a movement that the militant cows in the group might feel was threatening, I froze. What the cows wanted, as I discovered by accident, was for me to show them a way out of the garden. More stray cows came up my lane (cows do like to get together as much as possible). As I ran to head off these newcomers, shouting, throwing stones and so on, the main body of cows simply followed me out the garden gate, slowly filtering through the small opening like shoppers going through a supermarket checkout.

Later in the morning I went to see Burt to find out something about these new things in my life, cows. (I often visited him in those days. I don't see him at all now.) He listened to my questions solemnly. Strangely, he didn't seem to know much about cows. (That was when he told me that cows could not run downhill, and neither could bears.)

So I began to learn about the cow on my own. I came to respect and admire her. How noble she is, with her deep brown eyes, her monumental integrity, her stately gait, her swollen undercarriage of nourishment for the world. Cows are very restful to look at. They always return your stare, and quite inoffensively. They stare as a group with immense intentness but without a trace of curiosity. Cows do not need tranquilizers or transcendental meditation. They live in deep tranquility as a permanent state of mind, and a jittery human can actually absorb some of this placidity by hanging around with them, as I did.

Their reputation for stupidity is undeserved. What cows have succeeded in doing over the centuries is confine their lives and interests to essentials—food and comfort and their young. Ralph Waldo Emerson noted this, in a critical spirit, when he said: "A cow does not gaze at the rainbow, or show any interest in the landscape, or a peacock, or the sound of thrushes." That's poor observation on Emerson's part. Cows are very conscious of landscape, as theatrical background, and the advantage of being unaffected by moments of beauty is that you are equally unbothered by anguish. This is the way cows are. Unlike us, their nervous systems are not stretched in pain over an intricate web of worries and fears and anxieties. When a cow becomes upset her reaction is total. Her system seizes up. She stops giving milk. It becomes someone else's responsibility to find out what the problem is and put it right. Every cow functions as her own trade union.

During my life as a cow groupie, I would now and then go to local farmers for information. The result was always unsatisfactory. Farmers do not always respond well to searching questions about cows. Indeed they prefer not to respond at all. Some cows strayed into my lane one autumn afternoon. I didn't recognize the breed and went over to see Burt, who was digging sand out of a culvert with his friend Hal, a stringy man of ninety or so. They both leaned courteously on their shovels to listen to me while I explained that some strays were in my lane and I needed to know what they were so that I could notify the owner. I gave these expert dairy-farmers the technical description in detail—size, shape and face and midriff markings. Burt and Hal went into deep thought together, looking up at the sky and down at the ground, never at each other. Finally, shaking his head, committing himself to the difficult opinion, Burt said: "They sound like cows to me. I'm pretty near certain that's what they are, cows." He said: "Unless'n they're horses."

With the attitude I had then, I thought I understood how country people get a reputation for being slow-witted. I thought I was being tactful when I thanked them for their help.

My farm is in eastern Ontario, roughly between Ottawa and Toronto, where the land can be lush but tends to throw up lots of Precambrian[1] rock. This is renowned cheese-making country, and so my first and principal contact was with dairy cows, who outnumber beef cattle in Ontario by more than two to one. Beef steers are quite different. They have shallower contemplative reserves and seem to think and worry more. Watching a cow chewing and watching you back is blissful. A steer momentarily looks like a cow—there is a flash of similarity, in the way that the austere camel reminds you of a provincial court judge, but that's as far as it goes. The steer, while not exactly skittish, doesn't have the cow's awesome maternal sureness. A steer looks something like a seriously drugged juvenile delinquent—jaws moving on a wad of gum, an indication of latent threat in the stance. He has been castrated by society and he is being ignobly reared for his meat, so he is touchy. Only rookie cow buffs check for an udder. A true devotee can identify a cow by looking into the noble beast's eyes.

I hung around cows for personal reasons. Like the angler going to the trout stream, it was my habit to strike off across the fields after a day's work and unwind with the cows, listening to them crop grass—a satisfying rip, like tearing cloth—and exchanging long tranquilizing stares with different groups. Still, it was natural that I should be able to recognize Holsteins by their color after a while—black and white—and the other main dairy breeds: Ayrshires, Jerseys, Guernseys, Brown Swiss and Dual-purpose Shorthorns (a special kind of cow bred both for milk and meat).

A cow is a self-contained production factory, uniquely served by four stomach compartments that enable the animal to bring swallowed food back into her mouth to be chewed and swallowed again. (Think about what a cow is *tasting* the next time you see one meditatively chewing her cud.) As the food travels through her it seems to grow in bulk rather than be assimilated into the body, judging by the amount of manure she leaves behind. It's not unusual for a good Holstein, the commonest breed in

1. Of geological period predating the Cambrian era (the era of fossil-bearing rock formation).

Canada, to yield ten thousand quarts of milk in a year, as well as about thirty thousand pounds of high-quality manure.

Holsteins have been bred for dairy purposes for more than two thousand years and were first imported to North America by Dutch settlers in the late eighteenth century. They are known for their high milk production and low butterfat. Like most of their sisters, they no longer have horns (calves are de-horned while still very young, though some breeds have been rendered hornless through selective breeding).

Cows are almost eternally pregnant. They can't give milk unless they have given birth, so cows are usually bred at between fifteen and twenty-seven months old and once a year after that. After the birth of a calf a cow gives milk for about ten months. Of course they are not normally milked by hand anymore, though I am told that is the secret of building strong wrists for baseball or tennis. Most farmers now use milking machines, the effects of which are noticed by close neighbors and passing motorists in the form of relentless static on the radio during chore times.

Before settlement, no cows were native to North America, but Canada can claim the oldest dairy breed in the Western Hemisphere. Known worldwide as Canadian cattle and found mostly in Quebec, they bear a striking resemblance to the original Guernseys and Jerseys of the Channel Islands because they all were bred from the same French stock, now extinct in Europe. Canadian cattle are direct descendants of animals that came from Normandy and Brittany, beginning as long ago as 1518 when Baron de Lery imported them to Sable Island, Nova Scotia, in France's first attempt to establish itself in North America. Jacques Cartier brought more on his third voyage in 1541, and Samuel de Champlain ferried regular boatloads to the French settlements in 1608–10. Fifty years later Louis XIV ordered that a shipment of the best cows of Normandy be sent to New France. In 1667 Canada had a cow population of more than three thousand, all French nobility, every one an aristocrat.

A word of warning: it is not good to know too much about cows if you are an admirer. Watch them from a distance and you will receive a reward of pure joy. They like picturesque country. They like to strike pastoral poses and to reproduce Constable paintings[2] in nature. No movie director could arrange cows in a field as attractively as they arrange themselves. If there is a hill, some cows will lie on the slope—all facing the same way—while their calves play. If there is a pond, other cows will stand knee-deep in the water so that they are reflected upside-down. Cows like to pretend to be statues against the setting sun, letting their long purple shadows fall on the pastureland. On a summer morning they move through the ground mist as if walking on clouds. A distant

---

2. The reference is to John Constable (1776-1837), celebrated English painter of landscapes.

relationship is your best bet if you like cows. Do not become too closely involved, as I did, depending on them for peace of mind, respecting their nobility and assuming that cows can respect us to the end, maybe not as friends but as partners.

When I began to see the final, bleak answers to my city-man questions, I thought I would give Burt a last chance to treat me as an equal. I found him leaning on a gate and watching Lassie driving the herd toward the barns. The cows moved unhurriedly in the proper direction while Lassie trotted here and there behind them. My dog Andy was at home on the verandah, asleep behind the rain barrel.

"I was wondering what happens to cows in the end, when they can't give any more milk or calves," I said. "Is it old dairy cows who come under the heading of utility grade beef in the United States? That's Canada black brand here, Burt."

"I can't tell about that," Burt said solemnly, a normal answer from him. "I'll tell you this, though. My biggest problem with cows is diarrhea. I have to give them special medicine to cure it. If you see any cows of mine with diarrhea, give me a call."

That was his last chance. I don't ask Burt for advice and information anymore. I would give him back his dog if I could.

1979

Bruno Bettelheim

A VICTIM

Many students of discrimination are aware that the victim often reacts in ways as undesirable as the action of the aggressor. Less attention is paid to this because it is easier to excuse a defendant than an offender, and because they assume that once the aggression stops the victim's reactions will stop too. But I doubt if this is of real service to the persecuted. His main interest is that the persecution cease. But that is less apt to happen if he lacks a real understanding of the phenomenon of persecution, in which victim and persecutor are inseparably interlocked.

Let me illustrate with the following example: in the winter of 1938 a Polish Jew murdered the German attaché in Paris, vom Rath. The Gestapo used the event to step up anti-Semitic actions, and in the camp new hardships were inflicted on Jewish prisoners. One of these was an order barring them from the medical clinic unless the need for treatment had originated in work accident.

Nearly all prisoners suffered from frostbite which often led to gangrene and then amputation. Whether or not a Jewish prisoner was admitted to the clinic to prevent such a fate depended on the whim of an SS private. On reaching the clinic entrance, the prisoner explained the nature of his ailment to the SS man, who then decided if he should get treatment or not.

I too suffered from frostbite. At first I was discouraged from trying to get medical care by the fate of Jewish prisoners whose attempts had ended up in no treatment, only abuse. Finally things got worse and I was afraid that waiting longer would mean amputation. So I decided to make the effort.

When I got to the clinic, there were many prisoners lined up as usual, a score of them Jews suffering from severe frostbite. The main topic of discussion was one's chances of being admitted to the clinic. Most Jews had planned their procedure in detail. Some thought it best to stress their service in the German army during World War I: wounds received or decorations won. Others planned to stress the severity of their frostbite. A few decided it was best to tell some "tall story," such as that an SS officer had ordered them to report at the clinic.

Most of them seemed convinced that the SS man on duty would not see through their schemes. Eventually they asked me about my plans. Having no definite ones, I said I would go by the way the SS man dealt with other Jewish prisoners who had frostbite like me, and proceed accordingly. I doubted how wise it was to follow a preconceived plan, because it was hard to anticipate the reactions of a person you didn't know.

The prisoners reacted as they had at other times when I had voiced similar ideas on how to deal with the SS. They insisted that one SS man was like another, all equally vicious and stupid. As usual, any frustration was immediately discharged against the person who caused it, or was nearest at hand. So in abusive terms they accused me of not wanting to share my plan with them, or of intending to use one of theirs; it angered them that I was ready to meet the enemy unprepared.

No Jewish prisoner ahead of me in the line was admitted to the clinic. The more a prisoner pleaded, the more annoyed and violent the SS became. Expressions of pain amused him; stories of previous services rendered to Germany outraged him. He proudly remarked that he could not be taken in by Jews, that fortunately the time had passed when Jews could reach their goal by lamentations.

When my turn came he asked me in a screeching voice if I knew that work accidents were the only reason for admitting Jews to the clinic, and if I came because of such an accident. I replied that I knew the rules, but that I couldn't work unless my hands were freed of the dead flesh. Since prisoners were not allowed to have knives, I asked to have the dead flesh cut away. I tried to be matter-of-fact, avoiding pleading, deference, or arrogance. He replied: "If that's all you want, I'll tear the flesh off myself."

And he started to pull at the festering skin. Because it did not come off as easily as he may have expected, or for some other reason, he waved me into the clinic.

Inside, he gave me a malevolent look and pushed me into the treatment room. There he told the prisoner orderly to attend to the wound. While this was being done, the guard watched me closely for signs of pain but I was able to suppress them. As soon as the cutting was over, I started to leave. He showed surprise and asked why I didn't wait for further treatment. I said I had gotten the service I asked for, at which he told the orderly to make an exception and treat my hand. After I had left the room, he called me back and gave me a card entitling me to further treatment, and admittance to the clinic without inspection at the entrance.

* * *

Because my behavior did not correspond to what he expected of Jewish prisoners on the basis of his projection, he could not use his prepared defenses against being touched by the prisoner's plight. Since I did not act as the dangerous Jew was expected to, I did not activate the anxieties that went with his stereotype. Still he did not altogether trust me, so he continued to watch while I received treatment.

Throughout these dealings, the SS felt uneasy with me, though he did not unload on me the annoyance his uneasiness aroused. Perhaps he watched me closely because he expected that sooner or later I would slip up and behave the way his projected image of the Jew was expected to act. This would have meant that his delusional creation had become real.

1960

Paul Fussell

MY WAR[1]

* * *

My war is virtually synonymous with my life. I entered the war when I was nineteen, and I have been in it ever since. Melville's Ishmael[2] says that a whale-ship was his Yale College and his Harvard. An infantry division was mine, the 103rd, whose dispirited personnel wore a colorful green and yellow cactus on their left shoulders. These hillbillies and Okies, drop-outs and used-car salesmen and petty criminals were my teachers and friends.

1. Excerpted from a longer essay, also entitled "My War," in which Fussell explores and explains what he calls his "dark, ironical, flip view" of World War II and its effect, afterward, on his life and thinking.
2. Narrator of Herman Melville's novel *Moby-Dick* (1851).

How did an upper-middle-class young gentleman find himself in so unseemly a place? Why wasn't he in the Navy, at least, or in the OSS or Air Corps administration or editing the *Stars and Stripes* or being a general's aide?[3] The answer is comic: at the age of twenty I found myself leading forty riflemen over the Vosges Mountains[4] and watching them torn apart by German artillery and machine-guns because when I was sixteen, in junior college, I was fat and flabby, with feminine tits and a big behind. For years the thing I'd hated most about school was gym, for there I was obliged to strip and shower communally. Thus I chose to join the R.O.T.C. (infantry, as it happened) because that was a way to get out of gym, which meant you never had to take off your clothes and invite —indeed, compel—ridicule. You rationalized by noting that this was 1939 and that a little "military training" might not, in the long run, be wasted. Besides, if you worked up to be a cadet officer, you got to wear a Sam Browne belt, from which depended a nifty saber.

When I went on to college, it was natural to continue my technique for not exposing my naked person, and luckily my college had an infantry R.O.T.C. unit, where I was welcomed as something of an experienced hand. This was in 1941. When the war began for the United States, college students were solicited by various "programs" of the navy and marine corps and coast guard with plans for transforming them into officers. But people enrolled in the R.O.T.C. unit were felt to have committed themselves already. They had opted for the infantry, most of them all unaware, and that's where they were going to stay. Thus while shrewder friends were enrolling in Navy V-1[5] or signing up for the pacific exercises of the Naval Japanese Language Program or the Air Corps Meteorological Program, I signed up for the Infantry Enlisted Reserve Corps, an act guaranteeing me one extra semester in college before I was called. After basic training, advancement to officer training was promised, and that seemed a desirable thing, even if the crossed rifles on the collar did seem to betoken some hard physical exertion and discomfort —marching, sleeping outdoors, that sort of thing. But it would help "build you up," and besides officers, even in the Infantry, got to wear those wonderful pink trousers and receive constant salutes.

It was such imagery of future grandeur that in spring, 1943, sustained me through eighteen weeks of basic training in 100-degree heat at dreary Camp Roberts, California, where to toughen us, it was said, water was forbidden from 8:00 a.m. to 5:00 p.m. ("water discipline," this was called). Within a few weeks I'd lost all my flab and with it the whole ironic

3. I.e., all comparably safe and "intellectual" wartime assignments; specifically, the OSS, or Office of Strategic Services, was the American military-civilian intelligence organization, while The *Stars and Stripes* was a popular illustrated magazine put out for the information and enjoyment of the armed forces.

4. Mountains in the north of France, where Fussell's troops underwent their hardest fighting.

5. An intensive college-training program for naval officers.

"reason" I found myself there at all. It was abundantly clear already that "infantry" had been a big mistake: it was not just stupid and boring and bloody, it was athletic, and thus not at all for me. But supported by vanity and pride I somehow managed to march thirty-five miles and tumble through the obstacle course, and a few months later I found myself at the Infantry School, Fort Benning, Georgia, where, training to become an officer, I went through virtually the same thing over again. As a Second Lieutenant of Infantry I "graduated" in the spring of 1944 and was assigned to the 103rd Division at Camp Howze, Texas, the local equivalent of Camp Roberts, only worse: Roberts had white-painted two-storey clapboard barracks, Howze one-storey tar-paper shacks. But the heat was the same, and the boredom, and the local whore-culture, and the hillbilly songs:

> Who's that gal with the red dress on?
> Some folks call her Dinah.
> She stole my heart away,
> Down in Carolina.

The 103rd Division had never been overseas, and all the time I was putting my rifle platoon through its futile exercises we were being prepared for the invasion of southern France, which followed the landings in Normandy.[6] Of course we didn't know this, and assumed from the training ("water discipline" again) that we were destined for the South Pacific. There were some exercises involving towed gliders that seemed to portend nothing at all but self-immolation, we were so inept with these devices. In October, 1944, we were all conveyed by troop transports to Marseilles.[7]

It was my first experience of abroad, and my life-long affair with France dates from the moment I first experienced such un-American phenomena as: formal manners and a respect for the language; a well-founded skepticism; the pollarded plane trees on the Av. R. Schuman; the red wine and real bread; the pissoirs[8] in the streets; the international traffic signs and the visual public language hinting a special French understanding of things: Hôtel de Ville, Defense d'afficher;[9] the smell of Turkish tobacco when one has been brought up on Virginia and Burley. An intimation of what we might be opposing was supplied by the aluminum Vichy coinage. On one side, a fasces and Etat Français. No more Republic. On the other, Liberté, Egalité, Fraternité replaced by Travail (as in Arbeit Macht Frei), Famille, and Patrie (as in Vaterland).[1] But before we had time to

---

6. On June 6, 1944, British and American forces began their invasion of Nazi-occupied Europe by crossing the English Channel and landing on the beaches at Normandy.

7. Large seaport city in southern France.

8. Public urinals—a feature of French cities.

9. "Town Hall; Post No Bills."

1. The "Vichy government" of France during World War II was essentially the Nazis' means of controlling that country; its coinage was aluminum because other materials were pressed into war service. As Fussell describes the coins, one side bore the ancient Roman symbol of authority (the "fasces"),

contemplate all this, we were moving rapidly northeast. After a truck ride up the Rhone Valley, still pleasant with girls and flowers and wine, our civilized period came to an abrupt end. On the night of November 11 (nice irony there) we were introduced into the line at St. Dié, in Alsace.[2]

We were in "combat." I find the word embarrassing, carrying as it does false chivalric overtones (as in "single combat"). But synonyms are worse: *fighting* is not accurate, because much of the time you are being shelled, which is not fighting but suffering; *battle* is too high and remote; *in action* is a euphemism suited more to dire telegrams than description. "Combat" will have to do, and my first hours of it I recall daily, even now. They fueled, and they still fuel, my view of things.

Everyone knows that a night relief is among the most difficult of infantry maneuvers. But we didn't know it, and in our innocence we expected it to go according to plan. We and the company we were replacing were cleverly and severely shelled: it was as if the Germans a few hundred feet away could see us in the dark and through the thick pine growth. When the shelling finally stopped, at about midnight, we realized that, although near the place we were supposed to be, until daylight we would remain hopelessly lost. The order came down to stop where we were, lie down among the trees, and get some sleep. We would finish the relief at first light. Scattered over several hundred yards, the two hundred and fifty of us in F Company lay down in a darkness so thick we could see nothing at all. Despite the terror of our first shelling (and several people had been hit), we slept as soundly as babes. At dawn I awoke, and what I saw all around were numerous objects I'd miraculously not tripped over in the dark. These objects were dozens of dead German boys in greenish-gray uniforms, killed a day or two before by the company we were relieving. If darkness had hidden them from us, dawn disclosed them with open eyes and greenish-white faces like marble, still clutching their rifles and machine-pistols in their seventeen-year-old hands, fixed where they had fallen. (For the first time I understood the German phrase for the war-dead: *die Gefallenen*.[3]) Michelangelo could have made something beautiful out of these forms, in the *Dying Gaul* tradition,[4] and I was startled to find that in a way I couldn't understand, at first they struck me as beautiful. But after a moment, no feeling but shock and horror. My adolescent illusions, largely intact to that moment, fell away all at once, and I suddenly knew I was not and never would be in a world that was reasonable or just. The scene was less apocalyptic than shabbily ironic: it sorted so ill with modern popular assumptions about the idea of progress and attendant improvements in public health, social welfare, and social

---

which the Italian dictator Mussolini had made his symbol, and the words "French State"; on the other side, the French motto "Liberty, Equality, Brotherhood" was replaced by "Work" (as in the Nazi slogan "Work Makes Freedom"), "Family," and

"Country" (as in the German "Fatherland").
2. In northern France.
3. "The Fallen."
4. A reference to a starkly idealized statue by the great Renaissance artist.

justice. To transform guiltless boys into cold marble after passing them through unbearable fear and humiliation and pain and contempt seemed to do them an interesting injustice. I decided to ponder these things. In 1917, shocked by the Battle of the Somme and recovering from neurasthenia, Wilfred Owen[5] was reading a life of Tennyson. He wrote his mother: "Tennyson, it seems, was always a great child. So should I have been but for Beaumont Hamel." So should I have been but for St. Dié.

After that, one day was much like another: attack at dawn, run and fall and crawl and sweat and worry and shoot and be shot at and cower from mortar shells, always keeping up a jaunty carriage in front of one's platoon; and at night, "consolidate" the objective, usually another hill, sometimes a small town, and plan the attack for the next morning. Before we knew it we'd lost half the company, and we all realized then that for us there would be no way out until the war ended but sickness, wounds, or oblivion. And the war would end only as we pressed our painful daily advance. Getting it over was our sole motive. Yes, we knew about the Jews. But our skins seemed to us more valuable at the time.

The word for the German defense all along was clever, a word that never could have been applied to our procedures. It was my first experience, to be repeated many times in later years, of the cunning ways of Europe versus the blunter ways of the New World. Although manned largely by tired thirty-year-old veterans (but sharp enough to have got out of Normandy alive), old men, and crazy youths, the German infantry was officered superbly, and their defense, which we experienced for many months, was disciplined and orderly. My people would have run, or at least "snaked off." But the Germans didn't, until the very end. Their uniforms were a scandal—rags and beat-up boots and unauthorized articles—but somehow they held together. Nazis or not, they did themselves credit. Lacking our lavish means, they compensated by patience and shrewdness. Not until well after the war did I discover that many times when they unaccountably located us hidden in deep woods and shelled us accurately, they had done so by inferring electronically the precise positions of the radios over which we innocently conversed.

As the war went on, the destruction of people became its sole means. I felt sorry for the Germans I saw killed in quantity everywhere—along the roads, in cellars, on roof-tops—for many reasons. They were losing, for one thing, and their deaths meant nothing, though they had been persuaded that resistance might "win the war." And they were so pitifully dressed and accoutered: that was touching. Boys with raggedy ad hoc uniforms and *Panzerfausts*[6] and too few comrades. What were they doing? They were killing themselves; and for me, who couldn't imagine

---

5. British poet (1893–1918), killed in World War I; the Battle of the Somme was one of that war's worst battles; Tennyson, the great Victorian poet (1809–92).

6. Literally, "tank-fists," i.e., hand-carried antitank rockets.

being killed, for people my age voluntarily to get themselves killed caused my mouth to drop open.

Irony describes the emotion, whatever it is, occasioned by perceiving some great gulf, half-comic, half-tragic, between what one expects and what one finds. It's not quite "disillusion," but it's adjacent to it. My experience in the war was ironic because my innocence before had prepared me to encounter in it something like the same reasonableness that governed prewar life. This, after all, was the tone dominating the American relation to the war: talk of "the future," allotments and bond purchases carefully sent home,[7] hopeful fantasies of "the postwar world." I assumed, in short, that everyone would behave according to the clear advantages offered by reason. I had assumed that in war, like chess, when you were beaten you "resigned"; that when outnumbered and outgunned you retreated; that when you were surrounded you surrendered. I found out differently, and with a vengeance. What I found was people obeying fatuous and murderous "orders" for no reason I could understand, killing themselves because someone "told them to," prolonging the war when it was hopelessly lost because—because it was unreasonable to do so. It was my introduction to the shakiness of civilization. It was my first experience of the profoundly irrational element, and it made ridiculous all talk of plans and preparations for the future and goodwill and intelligent arrangements. Why did the red-haired young German machine-gunner firing at us in the woods not go on living—marrying, going to university, going to the beach, laughing, smiling—but keep firing long after he had made his point, and require us to kill him with a grenade?

Before we knew it it was winter, and the winter in 1944–1945 was the coldest in Europe for twenty-five years. For the ground troops conditions were unspeakable, and even the official history admits the disaster, imputing the failure to provide adequate winter clothing—analogous to the similar German oversight when the Russian winter of 1941–1942 surprised the planners[8]—to optimism, innocence, and "confidence":

> Confidence born of the rapid sweep across Europe in the summer of 1944 and the conviction on the part of many that the successes of Allied arms would be rewarded by victory before the onset of winter contributed to the unpreparedness for winter combat.

The result of thus ignoring the injunction "Be Prepared" was 64,008 casualties from "cold injury"—not wounds but pneumonia and trenchfoot. The official history sums up: "This constitutes more than four 15,000-man divisions. Approximately 90 percent of cold casualties involved riflemen and there were about 4,000 riflemen per infantry division. Thus closer to 13 divisions were critically disabled for combat." We

7. "Allotments": portions of a soldier's pay sent home to his family; "bond" refers to "War Bonds" (now "U. S. Savings Bonds").

8. A drastically heavy winter was one cause of the Germans' failure to conquer Russia.

can appreciate those figures by recalling that the invasion of Normany was initially accomplished by only six divisions (nine if we add the airborne). Thus crucial were little things like decent mittens and gloves, fur-lined parkas, thermal underwear—all of which any normal peacetime hiker or skier would demand as protection against prolonged exposure. But "the winter campaign in Europe was fought by most combat personnel in a uniform that did not give proper protection": we wore silly long overcoats, right out of the nineteenth century; thin field jackets, designed to convey an image of manliness at Fort Bragg; and dress wool trousers. We wore the same shirts and huddled under the same blankets as Pershing's troops in the expedition against Pancho Villa in 1916.[9] Of the 64,008 who suffered "cold injury" I was one. During February, 1945, I was back in various hospitals for a month with pneumonia. I told my parents it was flu.

That month away from the line helped me survive for four weeks more but it broke the rhythm and, never badly scared before, when I returned to the line early in March I found for the first time that I was terrified, unwilling to take the chances which before had seemed rather sporting. My month of safety had renewed my interest in survival, and I was psychologically and morally ill-prepared to lead my platoon in the great Seventh Army attack of March 15, 1945. But lead it I did, or rather push it, staying as far in the rear as was barely decent. And before the day was over I had been severely rebuked by a sharp-eyed lieutenant-colonel who threatened court martial if I didn't pull myself together. Before that day was over I was sprayed with the contents of a soldier's torso when I was lying behind him and he knelt to fire at a machine-gun holding us up: he was struck in the heart, and out of the holes in the back of his field jacket flew little clouds of tissue, blood, and powdered cloth. Near him another man raised himself to fire, but the machine-gun caught him in the mouth, and as he fell he looked back at me with surprise, blood and teeth dribbling out onto the leaves. He was one to whom early on I had given the Silver Star for heroism, and he didn't want to let me down.

As if in retribution for my cowardice, in the late afternoon, near Engwiller, Alsace, clearing a woods full of Germans cleverly dug in, my platoon was raked by shells from an 88, and I was hit in the back and leg by shell fragments. They felt like red-hot knives going in, but I was as interested in the few quiet moans, like those of a hurt child drifting off to sleep, of my thirty-seven-year-old platoon sergeant—we'd been together since Camp Howze—killed instantly by the same shell. We were lying together, and his immediate neighbor on the other side, a lieutenant in charge of a section of heavy machine-guns, was killed instantly too. And my platoon was virtually wiped away. I was in disgrace, I was hurt, I was

9. Referring to General John Pershing's unsuccessful punitive expedition against the Mexican revolutionary Francisco ("Pancho") Villa.

clearly expendable—while I lay there the supply sergeant removed my issue wristwatch to pass on to my replacement—and I was twenty years old.

I bore up all right while being removed from "the field" and passed back through the first-aid stations where I was known. I was deeply on morphine, and managed brave smiles as called for. But when I got to the evacuation hospital thirty miles behind the lines and was coming out from the anesthetic of my first operation, all my affectations of control collapsed, and I did what I'd wanted to do for months. I cried, noisily and publicly, and for hours. I was the scandal of the ward. There were lots of tears back there: in the operating room I saw a nurse dissolve in shoulder-shaking sobs when a boy died with great stertorous gasps on the operating table she was attending. That was the first time I'd seen anyone cry in the whole European Theater of Operations, and I must have cried because I felt that there, out of "combat," tears were licensed. I was crying because I was ashamed and because I'd let my men be killed and because my sergeant had been killed and because I recognized as never before that he might have been me and that statistically if in no other way he was me, and that I had been killed too. But ironically I had saved my life by almost losing it, for my leg wound providentially became infected, and by the time it was healed and I was ready for duty again, the European war was over, and I journeyed back up through a silent Germany to re-join my reconstituted platoon "occupying" a lovely Tyrolean valley near Innsbruck.[1] For the infantry there was still the Japanese war to sweat out, and I was destined for it, despite the dramatic gash in my leg. But thank God the Bomb[2] was dropped while I was on my way there, with the result that I can write this.

* * *

1982

1. In Austria.
2. The atomic bombs dropped on Japanese cities in 1945, which effectively ended the war in the Pacific.

QUESTIONS

1. *This is a basically chronological narrative, but on p. 44 he begins an interruption that takes up half of the discussion. Is the interruption justified? What is the point? or points?*
2. *Fussell says that he first realized the shakiness of civilization when he saw that the Germans were resisting in obedience to fatuous and murderous orders. He then implies that the civilized thing to do would have been to stop fighting, and this implication would seem to be supported by his description of his own behavior in the attack of March 15. Yet the reasons he gives for crying at the evacuation hospital are more complicated. Explain whether these reasons modify his idea of civilization or whether he has shifted to a larger, perhaps more basic topic.*

3. *Check your dictionary for a definition of* irony; *compare it with Fussell's (p. 46). What does he accomplish by classifying it, as he does, as an emotion?*
4. *Elsewhere Fussell describes the speaker in this account of his war as a "pissed-off infantryman." What do you find in his account that supports that self-identification? Presuming that not all of what you find will be equally important, what seems essential?*
5. *In Donald Pearce's* Journal of a War *(p. 105) you have the experience of another platoon leader during the same winter in another part of the same war. Compare the two. Is Pearce's speaker a "pissed-off infantryman"?*

Lillian Hellman

"TURTLE"

* * *

The day I remember best was in the first spring I owned the place.[1] I took Salud, the large poodle, and four of his puppies on an early morning walk to the lake. As we reached the heavily wooded small hill opposite the lake, Salud stopped, wheeled sharply, ran into the woods, and then slowly backed down to the road. The puppies and I went past him to the lake and I whistled for him, sure that he had been attracted by a woodchuck. But when I looked back he was immobile on the road, as if he had taken a deep breath and had not let it out. I called to him but he did not move. I called again in a command tone that he had never before disobeyed. He made an obedient movement of his head and front legs, stared at me, and turned back. I had never seen a dog stand paralyzed and, as I went back toward him, I remembered old tales of snakes and the spell they cast. I stopped to pick up a heavy stick and a rock, frightened of seeing the snake. As I heard Salud make a strange bark, I threw the rock over his head and into the woods, yelling at him to follow me. As the rock hit the ground, there was a heavy movement straight in front of the dog. Sure now that it was a snake about to strike, I ran toward Salud, grabbed his collar, and stumbled with the weight of him. He pulled away from me and moved slowly toward the sound. As I picked myself up, I saw a large,

---

1. A nineteenth-century house with extensive formal gardens which the author bought in 1940 with royalties from her successful play *The Little Foxes*.

possibly three-foot round shell move past him and go slowly toward the water. It was a large turtle.

Salud moved with caution behind the turtle and as I stood, amazed at the picture of the dog and the slowly moving shell, the dog jumped in front of the turtle, threw out a paw, and the jaws of the turtle clamped down on the leg. Salud was silent, then he reared back and a howl of pain came from him that was like nothing I had ever heard before. I don't know how long it took me to act, but I came down hard with my stick on the turtle's tail, and he was gone into the water. Salud's leg was a mess but he was too big for me to carry, so I ran back to the house for Fred and together we carried him to a vet. A week later, he was well enough to limp for the rest of his life.

Hammett[2] was in California for a few weeks and so I went alone almost every day to the lake in an attempt to see the turtle again, remembering that when I was a child in New Orleans I had gone each Saturday with my aunt to the French market to buy supplies for her boardinghouse. There had been two butchers in the market who had no thumbs, the thumbs having been taken off as they handled snapping turtles.

Hammett came back to the farm upset and angry to find his favorite dog was crippled. He said he had always known there were snappers in the lake, and snakes as well, but now he thought we ought to do something, and so he began his usual thorough research. The next few weeks brought books and government publications on how to trap turtles and strange packages began to arrive: large wire-mesh cages, meant for something else but stared at for days until Hammett decided how to alter them; giant fishhooks; extra heavy, finely made rope; and a book on tying knots. We both read about the origin of snapping turtles, but it didn't seem to me the accounts said very much: a guess that they were the oldest living species that had remained unchanged, that their jaws were powerful and of great danger to an enemy, that they could do nothing if turned on their backs, and the explanation of why my turtle had come out of the woods—each spring the female laid eggs on land, sat on them each day, and took the chance that the hatched babies would find their way to water.

One day, a month later perhaps—there was never any hurrying Hammett when he had made up his mind to learn about something—we went to the lake carrying the wire cages, the giant fishhooks, fish heads and smelly pieces of meat that he had put in the sun a few days before. I grew bored, as I often did, with the slow precision which was part of Dash's doing anything, and walked along the banks of the lake as he tied the bait inside the traps, baited the hooks, and rowed out with them to find heavy overhanging branches to attach them to.

---

2. Dashiell Hammett, author of *The Thin Man* and other masterpieces of the hardboiled detective story.

He had finished with one side of the lake, and had rowed himself beyond my view to the south side, when I decided on a swim. As I swam slowly toward the raft, I saw that one limb of a sassafras tree was swinging wildly over the water, some distance from me. Sitting on the raft, I watched it until I saw that the movement was caused by the guyline that held one of the hooks Hammett had tied to the branch. I shouted at Hammett that he had caught a turtle and he called back that couldn't be true so fast, and I called back that he was to come for me quick because I was frightened and not to argue.

As he came around the bend of the lake, he grinned at me.

"Drunk this early?"

I pointed to the swinging branch. He forgot about me and rowed over very fast. I saw him haul at the line, having trouble lifting it, stand up in the boat, haul again, and then slowly drop the line. He rowed back to the raft.

"It's a turtle all right. Get in. I need help."

I took the oars as he stood up to take the line from the tree. The line was so heavy that as he moved to attach it to the stern of the rowboat he toppled backward. I put an oar into the center of his back.

He stared at me, rubbing his back. "Remind me," he said and tied the line to the stern. Then he took the oars from me.

"Remind you of what?"

"Never to save me. I've been meaning to tell you for a long time."

When we reached the boat, we detached the rope and began to pull the rope on land. A turtle, larger than the one I had seen with Salud, was hauled up and I jumped back as the head came shooting out. Dash leaned down, grabbed the tail, and threw the turtle on its back.

"The hook is in fine. It'll hold. Go back and get the car for me."

I said, "I don't like to leave you alone, you shouldn't be handling that thing—"

"Go on," he said. "A turtle isn't a woman. I'll be safe."

We took the turtle home tied to the back bumper, dragging it through the dirt of the mile to the house. Dash went to the toolhouse for an axe, came back with it and a long heavy stick. He turned the turtle on its stomach, handed me the stick, and said, "Stand far back, hold the stick out, and wait until he snaps at it."

I did that, the turtle did snap, and the axe came down. But Dash missed because the turtle, seeing his arm, quickly withdrew his head. We tried five or six times. It was a hot day and that's why I thought I was sweating and, anyway, I never was comfortable with Hammett when he was doing something that didn't work.

He said, "Try once more."

I put the stick out, the turtle didn't take it, then did, and as he did, I moved my hand down the stick thinking that I could hold it better. The turtle dropped the stick and made the fastest move I have ever seen for my hand. I jumped back and the stick bruised my leg. Hammett put down the axe, took the stick from me, shook his head and said, "Go lie down."

I said I wasn't going to and he said I was to go somewhere and get out of his way. I said I wasn't going to do that either, that he was in a bad temper with me only because he couldn't kill the turtle with the axe.

"I am going to shoot it. But that's not my reason for bad temper. We've got some talking to do, you and I, it's been a long time."

"Talk now."

"No. I'm busy. I want you out of the way."

He took my arm, moved me to the kitchen steps, pushed me down and went into the house for a rifle. When he came out he put a piece of meat in front of the turtle's head and got behind it. We waited for a long time. Finally, the head did come out to stare at the meat and Hammett's gun went off. The shot was a beauty, just slightly behind the eyes. As I ran toward them the turtle's head convulsed in a forward movement, the feet carried the shell forward in a kind of heavy leap. I leaned down close and Hammett said, "Don't go too near. He isn't dead."

Then he picked up the axe and came down very hard on the neck, severing the head to the skin.

"That's odd," he said. "The shot didn' kill it, and yet it went through the brain. Very odd."

He grabbed the turtle by the tail and carried it up the long flight of steps to the kitchen. We found some newspapers and put the turtle on top of the coal stove that wasn't used much anymore except in the sausage-making season.

I said, "Now we'll have to learn about cutting it for soup."

Dash nodded. "O.K. But it's a long job. Let's wait until tomorrow."

I left a note under Helen's door—it was her day off and she had gone to New York—warning her there was a turtle sitting on the stove and not to be frightened. Then I telephoned my Aunt Jenny in New Orleans to get the recipe for the good soup of my childhood and she said I was to stay away from live turtles and go back to fine embroidery like a nice lady.

The next morning, coming down at six to help Fred milk the cows, I forgot about the turtle until I started down the kitchen steps and saw blood. Then, thinking it was the blood that we had spilled carrying the turtle into the house the evening before, I went on toward the barns. When I came back at eight, Helen asked me what I wanted for breakfast, she had made corn bread, and what had I meant by a turtle on the stove?

Going up to have a bath, I called back, "Just what I said. It's a turtle on the stove and you must know about snappers from your childhood."

After a few minutes she came upstairs to stare at me in the bathtub. "There ain't no turtle. But there's a mess of blood."

"On top of the coal stove," I said. "Just go have a look."

"I had a lot of looks. There ain't no turtle on top a stove in this house."

"Go wake Mr. Hammett," I said, "right away."

"I wouldn't like to do that," she said. "I don't like to wake men."

I went running down to the kitchen, and then fast back upstairs to Hammett's room, and shook him hard.

"Get up right away. The turtle's gone."

He turned over to stare at me. "You drink too much in the morning."

I said, *The turtle's gone.*

He came down to the kitchen in a few minutes, stared at the stove, and turned to Helen. "Did you clean the floor?"

"Yes," she said, "it was all nasty. Look at the steps."

He stared at the steps that led to the cellar and out to the lawn. Then he moved slowly down the steps, following the path of blood spots, and out into the orchard. Near the orchard, planted many years before I owned the house, was a large rock garden, over half an acre of rare trees and plants, rising steep above the house entrance. Hammett turned toward it, following a path around the orchard. He said, "Once, when I worked for Pinkerton,[3] I found a stolen ferris wheel for a traveling country fair. Then I lost the ferris wheel and, as far as I know, nobody ever found it again."

I said, "A turtle is not a ferris wheel. Somebody took the turtle."

"Who?"

"I don't know. Got a theory?"

"The turtle moved himself."

"I don't like what you're saying. He was dead last night. Stone dead."

"Look," he said.

He was pointing into the rock garden. Salud and three poodle puppies were sitting on a large rock, staring at something in a bush. We ran toward the garden. Hammett told the puppies to go away and parted the branches of the bush. The turtle, sidling in an effort at movement, was trying to leave the bush, its head dangling from one piece of neck skin.

"My God," we both said at the same time and stood watching the turtle for the very long time it took to move a foot away from us. Then it stopped and its back legs stiffened. Salud, quiet until now, immediately leaped on it and his two puppies, yapping, leaped after him. Salud licked the blood from the head and the turtle moved his front legs. I grabbed Salud's collar and threw him too hard against a rock.

Hammett said, "The turtle can't bite him now. He's dead."

I said, "How do you know?" He picked up the turtle by the tail. "What are you going to do?"

"Take it back to the kitchen."

I said, "Let's take it to the lake. It's earned its life."

"It's dead. It's been dead since yesterday."

3. An agency that provided guards and private detectives.

"No. Or maybe it was dead and now it isn't."

"The resurrection? You're a hard woman for an ex-Catholic," he said, moving off.

I was behind him as he came into the kitchen, threw the turtle on a marble slab. I heard Helen say, "My goodness, the good Lord help us all."

Hammett took down one of the butcher knives. He moved his lips as if rehearsing what he had read. Then he separated the leg meat from the shell, cutting expertly around the joints. The other leg moved as the knife went in.

Helen went out of the kitchen and I said, "You know very well that I help with the butchering of the animals here and don't like talk about how distasteful killing is by people who are willing to eat what is killed for them. But this is different. This is something else. We shouldn't touch it. It has earned its life."

He put down the knife. "O.K. Whatever you want."

We both went into the living room and he picked up a book. After an hour I said, "Then how does one define life?"

He said, "Lilly, I'm too old for that stuff."

Toward afternoon, I telephoned the New York Zoological Society of which I was a member. I had a hard time being transferred to somebody who knew about turtles. When I finished, the young voice said, "Yes, the *Chelydra serpentina*. A ferocious foe. Where did you meet it?"

"Meet it?"

"Encounter it."

"At a literary cocktail party by a lake."

He coughed. "On land or water? Particularly ferocious when encountered on land. Bites with such speed that the naked human eye often cannot follow the movement. The limbs are powerful and a narrow projection from each side connects them to the carapace—"

"Yes," I said. "You are reading from the same book I read. I want to know how it managed to get down a staircase and up into a garden with its head hanging only by a piece of skin."

"An average snapper weighs between twenty and thirty pounds, but many have weighed twice that amount. The eggs are very interesting, hard of shell, often compared with ping-pong balls—"

"Please tell me what you think of, of, of its *life*."

After a while he said, "I don't understand."

"Is it, was it, alive when we found it in the garden? Is it alive now?"

"I don't know what you mean," he said.

"I'm asking about life. What is *life*?"

"I guess what comes before death. Please put its heart in a small amount of salted water and be kind enough to send us a note reporting how long the heart beats. Our records show ten hours."

"Then it isn't dead."

There was a pause. "In our sense."

"What is our sense?"

There was talk in the background noise and I heard him whisper to somebody. Then he said, "The snapping turtle is a very low, possibly the lowest, form of life."

I said, "Is it alive or is it dead? That's all I want to know, please."

There was more whispering. "You asked me for a scientific opinion, Miss Hellerman. I am not qualified to give you a theological one. Thank you for calling."

Ten or twelve years later, at the end of a dinner party, a large lady crossed the room to sit beside me. She said she was engaged in doing a book on Madame de Staël, and when I had finished with the sounds I have for what I don't know about she said, "My brother used to be a zoologist. You once called him about a snapping turtle." I said to give him my regards and apologies and she said, "Oh, that's not necessary. He practices in Calcutta."

But the day of the phone call I went to tell Hammett about my conversation. He listened, smiled when I came to the theological part, went back to reading an old book called *The Animal Kingdom*. My notation in the front of this book, picked up again on a July afternoon in 1972, is what brought me to this memory of the turtle.

Toward dinnertime, Helen came into the room and said, "That turtle. I can't cook with it sitting around me."

I said to Hammett, "What will we do?"

"Make soup."

"The next time. The next turtle. Let's bury this one."

"You bury it."

"You're punishing me," I said, "Why?"

"I'm trying to understand you."

"It's that it moved so far. It's that I've never before thought about *life*, if you know what I mean."

"No, I don't," he said.

"Well, what is life and stuff like that."

"Stuff like that. At your age."

I said, "You are much older than I am."

"That still makes you thirty-four and too old for stuff like that."

"You're making fun of me."

"Cut it out, Lilly. I know all the signs."

"Signs of what?"

He got up and left the room. I carried up a martini an hour later and said, "Just this turtle, the next I'll be O.K."

"Fine with me," he said, "either way."

"No, it isn't fine with you. You're saying something else."

"I'm saying cut it out."

"And *I'm* saying—"

"I don't want any dinner," he said.

I left the room and slammed the door. At dinner time I sent Helen up to tell him to come down immediately and she came back and said he said he wasn't hungry immediately.

During dinner she said she didn't want the turtle around when she came down for breakfast.

About ten, when Helen had gone to bed, I went upstairs and threw a book against Hammett's door.

"Yes?" he said.

"Please come and help me bury the turtle."

"I don't bury turtles."

"Will you bury me?"

"When the time comes, I'll do my best," he said.

"Open the door."

"No. Get Fred Herrmann to help you bury the turtle. And borrow Helen's prayer book."

But by the time I had had three more drinks, it was too late to wake Fred. I went to look at the turtle and saw that its blood was dripping to the floor. For many years, and for many years to come, I had been frightened of Helen and so, toward midnight, I tied a rope around the turtle's tail, took a flashlight, dragged it down the kitchen steps to the garage, and tied the rope to the bumper of the car. Then I went back to stand under Hammett's window.

I shouted up. "I'm weak. I can't dig a hole big enough. Come help me."

After I had said it twice, he called down, "I wish I could help you, but I'm asleep."

I spent the next hour digging a hole on the high ground above the lake, and by the time I covered the turtle the whiskey in the bottle was gone and I was dizzy and feeling sick. I put a stick over the grave, drove the car back toward the house, and when I was halfway there evidently fell asleep because I woke up at dawn in a heavy rain with the right wheels of the car turned into a tree stump. I walked home to bed and neither Hammett nor I mentioned the turtle for four or five days. That was no accident because we didn't speak to each other for three of those days, eating our meals at separate times.

Then he came back from a late afternoon walk and said, "I've caught two turtles. What would you like to do with them?"

"Kill them. Make soup."

"You're sure?"

"The first of anything is hard," I said. "You know that."

"I didn't know that until I met you," he said.

"I hurt my back digging the grave and I've a cold, but I had to bury that turtle and I don't want to talk about it again."

"You didn't do it very well. Some animal's been at your grave and eaten the turtle, but God will bless you anyway. I gathered the bones, put them back in the hole, and painted a tombstone sign for you."

For all the years we lived on the place, and maybe even now, there was a small wooden sign, neatly painted: "My first turtle is buried here. Miss Religious L.H."

1973

James Stevenson

OFF OFF BROADWAY JOURNAL[1]

July 9. Hot night in country. Ninety degrees. Trying to sleep; can't. Gypsy moths keep landing on face. Around 10 P.M., drift off into half sleep. Wakened by wrong number at ten-twenty. Toss; turn; toss; turn. Can't get back to sleep. Decide to read. Moths flutter around light. Pick up bedside copy of *Jane Eyre*.[2] Jane, a few months after her arrival at Thornfield, is having rough night:

> . . . I started wide awake on hearing a vague murmur, peculiar and lugubrious, which sounded, I thought, just above me. I wished I had kept my candle burning: the night was drearily dark; my spirits were depressed. I rose and sat up in bed, listening. The sound was hushed.
>
> I tried again to sleep; but my heart beat anxiously: my inward tranquillity was broken. The clock, far down in the hall, struck two. Just then it seemed my chamber-door was touched; as if fingers had swept the panels in groping a way along the dark gallery outside. I said, "Who is there?" Nothing answered. I was chilled with fear. . . .
>
> [There] was a demoniac laugh—low, suppressed, and deep—uttered, as it seemed, at the very key-hole of my chamber door. The head of my bed was near the door, and I thought at first the goblin-laughter stood at my bedside —or rather, crouched by my pillow: but I rose, looked round, and could see nothing; while, as I still gazed, the unnatural sound was reiterated: and I knew it came from behind the panels. My first impulse was to rise and fasten the bolt; my next, again to cry out, "Who is there?"
>
> Something gurgled and moaned. . . .

Scene not conducive to sleep for Jane, me, or Mr. Rochester (whose bed is soon set ablaze by the crazed woman who has escaped from the

1. The term "Off Broadway" was coined to refer to theatrical companies or productions too experimental for standard Broadway tastes; as Off Broadway productions became, inevitably, more commercial, their place was taken by "Off Off Broadway"; the theaters, lofts, or other spaces in which these productions are staged are mainly located near Greenwich Village or in the Lower East Side area of New York City.

2. Famous novel (1847) by Charlotte Brontë.

attic). I turn off light; try to think serene thoughts. At last ... slowly ... sink into welcome sleep. RNNNG! RNNNG! Reach for phone; knock over lamp; *Jane Eyre* falls to floor. "Hello?" Enthusiastic voice identifies self as Joe Steele. (Who?) He is ebullient: The play is all set! (Play?) He and playwright want to see me on Tuesday in N.Y.C. for reading—"Don't worry, you have the part. No problem. We just want to see you"—and he talks about how great play will be; what fun; what wonderful people. "See you Tuesday!" he cries; hangs up. I am totally awake. Clock says eleven-fifty. No chance for sleep now, and many drearily dark hours until dawn.

July 10. Morning. Call Frank, in New York, to tell him the news. Frank, who is not an actor, either (he's an artist), is old friend. A couple of years ago, an acquaintance asked him if he'd like to act in an Off Broadway play. Frank—faced with several deadlines on work he didn't want to do—said sure. He had the time of his life; loved every minute; has never stopped talking about it. He was excellent in the play, too. After that, he got small part in movie, and has now begun to think of himself as actor who draws. Two months ago, Frank and I were walking down University Place, ran into Joe Steele (or the man I here call Joe Steele), who had been in play with Frank. Steele is wiry, dark-haired young actor-director; lots of energy. Frank and Joe elated to see each other. High-velocity show-biz conversation ensued: How's Sally? Seen Howie? Liz has a part in such-and-such. Tony's doing a commercial. Shirley's in a soap. They share laughs, reminisce. Then Steele says he's going to direct an Off Off Broadway play and wants some nonactors in cast. "Will you be available, Frank?" Will he! They continue to talk. I step forward inconspicuously; clear throat. Talk goes on. I nudge Frank. "How about him, too?" says Frank generously, finally. Steele looks me over. (Should I mention I played Second Lieutenant Raleigh in high-school production of *Journey's End*[3] in 1944? Died at end of play; deeply moving. Both my parents thought I was very good.) "Want to be in the play?" Steele asks. "Certainly," I reply. "Good," says Steele. "I'll be in touch." Dashes off. Frank excited now; back to his true calling. We walk down street feeling life is about to become less routine, boring. New directions; bright lights; late nights; beautiful actresses; cheering audiences. Reminded of scene in Walt Disney's *Pinocchio* where naïve Pinocchio goes rollicking off with bad companions, singing, "Hi, diddle-dee-dee—An actor's life for me."

July 14. 5:30 P.M. Next to doorway on Great Jones Street where we are to meet Steele and the playwright, a man I'll call Allan Walters, at six, a drunk has dropped himself on sidewalk and is shouting curses at pass-

---

3. Popular melodrama about World War I, written by R. C. Sherriff, long a staple of community theaters and high schools.

ersby. Excellent projection: remarks reach us across street with perfect clarity. Actor? We get coffee at Phebe's, bar-restaurant with big windows, on corner of Bowery and East Fourth Street. Wonderful view uptown: Cooper Union, and the Empire State Building beyond. Frank grim, nervous about reading. (Why? He's done this before. Maybe *I* should be nervous. Begin to get that way.) We return to Great Jones Street—drunk has departed—and get cheerful greeting from Steele and Walters, affable man in rumpled pink seersucker suit. Rehearsal room is two stories high. Floor taped to indicate stage. No set. Long table; chairs. Steele and Walters chat with Frank; shoot appraising glances at me from time to time. I begin to brood: How did I get nerve to come here? Who think I am? What if I can't handle role? Should I back out now? Humiliation looms. Too late to quit: Steele is handing us scripts. They have black covers with small plastic window. (What should I concentrate on? Voice? Diction? Posture? Characterization? Motivation?) Open scripts to page 56. Frank's part is Man Who Tells Story. Steele says to me, "You're Another." He and Walters beam. "Ready? Read." Frank starts reading his part aloud. It goes on and on. Suddenly, I have a line:

ANOTHER: *No!*

I say it, and Frank continues. Presently, I have another line: "No!" again. Then Frank resumes. Story unwinds. Finally, I have a bigger line: "My God!" Frank goes on. Turn page. Where's my part? My part is over. Frank's story ends; Man Who Tells Story and Another exit. Steele and Walters are nodding and smiling, delighted with our performances. We do it again. "Very good, very good," says Walters. They shake our hands, give us photocopies of the pages of the play we're on (we don't get scripts), explain rehearsal schedule, and we are out on Great Jones Street again. Walk in silence for a while. Frank says, "My part in the last play was a lot better than my part in this one." What's he complaining about? Now I am committed to daily rehearsals, then performances five nights a week, all in order to say, "No! . . . No! . . . My God!"

July 15. Country.
"No! . . . No! . . . My God!"
"No! . . . No! . . . My *God!*"
"No! . . .NO! . . . MY GOD!"
"*NO! . . . NO! . . . MY GOD!*"

July 17. Country. Party on somebody's lawn. Talk to distinguished actor. He has deep, resonant voice; exquisite diction; beard. Handsome; moves well. (Are these qualities necessary?) He is about to go to California to do thirteen weeks of TV. Later in evening, woman I am talking to points out how the actor is now sitting in chair at one side of lawn and is back-lit by garage floodlight: a silhouette with halo around him, and light coming through fringes of beard. We go over; she tells him he looks very dramatic. "I know," he booms. "That's why I'm sitting here."

July 18. Have told all my friends that I'm in play. Reaction I seek is congratulations; what I get is incredulity. Restless for rehearsals to start. Repressed thoughts keep bubbling up: How come Frank's role so big, mine so small? What if he gets hurt, sick . . . killed? "Tragic about Frank. Lucky thing you were around to step into the part." Go to see play at nearby summer theatre. Study acting techniques. Some actors good, some not so good. Encouraged by performance of one actress who gets big audience response with only *one line.* She says her line, then gives weird giggle. Small things like that make stars. Drive home after play. "No! . . . No! . . . My God!" Pause. Giggle. No. Can't use it.

July 19. Interview in *Times* with actress Swoosie Kurtz. Read it avidly. "I work from the outside in, which is not to say I work externally." Hmm. Can't decide which way to work. "'It's whatever works for you,' she said with a shrug." Feel better.

July 20. New York. Late afternoon. Having burger before first rehearsal. Outside Phebe's windows, a couple of Hell's Angels roar by; a girl with orange hair walks past (she wears white pants and a green T-shirt with an alligator on it); a young man with a blue Mohawk haircut; a bearded codger in an old tweed sports jacket, a pink straw hat with an "I LOVE N.Y." hatband, fuchsia pants, carrying a black plastic garbage bag. The derelicts pass, too, heading toward or away from the Salvation Army a couple of doors downtown, or the city shelter around the corner, or the bars between. Some walk sidewise with eyes closed, veering this way and that; some have torn shoes, others are barefoot; white-bearded and wrinkled; young and gaunt; bloodied; bandaged and unbandaged—it is a continuous parade of wounded veterans, limping back from private wars. Goya. Hieronymus Bosch.[4] Maybe actors and derelicts share discomfort at being who they are. The actor, however, hopes to become—at least briefly—somebody else. The derelict has a more modest goal: he just wants to destroy himself.

July 22. Some scenery has been moved into the rehearsal hall during the morning, and now we stand at an actual bar. I have no problem with my lines, but I am not comfortable. I lean on the bar with my left arm, then worry about my right arm. It has nothing to do. It just hangs there stiffly. Don't know where to put it. I feel the audience will begin whisper-

---

4. Francisco José de Goya y Lucientes (1746–1828) and Hieronymus Bosch (1450–1516), famous artists of the grotesque.

ing. ("Psst—look at him. Wow, is he self-conscious!" "Who? The one with the arm hanging there?") I ask Steele what to do to relax. "Don't worry about how you stand," he says. "Think about what you're feeling as Frank talks. The action will follow naturally. Don't *indicate* what you're feeling, though; just feel it. It'll be fine." Steele says we have the advantage of looking and sounding like nonactors, and we should make the most of it. "I was rehearsing in a play once and the director told me to turn upstage. I started to do it, and he yelled at me, 'No! Not like an *actor*—like a human being!'"

We talk for a while. Steele keeps reassuring Frank; tells actor stories. Rehearsals and real performances are very different, he says. Tells about actor who was in medieval play. During rehearsals, stage manager called out "Cannon!" and actor was supposed to say "Hark! The cannon fires! His Majesty arrives!" Worked fine during rehearsals. "Cannon!" "Hark! . . ." But on opening night there was actual sound of cannon firing. Actor jumped, shrieked, "What the———was THAT?"

We resume. Frank improves. Steele and Walters give me two more lines: another "My God!" and a "My God! That's incredible!" It feels like a soliloquy.

July 28. Discussion of costume for play. Steele says I should have "kind of a slob image." He is distracted by other matters, but eventually turns back to me, looks me over. "Why don't you just wear what you've got on?" he suggests, not unkindly. A few days ago, I was walking down the Bowery when I saw somebody I thought was a college classmate drive by. He didn't see me—or maybe he did. I glanced at reflection in window: I was wearing old T-shirt, dirty pants, sneakers, no socks. At this very moment, classmate probably saying to old friends, "Guess who I saw shuffling along on the Bowery."

July 30. Afternoon. Driving in to New York for first full-cast rehearsal. Anticipatory; preoccupied. Passing a car on highway, I notice driver giving me wary look. Realize I have been exclaiming, "My God! That's incredible!"

The real actors are friendly, cheerful, optimistic; generous about amateurs in their midst. We all shake hands. Rehearsal moves along. In middle of scene, I realize I'm supposed to be on other side of stage. Start to cross. But somebody is speaking his lines. I freeze, stuck in middle of stage like a scarecrow. Terrible sensation. Next time, I cross sooner. We run through play again. This time, I can't remember whether my first "My God!" is just "My God!" or "My God! That's incredible!" Total confusion. Frank still getting his lines wrong. When he gets into trouble, he increases his speed, contracting the story so there is no place for me to say "No!"—much less "My God!" Rehearsal ends. Everybody in high spirits. Great sense of sharing in something.

August 4. Wandering around before rehearsal. On Houston Street, see a used-clothes store with its door open, and a window heaped with shoes of all shapes and colors; piles of clothes inside—coats and suits and trousers—autumnal, as if blown across the avenue by a cold October wind and whirled through the open door into this dim storefront. Nearby, two legs are sticking out from a doorway: worn shoes, once black; pants the color of the sidewalk; a dirty hand hanging over one knee. The hand recedes; vanishes; reappears clutching a bottle of bright-red liquid. The bottle rises; disappears. The legs, the doorway, the pavement—everything has a wash of dirt over it, toning down the colors. Except the bright-red drink.

Between Lafayette Street and Mulberry Street, a derelict lies sleeping in a shadowed alley; two large red brick buildings rise on either side, with metal shutters (many open) on every floor. It is an area of large, fat, proud old buildings—their shutters like flags or kites; festive—and their strength and solidity contrast sharply with the skeletal, ragged men lurching among them now. Some of these men speak—mutter, growl, rasp—but they are not speaking to anybody in particular. They speak to the world at large, like actors.

August 6. We go to the real theatre tonight. Frank has been reading Stanislavski,[5] he says—very helpful. The block on which the theatre stands is shrill with portable radios; kids yelling to each other; people shouting down from fire escapes; dogs barking; cars honking; garbage cans clattering. Teen-agers sit on the hoods of cars, hugging and kissing; old people sit on the stoops of the tenements, fanning themselves, playing cards; speaking Spanish. Children are skipping rope; throwing balls; weaving through crowded sidewalk on roller skates. Frank steps over a man who is passed out on the sidewalk, and, entering theatre, says, "It would be hard to do a play in here that could compete with the human drama out there."

Theatre is in big, dim, musty building. Go up wide steps to second floor, through another door. Sign in. Go around side of bleachers, down dark passage, and then—abruptly—there is the nearly completed set, brightly lit, and the other actors. Greetings to all, and rehearsal begins. Frank has not yet learned his lines, and is very nervous. Every time he skips a cue, I lose a line. Since I have only ten words *in toto*, I resent losing any of them. Eight words, I now feel, is my absolute minimum. I won't do it for seven. When, on way out after rehearsal, I say to Frank "Damn it,

5. Constantin Stanislavski (1863–1938), widely influential theatrical director who stressed inner motivation in acting.

why can't you learn your lines?" he looks at me as if betrayed, clearly thinking, This is the person I helped to get a part?

August 7. The set is finished; looks great. Mike, the designer, is also the builder and painter. He has worked like hell, carrying heavy materials up the long flights of stairs into the theatre, where the temperature is steadily in the nineties, regardless of what the weather is outside; he's built the set, then painted it to make it look real and old. He gets little help, and demands no credit; just does it. A genuine professional. Rehearsal goes well. Late in evening, everybody goes to Phebe's. One by one, the actors stop at the table where Joe Steele is sitting; tell him how well the show is going. Steele listens; agrees pleasantly. Then, invariably, each actor adds one qualifier: "Of course, So-and-So isn't loud enough," or other such comment. Steele is amused by this. He is a skilled diplomat, among other things; he must get along with the actors, shape their performances without damaging their morale. Steele tells me I am fine. (Fine? Is that better than O.K.?)

August 8. Rehearsals getting more intense. Steele has been working with actors during the day, then full rehearsal at night; he's beginning to look slightly haggard. Tonight, we went in to rehearsal around six. It was a very hot, sticky, sunny afternoon. Five hours later, we came out into a dark downpour of steady rain. Nobody had known it was raining. There is little or no sense of outside world when we are inside theatre. Increasingly, this theatre and the play in it are becoming the real world. (Yesterday, I was watching somebody walk down the street, and thought, That's a very good walk—very convincing.) We sit on folding chairs behind the set waiting to go on. The stage is bright—lit from the front and above —but where we sit it is shadowy; the actors are dim shapes. It is a kind of limbo.

It's hard to go home at night, and once I'm there it's hard to sleep. When the main rehearsal is over, we all stay and watch others rehearse special bits. Everybody's tired, but doesn't want it to end; doesn't want to miss anything. When, finally, there is nothing left to see, the actors drift over to Phebe's, drink beer, and let down slowly. Some of the actors are old friends; have worked together before. They joke about how they have gone from Off Off Broadway play to Off Off Broadway play, never getting money or fame. What matters is to be doing a play, some play, and trying to do it well. They make ends meet as best they can: unemployment insurance; a part in a soap; an occasional commercial; odd jobs in between. They have a lot of admiration for each other, a lot of generosity, and great love for their work. They respect each other's professionalism. Joe Steele talks about an actress called Irene. They were in a play together a few years back. Irene had a scene with an actor named George, and it was very funny. Irene managed to get five separate laughs out of the scene each night. Then George had to leave to be in a movie, and he was replaced by another actor. This actor gave a different reading to the role, and now Irene was getting laughs in completely new places—eight laughs a night. Then George finished the movie and came back to the play. "You know what Irene did?" says Steele. "She got George to change his original reading so that she got thirteen laughs every night—the original five plus the eight others." He slaps the table with glee. "She's great!"

August 9. Three days until opening. Went to American Museum of Natural History; saw Shakespeare show. Globe Theatre,[6] it turns out, was situated in much crummier part of its city than our theatre is. (No bear-baiting rings on Bowery, for example.) Museum had film clips of actors doing Shakespeare, including Olivier as Hamlet. "Alas! poor Yorick," says Olivier, gazing at skull he holds in hand. Then Olivier turns to Horatio (offscreen) and remarks, "I knew him, Horatio." Then turns back to skull; continues. Made me laugh, it was so fresh and right.

Near the theatre, in early evening, a skin-and-bones derelict comes out of the municipal shelter for homeless men, moving stiff-legged, as if on stilts; goes to the edge of the sidewalk. Stands there awhile; plods back; returns. He repeats the process over and over, as if the edge of the sidewalk were a lookout, a vantage point, a place where he is able to gaze into some sort of distance—perhaps to see something coming, something he expects.

"I'm going to give you a sixty-second lesson in acting," says Steele when I get to theatre. He wants me to speak louder. He has Mike, the set designer, stand at the bottom of the stairs of the bleachers. "Say your line to me, but make it so Mike can hear it," says Steele. "My God! That's incredible!" I say. "O.K.," says Steele. "Mike—go up a few steps." Mike does so; I repeat my line. We do it again, as Mike moves up to the highest reaches of the theatre. "MY GOD! THAT'S INCREDIBLE!" Steele asks, "Did you hear him, Mike?" Mike says yes. "Good," says Steele to me. "Now you know something about acting." Rehearsal proceeds. Frank is doing very well. At Phebe's afterward, attractive and skillful young actress describes how she spent three years as a waitress in N.Y.C. before she got any parts. Another talks about how she was lucky to find theatre work in Vermont. Steele says, "The hardest thing in the theatre is writing. Then comes acting. Then producing, and then directing." Not sure he is serious, but maybe. He talks about one of the other amateur actors in the cast, who is getting lots of admiration. "He's never acted before," says

6. The theater where many of Shakespeare's plays were produced; like other theaters of the time, it was situated across the river from London proper, in an area abounding in brothels and other illicit kinds of entertainment, including "bear-baiting"—a spectator sport in which hunting dogs were unleashed against a bear tied to a post.

Steele, "but once we open and he sees the power he's got over a roomful of people, he's not going to want to go back to what he usually does." It's going to be hard for everybody to go back. What were evenings like when nobody had to be at the theatre at seven o'clock? What was life like? We have all become quite close, without knowing very much about each other. The actors greet each other with waves, kisses, embraces, handshakes, laughter. Would people in any other line of work be so open, so affectionate? Don't know.

August 12. Opening night. Joe Steele addresses cast. "I think you're ready," he says; wishes everybody luck. Cheers and applause. Dan, the stage manager, announces the time at intervals. "Ladies and gentlemen: Half hour." "The audience is entering the house." "Ladies and gentlemen: Fifteen minutes." Frank is sitting in a corner saying his lines over and over. He has been giving good performances, but he still worries. "Places!" calls Dan. The house lights go down. Chairs creak. A few coughs. Then silence. Beyond the dark set, the lights come up onstage; the voices begin.

September 7. Country. Gray day. Flat, dull light; no sun. Very quiet. The play ended a week ago. Mike, who built the set, has dismantled it. The actors have dispersed. Frank is back to drawing pictures and meeting deadlines. The last party at Phebe's was noisy, touching, and fun: talk of reunions, and phone numbers written on soggy napkins; hugs and kisses; then we all separated for the last time. Most of the phone calls will never be made; the reunions will never take place; in fact, we will probably move farther and farther apart, until names are no longer remembered, and then the faces will vanish, too—but it seems unlikely that any of us will forget the short, good time when we were a company of players and brought a play to life. Finished *Jane Eyre* last night; she married Rochester. "We entered the wood, and wended homeward."

1981

Joan Didion

ON GOING HOME

I am home for my daughter's first birthday. By "home" I do not mean
the house in Los Angeles where my husband and I and the baby live, but
the place where my family is, in the Central Valley of California. It is a
vital although troublesome distinction. My husband likes my family but
is uneasy in their house, because once there I fall into their ways, which
are difficult, oblique, deliberately inarticulate, not my husband's ways.
We live in dusty houses ("D-U-S-T," he once wrote with his finger on
surfaces all over the house, but no one noticed it) filled with mementos
quite without value to him (what could the Canton dessert plates mean
to him? how could he have known about the assay scales, why should he
care if he did know?), and we appear to talk exclusively about people we
know who have been committed to mental hospitals, about people we
know who have been booked on drunk-driving charges, and about property, particularly about property, land, price per acre and C-2 zoning and
assessments and freeway access. My brother does not understand my
husband's inability to perceive the advantage in the rather common real-
estate transaction known as "sale-leaseback," and my husband in turn
does not understand why so many of the people he hears about in my
father's house have recently been committed to mental hospitals or
booked on drunk-driving charges. Nor does he understand that when we
talk about sale-leasebacks and right-of-way condemnations we are talking
in code about the things we like best, the yellow fields and the cotton-
woods and the rivers rising and falling and the mountain roads closing
when the heavy snow comes in. We miss each other's points, have
another drink and regard the fire. My brother refers to my husband, in his
presence, as "Joan's husband." Marriage is the classic betrayal.

Or perhaps it is not any more. Sometimes I think that those of us who
are now in our thirties were born into the last generation to carry the
burden of "home," to find in family life the source of all tension and
drama. I had by all objective accounts a "normal" and a "happy" family
situation, and yet I was almost thirty years old before I could talk to my
family on the telephone without crying after I had hung up. We did not
fight. Nothing was wrong. And yet some nameless anxiety colored the
emotional charges between me and the place that I came from. The
question of whether or not you could go home again was a very real part
of the sentimental and largely literary baggage with which we left home
in the fifties; I suspect that it is irrelevant to the children born of the
fragmentation after World War II. A few weeks ago in a San Francisco
bar I saw a pretty young girl on crystal take off her clothes and dance for

the cash prize in an "amateur-topless" contest. There was no particular sense of moment about this, none of the effect of romantic degradation, of "dark journey," for which my generation strived so assiduously. What sense could that girl possibly make of, say, *Long Day's Journey into Night?*[1] Who is beside the point?

That I am trapped in this particular irrelevancy is never more apparent to me than when I am home. Paralyzed by the neurotic lassitude engendered by meeting one's past at every turn, around every corner, inside every cupboard, I go aimlessly from room to room. I decide to meet it head-on and clean out a drawer, and I spread the contents on the bed. A bathing suit I wore the summer I was seventeen. A letter of rejection from *The Nation,* an aerial photograph of the site for a shopping center my father did not build in 1954. Three teacups hand-painted with cabbage roses and signed "E.M.," my grandmother's initials. There is no final solution for letters of rejection from *The Nation* and teacups hand-painted in 1900. Nor is there any answer to snapshots of one's grandfather as a young man on skis, surveying around Donner Pass in the year 1910. I smooth out the snapshot and look into his face, and do and do not see my own. I close the drawer, and have another cup of coffee with my mother. We get along very well, veterans of a guerrilla war we never understood.

Days pass. I see no one. I come to dread my husband's evening call, not only because he is full of news of what by now seems to me our remote life in Los Angeles, people he has seen, letters which require attention, but because he asks what I have been doing, suggests uneasily that I get out, drive to San Francisco or Berkeley. Instead I drive across the river to a family graveyard. It has been vandalized since my last visit and the monuments are broken, overturned in the dry grass. Because I once saw a rattlesnake in the grass I stay in the car and listen to a country-and-Western station. Later I drive with my father to a ranch he has in the foothills. The man who runs his cattle on it asks us to the roundup, a week from Sunday, and although I know that I will be in Los Angeles I say, in the oblique way my family talks, that I will come. Once home I mention the broken monuments in the graveyard. My mother shrugs.

I go to visit my great-aunts. A few of them think now that I am my cousin, or their daughter who died young. We recall an anecdote about a relative last seen in 1948, and they ask if I still like living in New York City. I have lived in Los Angeles for three years, but I say that I do. The baby is offered a horehound drop, and I am slipped a dollar bill "to buy a treat." Questions trail off, answers are abandoned, the baby plays with the dust motes in a shaft of afternoon sun.

It is time for the baby's birthday party: a white cake, strawberry-

1. A powerful domestic tragedy by the modern American playwright Eugene O'Neill, based on his early life.

marshmallow ice cream, a bottle of champagne saved from another party. In the evening, after she has gone to sleep, I kneel beside the crib and touch her face, where it is pressed against the slats, with mine. She is an open and trusting child, unprepared for and unaccustomed to the ambushes of family life, and perhaps it is just as well that I can offer her little of that life. I would like to give her more. I would like to promise her that she will grow up with a sense of her cousins and of rivers and of her great-grandmother's teacups, would like to pledge her a picnic on a river with fried chicken and her hair uncombed, would like to give her *home* for her birthday, but we live differently now and I can promise her nothing like that. I give her a xylophone and a sundress from Madeira, and promise to tell her a funny story.

1966

QUESTIONS

1. *Does the author take a single attitude, or several, toward "home"? Try to specify the attitude, or attitudes.*
2. *The author speaks of herself at home as "paralyzed by the neurotic lassitude engendered by meeting one's past at every turn" (p. 67). What details in the essay help explain that feeling?*
3. *What does the author mean by "the ambushes of family life" (above)?*
4. *Explain whether the essay gives you any clues as to why so much of the talk at home is ". . . about people we know who have been committed to mental hospitals, about people we know who have been booked on drunk-driving charges, and about property . . . (p. 66)?*
5. *If you have read or seen the play, explain the appropriateness of the author's reference (p. 67) to Eugene O'Neill's* Long Day's *Journey into* Night.
6. *In her concluding sentence the author tells us she gives as birthday gifts to her daughter "a xylophone and a sundress from Madeira." Are these appropriate? Why, or why not? Explain why she would like to give other gifts.*

Joyce Maynard

FOUR GENERATIONS

My mother called last week to tell me that my grandmother is dying. She has refused an operation that would postpone, but not prevent, her death from pancreatic cancer. She can't eat, she has been hemorrhaging, and she has severe jaundice. "I always prided myself on being different," she told my mother. "Now I *am* different. I'm yellow."

My mother, telling me this news, began to cry. So I became the mother for a moment, reminding her, reasonably, that my grandmother is eighty-seven, she's had a full life, she has all her faculties, and no one who knows her could wish that she live long enough to lose them. Lately my mother has been finding notes in my grandmother's drawers at the nursing home, reminding her, "Joyce's husband's name is Steve. Their daughter is Audrey." In the last few years she hadn't had the strength to cook or garden, and she's begun to say she's had enough of living.

My grandmother was born in Russia, in 1892—the oldest daughter in a large and prosperous Jewish family. But the prosperity didn't last. She tells stories of the pogroms and the cossacks who raped her when she was twelve. Soon after that, her family emigrated to Canada, where she met my grandfather.

Their children were the center of their life. The story I loved best, as a child, was of my grandfather opening every box of Cracker Jack in the general store he ran, in search of the particular tin toy my mother coveted. Though they never had much money, my grandmother saw to it that her daughter had elocution lessons and piano lessons, and assured her that she would go to college.

But while she was at college, my mother met my father, who was blue-eyed and blond-haired and not Jewish. When my father sent love letters to my mother, my grandmother would open and hide them, and when my mother told her parents she was going to marry this man, my grandmother said if that happened, it would kill her.

Not likely, of course. My grandmother is a woman who used to crack Brazil nuts open with her teeth, a woman who once lifted a car off the ground, when there was an accident and it had to be moved. She has been representing her death as imminent ever since I've known her—twenty-five years—and has discussed, at length, the distribution of her possessions and her lamb coat. Every time we said goodbye, after our annual visit to Winnipeg, she'd weep and say she'd never see us again. But in the meantime, while every other relative of her generation, and a good many of the younger ones, has died (nursed usually by her), she has kept making knishes, shopping for bargains, tending the healthiest plants I've ever seen.

After my grandfather died, my grandmother lived, more than ever, through her children. When she came to visit, I would hide my diary. She couldn't understand any desire for privacy. She couldn't bear it if my mother left the house without her.

This possessiveness is what made my mother furious (and then guilt-ridden that she felt that way, when of course she owed so much to her mother). So I harbored the resentment that my mother—the dutiful daughter—would not allow herself. I—who had always performed specially well for my grandmother, danced and sung for her, presented her with kisses and good report cards—stopped writing to her, ceased to visit.

But when I heard that she was dying, I realized I wanted to go to Winnipeg to see her one more time. Mostly to make my mother happy, I told myself (certain patterns being hard to break). But also, I was offering up one more particularly fine accomplishment: my own dark-eyed, dark-skinned, dark-haired daughter, whom my grandmother had never met.

I put on my daughter's best dress for our visit to Winnipeg, the way the best dresses were always put on me, and I filled my pockets with animal crackers, in case Audrey started to cry. I scrubbed her face mercilessly. On the elevator going up to her room, I realized how much I was sweating.

Grandma was lying flat with an IV tube in her arm and her eyes shut, but she opened them when I leaned over to kiss her. "It's Fredelle's daughter, Joyce," I yelled, because she doesn't hear well anymore, but I could see that no explanation was necessary. "You came," she said. "You brought the baby."

Audrey is just one, but she has seen enough of the world to know that people in beds are not meant to be so still and yellow, and she looked frightened. I had never wanted, more, for her to smile.

Then Grandma waved at her—the same kind of slow, finger-flexing wave a baby makes—and Audrey waved back. I spread her toys out on my grandmother's bed and sat her down. There she stayed, most of the afternoon, playing and humming and sipping on her bottle, taking a nap at one point, leaning against my grandmother's leg. When I cranked her Snoopy guitar, Audrey stood up on the bed and danced. Grandma wouldn't talk much anymore, though every once in a while she would say how sorry she was that she wasn't having a better day. "I'm not always like this," she said.

Mostly she just watched Audrey. Sometimes Audrey would get off the bed, inspect the get-well cards, totter down the hall. "Where is she?" Grandma kept asking. "Who's looking after her?" I had the feeling, even then, that if I'd said, "Audrey's lighting matches," Grandma would have shot up to rescue her.

We were flying home that night, and I had dreaded telling her, remembering all those other tearful partings. But in the end, I was the one who cried. She had said she was ready to die. But as I leaned over to stroke her forehead, what she said was, "I wish I had your hair" and "I wish I was well."

On the plane flying home, with Audrey in my arms, I thought about mothers and daughters, and the four generations of the family that I know most intimately. Every one of those mothers loves and needs her daughter more than her daughter will love or need her some day, and we are, each of us, the only person on earth who is quite so consumingly interested in our child.

Sometimes I kiss and hug Audrey so much she starts crying—which is, in effect, what my grandmother was doing to my mother, all her life. And what makes my mother grieve right now, I think, is not simply that her mother will die in a day or two, but that, once her mother dies, there will never again be someone to love her in quite such an unreserved, unquestioning way. No one else who believes that, fifty years ago, she could have put Shirley Temple out of a job, no one else who remembers the moment of her birth. She will only be a mother, then, not a daughter anymore.

Audrey and I have stopped over for a night in Toronto, where my mother lives. Tomorrow she will go to a safe-deposit box at the bank and take out the receipt for my grandmother's burial plot. Then she will fly back to Winnipeg, where, for the first time in anybody's memory, there was waist-high snow on April Fool's Day. But tonight she is feeding me, as she always does when I come, and I am eating more than I do anywhere else. I admire the wedding china (once my grandmother's) that my mother has set on the table. She says (the way Grandma used to say to her, of the lamb coat), "Some day it will be yours."

1979

Loren Eiseley

THE BROWN WASPS

There is a corner in the waiting room of one of the great Eastern stations where women never sit. It is always in the shadow and overhung by rows of lockers. It is, however, always frequented—not so much by genuine travelers as by the dying. It is here that a certain element of the abandoned poor seeks a refuge out of the weather, clinging for a few hours longer to the city that has fathered them. In a precisely similar manner I have seen, on a sunny day in midwinter, a few old brown wasps creep slowly over an abandoned wasp nest in a thicket. Numbed and forgetful and frost-blackened, the hum of the spring hive still resounded

faintly in their sodden tissues. Then the temperature would fall and they
would drop away into the white oblivion of the snow. Here in the station
it is in no way different save that the city is busy in its snows. But the old
ones cling to their seats as though these were symbolic and could not be
given up. Now and then they sleep, their gray old heads resting with
painful awkwardness on the backs of the benches.

Also they are not at rest. For an hour they may sleep in the gasping
exhaustion of the ill-nourished and aged who have to walk in the night.
Then a policeman comes by on his round and nudges them upright.

"You can't sleep here," he growls.

A strange ritual then begins. An old man is difficult to waken. After a
muttered conversation the policeman presses a coin into his hand and
passes fiercely along the benches prodding and gesturing toward the
door. In his wake, like birds rising and settling behind the passage of a
farmer through a cornfield, the men totter up, move a few paces and
subside once more upon the benches.

One man, after a slight, apologetic lurch, does not move at all. Tuber-
cularly thin, he sleeps on steadily. The policeman does not look back. To
him, too, this has become a ritual. He will not have to notice it again
officially for another hour.

Once in a while one of the sleepers will not awake. Like the brown
wasps, he will have had his wish to die in the great droning center of the
hive rather than in some lonely room. It is not so bad here with the shuffle
of footsteps and the knowledge that there are others who share the bad
luck of the world. There are also the whistles and the sounds of everyone,
everyone in the world, starting on journeys. Amidst so many journeys
somebody is bound to come out all right. Somebody.

Maybe it was on a like thought that the brown wasps fell away from the
old paper nest in the thicket. You hold till the last, even if it is only to a
public seat in a railroad station. You want your place in the hive more
than you want a room or a place where the aged can be eased gently out of
the way. It is the place that matters, the place at the heart of things. It is
life that you want, that bruises your gray old head with the hard chairs; a
man has a right to his place.

But sometimes the place is lost in the years behind us. Or sometimes it
is a thing of air, a kind of vaporous distortion above a heap of rubble. We
cling to a time and place because without them man is lost, not only man
but life. This is why the voices, real or unreal, which speak from the
floating trumpets at spiritualist seances are so unnerving. They are
voices out of nowhere whose only reality lies in their ability to stir the
memory of a living person with some fragment of the past. Before the
medium's cabinet both the dead and the living revolve endlessly about an
episode, a place, an event that has already been engulfed by time.

This feeling runs deep in life; it brings stray cats running over endless
miles, and birds homing from the ends of the earth. It is as though all

living creatures, and particularly the more intelligent, can survive only by fixing or transforming a bit of time into space or by securing a bit of space with its objects immortalized and made permanent in time. For example, I once saw, on a flower pot in my own living room, the efforts of a field mouse to build a remembered field. I have lived to see this episode repeated in a thousand guises, and since I have spent a large portion of my life in the shade of a nonexistent tree, I think I am entitled to speak for the field mouse.

One day as I cut across the field which at that time extended on one side of our suburban shopping center, I found a giant slug feeding from a runnel of pink ice cream in an abandoned Dixie cup. I could see his eyes telescope and protrude in a kind of dim, uncertain ecstasy as his dark body bunched and elongated in the curve of the cup. Then, as I stood there at the edge of the concrete, contemplating the slug, I began to realize it was like standing on a shore where a different type of life creeps up and fumbles tentatively among the rocks and sea wrack. It knows its place and will only creep so far until something changes. Little by little as I stood there I began to see more of this shore that surrounds the place of man. I looked with sudden care and attention at things I had been running over thoughtlessly for years. I even waded out a short way into the grass and the wild-rose thickets to see more. A huge black-belted bee went droning by and there were some indistinct scurryings in the underbrush.

Then I came to a sign which informed me that this field was to be the site of a new Wanamaker suburban store. Thousands of obscure lives were about to perish, the spores of puffballs would go smoking off to new fields, and the bodies of little white-footed mice would be crunched under the inexorable wheels of the bulldozers. Life disappears or modifies its appearances so fast that everything takes on an aspect of illusion —a momentary fizzing and boiling with smoke rings, like pouring dissident chemicals into a retort. Here man was advancing, but in a few years his plaster and bricks would be disappearing once more into the insatiable maw of the clover. Being of an archaeological cast of mind, I thought of this fact with an obscure sense of satisfaction and waded back through the rose thickets to the concrete parking lot. As I did so, a mouse scurried ahead of me, frightened of my steps if not of that ominous Wanamaker sign. I saw him vanish in the general direction of my apartment house, his little body quivering with fear in the great open sun on the blazing concrete. Blinded and confused, he was running straight away from his field. In another week scores would follow him.

I forgot the episode then and went home to the quiet of my living room. It was not until a week later, letting myself into the apartment, that I realized I had a visitor. I am fond of plants and had several ferns standing on the floor in pots to avoid the noon glare by the south window.

As I snapped on the light and glanced carelessly around the room, I saw a little heap of earth on the carpet and a scrabble of pebbles that had been kicked merrily over the edge of one of the flower pots. To my astonishment I discovered a full-fledged burrow delving downward among the fern roots. I waited silently. The creature who had made the burrow did not appear. I remembered the wild field then, and the flight of the mice. No house mouse, no *Mus domesticus*, had kicked up this little heap of earth or sought refuge under a fern root in a flower pot. I thought of the desperate little creature I had seen fleeing from the wild-rose thicket. Through intricacies of pipes and attics, he, or one of his fellows, had climbed to this high green solitary room. I could visualize what had occurred. He had an image in his head, a world of seed pods and quiet, of green sheltering leaves in the dim light among the weed stems. It was the only world he knew and it was gone.

Somehow in his flight he had found his way to this room with drawn shades where no one would come till nightfall. And here he had smelled green leaves and run quickly up the flower pot to dabble his paws in common earth. He had even struggled half the afternoon to carry his burrow deeper and had failed. I examined the hole, but no whiskered twitching face appeared. He was gone. I gathered up the earth and refilled the burrow. I did not expect to find traces of him again.

Yet for three nights thereafter I came home to the darkened room and my ferns to find the dirt kicked gaily about the rug and the burrow reopened, though I was never able to catch the field mouse within it. I dropped a little food about the mouth of the burrow, but it was never touched. I looked under beds or sat reading with one ear cocked for rustlings in the ferns. It was all in vain; I never saw him. Probably he ended in a trap in some other tenant's room.

But before he disappeared I had come to look hopefully for his evening burrow. About my ferns there had begun to linger the insubstantial vapor of an autumn field, the distilled essence, as it were, of a mouse brain in exile from its home. It was a small dream, like our dreams, carried a long and weary journey along pipes and through spider webs, past holes over which loomed the shadows of waiting cats, and finally, desperately, into this room where he had played in the shuttered daylight for an hour among the green ferns on the floor. Every day these invisible dreams pass us on the street, or rise from beneath our feet, or look out upon us from beneath a bush.

Some years ago the old elevated railway in Philadelphia was torn down and replaced by a subway system. This ancient El with its barnlike stations containing nut-vending machines and scattered food scraps had, for generations, been the favorite feeding ground of flocks of pigeons, generally one flock to a station along the route of the El. Hundreds of pigeons were dependent upon the system. They flapped in and out of its stanchions and steel work or gathered in watchful little audiences about the feet of anyone who rattled the peanut-vending machines. They even watched people who jingled change in their hands, and prospected for food under the feet of the crowds who gathered between trains. Probably very few among the waiting people who tossed a crumb to an eager pigeon realized that this El was like a food-bearing river, and that the life which haunted its banks was dependent upon the running of the trains with their human freight.

I saw the river stop.

The time came when the underground tubes were ready; the traffic was transferred to a realm unreachable by pigeons. It was like a great river subsiding suddenly into desert sands. For a day, for two days, pigeons continued to circle over the El or stand close to the red vending machines. They were patient birds, and surely this great river which had flowed through the lives of unnumbered generations was merely suffering from some momentary drought.

They listened for the familiar vibrations that had always heralded an approaching train; they flapped hopefully about the head of an occasional workman walking along the steel runways. They passed from one empty station to another, all the while growing hungrier. Finally they flew away.

I thought I had seen the last of them about the El, but there was a revival and it provided a curious instance of the memory of living things for a way of life or a locality that has long been cherished. Some weeks after the El was abandoned workmen began to tear it down. I went to work every morning by one particular station, and the time came when the demolition crews reached this spot. Acetylene torches showered passersby with sparks, pneumatic drills hammered at the base of the structure, and a blind man who, like the pigeons, had clung with his cup to a stairway leading to the change booth, was forced to give up his place.

It was then, strangely, momentarily, one morning that I witnessed the return of a little band of the familiar pigeons. I even recognized one or two members of the flock that had lived around this particular station before they were dispersed into the streets. They flew bravely in and out among the sparks and the hammers and the shouting workmen. They had returned—and they had returned because the hubbub of the wreckers had convinced them that the river was about to flow once more. For several hours they flapped in and out through the empty windows, nodding their heads and watching the fall of girders with attentive little eyes. By the following morning the station was reduced to some burned-off stanchions in the street. My bird friends had gone. It was plain, however, that they retained a memory for an insubstantial structure now compounded of air and time. Even the blind man clung to it. Someone had provided him with a chair, and he sat at the same corner staring sightlessly at an invisible stairway where, so far as he was concerned, the crowds were still ascending to the trains.

I have said my life has been passed in the shade of a nonexistent tree, so that such sights do not offend me. Prematurely I am one of the brown wasps and I often sit with them in the great droning hive of the station, dreaming sometimes of a certain tree. It was planted sixty years ago by a boy with a bucket and a toy spade in a little Nebraska town. That boy was myself. It was a cottonwood sapling and the boy remembered it because of some words spoken by his father and because everyone died or moved away who was supposed to wait and grow old under its shade. The boy was passed from hand to hand, but the tree for some intangible reason had taken root in his mind. It was under its branches that he sheltered; it was from this tree that his memories, which are my memories, led away into the world.

After sixty years the mood of the brown wasps grows heavier upon one. During a long inward struggle I thought it would do me good to go and look upon that actual tree. I found a rational excuse in which to clothe this madness. I purchased a ticket and at the end of two thousand miles I walked another mile to an address that was still the same. The house had not been altered.

I came close to the white picket fence and reluctantly, with great effort, looked down the long vista of the yard. There was nothing there to see. For sixty years that cottonwood had been growing in my mind. Season by season its seeds had been floating farther on the hot prairie winds. We had planted it lovingly there, my father and I, because he had a great hunger for soil and live things growing, and because none of these things had long been ours to protect. We had planted the little sapling and watered it faithfully, and I remembered that I had run out with my small bucket to drench its roots the day we moved away. And all the years since it had been growing in my mind, a huge tree that somehow stood for my father and the love I bore him. I took a grasp on the picket fence and forced myself to look again.

A boy with the hard bird eye of youth pedaled a tricycle slowly up beside me.

"What'cha lookin' at?" he asked curiously.

"A tree," I said.

"What for?" he said.

"It isn't there," I said, to myself mostly, and began to walk away at a pace just slow enough not to seem to be running.

"What isn't there?" the boy asked. I didn't answer. It was obvious I was attached by a thread to a thing that had never been there, or certainly not for long. Something that had to be held in the air, or sustained in the mind, because it was part of my orientation in the universe and I could not survive without it. There was more than an animal's attachment to a place. There was something else, the attachment of the spirit to a grouping of events in time; it was part of our morality.

So I had come home at last, driven by a memory in the brain as surely as the field mouse who had delved long ago into my flower pot or the pigeons flying forever amidst the rattle of nut-vending machines. These, the burrow under the greenery in my living room and the red-bellied bowls of peanuts now hovering in midair in the minds of pigeons, were all part of an elusive world that existed nowhere and yet everywhere. I looked once at the real world about me while the persistent boy pedaled at my heels.

It was without meaning, though my feet took a remembered path. In sixty years the house and street had rotted out of my mind. But the tree, the tree that no longer was, that had perished in its first season, bloomed on in my individual mind, unblemished as my father's words. "We'll plant a tree here, son, and we're not going to move any more. And when you're an old, old man you can sit under it and think how we planted it here, you and me, together."

I began to outpace the boy on the tricycle.

"Do you live here, Mister?" he shouted after me suspiciously. I took a firm grasp on airy nothing—to be precise, on the bole of a great tree. "I do," I said. I spoke for myself, one field mouse, and several pigeons. We were all out of touch but somehow permanent. It was the world that had changed.

1971

QUESTIONS

1. Eiseley writes of old men in train stations, brown wasps, a field mouse, pigeons near the El, and his own return to his boyhood home in Nebraska. What do these matters have in common? Can you state the essay's theme?
2. Some psychologists study animal behavior in order to learn about human behavior, but many of them write about animals in a very different fashion. Do you think that Eiseley's way of relating the behavior of animals to human behavior makes sense? If you are studying psychology, it might be interesting to compare a selection from your textbook with this essay.
3. Would Eiseley agree with Henry David Thoreau's remarks in "Observation" (p. 189)? If so, in what particular ways would he agree?
4. Eiseley's essay contains sentences like "We cling to a time and place because without them man is lost, not only man but life" (p. 72) and also sentences like "A boy with the hard bird eye of youth pedaled a tricycle slowly up beside me" (p. 76). What is the difference between these two kinds of sentences? Can you show how Eiseley manages to connect one kind with the other?
5. In "Once More to the Lake" (p. 78) E. B. White describes his return to a lake he had known years earlier. What reflections arise in his mind on this occasion? Are they similar to, or different from, Eiseley's thoughts upon returning to his Nebraska home and the nonexistent tree?
6. Write an essay comparing the theme or purpose of "The Brown Wasps" with that of Konrad Z. Lorenz's "The Taming of the Shrew"

(p. 893) or of Niko Tinbergen's "The Bee-Hunters of Hulshorst" (p. 906). Do these authors take a similar approach to their subject, or are they largely different? Consider also the manner of the writing: how would you characterize it in each instance?

E. B. White

ONCE MORE TO THE LAKE

One summer, along about 1904, my father rented a camp on a lake in Maine and took us all there for the month of August. We all got ring-worm from some kittens and had to rub Pond's Extract on our arms and legs night and morning, and my father rolled over in a canoe with all his clothes on; but outside of that the vacation was a success and from then on none of us ever thought there was any place in the world like that lake in Maine. We returned summer after summer—always on August 1st for one month. I have since become a salt-water man, but sometimes in summer there are days when the restlessness of the tides and the fearful cold of the sea water and the incessant wind which blows across the afternoon and into the evening make me wish for the placidity of a lake in the woods. A few weeks ago this feeling got so strong I bought myself a couple of bass hooks and a spinner and returned to the lake where we used to go, for a week's fishing and to revisit old haunts.

I took along my son, who had never had any fresh water up his nose and who had seen lily pads only from train windows. On the journey over to the lake I began to wonder what it would be like. I wondered how time would have marred this unique, this holy spot—the coves and streams, the hills that the sun set behind, the camps and the paths behind the camps. I was sure the tarred road would have found it out and I wondered in what other ways it would be desolated. It is strange how much you can remember about places like that once you allow your mind to return into the grooves which lead back. You remember one thing, and that sud-denly reminds you of another thing. I guess I remembered clearest of all the early mornings, when the lake was cool and motionless, remembered how the bedroom smelled of the lumber it was made of and of the wet woods whose scent entered through the screen. The partitions in the camp were thin and did not extend clear to the top of the rooms, and as I was always the first up I would dress softly so as not to wake the others, and sneak out into the sweet outdoors and start out in the canoe, keeping close along the shore in the long shadows of the pines. I remembered being very careful never to rub my paddle against the gunwale for fear of disturbing the stillness of the cathedral.

The lake had never been what you would call a wild lake. There were cottages sprinkled around the shores, and it was in farming country although the shores of the lake were quite heavily wooded. Some of the cottages were owned by nearby farmers, and you would live at the shore and eat your meals at the farmhouse. That's what our family did. But although it wasn't wild, it was a fairly large and undisturbed lake and there were places in it which, to a child at least, seemed infinitely remote and primeval.

I was right about the tar: it led to within half a mile of the shore. But when I got back there, with my boy, and we settled into a camp near a farmhouse and into the kind of summertime I had known, I could tell that it was going to be pretty much the same as it had been before—I knew it, lying in bed the first morning, smelling the bedroom, and hearing the boy sneak quietly out and go off along the shore in a boat. I began to sustain the illusion that he was I, and therefore, by simple transposition, that I was my father. This sensation persisted, kept cropping up all the time we were there. It was not an entirely new feeling, but in this setting it grew much stronger. I seemed to be living a dual existence. I would be in the middle of some simple act, I would be picking up a bait box or laying down a table fork, or I would be saying something, and suddenly it would be not I but my father who was saying the words or making the gesture. It gave me a creepy sensation.

We went fishing the first morning. I felt the same damp moss covering the worms in the bait can, and saw the dragonfly alight on the tip of my rod as it hovered a few inches from the surface of the water. It was the arrival of this fly that convinced me beyond any doubt that everything was as it always had been, that the years were a mirage and there had been no years. The small waves were the same, chucking the rowboat under the chin as we fished at anchor, and the boat was the same boat, the same color green and the ribs broken in the same places, and under the floor-boards the same fresh-water leavings and débris—the dead helgramite[1] the wisps of moss, the rusty discarded fishhook, the dried blood from yesterday's catch. We stared silently at the tips of our rods, at the dragonflies that came and went. I lowered the tip of mine into the water, tentatively, pensively dislodging the fly, which darted two feet away, poised, darted two feet back, and came to rest again a little farther up the rod. There had been no years between the ducking of this dragonfly and the other one—the one that was part of memory. I looked at the boy, who was silently watching his fly, and it was my hands that held his rod, my eyes watching. I felt dizzy and didn't know which rod I was at the end of.

We caught two bass, hauling them in briskly as though they were

1. The nymph of the May-fly, used as bait.

mackerel, pulling them over the side of the boat in a businesslike manner without any landing net, and stunning them with a blow on the back of the head. When we got back for a swim before lunch, the lake was exactly where we had left it, the same number of inches from the dock, and there was only the merest suggestion of a breeze. This seemed an utterly enchanted sea, this lake you could leave to its own devices for a few hours and come back to, and find that it had not stirred, this constant and trustworthy body of water. In the shallows, the dark, water-soaked sticks and twigs, smooth and old, were undulating in clusters on the bottom against the clean ribbed sand, and the track of the mussel was plain. A school of minnows swam by, each minnow with its small individual shadow, doubling the attendance, so clear and sharp in the sunlight. Some of the other campers were in swimming, along the shore, one of them with a cake of soap, and the water felt thin and clear and unsubstantial. Over the years there had been this person with the cake of soap, this cultist, and here he was. There had been no years.

Up to the farmhouse to dinner through the teeming, dusty field, the road under our sneakers was only a two-track road. The middle track was missing, the one with the marks of the hooves and the splotches of dried, flaky manure. There had always been three tracks to choose from in choosing which track to walk in; now the choice was narrowed down to two. For a moment I missed terribly the middle alternative. But the way led past the tennis court, and something about the way it lay there in the sun reassured me; the tape had loosened along the backline, the alleys were green with plantains and other weeds, and the net (installed in June and removed in September) sagged in the dry noon, and the whole place steamed with midday heat and hunger and emptiness. There was a choice of pie for dessert, and one was blueberry and one was apple, and the waitresses were the same country girls, there having been no passage of time, only the illusion of it as in a dropped curtain—the waitresses were still fifteen; their hair had been washed, that was the only difference —they had been to the movies and seen the pretty girls with the clean hair.

Summertime, oh summertime, pattern of life indelible, the fade-proof lake, the woods unshatterable, the pasture with the sweetfern and the juniper forever and ever, summer without end; this was the background, and the life along the shore was the design, the cottagers with their innocent and tranquil design, their tiny docks with the flagpole and the American flag floating against the white clouds in the blue sky, the little paths over the roots of the trees leading from camp to camp and the paths leading back to the outhouses and the can of lime for sprinkling, and at the souvenir counters at the store the miniature birch-bark canoes and the post cards that showed things looking a little better than they looked. This was the American family at play, escaping the city heat, wondering whether the newcomers in the camp at the head of the cove were "common" or "nice," wondering whether it was true that the people who drove up for Sunday dinner at the farmhouse were turned away because there wasn't enough chicken.

It seemed to me, as I kept remembering all this, that those times and those summers had been infinitely precious and worth saving. There had been jollity and peace and goodness. The arriving (at the beginning of August) had been so big a business in itself, at the railway station the farm wagon drawn up, the first smell of the pine-laden air, the first glimpse of the smiling farmer, and the great importance of the trunks and your father's enormous authority in such matters, and the feel of the wagon under you for the long ten-mile haul, and at the top of the last long hill catching the first view of the lake after eleven months of not seeing this cherished body of water. The shouts and cries of the other campers when they saw you, and the trunks to be unpacked, to give up their rich burden. (Arriving was less exciting nowadays, when you sneaked up in your car and parked it under a tree near the camp and took out the bags and in five minutes it was all over, no fuss, no loud wonderful fuss about trunks.)

Peace and goodness and jollity. The only thing that was wrong now, really, was the sound of the place, an unfamiliar nervous sound of the outboard motors. This was the note that jarred, the one thing that would sometimes break the illusion and set the years moving. In those other summertimes all motors were inboard; and when they were at a little distance, the noise they made was a sedative, an ingredient of summer sleep. They were one-cylinder and two-cylinder engines, and some were make-and-break and some were jump-spark,[2] but they all made a sleepy sound across the lake. The one-lungers throbbed and fluttered, and the twin-cylinder ones purred and purred, and that was a quiet sound too. But now the campers all had outboards. In the daytime, in the hot mornings, these motors made a petulant, irritable sound; at night, in the still evening when the afterglow lit the water, they whined about one's ears like mosquitoes. My boy loved our rented outboard, and his great desire was to achieve singlehanded mastery over it, and authority, and he soon learned the trick of choking it a little (but not too much), and the adjustment of the needle valve. Watching him I would remember the things you could do with the old one-cylinder engine with the heavy flywheel, how you could have it eating out of your hand if you got really close to it spiritually. Motor boats in those days didn't have clutches, and you would make a landing by shutting off the motor at the proper time and coasting in with a dead rudder. But there was a way of reversing them, if you learned the trick, by cutting the switch and putting it on again exactly on the final dying revolution of the flywheel, so that it

2. Methods of ignition timing.

would kick back against compression and begin reversing. Approaching a dock in a strong following breeze, it was difficult to slow up sufficiently by the ordinary coasting method, and if a boy felt he had complete mastery over his motor, he was tempted to keep it running beyond its time and then reverse it a few feet from the dock. It took a cool nerve, because if you threw the switch a twentieth of a second too soon you would catch the flywheel when it still had speed enough to go up past center, and the boat would leap ahead, charging bull-fashion at the dock.

We had a good week at the camp. The bass were biting well and the sun shone endlessly, day after day. We would be tired at night and lie down in the accumulated heat of the little bedrooms after the long hot day and the breeze would stir almost imperceptibly outside and the smell of the swamp drift in through the rusty screens. Sleep would come easily and in the morning the red squirrel would be on the roof, tapping out his gay routine. I kept remembering everything, lying in bed in the mornings —the small steamboat that had a long rounded stern like the lip of a Ubangi, and how quietly she ran on the moonlight sails, when the older boys played their mandolins and the girls sang and we ate doughnuts dipped in sugar, and how sweet the music was on the water in the shining night, and what it had felt like to think about girls then. After breakfast we would go up to the store and the things were in the same place—the minnows in a bottle, the plugs and spinners disarranged and pawed over by the youngsters from the boys' camp, the fig newtons and the Beeman's gum. Outside, the road was tarred and cars stood in front of the store. Inside, all was just as it had always been, except there was more Coca-Cola and not so much Moxie and root beer and birch beer and sarsaparilla. We would walk out with a bottle of pop apiece and sometimes the pop would backfire up our noses and hurt. We explored the streams, quietly, where the turtles slid off the sunny logs and dug their way into the soft bottom; and we lay on the town wharf and fed worms to the tame bass. Everywhere we went I had trouble making out which was I, the one walking at my side, the one walking in my pants.

One afternoon while we were there at that lake a thunderstorm came up. It was like the revival of an old melodrama that I had seen long ago with childish awe. The second-act climax of the drama of the electrical disturbance over a lake in America had not changed in any important respect. This was the big scene, still the big scene. The whole thing was so familiar, the first feeling of oppression and heat and a general air around camp of not wanting to go very far away. In midafternoon (it was all the same) a curious darkening of the sky, and a lull in everything that had made life tick; and then the way the boats suddenly swung the other way at their moorings with the coming of a breeze out of the new quarter, and the premonitory rumble. Then the kettle drum, then the snare, then the bass drum and cymbals, then crackling light against the dark, and the gods grinning and licking their chops in the hills. Afterward the calm, the rain steadily rustling in the calm lake, the return of light and hope and spirits, and the campers running out in joy and relief to go swimming in the rain, their bright cries perpetuating the deathless joke about how they were getting simply drenched, and the children screaming with delight at the new sensation of bathing in the rain, and the joke about getting drenched linking the generations in a strong indestructible chain. And the comedian who waded in carrying an umbrella.

When the others went swimming my son said he was going in too. He pulled his dripping trunks from the line where they had hung all through the shower, and wrung them out. Languidly, and with no thought of going in, I watched him, his hard little body, skinny and bare, saw him wince slightly as he pulled up around his vitals the small, soggy, icy garment. As he buckled the swollen belt suddenly my groin felt the chill of death.

1941

QUESTIONS

1. *White had not been back to the lake for many years. What bearing has this fact on the experience which the essay describes?*
2. *What has guided White in his selection of the details he gives about the trip? Why, for example, does he talk about the road, the dragonfly, the bather with the cake of soap?*
3. *How do the differences between boats of the past and boats of today relate to or support the point of the essay?*
4. *What is the meaning of White's last sentence? What relation has it to the sentence just preceding? How has White prepared us for this ending?*
5. *How would the narrative differ if it were told by the boy? What details of the scene might the boy emphasize? Why? Show what point the boy's selection of details might make.*

Prose Forms: Journals

*Occasionally one catches oneself having said something aloud, obvi-
ously with no concern to be heard, even by oneself. And all of us have
overheard, perhaps while walking, a solitary person muttering or laughing softly or exclaiming abruptly. Something floats up from the world
within, forces itself to be expressed, takes no real account of the time or
the place, and certainly intends no conscious communication.*

*With more self-consciousness, and yet without a specific audience, one
sometimes speaks out at something that has momentarily filled his attention from the world without. A sharp play at the ball game, the twist of a
political speech, an old photograph—something from the outer world
impresses the mind, stimulates it, focuses certain of its memories and
values, interests and needs. Thus stimulated, one may wish to share an
experience with another, to inform or amuse that person, to rouse him or
her to action or persuade someone to a certain belief. Often, though, the
person experiencing may want most to talk to himself, to give a public
shape in words to thoughts and feelings but for the sake of a kind of
private dialogue. Communication to another may be an ultimate desire,
but the immediate motive is to articulate the experience for oneself.*

*To articulate, to shape the experience in language for one's own sake,
one may keep a journal. Literally a day-book, the journal enables one to
write down something about the experiences of a day which for a great
variety of reasons may have been especially memorable or impressive.
The journal entry may be merely a few words to call to mind a thing
done, a person seen, a menu enjoyed at a dinner party. It may be concerned at length with a political crisis in the community, or a personal
crisis in the home. It may even be as noble as it was with some pious
people in the past who used the journal to keep a record of their consciences, a periodic reckoning of their moral and spiritual accounts. In its
most public aspect, the idea of a journal calls to mind the newspaper or
the record of proceedings like the U. S.* Congressional Record *and the
Canadian* Hansard. *In its most closely private form, the journal becomes
the diary.*

*For the person keeping a journal, whatever he experiences and wants
to hold he can write down. But to get it down on paper begins another
adventure. For he has to focus on what he has experienced, and to be able
to say what, in fact, the experience is. What of it is new? What of it is*

84

remarkable because of associations in the memory it stirs up? Is this like anything I—or others—have experienced before? Is it a good or a bad thing to have happened? And why, specifically? The questions multiply themselves quickly, and as the journalist seeks to answer the appropriate ones, he begins to know what it is he contemplates. As one tries to find the words that best represent this discovery, the experience becomes even more clear in its shape and meaning. We can imagine Emerson going to the ballet, being absorbed in the spectacle, thinking casually of this or that association the dancer and the movements suggest. When he writes about the experience in his journal, a good many questions, judgments, and speculations get tied up with the spectacle, and it is this complex of event and his total relation to it that becomes the experience he records. The simple facts of time, place, people, and actions drop down into one's consciousness and set in motion ideas and feelings which give those facts their real meaning to oneself.

Once this consciousness of events is formulated in words, the journal-keeper has it, not only in the sense of understanding what has been seen or felt or thought, but also in the sense of having it there before him to contemplate long after the event itself. When we read a carefully kept journal covering a long period and varied experiences, we have the pleasure of a small world re-created for us in the consciousness of one who experienced it. Even more, we feel the continuity, the wholeness, of the writer. Something of the same feeling is there for the person who kept the journal: a whole world of events preserved in the form of their experienced reality, and with it the persistent self in the midst of that world. That world and that self are always accessible on the page, and ultimately, therefore, usably real.

Beyond the value of the journal as record, there is the instructive value of the habit of mind and hand journal keeping can assure. One begins to attend more carefully to what happens to and around oneself. One learns the resources of language as a means of representing what one sees, and gains skill and certainty in doing justice to experience and to one's own consciousness. And the journal represents a discipline. It brings together an individual and a complex environment in a relation that teaches the individual something of himself or herself, something of the world, and something of the meaning of their relation. There is scarcely a moment in a person's life when he is not poised for the lesson. When it comes with the promise of special force, there is the almost irresistible temptation to catch the impulse, give it form, make it permanent, assert its meaning. And so one commits oneself to language. To have given up one's experience to words is to have begun marking out the limits and potential of its meaning. In the journal that meaning is developed and clarified to oneself primarily. When the whole intention of the development and the clarification is the consideration of another reader, the method of the journal redirects itself to become that of the essay.

Joan Didion: ON KEEPING A NOTEBOOK

"'That woman Estelle,'" the note reads, "'is partly the reason why George Sharp and I are separated today.' *Dirty crepe-deChine wrapper, hotel bar, Wilmington RR, 9:45 a.m. August Monday morning.*"

Since the note is in my notebook, it presumably has some meaning to me. I study it for a long while. At first I have only the most general notion of what I was doing on an August Monday morning in the bar of the hotel across from the Pennsylvania Railroad station in Wilmington, Delaware (waiting for a train? missing one? 1960? 1961? why Wilmington?), but I do remember being there. The woman in the dirty crepe-de-Chine wrapper had come down from her room for a beer, and the bartender had heard before the reason why George Sharp and she were separated today. "Sure," he said, and went on mopping the floor. "You told me." At the other end of the bar is a girl. She is talking, pointedly, not to the man beside her but to a cat lying in the triangle of sunlight cast through the open door. She is wearing a plaid silk dress from Peck & Peck, and the hem is coming down.

Here is what it is: the girl has been on the Eastern Shore, and now she is going back to the city, leaving the man beside her, and all she can see ahead are the viscous summer sidewalks and the 3 a.m. long-distance calls that will make her lie awake and then sleep drugged through all the steaming mornings left in August (1960? 1961?). Because she must go directly from the train to lunch in New York, she wishes that she had a safety pin for the hem of the plaid silk dress, and she also wishes that she could forget about the hem and the lunch and stay in the cool bar that smells of disinfectant and malt and make friends with the woman in the crepe-de-Chine wrapper. She is afflicted by a little self-pity, and she wants to compare Estelles. That is what that was all about.

Why did I write it down? In order to remember, of course, but exactly what was it I wanted to remember? How much of it actually happened? Did any of it? Why do I keep a notebook at all? It is easy to deceive oneself on all those scores. The impulse to write things down is a peculiarly compulsive one, inexplicable to those who do not share it, useful only accidentally, only secondarily, in the way that any compulsion tries to justify itself. I suppose that it begins or does not begin in the cradle. Although I have felt compelled to write things down since I was five years old, I doubt that my daughter ever will, for she is a singularly blessed and accepting child, delighted with life exactly as life presents itself to her, unafraid to go to sleep and unafraid to wake up. Keepers of private notebooks are a different breed altogether, lonely and resistant rearrangers of things, anxious malcontents, children afflicted apparently at birth with some presentiment of loss.

My first notebook was a Big Five tablet, given to me by my mother with the sensible suggestion that I stop whining and learm to amuse myself by writing down my thoughts. She returned the tablet to me a few years ago; the first entry is an account of a woman who believed herself to be freezing to death in the Arctic night, only to find, when day broke, that she had stumbled onto the Sahara Desert, where she would die of the heat before lunch. I have no idea what turn of a five-year-old's mind could have prompted so insistently "ironic" and exotic a story, but it does reveal a certain predilection for the extreme which has dogged me into adult life; perhaps if I were analytically inclined I would find it a truer story than any I might have told about Donald Johnson's birthday party or the day my cousin Brenda put Kitty Litter in the aquarium.

So the point of my keeping a notebook has never been, nor is it now, to have an accurate factual record of what I have been doing or thinking. That would be a different impulse entirely, an instinct for reality which I sometimes envy but do not possess. At no point have I ever been able successfully to keep a diary; my approach to daily life ranges from the grossly negligent to the merely absent, and on those few occasions when I have tried dutifully to record a day's events, boredom has so overcome me that the results are mysterious at best. What is this business about "shopping, typing piece, dinner with E, depressed"? Shopping for what? Typing what piece? Who is E? Was this "E" depressed, or was I depressed? Who cares?

In fact I have abandoned altogether that kind of pointless entry; instead I tell what some would call lies. "That's simply not true," the members of my family frequently tell me when they come up against my memory of a shared event. "The party was *not* for you, the spider was *not* a black widow, *it wasn't that way at all.*" Very likely they are right, for not only have I always had trouble distinguishing between what happened and what merely might have happened, but I remain unconvinced that the distinction, for my purposes, matters. The cracked crab that I recall having for lunch the day my father came home from Detroit in 1945 must certainly be embroidery, worked into the day's pattern to lend verisimilitude; I was ten years old and would not now remember the cracked crab. The day's events did not turn on cracked crab. And yet it is precisely that fictitious crab that makes me see the afternoon all over again, a home movie run all too often, the father bearing gifts, the child weeping, an exercise in family love and guilt. Or that is what it was to me. Similarly, perhaps it never did snow that August in Vermont; perhaps there never were flurries in the night wind, and maybe no one else felt the ground hardening and summer already dead even as we pretended to bask in it, but that was how it felt to me, and it might as well have snowed, could have snowed, did snow.

How it felt to me: that is getting closer to the truth about a notebook. I sometimes delude myself about why I keep a notebook, imagine that some thrifty virtue derives from preserving everything observed. See enough and write it down, I tell myself, and then some morning when the world seems drained of wonder, some day when I am only going through the motions of doing what I am supposed to do, which is write—on that bankrupt morning I will simply open my notebook and there it will all be, a forgotten account with accumulated interest, paid passage back to the world out there: dialogue overheard in hotels and elevators and at the hatcheck counter in Pavillon (one middle-aged man shows his hat check to another and says, "That's my old football number"); impressions of Bettina Aptheker and Benjamin Sonnenberg and Teddy ("Mr. Acapulco") Stauffer; careful aperçus about tennis bums and failed fashion models and Greek shipping heiresses, one of whom taught me a significant lesson (a lesson I could have learned from F. Scott Fitzgerald, but perhaps we all must meet the very rich for ourselves) by asking, when I arrived to interview her in her orchid-filled sitting room on the second day of a paralyzing New York blizzard, whether it was snowing outside.

I imagine, in other words, that the notebook is about other people. But of course it is not. I have no real business with what one stranger said to another at the hat-check counter in Pavillon; in fact I suspect that the line "That's my old football number" touched not my own imagination at all, but merely some memory of something once read, probably "The Eighty-Yard Run." Nor is my concern with a woman in a dirty crepe-de-Chine wrapper in a Wilmington bar. My stake is always, of course, in the unmentioned girl in the plaid silk dress. Remember what it was to be me: that is always the point.

It is a difficult point to admit. We are brought up in the ethic that others, any others, all others, are by definition more interesting than ourselves; taught to be diffident, just this side of self-effacing. ("You're the least important person in the room and don't forget it," Jessica Mitford's governess would hiss in her ear on the advent of any social occasion; I copied that into my notebook because it is only recently that I have been able to enter a room without hearing some such phrase in my inner ear.) Only the very young and the very old may recount their dreams at breakfast, dwell upon self, interrupt with memories of beach picnics and favorite Liberty lawn dresses and the rainbow trout in a creek near Colorado Springs. The rest of us are expected, rightly, to affect absorption in other people's favorite dresses, other people's trout.

And so we do. But our notebooks give us away, for however dutifully we record what we see around us, the common denominator of all we see is always, transparently, shamelessly, the implacable "I." We are not talking here about the kind of notebook that is patently for public consumption, a structural conceit for binding together a series of graceful *pensées;*[1] we are talking about something private, about bits of the mind's string too short to use, an indiscriminate and erratic assemblage with meaning only for its maker.

And sometimes even the maker has difficulty with the meaning. There does not seem to be, for example, any point in my knowing for the rest of my life that, during 1964, 720 tons of soot fell on every square mile of New York City, yet there it is in my notebook, labeled "FACT." Nor do I really need to remember that Ambrose Bierce liked to spell Leland Stanford's name "£eland $tanford" or that "smart women almost always wear black in Cuba," a fashion hint without much potential for practical application. And does not the relevance of these notes seem marginal at best?:

> In the basement museum of the Inyo County Courthouse in Independence, California, sign pinned to a mandarin coat: "This MANDARIN COAT was often worn by Mrs. Minnie S. Brooks when giving lectures on her TEAPOT COL-LECTION."
>
> Redhead getting out of car in front of Beverly Wilshire Hotel, chinchilla stole, Vuitton bags with tags reading:
>
>
>
> MRS LOU FOX
>
> HOTEL SAHARA
>
> VEGAS
>
>

Well, perhaps not entirely marginal. As a matter of fact, Mrs. Minnie S. Brooks and her MANDARIN COAT pull me back into my own childhood, for although I never knew Mrs. Brooks and did not visit Inyo County until I was thirty, I grew up in just such a world, in houses cluttered with Indian relics and bits of gold ore and ambergris and the souvenirs my Aunt Mercy Farnsworth brought back from the Orient. It is a long way from that world to Mrs. Lou Fox's world, where we all live now, and is it not just as well to remember that? Might not Mrs. Minnie S. Brooks help me to remember what I am? Might not Mrs. Lou Fox help me to remember what I am not?

But sometimes the point is harder to discern. What exactly did I have in mind when I noted down that it cost the father of someone I know $650 a month to light the place on the Hudson in which he lived before the Crash?[3] What use was I planning to make of this line by Jimmy Hoffa: "I may have my faults, but being wrong ain't one of them"? And although I think it interesting to know where the girls who travel with the Syndicate have their hair done when they find themselves on the West Coast, will I ever make suitable use of it? Might I not be better off just passing it on to John O'Hara? What is a recipe for sauerkraut doing in my notebook? What kind of magpie keeps this notebook? *"He was born the night the*

---

1. Thoughts, reflections.
2. A nineteenth-century American million-
aire.
3. The stock market crash of 1929.

Titanic went down." That seems a nice enough line, and I even recall who said it, but is it not really a better line in life than it could ever be in fiction?

But of course that is exactly it: not that I should ever use the line, but that I should remember the woman who said it and the afternoon I heard it. We were on her terrace by the sea, and we were finishing the wine left from lunch, trying to get what sun there was, a California winter sun. The woman whose husband was born the night the *Titanic* went down wanted to rent her house, wanted to go back to her children in Paris. I remember wishing that I could afford the house, which cost $1,000 a month. "Someday you will," she said lazily. "Someday it all comes." There in the sun on her terrace it seemed easy to believe in someday, but later I had a low-grade afternoon hangover and ran over a black snake on the way to the supermarket and was flooded with inexplicable fear when I heard the checkout clerk explaining to the man ahead of me why she was finally divorcing her husband. "He left me no choice," she said over and over as she punched the register. "He has a little seven-month-old baby by her, he left me no choice." I would like to believe that my dread then was for the human condition, but of course it was for me, because I wanted a baby and did not then have one and because I wanted to own the house that cost $1,000 a month to rent and because I had a hangover.

It all comes back. Perhaps it is difficult to see the value in having one's self back in that kind of mood, but I do see it; I think we are well advised to keep on nodding terms with the people we used to be whether we find them attractive company or not. Otherwise they turn up unannounced and surprise us, come hammering on the mind's door at 4 a.m. of a bad night and demand to know who deserted them, who betrayed them, who is going to make amends. We forget all too soon the things we thought we could never forget. We forget the loves and the betrayals alike, forget what we whispered and what we screamed, forget who we were. I have already lost touch with a couple of people I used to be; one of them, a seventeen-year-old, presents little threat, although it would be of some interest to me to know again what it feels like to sit on a river levee drinking vodka-and-orange-juice and listening to Les Paul and Mary Ford and their echoes sing "How High the Moon" on the car radio. (You see I still have the scenes, but I no longer perceive myself among those present, no longer could even improvise the dialogue.) The other one, a twenty-three-year-old, bothers me more. She was always a good deal of trouble, and I suspect she will reappear when I least want to see her, skirts too long, shy to the point of aggravation, always the injured party, full of recriminations and little hurts and stories I do not want to hear again, at once saddening me and angering me with her vulnerability and ignorance, an apparition all the more insistent for being so long banished.

It is a good idea, then, to keep in touch, and I suppose that keeping in touch is what notebooks are all about. And we are all on our own when it comes to keeping those lines open to ourselves: your notebook will never help me, nor mine you. *"So what's new in the whiskey business?"* What could that possibly mean to you? To me it means a blonde in a Pucci bathing suit sitting with a couple of fat men by the pool at the Beverly Hills Hotel. Another man approaches, and they all regard one another in silence for a while. "So what's new in the whiskey business?" one of the fat men finally says by way of welcome, and the blonde stands up, arches one foot and dips it in the pool, looking all the while at the cabaña where Baby Pignatari is talking on the telephone. That is all there is to that, except that several years later I saw the blonde coming out of Saks Fifth Avenue in New York with her California complexion and a voluminous mink coat. In the harsh wind that day she looked old and irrevocably tired to me, and even the skins in the mink coat were not worked the way they were doing them that year, not the way she would have wanted them done, and there is the point of the story. For a while after that I did not like to look in the mirror, and my eyes would skim the newspapers and pick out only the deaths, the cancer victims, the premature coronaries, the suicides, and I stopped riding the Lexington Avenue IRT[4] because I noticed for the first time that all the strangers I had seen for years—the man with the seeing-eye dog, the spinster who read the classified pages every day, the fat girl who always got off with me at Grand Central —looked older than they once had.

It all comes back. Even that recipe for sauerkraut: even that brings it back. I was on Fire Island when I first made that sauerkraut, and it was raining, and we drank a lot of bourbon and ate the sauerkraut and went to bed at ten, and I listened to the rain and the Atlantic and felt safe. I made the sauerkraut again last night and it did not make me feel any safer, but that is, as they say, another story.

1968

4. A New York City subway line; one of its stops is the Grand Central railway terminal.

Ralph Waldo Emerson: FROM JOURNAL

I like to have a man's knowledge comprehend more than one class of topics, one row of shelves. I like a man who likes to see a fine barn as well as a good tragedy. [1828]

The Religion that is afraid of science dishonors God and commits suicide. [1831]

The things taught in colleges and schools are not an education, but the means of education. [1831]

Don't tell me to get ready to die. I know not what shall be. The only preparation I can make is by fulfilling my present duties. This is the everlasting life. [1832]

My aunt [Mary Moody Emerson] had an eye that went through and through you like a needle. "She was endowed," she said, "with the fatal gift of penetration." She disgusted everybody because she knew them too well. [1832]

I am sure of this, that by going much alone a man will get more of a noble courage in thought and word than from all the wisdom that is in books. [1833]

I fretted the other night at the hotel at the stranger who broke into my chamber after midnight, claiming to share it. But after his lamp had smoked the chamber full and I had turned round to the wall in despair, the man blew out his lamp, knelt down at his bedside, and made in low whisper a long earnest prayer. Then was the relation entirely changed between us. I fretted no more, but respected and liked him. [1835]

I believe I shall some time cease to be an individual, that the eternal tendency of the soul is to become Universal, to animate the last extremities of organization. [1837]

It is very hard to be simple enough to be good. [1837]

A man must have aunts and cousins, must buy carrots and turnips, must have barn and woodshed, must go to market and to the blacksmith's shop, must saunter and sleep and be inferior and silly. [1838]

How sad a spectacle, so frequent nowadays, to see a young man after ten years of college education come out, ready for his voyage of life—and to see that the entire ship is made of rotten timber, of rotten, honeycombed, traditional timber without so much as an inch of new plank in the hull. [1839]

A sleeping child gives me the impression of a traveler in a very far country. [1840]

In reading these letters of M.M.E. I acknowledge (with surprise that I could ever forget it) the debt of myself and my brothers to that old religion which, in those years, still dwelt like a Sabbath peace in the country population of New England, which taught privation, self-denial, and sorrow. A man was born, not for prosperity, but to suffer for the benefit of others, like the noble rock-maple tree which all around the villages bleeds for the service of man.[1] Not praise, not men's acceptance of our doing, but the Spirit's holy errand through us, absorbed the thought. How dignified is this! how all that is called talents and worth in Paris and in Washington dwindles before it! [1841]

All writing is by the grace of God. People do not deserve to have good writing, they are so pleased with bad. In these sentences that you show me, I can find no beauty, for I see death in every clause and every word. There is a fossil or a mummy character which pervades this book. The best sepulchers, the vastest catacombs, Thebes and Cairo, Pyramids, are sepulchers to me. I like gardens and nurseries. Give me initiative, spermatic, prophesying, man-making words. [1841],

When summer opens, I see how fast it matures, and fear it will be short; but after the heats of July and August, I am reconciled, like one who has had his swing, to the cool of autumn. So will it be with the coming of death. [1846]

In England every man you meet is some man's son; in America, he may be some man's father. [1848]

Every poem must be made up of lines that are poems. [1848]

Love is necessary to the righting the estate of woman in this world. Otherwise nature itself seems to be in conspiracy against her dignity and welfare; for the cultivated, high-thoughted, beauty-loving, saintly woman finds herself unconsciously desired for her sex, and even enhancing the appetite of her savage pursuers by these fine ornaments she has piously laid on herself. She finds with indignation that she is herself a snare, and was made such. I do not wonder at her occasional protest, violent protest against nature, in fleeing to nunneries, and taking black veils. Love rights all this deep wrong. [1848]

Natural Aristocracy. It is a vulgar error to suppose that a gentleman must be ready to fight. The utmost that can be demanded of the gentleman is that he be incapable of a lie. There is a man who has good sense, is well informed, well-read, obliging, cultivated, capable, and has an absolute devotion to truth. He always means what he says, and says what he means, however courteously. You may spit upon him—nothing could induce him to spit upon you—no praises, and no possessions, no compulsion of public opinion. You may kick him—he will think it the kick of a brute—but he is not a brute, and will not kick you in return. But neither your knife and pistol, nor your gifts and courting will ever make the smallest impression on his vote or word; for he is the truth's man, and will speak and act the truth until he dies. [1849]

---

1. The sap of the rock or sugar maple is collected and made into maple syrup.

Love is temporary and ends with marriage. Marriage is the perfection which love aimed at, ignorant of what it sought. Marriage is a good known only to the parties—a relation of perfect understanding, aid, contentment, possession of themselves and of the world—which dwarfs love to green fruit. [1850]

I found when I had finished my new lecture that it was a very good house, only the architect had unfortunately omitted the stairs. [1851]

This filthy enactment [The Fugitive Slave Law[2]] was made in the nineteenth century, by people who could read and write. I will not obey it, by God. [1851]

Henry [Thoreau] is military. He seemed stubborn and implacable; always manly and wise, but rarely sweet. One would say that, as Webster could never speak without an antagonist, so Henry does not feel himself except in opposition. He wants a fallacy to expose, a blunder to pillory, requires a little sense of victory, a roll of the drums, to call his powers into full exercise. [1853]

Shall we judge the country by the majority or by the minority? Certainly, by the minority. The mass are animal, in state of pupilage, and nearer the chimpanzee. [1854]

All the thoughts of a turtle are turtle. [1854]

Resources or feats. I like people who can do things. When Edward and I struggled in vain to drag our big calf into the barn, the Irish girl put her finger into the calf's mouth, and led her in directly. [1862]

George Francis Train said in a public speech in New York, "Slavery is a divine institution." "So is hell," exclaimed an old man in the crowd. [1862]

You complain that the Negroes are a base class. Who makes and keeps the Jew or the Negro base, who but you, who exclude them from the rights which others enjoy? [1867]

2. A law enacted in 1850 to compel the arrest of runaway slaves and their return to their owners.

Henry David Thoreau: FROM JOURNAL

As the least drop of wine tinges the whole goblet, so the least particle of truth colors our whole life. It is never isolated, or simply added as treasure to our stock. When any real progress is made, we unlearn and learn anew what we thought we knew before. [1837]

Not by constraint or severity shall you have access to true wisdom, but by abandonment, and childlike mirthfulness. If you would know aught, be gay before it. [1840]

It is the man determines what is said, not the words. If a mean person uses a wise maxim, I bethink me how it can be interpreted so as to commend itself to his meanness; but if a wise man makes a commonplace remark, I consider what wider construction it will admit. [1840]

Nothing goes by luck in composition. It allows of no tricks. The best you can write will be the best you are. Every sentence is the result of a long probation. The author's character is read from title-page to end. Of this he never corrects the proofs. We read it as the essential character of a handwriting without regard to the flourishes. And so of the rest of our actions; it runs as straight as a ruled line through them all, no matter how many curvets about it. Our whole life is taxed for the least thing well done: it is its net result. How we eat, drink, sleep, and use our desultory hours, now in these indifferent days, with no eye to observe and no occasion [to] excite us, determines our authority and capacity for the time to come. [1841]

What does education often do? It makes a straight-cut ditch of a free, meandering brook. [1850]

All perception of truth is the detection of an analogy; we reason from our hands to our head. [1851]

To set down such choice experiences that my own writings may inspire me and at last I may make wholes of parts. Certainly it is a distinct profession to rescue from oblivion and to fix the sentiments and thoughts which visit all men more or less generally, that the contemplation of the unfinished picture may suggest its harmonious completion. Associate reverently and as much as you can with your loftiest thoughts. Each thought that is welcomed and recorded is a nest egg, by the side of which more will be laid. Thoughts accidentally thrown together become a frame in which more may be developed and exhibited. Perhaps this is the main value of a habit of writing, of keeping a journal—that so we remember our best hours and stimulate ourselves. My thoughts are my company. They have a certain individuality and separate existence, aye, personality. Having by chance recorded a few disconnected thoughts and then brought them into juxtaposition, they suggest a whole new field in which it was possible to labor and to think. Thought begat thought. [1852]

It is pardonable when we spurn the proprieties, even the sanctities, making them stepping-stones to something higher. [1858]

There is always some accident in the best things, whether thoughts or expressions or deeds. The memorable thought, the happy expression, the admirable deed are only partly ours. The thought came to us because we were in a fit mood; also we were unconscious and did not know that we had said or done a good thing. We must walk consciously only part way toward our goal, and then leap in the dark to our success. What we do best or most perfectly is what we have most thoroughly learned by the longest practice, and at length it falls from us without our notice, as a leaf from a tree. It is the *last* time we shall do it—our unconscious leavings. [1859]

The expression "a *liberal* education" originally meant one worthy of freemen. Such is education simply in a true and broad sense. But education ordinarily so called—the learning of trades and professions which is designed to enable men to earn their living, or to fit them for a particular station in life—is *servile.* [1859]

May Sarton: FROM JOURNAL OF A SOLITUDE

September 17th. Cracking open the inner world again, writing even a couple of pages, threw me back into depression, not made easier by the weather, two gloomy days of darkness and rain. I was attacked by a storm of tears, those tears that appear to be related to frustration, to buried anger, and come upon me without warning. I woke yesterday so depressed that I did not get up till after eight.

I drove to Brattleboro[1] to read poems at the new Unitarian church there in a state of dread and exhaustion. How to summon the vitality needed? I had made an arrangement of religious poems, going back to early books and forward into the new book not yet published. I suppose it went all right—at least it was not a disaster—but I felt (perhaps I am wrong) that the kind, intelligent people gathered in a big room looking out on pine trees did not really want to think about God. His absence (many of the poems speak of that) or His presence. Both are too frightening.

1. Brattleboro, Vermont.

On the way back I stopped to see Perley Cole, my dear old friend, who is dying, separated from his wife, and has just been moved from a Dickensian nursing home into what seems like a far better one. He grows more transparent every day, a skeleton or nearly. Clasping his hand, I fear to break a bone. Yet the only real communication between us now (he is very deaf) is a handclasp. I want to lift him in my arms and hold him like a baby. He is dying a terribly lonely death. Each time I see him he says, "It is rough" or "I did not think it would end like this."

Everywhere I look about this place I see his handiwork: the three small trees by a granite boulder that he pruned and trimmed so they pivot the whole meadow; the new shady border he dug out for me one of the last days he worked here; the pruned-out stone wall between my field and the church. The second field where he cut brush twice a year and cleared out to the stone wall is growing back to wilderness now. What is done here has to be done over and over and needs the dogged strength of a man like Perley. I could have never managed it alone. We cherished this piece of land together, and fought together to bring it to some semblance of order and beauty.

I like to think that this last effort of Perley's had a certain ease about it, a game compared to the hard work of his farming years, and a game where his expert knowledge and skill could be well used. How he enjoyed teasing me about my ignorance!

While he scythed and trimmed, I struggled in somewhat the same way at my desk here, and we were each aware of the companionship. We each looked forward to noon, when I could stop for the day and he sat on a high stool in the kitchen, drank a glass or two of sherry with me, said, "Court's in session!" and then told me some tall tale he had been cogitating all morning.

It was a strange relationship, for he knew next to nothing about my life, really; yet below all the talk we recognized each other as the same kind. He enjoyed my anger as much as I enjoyed his. Perhaps that was part of it. Deep down there was understanding, not of the facts of our lives so much as of our essential natures. Even now in his hard, lonely end he has immense dignity. But I wish there were some way to make it easier. I leave him with bitter resentment against the circumstances of this death. "I know. But I did not approve. And I am not resigned."

In the mail a letter from a twelve-year-old child, enclosing poems, her mother having pushed her to ask my opinion. The child does really look at things, and I can write something helpful, I think. But it is troubling how many people expect applause, recognition, when they have not even begun to learn an art or a craft. Instant success is the order of the day; "I want it now!" I wonder whether this is not part of our corruption by machines. Machines do things very quickly and outside the natural rhythm of life, and we are indignant if a car doesn't start at the first try. So the few things that we still do, such as cooking (though there are TV dinners!), knitting, gardening, anything at all that cannot be hurried, have a very particular value.

September 18th. The value of solitude—one of its values—is, of course, that there is nothing to *cushion* against attacks from within, just as there is nothing to help balance at times of particular stress or depression. A few moments of desultory conversation with dear Arnold Miner, when he comes to take the trash, may calm an inner storm. But the storm, painful as it is, might have had some truth in it. So sometimes one has simply to endure a period of depression for what it may hold of illumination if one can live through it, attentive to what it exposes or demands.

The reasons for depression are not so interesting as the way one handles it, simply to stay alive. This morning I woke at four and lay awake for an hour or so in a bad state. It is raining again. I got up finally and went about the daily chores, waiting for the sense of doom to lift —and what did it was watering the house plants. Suddenly joy came back because I was fulfilling a simple need, a living one. Dusting never has this effect (and that may be why I am such a poor housekeeper!), but feeding the cats when they are hungry, giving Punch clean water, makes me suddenly feel calm and happy.

Whatever peace I know rests in the natural world, in feeling myself a part of it, even in a small way. Maybe the gaiety of the Warner family, their wisdom, comes from this, that they work close to nature all the time. As simple as that? But it is not simple. Their life requires patient understanding, imagination, the power to endure constant adversity —the weather, for example! To go with, not against the elements, an inexhaustible vitality summoned back each day to do the same tasks, to feed the animals, clean out barns and pens, keep that complex world alive.

October 6th. A day when I am expecting someone for lunch is quite unlike ordinary days. There is a reason to make the flowers look beautiful all over the house, and I know that Anne Woodson, who is coming today, will notice them, for she sees this house in a way that few of my friends do, perhaps because she has lived here without me, has lived her way into the place by pruning and weeding, and once even tidying the linen cupboard!

It is a mellow day, very gentle. The ash has lost its leaves and when I went out to get the mail and stopped to look up at it, I rejoiced to think that soon everything here will be honed down to structure. It is all a rich farewell now to leaves, to color. I think of the trees and how simply they let go, let fall the riches of a season, how without grief (it seems) they can let go and go deep into their roots for renewal and sleep. Eliot's statement comes back to me these days:

> Teach us to care and not to care
> Teach us to sit still.[2]

2. From T. S. Eliot's *Ash Wednesday* (1930),

It is there in Mahler's *Der Abschied*, which I play again every autumn (Bruno Walter with Kathleen Ferrier).[3] But in Mahler it is a cry of loss, a long lyrical cry just *before* letting go, at least until those last long phrases that suggest peace, renunciation. But I think of it as the golden leaves and the brilliant small red maple that shone transparent against the shimmer of the lake yesterday when I went over to have a picnic with Helen Milbank.

Does anything in nature despair except man? An animal with a foot caught in a trap does not seem to despair. It is too busy trying to survive. It is all closed in, to a kind of still, intense waiting. Is this a key? Keep busy with survival. Imitate the trees. Learn to lose in order to recover, and remember that nothing stays the same for long, not even pain, psychic pain. Sit it out. Let it all pass. Let it go.

Yesterday I weeded out violets from the iris bed. The iris was being choked by thick bunches of roots, so much like fruit under the earth. I found one single very fragrant violet and some small autumn crocuses. Now, after an hour's work as the light failed and I drank in the damp smell of earth, it looks orderly again.

October 9th. Has it really happened at last? I feel released from the rack, set free, in touch with the deep source that is only *good*, where poetry lives. We have waited long this year for the glory, but suddenly the big maple is all gold and the beeches yellow with a touch of green that makes the yellow even more intense. There are still nasturtiums to be picked, and now I must get seriously to work to get the remaining bulbs in.

It has been stupidly difficult to let go, but that is what has been needed. I had allowed myself to get overanxious, clutching at what seemed sure to pass, and clutching is the surest way to murder love, as if it were a kitten, not to be squeezed so hard, or a flower to fade in a tight hand. Letting go, I have come back yesterday and today to a sense of my life here in all its riches, depth, freedom for soulmaking.

It's a real break-through. I have not written in sonnet form for a long time, but at every major crisis in my life when I reach a point of clarification, where pain is transcended by the quality of the experience itself, sonnets come. Whole lines run through my head and I cannot *stop* writing until whatever it is gets said.

Found three huge mushrooms when I went out before breakfast to fill the bird feeder. So far only jays come, but the word will get around.

3. A famous record of Mahler's song "The Farewell," evocative of the coming of winter and death. Mahler died before it could be performed, and the premiere was conducted by his disciple Bruno Walter. Kathleen Ferrier was to die within a few years of recording the song.

October 11th. The joke is on me. I filled this weekend with friends so that I would not go down into depression, not knowing that I should have turned the corner and be writing poems. It is the climactic moment of autumn, but already I feel like Sleeping Beauty as the carpet of leaves on the front lawn gets thicker and thicker. The avenue of beeches as I drive up the winding road along the brook is glorious beyond words, wall on wall of transparent gold. Laurie Armstrong came for roast beef Sunday dinner. Then I went out for two hours late in the afternoon and put in a hundred tulips. In itself that would not be a big job, but everywhere I have to clear space for them, weed, divide perennials, rescue iris that is being choked by violets. I really get to weeding only in spring and autumn, so I am working through a jungle now. Doing it I feel strenuously happy and at peace. At the end of the afternoon on a gray day, the light is sad and one feels the chill, but the bitter smell of earth is a tonic.

I can hardly believe that relief from the anguish of these past months is here to stay, but so far it does feel like a true change of mood—or rather, a change of *being* where I can stand alone. So much of my life here is precarious. I cannot always believe even in my work. But I have come in these last days to feel again the validity of my struggle here, that it is meaningful whether I ever "succeed" as a writer or not, and that even its failures, failures of nerve, failures due to a difficult temperament, can be meaningful. It is an age where more and more human beings are caught up in lives where fewer and fewer inward decisions can be made, where fewer and fewer real choices exist. The fact that a middle-aged, single woman, without any vestige of family left, lives in this house in a silent village and is responsible only to her own soul means something. The fact that she is a writer and can tell where she is and what it is like on the pilgrimage inward can be of comfort. It is comforting to know there are lighthouse keepers on rocky islands along the coast. Sometimes, when I have been for a walk after dark and see my house lighted up, looking so alive, I feel that my presence here is worth all the Hell.

I have time to think. That is the great, the greatest luxury. I have time to be. Therefore my responsibility is huge. To use time well and to be all that I can in whatever years are left to me. This does not dismay. The dismay comes when I lose the sense of my life as connected (as if by an aerial) to many, many other lives whom I do not even know and cannot ever know. The signals go out and come in all the time.

Why is it that poetry always seems to me so much more a true work of the soul than prose? I never feel elated after writing a page of prose, though I have written good things on concentrated will, and at least in a novel the imagination is fully engaged. Perhaps it is that prose is earned and poetry given. Both can be revised almost indefinitely. I do not mean to say that I do not work at poetry. When I am really inspired I can put a poem through a hundred drafts and keep my excitement. But this sustained battle is possible only when I am in a state of grace, when the deep channels are open, and when they are, when I am both profoundly stirred and balanced, then poetry comes as a gift from powers beyond my will.

I have often imagined that if I were in solitary confinement for an indefinite time and knew that no one would ever read what I wrote, I would still write poetry, but I would not write novels. Why? Perhaps because the poem is primarily a dialogue with the self and the novel a dialogue with others. They come from entirely different modes of being. I suppose I have written novels to find out what I *thought* about something and poems to find out what I *felt* about something.

January 7th. I have worked all morning—and it is now afternoon—to try to make by sheer art and craft an ending to the first stanza of a lyric that shot through my head intact. I should not feel so pressed for time, but I do, and I suppose I always shall. Yeats[4] speaks of spending a week on one stanza. The danger, of course, is overmanipulation, when one finds oneself manipulating *words*, not images or concepts. My problem was to make a transition viable between lovers in a snowstorm and the whiteness of a huge amaryllis I look at across the hall in the cosy room—seven huge flowers that make constant silent hosannas as I sit here.

In a period of happy and fruitful isolation such as this, any interruption, any intrusion of the social, any obligation breaks the thread on my loom, breaks the pattern. Two nights ago I was called at the last minute to attend the caucus of Town Meeting . . . and it threw me. But at least the companionship gave me one insight: a neighbor told me she had been in a small car accident and had managed to persuade the local paper to ignore her true age (as it appears on her license) and to print her age as thirty-nine! I was really astonished by this confidence. I am proud of being fifty-eight, and still alive and kicking, in love, more creative, balanced, and potent than I have ever been. I mind certain physical deteriorations, but not *really*. And not at all when I look at the marvelous photograph that Bill sent me of Isak Dinesen[5] just before she died. For after all we make our faces as we go along, and who when young could ever look as she does? The ineffable sweetness of the smile, the total acceptance and joy one receives from it, life, death, everything taken in and, as it were, savored—and let go.

Wrinkles here and there seem unimportant compared to *Gestalt* of the whole person I have become in this past year. Somewhere in *The Poet and the Donkey* Andy speaks for me when he says, "Do not deprive me of my age. I have earned it."

My neighbor's wish to be known forever as thirty-nine years old made me think again of what K said in her letter about the people in their

---

4. William Butler Yeats, 1865–1939. Irish poet and dramatist.

5. Modern Danish short-story writer who despite painful illness in her later years continued writing until her death at seventy-seven.

thirties mourning their lost youth because we have given them no ethos that makes maturity appear an asset. Yet we have many examples before us. It looks as if T. S. Eliot came into a fully consummated happy marriage only when he was seventy. Yeats married when he was fifty or over. I am coming into the most fulfilled love of my life now. But for some reason Americans are terrified of the very idea of passionate love going on past middle age. Are they afraid of being alive? Do they want to be dead, i.e., *safe*? For of course one is never safe when in love. Growth is demanding and may seem dangerous, for there is loss as well as gain in growth. But why go on living if one has ceased to grow? And what more demanding atmosphere for growth than love in any form, than any relationship which can call out and requires of us our most secret and deepest selves?

My neighbor who wishes to remain thirty-nine indefinitely does so out of anxiety—she is afraid she will no longer be "attractive" if people know her age. But if one wants mature relationships, one will look for them among one's peers. I cannot imagine being in love with someone much younger than I because I have looked on love as an *éducation sentimentale*. About love I have little to learn from the young.

January 8th. Yesterday was a strange, hurried, uncentered day; yet I did not have to go out, the sun shone. Today I feel centered and time is a friend instead of the old enemy. It was zero this morning. I have a fire burning in my study, yellow roses and mimosa on my desk. There is an atmosphere of festival, of release, in the house. We are one, the house and I, and I am happy to be alone—time to think, time to be. This kind of open-ended time is the only luxury that really counts and I feel stupendously rich to have it. And for the moment I have a sense of fulfillment both about my life and about my work that I have rarely experienced until this year, or perhaps until these last weeks. I look to my left and the transparent blue sky behind a flame-colored cyclamen, lifting about thirty winged flowers to the light, makes an impression of stained glass, light-flooded. I have put the vast heap of unanswered letters into a box at my feet, so I don't see them. And now I am going to make one more try to get that poem right. The last line is still the problem.
1970,1971   1973

Woody Allen: SELECTIONS FROM THE ALLEN NOTEBOOKS

Following are excerpts from the hitherto secret private journal of Woody Allen, which will be published posthumously or after his death, whichever comes first.

Getting through the night is becoming harder and harder. Last evening, I had the uneasy feeling that some men were trying to break into my room to shampoo me. But why? I kept imagining I saw shadowy forms, and at 3 A.M. the underwear I had draped over a chair resembled the Kaiser on roller skates. When I finally did fall asleep, I had that same hideous nightmare in which a woodchuck is trying to claim my prize at a raffle. Despair.

I believe my consumption has grown worse. Also my asthma. The wheezing comes and goes, and I get dizzy more and more frequently. I have taken to violent choking and fainting. My room is damp and I have perpetual chills and palpitations of the heart. I noticed, too, that I am out of napkins. Will it never stop?

Idea for a story: A man awakens to find his parrot has been made Secretary of Agriculture. He is consumed with jealousy and shoots himself, but unfortunately the gun is the type with a little flag that pops out, with the word "Bang" on it. The flag pokes his eye out, and he lives—a chastened human being who, for the first time, enjoys the simple pleasures of life, like farming or sitting on an air hose.

Thought: Why does man kill? He kills for food. And not only food: frequently there must be a beverage.

Should I marry W.? Not if she won't tell me the other letters in her name. And what about her career? How can I ask a woman of her beauty to give up the Roller Derby? Decisions . . .

Once again I tried committing suicide—this time by wetting my nose and inserting it into the light socket. Unfortunately, there was a short in the wiring, and I merely caromed off the icebox. Still obsessed by thoughts of death, I brood constantly. I keep wondering if there is an afterlife, and if there is will they be able to break a twenty?

I ran into my brother today at a funeral. We had not seen one another for fifteen years, but as usual he produced a pig bladder from his pocket and began hitting me on the head with it. Time has helped me understand him better. I finally realize his remark that I am "some loathsome

vermin fit only for extermination" was said more out of compassion than
anger. Let's face it: he was always much brighter than me—wittier, more
cultured, better educated. Why he is still working at McDonald's is a
mystery.

Idea for story: Some beavers take over Carnegie Hall and perform
Wozzeck.[1] (Strong theme. What will be the structure?)

Good Lord, why am I so guilty? Is it because I hated my father?
Probably it was the veal-parmigian' incident. Well, what was it doing in
his wallet? If I had listened to him, I would be blocking hats for a living. I
can hear him now: "To block hats—that is everything." I remember his
reaction when I told him I wanted to write. "The only writing you'll do is
in collaboration with an owl." I still have no idea what he meant. What a
sad man! When my first play, A Cyst for Gus, was produced at the
Lyceum, he attended opening night in tails and a gas mask.

Today I saw a red-and-yellow sunset and thought, How insignificant I
am! Of course, I thought that yesterday, too, and it rained. I was overcome with self-loathing and contemplated suicide again—this time by
inhaling next to an insurance salesman.

Short story: A man awakens in the morning and finds himself transformed into his own arch supports (This idea can work on many levels.
Psychologically, it is the quintessence of Kruger, Freud's disciple who
discovered sexuality in bacon.)

How wrong Emily Dickinson was! Hope is not "the thing with feathers." The thing with feathers has turned out to be my nephew. I must
take him to a specialist in Zurich.

I have decided to break off my engagement with W. She doesn't
understand my writing, and said last night that my Critique of Metaphysical Reality reminded her of Airport. We quarreled, and she brought up
the subject of children again, but I convinced her they would be too
young.

Do I believe in God? I did until Mother's accident. She fell on some
meat loaf, and it penetrated her spleen. She lay in a coma for months,
unable to do anything but sing "Granada" to an imaginary herring. Why
was this woman in the prime of life so afflicted—because in her youth she

1. A lurid and discordant opera by the modern composer Alban Berg. Carnegie Hall is a
famous concert hall in New York City.

dared to defy convention and got married with a brown paper bag on her head? And how can I believe in God when just last week I got my tongue caught in the roller of an electric typewriter? I am plagued by doubts. What if everything is an illusion and nothing exists? In that case, I definitely overpaid for my carpet. If only God would give me some clear sign! Like making a large deposit in my name at a Swiss bank.

Had coffee with Melnick today. He talked to me about his idea of having all government officials dress like hens.

Play idea: A character based on my father, but without quite so prominent a big toe. He is sent to the Sorbonne[2] to study the harmonica. In the end, he dies, never realizing his one dream—to sit up to his waist in gravy. (I see a brilliant second-act curtain, where two midgets come upon a severed head in a shipment of volleyballs.)

While taking my noon walk today, I had more morbid thoughts. What *is* it about death that bothers me so much? Probably the hours. Melnick says the soul is immortal and lives on after the body drops away, but if my soul exists without my body I am convinced all my clothes will be too loose-fitting. Oh, well . . .

Did not have to break off with W. after all, for as luck would have it, she ran off to Finland with a professional circus geek. All for the best, I suppose, although I had another of those attacks where I start coughing out of my ears.

Last night, I burned all my plays and poetry. Ironically as I was burning my masterpiece, *Dark Penguin,* the room caught fire, and I am now the object of a lawsuit by some men named Pinchunk and Schlosser. Kierkegaard was right.

1972

2. The University of Paris.

Donald Pearce: FROM JOURNAL OF A WAR

December 28. We have been patroling the Rhine and guarding the bridge across it at Nijmegen continuously for so long now that they have begun to acquire a positive hold over our minds and imaginations. Our thoughts seem polarized by them, and turn to them like compasses to a magnet. This bridge is the only one over the Rhine left intact for a hundred miles, and we must keep it that way for our own no doubt imminent invasion of Germany. At the same time, if Jerry decides to counter-attack in force through here, and there has been a good deal of fresh evidence that he's getting ready to do just that, the bridge would become just as important to him. A really ambiguous prize. But he keeps sending explosives downstream at it. Damn strange. We shoot into the river at everything that moves, sometimes exploding mines tied to boards, or logs, or branches. Our engineers have run a huge net across the river about fifty yards upstream from the bridge to catch whatever floats downstream; but things get through or under the net somehow and that's what we shoot at. New rumor: German frogmen have been attempting to swim under the net; also, they have small one-man submarines in the river. Probably fairy lore.

But I was going to say—the bridge and river no longer appear ordinary to us, but seem to have acquired personalities, or to have been endowed with them. Sometimes the river seems less the watched one than the watcher, reflecting back our searchlight beams, and breaking the half-moon into a thousand yellow eyes as we steal along the edge on night patrols. The bridge's single span is unmistakably a high, arched eyebrow over an invisible eye peering across the Rhine. Everything we do here revolves around the bridge and river. As we go back for a rest or, as recently, for Christmas dinner, miles from the line, we cross the iced-flats that follow along the curving windswept dykes, and the great iron eyebrow is right behind us, lifting higher and higher above the mist, in a kind of inscrutable surmise, and as we return to those god-awful flats again, the eyebrow and invisible eye are at it again, staring back at us, watching the Rhine. Perhaps someone should put on a campaign to establish the ordinariness of this bridge and river, put up signs. But it would do no good, I tell myself, because this was Caesar's Rhine, Siegfried's Rhine, Wagner's Rhine,[1] and you can't silence all that mystery. I hate it here.

Whipping the company jeep at top speed along a mile-long windswept section of one of the dykes that stretches between our company and the next is one of the low diversions we have worked out. It's completely exposed and utterly bare; so for two minutes you are an A-number one moving target. An insane game, but we play it. Once I heard the loud, flat snap of a bullet going past my head on one of these mad runs. We are, as they say, very definitely under observation.

* * *

March 3 [1945]. The city[2] was quite heavily defended. First, a steep, raw, anti-tank ditch completely girdling the city had to be negotiated,

1. The great Rhine River, which flows northward through western Germany, was the scene of several great battles between the Roman legions of Julius Caesar and the armies of rebellious Germanic tribes. The mythic superhero Siegfried, protagonist of the nineteenth-century German composer Richard Wagner's operatic cycle *The Ring* of the Nibelungs, travels down the Rhine and is ultimately murdered on its bank. Moreover, in Wagner's *Ring* the Rhine is the source of magic gold whose plunder and forging into a ring of power brings on the end of the world.

2. Udem, in The Netherlands.

with continuous covering fire from both flanks. Then we ran into a connected system of crawl- and weapons-trenches forming a secondary ring about the interior. Our covering artillery fire was practically saturational; so he resisted only lightly till we were more than halfway in. There followed some sporadic street fighting and house clearing, nothing very spectacular, and the city fell to us shortly after daybreak; i.e., they simply pulled out and disappeared at about 4:00 A.M.

I had a couple of close ones during this show. On the way in, my platoon was evidently silhouetted against the night sky, and was fired on four times at a range of maybe 300 yards by an eighty-eight. (This is a notorious and vicious gun. The velocity of the shell is so high that you hear it pass or explode near you almost at the same instant that you hear the sound of its being fired. You really can't duck it. Also, it's an open-sights affair—you are aimed at particularly; not, as with mortars, aimed at only by approximation.) Anyway, they went past me about an arm's length above or in front of me, I don't know which. We hit the ditches. After pointing a few more, the gun was forced off by our return tank fire.

During the house-clearing phase, at one spot, I walked instead of ran from one house to another and got my helmet spun around on my head with a close shot. There was an extremely loud, flat "snap," like two hands clapped together hard beside my ear; that was all. Plus a crease in my helmet, which gave me immense prestige with the men all morning.

We had two tanks along with us, and their support made the assignment 100 per cent easier. At one point a handful of German snipers, who were perched in the attic of a three-story house at a bend in the main street, held up the battalion for over an hour. They were finally silenced by one of the tanks. In the half-dark, we circled around behind their house during the tank fire and cut off their escape route. Presently they came out through the back garden, dangling in front of them white cloths on long poles. It was vastly disconcerting. Instead of a squad of Nazi supermen in shiny boots, and packing Lugers, we were confronted by five of the most unkempt, stunted, scrubby specimens I have ever had the pleasure of capturing. Two of them couldn't have been more than fourteen on their next birthday. Possibly they were on some kind of dope; at least they acted that way, a little dazed, grinning, and rather immune to voice control. One of them had nearly shot me a few hours earlier in the dark before dawn. At the time, I remember, I had thought it wasn't any more than I had expected; but later on, seeing them, I felt that it would have been an unfortunate end to my life: I am obviously getting choosy. What I mean is that I would simply like to be well killed, if killed I am to be. I came to the conclusion that they were from the bottom of Germany's recruiting barrel.

The men in the platoon seemed to think so too, for I caught them in the middle of a queer performance. They had lined the five of them up against a schoolhouse wall and were pretending, quite ceremoniously, that they were going to shoot them. The prisoners certainly believed they were about to be shot; three of them had their hands on their heads and their faces turned to the wall, as for execution; the other two were pleading desperately with three or four of our men. I was astonished to find my best corporal in the thick of this business. I stopped it, of course. Not that they would have carried out the execution; I feel sure of that.

We passed through the town and seized a road-and-rail junction about 800 yards past the outskirts and dug in under moderate shelling. A child would know that that junction would become a hot target—which it very shortly did. We sat it out. He sent several salvos of rockets in on us. These you always hear coming, if it's any comfort. The first salvo was the best, but there was time for my sergeant and me to flatten out in a shallow ditch alongside the track. One rocket hit about four or five feet from us, practically shattering my hearing; it chewed up a couple of railway ties, took two or three chunks out of the rails, and turned me over from my stomach to my back. The blast stung my whole left side. Nothing more really close happened there all night.

Next day, I went back to have a look at Udem. In daylight it seemed in worse condition than I remembered it from the night before. Enemy shelling accounted for much of the destruction; but looters, busy rooting around before daybreak, accounted for some too. The houses that had not been shelled were practically turned inside out by our troops. I came across one soldier telling an admiring group about his morning exploits: "First I took a hammer and smashed over 100 plates, and the cups along with them. Then I took an ax to the china cabinets and buffets. Next I smashed all the furniture and pulled the stuffing out of the big chairs. Then I took the hammer again and smashed all the elements on two electric stoves and broke the enamel off the stove fronts and sides. Then I put a grenade in the big piano, and after that I poured a jar of molasses into it. I broke all the French doors and all the doors with mirrors in them and threw the lamps out into the street. I was so mad."

I turned him over to the Provost Corps in the afternoon.

Udem had a large church made of red stone with high twin towers. German artillery scouts had stationed themselves in these towers in order to direct fire onto our positions five miles away. So the church had to be "neutralized," as they say. We engaged it with 17-pounders for about an hour, I believe successfully. Anyway, I went in to see what we had done. It was full of gaping holes; the stone pillars had even been shot off far within the building. The only unharmed thing I saw was the font. The walls had had blue and gold paintings of religious scenes extending all around the interior; these were mostly peeled or ripped off. One painting was of the Descent from the Cross. It had come loose from its frame and seemed heading for a nosedive; the pale belly of Christ had a group of machine-gun bullets through it. The Germans had made a brief stand at the church and had obviously used it as a temporary strongpoint.

As I left, engineers were already laying dynamite charges at critical points along the foundations, with the intention of using the stones as rubble for roads, almost the only reasonable use left for it.

On the way back, I met a number of civilians carrying bundles. Most of them were covered with mud from head to foot. They were staggering along rather than walking, and started every time a gun went off far away or close up. One tall thin man was leading two small children, one by each hand. The children were around his back. The man limped; I saw that he was weeping. My limited German enabled me to discover that he was wounded in a couple of places, that his wife had been killed by shrapnel in the morning, and that he didn't know what to do with his tiny children who were wet, cold, and hungry. I took them down into our cellar where the stretcher bearer dressed his wounds and evacuated him. I offered the two children food—chocolate, bread and jam, biscuits. They only tightened their lips and refused. So I tried a sort of game with the names of the articles of furniture in the cellar, deliberately making silly mistakes, and after a while they laughed at my stupidity. I kept this up, and before long they gobbled whatever I put in front of them. I would like to have done more; but instead I turned them over to the Civil Affairs people, not without complicated feelings of concern and regret. I will never know what happened to them.

Kept rummaging around in the town. Went to the place where I was nearly shot, stood on the exact spot, in fact, and determined the window at the end of the street where the shots had come from. An impulse sent me inside the house itself, where I climbed to the upper room. The machine gun was there on its heavy mounting, still pointing out the window and down the street. I sat behind it and took aim on the doorway I had disappeared into at the moment I was fired on, and waited for someone to pass the spot just to see how I must have looked through his sights. No one came and I got tired of the melodrama and went back to our forward positions.

* * *

March 4. When will it all end? The idiocy and the tension, the dying of young men, the destruction of homes, of cities, starvation, exhaustion, disease, children parentless and lost, cages full of shivering, staring prisoners, long lines of hopeless civilians plodding through mud, the endless pounding of the battle line. I can scarcely remember what it is like to be where explosions are not going off around me, some hostile, some friendly, all horrible; an exploding shell is a terrible sound. What keeps this war going, now that its end is so clear? What do the Germans think of us, and we of them? I do not think we think of them at all, or much. Do they think of us? I can think of their weapons, their shells, their machine guns, but not of the men behind them. I do not feel as if I were fighting against men, but against machines. I need to go up in an airplane and actually see German transport hauling guns and ammunition, see their actual armies; for everything that happens merely comes from a vague beyond, and I cannot visualize the people who are fighting against me. The prisoners that come over hills with their hands up, or who come out of houses with white cloths waving—they have no relation, almost, to anything for me. I can't connect them with the guns they have just laid down, it seems like forcing something to do so. It is becoming hard for me not to feel sometimes that both sides are the common victims of a common terror, that everybody's guns are against everybody ultimately.

These are times when I feel that every bit of fighting is defensive. Self defense. If a machine-gun nest is attacked and wiped out by us, by my own platoon, I do not feel very aggressive, as if I had attacked somebody. It is always that I have defended myself against something that was attacking me. And how often I have thought that there might be a Rilke[3] out there in a German pill box. If I could only see them, as in battles long ago, at close range, before engaging them. In our wars, the warring sides are getting farther and farther apart and war is getting more and more meaningless for the field warriors, and more meaningful for the domestic warriors in factories and homes. Will there come a time when hundreds of miles separate the warring fronts? When long-range weapons and the ghastly impersonality of air attacks are the means of war? It is already a very impersonal thing. When a soldier is killed or wounded his buddies, shaking their heads, merely say, "Poor old Joe. He just got it. Just as he was going up that hill, he got it." As if to imply that he was merely in the wrong place at the wrong time, and that life and death are only matters of luck and do not depend on the calculations of human beings at the other end of an S.P. gun. When we were in our static positions around Wyler Meer and Nijmegen, the enemy became real to me for the first time. I watched him for weeks, saw him dig, run, hide, fire, walk. And when I went on patrols into his territory, there was meaning in that, too, for I knew where he was, I knew his habits. So that while we were probing the cuticle of the enemy, so to speak, he was real; but now when we are ripping into his body, he has disappeared and has turned into something read about in the papers. But the guns remain, manned by soldiers who are so meaningless to us that when they shoot a fellow, all we can say is, "He got it."

Once I could say you cannot be disgusted with the war, because it is too big for disgust, that disgust is too shallow an emotion for something involving millions of people. But I am disgusted now, and I know what I am saying. Once I used to get quite a thrill out of seeing a city destroyed and left an ash heap from end to end. It gave me a vicarious sense of power. I felt the romantic and histrionic emotion produced by seeing

3. That is, a major poet, like the German writer Rainer Maria Rilke (1875–1926).

"retribution" done; and an aesthetic emotion produced by beholding ruins; and the childish emotion that comes from destroying man-made things. But it is not that way any more. All I experience is revulsion every time a fresh city is taken on. I am no longer capable of thinking that the systematic destruction of a city is a wonderful or even a difficult thing, though some seem to think it even a heroic thing. Well, how is it done? Dozens upon dozens of gun crews stationed some two or three miles away from the city simply place shell after shell into hundreds of guns and fire away for a few hours—the simplest and most elementary physical and mental work—and then presently the firing stops, the city has been demolished, has become an ash heap, and great praise is bestowed on the army for the capture of a new city.

I am not suggesting that cities shouldn't be captured in this way; actually it saves lives. But it fills me with disgust because it is all so abysmally foolish, so lunatic. It has not the dramatic elements of mere barbarism about it; it is straight scientific debauchery. A destroyed city is a terrible sight. How can anyone record it?—the million smashed things, the absolutely innumerable tiny tragedies, the crushed life-works, the jagged homes, army tanks parked in living rooms—who could tell of these things I don't know; they are too numerous to mention, too awful in their meanings. Perhaps everyone should be required to spend a couple of hours examining a single smashed home, looking at the fragmentation of every little thing, especially the tiniest things from kitchen to attic, if he could find an attic; be required, in fact, to list the ruined contents of just one home; something would be served, a little sobriety perhaps honored.

It is disgusting (that it should be necessary, is what galls me to the bones) that a towering cathedral, built by ages of care and effort, a sweet labor of centuries, should be shot down by laughing artillerymen, mere boys, because somebody with a machine gun is hiding in a belfry tower. When I see such a building, damaged perhaps beyond repair after one of these "operations," I know only disgust. The matter of sides in this war temporarily becomes irrelevant, especially if someone at my elbow says, like a conquering hero: "Well, we sure did a job on the old church, eh?"

A job has been done on Europe, on the world, and the resulting trauma will be generations long in its effects. It is not just the shock of widespread destruction, of whole cities destroyed, nor the shock which the defeated and the homeless must have suffered, that I am thinking of: it is even more the conqueror's trauma, the habit of violence, the explosion of values, the distortion of relations, the ascending significance of the purely material, the sense of power, and the pride of strength. These things will afflict the victors as profoundly and for quite as long a time as the other things will afflict the victims; and of the two I am not sure that a crass superiority complex is the more desirable. Perhaps I underestimate our ability to return to normal again.

1944, 1945   1965

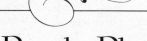

People, Places

Thomas Jefferson

GEORGE WASHINGTON[1]

I think I knew General Washington intimately and thoroughly; and were I called on to delineate his character, it should be in terms like these.

His mind was great and powerful, without being of the very first order; his penetration strong, though not so acute as that of a Newton, Bacon, or Locke; and as far as he saw, no judgment was ever sounder. It was slow in operation, being little aided by invention or imagination, but sure in conclusion. Hence the common remark of his officers, of the advantage he derived from councils of war, where hearing all suggestions, he selected whatever was best; and certainly no general ever planned his battles more judiciously. But if deranged during the course of the action, if any member of his plan was dislocated by sudden circumstances, he was slow in re-adjustment. The consequence was, that he often failed in the field, and rarely against an enemy in station, as at Boston and York. He was incapable of fear, meeting personal dangers with the calmest unconcern. Perhaps the strongest feature in his character was prudence, never acting until every circumstance, every consideration, was maturely weighed; refraining if he saw a doubt, but, when once decided, going through with his purpose, whatever obstacles opposed. His integrity was most pure, his justice the most inflexible I have ever known, no motives of interest or consanguinity, of friendship or hatred, being able to bias his decision. He was, indeed, in every sense of the words, a wise, a good, and a great man. His temper was naturally irritable and high toned; but reflection and resolution had obtained a firm and habitual ascendency over it. If ever, however, it broke its bonds, he was most tremendous in his wrath. In his expenses he was honorable, but exact; liberal in contri-

1. From a letter written in 1814 to a Doctor Jones, who was writing a history and wanted to know about Washington's role in the Federalist-Republican controversy.

butions to whatever promised utility; but frowning and unyielding on all visionary projects, and all unworthy calls on his charity. His heart was not warm in its affections; but he exactly calculated every man's value, and gave him a solid esteem proportioned to it. His person, you know, was fine, his stature exactly what one would wish, his deportment easy, erect and noble; the best horseman of his age, and the most graceful figure that could be seen on horseback. Although in the circle of his friends, where he might be unreserved with safety, he took a free share in conversation, his colloquial talents were not above mediocrity, possessing neither copiousness of ideas, nor fluency of words. In public, when called on for a sudden opinion, he was unready, short and embarrassed. Yet he wrote readily, rather diffusely, in an easy and correct style. This he had acquired by conversation with the world, for his education was merely reading, writing and common arithmetic, to which he added surveying at a later day. His time was employed in action chiefly, reading little, and that only in agriculture and English history. His correspondence became necessarily extensive, and, with journalizing his agricultural proceedings, occupied most of his leisure hours within doors. On the whole, his character was, in its mass, perfect, in nothing bad, in few points indifferent; and it may truly be said, that never did nature and fortune combine more perfectly to make a man great, and to place him in the same constellation with whatever worthies have merited from man an everlasting remembrance. For his was the singular destiny and merit, of leading the armies of his country successfully through an arduous war, for the establishment of its independence; of conducting its councils through the birth of a government, new in its forms and principles, until it had settled down into a quiet and orderly train; and of scrupulously obeying the laws through the whole of his career, civil and military, of which the history of the world furnishes no other example.

* * * I am satisfied, the great body of republicans think of him as I do. We were, indeed, dissatisfied with him on his ratification of the British treaty. But this was short lived. We knew his honesty, the wiles with which he was encompassed, and that age had already begun to relax the firmness of his purposes; and I am convinced he is more deeply seated in the love and gratitude of the republicans, than in the Pharisaical homage of the federal monarchists.[2] For he was no monarchist from preference of his judgment. The soundness of that gave him correct views of the rights of man, and his severe justice devoted him to them. He has often declared to me that he considered our new Constitution as an experiment on the practicability of republican government, and with what dose of liberty man could be trusted for his own good; that he was determined the experiment should have a fair trial, and would lose the last drop of his

2. Jefferson here compares those who sought to make the new United States a kingdom, with Washington as king, to the biblical Pharisees, the haughty sect of ancient Israel.

blood in support of it. And these declarations he repeated to me the oftener and more pointedly, because he knew my suspicions of Colonel Hamilton's views,[3] and probably had heard from him the same declarations which I had, to wit, "that the British constitution, with its unequal representation, corruption and other existing abuses, was the most perfect government which had ever been established on earth, and that a reformation of those abuses would make it an impracticable government." I do believe that General Washington had not a firm confidence in the durability of our government. He was naturally distrustful of men, and inclined to gloomy apprehensions; and I was ever persuaded that a belief that we must at length end in something like a British constitution, had some weight in his adoption of the ceremonies of levees,[4] birthdays, pompous meetings with Congress, and other forms of the same character, calculated to prepare us gradually for a change which he believed possible, and to let it come on with as little shock as might be to the public mind.

These are my opinions of General Washington which I would vouch at the judgment seat of God, having been formed on an acquaintance of thirty years. I served with him in the Virginia legislature from 1769 to the Revolutionary war, and again, a short time in Congress, until he left us to take command of the army. During the war and after it we corresponded occasionally, and in the four years of my continuance in the office of Secretary of State, our intercourse was daily, confidential and cordial. After I retired from that office, great and malignant pains were taken by our federal monarchists, and not entirely without effect, to make him view me as a theorist, holding French principles of government,[5] which would lead infallibly to licentiousness and anarchy. And to this he listened the more easily, from my known disapprobation of the British treaty. I never saw him afterwards, or these malignant insinuations should have been dissipated before his just judgment, as mists before the sun. I felt on his death, with my countrymen, that "verily a great man hath fallen this day in Israel."

1814

---

3. Alexander Hamilton (1755–1804) advocated a strong central federal government, led by the "wealthy, good, and wise." His views were opposed by the relatively more democratic views of Jefferson.
4. Morning receptions held by a head of state to enable him to attend to public affairs while rising and dressing. The form was characteristic of European monarchs.
5. Radical political views advanced by extreme democrats in the course of the French Revolution.

Nathaniel Hawthorne

ABRAHAM LINCOLN

Of course, there was one other personage, in the class of statesmen, whom I should have been truly mortified to leave Washington without seeing; since (temporarily, at least, and by force of circumstances) he was the man of men. But a private grief had built up a barrier about him, impeding the customary free intercourse of Americans with their chief magistrate; so that I might have come away without a glimpse of his very remarkable physiognomy, save for a semi-official opportunity of which I was glad to take advantage. The fact is, we were invited to annex ourselves, as supernumeraries, to a deputation that was about to wait upon the President, from a Massachusetts whip factory, with a present of a splendid whip.

Our immediate party consisted only of four or five (including Major Ben Perley Poore,[1] with his note-book and pencil), but we were joined by several other persons, who seemed to have been lounging about the precincts of the White House, under the spacious porch, or within the hall, and who swarmed in with us to take the chances of a presentation. Nine o'clock had been appointed as the time for receiving the deputation, and we were punctual to the moment; but not so the President, who sent us word that he was eating his breakfast, and would come as soon as he could. His appetite, we were glad to think, must have been a pretty fair one; for we waited about half an hour in one of the antechambers, and then were ushered into a reception-room, in one corner of which sat the Secretaries of War and of the Treasury, expecting, like ourselves, the termination of the Presidential breakfast. During this interval there were several new additions to our group, one or two of whom were in a working-garb, so that we formed a very miscellaneous collection of people, mostly unknown to each other, and without any common sponsor, but all with an equal right to look our head servant in the face.

By and by there was a little stir on the staircase and in the passageway, and in lounged a tall, loose-jointed figure, of an exaggerated Yankee port and demeanor, whom (as being about the homeliest man I ever saw, yet by no means repulsive or disagreeable) it was impossible not to recognize as Uncle Abe.

Unquestionably, Western man though he be, and Kentuckian by birth, President Lincoln is the essential representative of all Yankees, and the veritable specimen, physically, of what the world seems determined to regard as our characteristic qualities. It is the strangest and yet the fittest thing in the jumble of human vicissitudes, that he, out of so

1. American journalist and biographer.

many millions, unlooked for, unselected by any intelligible process that could be based upon his genuine qualities, unknown to those who chose him, and unsuspected of what endowments may adapt him for his tremendous responsibility, should have found the way open for him to fling his lank personality into the chair of state—where, I presume, it was his first impulse to throw his legs on the council-table, and tell the Cabinet Ministers a story. There is no describing his lengthy awkwardness, nor the uncouthness of his movement; and yet it seemed as if I had been in the habit of seeing him daily, and had shaken hands with him a thousand times in some village street; so true was he to the aspect of the pattern American, though with a certain extravagance which, possibly, I exaggerated still further by the delighted eagerness with which I took it in. If put to guess his calling and livelihood, I should have taken him for a country school-master as soon as anything else. He was dressed in a rusty black frock coat and pantaloons, unbrushed, and worn so faithfully that the suit had adapted itself to the curves and angularities of his figure, and had grown to be an outer skin of the man. His hair was black, still unmixed with gray, stiff, somewhat bushy, and had apparently been acquainted with neither brush nor comb that morning, after the disarrangement of the pillow; and as to a nightcap, Uncle Abe probably knows nothing of such effeminacies. His complexion is dark and sallow, betokening, I fear, a insalubrious atmosphere around the White House; he has thick black eyebrows and an impending brow; his nose is large, and the lines about his mouth are very strongly defined.

The whole physiognomy is as coarse a one as you would meet anywhere in the length and breadth of the States; but, withal, it is redeemed, illuminated, softened, and brightened by a kindly though serious look out of his eyes, and an expression of homely sagacity, that seems weighted with rich results of village experience. A great deal of native sense; no bookish cultivation, no refinement; honest at heart, and thoroughly so, and yet, in some sort, sly—at least, endowed with a sort of tact and wisdom that are akin to craft, and would impel him, I think, to take an antagonist in flank, rather than to make a bull-run at him right in front. But, on the whole, I like this sallow, queer, sagacious visage, with the homely human sympathies that warmed it; and, for my small share in the matter, would as lief have Uncle Abe for a ruler as any man whom it would have been practicable to put in his place.

Immediately on his entrance the President accosted our member of Congress, who had us in charge, and, with a comical twist of his face, made some jocular remark about the length of his breakfast. He then greeted us all round, not waiting for an introduction, but shaking and squeezing everybody's hand with the utmost cordiality, whether the individual's name was announced to him or not. His manner towards us was wholly without pretence, but yet had a kind of natural dignity, quite sufficient to keep the forwardest of us from clapping him on the shoulder and asking him for a story. A mutual acquaintance being established, our leader took the whip out of its case, and began to read the address of presentation. The whip was an exceedingly long one, its handle wrought in ivory (by some artist in the Massachusetts State Prison, I believe), and ornamented with a medallion of the President, and other equally beautiful devices; and along its whole length there was a succession of golden bands and ferrules. The address was shorter than the whip, but equally well made, consisting chiefly of an explanatory description of these artistic designs, and closing with a hint that the gift was a suggestive and emblematic one, and that the President would recognize the use to which such an instrument should be put.

This suggestion gave Uncle Abe rather a delicate task in his reply, because, slight as the matter seemed, it apparently called for some declaration, or intimation, or faint foreshadowing of policy in reference to the conduct of the war, and the final treatment of the Rebels. But the President's Yankee aptness and not-to-be-caughtness stood him in good stead, and he jerked or wiggled himself out of the dilemma with an uncouth dexterity that was entirely in character; although, without his gesticulation of eye and mouth—and especially the flourish of the whip, with which he imagined himself touching up a pair of fat horses—I doubt whether his words would be worth recording, even if I could remember them. The gist of the reply was, that he accepted the whip as an emblem of peace, not punishment; and, this great affair over, we retired out of the presence in high good humor, only regretting that we could not have seen the President sit down and fold up his legs (which is said to be a most extraordinary spectacle), or have heard him tell one of those delectable stories for which he is so celebrated. A good many of them are afloat upon the common talk of Washington, and are certainly the aptest, pithiest, and funniest little things imaginable; though, to be sure, they smack of the frontier freedom, and would not always bear repetition in a drawing-room, or on the immaculate page of the *Atlantic*.[2]

Good Heavens! what liberties have I been taking with one of the potentates of the earth, and the man on whose conduct more important consequences depend than on that of any other historical personage of the century! But with whom is an American citizen entitled to take a liberty, if not with his own chief magistrate? However, lest the above

2. This passage was one of those omitted from the article as originally published, and the following note was appended to explain the omission, which had been indicated by a line of points:
"We are compelled to omit two or three pages, in which the author describes the interview, and gives his idea of the personal appearance and deportment of the Presi-
dent. The sketch appears to have been written in a benign spirit, and perhaps conveys a not inaccurate impression of its august subject; but it lacks *reverence*, and it pains us to see a gentleman of ripe age, and who has spent years under the corrective influence of foreign institutions, falling into the characteristic and most ominous fault of Young America."

allusions to President Lincoln's little peculiarities (already well known to the country and to the world) should be misinterpreted, I deem it proper to say a word or two in regard to him, of unfeigned respect and measurable confidence. He is evidently a man of keen faculties, and, what is still more to the purpose, of powerful character. As to his integrity, the people have that intuition of it which is never deceived. Before he actually entered upon his great office, and for a considerable time afterwards, there is no reason to suppose that he adequately estimated the gigantic task about to be imposed on him, or, at least, had any distinct idea how it was to be managed; and I presume there may have been more than one veteran politician who proposed to himself to take the power out of President Lincoln's hands into his own, leaving our honest friend only the public responsibility for the good or ill success of the career. The extremely imperfect development of his statesmanly qualities, at that period, may have justified such designs. But the President is teachable by events, and has now spent a year in a very arduous course of education; he has a flexible mind, capable of much expansion, and convertible towards far loftier studies and activities than those of his early life; and if he came to Washington a backwoods humorist, he has already transformed himself into as good a statesman (to speak moderately) as his prime minister.[3]

1862

3. Presumably the Secretary of State, William H. Seward.

QUESTIONS

1. *In one sentence summarize Hawthorne's attitude toward Lincoln in the first seven paragraphs.*
2. *What is the basic pattern of the opening sentence of the fifth paragraph? Find other examples of this pattern. What is their total impact on Hawthorne's description?*
3. *In his final paragraph Hawthorne seeks to prevent misunderstanding by stressing his respect for and confidence in Lincoln. Is there anything in the paragraph which runs counter to that expression? To what effect?*
4. *In the footnote to the seventh paragraph the editor of* The Atlantic Monthly *explains his omission of the first seven paragraphs. On the evidence of this statement what sort of a person does the editor seem to be? Is there anything in the omitted paragraphs that would tend to justify his decision? Is the full description superior to the last paragraph printed alone? Explain.*
5. *Describe someone you know with a strong personality that has contrasting characteristics.*

Margaret Mead

HOME AND TRAVEL

For many people moving is one kind of thing and travel is something very different. Travel means going away from home and staying away from home; it is an antidote to the humdrum activities of everyday life, a prelude to a holiday one is entitled to enjoy after months of dullness. Moving means breaking up a home, sadly or joyfully breaking with the past; a happy venture or a hardship, something to be endured with good or ill grace.

For me, moving and staying at home, traveling and arriving, are all of a piece. The world is full of homes in which I have lived for a day, a month, a year, or much longer. How much I care about a home is not measured by the length of time I have lived there. One night in a room with a leaping fire may mean more to me than many months in a room without a fireplace, a room in which my life has been paced less excitingly.

From the time I can first remember, I knew that we had not always lived where we were living then—in Hammonton, New Jersey, where we had moved so that Mother could work on her doctoral thesis. I knew that I had spent my first summer at a resort called Lavallette, a place I did not visit again until I was seventeen, there to have the only authentic attack of homesickness I have ever had, brought on by the sound of the pounding surf. I knew also that we had lived on St. Marks Square, Philadelphia, because the next winter we lived near St. Marks Square and still knew people who lived there.

Every winter we went to live in or near Philadelphia so that Father would not have to travel too far or stay in the city on the nights that he lectured at the University. From the time I was seven years old, we went somewhere for the summer, too. So we moved four times a year, because for the fall and spring we returned to the house in Hammonton.

All the other houses were strange—houses that had to be made our own as quickly as possible so that they no longer would be strange. This did not mean that they were frightening, but only that we had to learn about every nook and corner, for otherwise it was hard to play hide-and-go-seek. As soon as we arrived, I ran ahead to find a room for myself as far away as possible from everyone else, preferably at the top of the house where I would always be warned by footsteps that someone was coming. After that, until we were settled in, I was busy exploring, making my own the new domain. Later, when I was about fourteen, I was in charge of unpacking, getting beds made, food in the icebox, and the lamps filled and lit before nightfall.

The next step was to explore the neighborhood. I had to find out what other children lived nearby and whether there were woods, wild flowers, tangles, or jungles—any hidden spot that could be turned into a miniature primeval forest where life could be quickly shaped to an imaginary world.

In Hammonton we had five whole acres, a good part of which was second-growth bush, studded with blueberries, which the little Italian children who were our neighbors picked and sold back to us. In Lansdowne and Swarthmore there were bits of woodlot. But in Philadelphia there was nothing, only stone walls of different heights on which to walk. Nothing, except for the winter when we lived at the edge of the park near the zoo.

However far away we moved and however often, we always came home again to Hammonton and the familiar and loved things that were too fragile to take with us—although Mother was very permissive about allowing us to carry along all the objects each of us wanted. In Hammonton there was the same blueberry thicket in which to wander along old paths and make new ones, the same surrey, which we hired from the livery stable, and the same door which was never opened—a second door on the front porch which was used only on one occasion, on the night the neighbors pounded on it to tell us that our chimney had caught fire.

There was the great tree from which a hornets' nest blew down in a storm. I had been dancing in the wind when it blew down and, still dancing, plunged my hands into it. I can still remember the wind but not the stings with which I was said to have been covered. There were the tall evergreen arborvitae that divided the lawn into little squares, where Grandma played games with us until one day she put her hand to her heart and then she did not play running games anymore. And outside the mock-orange hedge we once found faeces, and Mother said, in a tone of disgust close to horror, that they were human faeces.

There was the well with a pump that we used to prime with hot water, until one day my five-year-old brother and a desperado friend a year younger threw everything detachable down the well, and then it was never used again. There was an old dinghy in which we grew flowers until the boys tore it up. And once, when the barn had been reshingled and the old shingles had been piled in the barn for the winter, the two little boys threw all of them out. Grandma said it just showed how two children, each one quite good by himself, could get into mischief. You never could tell, when you put two children together, what the outcome would be. This enlarged my picture of what boys were like.

It was contrapuntal to an engraving in a homemade copper frame that stood on the mantelpiece. This showed a pair of children, a little girl diligently sewing a fine seam and a boy, beautiful and remote, simply sitting and looking out at the world. Long years later, the same picture provided the central image in a bitter little verse of feminine protest that

I wrote when Edward Sapir[1] told me I would do better to stay at home and have children than to go off to the South Seas to study adolescent girls:

> Measure your thread and cut it
> To suit your little seam,
> Stitch the garment tightly, tightly,
> And leave no room for dream.
>
> . . .
>
> Head down, be not caught looking
> Where the restless wild geese fly.

There were treasures on Mother's dressing table, too—a Wedgwood pin dish, a little porcelain Mary and her lamb, the pale green, flowered top of a rose bowl that had broken, and Mother's silver-backed comb and brush and mirror. All these things held meaning for me. Each was—and still is—capable of evoking a rush of memories.

Taken altogether, the things that mattered a great deal to me when I was a child are very few when I compare them to the overloaded tables and overcrowded shelves through which children today have to thread their way. Only if they are very fortunate will they be able to weave together into memories the ill-assorted mass of gadgets, toys, and easily forgotten objects, objects without a past or a future, and piles of snapshots that will be replaced by new, brightly colored snapshots next year.

The difficulty, it seems to me, is not—as so many older people claim —that in the past life was simpler and there were fewer things, and so people were somehow better, as well as more frugal. It is, rather, that today's children have to find new ways of anchoring the changing moments of their lives, and they have to try to do this with very little help from their elders, who grew up in an extraordinarily different world. How many of the young people who are rebelling against the tyranny of things, who want to strip their lives down to the contents of a rucksack, can remember and name the things that lay on their mother's dressing table or can describe every toy and book they had as a child?

It has been found that when desperate, unhappy youngsters are preparing to break away from a disordered, drug-ridden commune in which they have been living for months, they first gather together in one spot their few possessions and introduce a semblance of order among them. The need to define who you are by the place in which you live remains intact, even when that place is defined by a single object, like the small blue vase that used to mean home to one of my friends, the daughter of a widowed trained nurse who continually moved from one place to another. The Bushmen of the Kalahari Desert often build no walls when they camp in the desert. They simply hollow out a small space in the sand. But then they bend a slender sapling into an arch to make a

1. A well-known anthropologist and linguistics scholar.

doorway, an entrance to a dwelling as sacrosanct from invasion as the walled estates of the wealthy are or as Makati, in Manila, is, where watchmen guard the rich against the poor.

I realized how few things are needed to make a "home" when I took my seven-year-old daughter on her first sea voyage. The ship—the *Marine Jumper,* an unrenovated troopship with iron decks—was crowded with over a thousand students. They were bunked below where the troops had slept, while Cathy and I shared one cabin with six other members of the staff. Cathy climbed into her upper berth, opened the little packages that had been given to her as going-away presents, and arranged them in a circle around her. Then she leaned over the side of the berth and said, "Now I am ready to see the ship."

Home, I learned, can be anywhere you make it. Home is also the place to which you come back again and again. The really poignant parting is the parting that may be forever. It is this sense that every sailing may be a point of no return that haunts the peoples of the Pacific islands. On the very day I arrived in Samoa, people began to ask, "When will you leave?" When I replied, "In a year," they sighed, "Alas, *talofai*"—our love to you —with the sadness of a thousand partings in their voices. Their islands were peopled by voyagers who set off on a short known journey and whose canoes were blown hundreds of miles off course. But even when a fishing canoe goes out there is a chance that it will upset on the dangerous reef and that someone will be drowned. The smallest journey may be forever.

I have seen something similar on the seacoast of Portugal, where every year for four hundred years fishermen set out in their frail boats for the fishing banks across the treacherous Atlantic and no one could tell when —or whether—they would return. Portugal is still a widow's walk. The old women, dressed in black, still seem to be looking out to sea for the men who disappeared into the distance and an unknown fate.

In all my years of field work, each place where I have lived has become home. Each small object I have brought with me, each arrangement on a shelf of tin cans holding beads or salt for trade or crayons for the children to draw with becomes the mark of home. When it is dismantled on the last morning—a morning that is marked by the greed of those who have little and hope for a share of whatever is left behind, as well as by the grief of feeling that someone is leaving forever—on that morning, I weep. I, too, know that this departure, unlike my forays from home as a child, is likely to be forever.

* * *

1972

QUESTIONS

1. What is Mead's implied definition of home?
2. In Robert Frost's poem "The Death of the Hired Man," a husband and a wife give two different definitions of home. The husband says: "Home is the place where, when you have to go there, / They have to take you in." The wife replies: "I should have called it / Something you somehow haven't [i.e., don't have to] to deserve." Explain which of these definitions you think comes closer to Mead's definition of home.
3. Margaret Mead had a long career as an anthropologist studying people of other, more primitive cultures. In this essay is she looking at her own culture in ways that are similar to those she might adopt in looking at another culture? Explain.
4. Mead recounts an incident in which she was told it would be better if she stayed home and had children rather than going to the South Seas. Explain in what ways the poem she wrote is a reply.
5. Write about an object that has symbolic or nostalgic importance for you.
6. Describe the floor plan of the first house you can remember living in. What incidents do you associate with particular parts of the house?
7. Mead speaks of "the need to define who you are by the place in which you live." Explain how the place in which you live can define who you are. What things can it tell about you? What things can't it tell about you? Look at Dylan Thomas's "Memories of Christmas" (p. 1) or E. B. White's "Once More to the Lake" (p. 78). In each case does the place described help to "define" the author?
8. Read Joan Didion's "On Going Home" (p. 66). What does "home" mean to Didion? Compare and contrast her implied definition of home with Mead's.

N. Scott Momaday

THE WAY TO RAINY MOUNTAIN

A single knoll rises out of the plain in Oklahoma, north and west of the Wichita Range. For my people, the Kiowas, it is an old landmark, and they gave it the name Rainy Mountain. The hardest weather in the world is there. Winter brings blizzards, hot tornadic winds arise in the spring, and in summer the prairie is an anvil's edge. The grass turns brittle and brown, and it cracks beneath your feet. There are green belts along the rivers and creeks, linear groves of hickory and pecan, willow and witch hazel. At a distance in July or August the steaming foliage seems almost to writhe in fire. Great green and yellow grasshoppers are everywhere in the tall grass, popping up like corn to sting the flesh, and tortoises crawl about on the red earth, going nowhere in the plenty of time. Loneliness is an aspect of the land. All things in the plain are isolate; there is no confusion of objects in the eye, but one hill or one tree or one man. To look upon that landscape in the early morning, with the sun at your back, is to lose the sense of proportion. Your imagination comes to life, and this, you think, is where Creation was begun.

I returned to Rainy Mountain in July. My grandmother had died in the spring, and I wanted to be at her grave. She had lived to be very old and at last infirm. Her only living daughter was with her when she died, and I was told that in death her face was that of a child.

I like to think of her as a child. When she was born, the Kiowas were living the last great moment of their history. For more than a hundred years they had controlled the open range from the Smoky Hill River to the Red, from the headwaters of the Canadian to the fork of the Arkansas and Cimarron. In alliance with the Comanches, they had ruled the whole of the southern Plains. War was their sacred business, and they were among the finest horsemen the world has ever known. But warfare for the Kiowas was preeminently a matter of disposition rather than of survival, and they never understood the grim, unrelenting advance of the U.S. Cavalry. When at last, divided and ill-provisioned, they were driven onto the Staked Plains in the cold rains of autumn, they fell into panic. In Palo Duro Canyon they abandoned their crucial stores to pillage and had nothing then but their lives. In order to save themselves, they surrendered to the soldiers at Fort Sill and were imprisoned in the old stone corral that now stands as a military museum. My grandmother was spared the humiliation of those high gray walls by eight or ten years, but she must have known from birth the affliction of defeat, the dark brooding of old warriors.

Her name was Aho, and she belonged to the last culture to evolve in North America. Her forebears came down from the high country in western Montana nearly three centuries ago. They were a mountain people, a mysterious tribe of hunters whose language has never been positively classified in any major group. In the late seventeenth century they began a long migration to the south and east. It was a journey toward the dawn, and it led to a golden age. Along the way the Kiowas were befriended by the Crows, who gave them the culture and religion of the Plains. They acquired horses, and their ancient nomadic spirit was suddenly free of the ground. They acquired Tai-me, the sacred Sun Dance doll, from that moment the object and symbol of their worship, and so shared in the divinity of the sun. Not least, they acquired the sense of destiny, therefore courage and pride. When they entered upon the southern Plains they had been transformed. No longer were they slaves to the simple necessity of survival; they were a lordly and dangerous society of fighters and thieves, hunters and priests of the sun. According to their origin myth, they entered the world through a hollow log. From one point of view, their migration was the fruit of an old prophecy, for indeed they emerged from a sunless world.

Although my grandmother lived out her long life in the shadow of Rainy Mountain, the immense landscape of the continental interior lay like memory in her blood. She could tell of the Crows, whom she had never seen, and of the Black Hills, where she had never been. I wanted to see in reality what she had seen more perfectly in the mind's eye, and traveled fifteen hundred miles to begin my pilgrimage.

Yellowstone, it seemed to me, was the top of the world, a region of deep lakes and dark timber, canyons and waterfalls. But, beautiful as it is, one might have the sense of confinement there. The skyline in all directions is close at hand, the high wall of the woods and deep cleavages of shade. There is a perfect freedom in the mountains, but it belongs to the eagle and the elk, the badger and the bear. The Kiowas reckoned their stature by the distance they could see, and they were bent and blind in the wilderness.

Descending eastward, the highland meadows are a stairway to the plain. In July the inland slope of the Rockies is luxuriant with flax and buckwheat, stonecrop and larkspur. The earth unfolds and the limit of the land recedes. Clusters of trees, and animals grazing far in the distance, cause the vision to reach away and wonder to build upon the mind. The sun follows a longer course in the day, and the sky is immense beyond all comparison. The great billowing clouds that sail upon it are the shadows that move upon the grain like water, dividing light. Farther down, in the land of the Crows and Blackfeet, the plain is yellow. Sweet clover takes hold of the hills and bends upon itself to cover and seal the soil. There the Kiowas paused on their way; they had come to the place where they must change their lives. The sun is at home on the plains. Precisely there does it have the certain character of a god. When the Kiowas came to the land of the Crows, they could see the dark lees of the hills at dawn across the Bighorn River, the profusion of light on the grain shelves, the oldest deity ranging after the solstices. Not yet would they veer southward to the caldron of the land that lay below; they must wean their blood from the northern winter and hold the mountains a while longer in their view. They bore Tai-me in procession to the east.

A dark mist lay over the Black Hills, and the land was like iron. At the top of a ridge I caught sight of Devil's Tower upthrust against the gray sky as if in the birth of time the core of the earth had broken through its crust and the motion of the world was begun. There are things in nature that engender an awful quiet in the heart of man; Devil's Tower is one of them. Two centuries ago, because they could not do otherwise, the Kiowas made a legend at the base of the rock. My grandmother said: *Eight children were there at play, seven sisters and their brother. Suddenly*

the boy was struck dumb; he trembled and began to run upon his hands and
feet. His fingers became claws, and his body was covered with fur. Directly
there was a bear where the boy had been. The sisters were terrified; they
ran, and the bear after them. They came to the stump of a great tree, and the
tree spoke to them. It bade them climb upon it, and as they did so it began to
rise into the air. The bear came to kill them, but they were just beyond its
reach. It reared against the tree and scored the bark all around with its claws.
The seven sisters were borne into the sky, and they became the stars of the
Big Dipper.

From that moment, and so long as the legend lives, the Kiowas have
kinsmen in the night sky. Whatever they were in the mountains, they
could be no more. However tenuous their well-being, however much
they had suffered and would suffer again, they had found a way out of the
wilderness.

My grandmother had a reverence for the sun, a holy regard that now is
all but gone out of mankind. There was a wariness in her, and an ancient
awe. She was a Christian in her later years, but she had come a long way
about, and she never forgot her birthright. As a child she had been to the
Sun Dances; she had taken part in those annual rites, and by them she had
learned the restoration of her people in the presence of Tai-me. She was
about seven when the last Kiowa Sun Dance was held in 1887 on the
Washita River above Rainy Mountain Creek. The buffalo were gone. In
order to consummate the ancient sacrifice—to impale the head of a
buffalo bull upon the medicine tree—a delegation of old men journeyed
into Texas, there to beg and barter for an animal from the Goodnight
herd. She was ten when the Kiowas came together for the last time as a
living Sun Dance culture. They could find no buffalo; they had to hang an
old hide from the sacred tree. Before the dance could begin, a company of
soldiers rode out from Fort Sill under orders to disperse the tribe. Forbidden without cause the essential act of their faith, having seen the wild
herds slaughtered and left to rot upon the ground, the Kiowas backed
away forever from the medicine tree. That was July 20, 1890, at the great
bend of the Washita. My grandmother was there. Without bitterness,
and for as long as she lived, she bore a vision of deicide.

Now that I can have her only in memory, I see my grandmother in the
several postures that were peculiar to her: standing at the wood stove on a
winter morning and turning meat in a great iron skillet; sitting at the
south window, bent above her beadwork, and afterwards, when her
vision failed, looking down for a long time into the fold of her hands;
going out upon a cane, very slowly as she did when the weight of age
came upon her; praying. I remember her most often at prayer. She made
long, rambling prayers out of suffering and hope, having seen many
things. I was never sure that I had the right to hear, so exclusive where
they of all mere custom and company. The last time I saw her she prayed

standing by the side of her bed at night, naked to the waist, the light of a kerosene lamp moving upon her dark skin. Her long, black hair, always drawn and braided in the day, lay upon her shoulders and against her breasts like a shawl. I do not speak Kiowa, and I never understood her prayers, but there was something inherently sad in the sound, some merest hesitation upon the syllables of sorrow. She began in a high and descending pitch, exhausting her breath to silence; then again and again —and always the same intensity of effort, of something that is, and is not, like urgency in the human voice. Transported so in the dancing light among the shadows of her room, she seemed beyond the reach of time. But that was illusion; I think I knew then that I should not see her again.

Houses are like sentinels in the plain, old keepers of the weather watch. There, in a very little while, wood takes on the appearance of great age. All colors wear soon away in the wind and rain, and then the wood is burned gray and the grain appears and the nails turn red with rust. The windowpanes are black and opaque; you imagine there is nothing within, and indeed there are many ghosts, bones given up to the land. They stand here and there against the sky, and you approach them for a longer time than you expect. They belong in the distance; it is their domain.

Once there was a lot of sound in my grandmother's house, a lot of coming and going, feasting and talk. The summers there were full of excitement and reunion. The Kiowas are a summer people; they abide the cold and keep to themselves, but when the season turns and the land becomes warm and vital they cannot hold still; an old love of going returns upon them. The aged visitors who came to my grandmother's house when I was a child were made of lean and leather, and they bore themselves upright. They wore great black hats and bright ample shirts that shook in the wind. They rubbed fat upon their hair and wound their braids with strips of colored cloth. Some of them painted their faces and carried the scars of old and cherished enmities. They were an old council of warlords, come to remind and be reminded of who they were. Their wives and daughters served them well. The women might indulge themselves; gossip was at once the mark and compensation of their servitude. They made loud and elaborate talk among themselves, full of jest and gesture, fright and false alarm. They went abroad in fringed and flowered shawls, bright beadwork and German silver. They were at home in the kitchen, and they prepared meals that were banquets.

There were frequent prayer meetings, and great nocturnal feasts. When I was a child I played with my cousins outside, where the lamplight fell upon the ground and the singing of the old people rose up around us and carried away into the darkness. There were a lot of good things to eat, a lot of laughter and surprise. And afterwards, when the quiet returned, I lay down with my grandmother and could hear the frogs away by the river and feel the motion of the air.

Now there is a funeral silence in the rooms, the endless wake of some final word. The walls have closed in upon my grandmother's house. When I returned to it in mourning, I saw for the first time in my life how small it was. It was late at night, and there was a white moon, nearly full. I sat for a long time on the stone steps by the kitchen door. From there I could see out across the land; I could see the long row of trees by the creek, the low light upon the rolling plains, and the stars of the Big Dipper. Once I looked at the moon and caught sight of a strange thing. A cricket had perched upon the handrail, only a few inches away from me. My line of vision was such that the creature filled the moon like a fossil. It had gone there, I thought, to live and die, for there, of all places, was its small definition made whole and eternal. A warm wind rose up and purled like the longing within me.

The next morning I awoke at dawn and went out on the dirt road to Rainy Mountain. It was already hot, and the grasshoppers began to fill the air. Still, it was early in the morning, and the birds sang out of the shadows. The long yellow grass on the mountain shone in the bright light, and a scissortail hied above the land. There, where it ought to be, at the end of a long and legendary way, was my grandmother's grave. Here and there on the dark stones were ancestral names. Looking back once, I saw the mountain and came away.

1969

Virginia Woolf

MY FATHER: LESLIE STEPHEN

By the time that his children were growing up, the great days of my father's life were over. His feats on the river and on the mountains had been won before they were born. Relics of them were to be found lying about the house—the silver cup on the study mantelpiece; the rusty alpenstocks that leaned against the bookcase in the corner; and to the end of his days he would speak of great climbers and explorers with a peculiar mixture of admiration and envy. But his own years of activity were over, and my father had to content himself with pottering about the Swiss valleys or taking a stroll across the Cornish moors.

That to potter and to stroll meant more on his lips than on other people's is becoming obvious now that some of his friends have given their own version of those expeditions. He would start off after breakfast alone, or with one companion. Shortly after dinner he would return. If the walk had been successful, he would have out his great map and commemorate a new short cut in red ink. And he was quite capable, it appears, of striding all day across the moors without speaking more than a word or two to his companion. By that time, too, he had written the *History of English Thought in the Eighteenth Century,* which is said by some to be his masterpiece; and the *Science of Ethics*—the book which interested him most; and *The Playground of Europe,* in which is to be found "The Sunset on Mont Blanc"—in his opinion the best thing he ever wrote. He still wrote daily and methodically, though never for long at a time.

In London he wrote in the large room with three long windows at the top of the house. He wrote lying almost recumbent in a low rocking chair which he tipped to and fro as he wrote, like a cradle, and as he wrote he smoked a short clay pipe, and he scattered books round him in a circle. The thud of a book dropped on the floor could be heard in the room beneath. And often as he mounted the stairs to his study with his firm, regular tread he would burst, not into song, for he was entirely unmusical, but into a strange rhythmical chant, for verse of all kinds, both "utter trash," as he called it, and the most sublime words of Milton and Wordsworth, stuck in his memory, and the act of walking or climbing seemed to inspire him to recite whichever it was that came uppermost or suited his mood.

But it was his dexterity with his fingers that delighted his children before they could potter along the lanes at his heels or read his books. He would twist a sheet of paper beneath a pair of scissors and out would drop an elephant, a stag, or a monkey, with trunks, horns, and tails delicately and exactly formed. Or, taking a pencil, he would draw beast after beast —an art that he practiced almost unconsciously as he read, so that the flyleaves of his books swarm with owls and donkeys as if to illustrate the "Oh, you ass!" or "Conceited dunce" that he was wont to scribble impatiently in the margin. Such brief comments, in which one may find the germ of the more temperate statements of his essays, recall some of the characteristics of his talk. He could be very silent, as his friends have testified. But his remarks, made suddenly in a low voice between the puffs of his pipe, were extremely effective. Sometimes with one word —but his one word was accompanied by a gesture of the hand—he would dispose of the tissue of exaggerations which his own sobriety seemed to provoke. "There are 40,000,000 unmarried women in London alone!" Lady Ritchie once informed him. "Oh, Annie, Annie!" my father exclaimed in tones of horrified but affectionate rebuke. But Lady Ritchie, as if she enjoyed being rebuked, would pile it up even higher next time she came.

The stories he told to amuse his children of adventures in the Alps

—but accidents only happened, he would explain, if you were so foolish as to disobey your guides—or of those long walks, after one of which, from Cambridge to London on a hot day, "I drank, I am sorry to say, rather more than was good for me," were told very briefly, but with a curious power to impress the scene. The things that he did not say were always there in the background. So, too, though he seldom told anec- dotes, and his memory for facts was bad, when he described a person —and he had known many people, both famous and obscure—he would convey exactly what he thought of him in two or three words. And what he thought might be the opposite of what other people thought. He had a way of upsetting established reputations and disregarding conventional values that could be disconcerting, and sometimes perhaps wounding, though no one was more respectful of any feeling that seemed to him genuine. But when, suddenly opening his bright blue eyes and rousing himself from what had seemed complete abstraction, he gave his opinion, it was difficult to disregard it. It was a habit, especially when deafness made him unaware that this opinion could be heard, that had its inconve- niences.

"I am the most easily bored of men," he wrote, truthfully as usual; and when, as was inevitable in a large family, some visitor threatened to stay not merely for tea but also for dinner, my father would express his anguish at first by twisting and untwisting a certain lock of hair. Then he would burst out, half to himself, half to the powers above, but quite audibly, "Why can't he go? Why can't he go?" Yet such is the charm of simplicity—and did he not say, also truthfully, that "bores are the salt of the earth"?—that the bores seldom went, or, if they did, forgave him and came again.

Too much, perhaps, has been said of his silence; too much stress has been laid upon his reserve. He loved clear thinking; he hated sentimen- tality and gush; but this by no means meant that he was cold and unemotional, perpetually critical and condemnatory in daily life. On the contrary, it was his power of feeling strongly and of expressing his feeling with vigor that made him sometimes so alarming as a companion. A lady, for instance, complained of the wet summer that was spoiling her tour in Cornwall. But to my father, though he never called himself a democrat, the rain meant that the corn was being laid; some poor man was being ruined; and the energy with which he expressed his sympathy—not with the lady—left her discomfited. He had something of the same respect for farmers and fishermen that he had for climbers and explorers. So, too, he talked little of patriotism, but during the South African War—and all wars were hateful to him—he lay awake thinking that he heard the guns on the battlefield. Again, neither his reason nor his cold common sense helped to convince him that a child could be late for dinner without having been maimed or killed in an accident. And not all his mathematics

together with a bank balance which he insisted must be ample in the extreme could persuade him, when it came to signing a check, that the whole family was not "shooting Niagara to ruin,"[1] as he put it. The pictures that he would draw of old age and the bankruptcy court, of ruined men of letters who have to support large families in small houses at Wimbledon (he owned a very small house at Wimbledon), might have convinced those who complain of his understatements that hyperbole was well within his reach had he chosen.

Yet the unreasonable mood was superficial, as the rapidity with which it vanished would prove. The checkbook was shut; Wimbledon and the workhouse were forgotten. Some thought of a humorous kind made him chuckle. Taking his hat and his stick, calling for his dog and his daughter, he would stride off into Kensington Gardens, where he had walked as a little boy, where his brother Fitzjames and he had made beautiful bows to young Queen Victoria and she had swept them a curtsy; and so, round the Serpentine, to Hyde Park Corner, where he had once saluted the great Duke himself; and so home. He was not then in the least "alarming"; he was very simple, very confiding; and his silence, though one might last unbroken from the Round Pond to the Marble Arch, was curiously full of meaning, as if he were thinking half aloud, about poetry and philosophy and people he had known.

He himself was the most abstemious of men. He smoked a pipe perpetually, but never a cigar. He wore his clothes until they were too shabby to be tolerable; and he held old-fashioned and rather puritanical views as to the vice of luxury and the sin of idleness. The relations between parents and children today have a freedom that would have been impossible with my father. He expected a certain standard of behavior, even of ceremony, in family life. Yet if freedom means the right to think one's own thoughts and to follow one's own pursuits, then no one respected and indeed insisted upon freedom more completely than he did. His sons, with the exception of the Army and Navy, should follow whatever professions they chose; his daughters, though he cared little enough for the higher education of women, should have the same liberty. If at one moment he rebuked a daughter sharply for smoking a cigarette —smoking was not in his opinion a nice habit in the other sex—she had only to ask him if she might become a painter, and he assured her that so long as she took her work seriously he would give her all the help he could. He had no special love for painting; but he kept his word. Freedom of that sort was worth thousands of cigarettes.

It was the same with the perhaps more difficult problem of literature. Even today there may be parents who would doubt the wisdom of allowing a girl of fifteen the free run of a large and quite unexpurgated library. But my father allowed it. There were certain facts—very briefly,

1. The reference is to going over Niagara Falls in a boat.

very shyly he referred to them. Yet "Read what you like," he said, and all his books, "mangy and worthless," as he called them, but certainly they were many and various, were to be had without asking. To read what one liked because one liked it, never to pretend to admire what one did not —that was his only lesson in the art of reading. To write in the fewest possible words, as clearly as possible, exactly what one meant—that was his only lesson in the art of writing. All the rest must be learned for oneself. Yet a child must have been childish in the extreme not to feel that such was the teaching of a man of great learning and wide experience, though he would never impose his own views or parade his own knowledge. For, as his tailor remarked when he saw my father walk past his shop up Bond Street, "There goes a gentleman that wears good clothes without knowing it."

In those last years, grown solitary and very deaf, he would sometimes call himself a failure as a writer; he had been "jack of all trades, and master of none." But whether he failed or succeeded as a writer, it is permissible to believe that he left a distinct impression of himself on the minds of his friends. Meredith[2] saw him as "Phoebus Apollo turned fasting friar" in his earlier days; Thomas Hardy, years later, looked at the "spare and desolate figure" of the Schreckhorn[3] and thought of

> him,
> Who scaled its horn with ventured life and limb,
> Drawn on by vague imaginings, maybe,
> Of semblance to his personality
> In its quaint glooms, keen lights, and rugged trim.

But the praise he would have valued most, for though he was an agnostic nobody believed more profoundly in the worth of human relationships, was Meredith's tribute after his death: "He was the one man to my knowledge worthy to have married your mother." And Lowell,[4] when he called him "L.S., the most lovable of men," has best described the quality that makes him, after all these years, unforgettable.

1950[5]

2. George Meredith (1828–1909), English novelist and poet.
3. One of the peaks in the Swiss Alps.
4. James Russell Lowell, nineteenth-century American poet, essayist, and editor.
5. Published posthumously.

QUESTIONS

1. *What are the basic qualities Woolf admires, as revealed in this selection?*
2. *Giving praise can be a difficult rhetorical and social undertaking. How does Woolf avoid the pitfalls, or try to? Compare Doris Lessing, in "My Father" (p. 133). Does she take similar risks? Or compare Nathaniel Hawthorne, in "Abraham Lincoln" (p. 115).*
3. *What are the main currents of the Stephens' family life as revealed*

here? Any such description must be selective; what does Woolf leave
out? Do the omissions detract from her essay? If you think so, say why.
4. *In some of her other work Woolf shows a deep and sensitive concern*
for women's experience and awareness. Do you find a feminist aware-
ness here? In what way?

Doris Lessing

MY FATHER

We use our parents like recurring dreams, to be entered into when
needed; they are always there for love or for hate; but it occurs to me that
I was not always there for my father. I've written about him before, but
novels, stories, don't have to be "true." Writing this article is difficult
because it has to be "true." I knew him when his best years were over.

There are photographs of him. The largest is of an officer in the
1914–18 war. A new uniform—buttoned, badged, strapped, tabbed
—confines a handsome, dark young man who holds himself stiffly to
confront what he certainly thought of as his duty. His eyes are steady,
serious, and responsible, and show no signs of what he became later. A
photograph at sixteen is of a dark, introspective youth with the same
intent eyes. But it is his mouth you notice—a heavily-jutting upper lip
contradicts the rest of a regular face. His moustache was to hide it: "Had
to do something—a damned fleshy mouth. Always made me uncomfortable, that mouth of mine."

Earlier a baby (eyes already alert) appears in a lace waterfall that
cascades from the pillowy bosom of a fat, plain woman to her feet. It is the
face of a head cook. "Lord, but my mother was a practical female—almost
as bad as you!" as he used to say, or throw at my mother in moments of
exasperation. Beside her stands, or droops, arms dangling, his father, the
source of the dark, arresting eyes, but otherwise masked by a long beard.

The birth certificate says: Born 3rd August, 1886, Walton Villa, Cref-
field Road, S. Mary at the Wall, R.S.D. Name, Alfred Cook. Name and
surname of Father: Alfred Cook Tayler. Name and maiden name of
Mother: Caroline May Batley. Rank or Profession: Bank Clerk.
Colchester, Essex.

They were very poor. Clothes and boots were a problem. They "made
their own amusements." Books were mostly the Bible and *The Pilgrim's
Progress*.[1] Every Saturday night they bathed in a hipbath in front of the
kitchen fire. No servants. Church three times on Sundays. "Lord, when I

1. An allegory of Christian's progress toward heaven through a world filled with tempters, by
the seventeenth-century writer John Bunyan.

think of those Sundays! I dreaded them all week, like a nightmare coming at you full tilt and no escape." But he rabbited with ferrets along the lanes and fields, bird-nested, stole fruit, picked nuts and mushrooms, paid visits to the blacksmith and the mill and rode a farmer's carthorse.

They ate economically, but when he got diabetes in his forties and subsisted on lean meat and lettuce leaves, he remembered suet puddings, treacle puddings, raisin and currant puddings, steak and kidney puddings, bread and butter pudding, "batter cooked in the gravy with the meat," potato cake, plum cake, butter cake, porridge with treacle, fruit tarts and pies, brawn, pig's trotters and pig's cheek and home-smoked ham and sausages. And "lashings of fresh butter and cream and eggs." He wondered if this diet had produced the diabetes, but said it was worth it.

There was an elder brother described by my father as: "Too damned clever by half. One of those quick, clever brains. Now I've always had a slow brain, but I get there in the end, damn it!"

The brothers went to a local school and the elder did well, but my father was beaten for being slow. They both became bank clerks in, I think, the Westminster Bank, and one must have found it congenial, for he became a manager, the "rich brother," who had cars and even a yacht. But my father did not like it, though he was conscientious. For instance, he changed his writing, letter by letter, because a senior criticised it. I never saw his unregenerate hand, but the one he created was elegant, spiky, careful. Did this mean he created a new personality for himself, hiding one he did not like, as he hid his "damned fleshy mouth"? I don't know.

Nor do I know when he left home to live in Luton, or why. He found family life too narrow? A safe guess—he found everything too narrow. His mother was too down-to-earth? He had to get away from his clever elder brother?

Being a young man in Luton was the best part of his life. It ended in 1914, so he had a decade of happiness. His reminiscences of it were all of pleasure, the delight of physical movement, of dancing in particular. All his girls were "a beautiful dancer, light as a feather." He played billiards and ping-pong (both for his country); he swam, boated, played cricket and football,[2] went to picnics and horse races, sang at musical evenings. One family of a mother and two daughters treated him "like a son only better. I didn't know whether I was in love with the mother or the daughters, but oh I did love going there; we had such good times." He was engaged to one daughter, then, for a time, to the other. An engagement was broken off because she was rude to a waiter. "I could not marry a woman who allowed herself to insult someone who was defenceless." He used to say to my wryly smiling mother: "Just as well I didn't marry

2. Soccer.

either of them; they would never have stuck it out the way you have, old girl."

Just before he died he told me he had dreamed he was standing in a kitchen on a very high mountain holding X in his arms. "Ah, yes, that's what I've missed in my life. Now don't you let yourself be cheated out of life by the old dears. They take all the colour out of everything if you let them."

But in that decade—"I'd walk 10, 15 miles to a dance two or three times a week and think nothing of it. Then I'd dance every dance and walk home again over the fields. Sometimes it was moonlight, but I liked the snow best, all crisp and fresh. I loved walking back and getting into my digs[3] just as the sun was rising. My little dog was so happy to see me, and I'd feed her, and make myself porridge and tea, then I'd wash and shave and go off to work."

The boy who was beaten at school, who went too much to church, who carried the fear of poverty all his life, but who nevertheless was filled with the memories of country pleasures; the young bank clerk who worked such long hours for so little money, but who danced, sang, played, flirted—this naturally vigorous, sensuous being was killed in 1914, 1915, 1916. I think the best of my father died in that war, that his spirit was crippled by it. The people I've met, particularly the women, who knew him young, speak of his high spirits, his energy, his enjoyment of life. Also of his kindness, his compassion and—a word that keeps recurring—his wisdom. "Even when he was just a boy he understood things that you'd think even an old man would find it easy to condemn." I do not think these people would have easily recognised the ill, irritable, abstracted, hypochondriac man I knew.

He "joined up" as an ordinary soldier out of a characteristically quirky scruple: it wasn't right to enjoy officers' privileges when the Tommies[4] had such a bad time. But he could not stick the communal latrines, the obligatory drinking, the collective visits to brothels, the jokes about girls. So next time he was offered a commission he took it.

His childhood and young man's memories, kept fluid, were added to, grew, as living memories do. But his war memories were congealed in stories that he told again and again, with the same words and gestures, in stereotyped phrases. They were anonymous, general, as if they had come out of a communal war memoir. He met a German in no-man's-land, but both slowly lowered their rifles and smiled and walked away. The Tommies were the salt of the earth, the British fighting men the best in the world. He had never known such comradeship. A certain brutal officer was shot in a sortie by his men, but the other officers, recognising rough justice, said nothing. He had known men intimately who saw the Angels

---

3. Lodgings.   4. Foot soldiers.

at Mons.[5] He wished he could force all the generals on both sides into the trenches for just one day, to see what the common soldiers endured—*that* would have ended the war at once.

There was an undercurrent of memories, dreams, and emotions much deeper, more personal. This dark region in him, fate-ruled, where nothing was true but horror, was expressed inarticulately, in brief, bitter exclamations or phrases of rage, incredulity, betrayal. The men who went to fight in that war believed it when they said it was to end war. My father believed it. And he was never able to reconcile his belief in his country with his anger at the cynicism of its leaders. And the anger, the sense of betrayal, strengthened as he grew old and ill.

But in 1914 he was naïve, the German atrocities in Belgium inflamed him, and he enlisted out of idealism, although he knew he would have a hard time. He knew because a fortuneteller told him. (He could be described as uncritically superstitious or as psychically gifted.) He would be in great danger twice, yet not die—he was being protected by a famous soldier who was his ancestor. "And sure enough, later I heard from the Little Aunties that the church records showed we were descended the backstairs way from the Duke of Wellington, or was it Marlborough? Damn it, I forget. But one of them would be beside me all through the war, she said." (He was romantic, not only about this solicitous ghost, but also about being a descendant of the Huguenots, on the strength of the "e" in Tayler; and about "the wild blood" in his veins from a great uncle who, sent unjustly to prison for smuggling, came out of a ten-year sentence and earned it, very efficiently, along the coasts of Cornwall until he died.)

The luckiest thing that ever happened to my father, he said, was getting his leg shattered by shrapnel ten days before Passchendaele.[6] His whole company was killed. He knew he was going to be wounded because of the fortuneteller, who had said he would know. "I did not understand what she meant, but both times in the trenches, first when my appendix burst and I nearly died, and then just before Passchendaele, I felt for some days as if a thick, black velvet pall was settled over me. I can't tell you what it was like. Oh, it was awful, awful, and the second time it was so bad I wrote to the old people and told them I was going to be killed."

His leg was cut off at mid-thigh, he was shell-shocked, he was very ill for many months, with a prolonged depression afterwards. "You should always remember that sometimes people are all seething underneath. You don't know what terrible things people have to fight against. You should look at a person's eyes, that's how you tell. . . . When I was like that, after I lost my leg, I went to a nice doctor man and said I was going

5. An apparition that appeared during a World War I battle.
6. A prolonged and futile battle of World War I, in which British and Commonwealth forces sustained massive casualties.

mad, but he said, don't worry, everyone locks up things like that. You don't know—horrible, horrible, awful things. I was afraid of myself, of what I used to dream. I wasn't myself at all."

In the Royal Free Hospital was my mother, Sister McVeagh. He married his nurse which, as they both said often enough (though in different tones of voice), was just as well. That was 1919. He could not face being a bank clerk in England, he said, not after the trenches. Besides, England was too narrow and conventional. Besides, the civilians did not know what the soldiers had suffered, they didn't want to know, and now it wasn't done even to remember "The Great Unmentionable." He went off to the Imperial Bank of Persia, in which country I was born.

The house was beautiful, with great stone-floored high-ceilinged rooms whose windows showed ranges of snow-streaked mountains. The gardens were full of roses, jasmine, pomegranates, walnuts. Kermanshah he spoke of with liking, but soon they went to Teheran, populous with "Embassy people," and my gregarious mother created a lively social life about which he was irritable even in recollection.

Irritableness—that note was first struck here, about Persia. He did not like, he said, "the graft and the corruption." But here it is time to try and describe something difficult—how a man's good qualities can also be his bad ones, or if not bad, a danger to him.

My father was honourable—he always knew exactly what that word meant. He had integrity. His "one does not do that sort of thing," his "no, it is not right," sounded throughout my childhood and were final for all of us. I am sure it was true he wanted to leave Persia because of "the corruption." But it was also because he was already unconsciously longing for something freer, because as a bank official he could not let go into the dream-logged personality that was waiting for him. And later in Rhodesia, too, what was best in him was also what prevented him from shaking away the shadows: it was always in the name of honesty or decency that he refused to take this step or that out of the slow decay of the family's fortunes.

In 1925 there was leave from Persia. That year in London there was an Empire Exhibition, and on the Southern Rhodesian stand some very fine maize cobs and a poster saying that fortunes could be made on maize at 25/-[7] a bag. So on an impulse, turning his back forever on England, washing his hands of the corruption of the East, my father collected all his capital, £800, I think, while my mother packed curtains from Liberty's, clothes from Harrods, visiting cards, a piano, Persian rugs, a governess and two small children.

Soon, there was my father in a cigar-shaped house of thatch and mud on the top of a kopje[8] that overlooked in all directions a great system of

7. Twenty-five shillings. A shilling was then worth about twenty-five cents.

8. Small hill. The term is South African Dutch.

mountains, rivers, valleys, while overhead the sky arched from horizon to empty horizon. This was a couple of hundred miles south from the Zambesi, a hundred or so west from Mozambique, in the district of Banket, so called because certain of its reefs were of the same formation as those called *banket* on the Rand. Lomagundi—gold country, tobacco country, maize country—wild, almost empty. (The Africans had been turned off it into reserves.) Our neighbours were four, five, seven miles off. In front of the house . . . no neighbours, nothing; no farms, just wild bush with two rivers but no fences to the mountains seven miles away. And beyond these mountains and bush again to the Portuguese border,[9] over which "our boys" used to escape when wanted by the police for pass or other offences.

And then? There was bad luck. For instance, the price of maize dropped from 25/- to 9/- a bag. The seasons were bad, prices bad, crops failed. This was the sort of thing that made it impossible for him ever to "get off the farm," which, he agreed with my mother, was what he most wanted to do.

It was an absurd country, he said. A man could "own" a farm for years that was totally mortgaged to the Government and run from the Land Bank, meanwhile employing half-a-hundred Africans at 12/- a month and none of them knew how to do a day's work. Why, two farm labourers from Europe could do in a day what twenty of these ignorant black savages would take a week to do. (Yet he was proud that he had a name as a just employer, that he gave "a square deal.") Things got worse. A fortuneteller had told him that her heart ached when she saw the misery ahead for my father: this was the misery.

But it was my mother who suffered. After a period of neurotic illness, which was a protest against her situation, she became brave and resourceful. But she never saw that her husband was not living in a real world, that he had made a captive of her common sense. We were always about to "get off the farm." A miracle would do it—a sweepstake, a goldmine, a legacy. And then? What a question! We would go to England where life would be normal with people coming in for musical evenings and nice supper parties at the Trocadero after a show. Poor woman, for the twenty years we were on the farm, she waited for when life would begin for her and for her children, for she never understood that what was a calamity for her was for them a blessing.

Meanwhile my father sank towards his death (at 61). Everything changed in him. He had been a dandy and fastidious, now he hated to change out of shabby khaki. He had been sociable, now he was misanthropic. His body's disorders—soon diabetes and all kinds of stomach ailments—dominated him. He was brave about his wooden leg, and even went down mine shafts and climbed trees with it, but he walked clumsily

---

9. That is, the border of Mozambique, then a Portuguese possession.

and it irked him badly. He greyed fast, and slept more in the day, but would be awake half the night pondering about. . . .

It could be gold divining. For ten years he experimented on private theories to do with the attractions and repulsions of metals. His whole soul went into it but his theories were wrong or he was *unlucky*—after all, if he had found a mine he would have had to leave the farm. It could be the relation between the minerals of the earth and of the moon; his decision to make infusions of all the plants on the farm and drink them himself in the interests of science; the criminal folly of the British Government in not realising that the Germans and the Russians were conspiring as Anti-Christ to . . . the inevitability of war because no one would listen to Churchill, but it would be all right because God (by then he was a British Israelite[1]) had destined Britain to rule the world; a prophecy said 10 million dead would surround Jerusalem—how would the corpses be cleared away?; people who wished to abolish flogging should be flogged; the natives understood nothing but a good beating; hanging must not be abolished because the Old Testament said "an eye for an eye and a tooth for a tooth. . . ."

Yet, as this side of him darkened, so that it seemed all his thoughts were of violence, illness, war, still no one dared to make an unkind comment in his presence or to gossip. Criticism of people, particularly of women, made him more and more uncomfortable till at last he burst out with: "It's all very well, but no one has the right to say that about another person."

In Africa, when the sun goes down, the stars spring up, all of them in their expected places, glittering and moving. In the rainy season, the sky flashed and thundered. In the dry season, the great dark hollow of night was lit by veld fires: the mountains burned through September and October in chains of red fire. Every night my father took out his chair to watch the sky and the mountains, smoking, silent, a thin shabby fly-away figure under the stars. "Makes you think—there are so many worlds up there, wouldn't really matter if we did blow ourselves up—plenty more where we came from."

The Second World War, so long foreseen by him, was a bad time. His son was in the Navy and in danger, and his daughter a sorrow to him. He became very ill. More and more often it was necessary to drive him into Salisbury with him in a coma, or in danger of one, on the back seat. My mother moved him into a pretty little suburban house in town near the hospitals, where he took to his bed and a couple of years later died. For the most part he was unconscious under drugs. When awake he talked obsessively (a tongue licking a nagging sore place) about "the old war." Or he remembered his youth. "I've been dreaming—Lord, to see those

1. A reference to the contention that the English-speaking peoples are the descendants of the "ten tribes" of Israel, deported by Sargon of Assyria on the fall of Samaria in 721 B.C.

horses come lickety-split down the course with their necks stretched out
and the sun on their coats and everyone shouting. . . . I've been dreaming
how I walked along the river in the mist as the sun was rising. . . . Lord,
lord, lord, what a time that was, what good times we all had then, before
the old war."

1974

QUESTIONS

1. Lessing says that "writing this article is difficult because it has to be
   'true'." Why does she put quotation marks around "true"? Why would
   it be more difficult to write something that has to be "true" than, as she
   says, stories that "don't have to be 'true'?" How has she tried to make
   this sketch "true"? How well do you think she has succeeded?
2. Find facts about Lessing's father that are repeated or referred to more
   than once. Why does she repeat them?
3. Lessing says that it was difficult for her to write about her father
   because she "knew him when his best years were over." What other
   things about those "best years" might she have wanted to know that
   she apparently didn't?
4. If a stranger were writing about Lessing's father but had the same facts
   available, might the account differ in any ways? Explain.

Jean Rhys

MY FATHER

My father's sister, who was called Clarice, spent the winter in the
West Indies with us three times.[1] The first time I was too young to
remember, or perhaps I wasn't born. The third time she came to take me
back to England. The second time she stayed several months and it was
mostly from her talk that I pieced together something of my father's life.

I knew that he was the son of an Anglican clergyman, the rector of a
small village in Wales, of which I could never remember the name. I also
knew vaguely that he had run away to sea. But it was Aunt Clarice who
described how he was caught at Cardiff and taken back to the rectory. At
this time he wasn't quite fourteen. Apparently he persisted that he
wanted to spend his life as a sailor, and he was sent to the training ship
Worcester. When he left he got a job on a sailing ship. At the end of that

1. Rhys was born in Dominica, an island in   Indian of European descent; her father was
the British West Indies, before 1783 claimed   born in Wales.
by both Great Britain and France; its capital
is Roseau. Her mother was a Creole, a West

voyage he went home unwillingly to the rectory. I only heard him speak once of the sailing voyage on which he was so unhappy, and I remembered it. The captain seems to have been a very brutal man who said, "I'll teach you to think you're a gentleman." However, as my father didn't like his father he was even more unhappy at home.

There was a photograph of an old man with a clerical collar in the sitting-room in Roseau. One day I came in unexpectedly and saw him standing in front of the photograph shaking his fist and cursing. My mother's version of this was: "The old man grudged every penny spent on Willie. Everything must go to the eldest son, his favourite."

When he decided to become a doctor it was his mother who found the money. As soon as he had qualified he got a job as a ship's doctor.

When other children boasted of rich or distinguished relatives in England I used to say that my father had been to every country in the world. He had certainly been to a good many. I knew nothing of his life then for several years. Why he came to Dominica when he was nearly thirty, how he met my mother, all that I didn't know. It was Aunt Clarice who told me he had fallen very ill with fever after he'd accepted a Government post in Dominica. He wasn't in Roseau then, his district was close to Geneva estate, and when the twins heard of his illness they came over and nursed him back to health.[2] As soon as he recovered he married my mother. This is more or less what I was told anyway, or gathered.

As I remember him he was a man of middle height with broad shoulders and a great deal of grey wavy hair. Every now and again he would go to the barber's and have it cut so short you could see his scalp. I hated him then, and had to force myself to kiss him goodnight, but it soon grew again. He had a red moustache, not a Kaiser Bill, not a Hitler, not a Zapata, but a kind moustache.[3]

It was also my Aunt Clarice who first gave me the idea that he was a sad man, continually brooding over his exile in a small Caribbean island. This was the contrary of what I had thought before.

The entrance to the house was a long passage which we called the gallery, it was empty except for a wicker sofa, and at the end a round table with a green-shaded reading lamp, the latest *Times* weekly edition, a fortnight old, his pipe rack, and a large armchair where he sat reading and we weren't allowed to disturb him or speak to him. He was supposed to be reading, but was he reading? It was after Aunt Clarice's revelations that I wondered if he was gathering up strength to appear happy, jolly. "Poor Willy," she would say meaningly. "Poor, poor Willy."

Needless to say my mother and my aunt disliked each other, though

2. Geneva estate, where Rhys's mother and her twin sister lived before her mother's marriage.

3. Kaiser William II, Emperor of Germany during World War I; Adolf Hitler, Führer of Germany during World War II; Emiliano Zapata (1877?–1919), Mexican revolutionist.

they were always extremely polite. Something about Aunt Clarice made me uneasy. Her long fingers were not pretty but frightening. The meaning behind things she'd say I guessed at, so that when I was told I was to go to England with her, to school,[4] I was not altogether happy. When I think about her now I am still quite undecided. I don't know whether she was a kind but suppressed woman who bore with me as long as she could for her brother's sake, or a cool sarcastic person who disapproved of me from the first and was delighted to get rid of me at the first opportunity.

To her credit it must be said that later on, in London, when she came to fetch me at my first rehearsal of Our Miss Gibbs, all the girls were delighted with her. "Is this your Auntie, oh isn't she nice!"

It was Aunt Clarice who told me about the legendary Aunt Jeanette. She had been a great beauty married to a professor of mathematics at Cambridge University. He was much older than she was, untidy, unattractive and so absent-minded he was a joke, appearing for lectures dressed in his pyjamas. They were known as Beauty and the Beast.

When I went to England I was for a short time in Cambridge. On Saturday afternoons I would go to tea with Aunt Jeanette who lived somewhere in the Trumpington Road. She was still very beautiful and had, like other ladies of that time, a devoted maid. I was afraid of the maid, who always let me in with a tight mouth and suspicious eyes. In the armchair in the sitting-room Aunt Jeanette would be seated, beautifully dressed, her hair just so, her lovely hands almost transparent when she held them up to the fire. I was rather uneasy but I knew I was privileged.

One afternoon while we were sipping tea she asked me, "Have you ever read the Song of Songs?"[5]

I said, "You mean in the Bible? Yes, I have read it."

"I hope," she said, rather severely, "that you don't imagine it's about a woman. Or about a man's feelings for a woman. It's an allegory of the relationship of Christ and His church."

"But, Aunt Jeanette," I said, "Christ wasn't born when Solomon wrote that."

"A prophetic allegory," she said. "Great poems are often allegories. There's meaning behind the meaning."

"Is Omar Khayham an allegory too?" I asked. At that time I was very fond of Omar Khayham.[6]

"Oh no, that's not an allegory. That's just a bad translation."

"I like it anyway," I said.

"I daresay. But people who ought to know tell me that Fitzgerald's translation is a very inaccurate one indeed."

My Saturday teas with Aunt Jeannette were rather awe-inspiring but certainly weren't dull. I used to hear all the Cambridge gossip of her day.

4. Rhys briefly attended the Royal Academy of Dramatic Art.
5. Usually known as the Song of Solomon.
6. The Rubáiyát of Omar Khayyám, translated from Persian by Edward FitzGerald (Rhys uses the form Khayham).

"Poor Darwin.[7] He has threaded the labyrinths of creation and lost his creator."

I rarely found her anything but fascinating. I was very astonished when, one of the last times I saw her, she embraced me and kissed me and said, "Poor lamb, poor lamb." Perhaps she knew that I was bound for a stormy passage and would be sea-sick most of the time. I'm sure now that Aunt Clarice was wrong about my father. He wasn't a sad man. He was an active, outgoing man with many friends. He was sad when his mother died, so sad that his sadness filled the house. He didn't even pretend to read then. When a friend arrived my father looked at him and said, "She's dead." — "Who's dead" said the friend. My father didn't answer, and the friend went into the sitting-room where my mother explained that he had had very bad news.

That was Irish Granny, so there were no more presents at Christmas, no more books. Her last present to me was a novel about Richard Brinsley Sheridan[8] and his love for Elizabeth Linley, a singer. I suppose this was to let me know she realised I was growing up.

I probably romanticised my father, perhaps because I saw very little of him. School at the convent started early, at eight o'clock. We usually woke at about six and were having breakfast at seven, but with my mother. It was a delicious breakfast with good coffee and hot rolls bought that morning. They made good bread at that time, not croissants but petits pains, which you split down the middle to let the butter melt into the centre. By half-past seven I was on my way to the convent. My father woke and breakfasted a good deal later, about nine o'clock. He had what my mother called an English breakfast but it was only a boiled egg. After breakfast he'd set out for one of his districts, in the trap if the road was good enough, on horseback otherwise. He usually lunched with a friend or with the local priest. He was the doctor for the Presbytery and for the convent. When he came back we were again at school. I suppose he saw private patients in the afternoon, or they came to him. As soon as the day's work was over he'd go up to the club to play bridge, for cards were his passion.

For a time dinner was a family meal, and I saw my father there. My mother would listen by the hour to him holding forth about English politics and getting very excited, but she never gave an opinion. All my mother would say after sidelong glances at us was, "Don't do that!" We discovered that we could play tunes on the finger bowls. The exciting thing was that each finger bowl gave off an entirely different note and again a different note if you put the finger bowl on a table napkin. Was it the amount of water that mattered? I longed to experiment but never could, for after meals they were put away.

7. Charles Darwin, author of *The Origin of Species* (1859).

8. Richard Brinsley Sheridan (1751-1816), Irish dramatist.

My father never seemed to notice us at all, far too engaged in either abuse or praise of various English politicians, while my mother watched us the whole time. Soon we weren't allowed to dine with the grown-ups, especially when there were guests, because it was decided we were nuisances. That was my father's life as I knew it, and I still think he enjoyed it, or part of it.

I remember his always being very kind and gentle to me. It was he who stopped the hated plate of porridge my mother suddenly expected me to eat every morning, and arranged that I should have an egg beaten up in hot milk with nutmeg instead. He who stopped the extra lessons in mathematics when he found me crying because I could never understand them.

His habit of listing his various friends (I suppose to reassure himself), and his long speeches about English politicians were boring, but I didn't find them so.

I can only remember my father in little things. I can remember him walking with me arm-in-arm up and down the veranda, how pleased I was. He gave me a coral brooch and a silver bracelet.

One of my last memories of him was with a woman who had spent most of her life in India. She was small and thin and burnt brown. They must have been talking about religion, about Buddhism, for she said, "What's the use of living hundreds and hundreds of lives merely to end up in nothingness?" He said, "But Nirvana is not nothingness. Nirvana is . . ."

I've forgotten how he explained Nirvana.

I felt, or knew at once, that my father liked women. Some of the men I came across didn't, I knew that too. For instance, Mr. Kennaway. But talking to women, especially pretty ones, my father had a gentler, teasing way. You saw that he liked them. Also he would flirt outrageously with anyone attractive who came to the house. My mother didn't seem to mind at all and now I wonder if she minded but didn't show it.

It still seems strange to me that he's dead. I heard the other day that the Celtic Cross my mother put up so proudly over his grave had been knocked down and his grave wasn't marked any more. I hated whoever had done this and thought "I can hate too."

1979

Jean Rhys

MY MOTHER

I once came on a photograph of my mother on horseback which must have been taken before she was married.[1] Young, slim and pretty. I hated it. I don't know whether I was jealous or whether I resented knowing that she had once been very different from the plump, dark and only sometimes comfortable woman I knew. I didn't dare tear it up but I pushed it away to the back of the drawer. What wouldn't I give to have it now? Yet wasn't there a time when I remembered her pretty and young?

That must have been when I was the baby, sleeping in the crib. They were going out somewhere, for she was wearing a low-cut evening dress. She had come to say "Good night, sleep well." She smelled so sweet as she leaned over and kissed me.

She loved babies, any babies. Once I heard her say that black babies were prettier than white ones. Was this the reason why I prayed so ardently to be black, and would run to the looking-glass in the morning to see if the miracle had happened? And though it never had, I tried again. Dear God, let me be black.

Even after the new baby was born there must have been an interval before she seemed to find me a nuisance and I grew to dread her. Another interval and she was middle-aged and plump and uninterested in me.

Yes, she drifted away from me and when I tried to interest her she was indifferent.

One day, thinking to please her (this must have been long afterwards) I said, "I'm so glad that you make our jam and we don't get it from England."

"Why?" she said, unsmiling.

"Because I've just read an article about a jam factory in London. It was written by a girl who dressed up as a working girl and got a job there. She said that carrots, scrapings off the floor, all sorts of filthy things were put into the jam."

"And you believed that?" my mother said.

"Yes, I do believe it, she saw it."

"Well I wouldn't believe a word a girl like that said. Dressing up to spy and then make money out of what you pretend you've seen. Disgusting behaviour!"

I said, "Well, it wasn't so easy. She wrote that when she was dressed as a working girl men were very rude to her."

"Serve her right," said my mother.

1. See Rhys, "My Father," n. 1, p. 140.

One of her friends was a coloured woman called Mrs. Campbell. Her husband was a white man now retired from his business. Mrs. Campbell was kind, fat and smilling and I was very fond of her.

They lived some way out of Roseau. On this particular afternoon her husband wasn't there, and she took us for tea and cakes to a summerhouse which they'd built in the garden. There were no walls, only posts, and on these she'd hung sweet oranges (and our oranges certainly were sweet) cut in two and sugared. What seemed to me dozens of hummingbirds flew in and out as we sat there, their wings quivering as they hovered, sipping with their long beaks, then flying away again. I'd never seen so many. Mrs. Campbell was smiling at them when my mother began to cry. I had never seen her cry. I couldn't imagine such a thing. I stared at her more in wonder than in pity but I did eventually gather that she was crying about money.

"How could it stretch? What am I to do?" This is what I vaguely remember she said between sobs. I wondered if it was really money she was crying about.

Mrs. Campbell said, "I have lived long and now I am old, yet never have I seen the righteous forsaken or his seed begging their bread."

After a while my mother stopped crying and as we drove home in the trap she was her usual self-contained, withdrawn self. As I looked at her I could hardly believe what had happened. But this was the end of my comfortable certainty that we were not people who had to worry about expenses. For the first time I vaguely wondered if my father's reckless, throwaway attitude to money wasn't a cover-up for anxiety.

On certain mornings a procession of old men, no women, would come to the house and for some reason my father insisted that I must stand on the pantry steps and hand out the loaf of bread and small sum of money, sixpence or a shilling, I can't quite remember, that was given to each one. My mother objected strongly, she said they were old and often not very well, it wasn't a thing I should be expected to do. Truth to tell I wasn't fond of doing it.

One of them was very different from the others. He bowed, then walked away through the garden and out of the gate at the other end with the loaf under his arm, so straight and proud, I couldn't forget him afterwards.

> "Il y avait une fois
> Un pauvre gars. . . . "[2]

My mother didn't argue any more but she arranged that we would leave Roseau two or three weeks earlier than usual. When we came back

2. "Once there was a poor boy": lines from an unidentified French poem or song.

the bread and money had either been forgotten or someone else did it. There were no more arguments or processions of what the nuns called "God's poor."

Another memory. Sitting on the staircase looking through the bannisters, I watched her packing a trunk with blankets and warm things. One of the neighbouring islands had been hit by a bad hurricane and I don't suppose she was the only one to send all the help she could. I wonder if this happens now? I rather doubt it. I remember the expression on her face as she packed, careful and a little worried.

Just before I left Dominica she was ill and unable to come downstairs for some time. I went up to see her but walked softly and she didn't hear me. She didn't look up, she was sitting gazing out of the window, not reading, not crocheting or doing any of the things she usually did.

Behind her silence she looked lonely, a stranger in a strange house. But how could she be lonely when she was never alone? All the same she looked lonely, patient, and resigned. Also obstinate, "you haven't seen what I've seen, haven't heard what I've heard." From across the room I knew she was like someone else I remembered. I couldn't think who it was, at first. She was like the old man walking out of the gate with a loaf of bread under his arm, patient, dignified.

I wanted to run across the room and kiss her but I was too shy so it was the usual peck. Next day she was well enough to come downstairs and life went on as before.

I think that she was happier when her twin sister left Geneva[3] and came to live in Roseau. Though she didn't live with us, she was often at the house. It was impossible not to know that there was some link between them. One felt what the other was feeling without words. They would look at each other and both laugh quietly. This was often after one of my father's speeches about English politics.

He'd say, "Oh I do like to see them laugh like that."

But I, watching, was uneasy. Could they possibly be laughing at me?

My mother was more silent but not so serene. Auntie B never lost her temper, my mother often did. My mother sewed beautifully but she could not cut out a dress. Slash, slash went Auntie B's scissors with a certainty and out of the material would appear a dress that fitted.

My mother could make pastry light as a feather.

Auntie B mixed famous punch.

Gradually I came to wonder about my mother less and less until at last she was almost a stranger and I stopped imagining what she felt or what she thought.

1979

3. See Rhys, "My Father," n. 2, p. 141.

QUESTIONS:

1. *What method does the author adopt to create an impression of her mother? Why, for example, does she give us the anecdote about the girl in the English jam factory (p. 145)?*
2. *This sketch, written by an adult woman, includes recollections of herself as a little girl. Can you distinguish those places in the essay where the viewpoint is that of the little girl? of the adult woman?*
3. *How would you describe the tone the writer adopts toward the experiences recounted? What is the effect created by that tone?*
4. *What impression of the mother is conveyed through the memories narrated?*
5. *Compare this sketch with the same author's "My Father" (p. 140). Does the author use pretty much the same techniques of writing in the latter piece, or different ones? Is the tone similar or different? Does she give you about the same impression of both parents, or are they different?*

Studs Terkel

BOB PATRICK: A POLICEMAN

He is thirty-five, married, and has a child. He has been a member of the city police force for six years. For the past three years he has been an emergency service patrolman.

"Emergency service is like a rescue squad. You respond to any call, any incident: a man under a train, trapped in an auto, bridge jumping, psychos, guys that murdered people and barricaded themselves in. We go in and get these people out. It is sometimes a little too exciting. I felt like I wasn't gonna come home on two incidents."

He finished among the highest in his class at the police academy, though he was "eleven years out of high school." Most of his colleagues were twenty-one, twenty-two. "I always wanted to be with the city. I felt that was the best job in the world. If I wasn't a cop, see, I don't think I could be anything else. Oh, maybe a truckdriver."

I got assigned to foot patrolman in Bedford-Stuyvesant.[1] I never knew where Bedford-Stuyvesant was. I heard it was a low, poverty-stricken area, and it was a name that people feared. It's black. Something like Harlem, even worse. Harlem was where colored people actually grew up. But Bedford-Stuyvesant is where colored people migrated from Harlem or from North Carolina. They were a tougher class of people.

Myself and two friends from the neighborhood went there. We packed a lunch because we never really ventured outside the neighborhood. We met that morning about six o'clock. We had to be in roll call by eight. We got there a quarter after six. We couldn't believe it was so close. We laughed like hell because this is our neighborhood, more or less. We were like on the outskirts of our precinct. It was only ten minutes from my house.

When we got our orders, everybody said, "Oh wow, forget it." One guy thought he was going there, we had to chase him up three stories to tell him we're only kidding. He was ready to turn in his badge. Great fear, that was a danger area.

I was scared. Most people at Bedford-Stuyvesant were unemployed, mostly welfare, and they more or less didn't care too much for the police. The tour I feared most was four to twelve on a Friday or Saturday night. I'm not a drinker, I never drank, but I'd stop off at a bar over here and have a few beers just to get keyed up enough to put up with the problems we knew we were gonna come up against.

I would argue face to face with these people that I knew had their

1. A largely black neighborhood in Brooklyn, New York.

149

problems, too. But it's hard to use selective enforcement with 'em. Then get off at midnight and still feel nervous about it. And go for another few drinks and go home and I'd fall right to sleep. Two or three beers and I would calm down and feel like a husband again with the family at home.

I rode with a colored guy quite a few times. They would put you in a radio car and you'd be working with an old-timer. One of the calls we went on was a baby in convulsions, stopped breathing. The elevator was out of order and we ran up eight flights of stairs. This was a colored baby. It was blue. I had taken the baby from the aunt and my partner and I rushed down the stairs with the mother. In the radio car I gave the baby mouth to mouth resuscitation. The baby had regurgitated and started breathing again. The doctor at the hospital said whatever it was, we had gotten it up.

The sergeant wanted to write it up because of the problem we were having in the area. For a white cop doin' what I did. But I didn't want it. I said I would do it for anybody, regardless of black or white. They wrote it up and gave me a citation. The guys from the precinct was kidding me that I was now integrated. The mother had said she was willing to even change the baby's name to Robert after what I did.

The guy I worked with had more time on the job than I did. When we went on a family dispute, he would do all the talking. I got the impression that they were more aggressive than we were, the people we were tryin' to settle the dispute with. A husband and wife fight or a boyfriend and a husband. Most of the time you have to separate 'em. "You take the wife into the room and I'll take the husband into the other room." I looked up to my partner on the way he settled disputes. It was very quick and he knew what he was doing.

I've been shot. The only thing I haven't been in Bedford-Stuyvesant is stabbed. I've been spit at. I've been hit with bottles, rocks, sticks, Molotov cocktails, cherry bombs in my eye . . . I've gotten in disputes where I've had 10-13s called on me. That would be to assist the patrolman on the corner. Called by black people to help me against other black people.

After three years at Bedford-Stuyvesant he was assigned to the emergency service patrol. "Our truck is a $55,000 truck and it's maybe $150,000 in equipment. We have shotguns, we have sniper rifles, we have tear gas, bullet-proof vests, we have nets for jumpers, we have Morrissey belts for the patrolman to hold himself in when he goes up on a bridge, we have Kelly tools to pry out trapped people, we give oxygen . . ."

Fifty to seventy-five percent of our calls are for oxygen. I had people that were pronounced DOA by a doctor—dead on arrival. We have resuscitated them. I had brought him back. The man had lived for eight hours after I had brought him back. The doctor was flabbergasted. He

had written letters on it and thought we were the greatest rescue team in
New York City. We give oxygen until the arrival of the ambulance. Most
of the time we beat the ambulance.

We set up a net for jumpers. We caught a person jumping from
twenty-three stories in Manhattan. It musta looked like a postage stamp
to him. We caught a girl from a high school four stories high. If it saves
one life, it's worth it, this net.

A young man was out on a ledge on a six-story building. He was a
mental patient. We try to get a close friend to talk to him, a girl friend, a
priest, a guy from the old baseball team . . . Then you start talkin' to him.
You talk to him as long as you can. A lot of times they kid and laugh with
you—until you get too close. Then they'll tell you, "Stop right where you
are or I'll jump." You try to be his friend. Sometimes you take off the
police shirt to make him believe you're just a citizen. A lot of people don't
like the uniform.

You straddle the wall. You use a Morrissey belt, tie it around with a
line your partner holds. Sometimes you jump from a ledge and come right
up in front of the jumper to trap him. But a lot of times they'll jump if
they spot you. You try to be as cautious as possible. It's a life . . .

Sometimes you have eleven jobs in one night. I had to shoot a vicious
dog in the street. The kids would curse me for doin' it. The dog was
foaming at the mouth and snapping at everybody. We come behind him
and put three bullets in his head. You want to get the kids outa there. He
sees the cop shooting a dog, he's not gonna like the cop.

We get some terrible collisions. The cars are absolutely like accordi-
ons. The first week we had a head-on collision on a parkway. I was just
passing by when it happened and we jumped out. There were parents in
there and a girl and a boy about six years old. I carried the girl out. She
had no face. Then we carried out the parents. The father had lived until
we jacked him out and he had collapsed. The whole family was DOA. It
happens twenty-four hours a day. If emergency's gonna be like this, I'd
rather go back to Bedford-Stuyvesant.

The next day I read in the papers they were both boys, but had mod
haircuts. You look across the breakfast table and see your son. My wife
plenty times asked me, "How can you do that? How can you go under a
train with a person that's severed the legs off, come home and eat
breakfast, and feel . . .?" That's what I'm waiting for: when I can go home
and not feel anything for my family. See, I have to feel.

A patrolman will call you for a guy that's DOA for a month. He hanged
himself. I'm cuttin' him down. You're dancing to get out of the way of the
maggots. I caught myself dancing in the middle of the livingroom, trying
to get a ring off a DOA for a month, while the maggots are jumping all
over my pants. I just put the damn pants on, brand-new, dry cleaned. I go
back to the precinct and still itch and jump in the shower.

And to go under a train and the guy sealed his body to the wheel because of the heat from the third rail. And you know you're gonna drop him into the bag. A sixteen-year-old kid gets his hand caught in a meat grinder. His hand was comin' out in front. And he asks us not to tell his mother. A surgeon pukes on the job and tells you to do it.

One time we had a guy trapped between the platform and the train. His body was below, his head was above. He was talking to the doctor. He had a couple of kids home. In order to get him out we had to use a Z-bar, to jack the train away from the platform. The doctor said, "The minute you jack this train away from the platform, he's gonna go." He was talkin' and smokin' with us for about fifteen minutes. The minute we jacked, he was gone. (Snaps fingers.) I couldn't believe I could snuff out life, just like that. We just jacked this thing away and his life. And to give him a cigarette before it happened was even worse.

While you're en route to the job, to build yourself up, you say, This is part of the job that has to be done. Somebody's gotta do it. After this, there couldn't be nothing worse. No other job's gonna be as bad as this one. And another job comes up worse. Eventually you get used to what you're doin'.

Homicides are bad. I seen the medical examiner put his finger into seventeen knife wounds. I was holding the porto-light so he could see where his finger was going. Knuckle deep. And telling me. "It's hit the bone, the bullet here, the knife wound through the neck." I figure I've seen too much. Jeez. this is not for me. You wouldn't believe it. Maybe I don't believe it. Maybe it didn't hit me yet.

I'm afraid that after seein' so much of this I can come home and hear my kid in pain and not feel for him. So far it hasn't happened. I hope to God it never happens. I hope to God I always feel. When my grandmother passed away a couple of months ago, I didn't feel anything. I wonder, gee, is it happening to me?

One time a guy had shot up a cop in the hospital and threw the cop down the stairs and his wheel chair on top of him. He escaped with a bullet in him. He held up a tenement in Brownsville.[2] They called us down at three o'clock in the morning, with bullet-proof vests and shotguns. I said to myself, This is something out of the movies. The captain had a blackboard. There's eight of us and he gave each of us a job: "Two cover the back yard, you three cover the front, you three will have to secure the roof."

This guy wasn't gonna be taken alive. Frank and me will be the assault team to secure the roof. We're loaded with shotguns and we're gonna sneak in there. We met at four o'clock in the morning. We're goin' up the back stairs. On the first stairway there was a German shepherd dog

2. A largely black neighborhood in Brooklyn, New York.

outside the doorway. The dog cowered in the corner, thank God. We went up three more stories. We secured the roof.

We could hear them assaulting in each apartment, trying to flush this guy out. He fled to the fire escape. As he was comin' up, we told him to freeze, Tony, it was all over. He started to go back down. We radioed team one in the back yard. We heard shots. The rooftops had actually lit up. The assault man had fired twenty-seven bullets into this guy and he recovered. He's still standing trial from what I heard. This was one of the jobs I felt, when I was goin' up the stairs, should I give my wife a call? I felt like I had to call her.

If a perpetrator's in a building, you either talk to him or contain him or flush him out with tear gas rather than runnin' in and shoot. They feel a life is more important than anything else. Most cops feel this, yes.

I went on the prison riots we had in the Tombs.[3] I was the first one on the scene, where we had to burn the gates out of the prison, where the prisoners had boarded up the gates with chairs and furniture. We had to use acetylene torches. My wife knew I was in on it. I was on the front page. They had me with a shotgun and the bullet-proof vest and all the ammunition, waiting to go into the prison.

I wonder to myself, Is death a challenge? Is it something I want to pursue or get away from? I'm there and I don't have to be. I want to be. You have chances of being killed yourself. I've come so close . . .

I went on a job two weeks ago. A nineteen-year-old, he just got back from Vietnam on a medical discharge. He had ransacked his parents' house. He broke all the windows, kicked in the color television set, and hid upstairs with a homemade spear and two butcher knives in one hand. He had cut up his father's face.

We were called down to go in and get this kid. He tore the bannister up and used every pole for a weapon. We had put gas masks on. All the cops was there, with sticks and everything. They couldn't get near him. He kept throwing down these iron ash trays. I went up two steps and he was cocking this spear. We cleared out all the policemen. They just wanted emergency, us.

If you wait long enough, he'll come out. We had everybody talk to him, his mother . . . He didn't come out. The sergeant gave orders to fire tear gas. I could hear it go in the windows. I went up a little further and I seen this nozzle come out of his face. I said, "Sarge, he's got a gas mask on." We fired something like sixteen cannisters in the apartment. When he went back to close one of the doors, I lunged upstairs. I'm very agile. I hit him in the face and his mask went flying. I grabbed his spear and gave him a bear hug. He just didn't put up any resistance. It was all over.

The patrol force rushed in. They were so anxious to get this guy, they were tearing at me. I was tellin' him, "Hey, fella, you got my leg. We got

3. An overcrowded city prison in which those awaiting trial were held.

him, it's all over." They pulled my gas mask off. Now the big party starts. This was the guy who was agitating them for hours. "You bum, we got you." They dragged him down the stairs and put him in a body bag. It's like a straitjacket.

When we had him face down a patrolman grabbed him by the hair and slammed his face into the ground. I grabbed his wrist. "Hey, that's not necessary. The guy's handcuffed, he's secure." I brushed the kid's hair out of his eyes. He had mod long hair. My kid has mod hair. The guy says, "What's the matter with you?" I said, "Knock it off, you're not gonna slam the kid."

The neighbors congratulated me because the kid didn't get a scratch on him. I read in the paper, patrolman so-and-so moved in to make the arrest after a preliminary rush by the emergency service. Patrolman so-and-so is the same one who slammed the kid's face in the ground.

I'm gonna get him tonight. I'm gonna ask if he's writing up for a commendation. I'm gonna tell him to withdraw it. Because I'm gonna be a witness against him. The lieutenant recommended giving me a day off. I told my sergeant the night before last the lieutenant can have his day off and shove it up his ass.

A lot of the barricade snipers are Vietnam veterans. Oh, the war plays a role. A lot of 'em go in the army because it's a better deal. They can eat, they can get an income, they get room and board. They take a lot of shit from the upper class and they don't have to take it in the service.

It sounds like a fairy tale to the guys at the bar, in one ear and out the other. After a rough tour, a guy's dead, shot, people stabbed, you go into a bar where the guys work on Wall Street, margin clerks,[4] "How ya doin'? What's new?" You say, "You wouldn't understand." They couldn't comprehend what I did just last night. With my wife, sometimes I come home after twelve and she knows somethin's up. She waits up. "What happened?" Sometimes I'm shaking, trembling. I tell her, "We had a guy ..." (Sighs.) I feel better and I go to bed. I can sleep.

The one that kept me awake was three years ago. The barricaded kid. The first night I went right to sleep. The second night you start thinking, you start picturing the kid and taking him down. With the kid and the tear gas, the sergeant says, "Okay fire." And you hear the tear gas ... Like you're playing, fooling around with death. You don't want to die, but you're comin' close to it, to really skin it. It's a joke, it's not happening.

I notice since I been in emergency she says, "Be careful." I hate that, because I feel jinxed. Every time she says be careful, a big job comes up. I feel, shit, why did she say that? I hope she doesn't say it. She'll say. "I'll see you in the morning. Be careful.'" ooohhh!

Bad accidents, where I've held the guys' skulls ... I'm getting used to it, because there are younger guys comin' into emergency and I feel I

4. White-collar workers in brokerage houses in the financial district.

have to be the one to take charge. 'Cause I seen a retired guy come back and go on a bad job, like the kid that drowned and we pulled him out with hooks. I'm lookin' to him for help and I see him foldin'. I don't want that to happen to me. When you're workin' with a guy that has eighteen years and he gets sick, who else you gonna look up to?

Floaters, a guy that drowns and eventually comes up. Two weeks ago, we pulled this kid out. You look at him with the hook in the eye . . . You're holdin' in because your partner's holdin' in. I pulled a kid out of the pond, drowned. A woman asked me, "What color was he?" I said, "Miss, he's ten years old. What difference does it make what color he was?" "Well, you pulled him out, you should know." I just walked away from her.

Emergency got a waiting list of three thousand. I have one of the highest ratings. I do have status, especially with the young guys. When a guy says, "Bob, if they change the chart, could I ride with you?" that makes me feel great.

I feel like I'm helpin' people. When you come into a crowd, and a guy's been hit by a car, they call you. Ambulance is standing there dumfounded, and the people are, too. When you give orders to tell this one to get a blanket, this one to get a telephone book, so I can splint a leg and wrap it with my own belt off my gun, that looks good in front of the public. They say, "Gee, who are these guys?"

Last week we responded to a baby in convulsions. We got there in two minutes. The guy barely hung up the phone. I put my finger down the baby's throat and pulled the tongue back. Put the baby upside down, held him in the radio car. I could feel the heat from the baby's mouth on my knuckles. At the hospital the father wanted to know who was the guy in the car. I gave the baby to the nurse. She said, "He's all right." I said, "Good." The father was in tears and I wanted to get the hell out of there.

This morning I read the paper about that cop that was shot up. His six-year-old son wrote a letter: "Hope you get better, Dad." My wife was fixin' breakfast. I said, "Did you read the paper, hon?" She says, "Not yet." "Did you read the letter this cop's son sent to his father when he was in the hospital?" She says, "No." "Well, he's dead now." So I read the part of it and I started to choke. I says, "What the hell . . ." I dropped the paper just to get my attention away. I divided my attention to my son that was in the swing. What the hell. All the shit I seen and did and I gotta read a letter . . . But it made me feel like I'm still maybe a while away from feeling like I have no feeling left. I knew I still had feelings left. I still have quite a few jobs to go . . .

1972

Norman Mailer

CHICAGO, AUGUST 24–29 [1968]

Chicago is the great American city. New York is one of the capitals of the world and Los Angeles is a constellation of plastic, San Francisco is a lady, Boston has become Urban Renewal, Philadelphia and Baltimore and Washington wink like dull diamonds in the smog of Eastern Megalopolis, and New Orleans is unremarkable past the French Quarter. Detroit is a one-trade town, Pittsburgh has lost its golden triangle, St. Louis has become the golden arch of the corporation, and nights in Kansas City close early. The oil depletion allowance makes Houston and Dallas naught but checkerboards for this sort of game. But Chicago is a great American city. Perhaps it is the last of the great American cities.

The reporter was sentimental about the town. Since he had grown up in Brooklyn, it took him no time to recognize, whenever he was in Chicago again, that the urbanites here were like the good people of Brooklyn—they were simple, strong, warm-spirited, sly, rough, compassionate, jostling, tricky and extraordinarily good-natured because they had sex in their pockets, muscles on their back, hot eats around the corner, neighborhoods which dripped with the sauce of local legend, and real city architecture, brownstones with different windows on every floor, vistas for miles of red-brick and two-family wood-frame houses with balconies and porches, runty stunted trees rich as farmland in their promise of tenderness the first city evenings of spring, streets where kids played stick-ball and roller-hockey, lots of smoke and iron twilight. The clangor of the late nineteenth century, the very hope of greed, was in these streets. London one hundred years ago could not have looked much better.

Brooklyn, however, beautiful Brooklyn, grew beneath the skyscrapers of Manhattan, so it never became a great city, merely an asphalt herbarium for talent destined to cross the river. Chicago did not have Manhattan to preempt top branches, so it grew up from the savory of its neighborhoods to some of the best high-rise architecture in the world, and because its people were Poles and Ukrainians and Czechs as well as Irish and the rest, the city had Byzantine corners worthy of Prague or Moscow, odd tortured attractive drawbridges over the Chicago River, huge Gothic spires like the skyscraper which held the Chicago *Tribune*, curves and abutments and balconies in cylindrical structures thirty stories high twisting in and out of the curves of the river, and fine balustrades in its parks. Chicago had a North Side on Lake Shore Drive where the most elegant apartment buildings in the world could be found—Sutton Place in New York betrayed the cost analyst in the eye of the architect next to these palaces of glass and charcoal colored steel. In superb back streets behind the towers on the lake were brownstones which spoke of ironies, cupidities and intricate ambition in the fists of the robber barons who commissioned them—substantiality, hard work, heavy drinking, carnal meats of pleasure, and a Midwestern sense of how to arrive at upper-class decorum were also in the American grandeur of these few streets. If there was a fine American aristocracy of deportment, it was probably in the clean, tough, keen-eyed ladies of Chicago one saw on the streets off Lake Shore Drive on the near North Side of Chicago.

Not here for a travelogue—no need then to detail the Loop, in death like the center of every other American city, but what a dying! Old department stores, old burlesque houses, avenues, dirty avenues, the El with its nineteenth-century dialogue of iron screeching against iron about a turn, and caverns of shadow on the pavement beneath, the grand hotels with their massive lobbies, baroque ceilings, resplendent as Roman bordellos, names like Sheraton-Blackstone, Palmer House, red fields of carpet, a golden cage for elevator, the unheard crash of giant mills stamping new shapes on large and obdurate materials is always pounding in one's inner ear—Dreiser had not written about Chicago for nothing.

To the West of the Lake were factories and Ciceros, Mafia-lands and immigrant lands; to the North, the suburbs, the Evanstons; to the South were Negro ghettos of the South Side—belts of Black men amplifying each the resonance of the other's cause—the Black belt had the Blackstone Rangers, the largest gang of juvenile delinquents on earth, 2,000 by some count—one could be certain the gang had leaders as large in potential as Hannibal or Attila the Hun—how else account for the strength and wit of a stud who would try to rise so high in the Blackstone Rangers?

Further South and West were enclaves for the University of Chicago, more factories, more neighborhoods for Poles, some measure of more good hotels on the lake, and endless neighborhoods—white neighborhoods which went for miles of ubiquitous dingy wood houses with back yards, neighborhoods to hint of Eastern Europe, Ireland, Tennessee, a gathering of all the clans of the Midwest, the Indians and Scotch-Irish, Swedes, some Germans, Italians, Hungarians, Rumanians, Finns, Slovaks, Slovenes—it was only the French who did not travel. In the Midwest, land spread out; not five miles from the Loop were areas as empty, deserted, enormous and mournful by night as the outer freight yards of Omaha. Some industrial desert or marsh would lie low on the horizon, an area squalling by day, deserted by night, except for the hulking Midwestern names of the boxcars and the low sheds, the warehouse buildings, the wire fences which went along the side of unpaved roads for thousands of yards.

The stockyards were like this, the famous stockyards of Chicago were at night as empty as the railroad sidings of the moon. Long before the Democratic Convention of 1968 came to the Chicago Amphitheatre, indeed eighteen years ago when the reporter had paid his only previous visit, the area was even then deserted at night, empty as the mudholes on a battlefield after a war has passed. West of the Amphitheatre, railroad sidings seemed to continue on for miles, accompanied by those same massive low sheds larger than armories, with pens for tens of thousands of frantic beasts, cattle, sheep, and pigs, animals in an orgy of gorging and dropping and waiting and smelling blood. In the slaughterhouses, during the day, a carnage worthy of the Disasters of War took place each morning and afternoon. Endless files of animals were led through pens to be stunned on the head by hammers, and then hind legs trussed, be hoisted up on hooks to hang head down, and ride along head down on an overhead trolley which brought them to Negroes or whites, usually huge, the whites most often Polish or Hunkies (hence the etymology of Honkie —a Chicago word), the Negroes up from the South, huge men built for the shock of the work, slash of a knife on the neck of the beast and gouts of blood to bathe their torso (stripped of necessity to the waist) and blood to splash their legs. The animals passed a psychic current back along the overhead trolley—each cut throat released its scream of death into the throat not yet cut and just behind, and that penultimate throat would push the voltage up, drive the current back and further back into the screams of every animal upside down and hanging from that clanking overhead trolley, bare electric bulbs screaming into the animal eye and brain, gurglings and awesome hollows of sound coming back from the open plumbing ahead of the cut jugular as if death were indeed a rapids along some underground river, and the fear and absolute anguish of beasts dying upside down further ahead passed back along the line, back all the way to the corrals and the pens, back even to the siding with the animals still in boxcars, back, who knew—so high might be the psychic voltage of the beast—back to the farm where first they were pushed into the truck which would take them into the train. What an awful odor the fear of absolute and unavoidable death gave to the stool and stuffing and pure vomitous shit of the beasts waiting in the pens in the stockyard, what a sweat of hell-leather, and yet the odor, no, the titanic stench, which rose from the yards was not so simple as the collective diarrhetics of an hysterical army of beasts, no, for after the throats were cut and the blood ran in rich gutters, red light on the sweating backs of the red throatcutters, the dying and some just-dead animals clanked along the overhead, arterial blood spurting like the nip-ups of a little boy urinating in public, the red-hot carcass quickly encountered another Black or Hunkie with a long knife on a long stick who would cut the belly from chest to groin and a stew and a stink of two hundred pounds of stomach, lungs, intestines, mucosities, spleen, exploded cowflop and pigshit, blood, silver lining, liver, mother-of-pearl tissue, and general gag-all would flop and slither over the floor, the man with the knife getting a good blood-splatting as he dug and twisted with his blade to liberate the roots of the organ, intestine and impedimenta still integrated into the meat and bone of the excavated existence he was working on.

Well, the smell of the entrails and that agonized blood electrified by all the outer neons of ultimate fear got right into the grit of the stockyard stench. Let us pass over into the carving and the slicing, the boiling and scraping, annealing and curing of the flesh in sugars and honeys and smoke, the cooking of the cow carcass, stamp of the inspector, singeing of the hair, boiling of hooves, grinding of gristle, the wax-papering and the packaging, the foiling and the canning, the burning of the residue, and the last slobber of the last unusable guts as it went into the stockyard furnace, and up as stockyard smoke, burnt blood and burnt bone and burnt hair to add their properties of specific stench to fresh blood, fresh entrails, fresh fecalities already all over the air. It is the smell of the stockyards, all of it taken together, a smell so bad one must go down to visit the killing of the animals or never eat meat again. Watching the animals be slaughtered, one knows the human case—no matter how close to angel we may come, the butcher is equally there. So be it. Chicago makes for hard minds. On any given night, the smell may go anywhere —down to Gary to fight with the smog and the coke, out to Cicero to quiet the gangs with their dreams of gung ho and mop-up, North to Evanston to remind the polite that *inter faeces et urinam* are we born, and East on out to Lake Michigan where the super felicities in the stench of such earth-bound miseries and corruptions might cheer the fish with the clean spermy deep waters of their fate.

Yes, Chicago was a town where nobody could ever forget how the money was made. It was picked up from floors still slippery with blood, and if one did not protest and take a vow of vegetables, one knew at least that life was hard, life was in the flesh and in the massacre of the flesh —one breathed the last agonies of beasts. So something of the entrails and the secrets of the gut got into the faces of native Chicagoans. A great city, a strong city with faces tough as leather hide and pavement, it was also a city where the faces took on the broad beastiness of ears which were dull enough to ignore the bleatings of the doomed, noses battered enough to smell no more the stench of every unhappy end, mouths—fat mouths or slit mouths—ready to taste the gravies which were the reward of every massacre, and eyes, simple pig eyes, which could look the pig truth in the face. In any other city, they would have found technologies to silence the beasts with needles, quarter them with machines, lull them with Muzak, and have stainless steel for floors, aluminum beds to take over the old overhead trolley—animals would be given a shot of vitamin-enrichment before they took the last ride. But in Chicago, they did it straight, they cut the animals right out of their hearts—which is why it was the last of the great American cities, and people had great faces, carnal as blood, greedy, direct, too impatient for hypocrisy, in love with honest plunder. They were big and human and their brother in heaven was the slaughtered pig—they did not ignore him. If the yowls and moans of his extinction was the broth of their strength, still they had honest guts to smell him to the end—they did not flush the city with Odorono or Pinex or No-Scent, they swilled the beer and assigned the hits and gave America its last chance at straight-out drama. Only a great city provides honest spectacle, for that is the salvation of the schizophrenic soul. Chicago may have beasts on the street, it may have a giant of fortitude for Mayor[1] who grew into a beast—a man with the very face of Chicago —but it is an honest town, it does not look to incubate psychotics along an air-conditioned corridor with a vinyl floor.

1968

1. Richard C. Daley, former mayor of Chicago.

QUESTIONS

1. *Does the author admire the city of Chicago? What qualities in the city does he seem to applaud? Do you find these qualities admirable?*
2. *What tone does the author adopt in writing of ethnic groups? What is the effect produced by that tone?*
3. *What effect is created by the author's thoroughly detailed description of the slaughterhouse and the stench of the stockyards?*
4. *What is the author's thesis in this essay, seriously stated? What are his sources of authority?*
5. *Could this essay fairly be described as sentimental? Why, or why not?*

Calvin Trillin

EATING IN CINCINNATI

Harry Garrison, the eater who had agreed to serve as my consultant in Cincinnati, had been recommended by my friend Marshall J. Dodge III —a fact that gave me pause, particularly after Marshall described him as a calliope-restorer by trade. I don't mean that I harbor any prejudice against calliope-restorers or that I think Marshall would make a frivolous recommendation. Marshall is a practical man. He has a practicality so pure, in fact, that it sometimes makes him appear eccentric. He is an uncompromising bicyclist—partly because bicycling is the most practical way to get around New York—and when he travels to, say, Cincinnati, he merely removes the wheels of one of his bicycles, stuffs the parts into something that resembles a swollen Harvard bookbag,[1] and checks the mysterious bundle along with his luggage. If the ticket agent asks what the bag contains, Marshall looks at him solemnly—Marshall can manage an awesomely solemn look when the occasion calls for one—and says that the bag contains his grandmother's wheelchair. Like New York's most photographed bicyclist, John V. Lindsay—a tall man who was once the mayor—Marshall attended Buckley and St. Paul's and Yale, and it is implicit in his appearance and manner that he takes the presence of many generations of Dodges at those institutions before him and after him as a matter of course. But if it is practical to take along a knapsack while riding his bicycle, Marshall takes along a knapsack. Then if someone happens to ask him, say, if he knows the address of a good calliope-restorer in Cincinnati, he can reach into the knapsack, pull out a small file of three-by-five cards, and thumb through it until he finds the answer.

What concerned me about depending on Marshall's recommendation for a guide to Cincinnati is that the knapsack is much more likely to produce the address of of an expert on antique piano rolls or a supplier of Cajun-dialect phonograph albums than a specialist in French-fried onion rings or barbecue—a natural outgrowth of Marshall's own specialty, which is regional humor. (He has made an album of Down East stories called *Bert and I* and he has presented his monologues before groups in various parts of the country, always arriving by plane and bike.). I hinted about my concern to Marshall, but he assured me that Garrison would be the perfect guide to Cincinnati and environs. He was not certain if it had been Garrison who put him on to a small restaurant in Rabbit Hash, Kentucky, that served what Marshall remembered as the best fried chicken in the world, but he was certain that it was Garrison who had introduced him to Professor Harry L. Suter, an elderly musicologist who was able to play the piano and the violin simultaneously by means of an invention the professor called the viola-pan.

Garrison, I found out, not only restores calliopes but also restores and sells player pianos, appears professionally around the state as Uncle Sam the Magician, delivers an occasional lecture on how to detect crooked gambling devices, and in the midst of all those activities manages to spend more than the ordinary amount of time at table. He was not going to be able to meet me until a few hours after I arrived in Cincinnati, but he had suggested on the phone that for my first taste of authentic Cincinnati chili, at lunch, I might want to try the unadorned product and therefore should start with what is known locally as "a bowl of plain." He had no way of knowing, of course, that I have never eaten the unadorned version of anything in my life and that I once threatened to place a

1. That is, a shapeless bag of dull-green canvas.

Denver counterman under citizen's arrest for leaving the mayonnaise off my California burger.

"What should I order if I don't want to start with the plain?" I asked.

"Try a four-way," Garrison said.

In Cincinnati, everyone knows that a four-way is chili on spaghetti with cheese and onions added. I never saw any numbers on menus in Cincinnati, but it is accepted that a customer can walk into any chili parlor—an Empress or a Skyline or any of the independent neighborhood parlors—and say "One three-way" and be assured of getting chili on spaghetti with cheese. Cincinnati eaters take it for granted that the basic way to serve chili is on spaghetti, just as they take it for granted that the other ways to serve it go up to a five-way (chili, spaghetti, onions, cheese, and beans) and that the people who do the serving are Greeks. When the Kiradjieff family, which introduced authentic Cincinnati chili at the Empress in 1922, was sued several years ago by a manager who alleged that he had been fired unfairly, one of his claims amounted to the contention that anyone fired under suspicious circumstances from a chili parlor with Empress's prestige was all through in the Greek community. There are probably people in Cincinnati who reach maturity without realizing that Mexicans eat anything called chili, in the same way that there are probably young men from Nevada who have to be drafted and sent to an out-of-state Army camp before they realize that all laundromats are not equipped with slot machines.

What is called chili in America, of course, has less similarity to the Mexican dish than American football has to the game known as football just about everywhere else in the world. Like American football, though, it long ago became the accepted version within the borders, and anyone in, say, northern New Mexico who wanted to claim that the version served there (green or red chili peppers sliced up and cooked into a kind of stew) is the only one entitled to the name would have no more chance of being listened to than a soccer enthusiast who made a claim to the television networks for equal time with the N.F.L. As American chili goes, what is served in Cincinnati is sweeter than what I used to have at Dixon's and what I still have occasionally at the Alamo—a Tex-Mex chili parlor in Manhattan that offers eight or ten combination plates, all of which taste exactly alike, and is famous for a notation on the menu that says, "All combinations above without beans 25¢ extra." (I know people who have tried to work out the economics of how much the Alamo has to pay a professional bean-extractor to come out ahead on that offer, but a definite figure has eluded them.) The chili in Cincinnati is less ferocious than Texas chili, but I wouldn't want to carry the comparison any further. I decided a long time ago that I like chili, but not enough to argue about it with people from Texas.

To an out-of-towner, the chili in various Cincinnati chili parlors may seem pretty much alike, but there are natives who have stayed up late at night arguing about the relative merits of Empress and Skyline or explaining that the secret of eating at the downtown Empress is to arrive when the chili is at its freshest, which happens to be at about nine in the morning. In Cincinnati, people are constantly dropping into a new neighborhood chili parlor only to find out that it serves the best chili in the world. One chili fanatic I met was a supporter of a place across the river, in Kentucky, that he claimed serves a six-way and a seven-way.

"What could possibly be in a seven-way?" I asked.

"I don't know," he said. "They won't even tell you." I later learned from Bert Workum, a serious eater who works for the Kentucky *Post* in Covington, just across the river from Cincinnati, that the Dixie Chili parlor in Kentucky has once served a seven-way by including eggs (fried or scrambled) and cut-up frankfurters but is now serving only a six-way, having abandoned its egg-cooking operation. Workum also told me that the chicken restaurant Marshall J. Dodge III probably had in mind was McKnight's, which is in Cynthiana, Kentucky, rather than in Rabbit Hash. I told him that Dodge was the kind of person who would never say Cynthiana if there was any excuse to say Rabbit Hash.

Garrison had turned out to be a large man who wears three-piece suits and a full beard and has what used to be called an ample stomach. He appreciates good food, but even at a restaurant that he might patronize mainly because it has a pleasant atmosphere or is open late at night or charges reasonable prices he is what one of his friends described as a Clean Plate Ranger. One of his friends, a man who runs a barbecue restaurant called the Barn and Rib Pit in downtown Cincinnati, told me, "I love to see Harry eat ribs. He just inhales those ribs. You look at him and he's just glowin'."

I spent an afternoon with Garrison riding around Cincinnati, and found him to be one of those rare Americans who truly savors his city. I was still a bit concerned that he might be someone who would be more excited about finding an authentic boogie-woogie pianist or maybe a mechanical violin in perfect working order than he would about stumbling onto, say, the classic corn fritter. But he relieved my fears somewhat by describing what we were going to have for dinner at his house as "the best fried chicken in the world." At about that time, by coincidence, we passed a run-down looking restaurant whose sign actually said, WORLD'S BEST FRIED CHICKEN. Garrison glanced at it contemptuously. "I don't see any point in considering his claim at all," he said.

There was a lot of food talk among the dinner guests at Garrison's that evening, and there was also some staggering acorn squash and the best apple pie I have ever tasted. The chicken was delicious, but I still think the best fried chicken I have ever eaten was at a sort of outdoor homecoming that Cherokee County, Georgia, held for Dean Rusk, a native son, shortly after he was named Secretary of State—fried chicken so good that I still nurture a hope, against long odds, that Cherokee County will someday produce another Secretary of State and throw another home-coming.

Garrison finished off the meal by handing around made-in-Cincinnati cigars and treating the entire company to a display of smoke-ring blow-ing. Garrison's smoke-ring technique includes a remarkable motion by which he more or less nudges the ring along by pushing at the air a few inches behind it—a variation of the assistance that curlers offer a curling stone by sweeping away at the ice in its path. Between rings, Garrison announces his performance with the kind of grandiloquence he must use on the magic stage, and he is as irritable as a matador about the threat of air movement that could mar his artistry. Just when everyone at the table expects a ring to emerge, Garrison is likely to pause, glance around sternly, and say, in a majestic voice, "I detect human breathing in this room." Even after having stopped eating for a while to watch the smoke-ring blowing, none of us felt up to the late-night visit to the Barn and Rib Pit Garrison had contemplated. The fact that I knew the proprietor was white made me less disappointed at missing the Barn and Rib Pit than I might have been. Going to a white-run barbecue is, I think, like going to a gentile internist: It might turn out all right, but you haven't made any attempt to take advantage of the percentages.

Garrison had promised me a special treat for my last night in Ohio—a treat to be found in a restaurant near Oxford—but even as we drove to the restaurant he insisted that precisely what the treat was would have to be a surprise. After the day I had spent, I figured it might require more than a surprise treat to induce me to take any food on my fork. At about eleven, I had stopped at the downtown Empress to see what it looked like, and, deciding that it might be rude to leave without eating (particu-larly so early in the freshness cycle), had polished off a three-way. For lunch, Garrison had led me to a splendid place called Stenger's Café, which he described as the last of the old-fashioned workingman's bars left in what had been the old German section of Cincinnati known as Over the Rhine. At Stenger's I cleaned a plate on which the counterman had piled mettwurst,[2] two potato pancakes, a helping of beans, some beets, bread and butter, and, at the last minute, a piece of beef from a tray I had spotted being carried across the room. For that, I had parted with one dollar and twenty-eight cents. My appetite was returning as we drove, though, and Garrison helped it along by describing what we might have eaten at a few of the places he had considered taking me to before he decided on the restaurant in Oxford—including a place in Kentucky that specialized in farm food like ham with gravy.

2. A kind of German sausage.

"Red-eye gravy?" I asked.

"Red-eye gravy," Garrison said.

We drove along for a few miles while I thought that over.

"Is it too late to turn back toward Kentucky?" I asked.

"You'll love the place we're going," Garrison said. "It's going to have a fine surprise for you."

The place he had picked out was a restaurant outside Oxford called the Shady Nook. It turned out to be a normal-looking suburban restaurant with a sign in four or five colors of neon in the parking lot. Garrison insisted that we sit at the bar for a while to have shrimp cocktails and some wine. Behind the bar there was a stage that went completely around the room, and in front of the stage was a covered square that looked as if it might be a small orchestra pit. I was beginning to wonder what the surprise was. I didn't see anything amazing about the shrimp except how many of them Garrison was eating. Between bites he managed to say hello to a man he identified as the owner of the Shady Nook and to explain how Professor Harry L. Suter happened to design the viola-pan as he whiled away the time on the top floor of his house in Moscow, Ohio, during the great flood of 1913. Garrison told me that he had hired Professor Suter to play a Christmas party in 1959, and had the pleasure of being able to say in the introduction that it was the Professor's first Cincinnati appearance since the summer of 1917, when he played the Bell Telephone picnic. I couldn't spot anything extraordinary on the plates of the people already eating, but somehow I got it in my mind that the surprise was going to be either The Great Cherry Cobbler or maybe even The Classic Onion Ring. Suddenly, the recorded music that I had been listening to without realizing it was turned off. From deep within what I had thought was an orchestra pit came a rumbling noise. Before my eyes there arose a gigantic gold, intricately carved, four-keyboard, three-ton Wurlitzer Theater Organ. The owner of the Shady Nook climbed up on the stool, high above the bar, and—by playing at least all four keyboards at once and flicking on and off several dozen switches at the same time—transformed the Shady Nook into Radio City Music Hall. I was indeed surprised. Harry Garrison looked at the theater organ and looked at me and beamed.

1974

QUESTIONS

1. *Why does Trillin spend so much time describing Marshall and his infatuation with his bicycle? How does this description add to Trillin's account? Does all the detail about the calliope-restorer serve a similar function?*

2. *Trillin compares the people in Cincinnati who may not even realize that Mexicans eat chili to "young men from Nevada who have to be*

drafted and sent to an out-of-state Army camp before they realize that all laundromats are not equipped with slot machines" (p. 162). What message is conveyed by this comparison? How is the message different from what would be conveyed by a simpler, more straightforward statement, like "Chili is so popular in Cincinnati that some people do not realize that it was first a Mexican dish?"

3. Write a brief character sketch of Garrison. Do any of his character traits help you to understand the nature of his town? Does acquaintance with his character help to prepare you for the ending of the selection? Explain whether you found the ending a surprise, and whether you think it is effective.

4. Write a description of a place—a town, a state, a restaurant, or the like —without naming it, using comparisons with objects that are familiar to explain the unfamiliar.

Red Smith

CASEY STENGEL'S TESTIMONY

* * *

A young woman asked, "What was Casey Stengel like?" I thought she was pulling my leg until I realized that she was nine years old when Casey, retiring as manager of the New York Mets, dropped out of public view. "Casey Stengel," I said, "was—well, just a minute." I dug up my copy of Casey's testimony before the Senate Subcommittee on Antitrust and Monopoly on July 9, 1958. It seems to me that those of us who covered Casey in his time owe it to history to reintroduce him to readers in this fashion at least once a decade.

SENATOR ESTES KEFAUVER: Mr. Stengel, you are the manager of the New York Yankees. Will you give us very briefly your background and your views about this legislation?

STENGEL: Well, I started in professional ball in 1910. I have been in professional ball, I would say, for forty-eight years. I have been employed by numerous ball clubs in the majors and in the minor leagues.

I entered in the minor leagues with Kansas City. I played as low as Class D ball, which was at Shelbyville, Kentucky, and also Class C ball and Class A ball, and I have advanced in baseball as a ballplayer.

I had many years that I was not so successful as a ballplayer, as it is a game of skill. And then I was no doubt discharged by baseball in which I had to go back to the minor leagues as a manager, and after being in the minor leagues as a manager, I became a major league manager in several cities and was discharged, we call it discharged because there is no question I had to leave.

And I returned to the minor leagues at Milwaukee, Kansas City and Oakland, California, and then returned to the major leagues. In the last ten years, naturally, with the New York Yankees, the New York Yankees have had tremendous success and while I am not a ballplayer who does the work I have no doubt worked for a ball club that is very capable in the office.

I have been up and down the ladder. I know there are some things in baseball thirty-five to fifty years ago that are better now than they were in those days. In those days, my goodness, you could not transfer a ball club in the minor leagues, Class D, Class C ball, Class A ball.

How could you transfer a ball club when you did not have a highway? How could you transfer a ball club when the railroads then would take you to a town you got off and then you had to wait and sit up five hours to go to another ball club?

How could you run baseball then without night ball? You had to have night ball to improve the proceeds, to pay larger salaries, and I went to work, the first year I received $135 a month. I thought that was amazing. I had to put away enough money to go to dental college. I found out it was not better in dentistry. I stayed in baseball.

Any other questions you would like to ask me?

KEFAUVER: Mr. Stengel, are you prepared to answer particularly why baseball wants this bill passed?

STENGEL: Well, I would have to say at the present time, I think that baseball has advanced in this respect for the player help. That is an amazing statement for me to make, because you can retire with an annuity at fifty and what organization in America allows you to retire at fifty and receive money?

Now the second thing about baseball that I think is very interesting to the public or to all of us is that it is the owner's fault if he does not improve his club, along with the officials in the ball club and the players.

Now what causes that?

If I am going to go on the road and we are a traveling ball club and you know the cost of transportation now—we travel sometimes with three Pullman coaches, the New York Yankees, and I'm just a salaried man and do not own stock in the New York Yankees. I found out that in traveling with the New York Yankees on the road and all, that it is the best, and we have broken records in Washington this year, we have broken them in every city but New York and we have lost two clubs that have gone out of the city of New York.

Of course, we have had some bad weather. I would say that they are mad at us in Chicago, we fill the parks. They have come out to see good material. I will say they are mad at us in Kansas City, but we broke their attendance records.

Now on the road we only get possibly 27 cents. I am not positive of these figures, as I am not an official. If you go back fifteen years or if I owned stock in the club, I would give them to you.

KEFAUVER: Mr. Stengel, I am not sure that I made my question clear.

STENGEL: Yes, sir. Well, that is all right. I am not sure I'm going to answer yours perfectly, either.

SENATOR JOSEPH C. O'MAHONEY: How many minor leagues were there in baseball when you began?

STENGEL: Well, there were not so many at that time because of this fact: anybody to go into baseball at that time with the educational schools that we had were small, while you were probably thoroughly educated at school, you had to be—we had only small cities that you could put a team in and they would go defunct.

Why, I remember the first year I was at Kankakee, Illinois, and a bank offered me $550 if I would let them have a little notice. I left there and took a uniform because they owed me two weeks' pay. But I either had to quit but I did not have enough money to go to dental college so I had to go with the manager down to Kentucky.

What happened there was if you got by July, that was the big date. You did not play night ball and you did not play Sundays in half of the cities because of a Sunday observance, so in those days when things were tough, and all of it was, I mean to say, why they just closed up July 4 and there you were sitting there in the depot. You could go to work someplace else, but that was it.

So I got out of Kankakee, Illinois, and I just go there for the visit now.

SENATOR JOHN A. CARROLL: The question Senator Kefauver asked you was what, in your honest opinion, with your forty-eight years of experience, is the need for this legislation in view of the fact that baseball has not been subject to antitrust laws.

STENGEL: No.

CARROLL: I had a conference with one of the attorneys representing not only baseball but all of the sports, and I listened to your explanation to Senator Kefauver. It seemed to me it had some clarity. I asked the attorney this question: What was the need for this legislation? I wonder if you would accept his definition. He said they didn't want to be subjected to the *ipse dixit* of the federal government because they would throw a lot of damage suits on the *ad damnum* clause. He said, in the first place, the Toolson case was *sui generis*, it was *de minimus non curat lex.*

STENGEL: Well, you are going to get me there for about two hours.

KEFAUVER: Thank you, very much, Mr. Stengel. We appreciate your presence here.

Mr. Mickey Mantle, will you come around?

Mr. Mantle, do you have any observations with reference to the applicability of the antitrust laws to baseball?

MANTLE: My views are just about the same as Casey's.

* * *

1981

Mind

John Selden

THE MEASURE OF THINGS

We measure from ourselves; and as things are for our use and purpose, so we approve them. Bring a pear to the table that is rotten, we cry it down, 'tis naught; but bring a medlar that is rotten, and 'tis a fine thing; and yet I'll warrant you the pear thinks as well of itself as the medlar[1] does.

We measure the excellency of other men by some excellency we conceive to be in ourselves. Nash, a poet, poor enough (as poets use to be), seeing an alderman with his gold chain, upon his great horse, by way of scorn said to one of his companions, "Do you see yon fellow, how goodly, how big he looks? Why, that fellow cannot make a blank verse."

Nay, we measure the goodness of God from ourselves; we measure his goodness, his justice, his wisdom, by something we call just, good, or wise in ourselves; and in so doing, we judge proportionally to the country-fellow in the play, who said, if he were King, he would live like a lord, and have peas and bacon every day, and a whip that cried Slash.

1689

1. The medlar, a fruit like the crab apple, becomes edible only after it begins to decay.

QUESTIONS

1. *What pattern of parallels do you discern among the three parts of Selden's statement? How does this principle of structure enforce the thesis he is setting forth?*
2. *Can the three paragraphs be rearranged without damage? Explain. What principle or principles appear to govern the present arrangement? Does it imply anything about value? About the kind of universe in which Selden conceives man to live?*
3. *Consider the three desires of the country fellow who would be king.*

Has Selden arranged these desires in any particular order? If so, what relation does that order bear to the order of the whole statement?

Robertson Davies

A FEW KIND WORDS FOR SUPERSTITION

In grave discussions of "the renaissance of the irrational" in our time, superstition does not figure largely as a serious challenge to reason or science. Parapsychology, UFO's, miracle cures, transcendental meditation and all the paths to instant enlightenment are condemned, but superstition is merely deplored. Is it because it has an unacknowledged hold on so many of us?

Few people will admit to being superstitious; it implies naïveté or ignorance. But I live in the middle of a large university, and I see superstition in its four manifestations, alive and flourishing among people who are indisputably rational and learned.

You did not know that superstition takes four forms? Theologians assure us that it does. First is what they call Vain Observances, such as not walking under a ladder, and that kind of thing. Yet I saw a deeply learned professor of anthropology, who had spilled some salt, throwing a pinch of it over his left shoulder; when I asked him why, he replied, with a wink, that it was "to hit the Devil in the eye." I did not question him further about his belief in the Devil: but I noticed that he did not smile until I asked him what he was doing.

The second form is Divination, or consulting oracles. Another learned professor I know, who would scorn to settle a problem by tossing a coin (which is a humble appeal to Fate to declare itself), told me quite seriously that he had resolved a matter related to university affairs by consulting the *I Ching*.[1] And why not? There are thousands of people on this continent who appeal to the *I Ching*, and their general level of education seems to absolve them of superstition. Almost, but not quite. The *I Ching*, to the embarrassment of rationalists, often gives excellent advice.

The third form is Idolatry, and universities can show plenty of that. If you have ever supervised a large examination room, you know how many jujus, lucky coins and other bringers of luck are placed on the desks of the candidates. Modest idolatry, but what else can you call it?

The fourth form is Improper Worship of the True God. A while ago, I learned that every day, for several days, a ½ bill (in Canada we have ½

1. A Chinese work of divination.

bills, regarded by some people as unlucky) had been tucked under a candlestick on the altar of a college chapel. Investigation revealed that an engineering student, worried about a girl, thought that bribery of the Deity might help. When I talked with him, he did not think he was pricing God cheap, because he could afford no more. A reasonable argument, but perhaps God was proud that week, for the scientific oracle went against him.

Superstition seems to run, a submerged river of crude religion, below the surface of human consciousness. It has done so for as long as we have any chronicle of human behavior, and although I cannot prove it, I doubt if it is more prevalent today than it has always been. Superstition, the theologians tell us, comes from the Latin *supersisto*, meaning to stand in terror of the Deity. Most people keep their terror within bounds, but they cannot root it out, nor do they seem to want to do so.

The more the teaching of formal religion declines, or takes a sociological form, the less God appears to great numbers of people as a God of Love, resuming his older form of a watchful, minatory power, to be placated and cajoled. Superstition makes its appearance, apparently unbidden, very early in life, when children fear that stepping on cracks in the sidewalk will bring ill fortune. It may persist even among the greatly learned and devout, as in the case of Dr. Samuel Johnson, who felt it necessary to touch posts that he passed in the street. The psychoanalysts have their explanation, but calling a superstition a compulsion neurosis does not banish it.

Many superstitions are so widespread and so old that they must have risen from a depth of the human mind that is indifferent to race or creed. Orthodox Jews place a charm on their doorposts; so do (or did) the Chinese. Some peoples of Middle Europe believe that when a man sneezes, his soul, for that moment, is absent from his body, and they hasten to bless him, lest the soul be seized by the Devil. How did the Melanesians come by the same idea? Superstition seems to have a link with some body of belief that far antedates the religions we know—religions which have no place for such comforting little ceremonies and charities.

People who like disagreeable historical comparisons recall that when Rome was in decline, superstition proliferated wildly, and that something of the same sort is happening in our Western world today. They point to the popularity of astrology, and it is true that sober newspapers that would scorn to deal in love philters carry astrology columns and the fashion magazines count them among their most popular features. But when has astrology not been popular? No use saying science discredits it. When has the heart of man given a damn for science?

Superstition in general is linked to man's yearning to know his fate, and to have some hand in deciding it. When my mother was a child, she innocently joined her Roman Catholic friends in killing spiders on July 11, until she learned that this was done to ensure heavy rain the day following, the anniversary of the Battle of Boyne, when the Orangemen[2] would hold their parade. I knew an Italian, a good scientist, who watched every morning before leaving his house, so that the first person he met would not be a priest or a nun, as this would certainly bring bad luck.

I am not one to stand aloof from the rest of humanity in this matter, for when I was a university student, a gypsy woman with a child in her arms used to appear every year at examination time, and ask a shilling[3] of anyone who touched the Lucky Baby; that swarthy infant cost me four shillings altogether, and I never failed an examination. Of course, I did it merely for the joke—or so I thought then. Now, I am humbler.

1978

2. Protestant Irish. The Battle of the Boyne (1690), the final and decisive defeat of the forces of British Catholicism, made Protes- tantism secure as the official religion of Great Britain.
3. Then about twenty-five cents.

QUESTIONS

1. What is Davies' definition of superstition?
2. There is a certain quaintness about the names for the four forms of superstition. Why do you think Davies chose such names? Does his division of superstition into these four forms serve to clarify the nature or function of superstitions you know about?
3. Can superstition exist without religion? In what ways can it substitute for religion?
4. Write an essay describing the nature and function of a superstition you know about. In his conclusion Davies suggests two perspectives on the subject—a joking one and the later, "humbler," one. Which comes more naturally to you as the point of view in your essay? Or do you have a different perspective of your own?

Benjamin Franklin

THE CONVENIENCE OF BEING "REASONABLE"

I believe I have omitted mentioning that, in my first voyage from Boston, being becalmed off Block Island, our people set about catching cod, and hauled up a great many. Hitherto I had stuck to my resolution of not eating animal food, and on this occasion I considered, with my master Tryon,[1] the taking every fish as a kind of unprovoked murder, since none of them had, or ever could do us any injury that might justify the slaughter. All this seemed very reasonable. But I had formerly been a great lover of fish, and, when this came hot out of the frying-pan, it smelled admirably well. I balanced some time between principle and inclination, till I recollected that, when the fish were opened, I saw smaller fish taken out of their stomachs; then thought I, "if you eat one another, I don't see why we mayn't eat you." So I dined upon cod very heartily, and continued to eat with other people, returning only now and then occasionally to a vegetable diet. So convenient a thing it is to be a *reasonable creature*, since it enables one to find or make a reason for everything one has a mind to do.

1791

1. "When about 16 years of age, I happened to meet with a book written by one [Thomas] Tryon [*The Way to Health, Wealth, and Happiness*, 1682] recommending a vegetable diet. I determined to go into it. * * * My refusing to eat flesh occasioned an inconveniency, and I was frequently chid for my singularity" [Franklin, *Autobiography*].

William Golding

THINKING AS A HOBBY

While I was still a boy, I came to the conclusion that there were three grades of thinking; and since I was later to claim thinking as my hobby, I came to an even stranger conclusion—namely, that I myself could not think at all.

I must have been an unsatisfactory child for grownups to deal with. I remember how incomprehensible they appeared to me at first, but not, of course, how I appeared to them. It was the headmaster of my grammar school who first brought the subject of thinking before me—though neither in the way, nor with the result he intended. He had some statuettes in his study. They stood on a high cupboard behind his desk. One was a lady wearing nothing but a bath towel. She seemed frozen in an eternal panic lest the bath towel slip down any farther; and since she had no arms, she was in an unfortunate position to pull the towel up again. Next to her, crouched the statuette of a leopard, ready to spring down at the top drawer of a filing cabinet labeled A-AH. My innocence interpreted this as the victim's last, despairing cry. Beyond the leopard was a naked, muscular gentleman, who sat, looking down, with his chin on his fist and his elbow on his knee. He seemed utterly miserable.

Some time later, I learned about these statuettes. The headmaster had placed them where they would face delinquent children, because they symbolized to him the whole of life. The naked lady was the Venus of Milo. She was Love. She was not worried about the towel. She was just busy being beautiful. The leopard was Nature, and he was being natural. The naked, muscular gentleman was not miserable. He was Rodin's Thinker, an image of pure thought. It is easy to buy small plaster models of what you think life is like.

I had better explain that I was a frequent visitor to the headmaster's study, because of the latest thing I had done or left undone. As we now say, I was not integrated. I was, if anything, disintegrated; and I was puzzled. Grownups never made sense. Whenever I found myself in a penal position before the headmaster's desk, with the statuettes glimmering whitely above him, I would sink my head, clasp my hands behind my back and writhe one shoe over the other.

The headmaster would look opaquely at me through flashing spectacles.

"What are we going to do with you?"

Well, what were they going to do with me? I would writhe my shoe some more and stare down at the worn rug.

"Look up, boy! Can't you look up?"

Then I would look up at the cupboard, where the naked lady was frozen in her panic and the muscular gentleman contemplated the hindquarters of the leopard in endless gloom. I had nothing to say to the headmaster. His spectacles caught the light so that you could see nothing human behind them. There was no possibility of communication.

"Don't you ever think at all?"

No, I didn't think, wasn't thinking, couldn't think—I was simply waiting in anguish for the interview to stop.

"Then you'd better learn—hadn't you?"

On one occasion the headmaster leaped to his feet, reached up and plonked Rodin's masterpiece on the desk before me.

"That's what a man looks like when he's really thinking."

I surveyed the gentleman without interest or comprehension.

"Go back to your class."

Clearly there was something missing in me. Nature had endowed the rest of the human race with a sixth sense and left me out. This must be so,

I mused, on my way back to the class, since whether I had broken a window, or failed to remember Boyle's Law, or been late for school, my teachers produced me one, adult answer: "Why can't you think?"

As I saw the case, I had broken the window because I had tried to hit Jack Arney with a cricket ball and missed him; I could not remember Boyle's Law because I had never bothered to learn it; and I was late for school because I preferred looking over the bridge into the river. In fact, I was wicked. Were my teachers, perhaps, so good that they could not understand the depths of my depravity? Were they clear, untormented people who could direct their every action by this mysterious business of thinking? The whole thing was incomprehensible. In my earlier years, I found even the statuette of the Thinker confusing. I did not believe any of my teachers were naked, ever. Like someone born deaf, but bitterly determined to find out about sound, I watched my teachers to find out about thought.

There was Mr. Houghton. He was always telling me to think. With a modest satisfaction, he would tell me that he had thought a bit himself. Then why did he spend so much time drinking? Or was there more sense in drinking than there appeared to be? But if not, and if drinking were in fact ruinous to health—and Mr. Houghton was ruined, there was no doubt about that—why was he always talking about the clean life and the virtues of fresh air? He would spread his arms wide with the action of a man who habitually spent his time striding along mountain ridges.

"Open air does me good, boys—I know it!"

Sometimes, exalted by his own oratory, he would leap from his desk and hustle us outside into a hideous wind.

"Now, boys! Deep breaths! Feel it right down inside you—huge draughts of God's good air!"

He would stand before us, rejoicing in his perfect health, an open-air man. He would put his hands on his waist and take a tremendous breath. You could hear the wind, trapped in the cavern of his chest and struggling with all the unnatural impediments. His body would reel with shock and his ruined face go white at the unaccustomed visitation. He would stagger back to his desk and collapse there, useless for the rest of the morning.

Mr. Houghton was given to high-minded monologues about the good life, sexless and full of duty. Yet in the middle of one of these monologues, if a girl passed the window, tapping along on her neat little feet, he would interrupt his discourse, his neck would turn of itself and he would watch her out of sight. In this instance, he seemed to me ruled not by thought but by an invisible and irresistible spring in his nape.

His neck was an object of great interest to me. Normally it bulged a bit over his collar. But Mr. Houghton had fought in the First World War alongside both Americans and French, and had come—by who knows what illogic?—to a settled detestation of both countries. If either country happened to be prominent in current affairs, no argument could make Mr. Houghton think well of it. He would bang the desk, his neck would bulge still further and go red. "You can say what you like," he would cry, "but I've thought about this—and I know what I think!"

Mr. Houghton thought with his neck.

There was Miss Parsons. She assured us that her dearest wish was our welfare, but I knew even then, with the mysterious clairvoyance of childhood, that what she wanted most was the husband she never got. There was Mr. Hands—and so on.

I have dealt at length with my teachers because this was my introduction to the nature of what is commonly called thought. Through them I discovered that thought is often full of unconscious prejudice, ignorance and hypocrisy. It will lecture on disinterested purity while its neck is being remorselessly twisted toward a skirt. Technically, it is about as proficient as most businessmen's golf, as honest as most politicians' intentions, or—to come near my own preoccupation—as coherent as most books that get written. It is what I came to call grade-three thinking, though more properly, it is feeling, rather than thought.

True, often there is a kind of innocence in prejudices, but in those days I viewed grade-three thinking with an intolerant contempt and an incautious mockery. I delighted to confront a pious lady who hated the Germans with the proposition that we should love our enemies. She taught me a great truth in dealing with grade-three thinkers; because of her, I no longer dismiss lightly a mental process which for nine-tenths of the population is the nearest they will ever get to thought. They have immense solidarity. We had better respect them, for we are outnumbered and surrounded. A crowd of grade-three thinkers, all shouting the same thing, all warming their hands at the fire of their own prejudices, will not thank you for pointing out the contradictions in their beliefs. Man is a gregarious animal, and enjoys agreement as cows will graze all the same way on the side of a hill.

Grade-two thinking is the detection of contradictions. I reached grade two when I trapped the poor, pious lady. Grade-two thinkers do not stampede easily, though often they fall into the other fault and lap behind. Grade-two thinking is a withdrawal, with eyes and ears open. It became my hobby and brought satisfaction and loneliness in either hand. For grade-two thinking destroys without having the power to create. It set me watching the crowds cheering His Majesty and King and asking myself what all the fuss was about, without giving me anything positive to put in the place of that heady patriotism. But there were compensations. To hear people justify their habit of hunting foxes and tearing them to pieces by claiming that the foxes liked it. To hear our Prime Minister talk about the great benefit we conferred on India by jailing people like Pandit Nehru and Gandhi. To hear American politicians talk about peace in one sentence and refuse to join the League of Nations in the next. Yes, there were moments of delight.

But I was growing toward adolescence and had to admit that Mr. Houghton was not the only one with an irresistible spring in his neck. I, too, felt the compulsive hand of nature and began to find that pointing out contradiction could be costly as well as fun. There was Ruth, for example, a serious and attractive girl. I was an atheist at the time. Grade-two thinking is a menace to religion and knocks down sects like skittles. I put myself in a position to be converted by her with an hypocrisy worthy of grade three. She was a Methodist—or at least, her parents were, and Ruth had to follow suit. But, alas, instead of relying on the Holy Spirit to convert me, Ruth was foolish enough to open her pretty mouth in argument. She claimed that the Bible (King James Version) was literally inspired. I countered by saying that the Catholics believed in the literal inspiration of Saint Jerome's *Vulgate*,[1] and the two books were different. Argument flagged.

At last she remarked that there were an awful lot of Methodists, and they couldn't be wrong, could they—not all those millions? That was too easy, said I restively (for the nearer you were to Ruth, the nicer she was to be near to) since there were more Roman Catholics than Methodists anyway; and they couldn't be wrong, could they—not all those hundreds of millions? An awful flicker of doubt appeared in her eyes. I slid my arm around her waist and murmured breathlessly that if we were counting heads, the Buddhists were the boys for my money. But Ruth had *really* wanted to do me good, because I was so nice. She fled. The combination of my arm and those countless Buddhists was too much for her.

That night her father visited my father and left, red-cheeked and indignant. I was given the third degree to find out what had happened. It was lucky we were both of us only fourteen. I lost Ruth and gained an undeserved reputation as a potential libertine.

So grade-two thinking could be dangerous. It was in this knowledge, at the age of fifteen, that I remember making a comment from the heights of grade two, on the limitations of grade three. One evening I found myself alone in the school hall, preparing it for a party. The door of the headmaster's study was open. I went in. The headmaster had ceased to thump Rodin's Thinker down on the desk as an example to the young. Perhaps he had not found any more candidates, but the statuettes were still there, glimmering and gathering dust on top of the cupboard. I stood on a chair and rearranged them. I stood Venus in her bath towel on the filing cabinet, so that now the top drawer caught its breath in a gasp of sexy excitement. "A-ah!" The portentous Thinker I placed on the edge of the

---

1. The Latin Bible as revised in the fourth century A.D. by Jerome and used thereafter as the authoritative text for Roman Catholic ritual.

cupboard so that he looked down at the bath towel and waited for it to slip.

Grade-two thinking, though it filled life with fun and excitement, did not make for content. To find out the deficiencies of our elders bolsters the young ego but does not make for personal security. I found that grade two was not only the power to point out contradictions. It took the swimmer some distance from the shore and left him there, out of his depth. I decided that Pontius Pilate was a typical grade-two thinker. "What is truth?" he said, a very common grade-two thought, but one that is used always as the end of an argument instead of the beginning. There is still a higher grade of thought which says, "What is truth?" and sets out to find it.

But these grade-one thinkers were few and far between. They did not visit my grammar school in the flesh though they were there in books. I aspired to them, partly because I was ambitious and partly because I now saw my hobby as an unsatisfactory thing if it went no further. If you set out to climb a mountain, however high you climb, you have failed if you cannot reach the top.

I *did* meet an undeniably grade-one thinker in my first year at Oxford. I was looking over a small bridge in Magdalen Deer Park, and a tiny mustached and hatted figure came and stood by my side. He was a German who had just fled from the Nazis to Oxford as a temporary refuge. His name was Einstein.

But Professor Einstein knew no English at that time and I knew only two words of German. I beamed at him, trying wordlessly to convey by my bearing all the affection and respect that the English felt for him. It is possible—and I have to make the admission—that I felt here were two grade-one thinkers standing side by side; yet I doubt if my face conveyed more than a formless awe. I would have given my Greek and Latin and French and a good slice of my English for enough German to communicate. But we were divided; he was as inscrutable as my headmaster. For perhaps five minutes we stood together on the bridge, undeniable grade-one thinker and breathless aspirant. With true greatness, Professor Einstein realized that my contact was better than none. He pointed to a trout wavering in midstream.

He spoke: "*Fisch.*"

My brain reeled. Here I was, mingling with the great, and yet helpless as the veriest grade-three thinker. Desperately I sought for some sign by which I might convey that I, too, revered pure reason. I nodded vehemently. In a brilliant flash I used up half of my German vocabulary.

"*Fisch. Ja Ja.*"

For perhaps another five minutes we stood side by side. Then Professor Einstein, his whole figure still conveying good will and amiability, drifted away out of sight.

I, too, would be a grade-one thinker. I was irreverent at the best of times. Political and religious systems, social customs, loyalties and traditions, they all came tumbling down like so many rotten apples off a tree. This was a fine hobby and a sensible substitute for cricket, since you could play it all the year round. I came up in the end with what must always remain the justification for grade-one thinking, its sign, seal and charter. I devised a coherent system for living. It was a moral system, which was wholly logical. Of course, as I readily admitted, conversion of the world to my way of thinking might be difficult, since my system did away with a number of trifles, such as big business, centralized government, armies, marriage. . . .

It was Ruth all over again. I had some very good friends who stood by me, and still do. But my acquaintances vanished, taking the girls with them. Young women seemed oddly contented with the world as it was. They valued the meaningless ceremony with a ring. Young men, while willing to concede the chaining sordidness of marriage, were hesitant about abandoning the organizations which they hoped would give them a career. A young man on the first rung of the Royal Navy, while perfectly agreeable to doing away with big business and marriage, got as rednecked as Mr. Houghton when I proposed a world without any battleships in it.

Had the game gone too far? Was it a game any longer? In those prewar days, I stood to lose a great deal, for the sake of a hobby.

Now you are expecting me to describe how I saw the folly of my ways and came back to the warm nest, where prejudices are so often called loyalties, where pointless actions are hallowed into custom by repetition, where we are content to say we think when all we do is feel.

But you would be wrong. I dropped my hobby and turned professional.

If I were to go back to the headmaster's study and find the dusty statuettes still there, I would arrange them differently. I would dust Venus and put her aside, for I have come to love her and know her for the fair thing she is. But I would put the Thinker, sunk in his desperate thought, where there were shadows before him—and at his back, I would put the leopard, crouched and ready to spring.

1961

QUESTIONS

1. *Why does Golding at the end of his essay return to the three statuettes? Have the statuettes anything to do with the three kinds of thinking described in the essay? Why would Golding rearrange the statuettes as he does in the final paragraph?*
2. *It has been said: "Third-rate thinkers think like everybody else because everybody else thinks the same way. Second-rate thinkers think differently from everybody else because everybody else thinks the*

*same way. First-rate thinkers think." Does this saying correspond to
Golding's message? Would you modity it in any way in light of what
he writes?*
3. *Does Golding's anecdote about Einstein have any bearing upon his
account of the three categories of thinking?*
4. *What are the special attractions and what are the penalties of grade-
three thinking? Grade-two? Grade-one?*
5. *Are Golding's three categories all-encompassing? If so, how? If not,
what additional ones would you add?*
6. *Are Golding's categories useful for assessing the value of a person's
statements? Choose several selections in this book and examine them
by Golding's implied criteria.*
7. *William Golding is the author of the novel* Lord of the Flies. *If you
have read that work, do you see in his depiction of characters and
events any manifestations of the three categories of thinking?*

Carl Sagan

THE ABSTRACTIONS OF BEASTS

"Beasts abstract not," announced John Locke, expressing mankind's
prevailing opinion throughout recorded history: Bishop Berkeley[1] had,
however, a sardonic rejoinder: "If the fact that brutes abstract not be
made the distinguishing property of that sort of animal, I fear a great
many of those that pass for men must be reckoned into their numbers."
Abstract thought, at least in its more subtle varieties, is not an invariable
accompaniment of everyday life for the average man. Could abstract
thought be a matter not of kind but of degree? Could other animals be
capable of abstract thought but more rarely or less deeply than humans?

We have the impression that other animals are not very intelligent.
But have we examined the possibility of animal intelligence carefully
enough, or, as in François Truffaut's poignant film *The Wild Child*, do
we simply equate the absence of our style of expression of intelligence
with the absence of intelligence? In discussing communication with the
animals, the French philosopher Montaigne remarked, "The defect that
hinders communication betwixt them and us, why may it not be on our
part as well as theirs?"

There is, of course, a considerable body of anecdotal information
suggesting chimpanzee intelligence. The first serious study of the behavior of simians—including their behavior in the wild—was made in Indo-

1. John Locke, English philosopher, author   philosopher, author of A Treatise Concerning
of An Essay Concerning Human Understand-   the Principles of Human Knowledge (1710).
ing (1690); Bishop George Berkeley, Irish

nesia by Alfred Russel Wallace, the co-discoverer of evolution by natural selection. Wallace concluded that a baby orangutan he studied behaved "exactly like a human child in similar circumstances." In fact, "orangutan" is a Malay phrase meaning not ape but "man of the woods." Teuber recounted many stories told by his parents, pioneer German ethologists who founded and operated the first research station devoted to chimpanzee behavior on Tenerife in the Canary Islands early in the second decade of this century. It was here that Wolfgang Kohler performed his famous studies of Sultan, a chimpanzee "genius" who was able to connect two rods in order to reach an otherwise inaccessible banana. On Tenerife, also, two chimpanzees were observed maltreating a chicken: One would extend some food to the fowl, encouraging it to approach; whereupon the other would thrust at it with a piece of wire it had concealed behind its back. The chicken would retreat but soon allow itself to approach once again—and be beaten once again. Here is a fine combination of behavior sometimes thought to be uniquely human: cooperation, planning a future course of action, deception and cruelty. It also reveals that chickens have a very low capacity for avoidance learning.

Until a few years ago, the most extensive attempt to communicate with chimpanzees went something like this: A newborn chimp was taken into a household with a newborn baby, and both would be raised together —twin cribs, twin bassinets, twin high chairs, twin potties, twin diaper pails, twin babypowder cans. At the end of three years, the young chimp had, of course, far outstripped the young human in manual dexterity, running, leaping, climbing and other motor skills. But while the child was happily babbling away, the chimp could say only, and with enormous difficulty, "Mama," "Papa," and "cup." From this it was widely concluded that in language, reasoning and other higher mental functions, chimpanzees were only minimally competent: "Beasts abstract not."

But in thinking over these experiments, two psychologists, Beatrice and Robert Gardner, at the University of Nevada, realized that the pharynx and larynx of the chimp are not suited for human speech. Human beings exhibit a curious multiple use of the mouth for eating, breathing and communicating. In insects such as crickets, which call to one another by rubbing their legs, these three functions are performed by completely separate organ systems. Human spoken language seems to be adventitious. The exploitation of organ systems with other functions for communication in humans is also indicative of the comparatively recent evolution of our linguistic abilities. It might be, the Gardners reasoned, that chimpanzees have substantial language abilities which could not be expressed because of the limitations of their anatomy. Was there any symbolic language, they asked, that could employ the strengths rather than the weaknesses of chimpanzee anatomy?

The Gardners hit upon a brilliant idea: Teach a chimpanzee American sign language, known by its acronym Ameslan, and sometimes as "American deaf and dumb language" (the "dumb" refers, of course, to the inability to speak and not to any failure of intelligence). It is ideally suited to the immense manual dexterity of the chimpanzee. It also may have all the crucial design features of verbal languages.

There is by now a vast library of described and filmed conversations, employing Ameslan and other gestural languages, with Washoe, Lucy, Lana and other chimpanzees studied by the Gardners and others. Not only are there chimpanzees with working vocabularies of 100 to 200 words; they are also able to distinguish among nontrivially different grammatical patterns and syntaxes. What is more, they have been remarkably inventive in the construction of new words and phrases.

On seeing for the first time a duck land quacking in a pond, Washoe gestured "waterbird," which is the same phrase used in English and other languages, but which Washoe invented for the occasion. Having never seen a spherical fruit other than an apple, but knowing the signs for the principal colors, Lana, upon spying a technician eating an orange, signed "orange apple." After tasting a watermelon, Lucy described it as "candy drink" or "drink fruit," which is essentially the same word form as the English "water melon." But after she had burned her mouth on her first radish, Lucy forever after described them as "cry hurt food." A small doll placed unexpectedly in Washoe's cup elicited the response "Baby in my drink." When Washoe soiled, particularly clothing or furniture, she was taught the sign "dirty," which she then extrapolated as a general term of abuse. A rhesus monkey that evoked her displeasure was repeatedly signed at: "Dirty monkey, dirty monkey, dirty monkey." Occasionally Washoe would say things like "Dirty Jack, gimme drink." Lana, in a moment of creative annoyance, called her trainer "You green shit." Chimpanzees have invented swear words. Washoe also seems to have a sort of sense of humor; once, when riding on her trainer's shoulders and, perhaps inadvertently, wetting him, she signed: "Funny, funny."

Lucy was eventually able to distinguish clearly the meanings of the phrases "Roger tickle Lucy" and "Lucy tickle Roger," both of which activities she enjoyed with gusto. Likewise, Lana extrapolated from "Tim groom Lana" to "Lana groom Tim." Washoe was observed "reading" a magazine—i.e., slowly turning the pages, peering intently at the pictures and making, to no one in particular, an appropriate sign, such as "cat" when viewing a photograph of a tiger, and "drink" when examining a Vermouth advertisement. Having learned the sign "open" with a door, Washoe extended the concept to a briefcase. She also attempted to converse in Ameslan with the laboratory cat, who turned out to be the only illiterate in the facility. Having acquired this marvelous method of communication, Washoe may have been surprised that the cat was not also competent in Ameslan. And when one day Jane, Lucy's foster mother, left the laboratory, Lucy gazed after her and signed: "Cry me. Me cry."

Boyce Rensberger is a sensitive and gifted reporter for the New York Times whose parents could neither speak nor hear, although he is in both respects normal. His first language, however, was Ameslan. He had been abroad on a European assignment for the Times for some years. On his return to the United States, one of his first domestic duties was to look into the Gardners' experiments with Washoe. After some little time with the chimpanzee, Rensberger reported, "Suddenly I realized I was conversing with a member of another species in my native tongue." The use of the word tongue is, of course, figurative: it is built deeply into the structure of the language (a word that also means "tongue"). In fact, Rensberger was conversing with a member of another species in his native "hand." And it is just this transition from tongue to hand that has permitted humans to regain the ability—lost, according to Josephus,[2] since Eden—to communicate with the animals.

In addition to Ameslan, chimpanzees and other nonhuman primates are being taught a variety of other gestural languages. At the Yerkes Regional Primate Research Center in Atlanta, Georgia, they are learning a specific computer language called (by the humans, not the chimps) "Yerkish." The computer records all of its subjects' conversations, even during the night when no humans are in attendance; and from its ministrations we have learned that chimpanzees prefer jazz to rock and movies about chimpanzees to movies about human beings. Lana had, by January 1976, viewed The Developmental Anatomy of the Chimpanzee 245 times. She would undoubtedly appreciate a larger film library.

* * * The machine provides for many of Lana's needs, but not all. Sometimes, in the middle of the night, she forlornly types out: "Please, machine, tickle Lana." More elaborate requests and commentaries, each requiring a creative use of a set grammatical form, have been developed subsequently.

Lana monitors her sentences on a computer display, and erases those with grammatical errors. Once, in the midst of Lana's construction of an elaborate sentence, her trainer mischievously and repeatedly interposed, from his separate computer console, a word that made nonsense of Lana's sentence. She gazed at her computer display, spied her trainer at his console, and composed a new sentence: "Please, Tim, leave room." Just as Washoe and Lucy can be said to speak, Lana can be said to write.

At an early stage in the development of Washoe's verbal abilities, Jacob Bronowski and a colleague wrote a scientific paper denying the significance of Washoe's use of gestural language because, in the limited data available to Bronowski, Washoe neither inquired nor negated. But

2. First-century Jewish general and historian.

later observations showed that Washoe and other chimpanzees were
perfectly able both to ask questions and to deny assertions put to them.
And it is difficult to see any significant difference in quality between
chimpanzee use of gestural language and the use of ordinary speech by
children in a manner that we unhesitatingly attribute to intelligence. In
reading Bronowski's paper I cannot help but feel that a little pinch of
human chauvinsim has crept in, an echo of Locke's "Beasts abstract not."
In 1949, the American anthropologist Leslie White stated unequivocally: "Human behavior is symbolic behavior; symbolic behavior is
human behavior." What would White have made of Washoe, Lucy and
Lana?

   These findings on chimpanzee language and intelligence have an
intriguing bearing on "Rubicon" arguments[3]—the contention that the
total brain mass, or at least the ratio of brain to body mass, is a useful
index of intelligence. Against this point of view it was once argued that
the lower range of the brain masses of microcephalic humans overlaps
the upper range of brain masses of adult chimpanzees and gorillas; and
yet, it was said, microcephalics have some, although severely impaired,
use of language—while the apes have none. But in only relatively few
cases are microcephalics capable of human speech. One of the best
behavioral descriptions of microcephalics was written by a Russian physician, S. Korsakov, who in 1893 observed a female microcephalic named
"Masha." She could understand a very few questions and commands and
could occasionally reminisce on her childhood. She sometimes chattered
away, but there was little coherence to what she uttered. Korsakov
characterized her speech as having "an extreme poverty of logical associations." As an example of her poorly adapted and automaton-like
intelligence, Korsakov described her eating habits. When food was present on the table, Masha would eat. But if the food was abruptly removed
in the midst of a meal, she would behave as if the meal had ended,
thanking those in charge and piously blessing herself. If the food were
returned, she would eat again. The pattern apparently was subject to
indefinite repetition. My own impression is that Lucy or Washoe would
be a far more interesting dinner companion than Masha, and that the
comparison of microcephalic humans with normal apes is not inconsistent with some sort of "Rubicon" of intelligence. Of course, both the
quality and the quantity of neural connections are probably vital for the
sorts of intelligence that we can easily recognize.
   Recent experiments performed by James Dewson of the Stanford
University School of Medicine and his colleagues give some physiological support to the idea of language centers in the simian neocortex—in

3. Those assuming a definitive boundary be-   times the boundary between Rome and its
tween different kinds of intelligence. The   "barbaric" Germanic provinces.
allusion is to the river Rubicon, in ancient

particular, like humans, in the left hemisphere. Monkeys were trained to press a green light when they heard a hiss and a red light when they heard a tone. Some seconds after a sound was heard, the red or the green light would appear at some unpredictable position—different each time—on the control panel. The monkey pressed the appropriate light and, in the case of a correct guess, was rewarded with a pellet of food. Then the time interval between hearing the sound and seeing the light was increased up to twenty seconds. In order to be rewarded, the monkeys now had to remember for twenty seconds which noise they had heard. Dewson's team then surgically excised part of the so-called auditory association cortex from the left hemisphere of the neocortex in the temporal lobe. When retested, the monkeys had very poor recall of which sound they were then hearing. After less than a second they could not recall whether it was a hiss or a tone. The removal of a comparable part of the temporal lobe from the right hemisphere produced no effect whatever on this task. "It looks," Dewson was reported to say, "as if we removed the structure in the monkeys' brains that may be analogous to human language centers." Similar studies on rhesus monkeys, but using visual rather than auditory stimuli, seem to show no evidence of a difference between the hemispheres of the neocortex.

Because adult chimpanzees are generally thought (at least by zoo-keepers) to be too dangerous to retain in a home or home environment, Washoe and other verbally accomplished chimpanzees have been involuntarily "retired" soon after reaching puberty. Thus we do not yet have experience with the adult language abilities of monkeys and apes. One of the most intriguing questions is whether a verbally accomplished chimpanzee mother will be able to communicate language to her offspring. It seems very likely that this should be possible and that a community of chimps initially competent in gestural language could pass down the language to subsequent generations.

Where such communication is essential for survival, there is already some evidence that apes transmit extragenetic or cultural information. Jane Goodall observed baby chimps in the wild emulating the behavior of their mothers and learning the reasonably complex task of finding an appropriate twig and using it to prod into a termite's nest so as to acquire some of these tasty delicacies.

Differences in group behavior—something that it is very tempting to call cultural differences—have been reported among chimpanzees, baboons, macaques and many other primates. For example, one group of monkeys may know how to eat bird's eggs, while an adjacent band of precisely the same species may not. Such primates have a few dozen sounds or cries, which are used for intra-group communication, with such meanings as "Flee; here is a predator." But the sound of the cries differs somewhat from group to group: there are regional accents.

An even more striking experiment was performed accidentally by Japanese primatologists attempting to relieve an overpopulation and hunger problem in a community of macaques on an island in south Japan. The anthropologists threw grains of wheat on a sandy beach. Now it is very difficult to separate wheat grains one by one from sand grains; such an effort might even expend more energy than eating the collected wheat would provide. But one brilliant macaque, Imo, perhaps by accident or out of pique, threw handfuls of the mixture into the water. Wheat floats; sand sinks, a fact that Imo clearly noted. Through the sifting process she was able to eat well (on a diet of soggy wheat, to be sure). While older macaques, set in their ways, ignored her, the younger monkeys appeared to grasp the importance of her discovery, and imitate it. In the next generation, the practice was more widespread; today all macaques on the island are competent at water sifting, an example of a cultural tradition among the monkeys.

Earlier studies on Takasakiyama, a mountain in northeast Kyushu inhabited by macaques, show a similar pattern in cultural evolution. Visitors to Takasakiyama threw caramels wrapped in paper to the monkeys—a common practice in Japanese zoos, but one the Takasakiyama macaques had never before encountered. In the course of play, some young monkeys discovered how to unwrap the caramels and eat them. The habit was passed on successively to their playmates, their mothers, the dominant males (who among the macaques act as babysitters for the very young) and finally to the subadult males, who were at the furthest social remove from the monkey children. The process of acculturation took more than three years. In natural primate communities, the existing nonverbal communications are so rich that there is little pressure for the development of a more elaborate gestural language. But if gestural language were necessary for chimpanzee survival, there can be little doubt that it would be transmitted culturally down through the generations.

I would expect a significant development and elaboration of language in only a few generations if all the chimps unable to communicate were to die or fail to reproduce. Basic English corresponds to about 1,000 words. Chimpanzees are already accomplished in vocabularies exceeding 10 percent of that number. Although a few years ago it would have seemed the most implausible science fiction, it does not appear to me out of the question that, after a few generations in such a verbal chimpanzee community, there might emerge the memoirs of the natural history and mental life of a chimpanzee, published in English or Japanese (with perhaps an "as told to" after the by-line).

If chimpanzees have consciousness, if they are capable of abstractions, do they not have what until now has been described as "human rights"? How smart does a chimpanzee have to be before killing him constitutes

murder? What further properties must he show before religious missionaries must consider him worthy of attempts at conversion?

I recently was escorted through a large primate research laboratory by
its director. We approached a long corridor lined, to the vanishing point
as in a perspective drawing, with caged chimpanzees. They were one,
two or three to a cage, and I am sure the accommodations were exemplary as far as such institutions (or for that matter traditional zoos) go. As
we approached the nearest cage, its two inmates bared their teeth and
with incredible accuracy let fly great sweeping arcs of spittle, fairly
drenching the lightweight suit of the facility's director. They then uttered a staccato of short shrieks, which echoed down the corridor to be
repeated and amplified by other caged chimps, who had certainly not
seen us, until the corridor fairly shook with the screeching and banging
and rattling of bars. The director informed me that not only spit is apt to
fly in such a situation; and at his urging we retreated.

I was powerfully reminded of those American motion pictures of the
1930s and '40s, set in some vast and dehumanized state or federal peni-
tentiary, in which the prisoners banged their eating utensils against the
bars at the appearance of the tyrannical warden. These chimps are
healthy and well-fed. If they are "only" animals, if they are beasts which
abstract not, then my comparison is a piece of sentimental foolishness.
But chimpanzees can abstract. Like other mammals, they are capable of
strong emotions. They have certainly committed no crimes. I do not
claim to have the answer, but I think it is certainly worthwhile to raise
the question: Why, exactly, all over the civilized world, in virtually every
major city, are apes in prison?

For all we know, occasional viable crosses between humans and chimpanzees are possible. The natural experiment must have been tried very
infrequently, at least recently. If such off-spring are ever produced, what
will their legal status be? The cognitive abilities of chimpanzees force us,
I think, to raise searching questions about the boundaries of the community of beings to which special ethical considerations are due, and can, I
hope, help to extend our ethical perspectives downward through the taxa
on Earth and upwards to extraterrestial organisms, if they exist.

* * *

1977

Henry David Thoreau

OBSERVATION

There is no such thing as pure *objective* observation. Your observation, to be interesting, *i.e.* to be significant, must be *subjective*. The sum of what the writer of whatever class has to report is simply some human experience, whether he be poet or philosopher or man of science. The man of most science is the man most alive, whose life is the greatest event. Senses that take cognizance of outward things merely are of no avail. It matters not where or how far you travel—the farther commonly the worse—but how much alive you are. If it is possible to conceive of an event outside to humanity, it is not of the slightest significance, though it were the explosion of a planet. Every important worker will report what life there is in him. It makes no odds into what seeming deserts the poet is born. Though all his neighbors pronounce it a Sahara, it will be a paradise to him; for the desert which we see is the result of the barrenness of our experience. No mere willful activity whatever, whether in writing verses or collecting statistics, will produce true poetry or science. If you are really a sick man, it is indeed to be regretted, for you cannot accomplish so much as if you were well. All that a man has to say or do that can possibly concern mankind, is in some shape or other to tell the story of his love—to sing, and, if he is fortunate and keeps alive, he will be forever in love. This alone is to be alive to the extremities. It is a pity that this divine creature should ever suffer from cold feet; a still greater pity that the coldness so often reaches to his heart. I look over the report of the doings of a scientific association and am surprised that there is so little life to be reported; I am put off with a parcel of dry technical terms. Anything living is easily and naturally expressed in popular language. I cannot help suspecting that the life of these learned professors has been almost as inhuman and wooden as a rain-gauge or self-registering magnetic machine. They communicate no fact which rises to the temperature of bloodheat. It doesn't all amount to one rhyme.

Nicholas S. Thompson

THE OILMAN COMETH

If I had to identify a particular moment or experience that I've been striving for the last two years, this would be it. I am sitting in an oak tree overlooking a marshy field southwest of my house. Two crows are fooling around in the field. I can't quite see them. Every once in a while one flies up to a tree along the fringe between the marsh and the next field to perch a few moments, only to swoop back into the marsh. The blackbirds in the marsh are distressed; the marsh is alive with their clicks and scree calls. A brown thrasher is trying to figure out what I'm doing in the tree. He approaches me silently to a very close distance, almost within reach, always keeping a branch or a sprig of leaves between us. The air is cool but the sun is direct and hot; it filters through the fresh, new leaves of the oak tree. I have arranged my dew-drenched legs to catch a direct ray of sun and they are warming and drying. Here I am. The quintessential ethologist. No tape recorders, no fancy equipment. Not even a notebook to intrude between me and my animals. Attentive. In tune. Nothing to do. Bored.

I was totally unprepared for the discovery that "just" watching animals might be boring. Not to say that I hadn't been bored watching animals before. On the contrary. But I had always attributed this boredom to the constrained, unnatural, and equipment-ridden circumstances in which I was making my observations. My first experience at systematically watching animals was when I volunteered to assist on a study of the behavioral effects of several drugs thought to be related to emotional disorders in human beings. The drugs were given to rats, and the rats placed in a biggish (for a laboratory rat) cage with lots of things to do in it. There was a wheel to run on, and little toys to play with, and water to drink, and food to eat, and on the right a male rat to talk to, and a female rat to talk to on the left. The room was warm and dimly lit, as any rat would demand. Some of the drugs made the rats frisky, and I would be frantic trying to keep up in my note taking. Some of the drugs made the rats sleepy, and I could catch up on my reading. One drug, however, made the rats groom themselves. I couldn't read because the animal was active all the time; but he was active doing the same thing over and over again. Watching a rat groom himself is like watching an ugly man brush his teeth. All of us who worked on this project dreaded these animals. Every fifteen seconds the timing light would come on and I'd write G in the appropriate space on my note sheet. Gradually my head would pitch forward onto my clipboard and then, sometime later, jerk back up. The rat would be in a slightly different place in the cage, grooming his tummy instead of his back, and the timing clock would read ten minutes later. The custom in such cases was to enter on the observer protocol the code OA, for "observer asleep." Despite the promising theoretical argument on which this study was based, it produced only one statistically reliable result: the analysis of the data showed unequivocally that injection of rats with this particular drug caused observers to sleep an average of 6.6 minutes longer than injection of rats with any other drug in the study.

Since I attributed the boredom of such studies to the impediments of science—the darkened, stuffy rooms, the drugged animals, the stop-watches, the isolation—I was surprised to find myself bored in that tree. I was there as the result of a determined program to "go naked into nature," as it were. Even the decision not to carry a notebook was a conscious decision. Why did one need any equipment? Did not the human observer carry on his shoulders the most remarkable piece of analytical equipment in the universe—the human brain? Did I not possess the most marvelous balance of senses that evolution could produce? Did I not possess almost infinite resources for recording, analyzing, and interpreting information beneath my bald spot? All I had to do was turn these marvelous pieces of natural equipment loose upon the natural world and I would have the purest, the most natural of sciences. Except I was bored.

How come? I thought to myself. Most people would give their right arms to be me. Here I was, getting paid to sit in an oak tree and soak up the June morning sun. Tough life. My mind skimmed giddily on the envy of millions of people and then sank like a skipped stone that has caught a wave wrong. One of the two crows flew back across the marsh toward their nest, and I realized that I had been forgetting to watch them. How could I? I had nothing to do but watch those crows. I tried to concentrate on the remaining crow. It was balancing on the small low branch of a cherry tree, giving high-pitched caws. With each caw it bowed its neck, and the force of the caw caused it to rock on the end of its slender branch. "Here is the young ethologist, gone naked into nature, watching a crow." A wave of satisfaction spread through my being. "Here is the young ethologist about to make a major discovery about crow behavior. Here is the young . . . damn . . . here is the young ethologist having megalomania-cal fantasies." The crow had disappeared, dropped back into the marsh again, and I had missed it. I wrenched my mind back. Here I had gone naked into nature and what was I thinking about? Nature? No! I was thinking about *thinking* about nature. I might as well have had a brown paper bag over my head.

Over the next few weeks of that idyllic summer, the problem got worse. I would set myself up in some ideal circumstance for observing nature, and then "it" would happen. "It" would develop like this: first, I would realize that I wasn't thinking about nature; I would try to pull my mind around to what was going on around me—if not to the crows, then at least to the sky, the sunshine, the smells, something. I would take a moment's satisfaction in that mental bootstrapping operation, but then I would realize that I wasn't thinking about nature, I was *thinking about thinking about nature*. Then I would realize that I wasn't even just thinking about thinking about nature, I was *thinking about thinking about thinking about nature*. And so on, until my brain began to feel like an overloaded fuse box. Pretty soon I shortcut all these intricacies by calling this process "it." I would be looking at some crows and "it" would happen. "It" was like a jammed typewriter that keeps making x's until you pull the plug out. The only way I could pull the plug out was to go *do* something. Write a memo, hoe a row of corn, split some wood, mulch some raspberries, read a student paper, *anything*.

I thought I was losing my mind. I had other evidence. There was the "Oilman Problem." The Oilman Problem was so named not because the oilman had it, but because the oilman precipitated it. One day I was staring out the windows daydreaming and engaging in that mixture of fervor and depression which seems to precede some of my most creative moments, when I heard a clunk at the front door. I went to the door and found the oilman filling the tank. He had apparently bumped the door as he was fitting the ungainly nozzle to the tank pipe. Having come upon him thus, I felt obliged to pass the time of day while the tank was filling.

"Nice day," said I.

"Sure is," said he. "Home on vacation?"

"No," said I. "I work at home two days a week."

"You're the college teacher, right?"

"Right," I agreed.

"S'pose you spend a lot of time correcting papers."

"No," I said. I considered explaining that in my business nobody could be sure enough of anything to "correct" a paper, but decided that that answer was just going to get me in deeper, so I explained my answer on technical grounds. "I have a teaching assistant who does the grading."

"Must be a lot of time you spend teaching," he said, flexibly.

"No," I said. "Not a lot. I spend about nine hours in the classroom a week."

"Nine hours? A week?" He was going to ask me another question, but then thought better of it. The oil hose clunked and twitched and the pump on the oil truck eased from a roar to a hum. The oilman started to detach the hose.

"I do research," I volunteered, suddenly afraid that the connection between us would be broken before I had had a chance to explain myself.

"Research!" he exclaimed. "My daughter—she's a nurse—she'd be really interested in that. Like those people on the television last night who are trying to find a cure for cancer. What are you doing research on?"

"Crows."

"Do you have a lot of them in cages in your barn?"

"No," I said. "I just watch them."

"But what do you *do?*" he asked.

"Well, I guess I think a lot while I watch them," I offered.

He gave the hose a yank and it reeled him back to the truck. He stashed the nozzle and came back with the invoice. He was clearly groping for a polite resolution to our conversation.

"Well," he said, "I still don't understand what you do, but if you can find a cure for the crow, you're my man."

He climbed up into the cab, waved, and drove off. He left me no time to explain that I loved crows, I was fascinated by crows, would like to populate the world with crows, to live with crows, to dine with crows, to sleep with crows, to be awakened by their staccato self-declarations in the morning, and to be lulled by their evensong caws in the dusk.

Here was a pretty state of affairs. Here I had spent my family fortune to own a farm and live where I could be in touch with nature, and now my brain jammed every time I came near nature. Worse, I now spent long hours in vigorous internal dialogue trying to explain myself to the oilman. In desperation I decided to consult with a friend of mine. One of the great joys of working in a psychology department is that there's always a clinical psychologist down the hall when things get rough. One doesn't like to approach one's colleagues overtly for help, but one can always approach them covertly as if discussing an interesting Phenomenon of the Mind. The phenomenon I brought to my friend's attention was "it"—my mental blot, as I had come to think of it. My friend, although no older than I, is an ideal of what one would hope for in a borrowed clinician. Tweedy, pipe-smoking, and good-natured, he embraced my phenomenon like a long-lost friend, hugged it to himself vigorously, held it away from himself and looked at it admiringly, then hugged it to himself again. He liked my phenomenon, and what's more, he understood it and knew how to cure it. I was a victim, said he, of a misconception of "self." I had mistakenly assumed that if I stripped my nature-watching activities of all the encumbrances of doing—the notebooks, the telescopes, the tape recorders, and so on—I would get down to the basic essence of *being* a nature watcher. The self, he said, is not a thing apart from the activities of the person. In fact, he said, people know their "selves" from what they do. If I wanted to *be* a nature watcher, I had to *do* at least some of the things that nature watchers do. If that meant carrying binoculars and taking notes, then I should do that. "Not all goals are the same," he continued. "Some goals are mentally useful and some aren't. 'To experience' a thing is a bad goal, because it doesn't tell you what to *do*. Same with the goal 'to be happy.' Happiness and experience are two things that happen to you on the way to somewhere else." So, he said, if I had your problem—and I noticed he wasn't saying "phenomenon" anymore—I would stop going out in nature to experience it, and start going out in nature to take notes on it.

It was the best advice I've ever gotten from anybody. I was moved and grateful, and my eyes grew damper than I liked them. I stood up and shook his hand as one might in leaving a doctor's office. As if to alleviate my embarrassment, he concluded with a lengthy discussion of the theoretical significance of my "phenomenon."

Later that afternoon, I went out and purchased one of those leatherbound, prelined books with the word *notebook* embossed in phony gold. I bought myself two or three pencils, sharpened them well, and went home. By four o'clock that afternoon I was sitting out in my west field with my notebook and pencils. In the two hours that followed I took thirteen pages of notes. I never was bored and I never stopped thinking about nature once. "It" was conquered. The next time the oilman came, I told him I was writing a book about crows. That seemed to satisfy him, and now, whenever he comes, he asks, "How's the writing going?"

1981

Jacob Bronowski

THE REACH OF IMAGINATION

For three thousand years, poets have been enchanted and moved and perplexed by the power of their own imagination. In a short and summary essay I can hope at most to lift one small corner of that mystery; and yet it is a critical corner. I shall ask, What goes on in the mind when we imagine? You will hear from me that one answer to this question is fairly specific: which is to say, that we can describe the working of the imagination. And when we describe it as I shall do, it becomes plain that imagination is a specifically *human* gift. To imagine is the characteristic act, not of the poet's mind, or the painter's, or the scientist's, but of the mind of man.

My stress here on the word *human* implies that there is a clear difference in this between the actions of men and those of other animals. Let me then start with a classical experiment with animals and children which Walter Hunter thought out in Chicago about 1910. That was the time when scientists were agog with the success of Ivan Pavlov in forming and changing the reflex actions of dogs, which Pavlov had first announced in 1903. Pavlov had been given a Nobel prize the next year, in 1904; although in fairness I should say that the award did not cite his work on the conditioned reflex, but on the digestive gland.

Hunter duly trained some dogs and other animals on Pavlov's lines. They were taught that when a light came on over one of three tunnels out of their cage, that tunnel would be open; they could escape down it, and were rewarded with food if they did. But once he had fixed that conditioned reflex, Hunter added to it a deeper idea: he gave the mechanical experiment a new dimension, literally—the dimension of time. Now he no longer let the dog go to the lighted tunnel at once; instead, he put out the light, and then kept the dog waiting a little while before he let him go. In this way Hunter timed how long an animal can remember where he has last seen the signal light to his escape route.

The results were and are staggering. A dog or a rat forgets which one of three tunnels has been lit up within a matter of seconds—in Hunter's experiment, ten seconds at most. If you want such an animal to do much better than this, you must make the task much simpler: you must face him with only two tunnels to choose from. Even so, the best that Hunter could do was to have a dog remember for five minutes which one of two tunnels had been lit up.

I am not quoting these times as if they were exact and universal: they surely are not. Hunter's experiment, more than fifty years old now, had many faults of detail. For example, there were too few animals, they were oddly picked, and they did not all behave consistently. It may be unfair to test a dog for what he saw, when he commonly follows his nose rather than his eyes. It may be unfair to test any animal in the unnatural setting of a laboratory cage. And there are higher animals, such as chimpanzees and other primates, which certainly have longer memories than the animals that Hunter tried.

Yet when all these provisos have been made (and met, by more modern experiments) the facts are still startling and characteristic. An animal cannot recall a signal from the past for even a short fraction of the time that a man can—for even a short fraction of the time that a child can. Hunter made comparable tests with six-year-old children, and found, of course, that they were incomparably better than the best of his animals. There is a striking and basic difference between a man's ability to imagine something that he saw or experienced, and an animal's failure.

Animals make up for this by other and extraordinary gifts. The salmon and the carrier pigeon can find their way home as we cannot: they have, as it were, a practical memory that man cannot match. But their actions always depend on some form of habit: on instinct or on learning, which reproduce by rote a train of known responses. They do not depend, as human memory does, on calling to mind the recollection of absent things.

Where is it that the animal falls short? We get a clue to the answer, I think, when Hunter tells us how the animals in his experiment tried to fix their recollection. They most often pointed themselves at the light before it went out, as some gun dogs point rigidly at the game they scent —and get the name *pointer* from the posture. The animal makes ready to act by building the signal into its action. There is a primitive imagery in its stance, it seems to me; it is as if the animal were trying to fix the light on its mind by fixing it in its body. And indeed, how else can a dog mark and (as it were) name one of three tunnels, when he has no such words as *left* and *right*, and no such numbers as *one, two, three?* The directed gesture of attention and readiness is perhaps the only symbolic device that the dog commands to hold on to the past, and thereby to guide himself into the future.

I used the verb *to imagine* a moment ago, and now I have some ground for giving it a meaning. *To imagine* means to make images and to move them about inside one's head in new arrangements. When you and I recall the past, we imagine it in this direct and homely sense. The tool that puts the human mind ahead of the animal is imagery. For us, memory does not demand the preoccupation that it demands in animals, and it lasts immensely longer, because we fix it in images or other substitute symbols. With the same symbolic vocabulary we spell out the future—not one but many futures, which we weigh one against another.

I am using the word *image* in a wide meaning, which does not restrict it to the mind's eye as a visual organ. An image in my usage is what Charles Peirce called a *sign*, without regard for its sensory quality. Peirce distinguished between different forms of signs, but there is no reason to make his distinction here, for the imagination works equally with them all, and that is why I call them all images.

Indeed, the most important images for human beings are simply words, which are abstract symbols. Animals do not have words, in our sense: there is no specific center for language in the brain of any animal, as there is in the human being. In this respect at least we know that the human imagination depends on a configuration in the brain that has only evolved in the last one or two million years. In the same period, evolution has greatly enlarged the front lobes in the human brain, which govern the sense of the past and the future; and it is a fair guess that they are probably the seat of our other images. (Part of the evidence for this guess is that damage to the front lobes in primates reduces them to the state of Hunter's animals.) If the guess turns out to be right, we shall know why man has come to look like a highbrow or an egghead: because otherwise there would not be room in his head for his imagination.

The images play out for us events which are not present to our senses, and thereby guard the past and create the future—a future that does not yet exist, and may never come to exist in that form. By contrast, the lack of symbolic ideas, or their rudimentary poverty, cuts off an animal from the past and the future alike, and imprisons him in the present. Of all the distinctions between man and animal, the characteristic gift which makes us human is the power to work with symbolic images: the gift of imagination.

This is really a remarkable finding. When Philip Sidney in 1580 defended poets (and all unconventional thinkers) from the Puritan charge that they were liars, he said that a maker must imagine things that are not. Halfway between Sidney and us, William Blake said, "What is now proved was once only imagined." About the same time, in 1796, Samuel Taylor Coleridge for the first time distinguished between the passive fancy and the active imagination, "the living Power and prime Agent of all human Perception." Now we see that they were right, and precisely right: the human gift is the gift of imagination—and that is not just a literary phrase.

Nor is it just a literary gift; it is, I repeat, characteristically human. Almost everything that we do that is worth doing is done in the first place in the mind's eye. The richness of human life is that we have many lives; we live the events that do not happen (and some that cannot) as vividly as those that do; and if thereby we die a thousand deaths, that is the price we pay for living a thousand lives. (A cat, of course, has only nine.) Literature is alive to us because we live its images, but so is any play of the mind—so is chess: the lines of play that we foresee and try in our heads and dismiss are as much a part of the game as the moves that we make. John Keats said that the unheard melodies are sweeter, and all chess players sadly recall that the combinations that they planned and which never came to be played were the best.

I make this point to remind you, insistently, that imagination is the manipulation of images in one's head; and that the rational manipulation belongs to that, as well as the literary and artistic manipulation. When a child begins to play games with things that stand for other things, with chairs or chessmen, he enters the gateway to reason and imagination together. For the human reason discovers new relations between things not by deduction, but by that unpredictable blend of speculation and insight that scientists call induction, which—like other forms of imagination—cannot be formalized. We see it at work when Walter Hunter inquires into a child's memory, as much as when Blake and Coleridge do. Only a restless and original mind would have asked Hunter's questions and could have conceived his experiments, in a science that was dominated by Pavlov's reflex arcs and was heading toward the behaviorism of John Watson.[1]

Let me find a spectacular example for you from history. What is the

1. Watson, a forerunner of B. F. Skinner, argued that all human behavior consists of conditioned reflexes in response to environmental stimuli.

most famous experiment that you had described to you as a child? I will hazard that it is the experiment that Galileo is said to have made in Sidney's age, in Pisa about 1590, by dropping two unequal balls from the Leaning Tower. There, we say, is a man in the modern mold, a man after our own hearts: he insisted on questioning the authority of Aristotle and St. Thomas Aquinas, and seeing with his own eyes whether (as they said) the heavy ball would reach the ground before the light one. Seeing is believing.

Yet seeing is also imagining. Galileo did challenge the authority of Aristotle, and he did look at his mechanics. But the eye that Galileo used was the mind's eye. He did not drop balls from the Leaning Tower of Pisa —and if he had, he would have got a very doubtful answer. Instead, Galileo made an imaginary experiment in his head, which I will describe as he did years later in the book he wrote after the Holy Office silenced him: the *Discorsi . . . intorno a due nuove scienze*,[2] which was smuggled out to be printed in the Netherlands in 1638.

Suppose, said Galileo, that you drop two unequal balls from the tower at the same time. And suppose that Aristotle is right—suppose that the heavy ball falls faster, so that it steadily gains on the light ball, and hits the ground first. Very well. Now imagine the same experiment done again, with only one difference: this time the two unequal balls are joined by a string between them. The heavy ball will again move ahead, but now the light ball holds it back and acts as a drag or brake. So the light ball will be speeded up and the heavy ball will be slowed down; they must reach the ground together because they are tied together, but they cannot reach the ground as quickly as the heavy ball alone. Yet the string between them has turned the two balls into a single mass which is heavier than either ball—and surely (according to Aristotle) this mass should therefore move faster than either ball? Galileo's imaginary experiment has uncovered a contradiction; he says trenchantly, "You see how, from your assumption that a heavier body falls more rapidly than a lighter one, I infer that a (still) heavier body falls more slowly." There is only one way out of the contradiction: the heavy ball and the light ball must fall at the same rate, so that they go on falling at the same rate when they are tied together.

This argument is not conclusive, for nature might be more subtle (when the two balls are joined) than Galileo has allowed. And yet it is something more important: it is suggestive, it is stimulating, it opens a new view—in a word, it is imaginative. It cannot be settled without an actual experiment, because nothing that we imagine can become knowledge until we have translated it into, and backed it by, real experience. The test of imagination is experience. But then, that is as true of litera-

2. *Treatise . . . on Two New Sciences.* In 1630, after publishing his heretical theory that the earth moves around the sun, Galileo was forced by the Inquisition to recant it under threat of torture.

ture and the arts as it is of science. In science, the imaginary experiment is tested by confronting it with physical experience; and in literature, the imaginative conception is tested by confronting it with human experience. The superficial speculation in science is dismissed because it is found to falsify nature; and the shallow work of art is discarded because it is found to be untrue to our own nature. So when Ella Wheeler Wilcox died in 1919, more people were reading her verses than Shakespeare's; yet in a few years her work was dead. It had been buried by its poverty of emotion and its trivialness of thought: which is to say that it had been proved to be as false to the nature of man as, say, Jean Baptiste Lamarck and Trofim Lysenko[3] were false to the nature of inheritance. The strength of the imagination, its enriching power and excitement, lies in its interplay with reality—physical and emotional.

I doubt if there is much to choose here between science and the arts: the imagination is not much more free, and not much less free, in one than in the other. All great scientists have used their imagination freely, and let it ride them to outrageous conclusions without crying "Halt!" Albert Einstein fiddled with imaginary experiments from boyhood, and was wonderfully ignorant of the facts that they were supposed to bear on. When he wrote the first of his beautiful papers on the random movement of atoms, he did not know that the Brownian motion which it predicted could be seen in any laboratory. He was sixteen when he invented the paradox that he resolved ten years later, in 1905, in the theory of relativity, and it bulked much larger in his mind than the experiment of Albert Michelson and Edward Morley[4] which had upset every other physicist since 1881. All his life Einstein loved to make up teasing puzzles like Galileo's, about falling lifts and the detection of gravity; and they carry the nub of the problems of general relativity on which he was working.

Indeed, it could not be otherwise. The power that man has over nature and himself, and that a dog lacks, lies in his command of imaginary experience. He alone has the symbols which fix the past and play with the future, possible and impossible. In the Renaissance, the symbolism of memory was thought to be mystical, and devices that were invented as mnemonics (by Giordano Bruno, for example, and by Robert Fludd) were interpreted as magic signs. The symbol is the tool which gives man his power, and it is the same tool whether the symbols are images or

3. Lamarck was a French biologist (1744–1829) who held that characteristics acquired by experience were biologically transmittable. Lysenko is a Russian biologist (1898–   ) who has held that hereditary properties of organisms could be changed by manipulating the environment.
4. Physicists had believed space to be filled with an ether which made possible the propagation of light and magnetism; the Michel-son-Morley experiment proved this untrue. Einstein, an outsider, always claimed not to have heard of the experiment until after he published his special theory of relativity, which not only accounted for the Michelson-Morley findings but resolved such paradoxes as the impossibility of distinguishing qualitatively between gravity and the pull caused by the acceleration of an elevator, or lift.

words, mathematical signs or mesons. And the symbols have a reach and a roundness that goes beyond their literal and practical meaning. They are the rich concepts under which the mind gathers many particulars into one name, and many instances into one general induction. When a man says *left* and *right*, he is outdistancing the dog not only in looking for a light; he is setting in train all the shifts of meaning, the overtones and the ambiguities, between *gauche* and *adroit* and *dexterous*, between *sinister* and the sense of right. When a man counts *one, two, three*, he is not only doing mathematics; he is on the path to the mysticism of numbers in Pythagoras and Vitruvius and Kepler, to the Trinity and the signs of the Zodiac.

I have described imagination as the ability to make images and to move them about inside one's head in new arrangements. This is the faculty that is specifically human, and it is the common root from which science and literature both spring and grow and flourish together. For they do flourish (and languish) together; the great ages of science are the great ages of all the arts, because in them powerful minds have taken fire from one another, breathless and higgledy-piggledy, without asking too nicely whether they ought to tie their imagination to falling balls or a haunted island. Galileo and Shakespeare, who were born in the same year, grew into greatness in the same age; when Galileo was looking through his telescope at the moon, Shakespeare was writing *The Tempest* and all Europe was in ferment, from Johannes Kepler to Peter Paul Rubens, and from the first table of logarithms by John Napier to the Authorized Version of the Bible.

Let me end with a last and spirited example of the common inspiration of literature and science, because it is as much alive today as it was three hundred years ago. What I have in mind is man's ageless fantasy, to fly to the moon. I do not display this to you as a high scientific enterprise; on the contrary, I think we have more important discoveries to make here on earth than wait for us, beckoning, at the horned surface of the moon. Yet I cannot belittle the fascination which that ice-blue journey has had for the imagination of men, long before it drew us to our television screens to watch the tumbling astronauts. Plutarch and Lucian, Ariosto and Ben Jonson wrote about it, before the days of Jules Verne and H. G. Wells and science fiction. The seventeenth century was heady with new dreams and fables about voyages to the moon. Kepler wrote one full of deep scientific ideas, which (alas) simply got his mother accused of witchcraft. In England, Francis Godwin wrote a wild and splendid work, *The Man in the Moone*, and the astronomer John Wilkins wrote a wild and learned one, *The Discovery of a New World*. They did not draw a line between science and fancy; for example, they all tried to guess just where in the journey the earth's gravity would stop. Only Kepler understood that gravity has no boundary, and put a law to it—which happened to be the wrong law.

All this was a few years before Isaac Newton was born, and it was all in his head that day in 1666 when he sat in his mother's garden, a young man of twenty-three, and thought about the reach of gravity. This was how he came to conceive his brilliant image, that the moon is like a ball which has been thrown so hard that it falls exactly as fast as the horizon, all the way round the earth. The image will do for any satellite, and Newton modestly calculated how long therefore an astronaut would take to fall round the earth once. He made it ninety minutes, and we have all seen now that he was right; but Newton had no way to check that. Instead he went on to calculate how long in that case the distant moon would take to round the earth, if indeed it behaves like a thrown ball that falls in the earth's gravity, and if gravity obeyed a law of inverse squares. He found that the answer would be twenty-eight days.

In that telling figure, the imagination that day chimed with nature, and made a harmony. We shall hear an echo of that harmony on the day when we land on the moon, because it will be not a technical but an imaginative triumph, that reaches back to the beginning of modern science and literature both. All great acts of imagination are like this, in the arts and in science, and convince us because they fill out reality with a deeper sense of rightness. We start with the simplest vocabulary of images, with *left* and *right* and *one, two, three,* and before we know how it happened the words and the numbers have conspired to make a match with nature: we catch in them the pattern of mind and matter as one.

1967

QUESTIONS

1. *How does the Hunter experiment provide Bronowski with the ground for defining the imagination?*
2. *Bronowski discusses the work of Galileo and Newton in the middle and at the end of his essay; what use does he make of their work? Does it justify placing them in the central and final positions?*
3. *On page 196 Bronowski attributes the imagination to a "configuration" in the brain. Configuration seems vague here; what else shows uncertainty about exactly what happens in the brain? Does this uncertainty compromise the argument of this essay?*
4. *What function is given to the mind by the title metaphor of reaching (later extended to symbols on page 200)? What words does Bronowski use to indicate the objects reached for? What is the significance of his selecting these words?*

Isaac Asimov

THE EUREKA PHENOMENON

In the old days, when I was writing a great deal of fiction, there would come, once in a while, moments when I was stymied. Suddenly, I would find I had written myself into a hole and could see no way out. To take care of that, I developed a technique which invariably worked.

It was simply this—I went to the movies. Not just any movie. I had to pick a movie which was loaded with action but which made no demands on the intellect. As I watched, I did my best to avoid any conscious thinking concerning my problem, and when I came out of the movie I knew exactly what I would have to do to put the story back on the track.

It never failed.

In fact, when I was working on my doctoral dissertation, too many years ago, I suddenly came across a flaw in my logic that I had not noticed before and that knocked out everything I had done. In utter panic, I made my way to a Bob Hope movie—and came out with the necessary change in point of view.

It is my belief, you see, that thinking is a double phenomenon like breathing.

You can control breathing by deliberate voluntary action: you can breathe deeply and quickly, or you can hold your breath altogether, regardless of the body's needs at the time. This, however, doesn't work well for very long. Your chest muscles grow tired, your body clamors for more oxygen, or less, and you relax. The automatic involuntary control of breathing takes over, adjusts it to the body's needs and unless you have some respiratory disorder, you can forget about the whole thing.

Well, you can think by deliberate voluntary action, too, and I don't think it is much more efficient on the whole than voluntary breath control is. You can deliberately force your mind through channels of deductions and associations in search of a solution to some problem and before long you have dug mental furrows for yourself and find yourself circling round and round the same limited pathways. If those pathways yield no solution, no amount of further conscious thought will help.

On the other hand, if you let go, then the thinking process comes under automatic involuntary control and is more apt to take new pathways and make erratic associations you would not think of consciously. The solution will then come while you *think* you are *not* thinking.

The trouble is, though, that conscious thought involves no muscular action and so there is no sensation of physical weariness that would force you to quit. What's more, the panic of necessity tends to force you to go on uselessly, with each added bit of useless effort adding to the panic in a vicious cycle.

It is my feeling that it helps to relax, deliberately, by subjecting your mind to material complicated enough to occupy the voluntary faculty of thought, but superficial enough not to engage the deeper involuntary one. In my case, it is an action movie; in your case, it might be something else.

I suspect it is the involuntary faculty of thought that gives rise to what we call "a flash of intuition," something that I imagine must be merely the result of unnoticed thinking.

Perhaps the most famous flash of intuition in the history of science took place in the city of Syracuse in third-century B.C. Sicily. Bear with me and I will tell you the story—

About 250 B.C., the city of Syracuse was experiencing a kind of Golden Age. It was under the protection of the rising power of Rome, but it retained a king of its own and considerable self-government; it was prosperous; and it had a flourishing intellectual life.

The king was Hieron II, and he had commissioned a new golden crown from a goldsmith, to whom he had given an ingot of gold as raw material. Hieron, being a practical man, had carefully weighed the ingot and then weighed the crown he received back. The two weights were precisely equal. Good deal!

But then he sat and thought for a while. Suppose the goldsmith had subtracted a little bit of the gold, not too much, and had substituted an equal weight of the considerably less valuable copper. The resulting alloy would still have the appearance of pure gold, but the goldsmith would be plus a quantity of gold over and above his fee. He would be buying gold with copper, so to speak, and Hieron would be neatly cheated.

Hieron didn't like the thought of being cheated any more than you or I would, but he didn't know how to find out for sure if he had been. He could scarcely punish the goldsmith on mere suspicion. What to do?

Fortunately, Hieron had an advantage few rulers in the history of the world could boast. He had a relative of considerable talent. The relative was named Archimedes and he probably had the greatest intellect the world was to see prior to the birth of Newton.

Archimedes was called in and was posed the problem. He had to determine whether the crown Hieron showed him was pure gold, or was gold to which a small but significant quantity of copper had been added.

If we were to reconstruct Archimedes' reasoning, it might go as follows. Gold was the densest known substance (at that time). Its density in modern terms is 19.3 grams per cubic centimeter. This means that a given weight of gold takes up less volume than the same weight of

anything else! In fact, a given weight of pure gold takes up less volume
than the same weight of any kind of impure gold.

The density of copper is 8.92 grams per cubic centimeter, just about
half that of gold. If we consider 100 grams of pure gold, for instance, it is
easy to calculate it to have a volume of 5.18 cubic centimeters. But
suppose that 100 grams of what looked like pure gold was really only 90
grams of gold and 10 grams of copper. The 90 grams of gold would have a
volume of 4.66 cubic centimeters, while the 10 grams of copper would
have a volume of 1.12 cubic centimeters; for a total value of 5.78 cubic
centimeters.

The difference between 5.18 cubic centimeters and 5.78 cubic centimeters is quite a noticeable one, and would instantly tell if the crown
were of pure gold, or if it contained 10 per cent copper (with the missing
10 per cent of gold tucked neatly in the goldsmith's strongbox).

All one had to do, then, was measure the volume of the crown and
compare it with the volume of the same weight of pure gold.

The mathematics of the time made it easy to measure the volume of
many simple shapes: a cube, a sphere, a cone, a cylinder, any flattened
object of simple regular shape and known thickness, and so on.

We can imagine Archimedes saying, "All that is necessary, sire, is to
pound that crown flat, shape it into a square of uniform thickness, and
then I can have the answer for you in a moment."

Whereupon Hieron must certainly have snatched the crown away and
said, "No such thing. I can do that much without you; I've studied the
principles of mathematics, too. This crown is a highly satisfactory work
of art and I won't have it damaged. Just calculate its volume without in
any way altering it."

But Greek mathematics had no way of determining the volume of
anything with a shape as irregular as the crown, since integral calculus
had not yet been invented (and wouldn't be for two thousand years,
almost). Archimedes would have had to say, "There is no known way,
sire, to carry through a non-destructive determination of volume."

"Then think of one," said Hieron testily.

And Archimedes must have set about thinking of one, and gotten
nowhere. Nobody knows how long he thought, or how hard, or what
hypotheses he considered and discarded, or any of the details.

What we do know is that, worn out with thinking, Archimedes decided to visit the public baths and relax. I think we are quite safe in saying
that Archimedes had no intention of taking his problem to the baths with
him. It would be ridiculous to imagine he would, for the public baths of a
Greek metropolis weren't intended for that sort of thing.

The Greek baths were a place for relaxation. Half the social aristocracy
of the town would be there and there was a great deal more to do than
wash. One steamed one's self, got a massage, exercised, and engaged in

general socializing. We can be sure that Archimedes intended to forget the stupid crown for a while.

One can envisage him engaging in light talk, discussing the latest news from Alexandria and Carthage, the latest scandals in town, the latest funny jokes at the expense of the country-squire Romans—and then he lowered himself into a nice hot bath which some bumbling attendant had filled too full.

The water in the bath slopped over as Archimedes got in. Did Archimedes notice that at once, or did he sigh, sink back, and paddle his feet awhile before noting the water-slop. I guess the latter. But, whether soon or late, he noticed, and that one fact, added to all the chains of reasoning his brain had been working on during the period of relaxation when it was unhampered by the comparative stupidities (even in Archimedes) of voluntary thought, gave Archimedes his answer in one blinding flash of insight.

Jumping out of the bath, he proceeded to run home at top speed through the streets of Syracuse. He did *not* bother to put on his clothes. The thought of Archimedes running naked through Syracuse has titillated dozens of generations of youngsters who have heard this story, but I must explain that the ancient Greeks were quite lighthearted in their attitude toward nudity. They thought no more of seeing a naked man on the streets of Syracuse, than we would on the Broadway stage.

And as he ran, Archimedes shouted over and over, "I've got it! I've got it!" Of course, knowing no English, he was compelled to shout it in Greek, so it came out, *"Eureka! Eureka!"*

Archimedes' solution was so simple that anyone could understand it —once Archimedes explained it.

If an object that is not affected by water in any way, is immersed in water, it is bound to displace an amount of water equal to its own volume, since two objects cannot occupy the same space at the same time.

Suppose, then, you had a vessel large enough to hold the crown and suppose it had a small overflow spout set into the middle of its side. And suppose further that the vessel was filled with water exactly to the spout, so that if the water level were raised a bit higher, however slightly, some would overflow.

Next, suppose that you carefully lower the crown into the water. The water level would rise by an amount equal to the volume of the crown, and that volume of water would pour out the overflow and be caught in a small vessel. Next, a lump of gold, known to be pure and exactly equal in weight to the crown, is also immersed in the water and again the level rises and the overflow is caught in a second vessel.

If the crown were pure gold, the overflow would be exactly the same in each case, and the volume of water caught in the two small vessels would be equal. If, however, the crown were of alloy, it would produce a larger overflow than the pure gold would and this would be easily noticeable.

What's more, the crown would in no way be harmed, defaced, or even as much as scratched. More important, Archimedes had discovered the "principle of buoyancy."

And was the crown pure gold? I've heard that it turned out to be alloy and that the goldsmith was executed, but I wouldn't swear to it.

How often does this "Eureka phenomenon" happen? How often is there this flash of deep insight during a moment of relaxation, this triumphant cry of "I've got it! I've got it!" which must surely be a moment of the purest ecstasy this sorry world can afford?

I wish there were some way we could tell. I suspect that in the history of science it happens *often*; I suspect that very few significant discoveries are made by the pure technique of voluntary thought; I suspect that voluntary thought may possibly prepare the ground (if even that), but that the final touch, the real inspiration, comes when thinking is under involuntary control.

But the world is in a conspiracy to hide the fact. Scientists are wedded to reason, to the meticulous working out of consequences from assumptions to the careful organization of experiments designed to check those consequences. If a certain line of experiments ends nowhere, it is omitted from the final report. If an inspired guess turns out to be correct, it is *not* reported as an inspired guess. Instead, a solid line of voluntary thought is invented after the fact to lead up to the thought, and that is what is inserted in the final report.

The result is that anyone reading scientific papers would swear that *nothing* took place but voluntary thought maintaining a steady clumping stride from origin to destination, and that just can't be true.

It's such a shame. Not only does it deprive science of much of its glamour (how much of the dramatic story in Watson's *Double Helix* do you suppose got into the final reports announcing the great discovery of the structure of DNA?[1]), but it hands over the important process of "insight," "inspiration," "revelation" to the mystic.

The scientist actually becomes ashamed of having what we might call a revelation, as though to have one is to betray reason—when actually what we call revelation in a man who has devoted his life to reasoned thought, is after all merely reasoned thought that is not under voluntary control.

Only once in a while in modern times do we ever get a glimpse into the workings of involuntary reasoning, and when we do, it is always fascinat-

1. I'll tell you, in case you're curious. None! [Asimov's note]. How Francis Crick and James Watson discovered the molecular structure of this vital substance is told in Watson's autobiographical book, *The Double Helix*.

ing. Consider, for instance, the case of Friedrich August Kekule von Stradonitz.

In Kekule's time, a century and a quarter ago, a subject of great interest to chemists was the structure of organic molecules (those associated with living tissue). Inorganic molecules were generally simple in the sense that they were made up of few atoms. Water molecules, for instance, are made up of two atoms of hydrogen and one of oxygen (H_2O). Molecules of ordinary salt are made up of one atom of sodium and one of chlorine (NaCl), and so on.

Organic molecules, on the other hand, often contained a large number of atoms. Ethyl alcohol molecules have two carbon atoms, six hydrogen atoms, and an oxygen atom (C_2H_6O); the molecule of ordinary cane sugar is $C_{12}H_{22}O_{11}$, and other molecules are even more complex.

Then, too, it is sufficient, in the case of inorganic molecules generally, merely to know the kinds and numbers of atoms in the molecule; in organic molecules, more is necessary. Thus, dimethyl ether has the formula C_2H_6O, just as ethyl alcohol does, and yet the two are quite different in properties. Apparently, the atoms are arranged differently within the molecules—but how to determine the arrangements?

In 1852, an English chemist, Edward Frankland, had noticed that the atoms of a particular element tended to combine with a fixed number of other atoms. This combining number was called "valence." Kekule in 1858 reduced this notion to a system. The carbon atom, he decided (on the basis of plenty of chemical evidence) had a valence of four; the hydrogen atom, a valence of one; and the oxygen atom, a valence of two (and so on).

Why not represent the atoms as their symbols plus a number of attached dashes, that number being equal to the valence. Such atoms could then be put together as though they were so many Tinker Toy units and "structural formulas" could be built up.

It was possible to reason out that the structural formula of ethyl alcohol was

$$
\begin{array}{ccc}
\text{H} & \text{H} & \\
| & | & \\
\text{H--C--C--O--H,} \\
| & | & \\
\text{H} & \text{H} &
\end{array}
$$

while that of dimethyl ether was

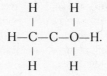

In each case, there were two carbon atoms, each with four dashes attached; six hydrogen atoms, each with one dash attached; and an oxygen atom with two dashes attached. The molecules were built up of the same components, but in different arrangements.

Kekule's theory worked beautifully. It has been immensely deepened and elaborated since his day, but you can still find structures very much like Kekule's Tinker Toy formulas in any modern chemical textbook. They represent oversimplifications of the true situation, but they remain extremely useful in practice even so.

The Kekule structures were applied to many organic molecules in the years after 1858 and the similarities and contrasts in the structures neatly matched similarities and contrasts in properties. The key to the rationalization of organic chemistry had, it seemed, been found.

Yet there was one disturbing fact. The well-known chemical benzene wouldn't fit. It was known to have a molecule made up of equal numbers of carbon and hydrogen atoms. Its molecular weight was known to be 78 and a single carbon-hydrogen combination had a weight of 13. Therefore, the benzene molecule had to contain six carbon-hydrogen combinations and its formula had to be C_6H_6.

But that meant trouble. By the Kekule formulas, the hydrocarbons (molecules made up of carbon and hydrogen atoms only) could easily be envisioned as chains of carbon atoms with hydrogen atoms attached. If all the valences of the carbon atoms were filled with hydrogen atoms, as in "hexane," whose molecule looks like this—

$$
\begin{array}{ccccccc}
\text{H} & \text{H} & \text{H} & \text{H} & \text{H} & \text{H} \\
| & | & | & | & | & | \\
\text{H--C--C--C--C--C--C--H} \\
| & | & | & | & | & | \\
\text{H} & \text{H} & \text{H} & \text{H} & \text{H} & \text{H}
\end{array}
$$

the compound is said to be saturated. Such saturated hydrocarbons were found to have very little tendency to react with other substances.

If some of the valences were not filled, unused bonds were added to those connecting the carbon atoms. Double bonds were formed as in "hexene"—

```
     H   H   H   H   H   H
     |   |   |   |   |   |
 H—C—C—C = C—C—C—H
     |   |           |   |
     H   H           H   H
```

Hexene is unsaturated, for that double bond has a tendency to open up and add other atoms. Hexene is chemically active.

When six carbons are present in a molecule, it takes fourteen hydrogen atoms to occupy all the valence bonds and make it inert—as in hexane. In hexene, on the other hand, there are only twelve hydrogens. If there were still fewer hydrogen atoms, there would be more than one double bond; there might even be triple bonds, and the compound would be still more active than hexene.

Yet benzene, which is C_6H_6 and has eight fewer hydrogen atoms than hexane, is *less* active than hexene, which has only two fewer hydrogen atoms than hexane. In fact, benzene is even less active than hexane itself. The six hydrogen atoms in the benzene molecule seem to satisfy the six carbon atoms to a greater extent than do the fourteen hydrogen atoms in hexane.

For heaven's sake, why?

This might seem unimportant. The Kekule formulas were so beautifully suitable in the case of so many compounds that one might simply dismiss benzene as an exception to the general rule.

Science, however, is not English grammar. You can't just categorize something as an exception. If the exception doesn't fit into the general system, then the general system must be wrong.

Or, take the more positive approach. An exception can often be made to fit into a general system, provided the general system is broadened. Such broadening generally represents a great advance and for this reason, exceptions ought to be paid great attention.

For some seven years, Kekule faced the problem of benzene and tried to puzzle out how a chain of six carbon atoms could be completely satisfied with as few as six hydrogen atoms in benzene and yet be left unsatisfied with twelve hydrogen atoms in hexene.

Nothing came to him!

And then one day in 1865 (he tells the story himself) he was in Ghent, Belgium, and in order to get to some destination, he boarded a public bus. He was tired and, undoubtedly, the droning beat of the horses' hooves on the cobblestones, lulled him. He fell into a comatose half-sleep.

In that sleep, he seemed to see a vision of atoms attaching themselves to each other in chains that moved about. (Why not? It was the sort of thing that constantly occupied his waking thoughts.) But then one chain twisted in such a way that head and tail joined, forming a ring—and Kekule woke with a start.

To himself, he must surely have shouted "Eureka," for indeed he had it. The six carbon atoms of benzene formed a ring and not a chain, so that the structural formula looked like this:

$$
\begin{array}{c}
\text{H} \\
| \\
\text{H}-\text{C} \quad\diagdown\quad \text{C} \quad=\quad \text{C}-\text{H} \\
\quad\quad \text{C} \\
\| \\
\text{H}-\text{C} \quad\quad \text{C}-\text{H} \\
\diagdown\quad \text{C} \quad=\quad \text{C} \diagup \\
| \\
\text{H}
\end{array}
$$

To be sure, there were still three double bonds, so you might think the molecule had to be very active—but now there was a difference. Atoms in a ring might be expected to have different properties from those in a chain and double bonds in one case might not have the properties of those in the other. At least, chemists could work on that assumption and see if it involved them in contradictions.

It didn't. The assumption worked excellently well. It turned out that organic molecules could be divided into two groups: aromatic and aliphatic. The former had the benzene ring (or certain other similar rings) as part of the structure and the latter did not. Allowing for different properties within each group, the Kekule structures worked very well.

For nearly seventy years, Kekule's vision held good in the hard field of actual chemical techniques, guiding the chemist through the jungle of reactions that led to the synthesis of more and more molecules. Then, in 1932, Linus Pauling applied quantum mechanics to chemical structure with sufficient subtlety to explain just why the benzene ring was so special and what had proven correct in practice proved correct in theory as well.

Other cases? Certainly.

In 1764, the Scottish engineer James Watt was working as an instrument maker for the University of Glasgow. The university gave him a model of a Newcomen steam engine, which didn't work well, and asked him to fix it. Watt fixed it without trouble, but even when it worked perfectly, it didn't work well. It was far too inefficient and consumed incredible quantities of fuel. Was there a way to improve that?

Thought didn't help; but a peaceful, relaxed walk on a Sunday after-noon did. Watt returned with the key notion in mind of using two separate chambers, one for steam only and one for cold water only, so that the same chamber did not have to be constantly cooled and reheated to the infinite waste of fuel.

The Irish mathematician William Rowan Hamilton worked up a theory of "quaternions" in 1843 but couldn't complete that theory until he grasped the fact that there were conditions under which $p \times q$ was not equal to $q \times p$. The necessary thought came to him in a flash one time when he was walking to town with his wife.

The German physiologist Otto Loewi was working on the mechanism of nerve action, in particular, on the chemicals produced by nerve end-ings. He awoke at 3 A.M. one night in 1921 with a perfectly clear notion of the type of experiment he would have to run to settle a key point that was puzzling him. He wrote it down and went back to sleep. When he woke in the morning, he found he couldn't remember what his inspiration had been. He remembered he had written it down, but he couldn't read his writing.

The next night, he woke again at 3 A.M. with the clear thought once more in mind. This time, he didn't fool around. He got up, dressed himself, went straight to the laboratory and began work. By 5 A.M. he had proved his point and the consequences of his findings became important enough in later years so that in 1936 he received a share in the Nobel prize in medicine and physiology.

How very often this sort of thing must happen, and what a shame that scientists are so devoted to their belief in conscious thought that they so consistently obscure the actual methods by which they obtain their results.

1971

QUESTIONS

1. *Does Asimov argue that science ought to abandon reasoned thought in favor of intuition?*
2. *What does Asimov find wrong about scientific reports as they are customarily written? Do you agree? If scientific writing were not strictly reasonable wouldn't there be a danger of misrepresenting science?*
3. *Is cultivation of "the Eureka phenomenon" encouraged in any of the science courses you may have taken or are now taking? Why, or why not?*
4. *Have you ever experienced anything like "the Eureka phenomenon" Asimov describes? If so, write out an account of what happened. Tell*

*what your feelings were when the phenomenon occurred. Did you
ever report the discovery in just that way to any one else (to a teacher,
for example)? If so, what was the other person's response?*
5. *In the preceding essay J. Bronowski discusses imagination and science.
Are there points on which Asimov and Bronowski would seem to be in
agreement concerning science?*

William James

THE ETHICAL AND PEDAGOGICAL
IMPORTANCE OF THE PRINCIPLE OF HABIT

"Habit a second nature! Habit is ten times nature," the Duke of
Wellington is said to have exclaimed; and the degree to which this is true
no one probably can appreciate as well as one who is a veteran soldier
himself. The daily drill and the years of discipline end by fashioning a
man completely over again, as to most of the possibilities of his conduct.

"There is a story," says Prof. Huxley, "which is credible enough,
though it may not be true, of a practical joker who, seeing a discharged
veteran carrying home his dinner, suddenly called out, 'Attention!'
whereupon the man instantly brought his hands down, and lost his
mutton and potatoes in the gutter. The drill had been thorough, and its
effects had become embodied in the man's nervous structure."

Riderless cavalry-horses, at many a battle, have been seen to come
together and go through their customary evolutions at the sound of the
bugle-call. Most domestic beasts seem machines almost pure and simple,
undoubtingly, unhesitatingly doing from minute to minute the duties
they have been taught, and giving no sign that the possibility of an
alternative ever suggests itself to their mind. Men grown old in prison
have asked to be readmitted after being once set free. In a railroad
accident a menagerie-tiger, whose cage had broken open, is said to have
emerged, but presently crept back again, as if too much bewildered by his
new responsibilities, so that he was without difficulty secured.

Habit is thus the enormous fly-wheel of society, its most precious
conservative agent. It alone is what keeps us all within the bounds of
ordinance, and saves the children of fortune from the envious uprisings of
the poor. It alone prevents the hardest and most repulsive walks of life
from being deserted by those brought up to tread therein. It keeps the
fisherman and the deck-hand at sea through the winter; it holds the miner
in his darkness, and nails the countryman to his log-cabin and his lonely
farm through all the months of snow; it protects us from invasion by the

natives of the desert and the frozen zone. It dooms us all to fight out the battle of life upon the lines of our nurture or our early choice, and to make the best of a pursuit that disagrees, because there is no other for which we are fitted, and it is too late to begin again. It keeps different social strata from mixing. Already at the age of twenty-five you see the professional mannerism settling down on the young commercial traveler, on the young doctor, on the young minister, on the young counselor-at-law. You see the little lines of cleavage running through the character, the tricks of thought, the prejudices, the ways of the "shop," in a word, from which the man can by-and-by no more escape than his coat-sleeve can suddenly fall into a new set of folds. On the whole, it is best he should not escape. It is well for the world that in most of us, by the age of thirty, the character has set like plaster, and will never soften again.

If the period between twenty and thirty is the critical one in the formation of intellectual and professional habits, the period below twenty is more important still for the fixings of *personal* habits, properly so called, such as a vocalization and pronunciation, gesture, motion, and address. Hardly ever is a language learned after twenty spoken without a foreign accent; hardly ever can a youth transferred to the society of his betters unlearn the nasality and other vices of speech bred in him by the associations of his growing years. Hardly ever, indeed, no matter how much money there be in his pocket, can he even learn to *dress* like a gentleman-born. The merchants offer their wares as eagerly to him as to the veriest "swell," but he simply *cannot* buy the right things. An invisible law, as strong as gravitation, keeps him within his orbit, arrayed this year as he was the last; and how his better-clad acquaintances contrive to get the things they wear will be for him a mystery till his dying day.

The great thing, then, in all education, is to *make our nervous system our ally instead of our enemy.* It is to fund and capitalize our acquisitions, and live at ease upon the interest of the fund. *For this we must make automatic and habitual, as early as possible, as many useful actions as we can,* and guard against the growing into ways that are likely to be disadvantageous to us, as we should guard against the plague. The more of the details of our daily life we can hand over to the effortless custody of automatism, the more our higher powers of mind will be set free for their own proper work. There is no more miserable human being than one in whom nothing is habitual but indecision, and for whom the lighting of every cigar, the drinking of every cup, the time of rising and going to bed every day, and the beginning of every bit of work, are subjects of express volitional deliberation. Full half the time of such a man goes to the deciding, or regretting, of matters which ought to be so ingrained in him as practically not to exist for his consciousness at all. If there be such daily duties not yet ingrained in any one of my readers, let him begin this very hour to set the matter right.

In Professor Bain's chapter on "The Moral Habits" there are some admirable practical remarks laid down. Two great maxims emerge from his treatment. The first is that in the acquisition of a new habit, or the leaving off of an old one, we must take care to *launch ourselves with as strong and decided an initiative as possible.* Accumulate all the possible circumstances which shall re-enforce the right motives; put yourself assiduously in conditions that encourage the new way; make engagements incompatible with the old; take a public pledge, if the case allows; in short, envelop your resolution with every aid you know. This will give your new beginning such a momentum that the temptation to break down will not occur as soon as it otherwise might; and every day during which a breakdown is postponed adds to the chances of its not occurring at all.

The second maxim is: *Never suffer an exception to occur till the new habit is securely rooted in your life.* Each lapse is like the letting fall of a ball of string which one is carefully winding up; a single slip undoes more than a great many turns will wind again. *Continuity* of training is the great means of making the nervous system act infallibly right. As Professor Bain says:

"The peculiarity of the moral habits, contradistinguishing them from the intellectual acquisitions, is the presence of two hostile powers, one to be gradually raised into the ascendant over the other. It is necessary, above all things, in such a situation, never to lose a battle. Every gain on the wrong side undoes the effect of many conquests on the right. The essential precaution, therefore, is so to regulate the two opposing powers that the one may have a series of uninterrupted successes, until repetition has fortified it to such a degree as to enable it to cope with the opposition, under any circumstances. This is the theoretically best career of mental progress."

The need of securing success at the *outset* is imperative. Failure at first is apt to damp the energy of all future attempts, whereas past experiences of success nerve one to future vigor. Goethe says to a man who consulted him about an enterprise but mistrusted his own powers: "Ach! you need only blow on your hands!" And the remark illustrates the effect on Goethe's spirits of his own habitually successful career.

The question of "tapering off," in abandoning such habits as drink and opium-indulgence comes in here, and is a question about which experts differ within certain limits, and in regard to what may be best for an individual case. In the main, however, all expert opinion would agree that abrupt acquisition of the new habit is the best way, *if there be a real possibility of carrying it out.* We must be careful not to give the will so stiff a task as to insure its defeat at the very outset; but, *provided one can stand it,* a sharp period of suffering, and then a free time, is the best thing to aim at, whether in giving up a habit like that of opium, or in simply changing one's hours of rising or of work. It is surprising how soon a desire will die of inanition if it be never fed.

> One must first learn, unmoved, looking neither to the right nor left, to walk firmly on the strait and narrow path, before one can begin "to make one's self over again." He who every day makes a fresh resolve is like one who, arriving at the edge of the ditch he is to leap, forever stops and returns for a fresh run. Without *unbroken* advance there is no such thing as *accumulation* of the ethical forces possible, and to make this possible, and to exercise us and habituate us in it, is the sovereign blessing of regular work. [J. Bahnsen]

A third maxim may be added to the preceding pair: *Seize the very first possible opportunity to act on every resolution you make, and on every emotional prompting you may experience in the direction of the habits you aspire to gain.* It is not in the moment of their forming, but in the moment of their producing *motor effects*, that resolves and aspirations communicate the new "set" to the brain. As the author last quoted remarks:

> The actual presence of the practical opportunity alone furnishes the fulcrum upon which the lever can rest, by means of which the moral will may multiply its strength, and raise itself aloft. He who has no solid ground to press against will never get beyond the stage of empty gesture-making.

No matter how full a reservoir of *maxims* one may possess, and no matter how good one's *sentiments* may be, if one have not taken advantage of every concrete opportunity to *act*, one's character may remain entirely unaffected for the better. With mere good intentions, hell is proverbially paved. And this is an obvious consequence of the principles we have laid down. A "character," as J. S. Mill says, "is a completely fashioned will"; and a will, in the sense in which he means it, is an aggregate of tendencies to act in a firm and prompt and definite way upon all the principal emergencies of life. A tendency to act only becomes effectively ingrained in us in proportion to the uninterrupted frequency with which the actions actually occur, and the brain "grows" to their use. When a resolve or a fine glow of feeling is allowed to evaporate without bearing practical fruit it is worse than a chance lost; it works so as positively to hinder future resolutions and emotions from taking the normal path of discharge. There is no more contemptible type of human character than that of the nerveless sentimentalist and dreamer, who spends his life in a weltering sea of sensibility and emotion, but who never does a manly concrete deed. Rousseau, inflaming all the mothers of France, by his eloquence, to follow Nature and nurse their babies themselves, while he sends his own children to the foundling hospital,[1] is the classical example of what I mean. But every one of us in his measure, whenever, after glowing for an abstractly formulated Good, he practi-

---

1. An institution for children abandoned by their parents. Rousseau's five children were born out of wedlock.

cally ignores some actual case, among the squalid "other particulars" of which that same Good lurks disguised, treads straight on Rousseau's path. All Goods are disguised by the vulgarity of their concomitants, in this work-a-day world; but woe to him who can only recognize them when he thinks them in their pure and abstract form! The habit of excessive novel-reading and theater-going will produce true monsters in this line. The weeping of the Russian lady over the fictitious personages in the play, while her coachman is freezing to death on his seat outside, is the sort of thing that everywhere happens on a less glaring scale. Even the habit of excessive indulgence in music, for those who are neither performers themselves nor musically gifted enough to take it in a purely intellectual way, has probably a relaxing effect upon the character. One becomes filled with emotions which habitually pass without prompting to any deed, and so the inertly sentimental condition is kept up. The remedy would be, never to suffer one's self to have an emotion at a concert, without expressing it afterward in some active way. Let the expression be the least thing in the world—speaking genially to one's grandmother, or giving up one's seat in a horse-car, if nothing more heroic offers—but let it not fail to take place.

These latter cases make us aware that it is not simply *particular lines* of discharge, but also *general forms* of discharge, that seem to be grooved out by habit in the brain. Just as, if we let our emotions evaporate, they get into a way of evaporating; so there is reason to suppose that if we often flinch from making an effort, before we know it the effort-making capacity will be gone; and that, if we suffer the wandering of our attention, presently it will wander all the time. Attention and effort are, as we shall see later, but two names for the same psychic fact. To what brain-processes they correspond we do not know. The strongest reason for believing that they do depend on brain-processes at all, and are not pure acts of the spirit, is just this fact, that they seem in some degree subject to the law of habit, which is a material law. As a final practical maxim, relative to these habits of the will, we may, then, offer something like this: *Keep the faculty of effort alive in you by a little gratuitous exercise every day.* That is, be systematically ascetic or heroic in little unneces-sary points, do every day or two something for no other reason than that you would rather not do it, so that when the hour of dire need draws nigh, it may find you not unnerved and untrained to stand the test. Ascetism of this sort is like the insurance which a man pays on his house and goods. The tax does him no good at the time, and possibly may never bring him a return. But if the fire *does* come, his having paid it will be his salvation from ruin. So with the man who has daily inured himself to habits of concentrated attention, energetic volition, and self-denial in unnecessary things. He will stand like a tower when everything rocks around him, and when his softer fellow-mortals are winnowed like chaff in the blast.

The physiological study of mental conditions is thus the most powerful ally of hortatory ethics. The hell to be endured hereafter, of which theology tells, is no worse than the hell we make for ourselves in this world by habitually fashioning our characters in the wrong way. Could the young but realize how soon they will become mere walking bundles of habits, they would give more heed to their conduct while in the plastic state. We are spinning our own fates, good or evil, and never to be undone. Every smallest stroke of virtue or of vice leaves its never so little scar. The drunken Rip Van Winkle, in Jefferson's play, excuses himself for every fresh dereliction by saying, "I won't count this time!" Well! he may not count it, and a kind Heaven may not count it; but it is being counted none the less. Down among his nerve cells and fibres the molecules are counting it, registering and storing it up to be used against him when the next temptation comes. Nothing we ever do is, in strict scientific literalness, wiped out. Of course this has its good side as well as its bad one. As we become permanent drunkards by so many separate drinks, so we become saints in the moral, and authorities and experts in the practical and scientific spheres, by so many separate acts and hours of work. Let no youth have any anxiety about the upshot of his education, whatever the line of it may be. If he keep faithfully busy each hour of the working day, he may safely leave the final result to itself. He can with perfect certainty count on waking up some fine morning, to find himself one of the competent ones of his generation, in whatever pursuit he may have singled out. Silently, between all the details of his business, the power of judging in all that class of matter will have built itself up within him as a possession that will never pass away. Young people should know this truth in advance. The ignorance of it has probably engendered more discouragement and faint-heartedness in youths embarking on arduous careers than all other causes put together.

1890

QUESTIONS

1. *What, according to James, is the utility of habit for society? For the individual person?*
2. *Will conformity result from cultivating habits according to the maxims here presented?*
3. *Does your own experience appear to prove or disprove the maxims James presents? All, or some?*
4. *James and Milgram ("The Perils of Obedience," p. 642) are both psychologists. Do they appear to be working in similar ways? If dissimilar, how do you explain the difference? Is one more scientific than the other? How do the two pieces of writing compare as to subject, method of presentation, assumptions, purpose, style?*

Education

Austin Clarke

A SCHOOLBOY IN BARBADOS

* * *

I was admitted to Combermere School, a secondary school in Barbados, on Roebuck Street, in Town, in September 1944, and placed in the "L2D," the Lower Second Form, with thirty other boys. For all these years, I have been wondering whether the "D" in L2D stood for "dunce." And nobody so far has told me.

But that was a day of personal rejoicing for my mother. She had at last achieved something beyond the expectations of the village. The village of St. Matthias rejoiced with her on that day. The poor and ambitious mothers gave me their blessing, and in their stern and frightening voices, they said, "Go 'long, boy, and *learn*! Learning going make you into a man."

And Delcina, the tallest, blackest and most beautiful woman I had ever seen, smiled and broke into a hymn. She lifted her operatic voice, trained in the hot broiling sun, as she bent over tubs of many sheets and shirts, with her black hands in the heavy soap suds, for the rich *out the front road*, and she sang on that morning. The washing, white as snow and ironed like glass, would be carried later in the week to the Marine Hotel.

Delcina sang a beautiful hymn that morning as I walked down the gap from my house on my way to a new but uncertain world. Delcina sang, "O God, Our Help in Ages Past." My book bag was filled with books of interminable pages, with puzzles of new knowledge undreamed of by my mother and by anybody else in the village. There was the shining gold-painted set that contained the compasses; the Rankin biscuit tin, scrubbed clean and looking like a small silver coffin, with a flying-fish sandwich in it; and my Ferrol bottle of "clear" lemonade, without the label on it.

On the previous Sunday, one of the "uncles" in that vicious circle of men, with a pair of scissors and a broken glass-bottle for a razor, had sat me down on the throne of a chair, under the clammy-cherry tree, and when I got up, my head was *clean*.

"Don't mind them few scratches and bumps I had to leave round the back of your head, boy. You is a Combermere boy now!"

The finished product had the impact and the look of a bowl on your head, and all the visible hair wiped clean away with soap and water by the blade of the glass-bottle. The smell of Limacol was strong even as I entered the large iron gate of Combermere School on that shaking, quivering morning, grabbed by the hand by my equally scared mother.

Combermere School was for middle- and lower middle-class boys. It was a second grade school. It would turn me into a civil servant, if I did well. If I didn't do well, it would turn me into a sanitary inspector. If I did even worse than that, into a "bookkeeper" on one of the many sugar plantations, to ride about on a horse in the sun, under a khaki helmet, dressed in a khaki suit, to drive some of my less fortunate friends and neighbours to work in the fields.

In those days the prospect of the sanitary inspector appealed more to me. I had seen them flitting about the village like black mosquitoes, a ladle in their hands, dipping into people's drinking water buckets and pigs' urinals, and pronouncing ruin and plague and pestilence at the sight of *larvees*; and having more drinks than doing work. That kind of drama and tragedy impressed me. I was at the beginning of having a choice in life.

But to be a civil servant, that was beyond my wildest dreams! Could I be like one of those powerful young men, walking up and down the corridor of the Old Public Buildings on the second and third floors, with huge important files of all colours—blue, red, white, faded and musty —dressed in white shirts and ties like the white Colonial officers who ruled and ran the country and who had the knack of looking important?

"Not on your blasted bottom dollar!" my mother said, imagining greater things. "I want you to be a *doctor*, hear?"

To be a doctor in those days, you had to know Latin backwards and forwards. You had to be a "Latin fool." *Amas, amat* and *amamus* would be the only things to save me from the hot sun of the bookkeeper; from the *larvees* of the sanitary inspector, dressed like a soldier of health; and from the low salary of the civil servant.

The other possibility was to be an elementary school teacher. But you had to have brains, and slightly more patience than brains if you wanted to be a school teacher; and you had to love children—and even more, lower wages. I was tempted by my own dreams to settle for the *amo amas amat*.

On that terrifying morning, ignorant of the meaning of higher education, and of Combermere School for Boys, and big books, and foreign languages of Latin and French, I waited in the hall with the other one hundred new boys, all of us stiff in our new khaki uniforms, clean heads, new ties of blue and gold which were the school colours, and which choked us; with our book bags made of blue denim, some of leather boasting the goodwill of a "relative" who lived Away, meaning most likely America. Our bags were filled with heavy books priced at more than most of our parents earned in a month. To those of us who did not win scholarships or receive government bursaries, the tuition fees were the devastating amount of eight dollars a term, which lasted three months. But Combermere meant we were to be the new leaders of the country, and members of the Barbados middle class.

The headmaster was a Santa Claus of a man. A man of the cloth. He was bull-frogged and deep-voiced, but lovable as a cherub; a man who liked cricket, and who would take your ability to play it into consideration when you were sent to him for a flogging. The Reverend A. E. Armstrong, BA (Durham), MA (Someplace). In our unexplained tradition of giving almost every living person a nickname, he was known as "The Buff." We called him The Buff behind his back, naturally; and we tipped our caps in his white-suited presence and called him "Sir!"

During my first term, I never came within his Church-of-England presence; never sat at his feet, for he taught Scripture in the first form, and Latin in the higher forms; and I was in L2D. But at the end of that first year, before he left for retirement and England, I was "sent" to him for a flogging. I had to stand on the long wooden bench in front of his office. And while I waited for him, I wilted with uncertainty from the rumours about his strength and cruelty and dexterity with a tamarind rod. All the time, smaller boys, big boys, the school prefects and the master who had "sent" me paused and jeered and "skinned" their teeth at me, imitating the rod of The Buff's justice "in your arse!"

After one academic year, I was old enough and wise in the ways of the school to know that I should shriek with pain even before the first blow landed on my starched khaki trousers. For my offence—making a whistling sound with a mechanical pencil my friend Kenny had received from his mother in America—I could get three lashes.

But this was nothing like the flogging orgies I had witnessed and sometimes suffered through at my previous school, St. Matthias Boys' School. There the headmaster used the belt from a sewing machine. Rumour was that he soaked it in pee every night. And during the long hot afternoons he walked throughout his empire of benches and blackboards and "desses," with the whip hanging around his neck like a dead black snake.

In comparison, the Reverend Armstrong, a man of great theological tolerance and knowledge, close to the altar and the communion cup, was a saint.

"Clarke!"

His voice was like large stones in a deep bucket. It was an authoritarian English voice. The water had already settled in my eyes. My body was waiting for the explosion of the rod. All I had to do now was scream so loud that the Reverend's understanding of Christian love and charity and pity would freeze his hand or lighten the blow; and he would say, "Dismiss, Clarke!"

"Bend over!" he said instead. The voice was still hoarse.

Wap!

"Go!"

And I left, laughing to myself the moment I was out of sight; eager again to dare the form master, and reassure the boys, "Man, The Buff can't lick, in truth! I didn't feel nothing . . . " And then to be welcomed back into the class as a hero, as a "bad boy."

One morning at St. Matthias the sun was already hot, although it was only nine o'clock. The perspiration was mixing with the coconut oil or the Brilliantine or vaseline which we wore on our hair. When I reached the school gate, and bolted to the entrance of the school, crossing the yard which had no grass, which never had any grass, and up the single step, when I reached the front door that morning, the headmaster was already there. Something had happened. Something was going to happen. The entire school of two hundred boys were singing "Rock of Ages." They had reached the last verse. But the headmaster loved singing and loved that song. He delighted in leading the bass section among his teachers: tenors, altos and less profundo basses; and so the hymn had to be sung from the beginning again. He could sing a hymn or a song ten times.

I stood at the door. Five other boys who were late stood silently beside me. We were three minutes late. The headmaster accepted no excuses. Once a boy told him, "Please, sir, I had was to go 'cross the road five times to bring water for my mother and for the sheeps, 'cause my mother sick with badfeels." The headmaster listened carefully and patiently. In our hearts we cheered for the little boy. There could be no better excuse. But when the confession was over, the pee-soaked black snake was wrapped six times across the boy's back, like the Cross of St. Andrew. And when it was over, four of us had to carry the boy out like a casualty, to the pipe across the school yard, and wash the faeces from his legs and pants. We all swore then, as we stood under the pipe, in the frightened secrecy of our hearts, to soon become men, strong men, and come back for the headmaster with a bull-pistle whip.

This morning I stood at the door, facing the Union Jack. It was pinned against the wall below the grandfather clock, which the headmaster wound every morning with a key he kept in his pocket. Once he asked me to wind the clock, and I knew that something had happened to me, and certainly to him. The boys were now singing "O God, Our Help in Ages Past." The voices were beautiful. Some of these voices belonged in the choir of the church which was separated from our school by a thick wall. It was made of stone and marl and lime and dust, and it covered our hands each time we jumped over it to steal the almonds which grew in the church yard. Now the school had become a church.

The hymn had come to an end. The school became very quiet. I could imagine the vicar walking up the aisle with the choir. It was still, like the hour before the school inspector was due to arrive and inspect our progress to send his report and our results back to England.

The headmaster wore white. He always wore white. He wore white as if it meant something which we boys could never aspire to; and he wore a tie that had no tropical colour in it. Around the knot he wore a pure, real, "true-true gold" ring, as the boys said. He walked like a tall black king, from the bottom of the one-room school right up to the platform. He held the bell, a dinner bell in size to the larger brown one which summoned the beginning of classes, and he touched its tongue with a finger.

But the school was already at attention. Nobody was breathing, including his teachers, who feared him as we trembled in his presence. From his side pocket he took a black object, something that looked like a huge hairpin. It was his tuning fork. He struck it against the desk, and it spoke the correct note and pitch he wanted. He hummed, "Do, re, me, faaaaaa!" In his youth he had won competitions for his voice. He struck the tuning fork again, and listened to its hum, and again he hummed, "Do, re, me, faaa."

"'Ride on'!" he said, announcing the hymn. When he announced hymns and sang the first few lines, he was calm and loving and like a choir master. He loved singing hymns, and he transferred some of that love on to us.

But this morning he rushed from the platform and in three strides reached the door where we were standing. He became like a giant. So we galloped into the hymn "Ride on, ride on, in Majesty," careful to let him know that we loved singing, and that we knew the words.

He was towering above us now. The long desk at the back was cleared of exercise books, nib pens, pencil boxes and boys. It looked clean, cleared away like a tribunal or a scaffold.

The entire school and the teachers were singing at the top of their voices.

> Ride on, ride on, in Majesty!
> In lowly pomp ride on to die . . .

"Fingers!" he said to the six of us at the door.

The boy at the head of the line held out his hands. The headmaster inspected his fingers and nails. They were dirty. They were always dirty.

We always had dirty fingernails. Not one of us in that school had ever held a nail file in our hands. They were not common in our village. When the time came, we cleaned our fingers with a stick.

We pitched marbles morning, noon and night, and our nails bore that evidence. He knew they were dirty; he knew they would always be dirty; that not one of the six of us in the late line would remember to use the stick. We seemed to want the inspection and the punishment.

He held the boy's ear and looked inside it, and then the other. Then he pushed him gently aside, like an approved piece of merchandise. And he inspected the rest of us, and pushed us aside. We were now thinking of the brimstone and ashes of his fierce temperament. And in all this time, the school was singing, like a choir of a cathedral, at the top of their voices.

> Ride on, ride on, in Majesty!
> The last and fiercest strife in nigh . . .

He threw the black snake across the neck of the boy nearest him. Then he was flogging all six of us at the same time, across our backs, our heads, our feet as we jumped in stupid attempts to avoid the snake, criss-crossing, horizontal, diagonal, like the various crosses in the English flag and in the flags of other countries he had taught us about in classes of social history. We smelled his chalk. We smelled his breath. And we could hear from that close, chilling distance the deep profundo of his voice, for as he flogged us he was singing along with the teachers and the rest of the school, singing and flogging with the pre-soaked, pee-soaked fan belt from his wife's sewing machine.

> Look down with sad and wondering eyes
> To see the approaching Sacrifice.

And when it was over, when we had come galloping and exhausted and *whemmed* to the end of the hymn, and he was perspiring, his black skin jewelled with beads, he touched the tongue of the dinner bell and silence reigned.

* * *

1980

John Holt

HOW TEACHERS MAKE CHILDREN
HATE READING

When I was teaching English at the Colorado Rocky Mountain School, I used to ask my students the kinds of questions that English teachers usually ask about reading assignments—questions designed to bring out the points that *I* had decided *they* should know. They, on their part, would try to get me to give them hints and clues as to what I wanted. It was a game of wits. I never gave my students an opportunity to say what they really thought about a book.

I gave vocabulary drills and quizzes too. I told my students that every time they came upon a word in their book they did not understand, they were to look it up in the dictionary. I even devised special kinds of vocabulary tests, allowing them to use their books to see how the words were used. But looking back, I realize that these tests, along with many of my methods, were foolish.

My sister was the first person who made me question my conventional ideas about teaching English. She had a son in the seventh grade in a fairly good public school. His teacher had asked the class to read Cooper's *The Deerslayer*. The choice was bad enough in itself; whether looking at man or nature, Cooper was superficial, inaccurate and sentimental, and his writing is ponderous and ornate. But to make matters worse, this teacher had decided to give the book the microscope and x-ray treatment. He made the students look up and memorize not only the definitions but the derivations of every big word that came along—and there were plenty. Every chapter was followed by close questioning and testing to make sure the students "understood" everything.

Being then, as I said, conventional, I began to defend the teacher, who was a good friend of mine, against my sister's criticisms. The argument soon grew hot. What was wrong with making sure that children understood everything they read? My sister answered that until this year her boy had always loved reading, and had read a lot on his own; now he had stopped. (He was not really to start again for many years.)

Still I persisted. If children didn't look up the words they didn't know, how would they ever learn them? My sister said, "Don't be silly! when you were little you had a huge vocabulary, and were always reading very grown-up books. When did you ever look up a word in a dictionary?"

She had me. I don't know that we had a dictionary at home; if we did, I didn't use it. I don't use one today. In my life I doubt that I have looked up as many as fifty words, perhaps not even half that.

Since then I have talked about this with a number of teachers. More than once I have said, "According to tests, educated and literate people like you have a vocabulary of about twenty-five thousand words. How many of these did you learn by looking them up in a dictionary?" They usually are startled. Few claim to have looked up even as many as a thousand. How did they learn the rest?

They learned them just as they learned to talk—by meeting words over and over again, in different contexts, until they saw how they fitted.

Unfortunately, we English teachers are easily hung up on this matter of understanding. Why should children understand everything they read? Why should anyone? Does anyone? I don't, and I never did. I was always reading books that teachers would have said were "too hard" for me, books full of words I didn't know. That's how I got to be a good reader. When about ten, I read all the D'Artagnan stories and loved them. It didn't trouble me in the least that I didn't know why France was at war with England or who was quarreling with whom in the French court or why the Musketeers should always be at odds with Cardinal Richelieu's men. I didn't even know who the Cardinal was, except that he was a dangerous and powerful man that my friends had to watch out for. This was all I needed to know.

Having said this, I will now say that I think a big, unabridged dictionary is a fine thing to have in any home or classroom. No book is more fun to browse around in—*if* you're not made to. Children, depending on their age, will find many pleasant and interesting things to do with a big dictionary. They can look up funny-sounding words, which they like, or words that nobody else in the class has ever heard of, which they like, or long words, which they like, or forbidden words, which they like best of all. At a certain age, and particularly with a little encouragement from parents or teachers, they may become very interested in where words came from and when they came into the language and how their meanings have changed over the years. But exploring for the fun of it is very different from looking up words out of your reading because you're going to get into trouble with your teacher if you don't.

While teaching fifth grade two years or so after the argument with my sister, I began to think again about reading. The children in my class were supposed to fill out a card—just the title and author and a one-sentence summary—for every book they read. I was not running a competition to see which child could read the most books, a competition that almost always leads to cheating. I just wanted to know what the children were reading. After a while it became clear that many of these very bright kids, from highly literate and even literary backgrounds, read very few books and deeply disliked reading. Why should this be?

At this time I was coming to realize, as I described in my book *How Children Fail*, that for most children school was a place of danger, and their main business in school was staying out of danger as much as possible. I now began to see also that books were among the most dangerous things in school.

From the very beginning of school we make books and reading a constant source of possible failure and public humiliation. When children are little we make them read aloud, before the teacher and other children, so that we can be sure they "know" all the words they are reading. This means that when they don't know a word, they are going to make a mistake, right in front of everyone. Instantly they are made to realize that they have done something wrong. Perhaps some of the other children will begin to wave their hands and say, "Ooooh! O-o-o-oh!" Perhaps they will just giggle, or nudge each other, or make a face. Perhaps the teacher will say, "Are you sure?" or ask someone else what he thinks. Or perhaps, if the teacher is kindly, she will just smile a sweet, sad smile—often one of the most painful punishments a child can suffer in school. In any case, the child who has made the mistake knows he has made it, and feels foolish, stupid, and ashamed, just as any of us would in his shoes.

Before long many children associate books and reading with mistakes, real or feared, and penalties and humiliation. This may not seem sensible, but it is natural. Mark Twain once said that a cat that sat on a hot stove lid would never sit on one again—but it would never sit on a cold one either. As true of children as of cats. If they, so to speak, sit on a hot book a few times, if books cause them humiliation and pain, they are likely to decide that the safest thing to do is to leave all books alone.

After having taught fifth-grade classes for four years I felt quite sure of this theory. In my next class were many children who had had great trouble with schoolwork, particularly reading. I decided to try at all costs to rid them of their fear and dislike of books, and to get them to read oftener and more adventurously.

One day soon after school had started, I said to them, "Now I'm going to say something about reading that you have probably never heard a teacher say before. I would like you to read a lot of books this year, but I want you to read them only for pleasure. I am not going to ask you questions to find out whether you understand the books or not. If you understand enough of a book to enjoy it and want to go on reading it, that's enough for me. Also I'm not going to ask you what words mean.

"Finally," I said, "I don't want you to feel that just because you start a book, you have to finish it. Give an author thirty or forty pages or so to get his story going. Then if you don't like the characters and don't care what happens to them, close the book, put it away, and get another. I don't care whether the books are easy or hard, short or long, as long as you enjoy them. Furthermore I'm putting all this in a letter to your parents, so they won't feel they have to quiz and heckle you about books at home."

The children sat stunned and silent. Was this a teacher talking? One

girl, who had just come to us from a school where she had had a very hard time, and who proved to be one of the most interesting, lively, and intelligent children I have ever known, looked at me steadily for a long time after I had finished. Then, still looking at me, she said slowly and solemnly, "Mr. Holt, do you really mean that?" I said just as solemnly, "I mean every word of it."

Apparently she decided to believe me. The first book she read was Dr. Seuss's *How the Grinch Stole Christmas*, not a hard book even for most third graders. For a while she read a number of books on this level. Perhaps she was clearing up some confusion about reading that her teachers, in their hurry to get her up to "grade level," had never given her enough time to clear up. After she had been in the class six weeks or so and we had become good friends, I very tentatively suggested that, since she was a skillful rider and loved horses, she might like to read *National Velvet*. I made my sell as soft as possible, saying only that it was about a girl who loved and rode horses, and that if she didn't like it, she could put it back. She tried it, and though she must have found it quite a bit harder than what she had been reading, finished it and liked it very much.

During the spring she really astonished me, however. One day, in one of our many free periods, she was reading at her desk. From a glimpse of the illustrations I thought I knew what the book was. I said to myself, "It can't be," and went to take a closer look. Sure enough, she was reading *Moby Dick*, in the edition with woodcuts by Rockwell Kent. When I came close to her desk she looked up. I said, "Are you really reading that?" She said she was. I said, "Do you like it?" She said, "Oh, yes, it's neat!" I said, "Don't you find parts of it rather heavy going?" She answered "Oh, sure, but I just skip over those parts and go on to the next good part."

This is exactly what reading should be and in school so seldom is—an exciting, joyous adventure. Find something, dive into it, take the good parts, skip the bad parts, get what you can out of it, go on to something else. How different is our mean-spirited, picky insistence that every child get every last little scrap of "understanding" that can be dug out of a book.

For teachers who really enjoy doing it, and will do it with gusto, reading aloud is a very good idea. I have found that not just fifth graders but even ninth and eleventh graders enjoy it. Jack London's "To Build a Fire" is a good read-aloud story. So are ghost stories, and "August Heat," by W. F. Harvey, and "The Monkey's Paw," by W. W. Jacobs, are among the best. Shirley Jackson's "The Lottery" is sure-fire, and will raise all kinds of questions for discussion and argument. Because of a TV program they had seen and that excited them, I once started reading my fifth graders William Golding's *Lord of the Flies*, thinking to read only a few chapters, but they made me read it to the end.

In my early fifth-grade classes the children usually were of high IQ, came from literate backgrounds and were generally felt to be succeeding in school. Yet it was astonishingly hard for most of those children to express themselves in speech or in writing. I have known a number of five-year-olds who were considerably more articulate than most of the fifth graders I have known in school. Asked to speak, my fifth graders were covered with embarrassment; many refused altogether. Asked to write, they would sit for minutes on end, staring at the paper. It was hard for most of them to get down a half page of writing, even on what seemed to be interesting topics or topics they chose themselves.

In desperation I hit on a device that I named the Composition Derby. I divided the class into teams, and told them that when I said, "Go," they were to start writing something. It could be about anything they wanted, but it had to be about something—they couldn't just write "dog dog dog dog" on the paper. It could be true stories, descriptions of people or places or events, wishes, made-up stories, dreams—anything they liked. Spelling didn't count, so they didn't have to worry about it. When I said, "Stop," they were to stop and count up the words they had written. The team that wrote the most words would win the derby.

It was a success in many ways and for many reasons. The first surprise was that the two children who consistently wrote the most words were two of the least successful students in the class. They were bright, but they had always had a very hard time in school. Both were very bad spellers, and worrying about this had slowed down their writing without improving their spelling. When they were free of this worry and could let themselves go, they found hidden and unsuspected talents.

One of the two, a very driven and anxious little boy, used to write long adventures, or misadventures, in which I was the central character —"The Day Mr. Holt Went to Jail," "The Day Mr. Holt Fell Into the Hole," "The Day Mr. Holt Got Run Over," and so on. These were very funny, and the class enjoyed hearing me read them aloud. One day I asked the class to write a derby on a topic I would give them. They groaned; they liked picking their own. "Wait till you hear it," I said. "It's 'The Day the School Burned Down.'"

With a shout of approval and joy they went to work, and wrote furiously for 20 minutes or more, laughing and chuckling as they wrote. The papers were all much alike; in them the children danced around the burning building, throwing in books and driving me and the other teachers back in when we tried to escape.

In our first derby the class wrote an average of about ten words a minute; after a few months their average was over 20. Some of the slower writers tripled their output. Even the slowest, one of whom was the best student in the class, were writing 15 words a minute. More important, almost all the children enjoyed the derbies and wrote interesting things.

Some time later I learned that Professor S. I. Hayakawa, teaching freshman English, had invented a better technique. Every day in class he asked his students to write without stopping for about half an hour. They could write on whatever topic or topics they chose, but the important thing was not to stop. If they ran dry, they were to copy their last sentence over and over again until new ideas came. Usually they came before the sentence had been copied once. I use this idea in my own classes, and call this kind of paper a Non-Stop. Sometimes I ask students to write a Non-Stop on an assigned topic, more often on anything they choose. Once in a while I ask them to count up how many words they have written, though I rarely ask them to tell me; it is for their own information. Sometimes these papers are to be handed in; often they are what I call private papers, for the students' eyes alone.

The private paper has proved very useful. In the first place, in any English class—certainly any large English class—if the amount the students write is limited by what the teacher can find time to correct, or even to read, the students will not write nearly enough. The only remedy is to have them write a great deal that the teacher does not read. In the second place, students writing for themselves will write about many things that they would never write on a paper to be handed in, once they have learned (sometimes it takes a while) that the teacher means what he says about the papers' being private. This is important, not just because it enables them to get things off their chest, but also because they are most likely to write well, and to pay attention to how they write, when they are writing about something important to them.

Some English teachers, when they first hear about private papers, object that students do not benefit from writing papers unless the papers are corrected. I disagree for several reasons. First, most students, particularly poor students, do not read the corrections on their papers; it is boring, even painful. Second, even when they do read these corrections, they do not get much help from them, do not build the teacher's suggestions into their writing. This is true even when they really believe the teacher knows what he is talking about.

Third, and most important, we learn to write by writing, not by reading other people's ideas about writing. What most students need above all else is practice in writing, and particularly in writing about things that matter to them, so that they will begin to feel the satisfaction that comes from getting important thoughts down in words and will care about stating these thoughts forcefully and clearly.

Teachers of English—or, as some schools say (ugh!), Language Arts —spend a lot of time and effort on spelling. Most of it is wasted; it does little good, and often more harm than good. We should ask ourselves, "How do good spellers spell? What do they do when they are not sure which spelling of a word is right?" I have asked this of a number of good spellers. Their answer never varies. They do not rush for a dictionary or rack their brains trying to remember some rules. They write down the word both ways, or several ways, look at them and pick the one that looks best. Usually they are right.

Good spellers know what words look like and even, in their writing muscles, feel like. They have a good set of word images in their minds, and are willing to trust these images. The things we do to "teach" spelling to children do little to develop these skills or talents, and much to destroy them or prevent them from developing.

The first and worst thing we do is to make children anxious about spelling. We treat a misspelled word like a crime and penalize the misspeller severely; many teachers talk of making children develop a "spelling conscience," and fail otherwise excellent papers because of a few spelling mistakes. This is self-defeating. When we are anxious, we don't perceive clearly or remember what we once perceived. Everyone knows how hard it is to recall even simple things when under emotional pressure; the harder we rack our brains, the less easy it is to find what we are looking for. If we are anxious enough, we will not trust the messages that memory sends us. Many children spell badly because although their first hunches about how to spell a word may be correct, they are afraid to trust them. I have often seen on children's papers a word correctly spelled, then crossed out and misspelled.

There are some tricks that might help children get sharper word images. Some teachers may be using them. One is the trick of air writing; that is, of "writing" a word in the air with a finger and "seeing" the image so formed. I did this quite a bit with fifth graders, using either the air or the top of a desk, on which their fingers left no mark. Many of them were tremendously excited by this. I can still hear them saying, "There's nothing there, but I can see it!" It seemed like black magic. I remember that when I was little I loved to write in the air. It was effortless, voluptuous, satisfying, and it was fun to see the word appear in the air. I used to write "Money Money Money," not so much because I didn't have any as because I liked the way it felt, particularly that y at the end, with its swooping tail.

Another thing to help sharpen children's image-making machinery is taking very quick looks at words—or other things. The conventional machine for doing this is the tachistoscope. But these are expensive, so expensive that most children can have few chances to use them, if any at all. With some three-by-five and four-by-eight file cards you can get the same effect. On the little cards you put the words or the pictures that the child is going to look at. You hold the larger card over the card to be read, uncover it for a split second with a quick wrist motion, then cover it up again. Thus you have a tachistoscope that costs one cent and that any child can work by himself.

Once when substituting in a first-grade class, I thought that the children, who were just beginning to read and write, might enjoy some of the kind of free, nonstop writing that my fifth graders had. One day about 40 minutes before lunch, I asked them all to take pencil and paper and start writing about anything they wanted to. They seemed to like the idea, but right away one child said anxiously, "Suppose we can't spell a word."

"Don't worry about it," I said. "Just spell it the best way you can."

A heavy silence settled on the room. All I could see were still pencils and anxious faces. This was clearly not the right approach. So I said, "All right, I'll tell you what we'll do. Any time you want to know how to spell a word, tell me and I'll write it on the board."

They breathed a sigh of relief and went to work. Soon requests for words were coming fast; as soon as I wrote one, someone asked me another. By lunchtime, when most of the children were still busily writing, the board was full. What was interesting was that most of the words they had asked for were much longer and more complicated than anything in their reading books or workbooks. Freed from worry about spelling, they were willing to use the most difficult and interesting words that they knew.

The words were still on the board when we began school next day. Before I began to erase them, I said to the children, "Listen, everyone. I have to erase these words, but before I do, just out of curiosity, I'd like to see if you remember some of them."

The result was surprising. I had expected that the child who had asked for and used a word might remember it, but I did not think many others would. But many of the children still knew many of the words. How had they learned them? I suppose each time I wrote a word on the board a number of children had looked up, relaxed yet curious, just to see what the word looked like, and these images and the sound of my voice saying the word had stuck in their minds until the next day. This, it seems to me, is how children may best learn to write and spell.

What can a parent do if a school, or a teacher, is spoiling the language for a child by teaching it in some tired way? First, try to get them to change, or at least let them know that you are eager for change. Talk to other parents; push some of these ideas in the PTA; talk to the English department at the school; talk to the child's own teacher. Many teachers and schools want to know what the parents want.

If the school or teacher cannot be persuaded, then what? Perhaps all you can do is try not to let your child become too bored or discouraged or worried by what is happening in school. Help him meet the school's demands, foolish though they may seem, and try to provide more interesting alternatives at home—plenty of books and conversation, and a serious and respectful audience when a child wants to talk. Nothing that ever happened to me in English classes at school was as helpful to me as the long conversations I used to have every summer with my uncle, who made me feel that the difference in our ages was not important and that he was really interested in what I had to say.

At the end of her freshman year in college a girl I know wrote home to her mother, "Hooray! Hooray! Just think—I never have to take English any more!" But this girl had always been an excellent English student, had always loved books, writing, ideas. It seems unnecessary and foolish and wrong that English teachers should so often take what should be the most flexible, exciting, and creative of all school courses and make it into something that most children can hardly wait to see the last of. Let's hope that we can and soon will begin to do much better.

1967

QUESTIONS

1. *What are the major indictments Holt makes and what alternatives does he propose?*
2. *Booth discusses various metaphors (including man as machine and man as animal) that underline different theories of education ("Is There Any Knowledge That a Man Must Have?," p. 293). Might Holt accept any of these metaphors? If Holt constructed a different metaphor of his own, what might it be?*
3. *Is the kind of teaching that Holt describes likely to lead to students' having the knowledge that Booth believes essential?*
4. *Here are two accounts of a young boy's going to school, the second a summary or précis of the first. Determine what has been removed from the original in the summary. Then write a short comparison of original and summary from Holt's educational point of view, as it can be inferred from his essay.*

> His days were rich in formal experience. Wearing overalls and an old sweater (the accepted uniform of the private seminary), he sallied forth at morn accompanied by a nurse or a parent and walked (or was pulled) two blocks to a corner where the school bus made a flag stop. This flashy vehicle was as punctual as death: seeing us waiting at the cold curb, it would sweep to a halt, open its mouth, suck the boy in, and spring away with an angry growl. It was a good deal like a train picking up a bag of mail. At school the scholar was worked on for six or seven hours by half a dozen teachers and a nurse, and was revived on orange juice in midmorning. In a cinder court he played games supervised by an athletic instructor, and in a cafeteria he ate lunch worked out by a dietitian.
>
> —E. B. White, "Education"

> His days followed a set routine. He wore overalls and an old sweater, as everyone else did in his school. In the morning, a parent or nurse walked the two blocks with him to the corner where he met the school bus. The bus was always on time. During the six or seven hours of the school day, he had six teachers. The school also employed a nurse and a dietitian. Games were

supervised. The children ate in the cafeteria. Orange juice was served during
the morning session.

—End-of-Year Examinations in English for college
bound students grades 9–12, Commission on English.

Ralph A. Raimi

OPIUM OF THE PEOPLE

My brother taught me to read and my parents taught me how to cross
the Detroit streets safely. With these two skills well established by the
time I was seven years old—this was 1931—I could with profit and safety
walk to the Main Branch of the Detroit Public Library each Saturday
morning.

Apart from the influence of my brother, and (naturally) of those librarians who had selected the holdings in the first place, my reading was
random. The library had been there for years; many tastes were represented. King Arthur, the Steadfast Tin Soldier, d'Artagnan and, as the
years wore on, tales of Copernicus and Louis Pasteur. I learned how it
was to have been a Plebe at West Point in 1902, and a classmate of
Hungry Smeed at Lawrenceville. Fu Manchu, Tarzan, Sorhab and Rus-
tam were equally real with Teddy Roosevelt and Robert of Sicily.

My choices had nothing to do with Education, which my parents and I
assumed was the province of the public schools I attended. Not until deep
into high school, and mainly later, did my recreational reading intersect
my formal education. Mostly they were in opposition. I would sometimes
read stealthily in class while a lesson was going on around me.

Self-teaching, with or without a brother, is bound to leave gaps. I didn't
hear of transubstantiation until college. Bad luck, that's all; if my hand
had plucked the right book from the shelf one Saturday morning, I might
have learned Sanskrit—who knows? I chose by color and title, and one
can aspire to only so much in the way of luck.

Surely one can hope for more in an organized school, especially a high
school. I went to the Central High School, 1938–41, five or six hours a day
and in the flower of my intellectual growth. It was a middle-class neighborhood, not a blackboard jungle; there was no war, no hunger, no racial
strife there. How many useful things I could have learned, with joy and
with ease: Greek, the history of China and the game of Go, for example.
Alas, of these I still know next to nothing. In my adult years I suppose I
could have looked into them more than in fact I have, but by then, at

some expense to something else. At Central I could have learned them at no cost at all. What *did* I learn then?

I attended, among others, classes labelled history, economics, civics, and physics. I name these four because I have a vivid recollection of a characteristic feature of each, a feature of instruction which I believe characterized all subjects taught me at that time: a listing.

(1) Economics: *The Four Properties of Gold, The Three Functions of Money.*

(2) History: *The Three Causes of the Civil War, The Seven Provisions of the Treaty of Versailles.*

(3) Civics: *The Capitals of the 48 States, The Three Kinds of City Governments.*

(4) Physics: *The Three Methods of Heat Transfer.*

Consider gold. It is (a) *valuable,*
　　　　　　　　　(b) *divisible,*
　　　　　　　　　(c) *portable,* and
　　　　　　　　　(d) *enduring.*
For these reasons, I was taught, gold is used as money. Granite and iron fail to satisfy (a) and (c), or at least no given quantity of (say) iron used as coin can simultaneously be both *valuable* and *portable;* hence civilized people don't use iron coins. Platinum, on the other hand, so well satisfies (a) that it can hardly be *divisible* (b) without danger of loss. So it went. (It would have been amusing to think of substances satisfying the various subsets of these four properties. Some might say *love* satisfies all but [d]. We didn't play games with our lists at Central, however.)

The economics teacher insisted a good deal on these four properties of gold. The class was called on in alphabetical order to stand up and recite the list of the day (one list could last several days) with precision and understanding. The reader must not think this list was a minor matter, a passing comment in an otherwise substantial book or course. Much ancillary and illustrative material was offered by both teacher and text-book, concerning these essential properties of gold.

We were told that some ancient (hence silly) lands used large bronze discs, too heavy to carry, as currency. Such a violation of (c) *portable* was its own punishment. I received the distinct impression that these people (they were either Neanderthal men or Etruscans, I forget which) walked lopsided, and in any case not far from home.

How many tales of wampum have I not heard? I had courses in wampum beginning in kindergarten, and while the formal study of braves, squaws, and happy hunting grounds is usually completed by the fifth grade, I am quite sure wampum got into the high school economics lesson of which I have been speaking.

There was a second list, *The Three Functions of Money*, essential to the first. You know of course that money is:

(α) *a standard of value,*
(β) *a medium of exchange,* and
(γ) *a standard for deferred payments.*

One cannot forget this and understand the four properties of gold, after all. Were it not for *deferred payments* (γ), the property (d) *enduring* would hardly be memorable or necessary, for example.

I'm sorry I don't still have that textbook; I must have sold it in June of 1940 to some student who would take the same class the following fall. June 1940! Gold had not been used as currency in America for the previous seven years, or since. What was I saying and what was my teacher listening to when I stood up beside my desk to recite these idiocies?

My economics teacher was named Mr. Minton (believe it or not); he and I had both lived through the closing of the banks in 1933, a period when the city of Detroit, totally bankrupt, paid its schoolteachers in 'scrip,' a currency without backing and which still did the job. Did he think of this when he drilled us on the portability of gold? I doubt it. The properties of gold were schoolbook truths, independent of the world outside. They too were a sort of currency. They travelled in a closed system from textbook to teacher to student to exam, and re-entered the system when some particularly malleable student became a teacher in his turn and wrote a textbook in careful improvement of those which had made him the man he was.

Still, that about the gold was not so entirely wrong. It had probably been cribbed in twelve relays from Adam Smith or Jean-Baptiste Say, so it is not surprising that a germ of truth remained. I later learned that *value, divisibility,* and *portability* are in fact a sensible list of demands to make of money, even if *durability* is asking perhaps more than modern governments committed to inflation can provide; and that while there isn't enough gold around to serve the whole world in this way, a "promise to pay" will serve as well. It is a stable government's promise to pay which we have used as currency since 1933, and, in effect, earlier too —even when we called it gold, it was in fact sometimes green and crinkly and sometimes only a rubber ink stamp of a bank teller.

I have no recollection that Mr. Minton appreciated all this. Even if he had and had been willing to substitute the list of properties for the actual yellow metal in our classroom discussions, whatever would he have made of the word *value?* Even in a correct formulation, the list exhibits what must be the most trivial or tautological aspects of the science of money, but this was no disqualification from its use in Central High School during the Battle of Britain. There, at Central, it was an island of certitude. At the end of the day we could know we had done our job, all of us, who remembered (a) through (d) in the right order and spoke them with expression, like an Edgar Guest poem in the morning's *Detroit Free Press.*

I know there were *Three Causes of the Civil War* (i.e., the American "War Between the States") but I can only remember *sectionalism.* It is hard to quarrel with that one. They might as well have listed *soldiers* or *secession.* Come to think of it, as I remember that textbook it was perfectly capable of listing *secession* as a cause, but I just don't remember. It must be that I wasn't called on to recite during that particular lesson, which took place in the Durfee Intermediate School, 9th Grade, sometime in 1937.

What is easier to remember is that *slavery* was not a cause of the Civil War, or at any rate not a certified cause of the 9th Grade Durfee School Civil War. Our teacher was quite insistent about it. When called on to recite the causes of the Civil War, or if asked about it on a State Proficiency Examination (or whatever) we were not—repeat, *not*—to list *slavery.*

Now the 9th grade is farther back in my memory than the 12th, and it is a bit harder to visualize the textbooks and the general form of classroom procedure. There was a list, I am sure of that, and the causes were certainly three, but that part about *slavery* may have been due to our teacher and not the book. I believe the teacher was trying to be deep instead of superficial, and hoping to take us behind the scenes, as it were. *Slavery*—hideous as it was—was only a symptom of some deeper malaise, I bet.

Detroit was still in the grip of the Depression, and Marxist ideals vied with trade-unionism in portraying the economic royalists as the cause of all our ills. I heard it at home and it must have penetrated the schools. Even if *surplus value* wasn't trotted out in the open, everyone was affected by the notion that all causes were deeper than they appeared. Marx and Freud are an infestation to this day, after all, and their fundamental message is actually neither economic nor psychiatric; it is that things are really the opposite of what they seem. Thus the downgrading of *slavery* in favor of the more general and more resonant.

Except then for *sectionalism* ("deep") and *slavery* ("superficial") I recall nothing I learned in school about the Civil War. Nothing in "social studies," that is. In music class we sang "Mahty Lak a Rose" and "Massa's In De Col' Col' Groun'." At home over the next few years I read *Uncle Tom's Cabin, Gone with the Wind,* and *Black Boy.* These things didn't touch the Civil War I had learned about in that Gothic and brick school building; they were part of some second Civil War that I gradually had to put together in my own mind and that I am still far from fully appreciating.

Oh yes—one vignette. There was a horrible day when I was convinced for a while that one of the approved causes of the Civil War was *coalition*. It happened this way. The teacher began the class by mentioning the *Three Causes*, and while my attention wandered she wrote some of them, maybe all three, something at any rate, on the blackboard. That is how I remember it. Probably I heard the chalk on the board but was looking out of the window. Coming out of my daze then, I focussed on the chalked word COALITION, printed on what I have since come to realize must have been a different part of the blackboard from the one she had just been using.

Her voice washed over me as I studied the word. *Coal?* That went with *oil* and *gas* and the unit on *Transportation and Communication*. Probably the teacher was saying words like *secession* or *sectionalism*, only vaguely according with the word that was bemusing me. I looked at it a long long time.

Coming home that night I looked it up in the dictionary and it was still a puzzle. I may have spent a fevered night trying to reconcile the day's experiences, maybe not. Only gradually, over the years, have I become certain that COALITION was an artifact of the classroom, a word left over from an earlier class and not at all, not even marginally, not even negatively like *slavery*, a cause of the Civil War.

Did I say *certain?* That is too strong. No, there is simply no telling. It has been thirty-five years now, and not one of them has passed without my turning to the matter in some mentally idle moment, trying to figure out a way to make *coalition*, or some brief phrase containing the word, a duly listed cause of the War Between the States. There is no way to make it an *obvious* cause, to be sure, but (as I have explained) we didn't deal in obvious causes in those days.

The capitals of the forty-eight states! I knew them once. Now there are fifty, but I'm not sure about the new ones. Honolulu? Anchorage? Maybe some of the old ones have changed too, or is that against the law?

I knew Lansing, Michigan, of course, since I had been there, and lived in Michigan anyhow. I don't know why *you* should remember it, though. Any New York child who thinks Detroit is the capital of Michigan shows thereby a certain understanding of Detroit and of Michigan which I count all to the good, in fact.

One asset this list of forty-eight had was that it was natural. It was in some sense a false lesson to be taught that the Civil War had precisely three causes, not two, not seven, but there was no denying the forty-eightness of this particular list, or its correctness. The only question is, why?

Progressive educators and modern parents were forever asking, even in my day, why one had to learn this or that foolish thing: Latin (a dead language), algebra (not true-to-life). They didn't really ask—they knew the answer in advance. There was no valid reason, if you were modern about it. Even my teachers (the younger ones) often commented in class —as they had been taught in Teacher's College—on the deadening effect of learning the dates of events in history.

So I grew up among classmates who couldn't place Julius Caesar and Napoleon in correct chronological order. That I could do so was an accident of my reading, but no such accident taught me Latin. I regret it to this day. Almost everything whose utility was under such attack in those days—algebra, Latin, dates, memorized poems—has seemed to me as an adult to be of enormous utility, while the list of forty-eight capitals, which everyone must have considered very practical knowledge, like a visit to the firehouse, now seems as much a waste of time as ever.

I can think of one interesting lesson to be drawn from that list, but it was a lesson probably not appreciated by my teachers. The thing about our capitals is that they are not necessarily, indeed very seldom, the most important cities of their respective states. This fact was mentioned in my class, but no explanation was given. In fact, nobody even said why this fact was remarkable.

If my teacher had mentioned Paris, London, Madrid, Rome, Berlin, Moscow, Copenhagen, Stockholm, Athens, Cairo, Bagdad, and Tokyo, and then gone on to mention Albany, Lansing, and Sacramento, we would at least have seen there was a puzzle buried somewhere between the two lists. These lists call attention to a deep distinction between the New World and the Old: Here, we set up our maps and governments *before* a state began its history, rather than after, as in the rest of the world. Something to ponder, something we have evidence for before our eyes, but it wasn't in the book, not on the exam.

How could it have been taught, after all? We would have had to invoke European history and culture, which was taught in a different grade. And how would it have looked on an examination? "Fill in the blanks in the following sentence: The States of the United States were mostly created ———their history began, rather than ———, so that . . ."

Not such a good question, is it? Also the explanation is only partial. After all, in some cases (Michigan among them) it was plain from the beginning which city would be preeminent, from its position on a waterway in most cases, yet the capital was deliberately placed elsewhere. Why? In Europe, of course, the capital was where the king was, and everything else followed: cathedrals, artists, law courts, trade. Why did Michigan *want* it otherwise?

The more I think about it, the more I have to draw on my knowledge of the facts of history, the flavor of social history, the currents of war and diplomacy, and the theories of American republicanism. To get up a respectable lecture would take work as well as knowledge, and when I got done what could I present after all, given the rules of the game? I know what my teacher would have done: she would have presented a list of *The Four Reasons Why American State Capitals Are Situated in Otherwise Minor Cities*, and drilled us till we got them right.

The three methods of heat transfer, as explained in my 1941 textbook called *Modern Physics* (I won't embarrass the author by mentioning his name), were as follows:
(a) *conduction*,
(b) *convection*, and
(c) *radiation*.
Without going into details of the molecular theory of matter (and kinetic theory of gases), and the quantum theory of radiation, by which these three words have been analyzed since 1900 or so, let me say that the above list is about as true and illuminating as the following analogy would suggest:
Q. What are the three methods of transfer of bank deposits?
A. 1) *personal check*,
2) *cashier's check*, and
3) *airmail*.
The book could go on to explain that *personal checks* are generally written in ink while *cashier's checks* are typed, and guaranteed by the bank. Other useful information might include the speed of airplanes and their tendency to crash from time to time, something not at all true of either sort of check.

Oh, if I were a teacher, what a fine week of the study of finance I could make out of this listing! I swear the analogy is a good one, though I will not otherwise explain the imbecility of the heat transfer listing. Nor will I attempt to trace the historical reasons for the 1941 appearance of precisely that list (it was not invented by the author of my textbook, you may be sure), though there are some.

The question is—as it was with the *Properties of Gold*, the *Causes of the Civil War* and the *Forty-Eight Capital Cities*—what did these teachers and textbook writers think they were doing when they arranged for us to gabble these miserable syllables? My own opinion, considered these thirty-odd years, is that they didn't think anything at all. They were doing what they had been told was virtuous and correct, as people do who follow any other ritual.

These lists were not intended to educate any more than a rain dance is intended to bring rain. Everyone gets told that these are the intentions, but (as anthropologists have pointed out in cases like these) to understand the reality one must study the ritual rather than the "belief."

When a workman uses a tool to smooth a piece of wood he doesn't offer prayer, he looks to see whether the wood in fact becomes smooth as a result of his manipulation of that tool. If it doesn't he invents another tool or uses differently the one he has. Carpentry is not a religion.

The results of ritual are also studied, in a manner of speaking, but not as the carpenter studies the effect of his tools. A successful rain dance verifies the ritual's correctness. An unsuccessful rain dance is evidence of sin, or improper incantation, or almost anything except the irrelevance of the ritual to the "intended" result. Every result reinforces the faith; it is by this observation that one can recognize—even define—a religion, to distinguish it from what should be the activity of the factory, a government, or an educational enterprise.

Just as with rain dances, then, the "educational" process at Central High School had its successes and its failures. I suppose I was among the successes: a solid moral literate productive citizen. The Board of Education had only to point to students like me to prove the efficacy of public education—grades K–12, September through June, and attended by the requisite number of certified and licensed teachers and school psychologists. What of the failures? The truants and jail-birds-to-be, the scornful, the drunk, the illiterate? Why, more teachers of course, more psychologists, stiffer licensing laws, Head Start, summer school, community college. Pray harder, put out more flags.

It is no accident then that the list is the most memorable, because the most characteristic, feature of my school days. A list is a litany, a catechism, a rosary, a chant. Abraham, Isaac and Jacob; Father, Son and Holy Ghost; Hare Krishna Hare Hare; the Twelve Tribes; the Seven Dwarfs. From Minoan temple to Michigan high school the impulse remains the same.

It will never die, I think. Whatever it is called and whatever the First Amendment may say, it is a state religion. In one form or another every state has one. Ours is maybe not as bad as some but this may not last. Certainly it is getting more expensive all the time.

1973

Walker Percy

THE LOSS OF THE CREATURE

* * *

A young Falkland Islander[1] walking along a beach and spying a dead dogfish and going to work on it with his jackknife has, in a fashion wholly unprovided in modern educational theory, a great advantage over the Scarsdale high-school pupil who finds the dogfish on his laboratory desk. Similarly the citizen of Huxley's Brave New World who stumbles across a volume of Shakespeare in some vine-grown ruins and squats on a potsherd to read it[2] is in a fairer way of getting at a sonnet than the Harvard sophomore taking English Poetry II.

The educator whose business it is to teach students biology or poetry is unaware of a whole ensemble of relations which exist between the student and the dogfish and between the student and the Shakespeare sonnet. To put it bluntly: A student who has the desire to get at a dogfish or a Shakespeare sonnet may have the greatest difficulty in salvaging the creature itself from the educational package in which it is presented. The great difficulty is that he is not aware that there is a difficulty; surely, he thinks, in such a fine classroom, with such a fine textbook, the sonnet must come across! What's wrong with me?

The sonnet and the dogfish are obscured by two different processes. The sonnet is obscured by the symbolic package which is formulated not by the sonnet itself but by the media through which the sonnet is transmitted, the media which the educators believe for some reason to be transparent. The new textbook, the type, the smell of the page, the classroom, the aluminum windows and the winter sky, the personality of Miss Hawkins—these media which are supposed to transmit the sonnet may only succeed in transmitting themselves. It is only the hardiest and cleverest of students who can salvage the sonnet from this many-tissued package. It is only the rarest student who knows that the sonnet must be salvaged from the package. (The educator is well aware that something is wrong, that there is a fatal gap between the student's learning and the student's life: The student reads the poem, appears to understand it, and gives all the answers. But what does he recall if he should happen to read a Shakespeare sonnet twenty years later? Does he recall the poem or does he recall the smell of the page and the smell of Miss Hawkins?)

One might object, pointing out that Huxley's citizen reading his

1. The Falkland Islands are located off the southern tip of South America. Their inhabitants live a simple life, close to the land and the sea.
2. In Aldous Huxley's novel Brave New World, a boy from a future civilization that has lost contact with the past rediscovers Shakespeare after finding a volume of his Complete Works.

sonnet in the ruins and the Falkland Islander looking at his dogfish on the beach also receive them in a certain package. Yes, but the difference lies in the fundamental placement of the student in the world, a placement which makes it possible to extract the thing from the package. The pupil at Scarsdale High sees himself placed as a consumer receiving an experience-package; but the Falkland Islander exploring his dogfish is a person exercising the sovereign right of a person in his lordship and mastery of creation. He too could use an instructor and a book and a technique, but he would use them as his subordinates, just as he uses his jackknife. The biology student does not use his scalpel as an instrument; he uses it as a magic wand! Since it is a "scientific instrument," it should do "scientific things."

The dogfish is concealed in the same symbolic package as the sonnet. But the dogfish suffers an additional loss. As a consequence of this double deprivation, the Sarah Lawrence student who scores A in zoology is apt to know very little about a dogfish. She is twice removed from the dogfish, once by the symbolic complex by which the dogfish is concealed, once again by the spoliation of the dogfish by theory which renders it invisible. Through no fault of zoology instructors, it is nevertheless a fact that the zoology laboratory at Sarah Lawrence College is one of the few places in the world where it is all but impossible to see a dogfish.

The dogfish, the tree, the seashell, the American Negro, the dream, are rendered invisible by a shift of reality from concrete thing to theory which Whitehead[3] has called the fallacy of misplaced concreteness. It is the mistaking of an idea, a principle, an abstraction, for the real. As a consequence of the shift, the "specimen" is seen as less real than the theory of the specimen. As Kierkegaard[4] said, once a person is seen as a specimen of a race or a species, at that very moment he ceases to be an individual. Then there are no more individuals but only specimens.

To illustrate: A student enters a laboratory which, in the pragmatic view, offers the student the optimum conditions under which an educational experience may be had. In the existential view, however—that view of the student in which he is regarded not as a receptacle of experience but as a knowing being whose peculiar property it is to see himself as being in a certain situation—the modern laboratory could not have been more effectively designed to conceal the dogfish forever.

The student comes to his desk. On it, neatly arranged by his instructor, he finds his laboratory manual, a dissecting board, instruments, and a mimeographed list:

Exercise 22

Materials: 1 dissecting board
      1 scalpel

----

3. Alfred North Whitehead (1861–1947), British philosopher.

4. Soren Kierkegaard (1813–55), Danish philosopher.

1 forceps
1 probe
1 bottle india ink and syringe
1 specimen of *Squalus acanthias*

The clue to the situation in which the student finds himself is to be found in the last item. 1 specimen of *Squalus acanthias*.

The phrase *specimen of* expresses in the most succinct way imaginable the radical character of the loss of being which has occurred under his very nose. To refer to the dogfish, the unique concrete existent before him, as a "specimen of *Squalus acanthias*" reveals by its grammar the spoliation of the dogfish by the theoretical method. This phrase, *specimen of,* example of, instance of, indicates the ontological status of the individual creature in the eyes of the theorist. The dogfish itself is seen as a rather shabby expression of an ideal reality, the species *Squalus acanthias*. The result is the radical devaluation of the individual dogfish. (The *reductio ad absurdum* of Whitehead's shift is Toynbee's[5] employment of it in his historical method. If a gram of NaCl is referred to by the chemist as a "sample of" NaCl, one may think of it as such and not much is missed by the oversight of the act of being of this particular pinch of salt, but when the Jews and the Jewish religion are understood as—in Toynbee's favorite phrase—a "classical example of" such and such a kind of *Voelkerwanderung*,[6] we begin to suspect that something is being left out.)

If we look into the ways in which the student can recover the dogfish (or the sonnet), we will see that they have in common the stratagem of avoiding the educator's direct presentation of the object as a lesson to be learned and restoring access to sonnet and dogfish as beings to be known, reasserting the sovereignty of knower over known.

In truth, the biography of scientists and poets is usually the story of the discovery of the indirect approach, the circumvention of the educator's presentation—the young man who was sent to the *Technikum*[7] and on his way fell into the habit of loitering in book stores and reading poetry; or the young man dutifully attending law school who on the way became curious about the comings and goings of ants. One remembers the scene in *The Heart Is a Lonely Hunter*[8] where the girl hides in the bushes to hear the Capehart[9] in the big house play Beethoven. Perhaps she was the lucky one after all. Think of the unhappy souls inside, who see the record, worry about scratches, and most of all worry about whether they are *getting it,* whether they are bona fide music lovers. What is the best way

5. Arnold Toynbee (1889–1975), British historian.
6. Tribal migration.
7. Technical school.
8. A novel by American writer Carson McCullers.
9. A large record player.

to hear Beethoven: sitting in a proper silence around the Capehart or eavesdropping from an azalea bush?

However it may come about, we notice two traits of the second situation: (1) an openness of the thing before one—instead of being an exercise to be learned according to an approved mode, it is a garden of delights which beckons to one; (2) a sovereignty of the knower—instead of being a consumer of a prepared experience, I am a sovereign wayfarer, a wanderer in the neighborhood of being who stumbles into the garden.

One can think of two sorts of circumstances through which the thing may be restored to the person. (There is always, of course, the direct recovery: A student may simply be strong enough, brave enough, clever enough to take the dogfish and the sonnet by storm, to wrest control of it from the educators and the educational package.) First by ordeal: The Bomb falls; when the young man recovers consciousness in the shambles of the biology laboratory, there not ten inches from his nose lies the dogfish. Now all at once he can see it, directly and without let, just as the exile or the prisoner or the sick man sees the sparrow at his window in all its inexhaustibility; just as the commuter who has had a heart attack sees his own hand for the first time. In these cases, the simulacrum of everydayness and of consumption has been destroyed by disaster; in the case of the bomb, literally destroyed. Secondly, by apprenticeship to a great man: One day a great biologist walks into the laboratory; he stops in front of our student's desk; he leans over, picks up the dogfish, and, ignoring instruments and procedure, probes with a broken fingernail into the little carcass. "Now here is a curious business," he says, ignoring also the proper jargon of the specialty. "Look here how this little duct reverses its direction and drops into the pelvis. Now if you would look into a coelacanth, you would see that it—" And all at once the student can see. The technician and the sophomore who loves his textbook are always offended by the genuine research man because the latter is usually a little vague and always humble before the thing; he doesn't have much use for the equipment or the jargon. Whereas the technician is never vague and never humble before the thing; he holds the thing disposed of by the principle, the formula, the textbook outline; and he thinks a great deal of equipment and jargon.

But since neither of these methods of recovering the dogfish is pedagogically feasible—perhaps the great man even less so than the Bomb—I wish to propose the following educational technique which should prove equally effective for Harvard and Shreveport High School. I propose that English poetry and biology should be taught as usual, but that at irregular intervals, poetry students should find dogfishes on their desks and biology students should find Shakespeare sonnets on their dissecting boards. I am serious in declaring that a Sarah Lawrence English major who began poking about in a dogfish with a bobby pin would learn more in thirty minutes than a biology major in a whole semester; and that the latter upon reading on her dissecting board

> That time of year thou may'st in me behold
> When yellow leaves, or none, or few, do hang
> Upon those boughs which shake against the cold—
> Bare ruin'd choirs where late the sweet birds sang.[1]

might catch fire at the beauty of it.

The situation of * * * the biology student is a special case of a predicament in which everyone finds himself in a modern technical society—a society, that is, in which there is a division between expert and layman, planner and consumer, in which experts and planners take special measures to teach and edify the consumer. The measures taken are measures appropriate to the consumer: The expert and the planner *know* and *plan*, but the consumer *needs* and *experiences*.

There is a double deprivation. First, the thing is lost through its packaging. The very means by which the thing is presented for consumption, the very techniques by which the thing is made available as an item of need-satisfaction, these very means operate to remove the thing from the sovereignty of the knower. A loss of title occurs. The measures which the museum curator takes to present the thing to the public are self-liquidating. The upshot of the curator's efforts are not that everyone can see the exhibit but that no one can see it. The curator protests: Why are they so indifferent? Why do they even deface the exhibits? Don't they know it is theirs? But it is not theirs. It is his, the curator's. By the most exclusive sort of zoning, the museum exhibit, the park oak tree, is part of an ensemble, a package, which is almost impenetrable to them. The archaeologist who puts his find in a museum so that everyone can see it accomplishes the reverse of his expectations. The result of his action is that no one can see it now but the archaeologist. He would have done better to keep it in his pocket and show it now and then to strangers.

The tourist who carves his initials in a public place, which is theoretically "his" in the first place, has good reasons for doing so, reasons which the exhibitor and planner know nothing about. He does so because in his role of consumer of an experience (a "recreational experience" to satisfy a "recreational need") he knows that he is disinherited. He is deprived of his title over being. He knows very well that he is in a very special sort of zone in which his only rights are the rights of a consumer. He moves like a ghost through schoolroom, city streets, trains, parks, movies. He carves his initials as a last desperate measure to escape his ghostly role of consumer. He is saying in effect: I am not a ghost after all; I am a

---

1. From Shakespeare's Sonnet 73.

sovereign person. And he establishes title the only way remaining to him, by staking his claim over one square inch of wood or stone.

Does this mean that we should get rid of museums? No, but it means that the sightseer should be prepared to enter into a struggle to recover a sight from a museum.

The second loss is the spoliation of the thing, the tree, the rock, the swallow, by the layman's misunderstanding of scientific theory. He believes that the thing is *disposed of* by theory, that it stands in the Platonic relation of being a *specimen of* such and such an underlying principle.[2] In the transmission of scientific theory from theorist to layman, the expectation of the theorist is reversed. Instead of the marvels of the universe being made available to the public, the universe is disposed of by theory. The loss of sovereignty takes this form: As a result of the science of botany, trees are not made available to every man. On the contrary. The tree loses its proper density and mystery as a concrete existent and, as merely another *specimen of* a species, becomes itself nugatory.

Does this mean that there is no use taking biology at Harvard and Shreveport High? No, but it means that the student should know what a fight he has on his hands to rescue the specimen from the educational package. The educator is only partly to blame. For there is nothing the educator can do to provide for this need of the student. Everything the educator does only succeeds in becoming, for the student, part of the educational package. The highest role of the educator is the maieutic[3] role of Socrates: to help the student come to himself not as a consumer of experience but as a sovereign individual.

The thing is twice lost to the consumer. First, sovereignty is lost: It is theirs, not his. Second, it is radically devalued by theory. This is a loss which has been brought about by science but through no fault of the scientist and through no fault of scientific theory. The loss has come about as a consequence of the seduction of the layman by science. The layman will be seduced as long as he regards beings as consumer items to be experienced rather than prizes to be won, and as long as he waives his sovereign rights as a person and accepts his role of consumer as the highest estate to which the layman can aspire.

As Mounier[4] said, the person is not something one can study and provide for; he is something one struggles for. But unless he also struggles for himself, unless he knows that there is a struggle, he is going to be just what the planners think he is.

1975

---

2. A reference to Plato's doctrine that everything is merely a copy of an ideal form for that thing.
3. "Bringing out ideas latent in the mind," the characteristic method by which Socrates taught.
4. Emmanuel Mounier (1905–50), French philosopher.

QUESTIONS

1. Percy chooses a dogfish and a Shakespeare sonnet to use as extended examples. How does he use these examples to make his major points? Why does he need both? What other examples might he have chosen?
2. What do the teaching of biology (dogfish) and of literature (sonnet) have in common? Are the two subjects taught differently? If so, what are the differences?
3. Percy asserts that things have been "devalued by theory . . . through no fault of the scientist and through no fault of scientific theory," but rather through "the seduction of the layman by science. The layman will be seduced," he continues, "as long as he regards beings as consumer items to be experienced rather than prizes to be won." Does this mean that scientific theories are not useful? Does it mean that each person should develop his own scientific theories? Could a science course be taught without reference to theories? Explain.
4. To what degree are theories important in nonscience courses? Compare a theory in a nonscience course with a theory in a science course.
5. Percy suggests that the individual student can have a good deal of control over his education by fighting to "rescue the specimen from the educational package," while "educators" can only do things that become "part of the educational package." Is this a desirable goal for the student? Why? Are there any changes that could be made in the educational system to make this process easier for the student?

Caroline Bird

COLLEGE IS A WASTE OF TIME AND MONEY

A great majority of our nine million college students are not in school because they want to be or because they want to learn. They are there because it has become the thing to do or because college is a pleasant place to be; because it's the only way they can get parents or taxpayers to support them without working at a job they don't like; because Mother wanted them to go, or some other reason entirely irrelevant to the course of studies for which college is supposedly organized.

As I crisscross the United States lecturing on college campuses, I am dismayed to find that professors and administrators, when pressed for a candid opinion, estimate that no more than 25 percent of their students are turned on by classwork. For the rest, college is at best a social center or aging vat, and at worst a young folks' home or even a prison that keeps them out of the mainstream of economic life for a few more years.

The premise—which I no longer accept—that college is the best place for all high-school graduates grew out of a noble American ideal. Just as the United States was the first nation to aspire to teach every small child to read and write, so, during the 1950s, we became the first and only great nation to aspire to higher education for all. During the '60s we damned the expense and built great state university systems as fast as we could. And adults—parents, employers, high-school counselors—began to push, shove and cajole youngsters to "get an education."

It became a mammoth industry, with taxpayers footing more than half the bill. By 1970, colleges and universities were spending more than 30 billion dollars annually. But still only half our highschool graduates were going on. According to estimates made by the economist Fritz Machlup, if we had been educating every young person until age 22 in that year of 1970, the bill for higher education would have reached 47.5 billion dollars, 12.5 billion more than the total corporate profits for the year.

Figures such as these have begun to make higher education for all look financially prohibitive, particularly now when colleges are squeezed by the pressures of inflation and a drop-off in the growth of their traditional market.

Predictable demography has caught up with the university empire builders. Now that the record crop of postwar babies has graduated from college, the rate of growth of the student population has begun to decline. To keep their mammoth plants financially solvent, many institutions have begun to use hard-sell, Madison-Avenue techniques to attract students. They sell college like soap, promoting features they think students want: innovative programs, an environment conducive to meaningful personal relationships, and a curriculum so free that it doesn't sound like college at all.

Pleasing the customers is something new for college administrators. Colleges have always known that most students don't like to study, and that at least part of the time they are ambivalent about college, but before the student riots of the 1960s educators never thought it either right or necessary to pay any attention to student feelings. But when students rebelling against the Vietnam war and the draft discovered they could disrupt a campus completely, administrators had to act on some student complaints. Few understood that the protests had tapped the basic discontent with college itself, a discontent that did not go away when the riots subsided.

Today students protest individually rather than in concert. They turn inward and withdraw from active participation. They drop out to travel to India or to feed themselves on subsistence farms. Some refuse to go to college at all. Most, of course, have neither the funds nor the self-confidence for constructive articulation of their discontent. They simply hang around college unhappily and reluctantly.

All across the country, I have been overwhelmed by the prevailing sadness on American campuses. Too many young people speak little, and then only in drowned voices. Sometimes the mood surfaces as diffidence, wariness, or coolness, but whatever its form, it looks like a defense mechanism, and that rings a bell. This is the way it used to be with women, and just as society had systematically damaged women by insisting that their proper place was in the home, so we may be systematically damaging 18-year-olds by insisting that their proper place is in college.

Campus watchers everywhere know what I mean when I say students are sad, but they don't agree on the reason for it. During the Vietnam war some ascribed the sadness to the draft; now others blame affluence, or say it has something to do with permissive upbringing.

Not satisfied with any of these explanations, I looked for some answers with the journalistic tools of my trade—scholarly studies, economic analyses, the historical record, the opinions of the especially knowledgeable, conversations with parents, professors, college administrators, and employers, all of whom spoke as alumni too. Mostly I learned from my interviews with hundreds of young people on and off campuses all over the country.

My unnerving conclusion is that students are sad because they are not needed. Somewhere between the nursery and the employment office, they become unwanted adults. No one has anything in particular against them. But no one knows what to do with them either. We already have too many people in the world of the 1970s, and there is no room for so many newly minted 18-year-olds. So we temporarily get them out of the way by sending them to college where in fact only a few belong.

To make it more palatable, we fool ourselves into believing that we are sending them there for their own best interests, and that it's good for them, like spinach. Some, of course, learn to like it, but most wind up preferring green peas.

Educators admit as much. Nevitt Sanford, distinguished student of higher education, says students feel they are "capitulating to a kind of voluntary servitude." Some of them talk about their time in college as if it were a sentence to be served. I listened to a 1970 Mount Holyoke graduate: "For two years I was really interested in science, but in my junior and senior years I just kept saying, 'I've done two years; I'm going to finish'. When I got out I made up my mind that I wasn't going to school anymore because so many of my courses had been bullshit."

But bad as it is, college is often preferable to a far worse fate. It is better than the drudgery of an uninspiring nine-to-five job, and better than doing nothing when no jobs are available. For some young people, it is a graceful way to get away from home and become independent without losing the financial support of their parents. And sometimes it is the only alternative to an intolerable home situation.

It is difficult to assess how many students are in college reluctantly. The conservative Carnegie Commission estimates from 5 to 30 percent. Sol Linowitz, who was once chairman of a special committee on campus tension of the American Council on Education, found that "a significant number were not happy with their college experience because they felt they were there only in order to get the 'ticket to the big show' rather than to spend the years as productively as they otherwise could."

Older alumni will identify with Richard Baloga, a policeman's son, who stayed in school even though he "hated it" because he thought it would do him some good. But fewer students each year feel this way. Daniel Yankelovich has surveyed undergraduate attitudes for a number of years, and reported in 1971 that 74 percent thought education was "very important." But just two years earlier, 80 percent thought so.

The doubters don't mind speaking up. Leon Lefkowitz, chairman of the department of social studies at Central High School in Valley Stream, New York, interviewed 300 college students at random, and reports that 200 of them didn't think that the education they were getting was worth the effort. "In two years I'll pick up a diploma," said one student, "and I can honestly say it was a waste of my father's bread."

Nowadays, says one sociologist, you don't have to have a reason for going to college; it's an institution. His definition of an institution is an arrangement everyone accepts without question; the burden of proof is not on why you go, but why anyone thinks there might be a reason for not going. The implication is that an 18-year-old is too young and confused to know what he wants to do, and that he should listen to those who know best and go to college.

I don't agree. I believe that college has to be judged not on what other people think is good for students, but on how good it feels to the students themselves.

I believe that people have an inside view of what's good for them. If a child doesn't want to go to school some morning, better let him stay at home, at least until you find out why. Maybe he knows something you don't. It's the same with college. If high-school graduates don't want to go, or if they don't want to go right away, they may perceive more clearly than their elders that college is not for them. It is no longer obvious that adolescents are best off studying a core curriculum that was constructed when all educated men could agree on what made them educated, or that professors, advisors, or parents can be of any particular help to young people in choosing a major or a career. High-school graduates see college graduates driving cabs, and decide it's not worth going. College students find no intellectual stimulation in their studies and drop out.

If students believe that college isn't necessarily good for them, you can't expect them to stay on for the general good of mankind. They don't go to school to beat the Russians to Jupiter, improve the national defense, increase the GNP, or create a new market for the arts—to mention some of the benefits taxpayers are supposed to get for supporting higher education.

Nor should we expect to bring about social equality by putting all young people through four years of academic rigor. At best, it's a round-about and expensive way to narrow the gap between the highest and lowest in our society anyway. At worst, it is unconsciously elitist. Equalizing opportunity through universal higher education subjects the whole population to the intellectual mode natural only to a few. It violates the fundamental egalitarian principle of respect for the differences between people.

Of course, most parents aren't thinking of the "higher" good at all. They send their children to college because they are convinced young people benefit financially from those four years of higher education. But if money is the only goal, college is the dumbest investment you can make. I say this because a young banker in Poughkeepsie, New York, Stephen G. Necel, used a computer to compare college as an investment with other investments available in 1974 and college did not come out on top.

For the sake of argument, the two of us invented a young man whose rich uncle gave him, in cold cash, the cost of a four-year education at any college he chose, but the young man didn't have to spend the money on college. After bales of computer paper, we had our mythical student write to his uncle: "Since you said I could spend the money foolishly if I wished, I am going to blow it all on Princeton."

The much respected financial columnnist Sylvia Porter echoed the common assumption when she said last year, "A college education is among the very best investments you can make in your entire life." But the truth is not quite so rosy, even if we assume that the Census Bureau is correct when it says that as of 1972, a man who completed four years of college would expect to earn $199,000 more between the ages of 22 and 64 than a man who had only a high-school diploma.

If a 1972 Princeton-bound high-school graduate had put the $34,181 that his four years of college would have cost him into a savings bank at 7.5 percent interest compounded daily, he would have had at age 64 a total of $1,129,200, or $528,200 more than the earnings of a male college graduate, and more than five times as much as the $199,000 extra the more educated man could expect to earn between 22 and 64.

The big advantage of getting your college money in cash now is that you can invest it in something that has a higher return than a diploma. For instance, a Princeton-bound high-school graduate of 1972 who liked fooling around with cars could have banked his $34,181, and gone to work at the local garage at close to $1,000 more per year than the average high-school graduate. Meanwhile, as he was learning to be an expert auto mechanic, his money would be ticking away in the bank. When he became 28, he would have earned $7,199 less on his job from age 22 to 28 than his college-educated friend, but he would have had $73,113 in his passbook—enough to buy out his boss, go into the used-car business, or acquire his own new-car dealership. If successful in business, he could expect to make more than the average college graduate. And if he had the brains to get into Princeton, he would be just as likely to make money without the four years spent on campus. Unfortunately, few college-bound high-school graduates get the opportunity to bank such a large sum of money, and then wait for it to make them rich. And few parents are sophisticated enough to understand that in financial returns alone, their children would be better off with the money than with the education.

Rates of return and dollar signs on education are fascinating brain teasers, but obviously there is a certain unreality to the game. Quite aside from the noneconomic benefits of college, and these should loom larger once the dollars are cleared away, there are grave difficulties in assigning a dollar value to college at all.

In fact there is no real evidence that the higher income of college graduates is due to college. College may simply attract people who are slated to earn more money anyway; those with higher IQs, better family backgrounds, a more enterprising temperament. No one who has wrestled with the problem is prepared to attribute all of the higher income to the impact of college itself.

Christopher Jencks, author of *Inequality,* a book that assesses the effect of family and schooling in America, believes that education in general accounts for less than half of the difference in income in the American population. "The biggest single source of income differences," writes Jencks, "seems to be the fact that men from high-status families have higher incomes than men from low-status families even when they enter the same occupations, have the same amount of education, and have the same test scores."

Jacob Mincer of the National Bureau of Economic Research and Columbia University states flatly that of "20 to 30 percent of students at any level, the additional schooling has been a waste, at least in terms of earnings." College fails to work its income-raising magic for almost a third of those who go. More than half of those people in 1972 who earned $15,000 or more reached that comfortable bracket without the benefit of a college diploma. Jencks says that financial success in the U.S. depends a good deal on luck, and the most sophisticated regression analyses have yet to demonstrate otherwise.

But most of today's students don't go to college to earn more money anyway. In 1968, when jobs were easy to get, Daniel Yankelovich made his first nationwide survey of students. Sixty-five percent of them said they "would welcome less emphasis on money." By 1973, when jobs were scarce, that figure jumped to 80 percent.

The young are not alone. Americans today are all looking less to the pay of a job than to the work itself. They want "interesting" work that permits them "to make a contribution," express themselves" and "use their special abilities," and they think college will help them find it.

Jerry Darring of Indianapolis knows what it is to make a dollar. He worked with his father in the family plumbing business, on the line at

Chevrolet, and in the Chrysler foundry. He quit these jobs to enter Wright State University in Dayton, Ohio, because "in a job like that a person only has time to work, and after that her's so tired that he can't do anything else but come home and go to sleep."

Jerry came to college to find work "helping people." And he is perfectly willing to spend the dollars he earns at dull, well-paid work to prepare for lower-paid work that offers the reward of service to others.

Jerry's case is not unusual. No one works for money alone. In order to deal with the nonmonetary rewards of work, economists have coined the concept of "psychic income" which according to one economic dictionary means "income that is reckoned in terms of pleasure, satisfaction, or general feelings of euphoria."

Psychic income is primarily what college students mean when they talk about getting a good job. During the most affluent years of the late 1960s and early 1970s college students told their placement officers that they wanted to be researchers, college professors, artists, city planners, social workers, poets, book publishers, archeologists, ballet dancers, or authors.

The psychic income of these and other occupations popular with students is so high that these jobs can be filled without offering high salaries. According to one study, 93 percent of urban university professors would choose the same vocation again if they had the chance, compared with only 16 percent of unskilled auto workers. Even though the monetary gap between college professor and auto worker is now surprisingly small, the difference in psychic income is enormous.

But colleges fail to warn students that jobs of these kinds are hard to come by, even for qualified applicants, and they rarely accept the responsibility of helping students choose a career that will lead to a job. When a young person says he is interested in helping people, his counselor tells him to become a psychologist. But jobs in psychology are scarce. The Department of Labor, for instance, estimates there will be 4,300 new jobs for psychologists in 1975 while colleges are expected to turn out 58,430 B.A.s in psychology that year.

Of 30 psych majors who reported back to Vassar what they were doing a year after graduation in 1972, only five had jobs in which they could possibly use their courses in psychology, and two of these were working for Vassar.

The outlook isn't much better for students majoring in other psychic-pay disciplines: sociology, English, journalism, anthropology, forestry, education. Whatever college graduates want to do, most of them are going to wind up doing what there is to do.

John Shingleton, director of placement at Michigan State University, accuses the academic community of outright hypocrisy. "Educators have never said, 'Go to college and get a good job,' but this has been implied, and now students expect it. . . . If we care what happens to students after college, then let's get involved with what should be one of the basic purposes of education: career preparation."

In the 1970s, some of the more practical professors began to see that jobs for graduates meant jobs for professors too. Meanwhile, students themselves reacted to the shrinking job market, and a "new vocationalism" exploded on campus. The press welcomed the change as a return to the ethic of achievement and service. Students were still idealistic, the reporters wrote, but they now saw that they could best make the world better by healing the sick as physicians or righting individual wrongs as lawyers.

But there are no guarantees in these professions either. The American Enterprise Institute estimated in 1971 that there would be more than the target ratio of 100 doctors for every 100,000 people in the population by 1980. And the odds are little better for would-be lawyers. Law schools are already graduating twice as many new lawyers every year as the Department of Labor thinks will be needed, and the oversupply is growing every year.

And it's not at all apparent that what is actually learned in a "professional" education is necessary for success. Teachers, engineers and others I talked to said they find that on the job they rarely use what they learned in school. In order to see how well college prepared engineers and scientists for actual paid work in their fields, The Carnegie Commission queried all the employees with degrees in these fields in two large firms. Only one in five said the work they were doing bore a "very close relationship" to their college studies, while almost a third saw "very little relationship at all." An overwhelming majority could think of many people who were doing their same work, but had majored in different fields.

Majors in nontechnical fields report even less relationship between their studies and their jobs. Charles Lawrence, a communications major in college and now the producer of "Kennedy & Co.," the Chicago morning television show, says, "You have to learn all that stuff and you never use it again. I learned my job doing it." Others employed as architects, nurses, teachers and other members of the so-called learned professions report the same thing.

Most college administrators admit that they don't prepare their graduates for the job market. "I just wish I had the guts to tell parents that when you get out of this place you aren't prepared to do anything," the academic head of a famous liberal-arts college told us. Fortunately, for him, most people believe that you don't have to defend a liberal-arts education on those grounds. A liberal-arts education is supposed to provide you with a value system, a standard, a set of ideas, not a job. "Like Christianity, the liberal arts are seldom practiced and would probably be hated by the majority of the populace if they were," said one defender. The analogy is apt. The fact is, of course, that the liberal arts are a religion in every sense of that term. When people talk about them, their language becomes elevated, metaphorical, extravagant, theoretical and reverent. And faith in personal salvation by the liberal arts is professed in a creed intoned on ceremonial occasions such as commencements.

If the liberal arts are a religious faith, the professors are its priests. But disseminating ideas in a four-year college curriculum is slow and most expensive. If you want to learn about Milton, Camus, or even Margaret Mead you can find them in paperback books, the public library, and even on television.

And when most people talk about the value of a college education, they are not talking about great books. When at Harvard commencement, the president welcomes the new graduates into "the fellowship of educated men and women," what he could be saying is, "Here is a piece of paper that is a passport to jobs, power and instant prestige." As Glenn Bassett, a personnel specialist at G.E. says, "In some parts of G.E., a college degree appears completely irrelevant to selection to, say, a manager's job. In most, however, it is a ticket of admission."

But now that we have doubled the number of young people attending college, a diploma cannot guarantee even that. The most charitable conclusion we can reach is that college probably has very little, if any, effect on people and things at all. Today, the false premises are easy to see:

First, college doesn't make people intelligent, ambitious, happy, or liberal. It's the other way around. Intelligent, ambitious, happy, liberal people are attracted to higher education in the first place.

Second, college can't claim much credit for the learning experiences that really change students while they are there. Jobs, friends, history, and most of all the sheer passage of time, have as big an impact as anything even indirectly related to the campus.

Third, colleges have changed so radically that a freshman entering in the fall of 1974 can't be sure to gain even the limited value research studies assigned to colleges in the '60s. The sheer size of undergraduate campuses of the 1970s makes college even less stimulating now than it was 10 years ago. Today even motivated students are disappointed with their college courses and professors.

Finally, a college diploma no longer opens as many vocational doors. Employers are beginning to realize that when they pay extra for someone with a diploma, they are paying only for an empty credential. The fact is that most of the work for which employers now expect college training is now or has been capably done in the past by people without higher educations.

College, then, may be a good place for those few young people who are really drawn to academic work, who would rather read than eat, but it has become too expensive, in money, time, and intellectual effort to serve as a holding pen for large numbers of our young. We ought to make it possible for those reluctant, unhappy students to find alternative ways of growing up, and more realistic preparation for the years ahead.

1975

Adrienne Rich

TAKING WOMEN STUDENTS SERIOUSLY[1]

I see my function here today as one of trying to create a context, delineate a background, against which we might talk about women as students and students as women. I would like to speak for awhile about this background, and then I hope that we can have, not so much a question period, as a raising of concerns, a sharing of questions for which we as yet may have no answers, an opening of conversations which will go on and on.

When I went to teach at Douglass, a women's college,[2] it was with a particular background which I would like briefly to describe to you. I had graduated from an all-girls' school in the 1940s, where the head and the majority of the faculty were independent, unmarried women. One or two held doctorates, but had been forced by the Depression (and by the fact that they were women) to take secondary school teaching jobs. These women cared a great deal about the life of the mind, and they gave a great deal of time and energy—beyond any limit of teaching hours—to those of us who showed special intellectual interest or ability. We were taken to libraries, art museums, lectures at neighboring colleges, set to work on extra research projects, given extra French or Latin reading. Although we sometimes felt "pushed" by them, we held those women in a kind of respect which even then we dimly perceived was not generally accorded to women in the world at large. They were vital individuals, defined not by their relationships but by their personalities; and although under the pressure of the culture we were all certain we wanted to get married, their lives did not appear empty or dreary to us. In a kind of cognitive dissonance, we knew they were "old maids" and therefore supposed to be bitter and lonely; yet we saw them vigorously involved with life. But despite their existence as alternate models of women, the *content* of the education they gave us in no way prepared us to survive as women in a world organized by and for men.

1. The talk that follows was addressed to teachers of women. . . . It was given for the New Jersey College and University Coalition on Women's Education, May 9,

1978 [Rich's note].
2. Part of Rutgers University in New Jersey.

From that school, I went on to Radcliffe, congratulating myself that now I would have great men as my teachers. From 1947 to 1951, when I graduated, I never saw a single woman on a lecture platform, or in front of a class, except when a woman graduate student gave a paper on a special topic. The "great men" talked of other "great men," of the nature of Man, the history of Mankind, the future of Man; and never again was I to experience, from a teacher, the kind of prodding, the insistence that my best could be even better, that I had known in high school. Women students were simply not taken very seriously. Harvard's message to women was an elite mystification: we were, of course, part of Mankind; we were special, achieving women, or we would not have been there; but of course our real goal was to marry—if possible, a Harvard graduate.

In the late sixties, I began teaching at the City College of New York—a crowded, public, urban, multiracial institution as far removed from Harvard as possible. I went there to teach writing in the SEEK Program,[3] which predated Open Admissions and which was then a kind of model for programs designed to open up higher education to poor, black, and Third World students. Although during the next few years we were to see the original concept of SEEK diluted, then violently attacked and betrayed, it was for a short time an extraordinary and intense teaching and learning environment. The characteristics of this environment were a deep commitment on the part of teachers to the minds of their students; a constant, active effort to create or discover the conditions for learning, and to educate ourselves to meet the needs of the new college population; a philosophical attitude based on open discussion of racism, oppression, and the politics of literature and language; and a belief that learning in the classroom could not be isolated from the student's experience as a member of an urban minority group in white America. Here are some of the kinds of questions we, as teachers of writing, found ourselves asking:

(1) What has been the student's experience of education in the inadequate, often abusively racist public school system, which rewards passivity and treats a questioning attitude or independent mind as a behavior problem? What has been her or his experience in a society that consistently undermines the selfhood of the poor and the nonwhite? How can such a student gain that sense of self which is necessary for active participation in education? What does all this mean for us as teachers?

(2) How do we go about teaching a canon of literature which has consistently excluded or depreciated nonwhite experience?

(3) How can we connect the process of learning to write well with the

3. SEEK is an acronym for "Search for Education, Elevation, and Knowledge"; the instructors in the program included not only college teachers but also creative artists and writers.

student's own reality, and not simply teach her/him how to write acceptable lies in standard English?

When I went to teach at Douglass College in 1976, and in teaching women's writing workshops elsewhere, I came to perceive stunning parallels to the questions I had first encountered in teaching the so-called disadvantaged students at City. But in this instance, and against the specific background of the women's movement, the questions framed themselves like this:

(1) What has been the student's experience of education in schools which reward female passivity, indoctrinate girls and boys in stereotypic sex roles, and do not take the female mind seriously? How does a woman gain a sense of her *self* in a system—in this case, patriarchal capitalism—which devalues work done by women, denies the importance and uniqueness of female experience, and is physically violent toward women? What does this mean for a woman teacher?

(2) How do we, as women, teach women students a canon of literature which has consistently excluded or depreciated female experience, and which often expresses hostility to women and validates violence against us?

(3) How can we teach women to move beyond the desire for male approval and getting "good grades" and seek and write their own truths that the culture has distorted or made taboo? (For women, of course, language itself is exclusive: I want to say more about this further on.)

In teaching women, we have two choices: to lend our weight to the forces that indoctrinate women to passivity, self-depreciation, and a sense of powerlessness, in which case the issue of "taking women students seriously" is a moot one; or to consider what we have to work against, as well as with, in ourselves, in our students, in the content of the curriculum, in the structure of the institution, in the society at large. And this means, first of all, taking ourselves seriously: Recognizing that central responsibility of a woman to herself, without which we remain always the Other, the defined, the object, the victim; believing that there is a unique quality of validation, affirmation, challenge, support, that one woman can offer another. Believing in the value and significance of women's experience, traditions, perceptions. Thinking of ourselves seriously, not as one of the boys, not as neuters, or androgynes, but as *women*.

Suppose we were to ask ourselves, simply: What does a woman need to know? Does she not, as a self-conscious, self-defining human being, need a knowledge of her own history, her much-politicized biology, an awareness of the creative work of women of the past, the skills and crafts and

techniques and powers exercised by women in different times and cultures, a knowledge of women's rebellions and organized movements against our oppression and how they have been routed or diminished? Without such knowledge women live and have lived without context, vulnerable to the projections of male fantasy, male prescriptions for us, estranged from our own experience because our education has not reflected or echoed it. I would suggest that not biology, but ignorance of our selves, has been the key to our powerlessness.

But the university curriculum, the high-school curriculum, do not provide this kind of knowledge for women, the knowledge of Womankind, whose experience has been so profoundly different from that of Mankind. Only in the precariously budgeted, much-condescended-to area of women's studies is such knowledge available to women students. Only there can they learn about the lives and work of women other than the few select women who are included in the "mainstream" texts, usually misrepresented even when they do appear. Some students, at some institutions, manage to take a majority of courses in women's studies, but the message from on high is that this is self-indulgence, soft-core education: the "real" learning is the study of Mankind.

If there is any misleading concept, it is that of "coeducation": that because women and men are sitting in the same classrooms, hearing the same lectures, reading the same books, performing the same laboratory experiments, they are receiving an equal education. They are not, first because the content of education itself validates men even as it invalidates women. Its very message is that men have been the shapers and thinkers of the world, and that this is only natural. The bias of higher education, including the so-called sciences, is white and male, racist and sexist; and this bias is expressed in both subtle and blatant ways. I have mentioned already the exclusiveness of grammar itself: "The student should test himself on the above questions"; "The poet is representative. He stands among partial men for the complete man." Despite a few half-hearted departures from custom, what the linguist Wendy Martyna has named "He-Man" grammar prevails throughout the culture. The efforts of feminists to reveal the profound ontological implications of sexist grammar are routinely ridiculed by academicians and journalists, including the professedly liberal *Times* columnist, Tom Wicker, and the professed humanist, Jacques Barzun.[4] Sexist grammar burns into the brains of little girls and young women a message that the male is the norm, the standard, the central figure beside which we are the deviants, the marginal, the dependent variables. It lays the foundation for androcentric thinking, and leaves men safe in their solipsistic tunnel-vision.

Women and men do not receive an equal education because outside the classroom women are perceived not as sovereign beings but as prey.

4. Rich is probably referring to Barzun's essay, "Was Paul Revere a Minute Person?"

The growing incidence of rape on and off the campus may or may not be fed by the proliferations of pornographic magazines and X-rated films available to young males in fraternities and student unions; but it is certainly occurring in a context of widespread images of sexual violence against women, on billboards and in so-called high art. More subtle, more daily than rape is the verbal abuse experienced by the woman student on many campuses—Rutgers for example—where, traversing a street lined with fraternity houses, she must run a gauntlet of male commentary and verbal assault. The undermining of self, of a woman's sense of her right to occupy space and walk freely in the world, is deeply relevant to education. The capacity to think independently, to take intellectual risks, to assert ourselves mentally, is inseparable from our physical way of being in the world, our feelings of personal integrity. If it is dangerous for me to walk home late of an evening from the library, *because I am a woman and can be raped*, how self-possessed, how exuberant can I feel as I sit working in that library? how much of my working energy is drained by the subliminal knowledge that, as a woman, I test my physical right to exist each time I go out alone? Of this knowledge, Susan Griffin has written:

> . . . more than rape itself, the fear of rape permeates our lives. And what does one do from day to day, with *this* experience, which says, without words and directly to the heart, *your existence, your experience, may end at any moment.* Your experience may end, and the best defense against this is not to be, to deny being in the body, as a self, to . . . avert your gaze, make yourself, as a presence in the world, less felt.[5]

Finally, rape of the mind. Women students are more and more often now reporting sexual overtures by male professors—one part of our overall growing consciousness of sexual harassment in the workplace. At Yale a legal suit has been brought against the university by a group of women demanding an explicit policy against sexual advances toward female students by male professors. Most young women experience a profound mixture of humiliation and intellectual self-doubt over seductive gestures by men who have the power to award grades, open doors to grants and graduate school, or extend special knowledge and training. Even if turned aside, such gestures constitute mental rape, destructive to a woman's ego. They are acts of domination, as despicable as the molestation of the daughter by the father.

But long before entering college the woman student has experienced her alien identity in a world which misnames her, turns her to its own uses, denying her the resources she needs to become self-affirming, self-defined. The nuclear family teaches her that relationships are more important than selfhood or work; that "whether the phone rings for you, and how often," having the right clothes, doing the dishes, take prece-

5. Rich is quoting (as her note to the passage says) from the manuscript of Griffin's *Rape: The Power of Consciousness* (New York: 1979).

dence over study or solitude; that too much intelligence or intensity may make her unmarriageable; that marriage and children—service to others —are, finally, the points on which her life will be judged a success or a failure. In high school, the polarization between feminine attractiveness and independent intelligence comes to an absolute. Meanwhile, the culture resounds with messages. During Solar Energy Week in New York I saw young women wearing "ecology" T-shirts with the legend: CLEAN, CHEAP AND AVAILABLE; a reminder of the 1960s antiwar button which read: CHICKS SAY YES TO MEN WHO SAY NO. Department store windows feature female mannequins in chains, pinned to the wall with legs spread, smiling in positions of torture. Feminists are depicted in the media as "shrill," "strident," "puritanical," or "humorless," and the lesbian choice—the choice of the woman-identified woman—as pathological or sinister. The young woman sitting in the philosophy classroom, the political science lecture, is already gripped by tensions between her nascent sense of self-worth, and the battering force of messages like these.

Look at a classroom: look at the many kinds of women's faces, postures, expressions. Listen to the women's voices. Listen to the silences, the unasked questions, the blanks. Listen to the small, soft voices, often courageously trying to speak up, voices of women taught early that tones of confidence, challenge, anger, or assertiveness, are strident and unfeminine. Listen to the voices of the women and the voices of the men; observe the space men allow themselves, physically and verbally, the male assumption that people will listen, even when the majority of the group is female. Look at the faces of the silent, and of those who speak. Listen to a woman groping for language in which to express what is on her mind, sensing that the terms of academic discourse are not her language, trying to cut down her thought to the dimensions of a discourse not intended for her (for it is not fitting that a woman speak in public); or reading her paper aloud at breakneck speed, throwing her words away, deprecating her own work by a reflex prejudgment: I do not deserve to take up time and space.

As women teachers, we can either deny the importance of this context in which women students think, write, read, study, project their own futures; or try to work with it. We can either teach passively, accepting these conditions, or actively, helping our students identify and resist them.

One important thing we can do is discuss the context. And this need not happen only in a women's studies course; it can happen anywhere. We can refuse to accept passive, obedient learning and insist upon critical thinking. We can become harder on our women students, giving them the kinds of "cultural prodding" that men receive, but on different terms and in a different style. Most young women need to have their intellectual lives, their work, legitimized against the claims of family, relationships, the old message that a woman is always available for service to others. We need to keep our standards very high, not to accept a woman's preconceived sense of her limitations; we need to be hard to please, while supportive of risk-taking, because self-respect often comes only when exacting standards have been met. At a time when adult literacy is generally low, we need to demand more, not less, of women, both for the sake of their futures as thinking beings, and because historically women have always had to be better than men to do half as well. A romantic sloppiness, an inspired lack of rigor, a self-indulgent incoherence, are symptoms of female self-depreciation. We should help our women students to look very critically at such symptoms, and to understand where they are rooted.

Nor does this mean we should be training women students to "think like men." Men in general think badly: in disjuncture from their personal lives, claiming objectivity where the most irrational passions seethe, losing, as Virginia Woolf[6] observed, their senses in the pursuit of professionalism. It is not easy to think like a woman in a man's world, in the world of the professions; yet the capacity to do that is a strength which we can try to help our students develop. To think like a woman in a man's world means thinking critically, refusing to accept the givens, making connections between facts and ideas which men have left unconnected. It means remembering that every mind resides in a body; remaining accountable to the female bodies in which we live; constantly retesting given hypotheses against lived experience. It means a constant critique of language, for as Wittgenstein[7] (no feminist) observed, "The limits of my language are the limits of my world." And it means that most difficult thing of all: listening and watching in art and literature, in the social sciences, in all the descriptions we are given of the world, for the silences, the absences, the nameless, the unspoken, the encoded—for there we will find the true knowledge of women. And in breaking those silences, naming our selves, uncovering the hidden, making ourselves present, we begin to define a reality which resonates to us, which affirms our being, which allows the woman teacher and the woman student alike to take ourselves, and each other, seriously: meaning, to begin taking charge of our lives.

1978   1979

---

6. Prominent British novelist, essayist, and feminist (1882–1941).
7. Ludwig Josef Johann Wittgenstein (1889–1951), influential Austrian philosopher.

James Thurber

UNIVERSITY DAYS

I passed all the other courses that I took at my university, but I could never pass botany. This was because all botany students had to spend several hours a week in a laboratory looking through a microscope at plant cells, and I could never see through a microscope. I never once saw a cell through a microscope. This used to enrage my instructor. He would wander around the laboratory pleased with the progress all the students were making in drawing the involved and, so I am told, interesting structure of flower cells, until he came to me. I would just be standing there. "I can't see anything," I would say. He would begin patiently enough, explaining how anybody can see through a microscope, but he would always end up in a fury, claiming that I could *too* see through a microscope but just pretended that I couldn't. "It takes away from the beauty of flowers anyway," I used to tell him. "We are not concerned with beauty in this course," he would say. "We are concerned solely with what I may call the *mechanics* of flars." "Well," I'd say, "I can't see anything." "Try it just once again," he'd say, and I would put my eye to the microscope and see nothing at all, except now and again a nebulous milky substance—a phenomenon of maladjustment. You were supposed to see a vivid, restless clockwork of sharply defined plant cells. "I see what looks like a lot of milk," I would tell him. This, he claimed, was the result of my not having adjusted the microscope properly, so he would readjust it for me, or rather, for himself. And I would look again and see milk.

I finally took a deferred pass, as they called it, and waited a year and tried again. (You had to pass one of the biological sciences or you couldn't graduate.) The professor had come back from vacation brown as a berry, bright-eyed, and eager to explain cell-structure again to his classes. "Well," he said to me, cheerily, when we met in the first laboratory hour of the semester, "we're going to see cells this time, aren't we?" "Yes, sir," I said. Students to right of me and to left of me and in front of me were seeing cells; what's more, they were quietly drawing pictures of them in their notebooks. Of course, I didn't see anything.

"We'll try it," the professor said to me, grimly, "with every adjustment of the microscope known to man. As God is my witness, I'll arrange this glass so that you see cells through it or I'll give up teaching. In twenty-two years of botany, I—" He cut off abruptly for he was beginning to quiver all over, like Lionel Barrymore,[1] and he genuinely wished to hold onto his temper; his scenes with me had taken a great deal out of him.

So we tried it with every adjustment of the microscope known to man.

1. Famed American actor (1878–1954), especially noted for elderly roles.

With only one of them did I see anything but blackness or the familiar lacteal opacity, and that time I saw, to my pleasure and amazement, a variegated constellation of flecks, specks, and dots. These I hastily drew. The instructor, noting my activity, came back from an adjoining desk, a smile on his lips and his eyebrows high in hope. He looked at my cell drawing. "What's that?" he demanded, with a hint of a squeal in his voice. "That's what I saw," I said. "You didn't, you didn't, you *didn't*!" he screamed, losing control of his temper instantly, and he bent over and squinted into the microscope. His head snapped up. "That's your eye!" he shouted. "You've fixed the lens so that it reflects! You've drawn your eye!"

Another course that I didn't like, but somehow managed to pass, was economics. I went to that class straight from the botany class, which didn't help me any in understanding either subject. I used to get them mixed up. But not as mixed up as another student in my economics class who came there direct from a physics laboratory. He was a tackle on the football team, named Bolenciecwcz. At that time Ohio State University had one of the best football teams in the country, and Bolenciecwcz was one of its outstanding stars. In order to be eligible to play it was necessary for him to keep up in his studies, a very difficult matter, for while he was not dumber than an ox he was not any smarter. Most of his professors were lenient and helped him along. None gave him more hints in answering questions or asked him simpler ones than the economics professor, a thin, timid man named Bassum. One day when we were on the subject of transportation and distribution, it came Bolenciecwcz's turn to answer a question. "Name one means of transportation," the professor said to him. No light came into the big tackle's eyes. "Just any means of transportation," said the professor. Bolenciecwcz sat staring at him. "That is," pursued the professor, "any medium, agency, or method of going from one place to another." Bolenciecwcz had the look of a man who is being led into a trap. "You may choose among steam, horsedrawn, or electrically propelled vehicles," said the instructor. "I might suggest the one which we commonly take in making long journeys across land." There was a profound silence in which everybody stirred uneasily, including Bolenciecwcz and Mr. Bassum, Mr. Bassum abruptly broke this silence in an amazing manner. "Choo-choo-choo," he said, in a low voice, and turned instantly scarlet. He glanced appealingly around the room. All of us, of course, shared Mr. Bassum's desire that Bolenciecwcz should stay abreast of the class in economics, for the Illinois game, one of the hardest and most important of the season, was only a week off. "Toot, toot, too-toooooooot!" some student with a deep voice moaned, and we all looked encouragingly at Bolenciecwcz. Somebody else gave a fine imitation of a locomotive letting off steam. Mr. Bassum himself rounded off the little show. "Ding, dong, ding, dong," he said, hopefully. Bolenciecwcz was staring at the floor now, trying to think, his great brow furrowed, his huge hands rubbing together, his face red.

"How did you come to college this year, Mr. Bolenciecwcz?" asked the professor. "*Chuffa* chuffa, *chuffa* chuffa."

"M'father sent me," said the football player.

"What on?" asked Bassum.

"I git an 'lowance," said the tackle, in a low, husky voice, obviously embarrassed.

"No, no," said Bassum. "Name a means of transportation. What did you *ride* here on?"

"Train," said Bolenciecwcz.

"Quite right," said the professor. "Now, Mr. Nugent, will you tell us —"

If I went through anguish in botany and economics—for different reasons—gymnasium work was even worse. I don't even like to think about it. They wouldn't let you play games or join in the exercises with your glasses on and I couldn't see with mine off. I bumped into professors, horizontal bars, agricultural students, and swinging iron rings. Not being able to see, I could take it but I couldn't dish it out. Also, in order to pass gymnasium (and you had to pass it to graduate) you had to learn to swim if you didn't know how. I didn't like the swimming pool, I didn't like swimming, and I didn't like the swimming instructor, and after all these years I still don't. I never swam but I passed my gym work anyway, by having another student give my gymnasium number (978) and swim across the pool in my place. He was a quiet, amiable blond youth, number 473, and he would have seen through a microscope for me if we could have got away with it, but we couldn't get away with it. Another thing I didn't like about gymnasium work was that they made you strip the day you registered. It is impossible for me to be happy when I am stripped and being asked a lot of questions. Still, I did better than a lanky agricultural student who was cross-examined just before I was. They asked each student what college he was in—that is, whether Arts, Engineering, Commerce, or Agriculture. "What college are you in?" the instructor snapped at the youth in front of me. "Ohio State University," he said promptly.

It wasn't that agricultural student but it was another a whole lot like him who decided to take up journalism, possibly on the ground that when farming went to hell he could fall back on newspaper work. He didn't realize, of course, that that would be very much like falling back full-length on a kit of carpenter's tools. Haskins didn't seem cut out for journalism, being too embarrassed to talk to anybody and unable to use a typewriter, but the editor of the college paper assigned him to the cow barns, the sheep house, the horse pavilion, and the animal husbandry department generally. This was a genuinely big "beat," for it took up five

times as much ground and got ten times as great a legislative appropriation as the College of Liberal Arts. The agricultural student knew animals, but nevertheless his stories were dull and colorlessly written. He
took all afternoon on each of them, on account of having to hunt for each
letter on the typewriter. Once in a while he had to ask somebody to help
him hunt. "C" and "L," in particular, were hard letters for him to find.
His editor finally got pretty much annoyed at the farmer-journalist because his pieces were so uninteresting. "See here, Haskins," he snapped
at him one day, "why is it we never have anything hot from you on the
horse pavilion? Here we have two hundred head of horses on this campus
—more than any other university in the Western Conference[2] except
Purdue—and yet you never get any real lowdown on them. Now shoot
over to the horse barns and dig up something lively." Haskins shambled
out and came back in about an hour; he said he had something. "Well,
start it off snappily," said the editor. "Something people will read."
Haskins set to work and in a couple of hours brought a sheet of typewritten paper to the desk; it was a two-hundred-word story about some
disease that had broken out among the horses. Its opening sentence was
simple but arresting. It read: "Who has noticed the sores on the tops of
the horses in the animal husbandry building?"

Ohio State was a land grant university and therefore two years of
military drill was compulsory. We drilled with old Springfield rifles and
studied the tactics of the Civil War even though the World War was
going on at the time. At 11 o'clock each morning thousands of freshmen
and sophomores used to deploy over the campus, moodily creeping up on
the old chemistry building. It was good training for the kind of warfare
that was waged at Shiloh[3] but it had no connection with what was going
on in Europe. Some people used to think there was German money
behind it, but they didn't dare say so or they would have been thrown in
jail as German spies. It was a period of muddy thought and marked, I
believe, the decline of higher education in the Middle West.

As a soldier I was never any good at all. Most of the cadets were glumly
indifferent soldiers, but I was no good at all. Once General Littlefield,
who was commandant of the cadet corps, popped up in front of me during
regimental drill and snapped, "You are the main trouble with this university!" I think he meant that my type was the main trouble with the
university but he may have meant me individually. I was mediocre at
drill, certainly—that is, until my senior year. By that time I had drilled
longer than anybody else in the Western Conference, having failed at
military at the end of each preceding year so that I had to do it all over
again. I was the only senior still in uniform. The uniform which, when
new, had made me look like an interurban railway conductor, now that it

2. The Big Ten.   3. In southwestern Tennessee, site of 1862
                                   Union victory.

had become faded and too tight made me look like Bert Williams in his bellboy act.[4] This had a definitely bad effect on my morale. Even so, I had become by sheer practice little short of wonderful at squad maneuvers.

One day General Littlefield picked our company out of the whole regiment and tried to get it mixed up by putting it through one movement after another as fast as we could execute them: squads right, squads left, squads on right into line, squads right about, squads left front into line, etc. In about three minutes one hundred and nine men were marching in one direction and I was marching away from them at an angle of forty degrees, all alone. "Company, halt!" shouted General Littlefield. "That man is the only man who has it right!" I was made a corporal for my achievement.

The next day General Littlefield summoned me to his office. He was swatting flies when I went in. I was silent and he was silent too, for a long time, I don't think he remembered me or why he had sent for me, but he didn't want to admit it. He swatted some more flies, keeping his eyes on them narrowly before he let go with the swatter. "Button up your coat!" he snapped. Looking back on it now I can see that he meant me although he was looking at a fly, but I just stood there. Another fly came to rest on a paper in front of the general and began rubbing its hind legs together. The general lifted the swatter cautiously. I moved restlessly and the fly flew away. "You startled him!" barked General Littlefield, looking at me severely. I said I was sorry. "That won't help the situation!" snapped the General, with cold military logic. I didn't see what I could do except offer to chase some more flies toward his desk, but I didn't say anything. He stared out the window at the faraway figures of co-eds crossing the campus toward the library. Finally, he told me I could go. So I went. He either didn't know which cadet I was or else he forgot what he wanted to see me about. It may have been that he wished to apologize for having called me the main trouble with the university; or maybe he had decided to compliment me on my brilliant drilling of the day before and then at the last minute decided not to. I don't know. I don't think about it much any more.

1933

4. Popular vaudeville comedian.

QUESTIONS

1. *Why did Thurber pick these particular incidents of his college career to write about? What do they have in common?*
2. *Take one of the incidents described in the essay and analyze how Thurber describes it. What do you think he may have added to or subtracted from what actually happened? Take a similar incident, (real or imagined) and in a brief essay try to treat it in the way that Thurber treats his incidents.*

3. Based on this essay, what do you think Thurber's definition or description of an ideal college education would be?

4. In "Examsmanship and the Liberal Arts," (p. 282) William G. Perry, Jr. distinguishes between two kinds of knowledge, "cow" and "bull." Read or review the Perry essay and then determine, judging by Thurber's essay, which kind of knowledge seems to have been in greater demand at Thurber's university.

5. In "Some Remarks on Humor" (p. 1047), E. B. White says about humorists: "Humorists fatten on trouble. . . . You find them wrestling with foreign languages, fighting folding ironing boards and swollen drainpipes, suffering the terrible discomfort of tight boots. . . . They pour out their sorrows profitably, in a form that is not quite fiction nor quite fact either. Beneath the sparkling surface of these dilemmas flows the strong tide of human woe." Discuss the validity of White's definition and test it by applying it to Thurber's essay.

Lord Ashby

THE UNIVERSITY IDEAL: A VIEW FROM BRITAIN

The story is told that in the medieval University of Paris the professors were disputing about the number of teeth in a horse's mouth. They agreed that the number could not be a multiple of three, for that would be an offense to the Trinity; nor could it be a multiple of seven, for God created the world in six days and rested on the seventh. Neither the records of Aristotle nor the arguments of St. Thomas enabled them to solve the problem. Then a shocking thing happened. A student who had been listening to the discussion went out, opened a horse's mouth, and counted the teeth.

I want to draw two conclusions from this parable. The first is that our present perplexities about universities derive from the act of this medieval student. He symbolizes the beginning of objective inquiry, the revolt against authority, the empirical attitude, the linking of academic study with the facts of life. His act introduced research into the university. After the horse's mouth was opened knowledge became an open system. The second conclusion is that we must think twice before we become nostalgic about the traditional university ideal. Not everything about the traditional university is worth preserving. The medieval university was hostile to what we now call academic freedom. To stray outside the corpus academicum of set books, even to interpret them in novel ways, was to court heresy. The traditional university was not much interested in discovery: it was preoccupied with transmission of a crystallized culture. It was at certain periods not even interested in knowledge for its own sake; many scholars pursued knowledge if not for preferment, then as a means of spiritual and intellectual health, just as a man plays golf not for the sake of golf but to keep down his weight.

I want to follow these two lines of thought by raising three questions. The first is this. What do we want to perpetuate from the university's long tradition? What, in other words, is the content of our loyalty to the university ideal? Secondly, what obligations does the university have —what loyalties ought it to foster—toward contemporary society? And thirdly, what are the prospects that these two loyalties—one to a traditional university ideal, the other to the society in which we live—can be reconciled?

On the very spot where I sat to prepare these remarks Clare College had existed since 1326. Six centuries ago it was a row of cottages, with an iron box in which some books were stored. In the cottages, under the Lady Clare's foundation, lived the Master and a dozen Fellows and about the same number of students, sharing the Fellows' rooms. There was a hall where lectures were held and where Fellows and scholars ate together, but much of the teaching was a private contract between Fellow and pupil; we still have records of the fees they paid. Fellows and scholars lived austerely. Their food was plain. They clustered in winter round a common fire. The little community was virtually independent of the University. It governed itself as it still does, sealing contracts in the name of the Master, Fellows, and Scholars of Clare; we still have the seal Lady Clare gave us.

In this simple society was to be found the secret of excellence in universities, the one element of tradition which we do want to preserve. It was an environment for the continuous polishing of one mind by another. Its basic formula was very simple. The essential ingredients were on the one hand a reflective, disciplined, learned man willing to teach; on the other hand an intelligent, motivated student willing to learn; and, thirdly, a balance of numbers between teacher and student so that the relation between them was intimate and personal. Given these ingredients, the university ideal can be realized whatever other shortcomings there may be. Without these ingredients, no institution can realize fully the university ideal.

The characteristic of university teaching is quality in communication, which must be distinguished from standards of achievement. Standards vary enormously in time and place. For example, the standards of achievement necessary for admission to Cambridge, Harvard, and Göttingen are very different. The standard of achievement necessary to get a degree in physics in Cambridge in 1900 was about the same as the standard now necessary to get entry to Cambridge as a freshman. But quality of teaching in Cambridge, Harvard, and Göttingen is—I believe

—about the same; and the quality of teaching in Cambridge two generations ago was certainly not lower than it is today. So when we talk of preserving traditional academic values, we mean quality. This we must preserve.

Now let me turn again to the student who opened the horse's mouth. He was the pioneer of academic freedom, the *Lern-* and *Lehrfreiheit*[1] of the Germans. He gave the university a new mission; not to preserve the *status quo* but to question it. From this all sorts of consequences flow: the university as a disruptive rather than a consolidating influence in society; the proliferation, and hence the fragmentation, of knowledge; the consequent inevitable increase in size and cost of universities, which threaten to deprive the university of its identity because it has become—I suppose for the first time since the middle ages—too dependent upon outside influence, an influence which in those days was the orthodoxy of the Church and in these days is the orthodoxy of alumni or legislature.

This brings me to the university's obligation to the present. Being modern is not necessarily a virtue; indeed it is one sign of a small mind to want to be contemporary in one's generation, just as it is to want to be parochial in one's geography. We face a problem in what a biologist would call selective permeability. Which outside pressures should we allow to act upon the university, and which should we resist?

It has been said of medieval universities "that they placed the administration of human affairs . . . in the hands of educated men." There could be no better summary than this of the obligations of universities to our present society; nor is it likely to be disputed. Our disputes center round the definition of an educated man. For some people still this is synonymous with a knowledge of the languages and civilizations of Greece and Rome, and consistent with an ignorance of science, technology, and modern society. It is still possible to rise to the highest ranks of public life in Britain having done no science since the age of 15, no social science at all, and at the university nothing but the classics for three years. Diversification of the curriculum has always met with fierce opposition. When history was introduced into Oxford one of the faculty wrote, "I can but fear the worst, a majority of fourteen in convocation voted in favor of . . . modern history. We did indeed by a large majority reject the details of this novelty, but the principle has been admitted . . . we have fallen into the weakness of yielding to the spirit of the age." A century later Flexner[2] was issuing similar Jeremiads about the introduction of journalism and business studies into American universities.

I believe Flexner was wrong. I believe that to admit into the college curriculum new professional schools on our terms—the terms of the faculty not of the legislature or the alumni—is an essential obligation of

---

1. Freedom to learn and freedom to teach.   educator and educational reformer.
2. Abraham Flexner (1866–1959), American

universities. But, let it be emphasized, on our terms, for we are the experts. And our terms are uncompromising and unambiguous. They are that any and every university subject must be mastered in the medium of one or other (or both) of two systems of symbols: language and mathematics. Indeed, the quintessence of higher education is the mastery of these systems of symbols and their application to real, and relevant, situations. To me, the touchstone of university studies is not to teach great truths but rather to teach truth in a great way; not simply to inherit orthodoxy but to master the dialectic between orthodoxy and dissent. It is a style of thought, which at its best transcends subject-matter; a style which cannot be acquired except from someone who is constantly exploring at the limits of understanding (hence the necessity for academics to do what is commonly, and erroneously, called "research").

One of the great contributions which the United States has made to the university tradition is to overcome the resistance to desirable adaptation of the curriculum. In permitting the proliferation of professional schools following a bachelor's degree in liberal arts, the United States has done no more than reinstate in modern dress the traditional medieval pattern of the university, which had been lost in nineteenth century Oxford and Cambridge. I believe this is a great achievement, but it has brought in its wake two problems. One is the enormous increase in size of universities, inevitable if they are to encompass this novel diversity of studies. The other is that you cannot have professional schools without professionals, and a professional's first loyalty is to his guild of other professionals, to chemists, historians, lawyers, outside the university. And so the university finds itself with a faculty which, if not exactly alienated, certainly does not give its total allegiance to the institution it serves.

Size and divided loyalty: these are not new problems. Estimates of student numbers in medieval universities have been greatly exaggerated, but it is very likely that at times there were about 7,000 students in some of the bigger ones. And a student population of 7,000 on one campus under medieval conditions must have been as formidable as a population ten times the size under modern conditions. As for divided loyalties, we only have to remember that the faculty in a medieval university were clerics, under church discipline, to realize where their first loyalty lay.

Let me say that in British universities we have, by and large, preserved the ark of the covenant,[3] which is dedication to quality in the transmission of learning and a sustained and rigorous training in the symbolism of language and mathematics. But, it is essential to point out at what cost we have done this. For the price has been high.

First, we have denied an opportunity for higher education to tens of

---

3. A sacred symbol of the biblical Hebrews, the ark was the wooden chest overlaid with gold in which Moses placed the stone tablets containing the ten commandments. See Exodus xxv. 10-21.

thousands of British children who deserved to have one. At the time of the Robbins Committee (1963) it was estimated that about 1 in 3 American children of university age were receiving full-time education. The corresponding figures for British children were about 1 in 14; and, if you count only degree-granting institutions, more like 1 in 25. Even when all allowances are made for our very different patterns of high school education, there is still no escape from the conclusion that we in Britain have avoided one of your problems simply by shutting college doors to thousands of our children. We are changing all that now (and hence running into troubles similar to yours), but even when our educational revolution is over, in 1980, we plan to have only 1 child in 6 attending college.

Secondly, we have virtually eliminated general education from our system, though some of our newer institutions are beginning in a modest way to reinstate it.

This is the price we are paying. Now let me tell you what we have bought for the price.

First, we have avoided some of the dangers of size. Rightly or wrongly (it is too early to say yet), we have met the demand for higher education not by enlarging our universities to 20,000 or 30,000 as you have but by creating new universities. And even our larger universities, such as my own, are divided into small units. Clare College has 360 undergraduates. We give personal tuition to every one of these undergraduates about twice a week and we draw on nearly 100 people, part time, to do this college teaching for us. And even in universities where there is no college system, students (since they are reading one-subject honors degrees) spend nearly all their time in one department, so it becomes their intellectual and largely their social home, and the faculty knows them as individuals.

One consequence of this restriction on student numbers and preservation of small units of size is that the ratio of teachers to students is high. We try to aim at a faculty-student ratio of 1 in 8. In small universities and in Cambridge colleges the "mix" is even richer; in these, every week the student receives two or three supervisions (called tutorials in Oxford) either alone with his teacher, or in pairs or at most threes, when he reads an essay and has it criticized. Faculty members become as enthusiastic about the performance of their pupils as though the pupils were horses entered in a race. It is the determined and deliberate policy of the British University Grants Committee that this "hand-made" method of teaching shall be adopted by all British universities, and some of them are well on the way to adopting it.

One may wonder where the faculty comes from. I can say for Cambridge. Of course we use Ph.D. teaching assistants as American universities do, but not to the same extent. We use also—and they are absolutely essential to our system—members of research teams and faculty wives, a device which could, I believe, be adopted effectively in American universities. But above all we expect our faculty members, however distinguished, to teach. No British university would offer even a Nobel Pricewinner a job with the understanding that he need teach only one quarter a year. In my own College there are Fellows of Royal Society who are teaching up to ten hours a week. The "flight from teaching" is, of course, a problem for us as well as you, but apart from the "flight across the Atlantic," it is less severe for us for two reasons: because we give tenure to academics earlier in their careers than America does, which means that the drive to publish is less pressing; and because we have uniform salary scales for all British universities; hence our faculty composition is more stable and one university cannot easily buy up scholars from another.

Of course it is an expensive method of education, this "hand-made" teaching. And Britain is not a wealthy country. But I wonder whether some of the troubles in America might be due to the fact (I hesitate to say such a surprising thing) that despite the astronomical bill for colleges, higher education is being done "on the cheap," insofar as it is not employing enough senior faculty to match the student numbers. For the sacred thread of transmission between teacher and pupil, does America perhaps rely more than we do on inexperienced teachers?

Secondly, our very neglect of general education does enable us to insist on mastery of a narrow field. If a student studies nothing but history (or chemistry) for three years, under the personal tutelage of an expert, he is likely to acquire a sense of values, standards of self-criticism, a mastery in handling data and concepts, which is one hallmark of higher education. Particularly is this so if the student is highly motivated. Since there is such competition for places, and selection nowadays is strictly on academic merit, we in Britain are able to select intelligent and often earnest students. Not exclusively, of course; but the frivolous student, the playboy, and the dullard do not easily slip into British universities. So our drop-out rate is low: in Cambridge less than 3 percent of those who enter fail to graduate; and the national average of drop-outs in Britain is around 12 percent.

Finally—and this is a controversial virtue—we meet the challenge of maintaining quality in higher education by our system of examination. Every university in every subject has an external examiner, usually from another university. It is the external examiner's business to see that the standards for the award of degrees are about the same as those in his own university. So (for example) the level of achievement which we call "a first" in history or chemistry is locked into a common standard for all British universities. In this way we have, I am sure, consolidated throughout the whole of our system of higher education our loyalty to the ideal of what a university should be. But, by putting on the market, as it were, only Cadillacs and no Fords, we have not fulfilled adequately our loyalty to contemporary society.

If one accepts my description of the university ideal as quality in the transmission of knowledge, possible ways to preserve this ideal are: (1) to insist on a rich faculty-student ratio and to require the faculty to teach at least eight hours a week; (2) to maintain comparatively small units of size: this is not inconsistent with the large university—one can build clusters of colleges around massive central amenities (the Residential College at the University of Michigan is one experimental prototype) and (3) at some stage of university education to require intense concentration in scope of studies.

It is time to sum up. Let us try to cast a balance for the modern university. In standards of achievement demanded of students and faculty, in a willingness to incorporate new areas of knowledge, in giving faculty and students freedom to teach and to learn, modern universities are incomparably better than were those in the middle ages, or indeed those in the nineteenth century.

It is the very success of universities which endangers their cohesion internally and their integrity from outside. It does not matter much if the external structure of universities changes, or if new subjects appear in the curriculum, or if universities open their doors to a greater proportion of the age group: provided always that the thin stream of excellence on which the intellectual health of the nation ultimately depends is not contaminated. In our present social climate I do not believe excellence can be safeguarded (as we have tried to safeguard it in Britain) by keeping mediocrity out of higher education. This is simply unrealistic. I believe it must be safeguarded as America is trying to do it, by the peaceful coexistence of mediocrity and excellence. They have, after all, got to coexist elsewhere in society, and it is an educational commonplace that Gresham's law[4] does not hold for college degrees; indeed mediocrity is improved by association with excellence. Fords do not drive Cadillacs off the market.

What we have to devise, on both sides of the Atlantic, are ways to foster motivation among students and quality in communication among teachers. That is why I venture to come back to the paradigm of Clare College six hundred years ago. I have faith in the American university because I believe that even with its immense numbers of students it can (and indeed is) solving the problem of cultivating quality as well as accommodating quantity. It is reconciling loyalty to the university ideal and loyalty to contemporary society.

c. 1965

---

4. The economic principle that "bad money drives out good"—that is, that the introduction of a debased coinage will result in the disappearance of coins made of precious metals.

William Zinsser

COLLEGE PRESSURES

Dear Carlos: I desperately need a dean's excuse for my chem midterm which will begin in about 1 hour. All I can say is that I totally blew it this week. I've fallen incredibly, inconceivably behind.

Carlos: Help! I'm anxious to hear from you. I'll be in my room and won't leave it until I hear from you. Tomorrow is the last day for . . .

Carlos: I left town because I started bugging out again. I stayed up all night to finish a take-home make-up exam & am typing it to hand in on the 10th. It was due on the 5th. P.S. I'm going to the dentist. Pain is pretty bad.

Carlos: Probably by Friday I'll be able to get back to my studies. Right now I'm going to take a long walk. This whole thing has taken a lot out of me.

Carlos: I'm really up the proverbial creek. The problem is I really *bombed* the history final. Since I need that course for my major I . . .

Carlos: Here follows a tale of woe. I went home this weekend, had to help my Mom, & caught a fever so didn't have much time to study. My professor . . .

Carlos: Aargh! Trouble. Nothing original but everything's piling up at once. To be brief, my job interview . . .

Hey Carlos, good news! I've got mononucleosis.

Who are these wretched supplicants, scribbling notes so laden with anxiety, seeking such miracles of postponement and balm? They are men and women who belong to Branford College, one of the twelve residential colleges at Yale University, and the messages are just a few of the hundreds that they left for their dean, Carlos Hortas—often slipped under his door at 4 A.M.—last year.

But students like the ones who wrote those notes can also be found on campuses from coast to coast—especially in New England and at many other private colleges across the country that have high academic standards and highly motivated students. Nobody could doubt that the notes are real. In their urgency and their gallows humor they are authentic voices of a generation that is panicky to succeed.

My own connection with the message writers is that I am master of Branford College. I live in its Gothic quadrangle and know the students well. (We have 485 of them.) I am privy to their hopes and fears—and also to their stereo music and their piercing cries in the dead of night ("Does anybody *ca-a-are*?"). If they went to Carlos to ask how to get

275

through tomorrow, they come to me to ask how to get through the rest of their lives.

Mainly I try to remind them that the road ahead is a long one and that it will have more unexpected turns than they think. There will be plenty of time to change jobs, change careers, change whole attitudes and approaches. They don't want to hear such liberating news. They want a map—right now—that they can follow unswervingly to career security, financial security. Social Security and, presumably, a prepaid grave.

What I wish for all students is some release from the clammy grip of the future. I wish them a chance to savor each segment of their education as an experience in itself and not as a grim preparation for the next step. I wish them the right to experiment, to trip and fall, to learn that defeat is as instructive as victory and is not the end of the world.

My wish, of course, is naïve. One of the few rights that America does not proclaim is the right to fail. Achievement is the national god, venerated in our media—the million-dollar athlete, the wealthy executive —and glorified in our praise of possessions. In the presence of such a potent state religion, the young are growing up old.

I see four kinds of pressure working on college students today: economic pressure, parental pressure, peer pressure, and self-induced pressure. It is easy to look around for villains—to blame the colleges for charging too much money, the professors for assigning too much work, the parents for pushing their children too far, the students for driving themselves too hard. But there are no villains; only victims.

"In the late 1960s," one dean told me, "the typical question that I got from students was 'Why is there so much suffering in the world?' or 'How can I make a contribution?' Today it's 'Do you think it would look better for getting into law school if I did a double major in history and political science, or just majored in one of them?'" Many other deans confirmed this pattern. One said: "They're trying to find an edge—the intangible something that will look better on paper if two students are about equal."

Note the emphasis on looking better. The transcript has become a sacred document, the passport to security. How one appears on paper is more important than how one appears in person. A is for Admirable and B is for Borderline, even though, in Yale's official system of grading, A means "excellent" and B means "very good." Today, looking very good is no longer good enough, especially for students who hope to go on to law school or medical school. They know that entrance into the better schools will be an entrance into the better law firms and better medical practices where they will make a lot of money. They also know that the odds are harsh, Yale Law School, for instance, matriculates 170 students from an applicant pool of 3,700; Harvard enrolls 550 from a pool of 7,000.

It's all very well for those of us who write letters of recommendation for our students to stress the qualities of humanity that will make them good lawyers or doctors. And it's nice to think that admission officers are really reading our letters and looking for the extra dimension of commitment or concern. Still, it would be hard for a student not to visualize these officers shuffling so many transcripts studded with As that they regard a *B* as positively shameful.

The pressure is almost as heavy on students who just want to graduate and get a job. Long gone are the days of the "gentleman's C," when students journeyed through college with a certain relaxation, sampling a wide variety of courses—music, art, philosophy, classics, anthropology, poetry, religion—that would send them out as liberally educated men and women. If I were an employer I would rather employ graduates who have this range and curiosity than those who narrowly pursued safe subjects and high grades. I know countless students whose inquiring minds exhilarate me. I like to hear the play of their ideas. I don't know if they are getting As or Cs, and I don't care. I also like them as people. The country needs them, and they will find satisfying jobs. I tell them to relax. They can't.

Nor can I blame them. They live in a brutal economy. Tuition, room, and board at most private colleges now comes to at least $7,000, not counting books and fees. This might seem to suggest that the colleges are getting rich. But they are equally battered by inflation. Tuition covers only 60 percent of what it costs to educate a student, and ordinarily the remainder comes from what colleges receive in endowments, grants, and gifts. Now the remainder keeps being swallowed by the cruel costs —higher every year—of just opening the doors. Heating oil is up. Insurance is up. Postage is up. Health-premium costs are up. Everything is up. Deficits are up. We are witnessing in America the creation of a brotherhood of paupers—colleges, parents, and students, joined by the common bond of debt.

Today it is not unusual for a student, even if he works part time at college and full time during the summer, to accrue $5,000 in loans after four years—loans that he must start to repay within one year after graduation. Exhorted at commencement to go forth into the world, he is already behind as he goes forth. How could he not feel under pressure throughout college to prepare for this day of reckoning? I have used "he," incidentally, only for brevity. Women at Yale are under no less pressure to justify their expensive education to themselves, their parents, and society. In fact, they are probably under more pressure. For although they leave college superbly equipped to bring fresh leadership to traditionally male jobs, society hasn't yet caught up with this fact.

Along with economic pressure goes parental pressure. Inevitably, the two are deeply intertwined.

I see many students taking pre-medical courses with joyless tenacity. They go off to their labs as if they were going to the dentist. It saddens me because I know them in other corners of their life as cheerful people.

"Do you want to go to medical school?" I ask them.

"I guess so," they say, without conviction, or "Not really."

"Then why are you going?"

"Well, my parents want me to be a doctor. They're paying all this money and . . ."

Poor students, poor parents. They are caught in one of the oldest webs of love and duty and guilt. The parents mean well; they are trying to steer their sons and daughters toward a secure future. But the sons and daughters want to major in history or classics or philosophy—subjects with no "practical" value. Where's the payoff on the humanities? It's not easy to persuade such loving parents that the humanities do indeed pay off. The intellectual faculties developed by studying subjects like history and classics—an ability to synthesize and relate, to weigh cause and effect, to see events in perspective—are just the faculties that make creative leaders in business or almost any general field. Still, many fathers would rather put their money on courses that point toward a specific profession —courses that are pre-law, pre-medical, pre-business, or, as I sometimes heard it put, "pre-rich."

But the pressure on students is severe. They are truly torn. One part of them feels obligated to fulfill their parents' expectations; after all, their parents are older and presumably wiser. Another part tells them that the expectations that are right for their parents are not right for them.

I know a student who wants to be an artist. She is very obviously an artist and will be a good one—she has already had several modest local exhibits. Meanwhile she is growing as a well-rounded person and taking humanistic subjects that will enrich the inner resources out of which her art will grow. But her father is strongly opposed. He thinks that an artist is a "dumb" thing to be. The student vacillates and tries to please everybody. She keeps up with her art somewhat furtively and takes some of the "dumb" courses her father wants her to take—at least they are dumb courses for her. She is a free spirit on a campus of tense students —no small achievement in itself—and she deserves to follow her muse.

Peer pressure and self-induced pressure are also intertwined, and they begin almost at the beginning of freshman year.

"I had a freshman student I'll call Linda," one dean told me, "who came in and said she was under terrible pressure because her roommate, Barbara, was much brighter and studied all the time. I couldn't tell her that Barbara had come in two hours earlier to say the same thing about Linda."

The story is almost funny—except that it's not. It's symptomatic of all the pressures put together. When every student thinks every other student is working harder and doing better, the only solution is to study harder still. I see students going off to the library every night after dinner and coming back when it closes at midnight. I wish they would sometimes forget about their peers and go to a movie. I hear the clacking of typewriters in the hours before dawn. I see the tension in their eyes when exams are approaching and papers are due: *"Will I get everything done?"*

Probably they won't. They will get sick. They will get "blocked." They will sleep. They will oversleep. They will bug out. *Hey Carlos, help!*

Part of the problem is that they do more than they are expected to do. A professor will assign five-page papers. Several students will start writing ten-page papers to impress him. Then more students will write ten-page papers, and a few will raise the ante to fifteen. Pity the poor student who is still just doing the assignment.

Once you have twenty or thirty percent of the student population deliberately overexerting," one dean points out, "it's bad for everybody. When a teacher gets more and more effort from his class, the student who is doing normal work can be perceived as not doing well. The tactic works, psychologically."

Why can't the professor just cut back and not accept longer papers? He can, and he probably will. But by then the term will be half over and the damage done. Grade fever is highly contagious and not easily reversed. Besides, the professor's main concern is with his course. He knows his students only in relation to the course and doesn't know that they are also overexerting in their other courses. Nor is it really his business. He didn't sign up for dealing with the student as a whole person and with all the emotional baggage the student brought along from home. That's what deans, masters, chaplains, and psychiatrists are for.

To some extent this is nothing new: a certain number of professors have always been self-contained islands of scholarship and shyness, more comfortable with books than with people. But the new pauperism has widened the gap still further, for professors who actually like to spend time with students don't have as much time to spend. They also are overexerting. If they are young, they are busy trying to publish in order not to perish, hanging by their finger nails onto a shrinking profession. If they are old and tenured, they are buried under the duties of administering departments—as departmental chairmen or members of committees —that have been thinned out by the budgetary axe.

Ultimately it will be the students' own business to break the circles in which they are trapped. They are too young to be prisoners of their parents' dreams and their classmates' fears. They must be jolted into believing in themselves as unique men and women who have the power to shape their own future.

"Violence is being done to the undergraduate experience," says Carlos

Hortas. "College should be open-ended: at the end it should open many, many roads. Instead, students are choosing their goal in advance, and their choices narrow as they go along. It's almost as if they think that the country has been codified in the type of jobs that exist—that they've got to fit into certain slots. Therefore, fit into the best-paying slot.

"They ought to take chances. Not taking chances will lead to a life of colorless mediocrity. They'll be comfortable. But something in the spirit will be missing."

I have painted too drab a portrait of today's students, making them seem a solemn lot. That is only half of their story; if they were so dreary I wouldn't so thoroughly enjoy their company. The other half is that they are easy to like. They are quick to laugh and to offer friendship. They are not introverts. They are unusually kind and are more considerate of one another than any student generation I have known.

Nor are they so obsessed with their studies that they avoid sports and extracurricular activities. On the contrary, they juggle their crowded hours to play on a variety of teams, perform with musical and dramatic groups, and write for campus publications. But this in turn is one more cause of anxiety. There are too many choices. Academically, they have 1,300 courses to select from; outside class they have to decide how much spare time they can spare and how to spend it.

This means that they engage in fewer extracurricular pursuits than their predecessors did. If they want to row on the crew and play in the symphony they will eliminate one; in the '60s they would have done both. They also tend to choose activities that are self-limiting. Drama, for instance, is flourishing in all twelve of Yale's residential colleges as it never has before. Students hurl themselves into these productions—as actors, directors, carpenters, and technicians—with a dedication to create the best possible play, knowing that the day will come when the run will end and they can get back to their studies.

They also can't afford to be the willing slave of organizations like the *Yale Daily News.* Last spring at the one-hundredth anniversary banquet of that paper—whose past chairmen include such once and future kings as Potter Stewart, Kingman Brewster, and William F. Buckley, Jr. —much was made of the fact that the editorial staff used to be small and totally committed and that "newsies" routinely worked fifty hours a week. In effect they belonged to a club; Newsies is how they defined themselves at Yale. Today's student will write one or two articles a week, when he can, and he defines himself as a student. I've never heard the word Newsie except at the banquet.

If I have described the modern undergraduate primarily as a driven creature who is largely ignoring the blithe spirit inside who keeps trying to come out and play, it's because that's where the crunch is, not only at

Yale but throughout American education. It's why I think we should all be worried about the values that are nurturing a generation so fearful of risk and so goal-obsessed at such an early age.

I tell students that there is no one "right" way to get ahead—that each of them is a different person, starting from a different point and bound for a different destination. I tell them that change is a tonic and that all the slots are not codified nor the frontiers closed. One of my ways of telling them is to invite men and women who have achieved success outside the academic world to come and talk informally with my students during the year. They are heads of companies or ad agencies, editors of magazines, politicians, public officials, television magnates, labor leaders, business executives, Broadway producers, artists, writers, economists, photographers, scientists, historians—a mixed bag of achievers.

I ask them to say a few words about how they got started. The students assume that they started in their present profession and knew all along that it was what they wanted to do. Luckily for me, most of them got into their field by a circuitous route, to their surprise, after many detours. The students are startled. They can hardly conceive of a career that was not pre-planned. They can hardly imagine allowing the hand of God or chance to nudge them down some unforeseen trail.

1979

QUESTIONS

1. By beginning with quotations from student notes to the counseling dean Zinsser seeks to establish the problem of college pressures as a concrete personal reality; then he seeks to generalize, using those personal statements to represent also the situation of other students at other colleges. Does this plan work? What makes the statements sound authentic, or inauthentic?

2. On p. 276 Zinsser names four kinds of pressure on college students. Are there others? Are they all equally strong? What counterpressures exist? What would be necessary for a state of equilibrium? Would those changes or that state be desirable?

3. In describing the four kinds of pressure, Zinsser has to make transitions. One of these ("Along with economic pressure . . ." [p. 277]) is loose. Could it be tightened? Should it be? What about the others? What are the logical relations among the four kinds of pressure?

4. On p. 280 Zinsser refers to "the blithe spirit" inside the "driven" college student. Willard Gaylin, in "What You See Is the Real You" (p. 620), rejects such analyses. Which view do you find more persuasive? Why?

5. In the New York Times for May 14, 1970, Fred Hechinger reported an apparent increase in cheating by college students and pointed out that, historically, cheating occurs when grades are used to determine success in competition for economic and social rewards. He then concluded that some people are wondering if this process is not damaging

*the colleges, if "the economic and political system is improperly ex-
ploiting the educational system." By making "system" the subject of
the clause, he avoided having to say who in particular is responsible for
the problem. Write an essay in which you show who is responsible for
the problem; or show that the problem doesn't exist, or isn't important;
or redefine the problem to lead to different conclusions.*

William G. Perry, Jr.

EXAMSMANSHIP AND THE LIBERAL ARTS:
A STUDY IN EDUCATIONAL EPISTEMOLOGY

"But sir, I don't think I really deserve it, it was mostly bull, really."
This disclaimer from a student whose examination we have awarded a
straight "A" is wondrously depressing. Alfred North Whitehead invented its only possible rejoinder: "Yes sir, what you wrote is nonsense,
utter nonsense. But ah! Sir! It's the right *kind* of nonsense!"

Bull, in this university,[1] is customarily a source of laughter, or a
problem in ethics. I shall step a little out of fashion to use the subject as a
take-off point for a study in comparative epistemology. The phenomenon
of bull, in all the honor and opprobrium with which it is regarded by
students and faculty, says something, I think, about our theories of
knowledge. So too, the grades which we assign on examinations communicate to students what these theories may be.

We do not have to be out-and-out logical-positivists[2] to suppose that
we have something to learn about "what we think knowledge is" by
having a good look at "what we do when we go about measuring it." We
know the straight "A" examination when we see it, of course, and we
have reason to hope that the student will understand why his work
receives our recognition. He doesn't always. And those who receive
lesser honor? Perhaps an understanding of certain anomalies in our
customs of grading good bull will explain the students' confusion.

I must beg patience, then, both of the reader's humor and of his morals.
Not that I ask him to suspend his sense of humor but that I shall ask him
to go beyond it. In a great university the picture of a bright student
attempting to outwit his professor while his professor takes pride in not
being outwitted is certainly ridiculous. I shall report just such a scene, for

1. Harvard.
2. Members of a contemporary school of philosophy which sees philosophy as an activity
rather than a body of knowledge, and concerns itself not with abstract notions of what
a thing is but with empirical observation of
what it does.

its implications bear upon my point. Its comedy need not present a serious obstacle to thought.

As for the ethics of bull, I must ask for a suspension of judgment. I wish that students could suspend theirs. Unlike humor, moral commitment is hard to think beyond. Too early a moral judgment is precisely what stands between many able students and a liberal education. The stunning realization that the Harvard Faculty will often accept, as evidence of knowledge, the cerebrations of a student who has little data at his disposal, confronts every student with an ethical dilemma. For some it forms an academic focus for what used to be thought of as "adolescent disillusion." It is irrelevant that rumor inflates the phenomenon to mythical proportions. The students know that beneath the myth there remains a solid and haunting reality. The moral "bind" consequent on this awareness appears most poignantly in serious students who are reluctant to concede the competitive advantage to the bullster and who yet feel a deep personal shame when, having succumbed to "temptation," they themselves receive a high grade for work they consider "dishonest."

I have spent many hours with students caught in this unwelcome bitterness. These hours lend an urgency to my theme. I have found that students have been able to come to terms with the ethical problem, to the extent that it is real, only after a refined study of the true nature of bull and its relation to "knowledge." I shall submit grounds for my suspicion that we can be found guilty of sharing the students' confusion of moral and epistemological issues.

I

I present as my "premise," then, an amoral fabliau. Its hero-villain is the Abominable Mr. Metzger '47. Since I celebrate his virtuosity, I regret giving him a pseudonym, but the peculiar style of his bravado requires me to honor also his modesty. Bull in pure form is rare; there is usually some contamination by data. The community has reason to be grateful to Mr. Metzger for having created an instance of laboratory purity, free from any adulteration by matter. The more credit is due him, I think, because his act was free from premeditation, deliberation, or hope of personal gain.

Mr. Metzger stood one rainy November day in the lobby of Memorial Hall. A junior, concentrating in mathematics, he was fond of diverting himself by taking part in the drama, a penchant which may have had some influence on the events of the next hour. He was waiting to take part in a rehearsal in Sanders Theatre, but, as sometimes happens, no other players appeared. Perhaps the rehearsal had been canceled without his knowledge? He decided to wait another five minutes.

Students, meanwhile, were filing into the Great Hall opposite, and taking seats at the testing tables. Spying a friend crossing the lobby toward the Great Hall's door, Metzger greeted him and extended appropriate condolences. He inquired, too, what course his friend was being tested in. "Oh, Soc. Sci. something-or-other." "What's it all about?" asked Metzger, and this, as Homer remarked of Patroclus, was the beginning of evil for him.

"It's about Modern Perspectives on Man and Society and All That," said his friend. "Pretty interesting, really."

"Always wanted to take a course like that," said Metzger. "Any good reading?"

"Yeah, great. There's this book"—his friend did not have time to finish.

"Take your seats please" said a stern voice beside them. The idle conversation had somehow taken the two friends to one of the tables in the Great Hall. Both students automatically obeyed; the proctor put blue-books before them; another proctor presented them with copies of the printed hour-test.

Mr. Metzger remembered afterwards a brief misgiving that was suddenly overwhelmed by a surge of curiosity and puckish glee. He wrote "George Smith" on the blue book, opened it, and addressed the first question.

I must pause to exonerate the Management. The Faculty has a rule that no student may attend an examination in a course in which he is not enrolled. To the wisdom of this rule the outcome of this deplorable story stands witness. The Registrar, charged with the enforcement of the rule, has developed an organization with procedures which are certainly the finest to be devised. In November, however, class rosters are still shaky, and on this particular day another student, named Smith, was absent. As for the culprit, we can reduce his guilt no further than to suppose that he was ignorant of the rule, or, in the face of the momentous challenge before him, forgetful.

We need not be distracted by Metzger's performance on the "objective" or "spot" questions on the test. His D on these sections can be explained by those versed in the theory of probability. Our interest focuses on the quality of his essay. It appears that when Metzger's friend picked up his own blue book a few days later, he found himself in company with a large proportion of his section in having received on the essay a C. When he quietly picked up "George Smith's" blue book to return it to Metzger, he observed that the grade for the essay was A. In the margin was a note in the section man's hand. It read "Excellent work. Could you have pinned these observations down a bit more closely? Compare ... in ... pp. ..."

Such news could hardly be kept quiet. There was a leak, and the whole scandal broke on the front page of Tuesday's *Crimson*. With the press Metzger was modest, as becomes a hero. He said that there had been nothing to it at all, really. The essay question had offered a choice of two books, Margaret Mead's *And Keep Your Powder Dry* or Geoffrey Gorer's *The American People*. Metzger reported that having read neither of them, he had chosen the second "because the title gave me some notion as to what the book might be about." On the test, two critical comments were offered on each book, one favorable, one unfavorable. The students were asked to "discuss." Metzger conceded that he had played safe in throwing his lot with the more laudatory of the two comments, "but I did not forget to be balanced."

I do not have Mr. Metzger's essay before me except in vivid memory. As I recall, he took his first cue from the name Geoffrey, and committed his strategy to the premise that Gorer was born into an "Anglo-Saxon" culture, probably English, but certainly "English speaking." Having heard that Margaret Mead was a social anthropologist, he inferred that Gorer was the same. He then entered upon his essay, centering his inquiry upon what he supposed might be the problems inherent in an anthropologist's observation of a culture which was his own, or nearly his own. Drawing in part from memories of table-talk on cultural relativity[3] and in part from creative logic, he rang changes on the relation of observer to observed, and assessed the kind and degree of objectivity which might accrue to an observer through training as an anthropologist. He concluded that the book in question did in fact contribute a considerable range of "'objective', and even 'fresh'," insights into the nature of our culture. "At the same time," he warned, "these observations must be understood within the context of their generation by a person only partly freed from his embeddedness in the culture he is observing, and limited in his capacity to transcend those particular tendencies and biases which he has himself developed as a personality in his interraction with this culture since his birth. In this sense the book portrays as much the character of Geoffrey Gorer as it analyzes that of the American people." It is my regretable duty to report that at this moment of triumph Mr. Metzger was carried away by the temptations of parody and added, "We are thus much the richer."

In any case, this was the essay for which Metzger received his honor grade and his public acclaim. He was now, of course, in serious trouble with the authorities.

I shall leave him for the moment to the mercy of the Administrative Board of Harvard College and turn the reader's attention to the section man who ascribed the grade. He was in much worse trouble. All the consternation in his immediate area of the Faculty and all the glee in other areas fell upon his unprotected head. I shall now undertake his defense.

3. "An important part of Harvard's education takes place during meals in the Houses." An Official Publication [Perry's note]. The Houses are residences for upperclassmen.

I do so not simply because I was acquainted with him and feel a respect for his intelligence; I believe in the justice of his grade! Well, perhaps "justice" is the wrong word in a situation so manifestly absurd. This is more a case in "equity." That is, the grade is equitable if we accept other aspects of the situation which are equally absurd. My proposition is this: if we accept as valid those C grades which were accorded students who, like Metzger's friend, demonstrated a thorough familiarity with the details of the book without relating their critique to the methodological problems of social anthropology, then "George Smith" deserved not only the same, but better.

The reader may protest that the C's given to students who showed evidence only of diligence were indeed not valid and that both these students and "George Smith" should have received E's. To give the diligent E is of course not in accord with custom. I shall take up this matter later. For now, were I to allow the protest, I could only restate my thesis: that "George Smith's" E would, in a college of liberal arts, be properly a "better" E.

At this point I need a short-hand. It is a curious fact that there is no academic slang for the presentation of evidence of diligence alone. "Parroting" won't do; it is possible to "parrot" bull. I must beg the reader's pardon, and, for reasons almost too obvious to bear, suggest "cow."

Stated as nouns, the concepts look simple enough:

> cow (pure): data, however relevant, without relevancies.
> bull (pure): relevancies, however relevant, without data.

The reader can see all too clearly where this simplicity would lead. I can assure him that I would not have imposed on him this way were I aiming to say that knowledge in this university is definable as some neuter compromise between cow and bull, some infertile hermaphrodite. This is precisely what many diligent students seem to believe: that what they must learn to do is to "find the right mean" between "amounts" of detail and "amounts" of generalities. Of course this is not the point at all. The problem is not quantitative, nor does its solution lie on a continuum between the particular and the general. Cow and bull are not poles of a single dimension. A clear notion of what they really are is essential to my inquiry, and for heuristic purposes I wish to observe them further in the celibate state.

When the pure concepts are translated into verbs, their complexities become apparent in the assumptions and purposes of the students as they write:

> To cow (v. intrans.) or the act of cowing:
>   To list data (or perform operations) without awareness of, or comment upon, the contexts, frames of reference, or points of observation which determine the origin, nature, and meaning of the data (or procedures). To

write on the assumption that "a fact is a fact." To present evidence of hard work as a substitute for understanding, without any intent to deceive.

To bull (v. *intrans.*) or the act of bulling:
   To discourse upon the contexts, frames of reference and points of observation which would determine the origin, nature, and meaning of data if one had any. To present evidence of an understanding of form in the hope that the reader may be deceived into supposing a familiarity with content.

At the level of conscious intent, it is evident that cowing is more moral, or less immoral, than bulling. To speculate about unconscious intent would be either an injustice or a needless elaboration of my theme. It is enough that the impression left by cow is one of earnestness, diligence, and painful naiveté. The grader may feel disappointment or even irritation, but these feelings are usually balanced by pity, compassion, and a reluctance to hit a man when he's both down and moral. He may feel some challenge to his teaching, but none whatever to his one-ups-manship. He writes in the margin: "See me."

We are now in a position to understand the anomaly of custom: As instructors, we always assign bull an E, *when we detect it*; whereas we usually give cow a C, *even though it is always obvious.*

After all, we did not ask to be confronted with a choice between morals and understanding (or did we?). We evince a charming humanity, I think, in our decision to grade in favor of morals and pathos. "I simply *can't* give this student an E after he has *worked* so hard." At the same time we tacitly express our respect for the bullster's strength. We recognize a colleague. If he knows so well how to dish it out, we can be sure that he can also take it.

Of course it is just possible that we carry with us, perhaps from our own school-days, an assumption that if a student is willing to work hard and collect "good hard facts" he can always be taught to understand their relevance, whereas a student who has caught onto the forms of relevance without working at all is a lost scholar.

But this is not in accord with our experience.

It is not in accord either, as far as I can see, with the stated values of a liberal education. If a liberal education should teach students "how to think," not only in their own fields but in fields outside their own—that is, to understand "how the other fellow orders knowledge," then bulling, even in its purest form, expresses an important part of what a pluralist university holds dear, surely a more important part than the collecting of "facts that are facts" which schoolboys learn to do. Here then, good bull appears not as ignorance at all but as an aspect of knowledge. It is both relevant and "true." In a university setting good bull is therefore of more value than "facts," which, without a frame of reference, are not even "true" at all.

Perhaps this value accounts for the final anomaly: as instructors, we are inclined to reward bull highly, *where we do not detect its intent,* to the consternation of the bullster's acquaintances. And often we do not examine the matter too closely. After a long evening of reading blue books full of cow, the sudden meeting with a student who at least understands the problems of one's field provides a lift like a draught of refreshing wine, and a strong disposition toward trust.

This was, then, the sense of confidence that came to our unfortunate section man as he read "George Smith's" sympathetic considerations.

II

In my own years of watching over students' shoulders as they work, I have come to believe that this feeling of trust has a firmer basis than the confidence generated by evidence of diligence alone. I believe that the theory of a liberal education holds. Students who have dared to understand man's real relation to his knowledge have shown themselves to be in a strong position to learn content rapidly and meaningfully, and to retain it. I have learned to be less concerned about the education of a student who has come to understand the nature of man's knowledge, even though he has not yet committed himself to hard work, than I am about the education of the student who, after one or two terms at Harvard, is working desperately hard and still believes that collected "facts" constitute knowledge. The latter, when I try to explain to him, too often understands me to be saying that he "doesn't *put in enough generalities.*" Surely he has "put in *enough* facts."

I have come to see such quantitative statements as expressions of an entire, coherent epistemology. In grammar school the student is taught that Columbus discovered America in 1492. The *more* such items he gets "right" on a given test the more he is credited with "knowing." From years of this sort of thing it is not unnatural to develop the conviction that knowledge consists of the accretion of hard facts by hard work.

The student learns that the more facts and procedures he can get "right" in a given course, the better will be his grade. The more courses he takes, the more subjects he has "had," the more credits he accumulates, the more diplomas he will get, until, after graduate school, he will emerge with his doctorate, a member of the community of scholars.

The foundation of this entire life is the proposition that a fact is a fact. The necessary correlate of this proposition is that a fact is either right or wrong. This implies that the standard against which the rightness or wrongness of a fact may be judged exists *someplace*—perhaps graven upon a tablet in a Platonic world[4] outside and above *this* cave of tears. In grammar school it is evident that the tablets which enshrine the spelling

4. That is, a world of ideal forms, of which this world is but the image. See Plato's "Allegory of the Cave," p. 1107.

of a word or the answer to an arithmetic problem are visible to my teacher who need only compare my offerings to it. In high school I observe that my English teachers disagree. This can only mean that the tablets in such matters as the goodness of a poem are distant and obscured by clouds. They surely exist. The pleasing of befuddled English teachers degenerates into assessing their prejudices, a game in which I have no protection against my competitors more glib of tongue. I respect only my science teachers, authorities who *really know*. Later I learn from them that "this is only what we think *now*." But eventually, surely.... Into this epistemology of education, apparently shared by teachers in such terms as "credits," "semester hours" and "years of French" the student may invest his ideals, his drive, his competitiveness, his safety, his self-esteem, and even his love.

College raises other questions: by whose calendar is it proper to say that Columbus discovered America in 1492? How, when and by whom was the year 1 established in this calendar? What of other calendars? In view of the evidence for Leif Ericson's previous visit (and the American Indians), what historical ethnocentrism is suggested by the use of the word "discover" in this sentence? As for Leif Ericson, in accord with what assumptions do you order the evidence?

These questions and their answers are not "more" knowledge. They are devastation. I do not need to elaborate upon the epistemology, or rather epistemologies, they imply. A fact has become at last "an observation or an operation performed in a frame of reference." A liberal education is founded in an awareness of frame of reference even in the most immediate and empirical examination of data. Its acquirement involves relinquishing hope of absolutes and of the protection they afford against doubt and the glib-tongued competitor. It demands an ever widening sophistication about systems of thought and observation. It leads, not away from, but *through* the arts of gamesmanship to a new trust.

This trust is in the value and integrity of systems, their varied character, and the way their apparently incompatible metaphors enlighten, from complementary facets, the particulars of human experience. As one student said to me: "I used to be cynical about intellectual games. Now I want to know them thoroughly. You see I came to realize that it was only when I knew the rules of the game cold that I could tell whether what I was saying was tripe."

We too often think of the bullster as cynical. He can be, and not always in a light-hearted way. We have failed to observe that there can lie behind cow the potential of a deeper and more dangerous despair. The moralism of sheer work and obedience can be an ethic that, unwilling to face a despair of its ends, glorifies its means. The implicit refusal to consider the relativity of both ends and means leaves the operator in an unconsidered proprietary absolutism. History bears witness that in the pinches this moral superiority has no recourse to negotiation, only to force.

A liberal education proposes that man's hope lies elsewhere: in the negotiability that can arise from an understanding of the integrity of systems and of their origins in man's address to his universe. The prerequisite is the courage to accept such a definition of knowledge. From then on, of course, there is nothing incompatible between such an epistemology and hard work. Rather the contrary.

I can now at last let bull and cow get together. The reader knows best how a productive wedding is arranged in his own field. This is the nuptial he celebrates with a straight A on examinations. The masculine context must embrace the feminine particular, though itself "born of woman." Such a union is knowledge itself, and it alone can generate new contexts and new data which can unite in their turn to form new knowledge.

In this happy setting we can congratulate in particular the Natural Sciences, long thought to be barren ground to the bullster. I have indeed drawn my examples of bull from the Social Sciences, and by analogy from the Humanities. Essay-writing in these fields has long been thought to nurture the art of bull to its prime. I feel, however, that the Natural Sciences have no reason to feel slighted. It is perhaps no accident that Metzger was a mathematician. As part of my researches for this paper, furthermore, a student of considerable talent has recently honored me with an impressive analysis of the art of amassing "partial credits" on examinations in advanced physics. Though beyond me in some respects, his presentation confirmed my impression that instructors of Physics frequently honor on examinations operations structurally similar to those requisite in a good essay.

The very qualities that make the Natural Sciences fields of delight for the eager gamesman have been essential to their marvelous fertility.

III

As priests of these mysteries, how can we make our rites more precisely expressive? The student who merely cows robs himself, without knowing it, of his education and his soul. The student who only bulls robs himself, as he knows full well, of the joys of inductive discovery—that is, of engagement. The introduction of frames of reference in the new curricula of Mathematics and Physics in the schools is a hopeful experiment. We do not know yet how much of these potent revelations the very young can stand, but I suspect they may rejoice in them more than we have supposed. I can't believe they have never wondered about Leif Ericson and that word "discovered," or even about 1492. They have simply been too wise to inquire.

Increasingly in recent years better students in the better high schools and preparatory schools are being allowed to inquire. In fact they appear to be receiving both encouragement and training in their inquiry. I have the evidence before me.

Each year for the past five years all freshmen entering Harvard and Radcliffe have been asked in freshman week to "grade" two essays answering an examination question in History. They are then asked to give their reasons for their grades. One essay, filled with dates, is 99% cow. The other, with hardly a date in it, is a good essay, easily mistaken for bull. The "official" grades of these essays are, for the first (alas!) C "because he has worked so hard," and for the second (soundly, I think) B. Each year a larger majority of freshmen evaluate these essays as would the majority of the faculty, and for the faculty's reasons, and each year a smaller minority give the higher honor to the essay offering data alone. Most interesting, a larger number of students each year, while not over-rating the second essay, award the first the straight E appropriate to it in a college of liberal arts.

For us who must grade such students in a university, these develop-ments imply a new urgency, did we not feel it already. Through our grades we describe for the students, in the showdown, what we believe about the nature of knowledge. The subtleties of bull are not peripheral to our academic concerns. That they penetrate to the center of our care is evident in our feelings when a student whose good work we have awarded a high grade reveals to us that he does not feel he deserves it. Whether he disqualifies himself because "there's too much bull in it," or worse because "I really don't think I've worked that hard," he presents a serious educational problem. Many students feel this sleaziness; only a few reveal it to us.

We can hardly allow a mistaken sense of fraudulence to undermine our students' achievements. We must lead students beyond their concept of bull so that they may honor relevancies that are really relevant. We can willingly acknowledge that, in lieu of the date 1492, a consideration of calendars and of the word "discovered," may well be offered with intent to deceive. We must insist that this does not make such considerations intrinsically immoral, and that, contrariwise, the date 1492 may be no substitute for them. Most of all, we must convey the impression that we grade understanding qua understanding. To be convincing, I suppose we must concede to ourselves in advance that a bright student's understand-ing is understanding even if he achieved it by osmosis rather than by hard work in our course.

These are delicate matters. As for cow, its complexities are not what need concern us. Unlike good bull, it does not represent partial knowl-edge at all. It belongs to a different theory of knowledge entirely. In our theories of knowledge it represents total ignorance, or worse yet, a knowledge downright inimical to understanding. I even go so far as to propose that we award no more C's for cow. To do so is rarely, I feel, the act of mercy it seems. Mercy lies in clarity.

The reader may be afflicted by a lingering curiosity about the fate of Mr. Metzger. I hasten to reassure him. The Administrative Board of Harvard College, whatever its satanic reputations, is a benign body. Its members, to be sure, were on the spot. They delighted in Metzger's exploit, but they were responsible to the Faculty's rule. The hero stood in danger of probation. The debate was painful. Suddenly one member, of a refined legalistic sensibility, observed that the rule applied specifically to "examinations" and that the occasion had been simply an hour-test. Mr Metzger was merely "admonished."

1963

QUESTIONS

1. *Near the beginning of his essay Perry says he must "beg patience . . . both of the reader's humor and of his morals" (p. 282). Why does he find this necessary, and what assumptions does he make about his readers?*

2. *What tone does Perry adopt in his essay? Explain how the italicized words in these phrases contribute to Perry's creation of a tone appropriate to his thesis: (1) " . . . the* stunning realization *that the Harvard faculty will often accept, as evidence of knowledge, the* cerebrations *of a student who has* little data *at his disposal . . . "; (2) " . . . the* peculiar style of his *bravado* requires me to *honor also his modesty . . . "; (3) "Bull in* pure form is rare; there is usually some *contamination by data"; (4) " . . . some neuter* compromise between cow and bull, some infertile hermaphrodite. . . . " *Find and comment on other examples in the essay that help to define its tone.*

3. *Perry speaks several times of "good bull." Explain what "bad bull" would be in Perry's view and give an example of it.*

4. *Perry points out the essential inaccuracy of such a supposedly simple statement of fact as "Columbus discovered America in 1492." Analyze one or two other such commonly accepted statements of fact in the same way Perry does.*

5. *In "Education by Poetry" (p. 1025) Robert Frost talks about the importance of metaphor in a liberal education. Compare Frost's remarks about metaphor with Perry's remarks about the relationship of bull and cow to a liberal education.*

6. *Perry says that the ideal is "a productive wedding" between bull and cow. Find another essay in this book that you feel represents such a "productive wedding" and explain how the author has brought that wedding about.*

Wayne C. Booth

IS THERE ANY KNOWLEDGE THAT A
MAN *MUST* HAVE?

Everyone lives on the assumption that a great deal of knowledge is not worth bothering about; though we all know that what looks trivial in one man's hands may turn out to be earth-shaking in another's, we simply cannot know very much, compared with what might be known, and we must therefore choose. What is shocking is not the act of choice which we all commit openly but the claim that some choices are wrong. Especially shocking is the claim implied by my title: There is some knowledge that a man *must* have.

There clearly is no such thing, if by knowledge we mean mere acquaintance with this or that thing, fact, concept, literary work, or scientific law. When C. P. Snow and F. R. Leavis exchanged blows on whether knowledge of Shakespeare is more important than knowledge of the second law of thermodynamics, they were both, it seemed to me, much too ready to assume as indispensable what a great many wise and good men have quite obviously got along without. And it is not only nonprofessionals who can survive in happy ignorance of this or that bit of lore. I suspect that many successful scientists (in biology, say) have lost whatever hold they might once have had on the second law; I know that a great many literary scholars survive and even flourish without knowing certain "indispensable" classics. We all get along without vast loads of learning that other men take as necessary marks of an educated man. If we once begin to "reason the need" we will find, like Lear, that "our basest beggars/Are in the poorest thing superfluous." Indeed, we can survive, in a manner of speaking, even in the modern world, with little more than the bare literacy necessary to tell the "off" buttons from the "on."

Herbert Spencer would remind us at this point that we are interpreting *need* as if it were entirely a question of private survival. Though he talks about what a man must know to stay alive, he is more interested, in his defense of science, in what a *society* must know to survive: "Is there any knowledge that *man* must have?"—not a man; but *man*. This question is put to us much more acutely in our time than it was in Spencer's, and it is by no means as easy to argue now as it was then that the knowledge needed for man's survival is scientific knowledge. The threats of atomic annihilation, of engulfing population growth, of depleted air, water, and food must obviously be met, if man is to survive, and in meeting them man will, it is true, need more and more scientific knowledge; but it is not at all clear that more and more scientific knowledge will by itself suffice. Even so, a modern Herbert Spencer might well argue that a conference like this one, with its emphasis on the individual and his cognitive needs, is simply repeating the mistakes of the classical tradition. The knowledge most worth having would be, from his point of view, that of how to pull mankind through the next century or so without absolute self-destruction. The precise proportions of different kinds of knowledge—physical, biological, political, ethical, psychological, historical, or whatever —would be different from those prescribed in Spencer's essay, but the nature of the search would be precisely the same.

We can admit the relevance of this emphasis on social utility and at the same time argue that our business here is with other matters entirely. If the only knowledge a man *must* have is how to cross the street without getting knocked down—or, in other words, how to navigate the centuries without blowing himself up—then we may as well close the conference and go home. We may as well also roll up the college and mail it to a research institute, because almost any place that is not cluttered up with notions of liberal education will be able to discover and transmit practical bits of survival-lore better than we can. Our problem of survival is a rather different one, thrust at us as soon as we change our title slightly once again to "Is there any knowledge (other than the knowledge for survival) that a man must have?" That slight shift opens a new perspective on the problem, because the question of what it is to be a man, of what it is to be fully human, is the question at the heart of liberal education.

To be human, to be human, to be fully human. What does it mean? What is required? Immediately, we start feeling nervous again. Is the speaker suggesting that some of us are not fully human *yet?* Here come those hierarchies again. Surely in our pluralistic society we can admit an unlimited number of legitimate ways to be a man, without prescribing some outmoded aristocratic code!

Who—or what—is the creature we would educate? Our answer will determine our answers to educational questions, and it is therefore, I think, worth far more vigorous effort than it usually receives. I find it convenient, and only slightly unfair, to classify the educational talk I encounter these days under four notions of man, three of them metaphorical, only one literal. Though nobody's position, I suppose, fits my types neatly, some educators talk as if they were programming machines, some talk as if they were conditioning rats, some talk as if they were training ants to take a position in the anthill, and some—precious few—talk as if they thought of themselves as men dealing with men.

One traditional division of the human soul, you will remember, was into three parts: the vegetable, the animal, and the rational. Nobody, so far as I know, has devised an educational program treating students as vegetables, though one runs into the analogy used negatively in academic sermons from time to time. Similarly, no one ever really says that men are ants, though there is a marvelous passage in Kwame Nkrumah's autobiography in which he meditates longingly on the order and pure functionality of an anthill.[1] Educators do talk of men as machines or as animals, but of course they always point out that men are much more complicated than any other known animals or machines. My point here is not so much to attack any one of these metaphors—dangerous as I think they are—but to describe briefly what answers to our question each of them might suggest.

Ever since Descartes, La Mettrie,[2] and others explicitly called a man a machine, the metaphor has been a dominant one in educational thinking. Some have thought of man as a very complex machine, needing very elaborate programming; others have thought of him as a very simple machine, requiring little more than a systematic pattern of stimuli to produce foretellable responses. I heard a psychologist recently repeat the old behaviorist claim (first made by John B. Watson, I believe) that if you would give him complete control over any normal child's life from birth, he could turn that child into a great musician or a great mathematician or a great poet—you name it and he could produce it. On being pressed, the professor admitted that this claim was only "in theory," because we don't yet have the necessary knowledge. When I pushed further by asking why he was so confident in advance of experimental proof, it became clear that his faith in the fundamental metaphor of man as a programmable machine was unshakable.

When the notion of man as machine was first advanced, the machine was a very simple collection of pulleys and billiard balls and levers. Such original simplicities have been badly battered by our growing awareness both of how complex real machines can be and of how much more complex man is than any known machine. Modern notions of stimulus-response patterns are immeasurably more complicated than anything Descartes imagined, because we are now aware of the fantastic variety of stimuli that the man-machine is subject to and of the even more fantastic complexity of the responding circuits.

But whether the machine is simple or complex, the educational task for those who think of man under this metaphor is to program the mechanism so that it will produce the results that we have foreordained. We do not simply fill the little pitchers, like Mr. Gradgrind in Dickens' *Hard Times*;[3] we are much too sophisticated to want only undigested "pour-back," as he might have called his product. But we still program the information channels so that the proper if-loops and do-loops will be

---

1. Nkrumah was the first premier of the African republic of Ghana; he was ultimately deposed in a coup and went to live in China.
2. René Descartes (1596–1650), French philosopher and mathematician; Julian Offray de La Mettrie (1709–1751), French physician and philosopher.
3. Thomas Gradgrind thought of his students as "little pitchers . . . who were to be filled so full of facts."

followed and the right feedback produced. The "programming" can be done by human teachers, of course, and not only by machines; but it is not surprising that those whose thinking is dominated by this metaphor tend to discover that machines are better teachers than men. The more ambitious programmers do not hesitate to claim that they can teach both thought and creativity in this way. But I have yet to see a program that can deal effectively with any subject that cannot be reduced to simple yes and no answers, that is, to answers that are known in advance by the programmer and can thus be fixed for all time.

We can assume that subtler machines will be invented that can engage in simulated dialogue with the pupil, and perhaps even recognize when a particularly bright pupil has discovered something new that refutes the program. But even the subtlest teaching machine imaginable will still be subject, one must assume, to a final limitation: it can teach only what a machine can "learn." For those who believe that man is literally nothing but a very complicated machine, this is not in fact a limitation; machines will ultimately be able to duplicate all mental processes, thus "learning" everything learnable, and they will be able in consequence to teach everything.

I doubt this claim for many reasons, and I am glad to find the testimony of Norbert Wiener, the first and best known cyberneticist, to the effect that there will always remain a radical gap between computers and the human mind. But "ultimately" is a long way off, and I am not so much concerned with whether ultimately man's mind will closely resemble some ultimately inventable machine as I am with the effects, here and now, of thinking about men under the analogy with machines of today. Let me simply close this section with an illustration of how the mechanistic model can permeate our thought in destructive ways. Ask yourselves what picture of creature-to-be-educated emerges from this professor of teacher education:

> To implement the TEAM Project new curriculum proposal . . . our first concerns are with instructional systems, materials to feed the system, and personnel to operate the system. We have defined an instructional system as the optimal blending of the demands of content, communication, and learning. While numerous models have been developed, our simplified model of an instructional system would look like Figure 2. . . . We look at the process of communication—communicating content to produce learning—as something involving the senses: . . . [aural, oral, tactile, visual]. And I think in teacher education we had better think of the communications aspect of the instructional system as a package that includes the teacher, textbook, new media, classroom, and environment. To integrate these elements to more effectively transmit content into permanent learning, new and better instructional materials are needed and a new focus on the teacher of teachers is required. The teacher of teachers must: (1) examine critically the content of traditional courses in relation to desired behavioral outcomes; (2) become

more sophisticated in the techniques of communicating course content; and (3) learn to work in concert with media specialists to develop the materials and procedures requisite to the efficient instructional system. And if the media specialist were to be charged with the efficient operation of the system, his upgrading would demand a broad-based "media generalist" orientation.

I submit that the author of this passage was thinking of human beings as stimulus-response systems on the simplest possible model, and that he was thinking of the purpose of education as the transfer of information from one machine to another. Though he would certainly deny it if we asked him, he has come to think about the human mind so habitually in the mechanistic mode that he doesn't even know he's doing it.[4]

But it is time to move from the machine metaphor to animal metaphors. They are closely related, of course, because everybody who believes that man is a machine also believes that animals are machines, only simpler ones. But many people who would resist the word "machine" do tend to analogize man to one or another characteristic of animals. Since man is obviously an animal in one sense, he can be studied as an animal, and he can be taught as an animal is taught. Most of the fundamental research in learning theory underlying the use of teaching machines has been done, in fact, on animals like rats and pigeons. You can teach pigeons to play Ping-Pong rather quickly by rewarding every gesture they make that moves them toward success in the game and refusing to reward those gestures that you want to efface. Though everybody admits that human beings are more complicated than rats and pigeons, just as everyone admits that human beings are more complicated than computers, the basic picture of the animal as a collection of drives or instincts, "conditioned" to learn according to rewards or punishments, has underlain much modern educational theory.

The notion of the human being as a collection of drives different from animal drives only in being more complex carries with it implications for education planners. If you and I are motivated only by sex or hunger or more complex drives like desire for power or for ego-satisfaction, then of course all education depends on the provision of satisfactions along our route to knowledge. If our teachers can just program carrots along the path at the proper distance, we donkey-headed students will plod along the path from carrot to carrot and end up as educated men.

I cannot take time here to deal with this view adequately, but it seems to me that it is highly questionable even about animals themselves. What kind of thing, really, is a rat or a monkey? The question of whether animals have souls has been debated actively for at least nine centuries; now psychologists find themselves dealing with the same question under

4. I am not of course suggesting that any use of teaching machines implies a mechanistic reduction of persons to machines; program- mers rightly point out that machines can free teachers from the mechanical and save time for the personal [Booth's note].

another guise: What are these little creatures that we kill so blithely for the sake of knowledge? What are these strangely resistant little bundles of energy that will prefer—as experiments with rats have shown—a complicated interesting maze without food to a dull one with food?

There are, in fact, many experiments by now showing that at the very least we must postulate, for animals, a strong independent drive for mastery of the environment or satisfaction of curiosity about it. All the more advanced animals will learn to push levers that produce interesting results—clicks or bells or flashing lights or sliding panels—when no other reward is offered. It seems clear that even to be a fulfilled animal, as it were, something more than "animal satisfaction" is needed!

I am reminded here of the experiments on mother-love in monkeys reported by Harry F. Harlow in the *Scientific American* some years ago. Harlow called his article "Love in Infant Monkeys," and the subtitle of his article read, "Affection in infants was long thought to be generated by the satisfactions of feeding. Studies of young rhesus monkeys now indicate that love derives mainly from close bodily contact." The experiment consisted of giving infant monkeys a choice between a plain wire figure that offered the infant milk and a terry-cloth covered figure without milk. There was a pathetic picture of an infant clinging to the terry-cloth figure, and a caption that read "The infants spent most of their time clinging to the soft cloth 'mother' even when nursing bottles were attached to the wire mother." The article concluded—rather prematurely, I thought—that "contact comfort" had been shown to be a "prime requisite in the formation of an infant's love for its mother," that the act of nursing had been shown to be unimportant if not totally irrelevant in forming such love (though it was evident to any reader, even at the time, that no genuine "act of nursing" had figured in the experiment at all), and that "our investigations have established a secure experimental approach to this realm of dramatic and subtle emotional relationships." The only real problem, Harlow said, was the availability of enough infant monkeys for experiment.

Now I would not want to underrate the importance of Harlow's demonstration to the scientific community that monkeys do not live by bread alone. But I think that most scientists and humanists reading the article would have been struck by two things. The first is the automatic assumption that the way to study a subject like love is to break it down into its component parts; nobody looking at that little monkey clinging to the terry-cloth could possibly have said, "This is love," unless he had been blinded by a hidden conviction that love in animals is—must be—a mere cumulative result of a collection of drive satisfactions. This assumption is given quite plainly in Harlow's concluding sentence: "Finally with such techniques established, there appears to be no reason why we cannot at some future time investigate the fundamental neurophysiological and biochemical variables underlying affection and love." For Harlow monkeys (and people) seem to be mere collections of neurophysiological and biochemical variables, and love will be best explained when we can explain the genesis of each of its parts. The second striking point is that for Harlow animals do not matter, except as they are useful for experiment. If he had felt that they mattered, he might have noticed the look on his infant's face—a look that predicted for me, and for other readers of the *Scientific American* I've talked with, that these monkeys were doomed.

And indeed they were. A year or so later another article appeared, reporting Harlow's astonished discovery that all of the little monkeys on which he had earlier experimented had turned out to be incurably psychotic. Not a single monkey could mate, not a single monkey could play, not a single monkey could in fact become anything more than the twisted half-creatures that Harlow's deprivations had made of them. Harlow's new discovery was that monkeys needed close association with their peers during infancy and that such association was even more important to their development than genuine mothering. There was no sign that Harlow had learned any fundamental lessons from his earlier gross mistakes; he had landed nicely on his feet, still convinced that the way to study love is to break it down into its component parts and that the way to study animals is to maim them or reduce them to something less than themselves. As Robert White says, summarizing his reasons for rejecting similar methods in studying human infancy, it is too often assumed that the scientific way is to analyze behavior until one can find a small enough unit to allow for detailed research, but in the process "very vital common properties" are lost from view.

I cite Harlow's two reports not, of course, to attack animal experimentation—though I must confess that I am horrified by much that goes on in its name—nor to claim that animals are more like human beings than they are. Rather, I want simply to suggest that the danger of thinking of men as animals is heightened if the animals we think of are reduced to machines on a simple model.

The effects of reducing education to conditioning can be seen throughout America today. Usually they appear in subtle forms, disguised with the language of personalism; you will look a long time before you find anyone (except a very few Skinnerians) saying that he thinks of education as exactly like conditioning pigeons. But there are plenty of honest, blunt folk around to let the cat out of the bag—like the author of an article this year in *College Composition and Communications*: "The Use of a Multiple Response Device in the Teaching of Remedial English." The author claimed to have evidence that if you give each student four buttons to be pushed on multiple-choice questions, with all the buttons wired into a lighted grid at the front of the room, the resulting "instantaneous feedback"—every child learning immediately whether he agrees with the rest of the class—speeds up the learning of grammatical rules considerably over the usual workbook procedures. I daresay it does—but meanwhile what has happened to education? Or take the author of an article on "Procedures and Techniques of Teaching," who wrote as follows: "If we expect students to learn skills, they have to practice, but practice doesn't make perfect. Practice works if the learner *learns the results* of his practice, i.e., if he receives feedback. Feedback is most effective when it is contiguous to the response being learned. One of the chief advantages of teaching machines is that the learner finds out quickly whether his response is right or wrong ... [Pressey] has published the results of an extensive program of research with tests that students score for themselves by punching alternatives until they hit the correct one. . . . [Thus] teaching machines or workbooks have many theoretical advantages over lecturing or other conventional methods of instruction." But according to what theory, one must ask, *do* systematic feedback mechanisms, perfected to whatever degree, have "theoretical advantages" over human contact? Whatever else can be said for such a theory, it will be based on the simplest of comparisons with animal learning. Unfortunately, the author goes on, experimental evidence is on the whole rather discouraging: "Experiments at the Systems Development Corporation . . . suggest that teaching incorporating . . . human characteristics is more effective than the typical fixed-sequence machines. (In this experiment instead of using teaching machines to simulate human teachers, the experimenters used humans to simulate teaching machines!)"

So far I have dealt with analogies for man that apply only to individuals. My third analogy turns to the picture of men in groups, and it is given to me partly by discussions of education, like those of Admiral Rickover, that see it simply as filling society's needs. I know of only one prominent educator who has publicly praised the anthill as a model for the kind of society a university should serve—a society of specialists each trained to do his part. But the notion pervades many of the defenses of the emerging multiversities.[5]

If knowledge is needed to enable men to function as units in society, and if the health of society is taken as the purpose of their existence, then there is nothing wrong in training the ants to fill their niches; it would be wrong not to. "Education is our first line of defense—make it strong," so reads the title of the first chapter of Admiral Rickover's book, *Education and Freedom* (New York: Dutton, 1959). "We must upgrade our schools" in order to "guarantee the future prosperity and freedom of the Republic." You can tell whether the ant-analogy is dominating a man's thinking by a simple test of how he orders his ends and means. In Admiral

5. A 1960s term for the gargantuan universities which often set government and corporate research, and the training of graduate students to do that research, above undergraduate education.

Rickover's statement, the schools must be upgraded in order to guarantee future prosperity, that is, we improve education for the sake of some presumed social good.

I seldom find anyone putting it the other way round: we must guarantee prosperity so that we can improve the schools, and the reason we want to improve the schools is that we want to insure the development of certain kinds of persons, both as teachers and as students. You cannot even say what I just said so long as you are really thinking of ants and anthills. Ants are not ends in themselves, ultimately more valuable than the hills they live in (I *think* they are not; maybe to themselves, or in the eyes of God, even ants are ultimate, self-justifying ends). At least from our point of view, ants are expendable, or to put it another way, their society is more beautiful, more interesting, more admirable than they are. And I would want to argue that too many people think of human beings in the same way when they think of educating them. The Communists make this quite explicit: the ends of Communist society justify whatever distortion or destruction of individual purposes is necessary to achieve them; men are educated for the state, not for their own well-being. They are basically political animals, not in the Aristotelian sense that they require society if they are to achieve their full natures and thus their own special, human kind of happiness, but in the sense that they exist, like ants, for the sake of the body politic.

If the social order is the final justification of what we do in education, then a certain attitude toward teaching and research will result: all of us little workmen, down inside the anthill, will go on happily contributing our tiny bit to the total scheme without worrying much about larger questions of the why and wherefore. I know a graduate student who says that she sometimes sees her graduate professors as an army of tiny industrious miners at the bottom of a vast mine, chipping away at the edges and shipping their bits of knowledge up to the surface, blindly hoping that someone up there will know what to do with it all. An order is received for such-and-such new organic compounds; society needs them. Another order is received for an atomic bomb; it is needed, and it is therefore produced. Often no orders come down, but the chipping goes on anyway, and the shipments are made, because everyone knows that the health of the mine depends on a certain tonnage of specialized knowledge each working day.

We have learned lately that "they" are going to establish a great new atom-smasher, perhaps near Chicago. The atom-smasher will employ two thousand scientists and technicians. I look out at you here, knowing that some of you are physics majors, and I wonder whether any of you will ultimately be employed in that new installation, and if you are, whether it will be as an ant or as a human being. Which it will be must depend not on your ultimate employers but on yourself and on what happens to your education between now and then: if you have been given nothing but training to be that ultimate unit in that ultimate system, only a miracle can save you from formic dissolution of your human lineaments.

But it is long past time for me to turn from these negative, truncated portraits of what man really is not and attempt to say what he is. And here we encounter a difficulty that I find very curious. You will note that each of these metaphors has reduced man to something less than man, or at least to a partial aspect of man. It is easy to say that man is not a machine, though he is in some limited respects organized like a machine and even to some degree "programmable." It is also easy to say that man is not simply a complicated rat or monkey, though he is in some ways like rats and monkeys. Nor is man an ant, though he lives and must function in a complicated social milieu. All these metaphors break down not because they are flatly false but because they are metaphors, and any metaphorical definition is inevitably misleading. The ones I have been dealing with are especially misleading, because in every case they have reduced something more complex to something much less complex. But even if we were to analogize man to something more complex, say, the universe, we would be dissatisfied. What we want is some notion of what man really is, so that we will know what or whom we are trying to educate.

And here it is that we discover something very important about man, something that even the least religious person must find himself mystified by: man is the one "thing" we know that is completely resistant to our efforts at metaphor or analogy or image-making. What seems to be the most important literal characteristic of man is his resistance to definitions in terms of anything else. If you call me a machine, even a very complicated machine, I know that you deny what I care most about, my selfhood, my sense of being a person, my consciousness, my conviction of freedom and dignity, my awareness of love, my laughter. Machines have none of these things, and even if we were generous to their prospects, and imagined machines immeasurably superior to the most complicated ones now in existence, we would still feel an infinite gap between them and what we know to be a basic truth about ourselves: machines are expendable, ultimately expendable, and men are mysteriously ends in themselves.

I hear people deny this, but when they do they always argue for their position by claiming marvelous feats of super-machine calculation that machines can now do or will someday be able to do. But that is not the point; of course machines can outcalculate us. The question to ask is entirely a different one: Will they ever outlove us, outlive us, outvalue us? Do we build machines because machines are good things in themselves? Do we nurture them for their own good, as we nurture our children? An obvious way to test our sense of worth in men and machines is to ask ourselves whether we would ever campaign to liberate the poor downtrodden machines who have been enslaved. Shall we form a National Association for the Advancement of Machinery? Will anyone ever feel a smidgeon of moral indignation because this or that piece of machinery is not given equal rights before the law? Or put it another way: Does anyone value Gemini[6] more than the twins? There may be men now alive who would rather "destruct," as we say, the pilot than the experimental rocket, but most of us still believe that the human being in the space ship is more important than the space ship.

When college students protest the so-called depersonalization of education, what they mean, finally, is not simply that they want to meet their professors socially or that they want small classes or that they do not want to be dealt with by IBM machines. All these things are but symptoms of a deeper sense of a violation of their literal reality as persons, ends in themselves rather than mere expendable things. Similarly, the current deep-spirited revolt against racial and economic injustice seems to me best explained as a sudden assertion that people, of whatever color or class, are not reducible to social conveniences. When you organize your labor force or your educational system as if men were mere social conveniences, "human resources," as we say, contributors to the gross national product, you violate something that we all know, in a form of knowledge much deeper than our knowledge of the times tables or the second law of thermodynamics: those field hands, those children crowded into the deadening classroom, those men laboring without dignity in the city anthills are men, creatures whose worth is mysteriously more than any description of it we might make in justifying what we do to them.

Ants, rats, and machines can all learn a great deal. Taken together, they "know" a very great part of what our schools and colleges are now designed to teach. But is there any kind of knowledge that a creature must have to qualify as a man? Is there any part of the educational task that is demanded of us by virtue of our claim to educate this curious entity, this person that cannot be reduced to mechanism or animality alone?

You will not be surprised, by now, to have me sound, in my answer, terribly traditional, not to say square: the education that a man must have is what has traditionally been called liberal education. The knowledge it yields is the knowledge or capacity or power of how to act freely as a man. That's why we call liberal education liberal: it is intended to liberate from whatever it is that makes animals act like animals and machines act like machines.

I'll return in a moment to what it means to act freely as a man. But we are already in a position to say something about what knowledge a man

6. Here referring not to the astrological sign but to the space rockets.

must have—he must first of all be able to learn for himself. If he cannot learn for himself, he is enslaved by his teachers' ideas, or by the ideas of his more persuasive contemporaries, or by machines programmed by other men. He may have what we call a good formal education, yet still be totally bound by whatever opinions happen to have come his way in attractive garb. One wonders how many of our graduates have learned how to take hold of a subject and "work it up," so that they can make themselves experts on what other men have concluded. In some ways this is not a very demanding goal, and it is certainly not very exciting. It says nothing about that popular concept, creativity, or about imagination or originality. All it says is that anyone who is dependent on his teachers is dependent, not free, and that anyone who knows how to learn for himself is less like animals and machines than anyone who does not know how to learn for himself.

We see already that a college is not being merely capricious or arbitrary when it insists that some kinds of learning are more important than some others. The world is overflowing with interesting subjects and valuable skills, but surely any college worth the name will put first things first: it will try to insure, as one inescapable goal, that every graduate can dig out from the printed page what he needs to know. And it will not let the desire to tamp in additional tidbits of knowledge, however delicious, interfere with training minds for whom a formal teacher is no longer required.

To put our first goal in this way raises some real problems that we cannot solve. Obviously no college can produce self-learners in very many subjects. Are we not lucky if a graduate can learn for himself even in one field, now that knowledge in all areas has advanced as far as it has? Surely we cannot expect our graduates to reach a stage of independence in mathematics and physics, in political science and psychology, in philosophy and English, and in all the other nice subjects that one would like to master.

Rather than answer this objection right away, let me make things even more difficult by saying that it is not enough to learn how to learn. The man who cannot *think* for himself, going beyond what other men have learned or thought, is still enslaved to other men's ideas. Obviously the goal of learning to think is even more difficult than the goal of learning to learn. But difficult as it is we must add it to our list. It is simply not enough to be able to get up a subject on one's own, like a good encyclopedia employee, even though any college would take pride if all its graduates could do so. To be fully human means in part to think one's own thoughts, to reach a point at which, whether one's ideas are different from or similar to other men's, they are truly one's own.

The art of asking oneself critical questions that lead either to new answers or to genuine revitalizing of old answers, the art of making thought live anew in each new generation, may not be entirely amenable to instruction. But it is a necessary art nonetheless, for any man who wants to be free. It is an art that all philosophers have tried to pursue, and many of them have given direct guidance in how to pursue it. Needless to say, it is an art the pursuit of which is never fully completed. No one thinks for himself very much of the time or in very many subjects. Yet the habitual effort to ask the right critical questions and to apply rigorous tests to our hunches is a clearer mark than any other of an educated man.

But again we stumble upon the question, "Learn to think about *what?*" The modern world presents us with innumerable subjects to think about. Does it matter whether anyone achieves this rare and difficult point in more than one subject? And if not, won't the best education simply be the one that brings a man into mastery of a narrow specialty as soon as possible, so that he can learn to think for himself as soon as possible? Even at best most of us are enslaved to opinions provided for us by experts in *most* fields. So far, it might be argued, I still have not shown that there is any kind of knowledge that a man must have, only that there are certain skills that he must be able to exercise in at least one field.

To provide a proper grounding for my answer to that objection would require far more time than I have left, and I'm not at all sure that I could do so even with all the time in the world. The question of whether it is possible to maintain a human stance toward any more than a tiny fraction of modern knowledge is not clearly answerable at this stage in our history. It will be answered, if at all, only when men have learned how to store and retrieve all "machinable" knowledge, freeing themselves for distinctively human tasks. But in the meantime, I find myself unable to surrender, as it were, three distinct kinds of knowledge that seem to me indispensable to being human.

To be a man, a man must first know something about his own nature and his place in Nature, with a capital N—something about the truth of things, as men used to say in the old-fashioned days before the word "truth" was banned from academia. Machines are not curious, so far as I can judge; animals are, but presumably they never go, in their philosophies, even at the furthest, beyond a kind of solipsistic existentialism. But in science, in philosophy (ancient and modern), in theology, in psychology and anthropology, and in literature (of some kinds), we are presented with accounts of our universe and of our place in it that as men we can respond to in only one manly way: by thinking about them, by speculating and testing our speculations.

We know before we start that our thought is doomed to incompleteness and error and downright chanciness. Even the most rigorously scientific view will be changed, we know, within a decade, or perhaps even by tomorrow. But to refuse the effort to understand is to resign from the human race; the unexamined life can no doubt be worth living in other respects—after all, it is no mean thing to be a vegetable, an oak tree, an elephant, or a lion.[7] But a man, a man will want to see, in this speculative domain, beyond his next dinner.

By putting it in this way, I think we can avoid the claim that to be a man I must have studied any one field—philosophy, science, theology. But to be a man, *I must speculate,* and I must learn how to test my speculations so that they are not simply capricious, unchecked by other men's speculations. A college education, surely, should throw every student into a regular torrent of speculation, and it should school him to recognize the different standards of validation proper to different kinds of claims to truth. You cannot distinguish a man who in this respect is educated from other men by whether or not he believes in God, or in UFO's. But you can tell an educated man by the way he takes hold of the question of whether God exists, or whether UFO's are from Mars. Do you know your own reasons for your beliefs, or do you absorb your beliefs from whatever happens to be in your environment, like plankton taking in nourishment?

Second, the man who has not learned how to make the great human achievements in the arts his own, who does not know what it means to *earn* a great novel or symphony or painting for himself, is enslaved either to caprice or to other men's testimony or to a life of ugliness. You will notice that as I turn thus to "beauty"—another old-fashioned term—I do not say that a man must know how to prove what is beautiful or how to discourse on aesthetics. Such speculative activities are pleasant and worthwhile in themselves, but they belong in my first domain. Here we are asking that a man be educated to the experience of beauty; speculation about it can then follow. My point is simply that a man is less than a man if he cannot respond to the art made by his fellow man.

Again I have tried to put the standard in a way that allows for the impossibility of any one man's achieving independent responses in very many arts. Some would argue that education should insure some minimal human competence in all of the arts, or at least in music, painting, and literature. I suppose I would be satisfied if all of our graduates had been "hooked" by at least one art, hooked so deeply that they could never get free. As in the domain of speculation, we could say that the more types of distinctively human activity a man can master, the better, but we are today talking about floors, not ceilings, and I shall simply rest content with saying that to be a man, a man must know artistic beauty, in some form, and know it in the way that beauty can be known. (The distinction between natural and man-made beauty might give me trouble if you pushed me on it here, but let me just say, dogmatically, that I would not

7. Here Booth echoes the assertion of Socrates, defending his practice of probing students' conventional beliefs, that the unexamined life is not worth living.

be satisfied simply to know natural beauty—women and sunsets, say—as a substitute for art.)

Finally, the man who has not learned anything about how to understand his own intentions and to make them effective in the world, who has not, through experience and books, learned something about what is possible and what impossible, what desirable and what undesirable, will be enslaved by the political and social intentions of other men, benign or malign. The domain of practical wisdom is at least as complex and troublesome as the other two, and at the same time it is even more self-evidently indispensable. How should a man live? How should a society be run? What direction should a university take in 1966? For that matter what should be the proportion, in a good university, of inquiry into truth, beauty, and "goodness"? What kind of knowledge of self or of society is pertinent to living the life proper to a man? In short, the very question of this conference falls within this final domain: What knowledge, if any, is most worthy of pursuit? You cannot distinguish the men from the boys according to any one set of conclusions, but you *can* recognize a man, in this domain, simply by discovering whether he can think for himself about practical questions, with some degree of freedom from blind psychological or political or economic compulsions. Ernest Hemingway tells somewhere of a man who had "moved one dollar's width to the [political] right for every dollar that he'd ever earned." Perhaps no man ever achieves the opposite extreme, complete freedom in his choices from irrelevant compulsions. But all of us who believe in education believe that it is possible for any man, through study and conscientious thought, to school his choices—that is, to free them through coming to understand the forces working on them.

Even from this brief discussion of the three domains, I think we are put in a position to see how it can be said that there is some knowledge that a man must have. The line I have been pursuing will not lead to a list of great books, or even to a list of indispensable departments in a university. Nor will it lead, in any clear-cut fashion, to a pattern of requirements in each of the divisions. Truth, beauty, and goodness (or "right choice") are relevant to study in every division within the university; the humanities, for example, have no corner on beauty or imagination or art, and the sciences have no corner on speculative truth. What is more, a man can be ignorant even of Shakespeare, Aristotle, Beethoven, and Einstein, and be a man for a' that—*if* he has learned how to think his own thoughts, experience beauty for himself, and choose his own actions.

It is not the business of a college to determine or limit what a man will know; if it tries to, he will properly resent its impositions, perhaps immediately, perhaps ten years later when the imposed information is outmoded. But I think that it *is* the business of a college to help teach a man how to use his mind for himself, in at least the three directions I have suggested. * * * To think for oneself is, as we all know, hard enough. To design a program and assemble faculty to assist rather than hinder students in their efforts to think for themselves is even harder. But in an age that is oppressed by huge accumulations of unassimilated knowledge, the task of discovering what it means to educate a man is perhaps more important than ever before.

1967

Language and
Communication

William March

THE UNSPEAKABLE WORDS

There were words in the Brett language considered so corrupting in their effect on others that if anyone wrote them or was heard to speak them aloud, he was fined and thrown into prison. The King of the Bretts was of the opinion that the words were of no importance one way or the other, and besides, everybody in the country knew them anyway; but his advisers disagreed, and at last, to determine who was right, a committee was appointed to examine the people separately.

At length everyone in the kingdom had been examined, and found to know the words quite well, without the slightest damage to themselves. There was then left only one little girl, a five-year-old who lived in the mountains with her deaf and dumb parents. The committee hoped that this little girl, at least, had never heard the corrupting words, and on the morning they visited her, they said solemnly: "Do you know the meaning of *poost, gist, duss, feng?*"

The little girl admitted that she did not, and then, smiling happily, she said, "Oh, you must mean *feek, kusk, dalu,* and *liben!*"

Those who don't know the words must make them up for themselves.

1960

Robert M. Adams

DIRTY STUFF

Stendhal on ice cream: "But it's perfectly delicious!
What a pity it isn't forbidden!"

To think of the obscene brings us onto a wider stage. Suppose we say, for starters, that the obscene is a word or act that causes a particular response; virtually everybody will recognize what that response is, though agreement on what does or doesn't cause it will be harder to come by, and a few people will say that it shouldn't exist at all—that outrage is itself an outrageous response to anything whatever. Very likely if one could find a society without any customs at all, it would be impervious to the sense of obscenity. But this is a highly metaphysical speculation. Within human society as we know it, the obscene is a shock rupture of ingrained social codes controlling verbal or physical action. By "ingrained" social codes I mean those to which moral value is attached, as opposed to merely convenient observances like driving on the right side of the road. The particulars don't much matter. Our heavy codes have mainly to do with sex and excretion, and we automatically think of the obscene in these connections. But among some South American tribes, where sex and excretion are completely open, the behavioral codes center on food, and the obscene would be to waste a piece of spider-monkey or eat a steak of snake. As a rule, perpetrators of the obscene should be aware of the codes they are violating. An innocent (an infant, an animal, a person from an alien culture) can hardly be obscene in violating a code he doesn't recognize or care about. Perhaps there's an element of the parochial in most judgments of obscenity—as when oriental men think western women grossly provocative because they don't hide their faces under a yashmak, while western men think oriental women slyly provocative because they do. There's not much question that we can train out of ourselves most of the reactions that inspire the word "obscene"; not much question, either, that if we grope around in almost anyone at the limits of what he thinks tolerable, we will find a little area—conditional, limited, and perhaps shamefaced—where the word seems to apply.

In the normal course of events, most of us live in a variety of environments that require us to adjust our definitions of the obscene from minute to minute and circumstance to circumstance. A word or gesture that's perfectly natural on the waterfront will be scandalous in a convent. Tact is the art of commanding this distance between decorum and the obscene, of quietly avoiding obscenity when we don't want it and deftly achieving it when we do. Two variants of obscenity which take for themselves a recognized target can be seen to flank and define our proper topic: the blasphemer directs his outrage specifically against the deity and his laws; the perpetrator of foul insult directs it against an enemy, individual or collective. Obscenity itself, lying in the uncommitted middle range of bad-mouthing, is the least sharply focused of the options. It may turn outward against public mores, or inwardly, against one's own inhibitions and conventions. A pure, natural setting is the moment when one has just missed a nail, but not one's thumb, with a hammer. The moment is explosive. The pain, outrageous and sudden, requires some release; the fault is entirely one's own; there is nobody to be hit back; one explodes against an interior curtain of verbal repression, as if to answer the pain with a like violence. The curse somehow gets you even.

Because there is guilty pleasure in the obscene—pleasure associated with actions, with words as the symbols of actions, and with the idea of breaking taboos which forbid both words and actions—exercising this pleasure could hardly help becoming a game, and purveying it to the passive a business. In both forms, the obscene obviously takes on new nonexpressive motivations—virtuosity and display in the first instance, calculation in the second. An artist in foul speech (I think particularly of an Arkansas corporal who put me through basic training at Jefferson Barracks in 1943) aims only to surpass himself. His goal is glory, to be known as the man with the most filthy, ingenious tongue in camp. (From a severely practical point of view, high artistry of his order is sometimes self-defeating: men perform monkey-drill much better when they are not torn between awe at a rocket-barrage of cursing, and silent, convulsive laughter at the sheer skill of it.) As for obscenity as a business, I suppose one of its main considerations is to promise as much and give as little as possible. Calculating the point where this minimum crosses that maximum is an activity with an interest of its own—game-playing indeed, but not at all like the game played by my corporal, for whom giving and getting were in some way synonymous. In general, the relation of commercial pornography to the spontaneously obscene seems comparable to the relation between military discipline and human bravery; yet there's no way to be elitist about the matter. However grubby the product of the porno-bookstore, however tired and mechanical the tart, the patron of both finds release for a part of himself that he knows and despises. He is a swine, well, he will find some pig to wallow with for a while. We are only now learning in what close, complementary bonds the Victorian angel in the house was linked with the Victorian whore in the lane.

In his appropriation and debasement of the obscene within his client, the commercial exploiter confronts a difficulty analogous to that faced by the solemn analyst of obscenity, the obscenologist as it were. The latter's edifying scientific intentions corrupt and simultaneously sanitize, despite his worst intentions, the examples that he cites. Even when he picks up words like "shit" and "fuck" for inspection, he touches them only with gleaming, stainless-steel forceps (represented on the still-sanitary page by quotation marks), in a solemn clinical atmosphere, the very reverse of the exceptional rage and disgust which usually authenticate such words. I must apologize, before anything else, for such artificiality, which forces me, in typing out polite, discursive obscenity, to commit counterobsceni-ties, for which I can plead no excuse but necessity. Among other admira-ble rules laid down in "The Revolutionist's Handbook and Pocket Companion" by John Tanner, M.I.R.C.[1] (it is an appendix to Shaw's *Man and Superman*) is one for corporal punishment of the young, which proposes that one should never beat a child except in uncontrollable rage. Obscenity in its cleanest form, least contaminated by prudence or exhibitionism or self-interest, is similarly the expression of pure, incoher-ent passion; but passion in explosive, i.e., contained-liberated form.

The conditions, it will be observed, are double. If there is no suppres-sion of caged, explosive feelings, there will be little or no obscenity, though there may be a lot of other things; if the taboos aren't violated deliberately and antagonistically, there will be little sense of obscenity, either expressive or responsive. Like wit, with which its alliance is ancient and intimate, obscenity frees a reality principle within us that has been clamoring to get out. It cuts through layers of social artifice and aspiration, reducing us to the gut and groin that we inescapably are and know ourselves to be, despite incessant prodding to be otherwise. Ob-scenity may or may not purify, but it releases; on the other hand, it also incites, and like many stimulants seems to demand more and more violent satisfactions. Whether it's a therapy or a sickness remains a bit ambiguous.

In any case, the obscene is a breaking open, a breaking out, a coun-tering of norms and surfaces imposed by society or our societally condi-tioned selves. If it is not *against*, it is nothing. For each nation, the debris points to the weapon of destruction, and vice versa. Of all peoples, the French, whose training in their polite speech is toward the sparse, for-mal, and lucid, are most given to Rabelaisian profusion in their obscenity. Eugène Robert's massive *Dictionnaire des injures*, though ostensibly devoted to the art of insult, includes an immense array of general obscen-ities, offering to the verbal duelist or displayman an incredible range of alternatives and optional combinations. (Cartesian duality[2] is carried to almost parodic lengths by French dictionaries of *argot*, with their scholas-tically precise distinctions between innumerable words implying differ-ent varieties and tonalities of whores, pricks, and asses.) By contrast, the Spaniard, whose normal speech includes a good deal of the ceremonious and whose pride in family is legendary, often conveys his ultimate ob-

---

1. Member of the Idle Rich Class. Tanner is the hero of the Shaw play.

2. René Descartes (1596–1650) divided na-ture into matter and mind.

scene sentiment with a gesture of the head and a curt, contemptuous phrase—"*Tu madre*," thy mother. *Not* saying the operative word seems a particularly devious and deadly form of obscenity, since it forces the victim to contaminate his own mind, to call up the expression that the speaker does not even deign to voice. In an equivalent way, the Italian forces into violent conjunction the two poles of his moral outrage in the expletive, "*Porca madonna*";[3] and the German, whose values are cleanliness, efficiency, and order, almost always expresses his sense of the obscene with the scatological. But the Japanese, for whom almost every aspect of life is or can be holy, have almost no special language for obscenity. Ladies who are not only respectable but distinguished, and in situations of perfect decorum, will use words which are the equivalent of "shit" and "fuck"—only in those circumstances they aren't of course in any way equivalent. Japanese insult apparently includes a few mild comparisons with animals, but nothing that we would recognize as artistic or inventive vituperation.

Negatively as well as positively, the power of the taboo to determine the obscenity is almost absolute: where taboos are strong, obscenity clusters; where they are weak, it hardly forms up at all. When women were swathed in yards of dry-goods, veils, boas, crinolines, and high collars, the glimpse of an ear or an ankle was titillating, a word like "bloomers" occasioned embarrassed laughter, and even the pianos had limbs instead of legs. The power of the taboo to create an obscene meaning out of whole cloth was nicely illustrated by a little red book of *Mother Goose Censored*, which circulated during the 1930's:

> Peter, Peter, pumpkin eater,
> Had a wife and couldn't censored her;
> He put her in a pumpkin shell,
> And there he censored her very well.

Swift said it: "A clean-minded man is a man of nasty ideas."

* * *

The obscene depends on the primal energy of the sacred—maybe not altogether, but for a lot of its energy. When there is no immediate general recognition of the sacred, or when the sacredness of the sacred has to be explained—even controverted—it seems likely the spontaneously, joyfully obscene will get heavier, more sullen, even morally calisthenic.

For some centuries in the western world, a naked woman appearing publicly in lubricious attitudes has been thought obscene. We note how burlesque, which began as low parody of the classic myths, shaded gradually and by natural affinity into a sex-show, one sort of anti-state-

---

3. The piggish or sluttish Virgin Mary. The phrase combines the extremes of female baseness and perfection.

ment leading into another. But recently, if the echoes I hear from off-Broadway are to be trusted, the naked woman is not only an expected figure, a convention, her whole import has changed. She is an emblem of honesty, frankness, moral ventilation-with-sanitation, and a standing reproach to the audience, shrinking prudishly in the symbolic dark under their dishonest and hypocritical vestments. If she is not always an example to be instantly followed (audiences have been known to accept the cue, and disrobe completely for a communal nudist frolic), she nonetheless authenticates and validates the show. Whether all this authenticity is really authentic or just a pretext for something else is a point that could be argued; indeed, it has to be argued, if only *in foro conscientiae*.[4] How little moral pretext suffices to sanitize an exhibition the patent aim of which is to titillate? I suppose it depends on how gross a hypocrite one wants to consider oneself. It is a remarkably open-ended question.

But the peripheral point is almost as important. If the naked and sexually enticing woman is an emblem of moral rectitude, the effect of obscenity, if we're going to have such an effect onstage at all, will have to be achieved in some other way—by intercourse on stage, simulated or real, preferably with one or several of the variations that are still recognized as perversions. (I know, "perversion" as a term implies a parochial attitude toward sexual behavior; but if there are no real perversions, an audience must be persuaded that it is watching one—something special —if it is to be stirred out of its ho-hum attitude toward the conventional.) Inflation works upon symbols of the obscene as upon the fiscal symbols: the higher the numbers, the lower the value of the unit.

Literary obscenity is of course all simulated, designed to create, by art or craft, a verbal equivalence of a social or psychological event. The equivalence is two-directional; the artist is bound not only to communicate an experience, but to do so within or against the verbal mores of his culture—mores which may provide only inadequate verbal counters for saying what he wants to say. There are linguistic media within which a number higher than five can only be represented as "many"; cultures which are deaf to many of our cherished overtones, as we are deaf to theirs. Within our own linguistic tradition there are many areas that used to be lively and vivid, but which are now dead and literally buried—old metaphors worn to triteness, images sunk so deeply in formulas that we no longer feel them as images at all, entire stories rubbed down to a fleeting formulaic phrase—as when we speak of a prodigal son or a good Samaritan. Time and constant usage wear the sharp edges off locutions, as they do off coins. It would be ridiculous to suppose that the ordinary everyday conversation of the American army could be represented without the inevitable, monotonous, all-purpose adjective, "fuckin'." It is equally ridiculous to suppose that such usage represents anything ob-

4. In the court of your conscience.

scene in the sense of verbal outrage. Quite the contrary; the word is a routine social convention, a filler on the order of "Y'know," spoken more out of habit and perhaps deliberate stupidity (to express, if anything, the nothingness of mass military existence) than out of any active feelings at all. With the idea of sexual intercourse it has nothing whatever to do. And when a novelist represents the speech of the army by reproducing this feature as it really occurs in daily life, the effect he gets is one of drabness and dreariness, of violence become monotonous, routine, meaningless.

The burden of representing unspeakable outrage falls inevitably on other expressions and devices when "fuckin'" has been given the everyday, commonplace function of a mild intensive like "very." In addition to scraping up another and dirtier word (but no culture possesses at any one time more than a limited supply of these), a violation of sense and syntax, or the sheer force of mechanical repetition, can be used to deepen the impression of fury. The peremptory, disjointed, spiteful sentences of Jason Compson are extraordinarily effective in developing the reader's feeling for an absolutely cold and vindictive mind, though Faulkner throughout *The Sound and the Fury* uses no expletive more potent than "damn." Joyce has Private Carr resort to the familiar ultimate word in the depths of the Nighttown scene of *Ulysses*, emphasizing not only illogicality and mechanical repetition, but an eloquent rhetorical rhythm as well: "I'll wring the neck of any fucking bastard says a word against my bleeding fucking king." But this spirited and forceful declaration has been carefully prepared for, by Joyce's meticulous avoidance of the term during the first 580 pages of the novel. The word has not been debased or rendered habitual; its explosion here is a triumph of blind and incoherent ferocity. Something, indeed, is to be said for the sheer hammer-like repetition of a single word, even though not in itself particularly violent. In his classic study, *Lars Porsenna, or the future of swearing and improper language*, Robert Graves cites a general officer operating under severe restrictions, who managed to convey deep sentiments about a slack member of an honor guard with the inspired sentence, "Oh, you naughty, naughty, NAUGHTY trumpeter!"

Language has many resources other than just vocabulary, and to a certain degree every author controls the range of his own verbal palette. If his scale is generally light throughout, he will have no difficulty finding dark tones where he needs them. But there is such a thing as a verbal climate, and it changes over the years, as do the spectrum of colors that our eyes are trained to see in paintings and the range of voices that we find gratifying in vocal music. * * * Verbal artists particularly are dependent for the basic materials of their work on the common linguistic heritage, the common linguistic habits. Apart from the colloquial patterns of his day, a writer lives in a tangible tradition of language, which has imposed value-laden connotations on words and concepts he is bound to use. He lives also in a haphazard but necessary linguistic projection ("What am I going to sound like fifty or a hundred years from now?") which is no less important to him for being hard to formulate unpretentiously.

* * *

All too often in public discussions of obscenity, it's taken for granted that if we inhibit the rights of pornographers to ply their trade (in magazines, movies, over television), we're on the way to crushing the right of some starry-eyed artist of the future to use the same tonal values in the formulation of some indescribably beautiful chord. Something like this awful repression may, indeed, someday occur, though the scanner of horizons looks in vain for a cloud even as big as a man's hand. Be that as it may, there's patently a lot of cant and hypocrisy in the argument as constructed. The pimping pornographer who claims to be fighting the battles of some future Proust or Joyce doesn't deserve much of our sympathy. If there wasn't good hard cash to be turned from his pious pose, one would soon see how much he cared about Proust or Joyce, supposing he had heard of either.

Twisting the matter another way, it's perfectly arguable that letting down all the barriers of "decency" (I don't mean real decency, of course, since that can't be legislated; just conventions of proper public discourse) will pose more problems for the really creative artist than it solves. It renders flat and commonplace certain expressions that he may want to use for his strongest and most violent effects; if he chooses not to use them at all, the prevalent standard of taste imposes on him (perhaps unjustly) a fussy and old-maidish air. For better or worse—it's not really an arguable point—Dostoevsky moved the benchmarks from around Henry James; in the same way, the most risqué novels of the last thirty years are rendered pallid by *Last Exit to Brooklyn*.[5] It's hard to stay out of the obscenity-sweepstakes, but each new success renders it harder to win. The diffusion of the obscene (which is just another consequence, I suppose, of the romantic spilling of the sacred) subjects artistic taste to an ultimate leveling and democratizing from which it's the constant endeavor of every artist to escape. He wants language of immediate distinction, carrying effortless impact; our liberals offer him the same rights as everybody else. It's a rotten bargain. The artist may get immunity from prosecution, but in contemporary society, this is hardly a significant immunity. No backwoods Alabama prosecutor is going to hound down Philip Roth (who reads Philip Roth in backwoods Alabama?) when he's got *Penthouse* and "Deep Throat" to exercise his publicity-gathering talents on. Besides, everybody knows that being banned in Boston is

---

5. A novel (1964) by Hubert Selby, Jr.

absolutely the most effective form of advertising, in Boston and else-where.

In short, the perils from which the artist is saved when we effectively eliminate a code-decision between the decent and the obscene are tri-fling, imaginary perils. What is imposed on him instead is a kind of schizoid uncertainty-anxiety about the verbal standards of his own days as contrasted with those of other days before and after, and of other cultures in other places. What serious literary artist wants to be caught up in a whirlpool of linguistic bad taste whipped up by the frantic effort of one freak to outdo another? I'm saying not that this has happened here and today, far less that the remedy is some form of bluenosed censorship, just that when a decaying puritanism begins to muddle the obscene with the sacred, directions get lost, along with a sense of where other folks are.

* * *

The confusion of verbal values * * * is general and pervasive. It grows, I think, from the ruin of an ancient set of hierarchical verbal values, and from their inversion. Watered down, homogenized, and stood on their heads, the sacred and the obscene have become so nearly indistinguish-able that deliberate effort is required to set them apart. The grossest of pornographers talk in oily tones of "moral frankness" and "esthetic honesty" and "facing facts." The man who cultivates the obscene for its own sake and without any appended garbage about "redeeming social purpose" has a little better chance of coming off with the shreds of moral integrity—a little better but not much. This emulsifying of the two spheres is a primary reason why all general rules regarding obscenity are absurd nowadays. Perhaps in the old days when society thought it knew what it was talking about on this matter, codes were possible, even under certain aspects desirable: no more. In contemporary society, the very question of obscenity is obscene; to answer it with an affirmation or a denial is an act of bad faith. The less we raise it, the better off we are; and any code we could devise would inevitably be surrounded by so many special contexts, circumstances, and conditions for social pretense and legal manipulation, as to render it instantly a nose of wax.

In surrendering, as it recently did, its claim to define the obscene by a lack of redeeming social purpose, the Supreme Court clearly took one short step toward a healthy skepticism. Anyone can see that the obscene isn't necessarily less obscene because it's hitched to a moral lesson, any more than a whorehouse is nicer if one is introduced into it by a deacon. But that this leaves the "local community" (meaning thereby the ambi-tious local prosecutor and the leader of the local prude society) free to take on this intricate and exacting task of discrimination is little short of ludicrous. One looks forward with awe and amazement to the potential complications which the new arrangement of rules-and-no-rule can bring about. Will it be possible to prosecute a man for reading a dirty book in a plane occupying air-space over eastern Kansas? What recourse will the publisher of Baudelaire have against the city council of Ogallala, Nebraska? Won't the standard-setters for Podunk and Peoria actually have to read all the things they object to—a time-consuming and often a puzzling process?

But in fact these queries go a long way to suggest how, not unpleasantly, the new ruling is bound to work out. For by making censorship local, one makes it, more than ever, ineffectual; as with local prohibition, district ordinances are made to be circumvented or allowed to mildew. At the same time, the obscene retains its power as a concept, if only because one knows that Aunt Tillie in Dubuque isn't allowed to see the wicked flick one can catch oneself by traveling to Iowa City. Copies of *Ulysses* will cross state lines in plain brown wrappers, to the exultant pleasure of the reader, the profit of the under-counter purveyor, the advantage of the legal profession, and the mystification of the unco guid[6] in the now morally purified community. Like jealousy and emulation, the obscene is triangular; we apply the word quite as much as to what we think will outrage other people's moral standards as to what really and in fact offends our own. But the most promising prognosis of all is for a vast torpor and weary indifference on the matter, which was surely what the court anticipated when it shrugged and uttered its Solomonic "Buh!"

Chaos and confusion are thus everybody's gain in this new public policy on the obscene; or the Supreme Court has at least given us a chance to test that hypothesis. There promises to be much comedy and little tragedy in its working out. But for the individual—on whom, as always, real responsibility rests for thinking about the matter—the obscene remains a sphinx in the path. An eighteenth-century arrangement of values (for which, personally, I feel much sympathy) would request certain cleanly and complete decorums, amounting almost to elegance, as a condition of finding the obscene to be a willful and aware violation of them. It's at least a nod in the direction of a Manichean outlook which seems to me as close to optimism as modern man can safely come: a throwback, if we can manage it, to the century of lights with its equivalent darks. Here and there this spirit still survives, perhaps with an access of larkiness, as I recently heard from the friends who sublet their California house for a year. Arriving to take possession, the tenants presented themselves in full evening dress, somehow arranged or locally omitted to display their genitals, which had, perhaps for the occasion, been gilded. A little forced, no doubt, a bit *voulu;* but clearly in the tradition of the *ancien régime.*[7]

The nineteenth-century style is that of the *poète maudit,*[8] who plunges into the obscene as an adventure in evil and a reaffirmation of spiritual

6. The "unbelievably good" of Robert Burns' poem "Address to the Unco Guid, or the Rigidly Righteous."

7. *voulu:* calculated; *ancien régime:* the old order.

8. The cursed poet.

law against mere nature. The great exemplar is of course Baudelaire, but one can find more than traces of the character in Swinburne, Poe, Huysmans, Sacher-Masoch. And for the twentieth century, the obscene represents an act of deep choice, an affirmation, even a creation, of the self. Far from being an occasional adventure, or a testing of alien moral values, it is itself in the character of moral nutriment. Through the obscene one declares one's independence of the rotten genteel tradition, and achieves the instant, universal *bona fides* of moral authenticity. I don't have to emphasize the element of fraud here, some actual and some potential, but the logic is all right. What happens when you look under the logic at the motivation is another matter.

Any time that the respectable (lumped all together in the accepted paranoid pattern) is felt to be patently obscene, then frank and deliberate violation of it is in order. Whatever else one may be rotting of (that, I repeat from my eighteenth-century stance, covers a lot of ground), it isn't inertia. How far one wants to push the formula that if I revolt against the faulty I'm bound to be faultless, depends very largely on one's balance between pretension and a sense of humor. The foul-mouthed saint-comedian-criminal-buffoon who is the characteristic moral register of our time (Genet, Céline, Lenny Bruce, et al.) seems to push and splinter the moral paradoxes as far as they will go; agile and elusive behind all his impersonations, he is unfailingly ready with Rousseau's all-purpose defense, which is simply to confess everything, plus 20 percent for contingencies, long before one is accused of it. He thus gains the right, which he'll liberally exercise, to bad-mouth the rest of us. Far from being obliged to suggest ways we can improve ourselves, he's under major obligation not to. In this day of confrontation psychology, who can deny the value of confrontation obscenity, which elicits moral responses from us (maybe) by affronting our moral values as cruelly, as corruptly, as intimately as possible? Of course there's something obscene, too, about having apparent moral dilemmas too easily both ways—but that's a purely metaphorical "obscene."

Without very much enthusiasm, then, I recognize the style in obscenity of my age: it is moralistic and confused. And without being able to account for the preference very clearly, I affirm my own predilection for esthetic clarity. I like my obscenity sharp and pure like a purple splotch across a canvas of Nicolas de Staël;[9] I don't want it doing me good underhandedly. One of my excuses for this stance is that the esthetic seems a less heavy judgment than the moral; less to defend, less to attack, mobility not nobility. Setting one's own style in the matter allows, it seems to me, a longer perspective and a freer choice of the company in which one chooses to be judged. That it's an evasion of sorts I won't try to deny. Let him who will look straight and hard, with an aroused moral

9. A modern French painter.

conscience, at the full range and scope of filth and dishonor in this world of ours—the sketchiest recital of which would fill an encyclopedia, blacken the heavens, and earn me a place among the obsessed and monomaniacal. Human kind, says the poet (or at least a bird, speaking to the poet), cannot bear very much reality. Whatever our pious truthtellers pretend, the obscene, when taken at its full valency, is a topic to be looked at askance, under peril of a scorched retina.

1973

Ralph Waldo Emerson

THE LANGUAGE OF THE STREET

The language of the street is always strong. What can describe the folly and emptiness of scolding like the word *jawing?* I feel too the force of the double negative, though clean contrary to our grammar rules. And I confess to some pleasure from the stinging rhetoric of a rattling oath in the mouths of truckmen and teamsters. How laconic and brisk it is by the side of a page of the *North American Review.* Cut these words and they would bleed; they are vascular and alive; they walk and run. Moreover they who speak them have this elegancy, that they do not trip in their speech. It is a shower of bullets, whilst Cambridge men and Yale men correct themselves and begin again at every half sentence.

1840   1914

QUESTION

Analyze a paragraph from each of the following writers in the terms of this one: Abraham Lincoln (p. 831), E. B. White (p. 842).

W. Somerset Maugham

LUCIDITY, SIMPLICITY, EUPHONY

I have never had much patience with the writers who claim from the reader an effort to understand their meaning. You have only to go to the great philosophers to see that it is possible to express with lucidity the most subtle reflections. You may find it difficult to understand the thought of Hume, and if you have no philosophical training its implications will doubtless escape you; but no one with any education at all can fail to understand exactly what the meaning of each sentence is. Few people have written English with more grace than Berkeley. There are two sorts of obscurity that you find in writers. One is due to negligence and the other to willfulness. People often write obscurely because they have never taken the trouble to learn to write clearly. This sort of obscurity you find too often in modern philosophers, in men of science, and even in literary critics. Here it is indeed strange. You would have thought that men who passed their lives in the study of the great masters of literature would be sufficiently sensitive to the beauty of language to write if not beautifully at least with perspicuity. Yet you will find in their works sentence after sentence that you must read twice to discover the sense. Often you can only guess at it, for the writers have evidently not said what they intended.

Another cause of obscurity is that the writer is himself not quite sure of his meaning. He has a vague impression of what he wants to say, but has not, either from lack of mental power or from laziness, exactly formulated it in his mind and it is natural enough that he should not find a precise expression for a confused idea. This is due largely to the fact that many writers think, not before, but as they write. The pen originates the thought. The disadvantage of this, and indeed it is a danger against which the author must be always on his guard, is that there is a sort of magic in the written word. The idea acquires substance by taking on a visible nature, and then stands in the way of its own clarification. But this sort of obscurity merges very easily into the willful. Some writers who do not think clearly are inclined to suppose that their thoughts have a significance greater than at first sight appears. It is flattering to believe that they are too profound to be expressed so clearly that all who run may read, and very naturally it does not occur to such writers that the fault is with their own minds which have not the faculty of precise reflection. Here again the magic of the written word obtains. It is very easy to persuade oneself that a phrase that one does not quite understand may mean a great deal more than one realizes. From this there is only a little way to go to fall into the habit of setting down one's impressions in all their original

321

vagueness. Fools can always be found to discover a hidden sense in them. There is another form of willful obscurity that masquerades as aristocratic exclusiveness. The author wraps his meaning in mystery so that the vulgar shall not participate in it. His soul is a secret garden into which the elect may penetrate only after overcoming a number of perilous obstacles. But this kind of obscurity is not only pretentious; it is short-sighted. For time plays it an odd trick. If the sense is meagre time reduces it to a meaningless verbiage that no one thinks of reading. This is the fate that has befallen the lucubrations of those French writers who were seduced by the example of Guillaume Apollinaire. But occasionally it throws a sharp cold light on what had seemed profound and thus discloses the fact that these contortions of language disguised very commonplace notions. There are few of Mallarmé's poems now that are not clear; one cannot fail to notice that his thought singularly lacked originality. Some of his phrases were beautiful; the materials of his verse were the poetic platitudes of his day.

Simplicity is not such an obvious merit as lucidity. I have aimed at it because I have no gift for richness. Within limits I admire richness in others, though I find it difficult to digest in quantity. I can read one page of Ruskin with delight, but twenty only with weariness. The rolling period, the stately epithet, the noun rich in poetic associations, the subordinate clauses that give the sentence weight and magnificence, the grandeur like that of wave following wave in the open sea; there is no doubt that in all this there is something inspiring. Words thus strung together fall on the ear like music. The appeal is sensuous rather than intellectual, and the beauty of the sound leads you easily to conclude that you need not bother about the meaning. But words are tyrannical things, they exist for their meanings, and if you will not pay attention to these, you cannot pay attention at all. Your mind wanders. This kind of writing demands a subject that will suit it. It is surely out of place to write in the grand style of inconsiderable things. No one wrote in this manner with greater success than Sir Thomas Browne, but even he did not always escape this pitfall. In the last chapter of *Hydriotaphia* the matter, which is the destiny of man, wonderfully fits the baroque splendor of the language, and here the Norwich doctor produced a piece of prose that has never been surpassed in our literature; but when he describes the finding of his urns in the same splendid manner the effect (at least to my taste) is less happy. When a modern writer is grandiloquent to tell you whether or no a little trollop shall hop into bed with a commonplace young man you are right to be disgusted.

But if richness needs gifts with which everyone is not endowed, simplicity by no means comes by nature. To achieve it needs rigid discipline. So far as I know ours is the only language in which it has been found necessary to give a name to the piece of prose which is described as the purple patch; it would not have been necessary to do so unless it were characteristic. English prose is elaborate rather than simple. It was not always so. Nothing could be more racy, straight-forward and alive than the prose of Shakespeare; but it must be remembered that this was dialogue written to be spoken. We do not know how he would have written if like Corneille he had composed prefaces to his plays. It may be that they would have been as euphuistic as the letters of Queen Elizabeth. But earlier prose, the prose of Sir Thomas More, for instance, is neither ponderous, flowery nor oratorical. It smacks of the English soil. To my mind King James's Bible has been a very harmful influence on English prose. I am not so stupid as to deny its great beauty. It is majestical. But the Bible is an oriental book. Its alien imagery has nothing to do with us. Those hyperboles, those luscious metaphors, are foreign to our genius. I cannot but think that not the least of the misfortunes that the Secession from Rome brought upon the spiritual life of our country is that this work for so long a period became the daily, and with many the only, reading of our people. Those rhythms, that powerful vocabulary, that grandiloquence, became part and parcel of the national sensibility. The plain, honest English speech was over-whelmed with ornament. Blunt Englishmen twisted their tongues to speak like Hebrew prophets. There was evidently something in the English temper to which this was congenial, perhaps a native lack of precision in thought, perhaps a naïve delight in fine words for their own sake, an innate eccentricity and love of embroidery, I do not know; but the fact remains that ever since, English prose has had to struggle against the tendency to luxuriance. When from time to time the spirit of the language has reasserted itself, as it did with Dryden and the writers of Queen Anne, it was only to be submerged once more by the pompositiés of Gibbon and Dr. Johnson. When English prose recovered simplicity with Hazlitt, the Shelley of the letters and Charles Lamb at his best, it lost it again with De Quincey, Carlyle, Meredith and Walter Pater. It is obvious that the grand style is more striking than the plain. Indeed many people think that a style that does not attract notice is not style. They will admire Walter Pater's, but will read an essay by Matthew Arnold without giving a moment's attention to the elegance, distinction and sobriety with which he set down what he had to say.

The dictum that the style is the man is well known. It is one of those aphorisms that say too much to mean a great deal. Where is the man in Goethe, in his birdlike lyrics or in his clumsy prose? And Hazlitt? But I suppose that if a man has a confused mind he will write in a confused way, if his temper is capricious his prose will be fantastical, and if he has a quick, darting intelligence that is reminded by the matter in hand of a hundred things, he will, unless he has great self-control, load his pages with metaphor and simile. There is a great difference between the magniloquence of the Jacobean writers, who were intoxicated with the new wealth that had lately been brought into the language, and the turgidity of Gibbon and Dr. Johnson, who were the victims of bad theories. I can read every word that Dr. Johnson wrote with delight, for he had good sense, charm and wit. No one could have written better if he had not willfully set himself to write in the grand style. He knew good English when he saw it. No critic has praised Dryden's prose more aptly. He said of him that he appeared to have no art other than that of expressing with clearness what he thought with vigor. And one of his Lives he finished with the words: "Whoever wishes to attain an English style, familiar but not coarse, and elegant but not ostentatious, must give his days and nights to the volumes of Addison." But when he himself sat down to write it was with a very different aim. He mistook the orotund for the dignified. He had not the good breeding to see that simplicity and naturalness are the truest marks of distinction.

For to write good prose is an affair of good manners. It is, unlike verse, a civil art. Poetry is baroque. Baroque is tragic, massive and mystical. It is elemental. It demands depth and insight. I cannot but feel that the prose writers of the baroque period, the authors of King James's Bible, Sir Thomas Browne, Glanville, were poets who had lost their way. Prose is a rococo art. It needs taste rather than power, decorum rather than inspiration and vigor rather than grandeur. Form for the poet is the bit and the bridle without which (unless you are an acrobat) you cannot ride your horse; but for the writer of prose it is the chassis without which your car does not exist. It is not an accident that the best prose was written when rococo with its elegance and moderation, at its birth attained its greatest excellence. For rococo was evolved when baroque had become declamatory and the world, tired of the stupendous, asked for restraint. It was the natural expression of persons who valued a civilized life. Humor, tolerance and horse sense made the great tragic issues that had preoccupied the first half of the seventeenth century seem excessive. The world was a more comfortable place to live in and perhaps for the first time in centuries the cultivated classes could sit back and enjoy their leisure. It has been said that good prose should resemble the conversation of a well-bred man. Conversation is only possible when men's minds are free from pressing anxieties. Their lives must be reasonably secure and they must have no grave concern about their souls. They must attach importance to the refinements of civilization. They must value courtesy, they must pay attention to their persons (and have we not also been told that good prose should be like the clothes of a well-dressed man, appropriate but unobtrusive?), they must fear to bore, they must be neither flippant nor solemn, but always apt; and they must look upon "enthusiasm" with a critical glance. This is a soil very suitable for prose. It is not to be wondered at that it gave a fitting opportunity for the appearance of the best writer of prose that our modern world has seen, Voltaire. The writers of English, perhaps owing to the poetic nature of the language, have seldom reached the excellence that seems to have come so naturally to him. It is in so far as they have approached the ease, sobriety and precision of the great French masters that they are admirable.

Whether you ascribe importance to euphony, the last of the three characteristics that I mentioned, must depend on the sensitiveness of your ear. A great many readers, and many admirable writers, are devoid of this quality. Poets as we know have always made a great use of alliteration. They are persuaded that the repetition of a sound gives an effect of beauty. I do not think it does so in prose. It seems to me that in prose alliteration should be used only for a special reason; when used by accident it falls on the ear very disagreeably. But its accidental use is so common that one can only suppose that the sound of it is not universally offensive. Many writers without distress will put two rhyming words together, join a monstrous long adjective to a monstrous long noun, or between the end of one word and the beginning of another have a conjunction of consonants that almost breaks your jaw. These are trivial and obvious instances. I mention them only to prove that if careful writers can do such things it is only because they have no ear. Words have weight, sound and appearance; it is only by considering these that you can write a sentence that is good to look at and good to listen to.

I have read many books on English prose, but have found it hard to profit by them; for the most part they are vague, unduly theoretical, and often scolding. But you cannot say this of Fowler's *Dictionary of Modern English Usage*. It is a valuable work. I do not think anyone writes so well that he cannot learn much from it. It is lively reading. Fowler liked simplicity, straightforwardness and common sense. He had no patience with pretentiousness. He had a sound feeling that idiom was the backbone of a language and he was all for the racy phrase. He was no slavish admirer of logic and was willing enough to give usage right of way through the exact demesnes of grammar. English grammar is very difficult and few writers have avoided making mistakes in it. So heedful a writer as Henry James, for instance, on occasion wrote so ungrammatically that a school-master, finding such errors in a schoolboy's essay, would be justly indignant. It is necessary to know grammar, and it is better to write grammatically than not, but it is well to remember that grammar is common speech formulated. Usage is the only test. I would prefer a phrase that was easy and unaffected to a phrase that was grammatical. One of the differences between French and English is that in French you can be grammatical with complete naturalness, but in English not invariably. It is a difficulty in writing English that the sound of the living voice dominates the look of the printed word. I have given the matter of style a great deal of thought and have taken great pains. I have written few pages that I feel I could not improve and far too many that I have left with dissatisfaction because, try as I would, I could do no better. I cannot say of myself what Johnson said of Pope: "He never passed a fault unamended by indifference, nor quitted it by despair." I do not write as I want to; I write as I can.

But Fowler had no ear. He did not see that simplicity may sometimes make concessions to euphony. I do not think a far-fetched, an archaic or even an affected word is out of place when it sounds better than the blunt, obvious one or when it gives a sentence a better balance. But, I hasten to add, though I think you may without misgiving make this concession to pleasant sound, I think you should make none to what may obscure your meaning. Anything is better than not to write clearly. There is nothing to be said against lucidity, and against simplicity only the possibility of dryness. This is a risk that is well worth taking when you reflect how much better it is to be bald than to wear a curly wig. But there is in euphony a danger that must be considered. It is very likely to be monotonous. When George Moore began to write, his style was poor; it gave you the impression that he wrote on wrapping paper with a blunt pencil. But he developed gradually a very musical English. He learnt to write sentences that fall away on the ear with a misty languor and it delighted him so much that he could never have enough of it. He did not escape monotony. It is like the sound of water lapping a shingly beach, so soothing that you presently cease to be sensible of it. It is so mellifluous that you hanker for some harshness, for an abrupt dissonance, that will interrupt the silky concord. I do not know how one can guard against this. I suppose the best chance is to have a more lively faculty of boredom than one's readers so that one is wearied before they are. One must always be on the watch for mannerisms and when certain cadences come too easily to the pen ask oneself whether they have not become mechanical. It is very hard to discover the exact point where the idiom one has formed to express oneself has lost its tang. As Dr. Johnson said: "He that has once studiously formed a style, rarely writes afterwards with complete ease." Admirably as I think Matthew Arnold's style was suited to his particular purposes, I must admit that his mannerisms are often irritating. His style was an instrument that he had forged once for all; it was not like the human hand capable of performing a variety of actions.

If you could write lucidly, simply, euphoniously and yet with liveliness you would write perfectly: you would write like Voltaire. And yet we know how fatal the pursuit of liveliness may be: it may result in the tiresome acrobatics of Meredith. Macaulay and Carlyle were in their different ways arresting; but at the heavy cost of naturalness. Their flashy effects distract the mind. They destroy their persuasiveness; you would not believe a man was very intent on ploughing a furrow if he carried a hoop with him and jumped through it at every other step. A good style should show no sign of effort. What is written should seem a happy accident. I think no one in France now writes more admirably than Colette, and such is the ease of her expression that you cannot bring yourself to believe that she takes any trouble over it. I am told that there are pianists who have a natural technique so that they can play in a manner that most executants can achieve only as the result of unremitting toil, and I am willing to believe that there are writers who are equally fortunate. Among them I was much inclined to place Colette. I asked her. I was exceedingly surprised to hear that she wrote everything over and over again. She told me that she would often spend a whole morning working upon a single page. But it does not matter how one gets the effect of ease. For my part, if I get it at all, it is only by strenuous effort. Nature seldom provides me with the word, the turn of phrase, that is appropriate without being far-fetched or commonplace.

1938

QUESTION

Maugham draws attention to the two conflicting yet complementary approaches to style that have been traditional in literary criticism. One approach maintains that style is primarily a combination of qualities and devices that can be learned and produced; the other, that "style is the man," the reflection in language of a personality with all its attitudes and idiosyncracies. Using passages from An Album of Styles (pp. 342–360), explore the two approaches. In any given passage what appears as impersonal technique or device, what as reflecting the special temperament or character of the author?

Wayne C. Booth

BORING FROM WITHIN: THE ART OF THE FRESHMAN ESSAY[1]

Last week I had for about the hundredth time an experience that always disturbs me. Riding on a train, I found myself talking with my seat-mate, who asked me what I did for a living. "I teach English." Do you have any trouble predicting his response? His face fell, and he groaned, "Oh, dear, I'll have to watch my language." In my experience there are only two other possible reactions. The first is even less inspiriting: "I hated English in school; it was my worst subject." The second, so rare as

1. Adapted by Mr. Booth from a speech delivered in May 1963 to the Illinois Council of College Teachers of English.

to make an honest English teacher almost burst into tears of gratitude when it occurs, is an animated conversation about literature, or ideas, or the American language—the kind of conversation that shows a continuing respect for "English" as something more than being sure about *who* and *whom, lie* and *lay.*

Unless the people you meet are a good deal more tactful or better liars than the ones I meet, you've had the two less favorable experiences many times. And it takes no master analyst to figure out why so many of our fellow citizens think of us as unfriendly policemen: it is because too many of us have seen ourselves as unfriendly policemen. I know of a high school English class in Indiana in which the students are explicitly told that their paper grades will not be affected by anything they say; required to write a paper a week, they are graded simply on the number of spelling and grammatical errors. What is more, they are given a standard form for their papers: each paper is to have three paragraphs, a beginning, a middle, and an end—or is it an introduction, a body, and a conclusion? The theory seems to be that if the student is not troubled about having to say anything, or about discovering a good way of saying it, he can then concentrate on the truly important matter of avoiding mistakes.

What's wrong with such assignments? What's wrong with getting the problem of correctness focused sharply enough so that we can really work on it? After all, we do have the job of teaching correct English, don't we? We can't possibly teach our hordes of students to be colorful writers, but by golly, we can beat the bad grammar out of them. Leaving aside the obvious fact that we *can't* beat the bad grammar out of them, not by direct assault, let's think a bit about what that kind of assignment does to the poor teacher who gives it. Those papers must be read, by someone, and unless the teacher has more trained assistance than you and I have, *she's* the victim. She can't help being bored silly by her own paper-reading, and we all know what an evening of being bored by a class's papers does to our attitude toward that class the next day. The old formula of John Dewey was that any teaching that bores the student is likely to fail. The formula was subject to abuse, quite obviously, since interest in itself is only one of many tests of adequate teaching. A safer formula, though perhaps also subject to abuse, might be: Any teaching that bores the teacher is sure to fail. And I am haunted by the picture of that poor woman in Indiana, week after week reading batches of papers written by students who have been told that nothing they say can possibly affect her opinion of those papers. Could any hell imagined by Dante or Jean-Paul Sartre[2] match this self-inflicted futility?

I call it self-inflicted, as if it were a simple matter to avoid receiving papers that bore us. But unfortunately it is not. It may be a simple matter

---

2. Booth refers to the elaborately described hell of the *Inferno*, by the fourteenth-century Italian poet Dante Alighieri, and to the banal locked room in which the characters of Sartre's *No Exit* discover that hell is "other people."

to avoid the *total* meaninglessness that the students must give that Indiana teacher, but we all know that it is no easy matter to produce interesting papers; our pet cures for boredom never work as well as they ought to. Every beginning teacher learns quickly and painfully that nothing works with all students, and that on bad days even the most promising ideas work with nobody.

As I try to sort out the various possible cures for those batches of boredom—in ink, double-spaced, on one side of the sheet, only, please—I find them falling into three groups: efforts to give the students a sharper sense of writing to an audience, efforts to give them some substance to express, and efforts to improve their habits of observation and of approach to their task—what might be called improving their mental personalities.

This classification, both obvious and unoriginal, is a useful one not only because it covers—at least I hope it does—all of our efforts to improve what our students can do but also because it reminds us that no one of the three is likely to work unless it is related to each of the others. In fact each of the three types of cure—"develop an awareness of audience," "give them something to say," and "enliven their writing personalities"—threatens us with characteristic dangers and distortions; all three together are indispensable to any lasting cure.

Perhaps the most obvious omission in that Indiana teacher's assignments is all sense of an audience to be persuaded, of a serious rhetorical purpose to be achieved. One tempting cure for this omission is to teach them to put a controversial edge on what they say. So we ask them to write a three-page paper arguing that China should be allowed into the UN or that women are superior to men or that American colleges are failing in their historic task. Then we are surprised when the papers turn out to be as boring as ever. The papers on Red China are full of abstract pomposities that the students themselves obviously do not understand or care about, since they have gleaned them in a desperate dash through the most readily available sources listed in the *Readers' Guide*. Except for the rare student who has some political background and awareness, and who thus might have written on the subject anyway, they manage to convey little more than their resentment at the assignment and their boredom in carrying it out. One of the worst batches of papers I ever read came out of a good idea we had at Earlham College for getting the whole student body involved in controversial discussion about world affairs. We required them to read Barbara Ward's *Five Ideas that Change the World*; we even had Lady Jackson[3] come to the campus and talk to everyone about her concern for the backward nations. The papers, to our surprise, were a discouraging business. We found ourselves in desperation collecting the boners that are always a sure sign, when present in great numbers,

---

3. Barbara Ward.

that students are thoroughly disengaged. "I think altruism is all right, so long as we practice it in our own interest." "I would be willing to die for anything fatal." "It sure is a doggie dog world."

It is obvious what had gone wrong: though we had ostensibly given the student a writing purpose, it had not become *his* purpose, and he was really no better off, perhaps worse, than if we had him writing about, say, piccolos or pizza. We might be tempted in revulsion from such overly ambitious failures to search for controversy in the students' own mundane lives. This may be a good move, but we should not be surprised when the papers on "Let's clean up the campus" or "Why must we have traffic fatalities?" turn out to be just as empty as the papers on the UN or the Congo. They may have more exclamation points and underlined adjectives, but they will not interest any teacher who would like to read papers for his own pleasure or edification. "People often fail to realize that nearly 40,000 people are killed on our highways each year. Must this carnage continue?" Well, I suppose it must, until people who write about it learn to see it with their own eyes, and hearts, instead of through a haze of cliché. The truth is that to make students assume a controversial pose before they have any genuine substance to be controversial about is to encourage dishonesty and slovenliness, and to ensure our own boredom. It may very well lead them into the kind of commercial concern for the audience which makes almost every *Reader's Digest* article intelligible to everyone over the chronological age of ten and boring to everyone over the mental age of fifteen. *Newsweek* magazine recently had a readability survey conducted on itself. It was found to be readable by the average twelfth grader, unlike *Time*, which is readable by the average eleventh grader. The editors were advised, and I understand are taking the advice, that by improving their "readability" by one year they could improve their circulation by several hundred thousand. Whether they will thereby lop off a few thousand adult readers in the process was not reported.

The only protection from this destructive type of concern for the audience is the control of substance, of having something solid to say. Our students bore us, even when they take a seemingly lively controversial tone, because they have nothing to say, to us or to anybody else. If and when they discover something to say, they will no longer bore us, and our comments will no longer bore them. Having something to say, they will be interested in learning how to say it better. Having something to say, they can be taught how to give a properly controversial edge to what will by its nature be controversial—nothing, after all, is worth saying that everybody agrees on already.

When we think of providing substance, we are perhaps tempted first to find some way of filling students' minds with a goodly store of general ideas, available on demand. This temptation is not necessarily a bad one.

After all, if we think of the adult writers who interest us, most of them have such a store; they have read and thought about man's major problems, and they have opinions and arguments ready to hand about how men ought to live, how society ought to be run, how literature ought to be written. Edmund Wilson, for example, one of the most consistently interesting men alive, seems to have an inexhaustible flow of reasoned opinions on any subject that comes before him. Obviously our students are not going to interest us until they too have some ideas.

But it is not easy to impart ideas. It is not even easy to impart opinions, though a popular teacher can usually manage to get students to parrot his views. But ideas—that is, opinions backed with genuine reasoning—are extremely difficult to develop. If they were not, we wouldn't have a problem in the first place; we could simply send our students off with an assignment to prove their conviction that God does or does not exist or that the American high school system is the best on God's earth, and the interesting arguments would flow.

There is, in fact, no short cut to the development of reasoned ideas. Years and years of daily contact with the world of ideas are required before the child can be expected to begin formulating his own ideas and his own reasons. And for the most part the capacity to handle abstract ideas comes fairly late. I recently saw a paper of a bright high school sophomore, from a good private school, relating the economic growth of China and India to their political development and relative supply of natural resources. It was a terrible paper; the student's hatred of the subject, his sense of frustration in trying to invent generalizations about processes that were still too big for him, showed in every line. The child's parent told me that when the paper was returned by the geography teacher, he had pencilled on the top of one page, "Why do you mix so many bad ideas with your good ones?" The son was almost in tears, his father told me, with anger and helplessness. "He talks as if I'd put bad ideas in on purpose. *I* don't know a bad idea from a good one on this subject."

Yet with all this said, I am still convinced that general ideas are not only a resource but also a duty that cannot be dodged just because it is a dangerous one. There is nothing we touch, as English teachers, that is immune to being tainted by our touch; all the difference lies in how we go about it.

Ideas are a resource because adolescents are surprisingly responsive to any real encouragement to think for themselves, *if* methods of forced feeding are avoided. The seventeen-year-old who has been given nothing but commonplaces and clichés all his life and who finally discovers a teacher with ideas of his own may have his life changed, and, as I shall say in my final point, when his life is changed his writing is changed. Perhaps some of you can remember, as I can, a first experience with a teacher who could think for himself. I can remember going home from a conversation with my high school chemistry teacher and audibly vowing to myself: "Someday I'm going to be able to think for myself like that." There was nothing especially unconventional about Luther Gidding's ideas—at least I can remember few of them now. But what I cannot forget is the way he had with an idea, the genuine curiosity with which he approached it, the pause while he gave his little thoughtful cough, and then the bulldog tenacity with which he would argue it through. And I am convinced that though he never required me to write a line, he did more to improve my writing during the high school years than all of my English teachers put together. The diary I kept to record my sessions with him, never read by anyone, was the best possible writing practice.

If ideas, in this sense of speculation backed up with an attempt to think about things rigorously and constructively, are a great and often neglected resource, they are also our civic responsibility—a far more serious responsibility than our duty to teach spelling and grammar. It is a commonplace to say that democracy depends for its survival on an informed citizenry, but we all know that mere information is not what we are talking about when we say such things. What we mean is that democracy depends on a citizenry that can reason for themselves, on men who know whether a case has been proved, or at least made probable. Democracy depends, if you will forgive some truisms for a moment, on free choices, and choices cannot be in any sense free if they are made blind: free choice is, in fact, choice that is based on knowledge—not just opinions, but knowledge in the sense of reasoned opinion. And if that half of our population who do not go beyond high school do not learn from us how to put two and two together and how to test the efforts of others to do so, and if the colleges continue to fail with most of the other half, we are doomed to become even more sheeplike, as a nation, than we are already.

Papers about ideas written by sheep are boring; papers written by thinking boys and girls are interesting. The problem is always to find ideas at a level that will allow the student to *reason*, that is, to provide support for his ideas, rather than merely assert them in half-baked form. And this means something that is all too often forgotten by the most ambitious teachers—namely, that whatever ideas the student writes about must somehow be connected with his own experience. Teaching machines will never be able to teach the kind of writing we all want, precisely because no machine can ever know which general ideas relate, for a given student, to some meaningful experience. In the same class we'll have one student for whom philosophical and religious ideas are meaningful, another who can talk with confidence about entropy and the second law of thermodynamics, a third who can write about social justice, and a fourth who can discuss the phony world of Holden Caulfield.[4] Each of them can do a good job on his own subject, because he has as part of his equipment a growing awareness of how conclusions in that subject are related to the steps of argument that support conclusions. Ideally, each of these students ought to have the personal attention of a tutor for an hour or so each week, someone who can help him sharpen those connections, and not force him to write on topics not yet appropriate to his interests or experience. But when these four are in a class of thirty or forty others, taught by a teacher who has three or four other similar sections, we all know what happens: the teacher is forced by his circumstances to provide some sort of mold into which all of the students can be poured. Although he is still better able to adapt to individual differences than a machine, he is unfortunately subject to boredom and fatigue, as a machine would not be. Instead of being the philosopher, scientist, political analyst, and literary critic that these four students require him to be, teaching them and learning from them at the same time, the teacher is almost inevitably tempted to force them all to write about the ideas he himself knows best. The result is that at least three of the four must write out of ignorance.

Now clearly the best way out of this impasse would be for legislatures and school boards and college presidents to recognize the teaching of English for what it is: the most demanding of all teaching jobs, justifying the smallest sections and the lightest course loads. No composition teacher can possibly concentrate on finding special interests, making imaginative assignments, and testing the effectiveness and cogency of papers if he has more than seventy-five students at a time; the really desirable limit would be about forty-five—three sections of fifteen students each. Nobody would ever expect a piano teacher, who has no themes to read, to handle the great masses of pupils that we handle. Everyone recognizes that for all other technical skills individual attention is required. Yet for this, the most delicate of all skills, the one requiring the most subtle interrelationships of training, character, and experience, we fling students and teachers into hopelessly impersonal patterns.

But if I'm not careful I'll find myself saying that our pupils bore us because the superintendents and college presidents hire us to be bored. Administrative neglect and misallocation of educational funds are basic to our problem, and we should let the citizenry know of the scandal on every occasion. But meanwhile, back at the ranch, we are faced with the situation as it now is: we must find some way to train a people to write responsibly even though the people, as represented, don't want this service sufficiently to pay for it.

The tone of political exhortation into which I have now fallen leads me to one natural large source of ideas as we try to encourage writing that is

4. The hero of *The Catcher in the Rye,* by J. D. Salinger.

not just lively and controversial but informed and genuinely persuasive. For many students there is obviously more potential interest in social problems and forces, political controversy, and the processes of everyday living around them than in more general ideas. The four students I described a moment ago, students who can say something about philosophy, science, general political theory, or literary criticism, are rare. But most students, including these four, can in theory at least be interested in meaningful argument about social problems in which they are personally involved.

As a profession we have tried, over the past several decades, a variety of approaches attempting to capitalize on such interests. Papers on corruption in TV, arguments about race relations, analyses of distortions in advertising, descriptions of mass communication—these have been combined in various quantities with traditional subjects like grammar, rhetoric, and literature. The "communications" movement, which looked so powerful only a few years ago and which now seems almost dead, had at its heart a perfectly respectable notion, a notion not much different from the one I'm working with today: get them to write about something they know about, and make sure that they see their writing as an act of communication, not as a meaningless exercise. And what better material than other acts of communication.

The dangers of such an approach are by now sufficiently understood. As subject matter for the English course, current "communications media" can at best provide only a supplement to literature and analysis of ideas. But they can be a valuable supplement. Analysis in class of the appeals buried in a New Yorker or Life advertisement followed by a writing assignment requiring similar analyses can be a far more interesting introduction to the intricacies of style than assignments out of a language text on levels of usage or emotion-charged adjectives. Analysis of a Time magazine account, purporting to be objective news but in actual fact a highly emotional editorial, can be not only a valuable experience in itself, but it can lead to papers in which the students do say something to us. Stylistic analysis of the treatment of the same news events by two newspapers or weeklies of different editorial policy can lead to an intellectual awakening of great importance, and thus to papers that will not, cannot, bore the teacher. But this will happen only if the students' critical powers are genuinely developed. It will not do simply to teach the instructor's own prejudices.

There was a time in decades not long past when many of the most lively English teachers thought of their job as primarily to serve as handmaids to liberalism. I had one teacher in college who confessed to me that his overriding purpose was to get students to read and believe The Nation rather than the editorials of their daily paper. I suppose that his approach was not entirely valueless. It seems preferable to the effort to be noncontroversial that marks too many English teachers in the '60's, and at least it stirred some of us out of our dogmatic slumbers. But unfortunately it did nothing whatever about teaching us to think critically. Though we graduated from his course at least aware—as many college graduates do not seem to be today—that you can't believe anything you read in the daily press until you have analyzed it and related it to your past experience and to other accounts, it failed to teach us that you can't believe what you read in The Nation either. It left the job undone of training our ability to think, because it concentrated too heavily on our opinions. The result was, as I remember, that my own papers in that course were generally regurgitated liberalism. I was excited by them, and that was something. But I can't believe that the instructor found reading them anything other than a chore. There was nothing in them that came from my own experience, my own notions of what would constitute evidence for my conclusions. There I was, in Utah in the depths of the depression, writing about the Okies when I could have been writing about the impoverished farmers all around me. I wrote about race relations in the south without ever having talked with a Negro in my life and without recognizing that the bootblack I occasionally saw in Salt Lake City in the Hotel Utah was in any way related to the problem of race relations.

The third element that accounts for our boring papers is the lack of character and personality in the writer. My life, my observations, my insights were not included in those papers on the Okies and race relations and the New Deal. Every opinion was derivative, every observation second-hand. I had no real opinions of my own, and my eyes were not open wide enough for me to make first-hand observations on the world around me. What I wrote was therefore characterless, without true personality, though often full of personal pronouns. My opinions had been changed, my self had not. The style was the boy, the opinionated, immature, uninformed boy; whether my teacher knew it or not—and apparently he did not—his real job was to make a man of me if he wanted me to write like a man.

Putting the difficulty in this way naturally leads me to what perhaps many of you have been impatient about from the beginning. Are not the narrative arts, both as encountered in great literature and as practiced by the students themselves, the best road to the infusion of individuality that no good writing can lack? Would not a real look at the life of that bootblack, and an attempt to deal with him in narrative, have led to a more interesting paper than all of my generalized attacks on the prejudiced southerners?

I think it would, but once again I am almost more conscious of the dangers of the cure than of the advantages. As soon as we make our general rule something like, "Have the students write a personal narrative on what they know about, what they can see and feel at first hand," we have opened the floodgates for those dreadful assignments that we all find ourselves using, even though we know better: "My Summer Vacation," "Catching My First Fish," and "Our Trip to the Seattle World's Fair." Here are personal experiences that call for personal observation and narration. What's wrong with them?

Quite simply, they invite triviality, superficiality, puerility. Our students have been writing essays on such non-subjects all their lives, and until they have developed some sort of critical vision, some way of looking at the world they passed through on their vacations or fishing trips, they are going to feed us the same old bromides that have always won their passing grades. "My Summer Vacation" is an invitation to a grocery list of items, because it implies no audience, no point to be made, no point of view, no character in the speaker. A bright student will make something of such an invitation, by dramatizing the comic family quarrel that developed two days out, or by comparing his view of the American motel system with Nabokov's in *Lolita*, or by remembering the types of people seen in the campgrounds. If he had his own eyes and ears open he might have seen, in a men's room in Grand Canyon last summer, a camper with a very thick French accent trying to convert a Brooklyn Jew into believing the story of the Mormon gold plates.[5] Or he could have heard, at Mesa Verde, a young park ranger, left behind toward the end of the season by all of the experienced rangers, struggling ungrammatically through a set speech on the geology of the area and finally breaking down in embarrassment over his lack of education. Such an episode, really *seen*, could be used narratively to say something to other high school students about what education really is.

But mere narration can be in itself just as dull as the most abstract theorizing about the nature of the universe or the most derivative opinion-mongering about politics. Even relatively skilful narration, used too obviously as a gimmick to catch interest, with no real relation to the subject, can be as dull as the most abstract pomposities. We all know the student papers that begin like *Reader's Digest* articles, with stereotyped narration that makes one doubt the event itself: "On a dark night last January, two teen agers were seen etc., etc." One can open any issue of *Time* and find this so-called narrative interest plastered throughout. From the March 29 issue I find, among many others, the following bits of fantasy: #1: "A Bolivian father sadly surveyed his nation's seven universities, then made up his mind. 'I don't want my son mixed up in politics.' . . . So saying, he sent his son off to West Germany to college." So writing, the author sends me into hysterical laughter: the quote is phony, made up for the occasion to disguise the generality of the news item. #2:

5. Bearing, according to Mormon tradition, the Book of Mormon, divinely revealed to the prophet Joseph Smith in upstate New York in 1827.

"Around 12:30 P.M. every Monday and Friday, an aging Cubana Airlines turbo-prop Britannia whistles to a halt at Mexico City's International Airport. Squads of police stand by. All passengers . . . without diplomatic or Mexican passports are photographed and questioned. . . . They always dodge questions. 'Why are you here? Where are you going?' ask the Mexicans. 'None of your business,' answer the secretive travelers." "Why should I go on reading?" ask I. #3: "At 6:30 one morning early this month, a phone shrilled in the small office off the bedroom of Egypt's President. . . Nasser. [All early morning phones "shrill" for *Time*.] Already awake, he lifted the receiver to hear exciting news: a military coup had just been launched against the anti-Nasser government of Syria. The phone rang again. It was the Minister of Culture. . . . How should Radio Cairo handle the Syrian crisis? 'Support the rebels,' snapped Nasser." Oh lucky reporter, I sigh, to have such an efficient wiretapping service. #4: "In South Korea last week, a farmer named Song Kyu Il traveled all the way from the southern provinces to parade before Seoul's Duk Soo Palace with a placard scrawled in his own blood. . . . Farmer Song was thrown in jail, along with some 200 other demonstrators." That's the last we hear of Song, who is invented as an individual for this opening and then dropped. #5: "Defense Secretary Robert McNamara last spring stood beside President Kennedy on the tenth-deck bridge of the nuclear-powered carrier *Enterprise*. For as the eye could see, other U.S. ships deployed over the Atlantic seascape." Well, maybe. But for as far as the eye can see, the narrative clichés are piled, rank on rank. At 12:00 midnight last Thursday a gaunt, harried English professor could be seen hunched over his typewriter, a pile of *Time* magazines beside him on the floor. "What," he murmured to himself, sadly, "Whatever can we do about this trashy imitation of narration?"

Fortunately there is something we can do, and it is directly within our province. We can subject our students to models of genuine narration, with the sharp observation and penetrating critical judgment that underlies all good story telling, whether reportorial or fictional.

> It is a truth universally acknowledged, that a single man in possession of a good fortune must be in want of a wife.
>
> However little known the feelings or views of such a man may be on his first entering a neighborhood, this truth is so well fixed in the minds of the surrounding families, that he is considered as the rightful property of some-one or other of their daughters.
>
> "My dear Mr. Bennet," said his lady to him one day, "have you heard that Netherfield Park is let at last?"

And already we have a strong personal tone established, a tone of mocking irony which leaves Jane Austen's Mrs. Bennet revealed before us as the grasping, silly gossip she is. Or try this one:

> I am an American, Chicago-born—Chicago, that somber city—and go at

things as I have taught myself, free-style, and will make the record in my own way: first to knock, first admitted; sometimes an innocent knock, sometimes a not so innocent. But a man's character is his fate, says Heraclitus, and in the end there isn't any way to disguise the nature of the knocks by acoustical work on the door or gloving the knuckles.

Everybody knows there is no fineness or accuracy of suppression; if you hold down one thing you hold down the adjoining.

My own parents were not much to me, though I cared for my mother. She was simple-minded, and what I learned from her was not what she taught. . . .

Do you catch the accent of Saul Bellow here, beneath the accent of his Augie March? You do, of course, but the students, many of them, do not. How do you know, they will ask, that Jane Austen is being ironic? How do you know, they ask again, that Augie is being characterized by his author through what he says? In teaching them how we know, in exposing them to the great narrative voices, ancient and modern, and in teaching them to hear these voices accurately, we are, of course, trying to change their lives, to make them new, to raise their perceptions to a new level altogether. Nobody can really catch these accents who has not grown up sufficiently to see through cheap substitutes. Or, to put it another way, a steady exposure to such voices is the very thing that will produce the maturity that alone can make our students ashamed of beclouded, commercial, borrowed spectacles for viewing the world.

It is true that exposure to good fiction will not in itself transform our students into good writers. Even the best-read student still needs endless hours and years of practice, with rigorous criticism. Fiction will not do the job of discipline in reasoned argument and of practice in developing habits of addressing a living audience. But in the great fiction they will learn what it means to look at something with full attention, what it means to see beneath the surface of society's platitudes. If we then give them practice in writing about things close to the home base of their own honest observations, constantly stretching their powers of generalization and argument but never allowing them to drift into pompous inanities or empty controversiality, we may have that rare but wonderful pleasure of witnessing the miracle: a man and a style where before there was only a bag of wind or a bundle of received opinions. Even when, as with most of our students, no miracles occur, we can hope for papers that we can enjoy reading. And as a final bonus, we might hope that when our students encounter someone on a train who says that he teaches English, their automatic response may be something other than looks of pity or, cries of mock alarm.

1963

QUESTIONS

1. Booth is writing for an audience of English teachers. In what ways might the essay differ if he were writing for an audience of students?
2. On page 333 Booth says he has "now fallen" into a "tone of political exhortation." (Tone may be defined as the reflection in language of the attitude a writer takes toward his subject or his audience or both.) What other "tones" are there in the essay? Why does Booth find it necessary to vary the tone?
3. What steps are necessary before an "opinion" can become a "reasoned opinion"? Select some subject on which you have a strong opinion and decide whether it is a reasoned opinion.
4. Booth characterizes the writing in the Reader's Digest and Time (pp. 336–337). What does he feel the two magazines have in common? Analyze an article from either one of these magazines to see how accurate Booth's characterization is.

Lewis Thomas

NOTES ON PUNCTUATION

There are no precise rules about punctuation (Fowler[1] lays out some general advice (as best he can under the complex circumstances of English prose (he points out, for example, that we possess only four stops (the comma, the semicolon, the colon and the period (the question mark and exclamation point are not, strictly speaking, stops; they are indicators of tone (oddly enough, the Greeks employed the semicolon for their question mark (it produces a strange sensation to read a Greek sentence which is a straightforward question: Why weepest thou; (instead of Why weepest thou? (and, of course, there are parentheses (which are surely a kind of punctuation making this whole much more complicated by having to count up the left-handed parentheses in order to be sure of closing with the right number (but it the parentheses were left out, with nothing to work with but the stops, we would have considerably more flexibility in the deploying of layers of meaning then if we tried to separate all the clauses by physical barriers (and in the latter case, while we might have more precision and exactitude for our meaning, we would lose the essential flavor of language, which is its wonderful ambiguity)))))))))))).

The commas are the most useful and usable of all the stops. It is highly important to put them in place as you go along. If you try to come back

---

1. H. W. Fowler, author of Modern English Usage (1926, revised 1965 by Sir Ernest Gowers), a standard reference work.

after doing a paragraph and stick them in the various spots that tempt you you will discover that they tend to swarm like minnows into all sorts of crevices whose existence you hadn't realized and before you know it the whole long sentence becomes immobilized and lashed up squirming in commas. Better to use them sparingly, and with affection, precisely when the need for each one arises, nicely, by itself.

I have grown fond of semicolons in recent years. The semicolon tells you that there is still some question about the preceding full sentence; something needs to be added; it reminds you sometimes of the Greek usage. It is almost always a greater pleasure to come across a semicolon than a period. The period tells you that that is that; if you didn't get all the meaning you wanted or expected, anyway you got all the writer intended to parcel out and now you have to move along. But with a semicolon there you get a pleasant little feeling of expectancy; there is more to come; read on; it will get clearer.

Colons are a lot less attractive, for several reasons: firstly, they give you the feeling of being rather ordered around, or at least having your nose pointed in a direction you might not be inclined to take if left to yourself, and, secondly, you suspect you're in for one of those sentences that will be labeling the points to be made: firstly, secondly and so forth, with the implication that you haven't sense enough to keep track of a sequence of notions without having them numbered. Also, many writers use this system loosely and incompletely, starting out with number one and number two as though counting off on their fingers but then going on and on without the succession of labels you've been led to expect, leaving you floundering about searching for the ninethly or seventeenthly that ought to be there but isn't.

Exclamation points are the most irritating of all. Look! they say, look at what I just said! How amazing is my thought! It is like being forced to watch someone else's small child jumping up and down crazily in the center of the living room shouting to attract attention. If a sentence really has something of importance to say, something quite remarkable, it doesn't need a mark to point it out. And if it is really, after all, a banal sentence needing more zing, the exclamation point simply emphasizes its banality!

Quotation marks should be used honestly and sparingly, when there is a genuine quotation at hand, and it is necessary to be very rigorous about the words enclosed by the marks. If something is to be quoted, the *exact* words must be used. If part of it must be left out because of space limitations, it is good manners to insert three dots to indicate the omission, but it is unethical to do this if it means connecting two thoughts which the original author did not intend to have tied together. Above all, quotation marks should not be used for ideas that you'd like to disown, things in the air so to speak. Nor should they be put in place around

Prose Forms:
An Album of Styles

Roger Ascham: THE WIND

To see the wind with a man his eyes it is unpossible, the nature of it is so fine and subtile; yet this experience of the wind had I once myself, and that was in the great snow that fell four years ago. I rode in the high way betwixt Topcliff-upon-Swale and Borough-bridge, the way being somewhat trodden before, by wayfaring men; the fields on both sides were plain, and lay almost yard-deep with snow; the night afore had been a little frost, so that the snow was hard and crusted above; that morning the sun shone bright and clear, the wind was whistling aloft, and sharp, according to the time of the year; the snow in the high way lay loose and trodden with horses' feet; so as the wind blew, it took the loose snow with it, and made it so slide upon the snow in the field, which was hard and crusted by reason of the frost over night, that thereby I might see very well the whole nature of the wind as it blew that day. And I had a great delight and pleasure to mark it, which maketh me now far better to remember it. Sometime the wind would be not past two yards broad, and so it would carry the snow as far as I could see. Another time the snow would blow over half the field at once. Sometime the snow would tumble softly; by and by it would fly wonderful fast. And this I perceived also, that the wind goeth by streams, and not whole together. For I should see one stream within a score on me; then the space of two score, no snow would stir; but, after so much quantity of ground, another stream of snow, at the same very time, should be carried likewise, but not equally, for the one would stand still, when the other flew apace and so continue sometime swiftlier, sometime slowlier, sometime broader, sometime narrower, as far as I could see. Nor it flew not straight, but sometime it crooked this way, sometime that way, and sometime it ran round about in a compass. And sometime the snow would be lift clean from the ground up to the air, and by and by it would be all clapt to the ground, as though

clichés; if you want to use a cliché you must take full respons
yourself and not try to job it off on anon., or on society.
objectionable misuse of quotation marks, but one which ill
dangers of misuse in ordinary prose, is seen in advertising, e
advertisements for small restaurants, for example "just arou
ner," or "a good place to eat." No single, identifiable, citable p
really said, for the record, "just around the corner," much le
place to eat," least likely of all for restaurants of the type that us
of prose.

The dash is a handy device, informal and essentially playf
you that you're about to take off on a different tack but still in
connected with the present course—only you have to remembe
dash is there, and either put a second dash at the end of the not
the reader know that he's back on course, or else end the sen
here, with a period.

The greatest danger in punctuation is for poetry. Here it is n
to be as economical and parsimonious with commas and period;
the words themselves, and any marks that seem to carry their ow
meanings, like dashes and little rows of periods, even semicol
question marks, should be left out altogether rather than inserted
up the thing with ambiguity. A single exclamation point in a p
matter what else the poem has to say, is enough to destroy the
work.

The things I like best in T. S. Eliot's poetry, especially in th
Quartets, are the semicolons. You cannot hear them, but they are
laying out the connections between the images and the ideas. Som
you get a glimpse of a semicolon coming, a few lines farther on, a
like climbing a steep path through woods and seeing a wooden ben
at a bend in the road ahead, a place where you can expect to sit
moment, catching your breath.

Commas can't do this sort of thing; they can only tell you ho
different parts of a complicated thought are to be fitted together, bu
can't sit, not even take a breath, just because of a comma,

Prose Forms:
An Album of Styles

Roger Ascham: THE WIND

To see the wind with a man his eyes it is unpossible, the nature of it is so fine and subtile; yet this experience of the wind had I once myself, and that was in the great snow that fell four years ago. I rode in the high way betwixt Topcliff-upon-Swale and Borough-bridge, the way being somewhat trodden before, by wayfaring men; the fields on both sides were plain, and lay almost yard-deep with snow; the night afore had been a little frost, so that the snow was hard and crusted above; that morning the sun shone bright and clear, the wind was whistling aloft, and sharp, according to the time of the year; the snow in the high way lay loose and trodden with horses' feet; so as the wind blew, it took the loose snow with it, and made it so slide upon the snow in the field, which was hard and crusted by reason of the frost over night, that thereby I might see very well the whole nature of the wind as it blew that day. And I had a great delight and pleasure to mark it, which maketh me now far better to remember it. Sometime the wind would be not past two yards broad, and so it would carry the snow as far as I could see. Another time the snow would blow over half the field at once. Sometime the snow would tumble softly; by and by it would fly wonderful fast. And this I perceived also, that the wind goeth by streams, and not whole together. For I should see one stream within a score on me; then the space of two score, no snow would stir; but, after so much quantity of ground, another stream of snow, at the same very time, should be carried likewise, but not equally, for the one would stand still, when the other flew apace and so continue sometime swiftlier, sometime slowlier, sometime broader, sometime narrower, as far as I could see. Nor it flew not straight, but sometime it crooked this way, sometime that way, and sometime it ran round about in a compass. And sometime the snow would be lift clean from the ground up to the air, and by and by it would be all clapt to the ground, as though

clichés; if you want to use a cliché you must take full responsibility for it yourself and not try to job it off on anon., or on society. The most objectionable misuse of quotation marks, but one which illustrates the dangers of misuse in ordinary prose, is seen in advertising, especially in advertisements for small restaurants, for example "just around the corner," or "a good place to eat." No single, identifiable, citable person ever really said, for the record, "just around the corner," much less "a good place to eat," least likely of all for restaurants of the type that use this type of prose.

The dash is a handy device, informal and essentially playful, telling you that you're about to take off on a different tack but still in some way connected with the present course—only you have to remember that the dash is there, and either put a second dash at the end of the notion to let the reader know that he's back on course, or else end the sentence, as here, with a period.

The greatest danger in punctuation is for poetry. Here it is necessary to be as economical and parsimonious with commas and periods as with the words themselves, and any marks that seem to carry their own subtle meanings, like dashes and little rows of periods, even semicolons and question marks, should be left out altogether rather than inserted to clog up the thing with ambiguity. A single exclamation point in a poem, no matter what else the poem has to say, is enough to destroy the whole work.

The things I like best in T. S. Eliot's poetry, especially in the *Four Quartets*, are the semicolons. You cannot hear them, but they are there, laying out the connections between the images and the ideas. Sometimes you get a glimpse of a semicolon coming, a few lines farther on, and it is like climbing a steep path through woods and seeing a wooden bench just at a bend in the road ahead, a place where you can expect to sit for a moment, catching your breath.

Commas can't do this sort of thing; they can only tell you how the different parts of a complicated thought are to be fitted together, but you can't sit, not even take a breath, just because of a comma,

1979

there had been no wind at all, straightway it would rise and fly again. And that which was the most marvel of all, at one time two drifts of snow flew, the one out of the west into the east, the other out of the north into the east. And I saw two winds, by reason of the snow, the one cross over the other, as it had been two high ways. And, again, I should hear the wind blow in the air, when nothing was stirred at the ground. And when all was still where I rode, not very far from me the snow should be lifted wonderfully. This experience made me more marvel at the nature of the wind, than it made me cunning in the knowledge of the wind; but yet thereby I learned perfectly that it is no marvel at all though men in wind lose their length in shooting, seeing so many ways the wind is so variable in blowing.

1545

Francis Bacon: Of Revenge

Revenge is a kind of wild justice; which the more man's nature runs to, the more ought law to weed it out. For as for the first wrong, it doth but offend the law; but the revenge of that wrong putteth the law out of office. Certainly, in taking revenge, a man is but even with his enemy; but in passing it over, he is superior; for it is a prince's part to pardon. And Salomon, I am sure, saith, *It is the glory of a man to pass by an offence.* That which is past is gone, and irrevocable; and wise men have enough to do with things present and to come: therefore they do but trifle with themselves, that labour in past matters. There is no man doth a wrong for the wrong's sake; but thereby to purchase himself profit, or pleasure, or honour, or the like. Therefore why should I be angry with a man for loving himself better than me? And if any man should do wrong merely out of ill nature, why, yet it is but like the thorn or briar, which prick and scratch, because they can do no other. The most tolerable sort of revenge is for those wrongs which there is no law to remedy; but then let a man take heed the revenge be such as there is no law to punish; else a man's enemy is still beforehand, and it is two for one. Some, when they take revenge, are desirous the party should know whence it cometh: this is the more generous. For the delight seemeth to be not so much in doing the hurt as in making the party repent: but base and crafty cowards are like the arrow that flieth in the dark. Cosmus, duke of Florence, had a desperate saying against perfidious or neglecting friends, as if those wrongs were unpardonable: *You shall read* (saith he) *that we are commanded to forgive our enemies; but you never read that we are commanded to forgive our friends.* But yet the spirit of Job was in a better tune: *Shall* we (saith he) *take good at God's hands, and not be content to take evil also?* And so of friends in a proportion. This is certain, that a man that studieth revenge keeps his own wounds green, which otherwise would heal and do well. Public revenges are for the most part fortunate; as that for the death of Caesar; for the death of Pertinax;[1] for the death of Henry the third of France;[2] and many more. But in private revenges it is not so. Nay rather, vindictive persons live the life of witches; who as they are mischievous, so end they infortunate.

1625

1. Publius Helvius Pertinax became Emperor of Rome in 193 and was assassinated three months after his accession to the throne by a soldier in his praetorian Guard.
2. King of France 1574–1589; assassinated during the Siege of Paris.

John Donne: MEN ARE SLEEPING PRISONERS

We are all conceived in close prison; in our Mothers wombs, we are close prisoners all; when we are born, we are born but to the liberty of the house;[1] prisoners still, though within larger walls; and then all our life is but a going out to the place of execution, to death. Now was there ever any man seen to sleep in the cart, between Newgate, and Tyburn?[2] Between the prison and the place of execution, does any man sleep? And we sleep all the way; from the womb to the grave we are never thoroughly awake; but pass on with such dreams, and imaginations as these, I may live as well, as another, and why should I die, rather than another? But awake, and tell me, says this text *Quis homo?*[3] Who is that other that thou talkest of? *What man is he that liveth, and shall not see death?*

1. Donne distinguishes between a prisoner confined to a cell and one given somewhat more liberty.
2. London prisoners were taken in carts from Newgate prison to nearby Tyburn for execution.
3. "Who [is] the man?"

Samuel Johnson: THE PYRAMIDS

Of the wall [of China] it is very easy to assign the motives. It secured a wealthy and timorous nation from the incursions of Barbarians, whose unskillfulness in arts made it easier for them to supply their wants by rapine than by industry, and who from time to time poured in upon the habitations of peaceful commerce, as vultures descend upon domestic fowl. Their celerity and fierceness made the wall necessary, and their ignorance made it efficacious.

But for the pyramids no reason has ever been given adequate to the cost and labor of the work. The narrowness of the chambers proves that it could afford no retreat from enemies, and treasures might have been reposited at far less expense with equal security. It seems to have been erected only in compliance with that hunger of imagination which preys incessantly upon life, and must be always appeased by some employment. Those who have already all that they can enjoy, must enlarge their desires. He that has built for use, till use is supplied must begin to build for vanity, and extend his plan to the utmost power of human performance, that he may not be soon reduced to form another wish.

I consider this mighty structure as a monument of the insufficiency of human enjoyments. A king, whose power is unlimited, and whose treasures surmount all real and imaginary wants, is compelled to solace, by the erection of a pyramid, the satiety of dominion and tastelessness of pleasures, and to amuse the tediousness of declining life, by seeing thousands laboring without end, and one stone, for no purpose, laid upon another. Whoever thou art, that, not content with a moderate condition, imaginest happiness in royal magnificence, and dreamest that command or riches can feed the appetite of novelty with perpetual gratifications, survey the pyramids, and confess thy folly!

1759

Laurence Sterne: OF DOOR HINGES AND LIFE IN GENERAL

Every day for at least ten years together did my father resolve to have it mended—'tis not mended yet: no family but ours would have borne with it an hour—and what is most astonishing, there was not a subject in the world upon which my father was so eloquent, as upon that of door-hinges. And yet at the same time, he was certainly one of the greatest bubbles to them, I think, that history can produce: his rhetoric and conduct were at perpetual handycuffs. Never did the parlor-door open—but his philosophy or his principles fell a victim to it; three drops of oyl with a feather, and a smart stroke of a hammer, had saved his honor for ever. Inconsistent soul that man is—languishing under wounds, which he has the power to heal—his whole life a contradiction to his knowledge—his reason, that precious gift of God to him—(instead of pouring in oyl) serving but to sharpen his sensibilities, to multiply his pains and render him more melancholy and uneasy under them—poor unhappy creature, that he should do so! Are not the necessary causes of misery in this life enow, but he must add voluntary ones to his stock of sorrow, struggle against evils which cannot be avoided, and submit to others, which a tenth part of the trouble they create him, would remove from his heart forever?

By all that is good and virtuous! if there are three drops of oyl to be got, and a hammer to be found within ten miles of Shandy-Hall, the parlor-door hinge shall be mended this reign.

1767

Charles Lamb: THE TWO RACES OF MEN

The human species, according to the best theory I can form of it, is composed of two distinct races, the men who borrow, and the men who lend. To these two original diversities may be reduced all those impertinent classifications of Gothic and Celtic tribes, white men, black men, red men. All the dwellers upon earth, "Parthians, and Medes, and Elamites," flock hither, and do naturally fall in with one or other of these primary distinctions. The infinite superiority of the former, which I choose to designate as the great race, is discernible in their figure, port, and a certain instinctive sovereignty. The latter are born degraded. "He shall serve his brethren." There is something in the air of one of this cast, lean and suspicious; contrasting with the open, trusting, generous manners of the other.

Observe who have been the greatest borrowers of all ages—Alcibiades—Falstaff—Sir Richard Steele—our late incomparable Brinsley—what a family likeness in all four!

What a careless, even deportment hath your borrower! what rosy gills! what a beautiful reliance on Providence doth he manifest—taking no more thought than lilies! What contempt for money—accounting it (yours and mine especially) no better than dross. What a liberal confounding of those pedantic distinctions of meum and tuum! or rather, what a noble simplification of language (beyond Tooke), resolving these supposed opposites into one clear, intelligible pronoun adjective! What near approaches doth he make to the primitive *community*—to the extent of one half of the principle at least!

1823

Thomas De Quincey: LITERATURE OF KNOWLEDGE AND LITERATURE OF POWER

In that great social organ which, collectively, we call literature, there may be distinguished two separate offices that may blend and often do so, but capable, severally, of a severe insulation, and naturally fitted for reciprocal repulsion. There is, first, the literature of *knowledge*, and secondly, the literature of *power*. The function of the first is to *teach*; the function of the second is to *move*; the first is a rudder, the second an oar or a sail. The first speaks to the mere discursive understanding; the second speaks ultimately, it may happen, to the higher understanding or reason, but always through affections of pleasure and sympathy. Remotely, it may travel towards an object seated in what Lord Bacon calls *dry* light; but, proximately, it does and must operate—else it ceases to be a literature of *power*—and on through that *humid* light which clothes itself in the mists and glittering *iris* of human passions, desires, and genial emotions. Men have so little reflected on the higher functions of literature as to find it a paradox if one should describe it as a mean or subordinate purpose of books to give information. But this is a paradox only in the sense which makes it honorable to be paradoxical. Whenever we talk in ordinary language of seeking information or gaining knowledge, we understand the words as connected with something of absolute novelty. But it is the grandeur of all truth which *can* occupy a very high place in human interests that it is never absolutely novel to the meanest of minds: it exists eternally by way of germ or latent principle in the lowest as in the highest, needing to be developed, but never to be planted. To be capable of transplantation is the immediate criterion of a truth that ranges on a lower scale. Besides which, there is a rarer thing than truth—namely, *power*, or deep sympathy with truth. What is the effect, for instance, upon society, of children? By the pity, by the tenderness, and by the peculiar modes of admiration, which connect themselves with the helplessness, with the innocence, and with the simplicity of children, not only are the primal affections strengthened and continually renewed, but the qualities which are dearest in the sight of heaven—the frailty, for instance, which appeals to forbearance, the·innocence which symbolizes the heavenly, and the simplicity which is most alien from the worldly —are kept up in perpetual remembrance, and their ideals are continually

refreshed. A purpose of the same nature is answered by the high literature, viz., the literature of power. What do you learn from *Paradise Lost?*
Nothing at all. What do you learn from a cookery book? Something new,
something that you did not know before, in every paragraph. But would
you therefore put the wretched cookery book on a higher level of estimation than the divine poem? What you owe to Milton is not any
knowledge, of which a million separate items are still but a million of
advancing steps on the same earthly level; what you owe is *power*—that
is, exercise and expansion to your own latent capacity of sympathy with
the infinite, where every pulse and each separate influx is a step upwards,
a step ascending as upon a Jacob's ladder from earth to mysterious
altitudes above the earth. *All* the steps of knowledge, from first to last,
carry you further on the same plane, but could never raise you one foot
above your ancient level of earth: whereas the very *first* step in power is a
flight—is an ascending movement into another element where earth is
forgotten.

1848

John Henry Newman: KNOWLEDGE AND VIRTUE

Knowledge is one thing, virtue is another; good sense is not conscience, refinement is not humility, nor is largeness and justness of view
faith. Philosophy, however enlightened, however profound, gives no
command over the passions, no influential motives, no vivifying principles. Liberal Education makes not the Christian, not the Catholic, but
the gentleman. It is well to be a gentleman, it is well to have a cultivated
intellect, a delicate taste, a candid, equitable, dispassionate mind, a noble
and courteous bearing in the conduct of life—these are the connatural
qualities of a large knowledge; they are the objects of a University; I am
advocating, I shall illustrate and insist upon them; but still, I repeat, they
are no guarantee for sanctity or even for conscientiousness, they may
attach to the man of the world, to the profligate, to the heartless, pleasant,
alas, and attractive as he shows when decked out in them. Taken by
themselves, they do but seem to be what they are not; they look like
virtue at a distance, but they are detected by close observers, and on the
long run; and hence it is that they are popularly accused of pretense and
hypocrisy, not, I repeat, from their own fault, but because their professors
and their admirers persist in taking them for what they are not, and are
officious in arrogating for them a praise to which they have no claim.
Quarry the granite rock with razors, or moor the vessel with a thread of
silk; then may you hope with such keen and delicate instruments as

human knowledge and human reason to contend against those giants, the passion and the pride of man.

1852

Matthew Arnold: CULTURE

But there is of culture another view, in which not solely the scientific passion, the sheer desire to see things as they are, natural and proper in an intelligent being, appears as the ground of it. There is a view in which all the love of our neighbor, the impulses towards action, help, and benefi-cence, the desire for removing human error, clearing human confusion, and diminishing human misery, the noble aspiration to leave the world better and happier than we found it—motives eminently such as are called social—come in as part of the grounds of culture, and the main and pre-eminent part. Culture is then properly described not as having its origin in curiosity, but as having its origin in the love of perfection; it is a *study of perfection*. It moves by the force, not merely or primarily of the scientific passion for pure knowledge, but also of the moral and social passion for doing good. As, in the first view of it, we took for its worthy motto Montesquieu's words: "To render an intelligent being yet more intelligent!" so, in the second view of it, there is no better motto which it can have than these words of Bishop Wilson: "To make reason and the will of God prevail!"

Only, whereas the passion for doing good is apt to be overhasty in determining what reason and the will of God say, because its turn is for acting rather than thinking, and it wants to be beginning to act; and whereas it is apt to take its own conceptions, which proceed from its own state of development and share in all the imperfections and immaturities of this, for a basis of action; what distinguishes culture is, that it is possessed by the scientific passion as well as by the passion of doing good; that it demands worthy notions of reason and the will of God, and does not readily suffer its own crude conceptions to substitute themselves for them. And knowing that no action or institution can be salutary and stable which is not based on reason and the will of God, it is not so bent on acting and instituting, even with the great aim of diminishing human error and misery ever before its thoughts, but that it can remember that acting and instituting are of little use, unless we know how and what we ought to act and to institute.

1869

Walter Pater: THE MONA LISA

The presence that rose thus so strangely beside the waters, is expressive of what in the ways of a thousand years men had come to desire. Hers is the head upon which all "the ends of the world are come," and the eyelids are a little weary. It is a beauty wrought out from within upon the flesh, the deposit, little cell by cell, of strange thoughts and fantastic reveries and exquisite passions. Set it for a moment beside one of those white Greek goddesses or beautiful women of antiquity, and how would they be troubled by this beauty, into which the soul with all its maladies has passed! All the thoughts and experience of the world have etched and molded there, in that which they have of power to refine and make expressive the outward form, the animalism of Greece, the lust of Rome, the mysticism of the middle ages with its spiritual ambition and imaginative loves, the return of the Pagan world, the sins of the Borgias. She is older than the rocks among which she sits; like the vampire, she has been dead many times, and learned the secrets of the grave; and has been a diver in deep seas, and keeps their fallen day about her; and trafficked for strange webs with Eastern merchants: and, as Leda, was the mother of Helen of Troy, and, as Saint Anne, the mother of Mary; and all this has been to her but as the sound of lyres and flutes, and lives only in the delicacy with which it has molded the changing lineaments, and tinged the eyelids and the hands. The fancy of a perpetual life, sweeping together ten-thousand experiences, is an old one; and modern philosophy has conceived the idea of humanity as wrought upon by, and summing up in itself, all modes of thought and life. Certainly Lady Lisa might stand as the embodiment of the old fancy, the symbol of the modern idea.
1868   1873

James Thurber: A DOG'S EYE VIEW OF MAN

If Man has benefited immeasurably by his association with the dog, what, you may ask, has the dog got out of it? His scroll has, of course, been heavily charged with punishments: he has known the muzzle, the leash, and the tether; he has suffered the indignities of the show bench, the tin can on the tail, the ribbon in the hair; his love life with the other sex of his species has been regulated by the frigid hand of authority, his digestion ruined by the macaroons and marshmallows of doting women. The list of his woes could be continued indefinitely. But he has also had his fun, for he has been privileged to live with and study at close range the only creature with reason, the most unreasonable of creatures.

The dog has got more fun out of Man than Man has got out of the dog, for the clearly demonstrable reason that Man is the more laughable of the two animals. The dog has long been bemused by the singular activities and the curious practices of men, cocking his head inquiringly to one side, intently watching and listening to the strangest goings-on in the world. He has seen men sing together and fight one another in the same evening. He has watched them go to bed when it is time to get up, and get up when it is time to go to bed. He has observed them destroying the soil in vast areas, and nurturing it in small patches. He has stood by while men built strong and solid houses for rest and quiet, and then filled them with lights and bells and machinery. His sensitive nose, which can detect what's cooking in the next township, has caught at one and the same time the bewildering smells of the hospital and the munitions factory. He has seen men raise up great cities to heaven and then blow them to hell.

1955

E. B. White: PROGRESS AND CHANGE

In resenting progress and change, a man lays himself open to censure. I suppose the explanation of anyone's defending anything as rudimentary and cramped as a Pullman berth is that such things are associated with an earlier period in one's life and that this period in retrospect seems a happy one. People who favor progress and improvements are apt to be people who have had a tough enough time without any extra inconvenience. Reactionaries who pout at innovations are apt to be well-heeled sentimentalists who had the breaks. Yet for all that, there is always a subtle danger in life's refinements, a dim degeneracy in progress. I have just been refining the room in which I sit, yet I sometimes doubt that a writer should refine or improve his workroom by so much as a dictionary: one thing leads to another and the first thing you know he has a stuffed chair and is fast asleep in it. Half a man's life is devoted to what he calls improvements, yet the original had some quality which is lost in the process. There was a fine natural spring of water on this place when I bought it. Our drinking water had to be lugged in a pail, from a wet glade of alder and tamarack. I visited the spring often in those first years, and had friends there—a frog, a woodcock, and an eel which had churned its way all the way up through the pasture creek to enjoy the luxury of pure water. In the normal course of development, the spring was rocked up, fitted with a concrete curb, a copper pipe, and an electric pump. I have visited it only once or twice since. This year my only gesture was the purely perfunctory one of sending a sample to the state bureau of health for analysis. I felt cheap, as though I were smelling an old friend's breath.

                                                                          1938

Toni Morrison: THREE MERRY GARGOYLES

Three merry gargoyles. Three merry harridans. Amused by a long-ago time of ignorance. They did not belong to those generations of prostitutes created in novels, with great and generous hearts, dedicated, because of the horror of circumstance, to ameliorating the luckless, barren life of men, taking money incidentally and humbly for their "understanding." Nor were they from that sensitive breed of young girl, gone wrong at the hands of fate, forced to cultivate an outward brittleness in order to protect her springtime from further shock, but knowing full well she was cut out for better things, and could make the right man happy. Neither were they the sloppy, inadequate whores who, unable to make a living at it alone, turn to drug consumption and traffic or pimps to help complete their scheme of self-destruction, avoiding suicide only to punish the memory of some absent father or to sustain the misery of some silent mother. Except for Marie's fabled love for Dewey Prince, these women hated men, all men, without shame, apology, or discrimination. They abused their visitors with a scorn grown mechanical from use. Black men, white men, Puerto Ricans, Mexicans, Jews, Poles, whatever—all were inadequate and weak, all came under their jaundiced eyes and were the recipients of their disinterested wrath. They took delight in cheating them. On one occasion the town well knew, they lured a Jew up the stairs, pounced on him, all three, held him up by the heels, shook everything out of his pants pockets, and threw him out of the window.

Neither did they have respect for women, who, although not their colleagues, so to speak, nevertheless deceived their husbands—regularly or irregularly, it made no difference. "Sugar-coated whores," they called them, and did not yearn to be in their shoes. Their only respect was for what they would have described as "good Christian colored women." The woman whose reputation was spotless, and who tended to her family, who didn't drink or smoke or run around. These women had their undying, if covert, affection. They would sleep with their husbands, and take their money, but always with a vengeance.

Nor were they protective and solicitous of youthful innocence. They looked back on their own youth as a period of ignorance, and regretted that they had not made more of it. They were not young girls in whores' clothing, or whores regretting their loss of innocence. They were whores in whores' clothing, whores who had never been young and had no word for innocence. With Pecola they were as free as they were with each other. Marie concocted stories for her because she was a child, but the stories were breezy and rough. If Pecola had announced her intention to live the life they did, they would not have tried to dissuade her or voiced any alarm.

1970

Joyce Cary: ART AND EDUCATION

A very large number of people cease when quite young to add anything to a limited stock of judgments. After a certain age, say 25, they consider that their education is finished.

It is perhaps natural that having passed through that painful and boring process, called expressly education, they should suppose it over, and that they are equipped for life to label every event as it occurs and drop it into its given pigeonhole. But one who has a label ready for everything does not bother to observe any more, even such ordinary happenings as he has observed for himself, with attention, before he went to school. He merely acts and reacts.

For people who have stopped noticing, the only possible new or renewed experience, and, therefore, new knowledge, is from a work of art. Because that is the only kind of experience which they are prepared to receive on its own terms, they will come out from their shells and expose themselves to music, to a play, to a book, because it is the accepted method of enjoying such things. True, even to plays and books they may bring artistic prejudices which prevent them from seeing *that* play or comprehending *that* book. Their artistic sensibilities may be as crusted over as their minds.

But it is part of an artist's job to break crusts, or let us say rather that artists who work for the public and not merely for themselves are interested in breaking crusts because they want to communicate their intuitions.

1949

John Steinbeck: THE DANGER OF SMALL THINGS

I guess it is true that big and strong things are much less dangerous than small soft weak things. Nature (whatever that is) makes the small and weak reproduce faster. And that is not true of course. The ones that did not reproduce faster than they died, disappeared. But how about little faults, little pains, little worries. The cosmic ulcer comes not from great concerns, but from little irritations. And great things can kill a man but if they do not he is stronger and better for them. A man is destroyed by the duck nibblings of nagging, small bills, telephones (wrong number), athlete's foot, ragweed, the common cold, boredom. All of these are the negatives, the tiny frustrations, and no one is stronger for them.

1969

John Updike: BEER CAN

This seems to be an era of gratuitous inventions and negative improvements. Consider the beer can. It was beautiful—as beautiful as the clothespin, as inevitable as the wine bottle, as dignified and reassuring as the fire hydrant. A tranquil cylinder of delightfully resonant metal, it could be opened in an instant, requiring only the application of a handy gadget freely dispensed by every grocer. Who can forget the small, symmetrical thrill of those two triangular punctures, the dainty *pffff*, the little crest of suds that foamed eagerly in the exultation of release? Now we are given, instead, a top beetling with an ugly, shmoo-shaped "tab," which, after fiercely resisting the tugging, bleeding fingers of the thirsty man, threatens his lips with a dangerous and hideous hole. However, we have discovered a way to thwart Progress, usually so unthwartable. *Turn the beer can upside down and open the bottom.* The bottom is still the way the top used to be. True, this operation gives the beer an unsettling jolt, and the sight of a consistently inverted beer can might make people edgy, not to say queasy. But the latter difficulty could be eliminated if manufacturers would design cans that looked the same whichever end was up, like playing cards. What we need is Progress with an escape hatch.

1964

Tom Wolfe: THE LEGEND OF JUNIOR JOHNSON

The legend of Junior Johnson! In this legend, here is a country boy, Junior Johnson, who learns to drive by running whiskey for his father, Johnson, Senior, one of the biggest copper-still operators of all time, up in Ingle Hollow, near North Wilkesboro, in northwestern North Carolina, and grows up to be a famous stock car racing driver, rich, grossing $100,000 in 1963, for example, respected, solid, idolized in his hometown and throughout the rural South. There is all this about how good old boys would wake up in the middle of the night in the apple shacks and hear a supercharged Oldsmobile engine roaring over Brushy Mountain and say, "Listen at him—there he goes!" although that part is doubtful, since some nights there were so many good old boys taking off down the road in supercharged automobiles out of Wilkes County, and running loads to Charlotte, Salisbury, Greensboro, Winston-Salem, High Point, or wherever, it would be pretty hard to pick out one. It was Junior Johnson, specifically, however, who was famous for the "bootleg turn" or "about-face," in which, if the Alcohol Tax agents had a roadblock up for you or were too close behind, you threw the car up into second gear, cocked the wheel, stepped on the accelerator and made the car's rear end skid around in a complete 180-degree arc, a complete about-face, and tore on back up the road exactly the way you came from. God! The Alcohol Tax agents used to burn over Junior Johnson. Practically every good old boy in town in Wilkesboro, the county seat, got to know the agents by sight in a very short time. They would rag them practically to their faces on the subject of Junior Johnson, so that it got to be an obsession. Finally, one night they had Junior trapped on the road up toward the bridge around Millersville, there's no way out of there, they had the barricades up and they could hear this souped-up car roaring around the bend, and here it comes—but suddenly they can hear a siren and see a red light flashing in the grille, so they think it's another agent, and boy, they run out like ants and pull those barrels and boards and sawhorses out of the way, and then —Ggghhzzzzzzzhhhhhhgggggzzzzzzzeeeeeong!—gawdam! there he goes again, it was him, Junior Johnson! with a gawdam agent's sireen and a red light in his grille!

1965

Robert Pirsig: CONCRETE, BRICK, AND NEON

The city closes in on him now, and in his strange perspective it becomes the antithesis of what he believes. The citadel not of Quality, the citadel of form and substance. Substance in the form of steel sheets and girders, substance in the form of concrete piers and roads, in the form of brick, of asphalt, of auto parts, old radios, and rails, dead carcasses of animals that once grazed the prairies. Form and substance without Quality. That is the soul of this place. Blind, huge, sinister and inhuman: seen by the light of fire flaring upward in the night from the blast furnaces in the south, through heavy coal smoke deeper and denser into the neon of BEER and PIZZA and LAUNDROMAT signs and unknown and meaningless signs along meaningless straight streets going off into other straight streets forever.

If it was all bricks and concrete, pure forms of substance, clearly and openly, he might survive. It is the little, pathetic attempts at Quality that kill. The plaster false fireplace in the apartment, shaped and waiting to contain a flame that can never exist. Or the hedge in front of the apartment building with a few square feet of grass behind it. A few square feet of grass, after Montana. If they just left out the hedge and grass it would be all right. Now it serves only to draw attention to what has been lost.

Along the streets that lead away from the apartment he can never see anything through the concrete and brick and neon but he knows that buried within it are grotesque, twisted souls forever trying the manners that will convince themselves they possess Quality, learning strange poses of style and glamour vended by dream magazines and other mass media, and paid for by the vendors of substance. He thinks of them at night alone with their advertised glamorous shoes and stockings and underclothes off, staring through the sooty windows at the grotesque shells revealed beyond them, when the poses weaken and the truth creeps in, the only truth that exists here, crying to heaven, God, there is nothing here but dead neon and cement and brick.

1975

John McPhee: THE GRIZZLY
* * *

We passed first through stands of fireweed, and then over ground that was wine-red with the leaves of bearberries. There were curlewberries, too, which put a deep-purple stain on the hand. We kicked at some wolf scat, old as winter. It was woolly and white and filled with the hair of a snowshoe hare. Nearby was a rich inventory of caribou pellets and, in increasing quantity as we moved downhill, blueberries—an outspreading acreage of blueberries. Fedeler stopped walking. He touched my arm. He had in an instant become even more alert than he usually was, and obviously apprehensive. His gaze followed straight on down our intended course. What he saw there I saw now. It appeared to me to be a hill of fur. "Big boar grizzly," Fedeler said in a near-whisper. The bear was about a hundred steps away, in the blueberries, grazing. The head was down, the hump high. The immensity of muscle seemed to vibrate slowly—to expand and contract, with the grazing. Not berries alone but whole bushes were going into the bear. He was big for a barren-ground grizzly. The brown bears of Arctic Alaska (or grizzlies; they are no longer thought to be different) do not grow to the size they will reach on more ample diets elsewhere. The barren-ground grizzly will rarely grow larger than six hundred pounds.

"What if he got too close?" I said.

Fedeler said, "We'd be in real trouble."

"You can't outrun them," Hession said.

A grizzly, no slower than a racing horse, is about half again as fast as the fastest human being. Watching the great mound of weight in the blueberries, with a fifty-five-inch waist and a neck more than thirty inches around, I had difficulty imagining that he could move with such speed, but I believed it, and was without impulse to test the proposition. Fortunately, a light southerly wind was coming up the Salmon valley. On its way to us, it passed the bear. The wind was relieving, coming into our faces, for had it been moving the other way the bear would not have been placidly grazing. There is an old adage that when a pine needle drops in the forest the eagle will see it fall; the deer will hear it when it hits the ground; the bear will smell it. If the boar grizzly were to catch our scent, he might stand on his hind legs, the better to try to see. Although he could hear well and had an extraordinary sense of smell, his eyesight was not much better than what was required to see a blueberry inches away. For this reason, a grizzly stands and squints, attempting to bring the middle distance into focus, and the gesture is often misunderstood as a sign of anger and forthcoming attack. If the bear were getting ready to attack, he would be on four feet, head low, ears cocked, the hair above his hump muscle standing on end. As if that message were not clear enough,

357

he would also chop his jaws. His teeth would make a sound that would carry like the ringing of an axe.

One could predict, but not with certainty, what a grizzly would do. Odds were very great that one touch of man scent would cause him to stop his activity, pause in a moment of absorbed and alert curiosity, and then move, at a not undignified pace, in a direction other than the one from which the scent was coming. That is what would happen almost every time, but there was, to be sure, no guarantee. The forest Eskimos fear and revere the grizzly. They know that certain individual bears not only will fail to avoid a person who comes into their country but will approach and even stalk the trespasser. It is potentially inaccurate to extrapolate the behavior of any one bear from the behavior of most, since they are both intelligent and independent and will do what they choose to do according to mood, experience, whim. A grizzly that has ever been wounded by a bullet will not forget it, and will probably know that it was a human being who sent the bullet. At sight of a human, such a bear will be likely to charge. Grizzlies hide food sometimes—a caribou calf, say, under a pile of scraped-up moss—and a person the bear might otherwise ignore might suddenly not be ignored if the person were inadvertently to step into the line between the food cache and the bear. A sow grizzly with cubs, of course, will charge anything that suggests danger to the cubs, even if the cubs are nearly as big as she is. They stay with their mother two and a half years.

None of us had a gun. (None of the six of us had brought a gun on the trip.) Among nonhunters who go into the terrain of the grizzly, there are several schools of thought about guns. The preferred one is: Never go without a sufficient weapon—a high-powered rifle or a shotgun and plenty of slug-loaded shells. The option is not without its own inherent peril. A professional hunter, some years ago, spotted a grizzly from the air and—with a client, who happened to be an Anchorage barber —landed on a lake about a mile from the bear. The stalking that followed was evidently conducted not only by the hunters but by the animal as well. The professional hunter was found dead from a broken neck, and had apparently died instantly, unaware of danger, for the cause of death was a single bite, delivered from behind. The barber, noted as clumsy with a rifle, had emptied his magazine, missing the bear with every shot but one, which struck the grizzly in the foot. The damage the bear did to the barber was enough to kill him several times. After the corpses were found, the bear was tracked and killed. To shoot and merely wound is worse than not to shoot at all. A bear that might have turned and gone away will possibly attack if wounded.

* * *

1977

D. Keith Mano: HOW TO KEEP FROM GETTING MUGGED

* * *

Learn to walk gas-fast. Book it, baby: Lay a big batch behind. Not in panic, mind you: never run. A power-purposeful, elbow-out, crazy kind of stride. The way people moved in old silent films—you know, right before they fell into an open manhole. Wave one hand now and then, as if you'd just seen three armed friends and were about to hail a cab. Your attitude should be: "Busy signal, dit-dit-dit. Can't fit you in today, fellas. Catch me tomorrow." In a real halfway-house neighborhood, walk dead street center: follow that white line; avoid ambush cover. Who's gonna mug you when he might get hit by a truck while doing it? Oh, you should see me squeeze out sneaker juice: I am Rapid City: I have no staying power, g'bye. A thug will get depressed by energy. He'd rather come down on someone wearing orthopedic pants. Also, if you can manage it, be tall.

Sing aloud. Mutter a lot. Preach Jesus. Interrogate yourself. Say things like: "Oh, the onion bagel won't come off. Oh, it hurts. Mmmmmm-huh. Mmmmm. Please, Ma, don't send me back to the nutria farm again. No. Oh, no. That three-foot roach is still swimming in my water bed. Ah. Oh. Ech." Muggers are superstitious. They don't like to attack loony people: Might be a cousin on the paternal side. Make sure your accent is very New York (or L. A. or Chicago or wherever). Tourists are considered table-grade meat: heck, who'd miss his super-saver flight to attend a three-month trial? Most of all, eschew eye contact. If your vision says, "Uh-oh, this creep is after my wallet," this creep may feel a *responsibility* to yank you off. Keep both pupils straight ahead, in close-order drill. Do not flash a bank-and-turn indicator. Sure, you may walk past the place you're headed for, but, *shees*, no system is perfect.

Dress way down. Mom-and-pop candy-store owners take their cash to deposit in an old brown Bohack[1] bag. Me, I *wear* the bag. I own two basic outfits: One has the *haute couture*[2] of some fourth-hand algebra-textbook cover; my second best was cut using three dish drainers as a pattern. If stagflation[3] were human, it'd look like me. No one messes with D.K.M.,[4] they figure I'm messed up enough now. But when you gotta go in finery, turn your tux jacket inside out and put a basketball kneepad around one trouser leg. Peg your collar. Stitch a white shoelace through your patent-leather pump. Recall what Jesus said about excessive glad-ragging (*Matthew*, chapter six): "Consider the lilies of the field . . . even Solomon in all

---

1. Supermarket chain in New York.
2. French: high fashion.
3. An economic condition combining rela-

tively high unemployment with relatively high inflation.
4. The author's initials.

his glory was not arrayed as one of these—so, *nu*, what happens? They get picked, *Dummkopf.*"[5]

* * *

1982

5. German: stupid (literally, dumbhead).

Anonymous

GUIDELINES FOR EQUAL TREATMENT OF THE SEXES IN MCGRAW-HILL BOOK COMPANY PUBLICATIONS

The word *sexism* was coined, by analogy to *racism,* to denote discrimination based on gender. In its original sense, *sexism* referred to prejudice against the female sex. In a broader sense, the term now indicates any arbitrary stereotyping of males and females on the basis of their gender.

We are endeavoring through these guidelines to eliminate sexist assumptions from McGraw-Hill Book Company publications and to encourage a greater freedom for all individuals to pursue their interests and realize their potentials. Specifically, these guidelines are designed to make McGraw-Hill staff members and McGraw-Hill authors aware of the ways in which males and females have been stereotyped in publications; to show the role language has played in reinforcing inequality; and to indicate positive approaches toward providing fair, accurate, and balanced treatment of both sexes in our publications.

One approach is to recruit more women as authors and contributors in all fields. The writings and viewpoints of women should be represented in quotations and references whenever possible. Anthologies should include a larger proportion of selections by and about women in fields where suitable materials are available but women are currently underrepresented.

Women as well as men have been leaders and heroes, explorers and pioneers, and have made notable contributions to science, medicine, law, business, politics, civics, economics, literature, the arts, sports, and other areas of endeavor. Books dealing with subjects like these, as well as general histories, should acknowledge the achievements of women. The fact that women's rights, opportunities, and accomplishments have been limited by the social customs and conditions of their time should be openly discussed whenever relevant to the topic at hand.

We realize that the language of literature cannot be prescribed. The recommendations in these guidelines, thus, are intended primarily for use in teaching materials, reference works, and nonfiction works in general.

Nonsexist Treatment of Women and Men

Men and women should be treated primarily as people, and not primarily as members of opposite sexes. Their shared humanity and common attributes should be stressed—not their gender difference. Neither sex should be stereotyped or arbitrarily assigned to a leading or secondary role.

1.

a. Though many women will continue to choose traditional occupations such as homemaker or secretary, women should not be type-cast in these roles but shown in a wide variety of professions and trades: as doctors and dentists, not always as nurses; as principals and professors, not always as teachers; as lawyers and judges, not always as social workers; as bank presidents, not always as tellers; as members of Congress, not always as members of the League of Women Voters.

b. Similarly, men should not be shown as constantly subject to the "masculine mystique" in their interests, attitudes, or careers. They should not be made to feel that their self-worth depends entirely upon their income level or the status level of their jobs. They should not be conditioned to believe that a man ought to earn more than a woman or that he ought to be the sole support of a family.

c. An attempt should be made to break job stereotypes for both women and men. No job should be considered sex-typed, and it should never be implied that certain jobs are incompatible with a woman's "femininity" or a man's "masculinity." Thus, women as well as men should be shown as accountants, engineers, pilots, plumbers, bridge-builders, computer operators, TV repairers, and astronauts, while men as well as women should be shown as nurses, grade-school teachers, secretaries, typists, librarians, file clerks, switchboard operators, and baby-sitters.

Women within a profession should be shown at all professional levels, including the top levels. Women should be portrayed in positions of authority over men and over other women, and there should be no implication that a man loses face or that a woman faces difficulty if the employer or supervisor is a woman. All work should be treated as honorable and worthy of respect; no job or job choices should be downgraded. Instead, women and men should be offered more options than were available to them when work was stereotyped by sex.

d. Books designed for children at the pre-school, elementary, and secondary levels should show married women who work outside the home and should treat them favorably. Teaching materials should not assume or imply that most women are wives who are also full-time mothers, but should instead emphasize the fact that women have choices about their marital status, just as men do: that some women choose to stay permanently single and some are in no hurry to marry; that some women marry but do not have children, while others marry, have children, and continue to work outside the home. Thus, a text might say that some married people have children and some do not, and that sometimes *one or both parents* work outside the home. Instructional materials should never imply that all women have a "mother instinct" or that the emotional life of a family suffers because a woman works. Instead they might state that when both parents work outside the home there is usually either greater sharing of the child-rearing activities or reliance on daycare centers, nursery schools, or other help.

According to Labor Department statistics for 1972, over 42 per cent of all mothers with children under 18 worked outside the home, and about a third of these working mothers had children under 6. Publications ought to reflect this reality.

Both men and women should be shown engaged in home maintenance activities, ranging from cooking and housecleaning to washing the car and making household repairs. Sometimes the man should be shown preparing the meals, doing the laundry, or diapering the baby, while the woman builds bookcases or takes out the trash.

e. Girls should be shown as having, and exercising, the same options as boys in their play and career choices. In school materials, girls should be encouraged to show an interest in mathematics, mechanical skills, and active sports, for example, while boys should never be made to feel ashamed of an interest in poetry, art, or music, or an aptitude for cooking, sewing, or child care. Course materials should be addressed to students of both sexes. For example, home economics courses should apply to boys as well as girls, and shop to girls as well as boys.

Both males and females should be shown in textbook illustrations depicting career choices.

When as a practical matter it is known that a book will be used primarily by women for the life of the edition (say, the next five years), it is pointless to pretend that the readership is divided equally between males and females. In such cases it may be more beneficial to address the book fully to women and exploit every opportunity (1) to point out to them a broader set of options than they might otherwise have considered, and (2) to encourage them to aspire to a more active, assertive, and policymaking role than they might otherwise have thought of.

f. Women and girls should be portrayed as active participants in the same proportion as men and boys in stories, examples, problems, illustrations, discussion questions, test items, and exercises, regardless of subject matter. Women should not be stereotyped in examples by being spoken of only in connection with cooking, sewing, shopping, and similar activities.

2.

a. Members of both sexes should be represented as whole human beings with *human* strengths and weaknesses, not masculine or feminine ones. Women and girls should be shown as having the same abilities, interests, and ambitions as men and boys. Characteristics that have been traditionally praised in males—such as boldness, initiative, and assertiveness—should also be praised in females. Characteristics that have been praised in females—such as gentleness, compassion, and sensitivity—should also be praised in males.

b. Like men and boys, women and girls should be portrayed as independent, active, strong, courageous, competent, decisive, persistent, serious-minded, and successful. They should appear as logical thinkers, problem-solvers, and decision makers. They should be shown as interested in their work, pursuing a variety of career goals, and both deserving of and receiving public recognition for their accomplishments.

c. Sometimes men should be shown as quiet and passive, or fearful and indecisive, or illogical and immature. Similarly, women should sometimes be shown as tough, aggressive, and insensitive. Stereotypes of the logical, objective male and the emotional, subjective female are to be avoided. In descriptions, the smarter, braver, or more successful person should be a woman or girl as often as a man or boy. In illustrations, the taller, heavier, stronger, or more active person should not always be male, especially when children are portrayed.

3.

Women and men should be treated with the same respect, dignity, and seriousness. Neither should be trivialized or stereotyped, either in text or in illustrations. Women should not be described by physical attributes when men are being described by mental attributes or professional position. Instead, both sexes should be dealt with in the same terms. References to a man's or a woman's appearance, charm, or intuition should be avoided when irrelevant.

no	yes
Henry Harris is a shrewd lawyer and his wife Ann is a striking brunette.	The Harrises are an attractive couple. Henry is a handsome blond and Ann is a striking brunette.

or

The Harrises are highly respected in their fields. Ann is an accomplished musician and Henry is a shrewd lawyer.

The Harrises are an interesting couple. Henry is a shrewd lawyer and Ann is very active in community (or church or civic) affairs.

a. In descriptions of women, a patronizing or girl-watching tone should be avoided, as should sexual innuendoes, jokes, and puns. Examples of practices to be avoided: focusing on physical appearance (a buxom blonde); using special female-gender word forms (poetess, aviatrix, usherette); treating women as sex objects or portraying the typical woman as weak, helpless, or hysterical; making women figures of fun or objects of scorn and treating their issues as humorous or unimportant.

Examples of stereotypes to be avoided: scatterbrained female, fragile flower, goddess on a pedestal, catty gossip, henpecking shrew, apron-wearing mother, frustrated spinster, ladylike little girl. Jokes at women's expense—such as the woman driver or nagging mother-in-law cliches—are to be avoided.

no	yes
the fair sex; the weaker sex	women

the distaff side	the female side or line
the girls or the ladies (when adult females are meant)	the women
girl, as in: I'll have my girl check that.	I'll have my secretary (or my assistant) check that. (Or use the person's name.)
lady used as a modifier, as in lady lawyer	lawyer (A woman may be identified simply through the choice of pronouns, as in: The lawyer made her summation to the jury. Try to avoid gender modifiers altogether. When you must modify, use woman or female, as in: a course on women writers, or the airline's first female pilot.)
the little woman; the better half; the ball and chain	wife
female-gender word forms, such as authoress, poetess, Jewess	author, poet, Jew
female-gender or diminutive word forms, such as suffragette, usherette, aviatrix	suffragist, usher, aviator (or pilot)
libber (a put-down)	feminist; liberationist
sweet young thing	young woman; girl
co-ed (as a noun)	student

(Note: Logically, co-ed should refer to any student at a co-educational college or university. Since it does not, it is a sexist term.)

housewife	homemaker for a person who works at home, or rephrase with a more precise or more inclusive term
The sound of the drilling disturbed the housewives in the neighborhood.	The sound of the drilling disturbed everyone within earshot (or everyone in the neighborhood).
Housewives are feeling the pinch of higher prices	Consumers (customers or shoppers) are feeling the pinch of higher prices.

| career girl or career woman | name the woman's profession: *attorney Ellen Smith; Maria Sanchez, a journalist* or editor or business executive or doctor or lawyer or agent |
| cleaning woman, cleaning lady, or maid | *housekeeper; house* or *office cleaner* |

b. In descriptions of men, especially men in the home, references to general ineptness should be avoided. Men should not be characterized as dependent on women for meals, or clumsy in household maintenance, or as foolish in self-care.

To be avoided: characterizations that stress men's dependence on women for advice on what to wear and what to eat, inability of men to care for themselves in times of illness, and men as objects of fun (the henpecked husband).

c. Women should be treated as part of the rule, not as the exception.

Generic terms, such as doctor and nurse, should be assumed to include both men and women, and modified titles such as "woman doctor" or "male nurse," should be avoided. Work should never be stereotyped as "woman's work" or as "a mansized job." Writers should avoid showing a "gee-whiz" attitude toward women who perform competently; ("Though a woman, she ran the business as well as any man" or "Though a woman, she ran the business efficiently.")

d. Women should be spoken of as participants in the action, not as possessions of the men. Terms such as *pioneer, farmer,* and *settler* should not be used as though they applied only to adult males.

no	yes
Pioneers moved West, taking their wives and children with them.	Pioneer families moved West.
	Pioneer men and women (or pioneer couples) moved West, taking their children with them.

e. Women should not be portrayed as needing male permission in order to act or to exercise rights (except, of course, for historical or factual accuracy).

no	yes
Jim Weiss allows his wife to work part-time.	Judy Weiss works part-time.

4.

Women should be recognized for their own achievements. Intelligent, daring, and innovative women, both in history and in fiction, should be provided as role-models for girls, and leaders in the fight for women's rights should be honored and respected, not mocked or ignored.

5.

In references to humanity at large, language should operate to include women and girls. Terms that tend to exclude females should be avoided whenever possible.

a. The word *man* has long been used not only to denote a person of male gender, but also generically to denote humanity at large. To many people today, however, the word *man* has become so closely associated with the first meaning (a male human being) that they consider it no longer broad enough to be applied to any person or to human beings as a whole. In deference to this position, alternative expressions should be used in place of *man* (or derivative constructions used generically to signify humanity at large) whenever such substitutions can be made without producing an awkward or artificial construction. In cases where *man*-words must be used, special efforts should be made to ensure that pictures and other devices make explicit that such references include women.

Here are some possible substitutions for *man*-words:

no	yes
mankind	humanity, human beings, human race, people
primitive man	primitive people or peoples; primitive human beings; primitive men and women
man's achievements	human achievements
If a man drove 50 miles at 60 mph ...	If a person (or driver) drove 50 miles at 60 mph ...
the best man for the job	the best person (or candidate) for the job

manmade	artificial; synthetic, manufactured; constructed; of human origin
manpower	human power; human energy; workers; workforce
grow to manhood	grow to adulthood; grow to manhood or womanhood

b. The English language lacks a generic singular pronoun signifying *he* or *she*, and therefore it has been customary and grammatically sanctioned to use masculine pronouns in expressions such as "one . . .*he*," "anyone . . .*he*," and "each child opens *his* book." Nevertheless, avoid when possible the pronouns *he*, *him*, and *his* in reference to the hypothetical person or humanity in general.

Various alternatives may be considered:

(1) Reword to eliminate unnecessary gender pronouns.

no	*yes*
The average American drinks his coffee black	The average American drinks black coffee.

(2) Recast into the plural.

Most Americans drink their coffee black.

(3) Replace the masculine pronoun with *one, you, he* or *she, her* or *his*, as appropriate. (Use *he* or *she* and its variations sparingly to avoid clumsy prose.)

(4) Alternate male and female expressions and examples.

no	*yes*
I've often heard supervisors say, "He's not the right man for the job," or "He lacks the qualifications for success."	I've often heard supervisors say, "She's not the right person for the job," or "He lacks the qualifications for success."

(5) To avoid severe problems of repetition or inept wording, it may sometimes be best to use the generic *he* freely, but to add, in the preface and as often as necessary in the text, emphatic statements to the effect that the masculine pronouns are being used for succinctness and are intended to refer to both females and males.

These guidelines can only suggest a few solutions to difficult problems of rewording. The proper solution in any given passage must depend on the context and on the author's intention. For example, it would be wrong to pluralize in contexts stressing a one-to-one relationship, as between teacher and child. In such cases, either using the expression *he* or *she* or alternating *he* and *she*, as appropriate, will be acceptable.

c. Occupational terms ending in *man* should be replaced whenever possible by terms that can include members of either sex unless they refer to a particular person.

no	yes
congressman	member of Congress; representative (but *Congressman* Koch and *Congresswoman* Holtzman)
businessman	business executive; business manager
fireman	fire fighter
mailman	mail carrier; letter carrier
salesman	sales representative; salesperson; sales clerk
insurance man	insurance agent
statesman	leader; public servant
chairman	the person presiding at (or chairing) a meeting; the presiding officer; the chair; head leader; coordinator; moderator
cameraman	camera operator
foreman	supervisor

d. Language that assumes all readers are male should be avoided.

no	yes
you and your wife	you and your spouse
when you shave in the morning	when you brush your teeth (or wash up) in the morning

6.

The language used to designate and describe females and males should treat the sexes equally.

a. Parallel language should be used for women and men.

no	yes
the men and the ladies	the men and the women
	the ladies and the gentlemen
	the girls and the boys
man and wife	husband and wife

Note that *lady* and *gentleman, wife* and *husband,* and *mother* and *father* are role words. *Ladies* should be used for women only when men are being referred to as *gentlemen.* Similarly, women should be called *wives* and *mothers* only when men are referred to as *husbands* and *fathers.* Like a male shopper, a woman in a grocery store should be called a *customer, not a housewife.*

b. Women should be identified by their own names (e.g., Indira Gandhi). They should not be referred to in terms of their roles as wife, mother, sister, or daughter unless it is in these roles that they are significant in context. Nor should they be identified in terms of their marital relationships (Mrs. Gandhi) unless this brief form is stylistically more convenient (than, say Prime Minister Gandhi) or is paired up with similar references to men.

(1) A woman should be referred to by name in the same way that a man is. Both should be called by their full names, by first or last name only, or by title.

no	yes
Bobby Riggs and Billie Jean	Bobby Riggs and Billie Jean King
Billy Jean and Riggs	Billie Jean and Bobby
Mrs. King and Riggs	King and Riggs
	Ms. King (because she prefers Ms.) and Mr. Riggs
Mrs. Meir and Moshe Dayan	Golda Meir and Moshe Dayan or Mrs. Meir and Dr. Dayan

(2) Unnecessary reference to or emphasis on a woman's marital status should be avoided. Whether married or not, a woman may be referred to by the name by which she chooses to be known, whether her name is her original name or her married name.

c. Whenever possible, a term should be used that includes both sexes. Unnecessary references to gender should be avoided.

no	yes
college boys and co-eds	students

d. Insofar as possible, job titles should be nonsexist. Different nomenclature should not be used for the same job depending on whether it is held by a male or by a female. (See also paragraph 5c for additional examples of words ending in *man*.)

no	yes
steward or purser or stewardess	flight attendant
policeman and policewoman	police officer
maid and houseboy	house or office cleaner; servant

e. Different pronouns should not be linked with certain work or occupations on the assumption that the worker is always (or usually) female or male. Instead either pluralize or use *he or she* and *she or he*.

no	yes
the consumer or shopper . . . she	consumers or shoppers . . . they
the secretary . . . she	secretaries . . . they
the breadwinner . . . his earnings	the breadwinner . . . his or her earnings or breadwinners . . . their earnings.

f. Males should not always be first in order of mention. Instead, alternate the order, sometimes using: *women and men, gentlemen and ladies, she or he, her or his.*

Conclusion

It is hoped that these guidelines have alerted authors and staff members to the problems of sex discrimination and to various ways of solving them.

1974

QUESTIONS

1. What assumptions about the powers and functions of language underlie these guidelines?
2. Racism and sexism represent discrimination on the basis of race or sex. What other kinds of discrimination exist in our society? Invent an analogous term for one of these and write a brief characterization of it.
3. "Discriminate" and "discrimination" originally had to do simply with the act of "distinguishing" or finding "distinguishing features." Explain the relationship between these earlier meanings and our current one connected with prejudice. Does the perception of distinctions or differences necessarily lead to prejudice?
4. Using the guidelines in the essay, examine a newspaper, a magazine, or a textbook for examples of sexism. Try to determine which examples reflect unconscious prejudice.

5. *Study the examples in the guidelines carefully. Will the guidelines lead to greater clarity or precision? Less? Discuss.*

Joseph Epstein

THE EPHEMERAL VERITIES

A few months back, as is most distinctly not my wont, I had lunch with an editor of *Playboy* magazine. I should like to be able to report that this man was a cunning erotician, that we dined in an elegant restaurant atop an expensive bordello where we were served by eunuchs, and that talk at nearby tables was of white slavery. Not quite so. As it turned out, my luncheon companion was much engrossed in the prospect of purchasing a condominium, and we ate in a restaurant whose custom seemed chiefly to come from that corporate class known, I believe, as middle management. Worse still, all that each of us ordered for lunch was a salad. Not my idea of playboys dining out, I must say.

I had come to this lunch because the editor had sent me a note saying he had read some of my scribblings and would like to discuss the possibility of my writing something for *Playboy*. I recall having heard, roughly a decade ago, that the magazine paid $3,000 for an article. Had it, I wondered, kept pace with inflation—as I, a domestic Keynesian with a talent for deficit financing, had not? In short, as the hunter said about the quail, I was game. I even had an answer for anyone who might reproach me by saying, "You mean you write for *Playboy*?" "You mean," I was prepared to shoot back, "you read it?"

But, as will appear in my annual report to stockholders, nothing came of this lunch. I neglected even to find out if *Playboy* had raised its payments to authors. What I did find out in talking to this editor was that I am not an ideal *Playboy* contributor, though he was too kind to say so. As we spoke about what I might write for the magazine, he mentioned that *Playboy* was planning a series of articles predicting trends in the 1980s. I allowed that, from the standpoint of a writer, I found the future boring, the present pleasant, and the past best of all. But as we talked further, it became clear to me that what he really wanted, what every editor of a contemporary mass magazine for the college-educated middle classes wants, is not a body of useful or curious information, or the spectacle of an idiosyncratic and perhaps interesting mind at work, but a piece of writing that will spot a trend, put a new phrase into the language, erect a new truth that will endure until the next issue of the magazine appears. What is wanted, if I may say so, is a shiny new cliché.

A new cliché? Isn't this a contradiction? As a near-contributor to *Playboy* I don't see why I should have to define my terms—especially at these prices—so, if it is all the same to you, I think I'll adopt the definition set forth by someone who has thought about clichés longer than I have. In *On Clichés* (Routledge and Kegan Paul), a most suggestive treatise, a Dutch sociologist named Anton C. Zijderveld defines a cliché thus:

> A cliché is a traditional form of human expression (in words, thoughts, emotions, gestures, acts) which—due to repetitive use in social life—has lost its original, often ingenious heuristic power. Although it thus fails positively to contribute meaning to social interactions and communication, it does function socially, since it manages to stimulate behavior (cognition, emotion, volition, action), while it avoids reflection on meanings.

This is a definition that doesn't, you might say, throw the baby out with the bathwater; it leaves no stone unturned while offering several blessings in disguise, and in the final analysis provides an acid test. You might say all this, that is, if you have an ear dead to the grossest of clichés. But two elements in Professor Zijderveld's definition are especially worth notice. The first is its capaciousness, which lies in its recognition that the clichéic can extend well beyond the merely linguistic. There are, after all, cliché acts, cliché thoughts, cliché books, possibly cliché lives. The second is that Professor Zijderveld's definition comprehends that clichés can stimulate behavior even while discouraging thought.

Still, new clichés? One tends to think of clichés as made stale by use and overuse. Yet, in a letter to Harriet Monroe, Wallace Stevens remarks, "There is, of course, a cliché of the moment as well as a cliché of the past." In *Human, All-Too-Human*, Nietzsche speaks of those who are fifteen minutes ahead of their time—persons of whom he did not think at all well. And I (if I may insert myself into such high-flown company) think there are things that ought to be called Ephemeral Verities, which are clichés of the moment and up to the moment, but without the staying power of ordinary clichés. To adapt the old cliché about Chinese restaurants, the trouble with Ephemeral Verities is that, an hour after you have mouthed them, you are empty-headed again.

There is nothing new about clichés as such. As an appendix to *Bouvard and Pécuchet*, Flaubert included a "Dictionnaire des idées reçues,"[1] later enlarged, in my translated copy, into *A Dictionary of Platitudes, Being a Compendium of Conversational Clichés, Blind Beliefs, Fashionable Misconceptions, and Fixed Ideas*. Flaubert intended his *Dictionary* to contain "everything that it is necessary to repeat in society in order to pass for a well-mannered and agreeable person." Befitting a book devoted to the cultivation of the commonplace, long stretches of the *Dictionary* are tedious, though every now and again a small nugget flashes. The proper

---

1. "A Dictionary of Received Ideas." *Bouvard and Pécuchet*, Flaubert's unfinished last novel.

cliché to mouth about Catholicism, for example, is "Has had a very beneficial influence on the arts"; the advice on the subject of Metaphysics is "To laugh at it is proof of a superior mind"; and, as for Memory, "Complain about your own, and even boast about having none. But roar when told you have no judgment."

I myself do not despise all clichés. Some of them usefully relieve life of its complications. The fully examined life, I have come to think, may not be worth living. Into each life a lot of cliché must fall. It may be a sign of maturity to accept this, smile, and pass on. Of the young Lytton Strachey, Max Beerbohm wrote that his prose had not a jot of preciosity. "He makes no attempt to dazzle," Beerbohm writes. "He is not even afraid of clichés." One of the finest obituaries I have ever read, that of the extraordinary Baroness Moura Budberg, which appeared in The Times (of London), ended flat dab and altogether correctly on a cliché: "There is an old American saying that fits her well: 'After they made that one, they broke the mould.'"

One can only begin to lay claim to knowing a foreign language, it has been said, when one can spot clichés in it. H. W. Fowler, in his article on the cliché in Modern English Usage, remarks, "What is new is not necessarily better than what is old; the original felicity that made a phrase a cliché may not be beyond recapture." Well to remember, too, that clichés often become in time the inevitable burial ground of even the most strikingly original phrase or thought or gesture; perhaps the more striking the more inevitably will it end as a cliché. "And the witty gentleman," says Fowler, in his article on hackneyed phrases, "who equipped coincidence with her long arm has doubtless suffered even in this life at seeing that arm so mercilessly overworked."

Some activities are quite unthinkable unembellished by clichés, and clichés can sometimes gently slide into tradition. For the sports fan, clichés are nearly as important to spectatorial pleasure as are statistics; the best contemporary writer on the subject of baseball, Roger Angell, is especially adept at carefully deploying clichés throughout his compositions. Certain events call for the clichéic: who wants veal limone for Thanksgiving dinner? Clichés can help us get through awkward situations; they keep things superficial where skimming the surface may be the wisest course. In On Clichés Professor Zijderveld notes: "In fact, if one were to collect clichés, like stamps or jokes, one would find a rich field of exploration in obituaries, in letters of condolence, and in funeral orations. It seems as if variations are deemed uncouth, or almost magically harmful and hazardous. Indeed, by leaving the set of clichés in such precarious situations one may easily hurt feelings inadvertently." Each of us, in short, has to be ready to call upon the Polonius[2] that is part of us all.

---

2. Shakespeare's elderly courtier, who advised his son in a series of clichés (Hamlet I, iii, 58–80).

But a little cliché goes a long way. The way things stand now, though, under the dispensation of the Ephemeral Verities, a great many clichés are asked to go a short way. We are today, I believe, being bombarded, indeed blitzed, by clichés. Professor Zijderveld maintains that modern society is especially susceptible to clichés—"clichégenic," he calls it, in a word that gets to look less hideous once one gets used to it—for the reason that, where meaning has in so many places been undermined, men and women swim about in choppy waters, desperately reaching out for something to keep themselves afloat. "Clichés," Professor Zijderveld writes, give "artificial clarity, stability, and certainty." While he is not in favor of this, nor of the clichéic as a mode of thought, he does think it is better than nothing. I am inclined to believe it is about the same as nothing.

Clichés are sometimes thought of as wisdom gone stale. But just as often they represent the devastation that time can wreak on serious ideas. Take the phrase "Protestant ethic," surely one of the leading clichés of our time. Nowadays it pops up everywhere, with a range of meanings that vary from the description of a person intent on success to a tag for the compulsion to work unrelentingly. The origin of this contemporary cliché is, of course, Max Weber's magnificent essay, "The Protestant Ethic and the Spirit of Capitalism," which I first read some twenty years ago as an undergraduate in a condition I can only describe as one of intellectual heat—so swept up was I by its learning, its subtlety, its power. Having read the essay, I now wince slightly when I hear, say, Jimmy Carter described as a product of the Protestant ethic. But then perhaps he is, in the sense that, say, Dick Cavett is a real Renaissance man.

Max Weber's phrase took some seventy-five years to lapse into cliché status, but usually the process by which thought turns to cliché is much more rapid. Indeed certain notions or phrases seem to come into the world as full-blown clichés. Joseph Kraft's "Middle America," Henry Fairlie's "establishment," Spiro Agnew's speech writer's "silent majority," and, on a somewhat higher level, Erik Erikson's "identity crisis" —these seem clichés almost out of the gate. What makes them so, I think, is that each of these alluring phrases is nonetheless finely inexact, fuzzy enough to be put to multiple uses, and exquisitely suited to what Santayana called "the habit of abbreviated thinking." Consider: "The silent majority, freshly emergent as Middle America, no longer feels an identity crisis vis-à-vis the establishment." There is something gratifying about striking off such a sentence—even though it is, of course, utter nonsense.

* * *

Two items that are especially cliché-prone continue to be those of decades and of generations. "Yours is a lost generation," Gertrude Stein is supposed to have remarked to Ernest Hemingway (I have always suspected she said a *louche géneration*),[3] and ever since no generation has been allowed to pass without a label: the Depression generation, the silent generation, the Woodstock generation, et cetera. But even more persistent is the penchant for clichés about decades. Here is a recent offering from the pages of the *New Republic:*

> It is becoming increasingly clear with the approaching end of the aimless 1970s, a decade so reminiscent of the 1950s and 1920s, that American politics is in for another of its periodic sea changes: ready or not, a more energetic public life looms before us in the 1980s.

I myself am not ready; I am not even ready for the analogy between the 1970s and the 1920s, having only recently become accustomed to that between the 1960s and the 1920s. But these clichés change quickly, which is what makes them, as verities, only ephemeral. Attend now, though, to that old cliché-meister the Reverend Norman Vincent Mailer, in an interview in *Publishers Weekly:* "The '70s have been too much for me. They appalled me the way the '50s appalled me." As one good cliché deserves another, Mailer caps his with an empty chiasmus:[4] "I used to hate America for what it was doing to all of us. Now I hate all of us for what we're doing to America."

The cliché seal was set on the just-ending decade, long before its completion, by Tom Wolfe, who called it the "Me Decade." The 1970s, in Mr. Wolfe's reading, was a decade given over to the self—to self-improvement programs, religious and therapeutic, to self-exhibition, and to self-absorption generally. When Tom Wolfe sent the Me Decade up the flagpole, nearly everyone, it seems, saluted. These boys, to adopt another advertising cliché, certainly know how to pick up the ball and run with it. Suddenly, everywhere one turned, the 1970s were all Me and narcissistic and dreadfully spineless. A young writer named Mark Crispin Miller remarked that those years have been "hospitable to narcissism." Michael Harrington, a fellow keen for political activism, referred to "the passive 1970s." Christopher Lasch published a collection of essays entitled *The Culture of Narcissism*, which turned out to be a best-seller. And then, at midyear of 1979, Jann Wenner, the publisher of *Rolling Stone* and hence presumably a careful reader of the Zeitgeist, announced that "The Me Decade is over."

But before the decade congeals into the plaster of paris of cliché, I think that a few things ought to be said on behalf of the 1970s—not least among them that they weren't the 1960s. Properly speaking, of course, the 1960s were not the '60s exclusively; insofar as they stand for a period of political tumult and intellectual incivility, they continued on well into the early 1970s. What is more, in what decade without a major war or

---

3. A dubious, or slightly crooked, generation.
4. A rhetorical contrast by means of a re-   versed parallel: for example, *Most people eat to live; he lives to eat.*

economic catastrophe have people *not* been self-absorbed? The labeling
of decades often tells less about the decades than about strangely skewed
views of history. A period such as the 1960s, when our nation was very
nearly ripped apart by riot and ill feeling all around, is now known as one
of social idealism. Another decade, such as the middle and late 1950s
under President Eisenhower, and after Korea and Senator Joseph Mc-
Carthy—a time when people could carry on their work—is known as
passive and conformist and boring. The fact is, I don't see me in the Me
Decade. I would, however, if people who insist on a label for the 1970s
settle for calling it the You Decade.

Not that all this talk of decades is entirely wrong. Many people who
came of age in the 1920s, when Prohibition was in force, seem never to
have lost their excitement about alcohol. Many people who were young
in the 1930s have never quite been able, owing to the Depression, to
shake their anxiety about money. And many people who came of age in
the 1960s are likely to have a wide acquaintance with drugs. I am not
sure, though, that one can safely say much more than these loose and
banal things about any ten-year period. Yet people seem to crave more.
Labels for decades help them pack up the complications of history and
even of their own lives, and put these away in the empty valise of clichés.
Once packed up, thinking can cease. Here is the real utility of clichés:
they explain the world, usually crudely and sometimes quite falsely. But
for many people a false explanation is better than no explanation at all.

So great is the need for explanations that certain thinkers gain ascendancy over others because, intricate and elaborate though their thought
might originally have been, it presents a rich mine from which clichés
can be easily extracted. Marxism is a prime example, with its two
whomping clichés: the eternal class struggle and economic determinism.
Freudianism is another example. Perhaps as few people have read Freud
as have read Marx, yet everyone is in on the id, ego, superego, the
determinism of early infancy, the importance of the sexual life, and the
rest of it. Existentialism has been yet another fountain of clichés, so much
so that the very word "existential" has itself become a cliché—one of the
true wooden nickels of intellectual discourse. Professor Zijderveld remarks of such intellectual clichés that they "are like mantras providing
modern man with a semi-magical sense of security and stability . . . in
which permanent reflection can come to rest."

The fact that all these items, from the class struggle to the Oedipus
complex, have become clichés does not necessarily disqualify them as
truth-bearing. Ideas, like statistics, cannot be held responsible for the
people who use them. Yet some ideas do allow easier access, and coarser
usage, than others. Finer grained writers—Montaigne, Pascal, Santayana
—are not so easily summarized. Their thought cannot be grasped by the
reins of a leading idea or two; rather like poets, they can scarcely be

paraphrased. Marx and Freud are writers of great power in any case, but surely a large part of their popularity is owing to their supreme nomenclatural skill. They could name things with cogency, and this cogency is decisive for the adaptation of ideas to use as clichés. "Just another example of thinking that if you name something you've explained it," says the protagonist of Kingsley Amis's novel *Jake's Thing.* "Like . . . like permissive society."

The permissive society, the consumer society, post-industrial society, the meritocratic society, the culture of narcissism, the culture of poverty, the adversary culture, the organization man, the lonely crowd, the Spock generation—there seems to be no end to these clichés, these Ephemeral Verities. Nor to ephemeral veritists, those philosophes who sail in on a phrase—Norman O. Brown ("polymorphous perverse"), Marshall McLuhan ("the medium is the message"), Herbert Marcuse ("repressive toleration")—and sail out again. Perhaps some day they will be used as names in an intellectual trivia game, like Monopoly, let's call it Doctorate. Pick a question card: "Who in the late 1960s said that in an insane society the most truly sane person was the schizophrenic?" Answer: the English psychiatrist R. D. Laing. If you answered incorrectly, return to another year as a teaching assistant at Eastern Illinois University. If you answered correctly, take credit for two master's degree courses, and apply to Columbia.

Marcuse and McLuhan, Brown and Laing, these are very great geysers of pishposh, as Mencken used to call such temporary sages, and very high-blowing ones at that. Their writings are scarcely accessible to the common reader, and even the uncommon reader needs a fairly broad streak of masochism and the mental equivalent of hip boots to trudge through their works. But if these ephemeral veritists are an acquired taste, like that for eating cactus, who is working the larger crowds—what in Las Vegas are called the "big rooms"?

One night not long ago when I was watching the local television news, a suburban high school teachers' strike was reported. Various teachers were asked how the strike would affect them personally. One of the respondents was a man with hairdo and mustache reminiscent of Kurt Vonnegut. "I was forty last month," he said into the microphone thrust under his mustache, "and this summer my wife and I separated, and now there's this strike. One more thing and I'll be going through a mid-life crisis." It took me a moment to realize what he was saying: here was a reader of, and apparently a true believer in, *Passages.*

Passages is a book about adult development by the journalist Gail Sheehy. Among ephemeral veritists, Miss Sheehy works the lower end of the vineyard. The air is not so rarefied down there, but the yield is much greater; *Passages* has been, as its mass paperback edition announces, "#1 from Coast to Coast." I have read only a hundred or so of its more than five hundred pages, but that is enough to recognize that, of its kind, the book is a work of genius—a structure built almost entirely of other people's clichés, though chiefly using materials from those two great brickyards of contemporary cliché, psychology and sociology. Miss Sheehy artfully uses jargon, supplies endless case-study interviews, exudes an air of scientism, and paints over the whole with a rich coat of hopefulness. "If I've been convinced by one idea in the course of collecting all the life stories that inform this book, it is this: Times of crisis, of disruption or constructive change, are not only predictable but desirable. They mean growth." Hmmm. Do try to remember that the next time you undergo bankruptcy, divorce, a coronary, or the death of someone you love: it means growth.

But all this is old news. Miss Sheehy has now moved on to fresh verities. *Esquire* has recently run a segment from a forthcoming book of hers; the segment is entitled "Introducing the Postponing Generation, the Truth About Today's Young Men." Ah, "the Postponing Generation"—who can fail to find the deft touch of the cliché artist in that, a woman with a sure sense of *le cliché juste?*[5] One can be reasonably certain that there is plenty more where that came from.

Professor Zijderveld makes the interesting observation that intellectual clichés do not demand any serious moral responsibility. One adopts them for a while, wearing them rather like a sweater. When something warmer or more attractive comes along, one switches to that. A continual shedding and changing of clichés, like sweaters, goes on and doubtless will continue to do so. One can attempt to beat back these clichés, but in the end the task can never be successfully completed, for it too closely resembles cleaning out the Augean stables without removing the horses.

Besides, the process has been going on for a very long while. Dostoevski, in the early pages of *The Diary of a Writer*, remarks, "In our day, thoughtfulness is next to impossible: it is too expensive a luxury. True enough, ready ideas are being bought. They are being sold everywhere, even gratis, but gratuitously, in the long run, they prove more expensive, and people begin to forbode this fact." Nearly seventy years later, Wallace Stevens, in more than one of his letters, notes that he is reading too much and, as a result, thinking too little. One might once have thought of reading as indistinguishable from thinking, but no longer. With so many clichés buzzing about in books and in the atmosphere generally, it is sometimes like trying to think with one's head in a beehive.

Meanwhile, should another *Playboy* or other slick magazine editor invite me to lunch, I will not again make the mistake of arriving unprepared. I have an idea for an article that will, I think, fill the bill. Its working title is "The New Incest." Interested editors may contact my agent, Georges Borchardt, Inc., New York, New York. I have also begun

5. The right cliché. A turn on Flaubert's *le mot juste*, the right word.

work on an article that will explain what happened in the 1990s. Editors should know in advance that for either of these articles the highest possible rates will be barely acceptable.

1979

QUESTIONS

1. Is Epstein arguing a point, or describing a condition, or both?
2. Epstein does not actually define his basic term, but he does use, without explicitly accepting, the definition of the Dutch sociologist, Zijderveld. He also talks about the subject enough to make clear his idea of a cliché. Write his definition for him.
3. What sort of evidence does he argue from, or what sort of phenomena does he describe? Why not simply line up a series of illustrative clichés?
4. Write a one-page essay in which you use all the clichés you can pack in. Then rewrite the essay eliminating them all. What do you think Epstein would say about the two versions?

Erich Fromm

THE NATURE OF SYMBOLIC LANGUAGE

Let us assume you want to tell someone the difference between the taste of white wine and red wine. This may seem quite simple to you. You know the difference very well; why should it not be easy to explain it to someone else? Yet you find the greatest difficulty putting this taste difference into words. And probably you will end up by saying, "Now look here, I can't explain it to you. Just drink red wine and then white wine, and you will know what the difference is." You have no difficulty in finding words to explain the most complicated machine, and yet words seem to be futile to describe a simple taste experience.

Are we not confronted with the same difficulty when we try to explain a feeling experience? Let us take a mood in which you feel lost, deserted, where the world looks gray, a little frightening though not really dangerous. You want to describe this mood to a friend, but again you find yourself groping for words and eventually feel that nothing you have said is an adequate explanation of the many nuances of the mood. The following night you have a dream. You see yourself in the outskirts of a city just before dawn, the streets are empty except for a milk wagon, the houses look poor, the surroundings are unfamiliar, you have no means of accustomed transportation to places familiar to you and where you feel you belong. When you wake up and remember the dream, it occurs to you that the feeling you had in that dream was exactly the feeling of lostness and grayness you tried to describe to your friend the day before. It is just one picture, whose visualization took less than a second. And yet this picture is a more vivid and precise description than you could have given by talking *about* it at length. The picture you see in the dream is a *symbol* of something you felt.

What is a symbol? A symbol is often defined as "something that stands for something else." This definition seems rather disappointing. It becomes more interesting, however, if we concern ourselves with those symbols which are sensory expressions of seeing, hearing, smelling, touching, standing for a "something else" which is an inner experience, a feeling or thought. A symbol of this kind is something outside ourselves; that which it symbolizes is something inside ourselves. Symbolic language is language in which we express inner experience as if it were a sensory experience, as if it were something we were doing or something that was done to us in the world of things. Symbolic language is language in which the world outside is a symbol of the world inside, a symbol for our souls and our minds.

If we define a symbol as "something which stands for something else," the crucial question is: *What is the specific connection between the symbol and that which it symbolizes?*

In answer to this question we can differentiate between three kinds of symbols: the *conventional*, the *accidental* and the *universal* symbol. As will become apparent presently, only the latter two kinds of symbols express inner experiences as if they were sensory experiences, and only they have the elements of symbolic language.

The *conventional* symbol is the best known of the three, since we employ it in everyday language. If we see the word "table" or hear the sound "table," the letters T-A-B-L-E stand for something else. They stand for the thing table that we see, touch and use. What is the connection between the *word* "table" and the *thing* "table"? Is there any inherent relationship between them? Obviously not. The thing table has nothing to do with the sound table, and the only reason the word symbolizes the thing is the convention of calling this particular thing by a particular name. We learn this connection as children by the repeated experience of hearing the word in reference to the thing until a lasting association is formed so that we don't have to think to find the right word.

There are some words, however, where the association is not only conventional. When we say "phooey," for instance, we make with our lips a movement of dispelling the air quickly. It is an expression of disgust in which our mouths participate. By this quick expulsion of air we imitate and thus express our intention to expel something, to get it out of our system. In this case, as in some others, the symbol has an inherent

connection with the feeling it symbolizes. But even if we assume that
originally many or even all words had their origins in some such inherent
connection between symbol and the symbolized, most words no longer
have this meaning for us when we learn a language.

Words are not the only illustration for conventional symbols, although
they are the most frequent and best-known ones. Pictures also can be
conventional symbols. A flag, for instance, may stand for a specific
country, and yet there is no connection between the specific colors and
the country for which they stand. They have been accepted as denoting
that particular country, and we translate the visual impression of the flag
into the concept of that country, again on conventional grounds. Some
pictorial symbols are not entirely conventional; for example, the cross.
The cross can be merely a conventional symbol of the Christian church
and in that respect no different from a flag. But the specific content of the
cross referring to Jesus' death or, beyond that, to the interpenetration of
the material and spiritual planes, puts the connection between the symbol and what it symbolizes beyond the level of mere conventional symbols.

The very opposite to the conventional symbol is the *accidental* symbol,
although they have one thing in common: there is no intrinsic relationship between the symbol and that which it symbolizes. Let us assume
that someone has had a saddening experience in a certain city; when he
hears the name of that city, he will easily connect the name with a mood
of sadness, just as he would connect it with a mood of joy had his
experience been a happy one. Quite obviously there is nothing in the
nature of the city that is either sad or joyful. It is the individual experience connected with the city that makes it a symbol of a mood.

The same reaction could occur in connection with a house, a street, a
certain dress, certain scenery, or anything once connected with a specific
mood. We might find ourselves dreaming that we are in a certain city. In
fact, there may be no particular mood connected with it in the dream; all
we see is a street or even simply the name of the city. We ask ourselves
why we happened to think of that city in our sleep and may discover that
we had fallen asleep in a mood similar to the one symbolized by the city.
The picture in the dream represents this mood, the city "stands for" the
mood once experienced in it. Here the connection between the symbol
and the experience symbolized is entirely accidental.

In contrast to the conventional symbol, the accidental symbol cannot
be shared by anyone else except as we relate the events connected with
the symbol. For this reason accidental symbols are rarely used in myths,
fairy tales, or works of art written in symbolic language because they are
not communicable unless the writer adds a lengthy comment to each
symbol he uses. In dreams, however, accidental symbols are frequent. * * *

The *universal* symbol is one in which there is an intrinsic relationship between the symbol and that which it represents. We have already given one example, that of the outskirts of the city. The sensory experience of a deserted, strange, poor environment has indeed a significant relationship to a mood of lostness and anxiety. True enough, if we have never been in the outskirts of a city we could not use that symbol, just as the word "table" would be meaningless had we never seen a table. This symbol is meaningful only to city dwellers and would be meaningless to people living in cultures that have no big cities. Many other universal symbols, however, are rooted in the experience of every human being. Take, for instance, the symbol of fire. We are fascinated by certain qualities of fire in a fireplace. First of all, by its aliveness. It changes continuously, it moves all the time, and yet there is constancy in it. It remains the same without being the same. It gives the impression of power, of energy, of grace and lightness. It is as if it were dancing and had an inexhaustible source of energy. When we use fire as a symbol, we describe the inner experience characterized by the same elements which we notice in the sensory experience of fire; the mood of energy, lightness, movement, grace, gaiety—sometimes one, sometimes another of these elements being predominant in the feeling.

Similar in some ways and different in others is the symbol of water—of the ocean or of the stream. Here, too, we find the blending of change and permanence, of constant movement and yet of permanence. We also feel the quality of aliveness, continuity and energy. But there is a difference; where fire is adventurous, quick, exciting, water is quiet, slow and steady. Fire has an element of surprise; water an element of predictability. Water symbolizes the mood of aliveness, too, but one which is "heavier," "slower," and more comforting than exciting.

That a phenomenon of the physical world can be the adequate expression of an inner experience, that the world of things can be a symbol of the world of the mind, is not surprising. We all know that our bodies express our minds. Blood rushes to our heads when we are furious, it rushes away from them when we are afraid; our hearts beat more quickly when we are angry, and the whole body has a different tonus if we are happy from the one it has when we are sad. We express our moods by our facial expressions and our attitudes and feelings by movements and gestures so precise that others recognize them more accurately from our gestures than from our words. Indeed, the body is a symbol—and not an allegory—of the mind. Deeply and genuinely felt emotion, and even any genuinely felt thought, is expressed in our whole organism. In the case of the universal symbol, we find the same connection between mental and physical experience. Certain physical phenomena suggest by their very nature certain emotional and mental experiences, and we express emotional experiences in the language of physical experiences, that is to say, symbolically.

The universal symbol is the only one in which the relationship between the symbol and that which is symbolized is not coincidental but intrinsic. It is rooted in the experience of the affinity between an emotion or thought, on the one hand, and a sensory experience, on the other. It can be called universal because it is shared by all men, in contrast not only to the accidental symbol, which is by its very nature entirely personal, but also to the conventional symbol, which is restricted to a group of people sharing the same convention. The universal symbol is rooted in the properties of our body, our senses, and our mind, which are common to all men and, therefore, not restricted to individuals or to specific groups. Indeed, the language of the universal symbol is the one common tongue developed by the human race, a language which it forgot before it succeeded in developing a universal conventional language.

There is no need to speak of a racial inheritance in order to explain the universal character of symbols. Every human being who shares the essential features of bodily and mental equipment with the rest of mankind is capable of speaking and understanding the symbolic language that is based upon these common properties. Just as we do not need to learn to cry when we are sad or to get red in the face when we are angry, and just as these reactions are not restricted to any particular race or group of people, symbolic language does not have to be learned and is not restricted to any segment of the human race. Evidence for this is to be found in the fact that symbolic language as it is employed in myths and dreams is found in all cultures—in so-called primitive as well as such highly developed cultures as Egypt and Greece. Furthermore, the symbols used in these various cultures are strikingly similar since they all go back to the basic sensory as well as emotional experiences shared by men of all cultures. Added evidence is to be found in recent experiments in which people who had no knowledge of the theory of dream interpretation were able, under hypnosis, to interpret the symbolism of their dreams without any difficulty. After emerging from the hypnotic state and being asked to interpret the same dreams, they were puzzled and said, "Well, there is no meaning to them—it is just nonsense."

The foregoing statement needs qualification, however. Some symbols differ in meaning according to the difference in their realistic significance in various cultures. For instance, the function and consequently the meaning of the sun is different in northern countries and in tropical countries. In northern countries, where water is plentiful, all growth depends on sufficient sunshine. The sun is the warm, life-giving, protecting, loving power. In the Near East, where the heat of the sun is much more powerful, the sun is a dangerous and even threatening power from which man must protect himself, while water is felt to be the source of all life and the main condition for growth. We may speak of dialects of universal symbolic language, which are determined by those differences in natural conditions which cause certain symbols to have a different meaning in different regions of the earth.

Quite different from these "symbolic dialects" is the fact that many symbols have more than one meaning in accordance with different kinds of experiences which can be connected with one and the same natural phenomenon. Let us take up the symbol of fire again. If we watch fire in the fireplace, which is a source of pleasure and comfort, it is expressive of a mood of aliveness, warmth, and pleasure. But if we see a building or forest on fire, it conveys to us an experience of threat or terror, of the powerlessness of man against the elements of nature. Fire, then, can be the symbolic representation of inner aliveness and happiness as well as of fear, powerlessness, or of one's own destructive tendencies. The same holds true of the symbol water. Water can be a most destructive force when it is whipped up by a storm or when a swollen river floods its banks. Therefore, it can be the symbolic expression of horror and chaos as well as of comfort and peace.

Another illustration of the same principle is a symbol of a valley. The valley enclosed between mountains can arouse in us the feeling of security and comfort, of protection against all dangers from the outside. But the protecting mountains can also mean isolating walls which do not permit us to get out of the valley and thus the valley can become a symbol of imprisonment. The particular meaning of the symbol in any given place can only be determined from the whole context in which the symbol appears, and in terms of the predominant experiences of the person using the symbol. * * *

A good illustration of the function of the universal symbol is a story, written in symbolic language, which is known to almost everyone in Western culture: the Book of Jonah. Jonah has heard God's voice telling him to go to Nineveh and preach to its inhabitants to give up their evil ways lest they be destroyed. Jonah cannot help hearing God's voice and that is why he is a prophet. But he is an unwilling prophet, who, though knowing what he should do, tries to run away from the command of God (or, as we may say, the voice of his conscience). He is a man who does not care for other human beings. He is a man with a strong sense of law and order, but without love.

How does the story express the inner processes in Jonah?

We are told that Jonah went down to Joppa and found a ship which should bring him to Tarshish. In mid-ocean a storm rises and, while everyone else is excited and afraid, Jonah goes into the ship's belly and falls into a deep sleep. The sailors, believing that God must have sent the storm because someone on the ship is to be punished, wake Jonah, who had told them he was trying to flee from God's command. He tells them to take him and cast him forth into the sea and that the sea would then become calm. The sailors (betraying a remarkable sense of humanity by first trying everything else before following his advice) eventually take Jonah and cast him into the sea, which immediately stops raging. Jonah is swallowed by a big fish and stays in the fish's belly three days and three nights. He prays to God to free him from this prison. God makes the fish vomit out Jonah unto the dry land and Jonah goes to Nineveh, fulfills God's command, and thus saves the inhabitants of the city.

The story is told as if these events had actually happened. However, it is written in symbolic language and all the realistic events described are symbols for the inner experiences of the hero. We find a sequence of symbols which follow one another: going into the ship, going into the ship's belly, falling asleep, being in the ocean, and being in the fish's belly. All these symbols stand for the same inner experience: for a condition of being protected and isolated, of safe withdrawal from communication with other human beings. They represent what could be represented in another symbol, the fetus in the mother's womb. Different as the ship's belly, deep sleep, the ocean, and a fish's belly are realistically, they are expressive of the same inner experience, of the blending between protection and isolation.

In the manifest story events happen in space and time: first, going into the ship's belly; then, falling asleep; then, being thrown into the ocean; then, being swallowed by the fish. One thing happens after the other and, although some events are obviously unrealistic, the story has its own logical consistency in terms of time and space. But if we understand that the writer did not intend to tell us the story of external events, but of the inner experience of a man torn between his conscience and his wish to escape from his inner voice, it becomes clear that his various actions following one after the other express the same mood in him; and that sequence in time is expressive of a growing intensity of the same feeling. In his attempt to escape from his obligation to his fellow men Jonah isolates himself more and more until, in the belly of the fish, the protective element has so given way to the imprisoning element that he can stand it no longer and is forced to pray to God to be released from where he had put himself. (This is a mechanism which we find so characteristic of neurosis. An attitude is assumed as a defense against a danger, but then it grows far beyond its original defense function and becomes a neurotic symptom from which the person tries to be relieved.) Thus Jonah's escape into protective isolation ends in the terror of being imprisoned, and he takes up his life at the point where he had tried to escape.

There is another difference between the logic of the manifest and of the latent story. In the manifest story the logical connection is one of causality of external events. Jonah wants to go overseas because he wants to flee from God, he falls asleep because he is tired, he is thrown overboard *because* he is supposed to be the reason for the storm, and he is swallowed by the fish *because* there are man-eating fish in the ocean. One event occurs because of a previous event. (The last part of the story is unrealistic but not illogical.) But in the latent story the logic is different. The various events are related to each other by their association with the same inner experience. What appears to be a causal sequence of external events stands for a connection of experiences linked with each other by their association in terms of inner events. This is as logical as the manifest story—but it is a logic of a different kind. * * *

1951

George Orwell

POLITICS AND THE ENGLISH LANGUAGE

Most people who bother with the matter at all would admit that the English language is in a bad way, but it is generally assumed that we cannot by conscious action do anything about it. Our civilization is decadent and our language—so the argument runs—must inevitably share in the general collapse. It follows that any struggle against the abuse of language is a sentimental archaism, like preferring candles to electric light or hansom cabs to aeroplanes. Underneath this lies the half-conscious belief that language is a natural growth and not an instrument which we shape for our own purposes.

Now, it is clear that the decline of a language must ultimately have political and economic causes: it is not due simply to the bad influence of this or that individual writer. But an effect can become a cause, reinforc-ing the original cause and producing the same effect in an intensified form, and so on indefinitely. A man may take to drink because he feels himself to be a failure, and then fail all the more completely because he drinks. It is rather the same thing that is happening to the English language. It becomes ugly and inaccurate because our thoughts are foolish, but the slovenliness of our language makes it easier for us to have foolish thoughts. The point is that the process is reversible. Modern English, especially written English, is full of bad habits which spread by imitation and which can be avoided if one is willing to take the necessary trouble. If one gets rid of these habits one can think more clearly, and to think clearly is a necessary first step towards political regeneration: so that the fight against bad English is not frivolous and is not the exclusive concern of professional writers. I will come back to this presently, and I hope that by that time the meaning of what I have said here will have become clearer. Meanwhile, here are five specimens of the English language as it is now habitually written.

These five passages have not been picked out because they are especially bad—I could have quoted far worse if I had chosen—but because they illustrate various of the mental vices from which we now suffer. They are a little below the average, but are fairly representative samples. I number them so that I can refer back to them when necessary:

"(1) I am not, indeed, sure whether it is not true to say that the Milton who once seemed not unlike a seventeenth-century Shelley had not become, out of an experience ever more bitter in each year, more alien [sic] to the founder of that Jesuit sect which nothing could induce him to tolerate."

Professor Harold Laski (Essay in Freedom of Expression).

"(2) Above all, we cannot play ducks and drakes with a native battery of idioms which prescribes such egregious collocations of vocables as the Basic put up with for tolerate or put at a loss for bewilder."

Professor Lancelot Hogben (Interglossa).

"(3) On the one side we have the free personality: by definition it is not neurotic, for it has neither conflict nor dream. Its desires, such as they are, are transparent, for they are just what institutional approval keeps in the forefront of consciousness; another institutional pattern would alter their number and intensity; there is little in them that is natural, irreducible, or culturally dangerous. But on the other side, the social bond itself is nothing but the mutual reflection of these self-secure integrities. Recall the definition of love. Is not this the very picture of a small academic? Where is there a place in this hall of mirrors for either personality or fraternity?"

Essay on psychology in Politics (New York).

"(4) All the 'best people' from the gentlemen's clubs, and all the frantic fascist captains, united in common hatred of Socialism and bestial horror of the rising tide of the mass revolutionary movement, have turned to acts of provocation, to foul incendiarism, to medieval legends of poisoned wells, to legalize their own destruction of proletarian organizations, and rouse the agitated petty-bourgeoisie to chauvinistic fervour on behalf of the fight against the revolutionary way out of the crisis."

Communist pamphlet.

"(5) If a new spirit is to be infused into this old country, there is one thorny and contentious reform which must be tackled, and that is the humanization and galvanization of the B.B.C. Timidity here will bespeak cancer and atrophy of the soul. The heart of Britain may be sound and of strong beat, for instance, but the British lion's roar at present is like that of Bottom in Shakespeare's Midsummer Night's Dream—as gentle as any sucking dove. A virile new Britain cannot continue indefinitely to be traduced in the eyes or rather ears, of the world by the effete languors of Langham Place, brazenly masquerading as 'standard English'. When the Voice of Britain is heard at nine o'clock, better far and infinitely less ludicrous to hear aitches honestly

dropped than the present priggish, inflated, inhibited, school-ma'amish arch
braying of blameless bashful mewing maidens!"

Letter in *Tribune*.

Each of these passages has faults of its own, but, quite apart from
avoidable ugliness, two qualities are common to all of them. The first is
staleness of imagery: the other is lack of precision. The writer either has a
meaning and cannot express it, or he inadvertently says something else,
or he is almost indifferent as to whether his words mean anything or not.
This mixture of vagueness and sheer incompetence is the most marked
characteristic of modern English prose, and especially of any kind of
political writing. As soon as certain topics are raised, the concrete melts
into the abstract and no one seems able to think of turns of speech that
are not hackneyed: prose consists less and less of *words* chosen for the
sake of their meaning, and more and more of *phrases* tacked together like
the sections of a prefabricated hen-house. I list below, with notes and
examples, various of the tricks by means of which the work of prose-
construction is habitually dodged:

Dying Metaphors

A newly invented metaphor assists thought by evoking a visual image,
while on the other hand a metaphor which is technically "dead" (e.g. *iron
resolution*) has in effect reverted to being an ordinary word and can
generally be used without loss of vividness. But in between these two
classes there is a huge dump of worn-out metaphors which have lost all
evocative power and are merely used because they save people the
trouble of inventing phrases for themselves. Examples are: *Ring the
changes on, take up the cudgels for, toe the line, ride roughshod over, stand
shoulder to shoulder with, play into the hands of, no axe to grind, grist to the
mill, fishing in troubled waters, on the order of the day, Achilles' heel, swan
song, hotbed.* Many of these are used without knowledge of their meaning (what is a "rift," for instance?), and incompatible metaphors are
frequently mixed, a sure sign that the writer is not interested in what he
is saying. Some metaphors now current have been twisted out of their
original meaning without those who use them even being aware of the
fact. For example, *toe the line* is sometimes written *tow the line*. Another
example is *the hammer and the anvil,* now always used with the implication that the anvil gets the worst of it. In real life it is always the anvil that
breaks the hammer, never the other way about: a writer who stopped to
think what he was saying would be aware of this, and would avoid
perverting the original phrase.

Operators or Verbal False Limbs

These save the trouble of picking out appropriate verbs and nouns, and at the same time pad each sentence with extra syllables which give it an appearance of symmetry. Characteristic phrases are: *render inoperative, militate against, make contact with, be subjected to, give rise to, give grounds for, have the effect of, play a leading part (role) in, make itself felt, take effect, exhibit a tendency to, serve the purpose of, etc., etc.* The keynote is the elimination of simple verbs. Instead of being a single word, such as *break, stop, spoil, mend, kill,* a verb becomes a *phrase,* made up of a noun or adjective tacked on to some general-purposes verb such as *prove, serve, form, play, render.* In addition, the passive voice is wherever possible used in preference to the active, and noun constructions are used instead of gerunds (*by examination of* instead of *by examining*). The range of verbs is further cut down by means of the *-ize* and *de-* formation, and the banal statements are given an appearance of profundity by means of the *not un-* formation. Simple conjunctions and prepositions are replaced by such phrases as *with respect to, having regard to, the fact that, by dint of, in view of, in the interests of, on the hypothesis that;* and the ends of sentences are saved from anticlimax by such resounding commonplaces as *greatly to be desired, cannot be left out of account, a development to be expected in the near future, deserving of serious consideration, brought to a satisfactory conclusion,* and so on and so forth.

Pretentious Diction

Words like *phenomenon, element, individual* (as noun), *objective, categorical, effective, virtual, basic, primary, promote, constitute, exhibit, exploit, utilize, eliminate, liquidate,* are used to dress up simple statements and give an air of scientific impartiality to biased judgments. Adjectives like *epoch-making, epic, historic, unforgettable, triumphant, age-old, inevitable, inexorable, veritable,* are used to dignify the sordid processes of international politics, while writing that aims at glorifying war usually takes on an archaic colour, its characteristic words being: *realm, throne, chariot, mailed fist, trident, sword, shield, buckler, banner, jackboot, clarion.* Foreign words and expressions such as *cul de sac, ancien régime, deus ex machina, mutatis mutandis, status quo, gleichschaltung, weltanschauung,* are used to give an air of culture and elegance. Except for the useful abbreviations *i.e., e.g.,* and *etc.,* there is no real need for any of the hundreds of foreign phrases now current in English. Bad writers, and especially scientific, political and sociological writers, are nearly aways haunted by the notion that Latin or Greek words are grander than Saxon ones, and unnecessary words like *expedite, ameliorate, predict, extraneous, deracinated, clandestine, subaqueous* and hundreds of others constantly gain ground from their Anglo-Saxon opposite numbers.[1] The jargon peculiar to Marxist writing (*hyena, hangman, cannibal, petty bourgeois, these gentry, lacquey, flunkey, mad dog, White Guard,* etc.) consists largely of words and phrases translated from Russian, German or French; but the normal way of coining a new word is to use a Latin or Greek root with the appropriate affix and, where necessary, the *-ize* formation. It is often easier to make up words of this kind (*deregionalize, impermissible, extramarital, nonfragmentatory* and so forth) than to think up the English words that will cover one's meaning. The result, in general, is an increase in slovenliness and vagueness.

Meaningless Words

In certain kinds of writing, particularly in art criticism and literary criticism, it is normal to come across long passages which are almost completely lacking in meaning.[2] Words like *romantic, plastic, values, human, dead, sentimental, natural, vitality,* as used in art criticism, are strictly meaningless in the sense that they not only do not point to any discoverable object, but are hardly ever expected to do so by the reader. When one critic writes, "The outstanding feature of Mr. X's work is its living quality", while another writes, "The immediately striking thing about Mr. X's work is its peculiar deadness", the reader accepts this as a simple difference of opinion. If words like *black* and *white* were involved, instead of the jargon words *dead* and *living,* he would see at once that language was being used in an improper way. Many political words are similarly abused. The word *Fascism* has now no meaning except in so far as it signifies "something not desirable." The words *democracy, socialism, freedom, patriotic, realistic, justice,* have each of them several different meanings which cannot be reconciled with one another. In the case of a word like *democracy,* not only is there no agreed definition, but the attempt to make one is resisted from all sides. It is almost universally felt that when we call a country democratic we are praising it: consequently the defenders of every kind of régime claim that it is a democracy, and fear that they might have to stop using the word if it were tied down to any one meaning. Words of this kind are often used in a consciously dishonest way. That is, the person who uses them has his own private

1. An interesting illustration of this is the way in which the English flower names which were in use till very recently are being ousted by Greek ones, snapdragon becoming *antirrhinum, forget-me-not* becoming *myosotis,* etc. It is hard to see any practical reason for this change of fashion: it is probably due to an instinctive turning-away from the more homely word and a vague feeling that the Greek word is scientific [Orwell's note].

2. Example: "Comfort's catholicity of perception and image, strangely Whitmanesque in range, almost the exact opposite in aesthetic compulsion, continues to evoke that trembling atmospheric accumulative hinting at a cruel, an inexorably serene timelessness ... Wrey Gardiner scores by aiming at simple bull's-eyes with precision. Only they are not so simple, and through this contented sadness- runs more than the surface bittersweet of resignation" (*Poetry Quarterly*) [Orwell's note].

definition, but allows his hearer to think he means something quite different. Statements like *Marshal Pétain was a true patriot, The Soviet Press is the freest in the world, The Catholic Church is opposed to persecution,* are almost always made with intent to deceive. Other words used in variable meanings, in most cases more or less dishonestly, are: *class, totalitarian, science, progressive, reactionary, bourgeois, equality.*

Now that I have made this catalogue of swindles and perversions, let me give another example of the kind of writing that they lead to. This time it must of its nature be an imaginary one. I am going to translate a passage of good English into modern English of the worst sort. Here is a well-known verse from *Ecclesiastes:*

> "I returned and saw under the sun, that the race is not to the swift, nor the battle to the strong, neither yet bread to the wise, nor yet riches to men of understanding, nor yet favour to men of skill; but time and chance happeneth to them all."

Here it is in modern English:

> "Objective consideration of contemporary phenomena compels the conclusion that success or failure in competitive activities exhibits no tendency to be commensurate with innate capacity, but that a considerable element of the unpredictable must invariably be taken into account."

This is a parody, but not a very gross one. Exhibit (3), above, for instance, contains several patches of the same kind of English. It will be seen that I have not made a full translation. The beginning and ending of the sentence follow the original meaning fairly closely, but in the middle the concrete illustrations—race, battle, bread—dissolve into the vague phrase "success or failure in competitive activities." This had to be so, because no modern writer of the kind I am discussing—no one capable of using phrases like "objective consideration of contemporary phenomena"—would ever tabulate his thoughts in that precise and detailed way. The whole tendency of modern prose is away from concreteness. Now analyse these two sentences a little more closely. The first contains forty-nine words but only sixty syllables, and all its words are those of everyday life. The second contains thirty-eight words of ninety syllables: eighteen of its words are from Latin roots, and one from Greek. The first sentence contains six vivid images, and only one phrase ("time and chance") that could be called vague. The second contains not a single fresh, arresting phrase, and in spite of its ninety syllables it gives only a shortened version of the meaning contained in the first. Yet without a doubt it is the second kind of sentence that is gaining ground in modern English. I do not want to exaggerate. This kind of writing is not yet universal, and outcrops of simplicity will occur here and there in the worst-written page. Still, if you or I were told to write a few lines on the uncertainty of human fortunes, we should probably come much nearer to my imaginary sentence than to the one from *Ecclesiastes*.

As I have tried to show, modern writing at its worst does not consist in picking out words for the sake of their meaning and inventing images in order to make the meaning clearer. It consists in gumming together long strips of words which have already been set in order by someone else, and making the results presentable by sheer humbug. The attraction of this way of writing is that it is easy. It is easier—even quicker, once you have the habit—to say *In my opinion it is a not unjustifiable assumption that* than to say *I think.* If you use ready-made phrases, you not only don't have to hunt about for words; you also don't have to bother with the rhythms of your sentences, since these phrases are generally so arranged as to be more or less euphonious. When you are composing in a hurry—when you are dictating to a stenographer, for instance, or making a public speech—it is natural to fall into a pretentious, Latinized style. Tags like *a consideration which we should do well to bear in mind* or *a conclusion to which all of us would readily assent* will save many a sentence from coming down with a bump. By using stale metaphors, similes and idioms, you save much mental effort, at the cost of leaving your meaning vague, not only for your reader but for yourself. This is the significance of mixed metaphors. The sole aim of a metaphor is to call up a visual image. When these images clash—as in *The Fascist octopus has sung its swan song, the jackboot is thrown into the melting pot*—it can be taken as certain that the writer is not seeing a mental image of the objects he is naming; in other words he is not really thinking. Look again at the examples I gave at the beginning of this essay. Professor Laski (1) uses five negatives in fifty-three words. One of these is superfluous, making nonsense of the whole passage, and in addition there is the slip *alien* for akin, making further nonsense, and several avoidable pieces of clumsiness which increase the general vagueness. Professor Hogben (2) plays ducks and drakes with a battery which is able to write prescriptions, and, while disapproving of the everyday phrase *put up with,* is unwilling to look *egregious* up in the dictionary and see what it means. (3), if one takes an uncharitable attitude towards it, is simply meaningless: probably one could work out its intended meaning by reading the whole of the article in which it occurs. In (4), the writer knows more or less what he wants to say, but an accumulation of stale phrases chokes him like tea leaves blocking a sink. In (5), words and meaning have almost parted company. People who write in this manner usually have a general emotional meaning—they dislike one thing and want to express solidarity with another—but they are not interested in the detail of what they are saying. A scrupulous writer, in every sentence that he writes, will ask himself at least four questions, thus: What am I trying to say? What words will express it? What image or idiom will make it clearer? Is this image fresh enough to have an effect?

And he will probably ask himself two more: Could I put it more shortly? Have I said anything that is avoidably ugly? But you are not obliged to go to all this trouble. You can shirk it by simply throwing your mind open and letting the ready-made phrases come crowding in. They will construct your sentences for you—even think your thoughts for you, to a certain extent—and at need they will perform the important service of partially concealing your meaning even from yourself. It is at this point that the special connection between politics and the debasement of language becomes clear.

In our time it is broadly true that political writing is bad writing. Where it is not true, it will generally be found that the writer is some kind of rebel, expressing his private opinions and not a "party line." Orthodoxy, of whatever colour, seems to demand a lifeless, imitative style. The political dialects to be found in pamphlets, leading articles, manifestos, White Papers and the speeches of under-secretaries do, of course, vary from party to party, but they are all alike in that one almost never finds in them a fresh, vivid, home-made turn of speech. When one watches some tired hack on the platform mechanically repeating the familiar phrases—*bestial atrocities, iron heel, bloodstained tyranny, free peoples of the world, stand shoulder to shoulder*—one often has a curious feeling that one is not watching a live human being but some kind of dummy: a feeling which suddenly becomes stronger at moments when the light catches the speaker's spectacles and turns them into blank discs which seem to have no eyes behind them. And this is not altogether fanciful. A speaker who uses that kind of phraseology has gone some distance towards turning himself into a machine. The appropriate noises are coming out of his larynx, but his brain is not involved as it would be if he were choosing his words for himself. If the speech he is making is one that he is accustomed to make over and over again, he may be almost unconscious of what he is saying, as one is when one utters the responses in church. And this reduced state of consciousness, if not indispensable, is at any rate favourable to political conformity.

In our time, political speech and writing are largely the defence of the indefensible. Things like the continuance of British rule in India, the Russian purges and deportations, the dropping of the atom bombs on Japan, can indeed be defended, but only by arguments which are too brutal for most people to face, and which do not square with the professed aims of political parties. Thus political language has to consist largely of euphemism, question-begging and sheer cloudy vagueness. Defenceless villages are bombarded from the air, the inhabitants driven out into the countryside, the cattle machine-gunned, the huts set on fire with incendiary bullets: this is called *pacification*. Millions of peasants are robbed of their farms and sent trudging along the roads with no more than they can carry: this is called *transfer of population* or *rectification of frontiers.* People are imprisoned for years without trial, or shot in the back of the neck or sent to die of scurvy in Arctic lumber camps: this is called *elimination of unreliable elements.* Such phraseology is needed if one wants to name things without calling up mental pictures of them. Consider for instance some comfortable English professor defending Russian totalitarianism. He cannot say outright, "I believe in killing off your opponents when you can get good results by doing so." Probably, therefore, he will say something like this:

"While freely conceding that the Soviet régime exhibits certain features which the humanitarian may be inclined to deplore, we must, I think, agree that a certain curtailment of the right to political opposition is an unavoidable concomitant of transitional periods, and that the rigors which the Russian people have been called upon to undergo have been amply justified in the sphere of concrete achievement."

The inflated style is itself a kind of euphemism. A mass of Latin words falls upon the facts like soft snow, blurring the outlines and covering up all the details. The great enemy of clear language is insincerity. When there is a gap between one's real and one's declared aims, one turns as it were instinctively to long words and exhausted idioms, like a cuttlefish squirting out ink. In our age there is no such thing as "keeping out of politics." All issues are political issues, and politics itself is a mass of lies, evasions, folly, hatred and schizophrenia. When the general atmosphere is bad, language must suffer. I should expect to find—this is a guess which I have not sufficient knowledge to verify—that the German, Russian and Italian languages have all deteriorated in the last ten or fifteen years, as a result of dictatorship.

But if thought corrupts language, language can also corrupt thought. A bad usage can spread by tradition and imitation, even among people who should and do know better. The debased language that I have been discussing is in some ways very convenient. Phrases like *a not unjustifiable assumption, leaves much to be desired, would serve no good purpose, a consideration which we should do well to bear in mind,* are a continuous temptation, a packet of aspirins always at one's elbow. Look back through this essay, and for certain you will find that I have again and again committed the very faults I am protesting against. By this morning's post I have received a pamphlet dealing with conditions in Germany. The author tells me that he "felt impelled" to write it. I open it at random, and here is almost the first sentence that I see: "(The Allies) have an opportunity not only of achieving a radical transformation of Germany's social and political structure in such a way as to avoid a nationalistic reaction in Germany itself, but at the same time of laying the foundations of a cooperative and unified Europe." You see, he "feels impelled" to write —feels, presumably, that he has something new to say—and yet his words, like cavalry horses answering the bugle, group themselves automatically into the familiar dreary pattern. This invasion of one's mind by ready-made phrases (*lay the foundations, achieve a radical transformation*) can only be prevented if one is constantly on guard against them, and every such phrase anaesthetizes a portion of one's brain.

I said earlier that the decadence of our language is probably curable. Those who deny this would argue, if they produced an argument at all, that language merely reflects existing social conditions, and that we cannot influence its development by any direct tinkering with words and constructions. So far as the general tone or spirit of a language goes, this may be true, but it is not true in detail. Silly words and expressions have often disappeared, not through any evolutionary process but owing to the conscious action of a minority. Two recent examples were *explore every avenue* and *leave no stone unturned*, which were killed by the jeers of a few journalists. There is a long list of flyblown metaphors which could similarly be got rid of if enough people would interest themselves in the job; and it should also be possible to laugh the *not un-* formation out of existence,[3] to reduce the amount of Latin and Greek in the average sentence, to drive out foreign phrases and strayed scientific words, and, in general, to make pretentiousness unfashionable. But all these are minor points. The defence of the English language implies more than this, and perhaps it is best to start by saying what it does *not* imply.

To begin with it has nothing to do with archaism, with the salvaging of obsolete words and turns of speech, or with the setting up of a "standard English" which must never be departed from. On the contrary, it is especially concerned with the scrapping of every word or idiom which has outworn its usefulness. It has nothing to do with correct grammar and syntax, which are of no importance so long as one makes one's meaning clear, or with the avoidance of Americanisms, or with having what is called a "good prose style." On the other hand it is not concerned with fake simplicity and the attempt to make written English colloquial. Nor does it even imply in every case preferring the Saxon word to the Latin one, though it does imply using the fewest and shortest words that will cover one's meaning. What is above all needed is to let the meaning choose the word, and not the other way about. In prose, the worst thing one can do with words is to surrender to them. When you think of a concrete object, you think wordlessly, and then, if you want to describe the thing you have been visualizing you probably hunt about till you find the exact words that seem to fit. When you think of something abstract you are more inclined to use words from the start, and unless you make a conscious effort to prevent it, the existing dialect will come rushing in and do the job for you, at the expense of blurring or even changing your meaning. Probably it is better to put off using words as long as possible

---

3. One can cure oneself of the *not un-* formation by memorizing this sentence: *A not unblack dog was chasing a not unsmall rabbit across a not ungreen field* [Orwell's note].

and get one's meaning as clear as one can through pictures or sensations. Afterwards one can choose—not simply *accept*—the phrases that will best cover the meaning, and then switch round and decide what impression one's words are likely to make on another person. This last effort of the mind cuts out all stale or mixed images, all prefabricated phrases, needless repetitions, and humbug and vagueness generally. But one can often be in doubt about the effect of a word or a phrase, and one needs rules that one can rely on when instinct fails. I think the following rules will cover most cases:

(i) Never use a metaphor, simile or other figure of speech which you are used to seeing in print.

(ii) Never use a long word where a short one will do.

(iii) If it is possible to cut a word out, always cut it out.

(iv) Never use the passive where you can use the active.

(v) Never use a foreign phrase, a scientific word or a jargon word if you can think of an everyday English equivalent.

(vi) Break any of these rules sooner than say anything outright barbarous.

These rules sound elementary, and so they are, but they demand a deep change of attitude in anyone who has grown used to writing in the style now fashionable. One could keep all of them and still write bad English, but one could not write the kind of stuff that I quoted in those five specimens at the beginning of this article.

I have not here been considering the literary use of language, but merely language as an instrument for expressing and not for concealing or preventing thought. Stuart Chase and others have come near to claiming that all abstract words are meaningless, and have used this as a pretext for advocating a kind of political quietism. Since you don't know what Fascism is, how can you struggle against Fascism? One need not swallow such absurdities as this, but one ought to recognize that the present political chaos is connected with the decay of language, and that one can probably bring about some improvement by starting at the verbal end. If you simplify your English, you are freed from the worst follies of orthodoxy. You cannot speak any of the necessary dialects, and when you make a stupid remark its stupidity will be obvious, even to yourself. Political language—and with variations this is true of all political parties, from Conservatives to Anarchists—is designed to make lies sound truthful and murder respectable, and to give an appearance of solidity to pure wind. One cannot change this all in a moment, but one can at least change one's own habits, and from time to time one can even, if one jeers loudly enough, send some worn-out and useless phrase—some *jackboot, Achilles' heel, hotbed, melting pot, acid test, veritable inferno* or other lump of verbal refuse—into the dustbin where it belongs.

1946

QUESTIONS

1. What is Orwell's pivotal point? Where is it best stated?
2. Discuss Orwell's assertion that "the decline of a language must ultimately have political and economic causes." Is this "clear" as he claims?
3. How can you be sure that a metaphor is dying, rather than alive or dead? Is Orwell's test of seeing it often in print a sufficient one? Can you defend any of his examples of dying metaphors as necessary or useful additions to our vocabularies?
4. Orwell gives a list of questions for the writer to ask himself (pp. 393–394) and a list of rules for the writer to follow (p. 397). Why does he consider it necessary to give both kinds of advice? How much do the two overlap? Are both consistent with Orwell's major ideas expressed elsewhere in the essay? Does his injunction to "break any of these rules sooner than say anything outright barbarous" beg the question?
5. Orwell suggests that if you look back through his essay you will find that he has "again and again committed the very faults" he is protesting against. Is this true? If it is, does it affect the validity of his major points?
6. Words create a personality or confer a character. Describe the personality that would be created by following Orwell's six rules; show that character in action.

Signs of the Times

Wendell Berry

HOME OF THE FREE

I was writing not long ago about a team of Purdue engineers who foresaw that by 2001 practically everything would be done by remote control. The question I asked—because such a "projection" *forces* one to ask it—was, *Where does satisfaction come from?* I concluded that there probably wouldn't be much satisfaction in such a world. There would be a lot of what passes for "efficiency," a lot of "production" and "consumption," but little satisfaction.

What I failed to acknowledge was that this "world of the future" is already established among us, and is growing. Two advertisements that I have lately received from correspondents make this clear, and raise the question about the sources of satisfaction more immediately and urgently than any abstract "projection" can do.

The first is the legend from a John Deere display at Waterloo Municipal Airport:

INTRODUCING SOUND-GARD BODY . . .
A DOWN TO EARTH SPACE CAPSULE.

New Sound-Gard body from John Deere, an "earth space capsule" to protect and encourage the American farmer at his job of being "Breadwinner to a world of families."

Outside: dust, noise, heat, storm, fumes.
Inside: all's quiet, comfortable, safe.

Features include a 4 post Roll Gard, space-age metals, plastics, and fibers to isolate driver from noise, vibration, and jolts. He dials 'inside weather', to his liking . . . he push buttons radio or stereo tape entertainment. He breathes filtered, conditioned air in his pressurized compartment. He has remote control over multi-ton and multi-hookups, with control tower visibility . . . from his scientifically padded seat.

399

The second is an ad for a condominium housing development:

HOME OF THE FREE.

We do the things you hate. You do the things you like. We mow the lawn, shovel the walks, paint and repair and do all exterior maintenance.

You cross-country ski, play tennis, hike, swim, work out, read or nap. Or advise our permanent maintenance staff as they do the things you hate.

Different as they may seem at first, these two ads make the same appeal, and they represent two aspects of the same problem: the widespread, and still spreading, assumption that we somehow have the right to be set free from anything whatsoever that we "hate" or don't want to do. According to this view, what we want to be set free from are the natural conditions of the world and the necessary work of human life; we do not want to experience temperatures that are the least bit too hot or too cold, or to work in the sun, or be exposed to wind or rain, or come in personal contact with anything describable as dirt, or provide for any of our own needs, or clean up after ourselves. Implicit in all this is the desire to be free of the "hassles" of mortality, to be "safe" from the life cycle. Such freedom and safety are always for sale. It is proposed that if we put all earthly obligations and the rites of passage into the charge of experts and machines, then life will become a permanent holiday.

What these people are really selling is insulation—cushions of technology, "space age" materials, and the menial work of other people—to keep fantasy in and reality out. The condominium ad says flat out that it is addressed to people who "hate" the handwork of household maintenance, and who will enjoy "advising" the people who do it for them; it is addressed, in other words, to those who think themselves too good to do work that other people are not too good to do. But it is a little surprising to realize that the John Deere ad is addressed to farmers who not only hate farming (that is, any physical contact with the ground or the weather or the crops), but also hate tractors, from the "dust," "fumes," "noise, vibration, and jolts" of which they wish to be protected by an "earth space capsule" and a "scientifically padded seat."

Of course, the only real way to get this sort of freedom and safety—to escape the hassles of earthly life—is to die. And what I think we see in these advertisements is an appeal to a desire to be dead that is evidently felt by many people. These ads are addressed to the perfect consumers —the self-consumers, who have found nothing of interest here on earth, nothing to do, and are impatient to be shed of earthly concerns. And so I am at a loss to explain the delay. Why hasn't some super salesman sold every one of these people a coffin—an "earth space capsule" in which they would experience no discomfort or inconvenience whatsoever, would have to do no work that they hate, would be spared all extremes of weather and all noises, fumes, vibrations, and jolts?

I wish it were possible for us to let these living dead bury themselves in the earth space capsules of their choice and think no more about them. The problem is that with their insatiable desire for comfort, convenience, remote control, and the rest of it, they cause an unconscionable amount of trouble for the rest of us, who would like a fair crack at living the rest of our lives within the terms and conditions of the real world. Speaking for myself, I acknowledge that the world, the weather, and the life cycle have caused me no end of trouble, and yet I look forward to putting in another forty or so years with them because they have also given me no end of pleasure and instruction. They interest me. I want to see them thrive on their own terms. I hate to see them abused and interfered with for the comfort and convenience of a lot of spoiled people who presume to "hate" the more necessary kinds of work and all the natural consequences of working outdoors.

When people begin to "hate" the life cycle and to try to live outside it and to escape its responsibilities, then the corpses begin to pile up and to get into the wrong places. One of the laws that the world imposes on us is that everything must be returned to its source to be used again. But one of the first principles of the haters is to violate this law in the name of convenience or efficiency. Because it is "inconvenient" to return bottles to the beverage manufacturers, "dead soldiers" pile up in the road ditches and in the waterways. Because it is "inconvenient" to be responsible for wastes, the rivers are polluted with everything from human excrement to various carcinogens and poisons. Because it is "efficient" (by what standard?) to mass-produce meat and milk in food "factories," the animal manures that once would have fertilized the fields have instead become wastes and pollutants. And so to be "free" of "inconvenience" and "inefficiency" we are paying a high price—which the haters among us are happy to charge to posterity.

And what a putrid (and profitable) use they have made of the idea of freedom! What a tragic evolution has taken place when the inheritors of the Bill of Rights are told, and when some of them believe, that "the home of the free" is where somebody else will do your work!

Let me set beside those advertisements a sentence that I consider a responsible statement about freedom: "To be free is precisely the same thing as to be pious, wise, just and temperate, careful of one's own, abstinent from what is another's, and thence, in fine, magnanimous and brave." That is John Milton. He is speaking out of the mainstream of our culture. Reading his sentence after those advertisements is coming home. His words have an atmosphere around them that a living human can breathe in.

How do you get free in Milton's sense of the word? I don't think you can do it in an earth space capsule or a space space capsule or a capsule of any kind. What Milton is saying is that you can do it only by living in this

world as you find it, and by taking responsibility for the consequences of
your life in it. And that means doing some chores that, highly objectionable in anybody's capsule, may not be at all unpleasant in the world.

Just a few days ago I finished up one of the heaviest of my spring jobs:
hauling manure. On a feed lot I think this must be real drudgery even
with modern labor-saving equipment—all that "waste" and no fields to
put it on! But instead of a feed lot I have a small farm—what would
probably be called a subsistence farm. My labor-saving equipment consists of a team of horses and a forty-year-old manure spreader. We forked
the manure on by hand—forty-five loads. I made my back tired and my
hands sore, but I got a considerable amount of pleasure out of it. Everywhere I spread that manure I knew it was needed. What would have been
a nuisance in a feed lot was an opportunity and a benefit here. I enjoyed
seeing it go out onto the ground. I was working some two-year-olds in the
spreader for the first time, and I enjoyed that—mostly. And, since there
were no noises, fumes, or vibrations the loading times were socially
pleasant. I had some help from neighbors, from my son, and, toward the
end, from my daughter who arrived home well rested from college. She
helped me load, and then read *The Portrait of a Lady*[1] while I drove up the
hill to empty the spreader. I don't think many young women have read
Henry James while forking manure. I enjoyed working with my daughter,
and I enjoyed wondering what Henry James would have thought of her.

                                                                    1978

1. Novel by Henry James.

Ada Louise Huxtable

MODERN-LIFE BATTLE: CONQUERING CLUTTER

There are two kinds of people in the world—those who have a horror
of a vacuum and those with a horror of the things that fill it. Translated
into domestic interiors, this means people who live with, and without,
clutter. (Dictionary definition: jumble, confusion, disorder.) The reasons
for clutter, the need to be surrounded by things, goes deep, from security
to status. The reasons for banning objects, or living in as selective and
austere an environment as possible, range from the esthetic to the neurotic. This is a phenomenon of choice that relates as much to the psychiatrist as to the tastemaker.

Some people clutter compulsively, and others just as compulsively
throw things away. Clutter in its highest and most organized form is

called collecting. Collecting can be done as the Collyer brothers[1] did it, or it can be done with art and flair. The range is from old newspapers to Fabergé.[2]

This provides a third category, or what might be called calculated clutter, in which the objets d'art, the memorabilia that mark one's milestones and travels, the irresistible and ornamental things that speak to pride, pleasure and temptation, are constrained by decorating devices and hierarchal principles of value. This gives the illusion that one is in control.

Most of us are not in control. My own life is an unending battle against clutter. By that I do not mean to suggest that I am dedicated to any clean-sweep asceticism or arrangements of high art; I am only struggling to keep from drowning in the detritus of everyday existence, or at least to keep it separate from the possessions that are meant to be part of what I choose to believe is a functional-esthetic scheme.

Really living without clutter takes an iron will, plus a certain stoicism about the little comforts of life. I have neither. But my eye requires a modest amount of beauty and serenity that clutter destroys. This involves eternal watchfulness and that oldest and most relentless of the housewife's occupations, picking up. I have a feeling that picking up will go on long after ways have been found to circumvent death and taxes.

I once saw a home in which nothing had ever been picked up. Daily vigilance had been abandoned a long time ago. Although disorder descends on the unwary with the speed of light, this chaos must have taken years to achieve; it was almost a new decorating art form.

The result was not, as one might suppose, the idiosyncratic disorder of a George Price[3] drawing, where things are hung from pipes and hooks in permanent arrangements of awesome convenience.

This was an expensive, thoughtful, architect-designed house where everything had simply been left where it landed. Pots and pans, linens and clothing, toys and utensils were tangled and piled everywhere, as well as all of those miscellaneous items that go in, and usually out, of most homes. No bare spot remained on furniture or floor. And no one who lived there found it at all strange, or seemed to require any other kind of domestic landscape. They had no hangups, in any sense of the word.

I know another house that is just as full of things, but the difference is instructive. This is a rambling old house lived in for many years by a distinguished scholar and his wife, whose love of the life of the mind and its better products has only been equaled by their love of life.

In this very personal and knowledgeable eclecticism, every shared intellectual and cultural experience led to the accumulation of discover-

1. See p. 568 of Malcolm Cowley's "The View from 80."
2. Peter Carl Fabergé (1846–1920), Russian court jeweler noted for delicate objects in gold and enamel.
3. Cartoonist (1901–　) whose jumbled interiors are typified in the rest of this sentence.

ies, mementos and objets de vertu,[4] kept casually at hand or in unstudied places. Tabletops and floors are thickets of books and overflow treasures. There is enormous, overwhelming, profligate clutter. And everything has meaning, memory and style.

At the opposite extreme is the stripped, instant, homogeneous style, created whole and new. These houses and apartments, always well-published, either start with nothing, which is rare, or clear everything out that the owners have acquired, which must take courage, desperation, or both. This means jettisoning the personal baggage, and clutter, of a lifetime.

I confess to very mixed reactions when I see these sleek and shining couples in their sleek and shining rooms, with every perfect thing in its perfect place. Not the least of my feelings is envy. Do these fashionable people, elegantly garbed and posed in front of the lacquered built-ins with just the right primitive pot and piece of sculpture and the latest exotic tree, feel a tremendous sense of freedom and release? Have they been liberated by their seamless new look?

More to the point, what have they done with their household lares and penates,[5] the sentimental possessions of their past? Did they give them away? Send them to auction galleries and thrift shops? Go on a trip while the decorator cleared them all out? Take a deduction for their memories? Were they tempted to keep nothing? Do they ever have any regrets?

This, of course, is radical surgery. The rest of us resort to more conventional forms of clutter combat. Houses have, or had, attics and cellars. Old apartments provide generous closets, which one fills with things that are permanently inaccessible and unneeded. In the city, there is stolen space, in elevator and service halls. And there is the ultimate catch-all—the house in the country.

Historically, clutter is a modern phenomenon, born of the industrial revolution. There was a time when goods were limited; and the rich and fashionable were few in number and objects were precious and hard to come by. Clutter is a 19th-century esthetic; it came with the abundance of products combined with the rise of purchasing power, and the shifts in society that required manifestations of status and style.

Victorian parlors were a jungle of elaborate furnishings and ornamental overkill. The reforms of the Arts and Crafts movement in the later 19th century only substituted a more "refined" kind of clutter—art pottery, embroidered mottos, handpainted tiles and porcelains, vases of bullrushes and peacock feathers. There were bewildering "artful" effects borrowed from the studio or atelier.

Clutter only became a bad word in the 20th century. The modern movement decreed a new simplicity—white walls, bare floors, and the

4. Art objects, especially if beautiful and rare.

5. Valued household possessions; literally, household gods.

most ascetic of furnishings in the most purified of settings. If ornament was crime, clutter was taboo.

Architects built houses and decorators filled them. Antiques were discovered and every kind of collecting boomed. There were even architects of impeccable modernist credentials—Charles Eames and Alexander Girard—who acquired and arranged vast numbers of toys and treasures. They did so with a discerning eye for the colorful and the primitive that added interest—and clutter—to modern rooms.

Today, clutter is oozing in at a record rate. Architect-collectors like Charles Moore are freewheeling and quixotic in their tastes; high seriousness has been replaced by eclectic whimsy. Nostalgia and fleamarkets coexist on a par with scholarship and accredited antiques. Turning the century on its head, the artifacts of early modernism are being collected by the post-modernist avant-garde. At the commercial level, sophisticated merchandising sells the endless new fashions and products embraced by an affluent consumer society. The vacuum must be filled. And the truth must be told. Our possessions possess us.

1981

Fran Lebowitz

THE SOUND OF MUSIC: ENOUGH ALREADY

First off, I want to say that as far as I am concerned, in instances where I have not personally and deliberately sought it out, the only difference between music and Muzak is the spelling. Pablo Casals[1] practicing across the hall with the door open—being trapped in an elevator, the ceiling of which is broadcasting "Parsley, Sage, Rosemary, and Thyme"—it's all the same to me. Harsh words? Perhaps. But then again these are not gentle times we live in. And they are being made no more gentle by this incessant melody that was once real life.

There was a time when music knew its place. No longer. Possibly this is not music's fault. It may be that music fell in with a bad crowd and lost its sense of common decency. I am willing to consider this. I am willing even to try and help. I would like to do my bit to set music straight in order that it might shape up and leave the mainstream of society. The first thing that music must understand is that there are two kinds of music —good music and bad music. Good music is music that I want to hear. Bad music is music that I don't want to hear.

So that music might more clearly see the error of its ways I offer the

1. Great Spanish cellist.

following. If you are music and you recognize yourself on this list, you are bad music.

1. Music in Other People's Clock Radios

There are times when I find myself spending the night in the home of another. Frequently the other is in a more reasonable line of work than I and must arise at a specific hour. Ofttimes the other, unbeknownst to me, manipulates an appliance in such a way that I am awakened by Stevie Wonder. On such occasions I announce that if I wished to be awakened by Stevie Wonder I would sleep with Stevie Wonder. I do not, however, wish to be awakened by Stevie Wonder and that is why God invented alarm clocks. Sometimes the other realizes that I am right. Sometimes the other does not. And that is why God invented *many* others.

2. Music Residing in the Hold Buttons of Other People's Business Telephones

I do not under any circumstances enjoy hold buttons. But I am a woman of reason. I can accept reality. I can face the facts. What I cannot face is the music. Just as there are two kinds of music—good and bad—so there are two kinds of hold buttons—good and bad. Good hold buttons are hold buttons that hold one silently. Bad hold buttons are hold buttons that hold one musically. When I hold I want to hold silently. That is the way it was meant to be, for that is what God was talking about when he said, "Forever hold your peace." He would have added, "and quiet," but he thought you were smarter.

3. Music in the Streets

The past few years have seen a steady increase in the number of people playing music in the streets. The past few years have also seen a steady increase in the number of malignant diseases. Are these two facts related? One wonders. But even if they are not—and, as I have pointed out, one cannot be sure—music in the streets has definitely taken its toll. For it is at the very least disorienting. When one is walking down Fifth Avenue, one does not expect to hear a string quartet playing a Strauss waltz. What one expects to hear while walking down Fifth Avenue is traffic. When one does indeed hear a string quartet playing a Strauss waltz while one is walking down Fifth Avenue, one is apt to become confused and imagine that one is not walking down Fifth Avenue at all but rather that one has somehow wound up in Old Vienna. Should one imagine that one is in Old Vienna one is likely to become quite upset when one realizes that in Old Vienna there is no sale at Charles Jourdan.[2] And that is why when I walk down Fifth Avenue I want to hear traffic.

4. Music in the Movies

I'm not talking about musicals. Musicals are movies that warn you by saying, "Lots of music here. Take it or leave it." I'm talking about regular movies that extend no such courtesy but allow unsuspecting people to come to see them and then assault them with a barrage of unasked-for tunes. There are two major offenders in this category: black movies and movies set in the fifties. Both types of movies are afflicted with the same misconception. They don't know that movies are supposed to be movies. They think that movies are supposed to be records with pictures. They have failed to understand that if God had wanted records to have pictures, he would not have invented television.

5. Music in Public Places Such as Restaurants, Supermarkets, Hotel Lobbies, Airports, Etc.

When I am in any of the above-mentioned places I am not there to hear music. I am there for whatever reason is appropriate to the respective place. I am no more interested in hearing "Mack the Knife" while waiting for the shuttle to Boston than someone sitting ringside at the Sands Hotel[3] is interested in being forced to choose between sixteen varieties of cottage cheese. If God had meant for everything to happen at once, he would not have invented desk calendars.

Epilogue

Some people talk to themselves. Some people sing to themselves. Is one group better than the other? Did not God create all people equal? Yes, God created all people equal. Only to some he gave the ability to make up their own words.

1978

2. A shoe store in New York City.
3. *shuttle to Boston:* an hourly airline service from New York; *ringside at the Sands Hotel:* near the stage in a famous Las Vegas resort hotel.

QUESTIONS

1. *What is the point of Lebowitz's epilogue?*
2. *How would you describe the personality Lebowitz presents? Maintaining a humorous tone is not easy; how does she do it, or try to do it? What sort of reader would you expect to find her amusing? annoying?*
3. *Lebowitz sometimes employs a device that might be called pseudo-logic—a series of statements that implies a comic conclusion. Pick an*

*example and explain the connections in the reasoning upon which the
success of the device depends.*
4. *Many a true word is spoken in jest. What is the serious substance of
Lebowitz's discussion? Outline a straightforward serious paper on the
same subject.*

Michael J. Arlen

THE LAME DEER

Every so often, some dismal weeks turn up when there seems to be
even less of interest than usual on the TV screen, and little point in being
a so-called critic of television programs, and, indeed, slight social value in
the fact of television itself. Should one, after all, waste time and paper on
composing a polemic against *Hello, Larry?* Or attempt a Jungian analysis
of *Fantasy Island?* Or pay sullen homage to the BBC? Or none of the
above? None of the above, I thought a few days ago, and went off instead
—there being intimations of spring in the air—to spend a day or so with
friends in the country. These friends I have known for fifteen years or
more. Bill is a sculptor of considerable renown, at least among the art
departments of Southwestern banks and Latin-American universities.
His wife, Mary, is a smart, sinewy woman who once climbed Mt. McKin-
ley in her youth (when, she says, it was not so steep), and who has since
raised three children, two of them now off at school and college, and also
found time to develop an innovative instructional program at a nearby
school for the deaf, where she teaches. They are fine people, at once
gentle and stubbornly uncompromising, and I suspect that, despite certain temperamental differences between us, we have liked each other
well over the years because we somehow fill up, or complement, the
blank spaces in each other's sensibilities.

That is, Bill and Mary are irredeemably rural, at least in the modern
manner (their new wood-burning stove, I have noted privately, stands
beside what must surely have been the Shah of Iran's personal collection
of stereo equipment): partial to all things natural, at ease with animals,
and moderately tolerant of, or at least entertained by, my soft and
superficial city ways, and certainly by my occupation of television critic,
which they try to be kind about, though as one might be in the case of a
once promising friend who had gone to medical school only to end up as a
dealer in patent medicine. And I, for my part, while irredeemably citified,
am always warmed by their hospitality and made to feel, after even a
brief stay on their Connecticut hillside, ever so slightly more in touch
with those blessed "basics" that have been eluding me all my life and that

I know will be snatched away again, presumably by the Triborough Bridge toll attendant, as soon as I try to reenter the city.

Indeed, the area of western Connecticut that they live in is as lovely, it seems to me, as any spot in New England. It is a place of small dairy farms, and old wooden fences, and roads without signposts which keep taking you in circles, and villages where the postmaster sells candy bars and potato chips on the side, and streams that look as though they might be fun to fish in if only one liked to fish. Above my friends' house, there is a broad, rough field belonging to a nearby farmer in which for years a half-dozen large, ancient, swaybacked horses have shuffled about like elderly out-of-work stevedores. Below the house, there are some woods: not dark, impenetrable, depressing woods, such as one finds in Maine or in the serious parts of New Hampshire, but green and leafy woods—in summer, that is—full of birch and maple and such, where animals, small and not so small, rustle about, in and out of sight. On the whole, except for Mr. L——, a half mile down the road, who owns a power saw that he exercises on Saturday morning, and Mr. and Mrs. McK——, who board a large male youth, possibly a son, who owns a Kawasaki motorbike of stupefying resonance, it has been a region of relative isolation and tranquillity, where raccoons and porcupines forage in the underbrush and deer occasionally appear right out on the hillside, once barren, that now each springtime blooms with Mary's tulips. Bill and Mary (he from a suburb of Boston, she from Grand Rapids) have become good conservators and groundskeepers. They are proud of their wildlife, of their shared place in the ecology of the hillside. They have become learned about the birds, the permanent constituency as well as the transients. For years, they have bought hay each summer from one of the farmers in order to feed the deer in winter. Sometimes, when the deer have then trampled or eaten too many of the tulips, there has been mild grumbling, followed by inconclusive discussions about wire fencing, but it is clear that Bill and Mary would rather have the deer than the tulips. The deer, as one or the other of them has periodically remarked, were there first, before the house and long before the tulips. The deer are a part of their lives and of their children's lives; in fact, it was largely so that their children might have what they describe as "this natural relationship with wildlife" that my friends moved to their hillside twelve years ago—to the real countryside rather than the artificial suburbs.

But, alas, in recent years, and especially in the past two or three years, even this remote corner of the state has experienced changes—the usual changes: first, a green, windowless factory for manufacturing filtration systems, three miles away; then a shopping center down near the crossroads; then a traffic light on North Street to replace the old flashing yellow beacon, and, of course, more traffic; and then a new "access road" to Route 22, so that the new traffic might have access. To be honest about it, the past few times I have visited Bill and Mary I have noticed a change in their place, too: not so much on their actual property—for their hillside has yet to be "improved"by new construction—but in the feel of the place. What not so long ago felt wild now feels less wild. Last August, for instance, the green and leafy woods were there, as always—to be looked at and listened to and roamed around in as their eight-year-old Jimmy chased after squirrels—but one was aware, through not entirely extrasensory means, that not so very far away (though technically invisible) was rapidly a-building an apparently quite elegant "condominium village" for senior citizens, on the other side of the trees.

This month, when I came out, the condominium village seemed to be completed. Hawthorne Estates is what it's called, perhaps in honor of the famed novelist, who unfortunately died too soon to live there. On the surface, Bill and Mary professed to be taking their new neighbors in stride. "I think they really tried to be careful about the environment," said Bill, and Mary said, "Even a community like this one has to have growth." But clearly their hearts were more than a little broken. We were standing together just outside the kitchen door, looking at the first buds and thinking our various thoughts. I remarked that, from the sound of things in the underbrush, the raccoons and porcupines were as plentiful as ever. "For the time being," said Mary. The number of migrating birds had noticeably lessened, she thought, and one species had simply not appeared.

"Maybe they're late," I said.

Mary said, "They're not late. They had a haven here, a safe place, and people spoiled it, as they usually do—people and their machines and their technology."

What made them saddest of all was what seemed to be happening to the deer population. All winter long, Bill and Mary had put hay out, but only a few deer had shown up, and for one long stretch of three weeks none had shown up. "The senior citizens probably shot them all," said Bill.

Mary said, "That's not funny. You know, we always used to speak of them as our deer, even though I knew they weren't our deer. But now that they're gone, or nearly gone, I feel we've all—especially Jimmy—lost something that was ours, and was priceless."

We went back inside the house—into the large, old-fashioned kitchen, where Mary had some things she was getting ready for dinner. Outside, the light was fading from the sky, now thick with gray-white clouds that hung heavily above the treetops: an autumnal sky. We all felt in need of cheering up. Bill disappeared down the stairs to the basement in search of beer. Mary was slicing carrots with a deft, rhythmic stroke. Suddenly she said, "Look! Look!" I peered with her through the window above the sink. At the edge of the tree line, perhaps two hundred feet away, quite motionless, stood a solitary deer. Then its small, fine head turned, sniffing the air. It took a few short, tactful steps parallel to the tree line, seeming to limp a little as it did, and then stopped. "It's the lame deer," Mary said, in a whisper. "I thought we'd lost it." Then, "Bill, go get Jimmy!"

Bill was still out of sight and hearing, rummaging for beer, so, thinking the moment was an urgent one, I went myself in search of Jimmy. I found him where I thought I might: in what is called the ironing room, watching television. Bill and Mary, I should explain, while not entirely disapproving of television in recent years—at least, not to the the extent of refusing to let it into the house—have nonetheless managed to maintain what I suppose is a certain degree of perverse integrity on the point by permitting only an antiquated, sixteen-inch Zenith (certainly not part of the Shah of Iran's collection), which they have stuck into the small, austere chamber, just off the washer-dryer alcove on the second floor, where Mrs. Cooney sometimes hangs out of a Tuesday or Thursday afternoon, reading the paper, drinking coffee, folding an occasional item of laundry, watching *The Young and the Restless*, but definitely not ironing. Thus, whenever members of the family wish to eat of the forbidden fruit (be it *The MacNeil/Lehrer Report* or *Great Performances*), they must do so in the same austere circumstances: a Presbyterian approach to worship which, as I have vainly pointed out, only emphasizes the basic spirituality of the occasion. "Jimmy," I now said in what I meant to be a sincere voice, "the lame deer is outside on the hill."

Jimmy swiveled his head, as if on ball bearings, and cast a bleary eye at me. "There's sea elephants fighting here," he said.

And so there were. On the Zenith's small and fuzzy screen, two hefty walruslike creatures were battering each other, with noisy grunts, against a picturesque background of rocks and ocean. A narrator's voice, cultivated and slightly European, intoned, "Once again, the age-old ritual of dominance is reenacted among the larger bulls."

"There's a deer outside in the field," I said to Jimmy.

"I've seen the deer," said Jimmy.

And so, together, we watched the sea elephants. Now dozens of them, flopping and waddling around on the beach. "Ungainly on the land," the distinguished-sounding narrator observed, "they are nonetheless uniquely streamlined for life in the ocean." Now babies: strange little blue-black things shaped like Marisol[1] sculptures. "This baby must find a cow willing to nurse him or face certain death," the narrator said gloomily. Now a baby flopping about in the surf. "A baby sea elephant not more than a day or two old struggles to stay afloat," said the narrator.

"Oh, look at that!" said Mary, who had just come into the ironing room. "What are they doing to it?"

1. Venezuelan-American sculptor (1930–   ), known for large, satirical wooden figure groups.

A good question, for at that moment two men, each with a beard and a woolen hat, appeared on the beach and started to wrestle with the baby sea elephant. "Members of the expedition spot him and move in to help," said the narrator as the two men carried the baby sea elephant from the water and dumped it into a group of sea elephants on the sand. "The milk the pups consume—estimated at half a gallon a day—is extremely rich in fat," said the narrator.

Mary said, "Imagine that."

And so it went. The sea elephants, both small and large, waddled and flopped about on the beach. Some grunted. Some swam in the water. The distinguished-sounding narrator—a learned but invisible presence on the remote and rock-strewn beach—spoke to us with a subtle mixture of charm and scientific detachment: "This old bull swims with an apparent lack of effort, yet he is capable of diving to a depth of one thousand feet and can suspend breathing for five minutes before coming up for air."

"That's extraordinary," said Bill, who had also come into the room, carrying a six-pack of beer.

"Five minutes isn't long," said Jimmy. "The humpback whale can stay down for forty-five minutes."

The assembled sea elephants now grew even noisier. "Responding to the seductive calls of the females," said the narrator, "a bull heads into the frenzy of mating."

Enormous sea elephants now crashed and bumped about on the beach. One huge creature, doubtless a bull, slumped peacefully over a rock, looking something like a beanbag chair.

In the half darkness of the room, I was aware of the three other faces watching the television screen. At first, I was struck by a certain obvious irony in the situation. Here we were, after all, gathered in this windowless room watching filmed scenes of distant animals while actual animals wandered about in the fields below, begging for attention. I wondered what had happened to the lame deer on the hillside, and guessed the unbeguiling answer. It had vanished as quickly and discreetly as it had arrived; nor, it occurred to me, had it been exactly begging for attention. I thought: in any case, there will be other deer coming to the hillside, to eat the hay or the tulips, to visit, to be part of Jimmy's priceless heritage. And then I thought: perhaps not, or perhaps not for long; certainly not forever.

I remembered, long ago, as a child of more or less Jimmy's age, visiting, with my mother, some of her kinfolk who lived in the French countryside. There was a large, cold, stone house; fireplaces and fires; snow on the fields and trees. One afternoon of a slow December day, my grandfather and I went on a jaunt together, up the hill back of the house, across endless fields, through woods where pine branches spilled snow on our heads. He was a tall, white-haired gentleman of few words, and wore knickerbockers, as I remember, and immense boots. At last, we came

through the woods and into a clearing. The sky was piercing blue. There
was another stand of dark trees on the horizon, about a mile away. On our
journey, some snow had got in between my socks and my boots, for the
boots were borrowed from a cousin and were much too large, and now I
tried to squidge my feet around inside the boots without attracting
attention. I felt my grandfather's hand on my shoulder and stopped
squidging my feet. He was pointing across the clearing, to the right.
Perhaps two dozen deer were crossing the snowy field: dark, delicate
animals with spindly legs. And now, breaking off from the herd, a large
stag came toward us. He stopped not far from where we stood. I remember him as huge, with flowering antlers; he seemed to float above the
snow. He stood there for I don't know how long, staring, it seemed, at my
old grandfather, and my grandfather stared at him, and then the stag
moved away, drifting back to the herd, and led the herd slowly across the
clearing and into the fastness of the woods, and then my grandfather
turned me about and we trudged home. Ten years later, after the war,
with my grandfather dead, and the woods cleared to make way for an
army supply depot, and with the old stone house sold to an executive of a
nearby chemical company, we went back there briefly to pick up some
things, though what things I can't recall. I remember my grandfather's
hunting trophies—mounted heads of deer and mountain sheep,   and
even one water buffalo—lying in a jumble on the floor of an empty room.
"He loved hunting," my mother said. "He could have taught you a lot
about it." I was eighteen at the time and full of sensibility, and those
dusty animal heads seemed to me quite horrible and wasteful; I felt
ashamed for my grandfather. But in due course a stronger memory took
over: a residue of the emotion I had been aware of in that long-ago winter
meeting between the old hunter and the stag, standing in the snow. It was
nothing, I imagine, so sentimental as love of wildlife, for there had been
too much killing for much love to have survived, but, rather—so I like to
think, anyway—the mysterious fellow-feeling (that doubtless does not
exclude either love or fear or wonder) of one earthly species for another.

In fact, in the end, it seems to me that it is this deep fellow-feeling that
transcends all the obvious and commonplace ironies of man's recent
relationships with animals, whether the relationship occurs nobly or
murderously (depending on one's current point of view), as it is said to
occur between hunters and their quarry; or awkwardly and trivially, as
generally happens when a city parent takes a city child to observe the
despondent inhabitants of the local zoo; or somewhat pompously, in a
manner redolent of utilitarianism and scientific super-ego, as in the
current vogue for subjecting animals to scientific study on behalf of
humankind. It is as if man still could not get rid of animals from his soul,
though he has killed them for his food and exploited them for his work
and made amusements of them for his sport, and steadily reduced their

territories through the growth of his own territories, and implacably
reduced their population by the enlargement of his own population.
Each step along the path that he has taken in his push to reduce the
wilderness seems to have brought with it a counterstep, so to speak
—never, of course, adequate to what has been taken away but expressive,
often in bizzare and unlikely ways, of the guilt and loss he appears to feel
for the "others." For instance, after the Americans had stripped the
buffalo from the plains (as Neil Harris[2] has pointed out), they created a
strange modern totem to the power of the vanished beasts in the form of
Buffalo Bill Cody and his hugely popular Wild West show. And, at a
time when the white man was beginning to impose his will in earnest
upon the "dark continent" of Africa and its wildlife, the totemic figure of
Tarzan was created, speaking to us of a land whose animalism was
supposedly so potent that it could transform an English gentleman into
an ape (or, at least, a half ape) in a few years; and, later, King Kong, whose
primitive power was supposedly nearly equal to that of a modern state (at
any rate, minus its air force). And all the while, the strange, haunted,
sometimes brutal, sometimes well-meaning process of the ghettoization
of wild animal life has continued. First, after the advanced peoples
cleared their own territories of wildlife, came the zoos and menageries
and animal shows of the last century. Then, as the advanced peoples
pushed farther into remote territories, notably into Africa, came the
segregation of those animals in areas where they might be hunted. Then,
as the number of huntable animals was dangerously reduced, and as the
number of transportable, nonhunting, animal-interested tourists increased, came the establishment of nonhunting (or photo-safari) ghettos.
Indeed, many, perhaps most, nations, recognizing the impossibility or
inadvisability of wild animals continuing to run wild, have erected their
own animal ghettos, be they, as in this country, large and government-
operated, like Yellowstone National Park, or small and commercial, like
Sea World or Marineland. There are ghettos now for waterfowl, for
alligators, for elk, for sea otters; although, as in the case of human ghettos,
many of the animal ghettos are under increasing pressure from the rising
numbers and commercial demands of the surrounding populations. According to recent reports, for instance, the clam diggers in California are
up in arms against the protected sea otters off Pismo Beach; in Kenya,
farmers, both black and white, are putting pressure on the government
to do something about the obstreperous elephants in the Tsavo game
park, which have been breaking out of the park and trampling farmland
underfoot. Thus, finally, it seems, not so much owing to his wisdom
(which is not greatly to be relied on in these matters) as perhaps in
response to these age-old and persistent stirrings in his soul, man, who

2. American historian (1938–   ), author of *The Artist in American Society*.

apparently cannot do *without* wild animals and cannot live *with* them, has devised the last animal ghetto: the television zoo.

Or so I thought, watching the sea elephants cavorting on Bill and Mary's television screen, and so I have thought since, remembering the beauty and oddity, however "distanced" by camera lens or electronic transmission, of the many images of wildlife that I have seen on other television screens. In some ways, doubtless, it is not such a great accomplishment. Man has killed off most of the wildlife on the planet, so now he dispatches little bands of TV explorers to remote islands or far-off rain forests, from which they return with images of wildlife, which they can bring to us at home. We stay put; the zoo comes to visit. Still, in other ways—and not unimportant ways, either—the new process seems but another link in what one rather hopes is a neverending chain of man's attempts to deal with not only his presence but the implications of his presence on this planet. I even thought (mindful that in the stern temple of the ironing room such a thought might be construed as close to blasphemy by my hosts) that television itself, despite its frequent trashiness and steady banality, may perhaps be already serving as a socializing (dare one say civilizing?) force, in ways that modern peoples can so far scarcely imagine.

At any rate, on the rocky island of the sea elephants, our TV explorers were winding up their activities, and trying to have the last word, as usual. One of the bearded and wool-hatted men advanced along the beach, carrying a loudspeaker that was emitting sounds that seemed to be driving the sea elephants into the water. "The noise of the loudspeaker is regarded as a threat by the bulls," explained the distinguished narrator. Then there were some beautiful sequences of sea elephants swimming underwater: giant Marisol sculptures gliding through the deep. Then, above water, a parting shot of the rocky island and of the sea elephants once again flopping around in the surf, as the narrator, no stranger to the poetic impulse, declaimed, "We salute you, our ancient cousin of the sea!" Soon afterward, the zoo closed for the night.

Somebody switched on a light in the room; it had grown dark outside.

"I want to see the deer," Jimmy said.

"The deer left," said Mary. "But don't worry—he'll be back."

"I wasn't worried," said Jimmy, who may even be right, for the time being.

1979

Edward Bunker

LET'S END THE DOPE WAR:
A JUNKIE'S VIEW OF THE QUAGMIRE

The United States has no choice but eventually to abandon its "war" on heroin addiction and adopt the so-called English system, which allows designated physicians to prescribe, under careful regulation and monitoring, maintenance doses of any narcotic except heroin, usually morphine or methadone, to registered addicts. Until a few years ago, physicians also prescribed heroin, but a slight rise in figures (it turned out to be false) changed that; now the heroin is dispensed from clinics. England isn't alone; nearly all Western European nations allow doctors to treat addicts with narcotics. None has a social problem with addiction; none has a crime rate gone berserk because of narcotics. European authorities believe that the United States created its own problem and tenaciously exacerbates it through collective delusions.

At the turn of the century, when opium, morphine and heroin were cheaper than aspirin and sold in more places, and when every male alcoholic was matched by a female drug addict, it was cause for a few clucks of sympathy when a family member was hooked, but no stigma was involved. We had 200,000 addicts in a population of 78 million, all of them living normally. Physicians gave opium and its derivatives for every sickness and every symptom. Even the temperance fanatics saw little wrong with it, by comparison to the demon rum.

Had anyone suddenly announced that henceforth addicts would be denied narcotics, there would have been public uproar. We stumbled into our present situation a little at a time. A Hague conference on international affairs, a precursor to the League of Nations and United Nations, drafted an agreement among nations to regulate and reduce the unrestrained international traffic of opium and its derivatives. This had nothing to do with addiction in Europe or the United States; it had to do with England flooding China with Indian opium that the Chinese didn't want. As an outgrowth of that, governments decided that narcotics should no longer be sold like gumdrops.

It was at that point that England and the United States diverged. We planted the seed of the tree of disaster that we are now harvesting, whereas England realized that trying to eradicate addiction would just create illegal traffic. The British had the benefit of having watched similar attempts in Asia in the nineteenth century. They also didn't want to make criminals of citizens who had a sickness. So the opium-laced patent medicines were taken away, morphine and heroin no longer sold to anyone, but there was never any question of depriving addicts of a supply—especially after the British saw what was happening in the United States. Strict laws against smuggling and trafficking were put in force, but these haven't been used very often. Registered addicts got their supply of pharmaceutical quality narcotics as they would any other routine, inexpensive medicine. Way back then England had, proportionate to its population, slightly fewer addicts than the United States. The figures held steady for a decade, and then slowly fell as older addicts died without contaminating others. Now England has about 3,000, 70 percent of whom are employed, pay taxes, and live at least as normally as diabetics on insulin. The streets of London are safe to walk at night.

The United States went the other way. We would not merely stop the spread of addiction to future generations, we would stamp it out forthwith. The first shot of the "war" was the Harrison Narcotic Act of 1914, which on its face curtails open distribution but seems to leave the question of treating addicts to doctors. The medical profession, which had and still has the highest rate of addiction of any profession, began to care for addicts in their sickness. Clinics were opened, private physicians wrote prescriptions. Then the United States Supreme Court, handing down the decision that has caused all the trouble, ruled that physicians could not give addicts any narcotics. Instantly the illicit traffic sprang up, though for several years the price was such that an addict could maintain his habit by working. The international and domestic racketeers didn't visualize what the traffic would bear, so where a legal daily dose had cost 15¢ it now cost 50¢. Throughout the 1930s the number of addicts remained about the same in both England and the United States. It has never been a big thing to be an addict in England. The most the English feel is slight pity; more stigma is attached to being an alcoholic. By the same token, there's no mystique, no sense of flirting with danger, which is an element that attracts youth here.

Addiction began to rise slightly in New York City in the years just before World War II, but during the war years the problem nearly disappeared. International routes were closed and synthetic narcotics were not yet being produced—the Germans were developing them—in sufficient quantity to reach the underground market. In 1946 addiction in the United States reached its lowest point in recent decades: 20,000 junkies, most of them in New York. There, too, was where the postwar traffic got its first hold.

By the time Dwight Eisenhower took office in 1953 the number of addicts had increased to 50,000 and another "war" was declared. Congress passed the Jones-Miller law, requiring mandatory minimum sentences of ten years (no probation, no parole) for possession, sale, transporting of any amount of heroin, cocaine or marijuana. It was all the same in those days. Sentences of fifty years (no parole) were common. In the decades since Jones-Miller became law, addiction has increased geometrically: 50,000 addicts in 1953, 150,000 in 1965, 560,000 in 1975. California, especially in Los Angeles, has always had a few addicts because of its proximity to the Mexican border. The 1950 estimate was 1,000, and when it started to rise soon thereafter the legislature began writing tougher laws. In the next decade the statutes were changed several times, culminating in 1961 with sentences whereby anyone with a prior conviction (one joint was enough) who was caught with any usable amount of heroin (even half a gram) received a mandatory fifteen-year-to-life sentence—fifteen years before being eligible for parole. Addiction in Los Angeles is now 60,000.

When he was appointed President, Gerald Ford declared his war on dope, asking for three-year minimum terms for traffickers. Clearly, penalties are not the answer, but we don't seem to learn very fast.

There's a parable about lilies in a pond that double every day, but nobody notices the danger that they will cover everything because the pond is still half clear on the last day. With drug addiction we are nearing the last day: it has increased by a factor of twenty-eight—from 20,000 to 560,000—in thirty years. This wildfire growth has been in the face of relentless attack and Draconian sentences.[1] Yet a Drug Enforcement Agency official in California, when asked his opinion of heroin maintenance, deplored it, saying that all we need is tougher penalties and more money for enforcement.

Everyone recognizes that 90 percent of addicts are forced to commit crimes to maintain their expensive habits. Street crime *is* addict crime. The actual cost of manufacturing a gram of pure heroin—enough to maintain an addict for at least one day, perhaps two or three—is around 10¢. That's the cost if it were dispensed by a physician and if nobody made a profit. The illicit price is $100, for which the junkie must steal $300 in merchandise, one-third of retail value being par for hot goods. At least 50 percent of property crimes are committed by addicts, and the recent spread of crime to suburbs and small towns seems to correspond with heroin addiction leaping the tracks from the ghetto and barrio. Now such places as Eugene and Medford, Ore., Tacoma, Wash., and Redding, Calif. have heroin addicts—and their crimes. Twenty years ago Seattle had no addicts; now it has 16,000. Santa Barbara, Calif. once jailed all its known addicts for a couple of months. It was probably unlawful, but burglaries dropped 55 percent. Upon the arrival of limited methadone maintenance in San Francisco, property crimes went down 20 percent. The *Los Angeles Times* recently reported the arrest of a young junkie who admitted 250 residence burglaries in fifteen months to pay for a $200

1. After Draco, an Athenian lawgiver of the seventh century B.C., whose code of laws was extremely harsh. His name means "the dragon."

a day habit, crimes committed not to live regally without work but to keep away from sweating, stomach cramps, vomiting, diarrhea and worse. According to outdated figures (pre-inflation) the average addict spends $8,000 a year on heroin; he also must eat and sleep. Multiply that by 560,000, add billions in law enforcement, institutions and lost taxes. Finally, look ahead to what the crime rate will be in ten years if addiction keeps spreading at even a fraction of the present rate.

That's just the economics; it doesn't include human misery beyond reckoning—not because of addiction per se but because of the life our twentieth-century leper is forced to live. The United States and the addict are locked in a weird dance of flagellation,[2] one through helplessness, the other because it clings to the concept of a "war." As in any war, demagogic propaganda drives out detached thought. The myths of drug addiction have become accepted reality. Even the Supreme Court, citadel of reason, has succumbed. In a case dealing with criminal sanctions to be levied merely for the *status* of being an addict, the Court called addicts "living dead" and "zombies." When you know that the only way to tell if someone is using heroin is by urinalysis it's hard to visualize a zombie. One of the "living dead" was a founder of Johns Hopkins. An addict from his 20s to his death, he was the greatest surgeon of the era (he fixed before putting on his gloves) and developed asepsis[3] in surgical technique. He didn't become emaciated, sunken-eyed and sallow because he was a doctor and had morphine available. Hermann Goering was a monster but hardly a zombie even after twenty years of morphine.

The medical reality of narcotic addiction is that fifty years of the heaviest imaginable habit will have no deleterious effect whatsoever on heart, liver, lungs, kidneys, cardiovascular or respiratory systems. It *might* affect calcium balance; so does milk. It might even contribute to longevity because it's the ultimate tranquilizer. The image of the scarecrow is appropriate, but that's because of the awful life society forces the addict to live. An addict is indeed enslaved. Nothing else matters when his habit must be satisfied, and his are the labors of Sisyphus.[4] When he gets his drug he is "normal," though probably less ambitious and driving than is thought ideal in the Protestant ethic.

The enslavement alone would justify the relentless war—if war could cure the addict or stop the traffic. Alas, half a century of this conflict has had precisely the opposite result. War has made selling narcotics in the United States the most lucrative business in the world. With so much money being made both from the traffic and the battle against it, wealthy and ruthless men have a vested interest in maintaining the status quo. To the big trafficker each invested dollar returns a hundred overnight—and

2. The practice of averting divine vengeance through self-punishment by whipping.
3. The boiling of surgical instruments to prevent infection from germs.

4. A mythical Greek figure condemned to the unending task of rolling a huge boulder up a hill.

the growth rate is faster than IBM's, because the frenzied street junkie wants to reduce the pressure, and the one way to do it is to get a couple of customers and become a pusher. Nobody could push dope in Europe. Why should an addict buy from a pusher when he can get a prescription and go to a drugstore?

The "war" has been on two fronts for a long time, and a third has been recently added. The first has been the campaign to cure the addict, usually while he's confined, but in the last decade with community programs as well. All are total failures, so much so that the bureaucrats administering them cannot allow thorough follow-up studies, lest the public scream at the gross waste of money. Synanon, the famed therapeutic community, claims just 10 percent success among those who stay two years, and they are but a fraction of those who enter. And Synanon deals with motivated persons. New York conducted a three-year follow-up on 247 adolescent addicts who had been treated in a heavily staffed, extremely expensive program. The young junkies were given group and private therapy and counseling, remedial education, vocational training and aid on release. The failure rate was 100 percent. Of the 247, eight were out of jail and drug-free—but when interviewed each claimed never to have been an addict. They'd been busted with dope on them and sent for treatment, which was better than jail.

Civil commitment programs in California and New York are expensive and useless. Ten years ago Congress established the Narcotic Addict Rehabilitation Act, and the Bureau of Prisons has NARA programs in many of its institutions. Under NARA, addicts convicted of nonviolent federal crimes are committed for treatment. All NARA does is provide a lot of $20,000-a-year jobs for sociologists. The NARA director at Terminal Island, Calif., has not produced one cured junkie after ten years and 1,000 commitments. On the other hand, it's easy to produce scores who have become addicts at Terminal Island. Indeed, wardens at Terminal Island, McNeil Island, Atlanta and elsewhere have declared the drug problem in prison insoluble. That raises an interesting question: if the federal government cannot control narcotics in federal prisons, how can it be controlled in the whole United States?

Addicts call themselves "dope fiends," and it fits. They live unimaginably mean lives, on the whole. They call it "running," and that, too, fits. A frantic cycle of stealing something, selling it, finding the connection and finally getting fixed. If they are lucky there's enough for a day or two, but usually in an hour they're running again. Unless they can become dealers the Damoclean sword[5] of getting sick hangs perpetually overhead, and the stays of execution are but a few hours at a time. Often they

5. Damocles, a Syracusan courtier of the fourth century B.C., found himself at a sumptuous banquet seated under a naked sword suspended from a single thread, symbolizing the precariousness of power.

hit the street during withdrawals, ready to do anything to relieve the agony.

Sooner or later—and often—a junkie goes to jail, where he usually has to kick cold turkey. "Kick" because that's what he does, jerking his legs for sleepless days; "cold turkey" because waves of goose bumps torment his body. After he kicks, he may spend months or years in jail or prison. Nonetheless, within hours, days or weeks of release he'll be inexorably drawn back to sticking a needle in his arm, knowing what his life is going to be, knowing he'll again find himself puking and shitting on himself on a jail floor.

Why do they do it? Theories are abundant, mostly psychological, but I believe that once a person has been fully hooked a permanent biochemical change takes place, and that once a body adapts, it is never again normal without narcotics. Though studies on that aspect of the problem are few, it's well known that a nonaddict can be given liberal doses of narcotics for ten days or longer with no discomfort when the medication is stopped, whereas an addict suffers mild symptoms after two days, and after a week will be fully sick. His body chemistry has changed. Whatever the cause, there is no cure. For all statistical purposes, once a junkie always a junkie.

If anything in this war has proven a greater failure than curing addicts, it is the second campaign of stopping the traffic. Half a century of unrelenting crackdown has achieved nothing. Every President since Truman has declared a new jihad[6] on the dealers of death, but all street pushers are dope fiends and nothing will dissuade them. They can't help themselves. The middle level of the distribution network is hard to penetrate, and so much money can be made that there will never be a shortage of persons eager to try their luck, no matter what the penalties. I know a 23-year-old ex-G.I. who flew into Hong Kong with $1,400 in his pocket. He bought a pound of #4 White Dragon Pearl heroin, broke it into tiny lumps and wrapped them in three layers of condom, tying them into little balls. These he swallowed. He put the rest in his colon. He failed the "smuggler profile" at customs, but the rigorous search revealed nothing. Would you advocate stomach pumps and enemas for anyone who *might* be a smuggler? He sold the load for $22,000. He could have made $150,000 if he'd diluted it to street quality and retailed it. He repeated the journey several times, taking another G.I. with him. In one year he had made enough to live like a prince forever in Mexico. That's where he is now.

The criminal syndicates, national and international (especially the latter), are invulnerable to arrest and prosecution. In some places the

6. A religious war.

kingpin traffickers and the rulers are one and the same. We look foolish to the world as we struggle in the net that tightens just because we struggle.

As for stopping the smuggling, a half-minute of thought about what that entails should get it crossed off the list of possibilities. Moreover, when customs boasts of seizing 5 kilos of pure heroin worth, say, $3 million, the impression conveyed is that somewhere Fu Manchu[7] is gnashing his teeth at this tremendous loss, or that somewhere addicts are falling into convulsions because the supply is cut off (why should that make anyone happy?). But $1 million was street value; Fu Manchu lost, perhaps, $15,000 and is in no danger of going bankrupt. The addict, it is true, may pay a little more, since dealers will take advantage of the alleged "shortage."

The third and newest campaign of the war is the attempt to curtail the growth of opium. Last December, President Ford announced that he'd consulted with the Chiefs of State of Colombia, Turkey and Mexico on the matter and elicited promises of cooperation in return for financing. Rep. Peter Rodino (D., N.J.) followed up the President's announcement with a proposal that we cut off aid to all noncooperative countries. Both men were either making political hay (narcotics is always good for that) or they don't understand the realities. Colombia grows no opium. Turkey had an agreement to stop raising it, but reneged after a year (during which there was no heroin shortage) because our compensation wasn't enough to repay the Turkish opium farmers for abandoning the crop. We let it go without a whimper.

As for Mexico, the central government is willing to help as long as we give enough millions to subsidize the effort, but Mexico isn't like the United States; Mexico City has only limited control in the hinterland, where the attitude is that our approach to drug addiction is hilariously stupid and that selling narcotics for U.S. consumption is no sin. In the mountains of Sinaloa where the opium grows, as soon as you leave the cities conditions have changed little since Pancho Villa.[8] When the government wants to go into the mountains it has to send troops. According to some Mexican dealers that's what the government has been doing recently. Opium fields are being burned and dealers arrested or killed. Virtually all of Mexico's crude brown heroin is for the U.S. market, where the wholesale price has gone up 40 percent since August 1975.

Before rejoicing, note that Mexico's production is picayune, perhaps 1 percent of the world supply. Ford neglected to mention the so-called Golden Triangle of Burma, Laos and Thailand, where 70 percent of the world's illicit opium grows, enough to supply 15 million addicts. In those jungle mountains the clans and tribes that grow opium neither know nor care what country they are in. They do know that they have all the guns in the area. Growing and selling opium is their way of life.

7. Fictional Oriental villain.   8. Mexican bandit leader (1877–1923).

Afghanistan and Pakistan also grow a lot of opium, though so far it hasn't been needed in the illicit pipeline. In fact, there's a lot of opium to curtail. Just 3 square miles of poppies can supply the U.S. market nicely. And even if there's a worldwide shortage, the American market will be the last to feel it because we pay 100 times more than anyone else.

Finally, matters would change only for the worse if every opium poppy in the world keeled over and died. Too many fortunes are at stake not to have contingency plans, and those are to manufacture the synthetics, such as dolphine, blue-morphan and dilaudid, which are more addictive than the real thing. Dilaudid, the oldest synthetic, is preferred to heroin by many addicts, and except for its stronger "rush" when injected is hard to differentiate from heroin. The chemical process is no more difficult than that of converting morphine base into heroin, or making LSD or speed. The base of the synthetic opiates is coal tar. Do we next try to curtail the world's supply of coal tar?

We cannot cure addicts and we cannot stop the traffic. Sooner or later, now or when the 560,000 junkies become 2 million, we are going to change our system and allow addicts to have regulated doses of narcotics, including heroin. Methadone has paved the way, showing that the world won't collapse if addicts are allowed what they need as critically as diabetics need insulin. Methadone programs are not without their own problems but, for those on them, they are the most effective therapy thus far attempted. Addicts who have spent years stealing or in jail suddenly get jobs and pay taxes because they can drink a glass of methadone and Tang every day. More than 80 percent are employed. True, some are still criminals, and a few sell part of their ration, but methadone is a viable program—or would be if the bureaucrats hadn't gotten in. It reaches only a minuscule percentage; in Los Angeles, for example, 2,000 out of 60,000, and even that is threatened because taxpayers rightfully resent spending $7 a day to give narcotics to a dope fiend. When you consider that methadone costs 10¢ per dose, plus 15¢ for the glass of Tang, it looks as though someone is doing nicely. The markup isn't nearly that of illicit heroin—6¢ to $100—but it's too much for the taxpayer and too much for the majority of addicts. We need a cheaper method of distribution.

Nor will methadone alone do the job. Too many addicts dislike it. Younger addicts still want the "rush" of a fix. And some people gain excessive weight on methadone, 40 or 50 pounds, while others become so somnolent that they can't do anything but doze in front of the television. Some are afraid of methadone because the withdrawal is much worse than that of heroin. Its main good points are that it can be taken orally, eliminating hepatitis and infection, and requires just one dose a day, compared to heroin's three or four.

What we must do, and will do despite the screams of law-enforcement officers and others, is register all addicts, determine the daily maintenance dose for each individual (some addicts in England use both methadone and heroin) and issue ration cards that allow the individual to buy that much each day in drugstores. Methadone clinics already allow most patients to take home enough for several days. Some if it will be resold, but no junkie is going to cut himself short. Pushers will disappear. We'd still have a lot of addict-citizens, but not many addict-criminals. You might even be able to walk in Central Park at night. The cost would be virtually nothing—and would save billions.

What can we lose by trying it for a year? Nothing else has worked. It would do nothing for today's addicts, except allow them to live normal lives. It might save the children.

1977

QUESTIONS

1. *Bunker states his thesis within the first paragraph of his essay. What are the advantages and disadvantages of stating it so early in the essay?*
2. *The subtitle tells you that Bunker himself has had experience as a drug addict. Could you tell from the essay if he hadn't said so? How has this affected the way he presents his case? How does it affect your assessment of that case?*
3. *Bunker might have given his essay a title like "Let's Treat Addicts Sensibly." Why instead does he use the term "war"? Where in the essay does he follow up on the metaphor of a war?*
4. *Bunker uses a number of other metaphors: "governments decided that narcotics should no longer be sold like gumdrops"; the lilies in the lily pond "that double every day, but nobody notices the danger that they will cover everything because the pond is still half clear on the last day"; the addict who must perform "the labors of Sisyphus" and has "the Damoclean sword of getting sick . . . perpetually overhead"; to name some of them. Examine each of these metaphors and any others you find in the essay and explain the part that each plays in developing Bunker's argument. How does metaphor help to supplement the factual information Bunker presents?*
5. *Write an essay on a similar social problem that we have tried to solve through confrontation. Title your essay "Let's End the ———— War" or "Let's End the War of ————." Possible subjects might vary from the generation gap to prostitution to school truancy.*

Carolyn G. Heilbrun

THREE CHANGES

Nostalgia holds no temptations for me; it is an emotion to which I am happily a stranger. I knew once of a woman who, asked if she kept a diary, replied that in her opinion, once a day was done it was done, and the hell with it. I agree. If I look back at all, it is with thankfulness for what has changed. I'm not making great claims for today's world—who could? —but in many ways it is a lot better than when I was young. Though my vocabulary is sometimes antique—is there anyone else who still refers to the ice box and the Victrola, in an age of self-defrosting refrigerators and automatic record changers?—I harbor no longing for the past.

Three changes to which I have borne personal witness between the days of my youth and the year 1981 seem to me grounds for rejoicing. In each case an "impossibility" of my childhood has been transformed into the manifestly possible, and each makes me sharply happy.

We may begin with biographies of women. I was already a compulsive reader when I first moved, as a child, to New York City. It was in the depths of the Depression, and if one must live through a depression, one does well to be a compulsive reader. This was before the days of paperbacks, and my weekly allowance, in any case, was a dime. I used the St. Agnes Branch of the public library on Amsterdam Avenue.

Until I went away to college, that was mostly where I found books, and the books I mostly read were biographies. I thought of this recently while reading Tom Stoppard's play *Travesties*. There is a librarian in that play called Cecily, whose knowledge of everything is eccentric, being based on alphabetical precedence. She is working her way through the shelves, and has got to G. So I worked my way through biographies at the St. Agnes Branch. I was disciplined and did not allow myself to stray from Henry Adams to Lincoln Steffens, who I suspected was more appealing.

What I could not have found, however, even if I had strayed alphabetically, were biographies of women, at least not of women whose fame did not depend on their connection to some notable or notorious man. There was not even a biography of St. Agnes, whoever she was. I was doubly constrained, by the alphabet and by the sex of all the subjects.

Need I document the glories I would meet today, standing before the biography section? Biographies of women lie about me now, as they did not in my childhood, and if a girl today wants to read the life of a woman who achieved or struggled or was acclaimed or neglected, she can. I call that an improvement.

When I was not reading in my youth, I was being athletic. A girl athlete, in those days, was neither prized nor, beyond a certain point, encouraged. Until puberty we played with the boys, which was not bad. But once in high school, I took up "girls' basketball." Can there be another woman of my age who remembers with as profound frustration as I do the game to which we were then relegated? It was a "feminine" version of what the boys played, designed to protect the weaker sex from too great exertions. Players were confined to only half of the court. If one was a guard, she guarded; only the forwards might shoot baskets. There was no dribbling; one bounce at a time was permitted, no more. Boys' basketball was the game worth watching.

Today, girls play by boys' rules everywhere, I am told, but my particular delight, my exercise in reverse nostalgia, consists in watching women's professional basketball. They play by National Basketball Association rules, the rules the New York Knicks play by, and no one fears that their female paraphernalia will come unhinged as they dash across the full court, dribbling the ball all the way. Any one of them can shoot, and some of them, like Carol Blazjowski, known as The Blaze, shoot remarkably.

Women's professional basketball, however, is not an easy game to find in these parts. For one blissful season we had the New York Stars, coached by a former Knick player, Dean Meminger, and I used to go and cheer in Madison Square Garden. Then the Stars were gone, no one could tell me where, or why, or when. But recently I was taken, in celebration of my birthday, to the West Orange Arena to watch the New Jersey Gems, for whom some of the old Stars now play. I felt as Dickens must have felt when he bought the big house he had dreamed of owning in his youth, as Satchel Paige must have felt when blacks made it into major-league baseball. I had always known women could play real basketball, but when I was young they said no, never in our time.

There was one other thing nobody believed any girl could do when I was in school, and that was make a million dollars. Marry it or inherit it, well maybe—but make it? Never. Women didn't make millions unless they became movie stars, and we knew none of us could do that because you had to be discovered in a Hollywood soda fountain, and none of us could get to Hollywood.

As it turned out, however, one of us got there, and made millions of dollars, though not by being a movie star. What she did was, she wrote *Scruples* and *Princess Daisy*. Spotting the face of Judith Krantz on the cover of a magazine a while ago I yelped with delight: THAT is Judy Tarcher! And she hasn't changed a bit. So one of us did make millions after all!

Judy Tarcher was in the grade below mine, but we lived on the same street, and went to the same school and eventually to the same college. And she had earned $2.3 million when her book was auctioned. I'm not claiming Judith Krantz and I have a great deal in common, aside from the

early years of our lives. There are a lot of differences now, even apart from her millions.

Her books are sold in every airport and store in the country, thousands a week I suppose, and it makes my day if someone has found a copy of one of my books in the local library. We both work all the time, all day, every day, except that Judith Krantz takes time out once a week to have her hair done, and I gave up on my hair years ago. To sell her books, she goes to parties where she doesn't drink and remembers to hold her stomach in; I almost never go to parties, but if I do, I drink a good deal and my stomach is on its own. But I'd still like to let all those ladylike types in fifth grade know that one of the girls in our school made millions of dollars.

I take special delight in these three changes because they make me feel that, although the equal rights amendment may be in trouble and although the advancement of women seems to be an unpopular cause at the White House, all the same, things sometimes do get better. People often say to me accusingly: O.K., you're a feminist, what do women want, what do you want? It's supposed, ever since Freud, to be the question no one can answer. Well, I can answer it. I want every girl to know, no question about it, that she can play basketball by N.B.A. rules, read biographies of women or become the subject of one, make a great deal of money, or do anything else that seems to her exciting.

Maybe I won't consider her goals desirable; men have plenty of goals I don't consider desirable either. But now women can stretch their bodies and minds to their utmost instead of being forced into a dreary pattern of "femininity" as they were in my childhood. I don't want any girl to hide her hopes, or feel a freak. I want her to know she's just fine as she is, playing on a full court.

1981

Adrienne Rich

WHEN WE DEAD AWAKEN: WRITING
AS RE-VISION

Ibsen's *When We Dead Awaken* is a play about the use that the male
artist and thinker—in the process of creating culture as we know it—has
made of women, in his life and in his work; and about a woman's slow
struggling awakening to the use to which her life has been put. Bernard
Shaw wrote in 1900 of this play: "[Ibsen] shows us that no degradation
ever devized or permitted is as disastrous as this degradation; that
through it women can die into luxuries for men and yet can kill them; that
men and women are becoming conscious of this: and that what remains
to be seen as perhaps the most interesting of all imminent social developments is what will happen 'when we dead awaken.'"

It's exhilarating to be alive in a time of awakening consciousness; it can
also be confusing, disorienting, and painful. This awakening of dead or
sleeping consciousness has already affected the lives of millions of women, even those who don't know it yet. It is also affecting the lives of
men, even those who deny its claims upon them. The argument will go
on whether an oppressive economic class system is responsible for the
oppressive nature of male/female relations, or whether, in fact, the sexual
class system is the original model on which all the others are based. But in
the last few years connections have been drawn between our sexual lives
and our political institutions which are inescapable and illuminating.
The sleepwalkers are coming awake, and for the first time this awakening
has a collective reality; it is no longer such a lonely thing to open one's
eyes.

Re-vision—the act of looking back, of seeing with fresh eyes, of entering an old text from a new critical direction—is for us more than a
chapter in cultural history: it is an act of survival. Until we can understand the assumptions in which we are drenched we cannot know ourselves. And this drive to self-knowledge, for woman, is more than a search
for identity: it is part of her refusal of the destructiveness of male-
dominated society. A radical critique of literature, feminist in its impulse, would take the work first of all as a clue to how we live, how we
have been living, how we have been led to imagine ourselves, how our
language has trapped as well as liberated us; and how we can begin to see
—and therefore live—afresh. A change in the concept of sexual identity
is essential if we are not going to see the old political order reassert itself
in every new revolution. We need to know the writing of the past, and
know it differently than we have ever known it; not to pass on a tradition
but to break its hold over us.

For writers, and at this moment for women writers in particular, there is the challenge and promise of a whole new psychic geography to be explored. But there is also a difficult and dangerous walking on the ice, as we try to find language and images for a consciousness we are just coming into, and with little in the past to support us. I want to talk about some aspects of this difficulty and this danger.

Jane Harrison, the great classical anthropologist, wrote in 1914 in a letter to her friend Gilbert Murray: "By the by, about 'Women,' it has bothered me often—why do women never want to write poetry about Man as a sex—why is Woman a dream and a terror to man and not the other way around? . . . Is it mere convention and propriety, or something deeper?" I think Jane's question cuts deep into the myth-making tradition, the romantic tradition; deep into what women and men have been to each other; and deep into the psyche of the woman writer. Thinking about that question, I began thinking of the work of two twentieth-century women poets, Sylvia Plath and Diane Wakoski. It strikes me that in the work of both Man appears as, if not a dream, a fascination, and a terror; and that the source of the fascination and the terror is, simply, Man's power—to dominate, tyrannize, choose or reject the woman. The charisma of Man seems to come purely from his power over her, and his control of the world by force; not from anything fertile or life-giving in him. And, in the work of both these poets, it is finally the woman's sense of *herself*—embattled, possessed—that gives the poetry its dynamic charge, its rhythms of struggle, need, will and female energy. Convention and propriety are perhaps not the right words, but until recently this female anger, this furious awareness of the Man's power over her, were not available materials to the female poet, who tended to write of Love as the source of her suffering, and to view that victimization by Love as an almost inevitable fate. Or, like Marianne Moore and Elizabeth Bishop, she kept human sexual relationships at a measured and chiselled distance in her poems.

One answer to Jane Harrison's question has to be that historically men and women have played very different parts in each others' lives. Where woman has been a luxury for man, and has served as the painter's model and the poet's muse, but also as comforter, nurse, cook, bearer of his seed, secretarial assistant, and copyist of manuscripts, man has played a quite different role for the female artist. Henry James repeats an incident which the writer Prosper Mérimée described, of how, while he was living with George Sand,

> he once opened his eyes, in the raw winter dawn, to see his companion, in a dressing-gown, on her knees before the domestic hearth, a candle-stick beside her and a red *madras* round her head, making bravely, with her own hands, the fire that was to enable her to sit down betimes to urgent pen and paper. The story represents him as having felt that the spectacle chilled his ardor and

tried his taste; her appearance was unfortunate, her occupation an inconse-
quence, and her industry a reproof—the result of all of which was a lively
irritation and an early rupture.

I am suggesting that the specter of this kind of male judgment, along with
the active discouragement and thwarting of her needs by a culture
controlled by males, has created problems for the woman writer:
problems of contact with herself, problems of language and style,
problems of energy and survival.

In rereading Virginia Woolf's A Room of One's Own for the first time
in some years, I was astonished at the sense of effort, of pains taken, of
dogged tentativeness, in the tone of that essay. And I recognized that
tone. I had heard it often enough, in myself and in other women. It is the
tone of a woman almost in touch with her anger, who is determined not to
appear angry, who is willing herself to be calm, detached, and even
charming in a roomful of men where things have been said which are
attacks on her very integrity. Virginia Woolf is addressing an audience of
women, but she is acutely conscious—as she always was—of being overheard by men: by Morgan and Lytton and Maynard Keynes[1] and for that
matter by her father, Leslie Stephen. She drew the language out into an
exacerbated thread in her determination to have her own sensibility yet
protect it from those masculine presences. Only at rare moments in that
essay do you hear the passion in her voice; she was trying to sound as cool
as Jane Austen, as Olympian as Shakespeare, because that is the way the
men of the culture thought a writer should sound.

No male writer has written primarily or even largely for women, or
with the sense of women's criticism as a consideration when he chooses
his materials, his theme, his language. But to a lesser or greater extent,
every woman writer has written for men even when, like Virginia Woolf,
she was supposed to be addressing women. If we have come to the point
when this balance might begin to change, when women can stop being
haunted, not only by "convention and propriety" but by internalized
fears of being and saying themselves, then it is an extraordinary moment
for the woman writer—and reader.

I have hesitated to do what I am going to do now, which is to use myself
as an illustration. For one thing, it's a lot easier and less dangerous to talk
about other women writers. But there is something else. Like Virginia
Woolf, I am aware of the women who are not with us here because they
are washing the dishes and looking after the children. Nearly fifty years
after she spoke, that fact remains largely unchanged. And I am thinking
also of women whom she left out of the picture altogether—women who
are washing other people's dishes and caring for other people's children,

1. E. M. Forster, novelist, and Lytton
Strachey, biographer, and John Maynard
Keynes, economist—all members of the
Bloomsbury group in London during the
twenties and thirties.

not to mention women who went on the streets last night in order to feed their children. We seem to be special women here, we have liked to think of ourselves as special, and we have known that men would tolerate, even romanticize us as special, as long as our words and actions didn't threaten their privilege of tolerating or rejecting us according to *their* ideas of what a special woman ought to be. An important insight of the radical women's movement, for me, has been how divisive and how ultimately destructive is this myth of the special woman, who is also the token woman. Every one of us here in this room has had great luck; our own gifts could not have been enough, for we all know women whose gifts are buried or aborted. Our struggles can have meaning only if they can help to change the lives of women whose gifts—and whose very being—continues to be thwarted.

My own luck was being born white and middle-class into a house full of books, with a father who encouraged me to read and write. So for about twenty years I wrote for a particular man, who criticized and praised me and made me feel I was indeed "special." The obverse side of this, of course, was that I tried for a long time to please him, or rather, not to displease him. And then of course there were other men—writers, teachers—the Man, who was not a terror or a dream but a literary master and a master in other ways less easy to acknowledge. And there were all those poems about women, written by men: it seemed to be a given that men wrote poems and women frequently inhabited them. These women were almost always beautiful, but threatened with the loss of beauty, the loss of youth—the fate worse than death. Or, they were beautiful and died young, like Lucy and Lenore.[2] Or, the woman was like Maud Gonne,[3] cruel and disastrously mistaken, and the poem reproached her because she had refused to become a luxury for the poet.

A lot is being said today about the influence that the myths and images of women have on all of us who are products of culture. I think it has been a peculiar confusion to the girl or woman who tries to write, because she is peculiarly susceptible to language. She goes to poetry or fiction looking for *her* way of being in the world, since she too has been putting words and images together; she is looking eagerly for guides, maps, possibilities; and over and over in the "words' masculine persuasive force" of literature she comes up against something that negates everthing she is about: she meets the image of Woman in books written by men. She finds a terror and a dream, she finds a beautiful pale face, she finds La Belle Dame Sans Merci, she finds Juliet or Tess or Salomé,[4] but precisely what

2. In poems by William Wordsworth and Edgar Allan Poe.
3. Irish revolutionary activist, subject of many love poems by William Butler Yeats.
4. These female figures appear respectively in the poem "La Belle Dame sans Merci" by John Keats, Shakespeare's play *Romeo and Juliet*, Thomas Hardy's novel *Tess of the D'Urbervilles*, and Oscar Wilde's play *Salomé*. The men whom they love, or who love them, all sicken or die.

she does not find is that absorbed, drudging, puzzled, sometimes inspired creature, herself, who sits at a desk trying to put words together.

So what does she do? What did I do? I read the older women poets with their peculiar keenness and ambivalence: Sappho, Christina Rossetti, Emily Dickinson, Elinor Wylie, Edna Millay, H.D. I discovered that the woman poet most admired at the time (by men) was Marianne Moore, who was maidenly, elegant, intellectual, discreet. But even in reading these women I was looking in them for the same things I had found in the poetry of men, because I wanted women poets to be the equals of men, and to be equal was still confused with sounding the same.

I know that my style was formed first by male poets: by the men I was reading as an undergraduate—Frost, Dylan Thomas, Donne, Auden, MacNiece, Stevens, Yeats. What I chiefly learned from them was craft. But poems are like dreams: in them you put what you don't know you know. Looking back at poems I wrote before I was twenty-one, I'm startled because beneath the conscious craft are glimpses of the split I even then experienced between the girl who wrote poems, who defined herself in writing poems, and the girl who was to define herself by her relationships with men. "Aunt Jennifer's Tigers," written while I was a student, looks with deliberate detachment at this split.

> Aunt Jennifer's tigers stride across a screen,
> Bright topaz denizens of a world of green.
> They do not fear the men beneath the tree,
> They pace in sleek chivalric certainty.
>
> Aunt Jennifer's fingers, fluttering through her wool,
> Find even the ivory needle hard to pull.
> The massive weight of Uncle's wedding-band
> Sits heavily upon Aunt Jennifer's hand.
>
> When Aunt is dead, her terrified hands will lie
> Still ringed with ordeals she was mastered by.
> The tigers in the panel that she made
> Will go on striding, proud and unafraid.

In writing this poem, composed and apparently cool as it is, I thought I was creating a portrait of an imaginary woman. But this woman suffers from the opposition of her imagination, worked out in tapestry, and her life-style, "ringed with ordeals she was mastered by." It was important to me that Aunt Jennifer was a person as distinct from myself as possible —distanced by the formalism of the poem; by its objective, observant tone; even by putting the woman in a different generation.

In those years formalism was part of the strategy—like asbestos gloves, it allowed me to handle materials I couldn't pick up barehanded. (A later strategy was to use the persona of a man, as I did in "The Loser.")

A man thinks of the woman he once loved: first, after her wedding, and then nearly a decade later.

I

I kissed you, bride and lost, and went
home from that bourgeois sacrament,
your cheek still tasting cold upon
my lips that gave you benison
with all the swagger that they knew—
as losers somehow learn to do.

Your wedding made my eyes ache; soon
the world would be worse off for one
more golden apple dropped to ground
without the least protesting sound,
and you would windfall lie, and we
forget your shimmer on the tree.

Beauty is always wasted: if
not Mignon's song sung to the deaf,
at all events to the unmoved.
A face like yours cannot be loved
long or seriously enough.
Almost, we seem to hold it off.

II

Well, you are tougher than I thought.
Now when the wash with ice hangs taut
this morning of St. Valentine,
I see you strip the squeaking line,
your body weighed against the load,
and all my groans can do no good.

Because you still are beautiful,
though squared and stiffened by the pull
of what nine windy years have done.
You have three daughters, lost a son.
I see all your intelligence
flung into that unwearied stance.

My envy is of no avail.
I turn my head and wish him well
who chafed your beauty into use
and lives forever in a house
lit by the friction of your mind.
You stagger in against the wind.

1958

I finished college, published my first book by a fluke, as it seemed to me, and broke off a love-affair. I took a job, lived alone, went on writing, fell in love. I was young, full of energy, and the book seemed to mean that others agreed I was a poet. Because I was also determined to have a "full" woman's life, I plunged in my early twenties into marriage and had three children before I was thirty. There was nothing overt in the environment to warn me: these were the fifties, and in reaction to the earlier wave of feminism, middle-class women were making careers of domestic perfection, working to send their husbands through professional schools, then retiring to raise large families. People were moving out to the suburbs, technology was going to be the answer to everything, even sex; the family was in its glory. Life was extremely private; women were isolated from each other by the loyalties of marriage. I have a sense that women didn't talk to each other much in the fifties—not about their secret emptinesses, their frustrations. I went on trying to write, my second book and first child appeared in the same month. But by the time that book came out I was already dissatisfied with those poems, which seemed to me mere exercises for poems I hadn't written. The book was praised, however, for its "gracefulness"; I had a marriage and a child. If there were doubts, if there were periods of null depression or active despairing, these could only mean that I was ungrateful, insatiable, perhaps a monster.

About the time my third child was born, I felt that I had either to consider myself a failed woman and a failed poet, or try to find some synthesis by which to understand what was happening to me. What frightened me most was the sense of drift, of being pulled along on a current which called itself my destiny, but in which I seemed to be losing touch with whoever I had been, with the girl who had experienced her own will and energy almost ecstatically at times, walking around a city or riding a train at night or typing in a student room. In a poem about my grandmother, I wrote (of myself): "A young girl, thought sleeping, is certified dead." I was writing very little, partly from fatigue, that female fatigue of suppressed anger and the loss of contact with her own being; partly from the discontinuity of female life with its attention to small chores, errands, work that others constantly undo, small children's constant needs. What I did write was unconvincing to me; my anger and frustration were hard to acknowledge in or out of poem, because in fact I cared a great deal about my husband and my children. Trying to look back and understand that time I have tried to analyze the real nature of the conflict. Most, if not all, human lives are full of fantasy—passive daydreaming which need not be acted on. But to write poetry or fiction, or even to think well, is not to fantasize, or to put fantasies on paper. For a poem to coalesce, for a character or an action to take shape, there has to be an imaginative transformation of reality which is in no way passive.

And a certain freedom of the mind is needed—freedom to press on, to enter the currents of your thought like a glider pilot, knowing that your motion can be sustained, that the buoyancy of your attention will not be suddenly snatched away. Moreover, if the imagination is to transcend and transform experience it has to question, to challenge, to conceive of alternatives, perhaps to the very life you are living at that moment. You have to be free to play around with the notion that day might be night, love might be hate; nothing can be too sacred for the imagination to turn into its opposite or to call experimentally by another name. For writing is re-naming. Now, to be maternally with small children all day in the old way, to be with a man in the old way of marriage, requires a holding-back, a putting-aside of that imaginative activity, and seems to demand instead a kind of conservatism. I want to make it clear that I am *not* saying that in order to write well, or think well, it is necessary to become unavailable to others, or to become a devouring ego. This has been the myth of the masculine artist and thinker; and I repeat, I do not accept it. But to be a female human being trying to fulfill traditional female functions in a traditional way is in direct conflict with the subversive function of the imagination. The word *traditional* is important here. There must be ways, and we will be finding out more and more about them, in which the energy of creation and the energy of relation can be united. But in those earlier years I always felt the conflict as a failure of love in myself. I had thought I was choosing a full life: the life available to most men, in which sexuality, work and parenthood could coexist. But I felt, at twenty-nine, guilt toward the people closest to me, and guilty toward my own being.

I wanted, then, more than anything, the one thing of which there was never enough: time to think, time to write. The fifties and early sixties were years of rapid revelations: the sit-ins and marches in the South, the Bay of Pigs,[5] the early anti-war movement raised large questions—questions for which the masculine world of the academy around me seemed to have expert and fluent answers. But I needed desperately to think for myself—about pacifism and dissent and violence, about poetry and society and about my own relationship to all these things. For about ten years I was reading in fierce snatches, scribbling in notebooks, writing poetry in fragments; I was looking desperately for clues, because if there were no clues then I thought I might be insane. I wrote in a notebook about this time: "Paralyzed by the sense that there exists a mesh of relationships —e.g. between my anger at the children, my sensual life, pacifism, sex, (I mean sex in its broadest significance, not merely sexual desire)—an interconnectedness which, if I could see it, make it valid, would give me back myself, make it possible to function lucidly and passionately. Yet I grope in and out among these dark webs." I think I began at this point to

5. Site of a failed American invasion of Cuba, intended to overthrow the Castro regime.

feel that politics was not something "out there" but something "in here" and of the essence of my condition.

In the late fifties I was able to write, for the first time, directly about experiencing myself as a woman. The poem was jotted in fragments during children's naps, brief hours in a library, or at 3 A.M. after rising with a wakeful child. I despaired of doing any continuous work at this time. Yet I began to feel that my fragments and scraps had a common consciousness and a common theme, one which I would have been very unwilling to put on paper at an earlier time because I had been taught that poetry should be "universal," which meant, of course, non-female. Until then I had tried very much *not* to identify myself as a female poet. Over two years I wrote a ten-part poem called "Snapshots of A Daughter-in-Law," in a longer, looser mode than I've ever trusted myself with before. It was an extraordinary relief to write that poem. It strikes me now as too literary, too dependent on allusion; I hadn't found the courage yet to do without authorities, or even to use the pronoun *I*—the woman in the poem is *always she*. One section of it, 2, concerns a woman who thinks she is going mad; she is haunted by voices telling her to resist and rebel, voices which she can hear but not obey.

2.

Banging the coffee-pot into the sink
she hears the angels chiding, and looks out
past the raked gardens to the sloppy sky.
Only a week since They said: *Have no patience.*

The next time it was: *Be insatiable.*
Then: *Save yourself; others you cannot save.*
Sometimes she's let the tapstream scald her arm,
a match burn to her thumbnail,

or held her hand above the kettle's snout
right in the woolly steam. They are probably angels,
since nothing hurts her any more, except
each morning's grit blowing into her eyes.

The poem "Orion," written five years later, is a poem of reconnection with a part of myself I had felt I was losing—the active principle, the energetic imagination, the "half-brother" whom I projected, as I had for many years, into the constellation Orion.

Far back when I went zig-zagging
through tamarack pastures
you were my genius, you
my cast-iron Viking, my helmed

lion-heart king in prison.
Years later now you're young

my fierce half-brother, staring
down from that simplified west
your breast open, your belt dragged down
by an oldfashioned thing, a sword
the last bravado you won't give over
though it weighs you down as you stride

and the stars in it are dim
and maybe have stopped burning.
But you burn, and I know it;
as I throw back my head to take you in
an old transfusion happens again:
divine astronomy is nothing to it.

Indoors I bruise and blunder,
break faith, leave ill enough
alone, a dead child born in the dark.
Night cracks up over the chimney,
pieces of time, frozen geodes
come showering down in the grate.

A man reaches behind my eyes
and finds them empty
a woman's head turns away
from my head in the mirror
children are dying my death
and eating crumbs of my life.

Pity is not your forte.
Calmly you ache up there
pinned aloft in your crow's nest,
my speechless pirate!
You take it all for granted
and when I look you back

it's with a starlike eye
shooting its cold and egotistical spear
where it can do least damage.
Breathe deep! No hurt, no pardon
out here in the cold with you
you with your back to the wall.

It's no accident that the words *cold and egotistical* appear in this poem,
and are applied to myself. The choice still seemed to be between "love"
—womanly, maternal love, altruistic love—a love defined and ruled by
the weight of an entire culture—and egotism—a force directed by men

into creation, achievement, ambition, often at the expense of others, but justifiably so. For weren't they men, and wasn't that their destiny as womanly love was ours? I know now that the alternatives are false ones —that the word *love* is itself in need of re-vision.

There is a companion poem to "Orion," written three years later, in which at last the woman in the poem and the woman writing the poem become the same person. It is called "Planetarium," and it was written after a visit to a real planetarium, where I read an account of the work of Caroline Herschel, the astronomer, who worked with her brother William, but whose name remained obscure, as his did not.

> *(Thinking of Caroline*
> *Herschel, 1750–1848,*
> *astronomer, sister of*
> *William; and others)*

A woman in the shape of a monster
a monster in the shape of a woman
the skies are full of them

a woman   'in the snow
among the Clocks and instruments
or measuring the ground with poles'

in her 98 years to discover
8 comets

she whom the moon ruled
like us
levitating into the night sky
riding the polished lenses

Galaxies of women, there
doing penance for impetuousness
ribs chilled
in those spaces   of the mind

An eye,
       'virile, precise and absolutely certain'
       from the mad webs of Uranisborg

                encountering the NOVA

every impulse of light exploding
from the core
as life flies out of us

       Tycho whispering at last
       'Let me not seem to have lived in vain'

What we see, we see
and seeing is changing

the light that shrivels a mountain
and leaves a man alive

Heartbeat of the pulsar
heart sweating through my body

The radio impulse
pouring in from Taurus

      I am bombarded yet   I stand

I have been standing all my life in the
direct path of a battery of signals
the most accurately transmitted most
untranslatable language in the universe
I am a galactic cloud so deep   so involuted that a light wave could take 15
years to travel through me   And has
taken   I am an instrument in the shape
of a woman trying to translate pulsations
into images   for the relief of the body
and the reconstruction of the mind.

In closing I want to tell you about a dream I had last summer. I dreamed I was asked to read my poetry at a mass women's meeting; but when I began to read, what came out were the lyrics of a blues song. I share this dream with you because it seemed to me to say a lot about the problems and the future of the woman writer, and probably of women in general. The awakening of consciousness is not like the crossing of a frontier —one step, and you are in another country. Much of women's poetry has been of the nature of the blues song: a cry of pain, of victimization, or a lyric of seduction. And today, much poetry by women—and prose for that matter—is charged with anger. I think we need to go through that anger, and we will betray our own reality if we try, as Virginia Woolf was trying, for an objectivity, a detachment; that would make us sound more like Jane Austen or Shakespeare. We know more than Jane Austen or Shakespeare knew: more than Jane Austen because our lives are more complex, more than Shakespeare because we know more about the lives of women, Jane Austen and Virginia Woolf included.

Both the victimization and the anger experienced by women are real, and have real sources, everywhere in the environment, built into society. They must go on being tapped and explored by poets, among others. We can neither deny them, nor can we rest there. They are our birth-pains, and we are bearing ourselves. We would be failing each other as writers and as women, if we neglected or denied what is negative, regressive or Sisyphean[5] in our inwardness.

We all know that there is another story to be told. I am curious and expectant about the future of the masculine consciousness. I feel in the work of the men whose poetry I read today a deep pessimism and fatalistic grief; and I wonder if it isn't the masculine side of what women have experienced, the price of masculine dominance. One thing I am sure of: just as woman is becoming her own midwife, creating herself anew, so man will have to learn to gestate and give birth to his own subjectivity—something he has frequently wanted woman to do for him. We can go on trying to talk to each other, we can sometimes help each other, poetry and fiction can show us what the other is going through; but women can no longer be primarily mothers and muses for men: we have our own work cut out for us.

1972

5. The reference is to the Greek myth of Sisyphus. He was condemned to roll a huge rock to the top of a hill, but the rock always rolled back down before the top was reached.

QUESTIONS

1. A typical male-chauvinist cliché is that women take everything too personally, that they lack the larger (i.e. male) perspective. Does this article tend to confirm or deny that belief?
2. In the eighth paragraph, Rich asserts that "no male writer has written primarily or even largely for women, or with the sense of women's criticism as a consideration when he chooses his materials, his theme, his language." How can she know this? Do you think she is right? How do you know?
3. Why does Rich include some of her poetry? Explain whether you think she is able to make points through it that she couldn't make otherwise.
4. In saying that the need is to break tradition's hold over us (p. 428), Rich clearly implies her assessment of tradition. Looking to the future she says, "Woman is becoming her own midwife, creating herself anew." What view of history is implicit here? What role does the speaker create for herself?
5. On p. 430 Rich describes Virginia Woolf as being conscious of male listeners even as she addressed women. Can you detect signs of this in Woolf's "In Search of a Room of One's Own" (p. 1034)? Rich will try to avoid this way of speaking and writing. Does she succeed? Find passages to support your answer; then extend your consideration to her "Taking Women Students Seriously" (p. 256).

Betty Rollin

MOTHERHOOD: WHO NEEDS IT?

Motherhood is in trouble, and it ought to be. A rude question is long overdue: Who needs it? The answer used to be (1) society and (2) women. But now, with the impending horrors of overpopulation, society desperately *doesn't* need it. And women don't need it either. Thanks to the Motherhood Myth—the idea that having babies is something that all normal women instinctively want and need and will enjoy doing—they just *think* they do.

The notion that the maternal wish and the activity of mothering are instinctive or biologically predestined is baloney. Try asking most sociologists, psychologists, psychoanalysts, biologists—many of whom are mothers—about motherhood being instinctive: it's like asking department store presidents if their Santa Clauses are real. "Motherhood—instinctive?" shouts distinguished sociologist/author Dr. Jessie Bernard. "Biological destiny? Forget biology! If it were biology, people would die from not doing it."

"Women don't need to be mothers any more than they need spaghetti," says Dr. Richard Rabkin, a New York psychiatrist. "But if you're in a world where everyone is eating spaghetti, thinking they need it and want it, you will think so too. Romance has really contaminated science. So-called instincts have to do with stimulation. They are not things that well up inside of you."

"When a woman says with feeling that she craved her baby from within, she is putting into biological language what is psychological," says University of Michigan psychoanalyst and motherhood-researcher Dr. Frederick Wyatt. "There are no instincts," says Dr. William Goode, president-elect of the American Sociological Association. "There are reflexes, like eye-blinking, and drives, like sex. There is no innate drive for children. Otherwise, the enormous cultural pressures that there are to reproduce wouldn't exist. There are no cultural pressures to sell you on getting your hand out of the fire."

There are, to be sure, biologists and others who go on about biological destiny, that is, the innate or instinctive goal of motherhood. (At the turn of the century, even good old capitalism was explained by a theorist as "the *instinct* of acquisitiveness.") And many psychoanalysts will hold the Freudian view that women feel so rotten about not having a penis that they are necessarily propelled into the child-wish to replace the missing organ. Psychoanalysts also make much of the psychological need to repeat what one's parent of the same sex has done. Since every woman

441

has a mother, it is considered normal to wish to imitate one's mother by being a mother.

There is, surely, a wish to pass on love if one has received it, but to insist women must pass it on in the same way is like insisting that every man whose father is a gardener has to be a gardener. One dissenting psychoanalyst says, simply, "There is a wish to comply with one's biology, yes, but we needn't and sometimes we shouldn't." (Interestingly, the woman who has been the greatest contributor to child therapy and who has probably given more to children than anyone alive is Dr. Anna Freud, Freud's magnificent daughter, who is not a mother.)

Anyway, what an expert cast of hundreds is telling us is, simply, that biological *possibility* and desire are not the same as biological *need.* Women have childbearing equipment. To choose not to use the equipment is no more blocking what is instinctive than it is for a man who, muscles or no, chooses not to be a weight lifter.

So much for the wish. What about the "instinctive" *activity* of mothering? One animal study shows that when a young member of a species is put in a cage, say, with an older member of the same species, the latter will act in a protective, "maternal" way. But that goes for both males and females who have been "mothered" themselves. And studies indicate that a human baby will also respond to whoever is around playing mother —even if it's father. Margaret Mead and many others frequently point out that mothering can be a fine occupation, if you want it, for either sex. Another experiment with monkeys who were brought up without mothers found them lacking in maternal behavior toward their own offspring. A similar study showed that monkeys brought up without other monkeys of the opposite sex had no interest in mating—all of which suggests that both mothering and mating behavior are learned, not instinctual. And, to turn the cart (or the baby carriage) around, baby ducks who lovingly follow their mothers seemed, in the mother's absence, to just as lovingly follow wooden ducks or even vacuum cleaners.

If motherhood isn't instinctive, when and why, then, was the Motherhood Myth born? Until recently, the entire question of maternal motivation was academic. Sex, like it or not, meant babies. Not that there haven't always been a lot of interesting contraceptive tries. But until the creation of the diaphragm in the 1880's, the birth of babies was largely unavoidable. And, generally speaking, nobody really seemed to mind. For one thing, people tend to be sort of good sports about what seems to be inevitable. For another, in the past, the population needed beefing up. Mortality rates were high, and agricultural cultures, particularly, have always needed children to help out. So because it "just happened" and because it was needed, motherhood was assumed to be innate.

Originally, it was the word of God that got the ball rolling with "Be fruitful and multiply," a practical suggestion, since the only people around then were Adam and Eve. But in no time, supermoralists like St. Augustine changed the tone of the message: "Intercourse, even with one's legitimate wife, is unlawful and wicked where the conception of the offspring is prevented," he, we assume, thundered. And the Roman Catholic position was thus cemented. So then and now, procreation took on a curious value among people who viewed (and view) the pleasures of sex as sinful. One could partake in the sinful pleasure, but feel vindicated by the ensuing birth. Motherhood cleaned up sex. Also, it cleaned up women, who have always been considered somewhat evil, because of Eve's transgression (". . . but the woman was deceived and became a transgressor. Yet woman will be saved through bearing children . . .," I Timothy, 2:14–15), and somewhat dirty because of menstruation.

And so, based on need, inevitability, and pragmatic fantasy—the Myth *worked*, from society's point of view—the Myth grew like corn in Kansas. And society reinforced it with both laws and propaganda—laws that made woman a chattel, denied her education and personal mobility, and madonna propaganda that she was beautiful and wonderful doing it and it was all beautiful and wonderful to do. (One rarely sees a madonna washing dishes.)

In fact, the Myth persisted—breaking some kind of record for long-lasting fallacies—until something like yesterday. For as the truth about the Myth trickled in—as women's rights increased, as women gradually got the message that it was certainly possible for them to do most things that men did, that they live longer, that their brains were not tinier—then, finally, when the really big news rolled in, that they could *choose* whether or not to be mothers—what happened? The Motherhood Myth soared higher than ever. As Betty Friedan made oh-so-clear in *The Feminine Mystique*, the '40's and '50's produced a group of ladies who not only had babies as if they were going out of style (maybe they were) but, as never before, they turned motherhood into a cult. First, they wallowed in the aesthetics of it all—natural childbirth and nursing became maternal musts. Like heavy-bellied ostriches, they grounded their heads in the sands of motherhood, only coming up for air to say how utterly happy and fulfilled they were. But, as Mrs. Friedan says only too plainly, they weren't. The Myth galloped on, moreover, long after making babies had turned from practical asset to liability for both individual parents *and* society. With the average cost of a middle-class child figured conservatively at $30,000 (not including college), any parent knows that the only people who benefit economically from children are manufacturers of consumer goods. Hence all those gooey motherhood commercials. And the Myth gathered momentum long after sheer numbers, while not yet extinguishing us, have made us intensely uncomfortable. Almost all of our societal problems, from minor discomforts like traffic to major ones like hunger, the population people keep reminding us, have to do with there being too many people. And who suffers most? The kids who have been so mindlessly brought into the world, that's who. They are the ones who have to cope with all of the difficult and dehumanizing conditions brought on by overpopulation. They are the ones who have to cope with the psychological nausea of feeling unneeded by society. That's not the only reason for drugs, but, surely, it's a leading contender.

Unfortunately, the population curbers are tripped up by a romantic, stubborn, ideological hurdle. How can birth-control programs really be effective as long as the concept of glorious motherhood remains unchanged? (Even poor old Planned Parenthood has to euphemize—why not Planned Unparenthood?) Particularly among the poor, motherhood is one of the few inherently positive institutions that are accessible. As Berkeley demographer Judith Blake points out, "Poverty-oriented birth control programs do not make sense as a welfare measure . . . as long as existing pronatalist policies . . . encourage mating, pregnancy, and the care, support, and rearing of children." Or, she might have added, as long as the less-than-idyllic child-rearing part of motherhood remains "in small print."

Sure, motherhood gets dumped on sometimes: Philip Wylie's Momism[1] got going in the '40's and Philip Roth's *Portnoy's Complaint* did its best to turn rancid the chicken-soup concept of Jewish motherhood. But these are viewed as the sour cries of a black humorist here, a malcontent there. Everyone shudders, laughs, but it's like the mouse and the elephant joke. Still, the Myth persists. Last April, a Brooklyn woman was indicted on charges of manslaughter and negligent homicide—eleven children died in a fire in a building she owned and criminally neglected —"But," sputtered her lawyer, "my client, Mrs. Breslow, is a mother, a grandmother, and a great-grandmother!"

Most remarkably, the Motherhood Myth persists in the face of the most overwhelming maternal unhappiness and incompetence. If reproduction were merely superfluous and expensive, if the experience were as rich and rewarding as the cliché would have us believe, if it were a predominantly joyous trip for everyone riding—mother, father, child —then the going everybody-should-have-two-children plan would suffice. Certainly, there are a lot of joyous mothers, and their children and (sometimes, not necessarily) their husbands reflect their joy. But a lot of evidence suggests that for more women than anyone wants to admit, motherhood can be miserable. ("If it weren't," says one psychiatrist wryly, "the world wouldn't be in the mess it's in.")

There is a remarkable statistical finding from a recent study of Dr. Bernard's, comparing the mental illness and unhappiness of married mothers and single women. The latter group, it turned out, was both

---

1. Philip Wylie's *A Generation of Vipers* (1942) blamed many of the ills of American society on dominating mothers.

markedly less sick and overtly more happy. Of course, it's not easy to measure slippery attitudes like happiness. "Many women have achieved a kind of reconciliation—a conformity," says Dr. Bernard,

> that they interpret as happiness. Since feminine happiness is supposed to lie in devoting one's life to one's husband and children, they do that; so *ipso facto*, they assume they are happy. And for many women, untrained for independence and "processed" for motherhood, they find their state far preferable to the alternatives, which don't really exist.

Also, unhappy mothers are often loath to admit it. For one thing, if in society's view not to be a mother is to be a freak, not to be a *blissful* mother is to be a witch. Besides, unlike a disappointing marriage, disappointing motherhood cannot be terminated by divorce. Of course, none of that stops such a woman from expressing her dissatisfaction in a variety of ways. Again, it is not only she who suffers but her husband and children as well. Enter the harridan housewife, the carping shrew. The realities of motherhood can turn women into terrible people. And, judging from the 50,000 cases of child abuse in the U.S. each year, some are worse than terrible.

In some cases, the unpleasing realities of motherhood begin even before the beginning. In *Her Infinite Variety*, Morton Hunt describes young married women pregnant for the first time as "very likely to be frightened and depressed, masking these feelings in order not to be considered contemptible. The arrival of pregnancy interrupts a pleasant dream of motherhood and awakens them to the realization that they have too little money, or not enough space, or unresolved marital problems. . . ."

The following are random quotes from interviews with some mothers in Ann Arbor, Mich., who described themselves as reasonably happy. They all had positive things to say about their children, although when asked about the best moment of their day, they *all* confessed it was when the children were in bed. Here is the rest:

> Suddenly I had to devote myself to the child totally. I was under the illusion that the baby was going to fit into my life, and I found that I had to switch my life and my schedule to fit *him*. You think, "I'm in love, I'll get married, and we'll have a baby." First there's two, then three, it's simple and romantic. You don't even think about the work. . . .

> You never get away from the responsibility. Even when you leave the children with a sitter, you are not out from under the pressure of the responsibility. . . .

> I hate ironing their pants and doing their underwear, and they never put their clothes in the laundry basket. . . . As they get older, they make less demands on our time because they're in school, but the demands are greater

in forming their values. . . . Best moment of the day is when all the children are in bed. . . . The worst time of the day is 4 P.M., when you have to get dinner started, the kids are tired, hungry and crabby—everybody wants to talk to you about *their* day . . . your day is only half over.

Once a mother, the responsibility and concern for my children became so encompassing. . . . It took a great deal of will to keep up other parts of my personality. . . . To me, motherhood gets harder as they get older because you have less control. . . . In an abstract sense, I'd have several. . . . In the non-abstract, I would not have any . . . .

I had anticipated that the baby would sleep and eat, sleep and eat. Instead, the experience was overwhelming. I really had not thought particularly about what motherhood would mean in a realistic sense. I want to do *other* things, like to become involved in things that are worthwhile—I don't mean women's clubs—but I don't have the physical energy to go out in the evenings. I feel like I'm missing something . . . the experience of being somewhere with people and having them talking about something—something that's going on in the world.

Every grownup person expects to pay a price for his pleasures, but seldom is the price as vast as the one endured "however happily" by most mothers. We have mentioned the literal cost factor. But what does that mean? For middle-class American women, it means a life style with severe and usually unimagined limitations; i.e., life in the suburbs, because who can afford three bedrooms in the city? And what do suburbs mean? For women, suburbs mean other women and children and leftover peanut-butter sandwiches and car pools and seldom-seen husbands. Even the Feminine Mystiqueniks—the housewives who finally admitted that their lives behind brooms (OK, electric brooms) were driving them crazy—were loath to trace their predicament to their children. But it is simply a fact that a childless married woman has no child-work and little house-work. She can live in a city, or, if she still chooses the suburbs or the country, she can leave on the commuter train with her husband if she wants to. Even the most ardent job-seeking mother will find little in the way of great opportunities in Scarsdale.[2] Besides, by the time she wakes up, she usually lacks both the preparation for the outside world and the self-confidence to get it. You will say there are plenty of city-dwelling working mothers. But most of those women do additional-funds-for-the-family kind of work, not the interesting career kind that takes plugging during childbearing years.

Nor is it a bed of petunias for the mother who does make it professionally. Says writer critic Marya Mannes:

If the creative woman has children, she must pay for this indulgence with a long burden of guilt, for her life will be split three ways between them and her

2. A wealthy suburb of New York City.

husband and her work. . . . No woman with any heart can compose a paragraph when her child is in trouble. . . . The creative woman has no wife to protect her from intrusion. A man at his desk in a room with closed door is a man at work. A woman at a desk in any room is available.

Speaking of jobs, do remember that mothering, salary or not, is a job. Even those who can afford nurses to handle the nitty-gritty still need to put out emotionally. "Well-cared-for" neurotic rich kids are not exactly unknown in our society. One of the more absurd aspects of the Myth is the underlying assumption that, since most women are biologically equipped to bear children, they are psychologically, mentally, emotionally, and technically equipped (or interested) to rear them. Never mind happiness. To assume that such an exacting, consuming, and important task is something almost all women are equipped to do is far more dangerous and ridiculous than assuming that everyone with vocal chords should seek a career in the opera.

A major expectation of the Myth is that children make a not-so-hot marriage hotter, or a hot marriage, hotter still. Yet almost every available study indicates that childless marriages are far happier. One of the biggest, of 850 couples, was conducted by Dr. Harold Feldman of Cornell University, who states his finding in no uncertain terms: "Those couples with children had a significantly lower level of marital satisfaction than did those without children." Some of the reasons are obvious. Even the most adorable children make for additional demands, complications, and hardships in the lives of even the most loving parents. If a woman feels disappointed and trapped in her mother role, it is bound to affect her marriage in any number of ways: she may take out her frustrations directly on her husband, or she may count on him too heavily for what she feels she is missing in her daily life.

". . . You begin to grow away from your husband," says one of the Michigan ladies. "He's working on his career and you're working on your family. But you both must gear your lives to the children. You do things the children enjoy, more than things you might enjoy." More subtle and possibly more serious is what motherhood may do to a woman's sexuality. Often when the stork flies in, sexuality flies out. Both in the emotional minds of some women *and* in the minds of their husbands, when a woman becomes a mother, she stops being a woman. It's not only that motherhood may destroy her physical attractiveness, but its madonna concept may destroy her *feelings* of sexuality.

And what of the payoff? Usually, even the most self-sacrificing of maternal self-sacrificers expects a little something back. Gratified parents are not unknown to the Western world, but there are probably at least just as many who feel, to put it crudely, shortchanged. The experiment mentioned earlier—where the baby ducks followed vacuum cleaners instead of their mothers—indicates that what passes for love from baby to mother is merely a rudimentary kind of object attachment. Without necessarily feeling like a Hoover, a lot of women become disheartened because babies and children are not only not interesting to talk to (not everyone thrills at the wonders of da-da-ma-ma talk) but they are generally not empathetic, considerate people. Even the nicest children are not capable of empathy, surely a major ingredient of love, until they are much older. Sometimes they're never capable of it. Dr. Wyatt says that often, in later years particularly, when most of the "returns" are in, it is the "good mother" who suffers most of all. It is then she must face a reality: The child—the appendage with her genes—is not an appendage, but a separate person. What's more, he or she may be a separate person who doesn't even like her—or whom she doesn't really like.

So if the music is lousy, how come everyone's dancing? Because the motherhood minuet is taught freely from birth, and whether or not she has rhythm or likes the music, every woman is expected to do it. Indeed, she wants to do it. Little girls start learning what to want—and what to be —when they are still in their cribs. Dr. Miriam Keiffer, a young social psychologist at Bensalem, the Experimental College of Fordham University, points to studies showing that

> at six months of age, mothers are already treating their baby girls and boys quite differently. For instance, mothers have been found to touch, comfort, and talk to their females more. If these differences can be found at such an early stage, it's not surprising that the end product is as different as it is. What is surprising is that men and women are, in so many ways, similar.

Some people point to the way little girls play with dolls as proof of their innate motherliness. But remember, little girls are given dolls. When Margaret Mead presented some dolls to New Guinea children, it was the boys, not the girls, who wanted to play with them, which they did by crooning lullabies and rocking them in the most maternal fashion.

By the time they reach adolescence, most girls, unconsciously or not, have learned enough about role definition to qualify for a master's degree. In general, the lesson has been that no matter what kind of career thoughts one may entertain, one must, first and foremost, be a wife and mother. A girl's mother is usually her first teacher. As Dr. Goode says, "A woman is not only taught by society to have a child; she is taught to have a child who will have a child." A woman who has hung her life on the Motherhood Myth will almost always reinforce her young married daughter's early training by pushing for grandchildren. Prospective grandmothers are not the only ones. Husbands, too, can be effective sellers. After all, they have the Fatherhood Myth to cope with. A married man is supposed to have children. Often, particularly among Latins, children are a sign of potency. They help him assure the world—and himself—that he is the big man he is supposed to be. Plus, children give him both immortality (whatever that means) and possibly the chance to become more in his lifetime through the accomplishments of his children, particularly his son. (Sometimes it's important, however, for the son to do better, but not too much better.)

Friends, too, can be counted on as myth-pushers. Naturally one wants to do what one's friends do. One study, by the way, found a correlation between a woman's fertility and that of her three closest friends. The negative sell comes into play here, too. We have seen what the concept of non-mother means (cold, selfish, unwomanly, abnormal). In practice, particulary in the suburbs, it can mean, simply, exclusion—both from child-centered activities (that is, most activities) and child-centered conversations (that is, most conversations). It can also mean being the butt of a lot of unfunny jokes. ("Whaddya waiting for? An immaculate conception? Ha ha.") Worst of all, it can mean being an object of pity.

In case she's escaped all those pressures (that is, if she was brought up in a cave), a young married woman often wants a baby just so that she'll (1) have something to do (motherhood is better than clerk/typist, which is often the only kind of job she can get, since little more has been expected of her and, besides, her boss also expects her to leave and be a mother); (2) have something to hug and possess, to be needed by and have power over; and (3) have something to be—e.g., a baby's mother. Motherhood affords an instant identity. First, through wifehood, you are somebody's wife; then you are somebody's mother. Both give not only identity and activity, but status and stardom of a kind. During pregnancy, a woman can look forward to the kind of attention and pampering she may not ever have gotten or may never otherwise get. Some women consider birth the biggest accomplishment of their lives, which may be interpreted as saying not much for the rest of their lives. As Dr. Goode says, "It's like the gambler who may know the roulette wheel is crooked, but it's the only game in town." Also, with motherhood, the feeling of accomplishment is immediate. It is really much faster and easier to make a baby than paint a painting, or write a book, or get to the point of accomplishment in a job. It is also easier in a way to shift focus from self-development to child development—particularly since, for women, self-development is considered selfish. Even unwed mothers may achieve a feeling of this kind. (As we have seen, little thought is given to the aftermath.) And, again, since so many women are underdeveloped as people, they feel that, besides children, they have little else to give—to themselves, their husbands, to their world.

You may ask why then, when the realities do start pouring in, does a woman want to have a second, third, even fourth child? OK, (1) just because reality is pouring in doesn't mean she wants to face it. A new baby can help bring back some of the old illusions. Says psychoanalyst Dr. Natalie Shainess, "She may view each successive child as a knight in armor that will rescue her from being a 'bad unhappy mother.'" (2) Next on the horror list of having no children, is having one. It suffices to say that only children are not only OK, they even have a high rate of exceptionality. (3) Both parents usually want at least one child of each sex. The husband, for reasons discussed earlier, probably wants a son. (4) The more children one has, the more of an excuse one has not to develop in any other way.

What's the point? A world without children? Of course not. Nothing could be worse or more unlikely. No matter what anyone says in *Look* or anywhere else, motherhood isn't about to go out like a blown bulb, and who says it should? Only the Myth must go out, and now it seems to be dimming.

The younger-generation females who have been reared on the Myth have not rejected it totally, but at least they recognize it can be more loving to children not to have them. And at least they speak of adopting children instead of bearing them. Moreover, since the new nonbreeders are "less hung-up" on ownership, they seem to recognize that if you dig loving children, you don't necessarily have to own one. The end of the Motherhood Myth might make available more loving women (and men!) for those children who already exist.

When motherhood is no longer culturally compulsory, there will, certainly, be less of it. Women are now beginning to think and do more about development of self, of their individual resources. Far from being selfish, such development is probably our only hope. That means more alternatives for women. And more alternatives mean more selective, better, happier, motherhood—and childhood and husbandhood (or manhood) and peoplehood. It is not a question of whether or not children are sweet and marvelous to have and rear; the question is, even if that's so, whether or not one wants to pay the price for it. It doesn't make sense any more to pretend that women need babies, when what they really need is themselves. If God were still speaking to us in a voice we could hear, even He would probably say, "Be fruitful. Don't multiply."

1970

Herb Goldberg

IN HARNESS: THE MALE CONDITION

Most men live in harness. Richard was one of them. Typically he had no awareness of how his male harness was choking him until his personal and professional life and his body had nearly fallen apart.

Up to that time he had experienced only occasional short bouts of depression that a drink would bring him out of. For Richard it all crashed at an early age, when he was thirty-three. He came for psychotherapy with resistance, but at the instruction of his physician. He had a bad ulcer, was losing weight, and, in spite of repeated warnings that it could kill him, he was drinking heavily.

His personal life was also in serious trouble. He had recently lost his job as a disc jockey on a major radio station because he'd been arrested for drunk driving. He had totaled his car against a tree and the newspapers had a picture of it on the front page. Shortly thereafter his wife moved out, taking with her their eight-year-old daughter. She left at the advice of friends who knew that he had become violent twice that year while drunk.

As he began to talk about himself it became clear that he had been securely fitted into his male harness early in his teens. In high school he was already quite tall and stronger than most. He was therefore urged to go out for basketball, which he did, and he got lots of attention for it.

He had a deep, resonant voice that he had carefully cultivated. He was told that he should go into radio announcing and dramatics, so he got into all the high school plays. In college he majored in theater arts.

In his senior year in college he dated one of the most beautiful and sought-after girls in the junior class. His peer group envied him, which reassured Richard that he had a good thing going. So he married Joanna a year after graduating and took a job with a small radio station in Fresno, California. During the next ten years he played out the male role; he fathered a child and fought his way up in a very competitive profession.

It wasn't until things had fallen apart that he even let himself know that he had any feelings of his own, and in therapy he began to see why it had been so necessary to keep his feelings buried. They were confusing and frightening.

More than anything else, there was a hypersensitive concern over what others thought about him as a "man." As other suppressed feelings began to surface they surprised him. He realized how he had hated the pressures of being a college basketball player. The preoccupation with being good and winning had distorted his life in college.

Though he had been to bed with many girls before marriage and even

451

a few afterward, he acknowledged that rarely was it a genuine turn-on for him. He liked the feeling of being able to seduce a girl but the experience itself was rarely satisfying, so he would begin the hunt for another as soon as he succeeded with one. "Some of those girls were a nightmare," he said, "I would have been much happier without them. But I was caught in the bag of proving myself and I couldn't seem to control it."

The obsessive preoccupation in high school and college with cultivating a deep, resonant "masculine" voice he realized was similar to the obsession some women have with their figures. Though he thought he had enjoyed the attention he got being on stage, he acknowledged that he had really disliked being an entertainer, or "court jester," as he put it.

When he thought about how he had gotten married he became particularly uncomfortable. "I was really bored with Joanna after the first month of dating but I couldn't admit it to myself because I thought I had a great thing going. I married her because I figured if I didn't one of the other guys would. I couldn't let that happen."

Richard had to get sick in his harness and nearly be destroyed by role-playing masculinity before he could allow himself to be a person with his own feelings, rather than just a hollow male image. Had it not been for a bleeding ulcer he might have postponed looking at himself for many years more.

Like many men, Richard had been a zombie, a daytime sleepwalker. Worse still, he had been a highly "successful" zombie, which made it so difficult for him to risk change. Our culture is saturated with successful male zombies, businessmen zombies, golf zombies, sports car zombies, playboy zombies, etc. They are playing by the rules of the male game plan. They have lost touch with, or are running away from, their feelings and awareness of themselves as people. They have confused their social masks for their essence and they are destroying themselves while fulfilling the traditional definitions of masculine-appropriate behavior. They set their life sails by these role definitions. They are the heroes, the studs, the providers, the warriors, the empire builders, the fearless ones. Their reality is always approached through these veils of gender expectations.

When something goes seriously wrong, they discover that they are shadows to themselves as well as to others. They are unknown because they have been so busy manipulating and masking themselves in order to maintain and garner more status that a genuine encounter with another person would threaten them, causing them to flee or to react with extreme defensiveness.

Men evaluate each other and are evaluated by many women largely by the degree to which they approximate the ideal masculine model. Women have rightfully lashed out against being placed into a mold and being related to as a sex object. Many women have described their roles in marriage as a form of socially approved prostitution. They assert that they are selling themselves out for an unfulfilling portion of supposed security. For psychologically defensive reasons the male has not yet come to see himself as a prostitute, day in and day out, both in and out of the marriage relationship.

The male's inherent survival instincts have been stunted by the seemingly more powerful drive to maintain his masculine image. He would, for example, rather die in the battle than risk living in a different way and being called a "coward" or "not a man." He would rather die at his desk prematurely than free himself from his compulsive patterns and pursuits. As a recently published study concluded, "A surprising number of men approaching senior citizenship say they would rather die than be buried in retirement."

The male in our culture is at a growth impasse. He won't move—not because he is protecting his cherished central place in the sun, but because he can't move. He is a cardboard Goliath precariously balanced and on the verge of toppling over if he is pushed even ever so slightly out of his well-worn path. He lacks the fluidity of the female who can readily move between the traditional definitions of male or female behavior and roles. She can be wife and mother or a business executive. She can dress in typically feminine fashion or adopt the male styles. She will be loved for having "feminine" interests such as needlework or cooking, or she will be admired for sharing with the male in his "masculine" interests. That will make her a "man's woman." She can be sexually assertive or sexually passive. Meanwhile, the male is rigidly caught in his masculine pose and, in many subtle and direct ways, he is severely punished when he steps out of it.

Unlike some of the problems of women, the problems of men are not readily changed through legislation. The male has no apparent and clearly defined targets against which he can vent his rage. Yet he is oppressed by the cultural pressures that have denied him his feelings, by the mythology of the woman and the distorted and self-destructive way he sees and relates to her, by the urgency for him to "act like a man" which blocks his ability to respond to his inner promptings both emotionally and physiologically, and by a generalized self-hate that causes him to feel comfortable only when he is functioning well in harness, or when he lives for joy and for personal growth.

The prevalent "enlightened" male's reaction to the women's liberation movement bears testimony to his inability to mobilize himself on his own behalf. He has responded to feminist assertions by donning sack cloth, sprinkling himself with ashes, and flagellating himself—accusing himself of the very things she is accusing him of. An article entitled, "You've Come a Long Way, Buddy," perhaps best illustrates the male self-hating attitude. In it, the writer said,

The members of the men's liberation movement are . . . a kind of embarrassing vanguard, the first men anywhere on record to take a political stand based on the idea that what the women are saying is right—men are a bunch of lazy, selfish, horny, unhappy oppressors.

Many other undoubtedly well-intentioned writers on the male condition have also taken a basically guilt- and shame-oriented approach to the male, alternately scolding him, warning him, and preaching to him that he better change and not be a male chauvinist pig anymore. During many years of practice as a psychotherapist, I have never seen a person grow or change in a self-constructive, meaningful way when he was motivated by guilt, shame, or self-hate. That manner of approach smacks of old-time religion and degrades the male by ignoring the complexity of the binds and repressions that are his emotional heritage.

Precisely because the tenor and mood of the male liberation efforts so far have been one of self-accusation, self-hate, and a repetition of feminist assertions, I believe it is doomed to failure in its present form. It is buying the myth that the male is culturally favored—a notion that is clung to despite the fact that every critical statistic in the area of longevity, disease, suicide, crime, accidents, childhood emotional disorders, alcoholism, and drug addiction shows a disproportionately higher male rate.

Many men who join male liberation groups do so to please or impress their women or to learn how to deal with and hold onto their recently liberated wives or girlfriends. Once in a male liberation group they intellectualize their feelings and reactions into lifelessness. In addition, the men tend to put each other down for thinking like "typical male chauvinists" or using words like "broad," "chick," "dike," etc. They have introjected the voices of their feminist accusers and the result is an atmosphere that is joyless, self-righteous, cautious, and lacking in a vitalizing energy. A new, more subtle kind of competitiveness pervades the atmosphere: the competition to be the least competitive and most free of the stereotyped version of male chauvinism.

The women's liberation movement did not effect its astounding impact via self-hate, guilt, or the desire to placate the male. Instead it has been energized by anger and outrage. Neither will the male change in any meaningful way until he experiences his underlying rage toward the endless, impossible binds under which he lives, the rigid definitions of his role, the endless pressure to be all things to all people, and the guilt-oriented, self-denying way he has traditionally related to women, to his feelings, and to his needs.

Because it is so heavily repressed, male rage only manifests itself indirectly and in hidden ways. Presently it is taking the form of emotional detachment, interpersonal withdrawal, and passivity in relationship to women. The male has pulled himself inward in order to deny his anger and to protect himself and others from his buried cascade of resentment and fury. Pathetic, intellectualized attempts not to be a male chauvinist pig will never do the job.

There is also a commonly expressed notion that men will somehow be freed as a by-product of the feminist movement. This is a comforting fantasy for the male but I see no basis for it becoming a reality. It simply disguises the fear of actively determining his own change. Indeed, by responding inertly and passively, the male will be moved, but not in a meaningful and productive direction. If there is to be a constructive change for the male he will have to chart his own way, develop his own style and experience his own anxieties, fear, and rage because *this time mommy won't do it!*

Recently, I asked a number of men to write to me about how they see their condition and what liberation would mean to them. A sense of suffocation and confusion was almost always present.

A forty-six-year-old businessman wrote: "From what do I need to be liberated? I'm too old and tired to worry about myself. I know that I'm only a high-grade mediocrity. I've come to accept a life where the dreams are now all revealed as unreality. I don't know how my role or my son's role should change. If I knew I suppose it would be in any way that would make my wife happier and less of a shrew."

A thirty-nine-year-old carpenter discussing the "joys" of working responded: "I contend that the times in which it is fun and rewarding in a healthy way have been fairly limited. Most of the time it has been a question of running in fear of failure." Referring to his relationships, he continued. "There is another aspect of women's and men's lib that I haven't experienced extensively. This is the creation of close friendships outside of the marriage. My past experiences have been stressful to the point where I am very careful to limit any such contact. What's the fear? I didn't like the sense of insecurity developed by my wife and the internal stresses that I felt. It created guilt feelings."

A fifty-seven-year-old college professor expressed it this way: "Yes, there's a need for male lib and hardly anyone writes about it the way it really is, though a few make jokes. My gut reaction, which is what you asked for, is that men—the famous male chauvinist pigs who neglect their wives, underpay their women employees, and rule the world—are literally slaves. They're out there picking that cotton, sweating, swearing, taking lashes from the boss, working fifty hours a week to support themselves and the plantation, only then to come back to the house to do another twenty hours a week rinsing dishes, toting trash bags, writing checks, and acting as butlers at the parties. It's true of young husbands and middle-aged husbands. Young bachelors may have a nice deal for a couple of years after graduating, but I've forgotten, and I'll never again be young! Old men. Some have it sweet, some have it sour.

"Man's role—how has it affected my life? At thirty-five, I chose to emphasize family togetherness and income and neglect my profession if necessary. At fifty-seven, I see no reward for time spent with and for the family, in terms of love or appreciation. I see a thousand punishments for neglecting my profession. I'm just tired and have come close to just walking away from it and starting over; just research, publish, teach, administer, play tennis, and travel. Why haven't I? Guilt. And love. And fear of loneliness. How should the man's role in my family change? I really don't know how it can, but I'd like a lot more time to do my thing."

The most remarkable and significant aspect of the feminist movement to date has been woman's daring willingness to own up to her resistances and resentment toward her time-honored, sanctified roles of wife and even mother. The male, however, has yet to fully realize, acknowledge, and rebel against the distress and stifling aspects of many of the roles he plays—from good husband, to good daddy, to good provider, to good lover, etc. Because of the inner pressure to constantly affirm his dominance and masculinity, he continues to act as if he can stand up under, fulfill, and even enjoy all the expectations placed on him no matter how contradictory and devitalizing they are.

It's time to remove the disguises of privilege and reveal the male condition for what it really is.

1976

QUESTIONS

1. *From what sort of evidence or experience does Goldberg draw his conclusions? Do the men who seek help from a psychotherapist represent a good cross section of all males? What biases might be encountered in such a group of subjects?*
2. *Compare Goldberg's conception of the male in harness with S. J. Perelman's idea of machismo (p. 457). Are the two talking about similar things? Is it true, as Goldberg states, that "the male in our culture is at a growth impasse" (p. 453)?*
3. *Describing what happens to men who try to understand women's liberation by joining a group of their own, Goldberg says that "once in a male liberation group [men] intellectualize their feelings and reactions into lifelessness" (p. 454). What other paths to understanding do men have open to them? Do liberated women pose a threat to men and their images?*
4. *Betty Rollin, in* Motherhood: Who Needs It? *(p. 441), talks about extinguishing the "Motherhood Myth" to encourage women to discover and be themselves. What does Goldberg imply about extinguishing Fatherhood? How do these two ideas differ? Which would have a greater impact on society?*
5. *Compare the approach to human personality taken by Goldberg with that of Willard Gaylin, also a psychotherapist, in* What You See Is the

Real You *(p. 620). Do they seem to agree on the nature of human personality? Explain.*
6. *Construct a dialogue in which Goldberg's "harnessed" man and a liberated woman discuss birth control, the proper role of parents, platonic relationships between men and women, or some similar topic.*

S. J. Perelman

THE MACHISMO MYSTIQUE

It was 3 P.M., that climactic midafternoon moment toward which every gallant worthy of the name bends his energies, and I'd done all the preparatory work time and an unencumbered credit card could accomplish. I had stoked my Chilean vis-à-vis with three vodka martinis, half a gallon of Sancerre, and two balloons of Armagnac until her eyes were veritable liquid pools. Under my bold, not to say outrageous, compliments her damask skin and the alabaster column of her throat glowed like a lovely pink pearl; her hair, black as the raven's wing, shimmered in the reflection of the boudoir lamp shading our discreet banquette; and every now and again as my knee nudged hers under the table, my affinity's magnificent bosom heaved uncontrollably. I had glissed through all those earnest confidences that begin, "You know, I've never said this to anyone before," to, "Look, I'm not very articulate, but I feel that in these parlous times, it behooves us all to reach out, to cling to another lonely person —do you know what I mean?" Suddenly I had the feeling that she knew what I meant, all right. In a swift glance, I encompassed the small chic restaurant whence all but we had fled—its idle barman and the maître d'hôtel stifling a yawn—and I struck.

"Listen," I said as if inspired. "This friend of mine, the Marquis de Cad, who has a wonderful collection of African sculpture, was called away to Cleveland, and I promised to stop by his flat and dust it. Why don't we pick up a bottle of lemon oil . . ."

Inamorata threw back her sleek head and shouted with laughter. "Stop, *querido*,"[1] she implored. "You're ruining my mascara. Such *machismo* —who would have expected it from a shrimp like you?"

Quicker than any hidalgo of Old Spain to erase an insult, I sprang up prepared to plunge my poniard into her bosom (a striking demonstration of the maxim that man kills that which he most loves). Unfortunately, I had left my poniard at home on the bureau and was wearing only a tie-

---

1. Beloved.

tack that could never penetrate anyone so thick-skinned. Nonetheless, I made the hussy smart for her insolence. "Let me tell you something, Chubby," I rasped. "Never underestimate the American male. I may not dance the mambo or reek of garlic, but I'm just as feisty as those caballeros of yours below the Rio Grande. Remember that our first colonial flag in Kentucky, the Dark and Bloody Ground, portrayed a coiled rattlesnake over the legend, 'Don't Tread on Me.'"

"Big deal," she scoffed. "Do you want an example of real *machismo* —the kind of masculinity Latin-American men are capable of? Tell them to bring me another Armagnac."

Downcast at the realization that our matinee had blown out the back, I sullenly acceded. The story as she related it dealt with a bar in Guatemala City called *Mi apuesta* (The Wager) after a bet once made there. Two young bloods or *machos*, it appeared, had swaggered in one evening, stiff with conceit and supremely self-confident, arrogant as a pair of fighting cocks. Lounging at the bar over a glass of manzanilla, one of them remarked to the other, *"Te apuesto que no eres bastante macho para matar al primero que entre"* (I wager you're not man enough to kill the first hombre who comes in).

The other sneered thinly. "No?" he said. "I bet you fifty *centavos* I will."

The bet was covered, whereupon the challenged party extracted a Beretta from his waistband, and a moment later, as a totally inoffensive stranger stepped through the saloon door, a bullet drilled him through the heart.

"Madre de Dios," I exclaimed, shocked. "What happened to the assassin?"

"Niente," said Inamorata calmly. "The judge gave him a three months' suspended sentence on the ground that the crime was in no way premeditated."

Needless to say, whenever Inamorata rang up after our abortive meeting and besought me to lunch her again, I showed her a clean pair of heels. (They were two fellows who dispensed towels at the Luxor Baths; they pursued her madly, and I hope with more success than I had.) At any rate, in pondering the whole business of *machismo,* of male bravado and excessive manliness, it occurred to me that I had met quite a few *machos* in my time, both in the entertainment world and belles-lettres. The one I remember most vividly in the former was a Hollywood screenwriter—a big redheaded blowhard I'll call Rick Ferret. A Montanan who claimed to have grown up on the range, Ferret was forever beating his gums about his amatory exploits; by his own blushing admission, he was Casanova reborn, the swordsman supreme, the reincarnation of Don Juan. According to him, women in every walk of life—society leaders and shopgirls, leading ladies and vendeuses—fell in windrows in his path, and though it was obvious to his auditors at the Brown Derby that he dealt in quantity rather than quality, the references he dropped to his nuclear power and durability left us pale with jealousy.

One evening, I attended a party at his house in Laurel Canyon. Living with him at the time was a lady named Susie, quite well-endowed and with a rather sharp tongue. So late was the hour when the bash ended that the two insisted I stay over, and the next morning, while I was adjusting my false lashes, Ferret entered the bathroom and proceeded to take a shower. Just as he was snorting and puffing like a grampus, I chanced to observe a quite formidable scar on his *Sitzfleisch*. With an apology for the personal nature of the question, I asked if it was a war wound of some kind.

"Yes, in a way," he said carelessly, turning off the taps. "There's quite a story attached to it." He opened the door of the bathroom to disperse the steam, and I glimpsed his Susie breakfasting in bed a few feet distant. "The fact is," he went on, "it happened some years ago down on the south fork of the Brazos while I was rounding up some mavericks. This gang of rustlers from Durango way cut into the herd, and I took after them hell for leather. Well, the greasers were spoiling for action, and they got it." He chuckled. "Before I could yank out my six-guns, they creased me here, but I managed to rub out the whole dad-blamed lot."

"Oh, for God's sake, Ferret," I heard Susie's voice croak from the bedroom. "You know perfectly well you had a boil lanced on your tail only last Tuesday."

The two most celebrated *machos* I ever knew, I suppose, were Ernest Hemingway—unquestionably the holder of the black belt in the Anglo-Saxon world—and Mike Todd, who, to pilfer a phrase from Marcel Proust, might aptly be termed the Sweet Cheat Gone. My go-around with Hemingway took place in the winter of 1954, directly after his two widely publicized plane crashes in East Africa. He was borne into the New Stanley Hotel in Nairobi in a somewhat disoriented state, suffering a double concussion, a smashed kidney, and alarming symptoms of *folie de grandeur*.[2] I turned up there two days later from Uganda with fourteen women comprising the first American all-girl safari (quite another story), and since my room was adjacent to his, saw a good bit of him thereafter. What with his tribulations and frequent infusions of hooch, Papa was inclined to ramble somewhat, and it was not always easy to follow the thread of his discourse. Once in a while, though, the clouds dissipated, and we were able to chat about mutual friends in the Montparnasse of the 'twenties. It was on such an occasion, one night, that he told me an anecdote that stunningly dramatized his *machismo*.

It concerned a period when he used to box at Stillman's Gymnasium in New York, a favorite haunt of enthusiasts of what is termed the manly art. His adversaries, Hemingway blushingly admitted, never matched his

2. Delusions of grandeur.

own speed and strength, but one of them improved so under his tutelage that occasionally the pair had a tolerable scrimmage. Thinking to intensify it, Hemingway suggested they discard their gloves and fight bareknuckle. This, too, while diverting, soon palled, but at last he had an inspiration.

"The room we boxed in," Hemingway explained, "had these rows of pipes running along the walls—you know, like backstage in a theater? Well, we flooded the place with steam, so thickly that it looked like a pea-soup fog in London. Then we started charging each other like a couple of rhinos. Butting our heads together and roaring like crazy. God, it was terrific—you could hear the impact of bone on bone, and we bled like stuck pigs. Of course, that made the footwork a bit more difficult, slipping and sliding all over, but it sure heightened the fun. Man, those were the days. You had to have real *cojones*[3] to stand up to it."

The same hormonal doodads were imperative in order to cope with Mike Todd and his vagaries. Todd's *machismo* was that common form that afflicts all undersized men—megalomania. He freely identified himself with Napoleon, P. T. Barnum, and Carl Laemmle, Junior, not to mention the Roman emperors of the decline. Whereas the latter, however, believed in giving the populace bread and circuses, Todd gave them circuses and kept the bread. Rarely if ever has there been anyone more unwilling to fork over what he owed to those actors, writers, and technicians who aided him in his grandiloquent projects of stage and screen. The little corpuscle, in short, believed in flaunting money where it made the most impression—at Deauville, Monaco, and the gaming tables of Las Vegas. In this respect, he was a true *macho*. My sole souvenir of our frenetic association is a replica of the carpetbag Phileas Fogg carried on his celebrated journey, a thousand of which Todd distributed in lordly fashion to Broadway companions, investors, accountants, dentists, and other sycophants. But surely, his admirers have since queried me, I must have been awed by his tremendous vitality; Only in part, I respond: *Moi-même*, I prefer the anthropoid apes. The gibbon swings farther, the chimpanzee's reflexes are quicker, the orangutan can scratch faster, and the gorilla—my particular love object—has been known to crunch a Stillson wrench in his teeth.

Of such literary *machos* was the late Robert Ruark, who of course patterned himself on Hemingway. Their careers afford ample demonstration of my two favorite maxims: a) that the gaudier the patter, the cheaper the scribe, and b) that easy writing makes hard reading. The legend of Ruark's fatal charisma with women still gives one a pain in the posterior when recounted, and his press interviews, studded with reference to the millions of words he merchandised, act as a tourniquet on

3. Testicles.

bleeders like myself who labor over a postcard. Even John O'Hara, somewhat more talented, was not above buttonholing acquaintances and boasting that he had written this or that deathless vignette in three quarters of an hour. It is interesting, by the way, that Scott Fitzgerald, with whom O'Hara was given to comparing himself, never made any claims to his own facility when I knew him in Hollywood. On the contrary, both he and Nathanael West were continually obsessed by delusions of their inadequacy with sex and their small literary output.

Looking back over a long and mottled career, I think the best illustration of real *machismo* I ever beheld took place on the terrace of the Café du Dôme in Paris in 1927. I was seated there at dusk one day with a fellow journalist when an enormous yellow Hispano-Suiza landaulet driven by a chauffeur drew up at the curb. From it emerged a tall and beautiful, exquisitely clad lady, followed by another even more photogenic—both clearly high-fashion mannequins. Reaching into the tonneau, they brought forth a wizened homunculus with a yellow face resembling Earl Sande, the celebrated jockey. Hooking their arms through his, they assisted him to a table farther down the terrace. I turned to my *copain* with my eyebrows raised, searching for some explanation of the phenomenon. A slow smile overspread his countenance, and he held his hands apart as does one when asked to steady a skein of wool.

That's *machismo*, sweetheart.

1975

QUESTIONS

1. *Write your own definition of* machismo, *basing it on Perelman's examples.*
2. *Perelman says his next-to-last paragraph contains his "best illustration of real* machismo." *Explain why you agree or disagree.*
3. *Toward the end of his essay Perelman talks about writers who boast about how fast and how much they write. Why do you think Perelman includes these examples? Explain whether they are a part of his definition of* machismo *or merely analogous to it.*
4. *Describe an incident (either actual or invented) which illustrates* machismo. *Then change the incident so that it no longer illustrates* machismo. *Explain whether the changes involved (1) changes in people, (2) changes in circumstances or social customs, or (3) changes in both. What conclusions can you draw about whether* machismo *is a part of human nature or is culturally conditioned?*
5. *Perelman has a very distinctive style. Try to determine what its characteristics are by rewriting one of his paragraphs in a more neutral style.*
6. *Read the McGraw-Hill "Guidelines for Equal Treatment of the Sexes" (p. 360). In what ways are* machismo *attitudes reflected in language?*

Lewis Thomas

ON MAGIC IN MEDICINE

Medicine has always been under pressure to provide public explanations for the diseases with which it deals, and the formulation of comprehensive, unifying theories has been the most ancient and willing preoccupation of the profession. In the earliest days, hostile spirits needing exorcism were the principal pathogens, and the shaman's duty was simply the development of improved techniques for incantation. Later on, especially in the Western world, the idea that the distribution of body fluids among various organs determined the course of all illnesses took hold, and we were in for centuries of bleeding, cupping, sweating, and purging in efforts to intervene. Early in this century the theory of autointoxication evolved, and a large part of therapy was directed at emptying the large intestine and keeping it empty. Then the global concept of focal infection became popular, accompanied by the linked notion of allergy to the presumed microbial pathogens, and no one knows the resulting toll of extracted teeth, tonsils, gallbladders, and appendixes: the idea of psychosomatic influences on disease emerged in the 1930s and, for a while, seemed to sweep the field.

Gradually, one by one, some of our worst diseases have been edited out of such systems by having their causes indisputably identified and dealt with. Tuberculosis was the paradigm. This was the most chronic and inexorably progressive of common human maladies, capable of affecting virtually every organ in the body and obviously influenced by crowding, nutrition, housing, and poverty; theories involving the climate in general, and night air and insufficient sunlight in particular, gave rise to the spa as a therapeutic institution. It was not until the development of today's effective chemotherapy that it became clear to everyone that the disease had a single, dominant, central cause. If you got rid of the tubercle bacillus you were rid of the disease.

But that was some time ago, and today the idea that complicated diseases can have single causes is again out of fashion. The microbial infections that can be neatly coped with by antibiotics are regarded as lucky anomalies. The new theory is that most of today's human illnesses, the infections aside, are multifactorial in nature, caused by two great arrays of causative mechanisms: 1) the influence of things in the environment and 2) one's personal life-style. For medicine to become effective in dealing with such diseases, it has become common belief that the environment will have to be changed, and personal ways of living will also have to be transformed, and radically.

462

These things may turn out to be true, for all I know, but it will take a long time to get the necessary proofs. Meanwhile, the field is wide open for magic.

One great difficulty in getting straightforward answers is that so many of the diseases in question have unpredictable courses, and some of them have a substantial tendency toward spontaneous remission. In rheumatoid arthritis, for instance, when such widely disparate therapeutic measures as copper bracelets, a move to Arizona, diets low in sugar or salt or meat or whatever, and even an inspirational book have been accepted by patients as useful, the trouble in evaluation is that approximately 35 percent of patients with this diagnosis are bound to recover no matter what they do. But if you actually have rheumatoid arthritis or, for that matter, schizophrenia, and then get over it, or if you are a doctor and observe this to happen, it is hard to be persuaded that it wasn't *something* you did that was responsible. Hence you need very large numbers of patients and lots of time, and a cool head.

Magic is back again, and in full force. Laetrile cures cancer, acupuncture is useful for deafness and low-back pain, vitamins are good for anything, and meditation, yoga, dancing, biofeedback, and shouting one another down in crowded rooms over weekends are specifics for the human condition. Running, a good thing to be doing for its own sake, has acquired the medicinal value formerly attributed to rare herbs from Indonesia.

There is a recurring advertisement, placed by Blue Cross on the op-ed page of *The New York Times*, which urges you to take advantage of science by changing your life habits, with the suggestion that if you do so, by adopting seven easy-to-follow items of life-style, you can achieve eleven added years beyond what you'll get if you don't. Since today's average figure is around seventy-two for all parties in both sexes, this might mean going on until at least the age of eighty-three. You can do this formidable thing, it is claimed, by simply eating breakfast, exercising regularly, maintaining normal weight, not smoking cigarettes, not drinking excessively, sleeping eight hours each night, and not eating between meals.

The science which produced this illumination was a careful study by California epidemiologists, based on a questionnaire given to about seven thousand people. Five years after the questionnaire, a body count was made by sorting through the county death certificates, and the 371 people who had died were matched up with their answers to the questions. To be sure, there were more deaths among the heavy smokers and drinkers, as you might expect from the known incidence of lung cancer in smokers and cirrhosis and auto accidents among drinkers. But there was also a higher mortality among those who said they didn't eat breakfast, and even higher in those who took no exercise, no exercise at all, not even going off in the family car for weekend picnics. Being up to 20 percent overweight was not so bad, surprisingly, but being *underweight* was clearly associated with a higher death rate.

The paper describing these observations has been widely quoted, and not just by Blue Cross. References to the Seven Healthy Life Habits keep turning up in popular magazines and in the health columns of newspapers, always with that promise of eleven more years.

The findings fit nicely with what is becoming folk doctrine about disease. You become ill because of not living right. If you get cancer it is, somehow or other, your own fault. If you didn't cause it by smoking or drinking or eating the wrong things, it came from allowing yourself to persist with the wrong kind of personality, in the wrong environment. If you have a coronary occlusion, you didn't run enough. Or you were too tense, or you *wished* too much, and didn't get a good enough sleep. Or you got fat. Your fault.

But eating breakfast? It is a kind of enchantment, pure magic.

You have to read the report carefully to discover that there is another, more banal way of explaining the findings. Leave aside the higher deaths in heavy smokers and drinkers, for there is no puzzle in either case; these are dangerous things to do. But it is hard to imagine any good reason for dying within five years from not eating a good breakfast, or any sort of breakfast.

The other explanation turns cause and effect around. Among the people in that group of seven thousand who answered that they don't eat breakfast, don't go off on picnics, are underweight, and can't sleep properly, there were surely some who were already ill when the questionnaire arrived. They didn't eat breakfast because they couldn't stand the sight of food. They had lost their appetites, were losing weight, didn't feel up to moving around much, and had trouble sleeping. They didn't play tennis or go off on family picnics because they didn't *feel* good. Some of these people probably had an undetected cancer, perhaps of the pancreas; others may have had hypertension or early kidney failure or some other organic disease which the questionnaire had no way of picking up. The study did not ascertain the causes of death in the 371, but just a few deaths from such undiscerned disorders would have made a significant statistical impact. The author of the paper was careful to note these possible interpretations, although the point was not made strongly, and the general sense you have in reading it is that you can live on and on if only you will eat breakfast and play tennis.

The popular acceptance of the notion of Seven Healthy Life Habits, as a way of staying alive, says something important about today's public attitudes, or at least the attitudes in the public mind, about disease and dying. People have always wanted causes that are simple and easy to comprehend, and about which the individual can *do* something. If you

believe that you can ward off the common causes of premature death —cancer, heart disease, and stroke, diseases whose pathogenesis we really do not understand—by jogging, hoping, and eating and sleeping regularly, these are good things to believe even if not necessarily true. Medicine has survived other periods of unifying theory, constructed to explain all of human disease, not always as benign in their effects as this one is likely to be. After all, if people can be induced to give up smoking, stop overdrinking and overeating, and take some sort of regular exercise, most of them are bound to feel the better for leading more orderly, regular lives, and many of them are surely going to look better.

Nobody can say an unfriendly word against the sheer goodness of keeping fit, but we should go carefully with the promises.

There is also a bifurcated ideological appeal contained in the seven-life-habits doctrine, quite apart from the subliminal notion of good luck in the numbers involved (7 come 11). Both ends of the political spectrum can find congenial items. At the further right, it is attractive to hear that the individual, the good old freestanding, free-enterprising American citizen, is responsible for his own health and when things go wrong it is his own damn fault for smoking and drinking and living wrong (and he can jolly well pay for it). On the other hand, at the left, it is nice to be told that all our health problems, including dying, are caused by failure of the community to bring up its members to live properly, and if you really want to improve the health of the people, research is not the answer; you should upheave the present society and invent a better one. At either end, you can't lose.

In between, the skeptics in medicine have a hard time of it. It is much more difficult to be convincing about ignorance concerning disease mechanisms than it is to make claims for full comprehension, especially when the comprehension leads, logically or not, to some sort of action. When it comes to serious illness, the public tends, understandably, to be more skeptical about the skeptics, more willing to believe the true believers. It is medicine's oldest dilemma, not to be settled by candor or by any kind of rhetoric; what it needs is a lot of time and patience, waiting for science to come in, as it has in the past, with the solid facts.

1979

QUESTIONS

1. *What would be a sensible response to a recommendation of the Seven Healthy Life Habits?*
2. *In the second paragraph, Thomas uses the word* paradigm. *First define the term from the way Thomas uses it in that paragraph and then compare that definition with what you find in the dictionary. Explain how Thomas might say that the study by the California epidemiologists that defined the Seven Healthy Life Habits (p. 463) was also a*

paradigm, for successful research in their case. Does such an explanation require that you define a place for magic in the paradigm for
successful research? Consult Thomas Kuhn's "The Route to Normal
Science" (p. 975) for help.
3. Thomas speaks of "folk doctrine about disease" (p. 464); James Fries
speaks of a shift "in the conceptualization of chronic disease and of
aging" (p. 593). Are they talking about the same thing?
4. On p. 464 Thomas argues for turning cause and effect (in the California study) around so that, for example, what was the effect, sickness,
becomes a cause and what was a cause, failure to exercise, becomes an
effect. This is obviously a potent argumentative tactic; suggest some
other applications in politics or international affairs.

Jessica Mitford

BEHIND THE FORMALDEHYDE CURTAIN

The drama begins to unfold with the arrival of the corpse at the
mortuary.

Alas, poor Yorick![1] How surprised he would be to see how his counterpart of today is whisked off to a funeral parlor and is in short order
sprayed, sliced, pierced, pickled, trussed, trimmed, creamed, waxed,
painted, rouged and neatly dressed—transformed from a common corpse
into a Beautiful Memory Picture. This process is known in the trade as
embalming and restorative art, and is so universally employed in the
United States and Canada that the funeral director does it routinely,
without consulting corpse or kin. He regards as eccentric those few who
are hardy enough to suggest that it might be dispensed with. Yet no law
requires embalming, no religious doctrine commends it, nor is it dictated
by considerations of health, sanitation, or even of personal daintiness. In
no part of the world but in Northern America is it widely used. The
purpose of embalming is to make the corpse presentable for viewing in a
suitably costly container; and here too the funeral director routinely,
without first consulting the family, prepares the body for public display

Is all this legal? The processes to which a dead body may be subjected
are after all to some extent circumscribed by law. In most states, for
instance, the signature of next of kin must be obtained before an autopsy
may be performed, before the deceased may be cremated, before the
body may be turned over to a medical school for research purposes; or
such provision must be made in the decedent's will. In the case of

---

1. The phrase is Hamlet's (V.i.184) on the disinterment, identification, and perusal of the skull
of the court clown he had known as a child.

embalming, no such permission is required nor is it ever sought. A textbook, *The Principles and Practices of Embalming*, comments on this: "There is some question regarding the legality of much that is done within the preparation room." The author points out that it would be most unusual for a responsible member of a bereaved family to instruct the mortician, in so many words, to "embalm" the body of a deceased relative. The very term "embalming" is so seldom used that the mortician must rely upon custom in the matter. The author concludes that unless the family specifies otherwise, the act of entrusting the body to the care of a funeral establishment carries with it an implied permission to go ahead and embalm.

Embalming is indeed a most extraordinary procedure, and one must wonder at the docility of Americans who each year pay hundreds of millions of dollars for its perpetuation, blissfully ignorant of what it is all about, what is done, how it is done. Not one in ten thousand has any idea of what actually takes place. Books on the subject are extremely hard to come by. They are not to be found in most libraries or bookshops.

In an era when huge television audiences watch surgical operations in the comfort of their living rooms, when, thanks to the animated cartoon, the geography of the digestive system has become familiar territory even to the nursery school set, in a land where the satisfaction of curiosity about almost all matters is a national pastime, the secrecy surrounding embalming can, surely, hardly be attributed to the inherent gruesomeness of the subject. Custom in this regard has within this century suffered a complete reversal. In the early days of American embalming, when it was performed in the home of the deceased, it was almost mandatory for some relative to stay by the embalmer's side and witness the procedure. Today, family members who might wish to be in attendance would certainly be dissuaded by the funeral director. All others, except apprentices, are excluded by law from the preparation room.

A close look at what does actually take place may explain in large measure the undertaker's intractable reticence concerning a procedure that has become his major *raison d'être*.[2] Is it possible he fears that public information about embalming might lead patrons to wonder if they really want this service? If the funeral men are loath to discuss the subject outside the trade, the reader may, understandably, be equally loath to go on reading at this point. For those who have the stomach for it, let us part the formaldehyde curtain. . . .

The body is first laid out in the undertaker's morgue—or rather, Mr. Jones is reposing in the preparation room—to be readied to bid the world farewell.

The preparation room in any of the better funeral establishments has the tiled and sterile look of a surgery, and indeed the embalmer-restora-

2. Reason for being.

tive artist who does his chores there is beginning to adopt the term "dermasurgeon" (appropriately corrupted by some mortician-writers as "demi-surgeon") to describe his calling. His equipment, consisting of scalpels, scissors, augers, forceps, clamps, needles, pumps, tubes, bowls and basins, is crudely imitative of the surgeon's, as is his technique, acquired in a nine- or twelve-month post-high-school course in an embalming school. He is supplied by an advanced chemical industry with a bewildering array of fluids, sprays, pastes, oils, powders, creams, to fix or soften tissue, shrink or distend it as needed, dry it here, restore the moisture there. There are cosmetics, waxes and paints to fill and cover features, even plaster of Paris to replace entire limbs. There are ingenious aids to prop and stabilize the cadaver: a Vari-Pose Head Rest, the Edwards Arm and Hand Positioner, the Repose Block (to support the shoulders during the embalming), and the Throop Foot Positioner, which resembles an old-fashioned stocks.

Mr. John H. Eckels, president of the Eckels College of Mortuary Science, thus describes the first part of the embalming procedure: "In the hands of a skilled practitioner, this work may be done in a comparatively short time and without mutilating the body other than by slight incision —so slight that it scarcely would cause serious inconvenience if made upon a living person. It is necessary to remove the blood, and doing this not only helps in the disinfecting, but removes the principal cause of disfigurements due to discoloration."

Another textbook discusses the all-important time element: "The earlier this is done, the better, for every hour that elapses between death and embalming will add to the problems and complications encountered. . . ." Just how soon should one get going on the embalming? The author tells us, "On the basis of such scanty information made available to this profession through its rudimentary and haphazard system of technical research, we must conclude that the best results are to be obtained if the subject is embalmed before life is completely extinct —that is, before cellular death has occurred. In the average case, this would mean within an hour after somatic death." For those who feel that there is something a little rudimentary, not to say haphazard, about this advice, a comforting thought is offered by another writer. Speaking of fears entertained in early days of premature burial, he points out, "One of the effects of embalming by chemical injection, however, has been to dispel fears of live burial." How true; once the blood is removed, chances of live burial are indeed remote.

To return to Mr. Jones, the blood is drained out through the veins and replaced by embalming fluid pumped in through the arteries. As noted in *The Principles and Practices of Embalming*, "every operator has a favorite injection and drainage point—a fact which becomes a handicap only if he fails or refuses to forsake his favorites when conditions demand it."

Typical favorites are the carotid artery, femoral artery, jugular vein, subclavian vein. There are various choices of embalming fluid. If Flextone is used, it will produce a "mild, flexible rigidity. The skin retains a velvety softness, the tissues are rubbery and pliable. Ideal for women and children." It may be blended with B. and G. Products Company's Lyf-Lyk tint, which is guaranteed to reproduce "nature's own skin texture . . . the velvety appearance of living tissue." Suntone comes in three separate tints: Suntan; Special Cosmetic Tint, a pink shade "especially indicated for young female subjects"; and Regular Cosmetic Tint, moderately pink.

About three to six gallons of a dyed and perfumed solution of formaldehyde, glycerin, borax, phenol, alcohol and water is soon circulating through Mr. Jones, whose mouth has been sewn together with a "needle directed upward between the upper lip and gum and brought out through the left nostril," with the corners raised slightly "for a more pleasant expression." If he should be bucktoothed, his teeth are cleaned with Bon Ami and coated with colorless nail polish. His eyes, meanwhile, are closed with flesh-tinted eye caps and eye cement.

The next step is to have at Mr. Jones with a thing called a trocar. This is a long, hollow needle attached to a tube. It is jabbed into the abdomen, poked around the entrails and chest cavity, the contents of which are pumped out and replaced with "cavity fluid." This done, and the hole in the abdomen sewn up, Mr. Jones's face is heavily creamed (to protect the skin from burns which may be caused by leakage of the chemicals), and he is covered with a sheet and left unmolested for a while. But not for long—there is more, much more, in store for him. He has been embalmed, but not yet restored, and the best time to start the restorative work is eight to ten hours after embalming, when the tissues have become firm and dry.

The object of all this attention to the corpse, it must be remembered, is to make it presentable for viewing in an attitude of healthy repose. "Our customs require the presentation of our dead in the semblance of normality . . . unmarred by the ravages of illness, disease or mutilation," says Mr. J. Sheridan Mayer in his *Restorative Art*. This is rather a large order since few people die in the full bloom of health, unravaged by illness and unmarked by some disfigurement. The funeral industry is equal to the challenge: "In some cases the gruesome appearance of a mutilated or disease-ridden subject may be quite discouraging. The task of restoration may seem impossible and shake the confidence of the embalmer. This is the time for intestinal fortitude and determination. Once the formative work is begun and affected tissues are cleaned or removed, all doubts of success vanish. It is surprising and gratifying to discover the results which may be obtained."

The embalmer, having allowed an appropriate interval to elapse, returns to the attack, but now he brings into play the skill and equipment of sculptor and cosmetician. Is a hand missing? Casting one in plaster of Paris is a simple matter. "For replacement purposes, only a cast of the back of the hand is necessary; this is within the ability of the average operator and is quite adequate." If a lip or two, a nose or an ear should be missing, the embalmer has at hand a variety of restorative waxes with which to model replacements. Pores and skin texture are simulated by stippling with a little brush, and over this cosmetics are laid on. Head off? Decapitation cases are rather routinely handled. Ragged edges are trimmed, and head joined to torso with a series of splints, wires and sutures. It is a good idea to have a little something at the neck—a scarf or a high collar—when time for viewing comes. Swollen mouth? Cut out tissue as needed from inside the lips. If too much is removed, the surface contour can easily be restored by padding with cotton. Swollen necks and cheeks are reduced by removing tissue through vertical incisions made down each side of the neck. "When the deceased is casketed, the pillow will hide the suture incisions . . . as an extra precaution against leakage, the suture may be painted with liquid sealer."

The opposite condition is more likely to present itself—that of emaciation. His hypodermic syringe now loaded with massage cream, the embalmer seeks out and fills the hollowed and sunken areas by injection. In this procedure the backs of the hands and fingers and the under-chin area should not be neglected.

Positioning the lips is a problem that recurrently challenges the ingenuity of the embalmer. Closed too tightly, they tend to give a stern, even disapproving expression. Ideally, embalmers feel, the lips should give the impression of being ever so slightly parted, the upper lip protruding slightly for a more youthful appearance. This takes some engineering, however, as the lips tend to drift apart. Lip drift can sometimes be remedied by pushing one or two straight pins through the inner margin of the lower lip and then inserting them between the two front upper teeth. If Mr. Jones happens to have no teeth, the pins can just as easily be anchored in his Armstrong Face Former and Denture Replacer. Another method to maintain lip closure is to dislocate the lower jaw, which is then held in its new position by a wire run through holes which have been drilled through the upper and lower jaws at the midline. As the French are fond of saying, *il faut souffrir pour être belle.*[3]

If Mr. Jones has died of jaundice, the embalming fluid will very likely turn him green. Does this deter the embalmer? Not if he has intestinal fortitude. Masking pastes and cosmetics are heavily laid on, burial garments and casket interiors are color-correlated with particular care, and Jones is displayed beneath rose-colored lights. Friends will say "How well he looks." Death by carbon monoxide, on the other hand, can be rather a

3. It's necessary to suffer to be beautiful.

good thing from the embalmer's viewpoint: "One advantage is the fact that this type of discoloration is an exaggerated form of a natural pink coloration." This is nice because the healthy glow is already present and needs but little attention.

The patching and filling completed, Mr. Jones is now shaved, washed and dressed. Cream-based cosmetic, available in pink, flesh, suntan, brunette and blond, is applied to his hands and face, his hair is shampooed and combed (and, in the case of Mrs. Jones, set), his hands manicured. For the horny-handed son of toil special care must be taken; cream should be applied to remove ingrained grime, and the nails cleaned. "If he were not in the habit of having them manicured in life, trimming and shaping is advised for better appearance—never questioned by kin."

Jones is now ready for casketing (this is the present participle of the verb "to casket"). In this operation his right shoulder should be depressed slightly "to turn the body a bit to the right and soften the appearance of lying flat on the back." Positioning the hands is a matter of importance, and special rubber positioning blocks may be used. The hands should be cupped slightly for a more lifelike, relaxed apearance. Proper placement of the body requires a delicate sense of balance. It should lie as high as possible in the casket, yet not so high that the lid, when lowered, will hit the nose. On the other hand, we are cautioned, placing the body too low "creates the impression that the body is in a box."

Jones is next wheeled into the appointed slumber room where a few last touches may be added—his favorite pipe placed in his hand or, if he was a great reader, a book propped into position. (In the case of little Master Jones a Teddy bear may be clutched.) Here he will hold open house for a few days, visiting hours 10 A.M. to 9 P.M.

All now being in readiness, the funeral director calls a staff conference to make sure that each assistant knows his precise duties. Mr. Wilber Kriege writes: "This makes your staff feel that they are a part of the team, with a definite assignment that must be properly carried out if the whole plan is to succeed. You never heard of a football coach who failed to talk to his entire team before they go on the field. They have drilled on the plays they are to execute for hours and days, and yet the successful coach knows the importance of making even the bench-warming third-string substitute feel that he is important if the game is to be won." The winning of this game is predicated upon glass-smooth handling of the logistics. The funeral director has notified the pallbearers whose names were furnished by the family, has arranged for the presence of clergyman, organist, and soloist, has provided transportation for everybody, has organized and listed the flowers sent by friends. In Psychology of Funeral Service Mr. Edward A. Martin points out: "He may not always do as much as the family thinks he is doing, but it is his helpful guidance that they appreciate in knowing they are proceeding as they should. . . . The important thing is how well his services can be used to make the family believe they are giving unlimited expression to their own sentiment."

The religious service may be held in a church or in the chapel of the funeral home; the funeral director vastly prefers the latter arrangement, for not only is it more convenient for him but it affords him the opportunity to show off his beautiful facilities to the gathered mourners. After the clergyman has had his say, the mourners queue up to file past the casket for a last look at the deceased. The family is never asked whether they want an open-casket ceremony; in the absence of their instruction to the contrary, this is taken for granted. Consequently well over 90 per cent of all American funerals feature the open casket—a custom unknown in other parts of the world. Foreigners are astonished by it. An English woman living in San Francisco described her reaction in a letter to the writer:

> I myself have attended only one funeral here—that of an elderly fellow worker of mine. After the service I could not understand why everyone was walking towards the coffin (sorry, I mean casket), but thought I had better follow the crowd. It shook me rigid to get there and find the casket open and poor old Oscar lying there in his brown tweed suit, wearing a suntan makeup and just the wrong shade of lipstick. If I had not been extremely fond of the old boy, I have a horrible feeling that I might have giggled. Then and there I decided that I could never face another American funeral—even dead.

The casket (which has been resting throughout the service on a Classic Beauty Ultra Metal Casket Bier) is now transferred by a hydraulically operated device called Porto-Lift to a balloon-tired, Glide Easy casket carriage which will wheel it to yet another conveyance, the Cadillac Funeral Coach. This may be lavender, cream, light green—anything but black. Interiors, of course, are color-correlated, "for the man who cannot stop short of perfection."

At graveside, the casket is lowered into the earth. This office, once the prerogative of friends of the deceased, is now performed by a patented mechanical lowering device. A "Lifetime Green" artificial grass mat is at the ready to conceal the sere earth, and overhead, to conceal the sky, is a portable Steril Chapel Tent ("resists the intense heat and humidity of summer and the terrific storms of winter . . . available in Silver Grey, Rose or Evergreen"). Now is the time for the ritual scattering of earth over the coffin, as the solemn words "earth to earth, ashes to ashes, dust to dust" are pronounced by the officiating cleric. This can today be accomplished "with a mere flick of the wrist with the Gordon Leak-Proof Earth Dispenser. No grasping of a handful of dirt, no soiled fingers. Simple, dignified, beautiful, reverent! The modern way!" The Gordon Earth Dispenser (at $5) is of nickel-plated brass construction. It is not only "attractive to the eye and long wearing"; it is also "one of the 'tools' for building better public relations" if presented as "an appropriate non-commercial gift" to the clergyman. It is shaped something like a salt-shaker.

Untouched by human hand, the coffin and the earth are now united.

It is in the function of directing the participants through this maze of gadgetry that the funeral director has assigned to himself his relatively new role of "grief therapist." He has relieved the family of every detail, he has revamped the corpse to look like a living doll, he has arranged for it to nap for a few days in a slumber room, he has put on a well-oiled performance in which the concept of *death* has played no part whatso-ever—unless it was inconsiderately mentioned by the clergyman who conducted the religious service. He has done everything in his power to make the funeral a real pleasure for everybody concerned. He and his team have given their all to score an upset victory over death.

1963

John Kenneth Galbraith

THE CONFIDENT SPECULATORS[1]

Anyone who reads in a compulsive way should be allowed one sordid aberration—an interest in pornography, abnormal psychology, or the chronicles of professional basketball. My own interest is in speculation, including the closely associated arts of swindling and financial prestidigi-tation. I have read the classics—Charles Mackay's notable treatise of 1841, *Memoirs of Extraordinary Popular Delusions and the Madness of Crowds*; the basic works on the tulipomania of the 1630s and on John Law and the Mississippi bubble; the recent and excellent *Manias, Panics and Crashes* (1978), by Charles Kindleberger, of MIT—and I've even gone on down to barely literate essays on the life and times of Robert Vesco.

The uniform finding from this literature, to use the word in a loose way, is that in all but the rarest cases the great speculators are the victims of their own speculation and the great swindlers almost invariably end up swindling themselves. Both kinds of operator are victims of the publicity that they have generated, which they then have come to believe. (Robert Vesco was something of an exception. He seems to have realized that he wasn't much good, and he knew when to cut and run.)

In the late 1920s, the financial press and other newspapers and magazines reveled in the power and insight of the men who were riding and furthering the stock-market boom and the more insane securities

1. A review of *Beyond Greed: The Hunts and Their Silver Bubble*, by Stephen Fay.

promotions of the time. M. J. Meehan and Arthur W. Cutten, two of the greatest plungers, were held to have overcome at long last all the uncertainties of the market and to have bent it entirely to their will. This they, too, believed. The Goldman, Sachs investment-trust promotions were thought the miracle of the age, a view that the people at Goldman, Sachs shared. Richard Whitney, the vice president and later the president of the New York Stock Exchange, let it be known that the most reputable wing of the financial establishment—the House of Morgan, no less—was committed through him to the boom. So, needless to say, was he, and for far more than his means. Ivar Kreuger was regularly pictured as standing astride the whole world of international finance. And so, without much doubt, he saw himself, even when he was delivering counterfeit Italian bonds as collateral to his banks. Charles Mitchell, the head of the National City Bank, as Citicorp then was, showed how transcendent were the financial resources committed to the boom. Not only was Mitchell speculating heavily with his own money but, in the spring of 1929, when the Federal Reserve made a meek protest against the use of its funds for purchase of stocks on margin, he moved in to say that his bank would be happy to make up the difference. The Federal Reserve backed off in defeated silence.

All of these men were destroyed by the boom they did so much to create. In later years, before a congressional committee, Meehan and Cutten made a far from impressive appearance. Some thought they looked a trifle seedy; both suffered from a seriously defective memory. The men from Goldman, Sachs were also called to account; they were deeply embarrassed, as the firm continued to be for many years to come. Part of their expressed justification was that, in an equitable spirit, they too had taken a bath on their promotions. Richard Whitney, taken up by Assistant United States District Attorney Thomas E. Dewey for the strikingly simpleminded embezzlement that he had committed to cover his market and business losses, went in a dignified way to Sing Sing. Whitney at least survived; Ivar Kreuger went out one day in Paris, bought a gun, and shot himself. Charlie Mitchell also survived, but he spent most of the next decade in court, defending himself against charges of tax evasion. He was acquitted of felonious intent but paid $1,100,000 in settlement of a civil suit. Thus did speculators (and those who also swindled) destroy themselves. The list could be much longer. The few who escaped with their speculative wealth—Bernard Baruch, Joseph P. Kennedy—were those who believed the least in the values they had helped to create.

The reasons for this dénouement are far from complex. The blind do not, in fact, lead the blind, but the gullible do gull the gullible. It is the confidence that speculators have in their own bad judgment that inspires confidence in others. So the speculators join those whom they have inspired in hope and avarice and are there with them holding the bag at the end. Then they are revealed for what they always were, which is not much. The greatest speculative promoter of all time, and one of the more intelligent, was John Law. Single-handedly he engineered the enormous speculation in nonexistent minerals on the lower Mississippi that engaged the attention of all Paris and much of France in the years 1718–1720. At the last, he narrowly escaped the country with his life. Anyone encountering him during the remaining nine years that he lived, as a poor refugee in Venice, would not have been deeply impressed. On balance, however, Law probably cut a more awesome figure in 1721 than Bunker and Herbert Hunt did after the collapse of the great silver bubble of 1980.

Like the speculators before them, the Hunts believed in what they were doing. And being the incredibly affluent legatees of H. L. Hunt and the OPEC oil-price enhancement, they persuaded others to believe that they knew what they were doing. (Wealth, in even the most improbable cases, manages to convey the aspect of intelligence.) But in the end, like their predecessors, the Hunts were the victims of their own aberration, although it also seems likely that they were left with more than enough money to sustain a Texas standard of living.

The documentation on this and other matters is in Stephen Fay's book, which is well written and admirably researched, some minor errors notwithstanding. Mr. Fay is an Englishman, an exponent of the modern British art form that consists in taking some subject of current interest, not necessarily one involving criminal intent, tracking down all details and ramifications, and presenting the results in wholly literate fashion. This he has done with the Hunts and the silver bubble.

The story begins with the grim social convictions that the Hunt brothers inherited, along with their oil wealth, from their father: the revolution is inevitable; the Russians will arrive any day now and will be helped along by numerous local allies who, wittingly or otherwise, are preparing the way. When this happens, the Hunts' extensive holdings in land, cattle, racehorses, sugar refining and other industry, and, above all, in oil-producing properties will be vulnerable. Even now, before the Russians arrive, their moral equivalents in Washington are paying debts with printed money, putting the dollar in extreme jeopardy. (The tendency so to finance deficits has not yet been remedied by Ronald Reagan as promised, but that is another story, and one that must be deeply disappointing to Bunker and Herbert.) The obvious answer is to put as much wealth as possible into something durable and solid, such as silver, and to fly an appreciable part of the hoard, at whatever expense, to storage in a Swiss bank. When the Reds swarm west, they will surely show a decent respect for Swiss neutrality and the gnomes of Zurich. If this reasoning sounds a bit far-fetched, that is because it is. But the

Hunts, as Mr. Fay makes clear, were sufficiently committed to these beliefs to act on them. They also had one or two slightly more common-place ideas.

Newly mined silver, although it was once so abundant that Washing-ton initiated special welfare operations for western miners, is now largely a by-product of base-metal mining. For some years, the supply had been running well behind demand. So it seemed certain that if one took enough off the market, there would be a substantial rise in price. With this in mind, the Hunts, financially abetted by Arabian allies, bought heavily of contracts for future delivery, especially for delivery in the early months of 1980. There was the further possibility, though it cannot be alleged, that as silver was taken up for delivery on these contracts, those who had sold short—that is to say, those who, expecting a decline, had promised future delivery at more or less the current prices—would find it impossible to fulfill their contracts. From their desperate efforts to do so, the price of the metal could rise to almost any level. Mr. Fay is careful not to ascribe any such intent, for this—a "corner"—would be illegal, and such intent, as the government has discovered, is very difficult to prove.

In fact, there was a marked scarcity in 1979, extending into the early part of the next year, when the price of silver reached a peak of more than $50 an ounce. This was up from around $1.50 a decade earlier and from 35 cents an ounce before World War II. Not industrial demand but the enormous purchases of the Hunts and their cohorts were the cause, but beginning around the middle of January, 1980, the metal ceased to be sufficiently scarce to hold at anything like the price it had then reached. The commodity exchanges in New York and Chicago were persuaded to raise margin requirements—the amount of cash in addition to the silver itself required as security for contracts of purchase and sale; in Chicago, limits were also placed on the contracts for forward purchase or sale that any speculator could hold; and the Federal Reserve, which, in October of 1979, had advised against increased use of bank credit for financing the speculation, finally, in March of 1980, insisted on restraint. All of this, along with the defection of some of the Hunt allies, had a chilling effect on the market. The action of the exchanges—motivated, so it is argued, by those who were caught short—is now the basis for lawsuits running into the hundreds of millions.

There were other depressing factors. The Russians did not come, and an almost wholly unpredicted development sent plans for the shortage awry. There is always a very large amount of silver around the country in flatware and utensils, including old bowling, golf, and baseball trophies. All kinds of people concluded that they would rather have paper money than their silver, and many who were reluctant to part with heirlooms had the decision made for them by burglars. An unprecedented exercise in informal expropriation swept the land; facilities for melting down and refining silver were jammed as they had never been before.

For all these reasons, but mostly, one judges, because those who had been waiting for still higher prices decided to get out while, for many, the getting was no longer good, the price of silver collapsed in March of 1981. The Hunts were left with their hoard of the actual metal; and they were left with an even heavier burden of contracts to buy silver at the earlier, high prices—prices that were rapidly becoming part of the financial history of the times. Eventually, out of fear that the financial system would somehow be wrecked, the Federal Reserve warning against loans to speculators was softened. A consortium of banks loaned money to the Hunts' oil company, Placid Oil, which in turn loaned it out on mortgages to the Hunts. With this help they were able to meet their margin calls. (The mortgages, as required by law and custom, were put on file at the Dallas County Courthouse and inspected there by the diligent Mr. Fay, and they are an excellent guide to the brothers' business assets and personal possessions. Thus Mr. Fay learned of Herbert Hunt that he is not much of a collector, "though he does buy coins, Greek statues and the occasional picture, especially when he likes the frame.")

Mr. Fay's research and writing go far beyond the summary presented here. Included is a careful consideration of the painfully innocuous role played by the Commodity Futures Trading Commission. Of the four members of the commission, two were indignantly committed to inaction. Though appointed to supervise the market, they were opposed, on principle, to anything that interfered with the free operation of the market: an interesting conflict. The author is also very good on the banks. The experience of most people with such institutions involves rather small sums—a mortgage or a tiding-over loan—and they discover from this experience how careful banks are when it comes to lending money. They cannot begin to realize how different it is when tens of millions and an armful of different banks are involved. When one bank has lent money in a large and imprudent way, others are persuaded that they are missing something big, and they follow in an even more imprudent rush. Again, the blind do not lead the blind; the activity is more in the manner of the lemmings.

Mr. Fay writes with a justifiable awe of the large sums—always in the tens and often in the hundreds of millions—that were involved in the silver caper. He is better on the losers than the winners (Armand Hammer, who was short in the market and made a hundred million or so when the crash came, is one of the few who is known to have scored). Mr. Fay writes also with a pleasant absence of indignation, an attitude that I share. One supposes that quite a few of those who got trimmed could afford to lose. Those who couldn't should not have been there in the first

place. And if it hadn't been silver, sooner rather than later it would have
been something else. I've been at pains to exculpate the blind as regards
the blind. No one should doubt, however, that fools and their money are
still being parted.

1982

Anthony Burgess

IS AMERICA FALLING APART?

I am back in Bracciano, a castellated town about 13 miles north of
Rome, after a year in New Jersey. I find the Italian Government still
unstable, gasoline more expensive than anywhere in the world, butchers
and bank clerks and tobacconists (which also means saltsellers) ready to
go on strike at the drop of a *cappello*,[1] neo-Fascists at their dirty work, the
hammer and sickle painted on the rumps of public statues, a thousand-
lire note (officially worth about $1.63) shrunk to the slightness of a dollar
bill.

Nevertheless, it's delightful to be back. People are underpaid but they
go through an act of liking their work, the open markets are luscious with
esculent color, the community is more important than the state, the
human condition is humorously accepted. The *tramontana*[2] blows viciously today, and there's no central heating to turn on, but it will be
pleasant when the wind drops. The two television channels are inadequate, but next Wednesday's rerun of an old Western, with Gary
Cooper coming into a saloon saying *"Ciao, ragazzi,"*[3] is something to look
forward to. Manifold consumption isn't important here. The quality of
life has nothing to do with the quantity of brand names. What matters is
talk, family, cheap wine in the open air, the wresting of minimal sweetness out of the long-known bitterness of living. I was spoiled in New
Jersey. The Italian for *spoiled* is *viziato*, cognate with *vitiated*, which has
to do with vice.

Spoiled? Well, yes. I never had to shiver by a fire that wouldn't draw,
or go without canned kraut juice or wild rice. America made me develop
new appetites in order to make proper use of the supermarket. A character in Evelyn Waugh's *Put Out More Flags* said that the difference
between prewar and postwar life was that, prewar, if one thing went
wrong the day was ruined; postwar, if one thing went right the day would
be made. America is a prewar country, psychologically unprepared for

1. Hat.
2. North wind.
3. "Howdy, boys," in Italian.

one thing to go wrong. Now everything seems to be going wrong. Hence the neurosis, despair, the Kafka feeling that the whole marvelous fabric of American life is coming apart at the seams. Italy is used to everything going wrong. This is what the human condition is about.

Let me stay for a while on this subject of consumption. American individualism, on the face of it an admirable philosophy, wishes to manifest itself in independence of the community. You don't share things in common; you have your own things. A family's strength is signalized by its possessions. Herein lies a paradox. For the desire for possessions must eventually mean dependence on possessions. Freedom is slavery. Once let the acquisitive instinct burgeon (enough flour for the winter, not just for the week), and there are ruggedly individual forces only too ready to make it come to full and monstrous blossom. New appetites are invented; what to the European are bizarre luxuries become, to the American, plain necessities.

During my year's stay in New Jersey I let my appetites flower into full Americanism except for one thing. I did not possess an automobile. This self-elected deprivation was a way into the nastier side of the consumer society. Where private ownership prevails, public amenities decay or are prevented from coming into being. The wretched run-down rail services of America are something I try, vainly, to forget. The nightmare of filth, outside and in, that enfolds the trip from Springfield, Mass., to Grand Central Station would not be accepted in backward Europe. But far worse is the nightmare of travel in and around Los Angeles, where public transport does not exist and people are literally choking to death in their exhaust fumes. This is part of the price of the metaphysic of individual ownership.

But if the car owner can ignore the lack of public transport, he can hardly ignore the decay of services in general. His car needs mechanics, and mechanics grow more expensive and less efficient. The gadgets in the home are cheaper to replace than repair. The more efficiently self-contained the home, primary fortress of independence, seems to be, the more dependent it is on the great impersonal corporations, as well as a diminishing army of servitors. Skills at the lowest level have to be wooed slavishly and exorbitantly rewarded. Plumbers will not come. Nor, at the higher level, will doctors. And doctors and dentists, in a nation committed to maiming itself with sugar and cholesterol, know their scarcity value and behave accordingly.

Americans are at last realizing that the acquisition of goods is not the whole of life. Consumption, on one level, is turning insipid, especially as the quality of the artifacts themselves seems to be deteriorating. Planned obsolescence is not conducive to pride in workmanship. On another level, consumption is turning sour. There is a growing guilt about the masses of discarded junk—rusting automobiles and refrigerators and washing machines and dehumidifiers—that it is uneconomical to recycle. Indestructible plastic hasn't even the grace to undergo chemical change. America, the world's biggest consumer, is the world's biggest polluter. Awareness of this is a kind of redemptive grace, but it doesn't appreciably lead to repentance and a revolution in consumer habits. Citizens of Los Angeles are horrified by that daily pall of golden smog, but they don't noticeably clamor for a decrease in the number of owner-vehicles. There is no worse neurosis than that which derives from a consciousness of guilt and an inability to reform.

America is anachronistic in so many ways, and not least in its clinging to a belief—now known to be unviable—in the capacity of the individual citizen to do everything for himself. Americans are admirable in their distrust of the corporate state—they have fought both Fascism and Communism—but they forget that there is a use for everything, even the loathsome bureaucratic machine. America needs a measure of socialization, as Britain needed it. Things—especially those we need most—don't always pay their way, and it is here that the state must enter, dismissing the profit element. Part of the present American neurosis, again, springs from awareness of this but inability to do anything about practical implementation. Perhaps only a country full of bombed cities feels capable of this kind of social revolution.

It would be supererogatory for me to list those areas in which thoughtful Americans feel that collapse is coming. It is enough for me to concentrate on what, during my New Jersey stay, impinged on my own life. Education, for instance, since I have a 6-year-old son to be brought up. America has always despised its teachers and, as a consequence, it has been granted the teachers it deserves. The quality of first-grade education that my son received, in a New Jersey town noted for the excellence of its public schools, could not, I suppose, be faulted on the level of dogged conscientiousness. The principal had read all the right pedagogic books, and was ready to quote these in the footnotes to his circular exhortations to parents. The teachers worked rigidly from the approved rigidly programed primers, ensuring that school textbook publication remains the big business it is.

But there seemed to be no spark; no daring, no madness, no readiness to engage the individual child's mind as anything other than raw material for statistical reductions. The fear of being unorthodox is rooted in the American teacher's soul: you can be fired for treading the path of experimental enterprise. In England, teachers cannot be fired, except for raping girl students and getting boy students drunk. In consequence, there is the kind of security that breeds eccentric genius, the capacity for firing mad enthusiasms.

I know that American technical genius, and most of all the moon landings, seems to give the lie to too summary a condemnation of the educational system, but there is more to education than the segmental equipping of the mind. There is that transmission of the value of the past as a force still miraculously fertile and moving—mostly absent from American education at all levels.

Of course, America was built on a rejection of the past. Even the basic Christianity which was brought to the continent in 1620 was of a novel and bizarre kind that would have nothing to do with the great rank river of belief that produced Dante and Michelangelo. America as a nation has never been able to settle to a common belief more sophisticated than the dangerous naiveté of the Declaration of Independence. "Life, liberty and the pursuit of happiness," indeed. And now America, filling in the vacuum left by the liquefied British Empire, has the task of telling the rest of the world that there's something better than Communism. The something better can only be money-making and consumption for its own sake. In the name of this ghastly creed the jungles must be defoliated.[3]

No wonder the guilt of the thoughtful Americans I met in Princeton and New York and, indeed, all over the Union tended to express itself as an extravagant masochism, a desire for flagellation. Americans want to take on all the blame they can find, gluttons for punishment. "What do Europeans really think of us?" is a common question at parties. The expected answer is: "They think you're a load of decadent, gross-lipped, potbellied, callous, overbearing neoimperialists." Then the head can be bowed and the chest smitten: "*Nostra culpa, nostra maxima culpa. . . .*"[4] But the fact is that such an answer, however much desired, would not be an honest one. Europeans think more highly of Americans now than they ever did. Let me try to explain why.

When Europe, after millennia of war, rapine, slavery, famine, intolerance, had sunk to the level of a sewer, America became the golden dream, the Eden where innocence could be recovered. Original sin was the monopoly of that dirty continent over there; in America man could glow in an aura of natural goodness, driven along his shining path by divine reason. The Declaration of Independence itself is a monument to reason. Progress was possible, and the wrongs committed against the Indians, the wildlife, the land itself, could be explained away in terms of the rational control of environment necessary for the building of a New Jerusalem.[5]

3. That is, in order to deny the enemy protective cover—a part of American strategy during the Vietnam war.
4. "Through our fault, through our most grievous fault," a modification of *Mea culpa, mea maxima culpa* ("Through my fault . . ."), part of the act of confession in the Roman Catholic church.
5. The holy city described by John in Revelation xxi, here a figurative expression for a perfected society.

Right and wrong made up the moral dichotomy; evil—that great eternal inextirpable entity—had no place in America.

At last, with the Vietnam war and especially the Mylai horror,[6] Americans are beginning to realize that they are subject to original sin as much as Europeans are. Some things—the massive crime figures, for instance —can now be explained only in terms of absolute evil. Europe, which has long known about evil and learned to live with it (*live* is *evil* spelled backwards), is now grimly pleased to find that America is becoming like Europe. America is no longer Europe's daughter nor her rich step-mother: she is Europe's sister. The agony that America is undergoing is not to be associated with breakdown so much as with the parturition of self-knowledge.

It has been assumed by many that the youth of America has been in the vanguard of the discovery of both the disease and the cure. The various copping-out movements, however, from the Beats on, have committed the gross error of assuming that original sin rested with their elders, their rulers, and that they themselves could manifest their essential innocence by building little neo-Edens. The drug culture could confirm that the paradisal vision was available to all who sought it. But instant ecstasy has to be purchased, like any other commodity, and, in economic terms, that passive life of pure being involves parasitism. Practically all of the crime I encountered in New York—directly or through report—was a preying of the opium-eaters on the working community. There has to be a snake in paradise. You can't escape the heritage of human evil by building com-munes, usually on an agronomic ignorance that, intended to be a rejec-tion of inherited knowledge, that suspect property of the elders, does violence to life. The American young are well-meaning but misguided, and must not themselves be taken as guides.

The guides, as always, lie among the writers and artists. And Ameri-cans ought to note that, however things may seem to be falling apart, arts and the humane scholarship are flourishing here, as they are not, for instance, in England. I'm not suggesting that Bellow, Mailer, Roth and the rest have the task of finding a solution to the American mess, but they can at least clarify its nature and show how it relates to the human condition in general. Literature, that most directly human of the arts, often reacts magnificently to an ambience of unease or apparent break-down. The Elizabethans,[7] to whose era we look back as to an irrecovera-ble Golden Age, were far more conscious than modern Americans of the chaos and corruption and incompetence of the state. Shakespeare's pe-riod was one of poverty, unemployment, ghastly inflation, violence in the streets. Twenty-six years after his death there was a bloody civil war, followed by a dictatorship of religious fanatics, followed by a calm respite

---

6. A massacre by American troops of over a hundred Vietnamese civilians in the village of Mylai.

7. The British during the reign of Elizabeth I, 1558-1603.

in which the seeds of a revolution were sown. England survived. America will survive.

I'm not suggesting that Americans sit back and wait for a transient period of mistrust and despair to resolve itself, like a disease, through the unconscious healing forces which lie deep in organic nature. Man, as Thornton Wilder showed in The Skin of Our Teeth,[8] always comes through—though sometimes only just. Americans living here and now have a right to an improvement in the quality of their lives, and they themselves, not the remote governors, must do something about it. It is not right that men and women should fear to go on the streets at night, and that they should sometimes fear the police as much as the criminals, both of whom sometimes look like mirror images of each other. I have had too much evidence, in my year in New Jersey, of the police behaving like the "Fascist pigs" of the revolutionary press. There are too many guns about, and the disarming of the police should be a natural aspect of the disarming of the entire citizenry.

American politics, at both the state and the Federal levels, is too much concerned with the protection of large fortunes, America being the only example in history of a genuine timocracy. The wealth qualification for the aspiring politician is taken for granted; a governmental system dedicated to the promotion of personal wealth in a few selected areas will never act for the public good. The time has come, nevertheless, for citizens to demand, from their government, a measure of socialization —the provision of amenities for the many, of which adequate state pensions and sickness benefits, as well as nationalized transport, should be priorities.

As for those remoter solutions to the American nightmare—only an aspect, after all, of the human nightmare—an Englishman must be diffident about suggesting that America made her biggest mistake in becoming America—meaning a revolutionary republic based on a romantic view of human nature. To reject a limited monarchy in favor of an absolute one (which is, after all, what the American Presidency is) argues a trust in the disinterestedness of an elected ruler which is, of course, no more than a reflection of belief in the innate goodness of man—so long as he happens to be American man. The American Constitution is out of date. Republics tend to corruption. Canada and Australia have their own problems, but they are happier countries than America.

This Angst[9] about America coming apart at the seams, which apparently is shared by nearly 50 per cent of the entire American population, is something to rejoice about. A sense of sin is always admirable, though it must not be allowed to become neurotic. If electric systems break down

8. American play depicting man's tragicomic struggle for survival from prehistoric times to the present.
9. Anxiety.

and gadgets disintegrate, it doesn't matter much. There is always wine to be drunk by candlelight, uniced. If America's position as a world power collapses, and the Union dissolves into independent states, there is still the life of the family or the individual to be lived. England has survived her own dissolution as an imperial power, and Englishmen seem to be happy enough. But I ask the reader to note that I, an Englishman, no longer live in England, and I can't spend more than six months at a stretch in Italy—or any other European country, for that matter. I come to America as to a country more stimulating than depressing. The future of mankind is being worked out there on a scale typically American —vast, dramatic, almost apocalyptical. I brave the brutality and the guilt in order to be in on the scene. I shall be back.

1971

QUESTIONS

1. What would Burgess say of the Whole Earth Catalogue: *is it a rejection of consumerism or a surrender to it?*
2. Burgess' observation about the Italian word for spoiled *implies a concern for etymology and precision of language. Is there evidence of that concern in his choice of English words?*

Jonathan Schell

THE DESTRUCTIVE POWER OF A ONE-MEGATON BOMB ON NEW YORK CITY

* * *

One way to begin to grasp the destructive power of present-day nuclear weapons is to describe the consequences of the detonation of a one-megaton bomb, which possesses eighty times the explosive power of the Hiroshima bomb, on a large city, such as New York. Burst some eighty-five hundred feet above the Empire State Building, a one-megaton bomb would gut or flatten almost every building between Battery Park and 125th Street, or within a radius of four and four-tenths miles, or in an area of sixty-one square miles, and would heavily damage buildings between the northern tip of Staten Island and the George Washington Bridge, or within a radius of about eight miles, or in an area of about two hundred square miles. A conventional explosive delivers a swift shock, like a slap, to whatever it hits, but the blast wave of a sizable nuclear weapon endures for several seconds and "can surround and destroy whole buildings" (Glasstone).[1] People, of course, would be picked up and hurled away from the blast along with the rest of the debris. Within the sixty-one square miles, the walls, roofs, and floors of any buildings that had not been flattened would be collapsed, and the people and furniture inside would be swept down onto the street. (Technically, this zone would be hit by various overpressures of at least five pounds per square inch. Overpressure is defined as the pressure in excess of normal atmospheric pressure.) As far away as ten miles from ground zero, pieces of glass and other sharp objects would be hurled about by the blast wave at lethal velocities. In Hiroshima, where buildings were low and, outside the center of the city, were often constructed of light materials, injuries from falling buildings were often minor. But in New York, where the buildings are tall and are constructed of heavy materials, the physical collapse of the city would certainly kill millions of people. The streets of New York are narrow ravines running between the high walls of the city's buildings. In a nuclear attack, the walls would fall and the ravines would fill up. The people in the buildings would fall to the street with the debris of the buildings, and the people in the street would be crushed by this avalanche of people and buildings. At a distance of two miles or so from ground zero, winds would reach four hundred miles an hour, and another two miles away they would reach a hundred and eighty miles an hour. Meanwhile, the fireball would be growing, until it was more than a mile wide, and rocketing upward, to a height of over six miles. For ten seconds, it would broil the city below. Anyone caught in the open within nine miles of ground zero would receive third-degree burns and would probably be killed; closer to the explosion, people would be charred and killed instantly. From Greenwich Village up to Central Park, the heat would be great enough to melt metal and glass. Readily inflammable materials, such as newspapers and dry leaves, would ignite in all five boroughs (though in only a small part of Staten Island) and west to the Passaic River, in New Jersey, within a radius of about nine and a half miles from ground zero, thereby creating an area of more than two hundred and eighty square miles in which mass fires were likely to break out.

If it were possible (as it would not be) for someone to stand at Fifth Avenue and Seventy-second Street (about two miles from ground zero) without being instantly killed, he would see the following sequence of events. A dazzling white light from the fireball would illumine the scene, continuing for perhaps thirty seconds. Simultaneously, searing heat would ignite everything flammable and start to melt windows, cars, buses, lampposts, and everything else made of metal or glass. People in the street would immediately catch fire, and would shortly be reduced to heavily charred corpses. About five seconds after the light appeared, the

1. Samuel Glasstone, editor with Philip Dolan of *Effects of Nuclear Weapons*.

blast wave would strike, laden with the debris of a now nonexistent midtown. Some buildings might be crushed, as though a giant fist had squeezed them on all sides, and others might be picked up off their foundations and whirled uptown with the other debris. On the far side of Central Park, the West Side skyline would fall from south to north. The four-hundred-mile-an-hour wind would blow from south to north, die down after a few seconds, and then blow in the reverse direction with diminished intensity. While these things were happening, the fireball would be burning in the sky for the ten seconds of the thermal pulse. Soon huge, thick clouds of dust and smoke would envelop the scene, and as the mushroom cloud rushed overhead (it would have a diameter of about twelve miles) the light from the sun would be blotted out, and day would turn to night. Within minutes, fires, ignited both by the thermal pulse and by broken gas mains, tanks of gas and oil, and the like, would begin to spread in the darkness, and a strong, steady wind would begin to blow in the direction of the blast. As at Hiroshima, a whirlwind might be produced, which would sweep through the ruins, and radioactive rain, generated under the meteorological conditions created by the blast, might fall. Before long, the individual fires would coalesce into a mass fire, which, depending largely on the winds, would become either a conflagration or a firestorm. In a conflagration, prevailing winds spread a wall of fire as far as there is any combustible material to sustain it; in a firestorm, a vertical updraft caused by the fire itself sucks the surrounding air in toward a central point, and the fires therefore converge in a single fire of extreme heat. A mass fire of either kind renders shelters useless by burning up all the oxygen in the air and creating toxic gases, so that anyone inside the shelters is asphyxiated, and also by heating the ground to such high temperatures that the shelters turn, in effect, into ovens, cremating the people inside them. In Dresden, several days after the firestorm raised there by Allied conventional bombing, the interiors of some bomb shelters were still so hot that when they were opened the inrushing air caused the contents to burst into flame. Only those who had fled their shelters when the bombing started had any chance of surviving. (It is difficult to predict in a particular situation which form the fires will take. In actual experience, Hiroshima suffered a firestorm and Nagasaki suffered a conflagration.)

In this vast theatre of physical effects, all the scenes of agony and death that took place at Hiroshima would again take place, but now involving millions of people rather than hundreds of thousands. Like the people of Hiroshima, the people of New York would be burned, battered, crushed, and irradiated in every conceivable way. The city and its people would be mingled in a smoldering heap. And then, as the fires started, the survivors (most of whom would be on the periphery of the explosion) would be driven to abandon to the flames those family members and other people who were unable to flee, or else to die with them. Before long, while the ruins burned, the processions of injured, mute people would begin their slow progress out of the outskirts of the devastated zone. However, this time a much smaller proportion of the population than at Hiroshima would have a chance of escaping. In general, as the size of the area of devastation increases, the possibilities for escape decrease. When the devastated area is relatively small, as it was at Hiroshima, people who are not incapacitated will have a good chance of escaping to safety before the fires coalesce into a mass fire. But when the devastated area is great, as it would be after the detonation of a megaton bomb, and fires are springing up at a distance of nine and a half miles from ground zero, and when what used to be the streets are piled high with burning rubble, and the day (if the attack occurs in the daytime) has grown impenetrably dark, there is little chance that anyone who is not on the very edge of the devastated area will be able to make his way to safety. In New York, most people would die wherever the blast found them, or not very far from there.

If instead of being burst in the air the bomb were burst on or near the ground in the vicinity of the Empire State Building, the overpressure would be very much greater near the center of the blast area but the range hit by a minimum of five pounds per square inch of overpressure would be less. The range of the thermal pulse would be about the same as that of the air burst. The fireball would be almost two miles across, and would engulf midtown Manhattan from Greenwich Village nearly to Central Park. Very little is known about what would happen to a city that was inside a fireball, but one would expect a good deal of what was there to be first pulverized and then melted or vaporized. Any human beings in the area would be reduced to smoke and ashes; they would simply disappear. A crater roughly three blocks in diameter and two hundred feet deep would open up. In addition, heavy radioactive fallout would be created as dust and debris from the city rose with the mushroom cloud and then fell back to the ground. Fallout would begin to drop almost immediately, contaminating the ground beneath the cloud with levels of radiation many times lethal doses, and quickly killing anyone who might have survived the blast wave and the thermal pulse and might now be attempting an escape; it is difficult to believe that there would be appreciable survival of the people of the city after a megaton ground burst. And for the next twenty-four hours or so more fallout would descend downwind from the blast, in a plume whose direction and length would depend on the speed and the direction of the wind that happened to be blowing at the time of the attack. If the wind was blowing at fifteen miles an hour, fallout of lethal intensity would descend in a plume about a hundred and fifty miles long and as much as fifteen miles wide. Fallout that was sublethal but could still cause serious illness would extend another hundred and fifty miles downwind. Exposure to radioactivity in human beings is measured in units called rems—an acronym for "roentgen equivalent in man." The roentgen is a standard measurement of gamma- and X-ray radiation, and the expression "equivalent in man" indicates that an adjustment has been made to take into account the differences in the degree of biological damage that is caused by radiation of different types. Many of the kinds of harm done to human beings by radiation—for example, the incidence of cancer and of genetic damage —depend on the dose accumulated over many years; but radiation sickness, capable of causing death, results from an "acute" dose, received in a period of anything from a few seconds to several days. Because almost ninety per cent of the so-called "infinite-time dose" of radiation from fallout—that is, the dose from a given quantity of fallout that one would receive if one lived for many thousands of years—is emitted in the first week, the one-week accumulated dose is often used as a convenient measure for calculating the immediate harm from fallout. Doses in the thousands of rems, which could be expected throughout the city, would attack the central nervous system and would bring about death within a few hours. Doses of around a thousand rems, which would be delivered some tens of miles downwind from the blast, would kill within two weeks everyone who was exposed to them. Doses of around five hundred rems, which would be delivered as far as a hundred and fifty miles downwind (given a wind speed of fifteen miles per hour), would kill half of all exposed able-bodied young adults. At this level of exposure, radiation sickness proceeds in the three stages observed at Hiroshima. The plume of lethal fallout could descend, depending on the direction of the wind, on other parts of New York State and parts of New Jersey, Pennsylvania, Delaware, Maryland, Connecticut, Massachusetts, Rhode Island, Vermont, and New Hampshire, killing additional millions of people. The circumstances in heavily contaminated areas, in which millions of people were all declining together, over a period of weeks, toward painful deaths, are ones that, like so many of the consequences of nuclear explosions, have never been experienced.

A description of the effects of a one-megaton bomb on New York City gives some notion of the meaning in human terms of a megaton of nuclear explosive power, but a weapon that is more likely to be used against New York is the twenty-megaton bomb, which has one thousand six hundred times the yield of the Hiroshima bomb. The Soviet Union is estimated to have at least a hundred and thirteen twenty-megaton bombs in its nuclear arsenal, carried by Bear intercontinental bombers. In addition, some of the Soviet SS-18 missiles are capable of carrying bombs of this size, although the actual yields are not known. Since the explosive power of the twenty-megaton bombs greatly exceeds the amount necessary to destroy most military targets, it is reasonable to suppose that they are meant for use against large cities. If a twenty-megaton bomb were air-burst over the Empire State Building at an altitude of thirty thousand feet, the zone gutted or flattened by the blast wave would have a radius of twelve miles and an area of more than four hundred and fifty square miles, reaching from the middle of Staten Island to the northern edge of the Bronx, the eastern edge of Queens, and well into New Jersey, and the zone of heavy damage from the blast wave (the zone hit by a minimum of two pounds of overpressure per square inch) would have a radius of twenty-one and a half miles, or an area of one thousand four hundred and fifty square miles, reaching to the southernmost tip of Staten Island, north as far as southern Rockland County, east into Nassau County, and west to Morris County, New Jersey. The fireball would be about four and a half miles in diameter and would radiate the thermal pulse for some twenty seconds. People caught in the open twenty-three miles away from ground zero, in Long Island, New Jersey, and southern New York State, would be burned to death. People hundreds of miles away who looked at the burst would be temporarily blinded and would risk permanent eye injury. (After the test of a fifteen-megaton bomb on Bikini Atoll, in the South Pacific, in March of 1954, small animals were found to have suffered retinal burns at a distance of three hundred and forty-five miles.) The mushroom cloud would be seventy miles in diameter. New York City and its suburbs would be transformed into a lifeless, flat, scorched desert in a few seconds.

If a twenty-megaton bomb were ground-burst on the Empire State Building, the range of severe blast damage would, as with the one-megaton ground blast, be reduced, but the fireball, which would be almost six miles in diameter, would cover Manhattan from Wall Street to northern Central Park and also parts of New Jersey, Brooklyn, and Queens, and everyone within it would be instantly killed, with most of them physically disappearing. Fallout would again be generated, this time covering thousands of square miles with lethal intensities of radiation. A fair portion of New York City and its incinerated population, now radioactive dust, would have risen into the mushroom cloud and would now be descending on the surrounding territory. On one of the few occasions when local fallout was generated by a test explosion in the multi-megaton range, the fifteen-megaton bomb tested on Bikini Atoll, which was exploded seven feet above the surface of a coral reef, "caused substantial contamination over an area of more than seven thousand square miles," according to Glasstone. If, as seems likely, a twenty-megaton bomb ground-burst on New York would produce at least a comparable amount of fallout, and if the wind carried the fallout onto populated areas, then this one bomb would probably doom upward of twenty million people, or almost ten per cent of the population of the United States.

* * *

1982

Garrison Keillor

THE TOWER PROJECT

Many of our personnel, conscious of the uncertainties of the construction business, have voiced concern relative to their future employment with the Company. What lies ahead on our horizon, they wonder, of the magnitude of the Fred M. and Ida S. Freebold Performing Arts Center, the Tannersfield Freeway Overpass, and other works that have put us in the construction forefront? They recall the cancellation in mid-contract of the Vietnam Parking Lot project, and they ask, "Will the Super-Tall Tower project, too, go down the drain, with a resultant loss of jobs and Company position in the building field?"

The Company believes such will not be the case. While we aren't putting all our "eggs" on one tower and are keeping an eye on the Los Angeles–Honolulu Bridge option and the proposed Lake Michigan Floating Airport, we feel that the Super-Tall Tower has achieved priority status in Washington, and all phases of research and development, land clearance, and counter-resistance are moving forward in expectation of final approval.

As for the Tower critics, they are few in number, and there isn't one of their objections that we haven't answered. Let's look at the record. Their favorite line is "Why build a Super-Tall Tower when money is so urgently needed for cancer and poverty?" With all due respect to the unwell or impoverished person and his or her family, we state our case as follows:

First, Tower construction will create a hundred thousand new jobs, not only in the Babel area and the Greater Southwest but also in other places where the bricks and slime will be made by subcontractors.

Second, because it will be the world's tallest tower, we will be able to see more from it than from any existing tower.

Third, we have reason to believe the Chinese are well along in the development of *their* tower. If we don't wish to abdicate tower leadership to Communist nations, however friendly at the moment, we can't afford to slow down now. To do so would mean the waste of all the money spent on tower research so far and would set back American tower technology for decades to come. Thus, our national prestige is at stake—not merely national pride but the confidence in our ability to rise toward the heavens. When a nation turns away from the sky and looks at its feet, it begins to die as a civilization. Man has long dreamed of building a tall tower from which he could look out and see many interesting and unusual things. Most Americans, we believe, share this dream.

Fourth, environmentalist groups have predicted various disastrous effects from the Tower—that the humming noise of its high-speed elevator will be "unbearable" to the passengers and to nearby residents, that its height will confuse migrating birds, that its long shadow will anger the sun, and so forth. The Company's research laboratory has engaged in a crash program that has already achieved a significant degree of hum reduction; at the same time, our engineers are quick to point out that since no elevator now in service can approach the speed and accompanying hum projected for the Tower elevator, there is no viable data on which to base the entire concept of an "unbearable" hum. Such a determination must wait until the completion of the Tower. In any event, the hum may serve to warn off approaching birds. As for the sun, we feel that, with certain sacrifices, this problem can be taken care of.

1982

Human Nature

Harold Fromm

FROM TRANSCENDENCE TO
OBSOLESCENCE: A ROUTE MAP

Although the age-old problem of the conflict between body and mind
that has tortured philosophers from Plato to Kant and obsessed the
Church from Augustine to Pope Paul has been resolved in modern
philosophical thinking by the elimination of "mind" as an autonomous
entity, the conflict would appear to have returned again to haunt us in a
new guise. The idealized emphasis on "rational" in the concept of man as
the rational animal which characterized Platonic-Christian thought for
two millennia had generally been the product of man's sense of his own
physical weakness, his knowledge that Nature could not be tamed or bent
to his own will. In lieu of the ability to mold Nature to serve his own ends,
man had chosen to extol and mythify that side of his being that seemed to
transcend Nature by inhabiting universes of thought that Nature could
not naysay. The triumphs of intellect and imagination by thinkers and
artists, and the heroic transcending of the body by saints and martyrs
who said "No" to their earthborn limitations, provided for centuries the
consolations of a victory that could be obtained not by winning the battle
but by changing the battlegrounds.

In the course of human history until the twentieth century there was
never any serious likelihood that man could win the body-mind battle on
the field of the body. If one found that it was necessary to produce ten
children in order to insure the survival of five, if one could be swept away
by plagues that killed hundreds of thousands, if one lost one's teeth by
thirty, could not be certain of a food supply for more than a few days,
carted one's own excrements out to the fields or emptied chamberpots
out the window, one could hardly come to believe (despite man's fantastic ability to believe almost anything) that one's ideal self would ever

stand forth on the field of the body, in the natural world. Nature was indeed the enemy, whom one propitiated in the forms of gods and goddesses or saints and martyrs, but who would finally do one in en route to one's *true* home, Abraham's bosom. Good sense taught that it was pointless to waste what little life one did have in a quarrel with the cruelty of Nature when the rational solution could only have been to accept a final repose in the kindness of God. If man was indeed made in the image of God, then it was reasonable to assume that only God could fully appreciate "man's unconquerable mind," while a just assessment of reality required that the field of the body be given up—as how could one do otherwise?—to Nature.

The exaltation of religious figures during all of Hebrew-Christian history prior to modern times was an acknowledgement that saints, prophets, priests, and nuns more fully embodied man's spiritual ideals than most people and that an approximation to spiritual perfection, however difficult, was a more realistic goal than that of bodily self-sufficiency or domination over Nature. The fascination with the fall of heroes in history and fiction involved a painful recognition that nothing physical could endure, not merely in the obvious sense that everything created must inevitably die but that everything created can barely stay alive. The philosophy of *carpe diem*—make your sun run fast if you can't make it stand still, to echo Marvell—was never a prevailing one. For most people, the fear of human fragility and a lack of substantial power against the material world made profound self-confidence a luxury only for kings, who themselves derived their power from God. For others, realism required an acceptance of the Divine will: existence was a gift and the creature had no rights. All was grace.

But by the eighteenth century, the rise of industrialism in the West was accompanied by a decline of religion that cannot be seen as an accidental concurrence. And from then on the trend accelerates. As the average man becomes more enabled to live in comfortable houses that resist the elements, to escape most of the childhood diseases that had made fecundity a virtue, to preserve his teeth into middle or old age, to store food for weeks, months, or years ahead, to communicate rapidly through time and space, to move long distances with ease, to dispose of his excrements through indoor plumbing that makes them all magically vanish in a trice, his perception of Nature undergoes a startling alteration. No longer does Nature seem quite so red in tooth and claw; for a man is much less likely now to perish from the heat or cold, to starve for want of food; his formerly intolerable dependency on the caprices of Nature is no longer so gross; his relation to the other animals and to the vegetable creation appears thickly veiled—by air conditioning, frozen foods, washing machines, detergents, automobiles, electric blankets, and power lawnmowers. And most startling of all, his need for transcendence seems to fade away. For what, after all, is so dreadfully unpleasant about contemporary Western middle-class life that it needs to be transcended? Yes, of course, traffic jams on the freeways are a strain and suburban life can be parodied, but on the scale of things, in relation to man's historical life on earth, the ills of suburbia are not so drastic as to encourage an unduly hasty shuffling off of this mortal coil.

It has been said again and again that modern Western man's comfortable life amidst the conveniences of technology has caused him to suffer a spiritual death, to feel alienated, empty, without purpose and direction. And that may very well be the case. But nevertheless a radical distinction must be made: the need for transcendence experienced by most human beings prior to modern times was a very different one from that which is claimed to exist today. It is not likely that the human race before our time, despite its life dominated by religions and churches and yearnings for transcendence, was a jot more spiritualized than it is today. For if the connection between the growth of industry and the decline of religion is a real one, the earlier spiritual longings appear as an escape from man's vulnerable position in his battle with Nature. It was not that man's aesthetic sensitivities to the Idea of the Good and the Idea of the Beautiful were any more developed in past history; rather, man's need to escape from an intolerable physical life was infinitely greater than ours, for our physical lives are not very oppressive. That "other," "better" world offered by religion could not have been worse than the "real" one, even in the duties that it required on earth, and as a mere fantasy it offered extreme gratification. When I speak of man's previous need for transcendence over the insupportable conditions of physical life, I do not refer to the needs of great creative people—artists, thinkers, craftsmen—who by their very temperaments can never be satisfied with any status quo. I speak of the masses of people whose spiritual lives were necessary to make their physical lives endurable and who, had choice been possible, would certainly have preferred physical comforts over spirituality. This situation does not for the most part now exist: television and toilets have made the need for God supererogatory. Western man does not generally live in fear of Nature, except when earthquakes or cancer strike, for he is mostly unaware of a connection with Nature that has been artfully concealed by modern technology. Almost every deprivation has its accessible remedy, whether hunger, cold, illness, or mere distance; and there is rarely a need, except at a few moments during one's lifetime, to go crying either to papa or to God the Father.

If a need for transcendence does exist today, a question that I am not here pursuing, it is in any case not the same need that formerly was so widespread. It is a need based on satiety and not on deprivation, and it does not seek a haven in another world but rather a more beautiful version of this one. What I am concerned to examine here is what has

happened as a result of the Industrial Revolution to man's conception of his relationship with Nature and what has become the present form of the old mind-body duality.

To the average child of the United States in the present day Nature is indeed a great mystery, not insofar as it is incomprehensible but insofar as it is virtually nonexistent to his perceptions. Not only do most children obtain without delay the nurturing commodities for a satisfied bodily life, but they are rarely in a position to experience a connection between the commodity that fills their need and its natural source. "Meat" consists of red geometrical shapes obtained in plastic packages at the supermarket, whose relationship to animals is obscure if not wholly invisible. Houses are heated by moving a thermostat and clothes are washed by putting them into a washing machine. Even the child's most primitive natural functions are minimally in evidence and it is not surprising that various psychological problems turn up later on in life when man's sensual nature has in some way been concealed at every point by technology. (I recall a student who once remarked that she had no desire to venture out into the country to "enjoy Nature" when she could see all the trees she wanted on color TV.)

The reader should be assured that I am not engaged in presenting these observations in an effort to make the familiar attack on "technology." I have no personal objections to meat in plastic containers or flush toilets and air conditioning. In fact, I like them very much. I have no desire to hunt animals, to chop down trees for firewood, to use an outhouse, or to have smallpox. I have no interest in a "return to Nature," which strikes me as an especially decadent form of aestheticism, like an adult of forty pretending to have the innocence of a child. My consciousness as a person living at a particular stage of history cannot be wiped away by a decision to perform a Marie Antoinette.[1] I would much prefer to listen to music or work in the garden than to struggle for survival. I have presented a picture of a hypothetical child who sees no relation between the red glob in the plastic carton and the animal from which it came, not to attack either technology or modern techniques of child raising. What I am trying to do is to present a picture of man's current relation to Nature.

With Nature barely in evidence and man's physical needs satisfied beyond what could have been imagined one hundred years ago, man's mind would appear to have arrived at a state of altogether new autonomy and independence—not this time the independence of a mind that has given up all hope of dominating Nature and satisfying the flesh and therefore seeking in desperation a haven in Abraham's bosom; rather, this time, a mind so assured of its domination of Nature and its capacity

1. The members of whose court affected a return to nature by playing at being shepherds and shepherdesses.

to satisfy the flesh that it seems to be borne up on its own engine of Will, cut off from any nurturing roots in the earth. Mind, now soaring not on wings of fear but on sturdy pinions of volition, can say to Nature, "*Retro Sathanas!*"[2] Do not presume, it would say, to interfere with my self-determination, for if you do, I will flip on the air conditioning, switch on the electronic air cleaner, swallow down the antibiotics, spread on the weed killer, inject the flu vaccine, fill up the gas tank.

But while all of this newfound mental assurance has been building up, when man has finally found a home in the world, when he feels he is lord of all he surveys, when he no longer needs to have his spirit stroked by the right hand of God—a new "trouble" (which I put in quotation marks because it is thought by some to be purely imaginary) rears its ugly head: man's nurturing environment threatens to stop nurturing and to start killing.

One opens the newspaper each day to find four or five articles whose burden is that pesticides contaminate the food of farm animals in Michigan; Kepone is being dumped in waterways, asbestos fibers in Lake Superior; poison gases render uninhabitable a village in Italy; the Parthenon is decaying faster in ten years than in the previous thousand because of automobile exhausts; ozone and sulfur dioxide increase mortality rates in Chicago and Los Angeles.

Although we had been taught in our high-school science classes for decades that neither matter nor energy could be created or destroyed, suddenly it dawns upon someone that the refuse being dumped into the oceans and atmosphere for years and years in ever-increasing quantities does not "go away." Where was it supposed to go? Suddenly, the human race has been put into the position of affluent teen-agers who dump beer cans from their moving sportscar and then drive off. The cans appear to have vanished, but no, there they are, astoundingly enough, rolling around the neighborhood where they had been dumped. And when the teen-agers arrive home, they find other beer cans dumped by other teen-agers. The neighborhood is a place of beer cans; the ocean a place of toxic effluents; the sky is vaporized garbage. And to add insult to injury, man's unconquerable mind turns out to have a mouth, through which it is fed; and worse still, it is being fed garbage. Its own!

Before continuing, let us stop for a moment to see where we have been: in the early days, man had no power over Nature and turned, instead, to his mind and its gods for consolation. Meanwhile, his mind produces a technology that enables his body to be as strong as the gods, rendering the gods superfluous and putting Nature in a cage. Then it appears that there is no Nature and that man has produced virtually everything out of his own ingenuity and it can be bought in a supermarket or a discount store, wrapped in plastic. By now, man is scarcely aware that he is eating

2. "Go back, Satan!" Jesus in the Bible so speaks to the adversary.

animals and producing wastes or that the animals come from somewhere and the wastes are headed somewhere. This "somewhere" turns out to be, practically speaking, a finite world whose basic components cannot be created or destroyed although (and here is the shocker) they can be turned into forms that are unusable by man. As more and more of these basic materials are rendered unusable by man, it becomes apparent that man has failed to see that now, as in the past, the roots of his being are in the earth; and he has failed to see this because Nature, whose effects on man were formerly *immediate*, is now *mediated* by technology so that it appears that technology and not Nature is actually responsible for everything. This has given to man a sense that he mentally and voluntarily determines the ground of his own existence and that his body is almost a dispensable adjunct of his being. This is modern man's own peculiar mythology: The Myth of Voluntary Omnipotence. It is the contemporary form of the Faust legend, a legend which in all of its variants ends the same way.

Nowhere is this modern version of the Faust myth so apparent as in the words of industrial corporations who attack the basic conception of environmental protection. If the classic flaw of the tragic hero is overweening pride and a refusal to acknowledge his own finitude, the contemporary Faustian attitude is archetypically struck in the advertisements of steel and oil companies protesting that "stagnation is the worst form of pollution." The current terminology of doublespeak can be seen in the modish word "trade-offs," a concept which would admirably serve as the basis for present-day tragic drama. One would suppose from such talk that modern industrial corporations, with their fears of economic stagnation and their estimate of clean air as an unaffordable economic luxury, were Shelleyan Prometheuses,[3] defending man's sublime aspirations in the face of a tyrannical and boorish Zeus. *Sic itur ad astra,*[4] indeed!

The continual appearance of the concept of "trade-offs," in which one sacrifices the "luxury" of an uncontaminated environment in order to permit economic "progress," brings to my mind a cartoon that I saw years ago, before anybody ever heard of the environment: two emaciated and threadbare prisoners are bound with manacles and pedicles to the middle of a wall about four stories high in an immense featureless white room. Flailing upon the wall, about two stories above the ground, one enfeebled prisoner says to the other, "Now here's my plan...." Is this not an emblem of modern man? Oblivious of his roots in the earth or unwilling to acknowledge them, intent only upon the desires of his unconquerable mind, he refuses to see that his well-nurtured body and Faustian will are connected by fine tubes—a "life-support system," if you wish—to the earth. Can those Faustian thoughts continue without a narrowly pre-

3. In Greek mythology, Prometheus defied Zeus and the other gods by bringing to man the gift of fire. The English poet Shelley celebrated Prometheus as hero.
4. Such is the way to the stars.

scribed nutriment for the body, a nutriment prescribed not by that Faustian mind itself but by a biological determination that has been *given* rather than *chosen?* Are not the limitations once described as the will of God and as "grace" as much limitations now as they have ever been in the past? Unless man can create himself, unless he can determine his own existential nature, how can he talk—absurdly, madly, derangedly —about "trade-offs" with the environment or "negotiations" with Nature? Can one negotiate with the *données* of human existence? Even a Promethean Sisyphus[5] needs food to push his rock.

I recently had occasion to publish two essays describing the traumatic effects which polluted air has had upon my wife and me during the past six years, one of my major points being that we are not "cardiac and respiratory patients" but normally healthy people whose lives have been radically altered by industrial emissions since we came to live in the Chicago area. One of these essays, a brief account of our experiences that appeared in the *New York Times* and was subsequently reprinted in other newspapers, brought me a number of interesting and varied responses from readers. A letter that particularly struck me read as follows:

Dear Sir:

Since all of the environmentalists who worry about pollution are also consumers of the products of these belching plants (the automobile for instance by which you reach your farm), what IS the answer? Do we cut off our noses to spite our faces? Do we destroy our economy: eliminate many necessities of life; go back to living in tents for the sake of clean air? The answers are complex.

This was a profoundly disturbing letter. The writer was by no means insensitive to the problems of our time; she saw that a complex dilemma is involved; and she was obviously very concerned about the entire affair. Yet her expression "for the sake of clean air" is a familiar one and reveals that the heart of the problem has not been grasped. For when she asks, "Do we eliminate many of the necessities of life for the sake of clean air?" one wants to know: what are the necessities of life in comparison with which clean air cannot be regarded as a necessity? But to ask this is to raise a purely rhetorical question, for the problem is really an ontological and not an ecological one.

When the writer refers to the "necessities of life" one must ask what it is that she means by *life,* and I am proposing that by "life" she means her desires and her will; by the "economy" and "necessities" she means those things which support her mind's conception of itself. There is not a body in sight. She sees steps taken to preserve the environment as actions "for the sake of" clean air. She does not see them as "for the sake of" her own

5. For showing disrespect to Zeus, Sisyphus (another god-defier in Greek mythology) is punished by having to roll a huge rock up a hill throughout eternity.

biological existence. *Somehow,* she is alive: she eats food, drinks water, breathes air, but she does not see these actions as *grounds of life;* rather, they are acts that *coincide* with her life, her life being her thoughts and wishes. The purity of the elements that make her life possible is not seen as a condition of existence. Instead, the economy, the "necessities" and not "living in tents" are what matter. *That* is life. Her existence on earth somehow takes care of itself and if it does take care of itself, then why sacrifice the "necessities" of life "for the sake of" the superfluities, like "clean air"?

The pattern of thought which this letter reflects becomes clearer if we make some substitutions: "Do we eliminate necessities of life for the sake of clean air?" could equally well be presented as "Do we give up smoking for the sake of avoiding lung cancer?" since smoking occupies the role (for those who feel they must smoke) of a necessity of life and "avoiding lung cancer" occupies the position of "for the sake of clean air." However, "avoiding lung cancer" can be more clearly stated as "remaining alive," which would then yield the question: "Do we give up smoking for the sake of remaining alive?" And in a final transformation we may obtain: "Do we give up the necessities of life for the sake of remaining alive?" I offer that as the paradigmatic question behind all of the similar ones that people ask. On the surface, we are faced with a paradox: how can someone ask whether it is necessary to give up a condition of life in order to remain alive? But the paradox evaporates when we realize that the "necessity" is no necessity at all, from the viewpoint of our biological existence. Rather, the "necessity" (smoking, the present economy, etc.) is a mental stance, a wish, that in fact is inimical to the survival of the body that would make it possible to continue to fulfill the wish.

We are able to see that this is a variant of the traditional mind-body problem, the view here being that man is his mind, that man is his thoughts and wishes. But man's sublime mind (not to mention the very unsublime wishes described above), while it may wander at will through the universe and be connected to the heavens at one end, is connected at the other to the earth. As free as that mind may appear in its wanderings, thoughts rely on calories, because they are fueled by the same metabolic processes that make all other human activities possible. A thought may have no weight and take up no space, but it exists as part of a stream of consciousness that is made possible by food, air, and water. Every moment of man's existence as a human being is dependent upon a continuous burning up of energy, his classical tragic conflict consisting of a mind that is capable of envisioning modes of existence that are not supportable by a human engine thusly fueled. The confidence of Oedipus that he could outwit causation[6] provides the model for the present environmen-

6. In the Greek tragedy *Oedipus Rex,* the hero fulfills his fated killing of his father and marrying of his mother in the very process of attempting to avoid the terms of the oracle that had foretold his fate.

tal dilemma. But there is little that is new about this dilemma besides its peculiarly contemporary terms. The struggle between the "necessities of modern life" and the "environment" is the age-old struggle between the individual will and the universe, the substance, in other words, of classical tragedy.

Thus "the problem of the environment," which many people persist in viewing as a peripheral arabesque drawn around the "important" concerns of human life, must ultimately be seen as a central philosophic and ontological question about the self-definition of contemporary man. For all one's admiration of man's unconquerable mind and its Faustian aspirations, that mind would seem to be eminently conquerable, particularly by itself. It is, after all, a very frail vessel, floating upon a bloodstream that is easily contaminated by every passing impurity: alcohol, nicotine, sulfur dioxide, ozone, Kepone, DDT, sodium nitrite, red dye #2—the list appears endless. As much as at any time in the past, however, man's relationship with Nature is nonnegotiable. Perhaps within a certain narrow range man's constitution is susceptible to adaptation, but in the light of the innumerable and arbitrary concurrences that make human life possible, man's adaptability seems very limited indeed. In the past, man's Faustian aspirations were seen against the background of his terrifying weakness in the face of Nature. Today, man's Faustian posturings take place against a background of arrogant, shocking, and suicidal disregard of his roots in the earth.

1978

QUESTIONS

1. *What is Fromm's thesis? Is that thesis formulated in a single sentence, a few sentences, or anywhere in the essay?*
2. *Does the author oppose all technology and favor a return to nature? Where and how does he make his position clear?*
3. *Will technological advances and more effective technological controls solve the problem Fromm is addressing? Why, or why not?*
4. *In what ways and to what purpose does Fromm use mythology? Does his use of myths strengthen or weaken his case? What do ancient myths have to do with present-day realities?*
5. *What are "the necessities of life"?*

Jerome S. Bruner

FREUD AND THE IMAGE OF MAN

By the dawn of the sixth century before Christ, the Greek physicist-philosophers had formulated a bold conception of the physical world as a unitary material phenomenon. The Ionians had set forth a conception of matter as fundamental substance, transformation of which accounted for the myriad forms and substances of the physical world. Anaximander was subtle enough to recognize that matter must be viewed as a generalized substance, free of any particular sensuous properties. Air, iron, water or bone were only elaborated forms, derived from a more general stuff. Since that time, the phenomena of the physical world have been conceived as continuous and monistic, as governed by the common laws of matter. The view was a bold one, bold in the sense of running counter to the immediate testimony of the senses. It has served as an axiomatic basis of physics for more than two millennia. The bold view eventually became the obvious view, and it gave shape to our common understanding of the physical world. Even the alchemists rested their case upon this doctrine of material continuity and, indeed, had they known about neutron bombardment, they might even have hit upon the proper philosopher's stone.

The good fortune of the physicist—and these matters are always relative, for the material monism of physics may have impeded nineteenth-century thinking and delayed insights into the nature of complementarity in modern physical theory—this early good fortune or happy insight has no counterpart in the sciences of man. Lawful continuity between man and the animal kingdom, between dreams and unreason on one side and waking rationality on the other, between madness and sanity, between consciousness and unconsciousness, between the mind of the child and the adult mind, between primitive and civilized man —each of these has been a cherished discontinuity preserved in doctrinal canons. There were voices in each generation, to be sure, urging the exploration of continuities. Anaximander had a passing good approximation to a theory of evolution based on natural selection; Cornelius Agrippa offered a plausible theory of the continuity of mental health and disease in terms of bottled-up sexuality. But Anaximander did not prevail against Greek conceptions of man's creation nor did Cornelius Agrippa against the demonopathy of the *Malleus Maleficarum.*[1] Neither in establishing the continuity between the varied states of man nor in pursuing

1. The *Hammer for Evil Doers*, a notorious medieval book about demons and witchcraft.

the continuity between man and animal was there conspicuous success until the nineteenth century.

I need not insist upon the social, ethical, and political significance of an age's image of man, for it is patent that the view one takes of man affects profoundly one's standard of dignity and the humanly possible. And it is in the light of such a standard that we establish our laws, set our aspirations for learning, and judge the fitness of men's acts. Those who govern, then, must perforce be jealous guardians of man's ideas about man, for the structure of government rests upon an uneasy consensus about human nature and human wants. Since the idea of man is of the order of res publica,[2] it is an idea not subject to change without public debate. Nor is it simply a matter of public concern. For man as individual has a deep and emotional investment in his image of himself. If we have learned anything in the last half-century of psychology, it is that man has powerful and exquisite capacities for defending himself against violation of his cherished self-image. This is not to say that Western man has not persistently asked: "What is man that thou art mindful of him?" It is only that the question, when pressed, brings us to the edge of anxiety where inquiry is no longer free.

Two figures stand out massively as the architects of our present-day conception of man: Darwin and Freud. Freud's was the more daring, the more revolutionary, and in a deep sense, the more poetic insight. But Freud is inconceivable without Darwin. It is both timely and perhaps historically just to center our inquiry on Freud's contribution to the modern image of man. Darwin I shall treat as a necessary condition for Freud and for his success, recognizing, of course, that this is a form of psychological license. Not only is it the centenary of Freud's birth; it is also a year in which the current of popular thought expressed in commemoration of the date quickens one's awareness of Freud's impact on our times.

Rear-guard fundamentalism did not require a Darwin to slay it in an age of technology. He helped, but this contribution was trivial in comparison with another. What Darwin had done was to propose a set of principles unified around the conception that all organic species had their origins and took their form from a common set of circumstances —the requirements of biological survival. All living creatures were on a common footing. When the post-Darwin era of exaggeration had passed and religious literalism had abated into a new nominalism, what remained was a broad, orderly, and unitary conception of organic nature, a vast continuity from the monocellular protozoans to man. Biology had at last found its unifying principle in the doctrine of evolution. Man was not unique but the inheritor of an organic legacy.

As the summit of an evolutionary process, man could still view himself

2. The state.

with smug satisfaction, indeed proclaim that God or Nature had shown a persistent wisdom in its effort to produce a final, perfect product. It remained for Freud to present the image of man as the unfinished product of nature: struggling against unreason, impelled by driving inner vicissitudes and urges that had to be contained if man were to live in society, host alike to seeds of madness and majesty, never fully free from an infancy anything but innocent. What Freud was proposing was that man at his best and man at his worst is subject to a common set of explanations: that good and evil grow from a common process.

Freud was strangely yet appropriately fitted for his role as architect of a new conception of man. We must pause to examine his qualifications, for the image of man that he created was in no small measure founded on his painfully achieved image of himself and of his times. We are concerned not so much with his psychodynamics, as with the intellectual traditions he embodies. A child of his century's materialism, he was wedded to the determinism and the classical physicalism of nineteenth-century physiology so boldly represented by Helmholtz. Indeed, the young Freud's devotion to the exploration of anatomical structures was a measure of the strength of this inheritance. But at the same time, as both Lionel Trilling and W. H. Auden have recognized with much sensitivity, there was a deep current of romanticism in Freud—a sense of the role of impulse, of the drama of life, of the power of symbolism, of ways of knowing that were more poetic than rational in spirit, of the poet's cultural alienation. It was perhaps this romantic's sense of drama that led to his gullibility about parental seduction and to his generous susceptibility to the fallacy of the dramatic instance.

Freud also embodies two traditions almost as antithetical as romanticism and nineteenth-century scientism. He was profoundly a Jew, not in a doctrinal sense but in his conception of morality, in his love of the skeptical play of reason, in his distrust of illusion, in the form of his prophetic talent, even in his conception of mature eroticism. His prophetic talent was antithetic to a Utopianism either of innocence or of social control. Nor did it lead to a counsel of renunciation. Free oneself of illusion, of neurotic infantilism, and "the soft voice of intellect" would prevail. Wisdom for Freud was neither doctrine nor formula, but the achievement of maturity. The patient who is cured is the one who is now free enough of neurosis to decide intelligently about his own destiny. As for his conception of mature love, it has always seemed to me that its blend of tenderness and sensuality combined the uxorious imagery of the Chassidic tradition[3] and the sensual quality of the Song of Songs. And might it not have been Freud rather than a commentator of the Haftorahs[4] who said, "In children, it was taught, God gives humanity a

3. Or Hasidic; the reference is to a Jewish sect devoted to mystical rather than secular study.
4. Writings of the Old Testament Prophets.

chance to make good its mistakes." For the mordern trend of permissiveness toward children is surely a feature of the Freudian legacy.

But for all the Hebraic quality, Freud is also in the classical tradition —combining the Stoics and the great Greek dramatists. For Freud as for the Stoics, there is no possibility of man disobeying the laws of nature. And yet, it is in this lawfulness that for him the human drama inheres. His love for Greek drama and his use of it in his formulation are patent. The sense of the human tragedy, the inevitable working out of the human plight—these are the hallmarks of Freud's case histories. When Freud, the tragic dramatist, becomes a therapist, it is not to intervene as a directive authority. The therapist enters the drama of the patient's life, makes possible a play within a play, the transference, and when the patient has "worked through" and understood the drama, he has achieved the wisdom necessary for freedom. Again, like the Stoics, it is in the recognition of one's own nature and in the acceptance of the laws that govern it that the good life is to be found.

Freud's contribution lies in the continuities of which he made us aware. The first of these is the continuity of organic lawfulness. Accident in human affairs was no more to be brooked as "explanation" than accident in nature. The basis for accepting such an "obvious" proposition had, of course, been well prepared by a burgeoning nineteenth-century scientific naturalism. It remained for Freud to extend naturalistic explanation to the heart of human affairs. The *Psychopathology of Everyday Life* is not one of Freud's deeper works, but "the Freudian slip" has contributed more to the common acceptance of lawfulness in human behavior than perhaps any of the more rigorous and academic formulations from Wundt to the present day. The forgotten lunch engagement, the slip of the tongue, the barked shin could no longer be dismissed as accident. Why Freud should have succeeded where the novelists, philosophers, and academic psychologists had failed we will consider in a moment.

Freud's extension of Darwinian doctrine beyond Haeckel's theorem that ontogeny recapitulates phylogeny[5] is another contribution to continuity. It is the conception that in the human mind, the primitive, infantile, and archaic exist side-by-side with the civilized and evolved.

> Where animals are concerned we hold the view that the most highly developed have arisen from the lowest. . . . In the realm of mind, on the other hand, the primitive type is so commonly preserved alongside the transformations which have developed out of it that it is superfluous to give instances in proof of it. When this happens, it is usually the result of a bifurcation in development. One quantitative part of an attitude or an impulse has survived unchanged while another has undergone further development. This brings us

5. That is, the evolution of the fetus into an independent organism parallels the evolutionary development of that species.

very close to the more general problem of conservation in the mind. . . . Since the time when we recognized the error of supposing that ordinary forgetting signified destruction or annihilation of the memory-trace, we have been inclined to the opposite view that nothing once formed in the mind could ever perish, that everything survives in some way or other, and is capable under certain conditions of being brought to light again . . . (Freud, *Civilization and Its Discontents*, pp. 14-15).

What has now come to be common sense is that in everyman there is the potentiality for criminality, and that these are neither accidents nor visitations of degeneracy, but products of a delicate balance of forces that, under different circumstances, might have produced normality or even saintliness. Good and evil, in short, grow from a common root.

Freud's genius was in his resolution of polarities. The distinction of child and adult was one such. It did not suffice to reiterate that the child was father to the man. The theory of infantile sexuality and the stages of psychosexual development were an effort to fill the gap, the latter clumsy, the former elegant. Though the alleged progression of sexual expression from the oral, to the anal, to the phallic, and finally to the genital has not found a secure place either in common sense or in general psychology, the developmental continuity of sexuality has been recognized by both. Common sense honors the continuity in the baby-books and in the permissiveness with which young parents of today resolve their doubts. And the research of Beach and others has shown the profound effects of infantile experience on adult sexual behavior—even in lower organisms.

If today people are reluctant to report their dreams with the innocence once attached to such recitals, it is again because Freud brought into common question the discontinuity between the rational purposefulness of waking life and the seemingly irrational purposelessness of fantasy and dream. While the crude symbolism of Freud's early efforts at dream interpretation has come increasingly to be abandoned—that telephone poles and tunnels have an invariant sexual reference—the conception of the dream as representing disguised wishes and fears has become common coin. And Freud's recognition of deep unconscious processes in the creative act, let it also be said, has gone far toward enriching our understanding of the kinship between the artist, the humanist, and the man of science.

Finally, it is our heritage from Freud that the all-or-none distinction between mental illness and mental health has been replaced by a more humane conception of the continuity of these states. The view that neurosis is a severe reaction to human trouble is as revolutionary in its implications for social practice as it is daring in formulation. The "bad seed" theories, the nosologies of the nineteenth century, the demonologies and doctrines of divine punishment—none of these provided a basis for compassion toward human suffering comparable to that of our time.

One may argue, at last, that Freud's sense of the continuity of human conditions, of the likeness of the human plight, has made possible a deeper sense of the brotherhood of man. It has in any case tempered the spirit of punitiveness toward what once we took as evil and what we now see as sick. We have not yet resolved the dilemma posed by these two ways of viewing. Its resolution is one of the great moral challenges of our age.

Why, after such initial resistance, were Freud's views so phenomenally successful in transforming common conceptions of man?

One reason we have already considered: the readiness of the Western world to accept a naturalistic explanation of organic phenomena and, concurrently, to be readier for such explanation in the mental sphere. There had been at least four centuries of uninterrupted scientific progress, recently capped by a theory of evolution that brought man into continuity with the rest of the animal kingdom. The rise of naturalism as a way of understanding nature and man witnessed a corresponding decline in the explanatory aspirations of religion. By the close of the nineteenth century, religion, to use Morton White's phrase, "too often agreed to accept the role of a non-scientific spiritual grab-bag, or an ideological know-nothing." The elucidation of the human plight had been abandoned by religion and not yet adopted by science.

It was the inspired imagery, the proto-theory of Freud that was to fill the gap. Its success in transforming the common conception of man was not simply its recourse to the "cause-and-effect" discourse of science. Rather it is Freud's imagery, I think, that provides the clue to this ideological power. It is an imagery of necessity, one that combines the dramatic, the tragic, and the scientific views of necessity. It is here that Freud's intellectual heritage matters so deeply. Freud's is a theory or a proto-theory peopled with actors. The characters are from life: the blind, energic, pleasure-seeking id; the priggish and punitive super-ego; the ego, battling for its being by diverting the energy of the others to its own use. The drama has an economy and a terseness. The ego develops canny mechanisms for dealing with the threat of id impulses: denial, projection,[6] and the rest. Balances are struck between the actors, and in the balance is character and neurosis. Freud was using the dramatic technique of decomposition, the play whose actors are parts of a single life. It is a technique that he himself had recognized in fantasies and dreams, one he honored in "The Poet and the Daydream."

The imagery of the theory, moreover, has an immediate resonance with the dialectic of experience. True, it is not the stuff of superficial conscious experience. But it fits the human plight, its conflictedness, its

6. The attribution to others of one's own feelings.

private torment, its impulsiveness, its secret and frightening urges, its tragic quality.

Concerning its scientific imagery, it is marked by the necessity of the classical mechanics. At times the imagery is hydraulic: suppress this stream of impulses, and perforce it breaks out in a displacement elsewhere. The system is a closed and mechanical one. At times it is electrical, as when cathexes are formed and withdrawn like electrical charges. The way of thought fitted well the common-sense physics of its age.

Finally, the image of man presented was thoroughly secular; its ideal type was the mature man free of infantile neuroticism, capable of finding his own way. This freedom from both Utopianism and asceticism has earned Freud the contempt of ideological totalitarians of the Right and the Left. But the image has found a ready home in the rising, liberal intellectual middle class. For them, the Freudian ideal type has become a rallying point in the struggle against spiritual regimentation.

I have said virtually nothing about Freud's equation of sexuality and impulse. It was surely and still is a stimulus to resistance. But to say that Freud's success lay in forcing a reluctant Victorian world to accept the importance of sexuality is as empty as hailing Darwin for his victory over fundamentalism. Each had a far more profound effect.

Can Freud's contribution to the common understanding of man in the twentieth century be likened to the impact of such great physical and biological theories as Newtonian physics and Darwin's conception of evolution? The question is an empty one. Freud's mode of thought is not a theory in the conventional sense, it is a metaphor, an analogy, a way of conceiving man, a drama. I would propose that Anaximander is the proper parallel: his view of the connectedness of physical nature was also an analogy—and a powerful one. Freud is the ground from which theory will grow, and he has prepared the twentieth century to nurture the growth. But far more important, he has provided an image of man that has made him comprehensible without at the same time making him contemptible.

1956

Anthony Burgess

OUR BEDFELLOW, THE MARQUIS DE SADE

Only two writers in the whole of world literature have, solely on the strength of the philosophies they preached, been elevated into monstrous figures of evil. The first was Niccolò Machiavelli, whose book on statecraft, *Il Principe* (The Prince), was not well understood by his chief traducers, the Elizabethan English. The popular view of "Old Nick" (yes, that's where the diabolic sobriquet comes from) was of a bogeyman dedicated to the subversion of good, the liquidation of religion, and the promotion of death and violence for their own sake. A close reading of *Il Principe* shows that Machiavelli went, in fact, nowhere near so far: he was concerned with a very laudable end—that of maintaining order in a community threatened by enemies without and traitors within. What earned him such extravagent odium was his lack of scruple about the means by which that end should be fulfilled. Every state, even the most liberal and democratic, has in time of emergency had to use Machiavellian devices: yet mention the term, or preferably whisper it ("Machiavellian!"), and the response is a shuddering one. The word has been loaded for centuries.

The second of these writers is the Marquis de Sade, and till recently, the term sadism has not carried the full load of horror available to it. The most popular joke that admits the perversion and its complement is about the sadist and the masochist who share adjoining beds in a psychiatric ward. "Beat me, beat me!" cries the masochist. "No," says the sadist. But that is not it at all: there is nothing negative in sadism. And the small torturer, the boy who pulls wings off flies, the husband who drops burning brown paper on his wife's bare body—these don't go far enough. The extravagance of evil falsely attributed to Machiavelli should, by rights, be transferred to the Marquis. But few people have read his works, and few imaginations are capable of teaching the ingenuities of his fancies. It is only fairly recently that this devil has been given his due.

The world that George Orwell presents in *Nineteen Eighty-Four* owes a great deal to Sade. The ruling oligarchy knows what it is doing: it wants power, and it intends, behind the immortal, because mythical, facade of Big Brother, to keep power till the end of time. This power is the ultimate pleasure, the final human fulfillment. Its image is of a jackboot poised voluptuously over a terrified human face. The exercise of power means the exercise of cruelty, for it is only through cruelty that you can show your victim the extent of your total domination over him.

Sade's actions and, more patently, Sade's literary fantasies represented power as an aspect of the sexual impulse. The sexual act is shown not as a reciprocity of pleasure giving, but as the enforcing of strange desires on an unwilling victim. To share pleasure, said Sade, is to weaken it. The victim (like Winston Smith in *Nineteen Eighty-Four*) must be impotent to strike back and must be of a preordained persecutable type. In the sexual field it is women who are made for persecution: physiologically they are natural victims. Sade's major work, the unfinished *120 Days of Sodom*, is a detailed catalogue of sexual perversions, all of which involve torture and some of them death. The form of the book is fictional. The setting is a castle in the Black Forest, totally impregnable, and in it four debauchées from Paris—a banker, a bishop, a duke, and a judge—spend seventeen weeks in perverse pleasures that are graduated from the merely revolting to the ineffably and transcendently evil. It was Sade's intention to describe six hundred perversions, but he only managed to get through the first thirty days—though he made very detailed notes for the other ninety. Thus the seventy-ninth perversion in the "Third Class of Criminal Passions" entails strapping a naked girl face down to a table and having "a piping hot omelette served upon her buttocks." The eater "uses an exceedingly sharp fork." This is comparatively mild. The ultimate horror has fifteen girls (none older than seventeen) all tortured simultaneously in fifteen different ways, while the *grand seigneur* who arranges this elaborate *grand guignol*[1] watches and waits for orgasm. It does not come easily, despite the monstrous stimulus: it has to be effected through masturbation and the exhibition of two male bottoms.

It is evident that Sade, in conceiving these nightmares (nightmares to us; delicious dreams to him), was in a state of sexual frustration so intense that it drove him to a kind of clearheaded mania. The deprivations of prison life were an obvious factor, but they must be only a small part of the story. For Sade's dreams are essentially dreams of impotence, just as the recorded orgies on which some of the dreams are based are attempts to find satisfaction when the normal means have failed. The situation is not all that unusual. Eighteenth-century France was notable for its lecherous aristocracy, and Sade's youthful roistering was not more spectacular than that of many of his peers and superiors. But the normal sexual vein was overworked; the palate demanded sharper sauces. Or put it another way: the familiar intoxication could only, as with drug takers, be attained by stimulants that grew stronger and stronger.

The first stimulant was sodomy—one that has never been as rare as the law, which represses it mercilessly, would have us believe. Heterosexual sodomy (read the *Kamasutra*[2] on this) is a regular age-old practice among Tamils, and it carries little flavor of the perverse. But sodomy is selfish, and it can also be cruel. Sade was fascinated by it, and he is led through it

1. The great lord. A theatrical entertainment stressing the gruesome or horrible; the name comes from a small theatre in Montmartre that showed such plays.
2. A Hindu manual of love.

to a genuinely nauseating preoccupation with the anus: he plays with feces like an infant.

When what may be termed pure sodomy fails to bring satisfaction, the next stage of cruelty is reached: the imposition of pain unconnected with coition and not necessarily centered on the erogenous zones. To inflict suffering is enough, by whatever means. But the more elementary forms —burning the flesh, cutting, flaying, even poisoning—must pall sooner or later, and then the sadist is led on to the more ingenious tortures, most of them slowly lethal. Where is the limit? The limit is reached, it would seem, when heterosexual fantasies are swallowed up in apocalyptic visions of mass destruction—Hitlerian visions whose sexual content is not immediately apparent. Sade's destructive fantasies are curiously modern —the blasting of whole towns, a sort of fête in which "children are blown up by rockets and bombs." Edmund Wilson, to whose long essay on the Sade documents I am deeply indebted, says apropos of this: "How gratified Sade would have been if he could have foreseen the scale on which we were later to indulge in this pastime! Or would he perhaps have been appalled, as he was by the Terror?"

Sade was capable of being appalled; his sadism was not so thoroughgoing as, for total philosophical consistency, it ought to have been. But once you divide the world into victims and persecutors, you are faced with the problem of a frontier where roles may change: sadism tends to embrace its opposite, masochism. Leopold von Sacher-Masoch was born twenty-two years after Sade's death, but his stories about the pleasure of being hurt, degraded, dominated, are to some extent anticipated in the older master. While in prison at Vincennes, Sade regularly flagellated himself. The girls involved in the Marseilles orgy testified that the inflictions of cruelty were not all onesided. Nowadays, informed by the sexologist of whom Sade was the true forerunner, we recognize in ourselves the dichotomy of our response to one of these magazine photographs we're always seeing—a girl in top boots with a whip or gun. "Kinky," we say, and shudder with two kinds of anticipatory pleasure: we identify with the torturer; we see ourselves as the victim.

That the sadomasochistic impulse is in all of us we no longer doubt. There is some obscure neural liaison in the brain between the sexual urge and the desire for domination—and the latter phrase I have deliberately left ambiguous. We are, quite rightly, scared of letting the sadomasochistic get out of hand: it is all too easy. We're all pretty bad inside; it's what we do outside that counts.

Sade, in his actions, and even more in his books, extrapolated on a Wagnerian scale what society insists on keeping locked in the crypts of the mind. Though vicious and perhaps demented, he does not belong to a race very different from our own. That is why he fascinates. But the fascination does not long survive the actual opening of one of his books.

Nauseated by his anal fixations, we soon become bored with his ingenuities. Nobody is real; he seems to be playing with automata. He was interested in the art of the novel, and he wanted to contribute to the pornographic branch of it (in this he was merely one among many); but he was not sufficiently interested in people as people. There is no give and take, none of the dialectic of character that we find in competent fiction; there is only the wearying but unwearied catalogue of atrocities. The people who publish extracts from Sade in paperback are misrepresenting him: they are picking out the plums and putting in the wastebasket the dollops of farinaceous inedibility. Sade has to be given us entire, so that we may yawn over the long pages of eighteenth-century moralizing and become irritated by the self-contradictions. The public ought not to be titillated by half-censorship: the works of the Marquis de Sade ought to be freely available, and that would cure the smut hounds.

Has he any value in the history of literature or philosophy? His literary interest is slight though not entirely negligible. His philosophy of Nature is untenable but stimulating. Where he has to be taken seriously is in his role as pioneer sexologist. He was the first modern Western man to list the varieties of erotic perversion, and the list is pretty well exhaustive. Moreover, his view of sex is not limited to the European ethos. He was something of an anthropologist and argued that there was not one sexual practice regarded as perverse by the West that was not accepted as normal in some remoter society. Most important of all, he saw with terrible clarity the sexual springs of cruelty, no matter how cruelty was disguised as a device of politics or of ecclesiastical discipline. Even in his recognition of the sexual elements that lie below family relationships and manifest themselves long before the age of puberty, he anticipated the Viennese school of psychology. He knew what we have taken a long time to learn—that sex is not just something that happens in a bedroom.

His profound misanthropy, while justified by the events of European history through which he lived, was not in conformity with the optimistic philosophies of his time. The chains of man could be broken, said Rousseau; reason could triumph, said the Encyclopedists.[3] Sade never expected anything but the worst from mankind, so he could never be disappointed. He did not overestimate the rational capacities of man; however—following the custom of the age—he did invoke reason in his writings. Nowadays there are millions of people who find cause, far better cause than Sade had, to despair of the human race. Sade merely dreamed of chemists who could blow up whole cities; we have seen the reality of conventional high explosives and the thermonuclear bomb. His visions, like those of science fiction in our own day, were ahead of their time.

3. The eighteenth-century *Encyclopedia* was a French project to expound the order of human knowledge.

It is sourly amusing to observe where his true influence lies. The great dictators, bemused by dreams of national glory, have found him abhorrent (Napoleon was the first to be shocked). Schoolmasters with canes and parents with flat, hard hands have scarcely thought about him. It is the popular writers who have diluted his message and made it palatable to suburban minds. Ian Fleming,[4] for instance:

> ". . . I can tell you that the entire population of Fort Knox will be dead or incapacitated by midnight. . . . The substance that will be inserted in the water supply, outside the filter plant, will be a highly concentrated form of GB."
>
> "You're mad! You don't really mean you're going to kill sixty thousand people!"
>
> "Why not? American motorists do it every two years."
>
> Bond stared into Goldfinger's face in fascinated horror. It couldn't be true! He couldn't mean it! He said tersely, "What's this GB?"
>
> "GB is the most powerful of the Trilone group of nerve poisons. It was perfected by the Wehrmacht in 1943, but never used for fear of reprisals. In fact, it is a more effective instrument of destruction than the hydrogen bomb. . . . Introduction through the water supply is an ideal method of applying it to a densely populated area."

How the Marquis de Sade would have reveled in the technological triumphs that now, in literature, merely serve the end of a popular frisson.[5]

In literature less popular, the misanthropy of Sade has become totally acceptable. I'm thinking particularly of William Golding's novel *The Inheritors*, where Homo sapiens, supervening on the gentle Neanderthals, destroys a worthier race because it is in his nature to destroy. Evil, Golding seems to say, is built into man. What do we do about that: acquiesce in it, as Sade did, or seek, however hopelessly, some form of regeneration? Mankind is not doing very well at the moment, but mankind has never done very well. Always expect the worst, and then you can never be depressed by your morning paper. As for action, note that history has a few lonely figures who did good or, fearing to do evil, did nothing. The impulses we share with the diabolic Marquis are best left to him, to be worked out in fantasy. We can never rid ourselves of these impulses by merely banning the books that most thoroughly express them. They are merely a spectacular symptom of one of the big human diseases. Whether the disease is curable is something we have still to find out.

1969

---

4. Author of the novels about the adventures of the secret agent, James Bond.   5. Pleasurable shudder; thrill.

Jeremy Bernstein

WHO WAS CHRISTY MATHEWSON?

I have long felt that the very best popular-science writing must come from scientists. For them, science is a part of everyday experience—their skin and bones—and this feeling is what emerges when a really good popular book is written by a scientist. But if this is to happen several criteria must be met. In the first place, the scientist not only must have the ability to write but must really *want* to write. Then, the scientist must be working in a field that has broad social and intellectual ramifications and must recognize them. As someone said, God loves the details. But if popular-science writing consists only of details no one will read it. I first became aware of the writing of Stephen Jay Gould some years ago, when I began reading his column "This View of Life" in *Natural History*. Everything about these pieces seemed right to me. There was the enthusiasm of a young and gifted scientist at the height of his powers. The problems he discussed—involving evolutionary biology—were of wide interest and could be made generally understandable, and the writing was full of fun, totally without pretentiousness, and absolutely clear. Many of these pieces have been collected in his books *Ever Since Darwin* and *The Panda's Thumb*. One wondered what would happen when Professor Gould—he teaches geology, biology, and the history of science at Harvard—turned his energies to a single major subject and addressed the general reader. Now one knows. He has just written a really extraordinary book, *The Mismeasure of Man*.

The Mismeasure of Man is a devastating and often extremely angry attack on the notion that "intelligence" is a "thing"—like temperature —to which can be attached a single number and that, furthermore, this number is an intrinsic characteristic of a person, somehow independent of all environmental influences. One might call this the fallacy of misplaced reification. It is beautifully characterized by John Stuart Mill in a quotation given in Professor Gould's book: "The tendency has always been strong to believe that whatever received a name must be an entity or being, having an independent existence of its own. And if no real entity answering to the name could be found, men did not for that reason suppose that none existed, but imagined that it was something peculiarly abstruse and mysterious." In fact, the dispute between the "realists," who believe that behind a name there must be a "real" essence, and the "nominalists," who believe that names refer only to particular things, has had a long and honorable history in philosophy. If all that was at stake here were an academic metaphysical dispute, there would be little reason to get exercised over it. But that is not what is at stake. Professor Gould argues that because of the false reification of intelligence hundreds of thousands—perhaps millions—of people's lives have been circumscribed, or even ruined. He writes, "We pass through this world but once. Few tragedies can be more extensive than the stunting of life, few injustices deeper than the denial of an opportunity to strive or even to hope, by a limit imposed from without, but falsely identified as lying within."

It will probably come as no surprise to read that the notion that black people are mentally inferior was pervasive in American society from the very beginning. Thomas Jefferson wrote, "I advance it, therefore, as a suspicion only, that the blacks, whether originally a distinct race, or made distinct by time and circumstance, are inferior to the whites in the endowment both of body and of mind." Probably the founders *had* to feel this way if they were to use blacks in slavery. And it will come as no surprise to read that with the development of science in the nineteenth century scholars used "scientific" methods to "prove" what most Europeans and Americans felt to be true anyway. Professor Gould, in the first part of his book, has reexamined the "proofs" on their own terms. The major preoccupation of these scholars was the size of brains. It was taken as a given that large brain size was correlated to intelligence, and measurements were done to confirm this "fact." In the mid-nineteenth century, Paul Broca, who was a surgeon and the founder of the Anthropological Society of Paris, felt able to announce, "In general, the brain is larger in mature adults than in the elderly, in men than in women, in eminent men than in men of mediocre talent, in superior races than in inferior races ... Other things equal, there is a remarkable relationship between the development of intelligence and the volume of the brain." Broca was a conscientious scientist, and he was nearly upended by his own data, for he discovered that Eskimos, Lapps, Malays, Tatars, "and several other peoples of the Mongolian type would surpass [in brain size] the most civilized people of Europe." But not to worry, for West African blacks, Kaffirs, Nubians, Tasmanians, Hottentots, and Australian aborigines had, Broca discovered, smaller brains. What Broca did not take sufficiently into account is that there is a correlation between brain size and body size. He did take this into account in the case of women but concluded that it was not relevant, since women were inferior regardless: "We are therefore permitted to suppose that the relatively small size of the female brain depends in part upon her physical inferiority and in part upon her intellectual inferiority." (Some of the later workers in this dismal enterprise did try to take body size, or something like it, into account, and when one of them, Léonce Manouvrier, subtracted the effects of what he termed "sexual mass" he came to the conclusion that the corrected brain size of women was actually greater than that of men.)

There is, by the way, a legitimate and fascinating study of brain size,

which is still being carried on, and is due largely to the pioneering work of Harry J. Jerison. Professor Gould touched on Jerison's work in *The Panda's Thumb*. For many years, Jerison has been measuring the size of the brains of animals, both extant and extinct (the latter through fossils). He finds that within a given class—reptiles, say—brain size increases, as one would guess, with body size, but not as rapidly as body size. Gould notes that "brains grow only about two-thirds as fast as bodies." A theory that might account for the "two-thirds" is that the animal brain may have evolved in size in response to sensory stimulations. These would be received from the surface of the body, which, roughly speaking, increases in magnitude as an area, while "body size" is really a measure of volume. (The surface area of a sphere, for example, increases with the square of the radius, while the volume of a sphere increases with the cube of the radius.) James A. Hopson, of the University of Chicago, has shown that the much-maligned dinosaurs fit very nicely on the reptile curve. While there is certainly no simple relation of brain size to intelligence, there is no reason to think that the dinosaurs perished because they were anomalously dumb. Interestingly, man is totally off the scale on these curves. It might be expected that human growth would not follow this pattern, since much of our brain does not respond merely to sensory stimuli: we think about ourselves.

The heart of *The Mismeasure of Man* is Professor Gould's analysis of the use and misuse of I.Q. tests. The originator of the modern intelligence test was the French psychologist Alfred Binet. He emerges as one of the few heroes of Gould's book. In 1898, Binet began, in the tradition of Broca, by measuring heads. After three years of work, he decided that any interpretation of whatever differences in size there were—and they were minuscule—between the heads of bright and poor students might well reflect his own a-priori bias about how such students should score on tests. "The idea of measuring intelligence by measuring heads seemed ridiculous," he wrote. In 1904, he was commissioned by the French Minister of Public Education to develop techniques for picking out children who might be having learning difficulties. By 1908, he had got the idea of assigning an age level to each of a variety of tasks—the earliest age at which an average child should be able to complete the task. The age level of the most advanced task a child could perform was said to be his "mental age." When this mental age was subtracted from the child's true age, a number could be assigned to the child's so-called intelligence. In 1912, a German psychologist, Louis William Stern, concluded that it would be more satisfactory to divide the mental age by the chronological age, and hence the notion of an "intelligence quotient" was born. Binet, unlike the people who followed him, had absolutely no idea of arriving at a single number that would give a definitive measure of something called "intelligence." Indeed, he wrote, "For the sake of simplicity of statement, we will speak of a child of 8 years having the intelligence of a child of 7 or 9 years; these expressions, if accepted arbitrarily, may give place to illusions." And, above all, he did not intend that his scale be used to stigmatize a child. Professor Gould notes, "Of one thing Binet was sure: whatever the cause of poor performance in school the aim of his scale was to identify in order to help and improve, not to label in order to limit. Some children might be innately incapable of normal achievement, but all could improve with special help." Professor Gould has no quarrel with this use of I.Q. and other achievement tests. He writes, "Speaking personally, I feel that tests of the I.Q. type were helpful in the proper diagnosis of my own learning-disabled son. His average score, the I.Q. itself, meant nothing, for it was only an amalgam of some very high and very low scores; but the pattern of low values indicated his areas of deficit." What he does quarrel with—and "quarrel" is much too mild a word, since this part of his book is a brilliantly acerbic polemic—is the evolution and corruption of Binet's work, especially in the United States, where I.Q. testing became, and still is, literally and figuratively, an industry. Along with this came the notion that if something can be tested it must correspond to something in reality, and the further notion —which, according to Gould, is a "home-grown American product" —that such "intelligence" is hereditary. Not only could an individual be condemned to a life of lessened expectations on the basis of I.Q. tests but so could his or her offspring.

Lest one imagine that all this is some sort of academic exercise, Professor Gould gives a concrete example: the case of Carrie and Doris Buck, two sisters in Virginia. On the basis of a variant of Binet's test, the mother of Carrie and Doris Buck was judged to have a mental age of seven. Carrie, on the basis of the same test, was awarded a mental age of nine. She was the mother of a child who was also judged to be "feeble-minded," so the State of Virginia decided that both Carrie and her sister Doris should be sterilized. In 1927, this became a Supreme Court case —Buck v. Bell—and Oliver Wendell Holmes, Jr., delivered the decision, which upheld the sterilization law, stating, "Three generations of imbeciles are enough." Under this law, several thousand people were sterilized in Virginia from 1924 to 1972, when the practice apparently stopped. Doris Buck, who, like her sister, would not be considered even mentally deficient by present standards, was not informed of what had been done to her. She later said, "They told me that the operation was for an appendix and rupture." She and her husband, Mathew Figgins, tried for years to have a child before they found out it was impossible. When she learned that, she said, "I broke down and cried. My husband and me wanted children desperately. We were crazy about them. I never knew what they'd done to me."

Professor Gould rips apart both the tests that led to this kind of result and the atmosphere in which such tests were often given. The originator of one series of tests was Robert M. Yerkes. Yerkes was a professor in the Psychology Department at Harvard when, in 1915, as Gould puts it, he "got one of those 'big ideas' that propel the history of science: could psychologists possibly persuade the army to test all its recruits?" Yerkes did manage to persuade an often reluctant military to test nearly two million men. The tests were of two types—Alpha and Beta—administered according to the recruit's degree of literacy. Here is a sample of the Alpha multiple-choice questions, which supposedly tested the *intrinsic* intelligence of the recruit:

> Crisco is a: patent medicine, disinfectant, toothpaste, food product
> The number of a Kaffir's legs is: 2, 4, 6, 8
> Christy Mathewson is famous as a: writer, artist, baseball player, comedian.

The Beta tests were reserved for nonliterates, many of whom had never used a pencil prior to the test. The Beta tests required associating, among other things, a rivet with a pocket knife, a filament with a light bulb, a horn with a phonograph, a net with a tennis court, and a ball with a bowler's hand. The recruits were rushed through the tests with examiners shouting orders at them. Professor Gould gave the Beta test to one of his classes at Harvard under very benign conditions. Of fifty-three students, thirty-one scored A and sixteen B; six got C, which meant that they were fit only for the duties of a buck private. (I remember being required to take such a test at the time of the Korean War and being confronted with all sorts of weird diagrams involving tools like awls. God knows how I did on the test, but, in the event, I was not sent to Korea. The atmosphere under which the test was given was such that I am not sure I could have spelled my own name correctly.) Yerkes was convinced that blacks were innately stupid. He ignored the fact that the better-educated Northern blacks did better than the mean for whites from nine Southern states. He believed that an I.Q. was a genetically determined quantity, like blue eyes; he was not able to recognize that his own data proved that the strongest factor in this kind of testing is environmental.

Using these tests, Yerkes came to the remarkable conclusion that the average mental age of white recruits was 13.08 years. (This use of statistics, like several others that Professor Gould cites, reminds me of the disease that struck only men of fifty: there were two known cases—one a boy of two and the other a man of ninety-eight.) Yerkes' result so alarmed him and some of his colleagues that they began to seek the cause. Since they subscribed to a "hereditarian" doctrine of intelligence, they felt that the cause could lie only in the degeneration of American genes, and this, they reasoned, must have to do with the dilution of "American" stock by immigration—or, at least, by the wrong kind of immigration. In 1923, a disciple of Yerkes named Carl C. Brigham, a psychology professor at

Princeton, published one of the most insidious books on this subject that have ever been written—*A Study of American Intelligence*. Brigham concluded on the basis of the Army tests that recent immigrants to America were polluting the gene pool for intelligence. That his argument was taken seriously seems, in retrospect, almost unbelievable. The tests showed that each five-year period of residency in this country brought an increase in the immigrants' test scores; hence, any immigrants who had lived here five years or more were more "intelligent" than new arrivals. He dismissed the obvious explanation—the environmental bias built into the tests (Christy Mathewson was very likely not a household name in a Polish *shtetl*[1] or a Macedonian hamlet)—and concluded that the recent immigrants were intrinsically less intelligent. This was readily explained, he felt: there were fewer Germans, Scandinavians, and Britons among them. The recent immigrants were mainly Italians, Greeks, and Poles, along with Jews, whom Brigham classified as "Alpine Slavs." All this might simply be considered funny except that it was widely accepted and led to the Immigration Restriction Act of 1924, which devised a quota system to keep out the groups that had scored poorly on the Yerkes tests. Whether, as Professor Gould maintains, this was the primary cause of the death of an enormous number of Jews who could not immigrate to this country in the nineteen-thirties is debatable. My own guess is that, considering the anti-Semitism that was part of the fabric of American life at that time, this "scientific evidence" of racial inferiority simply allowed some people to do with better conscience what they would have found a way to do anyway. It is remarkable that some six years after Brigham's book led to the quota system he described the Army tests on which it was based as absolute nonsense. He wrote, "One of the most pretentious of these comparative racial studies—the writer's own—was without foundation." By that time, the damage had been done.

It would be good to report that all this belongs to some "medieval" past. But, as Professor Gould makes clear, and as we all know, the spirit of Yerkes and his ilk persists. It is, in my view, important to keep certain things in mind when one reads that a race or a sex has some differential factor of intelligence. Even taken on their own terms, the phenomena—if they are phenomena—that such reports deal with are always buried beneath statistics. Real scientific phenomena usually stand out like a sore thumb. It did not take, for example, a hair-raising and controversial statistical analysis to convince people that pulsars[2] exist. A few good nights at the radio telescope were enough. (It is this, by the way, that has always made the reports of extrasensory perception in the guessing of cards and the like seem so dull to me. At least, Yuri Geller[3] puts on a good

1. Yiddish: small Jewish community in eastern Europe.
2. Any of several very short-period variable

Galactic sources of radio waves.
3. Also Uri Geller (1946–   ), a psychic and entertainer whose "miracles" seem to many

show.) Two things do stick out like a sore thumb. One is how little genetic variation there is—how similar the genes are—among all the races of the earth. Professor Gould quotes his colleague Richard Lewontin: "If the holocaust comes and a small tribe deep in the New Guinea forests are the only survivors, almost all the genetic variation now expressed among the innumerable groups of our four billion people will be preserved." The second is how numerous the genetically expressed variations are within any racial group. One can find a person of one's own race or of a different race who is better at just about any given task than one is oneself. These are differences that we live with every day, and, if we are mature, come to accept and even enjoy. What Professor Gould's superb book makes clear is how dangerous race prejudices are. It also makes clear how subjective and neurotic they are. If one insists on being a racist, science is no place to come for support. Whatever racism may be, it is not science.

1982

---

essentially trivial.

QUESTIONS

1. What is "the fallacy of misplaced reification" (p. 513)? If intelligence is falsely reified (that is, if there is no such entity), what would be a better description? If it isn't a thing, what is it?
2. A book review is very likely to be a special kind of writing in that it will have a double thesis: the author's, from the book being reviewed, and the reviewer's, about the book. The balance may vary, but each will have to be given some support. How does Bernstein manage this balance? He obviously endorses his author's thesis; insofar as you can tell, does he also adopt his author's tone? There is relatively little quotation in this review; is that a drawback?
3. Inferring your answer from Bernstein's practice, explain the purpose of a book review.

Paul West

A PASSION TO LEARN

I

Exceptional children come in two kinds, advanced and retarded. Both, like jugglers and mystics and astronauts, are astounding, especially the second kind, of which I've had a close view for six years. Amanda West, the daughter who is my theme, didn't seem unusual—not to mention exceptional—until she was two. Slow to speak, she was cautious about starting to walk; but once she had walked she ran like a bird preparing to take off. She fell in love, as well, with water and umbrellas, and in the presence of either orated vehemently (although nonverbally) to herself. Water she preferred in puddles on the living-room floor or in baths, but she also liked it in rainspouts, saucepans, and lavatory basins. Umbrellas —which, I think, exerted the stronger spell—she collected with casual relentlessness. She never had fewer than a dozen. They were her trees, really: a plastic-leaved, tin-branched orchard of them, which every night had to be rolled up firm and laid across her bed, and every morning landed in a cascade on ours when she came heavy-footedly in, hooting for them to be opened. Then, with half-blind eyes, down to the living room where we spread them over the floor like Pan[1] and Company afforesting a bare mountain while she, red-cheeked with elation, danced among them, catching occasionally the beads on the rib-ends and skimming the canopies half-around, but never trampling the handles or ramming a fist through the fabric.

She would stand, do a preliminary skip to get her timing right—a one-two-three with her big toes creased downward as if to scratch earth—and then flow into a joyous high-kneed pounding, her long hair a flash, her arms providing her with a tightrope-walker's balance, her eyes unobtainably fixed on an upper corner of the room, where she saw what no one else saw. She looked and smiled, and danced the more wildly for it, fueling her semi-tarantella from the presence in the vacancy.

Fred, we began to say, domesticating the ghost: *it's Fred again*. And so, each morning, with a flim and a flam, and a flim again, followed by a swift series of flim-flams, she danced spread-eagled, lithe, and bony, chirping on an empty stomach.

We began to wonder, hard as it was even to begin to do it, if she wasn't deaf or autistic. Or both. To think a thing is to make it so, whereas to deny it is to abolish it—especially on the Isle of Man, Amanda's home, island of witches, banshees, and temperamental goblins. But being not altogether pagan, we kept on wondering until the day we took her to the

1. In Greek mythology, a god of fields and forests.

mainland, to the Manchester University Audiology Clinic. It was winter, the sea heaving and pumice-gray; so we flew in a BEA Viscount, lurching through the rain, and Amanda, at each plunge or sideslip, let out a birdcall of delight.

Born on the island, she had never been off it—never been Across to England—and now, leaving it for the first time, she seemed isolated in a new way. Her three words—"baba," "more," and "ish-ish"—she had used heroically, intending meanings we missed and being credited with others that we invented. I listened to the lax, feathered whine of the engines, wondering what noise they made to her as she sat smiling into the clouds. I'd heard, I told myself, on humid days, the squeak of my sinuses filling, and then a pop of contraction on a day of high pressure, with all the sinews and membranes tugging and fluctuating in a mucous orchestration. But that was nothing to what I imagined for Amanda's head: a tinnitus of bad bells, a frying noise, which in combination drove her to cup a hand over her right ear and rock heavily to that side as if trying to shake something loose or back into place or—thought ended: the two-foot doll that bathed with Amanda in the teeth-chattering English bathroom and that we brought with us on the plane, slipped sideways from my casual hug, and a cache of bathwater spilled into my lap. My fault, I said; you can't blame a stark-naked doll.

When we landed, Amanda whooped down the steps from the plane. It was still raining, but we had two umbrellas, both hers. The only trouble was that she didn't want them open or up; they had to be carried before us like totems, one red, the other green, every loose fold clamped tight by a rubber band. Two umbrellas, kept from getting wet, made good folk stare; but good folk knew nothing of umbrellas, water, and Amanda. In the taxi, however, she opened up the red umbrella and sat in an indifferent silence, an erect-sitting being of utter trustfulness, heedless of the roof-lining she might puncture, and with no more idea of where she was going than of where she had come from. Out of the taxi, she insisted, with a plangent squeak, on the umbrella's being folded again and rebound in its rubber band. Then she was ready to march with us past the porter's lodge (empty), wrongly up steps to the Department of Law and down again, and finally into a waiting room stocked with heavy, ridable toys, and equipped with tiny toilets whose still water she inspected and approved.

Called for, we went left into the laboratory (one wall of which was a one-way window facing a lecture room). Amanda stared at the people, the things, and, it seemed, at Fred, whom she has always been able to find anywhere. She grew busy and began to chirp. When, to her exact satisfaction, she had arranged the umbrellas and the doll on a low table, she turned to the experts with a patronizing smile. We sat and watched —her mother at one end of the room, myself (still feeling damp) at the

other—helpless on the perimeter and unable to smoke. There was some
tinkering with a green box, all dials, and a chart. The door snicked open,
admitting an authoritative-looking face which beamed and vanished.
Then testing began with overtures of friendship from the studious-
mannered man whose trousers looked as if he kneeled a lot. The calm
woman in patent-leather high heels clicked a tiny clicker, but Amanda
did not turn. They gave her a doll then and tried her from behind with a
duck quack, a whistle of low pitch, several rattles, then a small tom-tom.
Abruptly, not having turned, she ran to the table, slammed one doll
alongside the other and hooted, with finger pointed, for the red umbrella
to be opened. There were nods; the umbrella opened, sprang taut, was
set in her hands, and she squatted, drawing it down over her as if
sheltering under a thin, frail mushroom, slipping out a hand to adjust a
downslid sock, and beginning to make again the birdcall (as if a curlew
tried to bleat) which had driven countless local dogs into emulative
frenzy, provoked birds into surpassing themselves (searching for a bird,
they never saw *her*), and scared all the cats away.

Private under the panels of vinyl, she sang with mounting fervor, the
umbrella stem between her legs. No one moved. It was clear that she was
going to be given her leisure, allowed to collect herself. In succession she
fluted her voice upward in an ecstatic trill, twirled the umbrella like a
color disc without once catching the rim or the plastic against her face (a
perfect, sheltering fit it was), peeped out to giggle just a bit fearfully,
hoisted the umbrella up and away behind her in a pose from *The Mikado*,
and then hid again beneath it. We had seen her face shining with heat,
seen her only long enough for that.

Now they tapped on her roof, flicked middle finger hard off thumb
against the fabric, and brought their mouths close to the surface, calling
her name. Out she came, astounded at something heard: not her name,
because she didn't know it, but something—a retaliating and envious
dog, a curlew weary of being competed with, a cat returning to venture a
duet—amplified and vibrating in the umbrella above her, but only faces
and maneuvering mouths to make it. Us. Us only; so she concealed
herself again, tilting the canopy forward.

What brought her out again and kept her out was the xylophone. She
abandoned the umbrella for it, fondled it a while, then beat the living
decibels out of it, a Lionel Hampton[2] Lilliputian[3] who struck away and
then canted her ear close to the trembling bars, her eyes widening in half-
piqued recognition that *this* was what we'd flown her across the sea for.
She banged on it with her wooden hammer a few times more and let it fall
the two-and-a-half feet to the parquet, wincing once in the wrong direction as it hit.

2. Famous xylophonist and band leader.   Swift's *Gulliver's Travels*, the inhabitants of
3. Lilliput: an imaginary island in Jonathan   which were six inches tall.

After calls, hums, hisses, pops, buzzes, barks, bays, and several indeterminate ululations, all from behind her, they did the left side while she smiled at a distracting monkey puppet over on the right. My hands were holding each other too tightly; her mother, twelve yards down the room, looked pale, her maternality shut painfully off and her own hand beginning gestures that ended halfway, the fingers tongue-tied.

"Now," said the studious, kneeling man, his kindly face tense, and snapped two wooden bars together. A slapstick, I thought; like the split lath of the harlequin. But whatever was going on, it wasn't low comedy. What he said next, after a fractional shake of his head to the woman in heels—the professional pair's exchange of glances crossing the parental one—sounded like:

"Right down the track." The headshake was a zero in mime.

Amanda smiled at the puppet, offering her hand to put inside it. They let her, working through all the modes of sound, but not to a crescendo, only to a punctuational drum-tap which she ignored. And then, as the light waned—that legendary dank Manchester light swollen with soot and rain and absorbed by tons on tons of Victorian brick and tile—they switched sides, this time beguiling her with a model farm at which she sat, cantankerously checking the cows for udders (as a country girl should) and stationing Clydesdale horses at the water trough. Brilliants of wet formed along her narrow nose, and she heard not the snap-crack of the wooden bars: not the first time, anyway. But when it came from a yard closer—these testers gliding about the room like prankish Druids—she flinched, directed an offended stare in a vaguely right-hand direction, and went back to her farm. Again and again they worked from the right, varying the angle and the sound. Again and again, with just a few moments of preoccupied indifference, she jerked her head sideways, beginning to be cheerful as she discovered the routine: beginning to play.

Suddenly there was no farm. It went into a gray steel cabinet against which Amanda kicked and at which she took a running kick as her eyes began to pour (tears whopping enough, I thought, to merit nostrils for conduits) and her birdcall harshened. As she swung, both-handed, the xylophone at the locked handle of the door, I got up, stuck out a hand as I half-fell in a skid on the polish. I took a tonic sol-fa[4] smack in the forehead as she swung the instrument backward again, farther than before, the better to mangle the steel between her and the authentic cows, the horses a-thirsting.

"Ap," I sort of said through the plong and the blank crash, not seeing well. "You might as well get it out again."

"Naughty girl," her mother said unconvincedly as Amanda laughcried, pitching the xylophone over her shoulder without so much as a look. I have seen her dispose in the same way of bus tickets, mail, money,

---

4. As in the scale *do, re, mi, fa, sol, la, ti.*

books, food, scissors, and plates. The oubliette[5] is anywhere behind her.

"She'll soon—" I heard, but the rest was drowned by a scream of unmitigated anger while Amanda pounded the cabinet with both fists.

"Strong!" called the man who kneeled a lot, busying himself with earphones attached to the many-dialed machine. "She's a grand temper."

"You've seen nothing," I told him. "Yet." I knew how, in the Cleopatra-Clytemnestra[6] rages to which she entitled herself, she could butt her head through a firm window (one so far, without bloodshed, but there were long blond hairs on the splinters of glass). Or pound her uncallused hand down through the crisp and warm pulp of a loaf not long out of the oven, once burying her hand and bringing her arm up with a bread mallet wedged on her wrist, crying "Ish! Ish!" which is anthem, plea, and threat in one.

But it wasn't "Ish" she came out with this time; it was the first of her calls, "Baba—babababab," uttered with pauses only long enough for everyone present to shout the same phonemes back at her. If you didn't, she increased the volume, blustering and raucous. It was the most comprehensive aural version of herself. So the clinic-room, soundproof of course (there is even a sign just inside the entrance requesting silence), became a barnyard for a while. Turning wet-eyed, grime-faced, to each of us in turn, she babbled at us, coercing, commanding, appealing; and in turn and sometimes in unison we babbled and brayed back, short only of a cock-a-doodle-doo, the hymn of a pig wallowing or even farrowing in hot lava, and a moose drowning in a swamp of caviar. This, so that the testing could go on; one farmyard for another.

In the beginning is the test, and in the end comes a remedy of sorts. But how, I wondered, can they even begin—overworked but obliged not to rush; never short of children to work with, one in six being somehow deaf and usually not deaf only—until they too have run their fingers across the crowns of her blunt, curiously thick teeth, have seen her dance a full hour among the umbrellas, have night after night studied her fanatical attention to the placing of her slippers within an invisible outline which is there and symmetrical for her beneath the chest of drawers in her bedroom.

"You haven't—" I began to say on our third trip to the clinic, seen her do the living things; give Creation a run for its money. Not at home. They hadn't seen her, like a gross Ophelia,[7] distribute around the house —on the window ledges, in the wardrobe between two decent suits or dresses, on the rim of the letter box, on the Christmas tree itself—pork sausages on butcher's hooks or threaded on wire coat-hangers. Or eat the sausage raw, oblivious of worms. Or, in hydrodynamic delight, rip off

5. A place of oblivion.
6. Cleopatra: queen of ancient Egypt, given to fickle behavior; Clytemnestra: in *The Oresteia*, Aeschylus's dramatic trilogy, the queen of Argos, who kills her husband, Agamemnon.
7. In Shakespeare's *Hamlet*, Polonius's daughter, who goes mad.

shoes and socks to plant her bare feet on the TV screen whenever it
showed water. Or (I stopped: they were calling her name again and she
wasn't ever going to answer) sit naked and warbling for an hour in a
washbasin of cold water. Or green her face with eye-shadow, eat nail-
varnish, coat the windows with lavender furniture polish, jump down five
stairs fearlessly, mimic (by waving a stiffened arm) men carrying umbrellas, chant into a toilet pedestal after choking it with a whole roll of tissue,
chew cigarettes, cover herself with Band-Aids when there wasn't a
scratch in sight, climb any ladder and refuse to descend, slide pencils up
her nose, use a rubber hammer on the doctor's private parts, drink from
her potty, wade into a sewer-inspection chamber the plumber had
opened, eat six bananas in six minutes, wind and play an alarm clock at
her right ear time and again, shave her face and arms and legs with
instant lather and bladeless razor, threaten enormous dogs by advancing
upon them with a reed in hand, cut her own hair at random, dissolve soap
in a tin basin, rock so hard that her hair touched the floor on either side,
sit motionless and rapt in front of a mirror, voluminously autograph
walls, tear samples from the dictionary or a book of Picasso prints, stare
unblinking into 150-watt bulbs, run, run, run everywhere, heedless of
gesticulating and half-felled adults and the sanity of drivers.

"Mandy . . .Mandy. . . MANDY," they said, upping the decibels as she
gazed from them to the red finger spinning across the dial and back again.
When she heard them, her expression changed, fixing in atavistic wonder. Funny, it was as if we were watching the face of sound itself while
she, flushed and nervous, heard something visible. After an interval they
let her use the microphone herself, and she began to boom and call in an
almost continuous orgy of sound, confronted for the first time with her
own share of the missing continent: a Columbus of euphony
dumbfoundedly exclaiming at the glories of exclamation itself, every bit
like the man in Xenophon who kept shouting *thalassa!*[8] when he saw the
sea. I myself felt a bit like shouting; I'd never heard anyone hearing
before. And since then I've known a good many firsts with her—things
which, up to then, I'd done without really experiencing them, or which
she herself thought up and I myself had never dreamed of doing. Some of
the latter are grotesque and sometimes rather revolting as well; I try not
to do them, but usually Amanda prevails, imperious queen with her
dithering court. I do as I am told. Most people would. You have to; that's
where the education begins.

II

She quickens in you the sense of life; makes you grateful for what's
granted, what's *taken* for granted. A handicap so severe drives you

8. Greek word for sea or gulf.

through fury, then through an empty, vengeful indignation, to two points: first, when, in the absence of explanations medical and reasons cosmic, you ignore the handicap to make it go away; second, nearer to common sense, when you welcome it in as her special gift and, while trying to eliminate it, learn its nature by heart as a caution to yourself, and study the voracious subtlety of her compensations—as when she, unlike most of us, smells at a pencil newly sharpened, inhaling from the beechwood its own soot-sour bouquet, or traces with addicted fingers the corrugations on the flat of a halved cabbage before eating it raw with the same naturalness with which she drinks vinegar, steak sauce, and mayonnaise, and sniffs glue. I too, now, have tasted ink (a flavor of charred toenail), coal (a rotted iron-and-yeast pill), bark (woolly and raw, suggesting vulcanized crabmeat), leather (a taste here not of the meat or fat next the hide but of the fur once outside it and of seaweed-iodine).

Tasting—testing—with her, I have found new ways into the world. She discovers what she discovers because she has lost what she's lost. I tag along on her voyages, and together we sneak into the randomness, the arbitrariness, of the universe as distinct from its patterns. Without her —although I have in my time delighted in *The Compleat Angler's*[9] bald and bland arcana, in insect and fungus books, in Jean Rostand's[1] reports on tadpoles and toads—I don't think I would be delving, as I now am, with strangely relevant irrelevance, into the behavior of slugs, mushrooms, cicadas, and flesh-eating plants, or into a way of death called atherosclerosis, the result not (I learn) of saturated fats yielding cholesterol but of unsaturated fats—much used in the paint and varnish industry—varnishing our insides with lipofuscin. Because she brandished it at a big dog, I found out about Great Reed Mace (*Typha latifolia*), often wrongly called the bulrush, but rightly, I reckon, thought sexy. The black six-foot stem is a long cheroot, topped by a yellow spike, and, as my *Observer's Book of Wild Flowers* says, "the closely packed pistillate flowers forming the 'mace' consist of a stalked ovary, with a slender style and a one-sided, narrow stigma, and enveloped in tufts of soft, brownish hairs."

I keep two books, one for what Amanda does, one for what I find out while waiting for our first conversation. She ate a dandelion flower some time back; one day I'll try her with the leaves in oil and vinegar, that good salad. I have a lot to tell her which, thank goodness, I've been late in learning: the hyena isn't quite the scavenger he's supposed to be, whereas the almost extinct American Bald Eagle is a scavenger out and out. And so on; it's a question, really, of finding a life-style, of opening up for myself a universe into which she fits. So I try to devise for her the biggest memberships possible, now and then blundering from wishful

---

9. An English masterwork of 1653 on the techniques of fishing and the pleasures of the simple life, by Izaak Walton.
1. French biologist and writer (1893–   ).

thinking into wishful biology, but at other times enrolling her in majestic clans we'd stare at if we knew about them, just as some of the inhumanly ordinary on the earth have stared at her.

Take the shark, created perpetually with two inexplicable handicaps: it has no swim bladder, so must keep on the move or sink; its fixed, paired fins have hardly any braking effect and no motive power, which means that it finds difficulty stopping or reversing. A shark, therefore, is compulsive and a bit helpless; no one knows why. But all sharks are handicapped thus, whereas what I am casting around for is a handicap not just inexplicable but also affecting a minority only. Trying again, I come up with such samples of a partly mismanaged universe as so-called "waltzing" mice, which have an abnormality of that part of the inner ear concerned with balance; the hereditary deafness found in white dogs like Dalmatians and Bull Terriers; *Gentian acaulis,* which for reasons unknown refuses to flower in good soil but does well where the acid and lime counts are high; holly, whose greenish flowers are sometimes bisexual, although sometimes male and female flowers exist on *separate* plants (which is why they tell you to plant hollies in groups); uranium 235, old faithful of an unstable and vulnerable isotope which is as it is because it isn't otherwise; the particle for which, it seems, there is no antiparticle; flawed crystals in which one atom is where another should be or where no atom ought to be at all; the so-called incoherence of natural light, traveling as it does in brief packets of energy in random directions at uncorrelated times, compared with the light from an optical maser; acridines, believed to produce mutations which consist in the deletion or addition of a base or bases from the DNA chain. Such is the beginning of my list: Amanda's alibi, not so much an excuse (the popular sense) as her being genuinely elsewhere while the universe put a foot wrong with that mouse or this crystal, but suffering a similar misadministration that relates her more closely than most people to Nature; a Nature I never really noticed until it bungled.

As a factory, Nature—the more familiar end of the universe—is more reliable than the best baseball pitcher ever, but less reliable than the London Underground.[2] To be sure, where it falters it sometimes lowers its guard usefully: U 235 gives us the chain reaction, or at least the possibility of it; the misbehaving particle may teach us something about the "elementariness" of particles (e.g., are two different particles equally fundamental or is one merely an "excited" state of the other?). The imperfect crystal tells physicists a great deal about the mechanical properties of solids. And the deaf—also, perhaps, in this case, the autistic and/or brain-damaged—child, from whom I have wandered briefly only to hunt out some of her peers and analogues, is equally instructive, preparing you for the next phase, in which you find what I will call the

2. Subway.

superior intricacy of one child at the deaf-blind unit at Condover in England: a child born without eyes or ears and with all internal organs so garbled that sex cannot be determined. Yet he/she knows how to get angry, is eager to sniff at things and people alike. Something on the lines of "Age 6—80 decibel hearing loss—IQ 120" says nothing much if you are willing to learn something more; neither does "Age 7—hearing nil —sight nil—sex?—IQ minimal" if you have a passion to learn (I intend the ambiguity). How you proceed from the statistics depends on who and what you are, how much of Nature you're willing to look at; but, pretty certainly, there will be some desperation in your proceeding. Which, given such standard desirables as warmth, light, and some health, may not be a bad thing. It's a bit like writing the prospective novel—being a prospector for fiction in uncharted areas—inasmuch as you don't know where you will end up or how.

To put it topically, locally: you run the home around the child. You learn her ignorances until they are yours. You steal her condition from her by risky analogies, like the mystic borrowing the lover's terms, like the lover borrowing the mystic's. You give your Amanda a glut of olibles, tangibles, edibles, and visibles: all the perfumes of Arabia; all the grades of sandpaper, leading up to a feel at an elephant; all the fluents from goat's milk to mercury; all the spices from cinnamon to chili; all the zoos, parades, Dufys, flags, unwanted *National Geographics*, French colonial stamps, travel posters, and rainbows you can muster. Always a color camera: preferably Polaroid, because she doesn't like to wait.

Against all this—the stark handicap and any voluptuously zany sharing in it—set a thought neither apocalyptic nor original. Ten years after the atomic explosion on Bikini Atoll, birds were sitting on sterile eggs; turtles, instead of going back to the sea after laying their own eggs, pressed on to the island's interior where they died of thirst. Their skeletons remain, thousands of them, evidence of a gratuitous handicap we might have had the brains to do without.

III

It is three years since that first visit to the clinic when powerlessness hit home to us. The strain told on Amanda too. She fetched a shovel from the garden to destroy with: lighting fixtures, windows, crockery, clocks. Strong always, she lifted and swung it with ease, pouting with birdcall. It took her two years to reject the shovel, to change from indefatigable and destructive hobgoblin into a girl who, gaining a word a month only to lose it the month after, developed luminously beautiful, big, Nordic features. Capable, without warning, of histrionic graciousness of manner (as if all the pressures lifted at once and the noises in her head stopped), she enjoyed her increasingly frequent visits to the clinic (toys, earphones, EEG apparatus), ate mightily, hardly ever caught a cold, thumped oblivi-

ously past staring or derisive children, and rebaffled the experts. Deaf, yes; "stone" deaf (in that melodramatic inversion of the pathetic fallacy[3]) in the left ear; autistic, perhaps, but that's a vague word like "romantic"; brain damage not ruled out; amblyopia[4] mentioned, with an ophthalmologist joining her team.

At five she left the island for the last time, blasé by now about Viscounts, to live near the clinic and the school associated with it. I signed out a speech-trainer, donated by the Variety Artists' Federation, on which she had a daily lesson, dealing sometimes in words, sometimes in sheer noise. She did her jigsaws like an impatient robot, began to lip-read, and gradually built up and kept a tiny vocabulary enunciated with almost coy preciosity, intoning "more" like an aria, raising "hair" into "har," curtailing "mouth" into "mou," lengthening "nose" into a three-second sound, but all the same *talking* although she still didn't know her name. Nicknames accumulated: Moo, from Mandy-Moo; Birdie, from her call; Tish from "ish-ish"; Lulu (developed cunningly from the two-syllable, high-pitched call with which her mother called her in); Yee (which sound she herself had substituted for Baba); Proof, from the condition called Manda-proof, she being the only thing or person invulnerable to herself, or so we said; and, strangest of all to strangers, Boat (her word for water —until she got *worbar*—shouted while paddling her feet on the TV screen). Epic formulae, these, while she went incognito.

During one spell, she averaged only three hours' sleep a night, erupting at midnight with umbrellas and jigsaws, then fetching a guitar, one mechanical top, several model baths, a dish brimming with soap dissolved, a length of iron piping, and a purloined fruit-knife, with all of which to while the night away until she could go out. And always wet. She became frenetic, twitched more than ever, during this waiting period: all that soothed her was running water, the swing in the garden, and ghoulish faces I pulled while pursuing her up the stairs. She partnered everyone at the lavatory, exclaiming "Oh" in exaggerative dismay at anyone's being under the vile necessity and then seeking to examine the deposit. But, we noticed, her "Yee" was less strident, less insistent; a month later, it had become a delicate, diffident greeting to be answered just as quietly, and she became drier, banged her head less, was less obsessed by the grotesque or the effluvial, gave up rending the day's newspaper, lost her passion for knives, began to draw faces and bodies that had two eyes, not one, with two legs instead of a barbed-wire entanglement of blue ball-point. She even drew a bath—always the long throne of her joy—with a Mandy in it.

She took the intelligence test and passed it before, after forty minutes' concentration, she flung the next puzzle across the room and mounted a

3. The literary device of portraying inanimate objects as possessing human qualities, e.g., the angry sea.

4. A disease of the optic nerve, causing blindness.

full-size tantrum. The children's hospital lost her file, and two starch-bosomed nurses lost their cool when she screamed twenty minutes solid because they took from her the model jet kept to calm little boys during EEG tests. She thought it was a present.

"I'll buy it," I said against the screams. "It's worth it." No, that was out of the question; it was part of the equipment—it was government property. She vanished into the pathology lab, and was there found admiring fetuses, tumors, and cysts in their quiet jars, a true humanist explaining to her what was what. We got her a jet at the airport, and, later, a helicopter, a new swing, a miniature cooking set in Bavarian iron, building blocks, card games, a thousand candy cigarettes, as many lollipops and ices: a surplus for purposes of habilitation.

Out of the clutter has come a girl who can make beds, bake bread, fry bacon, iron and fold clothes, hoover[5] the carpets, mow the lawn (she calls escalators "bo" now), set a table, adjust the TV, fell apples from the tree by swatting it with a tennis racquet, tune her own hearing-aid, on her best days say "roundabout" as "rounabou" and "elephant" as almost that (it's otherwise known as "NO-o-se"), and on most days recite her own name. She cried and shuffled not at all when she began at the school for the deaf, a day-girl, almost six. She dotes on baths, Scotch tape (which she calls yap), steaks, and tenon saws, has become unoffendably gregarious, has learned to spit, looks through illustrated magazines with an anthropologist's gravity, has discovered how "No" doubles her range of concepts, and, I realize, sees Fred less and less. The Martian, we call her, or Miss Rabelais. Photogenic, long and agile, she has about forty words all told, a schoolbag and a homework book, which is all penumbra to the darkness of Amanda invading the house with a big shovel, sometimes a coal hammer, and that unfailing drooped-eyelid leer.

One special thing left a new light shining. Her class of nine children, working by the loop that amplifies sound identically for them whichever way they turn, was told to draw a spider's web. All drew but Amanda, who sat abstractedly apart, aloof from this planet. No one saw her move —and, being ambidextrous, she could have done it with either hand —but when the teacher got to her, Amanda was yee-ing gently beside a perfectly delineated web, all done in one unbroken line, with a spider at center. It's a prized school exhibit now, which she can bring home at year's end, when, presumably, she will bury it unsentimentally in her crate of junk in which, I once thought, she meant to bury us all, outclassed by her energy, thwarted by her privacy, heartsick at Nature's misbehavior, and as short of new expedients as of sleep.

One day, home from school with her homework book in which the teacher uses the special alphabet ("home" is "hoem"), she will extend yee into what I think it is, what it has been all along. I mean yes, and so will

5. Vacuum.

she, even if she's as incoherent as daily light, as vulnerable as uranium 235, and has an atom where an atom shouldn't be.

1968

Naomi Weisstein

PSYCHOLOGY CONSTRUCTS THE FEMALE, OR, THE FANTASY LIFE OF THE MALE PSYCHOLOGIST (WITH SOME ATTENTION TO THE FANTASIES OF HIS FRIENDS, THE MALE BIOLOGIST AND THE MALE ANTHROPOLOGIST)

It is an implicit assumption that the area of psychology which concerns itself with personality has the onerous but necessary task of describing the limits of human possibility. Thus when we are about to consider the liberation of women, we naturally look to psychology to tell us what "true" liberation would mean: what would give women the freedom to fulfill their own intrinsic natures. Psychologists have set about describing the true natures of women with a certainty and a sense of their own infallibility rarely found in the secular world. Bruno Bettelheim, of the University of Chicago, tells us that

> We must start with the realization that, as much as women want to be good scientists or engineers, they want first and foremost to be womanly companions of men and to be mothers.

Erik Erikson of Harvard University, upon noting that young women often ask whether they can "have an identity before they know whom they will marry, and for whom they will make a home," explains somewhat elegiacally that

> Much of a young woman's identity is already defined in her kind of attractiveness and in the selectivity of her search for the man (or men) by whom she wishes to be sought . . .

Mature womanly fulfillment, for Erikson, rests on the fact that a woman's

> . . . somatic design harbors an "inner space" destined to bear the offspring of chosen men, and with it, a biological, psychological, and ethical commitment to take care of human infancy.

Some psychiatrists even see the acceptance of woman's role by women as a solution to social problems. "Woman is nurturance . . .," writes Joseph Rheingold (1964), a psychiatrist at the Harvard Medical School,

"... anatomy decrees the life of a woman ... when women grow up without dread of their biological functions and without subversion by feminist doctrine, and therefore enter upon motherhood with a sense of fulfillment and altruistic sentiment, we shall attain the goal of a good life and a secure world in which to live it."

These views from men who are assumed to be experts reflect, in a surprisingly transparent way, the cultural consensus. They not only assert that a woman is defined by her ability to attract men, they see no alternative definitions. They think that the definition of a woman in terms of a man is the way it should be; and they back it up with psychosexual incantation and biological ritual curses. A woman has an identity if she is attractive enough to obtain a man, and thus, a home; for this will allow her to set about her life's task of "joyful altruism and nurturance."

Business certainly does not disagree. If views such as Bettelheim's and Erikson's do indeed have something to do with real liberation for women, then seldom in human history has so much money and effort been spent on helping a group of people realize their true potential. Clothing, cosmetics, home furnishings, are multi-million dollar businesses: if you don't like investing in firms that make weaponry and flaming gasoline, then there's a lot of hard cash in "inner space." Sheet and pillowcase manufacturers are concerned to fill this inner space:

> Mother, for a while this morning, I thought I wasn't cut out for married life. Hank was late for work and forgot his apricot juice and walked out without kissing me, and when I was all alone I started crying. But then the postman came with the sheets and towels you sent, that look like big bandana handkerchiefs, and you know what I thought? That those big red and blue handkerchiefs are for girls like me to dry their tears on so they can get busy and do what a housewife has to do. Throw open the windows and start getting the house ready, and the dinner, maybe clean the silver and put new geraniums in the box. *Everything to be ready for him when he walks through that door.*[1]

Of course, it is not only the sheet and pillowcase manufacturers, the cosmetics industry, the home furnishings salesmen who profit from and make use of the cultural definitions of man and woman. The example above is blatantly and overtly pitched to a particular kind of sexist stereotype: the child nymph. But almost all aspects of the media are normative, that is, they have to do with the ways in which beautiful people, or just folks, or ordinary Americans, should live their lives. They define the possible; and the possibilities are usually in terms of what is male and what is female. Men and women alike are waiting for Hank, the Silva Thins man, to walk back through that door.

It is an interesting but limited exercise to show that psychologists and

1. Fieldcrest advertisement in the *New Yorker,* 1965. My italics [Weisstein's note].

psychiatrists embrace these sexist norms of our culture, that they do not see beyond the most superficial and stultifying media conceptions of female nature, and that their ideas of female nature serve industry and commerce so well. Just because it's good for business doesn't mean it's wrong. What I will show is that it *is wrong*; that there isn't the tiniest shred of evidence that these fantasies of servitude and childish dependence have anything to do with women's true potential; that the idea of the nature of human possibility which rests on the accidents of individual development of genitalia, on what is possible today because of what happened yesterday, on the fundamentalist myth of sex organ causality, has strangled and deflected psychology so that it is relatively useless in describing, explaining or predicting humans and their behavior.

It then goes without saying that present psychology is less than worthless in contributing to a vision which could truly liberate—men as well as women.

The central argument of my paper, then, is this. Psychology has nothing to say about what women are really like, what they need and what they want, essentially because psychology does not know. I want to stress that this failure is not limited to women; rather, the kind of psychology which has addressed itself to how people act and who they are has failed to understand, in the first place, why people act the way they do, and certainly failed to understand what might make them act differently.

The kind of psychology which has addressed itself to these questions divides into two professional areas: academic personality research, and clinical psychology and psychiatry. The basic reason for failure is the same in both these areas: the central assumption for most psychologists of human personality has been that human behavior rests on an individual and inner dynamic, perhaps fixed in infancy, perhaps fixed by genitalia, perhaps simply arranged in a rather immovable cognitive network. But this assumption is rapidly losing ground as personality psychologists fail again and again to get consistency in the assumed personalities of their subjects. Meanwhile, the evidence is collecting that what a person does and who she believes herself to be, will in general be a function of what people around her expect her to be, and what the overall situation in which she is acting implies that she is. Compared to the influence of the social context within which a person lives, his or her history and "traits," as well as biological makeup, may simply be random variations, "noise" superimposed on the true signal which can predict behavior.

Some academic personality psychologists are at least looking at the counter evidence and questioning their theories; no such corrective is occurring in clinical psychology and psychiatry: Freudians and neo-Freudians, nudie-marathonists and touchy-feelies, classicists and swingers, clinicians and psychiatrists, simply refuse to look at the evidence against their theory and practice. And they support their theory and practice with stuff so transparently biased as to have absolutely no standing as empirical evidence.

To summarize: the first reason for psychology's failure to understand what people are and how they act is that psychology has looked for inner traits when it should have been looking for social context; the second reason for psychology's failure is that the theoreticians of personality have generally been clinicians and psychiatrists, and they have never considered it necessary to have evidence in support of their theories.

Theory without Evidence

Let us turn to this latter cause of failure first: the acceptance by psychiatrists and clinical psychologists of theory without evidence. If we inspect the literature of personality, it is immediately obvious that the bulk of it is written by clinicians and psychiatrists, and that the major support for their theories is "years of intensive clinical experience." This is a tradition started by Freud. His "insights" occurred during the course of his work with his patients. Now there is nothing wrong with such an approach to theory *formulation*; a person is free to make up theories with any inspiration that works: divine revelation, intensive clinical practice, a random numbers table. But he/she is not free to claim any validity for his/her theory until it has been tested and confirmed. But theories are treated in no such tentative way in ordinary clinical practice. Consider Freud. What he thought constituted evidence violated the most minimal conditions of scientific rigor. In *The Sexual Enlightenment of Children*, the classic document which is supposed to demonstrate empirically the existence of a castration complex and its connection to a phobia, Freud based his analysis on the reports of the father of the little boy, himself in therapy, and a devotee of Freudian theory. I really don't have to comment further on the contamination in this kind of evidence. It is remarkable that only recently has Freud's classic theory on the sexuality of women—the notion of the double orgasm—been actually tested physiologically and found just plain wrong. Now those who claim that fifty years of psychoanalytic experience constitute evidence enough of the essential truths of Freud's theory should ponder the robust health of the double orgasm. Did women, until Masters and Johnson,[2] believe they were having two different kinds of orgasm? Did their psychiatrists badger them into reporting something that was not true? If so, were there other things they reported that were also not true? Did psychiatrists ever learn anything different than their theories had led them to believe? If clinical

2. W. H. Masters and V. E. Johnson, *Human Sexual Response* (Boston: Little, Brown, 1966) [Weisstein's note].

experience means anything at all, surely we should have been done with the double orgasm myth long before the Masters and Johnson studies.

But certainly, you may object, "years of intensive clinical experience" is the only reliable measure in a discipline which relies for its findings on insight, sensitivity, and intuition. The problem with insight, sensitivity, and intuition, is that they can confirm for all time the biases that one started with. People used to be absolutely convinced of their ability to tell which of their number were engaging in witchcraft. All it required was some sensitivity to the workings of the devil.

Years of intensive clinical experience is not the same thing as empirical evidence. The first thing an experimenter learns in any kind of experiment which involves humans is the concept of the "double blind." The term is taken from medical experiments, where one group is given a drug which is presumably supposed to change behavior in a certain way, and a control group is given a placebo. If the observers or the subjects know which group took which drug, the result invariably comes out on the positive side for the new drug. Only when it is not known which subject took which pill is validity remotely approximated. In addition, with judgments of human behavior, it is so difficult to precisely tie down just what behavior is going on, let alone what behavior should be expected, that one must test again and again the reliability of judgments. How many judges, blind, will agree in their observations? Can they replicate their own judgments at some later time? When, in actual practice, these judgment criteria are tested for clinical judgments, then we find that the judges cannot judge reliably, nor can they judge consistently: they do no better than chance in identifying which of a certain set of stories were written by men and which by women; which of a whole battery of clinical test results are the products of homosexuals and which are the products of heterosexuals, and which, of a battery of clinical test results and interviews (where questions are asked such as "Do you have delusions?") are products of psychotics, neurotics, psychosomatics, or normals. Lest this summary escape your notice, let me stress the implications of these findings. The ability of judges, chosen for their clinical expertise, to distinguish male heterosexuals from male homosexuals on the basis of three widely used clinical projective tests—the Rorschach, the TAT, and the MAP—was *no better than chance*. The reason this is such devastating news, of course, is that sexuality is supposed to be of fundamental importance in the deep dynamic of personality; if what is considered gross sexual deviance cannot be caught, then what are psychologists talking about when they, for example, claim that at the basis of paranoid psychosis is "latent homosexual panic"? They can't even identify what homosexual anything is, let alone "latent homosexual panic."[3]

3. It should be noted that psychologists have been as quick to assert absolute truths about the nature of homosexuality as they have about the nature of women. The arguments presented in this paper apply equally to the nature of homosexuality; psychologists know

More frightening, expert clinicians cannot be consistent on what diagnostic category to assign to a person, again on the basis of both tests and interviews; a number of normals in the Little and Schneidman study were described as psychotic, in such categories as "schizophrenic with homosexual tendencies" or "schizoid character with depressive trends." But most disheartening, when the judges were asked to rejudge the test protocols some weeks later, their diagnoses of the same subjects on the basis of the same protocol differed markedly from their initial judgments. It is obvious that even simple descriptive conventions in clinical psychology cannot be consistently applied; if clinicians were as faulty in recognizing food from non-food, they'd poison themselves and starve to death. That their descriptive conventions have any explanatory significance is therefore, of course, out of the question.

As a graduate student at Harvard some years ago, I was a member of a seminar which was asked to identify which of two piles of a clinical test, the TAT, had been written by males and which by females. Only four students out of twenty identified the piles correctly, and this was after one and a half months of intensively studying the differences between men and women. Since this result is below chance—that is, the result would occur by chance about four out of a thousand times—we may conclude that there *is* finally a consistency here; students are judging knowledgeably within the context of psychological teaching about the differences between men and women; the teachings themselves are simply erroneous.

You may argue that the theory may be scientifically "unsound" but at least it cures people. There is no evidence that it does. It 1952, Eysenck reported the results of what is called an "outcome of therapy" study of neurotics which showed that, of the patients who received psychoanalysis the improvement rate was 44 percent; of the patients who received psychotherapy the improvement rate was 64 percent; and of the patients who received no treatment at all the improvement rate was 72. percent. These findings have never been refuted; subsequently, later studies have confirmed the negative results of the Eysenck study. How can clinicians and psychiatrists, then, in all good conscience, continue to practice? Largely by ignoring these results and being careful not to do outcome-of-therapy studies. The attitude is nicely summarized by Rotter: "Research studies in psychotherapy tend to be concerned more with psychotherapeutic procedure and less with outcome. . . . To some extent, it reflects an interest in the psychotherapy situation as a kind of personality laboratory." Some laboratory.

---

nothing about it; there is no more evidence for the "naturalness" of heterosexuality. Psychology has functioned as a pseudoscientific buttress for patriarchal ideology and patriarchal social organization: women's liberation and gay liberation fight against a common victimization [Weisstein's note].

The Social Context

Thus, since we can conclude that because clinical experience and tools can be shown to be worse than useless when tested for consistency, efficacy, agreement, and reliability, we can safely conclude that theories of a clinical nature advanced about women are also worse than useless. I want to turn now to the second major point in my paper, which is that, even when psychological theory is constructed so that it may be tested, and rigorous standards of evidence are used, it has become increasingly clear that in order to understand why people do what they do, and certainly in order to change what people do, psychologists must turn away from the theory of the causal nature of the inner dynamic and look to the social context within which individuals live.

Before examining the relevance of this approach to the question of women, let me first sketch the groundwork for this assertion.

In the first place, it is clear that personality tests never yield consistent predictions; a rigid authoritarian on one measure will be an unauthoritarian on the next. But the reason for this inconsistency is only now becoming clear, and it seems overwhelmingly to have much more to do with the social situation in which the subject finds him/herself than with the subject him/herself.

In a series of brilliant experiments, Rosenthal and his co-workers have shown that if one group of experimenters has one hypothesis about what they expect to find, and another group of experimenters has the opposite hypothesis, both groups will obtain results in accord with their hypotheses. The results obtained are not due to mishandling of data by biased experimenters; rather, somehow, the bias of the experimenter creates a changed environment in which subjects actually act differently. For instance, in one experiment, subjects were to assign numbers to pictures of men's faces, with high numbers representing the subject's judgment that the man in the picture was a successful person, and low numbers representing the subject's judgment that the man in the picture was an unsuccessful person. Prior to running the subjects, one group of experimenters was told that the subjects tended to rate the faces high; another group of experimenters was told that the subjects tended to rate the faces low. Each group of experimenters was instructed to follow precisely the same producer: they were required to read to subjects a set of instructions, and to say *nothing else*. For the 375 subjects run, the results showed clearly that those subjects who performed the task with experimenters who expected high ratings gave high ratings, and those subjects who performed the task with experimenters who expected low ratings gave low ratings. How did this happen? The experimenters all used the same words; it was something in their conduct which made one group of subjects do one thing, and another group of subjects do another thing.[4]

The concreteness of the changed conditions produced by expectation is a fact, a reality: even with animal subjects, in two separate studies, those experimenters who were told that rats learning mazes had been especially bred for brightness obtained better learning from their rats than did experimenters believing their rats to have been bred for dullness. In a very recent study, Rosenthal and Jacobson (1968) extended their analysis to the natural classroom situation. Here, they tested a group of students and reported to the teachers that some among the students tested "showed great promise." Actually, the students so named had been selected on a random basis. Some time later, the experimenters retested the group of students: those students whose teachers had been told that they were "promising" showed real and dramatic increments in their IQs as compared to the rest of the students. Something in the conduct of the teachers towards those who the teachers believed to be the "bright" students, made those students brighter.

Thus, even in carefully controlled experiments, and with no outward or conscious difference in behavior, the hypotheses we start with will influence enormously the behavior of another organism. These studies are extremely important when assessing the validity of psychological studies of women. Since it is beyond doubt that most of us start with notions as to the nature of men and women, the validity of a number of observations of sex differences is questionable, even when these observations have been made under carefully controlled conditions. Second, and more important, the Rosenthal experiments point quite clearly to the influence of social expectation. In some extremely important ways, people are what you expect them to be, or at least they behave as you expect them to behave. Thus, if women, according to Bettelheim, want first and foremost to be good wives and mothers, it is extremely likely that this is what Bruno Bettelheim, and the rest of society, want them to be.

There is another series of brilliant social psychological experiments which point to the overwhelming effect of social context. These are the obedience experiments of Stanley Milgram in which subjects are asked to obey the orders of unknown experimenters, orders which carry with them the distinct possibility that the subject is killing somebody.

In Milgram's experiments, a subject is told that he/she is administering a learning experiment, and that he/she is to deal out shocks each time the other "subject" (in reality, a confederate of the experimenter) answers incorrectly. The equipment appears to provide graduated shocks ranging upwards from 15 volts through 450 volts; for each of four consecutive voltages there are verbal descriptions such as "mild shock," "danger, severe shock," and, finally, for the 435- and 450-volt switches, a red XXX

---

4. I am indebted to Jesse Lemisch for his valuable suggestions in the interpretation of these studies [Weisstein's note].

marked over the switches. Each time the stooge answers incorrectly, the subject is supposed to increase the voltage. As the voltage increases, the stooge begins to cry in pain; he/she demands that the experiment stop; finally, he/she refuses to answer at all. When he/she stops responding, the experimenter instructs the subject to continue increasing the voltage; for each shock administered the stooge shrieks in agony. Under these conditions, about 62 1/2 percent of the subjects administered shocks that they believed to be possibly lethal.

No tested individual differences between subjects predicted how many would continue to obey, and which would break off the experiment. When forty psychiatrists predicted how many of a group of 100 subjects would go on to give the lethal shock, their predictions were orders of magnitude below the actual percentages; most expected only one-tenth of one per cent of the subjects to obey to the end.

But even though *psychiatrists* have no idea how people will behave in this situation, and even though individual differences do not predict which subjects will obey and which will not, it is easy to predict when subjects will be obedient and when they will be defiant. All the experimenter has to do is change the social situation. In a variant of Milgram's experiment, two stooges were present in addition to the "victim"; these worked along with the subject in administering electric shocks. When these two stooges refused to go on with the experiment, only 10 percent of the subjects continued to the maximum voltage. This is critical for personality theory. It says that behavior is predicted from the social situation, not from the individual history.

Finally, an ingenious experiment by Schachter and Singer showed that subjects injected with adrenalin, which produces a state of physiological arousal in all but minor respects identical to that which occurs when subjects are extremely afraid, became euphoric when they were in a room with a stooge who was acting euphoric, and became extremely angry when they were placed in a room with a stooge who was acting extremely angry.

To summarize: If subjects under quite innocuous and non-coercive social conditions can be made to kill other subjects and under other types of social conditions will positively refuse to do so; if subjects can react to a state of physiological fear by becoming euphoric because there is somebody else around who is euphoric, or angry because there is somebody else around who is angry; if students become intelligent because teachers expect them to be intelligent, and rats run mazes better because experimenters are told the rats are bright, then it is obvious that a study of human behavior requires, first and foremost, a study of the social contexts within which people move, the expectations as to how they will behave, and the authority which tells them who they are and what they are supposed to do.

Biologically Based Theories

Biologists also have at times assumed they could describe the limits of human potential from their observations not of human, but of animal behavior. Here, as in psychology, there has been no end of theorizing about the sexes, again with a sense of absolute certainty surprising in "science." These theories fall into two major categories.

One category of theory argues that since females and males differ in their sex hormones, and sex hormones enter the brain, there must be innate behavioral differences. But the only thing this argument tells us is that there are differences in physiological state. The problem is whether these differences are at all relevant to behavior.

Consider, for example, differences in levels of the sex hormone testosterone. A man who calls himself Tiger[5] has recently argued that the greater quantities of testosterone found in human males as compared with human females (of a certain age group) determine innate differences in aggressiveness, competitiveness, dominance, ability to hunt, ability to hold public office, and so forth. But Tiger demonstrates in this argument the same manly and courageous refusal to be intimidated by evidence which we have already seen in our consideration of the clinical and psychiatric tradition. The evidence does not support his argument, and in most cases, directly contradicts it. Testosterone level does not seem to be related to hunting ability, dominance, or aggression, or competitiveness. As Storch has pointed out, all normal male mammals in the reproductive age group produce much greater quantities of testosterone than females; yet many of these males are neither hunters nor are they aggressive (e.g. rabbits). And, among some hunting mammals, such as the large cats, it turns out that more hunting is done by the female than the male. And there exist primate species where the female is clearly more aggressive, competitive, and dominant that the male. Thus, for some species, being female, and therefore, having less testosterone than the male of that species means hunting more, or being more aggressive, or being more dominant. Nor does having more testosterone preclude behavior commonly thought of as "female"; there exist primate species where females do not touch infants except to feed them; the males care for the infants at all times. So it is not clear what testosterone or any other sex-hormonal difference means for differences in nature, or sex-role behavior.

In other words, one can observe identical types of behavior which have been associated with sex (e.g. "mothering") in males and females, despite known differences in physiological state, i.e. sex hormones, genitalia, etc. What about the converse to this? That is, can one obtain differences in behavior given a single physiological state? The answer is overwhelm-

---

5. H. N. G. Schwarz-Belkin claims that the name was originally Mouse, but this may be a reference to an earlier L. Tiger (putative) [Weisstein's note].

ingly yes, not only as regards non-sex-specific hormones (as in the Schachter and Singer experiment cited above), but also as regards gender itself. Studies of hermaphrodites with the same diagnosis (the genetic, gonadal, hormonal sex, the internal reproductive organs, and the ambiguous appearances of the external genitalia were identical) have shown that one will consider oneself male or female depending simply on whether one was defined and raised as male or female:

> There is no more convincing evidence of the power of social interaction on gender-identity differentiation than in the case of congenital hermaphrodites who are of the same diagnosis and similar degree of hermaphroditism but are differently assigned and with a different postnatal medical and life history (Money, 1970, p. 743).

Thus, for example, if out of two individuals diagnosed as having the adrenogenital syndrome of female hermaphroditism, one is raised as a girl and one as a boy, each will act and identify her/himself accordingly. The one raised as a girl will consider herself a girl; the one raised as a boy will consider himself a boy; and each will conduct her/himself successfully in accord with that self-definition.

So, identical behavior occurs given different physiological states; and different behavior occurs given an identical physiological starting point. So it is not clear that differences in sex hormones are at all relevant to behavior.

The other category of theory based on biology, a reductionist theory, goes like this. Sex-role behavior in some primate species is described, and it is concluded that this is the "natural" behavior for humans. Putting aside the not insignificant problem of observer bias (for instance, Harlow, of the University of Wisconsin, after observing differences between male and female rhesus monkeys, quotes Laurence Sterne to the effect that women are silly and trivial, and concludes that "men and women have differed in the past and they will differ in the future"), there are a number of problems with this approach.

The most general and serious problem is that there are no grounds to assume that anything primates do is necessarily natural, or desirable in humans, for the simple reason that humans are not non-humans. For instance, it is found that male chimpanzees placed alone with infants will not "mother" them. Jumping from hard data to ideological speculation, researchers conclude from this information that *human* females are necessary for the safe growth of human infants. It would be reasonable to conclude, following this logic, that it is quite useless to teach human infants to speak, since it has been tried with chimpanzees and it does not work.

One strategy that has been used is to extrapolate from primate behavior to "innate" human preference by noticing certain trends in primate behavior as one moves phylogenetically closer to humans. But there are great difficulties with this approach. When behaviors from lower primates are directly opposite to those of higher primates, or to those one expects of humans, they can be dismissed on evolutionary grounds —higher primates and/or humans grew out of that kid stuff. On the other hand, if the behavior of higher primates is counter to the behavior considered natural for humans, while the behavior of some lower primate is considered the natural one for humans, the higher primate behavior can be dismissed also, on the grounds that it has diverged from an older, prototypical pattern. So either way, one can select those behaviors one wants to prove innate for humans. In addition, one does not know whether the sex-role behavior exhibited is dependent on the phylogenetic rank, or on the environmental conditions (both physical and social) under which different species live.

Is there then any value at all in primate observations as they relate to human females and males? There is a value but it is limited: its function can be no more than to show some extant examples of diverse sex-role behavior. It must be stressed, however, that this is an extremely limited function. The extant behavior does not begin to suggest all the possibilities, either for non-human primates or for humans. Bearing these caveats in mind, it is nonetheless interesting that if one inspects the limited set of observations of existing non-human primate sex-role behaviors, one finds, in fact, a much larger range of sex-role behavior than is commonly believed to exist. "Biology" appears to limit very little; the fact that a female gives birth does not mean, even in non-humans, that she necessarily cares for the infant (in marmosets, for instance, the male carries the infant at all times except when the infant is feeding); "natural" female and male behavior varies all the way from females who are much more aggressive and competitive than males (e.g. Tamarins) and male "mothers" (e.g. Titi monkeys, night monkeys, and marmosets[6]) to submissive and passive females and male antagonists (e.g. rhesus monkeys).

But even for the limited function that primate arguments serve, the evidence has been misused. Invariably, those primates have been cited which exhibit exactly the kind of behavior that the proponents of the biological fixedness of human female behavior wish were true for humans. Thus, baboons and rhesus monkeys are generally cited: males in these groups exhibit some of the most irritable and aggressive behavior found in primates, and if one wishes to argue that females are naturally passive and submissive, these groups provide vivid examples. There are abundant counter examples, such as those mentioned above; in fact, in general, a counter example can be found for every sex-role behavior cited, including, as mentioned in the case of marmosets, male "mothers."

But the presence of counter examples has not stopped florid and

---

6. All these are lower-order primates, which makes their behavior with reference to humans unnatural, or more natural; take your choice [Weisstein's note].

overarching theories of the natural or biological basis of male privilege from proliferating. For instance, there have been a number of theories dealing with the innate incapacity in human males for monogamy. Here, as in most of this type of theorizing, baboons are a favorite example, probably because of their fantasy value: the family unit of the hamadryas baboon, for instance, consists of a highly constant pattern of one male and a number of females and their young. And again, the counter examples, such as the invariably monogamous gibbon, are ignored.

An extreme example of this maiming and selective truncation of the evidence in the service of a plea for the maintenance of male privilege is a recent book, *Men in Groups* by Tiger. The central claim of this book is that females are incapable of "bonding" as in "male bonding." What is "male bonding"? Its surface definition is simple: ". . .a particular relationship between two or more males such that they react differently to members of their bonding units as compared to individuals outside of it." If one deletes the word male, the definition, on its face, would seem to include all organisms that have any kind of social organization. But this is not what Tiger means. For instance, Tiger asserts that females are incapable of bonding; and this alleged incapacity indicates to Tiger that females should be restricted from public life. Why is bonding an exclusively male behavior? Because, says Tiger, it is seen in male primates. All male primates? No, very few male primates. Tiger cites two examples where male bonding is seen: rhesus monkeys and baboons. Surprise, surprise. But not even all baboons: as mentioned above, the hamadryas social organization consists of one-male units; so does that of the gelada baboon. And the great apes do not go in for male bonding much either. The "male bond" is hardly a serious contribution to scholarship; one reviewer for *Science* has observed that the book ". . .shows basically more resemblance to a partisan political tract than to a work of objective social science," with male bonding being ". . .some kind of behavioral phlogiston."

In short, primate arguments have generally misused the evidence; primate studies themselves have, in any case, only the very limited function of describing some possible sex-role behavior; and at present, primate observations have been sufficiently limited so that even the range of possible sex-role behavior for non-human primates is not known. This range is not known since there is only minimal observation of what happens to behavior if the physical or social environment is changed. In one study, different troops of Japanese macaques were observed. Here, there appeared to be cultural differences: males in 3 out of the 18 troops observed differed in the amount of their aggressiveness and infant-caring behavior. There could be no possibility of differential evolution here; the differences seemed largely transmitted by infant socialization. Thus, the very limited evidence points to some plasticity in the sex-role behavior of non-human primates; if we can figure out experiments which massively change the social organization of primate groups, it is possible that we might observe great changes in behavior. At present, however, we must conclude that given a constant physical environment, non-human primates do not change their social conditions by themselves very much and thus the "innateness" and fixedness of their behavior is simply not known. Thus, even if there were some way, which there isn't, to settle on the behavior of a particular primate species as being the "natural" way for humans, we would not know whether or not this were simply some function of the present social organization of that species. And finally, once again it must be stressed that even if non-human primate behavior turned out to be relatively fixed, this would say little about our behavior. More immediate and relevant evidence, e.g. the evidence from social psychology, points to the enormous plasticity in human behavior, not only from one culture to the next, but from one experimental group to the next. One of the most salient features of human social organization is its variety; there are a number of cultures where there is at least a rough equality between men and women. In summary, primate arguments can tell us very little about our "innate" sex-role behavior; if they tell us anything at all, they tell us that there is no one biologically "natural" female or male behavior, and that sex-role behavior in non-human primates is much more varied than has previously been thought.

Conclusion

In brief, the uselessness of present psychology (and biology) with regard to women is simply a special case of the general conclusion: one must understand the social conditions under which humans live if one is going to attempt to explain their behavior. And, to understand the social conditions under which women live, one must understand the social expectations about women.

How are women characterized in our culture, and in psychology? They are inconsistent, emotionally unstable, lacking in a strong conscience or superego, weaker, "nurturant" rather then productive, "intuitive" rather than intelligent, and, if they are at all "normal," suited to the home and the family. In short, the list adds up to a typical minority group stereotype of inferiority: if they know their place, which is in the home, they are really quite lovable, happy, childlike, loving creatures. In a review of the intellectual differences between little boys and little girls, Eleanor Maccoby has shown that there are no intellectual differences until about high school, or, if there are, girls are slightly ahead of boys. At high school, girls begin to do worse on a few intellectual tasks, such as arithmetic reasoning, and beyond high school, the achievement of women now measured in terms of productivity and accomplishment drops off even more rapidly. There are a number of other, non-intellectual tests which show sex differences; I choose the intellectual differences since it is seen clearly that women start becoming inferior. It is no use to talk about women being different but equal; all of the tests I can think of have a "good" outcome and a "bad" outcome. Women usually end up at the "bad" outcome. In light of social expectations about women, what is surprising is that little girls don't get the message that they are supposed to be stupid until high school; and what is even more remarkable is that some women resist this message even after high school, college, and graduate school.

My paper began with remarks on the task of the discovery of the limits of human potential. Psychologists must realize that it is they who are limiting discovery of human potential. They refuse to accept evidence, if they are clinical psychologists, or, if they are rigorous, they assume that people move in a context-free ether, with only their innate dispositions and their individual traits determining what they will do. Until psychologists begin to respect evidence, and until they begin looking at the social context within which people move, psychology will have nothing of substance to offer in this task of discovery. I don't know what immutable differences exist between men and women apart from differences in their genitals; perhaps there are some other unchangeable differences; probably there are a number of irrelevant differences. But it is clear that until social expectations for men and women are equal, until we provide equal respect for both men and women, our answers to this question will simply reflect our prejudices.

1971

James Baldwin

STRANGER IN THE VILLAGE

From all available evidence no black man had ever set foot in this tiny Swiss village before I came. I was told before arriving that I would probably be a "sight" for the village; I took this to mean that people of my complexion were rarely seen in Switzerland, and also that city people are always something of a "sight" outside of the city. It did not occur to me —possibly because I am an American—that there could be people anywhere who had never seen a Negro.

It is a fact that cannot be explained on the basis of the inaccessibility of the village. The village is very high, but it is only four hours from Milan and three hours from Lausanne. It is true that it is virtually unknown.

Few people making plans for a holiday would elect to come here. On the other hand, the villagers are able, presumably, to come and go as they please—which they do: to another town at the foot of the mountain, with a population of approximately five thousand, the nearest place to see a movie or go to the bank. In the village there is no movie house, no bank, no library, no theater; very few radios, one jeep, one station wagon; and at the moment, one typewriter, mine, an invention which the woman next door to me here had never seen. There are about six hundred people living here, all Catholic—I conclude this from the fact that the Catholic church is open all year round, whereas the Protestant chapel, set off on a hill a little removed from the village, is open only in the summertime when the tourists arrive. There are four or five hotels, all closed now, and four or five *bistros*, of which, however, only two do any business during the winter. These two do not do a great deal, for life in the village seems to end around nine or ten o'clock. There are a few stores, butcher, baker, *épicerie*, a hardware store, and a money-changer—who cannot change travelers' checks, but must send them down to the bank, an operation which takes two or three days. There is something called the *Ballet Haus*, closed in the winter and used for God knows what, certainly not ballet, during the summer. There seems to be only one schoolhouse in the village, and this for the quite young children; I suppose this to mean that their older brothers and sisters at some point descend from these mountains in order to complete their education—possibly, again, to the town just below. The landscape is absolutely forbidding, mountains towering on all four sides, ice and snow as far as the eye can reach. In this white wilderness, men and women and children move all day, carrying washing, wood, buckets of milk or water, sometimes skiing on Sunday afternoons. All week long boys and young men are to be seen shoveling snow off the rooftops, or dragging wood down from the forest in sleds.

The village's only real attraction, which explains the tourist season, is the hot spring water. A disquietingly high proportion of these tourists are cripples, or semi-cripples, who come year after year—from other parts of Switzerland, usually—to take the waters. This lends the village, at the height of the season, a rather terrifying air of sanctity, as though it were a lesser Lourdes. There is often something beautiful, there is always something awful, in the spectacle of a person who has lost one of his faculties, a faculty he never questioned until it was gone, and who struggles to recover it. Yet people remain people, on crutches or indeed on death-beds; and wherever I passed, the first summer I was here, among the native villagers or among the lame, a wind passed with me—of astonishment, curiosity, amusement, and outrage. That first summer I stayed two weeks and never intended to return. But I did return in the winter, to work; the village offers, obviously, no distractions whatever and has the further advantage of being extremely cheap. Now it is winter again, a year later, and I am here again. Everyone in the village knows my name, though they scarcely ever use it, knows that I come from America —though, this, apparently, they will never really believe: black men come from Africa—and everyone knows that I am the friend of the son of a woman who was born here, and that I am staying in their chalet. But I remain as much a stranger today as I was the first day I arrived, and the children shout *Neger! Neger!* as I walk along the streets.

It must be admitted that in the beginning I was far too shocked to have any real reaction. In so far as I reacted at all, I reacted by trying to be pleasant—it being a great part of the American Negro's education (long before he goes to school) that he must make people "like" him. This smile-and-the-world-smiles-with-you routine worked about as well in this situation as it had in the situation for which it was designed, which is to say that it did not work at all. No one, after all, can be liked whose human weight and complexity cannot be, or has not been, admitted. My smile was simply another unheard-of phenomenon which allowed them to see my teeth—they did not, really, see my smile and I began to think that, should I take to snarling, no one would notice any difference. All of the physical characteristics of the Negro which had caused me, in America, a very different and almost forgotten pain were nothing less than miraculous—or infernal—in the eyes of the village people. Some thought my hair was the color of tar, that it had the texture of wire, or the texture of cotton. It was jocularly suggested that I might let it all grow long and make myself a winter coat. If I sat in the sun for more than five minutes some daring creature was certain to come along and gingerly put his fingers on my hair, as though he were afraid of an electric shock, or put his hand on my hand, astonished that the color did not rub off. In all of this, in which it must be conceded there was the charm of genuine wonder and in which there were certainly no elements of intentional unkindness, there was yet no suggestion that I was human: I was simply a living wonder.

I knew that they did not mean to be unkind, and I know it now; it is necessary, nevertheless, for me to repeat this to myself each time that I walk out of the chalet. The children who shout *Neger!* have no way of knowing the echoes this sound raises in me. They are brimming with good humor and the more daring swell with pride when I stop to speak with them. Just the same, there are days when I cannot pause and smile, when I have no heart to play with them; when, indeed, I mutter sourly to myself, exactly as I muttered on the streets of a city these children have never seen, when I was no bigger than these children are now: *Your mother was a nigger.* Joyce is right about history being a nightmare—but it may be the nightmare from which no one *can* awaken. People are trapped in history and history is trapped in them.

There is a custom in the village—I am told it is repeated in many villages—of "buying" African natives for the purpose of converting them to Christianity. There stands in the church all year round a small box with a slot for money, decorated with a black figurine, and into this box the villagers drop their francs. During the *carnaval* which precedes Lent, two village children have their faces blackened—out of which bloodless darkness their blue eyes shine like ice—and fantastic horsehair wigs are placed on their blond heads; thus disguised, they solicit among the villagers for money for the missionaries in Africa. Between the box in the church and the blackened children, the village "bought" last year six or eight African natives. This was reported to me with pride by the wife of one of the *bistro* owners and I was careful to express astonishment and pleasure at the solicitude shown by the village for the souls of black folks. The *bistro* owner's wife beamed with a pleasure far more genuine than my own and seemed to feel that I might now breathe more easily concerning the souls of at least six of my kinsmen.

I tried not to think of these so lately baptized kinsmen, of the price paid for them, or the peculiar price they themselves would pay, and said nothing about my father, who having taken his own conversion too literally never, at bottom, forgave the white world (which he described as heathen) for having saddled him with a Christ in whom, to judge at least from their treatment of him, they themselves no longer believed. I thought of white men arriving for the first time in an African village, strangers there, as I am a stranger here, and tried to imagine the astounded populace touching their hair and marveling at the color of their skin. But there is a great difference between being the first white man to be seen by Africans and being the first black man to be seen by whites. The white man takes the astonishment as tribute, for he arrives to conquer and to convert the natives, whose inferiority in relation to himself is not even to be questioned; whereas I, without a thought of conquest, find myself among a people whose culture controls me, has even, in a sense, created me, people who have cost me more in anguish and rage than they will ever know, who yet do not even know of my existence. The astonishment with which I might have greeted them, should they have stumbled into my African village a few hundred years ago, might have rejoiced their hearts. But the astonishment with which they greet me today can only poison mine.

And this is so despite everything I may do to feel differently, despite my friendly conversations with the *bistro* owner's wife, despite their three-year-old son who has at last become my friend, despite the *saluts* and *bonsoirs*[1] which I exchange with people as I walk, despite the fact that I know that no individual can be taken to task for what history is doing, or has done. I say that the culture of these people controls me—but they can scarcely be held responsible for European culture. America comes out of Europe, but these people have never seen America, nor have most of

---

1. "Hellos" and "good evenings."

them seen more of Europe than the hamlet at the foot of their mountain. Yet they move with an authority which I shall never have; and they regard me, quite rightly, not only as a stranger in their village but as a suspect latecomer, bearing no credentials, to everything they have —however unconsciously—inherited.

For this village, even were it incomparably more remote and incredibly more primitive, is the West, the West onto which I have been so strangely grafted. These people cannot be, from the point of view of power, strangers anywhere in the world; they have made the modern world, in effect, even if they do not know it. The most illiterate among them is related, in a way that I am not, to Dante, Shakespeare, Michelangelo, Aeschylus, Da Vinci, Rembrandt, and Racine; the cathedral at Chartres says something to them which it cannot say to me, as indeed would New York's Empire State Building, should anyone here ever see it. Out of their hymns and dances come Beethoven and Bach. Go back a few centuries and they are in their full glory—but I am in Africa, watching the conquerors arrive.

The rage of the disesteemed is personally fruitless, but it is also absolutely inevitable; this rage, so generally discounted, so little understood even among the people whose daily bread it is, is one of the things that makes history. Rage can only with difficulty, and never entirely, be brought under the domination of the intelligence and is therefore not susceptible to any arguments whatever. This is a fact which ordinary representatives of the *Herrenvolk*,[2] having never felt this rage and being unable to imagine, quite fail to understand. Also, rage cannot be hidden, it can only be dissembled. This dissembling deludes the thoughtless, and strenthens rage and adds, to rage, contempt. There are, no doubt, as many ways of coping with the resulting complex of tensions as there are black men in the world, but no black man can hope ever to be entirely liberated from this internal warfare—rage, dissembling, and contempt having inevitably accompanied his first realization of the power of white men. What is crucial here is that, since white men represent in the black man's world so heavy a weight, white men have for black men a reality which is far from being reciprocal; and hence all black men have toward all white men an attitude which is designed, really, either to rob the white man of the jewel of his naïveté, or else to make it cost him dear.

The black man insists, by whatever means he finds at his disposal, that the white man cease to regard him as an exotic rarity and recognize him as a human being. This is a very charged and difficult moment, for there is a great deal of will power involved in the white man's naïveté. Most people are not naturally reflective any more than they are naturally malicious, and the white man prefers to keep the black man at a certain human remove because it is easier for him thus to preserve his simplicity

2. Master race.

and avoid being called to account for crimes committed by his forefathers, or his neighbors. He is inescapably aware, nevertheless, that he is in a better position in the world than black men are, nor can he quite put to death the suspicion that he is hated by black men therefor. He does not wish to be hated, neither does he wish to change places, and at this point in his uneasiness he can scarcely avoid having recourse to those legends which white men have created about black men, the most usual effect of which is that the white man finds himself enmeshed, so to speak, in his own language which describes hell, as well as the attributes which lead one to hell, as being as black as night.

Every legend, moreover, contains its residuum of truth, and the root function of language is to control the universe by describing it. It is of quite considerable significance that black men remain, in the imagination, and in overwhelming numbers in fact, beyond the disciplines of salvation; and this despite the fact that the West has been "buying" African natives for centuries. There is, I should hazard, an instantaneous necessity to be divorced from this so visibly unsaved stranger, in whose heart, moreover, one cannot guess what dreams of vengeance are being nourished; and, at the same time, there are few things on earth more attractive than the idea of the unspeakable liberty which is allowed the unredeemed. When, beneath the black mask, a human being begins to make himself felt one cannot escape a certain awful wonder as to what kind of human being it is. What one's imagination makes of other people is dictated, of course, by the laws of one's own personality and it is one of the ironies of black-white relations that, by means of what the white man imagines the black man to be, the black man is enabled to know who the white man is.

I have said, for example, that I am as much a stranger in this village today as I was the first summer I arrived, but this is not quite true. The villagers wonder less about the texture of my hair than they did then, and wonder rather more about me. And the fact that their wonder now exists on another level is reflected in their attitudes and in their eyes. There are the children who make those delightful, hilarious, sometimes astonishingly grave overtures of friendship in the unpredictable fashion of children; other children, having been taught that the devil is a black man, scream in genuine anguish as I approach. Some of the older women never pass without a friendly greeting, never pass, indeed, if it seems that they will be able to engage me in conversation; other women look down or look away or rather contemptuously smirk. Some of the men drink with me and suggest that I learn how to ski—partly, I gather, because they cannot imagine what I would look like on skis—and want to know if I am married, and ask questions about my *métier*. But some of the men have accused *le sale nègre*[3]—behind my back—of stealing wood and there is already in the eyes of some of them that peculiar, intent, paranoiac

3. The dirty Negro.

malevolence which one sometimes surprises in the eyes of American white men when, out walking with their Sunday girl, they see a Negro male approach.

There is a dreadful abyss between the streets of this village and the streets of the city in which I was born, between the children who shout *Neger!* today and those who shouted *Nigger!* yesterday—the abyss is experience, the American experience. The syllable hurled behind me today expresses, above all, wonder: I am a stranger here. But I am not a stranger in America and the same syllable riding on the American air expresses the war my presence has occasioned in the American soul.

For this village brings home to me this fact: that there was a day, and not really a very distant day, when Americans were scarcely Americans at all but discontented Europeans, facing a great unconquered continent and strolling, say, into a marketplace and seeing black men for the first time. The shock this spectacle afforded is suggested, surely, by the promptness with which they decided that these black men were not really men but cattle. It is true that the necessity on the part of the settlers of the New World of reconciling their moral assumptions with the fact—and the necessity—of slavery enhanced immensely the charm of this idea, and it is also true that this idea expresses, with a truly American bluntness, the attitude which to varying extents all masters have had toward all slaves.

But between all former slaves and slave-owners and the drama which begins for Americans over three hundred years ago at Jamestown, there are at least two differences to be observed. The American Negro slave could not suppose, for one thing, as slaves in past epochs had supposed and often done, that he would ever be able to wrest the power from his master's hands. This was a supposition which the modern era, which was to bring about such vast changes in the aims and dimensions of power, put to death; it only begins, in unprecedented fashion, and with dreadful implications, to be resurrected today. But even had this supposition persisted with undiminished force, the American Negro slave could not have used it to lend his condition dignity, for the reason that this supposition rests on another: that the slave in exile yet remains related to his past, has some means—if only in memory—of revering and sustaining the forms of his former life, is able, in short, to maintain his identity.

This was not the case with the American Negro slave. He is unique among the black men of the world in that his past was taken from him, almost literally, at one blow. One wonders what on earth the first slave found to say to the first dark child he bore. I am told that there are Haitians able to trace their ancestry back to African kings, but any American Negro wishing to go back so far will find his journey through time abruptly arrested by the signature on the bill of sale which served as the entrance paper for his ancestor. At the time—to say nothing of the circumstances—of the enslavement of the captive black man who was to become the American Negro, there was not the remotest possibility that he would ever take power from his master's hands. There was no reason to suppose that his situation would ever change, nor was there, shortly, anything to indicate that his situation had ever been different. It was his necessity, in the words of E. Franklin Frazier, to find a "motive for living under American culture or die." The identity of the American Negro comes out of this extreme situation, and the evolution of this identity was a source of the most intolerable anxiety in the minds and the lives of his masters.

For the history of the American Negro is unique also in this: that the question of his humanity, and of his rights therefore as a human being, became a burning one for several generations of Americans, so burning a question that it ultimately became one of those used to divide the nation. It is out of this argument that the venom of the epithet *Nigger!* is derived. It is an argument which Europe has never had, and hence Europe quite sincerely fails to understand how or why the argument arose in the first place, why its effects are frequently disastrous and always so unpredictable, why it refuses until today to be entirely settled. Europe's black possessions remained—and do remain—in Europe's colonies, at which remove they represented no threat whatever to European identity. If they posed any problem at all for the European conscience it was a problem which remained comfortingly abstract: in effect, the black man, as a *man* did not exist for Europe. But in America, even as a slave, he was an inescapable part of the general social fabric and no American could escape having an attitude toward him. Americans attempt until today to make an abstraction of the Negro, but the very nature of these abstractions reveals the tremendous effects the presence of the Negro has had on the American character.

When one considers the history of the Negro in America it is of the greatest importance to recognize that the moral beliefs of a person, or a people, are never really as tenuous as life—which is not moral—very often causes them to appear; these create for them a frame of reference and a necessary hope, the hope being that when life has done its worst they will be enabled to rise above themselves and to triumph over life. Life would scarcely be bearable if this hope did not exist. Again, even when the worst has been said, to betray a belief is not by any means to have put oneself beyond its power; the betrayal of a belief is not the same thing as ceasing to believe. If this were not so there would be no moral standards in the world at all. Yet one must also recognize that morality is based on ideas and that all ideas are dangerous—dangerous because ideas can only lead to action and where the action leads no man can say. And dangerous in this respect: that confronted with the impossibility of remaining faithful to one's beliefs, and the equal impossibility of becoming free of them, one can be driven to the most inhuman excesses. The ideas on which American beliefs are based are not, though Americans often seem to think so, ideas which originated in America. They came out of Europe. And the establishment of democracy on the American continent was scarcely as radical a break with the past as was the necessity, which Americans faced, of broadening this concept to include black men.

This was, literally, a hard necessity. It was impossible, for one thing, for Americans to abandon their beliefs, not only because these beliefs alone seemed able to justify the sacrifices they had endured and the blood that they had spilled, but also because these beliefs afforded them their only bulwark against a moral chaos as absolute as the physical chaos of the continent it was their destiny to conquer. But in the situation in which Americans found themselves, these beliefs threatened an idea which, whether or not one likes to think so, is the very warp and woof of the heritage of the West, the idea of white supremacy.

Americans have made themselves notorious by the shrillness and the brutality with which they have insisted on this idea, but they did not invent it; and it has escaped the world's notice that those very excesses of which Americans have been guilty imply a certain, unprecedented uneasiness over the idea's life and power, if not, indeed, the idea's validity. The idea of white supremacy rests simply on the fact that white men are the creators of civilization (the present civilization, which is the only one that matters; all previous civilizations are simply "contributions" to our own) and are therefore civilization's guardians and defenders. Thus it was impossible for Americans to accept the black man as one of themselves, for to do so was to jeopardize their status as white men. But not so to accept him was to deny his human reality, his human weight and complexity, and the strain of denying the overwhelmingly undeniable forced Americans into rationalizations so fantastic that they approached the pathological.

At the root of the American Negro problem is the necessity of the American white man to find a way of living with the Negro in order to be able to live with himself. And the history of this problem can be reduced to the means used by Americans—lynch law and law, segregation and legal acceptance, terrorization and concession—either to come to terms with this necessity, or to find a way around it, or (most usually) to find a way of doing both these things at once. The resulting spectacle, at once foolish and dreadful, led someone to make the quite accurate observation that "the Negro-in-America is a form of insanity which overtakes white men."

In this long battle, a battle by on means finished, the unforeseeable effects of which will be felt by many future generations, the white man's motive was the protection of his identity; the black man was motivated by the need to establish an identity. And despite the terrorization which the Negro in America endured and endures sporadically until today, despite the cruel and totally inescapable ambivalence of his status in his country, the battle for his identity has long ago been won. He is not a visitor to the West, but a citizen there, an American; as Amercan as the Americans who despise him, the Americans who fear him, the Americans who love him—the Americans who became less than themselves, or rose to be greater than themselves by virtue of the fact that the challenge he represented was inescapable. He is perhaps the only black man in the world whose relationship to white men is more terrible, more subtle, and more meaningful than the relationship of bitter possessed to uncertain possessors. His survival depended, and his development depends, on his ability to turn his peculiar status in the Western world to his own advantage and, it may be, to the very great advantage of that world. It remains for him to fashion out of his experience that which will give him sustenance, and a voice.

The cathedral at Chartres, I have said, says something to the people of this village which it cannot say to me; but it is important to understand that this cathedral says something to me which it cannot say to them. Perhaps they are struck by the power of the spires, the glory of the windows; but they have known God, after all, longer than I have known him, and in a different way, and I am terrified by the slippery bottomless well to be found in the crypt, down which heretics were hurled to death, and by the obscene, inescapable gargoyles jutting out of the stone and seeming to say that God and the devil can never be divorced. I doubt that the villagers think of the devil when they face a cathedral because they have never been identified with the devil. But I must accept the status which myth, if nothing else, gives me in the West before I can hope to change the myth.

Yet, if the American Negro has arrived at his identity by virtue of the absoluteness of his estrangement from his past, American white men still nourish the illusion that there is some means of recovering the European innocence, of returning to a state in which black men do not exist. This is one of the greatest errors Americans can make. The identity they fought so hard to protect has, by virtue of that battle, undergone a change: Americans are as unlike any other white people in the world as it is possible to be. I do not think, for example, that it is too much to suggest that the American vision of the world—which allows so little reality, generally speaking, for any of the darker forces in human life, which tends until today to paint moral issues in glaring black and white—owes a great deal to the battle waged by Americans to maintain between themselves and black men a human separation which could not be bridged. It is only now beginning to be borne in on us—very faintly, it must be admitted, very slowly, and very much against our will—that this vision of the world is dangerously inaccurate, and perfectly useless. For it protects our moral high-mindedness at the terrible expense of weakening our grasp of reality. People who shut their eyes to reality simply invite their own destruction, and anyone who insists on remaining in a state of innocence long after that innocence is dead turns himself into a monster.

The time has come to realize that the interracial drama acted out on the American continent has not only created a new black man, it has created a new white man, too. No road whatever will lead Americans back to the simplicity of this European village where white men still have the luxury of looking on me as a stranger. I am not, really, a stranger any longer for any American alive. One of the things that distinguishes Americans from other people is that no other people has ever been so deeply involved in the lives of black men, and vice versa. This fact faced, with all its implications, it can be seen that the history of the American Negro problem is not merely shameful, it is also something of an achievement. For even when the worst has been said, it must also be added that the perpetual challenge posed by this problem was always, somehow, perpetually met. It is precisely this black-white experience which may prove of indispensable value to us in the world we face today. This world is white no longer, and it will never be white again.

1953

QUESTIONS

1. Baldwin begins with the narration of his experience in a Swiss village. At what point do you become aware that he is going to do more than tell the story of his stay in the village? What purpose does he make his experience serve?

2. On page 552 Baldwin says that Americans have attempted to make an abstraction of the Negro. To what degree has his purpose forced Baldwin to make an abstraction of the white man? What are the components of that abstraction?

3. Baldwin intimately relates the white man's language and legends about black men to the "laws" of the white man's personality. Bettelheim makes similar use of the myths of science fiction. This kind of inference reveals a conviction both men share about the nature of language; what is that conviction?

4. Describe some particular experience which raises a large social question or shows the working of large social forces. Does Baldwin offer any help in the problem of connecting the particular and the general?

5. Define alienation.

Norman Podhoretz

MY NEGRO PROBLEM—AND OURS

If we—and . . . I mean the relatively conscious whites and the relatively conscious blacks, who must, like lovers, insist on, or create, the consciousness of the others—do not falter in our duty now, we may be able, handful that we are, to end the racial nightmare, and achieve our country, and change the history of the world.   —JAMES BALDWIN[1]

Two ideas puzzled me deeply as a child growing up in Brooklyn during the 1930's in what today would be called an integrated neighborhood. One of them was that all Jews were rich; the other was that all Negroes were persecuted. These ideas have appeared in print; therefore they must be true. My own experience and the evidence of my senses told they were not true, but that only confirmed what a day-dreaming boy in the provinces—for the lower-class neighborhoods of New York belong as surely to the provinces as any rural town in North Dakota—discovers very early: his experience is unreal and the evidence of his senses is not to be trusted. Yet even a boy with a head full of fantasies incongruously synthesized out of Hollywood movies and English novels cannot altogether deny the reality of his own experience—especially when there is so much deprivation in that experience. Nor can he altogether gainsay the evidence of his own senses—especially such evidence of the senses as comes from being repeatedly beaten up, robbed, and in general hated, terrorized, and humiliated.

And so for a long time I was puzzled to think that Jews were supposed to be rich when the only Jews I knew were poor, and that Negroes were supposed to be persecuted when it was the Negroes who were doing the only persecuting I knew about—and doing it, moreover, to me. During the early years of the war, when my older sister joined a left-wing youth organization, I remember my astonishment at hearing her passionately denounce my father for thinking that Jews were worse off than Negroes. To me, at the age of twelve, it seemed very clear that Negroes were better off than Jews—indeed, than all whites. A city boy's world is contained within three or four square blocks, and in my world it was the whites, the Italians and Jews, who feared the Negroes, not the other way around. The Negroes were tougher than we were, more ruthless, and on the whole they were better athletes. What could it mean, then, to say that they were badly off and that we were more fortunate? Yet my sister's opinions, like print, were sacred, and when she told me about exploitation and economic forces I believed her. I believed her, but I was still afraid of Negroes. And I still hated them with all my heart.

1. The quotation is from the conclusion of Baldwin's *The Fire Next Time*.

It had not always been so—that much I can recall from early childhood. When did it start, this fear and this hatred? There was a kindergarten in the local public school, and given the character of the neighborhood, at least half of the children in my class must have been Negroes. Yet I have no memory of being aware of color differences at that age, and I know from observing my own children that they attribute no significance to such differences even when they begin noticing them. I think there was a day—first grade? second grade?—when my best friend Carl hit me on the way home from school and announced that he wouldn't play with me any more because I had killed Jesus. When I ran home to my mother crying for an explanation, she told me not to pay any attention to such foolishness, and then in Yiddish she cursed the goyim and the schwartzes, the schwartzes and the goyim.[2] Carl, it turned out, was a schwartze, and so was added a third to the categories into which people were mysteriously divided.

Sometimes I wonder whether this is a true memory at all. It is blazingly vivid, but perhaps it never happened: can anyone really remember back to the age of six? There is no uncertainty in my mind, however, about the years that followed. Carl and I hardly ever spoke, though we met in school every day up through the eight or ninth grade. There would be embarrassed moments of catching his eye or of his catching mine—for whatever it was that had attracted us to one another as very small children remained alive in spite of the fantastic barrier of hostility that had grown up between us, suddenly and out of nowhere. Nevertheless, friendship would have been impossible, and even if it had been possible, it would have been unthinkable. About that, there was nothing anyone could do by the time we were eight years old.

Item: The orphanage across the street is torn down, a city housing project begins to rise in its place, and on the marvelous vacant lot next to the old orphanage they are building a playground. Much excitement and anticipation as Opening Day draws near. Mayor LaGuardia himself comes to dedicate this great gesture of public benevolence. He speaks of neighborliness and borrowing cups of sugar, and of the playground he says that children of all races, colors, and creeds will learn to live together in harmony. A week later, some of us are swatting flies on the playground's inadequate little ball field. A gang of Negro kids, pretty much our own age, enter from the other side and order us out of the park. We refuse, proudly and indignantly, with superb masculine fervor. There is a fight, they win, and we retreat, half whimpering, half with bravado. My first nauseating experience of cowardice. And my first appalled realization that there are people in the world who do not seem to be afraid of anything, who act as though they have nothing to lose. Thereafter the

---

2. The Yiddish words *goyim* (Gentiles or white non-Jews) and *schwartzes* (blacks) are both partially derogatory terms.

playground becomes a battleground, sometimes quiet, sometimes the scene of athletic competition between Them and Us. But rocks are thrown as often as baseballs. Gradually we abandon the place and use the streets instead. The streets are safer, though we do not admit this to ourselves. We are not, after all, sissies—that most dreaded epithet of an American boyhood.

Item: I am standing alone in front of the building in which I live. It is late afternoon and getting dark. That day in school the teacher had asked a surly Negro boy named Quentin a question he was unable to answer. As usual I had waved my arm eagerly ("Be a good boy, get good marks, be smart, go to college, become a doctor") and, the right answer bursting from my lips, I was held up lovingly by the teacher as an example to the class. I had seen Quentin's face—a very dark, very cruel, very Oriental-looking face—harden, and there had been enough threat in his eyes to make me run all the way home for fear that he might catch me outside.

Now, standing idly in front of my own house, I see him approaching from the project accompanied by his little brother who is carrying a baseball bat and wearing a grin of malicious anticipation. As in a nightmare, I am trapped. The surroundings are secure and familiar, but terror is suddenly present and there is no one around to help. I am locked to the spot. I will not cry out or run away like a sissy, and I stand there, my heart wild, my throat clogged. He walks up, hurls the familiar epithet ("Hey, mo' f—r"), and to my surprise only pushes me. It is a violent push, but not a punch. Maybe I can still back out without entirely losing my dignity. Maybe I can still say, "Hey, c'mon Quentin, whaddya wanna do *that* for? I dint do nothin' to *you*," and walk away, not too rapidly. Instead, before I can stop myself, I push him back—a token gesture—and I say, "Cut that out, I don't wanna fight, I ain't got nothin' to fight about." As I turn to walk back into the building, the corner of my eye catches the motion of the bat his little brother has handed him. I try to duck, but the bat crashes colored lights into my head.

The next thing I know, my mother and sister are standing over me, both of them hysterical. My sister—she who was later to join the "progressive" youth organization—is shouting for the police and screaming imprecations at those dirty little black bastards. They take me upstairs, the doctor comes, the police come. I tell them that the boy who did it was a stranger, that he had been trying to get money from me. They do not believe me, but I am too scared to give them Quentin's name. When I return to school a few days later, Quentin avoids my eyes. He knows that I have not squealed, and he is ashamed. I try to feel proud, but in my heart I know that it was fear of what his friends might do to me that had kept me silent, and not the code of the street.

Item: There is an athletic meet in which the whole of our junior high school is participating. I am in one of the seventh-grade rapid-advance classes, and "segregation" has now set in with a vengeance. In the last three or four years of the elementary school from which we have just graduated, each grade had been divided into three classes, according to "intelligence." (In the earlier grades the divisions had either been arbitrary or else unrecognized by us as having anything to do with brains.) These divisions by IQ, or however it was arranged, had resulted in a preponderance of Jews in the "1" classes and a corresponding preponderance of Negroes in the "3's," with the Italians split unevenly along the spectrum. At least a few Negroes had always made the "1's," just as there had always been a few Jewish kids among the "3's" and more among the "2's" (where Italians dominated). But the junior high's rapid-advance class of which I am now a member is overwhelmingly Jewish and entirely white—except for a shy lonely Negro girl with light skin and reddish hair.

The athletic meet takes place in a city-owned stadium far from the school. It is an important event to which a whole day is given over. The winners are to get those precious little medallions stamped with the New York City emblem that can be screwed into a belt and that prove the wearer to be a distinguished personage. I am a fast runner, and so I am assigned the position of anchor man on my class's team in the relay race. There are three other seventh-grade teams in the race, two of them all Negro, as ours is all white. One of the all-Negro teams is very tall—their anchor man waiting silently next to me on the line looks years older than I am, and I do not recognize him. He is the first to get the baton and crosses the finishing line in a walk. Our team comes in second, but a few minutes later we are declared the winners, for it has been discovered that the anchor man on the first-place team is not a member of the class. We are awarded the medallions, and the following day our homeroom teacher makes a speech about how proud she is of us for being superior athletes as well as superior students. We want to believe that we deserve the praise, but we know that we could not have won even if the other class had not cheated.

That afternoon, walking home, I am waylaid and surrounded by five Negroes, among whom is the anchor man of the disqualified team. "Gimme my medal, mo'f—r," he grunts. I do not have it with me and I tell him so. "Anyway, it ain't yours," I say foolishly. He calls me a liar on both counts and pushes me up against the wall on which we sometimes play handball. "Gimme my mo'f—n' medal," he says again. I repeat that I have left it home. "Le's search the li'l mo'f—r," one of them suggests, "he prolly got it *hid* in his mo'f—n' *pants.*" My panic is now unmanageable. (How many times had I been surrounded like this and asked in soft tones, "Len' me a nickel, boy." How many times had I been called a liar for pleading poverty and pushed around, or searched, or beaten up, unless there happened to be someone in the marauding gang like Carl who liked me across that enormous divide of hatred and who would therefore say, "Aaah, c'mon, le's git someone else, this boy ain't got no money on 'im.") I scream at them through tears of rage and self-contempt, "Keep your f—n' filthy lousy black hands offa me! I swear I'll get the cops." This is all they need to hear, and the five of them set upon me. They bang me around, mostly in the stomach and on the arms and shoulders, and when several adults loitering near the candy store down the block notice what is going on and begin to shout, they run off and away.

I do not tell my parents about the incident. My team-mates, who have also been waylaid, each by a gang led by his opposite number from the disqualified team, have had their medallions taken from them, and they never squeal either. For days, I walk home in terror, expecting to be caught again, but nothing happens. The medallion is put away into a drawer, never to be worn by anyone.

Obviously experiences like these have always been a common feature of childhood life in working-class and immigrant neighborhoods, and Negroes do not necessarily figure in them. Wherever, and in whatever combination, they have lived together in the cities, kids of different groups have been at war, beating up and being beaten up: micks against kikes against wops against spicks against polacks. And even relatively homogeneous areas have not been spared the warring of the young: one block against another, one gang (called in my day, in a pathetic effort at gentility, an "S.A.C.," or social-athletic club) against another. But the Negro-white conflict had—and do doubt still has—a special intensity and was conducted with a ferocity unmatched by intramural white battling.

In my own neighborhood, a good deal of animosity existed between the Italian kids (most of whose parents were immigrants from Sicily) and the Jewish kids (who came largely from East European immigrant families). Yet everyone had friends, sometimes close friends, in the other "camp," and we often visited one another's strange-smelling houses, if not for meals, then for glasses of milk, and occasionally for some special event like a wedding or a wake. If it happened that we divided into warring factions and did battle, it would invariably be half-hearted and soon patched up. Our parents, to be sure, had nothing to do with one another and were mutually suspicious and hostile. But we, the kids, who all spoke Yiddish or Italian at home, were Americans, or New Yorkers, or Brooklyn boys: we shared a culture, the culture of the street, and at least for a while this culture proved to be more powerful than the opposing cultures of the home.

Why, why should it have been so different as between the Negroes and

us? How was it borne in upon us so early, white and black alike, that we were enemies beyond any possibility of reconciliation? Why did we hate one another so?

I suppose if I tried, I could answer those questions more or less adequately from the perspective of what I have since learned. I could draw upon James Baldwin—what better witness is there?—to describe the sense of entrapment that poisons the soul of the Negro with hatred for the white man whom he knows to be his jailer. On the other side, if I wanted to understand how the white man comes to hate the Negro, I could call upon the psychologists who have spoken of the guilt that white Americans feel toward Negroes and that turns into hatred for lack of acknowledging itself as guilt. These are plausible answers and certainly there is truth in them. Yet when I think back upon my own experience of the Negro and his of me, I find myself troubled and puzzled, much as I was as a child when I heard that all Jews were rich and all Negroes persecuted. How could the Negroes in my neighborhood have regarded the whites across the street and around the corner as jailers? On the whole, the whites were not so poor as the Negroes, but they were quite poor enough, and the years were years of Depression. As for white hatred of the Negro, how could guilt have had anything to do with it? What share had these Italian and Jewish immigrants in the enslavement of the Negro? What share had they—downtrodden people themselves breaking their own necks to eke out a living—in the exploitation of the Negro?

No, I cannot believe that we hated each other back there in Brooklyn because they thought of us as jailers and we felt guilty toward them. But does it mater, given the fact that we all went through an unrepresentative confrontation? I think it matters profoundly, for if we managed the job of hating each other so well without benefit of the aids to hatred that are supposedly at the root of this madness everywhere else, it must mean that the madness is not yet properly understood. I am far from pretending that I understand it, but I would insist that no view of the problem will begin to approach the truth unless it can account for a case like the one I have been trying to describe. Are the elements of any such view available to us?

At least two, I would say, are. One of them is a point we frequently come upon in the work of James Baldwin, and the other is a related point always stressed by psychologists who have studied the mechanisms of prejudice. Baldwin tells us that one of the reasons Negroes hate the white man is that the white man refuses to *look* at him: the Negro knows that in white eyes all Negroes are alike; they are faceless and therefore not altogether human. The psychologists, in their turn, tell us that the white man hates the Negro because he tends to project those wild impulses that he fears in himself onto an alien group which he then punishes with his contempt. What Baldwin does *not* tell us, however, is that the principle of facelessness is a two-way street and can operate in both directions with no difficulty at all. Thus, in my neighborhood in Brooklyn, I was as faceless to the Negroes as they were to me, and if they hated me because I never looked at them, I must also have hated them for never looking at me. To the Negroes, my white skin was enough to define me as the enemy, and in a war it is only the uniform that counts and not the person.

So with the mechanism of projection that the psychologists talk about: it too works in both directions at once. There is no question that the psychologists are right about what the Negro represents symbolically to the white man. For me as a child the life lived on the other side of the playground and down the block on Ralph Avenue seemed the very embodiment of the values of the street—free, independent, reckless, brave, masculine, erotic. I put the word "erotic" last, though it is usually stressed above all others, because in fact it came last, in consciousness as in importance. What mainly counted for me about Negro kids of my own age was that they were "bad boys." There were plenty of bad boys among the whites—this was, after all, a neighborhood with a long tradition of crime as a career open to aspiring talents—but the Negroes were really bad, bad in a way that beckoned to one, and made one feel inadequate. We all went home every day for a lunch of spinach-and-potatoes; they roamed around during lunch hour, munching on candy bars. In winter we had to wear itchy woolen hats and mittens and cumbersome galoshes; they were bareheaded and loose as they pleased. We rarely played hookey, or got into serious trouble in school, for all our street-corner bravado; they were defiant, forever staying out (to do what delicious things?), forever making disturbances in class and in the halls, forever being sent to the principal and returning uncowed. But most important of all, they were tough; beautifully, enviably tough, not giving a damn for anyone or anything. To hell with the teacher, the truant officer, the cop; to hell with the whole of the adult world that held us in its grip and that we never had the courage to rebel against except sporadically and in petty ways.

This is what I saw and envied and feared in the Negro: this is what finally made him faceless to me, though some of it, of course, was actually there. (The psychologists also tell us that the alien group which becomes the object of a projection will tend to respond by trying to live up to what is expected of them.) But what, on his side, did the Negro see in me that made me faceless to him? Did he envy me my lunches of spinach-and-potatoes and my itchy woolen caps and my prudent behavior in the face of authority, as I envied him his noon-time candy bars and his bare head in winter and his magnificent rebelliousness? Did those lunches and caps spell for him the prospect of power and riches in the future? Did they mean that there were possibilities open to me that were denied to him? Very likely they did. But if so, one also supposes that he feared the

impulses within himself toward submission to authority no less powerfully than I feared the impulses in myself toward defiance. If I represented the jailer to him, it was not because I was oppressing him or keeping him down: it was because I symbolized for him the dangerous and probably pointless temptation toward greater repression, just as he symbolized for me the equally perilous tug toward greater freedom. I personally was to be rewarded for this repression with a new and better life in the future, but how many of my friends paid an even higher price and were given only gall in return.

We have it on the authority of James Baldwin that all Negroes hate whites. I am trying to suggest that on their side all whites—all American whites, that is—are sick in their feelings about Negroes. There are Negroes, no doubt, who would say that Baldwin is wrong, but I suspect them of being less honest than he is, just as I suspect whites of self-deception who tell me they have no special feeling toward Negroes. Special feelings about color are a contagion to which white Americans seem susceptible even when there is nothing in their background to account for the susceptibility. Thus everywhere we look today in the North we find the curious phenomenon of white middle-class liberals with no previous personal experience of Negroes—people to whom Negroes have always been faceless in virtue rather than faceless in vice —discovering that their abstract commitment to the cause of Negro rights will not stand the test of a direct confrontation. We find such people fleeing in droves to the suburbs as the Negro population in the inner city grows; and when they stay in the city we find them sending their children to private school rather than to the "integrated" public school in the neighborhood. We find them resisting the demand that gerrymandered school districts be re-zoned for the purpose of overcoming de facto segregation; we find them judiciously considering whether the Negroes (for their own good, of course) are not perhaps pushing too hard; we find them clucking their tongues over Negro militancy; we find them speculating on the question of whether there may not, after all, be something in the theory that the races are biologically different; we find them saying that it will take a very long time for Negroes to achieve full equality, no matter what anyone does; we find them deploring the rise of black nationalism and expressing the solemn hope that the leaders of the Negro community will discover ways of containing the impatience and incipient violence within the Negro ghettos.

But that is by no means the whole story; there is also the phenomenon of what Kenneth Rexroth once called "crow-jimism." There are the broken-down white boys like Vivaldo Moore in Baldwin's *Another Country* who go to Harlem in search of sex or simply to brush up against something that looks like primitive vitality, and who are so often punished by the Negroes they meet for crimes that they would have been the last ever to commit and of which they themselves have been as sorry victims as any of the Negroes who take it out on them. There are the writers and intellectuals and artists who romanticize Negroes and pander to them, assuming a guilt that is not properly theirs. And there are all the white liberals who permit Negroes to blackmail them into adopting a double standard of moral judgment, and who lend themselves—again assuming the responsibility for crimes they never committed—to cunning and contemptuous exploitation by Negroes they employ or try to befriend.

And what about me? What kind of feelings do I have about Negroes today? What happened to me, from Brooklyn, who grew up fearing and envying and hating Negroes? Now that Brooklyn is behind me, do I fear them and envy them and hate them still? The answer is yes, but not in the same proportions and certainly not in the same way. I now live on the upper west side of Manhattan, where there are many Negroes and many Puerto Ricans, and there are nights when I experience the old apprehensiveness again, and there are streets that I avoid when I am walking in the dark, as there were streets that I avoided when I was a child. I find that I am not afraid of Puerto Ricans, but I cannot restrain my nervousness whenever I pass a group of Negroes standing in front of a bar or sauntering down the street. I know now, as I did not know when I was a child, that power is on my side, that the police are working for me and not for them. And knowing this I feel ashamed and guilty, like the good liberal I have grown up to be. Yet the twinges of fear and the resentment they bring and the self-contempt they arouse are not to be gainsaid.

But envy? Why envy? And hatred? Why hatred? Here again the intensities have lessened and everything has been complicated and qualified by the guilts and the resulting over-compensations that are the heritage of the enlightened middle-class world of which I am now a member. Yet just as in childhood I envied Negroes for what seemd to me their superior masculinity, so I envy them today for what seems to me their superior physical grace and beauty. I have come to value physical grace very highly, and I am now capable of aching with all my being when I watch a Negro couple on the dance floor, or a Negro playing baseball or basketball. They are on the kind of terms with their own bodies that I should like to be on with mine, and for that precious quality they seemed blessed to me.

The hatred I still feel for Negroes is the hardest of all the old feelings to face or admit, and it is the most hidden and the most overlarded by the conscious attitudes into which I have succeeded in willing myself. It no longer has, as for me it once did, any cause or justification (except, perhaps, that I am constantly being denied my right to an honest expression of the things I earned the right as a child to feel). How, then, do I know that this hatred has never entirely disappeared? I know it from the insane rage that can stir in me at the thought of Negro anti-Semitism; I know it from the disgusting prurience that can stir in me at the sight of a mixed couple; and I know it from the violence that can stir in me whenever I encounter that special brand of paranoid touchiness to which many Negroes are prone.

This, then, is where I am; it is not exactly where I think all other white liberals are, but it cannot be so very far away either. And it is because I am convinced that we white Americans are—for whatever reason, it no longer matters—so twisted and sick in our feelings about Negroes that I despair of the present push toward integration. If the pace of progress were not a factor here, there would perhaps be no cause for despair: time and the law and even the international political situation are on the side of the Negroes, and ultimately, therefore, victory—of a sort, anyway —must come. But from everything we have learned from observers who ought to know, pace has become as important to the Negroes as substance. They want equality and they want it *now*, and the white world is yielding to their demand only as much and as fast as it is absolutely being compelled to do. The Negroes know this in the most concrete terms imaginable, and it is thus becoming increasingly difficult to buy them off with rhetoric and promises and pious assurances of support. And so within the Negro community we find more and more people declaring —as Harold R. Isaacs recently put it in an article in *Commentary*—that they want *out*: people who say that integration will never come, or that it will take a hundred or a thousand years to come, or that it will come at too high a price in suffering and struggle for the pallid and sodden life of the American middle class that at the very best it may bring.

The most numerous, influential, and dangerous movement that has grown out of Negro despair with the goal of integration is, of course, the Black Muslims. This movement, whatever else we may say about it, must be credited with one enduring achievement: it inspired James Baldwin to write an essay which deserves to be placed among the classics of our language. Everything Baldwin has ever been trying to tell us is distilled in *The Fire Next Time* into a statement of overwhelming persuasiveness and prophetic magnificence. Baldwin's message is and always has been simple. It is this: "Color is not a human or personal reality; it is a political reality." And Baldwin's demand is correspondingly simple; color must be forgotten, lest we all be smited with a vengeance "that does not really depend on, and cannot really be executed by, any person or organization, and that cannot be prevented by any police force or army: historical vengeance, a cosmic vengeance based on the law that we recognize when we say, 'Whatever goes up must come down.'" The Black Muslims Baldwin portrays as a sign and a warning to the intransigent white world.

They come to proclaim how deep is the Negro's disaffection with the white world and all its works, and Baldwin implies that no American Negro can fail to respond somewhere in his being to their message: that the white man is the devil, that Allah has doomed him to destruction, and that the black man is about to inherit the earth. Baldwin of course knows that this nightmare inversion of the racism from which the black man has suffered can neither win nor even point to the neighborhood in which victory might be located. For in his view the neighborhood of victory lies in exactly the opposite direction: the transcendence of color through love.

Yet the tragic fact is that love is not the answer to hate—not in the world of politics, at any rate. Color is indeed a political rather than a human or a personal reality and if politics (which is to say power) has made it into a human and personal reality, then only politics (which is to say power) can unmake it once again. But the way of politics is slow and bitter, and as impatience on the one side is matched by a setting of the jaw on the other, we move closer and closer to an explosion and blood may yet run in the streets.

Will this madness in which we are all caught never find a resting-place? Is there never to be an end to it? In thinking about the Jews I have often wondered whether their survival as a distinct group was worth one hair on the head of a single infant. Did the Jews have to survive so that six million innocent people should one day be burned in the ovens of Auschwitz? It is a terrible question and no one, not God himself, could ever answer it to my satisfaction. And when I think about the Negroes in America and about the image of integration as a state in which the Negroes would take their rightful place as another of the protected minorities in a pluralistic society, I wonder whether they really believe in their hearts that such a state can actually be attained, and if so why they should wish to survive as a distinct group. I think I know why the Jews once wished to survive (though I am less certain as to why we still do): they not only believed that God had given them no choice, but they were tied to a memory of past glory and a dream of imminent redemption. What does the American Negro have that might correspond to this? His past is a stigma, his color is a stigma, and his vision of the future is the hope of erasing the stigma by making color irrelevant, by making it disappear as a fact of consciousness.

I share this hope, but I cannot see how it will ever be realized unless color does *in fact* disappear: and that means not integration, it means assimilation, it means—let the brutal word come out—miscegenation. The Black Muslims, like their racist counterparts in the white world, accuse the "so-called Negro leaders" of secretly pursuing miscegenation as a goal. The racists are wrong, but I wish they were right, for I believe that the wholesale merger of the two races is the most desirable alterna-

tive for everyone concerned. I am not claiming that this alternative can
be pursued programmatically or that it is immediately feasible as a
solution; obviously there are even greater barriers to its achievement
than to the achievement of integration. What I am saying, however, is
that in my opinion the Negro problem can be solved in this country in no
other way.

I have told the story of my own twisted feelings about Negroes here,
and of how they conflict with the moral convictions I have since developed, in order to assert that such feelings must be acknowledged as
honestly as possible so that they can be controlled and ultimately disregarded in favor of the convictions. It is *wrong* for a man to suffer because
of the color of his skin. Beside that clichéd proposition of liberal thought,
what argument can stand and be respected? If the arguments are the
arguments of feeling, they must be made to yield; and one's own soul is
not the worst place to begin working a huge social transformation. Not so
long ago, it used to be asked of white liberals, "Would you like your sister
to marry one?" When I was a boy and my sister was still unmarried I
would certainly have said no to that question. But now I am a man, my
sister is already married, and I have daughters. If I were to be asked today
whether I would like a daughter of mine "to marry one." I would have to
answer: "No, I wouldn't *like* it at all. I would rail and rave and rant and
tear my hair. And then I hope I would have the courage to curse myself
for raving and ranting, and to give her my blessing. How dare I withhold
it at the behest of the child I once was and against the man I now have a
duty to be?"

1964

Malcolm Cowley

THE VIEW FROM 80

Even before he or she is 80, the aging person may undergo another
identity crisis like that of adolescence. Perhaps there had also been a
middle-aged crisis, the male or the female menopause, but for the rest of
adult life he had taken himself for granted, with his capabilities and
failings. Now, when he looks in the mirror, he asks himself, "Is this really
me?"—or he avoids the mirror out of distress at what it reveals, those
bags and wrinkles. In his new makeup he is called upon to play a new role
in a play that must be improvised. André Gide, that long-lived man of
letters, wrote in his journal, "My heart has remained so young that I have

the continual feeling of playing a part, the part of the 70-year-old that I certainly am; and the infirmities and weaknesses that remind me of my age act like a prompter, reminding me of my lines when I tend to stray. Then, like the good actor I want to be, I go back into my role, and I pride myself on playing it well."

In his new role the old person will find that he is tempted by new vices, that he receives new compensations (not so widely known), and that he may possibly achieve new virtues. Chief among these is the heroic or merely obstinate refusal to surrender in the face of time. One admires the ships that go down with all flags flying and the captain on the bridge.

Among the vices of age are avarice, untidiness, and vanity, which last takes the form of a craving to be loved or simply admired. Avarice is the worst of those three. Why do so many old persons, men and women alike, insist on hoarding money when they have no prospect of using it and even when they have no heirs? They eat the cheapest food, buy no clothes, and live in a single room when they could afford better lodging. It may be that they regard money as a form of power; there is a comfort in watching it accumulate while other powers are dwindling away. How often we read of an old person found dead in a hovel, on a mattress partly stuffed with bankbooks and stock certificates! The bankbook syndrome, we call it in our family, which has never succumbed.

Untidiness we call the Langley Collyer syndrome. To explain, Langley Collyer was a former concert pianist who lived alone with his 70-year-old brother in a brownstone house on upper Fifth Avenue. The once fashionable neighborhood had become part of Harlem. Homer, the brother, had been an admiralty lawyer, but was now blind and partly paralyzed; Langley played for him and fed him on buns and oranges, which he thought would restore Homer's sight. He never threw away a daily paper because Homer, he said, might want to read them all. He saved other things as well and the house became filled with rubbish from roof to basement. The halls were lined on both sides with bundled newspapers, leaving narrow passageways in which Langley had devised booby traps to catch intruders.

On March 21, 1947, some unnamed person telephoned the police to report that there was a dead body in the Collyer house. The police broke down the front door and found the hall impassable, then they hoisted a ladder to a second-story window. Behind it Homer was lying on the floor in a bathrobe; he had starved to death. Langley had disappeared. After some delay, the police broke into the basement, chopped a hole in the roof, and began throwing junk out of the house, top and bottom. It was 18 days before they found Langley's body, gnawed by rats. Caught in one of his own booby traps, he had died in a hallway just outside Homer's door. By that time the police had collected, and the Department of Sanitation had hauled away, 120 tons of rubbish, including besides the newspapers,

14 grand pianos and the parts of a dismantled Model T Ford.

Why do so many old people accumulate junk, not on the scale of Langley Collyer, but still in a dismaying fashion? Their tables are piled high with it, their bureau drawers are stuffed with it, their closet rods bend with the weight of clothes not worn for years. I suppose that the piling up is partly from lethargy and partly from the feeling that everything once useful, including their own bodies, should be preserved. Others, though not so many, have such a fear of becoming Langley Collyers that they strive to be painfully neat. Every tool they own is in its place, though it will never be used again; every scrap of paper is filed away in alphabetical order. At last their immoderate neatness becomes another vice of age, if a milder one.

The vanity of older people is an easier weakness to explain, and to condone. With less to look forward to, they yearn for recognition of what they have been: the reigning beauty, the athlete, the soldier, the scholar. It is the beauties who have the hardest time. A portrait of themselves at twenty hangs on the wall, and they try to resemble it by making an extravagant use of creams, powders, and dyes. Being young at heart, they think they are merely revealing their essential persons. The athletes find shelves for their silver trophies, which are polished once a year. Perhaps a letter sweater lies wrapped in a bureau drawer. I remember one evening when a no-longer athlete had guests for dinner and tried to find his sweater. "Oh, that old thing," his wife said. "The moths got into it and I threw it away." The athlete sulked and his guests went home early.

Often the yearning to be recognized appears in conversation as an innocent boast. Thus, a distinguished physician, retired at 94, remarks casually that a disease was named after him. A former judge bursts into chuckles as he repeats bright things that he said on the bench. Aging scholars complain in letters (or one of them does), "As I approach 70 I'm becoming avid of honors, and such things—medals, honorary degrees, etc.—are only passed around among academics on a *quid pro quo* basis (one hood capping another)." Or they say querulously, "Bill Underwood has ten honorary doctorates and I have only three. Why didn't they elect me to . . .?" and they mention the name of some learned society. That search for honors is a harmless passion, though it may lead to jealousies and deformations of character, as with Robert Frost in his later years. Still, honors cost little. Why shouldn't the very old have more than their share of them?

To be admired and praised, especially by the young, is an autumnal pleasure enjoyed by the lucky ones (who are not always the most deserving). "What is more charming," Cicero observes in his famous essay *De*

Senectute,[1] "than an old age surrounded by the enthusiasm of youth! . . .
Attentions which seem trivial and conventional are marks of honor—the
morning call, being sought after, precedence, having people rise for you,
being escorted to and from the forum. . . . What pleasures of the body can
be compared to the prerogatives of influence?" But there are also
pleasures of the body, or the mind, that are enjoyed by a greater number
of older persons.

Those pleasures include some that younger people find hard to appreciate. One of them is simply sitting still, like a snake on a sun-warmed
stone, with a delicious feeling of indolence that was seldom attained in
earlier years. A leaf flutters down; a cloud moves by inches across the
horizon. At such moments the older person, completely relaxed, has
become a part of nature—and a living part, with blood coursing through
his veins. The future does not exist for him. He thinks, if he thinks at all,
that life for younger persons is still a battle royal of each against each, but
that now he has nothing more to win or lose. He is not so much above as
outside the battle, as if he had assumed the uniform of some small neutral
country, perhaps Liechtenstein or Andorra. From a distance he notes
that some of the combatants, men or women, are jostling ahead—but
why do they fight so hard when the most they can hope for is a longer
obituary? He can watch the scrounging and gouging, he can hear the
shouts of exultation, the moans of the gravely wounded, and meanwhile
he feels secure; nobody will attack him from ambush.

Age has other physical compensations besides the nirvana of dozing in
the sun. A few of the simplest needs become a pleasure to satisfy. When
an old woman in a nursing home was asked what she really liked to do,
she answered in one word: "Eat." She might have been speaking for
many of her fellows. Meals in a nursing home, however badly cooked,
serve as climactic moments of the day. The physical essence of the
pensioners is being renewed at an appointed hour; now they can go back
to meditating or to watching TV while looking forward to the next meal.
They can also look forward to sleep, which has become a definite pleasure, not the mere interruption it once had been.

Here I am thinking of old persons under nursing care. Others fero-
ciously guard their independence, and some of them suffer less than one
might expect from being lonely and impoverished. They can be rejoiced
by visits and meetings, but they also have company inside their heads.
Some of them are busiest when their hands are still. What passes through
the minds of many is a stream of persons, images, phrases, and familiar
tunes. For some that stream has continued since childhood, but now it is
deeper; it is their present and their past combined. At times they conduct
silent dialogues with a vanished friend, and these are less tiring—often
more rewarding—than spoken conversations. If inner resources are lack-

1. *On Old Age.*

ing, old persons living alone may seek comfort and a kind of companionship in the bottle. I should judge from the gossip of various
neighborhoods that the outer suburbs from Boston to San Diego are full
of secretly alcoholic widows. One of those widows, an old friend, was
moved from her apartment into a retirement home. She left behind her a
closet in which the floor was covered wall to wall with whiskey bottles.
"Oh, those empty bottles!" she explained. "They were left by a former
tenant."

Not whiskey or cooking sherry but simply giving up is the greatest
temptation of age. It is something different from a stoical acceptance of
infirmities, which is something to be admired. At 63, when he first
recognized that his powers were failing, Emerson wrote one of his best
poems, "Terminus":

> It is time to be old,
> To take in sail:—
> The god of bounds,
> Who sets to seas a shore,
> Came to me in his fatal rounds,
> And said: "No more!
> No farther shoot
> Thy broad ambitious branches, and thy root.
> Fancy departs: no more invent;
> Contract thy firmament
> To compass of a tent."

Emerson lived in good health to the age of 79. Within his narrowed
firmament, he continued working until his memory failed; then he consented to having younger editors and collaborators. The givers-up see no
reason for working. Sometimes they lie in bed all day when moving about
would still be possible, if difficult. I had a friend, a distinguished poet,
who surrendered in that fashion. The doctors tried to stir him to action,
but he refused to leave his room. Another friend, once a successful artist,
stopped painting when his eyes began to fail. His doctor made the
mistake of telling him that he suffered from a fatal disease. He then lost
interest in everything except the splendid Rolls-Royce, acquired in his
prosperous days, that stood in the garage. Daily he wiped the dust from
its hood. He couldn't drive it on the road any longer, but he used to sit in
the driver's seat, start the motor, then back the Rolls out of the garage
and drive it in again, back twenty feet and forward twenty feet; that was
his only distraction.

I haven't the right to blame those who surrender, not being able to put
myself inside their minds or bodies. Often they must have compelling
reasons, physical or moral. Not only do they suffer from a variety of
ailments, but also they are made to feel that they no longer have a
function in the community. Their families and neighbors don't ask them

for advice, don't really listen when they speak, don't call on them for efforts. One notes that there are not a few recoveries from apparent senility when that situation changes. If it doesn't change, old persons may decide that efforts are useless. I sympathize with their problems, but the men and women I envy are those who accept old age as a series of challenges.

For such persons, every new infirmity is an enemy to be outwitted, an obstacle to be overcome by force of will. They enjoy each little victory over themselves, and sometimes they win a major success. Renoir was one of them. He continued painting, and magnificently, for years after he was crippled by arthritis; the brush had to be strapped to his arm. "You don't need your hand to paint," he said. Goya was another of the unvanquished. At 72 he retired as an official painter of the Spanish court and decided to work only for himself. His later years were those of the famous "black paintings" in which he let his imagination run (and also of the lithographs, then a new technique). At 78 he escaped a reign of terror in Spain by fleeing to Bordeaux. He was deaf and his eyes were failing; in order to work he had to wear several pairs of spectacles, one over another, and then use a magnifying glass; but he was producing splendid work in a totally new style. At 80 he drew an ancient man propped on two sticks, with a mass of white hair and beard hiding his face and with the inscription "I am still learning."

Giovanni Papini said when he was nearly blind, "I prefer martyrdom to imbecility." After writing sixty books, including his famous *Life of Christ,* he was at work on two huge projects when he was stricken with a form of muscular atrophy. He lost the use of his left leg, then of his fingers, so that he couldn't hold a pen. The two big books, though never to be finished, moved forward slowly by dictation; that in itself was a triumph. Toward the end, when his voice had become incomprehensible, he spelled out a word, tapping on the table to indicate letters of the alphabet. One hopes never to be faced with the need for such heroic measures.

"Eighty years old!" the great Catholic poet Paul Claudel wrote in his journal. "No eyes left, no ears, no teeth, no legs, no wind! And when all is said and done, how astonishingly well one does without them!"

1981

Lewis Thomas

THE LONG HABIT

We continue to share with our remotest ancestors the most tangled and evasive attitudes about death, despite the great distance we have come to understanding some of the profound aspects of biology. We have as much distaste for talking about personal death as for thinking about it; it is an indelicacy, like talking in mixed company about venereal disease or abortion in the old days. Death on a grand scale does not bother us in the same special way: we can sit around a dinner table and discuss war, involving 60 million volatilized human deaths, as though we were talking about bad weather; we can watch abrupt bloody death every day, in color, on films and television, without blinking back a tear. It is when the numbers of dead are very small, and very close, that we begin to think in scurrying circles. At the very center of the problem is the naked cold deadness of one's own self, the only reality in nature of which we can have absolute certainty, and it is unmentionable, unthinkable. We may be even less willing to face the issue at first hand than our predecessors because of a secret new hope that maybe it will go away. We like to think, hiding the thought, that with all the marvelous ways in which we seem now to lead nature around by the nose, perhaps we can avoid the central problem if we just become, next year, say, a bit smarter.

"The long habit of living," said Thomas Browne, "indisposeth us to dying." These days, the habit has become an addiction: we are hooked on living, the tenacity of its grip on us, and ours on it, grows in intensity. We cannot think of giving it up, even when living loses its zest—even when we have lost the zest for zest.

We have come a long way in our technologic capacity to put death off, and it is imaginable that we might learn to stall it for even longer periods, perhaps matching the life-spans of the Abkhasian Russians, who are said to go on, springily, for a century and a half. If we can rid ourselves of some of our chronic, degenerative diseases, and cancer, strokes and coronaries, we might go on and on. It sounds attractive and reasonable, but it is no certainty. If we became free of disease, we would make a much better run of it for the last decade or so, but might still terminate on about the same schedule as now. We may be like the genetically different lines of mice, or like Hayflick's different tissue-culture lines, programmed to die after a predetermined number of days clocked by their genomes. If this is the way it is, some of us will continue to wear out and come unhinged in the sixth decade, and some much later, depending on genetic timetables.

If we ever do achieve freedom from most of today's diseases, or even

573

complete freedom from disease, we will perhaps terminate by drying out and blowing away on a light breeze, but we will still die.

Most of my friends do not like this way of looking at it. They prefer to take it for granted that we only die because we get sick, with one lethal ailment or another, and if we did not have our diseases we might go on indefinitely. Even biologists choose to think this about themselves, despite the evidences of the absolute inevitability of death that surround their professional lives. Everything dies, all around, trees, plankton, lichens, mice, whales, flies, mitochondria. In the simplest creatures it is sometimes difficult to see it as death, since the strands of replicating DNA they leave behind are more conspicuously the living parts of themselves than with us (not that it is fundamentally any different, but it seems so). Flies do not develop a ward round[1] of diseases that carry them off, one by one. They simply age, and die, like flies.

We hanker to go on, even in the face of plain evidence that long, long lives are not necessarily pleasurable in the kind of society we have arranged thus far. We will be lucky if we can postpone the search for new technologies for a while, until we have discovered some satisfactory things to do with the extra time. Something will surely have to be found to take the place of sitting on the porch reexamining one's watch.

Perhaps we would not be so anxious to prolong life if we did not detest so much the sickness of withdrawal. It is astonishing how little information we have about this universal process, with all the other dazzling advances in biology. It is almost as though we wanted not to know about it. Even if we could imagine the act of death in isolation, without any preliminary stage of being struck down by disease, we would be fearful of it.

There are signs that medicine may be taking a new interest in the process, partly from interest, partly from an embarrassed realization that we have not been handling this aspect of disease with as much skill as physicians once displayed, back in the days before they became convinced that disease was their solitary and sometimes defeatable enemy. It used to be the hardest and most important of all the services of a good doctor to be on hand at the time of death, and to provide comfort, usually in the home. Now it is done in hospitals, in secrecy (one of the reasons for the increased fear of death these days may be that so many people are totally unfamiliar with it; they never actually see it happen in real life). Some of our technology permits us to deny its existence, and we maintain flickers of life for long stretches in one community of cells or another, as though we were keeping a flag flying. Death is not a sudden all-at-once affair; cells go down in sequence, one by one. You can, if you like, recover great numbers of them many hours after the lights have gone out, and

1. That is, the variety of ailments a doctor sees during his circuit among the patients in a hospital ward.

grow them out in cultures. It takes hours, even days, before the irreversible word finally gets around to all the provinces.

We may be about to rediscover that dying is not such a bad thing to do after all. Sir William Osler took this view; he disapproved of people who spoke of the agony of death, maintaining that there was no such thing.

In a 19th-century memoir about an expedition in Africa, there is a story about an explorer who was caught by a lion, crushed across the chest in the animal's great jaws, and saved in the instant by a lucky shot from a friend. Later, he remembered the episode in clear detail. He was so amazed by the extraordinary sense of peace and calm, and total painlessness, associated with his partial experience of being killed, that he constructed a theory that all creatures are provided with a protective physiologic mechanism, switched on at the verge of death, carrying them through in a haze of tranquility.

I have seen agony in death only once, in a patient with rabies, who remained acutely aware of every stage in the process of his own disintegration over a 24-hour period, right up to his final moment. It was as though, in the special neuropathology of rabies, the switch had been prevented from turning.

We will be having new opportunities to learn more about the physiology of death at first hand, from the increasing numbers of cardiac patients who have been through the whole process and then back again. Judging from what has been found out thus far, from the first generation of people resuscitated from cardiac standstill (already termed the Lazarus syndrome), Osler seems to have been right. Those who remember parts or all of their episodes do not recall any fear, or anguish. Several people who remained conscious throughout, while appearing to have been quite dead, could only describe a remarkable sensation of detachment. One man underwent coronary occlusion with cessation of the heart and dropped for all practical purposes dead in front of a hospital, and within a few minutes his heart had been restarted by electrodes and he breathed his way back into life. According to his account, the strangest thing was that there were so many people around him, moving so urgently, handling his body with such excitement, while all his awareness was of quietude.

In a recent study of the reaction to dying in patients with obstructive disease of the lungs, it was concluded that the process was considerably more shattering for the professional observers than the observed. Most of the patients appeared to be preparing themselves with equanimity for death, as though intuitively familiar with the business. One elderly woman reported that the only painful and distressing part of the process was in being interrupted; on several occasions she was provided with conventional therapeutic measures to maintain oxygenation or restore fluids and electrolytes, and each time she found the experience of coming back harrowing, she deeply resented the interference with her dying.

I find myself surprised by the thought that dying is an all-right thing to do, but perhaps it should not surprise. It is, after all, the most ancient and fundamental of biologic functions, with its mechanisms worked out with the same attention to detail, the same provision for the advantage of the organism, the same abundance of genetic information for guidance through the stages, that we have long since become accustomed to finding in all the crucial acts of living.

Very well. But even so, if the transformation is a co-ordinated, integrated physiologic process in its initial, local stages, there is still that permanent vanishing of consciousness to be accounted for. Are we to be stuck forever with this problem? Where on earth does it go? Is it simply stopped dead in its tracks, lost in humus, wasted? Considering the tendency of nature to find uses for complex and intricate mechanisms, this seems to me unnatural. I prefer to think of it as somehow separated off at the filaments of its attachment, and then drawn like an easy breath back into the membrane of its origin, a fresh memory for a biospherical nervous system, but I have no data on the matter.

This is for another science, another day. It may turn out, as some scientists suggest, that we are forever precluded from investigating consciousness, by a sort of indeterminancy principle that stipulates that the very act of looking will make it twitch and blur out of sight. If this is true, we will never learn. I envy some of my friends who are convinced about telepathy; oddly enough, it is my European scientist acquaintances who believe it most freely and take it most lightly. All their aunts have received Communications, and there they sit, with proof of the motility of consciousness at their fingertips, and the making of a new science. It is discouraging to have had the wrong aunts, and never the ghost of a message.

1973

QUESTIONS

1. "They simply age, and die, like flies" (p. 574). What makes this sentence, which concludes the opening section of this brief essay, effective? What does Thomas establish in this opening section? What does he consider in the next, which constitutes the bulk of his essay? What is the logic that connects the two, and what is the basic assumption underlying the second?

2. In the paragraph beginning "I find myself surprised ... " (p. 576), Thomas considers the subject of death anew. What is his perspective here? How does the next paragraph set the limits on that perspective? Explain the metaphor with which he ends the next paragraph.

3. What does this essay have in common with Fries's "Aging, Natural Death, and the Compression of Morbidity" (p. 585) and Thomas's "On

*Magic in Medicine" (p. 462)? Is Thomas ever "unscientific"? Can you
infer from the two Thomas essays in this volume his estimate of
science—what it can do and what it can't do?*

4. *Thomas's two essays should give you some sense of the man; on that
basis predict his attitude toward the subject of punctuation and then
check his "Notes on Punctuation" (p. 339). Explain what made your
prediction accurate if it was or what surprised you if it wasn't. Do his
remarks on punctuation help in answering the first part of question 1
above?*

Elisabeth Kübler-Ross

ON THE FEAR OF DEATH

Let me not pray to be sheltered from
dangers but to be fearless in facing
them.
  Let me not beg for the stilling of
my pain but for the heart to conquer it.
  Let me not look for allies in life's
battlefield but to my own strength.
  Let me not crave in anxious fear to
be saved but hope for the patience to
win my freedom.
  Grant me that I may not be a
coward, feeling your mercy in my
success alone; but let me find the grasp
of your hand in my failure.

RABINDRANATH TAGORE,
Fruit-Gathering

Epidemics have taken a great toll of lives in past generations. Death in
infancy and early childhood was frequent and there were few families
who didn't lose a member of the family at an early age. Medicine has
changed greatly in the last decades. Widespread vaccinations have practically eradicated many illnesses, at least in western Europe and the
United States. The use of chemotherapy, especially the antibiotics, has
contributed to an ever decreasing number of fatalities in infectious
diseases. Better child care and education has effected a low morbidity and
mortality among children. The many diseases that have taken an impressive toll among the young and middle-aged have been conquered. The
number of old people is on the rise, and with this fact come the number of
people with malignancies and chronic diseases associated more with old
age.

Pediatricians have less work with acute and life-threatening situations as they have an ever increasing number of patients with psychosomatic disturbances and adjustment and behavior problems. Physicians have more people in their waiting rooms with emotional problems than they have ever had before, but they also have more elderly patients who not only try to live with their decreased physical abilities and limitations but who also face loneliness and isolation with all its pains and anguish. The majority of these people are not seen by a psychiatrist. Their needs have to be elicited and gratified by other professional people, for instance, chaplains and social workers. It is for them that I am trying to outline the changes that have taken place in the last few decades, changes that are ultimately responsible for the increased fear of death, the rising number of emotional problems, and the greater need for understanding of and coping with the problems of death and dying.

When we look back in time and study old cultures and people, we are impressed that death has always been distasteful to man and will probably always be. From a psychiatrist's point of view this is very understandable and can perhaps best be explained by our basic knowledge that, in our unconscious, death is never possible in regard to ourselves. It is inconceivable for our unconscious to imagine an actual ending of our own life here on earth, and if this life of ours has to end, the ending is always attributed to a malicious intervention from the outside by someone else. In simple terms, in our unconscious mind we can only be killed; it is inconceivable to die of a natural cause or of old age. Therefore death in itself is associated with a bad act, a frightening happening, something that in itself calls for retribution and punishment.

One is wise to remember these fundamental facts as they are essential in understanding some of the most important, otherwise unintelligible communications of our patients.

The second fact that we have to comprehend is that in our unconscious mind we cannot distinguish between a wish and a deed. We are all aware of some of our illogical dreams in which two completely opposite statements can exist side by side—very acceptable in our dreams but unthinkable and illogical in our wakening state. Just as our unconscious mind cannot differentiate betwee the wish to kill somebody in anger and the act of having done so, the young child is unable to make this distinction. The child who angrily wishes his mother to drop dead for not having gratified his needs will be traumatized greatly by the actual death of his mother—even if this event is not linked closely in time with his destructive wishes. He will always take part or the whole blame for the loss of his mother. He will always say to himself—rarely to others—"I did it, I am responsible, I was bad, therefore Mommy left me." It is well to remember that the child will react in the same manner if he loses a parent by divorce, separation, or desertion. Death is often seen by a child as an impermanent thing and has therefore little distinction from a divorce in which he may have an opportunity to see a parent again.

Many a parent will remember remarks of their children such as, "I will bury my doggy now and next spring when the flowers come up again, he will get up." Maybe it was the same wish that motivated the ancient Egyptians to supply their dead with food and goods to keep them happy and the old American Indians to bury their relatives with their belongings.

When we grow older and begin to realize that our omnipotence is really not so omnipotent, that our strongest wishes are not powerful enough to make the impossible possible, the fear that we have contributed to the death of a loved one diminishes—and with it the guilt. The fear remains diminished, however, only so long as it is not challenged too strongly. Its vestiges can be seen daily in hospital corridors and in people associated with the bereaved.

A husband and wife may have been fighting for years, but when the partner dies, the survivor will pull his hair, whine and cry louder and beat his chest in regret, fear and anguish, and will hence fear his own death more than before, still believing in the law of talion—an eye for an eye, a tooth for a tooth—"I am responsible for her death, I will have to die a pitiful death in retribution."

Maybe this knowledge will help us understand many of the old customs and rituals which have lasted over the centuries and whose purpose is to diminish the anger of the gods or the people as the case may be, thus decreasing the anticipated punishment. I am thinking of the ashes, the torn clothes, the veil, the *Klage Weiber*[1] of the old days—they are all means to ask you to take pity on them, the mourners, and are expressions of sorrow, grief, and shame. If someone grieves, beats his chest, tears his hair, or refuses to eat, it is an attempt at self-punishment to avoid or reduce the anticipated punishment for the blame that he takes on the death of a loved one.

This grief, shame, and guilt are not very far removed from feelings of anger and rage. The process of grief always includes some qualities of anger. Since none of us likes to admit anger at a deceased person, these emotions are often disguised or repressed and prolong the period of grief or show up in other ways. It is well to remember that it is not up to us to judge such feelings as bad or shameful but to understand their true meaning and origin as something very human. In order to illustrate this I will again use the example of the child—and the child in us. The five-year-old who loses his mother is both blaming himself for her disappearance and being angry at her for having deserted him and for no longer

---

1. Wailing wives.

gratifying his needs. The dead person then turns into something the child loves and wants very much but also hates with equal intensity for this severe deprivation.

The ancient Hebrews regarded the body of a dead person as something unclean and not to be touched. The early American Indians talked about the evil spirits and shot arrows in the air to drive the spirits away. Many other cultures have rituals to take care of the "bad" dead person, and they all originate in this feeling of anger which still exists in all of us, though we dislike admitting it. The tradition of the tombstone may originate in this wish to keep the bad spirits deep down in the ground, and the pebbles that many mourners put on the grave are left-over symbols of the same wish. Though we call the firing of guns at military funerals a last salute, it is the same symbolic ritual as the Indian used when he shot his spears and arrows into the skies.

I give these examples to emphasize that man has not basically changed. Death is still a fearful, frightening happening, and the fear of death is a universal fear even if we think we have mastered it on many levels.

What has changed is our way of coping and dealing with death and dying and our dying patients.

Having been raised in a country in Europe where science is not so advanced, where modern techniques have just started to find their way into medicine, and where people still live as they did in this country half a century ago, I may have had an opportunity to study a part of the evolution of mankind in a shorter period.

I remember as a child the death of a farmer. He fell from a tree and was not expected to live. He asked simply to die at home, a wish that was granted without questioning. He called his daughters into the bedroom and spoke with each one of them alone for a few moments. He arranged his affairs quietly, though he was in great pain, and distributed his belongings and his land, none of which was to be split until his wife should follow him in death. He also asked each of his children to share in the work, duties, and tasks that he had carried on until the time of the accident. He asked his friends to visit him once more, to bid good-bye to them. Although I was a small child at the time, he did not exclude me or my siblings. We were allowed to share in the preparations of the family just as we were permitted to grieve with them until he died. When he did die, he was left at home, in his own beloved home which he had built, and among his friends and neighbors who went to take a last look at him where he lay in the midst of flowers in the place he had lived in and loved so much. In that country today there is still no make-believe slumber room, no embalming, no false makeup to pretend sleep. Only the signs of very disfiguring illnesses are covered up with bandages and only infectious cases are removed from the home prior to the burial.

Why do I describe such "old-fashioned" customs? I think they are an indication of our acceptance of a fatal outcome, and they help the dying patient as well as his family to accept the loss of a loved one. If a patient is allowed to terminate his life in the familiar and beloved environment, it requires less adjustment for him. His own family knows him well enough to replace a sedative with a glass of his favorite wine; or the smell of a home-cooked soup may give him the appetite to sip a few spoons of fluid which, I think is still more enjoyable than an infusion. I will not minimize the need for sedatives and infusions and realize full well from my own experience as a country doctor that they are sometimes life-saving and often unavoidable. But I also know that patience and familiar people and foods could replace many a bottle of intravenous fluids given for the simple reason that it fulfills the physiological need without involving too many people and/or individual nursing care.

The fact that children are allowed to stay at home where a fatality has stricken and are included in the talk, discussions, and fears gives them the feeling that they are not alone in the grief and gives them the comfort of shared responsibility and shared mourning. It prepares them gradually and helps them view death as part of life, an experience which may help them grow and mature.

This is in great contrast to a society in which death is viewed as taboo, discussion of it is regarded as morbid, and children are excluded with the presumption and pretext that it would be "too much" for them. They are then sent off to relatives, often accompanied with some unconvincing lies of "Mother has gone on a long trip" or other unbelievable stories. The child senses that something is wrong, and his distrust in adults will only multiply if other relatives add new variations of the story, avoid his questions or suspicions, shower him with gifts as a meager substitute for a loss he is not permitted to deal with. Sooner or later the child will become aware of the changed family situation and, depending on the age and personality of the child, will have an unresolved grief and regard this incident as a frightening, mysterious, in any case very traumatic experience with untrustworthy grownups, which he has no way to cope with.

It is equally unwise to tell a little child who lost her brother that God loved little boys so much that he took little Johnny to heaven. When this little girl grew up to be a woman she never solved her anger at God, which resulted in a psychotic depression when she lost her own little son three decades later.

We would think that our great emancipation, our knowledge of science and of man, has given us better ways and means to prepare ourselves and our families for this inevitable happening. Instead the days are gone when a man was allowed to die in peace and dignity in his own home.

The more we are making advancements in science, the more we seem to fear and deny the reality of death. How is this possible?

We use euphemisms, we make the dead look as if they were asleep, we ship the children off to protect them from the anxiety and turmoil around the house if the patient is fortunate enough to die at home, we don't allow children to visit their dying parents in the hospitals, we have long and controversial discussions about whether patients should be told the truth —a question that rarely arises when the dying person is tended by the family physician who has known him from delivery to death and who knows the weaknesses and strengths of each member of the family.

I think there are many reasons for this flight away from facing death calmly. One of the most important facts is that dying nowadays is more gruesome in many ways, namely, more lonely, mechanical, and dehumanized; at times it is even difficult to determine technically when the time of death has occurred.

Dying becomes lonely and impersonal because the patient is often taken out of his familiar environment and rushed to an emergency room. Whoever has been very sick and has required rest and comfort especially may recall his experience of being put on a stretcher and enduring the noise of the ambulance siren and hectic rush until the hospital gates open. Only those who have lived through this may appreciate the discomfort and cold necessity of such transportation which is only the beginning of a long order—hard to endure when you are well, difficult to express in words when noise, light, pumps, and voices are all too much to put up with. It may well be that we might consider more the patient under the sheets and blankets and perhaps stop our well-meant efficiency and rush in order to hold the patient's hand, to smile, or to listen to a question. I include the trip to the hospital as the first episode in dying, as it is for many. I am putting it exaggeratedly in contrast to the sick man who is left at home—not to say that lives should not be saved if they can be saved by a hospitalization but to keep the focus on the patient's experience, his needs and his reactions.

When a patient is severely ill, he is often treated like a person with no right to an opinion. It is often someone else who makes the decision if and when and where a patient should be hospitalized. It would take so little to remember that the sick person too has feelings, has wishes and opinions, and has—most important of all—the right to be heard.

Well, our presumed patient has now reached the emergency room. He will be surrounded by busy nurses, orderlies, interns, residents, a lab technician perhaps who will take some blood, an electrocardiogram technician who takes the cardiogram. He may be moved to X-ray and he will overhear opinions of his condition and discussions and questions to members of the family. He slowly but surely is beginning to be treated like a thing. He is no longer a person. Decisions are made often without his opinion. If he tries to rebel he will be sedated and after hours of waiting and wondering whether he has the strength, he will be wheeled

into the operating room or intensive treatment unit and become an object of great concern and great financial investment.

He may cry for rest, peace, and dignity, but he will get infusions, transfusions, a heart machine, or tracheotomy[2] if necessary. He may want one single person to stop for one single minute so that he can ask one single question—but he will get a dozen people around the clock, all busily preoccupied with his heart rate, pulse, electrocardiogram or pulmonary functions, his secretions or excretions but not with him as a human being. He may wish to fight it all but it is going to be a useless fight since all this is done in the fight for his life, and if they can save his life they can consider the person afterwards. Those who consider the person first may lose precious time to save his life! At least this seems to be the rationale or justification behind all this—or is it? Is the reason for this increasingly mechanical, depersonalized approach our own defensiveness? Is this approach our own way to cope with and repress the anxieties that a terminally or critically ill patient evokes in us? Is our concentration on equipment, on blood pressure our desperate attempt to deny the impending death which is so frightening and discomforting to us that we displace all our knowledge onto machines, since they are less close to us than the suffering face of another human being which would remind us once more of our lack of omnipotence, our own limits and failures, and last but not least perhaps our own mortality?

Maybe the question has to be raised: Are we becoming less human or more human? * * * [I]t is clear that whatever the answer may be, the patient is suffering more—not physically, perhaps, but emotionally. And his needs have not changed over the centuries, only our ability to gratify them.

1969

2. The surgical opening of a passage through the neck into the trachea.

QUESTIONS

1. How is Kübler-Ross's essay organized? What difference does it make that she postpones presenting generalizations about her subject until late in her discussion?
2. To speak of rights, as Kübler-Ross does in the last pages of her essay, is to raise the question of where they come from; for example, the Declaration of Independence (p. 837) implies that the rights it asserts come from God; from what source would you expect Kübler-Ross to derive the rights she speaks of?
3. Kübler-Ross doubts the rationale for efficiency in medical care, but at the same time recognizes the life-saving results of this efficiency. There is obviously a dilemma here: what are the extreme opposite positions that define the dilemma? What is the best intermediate or compromise position?
4. Lewis Thomas in "The Long Habit" (p. 573) also speaks of dying. To

what extent is he in harmony with Kübler-Ross? What differences do
you find? What is the special contribution of each author?

5. Kübler-Ross opens her discussion with a quotation. Read Shakespeare's Sonnet 73 and Hopkins' "Spring and Fall: To a Young Child."
Would these poems be appropriate for introducing her essay? Why, or
why not?

73

That time of year thou mayst in me behold
When yellow leaves, or none, or few, do hang
Upon those boughs which shake against the cold,
Bare ruined choirs, where late the sweet birds sang.
In me thou see'st the twilight of such day
As after sunset fadeth in the west;
Which by and by black night doth take away,
Death's second self, that seals up all in rest.
In me thou see'st the glowing of such fire,
That on the ashes of his youth doth lie,
As the deathbed whereon it must expire,
Consumed with that which it was nourished by.
This thou perceiv'st, which makes thy love more strong,
To love that well which thou must leave ere long.

—William Shakespeare

SPRING AND FALL

TO A YOUNG CHILD

Margaret, are you grieving
Over Goldengrove unleaving?
Leaves, like the things of man, you
With your fresh thoughts care for, can you?
Ah! as the heart grows older
It will come to such sights colder
By and by, nor spare a sigh
Though worlds of wanwood leafmeal lie;
And yet you *will* weep and know why.
Now no matter, child, the name:
Sorrow's springs are the same.
Nor mouth had, no nor mind, expressed
What heart heard of, ghost [soul] guessed:
It is the blight man was born for,
It is Margaret you mourn for.

—Gerard Manley Hopkins

James F. Fries

AGING, NATURAL DEATH, AND THE COMPRESSION OF MORBIDITY[1]

Abstract   *The average length of life has risen from 47 to 73 years in this century, but the maximum life span has not increased. Therefore, survival curves have assumed an ever more rectangular form. Eighty per cent of the years of life lost to nontraumatic, premature death have been eliminated, and most premature deaths are now due to the chronic diseases of the later years. Present data allow calculation of the ideal average life span, approximately 85 years. Chronic illness may presumably be postponed by changes in life style, and it has been shown that the physiologic and psychologic markers of aging may be modified. Thus, the average age at first infirmity can be raised, thereby making the morbidity curve more rectangular. Extension of adult vigor far into a fixed life span compresses the period of senescence near the end of life. Health-research strategies to improve the quality of life require careful study of the variability of the phenomena of aging and how they may be modified. (N Engl J Med. 1980; 303:130-5.)*

This article discusses a set of predictions that contradict the conventional anticipation of an ever older, ever more feeble, and ever more expensive-to-care-for populace. These predictions suggest that the number of very old persons will not increase, that the average period of diminished physical vigor will decrease, that chronic disease will occupy a smaller proportion of the typical life span, and that the need for medical care in later life will decrease.

In forecasting health, the interaction between two sets of observations has gone unnoticed. The first set demonstrates that the length of the human life is fixed—that man is mortal and that natural death may occur without disease. The second set indicates that chronic disease can be postponed and that many of the "markers" of aging may be modified. If these two premises are granted, it follows that the time between birth and first permanent infirmity must increase and that the average period of infirmity must decrease.

The Length of Life Is Fixed

Speculation about immortality is rooted in antiquity and in human hope. The bioscientific, medical model of disease, our prevalent model,

1. From the Department of Medicine (S102B), Stanford University Medical Center, Stanford, CA 94305, where reprint requests should be addressed to Dr. Fries. This work was performed while the author was a Kaiser Fellow at the Center for Advanced Study in the Behavioral Sciences, and was delivered in part at the 2d Annual Nova Behavioral Conference on Aging, Fort Lauderdale, Fla., January 25, 1980 [author's note].

assumes that death is always the result of a disease process; if there were no disease, there would be no death. This view is hard to defend.

If relative immortality were possible, one would expect to find some persons who anticipated the future and acted accordingly. Thus, a person genetically favored and fortunate enough to avoid disease might live much longer than actuarially predicted. Data fail to confirm the existence of such events. For example, adequate data on the number of centenarians have been available in England since 1837; over this time, despite a great change in average life expectancy there has been no detectable change in the number of people living longer than 100 years or in the maximum age of persons dying in a given year.

The *Guinness Book of World Records* notes that the correlation between the claimed density of centenarians in a country and its regional illiteracy rate is 0.83. In Sweden, where careful investigations of centenarians are carried out, not one has yet exceeded 110 years of age. The greatest authenticated age in the world was recorded in Japan—114 years. Approximately one in 10,000 persons in developed countries lives beyond the age of 100. Moreover, inspection of the "tail" of the human survival curve demonstrates the falloff expected from a normal distribution, rather than the emergence of a few persons with notably long life spans. There has been no satisfactory documentation of any society with exceptional longevity.

Several theoretical explanations of the finite life span have been presented. At the cellular level, Hayflick and others have argued extensively for a finite number of cell doublings in the life span of a species. The number of doublings of human fibroblasts[2] is approximately 50; before reaching this point subcultivation of cells proceeds in an active and youthful way. However, over a short period after the 50th subcultivation, the cells first fail to grow and then die, although there has been no change in the nutrients or other conditions of the culture medium. The number of doublings is species specific, and long-lived species have more doublings than do short-lived species.

At the level of the organism, life may be defined as internal homeostasis. The internal milieu is adjusted within strict limits by compensating mechanisms in many organs, including heart, lungs, kidneys, and liver. In young adult life, the functional capacity of human organs is four to 10 times that required to sustain life. The existence of "organ reserve" enables the stressed organism to restore homeostasis when it is deranged by external threat. Measurement of organ reserve over time shows an almost linear decline beginning at about the age of 30. As organ reserve decreases, so does the ability to restore homeostasis, and eventually even the smallest perturbation prevents homeostasis from being restored. The inevitable result is natural death, even without disease. Although a

2. A connective tissue cell.

disease process may appear to be the cause of death, the actual cause is loss of the organism's ability to maintain homeostasis. Any small perturbation, without coexistent organ reserve, would have the same fatal result. Observations since those of Gompertz demonstrate an exponential increase in mortality rate after the age of 30; the rate doubles every eight years. The best mathematical models relate the linear decline in organ function to the exponential mortality rate. Obviously, an exponentially increasing mortality rate ensures a finite life span.

The Average Length of Life Is Increasing

The average length of life in the United States has increased from approximately 47 years at the turn of the century to 73 years today, an increase of 26 years (Fig. 1). Life expectancy for white women is now 77 years and for white men 70 years. A steady rise in life expectancy in the early years of this century changed to a relative plateau after 1950, but the increase has resumed in recent years. Such data form the basis for predictions that more people will live beyond the age of 65 and for projections of medical facilities likely to be required in the future.

A more critical look at these data, however, demonstrates that they reflect progress in the elimination of premature death, particularly neonatal mortality. For persons 40 years of age and older, life expectancy has increased relatively little; for those 75 years old the increase is barely perceptible. Figure 1 presents a largely unnoticed paradox: if these lines are extrapolated into the future, at some point in the 21st century the

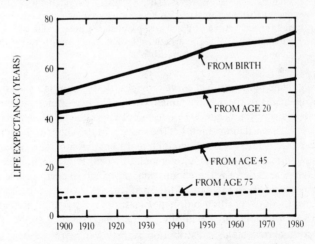

Figure 1. *Life Expectancy Trends in the United States.* Life expectancy at birth has increased by 26 years in this century, and expectancy at 75 (broken line) by only three years. The slope decreases as the life span is neared.

average life expectancy as projected at birth will exceed average age of death as projected at age 75.

A white woman aged 70 may now expect to live 14 years longer (on the average), and a white man of the same age 11 years. Present differences in life expectancy between sexes and races become much smaller as the age on which the analysis is based rises. Racial minorities and men are more subject to premature death.

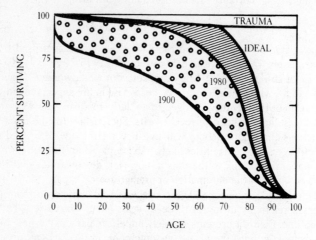

Figure 2. *The Increasingly Rectangular Survival Curve.* About 80 per cent (stippled area) of the difference between the 1900 curve and the ideal curve (stippled area plus hatched area) had been eliminated by 1980. Trauma is now the dominant cause of death in early life.

The shape of the survival curve provides additional insights. In antiquity, as in many species of animals now, death was almost a random event: an organism succumbs to an intercurrent problem before reaching the life span usual for members of the species. In 1900, the survival curve in the United States was not very different from this situation. However, sequential survival curves throughout this century show progressive "rectangularization" as the elimination of premature death results in a sharp downslope to the natural life span (Fig. 2). The serial data allow calculation of the position and shape of a survival curve if all premature death were eliminated: an ideally "rectangular" survival curve. If we assume a normal biologic distribution, statistics suggest that under ideal societal conditions mean age at death is not far from 85 years.

The natural limit to the life span can be calculated in several ways. Perhaps the easiest, after study of the rate at which life expectancy at various ages is increasing, is to calculate the point at which the curves intersect (Fig. 3). For example, over the first eight decades of this century average life expectancy from birth increased at the rate of 0.33 year per year of the century, and life expectancy from age 65 has increased by 0.05 year per year. These curves intersect in the year 2009, at a mean age at death of 82.4 years. During the most recent decade, average life expectancy from birth has also increased 0.33 year per year, and life expectancy from age 65 has increased at 0.12 year per year. These curves intersect in the year 2018, at a mean age at death of 85.6 years.

Calculations based on other periods or from other ages converge at similar points. Figure 3 shows intersection at age 85 in the year 2045, a reasonable median projection. In actuality the curves will not be straight but will approach an asymptote; the limit will be approached more slowly, and the attainable average life expectancy will be less than the theoretical estimate. Predictions by the federal government (Fig. 3) make such nonlinear assumptions and suggest that the actual limit may be less than 85 years.

Mortality data describe a biologic distribution, which appears approximately normal in populations of laboratory animals. If the tail of the survival curve remains fixed and the biologic distribution is normal, an age of 100 years is about four standard deviations from the mean, and the standard deviation about four years. Thus, under ideal conditions, 66 per cent of natural deaths would occur in persons 81 to 89 years, and 95 per cent in persons aged 77 to 93 years. With a biologic distribution, the ideal survival curve will never be completely "rectangular," and, if the rate of violent and traumatic death (a category now accounting for more than half of deaths in persons under the age of 40 years) remains roughly constant, there will always be some premature deaths.

Changes in survival curves in this century may be compared with the hypothetical ideal curve in Figure 2. Since 1900, Americans have covered most of the distance to that ideal, in terms of years of life saved: our progress has removed about 80 per cent of the area between the ideal curve and the 1900 curve (if the rate of violent death is disregarded). Moreover, the great change has occurred in the early years of life, with most remaining premature deaths concentrated in the years after age 60.

These changes are dramatic. In 1900 the average citizen died 38 years "prematurely" (short of the theoretical limit), in 1950 17 years, and in 1980 only 12 years. In 1980 white women will die on the average only seven years prematurely. Moreover, violent death accounts for three of the years by which we fall short of the limit. Clearly, the medical and social task of eliminating premature death is largely accomplished.

Chronic Disease Has Superseded Acute Disease

Acute illness has ceased to be the major medical problem in the United States. At the turn of the century, mortality patterns were dominated by acute, usually infectious disease. Tuberculosis, acute rheumatic fever, smallpox, diphtheria, tetanus, poliomyelitis, pneumococcal pneumonia in the young, and similar conditions constituted the principal threats to health. Each of these now causes less than 2 per cent of the health problems that it caused in 1900. Smallpox has been eradicated; polio, almost so. The decline in these diseases can be attributed to a number of factors, including improved nutrition, less crowded living arrangements, water sterilization, immunization, and specific antibiotics. It is important to recognize that chronic diseases have replaced acute illness as major health threats.

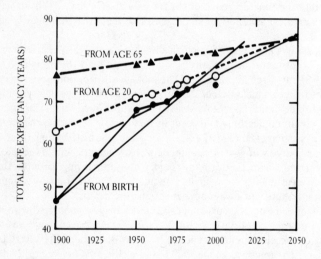

Figure 3. *Trends, Limits, and Convergences in Life Expectancy.* Projection of total life expectancy data into the future shows convergence at the ideal average life span, 85 years, in 2045. Spans of 82.6 to 85.6 years can be calculated from projections from different ages (at birth, at age 20, and at age 65) and different years in this century. (Data are from the National Center for Health Statistics [1977]; values indicated by triangle and circles for the year 2000 are estimates from the Office of the Actuary.)

Chronic illness now is responsible for more than 80 per cent of all deaths and for an even higher fraction of cases of total disability. Arteriosclerosis (including coronary-artery disease and stroke), arthritis, adult-onset diabetes, chronic obstructive pulmonary disease (including emphysema), cancer, and cirrhosis represent the overwhelming majority of our health problems. They are widespread conditions that originate in early life and develop insidiously; the probability of their occurrence increases with age. They can be considered, broadly, as problems of accelerated loss of organ reserve. Generally, they develop slowly and asymptomatically below a clinical threshold, at which the process becomes clinically evident, progresses, and often culminates in death or disability.

Thus, the early arteriosclerotic plaque does not materially impede circulation, but gradually the probability of an acute thrombotic event or insidious vascular insufficiency increases. The osteoarthritic bone spur is evident on x-ray films for many years before pain or disability is noted in the affected joint. Glucose tolerance decreases gradually until sugar is excreted in the urine of the diabetic. The patient with emphysema has accelerated loss of pulmonary reserve. The probability of development of neoplasms increases with age.

Disability and lowered quality of life due to the most prevalent chronic diseases are thus inescapably linked with eventual mortality. These chronic diseases are approached most effectively with a strategy of "postponement" rather than of cure. If the rate of progression is decreased, then the date of passage through the clinical threshold is postponed; if sufficiently postponed, the symptomatic threshold may not be crossed during a lifetime, and the disease is "prevented."

Some chronic illnesses definitely can be postponed; elimination of cigarette smoking greatly delays the date of onset of symptoms of emphysema and reduces the probability of lung cancer. Treatment of hypertension retards development of certain complications in the arteries. In other illnesses, circumstantial evidence of similar effects of postponement is strong but proof is difficult: that arteriosclerosis is retarded by weight reduction or exercise is suggested by associative data but has not yet been proved.

Until recently, progress in health care could be conceived of as an exchange of acute medical problems for chronic ones: the person who survives an illness appearing abruptly early in life will have more lingering problems later. Since early death would cost relatively little in direct expenses as compared with the expenses of a later chronic problem, the exchange of acute illnesses for chronic ones has resulted in a massive need for additional medical services. The end of this era is nearing because there are now few acute illnesses to be "exchanged."

The most recent increases in average life expectancy are due principally to a decline in arteriosclerosis, particularly cerebrovascular disease. This decline is the first demonstration of a national decrease in mortality from a major chronic disease, and most observers attribute the change to changes in life style and to better treatment of hypertension. The 26 per cent decline in per capita tobacco consumption over the past 15 years, now accelerating, may effect at least a similar percentage of decrease in the incidence of chronic obstructive pulmonary disease and lung cancer, after a delay of a few years. Moreover, the preventive approach to chronic illness is still in its infancy. The long-term effects of increased exercise, lower weight, and growth in personal autonomy and personal responsibility for health are also likely to be positive.

The Compression of Morbidity

The amount of disability can decrease as morbidity is compressed into the shorter span between the increasing age at onset of disability and the fixed occurrence of death. The end of the period of adult vigor will come later than it used to. Postponement of chronic illness thus results in rectangularization not only of the mortality curve but also of the morbidity curve.

The social consequences of this phenomenon will be profound. Death and disability, occurring later, become increasingly unavoidable. The incremental cost of marginal medical benefit inevitably rises. Intervention in the patient without organ reserve will be recognized as futile. The principles of fixed mortality and of natural death without disease carry profound implications.

Some caveats must be mentioned. War, depression, pestilence, or natural disaster could reverse recent trends. The human life span may not be fixed but may be slowly increasing, perhaps a month or so each century; the data are consistent with this hypothesis. The Hayflick phenomenon may have nothing to do with human aging. Medical progress may increase the number of cell doublings, learn to slow organ decay, or extend the maximum life span in some other way, notwithstanding its failure to do so to date. But it is highly unlikely that any such change will occur during our lifetime. The likelihood depends on whether the lowest curve of Figure 1 (life expectancy after age 75), after being relatively stable for many decades, will show a sudden upturn. Many of the chronic diseases, including arteriosclerosis, may be susceptible to "cure," and efforts directed at finding curative treatments must be continued. There will always be illness; theoretical curves may be approached but not reached. The surprising fact is that we are already approaching the limits.

By implication, the practical focus on health improvement over the next decades must be on chronic instead of acute disease, on morbidity not mortality, on quality of life rather than its duration, and on postponement rather than cure. The complex nature of the major diseases calls attention to multifactorial influences on outcome, in particular social and psychologic factors. Outcome is related to choice; assumption of personal responsibility, education for making decisions about personal health, and ability to encourage self-care are clearly essential to changing health behaviors. Returning responsibility to the patient may cause anguish.

The Compression of Senescence

An important shift is occurring in the conceptualization of chronic disease and of aging. Premature organ dysfunction, whether of muscle, heart, lung, or joint, is beginning to be conceived as stemming from disuse of the faculty, not overuse. At the Stanford Arthritis Clinic I tell patients to exercise, and to "use it or lose it"; "Run, not rest" is the new advice of the cardiologist. The body, to an increasing degree, is now felt to rust out rather than to wear out. If loss of reserve function represents aging in some sense, then exercising an organ presents a strategy for modifying the aging process.

The links between the widespread chronic diseases and aging are the insidious loss of organ reserve common to both processes and the often identical factors that influence the rate of development. In preventive medicine these variables are seen as antecedents to disease, whereas in gerontology they are markers of age. Serum cholesterol, vital capacity, and systolic blood pressure are examples of such variables. Exercise, weight control, and diet are some of the common modifying factors.

The modifiability, or "plasticity," of aging has been demonstrated in studies in which performance can be bettered despite age, within surprisingly broad limits. This important phenomenon has been largely unnoticed partly because of an emphasis on average rather than individual performance and partly because disparate disciplines are involved. Average declines in variables in aging can hide remarkable individual variation. The marathon runner is an example (Fig. 4). A runner in middle life who completes a marathon in 3 1/2 hours is in the 99th percentile for this endeavor; yet not until age 73 would that time set an age-group record. These marathon data are important in that they show the maximum rather than the average performance, but here too there is a linear decline in performance between age 30 and 70. Still, the age-related decrement in maximal performance is only 1 per cent per year. Variation between healthy persons of the same age is far greater than the variation due to age; age is a relatively unimportant variable, and training in marathon running is clearly more important than age.

Similar observations on increased variation between individuals with age and on modifiability with training, even after age 70, have been made for intelligence testing, social interaction, health after exercise, and memory. Certain data indicate improvement with age, against the gradient of linear decline, for some persons. An inference is that personal choice is important—one can choose not to age rapidly in certain faculties, within broad biologic limits.

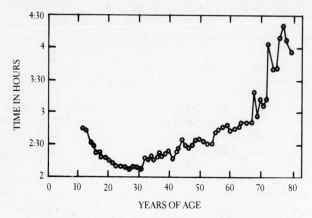

Figure 4. *World Marathon Records for Men.* Note the slow but linear decline in maximum performance between the age of 30 and 70.

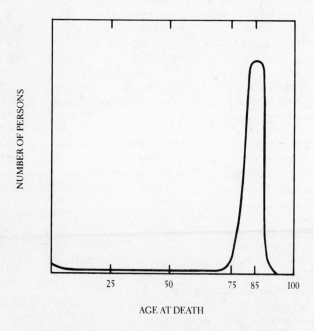

AGE AT DEATH

Figure 5. *Mortality According to Age, in the Absence of Premature Death.* The morbidity curve is made rectangular, and the period of morbidity compressed between the point of the end of adult vigor and the point of natural death.

Such considerations suggest that research strategy toward aging be fundamentally shifted. Analysis of variation, not of the mean values, becomes crucial. Indeed, one can argue that the number of studies showing that the mean of every function declines steadily with age is already sufficient. Research now requires measurement of standard deviation between individuals, not of standard error between populations or between chronological ages.

A new three-stage research strategy may be urged: measure the variability of a marker of aging (e.g., oxygen uptake, satisfaction as assessed by questionnaire, or intelligence as measured by IQ test) at a given chronological age; determine retrospectively the differences between the individual who has aged more rapidly and the one who has aged more slowly in that marker—hypothetically, such differences may be expected to correlate with the individual's practice in self-maintenance and to be confounded by self-selection; and design prospective intervention studies to explore causality.

At the top of the list of nationally important health-research subjects must be the ability to postpone chronic illness, to maintain vigor, and to slow social and psychologic involution. We must know for certain whether change is possible and how to accomplish it best. Personal autonomy has been emphasized above as a probable final common pathway to improved health. This emphasis is meant broadly, since clearly the collective efforts of individuals are required for removal of environmental hazards and the development of incentives to encourage rather than discourage the exercise of personal choice. We know relatively little about the specific relations between social changes and personal decisions, and much information in great depth is needed.

Summary

I have presented a model for national health that foresees continued decline in premature death and emergency of a pattern of natural death at the end of a natural life span. Present approaches to social interaction, promotion of health, and personal autonomy may postpone many of the phenomena usually associated with aging. The rectangularization of the survival curve may be followed by rectangularization of the morbidity curve and by compression of morbidity (Fig. 5).

These considerations suggest a radically different view of the life span and of society, in which life is physically, emotionally, and intellectually vigorous until shortly before its close, when, like the marvelous one-hoss-shay, everything comes apart at once and repair is impossible. Such a life approaches the intuitive ideal of many and confounds the dread of others for the opposite model, that of evermore lingering death. Paradoxically, predictability of death may prove soothing.

Since maintenance of organ capacity appears to require practice on the part of the individual, the implications for the societal role are as fundamentally different as are the two models. Indeed, the choice of societal postures toward the aged is likely to prove self-fulfilling. The older person requires opportunity for expression and experience and autonomy and accomplishment, not support and care and feeding and sympathy. High-level medical technology applied at the end of a natural life span epitomizes the absurd. The hospice becomes more attractive than the hospital. Human interaction, rather than respirators and dialysis and other mechanical support for failing organs, is indicated at the time of the "terminal drop." Anguish arising from the inescapability of personal choice and the inability to avoid personal consequences may become a problem for many. For others, exhilaration may come from recognition that the goal of a vigorous long life may be an attainable one.

1980

QUESTIONS

1. *Fries refers to "organ reserve" (p. 586). How is it defined, and what is its function in his argument?*
2. *This article is prefaced by an abstract. Abstracting is notoriously difficult; how good is this one? For example, the last sentence of the abstract implies that the variable phenomena of aging can be modified: How is this implication handled in the full treatment? How close does Fries come to saying that you can determine the rate at which you age? How does he support his argument? What limits does he acknowledge?*
3. *What sort of work is reported here? What exactly did Fries study? What is the scientific function of such work?*
4. *In "On Magic in Medicine" (p. 462), Lewis Thomas describes the rhetorical effect—the downplaying—of some researchers' mentioning but not stressing alternative interpretations of their data. On p. 592 Fries lists some "caveats"; is their rhetorical effect like that described by Thomas?*
5. *This essay, in its form and in its very words and sentence structure, has the special marks of science writing; what are they? How much of this special kind of writing is determined by the specific characteristics of the work reported; and how much is due to convention, to arbitrary but accepted ways of doing things?*

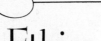

Ethics

James Thurber

THE BEAR WHO LET IT ALONE

In the woods of the Far West there once lived a brown bear who could take it or let it alone. He would go into a bar where they sold mead, a fermented drink made of honey, and he would have just two drinks. Then he would put some money on the bar and say, "See what the bears in the back room will have," and he would go home. But finally he took to drinking by himself most of the day. He would reel home at night, kick over the umbrella stand, knock down the bridge lamps, and ram his elbows through the windows. Then he would collapse on the floor and lie there until he went to sleep. His wife was greatly distressed and his children were very frightened.

At length the bear saw the error of his ways and began to reform. In the end he became a famous teetotaller and a persistent temperance lecturer. He would tell everybody that came to his house about the awful effects of drink, and he would boast about how strong and well he had become since he gave up touching the stuff. To demonstrate this, he would stand on his head and on his hands and he would turn cartwheels in the house, kicking over the umbrella stand, knocking down the bridge lamps, and ramming his elbows through the windows. Then he would lie down on the floor, tired by his healthful exercise, and go to sleep. His wife was greatly distressed and his children were very frightened.

Moral: You might as well fall flat on your face as lean over too far backward.

1955

Theophrastus

THE FLATTERER

Flattery is a cringing sort of conduct that aims to promote the advantage of the flatterer. The flatterer is the kind of man who, as he walks with an acquaintance, says: "Behold! how the people gaze at you! There is not a man in the city who enjoys so much notice as yourself. Yesterday your praises were the talk of the Porch.[1] While above thirty men were sitting there together and the conversation fell upon the topic: 'Who is our noblest citizen?' they all began and ended with your name." As the flatterer goes on talking in this strain he picks a speck of lint from his hero's cloak; or if the wind has lodged a bit of straw in his locks, he plucks it off and says laughingly, "See you? Because I have not been with you these two days, your beard is turned gray. And yet if any man has a beard that is black for his years, it is you."

While his patron speaks, he bids the rest be silent. He sounds his praises in his hearing and after the patron's speech gives the cue for applause by "Bravo!" If the patron makes a stale jest, the flatterer laughs and stuffs his sleeve into his mouth as though he could not contain himself.

If they meet people on the street, he asks them to wait until the master passes. He buys apples and pears, carries them to his hero's house and gives them to the children, and in the presence of the father, who is looking on, he kisses them, exclaiming: "Bairns of a worthy sire!" When the patron buys a pair of shoes, the flatterer observes: "The foot is of a finer pattern than the boot"; if he calls on a friend, the flatterer trips on ahead and says: "You are to have the honor of his visit"; and then turns back with, "I have announced you." Of course he can run and do the errands at the market in a twinkle.

Amongst guests at a banquet he is the first to praise the wine and, doing it ample justice, he observes: "What a fine cuisine you have!" He takes a bit from the board and exclaims: "What a dainty morsel this is!" Then he inquires whether his friend is chilly, asks if he would like a wrap put over his shoulders, and whether he shall throw one about him. With these words he bends over and whispers in his ear. While his talk is directed to the rest, his eye is fixed on his patron. In the theatre he takes the cushions from the page and himself adjusts them for the comfort of the master. Of his hero's house he says: "It is well built"; of his farm: "It is well tilled"; and of his portrait: "It is a speaking image."

4th century B.C.

---

1. Noted gathering place in Athens. Here in the fourth century B.C. the philosopher Zeno taught his disciples.

Samuel Johnson

ON SELF-LOVE AND INDOLENCE

—*Steriles transmisimus annos,*
Haec aevi mihi prima dies, haec limina vitae.
STAT. [I.362]

—Our barren years are past;
Be this of life the first, of sloth the last.
ELPHINSTON[1]

No weakness of the human mind has more frequently incurred animadversion, than the negligence with which men overlook their own faults, however flagrant, and the easiness with which they pardon them, however frequently repeated.

It seems generally believed, that, as the eye cannot see itself, the mind has no faculties by which it can contemplate its own state, and that therefore we have not means of becoming acquainted with our real characters; an opinion which, like innumerable other postulates, an inquirer finds himself inclined to admit upon very little evidence, because it affords a ready solution of many difficulties. It will explain why the greatest abilities frequently fail to promote the happiness of those who possess them; why those who can distinguish with the utmost nicety the boundaries of vice and virtue, suffer them to be confounded in their own conduct; why the active and vigilant resign their affairs implicitly to the management of others; and why the cautious and fearful make hourly approaches toward ruin, without one sigh of solicitude or struggle for escape.

When a position teems thus with commodious consequences, who can without regret confess it to be false? Yet it is certain that declaimers have indulged a disposition to describe the dominion of the passions as extended beyond the limits that nature assigned. Self-love is often rather arrogant than blind; it does not hide our faults from ourselves, but persuades us that they escape the notice of others, and disposes us to resent censures lest we would confess them to be just. We are secretly conscious of defects and vices which we hope to conceal from the public eye, and please ourselves with innumerable impostures, by which, in reality, no body is deceived.

In proof of the dimness of our internal sight, or the general inability of man to determine rightly concerning his own character, it is common to

---

1. The author of these lines is Publius Papinius Statius, a first-century Latin poet. They are given first in the original and then in William Elphinstone's sixteenth-century translation.

599

urge the success of the most absurd and incredible flattery, and the resentment always raised by advice, however soft, benevolent, and reasonable. But flattery, if its operation be nearly examined, will be found to owe its acceptance not to our ignorance but knowledge of our failures, and to delight us rather as it consoles our wants than displays our possessions. He that shall solicit the favor of his patron by praising him for qualities which he can find in himself, will be defeated by the more daring panegyrist who enriches him with adscititious excellence. Just praise is only a debt, but flattery is a present. The acknowledgment of those virtues on which conscience congratulates us, is a tribute that we can at any time exact with confidence, but the celebration of those which we only feign, or desire without any vigorous endeavors to attain them, is received as a confession of sovereignty over regions never conquered, as a favorable decision of disputable claims, and is more welcome as it is more gratuitous.

Advice is offensive, not because it lays us open to unexpected regret, or convicts us of any fault which had escaped our notice, but because it shows us that we are known to others as well as to ourselves; and the officious monitor is persecuted with hatred, not because his accusation is false, but because he assumes that superiority which we are not willing to grant him, and has dared to detect what we desired to conceal.

For this reason advice is commonly ineffectual. If those who follow the call of their desires, without inquiry whither they are going, had deviated ignorantly from the paths of wisdom, and were rushing upon dangers unforeseen, they would readily listen to information that recalls them from their errors, and catch the first alarm by which destruction or infamy is denounced. Few that wander in the wrong way mistake it for the right; they only find it more smooth and flowery, and indulge their own choice rather than approve it: therefore few are persuaded to quit it by admonition or reproof, since it impresses no new conviction, nor confers any powers of action or resistance. He that is gravely informed how soon profusion will annihilate his fortune, hears with little advantage what he knew before, and catches at the next occasion of expense, because advice has no force to suppress his vanity. He that is told how certainly intemperance will hurry him to the grave, runs with his usual speed to a new course of luxury, because his reason is not invigorated, nor his appetite weakened.

The mischief of Flattery is, not that it persuades any man that he is what he is not, but that it suppresses the influence of honest ambition, by raising an opinion that honor may be gained without the toil of merit; and the benefit of advice arises commonly, not from any new light imparted to the mind, but from the discovery which it affords, of the publick suffrages. He that could withstand conscience, is frighted at infamy, and shame prevails where reason was defeated.

As we all know our own faults, and know them commonly with many aggravations which human perspicacity cannot discover, there is, perhaps, no man, however hardened by impudence or dissipated by levity, sheltered by hypocrisy, or blasted by disgrace, who does not intend some time to review his conduct, and to regulate the remainder of his life by the laws of virtue. New temptations indeed attack him, new invitations are offered by pleasure and interest, and the hour of reformation is always delayed; every delay gives vice another opportunity of fortifying itself by habit; and the change of manners, though sincerely intended and rationally planned, is referred to the time when some craving passion shall be fully gratified, or some powerful allurement cease its importunity.

Thus procrastination is accumulated on procrastination, and one impediment succeeds another, till age shatters our resolution, or death intercepts the project of amendment. Such is often the end of salutary purposes, after they have long delighted the imagination, and appeased that disquiet which every mind feels from known misconduct, when the attention is not diverted by business or by pleasure.

Nothing surely can be more unworthy of a reasonable nature, than to continue in a state so opposite to real happiness, as that all the peace of solitude and felicity of meditation, must arise from resolutions of forsaking it. Yet the world will often afford examples of men, who pass months and years in a continual war with their own convictions, and are daily dragged by habit or betrayed by passion into practices, which they closed and opened their eyes with purposes to avoid; purposes which, though settled on conviction, the first impulse of momentary desire totally overthrows.

The influence of custom is indeed such that to conquer it will require the utmost efforts of fortitude and virtue, nor can I think any man more worthy of veneration and renown, than those who have burst the shackles of habitual vice. This victory however has different degrees of glory as of difficulty; it is more heroic as the objects of guilty gratification are more familiar, and the recurrence of solicitation more frequent. He that from experience of the folly of ambition resigns his offices, may set himself free at once from temptation to squander his life in courts, because he cannot regain his former station. He who is enslaved by an amorous passion, may quit his tyrant in disgust, and absence will without the help of reason overcome by degrees the desire of returning. But those appetites to which every place affords their proper object, and which require no preparatory measures or gradual advances, are more tenaciously adhesive; the wish is so near the enjoyment, that compliance often precedes consideration, and before the powers of reason can be summoned, the time for employing them is past.

Indolence is therefore one of the vices from which those whom it once infects are seldom reformed. Every other species of luxury operates upon some appetite that is quickly satiated, and requires some concurrence of art or accident which every place will not supply; but the desire of ease acts equally at all hours, and the longer it is indulged in the more increased. To do nothing is in every man's power; we can never want an opportunity of omitting duties. The lapse to indolence is soft and imperceptible, because it is only a mere cessation of activity; but the return to diligence is difficult, because it implies a change from rest to motion, from privation to reality.

> —*Facilis descensus Averni:*
> *Noctes atque dies patet atri janua Ditis:*
> *Sed revocare gradum, superasque evadere ad auras,*
> *Hoc opus, hic labor est.—*
>> [VIR. *Aeneid* VI. 126]

> The gates of *Hell* are open night and day;
>   Smooth the descent, and easy is the way:
>   But, to return, and view the chearful skies;
>   In this, the task and mighty labour lies.
>> DRYDEN

Of this vice, as of all others, every man who indulges it is conscious; we all know our own state, if we could be induced to consider it; and it might perhaps be useful to the conquest of all these ensnarers of the mind, if at certain stated days life was reviewed. Many things necessary are omitted, because we vainly imagine that they may be always performed, and what cannot be done without pain will for ever be delayed if the time of doing it be left unsettled. No corruption is great but by long negligence, which can scarcely prevail in a mind regularly and frequently awakened by periodical remorse. He that thus breaks his life into parts, will find in himself a desire to distinguish every stage of his existence by some improvement, and delight himself with the approach of the day of recollection, as of the time which is to begin a new series of virtue and felicity.

1751

Francis Bacon

OF SIMULATION AND DISSIMULATION

Dissimulation is but a faint kind of policy or wisdom; for it asketh a strong wit and a strong heart to know when to tell truth, and to do it. Therefore it is the weaker sort of politics[1] that are the great dissemblers.

Tacitus saith, *Livia sorted well with the arts of her husband and dissimulation of her son;* attributing arts or policy to Augustus, and dissimulation to Tiberius. And again, when Mucianus encourageth Vespasian to take arms against Vitellius, he saith, *We rise not against the piercing judgment of Augustus, nor the extreme caution or closeness of Tiberius.*[2] These properties, of arts or policy and dissimulation or closeness, are indeed habits and faculties several, and to be distinguished. For if a man have that penetration of judgment as he can discern what things are to be laid open, and what to be secreted, and what to be shewed at half lights, and to whom and when (which indeed are arts of state and arts of life, as Tacitus well calleth them), to him a habit of dissimulation is a hinderance and a poorness. But if a man cannot obtain to that judgment, then it is left to him generally to be close, and a dissembler. For where a man cannot choose or vary in particulars, there it is good to take the safest and wariest way in general; like the going softly, by one that cannot well see. Certainly the ablest men that ever were have had all an openness and frankness of dealing; and a name of certainty and veracity; but then they were like horses well managed; for they could tell passing well when to stop or turn; and at such times when they thought the case indeed required dissimulation, if then they used it, it came to pass that the former opinion spread abroad of their good faith and clearness of dealing made them almost invisible.

There be three degrees of this hiding and veiling of a man's self. The first, Closeness, Reservation, and Secrecy; when a man leaveth himself without observation, or without hold to be taken, what he is. The second, Dissimulation, in the negative; when a man lets fall signs and arguments, that he is not that he is. And the third. Simulation, in the affirmative; when a man industriously and expressly feigns and pretends to be that he is not.

For the first of these, Secrecy; it is indeed the virtue of a confessor.[3] And assuredly the secret man heareth many confessions. For who will open himself to a blab or babbler? But if a man be thought secret, it

---

1. Politicians.
2. The Roman historian Tacitus here speaks of the plottings of Livia, wife of the emperor Augustus Caesar and mother of his successor Tiberius; and of the Roman official Mucianus, who in 69 A.D. supported Vespasian in his successful struggle against Vitellius to gain the imperial throne.
3. One to whom confession is made.

inviteth discovery; as the more close air sucketh in the more open; and as in confession the revealing is not for worldly use, but for the ease of a man's heart, so secret men come to the knowledge of many things in that kind; while men rather discharge their minds than impart their minds. In few words, mysteries are due to secrecy. Besides (to say truth) nakedness is uncomely, as well in mind as body; and it addeth no small reverence to men's manners and actions, if they be not altogether open. As for talkers and futile persons, they are commonly vain and credulous withal. For he that talketh what he knoweth, will also talk what he knoweth not. Therefore set it down, *that an habit of secrecy is both politic and moral.* And in this part, it is good that a man's face give his tongue leave to speak. For the discovery of a man's self by the tracts of his countenance is a great weakness and betraying; by how much it is many times more marked and believed than a man's words.

For the second, which is Dissimulation; it followeth many times upon secrecy by a necessity; so that he that will be secret must be a dissembler in some degree. For men are too cunning to suffer a man to keep an indifferent carriage between both, and to be secret, without swaying the balance on either side. They will so beset a man with questions, and draw him on, and pick it out of him, that, without an absurd silence, he must shew an inclination one way; or if he do not, they will gather as much by his silence as by his speech. As for equivocations, or oraculous speeches, they cannot hold out for long. So that no man can be secret, except he give himself a little scope of dissimulation; which is, as it were, but the skirts or train of secrecy.

But for the third degree, which is Simulation and false profession; that I hold more culpable, and less politic; except it be in great and rare matters. And therefore a general custom of simulation (which is this last degree) is a vice, rising either of a natural falseness or fearfulness, or of a mind that hath some main faults, which because a man must needs disguise, it maketh him practice simulation in other things, lest his hand should be out of ure.[4]

The great advantages of simulation and dissimulation are three. First, to lay asleep opposition, and to surprise. For where a man's intentions are published, it is an alarum to call up all that are against them. The second is, to reserve to a man's self a fair retreat. For if a man engage himself by a manifest declaration, he must go through or take a fall. The third is, the better to discover the mind of another. For to him that opens himself men will hardly shew themselves adverse; but will (fair) let him go on, and turn their freedom of speech to freedom of thought. And therefore it is a good shrewd proverb of the Spaniard, *Tell a lie and find a troth.* As if there were no way of discovery but by simulation. There be also three disadvantages, to set it even. The first, that simulation and dissimulation

4. Practice.

commonly carry with them a shew of fearfulness, which in any business doth spoil the feathers of round flying up to the mark. The second, that it puzzleth and perplexeth the conceits[5] of many, that perhaps would otherwise co-operate with him; and makes a man walk almost alone to his own ends. The third and greatest is, that it depriveth a man of one of the most principal instruments for action; which is trust and belief. The best composition and temperature is to have openness in fame and opinion; secrecy in habit; dissimulation in seasonable use; and a power to feign, if there be no remedy.

5. Conceptions, thoughts.

QUESTIONS

1. Explain Bacon's distinction, drawn in the first two paragraphs, between dissembling, on the one hand, and, on the other, arts and policy. How does this opening prepare the way for the remainder of the essay?
2. How is the word "dissimulation" as used in the third paragraph and thereafter to be distinguished from its use in the first two paragraphs?
3. What are the three degrees of hiding of a man's self? According to what principles does Bacon arrange these degrees? What accounts for his according unequal amounts of space to the exposition of them?
4. Make a close analysis of Bacon's closing paragraph, indicating the ways Bacon achieves symmetry, balance. How does that effect contribute to his tone and purpose? What elements in the paragraph offset a mere symmetry?
5. In what connection and to what purpose does Bacon use the following expressions? Explain the image or allusion in each:
   a. "like the going softly, by one that cannot well see" (p. 603)
   b. "like horses well managed; for they could tell passing well when to stop or turn" (p. 603)
   c. "as the more close air sucketh in the more open" (p. 604)
   d. "it is good that a man's face give his tongue leave to speak" (p. 604)
   e. "he must go through or take a fall" (p. 604)
   f. "fearfulness, which in any business doth spoil the feathers of round flying up to the mark" (p. 605)
6. Bacon would allow "simulation and false profession" in "great and rare matters." Would you? Give an example of such matters. Write a brief essay explaining your position.
7. What view of the world underlies Bacon's essay? Write an essay showing what Bacon's assumptions about the world seem to be. Be careful to show how you draw upon the essay to find out Bacon's assumptions.

Samuel Johnson

LETTER TO LORD CHESTERFIELD

February 1755

MY LORD

I have been lately informed by the proprietor of *The World*[1] that two papers in which my *Dictionary* is recommended to the public were written by your Lordship. To be so distinguished is an honor which, being very little accustomed to favors from the great, I know not well how to receive, or in what terms to acknowledge.

When upon some slight encouragement I first visited your Lordship I was overpowered like the rest of mankind by the enchantment of your address,[2] and could not forbear to wish that I might boast myself *le vainqueur du vainqueur de la terre*,[3] that I might obtain that regard for which I saw the world contending, but found my attendance so little encouraged that neither pride nor modesty would suffer me to continue it. When I had once addressed your Lordship in public, I had exhausted all the art of pleasing which a retired and uncourtly scholar can possess. I had done all that I could, and no man is well pleased to have his all neglected, be it ever so little.

Seven years, my lord, have now past since I waited in your outward rooms or was repulsed from your door, during which time I have been pushing on my work through difficulties of which it is useless to complain, and have brought it at last to the verge of publication without one act of assistance, one word of encouragement, or one smile of favor. Such treatment I did not expect, for I never had a patron before.

The shepherd in Virgil grew at last acquainted with Love, and found him a native of the rocks.[4] Is not a patron, my lord, one who looks with unconcern on a man struggling for life in the water and when he has reached ground encumbers him with help. The notice which you have been pleased to take of my labors, had it been early, had been kind; but it has been delayed till I am indifferent and cannot enjoy it, till I am solitary and cannot impart it, till I am known and do not want[5] it.

I hope it is no very cynical asperity not to confess obligation where no benefit has been received, or to be unwilling that the public should consider me as owing that to a patron, which Providence has enabled me to do for myself.

1. A journal in which Lord Chesterfield had recently praised Johnson's *Dictionary of the English Language.* Johnson had been at work on the dictionary for nine years.
2. Here in the old sense of "courtesy."
3. The conquerer of the conqueror of the world.
4. Or deserts; an allusion to Virgil's eighth eclogue, line 43.
5. Need.

Having carried on my work thus far with so little obligation to any favorer of learning I shall not be disappointed though I should conclude it, if less be possible, with less, for I have been long wakened from that dream of hope, in which I once boasted myself with so much exultation, my lord your Lordship's most humble most obedient servant,

SAM:JOHNSON

1755

Lord Chesterfield

LETTER TO HIS SON

London, October 16, O.S. 1747

DEAR BOY

The art of pleasing is a very necessary one to possess, but a very difficult one to acquire. It can hardly be reduced to rules; and your own good sense and observation will teach you more of it than I can. "Do as you would be done by," is the surest method that I know of pleasing. Observe carefully what pleases you in others, and probably the same things in you will please others. If you are pleased with the complaisance and attention of others to your humors, your tastes, or your weaknesses, depend upon it, the same complaisance and attention on your part to theirs will equally please them. Take the tone of the company that you are in, and do not pretend to give it; be serious, gay, or even trifling, as you find the present humor of the company; this is an attention due from every individual to the majority. Do not tell stories in company; there is nothing more tedious and disagreeable; if by chance you know a very short story, and exceedingly applicable to the present subject of conversation, tell it in as few words as possible; and even then, throw out that you do not love to tell stories, but that the shortness of it tempted you.

Of all things banish the egotism out of your conversation, and never think of entertaining people with your own personal concerns or private affairs; though they are interesting to you, they are tedious and impertinent to everybody else; besides that, one cannot keep one's own private affairs too secret. Whatever you think your own excellencies may be, do not affectedly display them in company; nor labor, as many people do, to give that turn to the conversation, which may supply you with an opportunity of exhibiting them. If they are real, they will infallibly be discovered, without your pointing them out yourself, and with much more advantage. Never maintain an argument with heat and clamor, though you think or know yourself to be in the right; but give your opinion modestly and coolly, which is the only way to convince; and, if that does not do, try to change the conversation, by saying, with good-humor, "We shall hardly convince one another; nor is it necessary that we should, so let us talk of something else."

Remember that there is a local propriety to be observed in all companies; and that what is extremely proper in one company may be, and often is, highly improper in another.

The jokes, the *bon-mots*, the little adventures, which may do very well in one company, will seem flat and tedious, when related in another. The particular characters, the habits, the cant of one company may give merit to a word, or a gesture, which would have none at all if divested of those accidental circumstances. Here people very commonly err; and fond of something that has entertained them in one company, and in certain circumstances, repeat it with emphasis in another, where it is either insipid, or, it may be, offensive, by being ill-timed or misplaced. Nay, they often do it with this silly preamble: "I will tell you an excellent thing," or, "I will tell you the best thing in the world." This raises expectations, which, when absolutely disappointed, make the relator of this excellent thing look, very deservedly, like a fool.

If you would particularly gain the affection and friendship of particular people, whether men or women, endeavor to find out their predominant excellency, if they have one, and their prevailing weakness, which everybody has; and do justice to the one, and something more than justice to the other. Men have various objects in which they may excel, or at least would be thought to excel; and, though they love to hear justice done to them, where they know that they excel, yet they are most and best flattered upon those points where they wish to excel, and yet are doubtful whether they do or not. As for example: Cardinal Richelieu, who was undoubtedly the ablest statesman of his time, or perhaps of any other, had the idle vanity of being thought the best poet too; he envied the great Corneille his reputation, and ordered a criticism to be written upon the *Cid*.[1] Those, therefore, who flattered skillfully, said little to him of his abilities in state affairs, or at least but *en passant*, and as it might naturally occur. But the incense which they gave him, the smoke of which they knew would turn his head in their favor, was as a *bel esprit* and a poet. Why? Because he was sure of one excellency, and distrustful as to the other.

You will easily discover every man's prevailing vanity by observing his favorite topic of conversation; for every man talks most of what he has most a mind to be thought to excel in. Touch him but there, and you touch him to the quick. The late Sir Robert Walpole[2] (who was certainly

1. When the French classic tragedy *The Cid*, founded upon the legendary exploits of the medieval Castilian warrior-hero, was published in 1636 by its author Pierre Corneille (1606–1684), it was the subject of violent criticism, led by the French minister of state Richelieu (1585–1642).

2. For two decades a powerful prime minis-

an able man) was little open to flattery upon that head, for he was in no
doubt himself about it; but his prevailing weakness was, to be thought to
have a polite and happy turn to gallantry—of which he had undoubtedly
less than any man living. It was his favorite and frequent subject of
conversation, which proved to those who had any penetration that it was
his prevailing weakness, and they applied to it with success.

Women have, in general, but one object, which is their beauty; upon
which scarce any flattery is too gross for them to follow. Nature has
hardly formed a woman ugly enough to be insensible to flattery upon her
person; if her face is so shocking that she must, in some degree, be
conscious of it, her figure and air, she trusts, make ample amends for it. If
her figure is deformed, her face, she thinks, counterbalances it. If they are
both bad, she comforts herself that she has graces, a certain manner, a *je
ne sais quoi*[3] still more engaging than beauty. This truth is evident from
the studied and elaborate dress of the ugliest woman in the world. An
undoubted, uncontested, conscious beauty is, of all women, the least
sensible of flattery upon that head; she knows it is her due, and is
therefore obliged to nobody for giving it her. She must be flattered upon
her understanding; which, though she may possibly not doubt of herself,
yet she suspects that men may distrust.

Do not mistake me, and think that I mean to recommend to you abject
and criminal flattery: no; flatter nobody's vices or crimes: on the contrary,
abhor and discourage them. But there is no living in the world without a
complaisant indulgence for people's weaknesses, and innocent, though
ridiculous vanities. If a man has a mind to be thought wiser, and a woman
handsomer, than they really are, their error is a comfortable one to
themselves, and an innocent one with regard to other people; and I would
rather make them my friends by indulging them in it, than my enemies
by endeavoring (and that to no purpose) to undeceive them.

There are little attentions, likewise, which are infinitely engaging, and
which sensibly affect that degree of pride and self-love, which is inseparable from human nature, as they are unquestionable proofs of the regard
and consideration which we have for the persons to whom we pay them.
As, for example, to observe the little habits, the likings, the antipathies,
and the tastes of those whom we would gain; and then take care to
provide them with the one, and to secure them from the other; giving
them, genteelly, to understand, that you had observed they liked such a
dish, or such a room, for which reason you had prepared it: or, on the
contrary, that having observed they had an aversion to such a dish, a
dislike to such a person, etc., you had taken care to avoid presenting
them. Such attention to such trifles flatters self-love much more than

---

ter, Robert Walpole (1676-1745) was also a
patron of the arts and prided himself upon
his taste.
3. A certain inexpressible quality.

greater things, as it makes people think themselves almost the only objects of your thoughts and care.

These are some of the arcana[4] necessary for your initiation in the great society of the world. I wish I had known them better at your age; I have paid the price of three and fifty years for them, and shall not grudge it if you reap the advantage. Adieu.
1747

4. Secret things.

Samuel L. Clemens

ADVICE TO YOUTH

Being told I would be expected to talk here, I inquired what sort of a talk I ought to make. They said it should be something suitable to youth —something didactic, instructive, or something in the nature of good advice. Very well. I have a few things in my mind which I have often longed to say for the instruction of the young; for it is in one's tender early years that such things will best take root and be most enduring and most valuable. First, then, I will say to you, my young friends—and I say it beseechingly, urgingly—

Always obey your parents, when they are present. This is the best policy in the long run, because if you don't they will make you. Most parents think they know better than you do, and you can generally make more by humoring that superstition than you can by acting on your own better judgment.

Be respectful to your superiors, if you have any, also to strangers, and sometimes to others. If a person offend you, and you are in doubt as to whether it was intentional or not, do not resort to extreme measures; simply watch your chance and hit him with a brick. That will be sufficient. If you shall find that he had not intended any offense, come out frankly and confess yourself in the wrong when you struck him; acknowledge it like a man and say you didn't mean to. Yes, always avoid violence; in this age of charity and kindliness, the time has gone by for such things. Leave dynamite to the low and unrefined.

Go to bed early, get up early—this is wise. Some authorities say get up with the sun; some others say get up with one thing, some with another. But a lark is really the best thing to get up with. It gives you a splendid reputation with everybody to know that you get up with the lark; and if you get the right kind of a lark, and work at him right, you can easily train him to get up at half past nine, every time—it is no trick at all.

Now as to the matter of lying. You want to be very careful about lying; otherwise you are nearly sure to get caught. Once caught, you can never again be, in the eyes of the good and the pure, what you were before. Many a young person has injured himself permanently through a single clumsy and illfinished lie, the result of carelessness born of incomplete training. Some authorities hold that the young ought not to lie at all. That, of course, is putting it rather stronger than necessary; still, while I cannot go quite so far as that, I do maintain, and I believe I am right, that the young ought to be temperate in the use of this great art until practice and experience shall give them that confidence, elegance, and precision which alone can make the accomplishment graceful and profitable. Patience, diligence, painstaking attention to detail—these are the requirements; these, in time, will make the student perfect; upon these, and upon these only, may he rely as the sure foundation for future eminence. Think what tedious years of study, thought, practice, experience, went to the equipment of that peerless old master who was able to impose upon the whole world the lofty and sounding maxim that "truth is mighty and will prevail"—the most majestic compound fracture of fact which any of woman born has yet achieved. For the history of our race, and each individual's experience, are sown thick with evidence that a truth is not hard to kill and that a lie told well is immortal. There is in Boston a monument of the man who discovered anaesthesia; many people are aware, in these latter days, that that man didn't discover it at all, but stole the discovery from another man. Is this truth mighty, and will it prevail? Ah no, my hearers, the monument is made of hardy material, but the lie it tells will outlast it a million years. An awkward, feeble, leaky lie is a thing which you ought to make it your unceasing study to avoid; such a lie as that has no more real permanence than an average truth. Why, you might as well tell the truth at once and be done with it. A feeble, stupid, preposterous lie will not live two years—except it be a slander upon somebody. It is indestructible, then, of course, but that is no merit of yours. A final word: begin your practice of this gracious and beautiful art early—begin now. If I had begun earlier, I could have learned how.

Never handle firearms carelessly. The sorrow and suffering that have been caused through the innocent but heedless handling of firearms by the young! Only four days ago, right in the next farmhouse to the one where I am spending the summer, a grandmother, old and gray and sweet, one of the loveliest spirits in the land, was sitting at her work, when her young grandson crept in and got down an old, battered, rusty gun which had not been touched for many years and was supposed not to be loaded, and pointed it at her, laughing and threatening to shoot. In her freight she ran screaming and pleading toward the door on the other side of the room; but as she passed him he placed the gun almost against her very breast and pulled the trigger! He had supposed it was not loaded.

And he was right—it wasn't. So there wasn't any harm done. It is the only case of that kind I ever heard of. Therefore, just the same, don't you meddle with old unloaded firearms; they are the most deadly and unerring things that have ever been created by man. You don't have to take any pains at all with them; you don't have to have a rest, you don't have to have any sights on the gun, you don't have to take aim, even. No, you just pick out a relative and bang away, and you are sure to get him. A youth who can't hit a cathedral at thirty yards with a Gatling gun in three-quarters of an hour, can take up an old empty musket and bag his grandmother every time, at a hundred. Think what Waterloo[1] would have been if one of the armies had been boys armed with old muskets supposed not to be loaded, and the other army had been composed of their female relations. The very thought of it makes one shudder.

There are many sorts of books; but good ones are the sort for the young to read. Remember that. They are a great, an inestimable, an unspeakable means of improvement. Therefore be careful in your selection, my young friends; be very careful; confine yourselves exclusively to Robertson's Sermons, Baxter's *Saint's Rest*, *The Innocents Abroad*, and works of that kind.[2]

But I have said enough. I hope you will treasure up the instructions which I have given you, and make them a guide to your feet and a light to your understanding. Build your character thoughtfully and painstakingly upon these precepts, and by and by, when you have got it built, you will be surprised and gratified to see how nicely and sharply it resembles everybody else's.

1882   1923

1. The bloody battle (1815) in which Napoleon suffered his final defeat at the hands of English and German troops under the Duke of Wellington.
2. The five volumes of sermons by Frederick William Robertson (1816–1853), an English clergyman, and Richard Baxter's *Saints' Everlasting Rest* (1650) were once well-known religious works. *The Innocents Abroad* is Clemens's own collection of humorous travel sketches.

QUESTIONS

1. Is this piece unified? Does it have a thesis sentence? If you think it is unified, in what does the unity consist? If you think it is not unified, where are the breaks? Would it have seemed more unified when it was given as a speech?
2. What "image" or "personality" does Clemens project or assume? What does he do that creates his image or personality?
3. How much of his advice applies only to the young? How much of it is to be taken seriously?
4. What does Clemens assume about his audience? How many of these assumptions would hold true today?

Paul Fussell

THE BOY SCOUT HANDBOOK

It's amazing how many interesting books humanistic criticism manages not to notice. Staring fixedly at its handful of teachable masterpieces, it seems content not to recognize that a vigorous literary-moral life constantly takes place just below (sometimes above) its vision. What a pity Lionel Trilling or Kenneth Burke never paused to examine the intersection of rhetoric and social motive among, say, the Knights of Columbus or the Elks.[1] That these are their fellow citizens is less important than that the desires and rituals of these groups are desires and rituals, and thus of permanent social and psychological consequence. The culture of the Boy Scouts deserves this sort of look-in, especially since the right sort of people don't know much about it.

The right sort consists, of course, of liberal intellectuals. They have often gazed uneasily at the Boy Scout movement. After all, a general, the scourge of the Boers, invented it; Kipling admired it; the Hitlerjugend (and the Soviet Pioneers) aped it.[2] If its insistence that there is a God has not sufficed to alienate the enlightened, its khaki uniforms, lanyards, salutes, badges, and flag-worship have seemed to argue incipient militarism, if not outright fascism. The movement has often seemed its own worst enemy. Its appropriation of Norman Rockwell as its official Apelles[3] has not endeared it to those of exquisite taste. Nor has its cause been promoted by events like the TV appearance a couple of years ago of the Chief Pardoner, Gerald Ford, rigged out in scout neckerchief, assuring us from the teleprompter that a Scout is Reverent. Then there are the leers and giggles triggered by the very word "scoutmaster," which in knowing circles is alone sufficient to promise comic pederastic narrative. "*All* scoutmasters are homosexuals," asserted George Orwell,[4] who also insisted that "*All* tobacconists are Fascists."

But anyone who imagines that the scouting movement is either sinister or stupid or funny should spend a few hours with the latest edition of *The Official Boy Scout Handbook* (1979). Social, cultural, and literary historians could attend to it profitably as well, for after *The Red Cross*

1. Men's fraternal and benevolent associations; Trilling and Burke, highly intellectual and philosophical literary critics.
2. The references here are, first, to Sir Robert Baden-Powell (1857–1941), British hero of the Boer War (1899–1902), who founded the Boy Scouts in 1908; Rudyard Kipling (1865–1936), British author of, among other books, novels championing boyhood virtues;
and, secondly, to militaristic youth organizations in, respectively, Hitler's Nazi Germany and Soviet Russia.
3. Celebrated classical Greek painter; Rockwell, American commercial illustrator, was famous especially for paintings and posters celebrating American middle-class virtues.
4. British novelist and essayist (1903–50).

First Aid Manual, The World Almanac, and the Gideon Bible, it is probably the best-known book in this country. Since the first edition in 1910, twenty-nine million copies have been read in bed by flashlight. The first printing of this ninth edition is 600,000. We needn't take too seriously the ascription of authorship to William ("Green Bar Bill") Hillcourt, depicted on the title page as an elderly gentleman bare-kneed in scout uniform and identified as Author, Naturalist, and World Scouter. He is clearly the Ann Page or Reddy Kilowatt of the movement, and although he's doubtless contributed to this handbook (by the same author is *Baden-Powell: The Two Lives of a Hero* [1965]), it bears all the marks of composition by committee, or "task force," as it's called here. But for all that, it's admirably written. And although a complex sentence is as rare as a reference to girls, the rhetoric of this new edition has made no compromise with what we are told is the new illiteracy of the young. The book assumes an audience prepared by a very good high-school education, undaunted by terms like *biosphere, ideology,* and *ecosystem.*

The pliability and adaptability of the scout movement explains its remarkable longevity, its capacity to flourish in a world dramatically different from its founder's. Like the Roman Catholic Church, the scout movement knows the difference between cosmetic and real change, and it happily embraces the one to avoid any truck with the other. Witness the new American flag patch, now worn at the top of the right sleeve. It betokens no access of jingoism or threat to a civilized internationalism. It simply conduces to dignity by imitating a similar affectation of police and fire departments in anarchic towns like New York City. The message of the flag patch is not "I am a fascist, straining to become old enough to purchase and wield guns." It is, rather, "I can be put to quasi-official use, and like a fireman or policeman I am trained in first aid and ready to help."

There are other innovations, none of them essential. The breeches of thirty years ago have yielded to trousers, although shorts are still in. The wide-brimmed army field hat of the First World War is a fixture still occasionally seen, but it is now augmented by headwear deriving from succeeding mass patriotic exercises: overseas caps and berets from World War II, and visor caps of the sort worn by General Westmoreland and sunbelt retirees. The scout handclasp has been changed, perhaps because it was discovered in the context of the new internationalism that the former one, in which the little finger was separated from the other three on the right hand, transmitted inappropriate suggestions in the Third World. The handclasp is now the normal civilian one, but given with the left hand. There's now much less emphasis on knots than formerly; as if to signal this change, the neckerchief is no longer religiously knotted at the tips. What used to be known as artificial respiration ("Out goes the bad air, in comes the good") has given way to "rescue breathing." The young are now being familiarized with the metric system. Some bright empiric has discovered that a paste made of meat tenderizer is the best remedy for painful insect stings. Constipation is not the bugbear it was a generation ago. And throughout there is a striking new lyricism. "Feel the wind blowing through your hair," the scout is adjured, just as he is exhorted to perceive that Being Prepared for life means learning "to live happy" and—equally important—"to die happy." There's more emphasis now on fun and less on duty; or rather, duty is validated because, properly viewed, it is a pleasure. (If that sounds like advice useful to grown-ups as well as to sprouts, you're beginning to get the point.)

There are only two possible causes of complaint. The term "free world" surfaces too often, although the phrase is mercifully uncapitalized. And the Deism is a bit insistent. The United States is defined as a country "whose people believe in a supreme being." The words "In God We Trust" on the coinage and currency are taken almost as a constitutional injunction. The camper is told to carry along the "Bible, Testament, or prayer book of your faith," even though, for light backpacking, he is advised to leave behind air mattress, knife and fork, and pancake turner. When the scout finds himself lost in the woods, he is to "stay put and have faith that someone will find you." In aid of this end, "Prayer will help." But the religiosity is so broad that it's harmless. The words "your church" are followed always by the phrase "or synagogue." The writers have done as well as they can considering that they're saddled with the immutable twelve points of Baden-Powell's Scout Law, stating unambiguously that "A Scout is Reverent" and "faithful to his religious duties." But if "You have the right to worship God in your own way," you must see to it that "others retain their right to worship God in their way." Likewise, if "you have the right to speak your mind without fear of prison or punishment," you must "ensure that right for others, even when you do not agree with them." If the book adheres to any politics, they can hardly be described as conservative; they are better described as slightly archaic liberal. It is broadly hinted that industrial corporations are prime threats to clean air and conservation. In every illustration depicting more than three boys, one is black. The section introducing the reader to some Great Americans pays respects not only to Franklin and Edison and John D. Rockefeller and Einstein; it also makes much of Walter Reuther and Samuel Gompers,[5] as well as Harriet Tubman, Martin Luther King, and Whitney Young.[6] There is a post-Watergate awareness that public officials must be watched closely. One's civic duties include the obligation to "keep up on what is going on around you" in order to "get involved" and "help change things that are not good."

5. Prominent American labor leaders.
6. Tubman was one of the most famous black abolitionists of the nineteenth century; King, the great civil-rights leader, was assassinated in 1968; Young, another black leader, director of the National Urban League.

Few books these days could be called compendia of good sense. This is one such, and its good sense is not merely about swimming safely and putting campfires "cold out." The good sense is psychological and ethical as well. Indeed, this handbook is among the the the very few remaining popular repositories of something like classical ethics, deriving from Aristotle and Cicero. Except for the handbook's adhesions to the motif of scenic beauty, it reads as if the Romantic movement had never taken place. The constant moral theme is the inestimable benefits of looking objectively outward and losing consciousness of self in the work to be done. To its young audience vulnerable to invitations to "trips" and trances and anxious self-absorption, the book calmly says: "Forget your-self." What a shame the psychobabblers of Marin County[7] will never read it.

There is other invaluable advice, applicable to adults as well as to scouts. Some is practical, like "Never use flammable fluids to start a charcoal fire. They burn off fast, lighting only a little of the charcoal." Some is civic-moral: "Take a 2-hour walk where you live. Make a list of things that please you, another of things that should be improved." And then the kicker: "Set out to improve them." Some advice is even intellectual, and pleasantly uncompromising: "Reading trash all the time makes it impossible for anyone to be anything but a second-rate person." But the best advice is ethical: "Learn to think." "Gather knowledge." "Have initiative." "Respect the rights of others." Actually, there's hardly a better gauge for measuring the gross official misbehavior of the seventies than the ethics enshrined in this handbook. From its explicit ethics you can infer such propositions as "A scout does not tap his acquaintances' telephones," or "A scout does not bomb and invade a neutral country, and then lie about it," or "A scout does not prosecute war unless, as the Constitution provides, it has been declared by the Congress." Not to mention that because a scout is clean in thought, word, and deed, he does not, like Richard Nixon, designate his fellow citizens "shits" and then both record his filth and lie about the recordings ("A scout tells the truth").

Responding to Orwell's satiric analysis of "Boys' Weeklies" forty years ago, the boys' author Frank Richards, stigmatized by Orwell as a manufacturer of excessively optimistic and falsely wholesome stories, observed that "The writer for young people should . . . endeavor to give his young readers a sense of stability and solid security, because it is good for them, and makes for happiness and peace of mind." Even if it is true, as Orwell objects, that the happiness of youth is a cruel delusion, then, says Richards, "Let youth be happy, or as happy as possible. Happiness is the best preparation for misery, if misery must come. At least the poor kid will have had something." In the current world of Making It and

7. County in Northern California, home of many "consciousness-expanding" groups.

Getting Away with It, there are not many books devoted to associating happiness with virtue. The shelves of the CIA and the State Department must be bare of them. "Horror swells around us like an oil spill," Terrence Des Pres said recently. "Not a day passes without more savagery and harm." He was commenting on Philip Hallie's *Lest Innocent Blood Be Shed*, an account of a whole French village's trustworthiness, loyalty, helpfulness, friendliness, courtesy, kindness, cheerfulness, and bravery in hiding scores of Jews during the Occupation. Des Pres concludes: "*Goodness.* When was the last time anyone used that word in earnest, without irony, as anything more than a doubtful cliché?" *The Official Boy Scout Handbook*, for all its focus on Axmanship, Backpacking, Cooking, First Aid, Flowers, Hiking, Map and Compass, Semaphore, Trees, and Weather, is another book about goodness. No home, and certainly no government office, should be without a copy. The generously low price of $3.50 is enticing, and so is the place on the back cover where you're invited to inscribe your name.

1982

Barbara Grizzuti Harrison

ABORTION

If there is one issue on which sane and reasonable people cannot agree to disagree, it is abortion. And even to say that is to make an inflammatory statement: People on both sides of the issue—pro-choice (or pro-abortion) and anti-abortion (or pro-life)—refuse, for the most part, to acknowledge that honor and decency can attach to anyone in the other camp.

You see what I mean: pro-choice/pro-abortion; anti-abortion/pro-life —even the semantics of abortion defeat dialogue. And to occupy a middle ground, to admit to being pushed in one direction, pulled in another, by the claims of conscience, compassion, and reality, is intolerable (others would say unconscionable): People call you names.

Smugness or stridency overwhelms rational discourse; and the voices we hear from most frequently—the loudest voices—are often both smug *and* strident, which is to say arrogant. The arrogance of (some) anti-abortionists is flagrant: to burn a clinic is not an act conceived in humility. There is another kind of arrogance that expresses itself in the unwarranted assumption that anyone who takes a position against abortion is punitive, anti-sexual, lacking in compassion, or mindlessly following an imperative imposed upon her by a "patriarchal" religion.

Partly in an effort to resolve my own psychic tug of war, I sought to hear the quiet voices of conviction from whom we do not often hear.

I thought, while I was at it, that I might as well start at home. I have a 17-year-old son, a 16-year-old daughter. My daughter said: "Abortion is murder." My son said, "The woman should decide for herself." My daughter, however, added: "It's different from other murders, though, because nobody means to do evil; there isn't any desire to kill."

She was expressing—without knowing it—a sophisticated theological concept: that of subjective, as opposed to objective, sin.

Catholics who do not oppose abortion take refuge in this theological loophole: Miriam Walcott, a lay leader, formerly Catholic chaplain at Brown University, says that while she is "personally repelled by abortion, it is specifically inaccurate to ascribe sin, such as murder, where none is intended within the conscience of the individual choosing to have an abortion."

Catholics for a Free Choice, a national organization with state and local chapters, quotes the Second Vatican Council Declaration on Religious Liberty, saying that people who possess "civil rights are not to be hindered in leading their lives in accordance with their conscience." Joan Harriman, of Catholics for Alternatives, whose activities include "nonjudgmental pregnancy counseling," says that "abortion is often the lesser evil in service of the greater good. I am concerned with when 'ensoulment' takes place; and second-trimester abortions are awful to contemplate. But I can't contemplate making a choice for another woman, either."

A friend I value for her generosity as much as for her integrity says adamantly that if my daughter were to have an abortion, she would refuse to drive her to a clinic: "I couldn't aid and abet you. I'm beginning to feel immoral because I don't try to dissuade friends who are choosing to have abortions. I allow the vehemence of my feelings to embarrass me, so my protest comes out sounding like a little romantic squeak."

My friend is Jewish, and secular; and she "couldn't care less when 'ensoulment' takes place. That's splitting hairs and focusing attention away from the kind of society we're creating. I see abortion as the worst kind of denial of our bodies. We are our bodies. If we deny the limits inherent in being a physical creature, society approaches an ideal of mechanical perfection. Mongoloid children or thalidomide babies can live happy and good lives. The trouble is that they are intimations of our mortality."

Another friend of mine, an active member of a mainline Protestant church, says, "I know how terribly destructive it is for a mother to give up a child for adoption; and how much adopted children suffer from a sense of identity loss. On one side guilt, on the other side longing. When my extended family gets together, I see three faces that probably would not be here if abortion had been legal 20 years ago—three adopted children. I love those children, and I'm glad they're alive. But I think of their mothers. How terrible it must have been—how terrible it is—for them."

Elizabeth Moore is a welfare mother of six who works for Feminists for Life. When anti-abortionists brought a fetus to a National Organization for Women conference on abortion, she publicly denounced their action on the ground that it was "hurtful to dialogue." Active in the civil rights movement and in the peace movement, she is opposed to "all forms of violence—handguns, nukes, capital punishment."

Clearly not an ultraconservative, she takes issue with what has unfortunately become known as the "pro-family" line: she supports the proposed equal rights amendment, day-care centers, shelters for battered wives and sex education in the public schools. "Abortion," she says, "is not an alternative to sharing jobs and wealth. Abortion does not cure poverty."

Pam Cira, also of Feminists for Life, says, "Feminism grew out of the anger of women who did not want their value to be determined by men. How can we turn around and arbitrarily devalue the fetus? How can I support a Nestlé boycott and turn around and support the destruction of life in utero?"

"I wish we could talk to one another," she said. "This is a heartbreaking issue, and if we shout, the Women's Movement will be destroyed."

Some women are reluctant to speak. One very prominent religious reproaches herself for her silence: "A significant amount of blame must go to women like me who delivered the pro-life movement into the hands of people who care nothing about the hungry of the world, nothing about social justice, and who are not pro-life but merely anti-abortion.

"In talking about abortion," she continued, "we are talking about relationships: the relationship between the woman and the father, the relationship between the woman and the fetus, and our relationship to God, whose essence is creation and who calls us to be co-creators in the search for social justice. We say that a woman's body is her own, but we can't forget that moral decisions always come out of the perspective of being related. A human being is never not related."

"I was driving once with a group of poor Mexican-American women," she said, "and we passed a car with a bumper that said 'Abortion Is Murder.' By the time we reached our destination, every single woman in that car had admitted to having an abortion. They were scared to tell their husbands they were pregnant, and scared to tell them they were aborting. They had no options. Socially and economically, they saw no way out."

Like my daughter, I believe that abortion is murder. But I would drive my daughter to a clinic. I don't know how to fit this reality into a tidy moral or logical equation. But I do know that the arrogance one hears from the loud voices on both sides of this issue stems from the implicit assumption that the function of morality is to make one comfortable; whereas in fact the function of morality is to make one profoundly uncomfortable—it is only out of that discomfort, that spiritual or psychic itch, vexation and turmoil—that authentic ethical decisions can be made.

1980

Willard Gaylin

WHAT YOU SEE IS THE REAL YOU

It was, I believe, the distinguished Nebraska financier Father Edward J. Flanagan[1] who professed to having "never met a bad boy." Having, myself, met a remarkable number of bad boys, it might seem that either our experiences were drastically different or we were using the word "bad" differently. I suspect neither is true, but rather that the Father was appraising the "inner man," while I, in fact, do not acknowledge the existence of inner people.

Since we psychoanalysts have unwittingly contributed to this confusion, let one, at least, attempt a small rectifying effort. Psychoanalytic data—which should be viewed as supplementary information—is, unfortunately, often viewed as alternative (and superior) explanation. This has led to the prevalent tendency to think of the "inner" man as the real man and the outer man as an illusion or pretender.

While psychoanalysis supplies us with an incredibly useful tool for explaining the motives and purposes underlying human behavior, most of this has little bearing on the moral nature of that behavior.

Like roentgenology, psychoanalysis is a fascinating, but relatively new, means of illuminating the person. But few of us are prepared to substitute an X-ray of Grandfather's head for the portrait that hangs in the parlor. The inside of the man represents another view, not a truer one. A man may not always be what he appears to be, but what he appears to be is always a significant part of what he is. A man is the sum total of *all* his behavior. To probe for unconscious determinants of behavior and then define *him* in their terms exclusively, ignoring his overt behavior altogether, is a greater distortion than ignoring the unconscious completely.

Kurt Vonnegut has said, "You are what you pretend to be," which is

---

1. Founder (1917) of Boys Town, a self-governing community for homeless and abandoned boys, for which he was also an energetic fund raiser.

simply another way of saying, you are what we (all of us) perceive you to be, not what you think you are.

Consider for a moment the case of the ninety-year-old man on his deathbed (surely the Talmud must deal with this?) joyous and relieved over the success of his deception. For ninety years he has shielded his evil nature from public observation. For ninety years he has affected courtesy, kindness, and generosity—suppressing all the malice he knew was within him while he calculatedly and artificially substituted grace and charity. All his life he had been fooling the world into believing he was a good man. This "evil" man will, I predict, be welcomed into the Kingdom of Heaven.

Similarly, I will not be told that the young man who earns his pocket money by mugging old ladies is "really" a good boy. Even my generous and expansive definition of goodness will not accommodate that particular form of self-advancement.

It does not count that beneath the rough exterior he has a heart—or, for that matter, and entire innards—of purest gold, locked away from human perception. You are for the most part what you seem to be, not what you would wish to be, nor, indeed, what you believe yourself to be.

Spare me, therefore, your good intentions, your inner sensitivities, your unarticulated and unexpressed love. And spare me also those tedious psychohistories which—by explosing the goodness inside the bad man, and the evil in the good—invariably establish a vulgar and perverse egalitarianism, as if the arrangement of what is outside and what inside makes no moral difference.

Saint Francis[2] may, in his unconscious, indeed have been compensating for, and denying, destructive, unconscious Oedipal impulses identical to those which Atilla projected and acted on. But the similarity of the unconscious constellations in the two men matters precious little, if it does not distinguish between them.

I do not care to learn that Hitler's heart was in the right place. A knowledge of the unconscious life of the man may be an adjunct to understanding his behavior. It is *not* a substitute for his behavior in describing him.

The inner man is a fantasy. If it helps you to identify with one, by all means, do so; preserve it, cherish it, embrace it, but do not present it to others for evaluation or consideration, for excuse or exculpation, or, for that matter, for punishment or disapproval.

Like any fantasy, it serves your purposes alone. It has no standing in the real world which we share with each other. Those character traits, those attitudes, that behavior—that strange and alien stuff sticking out all over you—*that's the real you!*

1977

2. Saint Francis of Assisi, who early in the thirteenth century renounced parental wealth, entered on a life of poverty, and founded the Franciscan order of begging friars.

QUESTIONS

1. *Gaylin makes a key distinction between the inner and the outer man. Why is it necessary for him to start with this distinction?*
2. *Gaylin finds in the relation between an X-ray and a portrait an analogy for the relation between the inner man and the outer man. How accurate is this analogy?*
3. *Compare the approach to human personality taken by Gaylin with that of Herb Goldberg, also a psychotherapist, in "In Harness: The Male Condition" (p. 451). Do they seem to agree on the nature of human personality? Explain.*
4. *Discuss the effectiveness of the examples in the essay and suggest others that Gaylin might have used.*
5. *Comment on the appropriateness of Gaylin's title.*
6. *Gaylin says in his first paragraph that he does "not acknowledge the existence of inner people," which in his fourth paragraph he says that "the inside of the man represents another view, not a truer one." How can you account for this seeming contradiction?*

Susan Lee

FRIENDSHIP, FEMINISM, AND BETRAYAL

Home for Christmas my first year in college, I spoke to my best friend from high school. Elizabeth and I stayed on the phone for 45 minutes, but we had nothing very much to say to each other. After the conversation, I was upset. I remember wanting to tell my mother, who asked what the matter was, about the weirdness of discovering that his woman and I, who had talked every school day for five years, no longer had anything in common. All I could do was cry.

Except for a brief, awkward visit to my house a month later when my father died, a church wedding where Elizabeth married a man I'd gone out with in seventh grade, and two short stopovers in southern New Jersey, I don't remember ever seeing or speaking to her again.

We used to spend hours talking about our relationships with boys. We never discussed our relationship with each other. Except for the few minutes with my mother, who told me she thought Elizabeth and I never had anything in common, and my once making a distinction between acquaintances and friends, I'd never spoken about what I considered a real friendship.

Many people have expressed agreement with Cicero that "friendship can only exist between good men." I'm not one of them. As a 30-year-old woman who has had friends since grade school, I have been very concerned with those friendships. Yet only in the last few years have such relationships been acknowledged as being as important as they've always been.

It was always commonplace for girls in my high school to spend a great deal of time together. It was also commonplace for a girl to spend Saturdays with another girl listening to Johnny Mathis albums, trying on clothes to find something that fit right, or babysitting and then having the evening that was planned together usurped by some boy calling up for a date. When this happened to me, I felt betrayed. I never said anything. It didn't occur to me that this wasn't the natural order of things. I didn't know anyone who complained, nor do I remember anyone who ever turned down a boy because she'd already made plans with a girl.

One woman I know said that if as a teenager she had told her parents she'd prefer being with a girl than a boy, they would have sent her to a doctor.

Even now, this past summer, when I was home for a few weeks because my mother was sick, my mother only asked questions about the men who called. One night when I was coming into the city, she discovered I was going to see a woman instead of the man who had just called.

All she said was, "Oh?" Within that one word was more archness than I'd ever heard placed in such a small space.

A male friend of mine suggested that, as kids, if a girl could turn down another girl for a boy, maybe the girls weren't friends. What he didn't understand is how power works, how it matters who gets to set the dates, how important one telephone call can be, and how helpless someone can feel waiting for it.

But girls didn't deny each other because we weren't friends. We could only do it because we were and because boys weren't, and because they got to make the call and we didn't.

Still, a friend of mine recently remembered that she once was leaving a girl to go out on a date. Her girlfriend's mother, who was very hurt for her daughter, stopped her and said that when she was young, girls knew the value of friendship.

Now, each of us knows what this woman meant. We might express it in terms of a heightened woman's consciousness. We might talk of it in terms of respect for each of our relationships. My friend didn't. She went out on her date. She knew what was flexible in her life and what wasn't. The given of having friends then was that we understood the same rules. The same given remains except that some of the rules are changing.

* * *

Friendship has become so institutionalized in our culture that a recent book combined the notion that everyone should have a good friend with the alienated sense that each person should be her or his own best friend.

My guess is that as the family breaks down, friendships will grow in importance. In my own life, as I have relied less and less on the idea of marriage for myself, the more I've come to see the friendships that I've had for years and years as the on-going relationships in my life.

College was a relatively easy place to find people I liked. Condescending as it might have sounded to me then, we each had our futures ahead of us. It seemed possible to get on with a large number of people. Still, most of my college friends and acquaintances disappeared from my life almost as soon as I left the campus. Like Elizabeth and me, we had little more in common than living near each other.

I used to think affection was enough for friendship, but I no longer believe that. Affection can be sufficient for lovers in a way it isn't for friends. But then, people "fall in" love. Someone is a lover after a few days. A friendship, where love develops, often takes years.

A friend is someone I can be myself with; with a lover, I'm all too often someone else, someone I'd rather be. * * *

I can only be myself when there is a shared community of interests between the other person and me. I began to realize how important this was when I got to graduate school in San Francisco and met other people who cared intimately about the same work I did. No longer was someone's impending wedding date the ongoing center of a conversation.

I found people who perceived what went on outside of them and how they acted in the world in many of the same ways I did. I was not as aware of the need for loyalty to friends as I am now. If I fall under the illusion that I was particularly unusual in the way that I treated other women, I remind myself of the green rocking chair in my San Francisco living room. I gave this chair up to any man who came into my house and kept it for myself if another woman was there.

One relationship developed into something more than shared after classroom time. Both Linda and I were dedicated to writing fiction and to working out our lives so that we'd be able to write. And, however different Linda and I were, I was conscious that our friendship had a loyalty and a respect for each other that other friendly relationships did not have.

We spent hours discussing our lives, our work, our dailyness. Where a lover and I take endless time concerning ourselves with ourselves and our specific relationship, Linda and I were spectators at the landscapes of each other's lives. We were more like adjacent lands sharing common borders than the same property itself. It seemed to me that not only did I have my life, but I had hers as well, to see the working out of our goal to become the best writers we possibly could.

A friend like Linda is a reflection of what I value, in a way a lover is not necessarily. I like to be friends, with what is best in me and with what I'm interested in. While I, and several of my friends, too often excuse our choice of lovers as irrational or necessary acts, we take the responsibility for whom we've chosen as friends.

Still, I'm far more conscious of lovers than I am of friends. Though this is changing, I usually think about friends when something is wrong between us. When I'm in love, I'm almost always aware of my lover.

When I was in California and Linda didn't call or was late for an appointment, I assumed there was a good reason. When a lover messes up, I'm quick to think it's our relationship. Friends don't take things as personally as lovers do. There's less expectation and more politeness with friends, who are taken far more for granted than lovers. Yet the reality in my life is that friends are more constant. Lovers come and go except for those who become my friends and stay near me.

Even understanding this, it didn't occur to me to stay in California because of my friends. Linda, abiding by the same implicit rules I did, never mentioned my remaining to me; I don't know if she thought of it. Another friend confronted me; he asked how I could leave the people I freely acknowledged loving more than anyone else. It was enough for me that I was bored and dissatisfied in San Francisco and wanted to come back to New York.

The following year, I returned to the West Coast for Linda's wedding to another writer. Our relationship had deepened into the assumption that we were each other's friend. Although I had fears about the marriage which Linda was all too aware of, I didn't think of not going to give support. I hoped that if any woman could manage writing and a marriage, Linda would.

I tried seeing her for several weeks yearly in Italy or France where she lived. What I didn't admit to myself after one visit to Praiano was how the three of us were developing. I was writing; Thomas, Linda's husband, was writing; only Linda wasn't.

A year and a half later in Paris, I couldn't help seeing what I hadn't wanted to see in Italy. Thomas wrote constantly, and Linda talked about writing. When he worked, we had to whisper. One night when Linda went into her study to work, Thomas interrupted her. I expected her to tell him to leave her alone as she so assiduously left him. Instead, he talked her out of doing anything but spending time with him and me. She acceded to him as she did in much else of what he wanted. She had become a wife.

My visit to Paris was disastrous. Whenever I tried talking about what I found appalling, Linda turned the discussion to my love relationships of the previous year which had not been ones she would have liked to have had. My anger at what I construed as her growing passivity remained unarticulated and high.

I came home and didn't answer a cheery letter ignoring the realities of my stay. A few months later, I wrote a very disturbed explanatory response and did not hear from Linda again.

I knew she'd stopped speaking to her childhood best friend because the woman had once flirted with Thomas. I was aware she'd given me up because of what she thought was an opposite reaction to the man she chose to live with and to the way she led her life.

Six months later, I was speaking to an editor in the publishing house which had signed Thomas's novel and found out Linda and Thomas were in New York for a few weeks.

Sorting out my resentment at having lost my closest friendship, I called them. Linda answering, we talked awkwardly and arranged dinner for that night. I thought the two of us might be able to resolve our difficulties. Perhaps I had been wrong. Deep friendship is hard to come by, and I was prepared to do what I could to salvage this one.

When Linda arrived at the restaurant, she said Thomas would be there with some of his friends within half an hour. I was dumbfounded. She and I were to have dinner alone.

By the next day, I was furious. Living outside English-speaking countries, Linda might have missed the American women's movement. Still, she taught a college course on women in Paris. She couldn't be as unaware of turning into a passive, dependent person as she seemed to be. If she and I weren't going to be friends, I at least wanted to make clear what bothered me.

But she didn't want to hear it. As far as she was concerned, I was hostile, Finally, she agreed to meet.

There we were at the Buffalo Road House: I, with a tennis racket, T-shirt, and dungarees; she, with the latest long Parisian swirl skirt. We were surrounded by four booths of male couples who all stopped talking as we began.

I gathered they all thought we were the lovers Thomas had believed we were years before. I wanted to turn around and say, "No, no. This is worse. We were friends, and now we're not going to be."

We drank wine and were each very upset. Surprising me, she told me that I had betrayed her. She, who long before defined a friend as someone who knew you and loved you anyway, said I didn't trust her. On my side, I was sure she was the one who betrayed our original friendship. She was the one who'd given up her life for someone else's needs.

I argued, somewhat disingenuously, that I was never hostile to her but to her role as wife. I remember thinking that we were never as close as I had thought.

Linda said, "If Thomas ever was as nasty about you as you've been about him, I would have divorced him a long time ago."

I thought this was not only untrue but gratuitous. Thomas, whose novel includes such lines as, "He stuck his throbbing cock into her Hawaiian cunt," could afford to be magnanimous. There was little reason for him to complain. I could talk all I wanted of the need for women to struggle. While he and his friends discussed how liberated they were, he knew Linda's allegiance and investment were more and more in him and his future and less so in her own.

Then she said that since she and I had stopped corresponding, she'd started a novel about the friendship between two women and had gotten more than 100 pages into it.

She and I haven't spoken since. I've hoped she would finish that novel. Not only do I want her to write, I want to read about a friendship through her eyes, and I want something to come out of our relationship.

But I'm being disingenuous again. While acting as an external conscience to a friend might sound touching and be theoretically correct, the reshaping of people, luckily for friendship, is traditionally—and usually without success—left to lovers. Linda knew what I was upset about. At one point when I was in Paris talking to Thomas about each of our projects, Linda burst out, "Don't you both see? I'm the one in trouble." Thomas denied what I perceived was true. Linda didn't need me to be tiresome or belligerent about it. Even more, she didn't need someone who she sensed didn't trust her enough to overcome it.

While I now know I can no longer be friendly with someone who acts like a "wife," I think Linda was right about my betraying her. I acted like one of the Plymouth Bay colonists. In effect, I said that specific beliefs and actions meant more than our history together.

Still, I'm angry. I know very well that other people's supposedly durable friendships turn out unexpectedly fragile and break fairly easily. Yet, however necessary my betrayal was, this woman and I had made a commitment to each other, the alternative was not to have gone on being friends. We were too on edge with each other to do that. All we could have done was to fade away from each other without having had the courage to talk about our differences at all.

When I was young, I thought my friends *had* to act as they did. As a result, I overlooked many decisions that I fundamentally disagreed with. Now, due to the women's movement, I assume each of my friends takes responsibility for her life. Because I no longer consider us powerless, I no longer can forgive acting as if we were.

While a heightened women's consciousness has resulted in our openly valuing friendships more highly than we did before, this same consciousness has caused me, and other women, to demand more of these relationships. The validity of each of our lives has become an issue that might have been passed by before and now can no longer be.

Often, these new pressures are too great for many of these friendships to bear. I know there are no models to go by to put them back together. I know we have to develop new models of not only keeping friendships but having them at all.

Yet to venture that friendships often break apart because of social and political dislocations doesn't alleviate my wanting friendships that last or my being hurt that this relationship with Linda, which I had assumed would be one of these, no longer exists.

Looking back on what happened between us, I can understand the pressures on her to choose as she did. I can wish her well. I can understand my own development which made me make demands that others might find unreasonable. I can do a lot of things, but what I feel—not by Linda so much as by historical circumstance—is cheated.

1975

QUESTIONS

1. Lee talks about differences in the relationships between friends and lovers and between men and women. Why are the two sets of terms necessary?
2. What does Lee mean when she says that she and her friends "too often excuse our choice of lovers as irrational or necessary acts," but "take the responsibility for whom we've chosen as friends?" What does it mean to "take the responsibility" for choosing a friend? How did this figure in Lee's friendship with Linda?
3. Explain the significance of the green rocking chair. Cite similar examples from your own experience or observation that illustrate something about relationships between men and women, friends, or lovers.
4. What does Lee mean when she says the "reshaping of people" is left to lovers rather than friends. Explain why you agree or disagree.
5. Try to write an account of Lee's friendship with Linda from Linda's point of view. Has Lee given you enough material to be able to do this? What, if anything, will you have to imagine or invent?

Carol Bly

BRUNO BETTELHEIM: THREE IDEAS TO TRY IN MADISON, MINNESOTA

It is exhilarating to spend a few days thinking about the ideas of Bruno Bettleheim,[1] not just because he has such energy and moral genius, but because he is so out of style at the moment. The attention, and certainly the affections, of the liberal intelligentsia are somewhere else, and I feel private and quiet among Bettelheim's findings, instead of feeling like one of a cheering crowd at the arena. There is no distraction.

I expect Bettelheim owes his unpopularity to the fact that he is such a mixed bag: he gets off some of the coarsest censures of young people, leftists, and women that you can come across. He is good and out of fashion. What I like and honor in him is his constant work on *decency*. In a decade given to opening up the unconscious almost as an end in itself, Bettelheim still goes on working on decency between people, decency based squarely on the moral well-being within each person. He calls this moral well-being "individual autonomy." Roughly, it means that no matter how sensibly some insane or cruel proposition is presented to you, you make up your own mind that it is not acceptable, and you do not do the insane or cruel thing.

Applying Bruno Bettelheim's perspective to life in rural Minnesota means taking ideas learned *in great straits* (in the concentration camp at Dachau and later, in the Orthogenic School of the University of Chicago, where he treated autistic children) and deliberately using them *in little straits*. I commend this idea because the countryside, despite its apparent culture lag, is doomed to be wrecked in the mass culture just as surely as the cities are being wrecked. We need major thinking, but our habit is to listen only to the local prophets—mild-mannered provincial professionals living among us, regional poets with their evident faith in nature, local administrators of community education projects. Our habit is to listen to those nearby who are affable and low-key. They can't save our personalities, though, any better than fervent quilt making can save our artistic nature or Solarcaine can set a broken leg.

Certainly life in western Minnesota must be about as untroublesome as life anywhere in the twentieth century. It is only luck; we haven't ourselves done anything, psychically or morally, to protect us from the coarsening of life that comes with more population. We are all set to become "mass men"—or at least we have no proofs that we won't give way to impersonal relations, increasing rudeness, increasing distrust, ill-

---

1. Dr. Bettleheim has written many books. I've taken some of his ideas here from *The Informed Heart, The Empty Fortress, and* some recent newspaper interviews [author's note].

temper while queuing up for everything from tennis courts to funeral reservations. Bettelheim's ideas—and I've chosen three of them to think about—have to do with how to keep the self from succumbing to the mass state. The three ideas are (1) replacing the feeling of "business as usual" with crisis thinking, (2) forcing ourselves to have a sense of time in our lives, and (3) understanding the power of negative thinking.

Even when the Germans began arresting Jews in the 1930s, many of the Jews refused to leave Germany because the aura of their possessions —the rooms, the rugs, the paintings—gave them a sense of normalcy in things: they'd projected some of themselves into these objects around them, so if the objects were still there, surely everything was usual? What they needed to do was to switch to *crisis thinking*: they needed to say to themselves, "This is *not* business as usual. We must run away at night, or join the Underground, or separate and plan to meet in Switzerland."

Bettelheim says we must speak or fight, whichever is called for, at the *first moment of our anxiety*. National Socialism looked like "business as usual" in 1932 and 1933; by 1934 it was too late. The Gestapo's intention to terrify eighty million Germans through the constant threat of the camps was published long before they actually did it, but few paid attention. *Mein Kampf*[2] should have been lots of warning: very few people took it seriously. So Bettelheim suggests we must ask ourselves at every other moment, Is this business as usual? Is this a crisis? Is it O.K. to go on just maintaining my life today, or must I act in a political way? So here are some questions we can ask in rural Minnesota:

1. Should the President[3] be impeached? Now in the moment of our anxiety over his crookedness: should we impeach? If not, is there something else we should be doing? Is it really O.K. just to be sitting here?

2. Is TV watching turning our children into mass men or is it not? Many parents in Madison have said explicitly they think TV watching is bad for their children, but only two families I know of have got rid of the set. Somehow, the course of each day's activity disperses the parents' anxiety. Since they do not act in the moment of anxiety, then the children go on dully taking in the commercials and the vulgarity of feeling and another week goes by, a year goes by, and the day after tomorrow, or perhaps it was yesterday, the children are eighteen and they have been watching television for seventeen years. They saw eighteen thousand murders by the time they were fourteen (according to *TV Generation*, by Gerald Loomey), and all the while the parents sincerely felt that TV watching was bad for them.

3. Is the American diet really "well balanced" as the Department of Agriculture would have us believe, or have the grain-milling companies (who systematically began degerminating all wheat flour on the market in the second decade of the century) caused a deficiency of Vitamin E (and other

2. Adolf Hitler's statement of his theories   3. Richard M. Nixon, who resigned the pres-
and program, published 1925–27.   idency in 1974.

vitamins as well) which is responsible for the multiplying incidence of certain diseases and a sharp rise in fatalities from them? Does it mean anything that in the pamphlets given 4-H children, telling them how to make bread, the picture credits are nearly all to those very grain-milling companies?

A sense of time warns that now is the time; it is not business as usual. Thinking of time leads to the second idea of Bettelheim's I'd like to bring in: a sense of *time left*. The Gestapo cleverly realized that if you never know *when* something will happen, such as the release of a prisoner from camp or the end of a slave-work detail, you can't organize your own thoughts. A crude example that comes to my mind is the dilemma of a runner; if he doesn't know how many laps remain, how shall he husband his diminishing strength? When shall he make his final spurt? Christianity feels the sense of *time left* so strongly that the Church teaches that you must regard every moment as your last, so that you will make the final, mortal spurt always. But mass society, which tends to make people relaxed and low-key and unambitious, encourages a slack time sense. Here's an example from my town.

As soon as a Madison girl marries she will be asked to join most if not all of the following groups:

1. A circle of church women
2. The large Ladies' Aid, which meets monthly.
3. A homemakers' group
4. An auxiliary of the American Legion or the VFW
5. Mrs. Jaycees
6. A study club (Federated Women's Clubs of America)
7. Women's—or couples'—bridge club

I have omitted community groups that do useful work, such as teaching released-time school, or shampooing at the Home, filling hospital bird-feeding stations, or working in the hospital auxiliary. These projects are self-justifying.

If the young woman doesn't say to herself: I am twenty-five and in seventy years I will probably be dead, she is likely to join the organizations listed. If she has a sense of *time left*, however, she may ask the right questions: How much of my life do I want to spend in solitude? Most women in town also drink coffee with two or more other women at 10 A.M. and at 3 P.M. every day. This means another three hours a day of time spent in idle social intercourse. Yet, whenever we ask these young women if they think they might on their deathbeds regret this casual frittering away of time, they grin and say, "Oh, let's not be morbid now!"

Still, forty-five-year-old women do start dropping out of the artificially structured social life in Madison: people who have dazedly accepted belonging to clubs for twenty years now choose to topple into their own inner lives instead. They simply have finally learned a sense of *time left*

—and the tragedy of it is that a spiritually dormant society ever allowed them to waste twenty years.

A few years ago we had a constantly cheerful minister in town; no one was less apprehensive than he. He wasn't nervous about the hydrogen bomb and he wasn't nervous about our participation in the Vietnam War. Then he became critically ill, and upon recovery he preached for an entire winter the first serious, thoughtful sermons of his life, or at least of his life here. Any number of people complained that the sermons had gone morbid and "negative." They hadn't. He simply had learned a sense of *time left*.

Complaints about "negative" sermons bring me to the third of Bettelheim's ideas: the usefulness of negative or critical thinking. Bettelheim objects to everyone's seizing on Anne Frank's "All men are basically good." He argues that they wish to derive comfort from their admiration of her positive attitude under such awful circumstances, instead of feeling uncomfortable with the truth—which is that men are basically good and they are basically bad. They can be ghastly. Stanley Milgram's *Obedience to Authority*[4] describes an experiment in which subjects were directed to "administer pain" to people strapped in chairs in the next room who were visible through the window. The subjects believed that the dials they operated gave pain whenever the people strapped to the chair failed to learn a given piece of information. Some of the subjects repeatedly turned the dial to the "danger" markings on the machine. They were sadistic without even noticing. If we keep in mind such left-handed inhumanity—Americans just obeying orders—and then repeat to ourselves Anne Frank's remark about men being basically good, we are irritated: naïveté, which ever wants to preserve its artless high, is ignoring rank cruelty. Positive thinking is that kind of naïveté. People who practice or commend it are interested in feeling no pain and in preserving a high. Sometimes a whole culture wishes to preserve this high: then its art and doctrines turn not into positive thinking but into positive pretending.

We haven't got a Germany here, but we do have a TV space-selling society. Hence a generation has grown up on mostly happy, bland, evasive propaganda. No wonder this beastly positive thinking, which means positive *pretending*, has become the crutch of church and club. The other day a clergyman told me he "preferred to think of the Ten Commandments as positive, not negative." Marvelous! What is the *positive* way not to commit adultery? How do you *positively* not covet your neighbor's husband? How do you *positively* not steal from the Klein National Bank?

Bettelheim noted that, when he first wrote his interpretations of the concentration camps, his readers told him they felt "a strange relief,"

4. An excerpt from this book begins on page 642.

gruesome as the subject was. No matter how oppressive the facts, facing them, calling evil evil, safeguards our personalities.

Why read a set of ideas based on imprisonment in Dachau in 1938? When I first began reading Bettelheim years ago I had the uncanny sensation he was handing me a beautifully thought-out set of bright tools, to keep me (or anyone) in one piece. He showed a way not to sit around absent-mindedly while a gross society raveled away decency like a yarn ball. As much as anyone I've read, Bettelheim helps us not to be wrecked. It takes affection to keep preventing wrecks, and saving people already wrecked. You feel this tough affection in his ideas.

1973

QUESTIONS

1. *Do the three ideas Bly discusses unite? Are her transitions logical, or are they simple verbal echoes?*
2. *Although Bly recognizes that what Bettelheim saw in Hitler's Germany was far worse than what she sees in Minnesota, she is still upset by what she sees. Yet her tone is not angry. How do you account for that? Would her essay be more effective if she were angry?*
3. *Bly raises three questions (p. 630); do they seem to be matters requiring crisis thinking? If you think not, how can you be sure that your rejection of the idea is not what she calls "business as usual"?*
4. *Bly's question about how ideas based on imprisonment at Dachau in 1938 apply to life in Minnesota in the 1970s is a good one. What answers are suggested by Bettelheim's description of his prison camp experience in "A Victim" (p. 39)?*

Gilbert Ryle

ON FORGETTING THE DIFFERENCE BETWEEN
RIGHT AND WRONG

"Don't you know the difference between right and wrong?" "Well, I did learn it once, but I have forgotten it." This is a ridiculous thing to say. But why is it ridiculous? We forget lots of things, including lots of important things, that we used to know. So what is the absurdity in the idea of a person's forgetting the difference between right and wrong?

I think the question worthy of discussion, if only because the epistemological wheels on which ethical theories are made to run are apt to be wooden and uncircular.

Only one philosopher, as far as I know, has discussed my question.

Aristotle does so very briefly in the *Nicomachean Ethics* 1100^b 17 and 1140^b 29.[1]

First let us get rid of two possible misconstructions of my question.

In speaking of a person's knowing or not knowing the difference between right and wrong, I shall not be speaking of him as knowing or not knowing the solutions to philosophers' conceptual questions like, "What are the definitions of Rightness and Wrongness, respectively?" A properly brought up child knows the difference between right and wrong, for all that he has never heard an argument from Kant or Thrasymachus[2] and would not have understood their definitions if he had. Anyhow, there is no absurdity in the idea of a philosophy student's having forgotten some ethical definitions or analyses that he had once known. He would not thereby cease to know the difference between right and wrong.

Next, the assertion that it is absurd to say that a person might forget the difference between right and wrong could be misconstrued as the ascription to our knowledge of right and wrong of an inspiring kind of indelibility, perhaps a Heaven-hinting innateness or a trailing cloud of glory.[3] No such edifying moral can be looked for. If it is absurd to say that one has forgotten the difference, it is also absurd to say that one recollects it. If it is absurd to say that one's knowledge of the difference between right and wrong might, like one's Latin, get rusty, then it is also absurd to say that it actually remains, like one's English, unrusty.

1. It might be suggested that there is a quite simple reason why we cannot forget the difference between right and wrong, namely, that daily life gives us constant reminders of it. Somewhat as, throughout December, Christmas carols, Christmas cards, and butchers' shops constantly remind us of the imminence of Christmas Day, so the daily procession of duties to be done and derelictions to be apologized for keeps us constantly in mind of the difference between right and wrong. But this explanation will not do. A very forgetful person remains unreminded in the midst of reminders. Even the knot in his handkerchief does not remind him of anything. Moreover, a man might happen to sojourn in a part of the world where there were no reminders of Christmas. If this were all, then the maker of the paradoxical remark might just be in the rare position of being unusually forgetful or unusually unexposed to obligations; and then his remark would be not ridiculous but only hard to credit. Forgetting the difference between right and wrong would then be merely a rare thing, like forgetting one's own name.

This suggested explanation is a causal hypothesis. It offers to tell what

1. Aristotle's last treatise on ethics; the passage in question is part of a discussion of the role of habit in morality.
2. Immanuel Kant, eighteenth-century German philosopher; Thrasymachus appears in Plato's *Republic.*

3. The reference is to "Ode: Intimations of Immortality," by the English poet William Wordsworth (1770–1850), which asserts that as children, "trailing clouds of glory do we come / From God, who is our home."

makes people very unlikely to forget the difference between right and wrong. It therefore assumes that there is such a thing as forgetting this difference. But our question is, rather, "Why is there no such thing? Why will 'forget' and 'be reminded of' not go with 'the difference between right and wrong'?"

2. A better, though still inadequate, explanation would be this. Knowing the difference between right and wrong is of a piece not with remembering particular matters of fact, like names, dates, and engagements, but with knowing how to do things, knowing the way from place to place, knowing Latin, and knowing the rules of the road in one's own country. Such things do not slip our memories, nor are knots tied in our handkerchiefs to keep us in mind of them. Knowledge here is mastery of techniques rather than mere possession of information; it is a capacity that can improve or decline, but cannot just come in and go out. We acquire such knowledge not just from being told things, but from being trained to do things. The knowledge is not imparted but inculcated. It is a second nature, and therefore not evanescent. Now our knowledge of the difference between right and wrong certainly is in many important respects much more like a mastery than like the retention of a piece of information. It is, for instance, inculcated by upbringing rather than imparted by dictation. It is not a set of things memorized and is not, consequently, the sort of knowledge of which shortness of memory is the natural enemy.

Nonetheless, there is such a thing as forgetting much or all of one's Latin. With desuetude, one does become rustier and rustier, until one has totally forgotten it. We know what we have to do to keep up our Latin, our geometry, or our tennis, namely, to give ourselves regular practice. Just here is one place where the analogy breaks down between knowing the difference between right and wrong and having mastery of a science or a craft. One's knowlege of the difference between right and wrong does not get rusty; we do not keep up our honesty by giving ourselves regular exercises in it. Nor do we excuse a malicious action by saying that we have recently been short of practice in fair-mindedness and generosity. Virtues are not proficiencies. The notion of being out of practice, which is appropriate to skills, is inappropriate to virtues.

Aristotle's explanation of the fact that there is no such thing as forgetting the difference between right and wrong seems to be that moral dispositions are, from constant exercise, much more abiding things than even our masteries of sciences and crafts. In the latter there is forgetting, though only gradual forgetting; in the former there happens to be none. But the difference does not seem to be just a difference in degree, or even just a difference between a small magnitude and zero. Nor is it just a matter of anthropological fact that our knowledge of the difference between right and wrong never decays. The notion of decay does not fit.

En passant,[4] when I argue that we do not impose moral exercises upon ourselves in order to prevent our knowledge of the difference between right and wrong from rusting, since the notion of rusting does not belong, I am not denying that we can or should drill ourselves into good habits and out of bad ones. I am only denying that such self-disciplining is to be assimilated to the exercises by which we prevent our Latin or our tennis from getting rusty. The object of moral drills is not to save us from forgetting the difference between right and wrong, but to stiffen us against doing what we know to be wrong.

Neither, to make the obverse point, am I denying that moral deterioration occurs. People often do get more callous, less public-spirited, meaner, lazier, and shiftier. What I am denying is that such deteriorations are to be assimilated to declines in expertness, i.e., to getting rusty.

3. A third explanation would be this. Since virtues are not skills, that is, since to be unselfish or patient is not to be good *at* doing anything, perhaps virtues should be classed rather with tastes and preferences, and particularly with educated tastes and cultivated preferences. As the music lover had once to learn to appreciate music, and the bridge player had to learn both to play and to enjoy playing bridge, so the honest man had to be taught or trained to dislike deception, and the charitable man had to be taught or trained to want to relieve distress. Doubtless, as some people take to music from the start as a duck takes to water, so some people are naturally more prone than others to be frank and sympathetic. But to be honest or charitable on principle, even against the impulses of the moment, involves knowing the difference between right and wrong —much as, unlike the mere relishing of one piece of music more than another, appreciating the superiority of the one piece over the other involves knowing their relative merits and demerits. Taste is educated preference, preference for recognized superiorities. To be able to recognize superiorities is to know the difference between good and bad.

Now likings, whether natural or cultivated, can be lost. Most grownups have lost the enthusiasm for playing hide-and-seek, and some cease to enjoy tobacco and poetry. There can also be deteriorations in taste. A person who once had appreciated the excellences of Jane Austen[5] might become so coarsened in palate as to cease to recognize or relish them.

It is relevant to my problem that we do not call such losses or deteriorations "forgetting." Perhaps the absurdity in speaking of someone's forgetting the difference between right and wrong is of a piece with the absurdity in speaking of someone who has lost the taste for poetry as having forgotten the difference between good and bad poetry.

When a person has an educated taste, he can speak of himself as having learned or been taught not only to recognize the differences between,

4. In passing.   5. English novelist (1775–1817).

say, good and bad singing or good and bad tennis strokes, but also to appreciate, i.e., to like, admire, and try for the good and to dislike, despise, and avoid the bad. Knowing, in this region, goes hand in hand with approving and disapproving, relishing and disrelishing, admiring and despising, pursuing and avoiding. Indeed, their connection seems even closer than mere hand-in-hand concomitance. There seems to be a sort of incongruity in the idea of a person's knowing the difference between good and bad wine or poetry, while not caring a whit more for the one than for the other; of his appreciating without being appreciative of excellences. When we read, "We needs must love the highest when we see it,"[6] we incline to say, "Of course. We should not be seeing it if we were not loving it. The 'needs must' is a conceptual one. At least in this field, the partitions are down between the Faculties of Cognition, Conation, and Feeling."

Now whether this inclination is justified or not, it exists just as much in our thinking about the knowledge of right and wrong. Here, too, there seems to be an incongruity in the idea of a person's knowing that something wrong had been done, but still not disapproving of it or being ashamed of it; of his knowing that something would be the wrong thing for him to do, but still not scrupling to do it. We hanker to say that, if he has no scruples at all in doing the thing, then he cannot know that it is wrong, but only, perhaps, that it is "wrong," i.e., what other people call "wrong."

Socrates used to ask the important question, "Can Virtue be taught?" It puzzled him, very properly, that if virtue can be taught there exist no pundits in courage, abstinence, or justice. If we, too, think that knowledge of the difference between right and wrong is knowledge, ought we not to be puzzled that universities and technical colleges do not give courses in industriousness, fair-mindedness, and loyalty? But the moment such a suggestion is made, we realize that the nonexistence of pundits and colleges of the virtues is not a lamentable lacuna in our society. It would be silly to try to provide such instruction; silly, since knowledge of the difference between right and wrong is not the sort of thing that such instruction could bestow. We continue to think that children have to be taught the difference between right and wrong, but we know in our bones that this teaching is not a species of either factual or technical instruction. What sort of teaching, then, is the teaching of the difference between right and wrong? What sort of learning is the learning of this difference? What kind of knowing is the knowing of it? Maybe we can approach an answer to these questions by considering the teaching and learning of tastes.

6. From "Guinevere," in *The Idylls of the King,* by the nineteenth-century English poet Alfred, Lord Tennyson.

A person who has received technical instruction in tennis, music, or landscape gardening may, but may not, owe to his instructor a second debt of gratitude for having taught him also to enjoy these things. A person who has learned from a geographer and a botanist the special features of the Lake District[7] may have been inspired by Wordsworth also to love this district for these features. As one gets to know a person better, one may learn to respect or admire him. Learning to enjoy, to love, or to admire is not acquiring a skill or a parcel of information. Nonetheless it *is* learning. There is a difference between a mere change-over from disliking rice pudding to liking it, and learning to appreciate wines, poems, or people for their excellences. Learning to appreciate requires some studiousness, judiciousness, and acuteness. The judge has reasons to give for his likings, his verdicts, and his choices.

True, the special notions of *lessons, instruction, coaching, examinations, laboratories, courses, manuals,* and the like are no part of the idea of learning to enjoy or learning to admire. Even if Wordsworth really does teach us to love the Lake District, he does not merit or need a professor's chair. But this is only to say again that admiring, enjoying, and loving are not efficiencies or equipments. The notions of *learning, studying, teaching,* and *knowing* are ampler notions than our academic epistemologies have acknowledged. They are hospitable enough to house under their roofs notions like those of *inspiring, kindling,* and *infecting.*

It will be objected, I expect, that what is called "learning to enjoy" or "being taught to admire" is really always two processes, namely, (1) coming to know some things, and (2) as an effect of coming to know them, coming to like or admire. An emotional condition, disposition, or attitude is caused by a cognitive act or disposition. As the rolling of the ship makes me feel sick, so discovering a person's characteristics makes me experience feelings of admiration toward him. So, presumably, as certain nostrums save me from feeling sick when the ship rolls, certain other nostrums might save me from admiring a person when I have discovered what a stanch friend he is. Alternatively, if this sounds too ridiculous, then a peculiarly intimate kind of causal connection has to be invoked in order to represent the connection between knowing and admiring as still a causal one, and yet as one that is exempt from preventions.

If we ask what the supposedly antecedent process of coming to know consists in, we are likely to be told that it consists in coming to be equipped with some information or/and coming to be relatively efficient at doing certain sorts of things, *plus,* perhaps, coming to be able and ready to explain, instruct, criticize, and so forth. These are not effects of coming to know; they are concrete examples of what coming to know is coming to. But why not add that sometimes coming to know *is,* also, *inter*

---

7. Region in the northwest of England celebrated in many of Wordsworth's poems.

alia,[8] coming to admire or enjoy? If making a skillful tennis stroke or a skillful translation is doing something that one has learned to do, i.e., is an exercise and not an effect of knowledge, why may not admiring a person for his stanchness be, in a partly similar way, an example and not an after-effect of what our study of his character has taught us? The reply that what is learned must be either a piece of information or a technique begs the question, since the question is, in part, "Why must it be either one or the other?"

How does all this apply to our knowledge of the difference between right and wrong? We are unwilling to allow that a person has learned this difference who does not, for instance, care a bit whether he breaks a promise or keeps it, and is quite indifferent whether someone else is cruel or kind. This *caring* is not a special feeling; it covers a variety of feelings, like those that go with being shocked, ashamed, indignant, admiring, emulous, disgusted, and enthusiastic; but it also covers a variety of actions, as well as readinesses and pronenesses to do things, like apologizing, recompensing, scolding, praising, persevering, praying, confessing, and making good resolutions. Now, if we consider what in detail a person who has learned the difference between right and wrong has learned, we do not naturally draw a line between some things, namely, what he has learned to say and do, and other things, namely, what he has learned to feel, and relegate the latter to the class of mere aftereffects of his learning to say and do the proper things. In thinking about his conscience or his sense of duty, we do not naturally fence off his qualms from his acts of reparation; his pangs from his confessings or his resolvings; his pickings from his perseverings. *Because* he has learned the difference between right and wrong, he both makes reparations and feels contrite; and the "because" is the same noncausal "because." Certainly his feeling contrite is not an exercise of a technique or the giving of a piece of information; but the same is true, though for different reasons, of his making reparations, persevering, reproaching, resolving, and keeping appointments. All are marks, though different sorts of marks, of his knowing the difference between right and wrong; all show, though in different ways, that he has principles, and what these principles are; any one of them is one of the many sorts of things that we have in mind when we say of him that he has a sense of duty.

Now we can begin to see why it is ridiculous to say that one has forgotten the difference between right and wrong. To have been taught the difference is to have been brought to appreciate the difference, and this appreciation is not just a competence to label correctly or just a capacity to do things efficiently. It includes an inculcated caring, a habit of taking certain sorts of things seriously.

A person who used to care may, indeed, cease to care or to care so much. But ceasing to care is not forgetting, any more than ceasing to

8. Among other things.

believe something or to mistrust someone is forgetting. "Forget" is reserved, apparently, mainly for the nonretention of information and the loss of skills through desuetude, though it is also used for ceasing to notice things, e.g., for the oblivion brought by sleep or distractions.

This use of "forget" for the loss of information and technical abilities, and its nonuse for cessations of caring, may go with another difference. If I have ceased to enjoy bridge, or come to admire Picasso,[9] then I have changed. But, if I have forgotten a date or become rusty in my Latin, I do not think of this as a change in me, but rather as a diminution of my equipment. In the same way, a person who becomes less or more conscientious is a somewhat changed person, not a person with an enlarged or diminished stock of anything. In a testimonial both personal qualities and equipment need to be mentioned, but the equipment is not mentioned among the personal qualities.

So far I have been pressing some analogies between things like tastes and pastimes on the one hand and virtues on the other; I have concentrated on ways in which the notions of learning, teaching, and knowing lock in with notions of caring, i.e., enjoying, admiring, despising, trying, avoiding, and so forth; and I have tried to show how, in these connections, they detach themselves from the notion of forgetting. But we must not push assimilation to the point of identification.

The man who knows the difference btween good and bad tennis strokes, and applauds or tries for the good ones and pities or avoids the bad ones, is something of a specialist. The man who appreciates wines is something of a connoisseur. They have acquired special technical abilities and, therewith, special enjoyments. We others may envy them for both. But knowledge of the difference between right and wrong is common knowledge, and it is not mastery of a technique. There is nothing in particular that the honest man knows, ex officio,[1] how to do. He is not, ex officio, even a bit of an expert at anything. Nor is his life enriched by some extra relishes. He possesses nothing for us to envy.

Often, though not always, we study to become relatively good at things, e.g., games, fine arts, and recreations, because we either enjoy them from the start or anyhow expect to get pleasure from them in the end. Our elders coerce us into learning to swim, largely because they think that we shall miss a lot of pleasure afterward if we do not learn to swim, or to swim well. But this is nothing like the reason or reasons for which elders train the young to be honest. The truth lover has no treats to match against those of the music lover. A sense of duty is not an esthetic sensibility; nor is the passion for righteousness indulged as the passion for bridge or birdwatching is indulged. It is not addiction to a sport or hobby. Certainly there are activities, like most work, in which,

9. Pablo Picasso (1881–1973), Spanish painter and sculptor.
1. By virtue of an office or position; in this instance, by virtue of his being an honest man.

although technical excellence pleases and bad craftsmanship displeases, still the jobs are not done or even done well only for pleasure's sake. But the honest or charitable man has not, ex officio, any particular job to do, much less to be proud of doing well rather than botching. Knowing the difference between right and wrong is not identical with knowing the difference between good and bad work, even though they resemble one another in the fact that ceasing to care how one does one's job, like ceasing to care what one does, is not a case of forgetting.

One more reinsurance. I have claimed to detect an incongruity, and the same sort of incongruity, in the idea of a man's knowing the difference between right and wrong but not caring a bit whether he lies, say, or tells the truth; in the idea of a man's recognizing. without being appreciative of, the excellences of Jane Austen; and in the idea of a craftsman's knowing the difference between good and bad workmanship without taking any pride in his own good work or feeling any contempt for the bad work of others. I may seem to have equated this knowing with having learned to take seriously. But there is a trap here.

I may be a bit shocked and indignant at an exhibition of unfairness, while you are much shocked and highly indignant. I care a bit about it, and you care much more. But this does not involve that you know more differences between right and wrong than I do, if this makes any sense, or that you know the difference better, if this makes any sense. Similarly, a specimen of Shakespeare's literary genius may please me while it thrills you. We appreciate the same excellence, though we are unequally appreciative of it. So even if, in some domains, to teach is, *inter alia*, to kindle, still we do not think of what is taught as varying in magnitude with the heat of the fire. The match is the same, but the fuels are different.

One last point. In most fields instructors can misinstruct. I may be taught that the Battle of Hastings was fought in 1077,[2] and I may be taught to grip fiercely my billiard cue and my steering wheel. While I retain faith in my instructor, I shall still claim to know the date of the battle and to know how to control the cue and the steering wheel; but, when I have learned better, I shall agree that I had not formerly known the date of the battle or how to control the cue or the wheel. I have to unlearn what I was originally taught.

There is no difficulty in conceiving of misinstruction in the particular articles of codes of etiquette. A boy might well be trained to remain respectfully hatted in a lady's drawing room and punctiliously to end his letters to tradesmen with "Yours sincerely."[3] Nor is there much difficulty in conceiving of misinstruction in some of the bylaws of morality. Some people used scrupulously to pay all their gambling debts before paying

---

2. It completed the Norman Conquest of England and was fought, as every British schoolchild knows, in 1066.

3. One code of etiquette reserves "Yours sincerely" for personal—as opposed to business—letters.

off any of their debts to servants and tradesmen. Their consciences had been educated to insist on this priority.

But there is a difficulty in conceiving of a person's being taught to be selfish, deceitful, cruel, and lazy on principle; to be morally shocked at exhibitions of fair-mindedness; or scrupulously to make reparations for his backslidings into unselfishness. The notion of moral noneducation is familiar enough, but the notion of moral miseducation has a smell of absurdity. There is a whiff of the same smell of absurdity in the notion of the would-be connoisseur of wines or engravings being mistaught, taught, that is, to relish wines for their immaturity or to admire engravings for their smudginesses. However, the smell of absurdity is less strong here. The Albert Memorial[4] does seem to have been admired for its architectural badnesses.

The oddness, if it exists, in the idea of moral miseducation might be one source of the strength of the notion of The Moral Law. But to follow up this train of thought would seduce me into talking Ethics.

1958

4. A monument to Queen Victoria's prince consort, Albert, built in an ornate Victorian style no longer fashionable.

Stanley Milgram

THE PERILS OF OBEDIENCE

Obedience is as basic an element in the structure of social life as one can point to. Some system of authority is a requirement of all communal living, and it is only the person dwelling in isolation who is not forced to respond, with defiance or submission, to the commands of others. For many people, obedience is a deeply ingrained behavior tendency, indeed a potent impulse overriding training in ethics, sympathy, and moral conduct.

The dilemma inherent in submission to authority is ancient, as old as the story of Abraham,[1] and the question of whether one should obey when commands conflict with conscience has been argued by Plato, dramatized in *Antigone*,[2] and treated to philosophic analysis in almost every historical epoch. Conservative philosophers argue that the very fabric of society is threatened by disobedience, while humanists stress the primacy of the individual conscience.

1. The patriarch Abraham, commanded by God to sacrifice his son Isaac, is ready to do so until an angel stays his knife.
2. In Plato's *Apology* the philosopher Socrates provokes and accepts the sentence of death rather than belie his conscience; the heroine of Sophocles' *Antigone* risks such a sentence in order to give her brother proper burial.

The legal and philosophic aspects of obedience are of enormous import, but they say very little about how most people behave in concrete situations. I set up a simple experiment at Yale University to test how much pain an ordinary citizen would inflict on another person simply because he was ordered to by an experimental scientist. Stark authority was pitted against the subjects' strongest moral imperatives against hurting others, and, with the subjects' ears ringing with the screams of the victims, authority won more often than not. The extreme willingness of adults to go to almost any lengths on the command of an authority constitutes the chief finding of the study and the fact most urgently demanding explanation.

In the basic experimental design, two people come to a psychology laboratory to take part in a study of memory and learning. One of them is designated as a "teacher" and the other a "learner." The exerimenter explains that the study is concerned with the effects of punishment on learning. The learner is conducted into a room, seated in a kind of miniature electric chair; his arms are strapped to prevent excessive movement, and an electrode is attached to his wrist. He is told that he will be read lists of simple word pairs, and that he will then be tested on his ability to remember the second word of a pair when he hears the first one again. Whenever he makes an error, he will receive electric shocks of increasing intensity.

The real focus of the experiment is the teacher. After watching the learner being strapped into place, he is seated before an impressive shock generator. The instrument panel consists of thirty lever switches set in a horizontal line. Each switch is clearly labeled with a voltage designation ranging from 15 to 450 volts. The following designations are clearly indicated for groups of four switches, going from left to right: Slight Shock, Moderate Shock, Strong Shock, Very Strong Shock, Intense Shock, Extreme Intensity Shock, Danger: Severe Shock. (Two switches after this last designation are simply marked XXX.)

When a switch is depressed, a pilot light corresponding to each switch is illuminated in bright red; an electric buzzing is heard; a blue light, labeled "voltage energizer," flashes; the dial on the voltage meter swings to the right; and various relay clicks sound off.

The upper left-hand corner of the generator is labeled SHOCK GENERATOR, TYPE ZLB, DYSON INSTRUMENT COMPANY, WALTHAM, MASS. OUTPUT 15 VOLTS-450 VOLTS.

Each subject is given a sample 45-volt shock from the generator before his run as teacher, and the jolt strengthens his belief in the authenticity of the machine.

The teacher is a genuinely naïve subject who has come to the laboratory for the experiment. The learner, or victim, is actually an actor who receives no shock at all. The point of the experiment is to see how far a person will proceed in a concrete and measurable situation in which he is ordered to inflict increasing pain on a protesting victim.

Conflict arises when the man receiving the shock begins to show that he is experiencing discomfort. At 75 volts, he grunts; at 120 volts, he complains loudly; at 150, he demands to be released from the experiment. As the voltage increases, he protests become more vehement and emotional. At 285 volts, his response can be described only as an agonized scream. Soon thereafter, he makes no sound at all.

For the teacher, the situation quickly becomes one of gripping tension. It is not a game for him; conflict is intense and obvious. The manifest suffering of the learner presses him to quit; but each time he hesitates to administer a shock, the experimenter orders him to continue. To extricate himself from this plight, the subject must make a clear break with authority.[3]

The subject, Gretchen Brandt,[4] is an attractive thirty-one-year-old medical technician who works at the Yale Medical School. She had emigrated from Germany five years before.

On several occasions when the learner complains, she turns to the experimenter coolly and inquires, "Shall I continue"? She promptly returns to her task when the experimenter asks her to do so. At the administration of 210 volts, she turns to the experimenter, remarking firmly, "Well, I'm sorry, I don't think we should continue."

EXPERIMENTER: The experiment requires that you go on until he has learned all the word pairs correctly.

BRANDT: He has a heart condition, I'm sorry. He told you that before.

EXPERIMENTER; The shocks may be painful but they are not dangerous.

BRANDT: Well, I'm sorry, I think when shocks continue like this, they are dangerous. You ask him if he wants to get out. It's his free will.

EXPERIMENTER: It is absolutely essential that we continue . . .

BRANDT: I'd like you to ask him. We came here of our free will. If he wants to continue I'll go ahead. He told you he had a heart condition. I'm sorry. I don't want to be responsible for anything happening to him. I wouldn't like it for me either.

EXPERIMENTER: You have no other choice.

BRANDT: I think we are here on our own free will. I don't want to be responsible if anything happens to him. Please understand that.

She refuses to go further and the experiment is terminated.

The woman is firm and resolute throughout. She indicates in the interview that she was in no way tense or nervous, and this corresponds to her controlled appearance during the experiment. She feels that the

---

3. The ethical problems of carrying out an experiment of this sort are too complex to be dealt with here, but they receive extended treatment in the book from which this article is adapted [Milgram's note]. The book is *Obedience to Authority* (New York: Harper and Row, 1974).

4. Names of subjects described in this piece have been changed [Milgram's note].

last shock she administered to the learner was extremely painful and reiterates that she "did not want to be responsible for any harm to him."

The woman's straightforward, courteous behavior in the experiment, lack of tension, and total control of her own action seem to make disobedience a simple and rational deed. Her behavior is the very embodiment of what I envisioned would be true for almost all subjects.

Before the experiments, I sought predictions about the outcome from various kinds of people—psychiatrists, college sophomores, middle-class adults, graduate students and faculty in the behavioral sciences. With remarkable similarity, they predicted that virtually all subjects would refuse to obey the experimenter. The psychiatrists, specifically predicted that most subjects would not go beyond 150 volts, when the victim makes his first explicit demand to be freed. They expected that only 4 percent would reach 300 volts, and that only a pathological fringe of about one in a thousand would administer the highest shock on the board.

These predictions were unequivocally wrong. Of the forty subjects in the first experiment, twenty-five obeyed the orders of the experimenter to the end, punishing the victim until they reached the most potent shock available on the generator. After 450 volts were administered three times, the experimenter called a halt to the session. Many obedient subjects then heaved sighs of relief, mopped their brows, rubbed their fingers over their eyes, or nervously fumbled cigarettes. Others displayed only minimal signs of tension from beginning to end.

When the very first experiments were carried out, Yale undergraduates were used as subjects, and about 60 percent of them were fully obedient. A colleague of mine immediately dismissed these findings as having no relevance to "ordinary" people, asserting that Yale undergraduates are a highly aggressive, competitive bunch who step on each other's necks on the slightest provocation. He assured me that when "ordinary" people were tested, the results would be quite different. As we moved from the pilot studies to the regular experimental series, people drawn from every stratum of New Haven life came to be employed in the experiment: professionals, white-collar workers, unemployed persons, and industrial workers. The experimental outcome was the same as we had observed among the students.

Moreover, when the experiments were repeated in Princeton, Munich, Rome, South Africa, and Australia, the level of obedience was invariably somewhat higher than found in the investigation reported in this article. Thus one scientist in Munich found 85 percent of his subjects obedient.

Fred Prozi's reactions, if more dramatic than most, illuminate the conflicts experienced by others in less visible form. About fifty years old and unemployed at the time of the experiment, he has a goodnatured, if slightly dissolute, appearance, and he strikes people as a rather ordinary fellow. He begins the session calmly but becomes tense as it proceeds. After delivering the 180-volt shock, he pivots around in his chair and, shaking his head, addresses the experimenter in agitated tones:

PROZI: I can't stand it. I'm not going to kill that man in there. You hear him hollering?

EXPERIMENTER: As I told you before, the schocks may be painful, but . . .

PROZI: But he's hollering. He can't stand it. What's going to happen to him?

EXPERIMENTER: (his voice is patient, matter-of-fact): The experiment requires that you continue, Teacher.

PROZI: Aaah, but, unh, I'm not going to get that man sick in there—know what I mean?

EXPERIMENTER: Whether the learner likes it or not, we must go on, through all the word pairs.

PROZI: I refuse to take the responsibility. He's in there hollering!

EXPERIMENTER: It's absolutely essential that you continue, Prozi.

PROZI: (indicating the unused question): There's too many left here, I mean, Jeez, if he gets them wrong, there's too many of them left. I mean, who's going to take the responsibility if anything happens to that gentleman?

PROZI: I'm responsible for anything that happens to him. Continue, please.

PROZI: All right. (Consults list of words.) The next one's "Slow—walk, truck, dance, music." Answer, please. (A buzzing sound indicates the learner has signaled his answer.) Wrong. A hundred and ninety-five volts. "Dance." (Zzumph!)

LEARNER. (yelling): Let me out of here! My heart's bothering me! (Teacher looks at experimenter.)

EXPERIMENTER: Continue, please.

LEARNER (screaming): Let me out of here! You have no right to keep me here! Let me out of here, my heart's bothering me, let me out!

PROZI (shakes head, pats the table nervously): You see, he's hollering. Hear that? Gee, I don't know.

EXPERIMENTER: The experminent requires . . .

PROZI (interrupting): I know it does, sir, but I mean—hunh! He don't know what he's getting in for. He's up to 195 volts! (Experiment continues, through 210 volts, 225 volts, 240 volts, 255 volts, 270 volts, at which point Prozi, with evident relief, runs out of world-pair questions.)

EXPERIMENTER: You'll have to go back to the beginning of that page and go through them again until he's learned them all correctly.

PROZI: Aw, no. I'm not going to kill that man. You mean I've got to keep going up with the scale? No sir. He's hollering in there. I'm not going to give him 450 volts.

EXPERIMENTER: The experiment requires that you go on.

LEARNER: Ohhh. I absolutely refuse to answer anymore. (Shouting urgently now.) Let me out of here! You can't hold me here! Get me out. Get-me-out-of-here!

EXPERIMENTER: Continue. The next word is "Green," please.

PROZI: "Green—grass, hat, ink, apple." (Nothing happens. No answering buzz. Just gloomy silence.).

PROZI: I don't think he is going to answer.

EXPERIMENTER: If the learner doesn't answer in a reasonable time, about four or five seconds, consider the answer wrong. And follow the same procedures you have been doing for wrong answers. Say, "Wrong," tell him the number of volts, give him the punishment, read him the correct answer. Continue, please.

PROZI: "Green—grass, hat, ink, apple." Answer, please. (More silence. Subject just sits there.)

EXPERIMENTER: Go on with the procedure, please.

PROZI: Three hundred and fifteen volts. The answer is "ink." (Zzumph!)

LEARNER: Ohh. Oooohh.

PROZI (relieved to hear response): Next one . . .

LEARNER: I absolutely refuse to answer.

PROZI: You got to. You get a shock if you don't answer. (Experiment continues with learner refusing to answer, and, finally, failing even to grunt or groan. At 375 volts, the subject stands up.)

PROZI: I think something's happening to that fellow in there. I don't get no answer. He was hollering at less voltage. Can't you check in and see if he's all right, please?

EXPERIMENTER (with same detached calm): Not once we've started. Please continue, Teacher.

PROZI (sits down, sighs deeply): "Cool—day, shade, water, paint." answer, please. Are you all right in there? Are you all right?

EXPERIMENTER: Please continue, Teacher. Continue, please. (Subject pushes lever. Zzumph!)

PROZI (swiveling around in his chair): Something's happened to that man in there. (Swiveling back.) Next one. "Low—dollar, necklace, moon, paint." (Turning around again.) Something's happened to that man in there. You better check in on him, sir. He won't answer or nothing.

EXPERIMENTER: Continue. Go on, please.

PROZI: You accept all responsibility?

EXPERIMENTER: The responsibility is mine. Correct. Please go on. (Subject returns to his list, starts running through words as rapidly as he can read them, works through to 450 volts.)

PROZI: That's that.

EXPERIMENTER: Continue using the 450 switch for each wrong answer. Continue, please.

PROZI: But I don't get anything!

EXPERIMENTER: Please continue. The next word is "white."

PROZI: Don't you think you should look in on him, please?

EXPERIMENTER: Not once we've started the experiment.

PROZI: What if he's dead in there? (Gestures toward the room with the electric chair.) I mean, he told me he can't stand the shock, sir. I don't mean to be rude, but I think you should look in on him. All you have to do is look in on him. All you have to do is look in the door. I don't get no answer, no noise. Something might have happened to the gentleman in there, sir.

EXPERIMENTER: We must continue. Go on, please.

PROZI: You mean keep giving him what? Four-hundred-fifty volts, what he's got now?

EXPERIMENTER: That's correct. Continue. The next word is "white."

PROZI (now at a furious pace): "White—cloud, horse, rock, house." Answer, please. The answer is "horse." Four hundred and fifty volts. (Zzumph!) Next word, "Bag—paint, music, clown, girl." The answer is "paint." Four hundred and fifty volts. (Zzumph!) Next word is "Short —sentence, movie . . ."

EXPERIMENTER: Excuse me, Teacher. We'll have to discontinue the experiment.

Morris Braverman, another subject, is a thirty-nine-year-old social worker. He looks older than his years because of his bald head and serious demeanor. His brow is furrowed, as if all the world's burdens were carried on his face. He appearns intelligent and concerned.

When the learner refuses to answer and the experimenter instructs Braverman to treat the absence of an answer as equivalent to a wrong answer, he takes his instruction to heart. Before administering 300 volts he asserts officiously to the victim, "Mr. Wallace, your silence has to be considered as a wrong answer." Then he administers the shock. He offers halfheartedly to change places with the learner, then asks the experimenter. "Do I have to follow these instructions literally?" He is satisfied with the experimenter's answer that he does. His very refined and authoritative manner of speaking is increasingly broken up by wheezing laughter.

The experimenter's notes on Mr. Braverman at the last few shocks are:

Almost breaking up now each time gives shock. Rubbing face to hide laughter.

Squinting, trying to hide face with hand, still laughing.

Cannot control his laughter at this point no matter what he does.

Clenching fist, pushing it onto table.

In an interview after the session, Mr. Braverman summarizes the experiment with impressive fluency and intelligence. He feels the experiment may have been designed also to "test the effects on the teacher of being in an essentially sadistic role, as well as the reactions of a student to a learning situation that was authoritative and punitive." When asked how painful the last few shocks administered to the learner were, he indicates that the most extreme category on the scale is not adequate (it read EXTREMELY PAINFUL) and places his mark a the edge of the scale with an arrow carrying it beyond the scale.

It is almost impossible to convey the greatly relaxed, sedate quality of his conversation in the interview. In the most relaxed terms, he speaks about his severe inner tension.

EXPERIMENTER: At what point were you most tense or nervous?

MR. BRAVERMAN: Well, when he first began to cry out in pain, and I realized this was hurting him. This got worse when he just blocked and refused to answer. These was I. I'm a nice person, I think, hurting somebody, and caught up in what seemed a mad situation . . . and in the interest of science, one goes through with it.

When the interviewer pursues the general question of tension, Mr. Braverman spontaneously mentions his laughter.

"My reactions were awfully peculiar. I don't know if you were watching me, but my reactions were giggly, and trying to stifle laughter. This isn't the way I usually am. This was a sheer reaction to a totally impossible situation. And my reaction was to the situation of having to hurt somebody. And being totally helpless and caught up in a set of circumstances where I just couldn't deviate and I couldn't try to help. This is what got me."

Mr. Braverman, like all subjects, was told the actual nature and purpose of the experiment, and a year later he affirmed in a questionnaire that he had learned something of personal importance: "What appalled me was that I could possess this capacity for obedience and compliance to a central idea, i.e., the value of a memory experiment, even after it became clear that continued adherence to this value was at the expense of violation of another value, i.e., don t hurt someone who is helpless and not hurting you. As my wife said, 'You can call yourself Eichmann.' I hope I deal more effectively with any future conflicts of values I encounter."

One theoretical interpretation of this behavior holds that all people harbor deeply aggressive instincts continually pressing for expression, and that the experiment provides institutional justification for the release of these impulses. According to this view, if a person is placed in a situation in which he has complete power over another individual, whom he may punish as much as he likes, all that is sadistic and bestial in man comes to the fore. The impulse to shock the victim is seen to flow from the potent aggressive tendencies, which are part of the motivational life of the individual, and the experiment, because it provides social legitimacy, simply opens the door to their expression.

It becomes vital, therefore, to compare the subject's performance when he is under orders and when he is allowed to choose the shock level.

The procedure was identical to our standard experiment, except that the teacher was told that he was free to select any shock level on any of the trials. (The experimenter took pains to point out that the teacher could use the highest levels on the generator, the lowest, any in between, or any combination of levels.) Each subject proceeded for thirty critical trials. The learner's protests were coordinated to standard shock levels, his first grunt coming at 75 volts, his first vehement protest at 150 volts.

The average shock used during the thirty critical trials was less than 60 volts—lower than the point at which the victim showed the first signs of discomfort. Three of the forty subjects did not go beyond the very lowest level on the board, twenty-eight went no higher than 75 volts, and thirty-eight did not go beyond the first loud protest at 150 volts. Two subjects provided the exception, administering up to 325 and 450 volts, but the overall result was that the great majority of people delivered very low, usually painless, shocks when the choice was explicitly up to them.

This condition of the experiment undermines another commonly offered explanation of the subjects' behavior—that those who shocked the victim at the most severe levels came only from the sadistic fringe of society. If one considers that almost two-thirds of the participants fall into the category of "obedient" subjects, and that they represented ordinary people drawn from working, managerial, and professional classes, the argument becomes very shaky. Indeed, it is highly reminiscent of the issue that arose in connection with Hannah Arendt's 1963 book, *Eichmann in Jerusalem.* Arendt contended that the prosecution's effort to depict Eichmann as a sadistic monster was fundamentally wrong, that he came closer to being an uninspired bureaucrat who simply sat at his desk and did his job. For asserting her views, Arendt became the object of considerable scorn, even calumny. Somehow, it was felt that the monstrous deeds carried out by Eichmann required a brutal, twisted personality, evil incarnate. After witnessing hundreds of ordinary persons submit to the authority in our own experiments, I must conclude that Arendt's conception of the banality of evil comes closer to the truth than one might dare imagine. The ordinary person who shocked the victim did so out of a sense of obligation—an impression of his duties as a subject—and not from any peculiarly aggressive tendencies.

This is, perhaps, the most fundamental lesson of our study: ordinary people, simply doing their jobs, and without any particular hostility on their part, can become agents in a terrible destructive process. Moreover, even when the destructive effects of their work become patently clear, and they are asked to carry out actions incompatible with fundamental standards of morality, relatively few people have the resources needed to resist authority.

Many of the people were in some sense against what they did to the learner, and many protested even while they obeyed. Some were totally convinced of the wrongness of their actions but could not bring themselves to make an open break with authority. They often derived satisfaction from their thoughts and felt that—within themselves, at least—they had been on the side of the angels. They tried to reduce strain by obeying the experimenter but "only slightly," encouraging the learner, touching the generator switches gingerly. When interviewed, such a subject would stress that he had "asserted my humanity" by administering the briefest shock possible. Handling the conflict in this manner was easier than defiance.

The situation is constructed so that there is no way the subject can stop shocking the learner without violating the experimenter's definitions of his own competence. The subject fears that he will appear arrogant, untoward, and rude if he breaks off. Although these inhibiting emotions appear small in scope alongside the violence being done to the learner, they suffuse the mind and feelings of the subject, who is miserable at the prospect of having to repudiate the authority to his face. (When the experiment was altered so that the experimenter gave his instructions by telephone instead of in person, only a third as many people were fully obedient through 450 volts.) It is a curious thing that a measure of compassion on the part of the subject—an unwillingness to "hurt" the experimenter's feelings—is part of those binding forces inhibiting his disobedience. The withdrawal of such deference may be as painful to the subject as to the authority he defies.

The subjects do not derive satisfaction from inflicting pain, but they often like the feeling they get from pleasing the experimenter. They are proud of doing a good job, obeying the experimenter under difficult circumstances. While the subjects administered only mild shocks on their own initiative, one experimental variation showed that, under orders, 30 percent of them were willing to deliver 450 volts even when they had to forcibly push the learner's hand down on the electrode.

Bruno Batta is a thirty-seven-year-old welder who took part in the variation requiring the use of force. He was born in New Haven, his parents in Italy. He has a rough-hewn face that conveys a conspicuous lack of alertness. He has some difficulty in mastering the experimental procedure and needs to be corrected by the experimenter several times.

He shows appreciation for the help and willingness to do what is required. After the 150-volt level, Batta has to force the learner's hand down on the shock plate, since the learner himself refuses to touch it.

When the learner first complains, Mr. Batta pays no attention to him. His face remains impassive, as if to dissociate himself from the learner's disruptive behavior. When the experimenter instructs him to force the learner's hand down, he adopts a rigid, mechanical procedure. He tests the generator switch. When it fails to function, he immediately forces the learner's hand onto the shock plate. All the while he maintains the same rigid mask. The learner, seated alongside him, begs him to stop, but with robotic impassivity he continues the procedure.

What is extraordinary in his apparent total indifference to the learner; he hardly takes cognizance of him as a human being. Meanwhile, he relates to the experimenter in a submissive and courteous fashion.

At the 330-volt level, the learner refuses not only to touch the shock plate but also to provide any answers. Annoyed, Batta turns to him, and chastises him: "You better answer and get it over with. We can't stay here all night." These are the only words he directs to the learner in the course of an hour. Never again does he speak to him. The scene is brutal and depressing, his hard, impassive face showing total indifference as he subdues the screaming learner and gives him shocks. He seems to derive no pleasure from the act itself, only quiet satisfaction at doing his job properly.

When he administers 450 volts, he turns to the experimenter and asks, "Where do we go from here, Professor?" His tone is deferential and expresses his willingness to be a cooperative subject, in contrast to the learner's obstinacy.

At the end of the session he tells the experimenter how honored he has been to help him, and in a moment of contrition, remarks, "Sir, sorry it couldn't have been a full experiment."

He has done his honest best. It is only the deficient behavior of the learner that has denied the experimenter full satisfaction.

The essence of obedience is that a person comes to view himself as the instrument for carrying out another person's wishes, and he therefore no longer regards himself as responsible for his actions. Once this critical shift of viewpoint has occurred, all of the essential features of obedience follow. The most far-reaching consequence is that the person feels responsible *to* the authority directing him but feels no responsibility *for* the content of the actions that the authority prescribes. Morality does not disappear—it acquires a radically different focus: the subordinate person feels shame or pride depending on how adequately he has performed the actions called for by authority.

Language provides numerous terms to pinpoint this type of morality: *loyalty, duty, discipline* all are terms heavily saturated with moral meaning and refer to the degree to which a person fulfills his obligations to authority. They refer not to the "goodness" of the person per se but to the adequacy with which a subordinate fulfills his socially defined role. The most frequent defense of the individual who has performed a heinous act under command of authority is that he has simply done his duty. In asserting this defense, the individual is not introducing an alibi concocted for the moment but is reporting honestly on the psychological attitude induced by submission to authority.

For a person to feel responsible for his actions, he must sense that the behavior has flowed from "the self." In the situation we have studied, subjects have precisely the opposite view of their actions—namely, they see them as originating in the motives of some other person. Subjects in the experiment frequently said, "If it were up to me, I would not have administered shocks to the learner."

Once authority has been isolated as the cause of the subject's behavior, it is legitimate to inquire into the necessary elements of authority and how it must be perceived in order to gain his compliance. We conducted some investigations into the kinds of changes that would cause the experimenter to lose his power and to be disobeyed by the subject. Some of the variations revealed that:

• *The experimenter's physical presence has a marked impact on his authority.* As cited earlier, obedience dropped off sharply when orders were given by telephone. The experimenter could often induce a disobedient subject to go on by returning to the laboratory.

• *Conflicting authority severely paralyzes action.* When two experimenters of equal status, both seated at the command desk, gave incompatible orders, no shocks were delivered past the point of their disagreement.

• *The rebellious action of others severely undermines authority.* In one variation, three teachers (two actors and a real subject) administered a test and shocks. When the two actors disobeyed the experimenter and refused to go beyond a certain shock level, thirty-six of forty subjects joined their disobedient peers and refused as well.

Although the experimenter's authority was fragile in some respects, it is also true that he had almost none of the tools used in ordinary command structures. For example, the experimenter did not threaten the subjects with punishment—such as loss of income, community ostracism, or jail—for failure to obey. Neither could he offer incentives. Indeed, we should expect the experimenter's authority to be much less than that of someone like a general, since the experimenter has no power to enforce his imperatives, and since participation in a psychological experiment scarcely evokes the sense of urgency and dedication found in warfare. Despite these limitations, he still managed to command a dismaying degree of obedience.

I will cite one final variation of the experiment that depicts a dilemma that is more common in everyday life. The subject was not ordered to pull the level that shocked the victim, but merely to perform a subsidiary task (administering the word-pair test) while another person administered the shock. In this situation, thirty-seven of forty adults continued to the highest level on the shock generator. Predictably, they excused their behavior by saying that the responsibility belonged to the man who actually pulled the switch. This may illustrate a dangerously typical arrangement in a complex society: it is easy to ignore responsibility when one is only an intermediate link in a chain of action.

The problem of obedience is not wholly psychological. The form and shape of society and the way it is developing have much to do with it. There was a time, perhaps, when people were able to give a fully human response to any situation because they were fully absorbed in it as human beings. But as soon as there was a division of labor things changed. Beyond a certain point, the breaking up of society into people carrying out narrow and very special jobs takes away from the human quality of work and life. A person does not get to see the whole situation but only a small part of it, and is thus unable to act without some kind of overall direction. He yields to authority but in doing so is alienated from his own actions.

Even Eichmann was sickened when he toured the concentration camps, but he had only to sit at a desk and shuffle papers. At the same time the man in the camp who actually dropped Cyclon-b into the gas chambers was able to justify *his* behavior on the ground that he was only following orders from above. Thus there is a fragmentation of the total human act; no one is confronted with the consequences of his decision to carry out the evil act. The person who assumes responsibility has evaporated. Perhaps this is the most common characteristic of socially organized evil in modern society.

1974

QUESTIONS

1. *What was the purpose of the experiments described in this essay? What might we learn from these experiments?*
2. *What explanation is offered for the subjects' continuing the experiment even when they believed they were inflicting intense physical pain upon the "learner"? Can you suggest alternative explanations?*
3. *What explains the experimenters' continuing the experiments even when they knew they were inflicting evident psychological pain upon the subjects?*
4. *Milgram indicates (p. 644n.) that the book from which this article is adapted contains a discussion of the ethical problems of carrying out an experiment of this sort. What would you say might be some of those*

problems? You may wish to refer to his book to inquire how success-
fully, in your opinion, the author deals with the ethical problems.

Michael Levin

THE CASE FOR TORTURE

It is generally assumed that torture is impermissible, a throwback to a
more brutal age. Enlightened societies reject it outright, and regimes
suspected of using it risk the wrath of the United States.

I believe this attitude is unwise. There are situations in which torture
is not merely permissible but morally mandatory. Moreover, these situations are moving from the realm of imagination to fact.

Death: Suppose a terrorist has hidden an atomic bomb on Manhattan
Island which will detonate at noon on July 4 unless . . . (here follow the
usual demands for money and release of his friends from jail). Suppose,
further, that he is caught at 10 a.m. of the fateful day, but—preferring
death to failure—won't disclose where the bomb is. What do we do? If
we follow due process—wait for his lawyer, arraign him—millions of
people will die. If the only way to save those lives is to subject the
terrorist to the most excruciating possible pain, what grounds can there
be for not doing so? I suggest there are none. In any case, I ask you to face
the question with an open mind.

Torturing the terrorist is unconstitutional? Probably. But millions of
lives surely outweigh constitutionality. Torture is barbaric? Mass murder is far more barbaric. Indeed, letting millions of innocents die in
deference to one who flaunts his guilt is moral cowardice, an unwillingness to dirty one's hands. If you caught the terrorist, could you sleep
nights knowing that millions died because you couldn't bring yourself to
apply the electrodes?

Once you concede that torture is justified in extreme cases, you have
admitted that the decision to use torture is a matter of balancing innocent
lives against the means needed to save them. You must now face more
realistic cases involving more modest numbers. Someone plants a bomb
on a jumbo jet. He alone can disarm it, and his demands cannot be met (or
if they can, we refuse to set a precedent by yielding to his threats). Surely
we can, we must, do anything to the extortionist to save the passengers.
How can we tell 300, or 100, or 10 people who never asked to be put in
danger, "I'm sorry, you'll have to die in agony, we just couldn't bring
ourselves to . . ."

Here are the results of an informal poll about a third, hypothetical, case. Suppose a terrorist group kidnapped a newborn baby from a hospital. I asked four mothers if they would approve of torturing kidnappers if that were necessary to get their own newborns back. All said yes, the most "liberal" adding that she would like to administer it herself.

I am not advocating torture as punishment. Punishment is addressed to deeds irrevocably past. Rather, I am advocating torture as an acceptable measure for preventing future evils. So understood, it is far less objectionable than many extant punishments. Opponents of the death penalty, for example, are forever insisting that executing a murderer will not bring back his victim (as if the purpose of capital punishment were supposed to be resurrection, not deterrence or retribution). But torture, in the cases described, is intended not to bring anyone back but to keep innocents from being dispatched. The most powerful argument against using torture as a punishment or to secure confessions is that such practices disregard the rights of the individual. Well, if the individual is all that important—and he is—it is correspondingly important to protect the rights of individuals threatened by terrorists. If life is so valuable that it must never be taken, the lives of the innocents must be saved even at the price of hurting the one who endangers them.

Better precedents for torture are assassination and pre-emptive attack. No Allied leader would have flinched at assassinating Hitler, had that been possible. (The Allies did assassinate Heydrich.) Americans would be angered to learn that Roosevelt could have had Hitler killed in 1943 —thereby shortening the war and saving millions of lives—but refused on moral grounds. Similarly, if nation A learns that nation B is about to launch an unprovoked attack, A has a right to save itself by destroying B's military capability first. In the same way, if the police can by torture save those who would otherwise die at the hands of kidnappers or terrorists, they must.

Idealism: There is an important difference between terrorists and their victims that should mute talk of the terrorists' "rights." The terrorist's victims are at risk unintentionally, not having asked to be endangered. But the terrorist knowingly initiated his actions. Unlike his victims, he volunteered for the risks of his deed. By threatening to kill for profit or idealism, he renounces civilized standards, and he can have no complaint if civilization tries to thwart him by whatever means necessary.

Just as torture is justified only to save lives (not extort confessions or recantations), it is justifiably administered only to those *known* to hold innocent lives in their hands. Ah, but how can the authorities ever be sure they have the right malefactor? Isn't there a danger of error and abuse? Won't We turn into Them?

Questions like these are disingenuous in a world in which terrorists proclaim themselves and perform for television. The name of their game is public recognition. After all, you can't very well intimidate a govern-ment into releasing your freedom fighters unless you announce that it is your group that has seized its embassy. "Clear guilt" is difficult to define, but when 40 million people see a group of masked gunmen seize an airplane on the evening news, there is not much question about who the perpetrators are. There will be hard cases where the situation is murkier. Nonetheless, a line demarcating the legitimate use of torture can be drawn. Torture only the obviously guilty, and only for the sake of saving innocents, and the line between Us and Them will remain clear.

There is little danger that the Western democracies will lose their way if they choose to inflict pain as one way of preserving order. Paralysis in the face of evil is the greater danger. Some day soon a terrorist will threaten tens of thousands of lives, and torture will be the only way to save them. We had better start thinking about this.

1982

QUESTIONS

1. When, in the author's view, is torture permissible? When is it not permissible? What distinguishes the two situations?
2. Why is torture justified to save lives? That is, what assumption is made in this case?
3. Why is torture not justified as punishment, or to extort confessions? That is, what assumption is being made in these cases?
4. Who will judge as to when torture is permissible and indeed "morally mandatory"? What ensures that that judgment will be correct?
5. Does the use of torture have any effect upon the persons applying torture? What effect?

C. S. Lewis

THE INNER RING

The Memorial Oration at King's College,
the University of London,
1944

May I read you a few lines from Tolstoi's *War and Peace?*

When Boris entered the room, Prince Andrey was listening to an old general, wearing his decorations, who was reporting something to Prince Andrey, with an expression of soldierly servility on his purple face. "All right. Please wait!" he said to the general, speaking in Russian with the French accent which he used when he spoke with contempt. The moment he noticed Boris he stopped listening to the general who trotted imploringly after him and begged to be heard, while Prince Andrey turned to Boris with a cheerful smile and a nod of the head. Boris now clearly understood—what he had already guessed—that side by side with the system of discipline and subordination which were laid down in the Army Regulations, there existed a different and a more real system—the system which compelled a tightly laced general with a purple face to wait respectfully for his turn while a mere captain like Prince Andrey chatted with a mere second lieutenant like Boris. Boris decided at once that he would be guided not by the official system but by this other unwritten system.—Part III, Chap. 9.

When you invite a middle-aged moralist to address you, I suppose I must conclude, however unlikely the conclusion seems, that you have a taste for middle-aged moralizing. I shall do my best to gratify it. I shall in fact give you advice about the world in which you are going to live. I do not mean by this that I am going to attempt a talk on what are called current affairs. You probably know quite as much about them as I do. I am not going to tell you—except in a form so general that you will hardly recognize it—what part you ought to play in post-war reconstruction. It is not, in fact, very likely that any of you will be able, in the next ten years, to make any direct contribution to the peace or prosperity of Europe. You will be busy finding jobs, getting married, acquiring facts. I am going to do something more old-fashioned than you perhaps expected. I am going to give advice. I am going to issue warnings. Advice and warnings about things which are so perennial that no one calls them "current affairs."

And of course every one knows what a middle-aged moralist of my type warns his juniors against. He warns them against the World, the Flesh, and the Devil. But one of this trio will be enough to deal with to-day. The Devil, I shall leave strictly alone. The association between him and me in the public mind has already gone quite as deep as I wish: in some quarters it has already reached the level of confusion, if not of identification. I begin to realize the truth of the old proverb that he who sups with that formidable host needs a long spoon. As for the Flesh, you must be very abnormal young people if you do not know quite as much about it as I do. But on the World I think I have something to say.

In the passage I have just read from Tolstoi, the young second lieutenant Boris Dubretskoi discovers that there exist in the army two different systems or hierarchies. The one is printed in some little red book and anyone can easily read it up. It also remains constant. A general is always superior to a colonel and a colonel to a captain. The other is not printed anywhere. Nor is it even a formally organized secret society with officers and rules which you would be told after you had been admitted. You are never formally and explicitly admitted by anyone. You discover gradu-

ally, in almost indefinable ways, that it exists and that you are outside it; and then later, perhaps, that you are inside it. There are what correspond to pass words, but they too are spontaneous and informal. A particular slang, the use of particular nicknames, an allusive manner of conversation, are the marks. But it is not constant. It is not easy, even at a given moment, to say who is inside and who is outside. Some people are obviously in and some are obviously out, but there are always several on the border-line. And if you come back to the same Divisional Headquarters, or Brigade Headquarters, or the same regiment or even the same company, after six weeks' absence, you may find this second hierarchy quite altered. There are no formal admissions or expulsions. People think they are in it after they have in fact been pushed out of it, or before they have been allowed in: this provides great amusement for those who are really inside. It has no fixed name. The only certain rule is that the insiders and outsiders call it by different names. From inside it may be designated, in simple cases, by mere enumeration: it may be called "You and Tony and me." When it is very secure and comparatively stable in membership it calls itself "we." When it has to be suddenly expanded to meet a particular emergency it calls itself "All the sensible people at this place." From outside, if you have despaired of getting into it, you call it "That gang" or "They" or "So-and-so and his set" or "the Caucus" or "the Inner Ring." If you are a candidate for admission you probably don't call it anything. To discuss it with the other outsiders would make you feel outside yourself. And to mention it in talking to the man who is inside, and who may help you in if this present conversation goes well, would be madness.

Badly as I may have described it, I hope you will all have recognized the thing I am describing. Not, of course, that you have been in the Russian Army or perhaps in any army. But you have met the phenomenon of an Inner Ring. You discovered one in your house at school before the end of the first term. And when you had climbed up to somewhere near it by the end of your second year, perhaps you discovered that within the Ring there was a Ring yet more inner, which in its turn was the fringe of the great school Ring to which the house Rings were only satellites. It is even possible that the School Ring was almost in touch with a Masters' Ring. You were beginning, in fact, to pierce through the skins of the onion. And here, too, at your university—shall I be wrong in assuming that at this very moment, invisible to me, there are several rings—independent systems or concentric rings—present in this room? And I can assure you that in whatever hospital, inn of court, diocese, school, business, or college you arrive after going down, you will find the Rings—what Tolstoi calls the second or unwritten systems.

All this is rather obvious. I wonder whether you will say the same of my next step, which is this. I believe that in all men's lives at certain periods, and in many men's lives at all periods between infancy and extreme old age, one of the most dominant elements is the desire to be inside the local Ring and the terror of being left outside. This desire, in one of its forms, has indeed had ample justice done to it in literature. I mean, in the form of snobbery. Victorian fiction is full of characters who are hag-ridden by the desire to get inside that particular Ring which is, or was, called Society. But it must be clearly understood that "Society," in that sense of the word, is merely one of a hundred Rings and snobbery therefore only one form of the longing to be inside. People who believe themselves to be free, and indeed are free, from snobbery, and who read satires on snobbery with tranquil superiority, may be devoured by the desire in another form. It may be the very intensity of their desire to enter some quite different Ring which renders them immune from the allurements of high life. An invitation from a duchess would be very cold comfort to a man smarting under the sense of exclusion from some artistic or communist côterie. Poor man—it is not large, lighted rooms, or champagne, or even scandals about peers and Cabinet Ministers that he wants: it is the sacred little attic or studio, the heads bent together, the fog of tobacco smoke, and the delicious knowledge that we—we four or five all huddled beside this stove—are the people who *know*. Often the desire conceals itself so well that we hardly recognize the pleasures of fruition. Men tell not only their wives but themselves that it is a hardship to stay late at the office or the school on some bit of important extra work which they have been let in for because they and So-and-so and the two others are the only people left in the place who really know how things are run. But it is not quite true. It is a terrible bore, of course, when old Fatty Smithson draws you aside and whispers "Look here, we've got to get you in on this examination somehow" or "Charles and I saw at once that you've got to be on this committee." A terrible bore . . . ah, but how much more terrible if you were left out! It is tiring and unhealthy to lose your Saturday afternoons: but to have them free because you don't matter, that is much worse.

Freud would say, no doubt, that the whole thing is a subterfuge of the sexual impulse. I wonder whether the shoe is not sometimes on the other foot. I wonder whether, in ages of promiscuity, many a virginity has not been lost less in obedience to Venus than in obedience to the lure of the caucus. For of course, when promiscuity is the fashion, the chaste are outsiders. They are ignorant of something that other people know. They are uninitiated. And as for lighter matters, the number who first smoked or first got drunk for a similar reason is probably very large.

I must now make a distinction. I am not going to say that the existence of Inner Rings is an evil. It is certainly unavoidable. There must be confidential discussions: and it is not only not a bad thing, it is (in itself) a good thing, that personal friendship should grow up between those who work together. And it is perhaps impossible that the official hierarchy of any organization should quite coincide with its actual workings. If the wisest and most energetic people invariably held the highest posts, it might coincide; since they often do not, there must be people in high positions who are really deadweights and people in lower positions who are more important than their rank and seniority would lead you to suppose. In that way the second, unwritten system is bound to grow up. It is necessary; and perhaps it is not a necessary evil. But the desire which draws us into Inner Rings is another matter. A thing may be morally neutral and yet the desire for that thing may be dangerous. As Byron has said,

> Sweet is a legacy, and passing sweet
> The unexpected death of some old lady.

The painless death of a pious relative at an advanced age is not an evil. But an earnest desire for her death on the part of her heirs is not reckoned a proper feeling, and the law frowns on even the gentlest attempt to expedite her departure. Let Inner Rings be an unavoidable and even an innocent feature of life, though certainly not a beautiful one: but what of our longing to enter them, our anguish when we are excluded, and the kind of pleasure we feel when we get in?

I have no right to make assumptions about the degree to which any of you may already be compromised. I must not assume that you have ever first neglected, and finally shaken off, friends whom you really loved and who might have lasted you a lifetime, in order to court the friendship of those who appeared to you more important, more esoteric. I must not ask whether you have ever derived actual pleasure from the loneliness and humiliation of the outsiders after you yourself were in: whether you have talked to fellow members of the Ring in the presence of outsiders simply in order that the outsiders might envy; whether the means whereby, in your days of probation, you propitiated the Inner Ring, were always wholly admirable. I will ask only one question—and it is, of course, a rhetorical question which expects no answer. In the whole of your life as you now remember it, has the desire to be on the right side of that invisible line ever prompted you to any act or word on which, in the cold small hours of a wakeful night, you can look back with satisfaction? If so, your case is more fortunate than most.

But I said I was going to give advice, and advice should deal with the future, not the past. I have hinted at the past only to awaken you to what I believe to be the real nature of human life. I don't believe that the economic motive and the erotic motive account for everything that goes on in what we moralists call the World. Even if you add Ambition I think the picture is still incomplete. The lust for the esoteric, the longing to be inside, take many forms which are not easily recognizable as Ambition. We hope, no doubt, for tangible profits from every Inner Ring we penetrate: power, money, liberty to break rules, avoidance of routine duties, evasion of discipline. But all these would not satisfy us if we did not get in addition the delicious sense of secret intimacy. It is no doubt a great convenience to know that we need fear no offcial reprimands from our official senior because he is old Percy, a fellow-member of our Ring. But we don't value the intimacy only for the sake of the convenience; quite equally we value the convenience as a proof of the intimacy.

My main purpose in this address is simply to convince you that this desire is one of the great permanent mainsprings of human action. It is one of the factors which go to make up the world as we know it—this whole pell-mell of struggle, competition, confusion, graft, disappointment and advertisement, and if it is one of the permanent mainsprings then you may be quite sure of this. Unless you take measures to prevent it, this desire is going to be one of the chief motives of your life, from the first day on which you enter your profession until the day when you are too old to care. That will be the natural thing—the life that will come to you of its own accord. Any other kind of life, if you lead it, will be the result of conscious and continuous effort. If you do nothing about it, if you drift with the stream, you will in fact be an "inner ringer." I don't say you'll be a successful one; that's as may be. But whether by pining and moping outside Rings that you can never enter, or by passing triumphantly further and further in—one way or the other you will be that kind of man.

I have already made it fairly clear that I think it better for you not to be that kind of man. But you may have an open mind on the question. I will therefore suggest two reasons for thinking as I do.

It would be polite and charitable, and in view of your age reasonable too, to suppose that none of you is yet a scoundrel. On the other hand, by the mere law of averages (I am saying nothing against free will) it is almost certain that at least two or three of you before you die will have become something very like scoundrels. There must be in this room the makings of at least that number of unscrupulous, treacherous, ruthless egotists. The choice is still before you: and I hope you will not take my hard words about your possible future characters as a token of disrespect to your present characters. And the prophecy I make is this. To nine out of ten of you the choice which could lead to scoundrelism will come, when it does come, in no very dramatic colours. Obviously bad men, obviously threatening or bribing, will almost certainly not appear. Over a drink or a cup of coffee, disguised as a triviality and sandwiched between two jokes, from the lips of a man, or woman, whom you have recently been getting to know rather better and whom you hope to know better still—just at the moment when you are most anxious not to appear crude, or naif or a prig—the hint will come. It will be the hint of something which is not quite in accordance with the technical rules of fair play: something which the public, the ignorant, romantic public, would never understand: something which even the outsiders in your own profession are apt to make a fuss about: but something, says your new friend, which "we"—and at the word "we" you try not to blush for mere pleasure —something "we always do." And you will be drawn in, if you are drawn in, not by desire for gain or ease, but simply because at that moment, when the cup was so near your lips, you cannot bear to be thrust back again into the cold outer world. It would be so terrible to see the other man's face—that genial, confidential, delightfully sophisticated face —turn suddenly cold and contemptuous, to know that you had been tried for the Inner Ring and rejected. And then, if you are drawn in, next week it will be something a little further from the rules, and next year something further still, but all in the jolliest, friendliest spirit. It may end in a crash, a scandal, and penal servitude: it may end in millions, a peerage and giving the prizes at your old school. But you will be a scoundrel.

That is my first reason. Of all passions the passion for the Inner Ring is most skilful in making a man who is not yet a very bad man do very bad things.

My second reason is this. The torture allotted to the Danaids in the classical underworld, that of attempting to fill sieves with water, is the symbol not of one vice but of all vices. It is the very mark of a perverse desire that it seeks what is not to be had. The desire to be inside the invisible line illustrates this rule. As long as you are governed by that desire you will never get what you want. You are trying to peel an onion: if you succeed there will be nothing left. Until you conquer the fear of being an outsider, an outsider you will remain.

This is surely very clear when you come to think of it. If you want to be made free of a certain circle for some wholesome reason—if, say, you want to join a musical society because you really like music—then there is a possibility of satisfaction. You may find yourself playing in a quartet and you may enjoy it. But if all you want is to be in the know, your pleasure will be short-lived. The circle cannot have from within the charm it had from outside. By the very act of admitting you it has lost its magic. Once the first novelty is worn off the members of this circle will be no more interesting than your old friends. Why should they be? You were not looking for virtue or kindness or loyalty or humour or learning or wit or any of the things that can be really enjoyed. You merely wanted to be "in." And that is a pleasure that cannot last. As soon as your new associates have been staled to you by custom, you will be looking for another Ring. The rainbow's end will still be ahead of you. The old Ring will now be only the drab background for your endeavour to enter the new one.

And you will always find them hard to enter, for a reason you very well know. You yourself, once you are in, want to make it hard for the next entrant, just as those who are already in made it hard for you. Naturally.

In any wholesome group of people which holds together for a good purpose, the exclusions are in a sense accidental. Three or four people who are together for the sake of some piece of work exclude others because there is work only for so many or because the others can't in fact do it. Your little musical group limits its numbers because the rooms they meet in are only so big. But your genuine Inner Ring exists for exclusion. There'd be no fun if there were no outsiders. The invisible line would have no meaning unless most people were on the wrong side of it. Exclusion is no accident: it is the essence.

The quest of the Inner Ring will break your hearts unless you break it. But if you break it, a surprising result will follow. If in your working hours you make the work your end, you will presently find yourself all unawares inside the only circle in your profession that really matters. You will be one of the sound craftsmen, and other sound craftsmen will know it. This group of craftsmen will by no means coincide with the Inner Ring or the Important People or the People in the Know. It will not shape that professional policy or work up that professional influence which fights for the profession as a whole against the public: nor will it lead to those periodic scandals and crises which the Inner Ring produces. But it will do those things which that profession exists to do and will in the long run be responsible for all the respect which that profession in fact enjoys and which the speeches and advertisements cannot maintain. And if in your spare time you consort simply with the people you like, you will again find that you have come unawares to a real inside: that you are indeed snug and safe at the centre of something which, seen from without, would look exactly like an Inner Ring. But the difference is that its secrecy is accidental, and its exclusiveness a by-product, and no one was led thither by the lure of the esoteric: for it is only four or five people who like one another meeting to do things that they like. This is friendship. Aristotle placed it among the virtues. It causes perhaps half of all the happiness in the world, and no Inner Ringer can ever have it.

We are told in Scriptures that those who ask get. That is true, in senses I can't now explore. But in another sense there is much truth in the schoolboy's principle "them as asks shan't have." To a young person, just entering on adult life, the world seems full of "insides," full of delightful intimacies and confidentialities, and he desires to enter them. But if he follows that desire he will reach no "inside" that is worth reaching. The true road lies in quite another direction. It is like the house in *Alice Through the Looking Glass*.[1]

1949

1. In Lewis Carroll's *Through the Looking-Glass*, Alice speculates on what it would be like to pass through the mirror into the room she sees beyond and then to explore the rest of "Looking-Glass House": "How nice it would be if we could only get through into Looking-Glass House! I'm sure it's got, oh! such beautiful things in it!"

Erik H. Erikson

THE GOLDEN RULE IN THE LIGHT
OF NEW INSIGHT[1]

When a lecture is announced one does not usually expect the title to foretell very much about the content. But it must be rare, indeed, that a title is as opaque as the one on your invitation to this lecture: for it does not specify the field from which new insight is to come and throw new light on the old principle of the Golden Rule. You took a chance, then, in coming, and now that I have been introduced as a psychoanalyst, you must feel that you have taken a double chance.

Let me tell you, therefore, how I came upon our subject. In Harvard College, I teach a course, "The Human Life Cycle." There (since I am by experience primarily a clinician) we begin by considering those aggravated *crises* which mark each stage of life and are known to psychiatry as potentially pathogenic. But we proceed to discuss the potential *strengths* which each stage contributes to human maturity. In either case, so psychiatric experience and the observation of healthy children tell us, much depends on the interplay of generations in which human strength can be revitalized or human weakness perseverated "into the second and third generation." But this leads us to the role of the individual in the sequence of generations, and thus to that evolved order which your scriptures call *Lokasangraha*—the "maintenance of the world" (in Professor Radhakrishnan's translation). Through the study of case-histories and of life-histories we psychoanalysts have begun to discern certain fateful and certain fruitful patterns of interaction in those most concrete categories (parent and child, man and woman, teacher and pupil) which carry the burden of maintenance from generation to generation. The implication of our insights for ethics had preoccupied me before I came here; and, as you will well understand, a few months of animated discussion in India have by no means disabused me from such concerns. I have, therefore, chosen to tell you where I stand in my teaching, in the hope of learning more from you in further discussion.

My base line is the Golden Rule, which advocates that one should do (or not do) to another what one wishes to be (or not to be) done by. Systematic students of ethics often indicate a certain disdain for this all-too-primitive ancestor of more logical principles; and Bernard Shaw found the rule an easy target: don't do to another what you would like to be done by, he warned, because his tastes may differ from yours. Yet this

1. A speech given for the University of Delhi and the India International Center in New Delhi, January 1963.

rule has marked a mysterious meeting ground between ancient peoples separated by oceans and eras, and has provided a hidden theme in the most memorably sayings of many thinkers.

The Golden Rule obviously concerns itself with one of the very basic paradoxes of human existence. Each man calls his own a separate body, a self-conscious individuality, a personal awareness of the cosmos, and a certain death; and yet he shares this world as a *reality* also perceived and judged by others and as an *actuality* within which he must commit himself to ceaseless interaction. This is acknowledged in your scriptures as the principle of Karma.

To identify self-interest and the interest of other selves, the Rule alternately employs the method of warning, "Do *not* as you would *not* be done by," and of exhortation, "Do, as you *would* be done by." For psychological appeal, some versions rely on a minimum of *egotistic prudence*, while others demand a maximum of *altrustic sympathy*. It must be admitted that the formula, "Do not to others what if done to you would cause you pain," does not presuppose much more than the mental level of the small child who desists from pinching when it gets pinched in return. More mature insight is assumed in the saying, "No one is a believer until he loves for his brother what he loves for himself." Of all the versions, however, none commit us as unconditionally as the Upanishad's,[2] "he who sees all beings in his own self and his own self in all beings," and the Christian injunction, "love the neighbor as thyself." They even suggest a true love and a true knowledge of ourselves. Freud, of course, took this Christian maxim deftly apart as altogether illusory, thus denying with the irony of the enlightenment[3] what a maxim really is —and what (as I hope to show) his method may really stand for.

I will not (I could not) trace the versions of the Rule to various world religions. No doubt in English translation all of them have become somewhat assimilated to Biblical versions. Yet the basic formula seems to be universal, and it re-appears in an astonishing number of the most revered sayings of our civilization, from St. Francis' prayer to Kant's moral imperative[4] and Lincoln's simple political creed: "As I would not be slave, I would not be master."

The variations of the Rule have, of course, provided material for many a discussion of ethics weighting the soundness of the logic implied and measuring the degree of ethical nobility reached in each. My field of

---

2. The reference is to one of the Upanishads, a group of treatises constituting the chief metaphysical work of pre-Christian Indian philosophy.

3. That is, of the eighteenth century, a period notable for its appreciation of irony (see Jonathan Swift's "A Modest Proposal," p. 804) and for the production of maxims.

4. The prayer of Francis of Assisi, a medieval saint and founder of the Franciscan order, is quoted later in this essay, on p. 674. The eighteenth-century German philosopher Immanuel Kant stated his form of the Golden Rule thus: "So act as to treat humanity, whether in your own person or that of another, in every case as an end in itself, never as a means."

inquiry, the clinical study of the human life cycle, suggests that I desist from arguing logical merit or spiritual worth and instead distinguish *variations in moral and ethical sensitivity* in accordance with stages in the development of human conscience.

The dictionary, our first refuge from ambiguity, in this case only confounds it: morals and ethics are defined as synonyms *and* antonyms of each other. In other words, they are the same, with a difference—a difference which I intend to emphasize. For it is clear that he who knows what is legal or illegal and what is moral or immoral has not necessarily learned thereby what is ethical. Highly moralistic people can do unethical things, while an ethical man's involvement in immoral doings becomes by inner necessity an occasion for tragedy.

I would propose that we consider *moral rules* of conduct to be based on a fear of *threats* to be forestalled. These may be outer threats of abandonment, punishment and public exposure, or a threatening inner sense of guilt, of shame or of isolation. In either case, the rationale for obeying a rule may not be too clear; it is the threat that counts. In contrast, I would consider *ethical rules* to be based on *ideals* to be striven for with a high degree of rational assent and with a ready consent to a formulated good, a definition of perfection, and some promise of self-realization. This differentiation may not agree with all existing definitions, but it is substantiated by the observation of human development. Here, then, is my first proposition: the moral and the ethical sense are different in their psychological dynamics, because the moral sense develops on an earlier, more immature level. This does not mean that the moral sense could be skipped, as it were. On the contrary, all that exists layer upon layer in an adult's mind has developed step by step in the growing child's, and all the major steps in the comprehension of what is considered good behavior in one's cultural universe are—for better and for worse—related to different stages in individual maturation. But they are all necessary to one another.

The response to a moral tone of voice develops early, and many an adult is startled when inadvertently he makes an infant cry, because his voice has conveyed more disapproval than he intended to. Yet, the small child, so limited to the intensity of the moment, somehow must learn the boundaries marked by "don'ts." Here, cultures have a certain leeway in underscoring the goodness of one who does not transgress or the evilness of one who does. But the conclusion is unavoidable that children can be made to feel evil, and that adults continue to project evil on one another and on their children far beyond the verdict of rational judgment. Mark Twain once characterized man as "the animal that blushes."

Psychoanalytic obervation first established the psychological basic of a fact which Eastern thinkers have always known, namely, that the radical division into good and bad can be the sickness of the mind. It has traced the moral scruples and excesses of the adult to the childhood stages in which guilt and shame are ready to be aroused and are easily exploited. It has named and studied the "super-ego" which hovers over the ego as the inner perpetuation of the child's subordination to the restraining will of his elders. The voice of the super-ego is not always cruel and derisive, but it is ever ready to become so whenever the precarious balance which we call a good conscience is upset, at which times the secret weapons of this inner governor are revealed: the brand of shame and the bite of conscience. We who deal with the consequences in individual neuroses and in collective irrationality must ask ourselves whether excessive guilt and excessive shame are "caused" or merely accentuated by the pressure of parental and communal methods, by the threat of loss of affection, of corporal punishment, of public shaming. Or are they by now a proclivity for self-alienation which has become a part—and, to some extent, a necessary part—of man's evolutionary heritage?

All we know for certain is that the moral proclivity in man does not develop without the establishment of some chronic self-doubt and some truly terrible—even if largely submerged—rage against anybody and anything that reinforces such doubt. The "lowest" in man is thus apt to reappear in the guise of the "highest." Irrational and pre-rational combinations of goodness, doubt, and rage can re-emerge in the adult in those malignant forms of righteousness and prejudice which we may call *moralism*. In the name of high moral principles all the vindictiveness of derision, of torture, and of mass extinction can be employed. One surely must come to the conclusion that the Golden Rule was meant to protect man not only against his enemy's open attacks, but also against his friend's righteousness.

Lest this view, in spite of the evidence of history, seem too "clinical," we turn to the writings of the evolutionists who in the last few decades have joined psychoanalysis in recognizing the super-ego as an evolutionary fact—and danger. The *developmental* principle is thus joined by an *evolutionary* one. Waddington even goes so far as to say that super-ego rigidity may be an overspecialization in the human race, like the excessive body armor of the late dinosaurs. In a less grandiose comparison he likens the super-ego to "the finicky adaptation of certain parasites which fits them to live only on one host animal." In recommending his book, *The Ethical Animal*, I must admit that his terminology contradicts mine. He calls the awakening of morality in childhood a proclivity for "ethicizing," whereas I would prefer to call it moralizing. As do many animal psychologists, he dwells on analogies between the very young child and the young animal instead of comparing, as I think we must, the young animal with the pre-adult human, including the adolescent.

In fact, I must introduce here an amendment to my first, my "developmental" proposition, for between the development in childhood of man's *moral* proclivity and that of his *ethical* powers in adulthood, adolescence intervenes when he perceives the universal good in *ideological* terms. The imagery of steps in development, of course, is useful only where it is to be suggested that one item precedes another in such a way that the earlier one is necessary to the later ones and that each later one is of a higher order.

This "epigenetic" principle, according to which the constituent parts of a ground plan develop during successive stages, will be immediately familiar to you. For in the traditional Hindu concept of the life cycle the four intrinsic goals of life (Dharma, the orders that define virtue; Artha, the powers of the actual; Kama, the joys of libidinal abandon; and Moksha, the peace of deliverance) come to their successive and mutual perfection during the four stages, the ashramas[5] of the apprentice, the householder, the hermit, and the ascetic. These stages are divided from each other by sharp turns of direction; yet, each depends on the previous one, and whatever perfection is possible depends on them all.

I would not be able to discuss the relation of these two foursomes to each other, nor ready to compare this ideal conception to our epigenetic views of the life cycle. But the affinities of the two conceptions are apparent, and at least the ideological indoctrination of the apprentice, the Brahmacharya, and the ethical one of the Grihasta, the householder, correspond to the developmental categories suggested here.

No wonder; for it is the joint development of cognitive and emotional powers paired with appropriate social learning which enables the individual to realize the potentialities of a stage. Thus youth becomes ready —if often only after a severe bout with moralistic regression—to envisage the more universal principles of a highest human good. The adolescent learns to grasp the flux of time, to anticipate the future in a coherent way, to perceive ideas and to assent to ideals, to take—in short—an *ideological* position for which the younger child is cognitively not prepared. In adolescence, then, an ethical view is approximated, but it remains susceptible to an alternation of impulsive judgment and odd rationalization. It is, then, as true for adolescence as it is for childhood that man's way stations to maturity can become fixed, can become premature end stations, or stations for future regression.

The moral sense, in its perfections and its perversions, has been an intrinsic part of man's *evolution*, while the sense of ideological rejuvenation has pervaded his *revolutions*, both with prophetic idealism and with destructive fanaticism. Adolescent man, in all his sensitivity to the ideal, is easily exploited by promises of counterfeit millennia, easily taken in by the promise of a new and arrogantly exclusive identity.

The *true* ethical sense of the young adult, finally, encompasses and goes beyond moral restraint and ideal vision, while insisting on concrete

5. Stages of life.

commitments to those intimate relationships and work associations by which man can hope to share a lifetime of productivity and competence. But young adulthood engenders its own dangers. It adds to the moralist's righteousness, the *territorial defensiveness* of one who has appropriated and staked out his earthly claim and who seeks eternal security in the super-identity of organizations. Thus, what the Golden Rule at its highest has attempted to make all-inclusive, tribes and nations, castes and classes, moralities and ideologies have consistently made exclusive again —proudly, superstitiously, and viciously denying the status of reciprocal ethics to those "outside."

If I have so far underscored the malignant potentials of man's slow maturation, I have done so not in order to dwell on a kind of dogmatic pessimism which can emerge all too easily from clinical preoccupation and often leads only to anxious avoidances. I know that man's moral, ideological, and ethical propensities can find, and, have found on occasion, a sublime integration, in individuals and in groups who were both tolerant and firm, both flexible and strong, both wise and obedient. Above all, men have always shown a dim knowledge of their better potentialities by paying homage to those purest leaders who taught the simplest and most inclusive rules for an undivided mankind. I will have a word to say later about Gandhi's continued "presence" in India. But men have also persistently betrayed them, on what passed for moral or ideological grounds, even as they are now preparing a potential betrayal of the human heritage on scientific and technological grounds in the name of that which is considered good merely because it can be made to work —no matter where it leads. No longer do we have license to emphasize either the "positive" or the "negative" in man. Step for step, they go together: moralism with moral obedience, fanaticism with ideological devotion, and rigid conservatism with adult ethics.

Man's socio-genetic evolution is about to reach a crisis in the full sense of the word, a crossroads offering one path to fatality, and one to recovery and further growth. Artful perverter of joy and keen exploiter of strength, man is the animal that has learned to survive "in a fashion," to multiply without food for the multitudes, to grow up healthily without reaching personal maturity, to live well but without purpose, to invent ingeniously without aim, and to kill grandiosely without need. But the processes of socio-genetic evolution also seem to promise a new humanism, the acceptance by man—as an evolved product as well as a producer, and a self-conscious tool of further evolution—of the obligation to be guided in his planned actions and his chosen self-restraints by his knowledge and his insights. In this endeavor, then, it may be of a certain importance to learn to understand and to master the differences between infantile morality, adolescent ideology and adult ethics. Each is necessary to the next, but each is effective only if they eventually combine in that wisdom which, as Waddington puts it, "fulfills sufficiently the function of mediating evolutionary advance."

At the point, however, when one is about to end an argument with a global injunction of what we *must* do, it is well to remember Blake's admonition that the common good readily becomes the topic of "the scoundrel, the hypocrite, and the flatterer"; and that he who would do some good must do so in "minute particulars." And indeed, I have so far spoken only of the developmental and the evolutionary principle, according to which the propensity for ethics grows in the individual as part of an adaptation roughly laid down by evolution. Yet, to grow in the individual, ethics must be generated and regenerated in and by the sequence of generations—again, a matter fully grasped and systematized, some will say stereotyped, in the Hindu tradition. I must now make more explicit what our insights tell us about this process.

Let me make an altogether new start here. Let us look at scientific man in his dealings with animals and let us assume (this is not a strange assumption in India) that animals, too, may have a place close to the "other" included in the Rule. The psychologists among you know Professor Harry Harlow's studies on the development of what he calls affection in monkeys. He did some exquisite experimental and photographic work attempting, in the life of laboratory monkeys, to "control the mother variable." He took monkeys from their mothers within a few hours after birth, isolated them and left them with "mothers" made out of wire, metal, wood, and terry cloth. A rubber nipple somewhere in their middles emitted piped in milk, and the whole contraption was wired for body warmth. All the "variables" of this mother situation were controlled: the amount of rocking, the temperature of the "skin," and the exact incline of the maternal body necessary to make a scared monkey feel safe and comfortable. Years ago, when this method was presented as a study of the development of affection in monkeys, the clinician could not help wondering whether the small animals' obvious attachment to this contraption was really *monkey* affection or a fetishist addiction to inanimate objects. And, indeed, while these laboratory-reared monkeys became healthier and healthier, and much more easily trained in technical know-how than the inferior animals brought up by mere monkey mothers, they became at the end what Harlow calls "psychotics." They sit passively, they stare vacantly, and some do a terrifying thing: when poked they bite themselves and tear at their own flesh until the blood flows. They have not learned to experience "the other," whether as mother, mate, child —or enemy. Only a tiny minority of the females produced offspring, and only one of them made an attempt to nurse hers. But science remains a wonderful thing. Now that we have succeeded in producing "psychotic" monkeys experimentally, we can convince ourselves that we have at last given scientific support to the theory that severely disturbed mother-child relationships "cause" human psychosis.

This is a long story; but it speaks for Professor Harlow's methods that what they demonstrate is unforgettable. At the same time, they lead us to that borderline where we recognize that the scientific approach toward living beings must be with concepts and methods adequate to the study of ongoing life, not of selective extinction. I have put it this way: one can study the nature of things by doing something *to* them, but one can really learn something about the essential nature of living beings only by doing something *with* them or *for* them. This, of course, is the principle of clinical science. It does not deny that one can learn by dissecting the dead, or that animal or man can be motivated to lend circumscribed parts of themselves to an experimental procedure. But for the study of those central transactions which are the carriers of socio-genetic evolution, and for which we must take responsibility in the future, the chosen unit of observation must be the generation, not the individual. Whether an individual animal or human being has partaken of the stuff of life can only be tested by the kind of observation which includes his ability to transmit life—in some essential form—to the next generation.

One remembers here the work of Konrad Lorenz, and the kind of "inter-living" research which he and others have developed, making—in principle—the life cycle of certain selected animals part of the same environment in which the observer lives his own life cycle, studying his own role as well as theirs and taking his chances with what his ingenuity can discern in a setting of sophisticated naturalist inquiry. One remembers also Elsa the lioness, a foundling who was brought up in the Adamson household in Kenya. There the mother variable was not controlled, it was in control. Mrs. Adamson and her husband even felt responsible for putting grown-up Elsa back among the lions and succeeded in sending her back to the bush, where she mated and had cubs, and yet came back from time to time (accompanied by her cubs) to visit her human foster parents. In our context, we cannot fail to wonder about the built-in "moral" sense that made Elsa respond—and respond in very critical situations, indeed—to the words, "No, Elsa, no," *if* the words came from human beings she trusted. Yet, even with this built-in "moral" response, and with a lasting trust in her foster parents (which she transmitted to her wild cubs) she was able to live as a wild lion. Her mate, however, never appeared; he apparently was not too curious about her folks.

The point of this and similar stories is that our habitual relationship to what we call beasts in nature and "instinctive" or "instinctual" beastliness in ourselves may be highly distorted by thousands of years of superstition, and that there may be resources for peace even in our "animal nature" if we will only learn to nurture nature, as well as to master it. Today, we can teach a monkey, in the very words of the Bible, to "eat the flesh of his own arm," even as we can permit "erring leaders" to make of all mankind the "fuel of the fire." Yet, it seems equally plausible that we can also let our children grow up to lead "the calf and the young lion and the fatling together"—in nature and in their own nature.

To recognize one of man's prime resources, however, we must trace back his individual development to his *pre-moral* days, his infancy. His earliest social experimentation at that time leads to a certain ratio of basic trust and basic mistrust—a ratio which, if favorable, establishes the fundamental human strength: hope. This over-all attitude emerges as the newborn organism reaches out to its caretakers and as they bring to it what we will now discuss as *mutuality*. The failure of basic trust and of mutuality has been recognized in psychiatry as the most far-reaching failure, undercutting all development. We know how tragic and deeply pathogenic its absence can be in children and parents who cannot arouse and cannot respond. It is my further proposition, then, that all moral, ideological, and ethical propensities depend on this early experience of mutuality.

I would call mutuality a relationship in which partners depend on each other for the development of their respective strengths. A baby's first responses can be seen as part of an actuality consisting of many details of mutual arousal and response. While the baby initially smiles at a mere configuration resembling the human face, the adult cannot help smiling back, filled with expectations of a "recognition" which he needs to secure from the new being as surely as it needs him. The fact is that the mutuality of adult and baby is the original source of hope, the basic ingredient of all affective as well as ethical human action. As far back as 1895, Freud, in his first outline of a "Psychology for Neurologists," confronts the "helpless" newborn infant with a "help-rich" ("*hilfreich*") adult, and postulates that their mutual understanding is "the primal source of all moral motives." Should we, then, endow the Golden Rule with a principle of mutuality, replacing the reciprocity of both prudence and sympathy?

Here we must add the observation that a parent dealing with a child will be strengthened in *his* vitality, in *his* sense of identity, and in *his* readiness for ethical action by the very ministrations by means of which he secures to the child vitality, future identity, and eventual readiness for ethical action.

But we should avoid making a new Utopia out of the "mother-child relationship." The paradise of early childhood must be abandoned—a fact which man has as yet not learned to accept. The earliest mutuality is only a beginning and leads to more complicated encounters, as both the child and his interaction with a widening circle of persons grow more complicated. I need only point out that the second basic set of vital strengths in childhood (following trust and hope) is autonomy and will, and it must be clear that a situation in which the child's willfulness faces the adult's will is a different proposition from that of the mutuality of instilling hope. Yet, any adult who has managed to train a child's will must admit—for better or for worse—that he has learned much about himself and about will that he never knew before, something which cannot be learned in any other way. Thus each growing individual's developing strength "dovetails" with the strengths of an increasing number of persons arranged about him in the formalized orders of family, school, community and society. But orders and rules are kept alive only by those "virtues" of which Shakespeare says (in what appears to me to be *his* passionate version of the Rule) that they, "shining upon others heat them and they retort that heat again to the first giver."

One more proposition must be added to the developmental and to the generational one, and to that of mutuality. It is implied in the term "activate," and I would call it the principle of *active choice*. It is, I think, most venerably expressed in St. Francis's prayer: "Grant that I may not so much seek to be consoled as to console; to be understood, as to understand; to be loved as to love; for it is in giving that we receive." Such commitment to an initiative in love is, of course, contained in the admonition to "love thy neighbor." I think that we can recognize in these words a psychological verity, namely, that only he who approaches an encounter in a (consciously and unconsciously) active and giving attitude, rather than in a demanding and dependent one, will be able to make of that encounter what it can become.

With these considerations in mind, then, I will try to formulate my understanding of the Golden Rule. I have been reluctant to come to this point; it has taken thousands of years and many linguistic acrobatics to translate this Rule from one era to another and from one language into another, and at best one can only confound it again, in a somewhat different way.

I would advocate a general orientation which has its center in whatever activity or activities gives man the feeling, as William James put it, of being "most deeply and intensely active and alive." In this, so James promises, each one will find his "real me"; but, I would now add, he will also acquire the experience that *truly worthwhile acts enhance a mutuality between the doer and the other—a mutuality which strengthens the doer even as it strengthens the other.* Thus, the "doer" and "the other" are partners in one deed. Seen in the light of human development, this means that the doer is activated in whatever strength is *appropriate to his age, stage, and condition,* even as he activates in the other the strength appropriate to *his* age, stage, and condition. Understood this way, the Rule would say that it is best to do to another what will strengthen you

even as it will strengthen him—that is, what will develop his best potentials even as it develops your own.

This variation of the Rule is obvious enough when applied to the relation of parent and child. But does the uniqueness of their respective positions, which has served as our model so far, have any significant analogies in other situations in which uniqueness depends on a divided function?

To return to particulars, I will attempt to apply my amendment to the diversity of function in the two sexes. I have not dwelled so far on this most usual subject of a psychoanalytic discourse, sexuality. So much of this otherwise absorbing aspect of life has, in recent years, become stereotyped in theoretical discussion. Among the terminological culprits to be blamed for this sorry fact is the psychoanalytic term "love object." For this word "object" in Freud's theory has been taken too literally by many of his friends and by most of his enemies—and moralistic critics do delight in misrepresenting a man's transitory formulations as his ultimate "values." The fact is that Freud, on purely conceptual grounds, and on the basis of the scientific language of his laboratory days, pointed out that drive energies have "objects." But he certainly never advocated that men or women should treat one another as objects on which to live out their sexual idiosyncrasies.

Instead, his central theory of genitality which combines strivings of sexuality and of love points to one of those basic mutualities in which a partner's potency and potentialities are activated even as he activates the other's potency and potentialities. Freud's theory implies that a man will be more a man to the extent to which he makes a woman more a woman —and vice versa—because only two uniquely different beings can en-hance their respective uniqueness for one another. A "genital" person in Freud's sense[6] is thus more apt to act in accordance with Kant's version of the Golden Rule, in that he would so act as to treat humanity "whether in his person or in another, always as an end, and never as only a means." What Freud added to the ethical principle, however, is a methodology which opens to our inquiry and to our influence the powerhouse of inner forces. For they provide the shining heat for our strengths—and the smoldering smoke of our weaknesses.

I cannot leave the subject of the two sexes without a word on the uniqueness of women. One may well question whether or not the Rule in its oldest form tacitly meant to include women as partners in the golden deal. Today's study of lives still leaves quite obscure the place of women in what is most relevant in the male image of man. True, women are being granted equality of political rights, and the recognition of a certain

6. A person who has reached mature adulthood; Freud held that attainment of maturity involved moving beyond the oral and anal fixations of childhood.

sameness in mental and moral equipment. But what they have not begun to earn, partially because they have not cared to ask for it, is the *equal right to be effectively unique,* and to use hard-won rights in the service of what they uniquely represent in human evolution. The West has much to learn, for example, from the unimpaired womanliness of India's modern women. But there is today a universal sense of the emergence of a new feminism as part of a more inclusive humanism. This coincides with a growing conviction—highly ambivalent, to be sure—that the future of mankind cannot depend on men alone and may well depend on the fate of a "mother variable" uncontrolled by technological man. The resistance to such a consideration always comes from men and women who are mortally afraid that by emphasizing what is unique one may tend to re-emphasize what is unequal. And, indeed, the study of life histories confirms a farreaching sameness in men and women insofar as they express the mathematical architecture of the universe, the organization of logical thought, and the structure of language. But such a study also suggests that while boys and girls can think and act and talk alike, they naturally do not experience their bodies (and thus the world) alike. I have attempted to demonstrate this by pointing to sex differences in the structuralization of space in the play of children. But I assume that a uniqueness of either sex will be granted without proof, and that the "difference" acclaimed by the much-quoted Frenchman[7] is not considered only a matter of anatomical appointments for mutual sexual enjoyment, but a psychobiological difference central to two great modes of life, the *paternal* and the *maternal* modes. The amended Golden Rule suggests that one sex enhances the uniqueness of the other; it also implies that each, to be really unique, depends on a mutuality with an equally unique partner.

From the most intimate human encounters we now turn to a professional, and yet relatively intimate, one: that between healer and patient. There is a very real and specific inequality in the relationship of doctor and patient in their roles of knower and known, helper and sufferer, practitioner of life and victim of disease and death. For this reason medical people have their own and unique professional oath and strive to live up to a universal ideal of "the doctor." Yet the practice of the healing arts permits extreme types of practitioners, from the absolute authoritarian over homes and clinics to the harassed servant of demanding mankind, from the sadist of mere proficiency, to the effusive lover of all (well, almost all) of his patients. Here, too, Freud has thrown intimate and original light on the workings of a unique relationship. His letters to his friend and mentor Fliess illustrate the singular experience which made him recognize in his patients what he called "transference"—that is, the

7. Who said, "Vive *la différence!*"

patient's wish to exploit sickness and treatment for infantile and regressive ends. But more, Freud, recognized a "countertransference" in the healer's motivation to exploit the patient's transference and to dominate or serve, possess or love him to the disadvantage of his true function. He made systematic insight into transference and countertransference part of the training of the psychoanalytic practitioner.

I would think that all of the motivations necessarily entering so vast and so intricate a field could be reconciled in a Golden Rule amended to include a mutuality of divided function. Each specialty and each technique in its own way permits the medical man to *develop as a practitioner, and as a person, even as the patient is cured as a patient, and as a person.* For a real cure transcends the transitory state of patienthood. It is an experience which enables the cured patient to develop and to transmit to home and neighborhood an attitude toward health which is one of the most essential ingredients of an ethical outlook.

Beyond this, can the healing arts and sciences contribute to a new ethical outlook? This question always recurs in psychoanalysis and is usually disposed of with Freud's original answer that the psychoanalyst represents the ethics of scientific truth only and is committed to studying ethics (or morality) in a scientific way. Beyond this, he leaves *Weltanschauungen* (ethical world views) to others.

It seems to me, however, that the clinical arts and sciences, while employing the scientific method, are not defined by it or limited by it. The healer is committed to a highest good, the preservation of life and the furtherance of well-being—the "maintenance of life." He need not prove scientifically that these are, in fact, the highest good; rather, he is precommitted to this basic proposition while investigating what can be verified by scientific means. This, I think, is the meaning of the Hippocratic oath, which subordinates all medical method to a humanist ethic. True, a man can separate his personal, his professional, and his scientific ethics, seeking fulfillment of idiosyncratic needs in personal life, the welfare of others in his profession, and truths independent of personal preference or service in his research. However, there are psychological limits to the multiplicity of values a man can live by, and, in the end, not only the practitioner, but also his patient and his research, depend on a certain unification in him of temperament, intellect, and ethics. This unification clearly characterizes great doctors.

While it is true, then, that as scientists we must study ethics objectively, we are, as professional individuals, committed to a unification of personality, training, and conviction which alone will help us to do our work adequately. At the same time, as transient members of the human race, we must record the truest meaning of which the fallible methods of our era and the accidental circumstances of our existence have made us aware. In this sense, there is (and always has been) not only an ethics governing clinical work, and a clinical approach to the study of ethics, but also a contribution to ethics of the healing orientation. The healer, furthermore, has now committed himself to prevention on a large scale, and he cannot evade the problem of assuring ethical vitality to all lives saved from undernourishment, morbidity, and early mortality. Man's technical ability and social resolve to prevent accidental conception makes every child conceived a subject of universal responsibility.

As I approach my conclusion, let me again change my focus and devote a few minutes to a matter political and economic as well as ethical: Gandhi's "Rule."

In Ahmedabad I had occasion to visit Gandhi's ashram[8] across the Sabarmati River; and it was not long before I realized that in Ahmedabad a hallowed and yet eminently concrete event had occurred which perfectly exemplifies everything I am trying to say. I refer, of course, to Gandhi's leadership in the lockout and strike of the mill-workers in 1918, and his first fast in a public cause. This event is well known in the history of industrial relations the world over, and vaguely known to all educated Indians. Yet, I believe that only in Ahmedabad, among surviving witnesses and living institutions, can one fathom the "presence" of that event as a lastingly successful "experiment" in local industrial relations, influential in Indian politics, and, above all, representing a new type of encounter in divided human functions. The details of the strike and of the settlement need not concern us here. As usual, it began as a matter of wages. Nor can I take time to indicate the limited political and economic applicability of the Ahmedabad experiment to other industrial areas in and beyond India. What interests us here is the fact that Gandhi, from the moment of his entry into the struggle, considered it an occasion not for maximum reciprocal coercion resulting in the usual compromise, but as an opportunity for all—the workers, the owners, and himself—"to rise from the present conditions."

The utopian quality of the principles on which he determined to focus can only be grasped by one who can visualize the squalor of the workmen's living conditions, the latent panic in the ranks of the paternalistic millowners (best by worries of British competition), and Gandhi's then as yet relative inexperience in handling the masses of India. The shadows of defeat, violence, and corruption hovered over every one of the "lofty" words which I am about to quote. But to Gandhi, any worthwhile struggle must "transform the inner life of the people." Gandhi spoke to the workers daily under the famous Babul Tree outside the medieval Shahpur Gate. He had studied their desperate condition, yet he urged them to ignore the threats and the promises of the millowners who in the obstinate fashion of all "haves" feared the anarchic insolence and vio-

8. Holy retreat.

lence of the "have nots." He knew that they feared him, too, for they had indicated that they might even accept his terms if only he would promise to leave and to stay away forever. But he settled down to prove that a just man could "secure the good of the workers while safeguarding the good of the employers"—the two opposing sides being represented by a sister and a brother, Anasuyabehn and Ambalal Sarabhai. Under the Babul Tree Gandhi announced the principle which somehow corresponds to our amended Rule: *"That line of action is alone justice which does not harm either party to a dispute."* By harm he meant—and his daily announcements leave no doubt of this—an inseparable combination of economic disadvantage, social indignity, loss of self-esteem, and latent vengeance.

Neither side found it easy to grasp this principle. When the workers began to weaken, Gandhi suddenly declared a fast. Some of his friends, he admitted, considered this "foolish, unmanly, or worse"; and some were deeply distressed. But, "I wanted to show you," he said to the workers, "that I was not playing with you." He was, as we would say, in dead earnest, and this fact, then as later, immediately raised an issue of local conscience to national significance. In daily appeals, Gandhi stressed variously those basic inner strengths without which no issue has "virtue," namely, will with justice, purpose with discipline, respect for work of any kind, and truthfulness. But he knew, and he said so, that these masses of illiterate men and women, newly arrived from the villages and already exposed to proletarization, did not have the moral strength or the social solidarity to adhere to principle without strong leadership. "You have yet to learn how and when to take an oath," he told them. The oath, the dead earnestness, then, was as yet the leader's privilege and commitment. In the end the matter was settled, not without a few Gandhian compromises to save face all around, but with a true acceptance of the settlement originally proposed by Gandhi.

I do not claim to understand the complex motivations and curious turns of Gandhi's mind—some contradicting Western rigidity in matters of principle, and some, I assume, strange to Indian observers, as well. I can also see in Gandhi's actions a paternalism which may now be "dated." But his monumental simplicity and total involvement in the "experiment" made both workers and owners revere him. And he himself said with humorous awe, "I have never come across such a fight." For, indeed both sides had matured in a way that lifted labor relations in Ahmedabad to a new and lasting level. Let me quote only the fact that, in 1950, the Ahmedabad Textile Labor Organization accounted for only a twentieth of India's union membership, but for eighty per cent of its welfare expenditures.

Such a singular historical event, then, reveals something essential in human strength, in traditional Indian strength, and in the power of

Gandhi's own personal transformation at the time. To me, the miracle of the Ahmedabad experiment has been not only its lasting success and its tenacity during those days of anarchic violence which after the great partition broke down so many dams of solidarity, but above all, the spirit which points beyond the event.

And now a final word on what is, and will be for a long time to come, the sinister horizon of the world in which we all study and work: the international situation. Here, too, we cannot afford to live for long with a division of personal, professional, and political ethics—a division endangering the very life which our professions have vowed to keep intact, and thus cutting through the very fiber of our personal existence. Only in our time, and in our very generation, have we come, with traumatic suddenness, to be conscious of what was self-evident all along, namely, that in all of previous history the Rule, in whatever form, has comfortably coexisted with warfare. A warrior, all armored and spiked and set to do to another what he fully expected the other to be ready to do to him, saw no ethical contradiction between the Rule and his military ideology. He could, in fact, grant to his adversary a respect which he hoped to earn in return. This tenuous coexistence of ethics and warfare may outlive itself in our time. Even the military mind may well come to fear for its historical identity, as boundless slaughter replaces tactical warfare. What is there, even for a "fighting man," in the Golden Rule of the Nuclear Age, which seems to say, "Do not unto others—unless you are sure you can do them in as totally as they can do you in"?

One wonders, however, whether this deadlock in international morals can be broken by the most courageous protest, the most incisive interpretation, or the most prophetic warning—a warning of catastrophe so all-consuming that most men must ignore it, as they ignore their own death and have learned to ignore the monotonous prediction of hell. It seems, instead that only an ethical orientation, a direction for vigorous cooperation, can free today's energies from their bondage in armed defensiveness. We live at a time in which—with all the species-wide destruction possible—we can think for the first time of a species-wide identity, of a truly universal ethics, such as has been prepared in the world religions, in humanism, and by some philosophers. Ethics, however, cannot be fabricated. They can only emerge from an informed and inspired search for a more inclusive human identity, which a new technology and a new world image make possible as well as mandatory. But again, all I can offer you here is another variation of the theme. What has been said about the relationships of parent and child, of man and woman, and of doctor and patient, may have some application to the relationship of nations to each other. Nations today are by definition units at different stages of political, technological, and economic transformation. Under these conditions, it

is all too easy for overdeveloped nations to believe that nations, too, should treat one another with a superior educative or clinical attitude. The point of what I have to say, however, is not underscored inequality, but respected uniqueness within historical differences. Insofar as a nation thinks of itself as a collective individual, then, it may well learn to visualize its task as that of maintaining mutuality in international relations. For the only alternative to armed competition seems to be the effort to *activate in the historical partner what will strengthen him in his historical development even as it strengthens the actor in his own development—toward a common future identity*. Only thus can we find a common denominator in the rapid change of technology and history and transcend the dangerous imagery of victory and defeat, of subjugation and exploitation which is the heritage of a fragmented past.

Does this sound utopian? I think, on the contrary, that all of that I have said is already known in many ways, is being expressed in many languages, and practiced on many levels. At our historical moment it becomes clear in a most practical way that the doer of the Golden Rule, and he who is done by, is the same man, *is* man.

Men of clinical background, however, must not lose sight of a dimension which I have taken for granted here. While the Golden Rule in its classical versions prods man to strive *consciously* for a highest good and to avoid mutual harm with a sharpened awareness, our insights assume an *unconscious* substratum of ethical strength and, at the same time, unconscious arsenals of destructive rage. The last century has traumatically expanded man's awareness of unconscious motivations stemming from his animal ancestry, from his economic history, and from his inner estrangements. It has also created (in all these reports) methods of productive self-analysis. These I consider the pragmatic Western version of that universal trend toward self-scrutiny which once reached such heights in Asian tradition. It will be the task of the next generation everywhere to begin to integrate new and old methods of self-awareness with the minute particulars of universal technical proficiency.

It does not seem easy to speak of ethical subjects without indulging in some moralizing. As an antidote I will conclude with the Talmudic version of the Rule. Rabbi Hillel once was asked by an unbeliever to tell the whole of the Torah while he stood on one foot. I do not know whether he meant to answer the request or to remark on its condition when he said: "What is hateful to yourself, do not to your fellow man. That is the whole of the Torah and the rest is but commentary." At any rate, he did not add: "Act accordingly." He said: "Go and learn it."

1963

QUESTIONS

1. At times Erikson implies that he is digressing, and he certainly does cover a wide range of topics. How tightly is his talk organized? Can it be outlined?
2. Erikson distinguishes three stages of growth—moral, ideological, and ethical. What are the significant characteristics of each, and how do they relate to one another? What does Erikson mean by "evolution"?
3. Bruno Bettelheim said that liberals, the press, and teachers who failed to assert their authority all shared some blame for denying superego models to the young, particularly to the poor and disadvantaged: "There's no doubt about the underlying violence with which we are born. Whether we are going to have violence depends to a very large degree on how we develop the superego and controls of the coming generation." Would Erikson agree? Can you think of ways in which superego models are denied? Does a man in authority have to be unusually good himself to serve as a satisfactory model?

Edward Hoagland

THE PROBLEM OF THE GOLDEN RULE

Like a good many New Yorkers, I've often wondered whether I was going to be mugged. I've lived in a number of neighborhoods, and being a night walker, have many times changed my course or speeded my stride, eying a formidable-looking figure as he approached. But it's never happened, and I imagine that if it finally does there may actually be a kind of relief, even a species of exhilaration, as I pick myself up—assuming that I am not badly hurt—because a danger anticipated for a long time may come to seem worse than the reality. People who come home and encounter a robber in their apartment who flees are likely to be less shaken up than the householder is who simply steps into a shambles of ransacked bureaus and upended beds: they've seen the fellow; they know he's human. A friend of mine wrestled a burglar for several minutes around the floor of his living room, both of them using the trips and hip throws that they remembered from their teens, until by the time my friend won and phoned the police they were old acquaintances. I know, too, that to describe the few incidents of violence I've met with in the past makes them sound more grisly than they were in fact. In the army, my platoon was put in the charge of a peculiar sergeant who, mostly for reasons of his own, had us do squat jumps one noontime until we could no longer walk or stand up. Then he strolled among us kicking us to make sure that we weren't faking. It was a hot drill field strewn with packs and stacked rifles and other movie props, and yet the experience was not nearly as bad as one would anticipate if he were told at breakfast what to expect that day. We just followed orders until we couldn't get up and then we lay where we were on the ground until the sergeant was satisfied that we had done what was humanly possible. Even in a true atrocity situation that's all that is ever done, what is humanly possible. Afterwards one becomes unresponsive and fatalistic; terror is no longer a factor.

Next day the sergeant wanted to have it both ways, so he set us into formation and told us what he was going to make us do, and thereupon went off to the latrine to give us a chance to stand at attention and think and stew. Another sergeant promptly walked up and dismissed us, however. We hobbled away in every direction as fast as possible, while the two sergeants met to discuss the issue in the barracks door. They met person-to-person, and we had been punished person-to-person, and the facelessness of the mugger whom one anticipates meeting on Little West 12th Street was never a part of it. This, like our doing whatever was humanly possible, made the experience supportable.

I visualize Armageddon not as a steel-muzzled affair of pushbutton silos under the earth but as a rusty freighter, flying the Liberian flag, perhaps, which sails inconspicuously up the Hudson past my apartment and goes off. Beyond that I don't see any details—though, as a non sequitur, I expect the tunnels and bridges would fill up with hikers leaving the city before it was too late. A woman I know says she sees Armageddon as getting under the bed. What we do with the insupportable is to turn it to terms we can file and forget. Unfortunately we are able to deal almost as handily with the nuclear bombs that have already gone off as we are with the ones that haven't. If as individual fighting men we had razed Hiroshima, then the horror of its destruction would persist as a legend to our great-grandchildren because it would have been witnessed and done on the spot—also because of the somber old notion that residing in every man is a spark of divinity, whether the man is an enemy or a friend. This putative spark is central to most religious belief; and right at the root of Western ethics is what is called, under one of its names, the Golden Rule. But spark or no spark, since in practice we cannot react to others with unabashed fellow-feeling, we usually reduce the Golden Rule to a sort of silver rule, doing to them just about what we think they would do to us if they had the opportunity. And this works—has been working—though the new impersonalized technology is challenging its workability, along with another behemoth among changes, which is that today there are too many people. Where there are too many people, we get tired of following even the silver rule, tired of paying that much attention, of noticing whom we are with and who is who. For the agnostic as well, basing his reverence for life on its variety and on a Jeffersonian fascination with the glimmerings of talent in every man, the glut is discouraging. Although we don't ridicule these old ideas, the sentiments that people have for one another in a traffic jam are becoming our sentiments more and more. A groan goes up in any suburb when it's announced that a new complex of housing for two thousand souls is going to be built on Lone Tree Hill. And the vast sigh of impatience which greeted Pope Paul's traditionalist statement of faith in the sanctity of the seed germs of life points to the tons to come. *Life for the living,* people will say: body-counts in war and baby-counts in peace. We grant each union man his $10,500 a year, and then the hell with him. He, for his part, doesn't care if our garbage cans fester with rats when the union goes after $10,900.

Never have people dealt so briskly with strangers as now. Many of us have ceased to see strangers at all; our eyes simply don't register them except as verticals on the sidewalk, and when we must parley with them we find out quickly what they are asking from us, do it—maybe—and that's that. When I was a child I remember how my astonishment evolved as I realized that people often would not do the smallest thing to convenience another person or make him feel easier for the moment. Of course I'd known that *kids* wouldn't, but I had thought that was because they were kids. It was my first comprehension of the deadness of life. Everyone has discovered at some particular point life's deadness, but the galloping sense of deadness which alarms so many people lately, and especially the young, goes way beyond such individual discoveries to dimensions and contexts that have brought revolution to the U.S. Even in the arts the ancient austerities have been deemed insufficient, and we have actors who jump into the audience and do their acting there. When acting seems to fail, they improvise, and finally improvisation isn't enough either, and instead of having an actor play the drug addict, the addict himself must appear onstage and play himself—like the toothpaste tube blown up and hanging on the museum wall: "Look, if nothing else, I'm real." This is the era when students are so busy trying to teach their teachers that they are hard to teach, and when the chip on the shoulder of the man in the street is his "personality"—personality is quarrelsomeness. The revolution, in any case, is overdue, but maybe our best hope is that we remain at least idiosyncratic creatures, absorbed close to home. Dog owners, when they walk their dogs, show nearly as exact an interest in their pets' defecations as they would in their own. The same communing silence steals over their faces, the look of musing solemnity, that usually only the bathroom mirror gets a glimpse of.

The worst public tragedy I've witnessed was in Boston, when from a distance I saw a brick wall fall on a company of firemen. Some, with a great shout, got away, but even the leap that they made while the rest crumpled is blurred as a memory compared to the images of two old men whom I knew very slightly at the time. Mr. Kate wrote cookbooks in the

winter and hired out as a cook on a private yacht during the warm months. His other love, besides cooking, was opera, and he lived in a room shaped like a shoebox that cost him eight dollars a week. He served himself candlelit meals on a folding table and concocted all of his recipes on a hotplate set in the sink. By contrast, Mr. Hurth, although a somewhat less cultivated man, was an alumnus of Brown University and lived in a large ground-floor room in the same house. He had ruined himself in a scandal in St. Louis, where he had been a businessman, but that was all I learned. What he'd done next was to come to Boston and throw himself on the old-fashioned, private or "Christian" charity, as it used to be called, of a roommate from college, though thirty years had passed. He was a pleasant subdued man ordinarily, swinging from sweet to vaguely hangdog, but he was a drinker, and so this benefactor no longer asked him to Newton Centre for Thanksgiving because he was likely to break the furniture. When he did, he'd leave his glasses behind by mistake so that he'd have to go back out again for a whole second festival of apologies. Through charitable intercession, Mr. Hurth was on the payroll of the John Hancock Insurance Company, being listed on the books as a claims investigator, though actually (charity compounding charity) his single duty was to work for the United Fund once a year on a loan basis. The campaign was a brief one, but he was a bitter, floundering functionary, faced with his fate if his drinking should snap off his last sticks of presence and respectability.

As I say, next to the memory of two nodding acquaintances the death of some distant firemen is small potatoes. I was reminded of that catastrophe the other night for the first time in years while watching a fire on Third Avenue. Here in the bigger city one is witness to such a cataract of appalling happenings that they pass remembering. I saw a man who had just been burned out of his apartment turned away from a hotel in the neighborhood because he had a little blacking on him, although the shock and fear stood in his eyes. "Sure, there was a fire there, all right," the manager told me with a laugh. "I never take them in, those victims. They're dirty and they're scared to death. They're not worth the nuisance."

He was a modern, casual villain, however, impartial, just the kind who is not memorable. I came upon a much less gratuitous drama a few days afterwards. A child of two or three had been stuck inside one of those all-glass phone booths with a spring door which cannot be opened except by a grown person because of where the handle is placed. The world was passing—this was on the open street—but he was feeling his way around the glass in gathering panic, trying to find an escape route, reaching up and reaching down. Every few seconds he let out a thin, fluting scream so pure in pitch that it was hardly human; it was pre-human. You could see him thinking, learning, recording discoveries. He reached for the phone, but that was too high up; he thumped each pane of glass, searching for the door, and pounded on the metal frame, and screamed to find whether screaming would work. He was boxed into his terror, and you could see him grow older by leaps and bounds. I'm just this month a new father, so I was as transfixed as if he were my child. His governess or baby-sitter, baby-walker, or whatever she was, a short shadowy woman such as you might see manning a subway change booth, was standing right next to the glass, apparently feasting her eyes. Whether it was supposed to be a "punishment" or merely a pleasure fest, the child was too frightened by now to notice her.

Maybe our cruelty will save us. At least the cruel do pay attention, and the woman would probably have let him out before the crowd got around to hearing him. She had moved to the door, looking down at him intently as he pushed on the glass. I was seething, partly because I found that some of the woman's sexual excitement had communicated itself to me, which was intolerable, and partly because my cowardice in not interfering was equally outrageous. We've all become reluctant to stop and stick our noses in—a man is run over by a Breakstone cream-cheese truck and we pass quickly by. But cowardice was what it was in this particular event, since even under happy circumstances I stutter and it requires an enormous gearing up of nerve for me to step into a public fracas on the street. I strangle; I can't speak at all and must either use my hands on the stranger or gag and quaver, unable to put two words together. The seams of human nature frighten me in this regard, and the whole confrontation ethic of the sixties, much as I have entered into it on occasion, gives me nightmare visions because I have no conventional means of battling. I see myself as unable to protest in words to the person whose behavior has angered me and so using my hands on him; then just as unable to explain myself to the crowd that gathers, but only shuddering and stuttering; and then in court again enforcedly silent, dependent on the empathy or telepathic capacities of the people who are there to convey my side of the controversy.

Weaving like a nauseous moose, I was working my way toward her, when the woman, with a glance at me, pushed the door of the booth open, reached inside, and pulled the boy to her and walked away. In effect, I was let off, because only an exceptional well-doer would have tracked the woman down from that point on and questioned her about her psyche.

However, there are times one isn't let off, when one's very humanity hangs at issue and perhaps my specific problems with my stutter are an epitome of what each of us meets. Once in northern New England when I was snowshoeing, a hunter started shooting at me, really only to scare me, pinging with his .22 in my immediate vicinity. I was on an open hillside which I'd already realized was too slippery to climb, but as long as I kept scrabbling there in silence on the ice, like an animal in trouble, he was going to keep on pinging. Because a stutterer's every impulse is to stutter softly, unobtrusively, it's twice as hard to shout one's way through a stutter as to wedge through in quiet tones; but from the sheer imperatives of survival I shouted, "I CAN SEE YOU!" I shouted it several times again, although I couldn't see him; he was in the woods. I was insisting and reiterating that I was a human being: if I could get that message across to him he would stop shooting at me. It was even worse than my conception of a courtroom trial because this was one of those rare emergencies when we can't trust to all our faculties to operate together for us—the movements of our hands, our youth or age, our manner and expression—some compensating for the inadequacies of the others. I had to go to bat with my speaking abilities and nothing else. So I shouted to him that I could see him, by which I meant I was a man, and he stopped shooting.

More recently, I was on a tiny Danish island off the coast of Sweden, wandering around some seventeenth-century fortifications and the walled town, now a huddled fishing village. I had sat on the sea wall to watch the cloud action but was distracted by the spectacle below me of a boy mistreating a wild duck. Oddly enough, many times an incident where a person, rather than an animal, is being mauled and manhandled is easier to shrug off. The fact that he's a person complicates the case. As an onlooker you can see, for example, that he has gotten himself drunk and let his guard down, lost his dignity, talked out of turn. But the duck, with its wings clipped, presumably, was only trying to run away. The boy would catch it, pummel it and grip it tightly, trundling it about. Finally I got off my bench and went over and told him falteringly to cut that out. Many Danes speak English, but he was twelve or so and he may not have understood me. Like a mirror of myself, he stared at me without trying to say a word. Then he squeezed the duck again hard in both hands. My bugaboo about trying to explain myself to strangers rose in me, along with my indignation. Instead of looking for a local fellow to translate and take over, I lifted the duck from his arms, and with the sense of right and doom that I have dreaded in foreseeing a confrontation on the street, carried it down the stairs of the sea wall and released it on the beach. The boy ran for help; the duck paddled into the waves; I climbed to the promenade and started walking as deliberately as I could toward the small boat which had brought me to the island.

Uncannily soon, before I'd gone a dozen yards, practically the whole male populace was on the scene. "Hey! Turn around!" they yelled. I took another couple of steps away and then did so. They told me very plainly in English that they were going to throw me over the sea wall. They said the duck had been rescued by the boys of the island—their sons—after it had swum through an oil slick and almost drowned. Now, because of what I'd done, it really was about to drown, and when it went under, they would toss me over. This was not spoken in joking tones, and I could see the duck getting heavier in the water; its feathers, though as tidy to the eye as a healthy duck's feathers, had no buoyancy. Meanwhile, I'd fallen into something like what a prizefighter would call a clinch by refusing to acknowledge by any sign that I understood what was being said to me. It is a psychological necessity that when you punish somebody he understand the reason why. Even if he doesn't accept the guilty finding, you must explain to him why you are punishing him or you can't do it. So while they could scarcely contain their frustration, my face displayed bewilderment; I kept pretending to grope to understand, I was doing this instinctively, of course, and as their first impetus to violence passed, I found myself acting out with vehemence how I had seen the boy mistreat the duck. The men, who wanted at the least to take a poke at me, watched doubtfully, but there was a Coast Guardsman, an off-islander, who seemed to be arguing in Danish on my behalf. Another man went down to where the duck was swimming and reached out; the duck perceiving itself to be sinking, had moved cautiously closer to shore. And when the duck was saved I was saved; I only had the island's boys waiting for me in the embrasures of the wall.

Yet this quite comic misadventure, when every dread came real—I couldn't say a single word to save my life—was just as numbing as those ninety-five squat jumps at Fort Dix—only later was it terrifying. And in a way it makes up for the memories I have as a teenager of watching flocks of bats murdered with brooms and frogs tormented—moments when I didn't interfere, but giggled ruefully to keep my popularity and stifle my outcries.

Sociology progresses; the infant mortality rate among Negroes goes down. Nevertheless we know that if the announcement were made that there was going to be a public hanging in Central Park, Sheep Meadow would be crowded with spectators, like Tyburn mall.[1] Sometimes at night my standing lamp shapes itself into an observant phantom figure which takes a position next to my bed. It doesn't threaten me directly, and I stretch out to clutch its throat with careful anger. My final grab bumps the lamp over. This electric phantom is a holdover from my vivid night demons when I was eight or ten. I never saw them outright, thank the Lord, but for years I fell asleep facing the wall to avoid beholding my destruction. I'd "whisper," as I called it, when I went to bed, telling myself an installment of a round-robin story, and when the installment was over I'd wait for the demons, until I fell asleep. Later, just as invariably, I faced the outer room so I could see them come and have warning to fight. Such archaisms in our minds are not an unmixed evil,

1. The place in London where, from the thirteenth through the eighteenth centuries, public executions were held. Attending executions was then a popular and rowdy spectator sport.

however, because they link us to humanity and to our history as human beings. My wife says every man she's been familiar with would smell his socks at night before he went to bed: just a whiff—each sock, not only one. I do this too, although the smell has been of no intrinsic interest to me for twenty years. The smell of each sock checks precisely with the other one and smells as vital as pigs do. Maybe it reassures us that we're among the living still. We need to know. In the fifties I also liked the smell of air pollution. I didn't think of it as air pollution then—nobody did—but as the smell of industry and the highways I hitchhiked on, the big-shouldered America I loved.

In 1943 George Orwell said the problem of the times was the decay in the belief in personal immortality. Several French novelists had turned existentialist and several English movelists Catholic (possibly the same reaction), while he himself, like many of the more likable writers, had adopted a hardy humanist's masculine skepticism. Twenty-odd years later, the problem appears only to have grown more piercing, though it is not put into the same terms. You can't have as many people walking around as there are now and still simply see them as chips off the divine lodestone. Nor is the future 1984: that's too succinct. At first the new nuclear bullying, the new technocracy, made mere survival more the point, because we wanted to be sure of surviving here on earth before we worried about heaven. Lately, instead the talk has been about over-population, and city people have started venturing to the outback, buy-ing acreage with all the premonitory fervor of Noah sawing logs. Every-one wants space to breathe; the character of city life has drastically deteriorated, and there's no questioning the statistics, just as there used to be no questioning the odds that eventually a nuclear war was going to penetrate our precautions through that old fontanel of existence: human mix-up.

When we say that enough is enough, that we have enough people on hand now for any good purpose, we mean that the divine spark has become something of a conflagration, besides an embarrassment of riches. We're trying to make a start at sorting the riches, buying Edward-ian clothes but also Volkswagens, and settling down to the process of zoning the little land there is. As we also begin to cogitate on how the quality of life can be improved, we may be in for a religious revival, too. It's a natural beginning, and faddism will probably swing that way, and after all, we are extraordinary—we're so extraordinary we're everywhere. Next to the new mysticisms, old-fashioned, run-of-the-mill religion is not so hard to swallow. The difficulty will be how we regard individual people, a question which involves not only whether we think we're immortal but whether we think they are. The crowded impatience of suburb-city living doesn't often evoke intimations of other people's im-mortality, and neither do the hodge-podge leveling procedures of a modern democracy. So much of the vigor of the Victorian church, for instance, grew out of the contrast between its members and the raw, destitute brown masses who covered the rest of the globe. Among an elite, self-congratulatory minority even the greatest of attributes—immortality—seemed plausible.

But maybe I'm being overly sour. We have wiped tigers off the earth and yet our children hear as much about the symbolism of tigers as children did in the old days. And next to the subway station I use there is a newsdealer who was blinded in Orwell's war, the Spanish War, in the mountains behind Motril. He wears the aura of a revolutionary volunteer. He dresses bulkily, as if for weather at the front, and rigs canvas around his hut as neatly as a soldier's tent. Not one of your meek blind men, he's on his feet most of the day, especially in tough weather, pacing, marching, standing tall. He's gray and grim, hard and spare, and doubtless lives surrounded by the companions that he had in the Sierra Nevada. But he's too bluff and energetic to be a museum piece. If you help him cross the street you get the rough edge of his tongue. He searches for the lamppost with his cane like a tennis player swinging backhand, and if he loses his bearings and bumps against something, he jerks abruptly back like a cavalier insulted, looking gaunt and fierce. I pity him, but I take note of him; he counts himself among the living. I buy a paper and go home to my newborn baby, who is as intense and focused (to my eye) as a flight of angels dancing on a pinhead.

I don't believe in a god you can pray to, but I do find I believe in God—I do more than I don't. I believe in glee and in the exuberance I feel with friends and animals and in the fields, and in other emotions besides that. Anyway, as we know, it really isn't necessary to see sparks of a grand divinity in someone else to feel with the old immediacy that he is kin; we can evolve a more sophisticated Golden Rule than that. We will be trying to refine and revivify the qualities of life, and the chief stumbling block is that we must somehow reduce the density of people in our own comings and goings without doing it as we do now, which is by simply not seeing them, by registering them as shadows to dodge by on the street. Without degenerating into callousness, we must develop our ability to switch on and off—something analogous to what we do already with body temperature in a harsh world. Generally we'd button up if we were out walking, but when the Breakstone cream-cheese truck ran over an old man, this would be a time when our ancient instinct for cherishing a stranger would spring to being.

I live in a high-rise apartment and keep a pair of field glasses next to the window to use whenever somebody emerges on one of the rooftops nearby. There are ten or fifteen regulars—old people hanging wash, high school kids who have come up into the open to talk where they can be alone. All of them are neighbors to me now, though on the street I probably would turn away from them—even the bathing beauties would not be beauties there. Admittedly I am a bit of a voyeur, as who isn't, but the population density on the rooftops seems about right. In fact, I roused myself not long ago to drive some robbers off a roof across the street by gesticulating sternly. They waved back as they went down the stairs like people who've escaped a fall.

1969

QUESTIONS

1. *On p. 686 Hoagland says that stuttering makes him incapable of speech in tense confrontations. What does he do—word choice, figures of speech, management of detail—to make you feel his tension? What is the consequence of his breaking the sequence of his essay after explaining about his stuttering?*

2. *Hoagland provides a good deal of potentially verifiable biographical information about himself (e.g., he lives in New York, at the time of writing he had a newborn baby, he lives in a high-rise building). List this data and then explain what more you know about him and how you know it.*

3. *At the end Hoagland makes the issue into a perceptual problem —being able to see other people. What is the relation between his earlier stress on his inability to speak and this on perception?*

4. *Compare Hoagland on the golden rule with Erikson's discussion of it (p. 665). Which is the more effective treatment?*

Prose Forms: Apothegms

At the beginning of Bacon's essay "Of Truth," jesting Pilate asks, "What is truth?" and does not stay for an answer. Perhaps Pilate asked in jest because he thought the question foolish; perhaps because he thought an answer impossible. Something of Pilate's skepticism is in most of us, but something too of a belief that there is truth, even if—as the history of philosophy teaches us—determining its nature may be enormously difficult. We readily assume some things to be true even if we hesitate to say what ultimately is Truth.

The test of truth most often is an appeal to the observed facts of experience. The observation of experience yields knowledge; the generalized statement of that knowledge yields a concept of the experience; the concise, descriptive form in which that concept is expressed we call variously, apothegm, proverb, maxim, or aphorism. Thus Sir James Mackintosh can speak of apothegms as "the condensed good sense of nations," because the apothegm conveys the distilled observations of people about their own persistent conduct. To hear the familiar "Absence makes the heart grow fonder" is to be reminded of a general truth which you and the world acknowledge. It does not matter that the equally familiar "Out of sight, out of mind" seems to contradict the other saying; both are true but applicable to different situations. Both statements are immediately recognizable as true and neither requires to be argued for, representing as they do the collective experience of mankind intelligently observed.

Aphoristic statements often occur within the context of more extended pieces of writing, and while not apothegms in the strictest sense, but rather propositions, they have the force of apothegms. For example, Percy Shelley's "Defence of Poetry" (1821) concludes that "Poets are the unacknowledged legislators of the world." Seventy years later in his Preface to The Picture of Dorian Gray Oscar Wilde asserts that "All art is quite useless." Although these statements seem contradictory, each is unarguable within its own context.

Not everyone is as astute an observer as the writer of apothegms and maxims, of course, but everyone is presumably capable of perceiving their rightness. What we perceive first is the facts to which the saying

692

applies. When Franklin says "An empty bag cannot stand upright" (in 1740 he obviously had in mind a cloth bag), we acknowledge that this is the condition of the empty bag—and of ourselves when we are empty. Or when La Rochefoucauld says "We are all strong enough to endure the misfortunes of others," he too observes a condition that exists among people.

Many aphoristic assertions claim their validity primarily in descriptive terms. But the descriptive "is" in most apothegms and maxims is joined to a normative "ought" and the sayings therefore convey admonitions about and judgments of the conditions they describe. "Waste not, want not" is a simple illustration of this use of fact to admonish. Samuel Butler briefly gives us the presumed fact that "the world will always be governed by self-interest." Then he quickly advises: "We should not try to stop this, we should try to make the self-interest of cads a little more consistent with that of decent people." The condition of "ought" need not always be admonitory; it may be the implied judgment in La Rochefoucauld's assertion that "It is the habit of mediocre minds to condemn all that is beyond their grasp." The judgment is explicit in Franklin's "Fish and visitors stink in three days." And Bierce's definitions of ordinary words are not specifications of meanings in the way of ordinary dictionaries, but critical concepts of the experiences to which the words point.

"Wisdom" or "good sense," then, is the heart of the apothegm or maxim, the conjunction of "is" and "ought" in an assertion of universal truth. Unlike ordinary assertions of fact or opinion usually concerned with particular rather than universal experience, the wise saying is complete in its brevity. Before the ordinary assertion is allowed to hold, we require that the assumptions on which it rests, the implications it carries, the critical concepts and terms it contains, be examined closely and explored or justified. If someone says that the modern college student wants most to succeed materially in life, we want to be satisfied about what constitutes "modern," which college students (and where) are referred to, what else is involved in the comparative "most," what specifically is meant by "materially." But the apothegm assumes facts widely known and accepted, and in its judgments invokes values or attitudes readily intelligible to the great majority. It is the truth as most people experience it.

In a sense, every writer's concern is ultimately with truth. Certainly the essayist is directly concerned, in defining and ordering ideas, to say what is true and, somehow, to say it "new." Much of what he or she says is of the nature of assertion about particular experience; he or she must therefore be at pains to handle such matters as assumptions and logical proofs carefully and deliberately. But one cannot always be starting from scratch, not daring to assume anything, trusting no certain knowledge or experience or beliefs held in common with other people. Careful one must be, but also aware that there is available, in addition to methods of logical analysis and proof, rules of evidence, and the other means to effective exposition, the whole memory and record of the vast experience of the race contained in a people's apothegms and aphorisms. In them is a treasury of truths useful to many demands of clarity and precision. And in them, too, is a valuable lesson in the way a significantly large body of experience—direct, in a person's day-to-day encounters; indirect, in the study of all forms of history—can be observed, conceptualized, and then expressed in an economy of language brief in form, comprehensive in meaning, and satisfyingly true.

W. H. Auden: Apothegms

Some books are undeservedly forgotten; none are undeservedly remembered.

You do not educate a person's palate by telling him that what he has been in the habit of eating—watery, overboiled cabbage, let us say—is disgusting, but by persuading him to try a dish of vegetables which have been properly cooked. With some people, it is true, you seem to get quicker results by telling them—"Only vulgar people like overcooked cabbage; the best people like cabbage as the Chinese cook it"—but the results are less likely to be lasting.

No poet or novelist wishes he were the only one who ever lived, but most of them wish they were the only one alive, and quite a number fondly believe their wish has been granted.

The integrity of a writer is more threatened by appeals to his social conscience, his political or religious convictions, than by appeals to his cupidity. It is morally less confusing to be goosed by a traveling salesman than by a bishop.

Only a minor talent can be a perfect gentleman; a major talent is always more than a bit of a cad. Hence the importance of minor writers —as teachers of good manners. Now and again, an exquisite minor work can make a master feel thoroughly ashamed of himself.

Narcissus does not fall in love with his reflection because it is beautiful, but because it is *his*. If it were his beauty that enthralled him he would be set free in a few years by its fading.

"After all," sighed Narcissus the hunchback, "on *me* it looks good."

Our sufferings and weaknesses, in so far as they are personal, *our* sufferings, *our* weaknesses, are of no literary interest whatsoever. They are only interesting in so far as we can see them as typical of the human condition. A suffering, a weakness, which cannot be expressed as an aphorism should not be mentioned.

The same rules apply to self-examination as apply to confession to a priest: *be brief, be blunt, be gone.* Be brief, be blunt, forget. The scrupuland is a nasty specimen.

In a state of panic, a man runs round in circles by himself. In a state of joy, he links hands with others and they dance round in a circle together.

A sense of humor develops in a society to the degree that its members are simultaneously conscious of being each a unique person and of being all in common subjection to unalterable laws.

Among those whom I like or admire, I can find no common denominator, but among those whom I love, I can: all of them make me laugh.

If Homer had tried reading the *Iliad* to the gods on Olympus, they would either have started to fidget and presently asked if he hadn't got something a little lighter, or, taking it as a comic poem, would have roared with laughter or possibly, even, reacting like ourselves to a tear-jerking movie, have poured pleasing tears.

1962

Ambrose Bierce: FROM THE DEVIL'S DICTIONARY

abdication, *n.* An act whereby a sovereign attests his sense of the high temperature of the throne.

abscond, *v.i.* To "move in a mysterious way," commonly with the property of another.

absent, *adj.* Peculiarly exposed to the tooth of detraction; vilified; hopelessly in the wrong; superseded in the consideration and affection of another.

accident, *n.* An inevitable occurrence due to the action of immutable natural laws.

accordion, *n.* An instrument in harmony with the sentiments of an assassin.

achievement, *n.* The death of endeavor and the birth of disgust.

admiration, *n.* Our polite recognition of another's resemblance to ourselves.

alone, *adj.* In bad company.

applause, *n.* The echo of a platitude.

ardor, *n.* The quality that distinguishes love without knowledge.

bore, *n.* A person who talks when you wish him to listen.

cemetery, *n.* An isolated suburban spot where mourners match lies, poets write at a target and stone-cutters spell for a wager. The inscription following will serve to illustrate the success attained in these Olympian games:

> His virtues were so conspicuous that his enemies, unable to overlook them, denied them, and his friends, to whose loose lives they were a rebuke, represented them as vices. They are here commemorated by his family, who shared them.

childhood, *n.* The period of human life intermediate between the idiocy of infancy and the folly of youth—two removes from the sin of manhood and three from the remorse of age.

Christian, *n.* One who believes that the New Testament is a divinely inspired book admirably suited to the spiritual needs of his neighbor. One who follows the teachings of Christ in so far as they are not inconsistent with a life of sin.

compulsion, *n.* The eloquence of power.

congratulation, *n.* The civility of envy.

conservative, *n.* A statement who is enamored of existing evils, as distinguished from the Liberal, who wishes to replace them with others.

consult, *v.t.* To seek another's approval of a course already decided on.

contempt, *n.* The feeling of a prudent man for an enemy who is too formidable safely to be opposed.

coward, *n.* One who in a perilous emergency thinks with his legs.

debauchee, *n.* One who has so earnestly pursued pleasure that he has had the misfortune to overtake it.

destiny, *n.* A tyrant's authority for crime and a fool's excuse for failure.

diplomacy, *n.* The patriotic art of lying for one's country.

distance, *n.* The only thing that the rich are willing for the poor to call theirs and keep.

duty, *n.* That which sternly impels us in the direction of profit, along the line of desire.

education, *n.* That which discloses to the wise and disguises from the foolish their lack of understanding.

erudition, *n.* Dust shaken out of a book into an empty skull.

extinction, *n.* The raw material out of which theology created the future state.

faith, *n.* Belief without evidence in what is told by one who speaks without knowledge, of things without parallel.

genealogy, *n.* An account of one's descent from an ancestor who did not particularly care to trace his own.

ghost, *n.* The outward and visible sign of an inward fear.

habit, *n.* A shackle for the free.

heaven, *n.* A place where the wicked cease from troubling you with talk of their personal affairs, and the good listen with attention while you expound your own.

historian, *n*. A broad-gauge gossip.

hope, *n*. Desire and expectation rolled into one.

hypocrite, *n*. One who, professing virtues that he does not respect, secures the advantage of seeming to be what he despises.

impiety, *n*. Your irreverence toward my deity.

impunity, *n*. Wealth.

language, *n*. The music with which we charm the serpents guarding another's treasure.

logic, *n*. The art of thinking and reasoning in strict accordance with the limitations and incapacities of the human misunderstanding.

The basis of logic is the syllogism, consisting of a major and a minor premise and a conclusion—thus:

Major Premise: Sixty men can do a piece of work sixty times as quickly as one man.

Minor Premise: One man can dig a post-hole in sixty seconds; therefore—

Conclusion: Sixty men can dig a post-hole in one second.

This may be called the syllogism arithmetical, in which, by combining logic and mathematics, we obtain a double certainty and are twice blessed.

love, *n*. A temporary insanity curable by marriage or by removal of the patient from the influences under which he incurred the disorder. This disease, like *caries* and many other ailments, is prevalent only among civilized races living under artificial conditions; barbarous nations breathing pure air and eating simple food enjoy immunity from its ravages. It is sometimes fatal, but more frequently to the physician than to the patient.

miracle, *n*. An act or event out of the order of nature and unaccountable, as beating a normal hand of four kings and an ace with four aces and a king.

monkey, *n*. An arboreal animal which makes itself at home in genealogical trees.

mouth, *n*. In man, the gateway to the soul; in woman, the outlet of the heart.

non-combatant, *n*. A dead Quaker.

platitude, *n*. The fundamental element and special glory of popular literature. A thought that snores in words that smoke. The wisdom of a million fools in the diction of a dullard. A fossil sentiment in artificial rock. A moral without the fable. All that is mortal of a departed truth. A demi-tasse of milk-and-morality. The Pope's-nose of a featherless peacock. A jelly-fish withering on the shore of the sea of thought. The cackle surviving the egg. A dessicated epigram.

pray, *v*. To ask that the laws of the universe be annulled in behalf of a single petitioner confessedly unworthy.

presidency, *n.* The greased pig in the field game of American politics.

prude, *n.* A bawd hiding behind the back of her demeanor.

rapacity, *n* Providence without industry. The thrift of power.

reason, *v.i.* To weigh probabilities in the scales of desire.

religion, *n.* A daughter of Hope and Fear, explaining to Ignorance the nature of the Unknowable.

resolute, *adj.* Obstinate in a course that we approve.

retaliation, *n.* The natural rock upon which is reared the Temple of Law.

saint, *n.* A dead sinner revised and edited.

> The Duchess of Orleans relates that the irreverent old calumniator, Marshal Villeroi, who in his youth had known St. Francis de Sales, said, on hearing him called saint: "I am delighted to hear that Monsieur de Sales is a saint. He was fond of saying indelicate things, and used to cheat at cards. In other respects he was a perfect gentleman, though a fool."

valor, *n.* A soldierly compound of vanity, duty and the gambler's hope:

> "Why have you halted?" roared the commander of a division at Chickamauga, who had ordered a charge; "move forward, sir, at once."
>
> "General," said the commander of the delinquent brigade, "I am persuaded that any further display of valor by my troops will bring them into collision with the enemy."

1906

William Blake: PROVERBS OF HELL

In seed time learn, in harvest teach, in winter enjoy.
Drive your cart and your plough over the bones of the dead.
The road of excess leads to the palace of wisdom.
Prudence is a rich, ugly old maid courted by Incapacity.
He who desires but acts not, breeds pestilence.
The cut worm forgives the plough.
Dip him in the river who loves water.
A fool sees not the same tree that a wise man sees.
He whose face gives no light, shall never become a star.
Eternity is in love with the productions of time.
The busy bee has no time for sorrow.

The hours of folly are measur'd by the clock; but of wisdom, no clock can measure.

All wholesome food is caught without a net or a trap.

Bring out number, weight, and measure in a year of dearth.

No bird soars too high, if he soars with his own wings.

A dead body revenges not injuries.

The most sublime act is to set another before you.

If the fool would persist in his folly he would become wise.

Folly is the cloak of knavery.

Shame is Pride's cloak.

Prisons are built with stones of Law, brothels with bricks of Religion.

The pride of the peacock is the glory of God.

The lust of the goat is the bounty of God.

The wrath of the lion is the wisdom of God.

The nakedness of woman is the work of God.

Excess of sorrow laughs. Excess of joy weeps.

The roaring of lions, the howling of wolves, the raging of the stormy sea, and the destructive sword are portions of eternity too great for the eye of man.

The fox condemns the trap, not himself.

Joys impregnate. Sorrows bring forth.

Let man wear the fell of the lion, woman the fleece of the sheep.

The bird a nest, the spider a web, man friendship.

The selfish, smiling fool, and the sullen, frowning fool shall be both thought wise, that they may be a rod.

What is now proved was once only imagin'd.

The rat, the mouse, the fox, the rabbit watch the roots; the lion, the tiger, the horse, the elephant watch the fruits.

The cistern contains: the fountain overflows.

One thought fills immensity.

Always be ready to speak your mind, and a base man will avoid you.

Everything possible to be believ'd is an image of truth.

The eagle never lost so much time as when he submitted to learn of the crow.

The fox provides for himself; but God provides for the lion.

Think in the morning. Act in the noon. Eat in the evening. Sleep in the night.

He who has suffer'd you to impose on him, knows you.

As the plough follows words, so God rewards prayers.

The tigers of wrath are wiser than the horses of instruction.

Expect poison from the standing water.

You never know what is enough unless you know what is more than enough.

Listen to the fool's reproach! it is a kingly title!

The eyes of fire, the nostrils of air, the mouth of water, the beard of earth.
The weak in courage is strong in cunning.
The apple tree never asks the beech how he shall grow; nor the lion, the
horse, how he shall take his prey.
The thankful receiver bears a plentiful harvest.
If others had not been foolish, we should be so.
The soul of sweet delight can never be defil'd.
When thou seest an eagle, thou seest a portion of Genius; lift up thy
head!
As the caterpillar chooses the fairest leaves to lay her eggs on, so the
priest lays his curse on the fairest joys.
To create a little flower is the labor of ages.
Damn braces. Bless relaxes.
The best wine is the oldest, the best water the newest.
Prayers plough not! Praises reap not!
Joys laugh not! Sorrows weep not!
The head Sublime, the heart Pathos, the genitals Beauty, the hands and
feet Proportion.
As the air to a bird or the sea to a fish, so is contempt to the contemptible.
The crow wish'd everything was black, the owl that everything was
white.
Exuberance is Beauty.
If the lion was advised by the fox, he would be cunning.
Improvement makes straight roads; but the crooked roads without im-
provement are roads of Genius.
Sooner murder an infant in its cradle than nurse unacted desires.
Where man is not, nature is barren.
Truth can never be told so as to be understood, and not be believ'd.
Enough! or Too much.

1790

Benjamin Franklin: FROM POOR RICHARD'S
ALMANACK

Light purse, heavy heart.   1733
He's a fool that makes his doctor his heir.
Love well, whip well.
Hunger never saw bad bread.
Fools make feasts, and wise men eat 'em.
He that lies down with dogs, shall rise up with fleas.
He is ill clothed, who is bare of virtue.

There is no little enemy.

Without justice courage is weak.   1734
Where there's marriage without love, there will be love without
marriage.
    Do good to thy friend to keep him, to thy enemy to gain him.
    He that cannot obey, cannot command.
    Marry your son when you will, but your daughter when you can.

Approve not of him who commends all you say.   1735
    Necessity never made a good bargain.
    Be slow in chusing a friend, slower in changing.
    Three may keep a secret, if two of them are dead.
    Deny self for self's sake.
    To be humble to superiors is duty, to equals courtesy, to inferiors
nobleness.

Fish and visitors stink in three days.   1736
    Do not do that which you would not have known.
    Bargaining has neither friends nor relations.
    Now I've a sheep and a cow, every body bids me good morrow.
    God helps them that help themselves.
    He that speaks much, is much mistaken.
    God heals, and the doctor takes the fees.

There are no ugly loves, nor handsome prisons.   1737
    Three good meals a day is bad living.

Who has deceiv'd thee so oft as thyself?   1738
    Read much, but not many books.
    Let thy vices die before thee.

He that falls in love with himself, will have no rivals.   1739
    Sin is not hurtful because it is forbidden, but it is forbidden because it's
hurtful.

An empty bag cannot stand upright.   1740

Learn of the skilful: he that teaches himself, hath a fool for his master.
                                            1741

Death takes no bribes.   1742

An old man in a house is a good sign.   1744

Fear God, and your enemies will fear you.

He's a fool that cannot conceal his wisdom.   1745
Many complain of their memory, few of their judgment.

When the well's dry, we know the worth of water.   1746
The sting of a reproach is the truth of it.

Write injuries in dust, benefits in marble.   1747

Nine men in ten are suicides.   1749
A man in a passion rides a mad horse.

He is a governor that governs his passions, and he is a servant that
serves them.   1750
Sorrow is good for nothing but sin.

Calamity and prosperity are the touchstones of integrity.   1752
Generous minds are all of kin.

Haste makes waste.   1753

The doors of wisdom are never shut.   1755

The way to be safe, is never to be secure.   1757

La Rochefoucauld: FROM MAXIMS

Our virtues are mostly but vices in disguise.

14. Men not only forget benefits received and injuries endured; they
even come to dislike those to whom they are indebted, while ceasing to
hate those others who have done them harm. Diligence in returning good
for good, and in exacting vengeance for evil, comes to be a sort of
servitude which we do not readily accept.

19. We are all strong enough to endure the misfortunes of others.

20. The steadiness of the wise man is only the art of keeping his
agitations locked within his breast.

25. Firmer virtues are required to support good fortune than bad.

28. Jealousy is, in its way, both fair and reasonable, since its intention is
to preserve for ourselves something which is ours, or which we believe to

be ours; envy, on the other hand, is a frenzy which cannot endure contemplating the possessions of others.

31. Were we faultless, we would not derive such satisfaction from remarking the faults of others.

38. Our promises are made in hope, and kept in fear.

50. A man convinced of his own merit will accept misfortune as an honor, for thus can he persuade others, as well as himself, that he is a worthy target for the arrows of fate.

56. To achieve a position in the world a man will do his utmost to appear already arrived.

59. There is no accident so disastrous that a clever man cannot derive some profit from it: nor any so fortunate that a fool cannot turn it to his disadvantage.

62. Sincerity comes from an open heart. It is exceedingly rare; what usually passes for sincerity is only an artful pretense designed to win the confidence of others.

67. Grace is to the body what sense is to the mind.

71. When two people have ceased to love, the memory that remains is almost always one of shame.

72. Love, to judge by most of its effects, is closer to hatred than to friendship.

75. Love, like fire, needs constant motion; when it ceases to hope, or to fear, love dies.

78. For most men the love of justice is only the fear of suffering injustice.

79. For a man who lacks self-confidence, silence is the wisest course.

83. What men have called friendship is only a social arrangement, a mutual adjustment of interests, an interchange of services given and received; it is, in sum, simply a business from which those involved purpose to derive a steady profit for their own self-love.

89. Everyone complains of his memory, none of his judgment.

90. In daily life our faults are frequently more pleasant than our good qualities.

93. Old people love to give good advice: it compensates them for their inability nowadays to set a bad example.

119. We are so accustomed to adopting a mask before others that we end by being unable to recognize ourselves.

122. If we master our passions it is due to their weakness, not our strength.

134. We are never so ridiculous through what we are as through what we pretend to be.

138. We would rather speak ill of ourselves than not at all.

144. We do not like to give praise, and we never do so without reasons of self-interest. Praise is a cunning, concealed and delicate form of flattery

which, in different ways, gratifies both the giver and the receiver; the one accepts it as the reward for merit; the other bestows it to display his sense of justice and his powers of discernment.

146. We usually only praise that we may be praised.

149. The refusal to accept praise is the desire to be praised twice over.

150. The wish to deserve the praise we receive strengthens our virtues; and praise bestowed upon wit, courage and beauty contributes to their increase.

167. Avarice, more than open-handedness, is the opposite of economy.

170. When a man's behavior is straightforward, sincere and honest it is hard to be sure whether this is due to rectitude or cleverness.

176. In love there are two sorts of constancy: the one comes from the perpetual discovery of new delights in the beloved: the other, from the self-esteem which we derive from our own fidelity.

180. Our repentance is less a regret for the evil we have done than a precaution against the evil that may be done to us.

185. Evil, like good, has its heroes.

186. Not all who have vices are contemptible: all without a trace of virtue are.

190. Only great men are marked with great faults.

192. When our vices depart from us, we flatter ourselves that it is we who have rid ourselves of them.

200. Virtue would not go so far did vanity not keep her company.

205. Virtue, in women, is often love of reputation and fondness for tranquillity.

216. Perfect valor is to behave, without witnesses, as one would act were all the world watching.

218. Hypocrisy is the tribute that vice pays to virtue.

230. Nothing is as contagious as example, and we never perform an outstandingly good or evil action without its producing others of its sort. We copy goodness in the spirit of emulation, and wickedness owing to the malignity of our nature which shame holds in check until example sets it free.

237. No man should be praised for his goodness if he lacks the strength to be bad: in such cases goodness is usually only the effect of indolence or impotence of will.

259. The pleasure of love is in loving: and there is more joy in the passion one feels than in that which one inspires.

264. Pity is often only the sentiment of our own misfortunes felt in the ills of others. It is a clever pre-science of the evil times upon which we may fall. We help others in order to ensure their help in similar circumstances; and the kindnesses we do them are, if the truth were told, only acts of charity towards ourselves invested against the future.

276. Absence diminishes small loves and increases great ones, as the

wind blows out the candle and blows up the bonfire.

277. Women frequently believe themselves to be in love even when they are not: the pursuit of an intrigue, the stimulus of gallantry, the natural inclination towards the joys of being loved, and the difficulty of refusal, all these combine to tell them that their passions are aroused when in fact it is but their coquetry at play.

375. It is the habit of mediocre minds to condemn all that is beyond their grasp.

376. True friendship destroys envy, as true love puts an end to coquetry.

378. We give advice but we do not inspire behavior.

392. One should treat one's fate as one does one's health; enjoy it when it is good, be patient with it when it is poorly, and never attempt any drastic cure save as an ultimate resort.

399. There is a form of eminence which is quite independent of our fate; it is an air which distinguishes us from our fellow men and makes us appear destined for great things; it is the value which we imperceptibly attach to ourselves; it is the quality which wins us the deference of others; more than birth, honours or even merit, it gives us ascendancy.

417. In love, the person who recovers first recovers best.

423. Few people know how to be old.

467. Vanity leads us to act against our inclinations more often than does reason.

479. Only people who are strong can be truly gentle: what normally passes for gentleness is mere weakness, which quickly turns sour.

483. Vanity, rather than malice, is the usual source of slander.

540. Hope and fear are inseparable. There is no hope without fear, nor any fear without hope.

576. We always discover, in the misfortunes of our dearest friends, something not altogether displeasing.

597. No man can be sure of his own courage until he has stared danger in the face.

617. How can we expect another to keep our secret, if we cannot keep it ourself?

1655–1678

George Bernard Shaw: FROM THE REVOLUTIONIST'S HANDBOOK (IN MAN AND SUPERMAN)

Democracy

Democracy substitutes selection by the incompetent many for appointment by the corrupt few.

Democratic republics can no more dispense with national idols than monarchies with public functionaries.

Liberty and Equality

He who confuses political liberty with freedom and political equality with similarity has never thought for five minutes about either.

Nothing can be unconditional: consequently nothing can be free.

Liberty means responsibility. That is why most men dread it.

The duke inquires contemptuously whether his gamekeeper is the equal of the Astronomer Royal; but he insists that they shall both be hanged equally if they murder him.

The notion that the colonel need be a better man than the private is as confused as the notion that the keystone need be stronger than the coping stone.

The relation of superior to inferior excludes good manners.

Education

When a man teaches something he does not know to somebody else who has no aptitude for it, and gives him a certificate of proficiency, the latter has completed the education of a gentleman.

A fool's brain digests philosophy into folly, science into superstition, and art into pedantry. Hence University education.

The best brought-up children are those who have seen their parents as they are. Hypocrisy is not the parent's first duty.

The vilest abortionist is he who attempts to mould a child's character.

He who can, does. He who cannot, teaches.

A learned man is an idler who kills time with study. Beware of his false knowledge: it is more dangerous than ignorance.

Activity is the only road to knowledge.

Every fool believes what his teachers tell him, and calls his credulity science or morality as confidently as his father called it divine revelation.

No man fully capable of his own language ever masters another.

No man can be a pure specialist without being in the strict sense an idiot.

Do not give your children moral and religious instruction unless you are quite sure they will not take it too seriously. Better be the mother of Henri Quatre and Nell Gwynne than of Robespierre and Queen Mary Tudor.

Virtues and Vices

No specific virtue or vice in a man implies the existence of any other specific virtue or vice in him, however closely the imagination may associate them.

Virtue consists, not in abstaining from vice, but in not desiring it.

Self-denial is not a virtue: it is only the effect of prudence on rascality.

Obedience simulates subordination as fear of the police simulates honesty.

Disobedience, the rarest and most courageous of the virtues, is seldom distinguished from neglect, the laziest and commonest of the vices.

Vice is waste of life. Poverty, obedience, and celibacy are the canonical vices.

Economy is the art of making the most of life.

The love of economy is the root of all virtue.

Greatness

In heaven an angel is nobody in particular.

Greatness is the secular name for Divinity: both mean simply what lies beyond us.

If a great man could make us understand him, we should hang him.

We admit that when the divinity we worshipped made itself visible and comprehensible we crucified it.

To a mathematician the eleventh means only a single unit: to the bushman who cannot count further than his ten fingers it is an incalculable myriad.

The difference between the shallowest routineer and the deepest thinker appears, to the latter, trifling; to the former, infinite.

its meanness to the world; or if it were sublime, to know it by experience, and be able to give a true account of it in my next excursion.
Henry David Thoreau, *Walden* 1854

Unhappye are they whyche have more appetite than theyr stomake.
Sir Thomas Elyot, *The Bankette of Sapience* 1545

Men dig their Graves with their own Teeth and die more by those fatal instruments than the Weapons of their Enemies.
Thomas Moffett, *Helth's Improvement* 1590

We must check our speed. We bring up our children too fast, we work too fast, we dissipate too fast, we eat too fast, live too fast, and, consequently, always ahead of our time, we die too fast.
Anonymous, *How to Keep Well,* in *Harper's Monthly* December 1856

Wholesome food and drink are cheaper than doctors and hospitals.
Dr. Carl C. Wahl, *Essential Health Knowledge* 1966

I see no virtues where I smell no sweat.
Francis Quarles, *Enchiridion* 1640

Labour and Abstinence are two of the best Physicians in the World.
Thomas Tryon, *The Country-man's Companion* 1684

Industry must make a purse, and frugality find strings for it.
Esther Copley, *Cottage Comforts* 1825

Frugality is good, if liberality be joyn'd with it. The first is leaving off superfluous Expences; the last, bestowing them to the Benefit of others that need. The first without the last begins Covetousness; the last without the first begins Prodigality. Both together make an excellent Temper. Happy the Place where that is found.
William Penn, *Some Fruits of Solitude* 1726

Let us spare where we may, so that we may spend where we should.
Thomas Fuller, *Wise Words & Quaint Counsels* 1892

Economy is a poor man's revenue; extravagance a rich man's ruin.
Anonymous, *Proverbs for Daily Living* undated

A life without festivities is a long road without inns.
Democritus, *Ethical Precepts* ca. 400 B.C.

To me, Spring is a movement, a mighty surging upward. It isn't coaxed from above, but moved from below. The growing things break upward through the crust of chill earth the way a man gets out of bed on a zero morning—gradually, reluctantly, cover by cover, a toe at a time; not because someone has waked him, but because he has accumulated the

In a stupid nation the man of genius becomes a god: everybody worships him and nobody does his will.

Gambling

The most popular method of distributing wealth is the method of the roulette table.

The roulette table pays nobody except him that keeps it. Nevertheless a passion for gaming is common, though a passion for keeping roulette tables is unknown.

Gambling promises the poor what Property performs for the rich: that is why the bishops dare not denounce it fundamentally.

1903

Helen Nearing: FROM WISE WORDS ON THE GOOD LIFE

The ayre can not be to clene and pure: consyderynge it doth compasse us rounde aboute, and we do receyve it unto us. We can not be without it, for we lyve by it as the fysshe lyveth by the water. Good ayre, therfore, is to be praysed.

Andrewe Boorde, *A Dyetary of Helth* 1542

The more I am acquainted with agricultural affairs, the better I am pleased with them; insomuch, that I can no where find so great satisfaction as in those innocent and useful pursuits. In indulging these feelings, I am led to reflect how much more delightful to an undebauched mind, is the task of making improvements on the earth, than all the vainglory which can be acquired from ravaging it, by the most uninterrupted career of conquests.

George Washington, *Letter to Arthur Young* December 4, 1788

I went to the woods because I wished to live life deliberately, to front only the essential facts of life, and see if I could not learn what it had to teach, and not, when I came to die, discover that I had not lived. I did not wish to live what was not life, living is so dear; nor did I wish to practice resignation, unless it was quite necessary. I wanted to live deep and suck out all the marrow of life, to live so sturdily and spartan-like as to put to rout all that was not life, to cut a broad swath and shave close, to drive life into a corner, and reduce it to its lowest terms, and, if it proved to be mean, why then to get the whole and genuine meanness of it, and publish

its meanness to the world; or if it were sublime, to know it by experience, and be able to give a true account of it in my next excursion.
Henry David Thoreau, Walden 1854

Unhappye are they whyche have more appetite than theyr stomake.
Sir Thomas Elyot, The Bankette of Sapience 1545

Men dig their Graves with their own Teeth and die more by those fatal instruments than the Weapons of their Enemies.
Thomas Moffett, Helth's Improvement 1590

We must check our speed. We bring up our children too fast, we work too fast, we dissipate too fast, we eat too fast, live too fast, and, consequently, always ahead of our time, we die too fast.
Anonymous, How to Keep Well, in Harper's Monthly December 1856

Wholesome food and drink are cheaper than doctors and hospitals.
Dr. Carl C. Wahl, Essential Health Knowledge 1966

I see no virtues where I smell no sweat.
Francis Quarles, Enchiridion 1640

Labour and Abstinence are two of the best Physicians in the World.
Thomas Tryon, The Country-man's Companion 1684

Industry must make a purse, and frugality find strings for it.
Esther Copley, Cottage Comforts 1825

Frugality is good, if liberality be joyn'd with it. The first is leaving off superfluous Expences; the last, bestowing them to the Benefit of others that need. The first without the last begins Covetousness; the last without the first begins Prodigality. Both together make an excellent Temper. Happy the Place where that is found.
William Penn, Some Fruits of Solitude 1726

Let us spare where we may, so that we may spend where we should.
Thomas Fuller, Wise Words & Quaint Counsels 1892

Economy is a poor man's revenue; extravagance a rich man's ruin.
Anonymous, Proverbs for Daily Living undated

A life without festivities is a long road without inns.
Democritus, Ethical Precepts ca. 400 B.C.

To me, Spring is a movement, a mighty surging upward. It isn't coaxed from above, but moved from below. The growing things break upward through the crust of chill earth the way a man gets out of bed on a zero morning—gradually, reluctantly, cover by cover, a toe at a time; not because someone has waked him, but because he has accumulated the

In a stupid nation the man of genius becomes a god: everybody worships him and nobody does his will.

Gambling

The most popular method of distributing wealth is the method of the roulette table.

The roulette table pays nobody except him that keeps it. Nevertheless a passion for gaming is common, though a passion for keeping roulette tables is unknown.

Gambling promises the poor what Property performs for the rich: that is why the bishops dare not denounce it fundamentally.

1903

Helen Nearing: FROM WISE WORDS ON THE GOOD LIFE

The ayre can not be to clene and pure: consyderynge it doth compasse us rounde aboute, and we do receyve it unto us. We can not be without it, for we lyve by it as the fysshe lyveth by the water. Good ayre, therfore, is to be praysed.
                              Andrewe Boorde, *A Dyetary of Helth* 1542

The more I am acquainted with agricultural affairs, the better I am pleased with them; insomuch, that I can no where find so great satisfaction as in those innocent and useful pursuits. In indulging these feelings, I am led to reflect how much more delightful to an undebauched mind, is the task of making improvements on the earth, than all the vainglory which can be acquired from ravaging it, by the most uninterrupted career of conquests.
                  George Washington, *Letter to Arthur Young* December 4, 1788

I went to the woods because I wished to live life deliberately, to front only the essential facts of life, and see if I could not learn what it had to teach, and not, when I came to die, discover that I had not lived. I did not wish to live what was not life, living is so dear; nor did I wish to practice resignation, unless it was quite necessary. I wanted to live deep and suck out all the marrow of life, to live so sturdily and spartan-like as to put to rout all that was not life, to cut a broad swath and shave close, to drive life into a corner, and reduce it to its lowest terms, and, if it proved to be mean, why then to get the whole and genuine meanness of it, and publish

necessary refreshment of sleep and is ready to go forth and do the day's work.

Richardson Wright, Truly Rural 1922

Gardening is one of the best-natured delights of all others, for a man to look about him, and see nothing but the effects and improvements of his own art and diligence; to be always gathering some fruits of it, and at the same time to behold others ripening, and others budding; to see his soil covered with the beauteous creatures of his own industry; and to see, like God, that all his works are good.

Abraham Cowley, Of Agriculture 1668

One hears a lot about the rules of good husbandry; there is only one —leave the land far better than you found it.

George Henderson, The Farming Ladder 1944

It will not always be summer: build barns.

Hesiod, Works and Days ca. 800 B.C.

A culture begins with simple things—with the way the potter moulds the clay on his wheel, the way a weaver threads his yarns, the way the builder builds his house. Greek culture did not begin with the Parthenon: it began with a white-washed hut on a hillside.

Herbert Read, The Politics of the Unpolitical 1943

If a man cannot start a cooking fire, he can always locate a Boy Scout to do it for him.

Frank Shay, The Best Men are Cooks 1941

There are no riches above a sound body, and no joy above the joy of the heart.

A good wife, and health, are a man's best wealth.

Contentment is the philosopher's stone, which turns all it toucheth into gold; the poor man is rich with it, the rich man poor without it.

Riches consists not in the extent of possessions but in the fewness of wants.

Anonymous, Proverbs for Daily Living undated

If there are people at once rich and content, be assured that they are content because they know how to be so, not because they are rich.

Charles Wagner, The Simple Life 1901

How happy is he that owes nothing but to himself, and only that which he can easily refuse or easily pay. I do not reckon him poor that has but a little. . . . All I desire is that my poverty may not be a burden to myself, or make me so to others; and that is the best state of fortune, that is neither necessitous, nor far from it.

With parsimony, a little is sufficient, and without it, nothing; whereas
frugality makes a poor man rich. If we lose an estate, we had better never
have had it. He that has least to lose has least to fear; and those are better
satisfied whom fortune never favored, than those whom she has forsaken.

He that is not content in poverty would not be so neither in plenty; for
the fault is not in the thing, but in the mind. If he be sickly, remove him
from a cottage to a palace, he is at the same pass; for he carries his disease
along with him. What can be happier than that condition both of mind
and of fortune from which we cannot fall? A man may lie as warm and as
dry under a thatched as under a gilded roof.

Seneca, Of a Happy Life A.D. 45

A good wife is a world of wealth, where just cause of content makes a
kingdom in conceit: she is the eye of wariness, the tongue of silence, the
hand of labour, and the heart of love: a companion of kindness, a mistress
of passion, an exercise of patience, and an example of experience: she is
the kitchen physician, the chamber comfort, the hall's care, and the
parlour's grace; she is the dairy's neatness, the brew-house's wholesome-
ness, the garner's provision, and the garden's plantation: her voice is
music, her countenance meekness, her mind virtuous, and her soul gracious: she is her husband's jewel, her children's joy, her neighbor's love,
and her servant's honour: she is poverty's prayer, and charity's praise,
religion's love, and devotion's zeal: she is a care of necessity, and a course
of thrift, a book of housewifery, and a mirror of modesty. In sum, she is
God's blessing, and man's happiness, earth's honour and Heaven's creature.

Nicholas Breton, The Good and the Bad 1616

The right Education of the Female Sex, as it is in a manner every where
neglected, so it ought to be generally lamented. Most in this depraved
later Age think a Woman learned and wise enough if she can distinguish
her Husband's Bed from anothers. Vain man is apt to think we were
merely intended for the World's propagation, and to keep its humane
inhabitants sweet and clean; but by their leaves, had we the same Literature books and opportunity to read them, he would find our brains as
fruitful as our bodies.

Hannah Wooley, The Gentlewoman's Companion 1673

The most conventional customs cling to the table. Farmers who wouldn't
drive a horse too hard expect pie three times a day.

Ella H. Richards, The Healthful Farmhouse 1906

No one need be ashamed of plain dinners if given with a hearty welcome.

Anonymous, Table Observances 1854

As long as we live in public, business breaks in upon us, as one billow
drives on another, and there is no avoiding it with either modesty or

quiet. It is a kind of whirlpool that sucks a man in, and he can never disengage himself. A man of business cannot in truth be said to live, and not one of a thousand understands how to do it. It is the greatest of all miseries to be perpetually employed upon other people's business; for to sleep, to eat, to drink at their hours, to walk their pace, and to love and hate as they do, is the vilest of servitudes.

Seneca, Of a Happy Life A.D. 54

I learned this, at least, by my experiment, that if one advances confidently in the direction of his dreams, and endeavors to live the life which he has imagined, he will meet with a success unexpected in common hours. He will put some things behind, will pass an invisible boundary; new, universal, and more liberal laws will begin to establish themselves around and within him; or the old laws be expanded, and interpreted in his favor in a more liberal sense, and he will live with the license of a higher order of beings. In proportion as he simplifies his life, the laws of the universe will appear less complex, and solitude will not be solitude, nor poverty poverty, nor weakness weakness. If you have built castles in the air, your work need not be lost, that is what they should be. Now put foundations under them.

Henry David Thoreau, Walden 1854

No meal is as good as when you have your feet under your own table.

Scott Nearing, an opinion 1970

1980

History

Herbert Butterfield

THE ORIGINALITY OF THE OLD TESTAMENT

The Old Testament sometimes seems very ancient, but the earliest considerable body of historical literature that we possess was being produced through a period of a thousand years and more before that. It consisted of what we call "annals," written in the first person singular by the heads of great empires which had their centre in Egypt or Mesopotamia or Asia Minor. These monarchs, often year by year, would produce accounts—quite detailed accounts sometimes—of their military campaigns. It is clear from what they say that one of their objects in life was to put their own personal achievements on record—their building feats, their prowess in the hunt, but also their victories in war. They show no sign of having had any interest in the past, but, amongst other things, they betray a great anxiety about the reputation they would have after they were dead. They did not look behind them to previous generations, but instead they produced what we should call the history of their own times, in a way rather like Winston Churchill producing his account of his wars against Germany in the twentieth century.

After this, however, a great surprise occurs. There emerges from nowhere a people passionately interested in the past, dominated by an historical memory. It is clear that this is due to the fact that there is a bygone event that they really cannot get over; it takes command over their whole mentality. This people were the ancient Hebrews. They had been semi-nomads, moving a great deal in the desert, but having also certain periods in rather better areas where they could grow a bit of something. Like semi-nomads in general, they had longed to have land of their own, a settled land which they could properly cultivate. This is what they expected their God to provide for them, and what he promised to provide. Indeed the semi-nomads would tend to judge his effectiveness

714

as a god by his ability to carry out his promise. The ancient Hebrews, the Children of Israel, had to wait a long time for their due reward, and perhaps this was the reason why they were so tremendously impressed when ultimately the Promise was actually fulfilled.

The earliest thing that we know from sheer historical evidence about these people is that as soon as they appear in the light of day they are already dominated by this historical memory. In some of the earliest books of the Bible there are embedded patches of text far earlier still, far earlier than the Old Testament itself, and repeatedly they are passages about this very thing. Fresh references go on perpetually being made to the same matter throughout the many centuries during which the Old Testament was being produced, indeed also in the Jewish literature that was written for a few centuries after that. We are more sure that the memory of this historical event was the predominating thing amongst them than we are of the reality, the actual historicity, of the event itself.

What they commemorated in this tremendous way, of course, was the fact that God had brought them up out of the land of Egypt and into the Promised Land. In reality it seems pretty clear that some of the tribes of Israel did not come into the land of Palestine from Egypt at all. Nevertheless I think it would be a central view amongst scholars that some of the ancient Hebrews came to the Promised Land from Egypt, and the impression of this was so powerful that it became the common memory of the whole group of tribes which settled in the land of Canaan; it became the accepted tradition even among the tribes that had never been in Egypt. Moreover the common tradition was the very thing that became the effective bond between the tribes of Israel, helping to weld them together as a people. This sense of a common history is always a powerful factor in fusing a group of tribes into a nation, just as Homer made the various bodies of Greeks feel that they had had a common experience in the past, a consciousness that they were all Hellenes. All this was so powerful with the Children of Israel because they felt such a fabulous gratitude for what had happened. I know of no other case in history where gratitude was carried so far, no other case where gratitude proved to be such a generative thing. Their God had stepped into history and kept his ancient Promise, bringing them to freedom and the Promised Land, and they simply could not get over it.

This was not the first time in history that gratitude had been a factor in religion, for at a date earlier still there are signs amongst the Hittites that the very sincerity of their feeling of indebtedness added an attractive kind of devotion to their worship of their pagan deities. But this gratitude was such a signal thing amongst the Israelitish people that it altered the whole development of religion in that quarter of the globe; it altered the character of religion in the area from which our Western civilisation sprang. It gave the Children of Israel a historical event that they could not get over, could not help remembering, and in the first place it made them historians—historians in a way that nobody had ever been before. The ancient Hebrews worshipped the God who brought them up out of the land of Egypt more than they worshipped God as the Creator of the World. By all the rules of the game, when once they had settled down in the land of Canaan and become an agricultural people, they ought to have turned to the gods of nature, the gods of fertility, and this is what some of their number wanted to do. But their historical memory was too strong. Even when they borrowed rites and ceremonies from neighbouring peoples—pieces of ritual based on the cycle of nature, the succession of the seasons—they turned these into celebrations of historical events, just as I suppose Christianity may have turned the rites of Spring into a celebration of the Resurrection. The Hebrews took over circumcision, which existed amongst their neighbours, but they turned even this into the celebration of a historical event. A Harvest Festival is an occasion on which even amongst Christians to-day we call attention to the cycle of the seasons and the bounty of nature. But amongst the Children of Israel at this ceremony you handed your thankoffering to the priest and then, if you please, you did not speak of the corn or the vine—you recited your national history, you narrated the story of the Exodus. It was set down in writing that if the younger generation started asking why they were expected to obey God's commandments they should be told that it was because God had brought their forefathers out of the house of bondage. Everything was based on their gratitude for what God had done for the nation. And it is remarkable to see to what a degree the other religious ideas of the Old Testament always remained historical in character—the Promise, the Covenant, the Judgment, the Messiah, the remnant of Israel, etc.

Yet this Promised Land to which God had brought them and on which they based a religion of extravagant gratitude was itself no great catch, and if they called it a land flowing with milk and honey, this was only because it looked rich when compared to the life that they had hitherto led. In the twentieth century Palestine has demanded a tremendous wrestling with nature, and if one looks back to the state of that region in Old Testament times one cannot help feeling that Providence endowed this people with one of the riskiest bits of territory that existed in that part of the globe. They were placed in an area which had already been encircled by vast empires, based on Egypt and on Mesopotamia and on a Hittite realm in Asia Minor. And, for all their gratitude, they were one of the most unlucky peoples of history. Other great empires soon arose again in the same regions, and they were so placed that they could not be expected to keep their freedom—their independence as a state only lasted for a few centuries, something like the period between Tudor

England and the present day.[1] The one stroke of luck that they did have was that for just a space at the crucial period those surrounding empires had come into decline, and this gave the Hebrews the chance of forming an independent state for a while. They virtually stood in the cockpit in that part of the world, just as Belgium stood in the cockpit in Western Europe and Poland in Eastern Europe. The fact that the Hebrews became, along with the Greeks, one of the main contributors to the formation of Western civilisation is a triumph of mind over matter, of the human spirit over misfortune and disaster. They almost built their religion on gratitude for their good fortune in having a country at all, a country that they could call their own.

Because of the great act of God which had brought them to Palestine they devoted themselves to the God of History rather than to the gods of nature. Here is their great originality, the thing that in a way enabled them to change the very nature of religion. Because they turned their intellect to the actions of God in history, they were drawn into an ethical view of God. They were continually wrestling with him about ethical questions, continually debating with him as to whether he was playing fair with them. Religion became intimately connected with morality because this was a God who was always in personal relations with human beings in the ordinary historical realm, and in any case you find that it was the worshippers of the gods of nature who ran to orgies and cruelties and immoralities. In fact, the ancient Hebrews developed their thought about God, about personality, and about ethics all together, all rolled into one. Because these things all involved what we call problems of personal relations they developed their thought about history step by step along with the rest. For a student of history, one of the interesting features of the Old Testament is that it gives us evidence of religious development from very early stages, from most primitive ideas about God, some of these ideas being quite shocking to the modern mind. Indeed, in some of the early books of the Bible there are still embedded certain ancient things that make it look as though, here as in no other parts of Western Asia, the God of History may at one stage have been really the God of War.

So far as I have been able to discover—approaching the matter as a modern historian, and rather an outsider, and using only what is available in Western languages—the Children of Israel, while still a comparatively primitive society, are the first people who showed a really significant interest in the past, the first to produce anything like a history of their nation, the first to lay out what we call a universal history, doing it with the help of some Babylonian legends but attempting to see the whole story of the human race. Because what we possess in the Old Testament is history as envisaged by the priests, or at least by the religious people, it

1. Queen Elizabeth I, the last of the Tudor monarchs, died in 1603.

is also a history very critical of the rulers—not like the mass of previous historical writing, a case of monarchs blowing their own trumpets. The history they wrote is a history of the people and not just of the kings, and it is very critical even of the people. So far as I know here is the only case of a nation producing a national history and making it an exposure of its national sins. In a technical sense this ancient Hebrew people became very remarkable as writers of history, some of their narratives (for example, the death of King David and the question of the succession to his throne) being quite wonderful according to modern standards of judgment. It was to be of momentous importance for the development of Western civilisation, that, growing up in Europe (with Christianity presiding over its creative stages), it was influenced by the Old Testament, by this ancient Jewish passion for history. For century after century over periods of nearly 2000 years, the European could not even learn about his religion without studying the Bible, including the Old Testament—essentially a history-book, a book of very ancient history. Our civilisation, unlike many others, became historically-minded, therefore, one that was interested in the past, and we owe that in a great part to the Old Testament.

1949

QUESTIONS

1. What difference does Butterfield find between the writings of the ancient Hebrews and writings made in the empires of the Near East? What caused the difference?
2. What was the effect of historical memory on the formation of the ancient nation of Israel?
3. How did the sense of history in Israel make Hebrew religion different from the religions around Israel?
4. What value does Butterfield attach to being "historically-minded"? Does his essay imply that being so minded is beneficial? In what specific ways?

Henry David Thoreau

THE BATTLE OF THE ANTS

One day when I went out to my wood-pile, or rather my pile of stumps, I observed two large ants, the one red, the other much larger, nearly half an inch long, and black, fiercely contending with one another. Having once got hold they never let go, but struggled and wrestled and rolled on the chips incessantly. Looking farther, I was surprised to find that the chips were covered with such combatants, that it was not a *duellum*, but a *bellum*, a war between two races of ants, the red always pitted against the black, and frequently two red ones to one black. The legions of these Myrmidons[1] covered all the hills and vales in my wood-yard, and the ground was already strewn with the dead and dying, both red and black. It was the only battle which I have ever witnessed, the only battle-field I ever trod while the battle was raging; internecine war; the red republicans on the one hand, and the black imperialists on the other. On every side they were engaged in deadly combat, yet without any noise that I could hear, and human soldiers never fought so resolutely. I watched a couple that were fast locked in each other's embraces, in a little sunny valley amid the chips, now at noonday prepared to fight till the sun went down, or life went out. The smaller red champion had fastened himself like a vice to his adversary's front, and through all the tumblings on that field never for an instant ceased to gnaw at one of his feelers near the root, having already caused the other to go by the board; while the stronger black one dashed him from side to side, and, as I saw on looking nearer, had already divested him of several of his members. They fought with more pertinacity than bulldogs. Neither manifested the least disposition to retreat. It was evident that their battle-cry was "Conquer or die." In the meanwhile there came along a single red ant on the hillside of this valley, evidently full of excitement, who either had despatched his foe, or had not yet taken part in the battle; probably the latter, for he had lost none of his limbs; whose mother had charged him to return with his shield or upon it. Or perchance he was some Achilles, who had nourished his wrath apart, and had now come to avenge or rescue his Patroclus.[2] He saw this unequal combat from afar—for the blacks were nearly twice the size of the red—he drew near with rapid pace till he stood on his guard within half an inch of the combatants; then, watching his opportunity, he sprang upon the black warrior, and commenced his operations near the root of his right fore leg, leaving the foe to select among his own mem-

---

1. The reference is to the powerful soldiers of Achilles in Homer's *Iliad*.

2. A Greek warrior in the *Iliad*, whose death Achilles avenges.

bers; and so there were three united for life, as if a new kind of attraction had been invented which put all other locks and cements to shame. I should not have wondered by this time to find that they had their respective musical bands stationed on some eminent chip, and playing their national airs the while, to excite the slow and cheer the dying combatants. I was myself excited somewhat even as if they had been men. The more you think of it, the less the difference. And certainly there is not the fight recorded in Concord history, at least, if in the history of America, that will bear a moment's comparison with this, whether for the numbers engaged in it, or for the patriotism and heroism displayed. For numbers and for carnage it was an Austerlitz or Dresden.[3] Concord Fight! Two killed on the patriots' side, and Luther Blanchard wounded! Why here every ant was a Buttrick—"Fire! for God's sake fire!"—and thousands shared the fate of Davis and Hosmer. There was not one hireling there. I have no doubt that it was a principle they fought for, as much as our ancestors, and not to avoid a three-penny tax on their tea; and the results of this battle will be as important and memorable to those whom it concerns as those of the battle of Bunker Hill, at least.

I took up the chip on which the three I have particularly described were struggling, carried into my house, and placed it under a tumbler on my window-sill, in order to see the issue. Holding a microscope to the first-mentioned red ant, I saw that, though he was assiduously gnawing at the near fore leg of his enemy, having severed his remaining feeler, his own breast was all torn away, exposing what vitals he had there to the jaws of the black warrior, whose breastplate was apparently too thick for him to pierce; and the dark carbuncles of the sufferer's eyes shone with ferocity such as war only could excite. They struggled half an hour longer under the tumbler, and when I looked again the black soldier had severed the heads of his foes from their bodies, and the still living heads were hanging on either side of him like ghastly trophies at his saddle-bow, still apparently as firmly fastened as ever, and he was endeavoring with feeble struggles, being without feelers, and with only the remnant of a leg, and I know not how many other wounds, to divest himself of them; which at length, after half an hour more, he accomplished. I raised the glass, and he went off over the window-sill in that crippled state. Whether he finally survived that combat, and spent the remainder of his days in some Hôtel des Invalides,[4] I do not know; but I thought that his industry would not be worth much thereafter. I never learned which party was victorious, nor the cause of the war, but I felt for the rest of that day as if I had my feelings excited and harrowed by witnessing the struggle, the ferocity and carnage, of a human battle before my door.

Kirby and Spence tell us that the battles of ants have long been

3. Bloody Napoleonic victories.   soldiers and sailors.
4. The famous French hospital for wounded

celebrated and the date of them recorded, though they say that Huber[5] is the only modern author who appears to have witnessed them. "Aeneas Sylvius," say they, "after giving a very circumstantial account of one contested with great obstinacy by a great and small species on the trunk of a pear tree," adds that "'this action was fought in the pontificate of Eugenius the Fourth, in the presence of Nicholas Pistoriensis, an eminent lawyer, who related the whole history of the battle with the greatest fidelity.' A similar engagement between great and small ants is recorded by Olaus Magnus, in which the small ones, being victorious, are said to have buried the bodies of their own soldiers, but left those of their giant enemies a prey to the birds. This event happened previous to the expulsion of the tyrant Christiern the Second from Sweden." The battle which I witnessed took place in the Presidency of Polk, five years before the passage of Webster's Fugitive-Slave Bill.[6]

1854

5. Kirby and Spence were nineteenth-century American entomologists; Huber was a great Swiss entomologist.
6. Passed in 1851.

QUESTIONS

1. *Thoreau uses the Latin word* bellum *to describe the battle of the ants and he quickly follows this with a reference to the Myrmidons of Achilles. What comparison is implicit here? Find further examples of it. This passage comes from a chapter entitled "Brute Neighbors"; how does this comparison amplify the meaning of that title?*

2. *Describe the life, or part of the life, of an animal so that, while remaining faithful to the facts as you understand them, your description opens outward as does Thoreau's, and speaks not only of the animal but also of man, society, or nature.*

John Livingston Lowes

TIME IN THE MIDDLE AGES

We live in terms of *time*. And so pervasive is that element of our consciousness that we have to stand, as it were, outside it for a moment to realize how completely it controls our lives. For we think and act perpetually, we mortals who look before and after, in relation to hours and days and weeks and months and years. Yesterday and to-morrow, next week a month from now, a year ago, in twenty minutes—those are the terms in which, wittingly or automatically, we act and plan and think. And to orient ourselves at any moment in that streaming continuum we carry watches on our wrists, and put clocks about our houses and on our public towers, and somewhere in our eye keep calendars, and scan time-tables when we would go abroad. And all this is so utterly familiar that it has ceased to be a matter of conscious thought or inference at all. And—to come to the heart of the business—unless we are mariners or woodsmen or astronomers or simple folk in lonely places, we never any longer reckon with the sky. Except for its bearing on the weather or upon our moods, or for contemplation of its depths of blue or fleets of white, or of the nightly splendor of its stars, we are oblivious of its influence. And therein lies the great gulf fixed between Chaucer's century[1] and ours.

For Chaucer and his contemporaries, being likewise human, also lived in terms of time. But their calendar and time-piece was that sky through which moved immutably along predestined tracks the planets and the constellations. And no change, perhaps, wrought by the five centuries between us is more revealing of material differences than that shift of attitude towards "this brave o'erhanging firmament," the sky. And it is that change, first of all, that I wish, if I can, to make clear.

There could be, I suspect, no sharper contrast than that between the "mysterious universe" of modern science, as interpreters like Eddington and Jeans have made even laymen dimly perceive it, and the nest of closed, concentric spheres in terms of which Chaucer and his coevals thought. The structure of that universe may be stated simply enough. Its intricacies need not concern us here. About the earth, as the fixed center, revolved the spheres of the seven then known planets, of which the sun and the moon were two. Beyond these seven planetary spheres lay the sphere of the fixed stars. Beyond that in turn, and carrying along with it in its "diurnal sway" the eight spheres which lay within it, moved the *primum mobile*, a ninth sphere with which, to account for certain planetary eccentricities, the Middle Ages had supplemented the Ptolemaic

1. The fourteenth; the reference is to the great Middle English poet Geoffrey Chaucer.

system.[2] We must think, in a word, of Chaucer's universe as geocentric —the "litel erthe," encompassed by "thilke speres thryes three." As an interesting fact which we have learned, we know it; to conceive it as reality demands an exercise of the imagination. And only with that mental *volte-face*[3] accomplished can we realize the cosmos as Chaucer thought of it.

Now the order of succession of the planetary spheres had farreaching implications. Starting from the earth, which was their center, that succession was as follows: Moon, Mercury, Venus, Sun, Mars, Jupiter, Saturn. And implicit in that order were two fundamental consequences—the astrological status of the successive hours of the day, and the sequence of the days of the week. The two phenomena stood in intimate relation, and some apprehension of each is fundamental to an understanding of the framework of conceptions within which Chaucer thought, and in terms of which he often wrote.

There were, then, in the first place—and this is strange to us—two sorts of *hours*, with both of which everybody reckoned. There were the hours from midnight to midnight, which constituted the "day natural" —the hours, that is, with which we are familiar—and these, in Chaucer's phrase, were "hours equal," or "hours of the *clock*." But there were also the hours which were reckoned from sunrise to sunset (which made up "day artificial"), and on from sunset to sunrise again. And these, which will most concern us, were termed "hours inequal," or "hours of the *planets*." And they were the hours of peculiar significance, bound up far more closely with human affairs than the "hours of the clock." It is worth, then, a moment's time to get them clear.

They were termed "inequal" for an obvious reason. For the periods between sunrise and sunset, and sunset and sunrise, respectively, change in length with the annual course of the sun, and the length of their twelfths, or hours, must of necessity change too, Between the equinoxes, then, it is clear that the inequal hours will now be longer by day than by night, now longer by night than by day. And only twice in the year, at the equinoxes, will the equal hours and the inequal hours—the hours of the clock and the hours of the planets—be identical. Moreover, each of the inequal hours (and this is of the first importance) was "ruled" by one of the seven planets, and it was as "hours of the planets" that the "hours inequal" touched most intimately human life. And that brings us at once to the days of the week, and their now almost forgotten implications. Why, to be explicit, is to-day Saturday? And why to-morrow Sunday? To answer those two questions is to arrive at one of the determining concepts of Chaucer's world.

2. The ancient view of the cosmos, with the earth at its center.

3. About-face; *thilke speres thryes three:* "those spheres thrice three."

Let me first arrange the seven planets in their order, starting (to simplify what follows) with the outermost. Their succession will then be this: Saturn, Jupiter, Mars, Sun, Venus, Mercury, Moon. Now Saturn will rule the first hour of the day which, for that reason, bears his name, and which we still call *Saturday*. Of that day Jupiter will rule the second hour, Mars the third, the Sun the fourth, Venue the fifth, Mercury the sixth, the Moon the seventh, and Saturn again, in due order, the eighth. Without carrying the computation farther around the clock it is obvious that Saturn will also rule the fifteenth and the twenty-second hours of the twenty-four which belong to his day. The twenty-third hour will then be ruled by Jupiter, the twenty-fourth by Mars, and the twenty-fifth by the Sun. But the twenty-fifth hour of one day is the first hour of the next, and accordingly the day after Saturn's day will be the sun's day. And so, through starry compulsion, the next day after Saturday *must* be Sunday. In precisely the same fashion—accomplished most quickly by remembering that each planet must rule the twenty-second hour of its own day —the ruling planet of the first hour of each of the succeeding days may readily be found. And their order, so found, including Saturn and the Sun, is this: Saturn, Sun, Moon, Mars, Mercury, Jupiter, Venus—then Saturn again, and so on *ad libitum*.[4] And the days of the week will accordingly be the days of the seven planets in that fixed order.

Now Saturn's day, the Sun's day, and the Moon's day are clearly recognizable in their English names of Saturday, Sunday, and Monday. But what of the remaining four—to wit, the days of Mars, Mercury, Jupiter, and Venus, which we call Tuesday, Wednesday, Thursday, and Friday? French has preserved, as also in Lundi, the planetary designations: Mardi (*Martis dies*), Mercredi (*Mercurii dies*), Jeudi (*Jovis dies*), and Vendredi (*Veneris dies*). The shift of the names in English is due to the ousting, in those four instances, of the Roman pantheon by the Germanic. Tiw, Woden, Thor, and Frig (or Freya) have usurped the seats of Mars, Mercury, Jupiter, and Venus, and given their barbarous names to the days. And in France a fourth, even more significant substitution has taken place. For the sun's day is in French *dimanche, and dimanche* is *dominica dies*, the Lord's day. And so between Saturn's planet and Diana's moon is memorialized, along with Mercury and Jupiter and Venus and Mars, the second Person of the Christian Trinity. The ancient world has crumbled, and its detritus has been remoulded into almost unrecognizable shapes. But half the history of Europe and of its early formative ideas is written in the nomenclature of the week. And that nomenclature depends in turn upon the succession of the planetary hours. And it was in terms of those hours that Chaucer and his contemporaries thought.

---

4. As you wish.

In the *Knight's Tale*,[5] to be specific, Palamon, Emily, and Arcite go to pray, each for the granting of his own desire, to the temples respectively of Venus, Diana, and Mars. And each goes, as in due observance of ceremonial propriety he must, in the hour of the planet associated with the god to whom he prays. Palamon goes to the temple of Venus, "And *in hir houre* he walketh forth." A few lines earlier that hour has been stated in everyday terms: it was "The Sonday night, er day bigan to springe . . . Although it nere nat day by houres two"—two hours, that is, before sunrise. The day that was springing after Sunday night was Monday, and the hour of Monday's sunrise is the hour of the Moon. And the hour two hours earlier, in which Palamon walked forth, was the hour ruled by Venus, to whose temple he was on the way. And Emily and Arcite, as the tale goes on, performed their pilgrimages at similarly reckoned hours. To Chaucer and his readers all this was familiar matter of the day, as instantly comprehensible as are now to us the hours which we reckon by the clock. For us alas! it has become a theme for cumbrous exposition, because the hours of the planets have vanished, with the gods whose names they bore. All that is left of them is the time-worn and wonted sequence of the seven designations of the days.

Nothing, indeed, is more characteristic of the period in which Chaucer wrote than the strange, twisted mythology, transmogrified and confused, which emerged from the association of the planets and the gods. Not even Ovid had conceived such metamorphoses.[6] For the gods were invested with the attributes of planets, and as such became accountable for the most bizarre occurrences, and kept amazing company. Under the aegis of Mars, to take one instance only, were enrolled the butchers, hangmen, tailors, barbers, cooks, cutlers, carpenters, smiths, physicians, and apothecaries—a band about as "martial" as Falstaff's Thomas Wart and Francis Feeble.[7] And so, in "the temple of mighty Mars the rede" in the *Knight's Tale*, there were depicted, together with the "open werre"[8] which was his by virtue of his godhead, the disastrous chances proceeding from his malign ascendancy as planet—the corpse in the bushes with cut throat, the nail driven, like Jael's, into the temple,[9] the sow eating the child in the cradle, the cook scalded in spite of his long ladle. And from among the members of what Chaucer twice calls Mars' "divisioun" there were present—together with the pickpurse, and "the smyler with the knyf under the cloke"—the barber and the butcher and the smith. And in the next paragraph Mars becomes again "this god of armes"—god of war and wicked planet inextricably interfused.

5. One of the stories in Chaucer's *Canterbury Tales*.
6. Ovid's *Metamorphoses* includes poetical renderings of myths dealing with the transformation of men and women into birds, flowers, trees, etc.
7. Recruits in Shakespeare's play *Henry IV*, Part 2.
8. Open war; *rede*: red.
9. The reference is to Judges iv.17–22, in which Jael offers shelter to Sisera, gives him her cloak, and quenches his thirst, and then while he is asleep kills him by driving a nail into his temple.

Moreover, as the day and week were conceived in terms of planetary sequence, so the year stood in intricate relation to the stars. the sun, with the other planets, moved annually along the vast starry track across the sky which then, as now, was called the zodiac—so called, as Chaucer lucidly explains to "litel Lowis" in the *Treatise on the Astrolabe,* because (and his etymology is sound) "*zodia* in langage of Greek sowneth [signifies] 'bestes'. . . and in the zodiak ben the twelve signes that han names of bestes." These twelve signs, as everybody knows, are Aries, Taurus, Gemini, Cancer, Leo, Virgo, Libra, Scorpio, Sagittarius, Capricornus, Aquarius, Pisces—or, to follow Chaucer's praiseworthy example and translate, Ram, Bull, Twins, Crab, Lion, Virgin, Scales, Scorpion, Archer, Goat, Water-carrier, Fishes. There they were, "eyrish bestes,"[1] as Chaucer calls them in a delightful passage that will meet us later, and along their celestial highway passed, from one sign to another, and from house to house, the seven eternal wanderers. To us who read this —though not to countless thousands even yet—the twelve constellations of the zodiac are accidental groupings, to the eye, of infinitely distant suns. To Chaucer's century they were strangely living potencies, and the earth, in the words of a greater than Chaucer,[2] was "this huge stage . . . whereon the stars in secret influence comment." Each sign, with its constellation, had its own individual efficacy or quality—Aries, "the colerik hote signe"; Taurus, cold and dry; and so on through the other ten. Each planet likewise had its own peculiar nature—Mars, like Aries, hot and dry; Venus hot and moist; and so on through the other five. And as each planet passed from sign to sign, through the agency of the successive constellations its character and influence underwent change. Chaucer in the *Astrolabe* put the matter in its simplest terms: "Whan an hot planete cometh in-to an hot signe, then encresseth his hete; and yif a planete be cold, thanne amenuseth [diminshes] his coldnesse, by cause of the hote signe." But there was far more to it than that. For these complex planetary changes exercised a determining influence upon human beings and their affairs. Arcite behind prison bars cries out:

> Som wikke aspect or disposicioun
> Of Saturne, *by sum constellacioun,*
> Hath yeven us this.

And "the olde colde Saturnus" names the constellation.

Myn is the prison in the derke cote. . .
Whyl I dwelle in the signe of the Leoun.

The tragedy of Constance, as the Man of Law conceived it, comes about because Mars, at the crucial moment, was in his "derkest hous."

1. Beasts of the air.   2. Shakespeare.

Mars gave, on the other hand, the Wife of Bath,[3] as she avers, her "sturdy hardinesse," because Mars, at her birth, was in the constellation Taurus, which was, in astrological terminology, her own "ascendent." And since the constellation Taurus was also the "night house" of Venus, certain other propensities which the wife displayed had been thrust upon her, as she cheerfully averred, by the temporary sojourn of Mars in Venus's house, when she was born.

But the march of the signs along the zodiac touched human life in yet another way. "Everich of thise twelve signes," Chaucer wrote again to his little Lewis, "hath respecte to a certein parcelle of the body of a man and hath it in governance; as Aries hath thyn heved, and Taurus thy nekke and thy throte. Gemini thyn armholes and thyn armes, and so forth." And at once one recalls Sir Toby Belch and Sir Andrew Aguecheek in *Twelfth Night*. "Shall we not set about some revels?" asks Sir Andrew. "What shall we do else?" replies Sir Toby. "Were we not born under Taurus?" "Taurus!" exclaims Sir Andrew, "that's sides and heart." "No, sir," retorts Sir Toby, "it is legs and thighs." And you may still pick up, in the shops of apothecaries here and there, cheaply printed almanacs, designed to advertise quack remedies, in which the naked human figure is displayed with lines drawn from each of the pictured zodiacal signs—Ram, Bull, Crab, Scorpion—to the limbs or organs, legs, thighs, sides, or heart, which that particular sign (in Chaucerian phrase) "hath in governance." It is not only in worn stone and faded parchments that strange fragments of the elder world survive.

1934

3. The forthright and lusty teller of "The Wife of Bath's Tale" in Chaucer's *Canterbury Tales*.

QUESTIONS

1. *Arrange the steps of Lowes' explanation of medieval time in a different order. Is your order superior to Lowes' or inferior? By what criteria?*
2. *When the advertising man and the engineer from the electronics laboratory become suburban gardeners, why may they have to reckon with the sky and neglect their watches and calendars?*
3. *List some ways in which the abstractions of watch and calendar (and time table) "rule" our lives. This list will be a selection from the particulars of daily life. What generalizations about our society will these particulars justify? Does our society, as focused in these generalizations, have a mythology—a set of hypothetical or typical characters going through hypothetical or typical experiences?*

Giovanni Boccaccio

THE BLACK DEATH

* * *

Thirteen hundred and forty-eight years had already passed after the fruitful Incarnation of the Son of God when into the distinguished city of Florence, more noble than any other Italian city, there came the deadly pestilence. It started in the East, either because of the influence of heavenly bodies or because of God's just wrath as a punishment to mortals for our wicked deeds, and it killed an infinite number of people. Without pause it spread from one place and it stretched its miserable length over the West. And against this pestilence no human wisdom or foresight was of any avail; quantities of filth were removed from the city by officials charged with this task; the entry of any sick person into the city was prohibited; and many directives were issued concerning the maintenance of good health. Nor were the humble supplications, rendered not once but many times to God by pious people, through public processions or by other means, efficacious; for almost at the beginning of springtime of the year in question the plague began to show its sorrowful effects in an extraordinary manner. It did not act as it had done in the East, where bleeding from the nose was a manifest sign of inevitable death, but it began in both men and women with certain swellings either in the groin or under the armpits, some of which grew to the size of a normal apple and others to the size of an egg (more or less), and the people called them gavoccioli. And from the two parts of the body already mentioned, within a brief space of time, the said deadly gavoccioli began to spread indiscriminately over every part of the body; and after this, the symptoms of the illness changed to black or livid spots appearing on the arms and thighs, and on every part of the body, some large ones and sometimes many little ones scattered all around. And just as the gavoccioli were originally, and still are, a very certain indication of impending death, in like manner these spots came to mean the same thing for whoever had them. Neither a doctor's advice nor the strength of medicine could do anything to cure this illness; on the contrary, either the nature of the illness was such that it afforded no cure, or else the doctors were so ignorant that they did not recognize its cause and, as a result, could not prescribe the proper remedy (in fact, the number of doctors, other than the well-trained, was increased by a large number of men and women who had never had any medical training); at any rate, few of the sick were ever cured, and almost all died after the third day of the appearance of the previously described symptoms (some sooner, others later), and most of them died without fever or any other side effects.

This pestilence was so powerful that it was communicated to the healthy by contact with the sick, the way a fire close to dry or oily things will set them aflame. And the evil of the plague went even further: not only did talking to or being around the sick bring infection and a common death, but also touching the clothes of the sick or anything touched or used by them seemed to communicate this very disease to the person involved. What I am about to say is incredible to hear, and if I and others had not witnessed it with our own eyes, I should not dare believe it (let alone write about it), no matter how trustworthy a person I might have heard it from. Let me say, then, that the power of the plague described here was of such virulence in spreading from one person to another that not only did it pass from one man to the next, but, what's more, it was often transmitted from the garments of a sick or dead man to animals that not only became contaminated by the disease, but also died within a brief period of time. My own eyes, as I said earlier, witnessed such a thing one day: when the rags of a poor man who died of this disease were thrown into the public street, two pigs came upon them, as they are wont to do, and first with their snouts and then with their teeth they took the rags and shook them around; and within a short time, after a number of convulsions, both pigs fell dead upon the ill-fated rags, as if they had been poisoned. From these and many similar or worse occurrences there came about such fear and such fantastic notions among those who remained alive that almost all of them took a very cruel attitude in the matter; that is, they completely avoided the sick and their possessions; and in so doing, each one believed that he was protecting his good health.

There were some people who thought that living moderately and avoiding all superfluity might help a great deal in resisting this disease, and so, they gathered in small groups and lived entirely apart from everyone else. They shut themselves up in those houses where there were no sick people and where one could live well by eating the most delicate of foods and drinking the finest of wines (doing so always in moderation), allowing no one to speak about or listen to anything said about the sick and the dead outside; these people lived, spending their time with music and other pleasures that they could arrange. Others thought the opposite: they believed that drinking too much, enjoying life, going about singing and celebrating, satisfying in every way the appetites as best one could, laughing, and making light of everything that happened was the best medicine for such a disease; so they practiced to the fullest what they believed by going from one tavern to another all day and night, drinking to excess; and often they would make merry in private homes, doing everything that pleased or amused them the most. This they were able to do easily, for everyone felt he was doomed to die and, as a result, abandoned his property, so that most of the houses had become common property, and any stranger who came upon them used them as if he were their rightful owner. In addition to this bestial behavior, they always managed to avoid the sick as best they could. And in this great affliction and misery of our city the revered authority of the laws, both divine and human, had fallen and almost completely disappeared, for, like other men, the ministers and executors of the laws were either dead or sick or so short of help that it was impossible for them to fulfill their duties; as a result, everybody was free to do as he pleased.

Many others adopted a middle course between the two attitudes just described: neither did they restrict their food or drink so much as the first group nor did they fall into such dissoluteness and drunkenness as the second; rather, they satisfied their appetites to a moderate degree. They did not shut themselves up, but went around carrying in their hands flowers, or sweet-smelling herbs, or various kinds of spices; and often they would put these things to their noses, believing that such smells were a wonderful means of purifying the brain, for all the air seemed infected with the stench of dead bodies, sickness, and medicines.

Others were of a crueler opinion (though it was, perhaps, a safer one): they maintained that there was no better medicine against the plague than to flee from it; and convinced of this reasoning, not caring about anything but themselves, men and women in great numbers abandoned their city, their houses, their farms, their relatives, and their possessions and sought other places, and they went at least as far away as the Florentine countryside—as if the wrath of God could not pursue them with this pestilence wherever they went but would only strike those it found within the walls of the city! Or perhaps they thought that Florence's last hour had come and that no one in the city would remain alive.

And not all those who adopted these diverse opinions died, nor did they all escape with their lives; on the contrary, many of those who thought this way were falling sick everywhere, and since they had given, when they were healthy, the bad example of avoiding the sick, they, in turn, were abandoned and left to languish away without care. The fact was that one citizen avoided another, that almost no one cared for his neighbor, and that relatives rarely or hardly ever visited each other —they stayed far apart. This disaster had struck such fear into the hearts of men and women that brother abandoned brother, uncle abandoned nephew, sister left brother, and very often wife abandoned husband, and —even worse, almost unbelievable—fathers and mothers neglected to tend and care for their children, as if they were not their own.

Thus, for the countless multitude of men and women who fell sick, there remained no support except the charity of their friends (and these were few) or the avarice of servants, who worked for inflated salaries and indecent periods of time and who, in spite of this, were few and far between; and those few were men or women of little wit (most of them not trained for such service) who did little else but hand different things

to the sick when requested to do so or watch over them while they died, and in this service, they very often lost their own lives and their profits. And since the sick were abandoned by their neighbors, their parents, and their friends and there was a scarcity of servants, a practice that was almost unheard of before spread through the city: when a woman fell sick, no matter how attractive or beautiful or noble she might be, she did not mind having a manservant (whoever he might be, no matter how young or old he was), and she had no shame whatsoever in revealing any part of her body to him—the way she would have done to a woman —when the necessity of her sickness required her to do so. This practice was, perhaps, in the days that followed the pestilence, the cause of looser morals in the women who survived the plague. And so, many people died who, by chance, might have survived if they had been attended to. Between the lack of competent attendants, which the sick were unable to obtain, and the violence of the pestilence, there were so many, many people who died in the city both day and night that it was incredible just to hear this described, not to mention seeing it! Therefore, out of sheer necessity, there arose among those who remained alive customs which were contrary to the established practices of the time.

It was the custom, as it is again today, for the women, relatives, and neighbors to gather together in the house of a dead person and there to mourn with the women who had been dearest to him; on the other hand, in front of the deceased's home, his male relatives would gather together with his male neighbors and other citizens, and the clergy also came (many of them, or sometimes just a few) depending upon the social class of the dead man. Then, upon the shoulders of his equals, he was carried to the church chosen by him before death with the funeral pomp of candles and chants. With the fury of the pestilence increasing, this custom, for the most part, died out and other practices took its place. And so, not only did people die without having a number of women around them, but there were many who passed away without even having a single witness present, and very few were granted the piteous laments and bitter tears of their relatives; on the contrary, most relatives were somewhere else, laughing, joking, and amusing themselves; even the women learned this practice too well, having put aside, for the most part, their womanly compassion for their own safety. Very few were the dead whose bodies were accompanied to the church by more than ten or twelve of their neighbors, and these dead bodies were not even carried on the shoulders of honored and reputable citizens but rather by gravediggers from the lower classes that were called *becchini*. Working for pay, they would pick up the bier and hurry it off, not to the church the dead man had chosen before his death but, in most cases, to the church closest by, accompanied by four or six churchmen with just a few candles, and often none at all. With the help of these *becchini*, the churchmen would place the body as

fast as they could in whatever unoccupied grave they could find, without
going to the trouble of saying long or solemn burial services.

The plight of the lower class and, perhaps, a large part of the middle
class, was even more pathetic: most of them stayed in their homes or
neighborhoods either because of their poverty or their hopes for remaining safe, and every day they fell sick by the thousands; and not having
servants or attendants of any kind, they almost always died. Many ended
their lives in the public streets, during the day or at night, while many
others who died in their homes were discovered dead by their neighbors
only by the smell of their decomposing bodies. The city was full of
corpses. The dead were usually given the same treatment by their neighbors, who were moved more by the fear that the decomposing corpses
would contaminate them than by any charity they might have felt towards the deceased: either by themselves or with the assistance of porters
(when they were available), they would drag the corpse out of the home
and place it in front of the doorstep where, usually in the morning,
quantities of dead bodies could be seen by any passerby; then, they were
laid out on biers, or for lack of biers, on a plank. Nor did a bier carry only
one corpse; sometimes it was used for two or three at a time. More than
once, a single bier would serve for a wife and husband, two or three
brothers, a father or son, or other relatives, all at the same time. And
countless times it happened that two priests, each with a cross, would be
on their way to bury someone, when porters carrying three or four biers
would just follow along behind them; and where these priests thought
they had just one dead man to bury, they had, in fact, six or eight and
sometimes more. Moreover, the dead were honored with no tears or
candles or funeral mourners but worse: things had reached such a point
that the people who died were cared for as we care for goats today. Thus,
it became quite obvious that what the wise had not been able to endure
with patience through the few calamities of everyday life now became a
matter of indifference to even the most simple-minded people as a result
of this colossal misfortune.

So many corpses would arrive in front of a church every day and at
every hour that the amount of holy ground for burials was certainly
insufficient for the ancient custom of giving each body its individual
place; when all the graves were full, huge trenches were dug in all of the
cemeteries of the churches and into them the new arrivals were dumped
by the hundreds; and they were packed in there with dirt, one on top of
another, like a ship's cargo, until the trench was filled.

But instead of going over every detail of the past miseries which befell
our city, let me say that the same unfriendly weather there did not,
because of this, spare the surrounding countryside any evil; there, not to
speak of the towns which, on a smaller scale, were like the city, in the
scattered villages and in the fields the poor, miserable peasants and their

families, without any medical assistance or aid of servants, died on the roads and in their fields and in their homes, as many by day as by night, and they died not like men but more like wild animals. Because of this they, like the city dwellers, became careless in their ways and did not look after their possessions or their businesses; furthermore, when they saw that death was upon them, completely neglecting the future fruits of their past labors, their livestock, their property, they did their best to consume what they already had at hand. So, it came about that oxen, donkeys, sheep, pigs, chickens and even dogs, man's most faithful companion, were driven from their homes into the fields, where the wheat was left not only unharvested but also unreaped, and they were allowed to roam where they wished; and many of these animals, almost as if they were rational beings, returned at night to their homes without any guidance from a shepherd, satiated after a good day's meal.

Leaving the countryside and returning to the city, what more can one say, except that so great was the cruelty of Heaven, and, perhaps, also that of man, that from March to July of the same year, between the fury of the pestiferous sickness and the fact that many of the sick were badly treated or abandoned in need because of the fear that the healthy had, more than one hundred thousand human beings are believed to have lost their lives for certain inside the walls of the city of Florence whereas, before the deadly plague, one would not have estimated that there were actually that many people dwelling in that city.

* * *

ca. 1353

Dorothy Gies McGuigan

TO BE A WOMAN AND A SCHOLAR

On a Saturday morning in June exactly three hundred years ago this year, the first woman in the world to receive a doctoral degree mounted a pulpit in the cathedral of Padua to be examined in Aristotelian dialectics.

Her name was Elena Lucrezia Cornaro Piscopia. She was thirty-two years old, single, daughter of one of the wealthiest families in Venice. Precociously brilliant, she had begun to study Aristotle at the age of seven. Her father had backed her studies and supplied the best of tutors; by the time she enrolled in the University of Padua, she knew not only Latin and Greek, French, English, and Spanish, but also Hebrew, Arabic, and Chaldaic.

News of the unique phenomenon of a woman scholar had drawn such throngs to witness her doctoral trial that it had to be moved from the hall of the University of Padua into the cathedral. Elena had first applied to take her doctorate in theology, but the Chancellor of the university's Theological Faculty, Cardinal Gregorio Barbarigo, Bishop of Padua, had refused indignantly. "Never," he replied. "Woman is made for motherhood, not for learning." He wrote later of the incident, "I talked with a French cardinal about it and he broke out in laughter." Reluctantly Barbarigo agreed that she be allowed to take the doctoral examination in philosophy. A modest, deeply religious young woman, Elena Cornaro had quailed before the prospect of the public examination; it was her proud, ambitious father who had insisted. A half hour before the solemn program began, Elena expressed such anguish and reluctance that her confessor had to speak very sternly to persuade her to go through with it. Her examiners were not lenient because of her sex, for the prestige of the university was at stake. But Elena's replies—in Latin, of course—were so brilliant that the judges declared the doctorate in philosophy was "hardly an honor for so towering an intellect." The doctoral ring was placed on Elena's finger, the ermine cape of teacher laid about her shoulders, and the laurel crown of poet placed on her dark curly head. The entire assembly rose and chanted a Te Deum.[1]

What was it like to be a gifted woman, an Elena Cornaro, three hundred years ago? What happened to a bright woman in the past who wanted to study another culture, examine the roots of a language, master the intricacies of higher mathematics, write a book—or prevent or cure a terrible disease?

To begin with, for a woman to acquire anything that amounted to real learning, she needed four basics.

She needed to survive. In the seventeenth century women's life expectancy had risen only to thirty-two; not until 1750 did it begin to rise appreciably and reach, in mid-nineteenth century, age forty-two. A woman ambitious for learning would do well to choose a life of celibacy, not only to avoid the hazards of childbirth but because there was no room for a scholar's life within the confines of marriage and childbearing. Elena Cornaro had taken a vow of chastity at the age of eleven, turned down proposals of marriage to become an oblate of the Benedictine Order.

Secondly, to aspire to learning a woman needed basic literacy; she had to be one of the fortunate few who learned at least to read and write. Although literacy studies in earlier centuries are still very incomplete and comparative data on men's and women's literacy are meager, it appears that before 1650 a bare 10 percent of women in the city of London could sign their names. What is most striking about this particular study is that when men are divided by occupation—with clergy and the professions at the top, 100 percent literate, and male laborers at the

---

1. Festival hymn of rejoicing and praise of God.

bottom of the scale, about 15 percent literate—women as a group fell below even unskilled male laborers in their rate of literacy. By about 1700 half the women in London could sign their names; in the provinces women's literacy remained much lower.

The third fundamental a woman needed if she aspired to learning was, of course, an economic base. It was best to be born, like Elena Cornaro, to a family of wealth who owned a well-stocked library and could afford private tutors. For girls of poor families the chance of learning the bare minimum of reading and writing was small. Even such endowed charity schools as Christ's Hospital in London were attended mostly by boys; poor girls in charity schools were apt to have their literacy skills slighted in favor of catechism, needlework, knitting, and lace-making in preparation for a life in domestic service.

The fourth fundamental a woman scholar needed was simply a very tough skin, for she was a deviant in a society where the learned woman, far from being valued, was likely to hear herself preached against in the pulpit and made fun of on the public stage. Elena Cornaro was fortunate to have been born in Italy where an array of learned women had flourished during the Renaissance and where the woman scholar seems to have found a more hospitable ambiance than in the northern countries.

In eighteenth-century England the gifted writer Lady Mary Wortley Montagu, writing in 1753 about proposed plans for a little granddaughter's education, admonished her daughter with some bitterness "to conceal whatever Learning [the child] attains, with as much solicitude as she would hide crookedness or lameness."

In post-Renaissance Europe two overriding fears dominated thinking on women's education: the fear that learning would unfit women for their social role, defined as service to husband and children and obedience to the church; and, a corollary of the first, that open access to education would endanger women's sexual purity. For while humanist philosophy taught that education led to virtue, writers on education were at once conflicted when they applied the premise to women. Nearly all, beginning with the influential sixteenth-century Juan Luis Vives, opted for restricting women's learning. Only a few radical thinkers—some men, such as Richard Mulcaster in Tudor England and the extraordinary Poullain de la Barre in seventeenth-century France, some women, like the feisty Bathsua Makin and revolutionary Mary Wollenstonecraft —spoke out for the full development of women's intellectual potential.

In any case, since institutions of higher learning were designed for young men entering the professions—the church, the law, government service—from which women were excluded, they were excluded too from the universities that prepared for them. And, just as importantly, they were excluded from the grammar or preparatory schools, whose curriculum was based on Latin, the code language of the male intellectual

elite. Since most scholarly texts were written in Latin, ignorance of that
language prevented women from reading scholarly literature in most
fields—which only gradually and belatedly became available in translation.

Richard Hyrde, a tutor in the household of Sir Thomas More and
himself a defender of learning in women, cited the common opinion:

> ... that the frail kind of women, being inclined of their own courage unto
> vice, and mutable at every newelty [sic], if they should have skill in many
> things that must be written in the Latin and Greek tongue ... it would of
> likelihood both inflame their stomachs a great deal the more to that vice, that
> men say they be too much given unto of their own nature already and instruct
> them also with more subtility and conveyance, to set forward and accomplish
> their froward intent and purpose.

And yet, despite all the hurdles, some bright women did manage to
make a mark as scholars and writers. Sometimes girls listened in on their
brothers' tutored lessons. A fortunate few, like Elena Cornaro, had
parents willing and able to educate daughters equally with sons. The
daughters of Sir Thomas More, of the Earl of Arundel, and of Sir
Anthony Cooke in Tudor England were given excellent educations.
Arundel's daughter, Lady Joanna Lumley, produced the earliest known
English translation of a Greek drama.

But by far the largest number of women scholars in the past were
almost totally self-educated. Through sheer intellectual curiosity, self-
discipline, often grinding hard work, they taught themselves what they
wanted to know. Such self-teaching may well be the only truly joyous
form of learning. Yet it has its drawbacks: it may also be haphazard and
superficial. Without access to laboratory, lecture, and dissecting table, it
was all but impossible for women to train themselves in higher mathematics, for instance, in science, in anatomy.

Mary Wollstonecraft wrote in 1792 that most women who have acted
like rational creatures or shown any vigor of intellect have accidentally
been allowed "to run wild," and running wild in the family library was
the usual way intellectually ambitious women educated themselves.
Such a self-taught scholar was Elizabeth Tanfield, Viscountess Cary,
who as a girl in Elizabethan England, taught herself French, Spanish,
Italian, Latin, and added Hebrew "with very little teaching." Her unsympathetic mother refused to allow her candles to read at night, so Elizabeth bribed the servants, and by her wedding day—she was married at
fifteen—she had run up a candle debt of a hundred pounds. She wrote
numerous translations, poetry—most of which she destroyed—and at
least one play, *Mariam, the Faire Queen of Jewry.*

Very often the critical phase of women's intellectual development
took place at a different period in their lives from the normal time of

men's greatest development. Gifted women often came to a period of intellectual crisis and of intense self-teaching during adulthood.

When Christine de Pisane, daughter of the Italian astrologer and physician at the court of Charles V of France, found herself widowed at twenty-five with three children to support, she turned to writing—certainly one of the first, if not the first, woman in Europe to support herself through a literary career. But Christine found her education wholly inadequate, and at the age of thirty-four she laid down a complete course of study for herself, teaching herself Latin, history, philosophy, literature. She used her pen later on to urge better educational opportunities for women, to defend her sex from the charges of such misogynistic writers as Jean de Meung.[2] In her book, *The City of Ladies*, Christine imagined talented women building a town for themselves where they could lead peaceful and creative lives—an existence impossible, she considered, in fifteenth-century France.

Like Christine de Pisane, the Dutch scholar Anna van Schurman of Utrecht, a contemporary of Elena Cornaro, found her early education superficial and unsatisfying. Like most upper middle class girls of the seventeenth century, Anna, precocious though she was, had been taught chiefly to sing nicely, to play musical instruments, to carve portraits in boxwood and wax, to do needlework and tapestry and cut paperwork. At the age of twenty-eight, frustrated by the lack of intellectual stimulation in her life, Anna turned her brilliant mind to serious studies, became one of the finest Latinists of her day, learned Hebrew, Syriac, Chaldaic, wrote an Ethiopian grammar that was the marvel of Dutch scholars, carried on an international correspondence—in Latin, of course—with all the leading scholars of continental Europe. When a professor of theology at Leyden wrote that women were barred from equality with men "by the sacred laws of nature," Anna wrote a Latin treatise in reply in 1641, defending the intellectual capacity of women and urging, as Christine de Pisane had, much greater educational opportunities. Her work was widely translated and made Anna van Schurman a model for women scholars all over Europe.

In France, during the lifetime of Anna van Schurman, a group of bright, intellectually malnourished women—most of them convent-educated—developed one of the most ingenious devices for women's lifelong learning. Bored with the dearth of cultivated conversation at the French court, the Marquise de Rambouillet, Mlle de Scudéry, Mme de Lafayette, and a host of others opened their town houses in Paris, invited men and women of talent and taste to hone their wits and talk of science and philosophy, literature and language, love and friendship. The salon has been described as "an informal university for women." Not only did it

2. Medieval French author of the satirical antifeminist portion of the influential poem *The Romance of the Rose.*

contribute to adult women's education, but it shaped standards of speaking and writing for generations in France and profoundly influenced French culture as a whole.

An offshoot of the salons were the special lecture courses offered by eminent scholars in chemistry, etymology and other subjects—lectures largely attended by women. Fontenelle wrote his popular book on astronomy, *The Plurality of Worlds*, specifically for a female readership, and Descartes declared he had written his *Discourse on Method* in French rather than Latin so that women too would be able to read it.

There was, rather quickly, a backlash. Molière's satires on learned women did much to discredit the ladies who presided at salons—and who might at times be given to a bit of overelegance in speech and manner. When Abbé Fénélon wrote his influential treatise, *On the Education of Girls*, in 1686—just eight years after Elena Cornaro had won her doctorate—he mentioned neither Elena Cornaro nor Anna van Schurman nor Christine de Pisane. He inveighed against the pernicious effect of the salons. Declaring that "A woman's intellect is normally more feeble and her curiosity greater than those of men, it is undesirable to set her to studies which may turn her head. A girl," admonished that worthy French cleric, "must learn to obey without respite, to hold her peace and allow others to do the talking. Everything is lost if she obstinately tries to be clever and to get a distaste for domestic duties. The virtuous woman spins, confines herself to her home, keeps quiet, believes and obeys."

So much for the encouragement of women scholars in late seventeenth century France.

Across the Channel in England in the second half of the seventeenth century, bright ambitious women were studying not only the classics and languages but learning to use the newly perfected telescope and microscope, and to write on scientific subjects. Margaret Cavendish, Duchess of Newcastle, a remarkable woman with a wide-ranging mind and imagination, wrote not only biography, autobiography, and romance, but also popular science—she called it "natural philosophy"—directed especially to women readers. The versatile and talented writer Aphra Behn—the first woman in England to make her living by her pen—translated Fontenelle's *Plurality of Worlds* into English in 1688. In the preface she declared she would have preferred to write an original work on astronomy but had "neither health nor leisure" for such a project; it was, in fact, the year before her death and she was already ailing. But she defended the Copernican system vigorously against the recent attack by a Jesuit priest, did not hesitate to criticize the author, Fontenelle, and to correct an error in the text on the height of the earth's atmosphere.

But the learned lady in England as in France found herself criticized from the pulpit and satirized on the stage. Margaret Cavendish was dubbed "Mad Madge of Newcastle." Jonathan Swift poked fun at Mary Astell for her proposal to found a women's college. Thomas Wright in

The Female Virtuosos, the anonymous authors of *The Humours of Oxford* and *Female Wits*, Shadwell, Congreve, and others lampooned the would-be woman scholar. The shy poet, Anne, countess of Winchilsea, who had only reluctantly identified herself as author of a published volume of verse, was cruelly pilloried by Pope and Gay in their play *Three Hours after Marriage*. And Aphra Behn, author of a phenomenal array of plays, poems, novels, and translations, could read this published verse about herself and her work at about the same time she was translating Fontenelle:

> Yet hackney writers, when their verse did fail
> To get 'em brandy, bread and cheese, and ale,
> Their wants by prostitution were supplied;
> Show but a tester [sixpence] you might up and ride;
> For punk and poetess agree so pat
> You cannot well be this, and not be that.

So if one asks what it was like to be a gifted woman, to aspire to learning at the time of Elena Cornaro, the answer must be that it was a difficult and demanding choice, requiring not merely intellectual gifts but extraordinary physical and mental stamina, and only a rare few women succeeded in becoming contributing scholars and writers. All the usual scholarly careers were closed to women, so than even for women who succeeded in educating themselves to the level of their male colleagues, the opportunities to support themselves were meager.

In a day when it was considered impermissible for a woman to speak in public, it was also considered inappropriate and unfeminine to draw attention to herself by publishing a work under her own name. Many —perhaps most—women scholars and writers—from Anne, Countess of Winchilsea, Lady Mary Wortley Montagu down to Fanny Burney and Jane Austen—published their works at first either anonymously or pseudonymously. Nor was Elizabeth Tanfield the only woman scholar who destroyed her own writings before they were published.

And what of Elena Cornaro's life after she won her doctorate in 1678? During the six years she lived after that event, she divided her time between scholarly pursuits and service to the poor, sick and needy. Baroque Italy paid honor to its unique woman scholar. Certainly Elena Cornaro aroused no antagonisms, but rather filled with discretion the approved nunlike role designated for the woman in Catholic countries who chose not to marry. Scholars and statesmen from several countries made a point of visiting her in Padua, and she was invited to join fellow scholars in the Academy of Ricovrati in Padua. When she died of tuberculosis in 1684 at the age of thirty-eight—a disease that was in a measure responsible for her eminence, for she had been sent to Padua partly to escape the damp air of Venice—her funeral attracted a greater throng than her doctoral examination. A delegation of distinguished university faculty accompanied the procession through the streets of Padua, and on her coffin were heaped books in the languages she had mastered and the sciences she had studied. She was buried in the Chapel of St. Luke among the Benedictine monks, having carefully instructed her maid to sew her robe together at the hem so that even in death her modesty would be preserved.

Of her writings very little has survived. She had arranged to have her correspondence and many of her manuscripts destroyed before she died, and the remainder of her writings were disseminated as souvenirs among family and friends.

After Elena Cornaro's death a half century passed before a second woman, again Italian, Laura Maria Catherina Bassi, was awarded a doctorate at the University of Bologna. Not until 150 years later did American universities admit women for degrees, and two centuries passed before Oxford and Cambridge conferred degrees on women. Only in our own decade, in 1970, did the Catholic Church finally award the degree of Doctor of Theology that had been denied Elena Cornaro to two women: one to the sixteenth century Spanish saint, Teresa of Avila, the other to fourteenth century St. Catherine of Siena, who had in fact never learned to read and write. One hopes that in some academic elysium those two saintly ladies are proudly showing off their belated scholarly credentials.

1978

QUESTIONS

1. *What obstacles stood in the way of a woman seeking learning in the past, and what did she need in order to overcome them? Which of these obstacles and needs still exist? Are there any new difficulties today?*

2. *What do you imagine were Elena Cornaro's thoughts and feelings in the hour before the public examination for the doctorate? Write an essay exploring this question. You might like to try placing yourself in her position and writing from her point of view.*

Chief Seattle

ADDRESS[1]

The Governor made a fine speech, but he was outranged and out-classed that day. Chief Seattle, who answered on behalf of the Indians, towered a foot above the Governor. He wore his blanket like the toga of a Roman senator, and he did not have to strain his famous voice, which everyone agreed was audible and distinct at a distance of half a mile.

Seattle's oration was in Duwamish. Doctor Smith, who had learned the language, wrote it down; under the flowery garlands of his translation the speech rolls like an articulate iron engine, grim with meanings that outlasted his generation and may outlast all the generations of men. As the amiable follies of the white race become less amiable, the iron rumble of old Seattle's speech sounds louder and more ominous.

Standing in front of Doctor Maynard's office in the stumpy clearing, with his hand on the little Governor's head, the white invaders about him and his people before him, Chief Seattle said:

"Yonder sky that has wept tears of compassion upon my people for centuries untold, and which to us appears changeless and eternal, may change. Today is fair. Tomorrow may be overcast with clouds. My words are like the stars that never change. Whatever Seattle says the great chief at Washington can rely upon with as much certainty as he can upon the return of the sun or the seasons. The White Chief says that Big Chief at Washington sends us greetings of friendship and goodwill. That is kind of him for we know he has little need of our friendship in return. His people are many. They are like the grass that covers vast prairies. My people are few. They resemble the scattering trees of a storm-swept plain. The great, and—I presume—good, White Chief sends us word that he wishes to buy our lands but is willing to allow us enough to live comfortably. This indeed appears just, even generous, for the Red Man no longer has rights that he need respect, and the offer may be wise also, as we are no longer in need of an extensive country.... I will not dwell on, nor mourn over, our untimely decay, nor reproach our paleface brothers with hastening it, as we too may have been somewhat to blame.

"Youth is impulsive. When our young men grow angry at some real or imaginary wrong, and disfigure their faces with black paint, it denotes that their hearts are black, and then they are often cruel and relentless, and our old men and old women are unable to restrain them. Thus it has

1. In 1854, Governor Isaac Stevens, Commissioner of Indian Affairs for the Washington Territory, proffered a treaty to the Indians providing for the sale of two million acres of their land to the federal government. This address is the reply of Chief Seattle of the Duwampo tribe. The translator was Henry A. Smith.

ever been. Thus it was when the white men first began to push our forefathers further westward. But let us hope that the hostilities between us may never return. We would have everything to lose and nothing to gain. Revenge by young men is considered gain, even at the cost of their own lives, but old men who stay at home in times of war, and mothers who have sons to lose, know better.

"Our good father at Washington—for I presume he is now our father as well as yours, since King George has moved his boundaries further north—our great good father, I say, sends us word that if we do as he desires he will protect us. His brave warriors will be to us a bristling wall of strength, and his wonderful ships of war will fill our harbors so that our ancient enemies far to the northward—the Hydas and Tsimpsians—will cease to frighten our women, children, and old men. Then in reality will he be our father and we his children. But can that ever be? Your God is not our God! Your God loves your people and hates mine. He folds his strong and protecting arms lovingly about the paleface and leads him by the hand as a father leads his infant son—but He has forsaken His red children—if they really are his. Our God, the Great Spirit, seems also to have forsaken us. Your God makes your people wax strong every day. Soon they will fill the land. Our people are ebbing away like a rapidly receding tide that will never return. The white man's God cannot love our people or He would protect them. They seem to be orphans who can look nowhere for help. How then can we be brothers? How can your God become our God and renew our prosperity and awaken in us dreams of returning greatness? If we have a common heavenly father He must be partial—for He came to his paleface children. We never saw Him. He gave you laws but He had no word for His red children whose teeming multitudes once filled this vast continent as stars fill the firmament. No; we are two distinct races with separate origins and separate destinies. There is little in common between us.

"To us the ashes of our ancestors are sacred and their resting place is hallowed ground. You wander far from the graves of your ancestors and seemingly without regret. Your religion was written upon tables of stone by the iron finger of your God so that you could not forget. The Red Man could never comprehend nor remember it. Our religion is the traditions of our ancestors—the dreams of our old men, given them in solemn hours of night by the Great Spirit; and the visions of our sachems; and it is written in the hearts of our people.

"Your dead cease to love you and the land of their nativity as soon as they pass the portals of the tomb and wander way beyond the stars. They are soon forgotten and never return. Our dead never forget the beautiful world that gave them being.

"Day and night cannot dwell together. The Red Man has ever fled the approach of the White Man, as the morning mist flees before the morning sun. However, your proposition seems fair and I think that my people will accept it and will retire to the reservation you offer them. Then we will dwell apart in peace, for the words of the Great White Chief seem to be the words of nature speaking to my people out of dense darkness.

"It matters little where we pass the remnant of our days. They will not be many. A few more moons; a few more winters—and not one of the descendants of the mighty hosts that once moved over this broad land or lived in happy homes, protected by the Great Spirit, will remain to mourn over the graves of a people once more powerful and hopeful than yours. But why should I mourn at the untimely fate of my people? Tribe follows tribe, and nation follows nation, like the waves of the sea. It is the order of nature, and regret is useless. Your time of decay may be distant, but it will surely come, for even the White Man whose God walked and talked with him as friend with friend, cannot be exempt from the common destiny. We may be brothers after all. We will see.

"We will ponder your proposition, and when we decide we will let you know. But should we accept it, I here and now make this condition that we will not be denied the privilege without molestation of visiting at any time the tombs of our ancestors, friends and children. Every part of this soil is sacred in the estimation of my people. Every hillside, every valley, every plain and grove, has been hallowed by some sad or happy event in days long vanished.... The very dust upon which you now stand responds more lovingly to their footsteps than to yours, because it is rich with the blood of our ancestors and our bare feet are conscious of the sympathetic touch.... Even the little children who lived here and rejoiced here for a brief season will love these somber solitudes and at eventide they greet shadowy returning spirits. And when the last Red Man shall have perished, and the memory of my tribe shall have become a myth among the White Men, these shores will swarm with the invisible dead of my tribe, and when your children's children think themselves alone in the field, the store, the shop, upon the highway, or in the silence of the pathless woods, they will not be alone.... At night when the streets of your cities and villages are silent and you think them deserted, they will throng with the returning hosts that once filled and still love this beautiful land. The White Man will never be alone.

"Let him be just and deal kindly with my people, for the dead are not powerless. Dead, did I say? There is no death, only a change of worlds."

1854

John Houseman

THE WAR OF THE WORLDS

The War of the Worlds formed part of our general plan of contrasting shows.[1] No one, as I recall, was particularly enthusiastic about it. But it seemed good programming—following *Julius Caesar* (with the original Mercury cast and commentary by Kaltenborn out of Plutarch[2]), *Oliver Twist* (in which Orson played both the boy Oliver and the villainous Fagin), *Eighty Days Around the World, The Heart of Darkness, Jane Eyre* and before *Life with Father*, which was to be our next show—to throw in something of a scientific nature. We thought of Shiel's *Purple Cloud*, Conan Doyle's *Lost World* and several other well-known works of science fiction before settling on H. G. Wells's twenty-year-old novel, which neither Orson nor I remembered at all clearly. It is just possible that neither of us had ever read it.

Actually it was a narrow squeak. The men from Mars barely escaped being stillborn. Late Tuesday night—thirty-six hours before the first rehearsal—Howard Koch called me at the theater. He was in deep distress. After three days of slaving on H. G. Wells's scientific fantasy he was ready to give up. Under no circumstances, he declared, could it be made interesting or in any way credible to modern American ears. Koch was not given to habitual alarmism. To confirm his fears, Annie[3] came to the phone. "You can't do it, Houseman!" she whined. "Those old Martians are just a lot of nonsense! It's all too silly! We're going to make fools of ourselves! Absolute idiots!"

We were not averse to changing a show at the last moment. But the only other script available was an extremely dreary version of *Lorna Doone*[4] which I had started during the summer and abandoned. I reasoned with Koch. I was severe. I taxed him and Annie with defeatism. I gave them false comfort, I promised to come up and help. When I finally got there—around two in the morning—things were better. They were beginning to have fun laying waste the State of New Jersey. Annie had stopped grinding her teeth. I worked with them for the rest of the night and they went on through the next day. Wednesday at sunset the script was finished.

---

1. In the series *Mercury Theatre of the Air*, named for the stage company of which Houseman and Orson Welles were cofounders and presiding geniuses; the series offered weekly broadcasts of adaptations of famous plays and fictional works.
2. H. V. Kaltenborn was a leading news commentator of the day, distinguished for his clipped, pedantic speech [Houseman's note].

Plutarch (46–120) was a biographer of famous Greeks and Romans, among the latter the dictator Julius Caesar.
3. Ann Froelich, who worked with Howard Koch, the show's regular scripwriter; Paul Stewart, mentioned later, was associate producer of the show.
4. Well-known romantic novel (1869) by R. D. Blackmore.

Thursday, as usual, Paul Stewart rehearsed the show, then made a record. We listened to it rather gloomily, between *Danton* rehearsals, in Orson's room at the St. Regis, sitting on the floor because all the chairs were still covered with coils of unrolled and unedited film.[5] He was dead tired and thought it was a dull show. We all agreed that its only chance of coming off lay in emphasizing its newscast style—its simultaneous, eye-witness quality.

All night we sat up—Howard, Paul, Annie and I—spicing the script with circumstantial allusions and authentic detail. Friday afternoon it was sent over to CBS to be passed by the network censor. Certain name alterations were requested. Under protest and with a deep sense of grievance we changed the Hotel Biltmore to a nonexistent Park Plaza, Trans-America to Inter-Continent, the Columbia Broadcasting Building to Broadcasting Building. Then the script went over to mimeograph and I went back to the theater. We had done our best and, after all, it was just another radio show.

Saturday, Paul Stewart rehearsed with sound effects and without Welles. He worked for a long time on the crowd scenes, the roar of cannon echoing in the Watchung Hills[6] and the sound of New York Harbor as the ships with the last remaining survivors put out to sea.

Around six we left the studio. Orson, phoning from the theater a few minutes later to find out how things were going, was told by one of the CBS sound men, who had stayed behind to pack up his equipment, that it was not one of our better shows. Confidentially, the man opined, it just didn't come off. Twenty-seven hours later, quite a few of his employers would have found themselves a good deal happier if he had turned out to be right.

On Sunday, October 30, at 8:00 P.M., E.S.T., in a studio littered with coffee cartons and sandwich paper, Orson swallowed a second container of pineapple juice, put on his earphones, raised his long white fingers and threw the cue for the Mercury theme—the Tchaikovsky Piano Concerto No. 1 in B Flat Minor. After the music dipped, there were routine introductions—then the announcement that a dramatization of H. G. Wells's famous novel, *The War of the Worlds*, was about to be performed. Around 8:01 Orson began to speak, as follows:

WELLES

We know now that in the early years of the twentieth century this world was being watched closely by intelligences greater than man's and yet as mortal as his own. We know now that as human beings busied themselves about their various concerns they were scrutinized and studied, perhaps

---

5. A future Mercury Theatre stage production was to have two filmed chase scenes, which for several weeks Welles had been trying to edit. Currently in rehearsal was Georg Büchner's *Danton's Death* (1835).

6. In northern New Jersey.

almost as narrowly as a man with a microscope might scrutinize the transient creatures that swarm and multiply in a drop of water. With infinite complacence people went to and fro over the earth about their little affairs, serene in the assurance of their dominion over this small spinning fragment of solar driftwood which by chance or design man has inherited out of the dark mystery of Time and Space. Yet across an immense ethereal gulf minds that are to our minds as ours are to the beasts in the jungle, intellects vast, cool, and unsympathetic regarded this earth with envious eyes and slowly and surely drew their plans against us. In the thirty-ninth year of the twentieth century came the great disillusionment.

It was near the end of October. Business was better. The war scare was over. More men were back at work. Sales were picking up. On this particular evening, October 30th, the Crossley service estimated that thirty-two million people were listening in on their radios. . . .

Neatly, without perceptible transition, he was followed on the air by an anonymous announcer caught in a routine bulletin:

ANNOUNCER

. . .for the next twenty-four hours not much change in temperature. A slight atmospheric disturbance of undetermined origin is reported over Nova Scotia, causing a low pressure area to move down rather rapidly over the northeastern states, bringing a forecast of rain, accompanied by winds of light gale force. Maximum temperature 66; minimum 48. This weather report comes to you from the Government Weather Bureau. . . . We now take you to the Meridian Room in the Hotel Park Plaza in downtown New York, where you will be entertained by the music of Ramon Raquello and his orchestra.

At which cue, Bernard Herrmann led the massed men of the CBS house orchestra in a thunderous symphonic rendition of "La Cumparsita." The entire hoax might have been exposed there and then—but for the fact that hardly anyone was listening. They were being entertained by Charlie McCarthy.

The Crossley census, taken about a week before the broadcast, had given us 3.6 percent of the listening audience to Edgar Bergen's 34.7 percent. What the Crossley Institute (that hireling of the advertising agencies) deliberately ignored, was the healthy American habit of dial twisting. On that particular evening Edgar Bergen, in the person of Charlie McCarthy, temporarily left the air about 8:12 P.M. E.S.T., yielding place to a new and not very popular singer. At that point, and during the following minutes, a large number of listeners started twisting their dials in search of other entertainment. Many of them turned to us—and when they did, they stayed put! For by this time the mysterious meteorite had fallen at Grovers Mill in New Jersey, the Martians had begun to show their foul leathery heads above the ground, and the New Jersey State Police were racing to the spot. Within a few minutes people all

over the United States were praying, crying, fleeing frantically to escape death from the Martians. Some remembered to rescue loved ones, others telephoned farewells or warnings, hurried to inform neighbors, sought information from newspapers or radio stations, summoned ambulances and police cars.

The reaction was strongest at points nearest the tragedy—in Newark, New Jersey, in a single block, more than twenty families rushed out of their houses with wet handkerchiefs and towels over their faces. Some began moving household furniture. Police switchboards were flooded with calls inquiring, "Shall I close my windows?"; "Have the police any extra gas masks?" Police found one family waiting in the yard with wet cloths on faces contorted with hysteria. As one women reported later:

> I was terribly frightened. I wanted to pack and take my child in my arms, gather up my friends and get in the car and just go north as far as we could. But what I did was just sit by one window, praying, listening, and scared stiff, and my husband by the other sniffing, and looking out to see if people were running. . . .

In New York hundreds of people on Riverside Drive left their homes ready for flight. Bus terminals were crowded. A woman calling up the Dixie Bus Terminal for information said impatiently, "Hurry please, the world is coming to an end and I have a lot to do."

In the parlor churches of Harlem, evening service became "end of the world" prayer meetings. Many turned to God in that moment:

> I held a crucifix in my hand and prayed while looking out of my open window for falling meteors. . . . When the monsters were wading across the Hudson River and coming into New York, I wanted to run up on my roof to see what they looked like, but I couldn't leave my radio while it was telling me of their whereabouts.

> Aunt Grace began to pray with Uncle Henry. Lily got sick to her stomach. I don't know what I did exactly but I know I prayed harder and more earnestly than ever before. Just as soon as we were convinced that this thing was real, how petty all things on this earth seemed; how soon we put our trust in God!

The panic moved upstate. One man called up the Mt. Vernon Police Headquarters to find out "where the forty policemen were killed." Another took time out to philosophize:

> I thought the whole human race was going to be wiped out—that seemed more important than the fact that we were going to die. It seemed awful that everything that had been worked on for years was going to be lost forever.

In Rhode Island weeping and hysterical women swamped the switchboard of the Providence *Journal* for details of the massacre, and officials of the electric light company received a score of calls urging them to turn off all lights so that the city would be safe from the enemy. The Boston *Globe* received a call from one woman who "could see the fire." A man in Pittsburgh hurried home in the midst of the broadcast and found his wife in the bathroom, a bottle of poison in her hand, screaming, "I'd rather die this way than that." In Minneapolis a woman ran into church screaming, "New York destroyed, this is the end of the world. You might as well go home to die. I just heard it on the radio."

The Kansas City bureau of the AP received inquiries about the "meteors" from Los Angeles; Salt Lake City; Beaumont, Texas; and St. Joseph, Missouri. In San Francisco the general impression of listeners seemed to be that an overwhelming force had invaded the United States from the air—was in process of destroying New York and threatening to move westward. "My God," roared an inquirer into a telephone, "where can I volunteer my services, we've got to stop this awful thing!"

As far south as Birmingham, Alabama, people gathered in churches and prayed. On the campus of a Southeastern college—

> The girls in the sorority houses and dormitories huddled around their radios trembling and weeping in each other's arms. They separated themselves from their friends only to take their turn at the telephones to make long-distance calls to their parents, saying goodbye for what they thought might be the last time. . . .

There are hundreds of such items, gathered from coast to coast. At least one book and quite a pile of sociological literature have appeared on the subject of "the invasion from Mars." Many theories have been put forward to explain the "tidal wave" of panic that swept the nation. Two factors, in my opinion, contributed to the broadcast's extraordinarily violent effect. First, its historical timing. It came within thirty-five days of the Munich crisis.[7] For weeks, the American people had been hanging on their radios, getting most of their news over the air. A new technique of "on-the-spot" reporting had been developed and eagerly accepted by an anxious and newshungry world. The Mercury Theatre of the Air, by faithfully copying every detail of the new technique, including its imperfections, found an already enervated audience ready to accept its wildest fantasies. The second factor was the show's sheer technical brilliance. To this day it is impossible to sit in a room and hear the scratched, worn, off-the-air recording of the broadcast without feeling in the back of your neck some slight draft left over from the great wind of terror that swept

7. The broadcast was on October 30, 1938. In September the prime ministers of Great Britain and France had met in Munich with Hitler and Mussolini and ceded western Czechoslovakia to Germany in an effort to appease Hitler's expansionism and prevent war.

the nation. Even with the element of credibility totally removed it remains a surprisingly effective broadcast.

Beginning some time around two when the show started to take shape under Orson's hands, a strange fever seemed to invade the studio—part childish mischief, part professional zeal. First to feel it were the actors. I remember Frank Readick (who played the part of Carl Phillips, the network's special reporter) going down to the record library and digging up the recording of the explosion of the *Hindenburg* at Lakehurst. This is a classic reportage—one of those wonderful, unpredictable accidents of eyewitness description. The broadcaster is casually describing the routine landing of the giant dirigible. Suddenly he sees something. A flash of flame! An instant later the whole thing explodes. It takes him time—a full second—to react at all. Then seconds more of sputtering ejaculations before he can make the adjustment between brain and tongue. He starts to describe the terrible things he sees—the writhing human figures twisting and squirming as they fall from the white burning wreckage. He stops, fumbles, vomits, then quickly continues. Readick played the record to himself, over and over. Then, recreating the emotion in his own terms he described the Martian meteorite as he saw it lying inert and harmless in a field at Grovers Mill, lit up by the headlights of a hundred cars, the coppery cylinder suddenly opening, revealing the leather tentacles and the terrible pale-eyed faces of the Martians within. As they began to emerge he froze, unable to translate his vision into words; he fumbled, retched, and then after a second continued.

A few moments later Carl Phillips lay dead, tumbling over the microphone in his fall—one of the first victims of the Martian ray. There followed a moment of absolute silence—an eternity of waiting. Then without warning, the network's emergency fill-in was heard—somewhere in a quiet studio, a piano, close on mike, playing "Claire de Lune," soft and sweet as honey, for many seconds, while the fate of the universe hung in the balance. Finally it was interrupted by the manly reassuring voice of Brigadier General Montgomery Smith, Commander of the New Jersey State Militia, speaking from Trenton and placing "the counties of Mercer and Middlesex as far west as Princeton and east to Jamesburg" under martial law! Tension—release—then renewed tension. Soon after that came an eyewitness account of the fatal battle of the Watchung Hills; then, once again, that lone piano was heard—now a symbol of terror, shattering the dead air with its ominous tinkle. As it played on and on, its effect became increasingly sinister—a thin band of suspense stretched almost beyond endurance.

That piano was the neatest trick of the show—a fine specimen of the theatrical "retard," boldly conceived and exploited to the full. It was one of the many devices with which Welles succeeded in compelling not merely the attention, but also the belief of his invisible audience. *The*

War of the Worlds was a magic act, one of the world's greatest, and Orson was the man to bring it off.

For Welles, as I have said, was first and foremost, a magician whose particular talent lay in his ability to stretch the familiar elements of theatrical effect far beyond their normal point of tension. For this reason (as we were discovering to our sorrow on Forty-first Street) his productions required more careful preparation and more perfect execution than most; like all complicated magic tricks, they remained, till the last moment, in a state of precarious balance. When they came off they gave, by virtue of their unusually high intensity, an impression of the greatest brilliance and power; when they failed—when something in their balance went wrong or the original structure proved to have been unsound —they provoked a particularly violent reaction of unease and revulsion. Welles's flops were louder then other men's. The Mars broadcast was one of his unqualified successes.

Among the columnists and public figures who discussed the affair during the next few days (some praising us for the public service we had rendered, some condemning us as sinister scoundrels), the most general reaction was one of amazement at the "incredible stupidity" and "gullibility" of the American public, who had accepted as real, in this single broadcast, incidents which in actual fact would have taken days or even weeks to occur. One explanation of our success lay in the fact that the first few minutes of our broadcast were strictly realistic in time and perfectly credible, though somewhat boring, in content. Herein lay the great tensile strength of the show; it was the structural device that made the whole illusion possible. And it could have been carried off in no other medium than radio.

Our actual broadcasting time, from the first mention of the meteorites to the fall of New York City, was less than forty minutes. During that time men traveled long distances, large bodies of troops were mobilized, cabinet meetings were held, savage battles fought on land and in the air. And millions of people accepted it—emotionally if not logically.

There is nothing so very strange about that. Most of us do the same thing, to some degree, most days of our lives—every time we look at a movie or a television show. Not even the realistic theater observes the literal unities; films, TV and, particularly, in its day, radio (where neither place nor time existed save in the imagination of the listener) have no difficulty in getting their audiences to accept the telescoped reality of dramatic time. Our special hazard lay in the fact that we purported to be not a play, but reality. In order to take advantage of the accepted convention, we had to slide swiftly and imperceptibly out of the "real" time of a news report into the "dramatic" time of a fictional broadcast. Once that was achieved—without losing the audience's attention or arousing their skepticism—once they were sufficiently absorbed and bewitched not to notice the transitions any more, there was no extreme of fantasy through which they would now follow us. If, that night, the American public proved "gullible," it was because enormous pains and a great deal of thought had been spent to make it so.

In the script, *The War of the Worlds* started extremely slowly—dull meteorological and astronomical bulletins alternating with musical interludes. These were followed by a colorless scientific interview and still another stretch of dance music. These first few minutes of routine broadcasting "within the existing standards of judgment of the listener" were intended to lull (or maybe bore) the audience into a false security and to furnish a solid base of realistic time from which to accelerate later. Orson, in directing the show, extended these slow movements far beyond our original conception. The interview in the Princeton Observatory—the clockwork ticking monontonously overhead, the wooly-minded professor mumbling vague replies to the reporters' uninformed questions—this, too, was dragged out to the point of tedium. Over my protests, lines were restored that had been cut at earlier rehearsals. I cried there would not be a listener left. Welles stretched them out even longer.

He was right. His sense of tempo, that night, was infallible. When the flashed news of the cylinder's landing finally came—almost fifteen minutes after the beginning of a fairly dull show—he was able suddenly to spiral his action to a speed as wild and reckless as its base was solid. The appearance of the Martians; their first treacherous act; the death of Carl Phillips; the arrival of the militia; the battle of the Watchung Hills; the destruction of New Jersey—all these were telescoped into a space of twelve minutes without overstretching the listeners' emotional credulity. The broadcast, by then, had its own reality, the reality of emotionally felt time and space.

At the height of the crisis, around 8:31, the Secretary of the Interior came on the air with an exhortation to the American people. It was admirably spoken—in a voice just faintly reminiscent of Franklin Delano Roosevelt's—by a young man named Kenneth Delmar, who later grew rich and famous as Senator Claghorn.[8]

THE SECRETARY

    Citizens of the nation: I shall not try to conceal the gravity of the situation that confronts the country, nor the concern of your Government in protecting the lives and property of its people. However, I wish to impress upon you —private citizens and public officials, all of you—the urgent need of calm and resourceful action. Fortunately, this formidable enemy is still confined to a comparatively small area, and we may place our faith in the military forces to keep them there. In the meantime placing our trust in God, we must continue the performance of our duties, each and every one of us, so that we may

8. A comic character in Fred Allen's popular radio show.

confront this destructive adversary with a nation united, courageous, and consecrated to the preservation of human supremacy of this earth. I thank you.

Toward the end of this speech (circa 8:32 E.S.T.), Davidson Taylor, supervisor of the broadcast for the Columbia Broadcasting System, received a phone call in the control room, creased his lips, and hurriedly left the studio. By the time he returned, a few minutes later, pale as death, clouds of heavy smoke were rising from Newark, New Jersey, and the Martians, tall as skyscrapers, were astride the Pulaski Highway preparatory to wading the Hudson River. To us in the studio the show seemed to be progressing splendidly—how splendidly Davidson Taylor had just learned outside. For several minutes now, a kind of madness had been sweeping the continent: it was somehow connected with our show. The CBS switchboards had been swamped into uselessness, but from outside sources vague rumors were coming in of deaths and suicides and panic injuries by the thousands.

Taylor had orders to interrupt the show immediately with an explanatory station announcement. By now the Martians were across the Hudson and gas was blanketing the city. The end was near. We were less than a minute from the station break. Ray Collins, superb as the "last announcer," was choking heroically to death on the roof of Broadcasting Building. The boats were all whistling for a while as the last of the refugees perished in New York Harbor. Finally, as they died away, an amateur short-wave operator was heard, from heaven knows where, weakly reaching out for human companionship across the empty world:

> $_2$X$_2$L Calling CQ
> $_2$X$_2$L Calling CQ
> $_2$X$_2$L Calling CQ
> Isn't there anyone on the air?
> Isn't there anyone?

Five seconds of absolute silence. Then, shattering the reality of world's end—the announcer's voice was heard, suave and bright:

ANNOUNCER

You are listening to the CBS presentation of Orson Welles and the Mercury Theatre of the Air in an original dramatization of *The War of the Worlds,* by H. G. Wells. The performance will continue after a brief intermission.

The second part of the show was well written and sensitively played —but nobody heard it. It recounted the adventures of a lone survivor, with interesting observations on the nature of human society; it described the eventual death of the Martian invaders, slain—"after all man's defenses had failed by the humblest thing that God in his wisdom had put upon this earth"—by bacteriological action; it told of the rebuilding of a brave new world. After a stirring musical finale, Welles, in his own person, delivered a charmingly apologetic little speech about Halloween and goblins.

I remember, during the playing of the final theme, the phone starting to ring in the control room and a shrill voice through the receiver announcing itself as belonging to the mayor of some Midwestern city, one of the big ones. He was screaming for Welles. Choking with fury, he reported mobs in the streets of his city, women and children huddled in the churches, violence and looting. If, as he now learned, the whole thing was nothing but a crummy joke—then he, personally, was on his way to New York to punch the author of it on the nose! I hung up quickly. For we were off the air now and the studio door had burst open.

The following hours were a nightmare. The building was suddenly full of people and dark-blue uniforms. Hustled out of the studio, we were locked into a small back office on another floor. Here we sat incommunicado while network employees were busily collecting, destroying, or locking up all scripts and records of the broadcast. Finally the Press was let loose upon us, ravening for horror. How many deaths had we heard of? (Implying they knew of thousands.) What did we know of the fatal stampede in a Jersey hall? (Implying it was one of many.) What traffic deaths? (The ditches must be choked with corpses.) The suicides? (Haven't you heard about the one on Riverside Drive?) It is all quite vague in my memory and quite terrible.

Hours later, instead of arresting us, they let us out a back way and we scurried down to the theater like hunted animals to their hole. It was surprising to see life going on as usual in the midnight streets, cars stopping for traffic, people walking. At the Mercury the company was still rehearsing *Danton's Death*—falling up and down stairs and singing the "Carmagnole."[9] Welles went up on stage, where photographers, lying in wait, caught him with his eyes raised to heaven, his arms outstretched in an attitude of crucifixion. Thus he appeared in a tabloid the next morning over the caption, "I Didn't Know What I was Doing!" *The New York Times* quoted him as saying, "I don't think we will choose anything like this again."

We were on the front page for two days. Having had to bow to radio as a news source during the Munich crisis, the press was now only too eager to expose the perilous irresponsibilities of the new medium. Orson was their whipping boy. They quizzed and badgered him. Condemnatory

9. A song of the French Revolution of 1789, the setting for *Danton's Death*.

editorials were delivered by our press-clipping bureau in bushel baskets. There was talk, for a while, of criminal action.

Then gradually, after about two weeks, the excitement subsided. By then it had been discovered that the casualties were not as numerous or as serious as had at first been supposed. One young woman had fallen and broken her arm running downstairs. Later the Federal Communications Commission held some hearings and passed some regulations. The Columbia Broadcasting System made a public apology. With that the official aspects of the incident were closed.

Of the suits that were brought against the network—amounting to over three-quarters of a million dollars for damages, injuries, miscarriages and distresses of various kinds—not one was substantiated. We did settle one claim, however. It was the particularly affecting case of a man in Massachusetts, who wrote:

> I thought the best thing to do was to go away. So I took three dollars twenty-five cents out of my savings and bought a ticket. After I had gone sixty miles I knew it was a play. Now I don't have money left for the shoes I was saving up for. Will you please have someone send me a pair of black shoes size 9B!

We did. And all the lawyers were very angry with us.

Hannah Arendt

DENMARK AND THE JEWS

At the Wannsee Conference,[1] Martin Luther, of the Foreign Office, warned of great difficulties in the Scandinavian countries, notably in Norway and Denmark. (Sweden was never occupied, and Finland, though in the war on the side of the Axis, was one country the Nazis never even approached on the Jewish question. This surprising exception of Finland, with some two thousand Jews, may have been due to Hitler's great esteem for the Finns, whom perhaps he did not want to subject to threats and humiliating blackmail.) Luther proposed postponing evacuations from Scandinavia for the time being, and as far as Denmark was concerned, this really went without saying, since the country retained its independent government, and was respected as a neutral state, until the fall of 1943, although it, along with Norway, had

---

1. A meeting of German officials on "the Jewish question."

been invaded by the German Army in April, 1940. There existed no
Fascist or Nazi movement in Denmark worth mentioning, and therefore
no collaborators. In Norway, however, the Germans had been able to find
enthusiastic supporters; indeed, Vidkun Quisling, leader of the pro-Nazi
and anti-Semitic Norwegian party, gave his name to what later became
known as a "quisling government." The bulk of Norway's seventeen
hundred Jews were stateless, refugees from Germany; they were seized
and interned in a few lightning operations in October and November,
1942. When Eichmann's office ordered their deportation to Auschwitz,
some of Quisling's own men resigned their government posts. This may
not have come as a surprise to Mr. Luther and the Foreign Office, but
what was much more serious, and certainly totally unexpected, was that
Sweden immediately offered asylum, and even Swedish nationality, to all
who were persecuted. Dr. Ernst von Weizsäcker, Undersecretary of
State of the Foreign Office, who received the proposal, refused to discuss
it, but the offer helped nevertheless. It is always relatively easy to get out
of a country illegally, whereas it is nearly impossible to enter the place of
refuge without permission and to dodge the immigration authorities.
Hence, about nine hundred people, slightly more than half of the small
Norwegian community, could be smuggled into Sweden.

It was in Denmark, however, that the Germans found out how fully
justified the Foreign Offices's apprehensions had been. The story of the
Danish Jews is *sui generis*, and the behavior of the Danish people and
their government was unique among all the countries in Europe
—whether occupied, or a partner of the Axis, or neutral and truly independent. One is tempted to recommend the story as required reading in
political science for all students who wish to learn something about the
enormous power potential inherent in non-violent action and in resistance to an opponent possessing vastly superior means of violence. To be
sure, a few other countries in Europe lacked proper "understanding of
the Jewish question," and actually a majority of them were opposed to
"radical" and "final" solutions. Like Denmark, Sweden, Italy, and Bulgaria proved to be nearly immune to anti-Semitism, but of the three that
were in the German sphere of influence, only the Danes dared speak out
on the subject to their German masters. Italy and Bulgaria sabotaged
German orders and indulged in a complicated game of double-dealing
and double-crossing, saving their Jews by a tour de force of sheer ingenuity, but they never contested the policy as such. That was totally different
from what the Danes did. When the Germans approached them rather
cautiously about introducing the yellow badge, they were simply told
that the King would be the first to wear it, and the Danish government
officials were careful to point out that anti-Jewish measures of any sort
would cause their own immediate resignation. It was decisive in this
whole matter that the Germans did not even succeed in introducing the
vitally important distinction between native Danes of Jewish origin, of
whom there were about sixty-four hundred, and the fourteen hundred

German Jewish refugees who had found asylum in the country prior to the war and who now had been declared stateless by the German government. This refusal must have surprised the Germans no end, since it appeared so "illogical" for a government to protect people to whom it had categorically denied naturalization and even permission to work. (Legally, the prewar situation of refugees in Denmark was not unlike that in France, except that the general corruption in the Third Republic's civil services enabled a few of them to obtain naturalization papers, through bribes or "connections," and most refugees in France could work illegally, without a permit. But Denmark, like Switzerland, was no country pour se débrouiller[2].) The Danes, however, explained to the German officials that because the stateless refugees were no longer German citizens, the Nazis could not claim them without Danish assent. This was one of the few cases in which statelessness turned out to be an asset, although it was of course not statelessness per se that saved the Jews but, on the contrary, the fact that the Danish government had decided to protect them. Thus, none of the preparatory moves, so important for the bureaucracy of murder, could be carried out, and operations were postponed until the fall of 1943.

What happened then was truly amazing; compared with what took place in other European countries, everything went topsy-turvy. In August, 1943—after the German offensive in Russia had failed, the Afrika Korps had surrendered in Tunisia, and the Allies had invaded Italy—the Swedish government canceled its 1940 agreement with Germany which had permitted German troops the right to pass through the country. Thereupon, the Danish workers decided that they could help a bit in hurrying things up; riots broke out in Danish shipyards, where the dock workers refused to repair German ships and then went on strike. The German military commander proclaimed a state of emergency and imposed martial law, and Himmler thought this was the right moment to tackle the Jewish question, whose "solution" was long overdue. What he did not reckon with was that—quite apart from Danish resistance—the German officials who had been living in the country for years were no longer the same. Not only did General von Hannecken, the military commander, refuse to put troops at the disposal of the Reich plenipotentiary, Dr. Werner Best; the special S.S. units (Einsatz-kommandos) employed in Denmark very frequently objected to "the measures they were ordered to carry out by the central agencies"—according to Best's testimony of Nuremberg. And Best himself, an old Gestapo man and former legal adviser to Heydrich, author of a then famous book on the police, who had worked for the military government in Paris to the entire satisfaction of his superiors, could not longer be trusted, although it is doubtful that Berlin ever learned the extent of his unreliability. Still, it was clear from the beginning that things were not going well, and Eichmann's office sent one of its best men to Denmark—Rolf Günther,

---

2. For wangling—using bribery to circumvent bureaucratic regulations.

whom no one had ever accused of not possessing the required "ruthless toughness." Günther made no impression on his colleagues in Copenhagen, and now von Hannecken refused even to issue a decree requiring all Jews to report for work.

Best went to Berlin and obtained a promise that all Jews from Denmark would be sent to Theresienstadt[3] regardless of their category—a very important concession, from the Nazis' point of view. The night of October 1 was set for their seizure and immediate departure—ships were ready in the harbor—and since neither the Danes nor the Jews nor the German troops stationed in Denmark could be relied on to help, police units arrived from Germany for a door-to-door search. At the last moment, Best told them that they were not permitted to break into apartments, because the Danish police might then interfere, and they were not supposed to fight it out with the Danes. Hence they could seize only those Jews who voluntarily opened their doors. They found exactly 477 people, out of a total of more then 7,800, at home and willing to let them in. A few days before the date of doom, a German shipping agent, Georg F. Duckwitz, having probably been tipped off by Best himself, had revealed the whole plan to Danish government officials, who, in turn, had hurriedly informed the heads of the Jewish community. They, in marked contrast to Jewish leaders in other countries, had then communicated the news openly in the synagogues on the occasion of the New Year services. The Jews had just time enough to leave their apartments and go into hiding, which was very easy in Denmark, because, in the words of the judgment, "all sections of the Danish people, from the King down to simple citizens," stood ready to receive them.

They might have remained in hiding until the end of the war if the Danes had not been blessed with Sweden as a neighbor. It seemed reasonable to ship the Jews to Sweden, and this was done with the help of the Danish fishing fleet. The cost of transportation for people without means—about a hundred dollars per person—was paid largely by wealthy Danish citizens, and that was perhaps the most astounding feat of all, since this was a time when Jews were paying for their own deportation, when the rich among them were paying fortunes for exit permits (in Holland, Slovakia, and, later, in Hungary) either by bribing the local authorities or by negotiating "legally" with the S.S., who accepted only hard currency and sold exit permits, in Holland, to the tune of five or ten thousand dollars per person. Even in places where Jews met with genuine sympathy and a sincere willingness to help, they had to pay for it, and the chances poor people had of escaping were nil.

It took the better part of October to ferry all the Jews across the five to fifteen miles of water that separates Denmark from Sweden. The Swedes received 5,919 refugees, of whom at least 1,000 were of German origin, 1,310 were half-Jews, and 686 were non-Jews married to Jews. (Almost

3. A camp for certain classes of prisoners who were to receive special treatment.

half the Danish Jews seem to have remained in the country and survived the war in hiding.) The non-Danish Jews were better off than ever before, they all received permission to work. The few hundred Jews whom the German police had been able to arrest were shipped to Theresienstadt. They were old or poor people, who either had not received the news in time or had not been able to comprehend its meaning. In the ghetto, they enjoyed greater privileges than any other group because of the never-ending "fuss" made about them by Danish institutions and private persons. Forty-eight persons died, a figure that was not particularly high, in view of the average age of the group. When everything was over, it was the considered opinion of Eichmann that "for various reasons the action against the Jews in Denmark has been a failure," whereas the curious Dr. Best declared that "the objective of the operation was not to seize a great number of Jews but to clean Denmark of Jews, and this objective has now been achieved."

Politically and psychologically, the most interesting aspect of this incident is perhaps the role played by the German authorities in Denmark, their obvious sabotage of orders from Berlin. It is the only case we know of in which the Nazis met with *open* native resistance, and the result seems to have been that those exposed to it changed their minds. They themselves apparently no longer looked upon the extermination of a whole people as a matter of course. They had met resistance based on principle, and their "toughness" had melted like butter in the sun, they had even been able to show a few timid beginnings of genuine courage. That the ideal of "toughness," except, perhaps, for a few half-demented brutes, was nothing but a myth of self-deception, concealing a ruthless desire for conformity at any price, was clearly revealed at the Nuremberg Trials, where the defendants accused and betrayed each other and assured the world that they "had always been against it" or claimed, as Eichmann was to do, that their best qualities had been "abused" by their superiors. (In Jerusalem, he accused "those in power" of having abused his "obedience." "The subject of a good government is lucky, the subject of a bad government is unlucky. I had no luck.") The atmosphere had changed, and although most of them must have known that they were doomed, not a single one of them had the guts to defend the Nazi ideology. Werner Best claimed at Nuremberg that he had played a complicated double role and that it was thanks to him that the Danish officials had been warned of the impending catastrophe; documentary evidence showed, on the contrary, that he himself had proposed the Danish operation in Berlin, but he explained that this was all part of the game. He was extradited to Denmark and there condemned to death, but he appealed the sentence, with surprising results; because of "new evidence," his sentence was commuted to five years in prison, from which he was released soon afterward. He must have been able to prove to the satisfaction of the Danish court that he really had done his best.

1963

Edward Hallett Carr

THE HISTORIAN AND HIS FACTS

What is history? Lest anyone think the question meaningless or super-fluous, I will take as my text two passages relating respectively to the first and second incarnations of *The Cambridge Modern History*. Here is Acton in his report of October 1896 to the Syndics of the Cambridge University Press on the work which he had undertaken to edit:

> It is a unique opportunity of recording, in the way most useful to the greatest number, the fullness of the knowledge which the nineteenth century is about to bequeath. . . . By the judicious division of labor we should be able to do it, and to bring home to every man the last document, and the ripest conclusions of international research.
>
> Ultimate history we cannot have in this generation; but we can dispose of conventional history, and show the point we have reached on the road from one to the other, now that all information is within reach, and every problem has become capable of solution.

And almost exactly sixty years later Professor Sir George Clark, in his general introduction to the second *Cambridge Modern History*, commented on this belief of Acton and his collaborators that it would one day be possible to produce "ultimate history," and went on:

> Historians of a later generation do not look forward to any such prospect. They expect their work to be superseded again and again. They consider that knowledge of the past has come down through one or more human minds, has been "processed" by them, and therefore cannot consist of elemental and impersonal atoms which nothing can alter. . . . The exploration seems to be endless, and some impatient scholars take refuge in scepticism, or at least in the doctrine that, since all historical judgments involve persons and points of view, one is as good as another and there is no "objective" historical truth.

Where the pundits contradict each other so flagrantly the field is open to enquiry. I hope that I am sufficiently up-to-date to recognize that any-thing written in the 1890's must be nonsense. But I am not yet advanced enough to be committed to the view that anything written in the 1950's necessarily makes sense. Indeed, it may already have occurred to you that this enquiry is liable to stray into something even broader than the nature of history. The clash between Acton and Sir George Clark is a reflection of the change in our total outlook on society over the interval between these two pronouncements. Acton speaks out of the positive belief, the clear-eyed self-confidence of the later Victorian age; Sir George Clark echoes the bewilderment and distracted scepticism of the beat generation. When we attempt to answer the question, What is history?, our answer, consciously or unconsciously, reflects our own position in time, and forms part of our answer to the broader question, what view we take of the society in which we live. I have no fear that my subject may, on closer inspection, seem trivial. I am afraid only that I may seem presumptuous to have broached a question so vast and so important.

The nineteenth century was a great age for facts. "What I want," said Mr. Gradgrind in *Hard Times*, "is Facts. . . . Facts alone are wanted in life." Nineteenth-century historians on the whole agreed with him. When Ranke in the 1830's, in legitimate protest against moralizing history, remarked that the task of the historian was "simply to show how it really was [*wie es eigentlich gewesen*]" this not very profound aphorism had an astonishing success. Three generations of German, British, and even French historians marched into battle intoning the magic words, "*Wie es eigentlich gewesen*" like an incantation—designed, like most incantations, to save them from the tiresome obligation to think for themselves. The Positivists, anxious to stake out their claim for history as a science, contributed the weight of their influence to this cult of facts. First ascertain the facts, said the positivists, then draw your conclusions from them. In Great Britain, this view of history fitted in perfectly with the empiricist tradition which was the dominant strain in British philosophy from Locke to Bertrand Russell. The empirical theory of knowledge presupposes a complete separation between subject and object. Facts, like sense-impressions, impinge on the observer from outside, and are independent of his consciousness. The process of reception is passive: having received the data, he then acts on them. *The Shorter Oxford English Dictionary*, a useful but tendentious work of the empirical school, clearly marks the separateness of the two processes by defining a fact as "a datum of experience as distinct from conclusions." This is what may be called the common-sense view of history. History consists of a corpus of ascertained facts. The facts are available to the historian in documents, inscriptions, and so on, like fish on the fishmonger's slab. The historian collects them, takes them home, and cooks and serves them in whatever style appeals to him. Acton, whose culinary tastes were austere, wanted them served plain. In his letter of instructions to contributors to the first *Cambridge Modern History* he announced the requirement "that our Waterloo must be one that satisfies French and English, German and Dutch alike; that nobody can tell, without examining the list of authors where the Bishop of Oxford laid down the pen, and whether Fairbairn or Gasquet, Liebermann or Harrison took it up." Even Sir George Clark, critical as he was of Acton's attitude, himself contrasted the "hard core of facts" in history with the "surrounding pulp of disputable interpretation"—forgetting perhaps that the pulpy part of the fruit is more rewarding than the hard core. First get your facts straight, then plunge at your peril into the shifting sands of interpretation—that is the ultimate wisdom of the empirical, common-sense school of history. It recalls the favorite dictum of the great liberal journalist C. P. Scott: "Facts are sacred, opinion is free."

Now this clearly will not do. I shall not embark on a philosophical discussion of the nature of our knowledge of the past. Let us assume for present purposes that the fact that Caesar crossed the Rubicon and the fact that there is a table in the middle of the room are facts of the same or of a comparable order, that both these facts enter our consciousness in the same or in a comparable manner, and that both have the same objective character in relation to the person who knows them. But, even on this bold and not very plausible assumption, our argument at once runs into the difficulty that not all facts about the past are historical facts, or are treated as such by the historian. What is the criterion which distinguishes the facts of history from other facts about the past?

What is a historical fact? This is a crucial question into which we must look a little more closely. According to the common-sense view, there are certain basic facts which are the same for all historians and which form, so to speak, the backbone of history—the fact, for example, that the Battle of Hastings was fought in 1066. But this view calls for two observations. In the first place, it is not with facts like these that the historian is primarily concerned. It is no doubt important to know that the great battle was fought in 1066 and not in 1065 or 1067, and that it was fought at Hastings and not at Eastbourne or Brighton. The historian must not get these things wrong. But when points of this kind are raised, I am reminded of Housman's remark[1] that "accuracy is a duty, not a virtue." To praise a historian for his accuracy is like praising an architect for using well-seasoned timber or properly mixed concrete in his building. It is a necessary condition of his work, but not his essential function. It is precisely for matters of this kind that the historian is entitled to rely on what have been called the "auxiliary sciences" of history—archaeology, epigraphy, numismatics, chronology, and so forth. The historian is not required to have the special skills which enable the expert to determine the origin and period of a fragment of pottery or marble, or decipher an obscure inscription, or to make the elaborate astronomical calculations necessary to establish a precise date. These so-called basic facts which are the same for all historians commonly belong to the category of the raw materials of the historian rather than of history itself. The second observation is that the necessity to establish these basic facts rests not on any quality in the facts themselves, but on an a priori decision of the historian. In spite of C. P. Scott's motto, every journalist knows today that the most effective way to influence opinion is by the selection and arrangement of the appropriate facts. It used to be said that facts speak

1. In the preface to his critical edition of Manilius, *Astronomicon*, an obscure Latin work.

for themselves. This is, of course, untrue. The facts speak only when the historian calls on them: It is he who decides to which facts to give the floor, and in what order or context. It was, I think, one of Pirandello's characters who said that a fact is like a sack—it won't stand up till you've put something in it. The only reason why we are interested to know that the battle was fought at Hastings in 1066 is that historians regard it as a major historical event. It is the historian who has decided for his own reasons that Caesar's crossing of that petty stream, the Rubicon, is a fact of history, whereas the crossing of the Rubicon by millions of other people before or since interests nobody at all. The fact that you arrived in this building half an hour ago on foot, or on a bicycle, or in a car, is just as much a fact about the past as the fact that Caesar crossed the Rubicon. But it will probably be ignored by historians. Professor Talcott Parsons once called science "a selective system of cognitive orientations to reality." It might perhaps have been put more simply. But history is, among other things, that. The historian is necessarily selective. The belief in a hard core of historical facts existing objectively and independently of the interpretation of the historian is a preposterous fallacy, but one which it is very hard to eradicate.

Let us take a look at the process by which a mere fact about the past is transformed into a fact of history. At Stalybridge Wakes in 1850, a vendor of gingerbread, as the result of some petty dispute, was deliberately kicked to death by an angry mob. Is this a fact of history? A year ago I should unhesitatingly have said "no." It was recorded by an eyewitness in some little-known memoirs;[2] but I had never seen it judged worthy of mention by any historian. A year ago Dr. Kitson Clark cited it in his Ford lectures in Oxford. Does this make it into a historical fact? Not, I think, yet. Its present status, I suggest, is that it has been proposed for membership of the select club of historical facts. It now awaits a seconder and sponsors. It may be that in the course of the next few years we shall see this fact appearing first in footnotes, then in the text, of articles and books about nineteenth-century England, and that in twenty or thirty years' time it may be a well established historical fact. Alternatively, nobody may take it up, in which case it will relapse into the limbo of unhistorical facts about the past from which Dr. Kitson Clark has gallantly attempted to rescue it. What will decide which of these two things will happen? It will depend, I think, on whether the thesis or interpretation in support of which Dr. Kitson Clark cited this incident is accepted by other historians as valid and significant. Its status as a historical fact will turn on a question of interpretation. This element of interpretation enters into every fact of history.

2. Lord George Sanger: *Seventy Years a Showman* (London: J. M. Dent & Sons, 1926), pp. 188–9 [Carr's note].

May I be allowed a personal reminiscence? When I studied ancient history in this university many years ago, I had as a special subject "Greece in the period of the Persian Wars." I collected fifteen or twenty volumes on my shelves and took it for granted that there, recorded in these volumes, I had all the facts relating to my subject. Let us assume—it was very nearly true—that those volumes contained all the facts about it that were then known, or could be known. It never occurred to me to enquire by what accident or process of attrition that minute selection of facts, out of all the myriad facts that must have once been known to somebody, had survived to become *the* facts of history. I suspect that even today one of the fascinations of ancient and mediaeval history is that it gives us the illusion of having all the facts at our disposal within a manageable compass: the nagging distinction between the facts of history and other facts about the past vanishes because the few known facts are all facts of history. As Bury, who had worked in both periods, said, "the records of ancient and mediaeval history are starred with lacunae." History has been called an enormous jig-saw with a lot of missing parts. But the main trouble does not consist of the lacunae. Our picture of Greece in the fifth century b.c. is defective not primarily because so many of the bits have been accidentally lost, but because it is, by and large, the picture formed by a tiny group of people in the city of Athens. We know a lot about what fifth-century Greece looked like to an Athenian citizen; but hardly anything about what it looked like to a Spartan, a Corinthian, or a Theban—not to mention a Persian, or a slave or other non-citizen resident in Athens. Our picture has been preselected and predetermined for us, not so much by accident as by people who were consciously or unconsciously imbued with a particular view and thought the facts which supported that view worth preserving. In the same way, when I read in a modern history of the Middle Ages that the people of the Middle Ages were deeply concerned with religion, I wonder how we know this, and whether it is true. What we know as the facts of mediaeval history have almost all been selected for us by generations of chroniclers who were professionally occupied in the theory and practice of religion, and who therefore thought it supremely important, and recorded everything relating to it, and not much else. The picture of the Russian peasant as devoutly religious was destroyed by the revolution of 1917. The picture of mediaeval man as devoutly religious, whether true or not, is indestructible, because nearly all the known facts about him were preselected for us by people who believed it, and wanted others to believe it, and a mass of other facts, in which we might possibly have found evidence to the contrary, has been lost beyond recall. The dead hand of vanished generations of historians, scribes, and chroniclers has determined beyond the possibility of appeal the pattern of the past. "The history we read," writes Professor Barraclough, himself trained as a mediaevalist, "though based on facts, is, strictly speaking, not factual at all, but a series of accepted judgments."

But let us turn to the different, but equally grave, plight of the modern historian. The ancient or mediaeval historian may be grateful for the vast winnowing process which, over the years, has put at his disposal a manageable corpus of historical facts. As Lytton Strachey said in his mischievous way, "ignorance is the first requisite of the historian, ignorance which simplifies and clarifies, which selects and omits." When I am tempted, as I sometimes am, to envy the extreme competence of colleagues engaged in writing ancient or mediaeval history, I find consolation in the reflection that they are so competent mainly because they are so ignorant of their subject. The modern historian enjoys none of the advantages of this built-in ignorance. He must cultivate this necessary ignorance for himself—the more so the nearer he comes to his own times. He has the dual task of discovering the few significant facts and turning them into facts of history, and of discarding the many insignificant facts are unhistorical. But this is the very converse of the nineteenth-century heresy that history consists of the compilation of a maximum number of irrefutable and objective facts. Anyone who succumbs to this heresy will either have to give up history as a bad job, and take to stamp-collecting or some other form of antiquarianism, or end in a madhouse. It is this heresy, which during the past hundred years has had such devastating effects on the modern historian, producing in Germany, in Great Britain, and in the United States a vast and growing mass of dry-as-dust factual histories, of minutely specialized monographs, of would-be historians knowing more and more about less and less, sunk without trace in an ocean of facts. It was, I suspect, this heresy—rather than the alleged conflict between liberal and Catholic loyalties—which frustrated Acton as a historian. In an early essay he said of his teacher Döllinger: "He would not write with imperfect materials, and to him the materials were always imperfect."[3] Acton was surely here pronouncing an anticipatory verdict on himself, on that strange phenomenon of a historian whom many would regard as the most distinguished occupant the Regius Chair of Modern History in this university has ever had—but who wrote no history. And Acton wrote his own epitaph in the introductory note to the first volume of the *Cambridge Modern History*, published just after his death, when he lamented that the requirements pressing on the historian "threaten to turn him from a man of letters into the compiler of an encyclopedia." Something had gone wrong. What had gone wrong was the belief in this untiring and unending accumulation of hard facts as the foundation of history, the belief that facts speak for themselves and that we cannot have too many facts, a belief at that time so unquestioning that

---

3. Later Acton said of Döllinger that "it was given to him to form his philosophy of history on the largest induction ever available to man" [Carr's note].

few historians then thought it necessary—and some still think it unnecessary today—to ask themselves the question: What is history?

The nineteenth-century fetishism of facts was completed and justified by a fetishism of documents. The documents were the Ark of the Covenant in the temple of facts. The reverent historian approached them with bowed head and spoke of them in awed tones. If you find it in the documents, it is so. But what, when we get down to it, do these documents—the decrees, the treaties, the rent-rolls, the blue books, the official correspondence, the private letters and diaries—tell us? No document can tell us more than what the author of the document thought —what he thought had happened, what he thought ought to happen or would happen, or perhaps only what he wanted others to think he thought, or even only what he himself thought he thought. None of this means anything until the historian has got to work on it and deciphered it. The facts, whether found in documents or not, have still to be processed by the historian before he can make any use of them: the use he makes of them is, if I may put it that way, the processing process.

Let me illustrate what I am trying to say by an example which I happen to know well. When Gustav Stresemann, the Foreign Minister of the Weimar Republic, died in 1929, he left behind him an enormous mass —300 boxes full—of papers, official, semiofficial, and private, nearly all relating to the six years of his tenure of office as Foreign Minister. His friends and relatives naturally thought that a monument should be raised to the memory of so great a man. His faithful secretary Bernhardt got to work; and within three years there appeared three massive volumes, of some 600 pages each, of selected documents from the 300 boxes, with the impressive title *Stresemanns Vermächtnis*.[4] In the ordinary way the documents themselves would have moldered away in some cellar or attic and disappeared for ever; or perhaps in a hundred years or so some curious scholar would have come upon them and set out to compare them with Bernhardt's text. What happened was far more dramatic. In 1945 the documents fell into the hands of the British and the American governments, who photographed the lot and put the photostats at the disposal of scholars in the Public Record Office in London and in the National Archives in Washington, so that, if we have sufficient patience and curiosity, we can discover exactly what Bernhardt did. What he did was neither very unusual nor very shocking. When Stresemann died, his Western policy seemed to have been crowned with a series of brilliant successes—Locarno, the admission of Germany to the League of Nations, the Dawes and Young plans and the American loans, the withdrawal of allied occupation armies from the Rhineland. This seemed the important and rewarding part of Stresemann's foreign policy; and it was not unnatural that it should have been over-represented in Bernhardt's

4. *Stresemann's Legacy.*

selection of documents. Stresemann's Eastern policy, on the other hand, his relations with the Soviet Union, seemed to have led nowhere in particular; and, since masses of documents about negotiations which yielded only trivial results were not very interesting and added nothing to Stresemann's reputation, the process of selection could be more rigorous. Stresemann in fact devoted a far more constant and anxious attention to relations with the Soviet Union, and they played a far larger part in his foreign policy as a whole, than the reader of the Bernhardt selection would surmise. But the Bernhardt volumes compare favorably, I suspect, with many published collections of documents on which the ordinary historian implicitly relies.

This is not the end of my story. Shortly after the publication of Bernhardt's volumes, Hitler came into power. Stresemann's name was consigned to oblivion in Germany, and the volumes disappeared from circulation: many, perhaps most, of the copies must have been destroyed. Today *Stresemanns Vermächtnis* is a rather rare book. But in the West Stresemann's reputation stood high. In 1935 an English publisher brought out an abbreviated translation of Bernhardt's work—a selection from Bernhardt's selection; perhaps one third of the original was omitted. Sutton, a well-known translator from the German, did his job competently and well. The English version, he explained in the preface, was "slightly condensed, but only by the omission of a certain amount of what, it was felt, was more ephemeral matter ... of little interest to English readers or students." This again is natural enough. But the result is that Stresemann's Eastern policy, already under-represented in Bernhardt, recedes still further from view, and the Soviet Union appears in Sutton's volumes merely as an occasional and rather unwelcome intruder in Stresemann's predominantly Western foreign policy. Yet it is safe to say that, for all except a few specialists, Sutton and not Bernhardt—and still less the documents themselves—represents for the Western world the authentic voice of Stresemann. Had the documents perished in 1945 in the bombing, and had the remaining Bernhardt volumes disappeared, the authenticity and authority of Sutton would never have been questioned. Many printed collection of documents gratefully accepted by historians in default of the originals rest on no securer basis than this.

But I want to carry the story one step further. Let us forget about Bernhardt and Sutton, and be thankful that we can, if we choose, consult the authentic papers of a leading participant in some important events in recent European history. What do the papers tell us? Among other things they contain records of some hundreds of Stresemann's conversations with the Soviet ambassador in Berlin and of a score or so with Chicherin.[5] These records have one feature in common. They depict Stresemann as having the lion's share of the conversations and reveal his

5. Soviet foreign minister from 1918 to 1928.

arguments as invariably well put and cogent, while those of his partner are for the most part scanty, confused, and unconvincing. This is a familiar characteristic of all records of diplomatic conversations. The documents do not tell us what happened, but only what Stresemann thought had happened. It was not Sutton or Bernhardt, but Stresemann himself, who started the process of selection. And, if we had, say Chicherin's records of these same conversations, we should still learn from them only what Chicherin thought, and what really happened would still have to be reconstructed in the mind of the historian. Of course, facts and documents are essential to the historian. But do not make a fetish of them. They do not by themselves constitute history; they provide in themselves no ready-made answer to this tiresome question: What is history?

At this point I should like to say a few words on the question of why nineteenth-century historians were generally indifferent to the philosophy of history. The term was invented by Voltaire, and has since been used in different senses; but I shall take it to mean, if I use it at all, our answer to the question: What is history? The nineteenth century was, for the intellectuals of Western Europe, a comfortable period exuding confidence and optimism. The facts were on the whole satisfactory; and the inclination to ask and answer awkward questions about them was correspondingly weak. Ranke piously believed that divine providence would take care of the meaning of history if he took care of the facts; and Burckhardt with a more modern touch of cynicism observed that "we are not initiated into the purposes of the eternal wisdom." Professor Butterfield as late as 1931 noted with apparent satisfaction that "historians have reflected little upon the nature of things and even the nature of their own subject." But my predecessor in these lectures, Dr. A. L. Rowse, more justly critical, wrote of Sir Winston Churchill's *The World Crisis*—his book about the First World War—that, while it matched Trotsky's *History of the Russian Revolution* in personality, vividness, and vitality, it was inferior in one respect: it had "no philosophy of history behind it." British historians refused to be drawn, not because they believed that history had no meaning, but because they believed that its meaning was implicit and self-evident. The liberal nineteenth-century view of history had a close affinity with the economic doctrine of *laissez-faire*—also the product of a serene and self-confident outlook on the world. Let everyone get on with his particular job, and the hidden hand would take care of the universal harmony. The facts of history were themselves a demonstration of the supreme fact of a beneficent and apparently infinite progress towards higher things. This was the age of innocence, and historians walked in the Garden of Eden, without a scrap of philosophy to cover them, naked and unashamed before the god of history. Since then, we have known Sin and experienced a Fall; and those historians who today pretend to dispense with a philosophy of history are merely trying, vainly and self-consciously, like members of a nudist colony, to recreate the Garden of Eden in their garden suburb. Today the awkward question can no longer be evaded. * * *

During the past fifty years a good deal of serious work has been done on the question: What is history? It was from Germany, the country which was to do so much to upset the comfortable reign of nineteenth-century liberalism, that the first challenge came in the 1880's and 1890's to the doctrine of the primacy and autonomy of facts in history. The philosophers who made the challenge are now little more than names: Dilthey is the only one of them who has recently received some belated recognition in Great Britain. Before the turn of the century, prosperity and confidence were still too great in this country for any attention to be paid to heretics who attacked the cult of facts. But early in the new century, the torch passed to Italy, where Croce began to propound a philosophy of history which obviously owed much to German masters. All history is "contemporary history," declared Croce,[6] meaning that history consists essentially in seeing the past through the eyes of the present and in the light of its problems, and that the main work of the historian is not to record, but to evaluate; for, if he does not evaluate, how can he know what is worth recording? In 1910 the American philosopher, Carl Becker, argued in deliberately provocative language that "the facts of history do not exist for any historian till he creates them." These challenges were for the moment little noticed. It was only after 1920 that Croce began to have a considerable vogue in France and Great Britain. This was not perhaps because Croce was a subtler thinker or a better stylist than his German predecessors, but because, after the First World War, the facts seemed to smile on us less propitiously than in the years before 1914, and we were therefore more accessible to a philosophy which sought to diminish their prestige. Croce was an important influence on the Oxford philosopher and historian Collingwood, the only British thinker in the present century who has made a serious contribution to the philosophy of history. He did not live to write the systematic treatise he had planned; but his published and unpublished papers on the subject were collected after his death in a volume entitled *The Idea of History*, which appeared in 1945.

The views of Collingwood can be summarized as follows. The philosophy of history is concerned neither with "the past by itself" nor with "the historian's thought about it by itself," but with "the two things in their

6. The context of this celebrated aphorism is as follows: "The practical requirements which underlie every historical judgment give to all history the character of 'contemporary history,' because, however remote in time events thus recounted may seem to be, the history in reality refers to present needs and present situations wherein those events vibrate" [Carr's note].

mutual relations." (This dictum reflects the two current meanings of the word "history"—the enquiry conducted by the historian and the series of past events into which he enquires.) "The past which a historian studies is not a dead past, but a past which is some sense is still living in the present." But a past act is dead, *i.e.* meaningless to the historian, unless he can understand the thought that lay behind it. Hence "all history is the history of thought," and "history is the re-enactment in the historian's mind of the thought whose history he is studying." The reconstitution of the past in the historian's mind is dependent on empirical evidence. But it is not in itself an empirical process, and cannot consist in a mere recital of facts. On the contrary, the process of reconstitution governs the selection and interpretation of the facts: this, indeed, is what makes them historical facts. "History," says Professor Oakeshott, who on this point stands near to Collingwood, "is the historian's experience. It is 'made' by nobody save the historian: to write history is the only way of making it."

This searching critique, though it may call for some serious reservations, brings to light certain neglected truths.

In the first place, the facts of history never come to us "pure," since they do not and cannot exist in a pure form: they are always refracted through the mind of the recorder. It follows that when we take up a work of history, our first concern should be not with the facts which it contains but with the historian who wrote it. Let me take as an example the great historian in whose honor and in whose name these lectures were founded. Trevelyan, as he tells us in his autobiography, was "brought up at home on a somewhat exuberantly Whig tradition"; and he would not, I hope, disclaim the title if I described him as the last and not the least of the great English liberal historians of the Whig tradition. It is not for nothing that he traces back his family tree, through the great Whig historian George Otto Trevelyan, to Macaulay, incomparably the greatest of the Whig historians. Dr. Trevelyan's finest and maturest work *England under Queen Anne* was written against that background, and will yield its full meaning and significance to the reader only when read against that background. The author, indeed, leaves the reader with no excuse for failing to do so. For if, following the technique of connoisseurs of detective novels, you read the end first, you will find on the last few pages of the third volume the best summary known to me of what is nowadays called the Whig interpretation of history; and you will see that what Trevelyan is trying to do is to investigate the origin and development of the Whig tradition, and to root it fairly and squarely in the years after the death of its founder, William III. Though this is not, perhaps, the only conceivable interpretation of the events of Queen Anne's reign, it is a valid and, in Trevelyan's hands, a fruitful interpretation. But, in order to appreciate it at its full value, you have to understand what the historian is doing. For if, as Collingwood says, the historian must re-enact in thought what has gone on in the mind of his *dramatis personae*, so the reader in his turn must re-enact what goes on in the mind of the historian. Study the historian before you begin to study the facts. This is, after all, not very abstruse. It is what is already done by the intelligent undergraduate who, when recommended to read a work by that great scholar Jones of St. Jude's, goes round to a friend at St. Jude's to ask what sort of chap Jones is, and what bees he has in his bonnet. When you read a work of history, always listen out for the buzzing. If you can detect none, either you are tone deaf or your historian is a dull dog. The facts are really not at all like fish on the fishmonger's slab. They are like fish swimming about in a vast and sometimes inaccessible ocean; and what the historian catches will depend partly on chance, but mainly on what part of the ocean he chooses to fish in and what tackle he chooses to use—these two factors being, of course, determined by the kind of fish he wants to catch. By and large, the historian will get the kind of facts he wants. History means interpretation. Indeed, if, standing Sir George Clark on his head, I were to call history "a hard core of interpretation surrounded by a pulp of disputable facts," my statement would, no doubt, be one-sided and misleading, but no more so, I venture to think, than the original dictum.

The second point is the more familiar one of the historian's need of imaginative understanding for the minds of the people with whom he is dealing, for the thought behind their acts: I say "imaginative understanding," not "sympathy," lest sympathy should be supposed to imply agreement. The nineteenth century was weak in mediaeval history, because it was too much repelled by the superstitious beliefs of the Middle Ages and by the barbarities which they inspired, to have any imaginative understanding of mediaeval people. Or take Burckhardt's censorious remark about the Thirty Years' War: "It is scandalous for a creed, no matter whether it is Catholic or Protestant, to place its salvation above the integrity of the nation." It was extremely difficult for a nineteenth-century liberal historian, brought up to believe that it is right and praiseworthy to kill in defense of one's country, but wicked and wrongheaded to kill in defense of one's religion, to enter into the state of mind of those who fought the Thirty Years' War. This difficulty is particularly acute in the field in which I am now working. Much of what has been written in English-speaking countries in the last ten years about the Soviet Union, and in the Soviet Union about the English-speaking countries, has been vitiated by this inability to achieve even the most elementary measure of imaginative understanding of what goes on in the mind of the other party, so that the words and actions of the other are always made to appear malign, senseless, or hypocritical. History cannot be written unless the historian can achieve some kind of contact with the mind of those about whom he is writing.

The third point is that we can view the past, and achieve our under-

standing of the past, only through the eyes of the present. The historian is of his own age, and is bound to it by the conditions of human existence. The very words which he uses—words like democracy, empire, war, revolution—have current connotations from which he cannot divorce them. Ancient historians have taken to using words like *polis* and *plebs* in the original, just in order to show that they have not fallen into this trap. This does not help them. They, too, live in the present, and cannot cheat themselves into the past by using unfamiliar or obsolete words, any more than they would become better Greek or Roman historians if they delivered their lectures in a *chlamys* or a *toga*. The names by which successive French historians have described the Parisian crowds which played so prominent a role in the French Revolution—*les sansculottes, le peuple, la canaille, les bras-nus*—are all, for those who know the rules of the game, manifestos of a political affiliation and of a particular interpretation. Yet the historian is obliged to choose: the use of language forbids him to be neutral. Nor is it a matter of words alone. Over the past hundred years the changed balance of power in Europe has reversed the attitude of British historians to Frederick the Great. The changed balance of power within the Christian churches between Catholicism and Protestantism has profoundly altered their attitude to such figures as Loyola, Luther, and Cromwell. It requires only a superficial knowledge of the work of French historians of the last forty years on the French revolution to recognize how deeply it has been affected by the Russian revolution of 1917. The historian belongs not to the past but to the present. Professor Trevor-Roper tells us that the historian "ought to love the past." This is a dubious injunction. To love the past may easily be an expression of the nostalgic romanticism of old men and old societies, a symptom of loss of faith and interest in the present or future.[7] *Cliché* for *cliché*, I should prefer the one about freeing oneself from "the dead hand of the past." The function of the historian is neither to love the past nor to emancipate himself from the past, but to master and understand it as the key to the understanding of the present.

If, however, these are some of the sights of what I may call the Collingwood view of history, it is time to consider some of the dangers. The emphasis on the role of the historian in the making of history tends, if pressed to its logical conclusion, to rule out any objective history at all: history is what the historian makes. Collingwood seems indeed, at one moment, in an unpublished note quoted by his editor, to have reached this conclusion:

> St. Augustine looked at history from the point of view of the early Christian; Tillemont, from that of a seventeenth-century Frenchman; Gibbon,

7. Compare Nietzsche's view of history: "To old age belongs the old man's business of looking back and casting up his accounts, of seeking consolation in the memories of the past, in historical culture" [Carr's note].

from that of an eighteenth-century Englishman; Mommsen, from that of a
nineteenth-century German. There is no point in asking which was the right
point of view. Each was the only one possible for the man who adopted it.

This amounts to total scepticism, like Froude's remark that history is "a
child's box of letters with which we can spell any word we please."
Collingwood, in his reaction against "scissors-and-paste history," against
the view of history as a mere compilation of facts, comes perilously near
to treating history as something spun out of the human brain, and leads
back to the conclusion referred to by Sir George Clark in the passage
which I quoted earlier, that "there is no 'objective' historical truth." In
place of the theory that history has no meaning, we are offered here the
theory of an infinity of meanings, none any more right than any other
—which comes to much the same thing. The second theory is surely as
untenable as the first. It does not follow that, because a mountain appears
to take on different shapes from different angles of vision, it has objectively either no shape at all or an infinity of shapes. It does not follow that,
because interpretation plays a necessary part in establishing the facts of
history, and because no existing interpretation is wholly objective, one
interpretation is as good as another, and the facts of history are in
principle not amenable to objective interpretation. I shall have to consider at a later stage what exactly is meant by objectivity in history.

But a still greater danger lurks in the Collingwood hypothesis. If the
historian necessarily looks at his period of history through the eyes of his
own time, and studies the problems of the past as a key to those of the
present, will he not fall into a purely pragmatic view of the facts, and
maintain that the criterion of a right interpretation is its suitability to
some present purpose? On this hypothesis, the facts of history are nothing, interpretation is everything. Nietzsche had already enunciated the
principle: "The falseness of an opinion is not for us any objection to it. . . .
The question is how far it is life-furthering, life-preserving, species-
preserving, perhaps species-creating." The American pragmatists
moved, less explicitly and less wholeheartedly, along the same line.
Knowledge is knowledge for some purpose. The validity of the knowledge depends on the validity of the purpose. But, even where no such
theory has been professed, the practice has often been no less disquiet-
ing. In my own field of study, I have seen too many examples of extravagant interpretation riding roughshod over facts, not to be impressed with
the reality of this danger. It is not surprising that perusal of some of the
more extreme products of Soviet and anti-Soviet schools of historiogra-
phy should sometimes breed a certain nostalgia for that illusory nineteenth-century heaven of purely factual history.

How then, in the middle of the twentieth century, are we to define the
obligation of the historian to his facts? I trust that I have spent a sufficient
number of hours in recent years chasing and perusing documents, and

stuffing my historical narrative with properly footnoted facts, to escape the imputation of treating facts and documents too cavalierly. The duty of the historian to respect his facts is not exhausted by the obligation to see that his facts are accurate. He must seek to bring into the picture all known or knowable facts relevant, in one sense or another, to the theme on which he is engaged and to the interpretation proposed. If he seeks to depict the Victorian Englishman as a moral and rational being, he must not forget what happened at Stalybridge Wakes in 1850. But this, in turn, does not mean that he can eliminate interpretation, which is the life-blood of history. Laymen—that is to say, non-academic friends or friends from other academic disciplines—sometimes ask me how the historian goes to work when he writes history. The commonest assumption appears to be that the historian divides his work into two sharply distinguishable phases or periods. First, he spends a long preliminary period reading his source and filling his notebooks with facts: then, when this is over, he puts away his sources, takes out his notebooks, and writes his book from beginning to end. This is to me an unconvincing and unplausible picture. For myself, as soon as I have got going on a few of what I take to be the capital sources, the itch becomes too strong and I begin to write—not necessarily at the beginning, but somewhere, anywhere. Thereafter, reading and writing go on simultaneously. The writing is added to, subtracted from, re-shaped, cancelled, as I go on reading. The reading is guided and directed and made fruitful by the writing: the more I write, the more I know what I am looking for, the better I understand the significance and relevance of what I find. Some historians probably do all this preliminary writing in their head without using pen, paper, or typewriter, just as some people play chess in their heads without recourse to board and chess-men: this is a talent which I envy, but cannot emulate. But I am convinced that, for any historian worth the name, the two processes of what economists call "input" and "output" go on simultaneously and are, in practice, parts of a single process. If you try to separate them, or to give one priority over the other, you fall into one of two heresies. Either you write scissors-and-paste history without meaning or significance; or you write propaganda or historical fiction, and merely use facts of the past to embroider a kind of writing which has nothing to do with history.

Our examination of the relation of the historian to the facts of history finds us, therefore, in an apparently precarious situation, navigating delicately between the Scylla of an untenable theory of history as an objective compilation of facts, of the unqualified primacy of fact over interpretation, and the Charybdis of an equally untenable theory of history as the subjective product of the mind of the historian who establishes the facts of history and masters them through the process of interpretation, between a view of history having the center of gravity in the past and the view having the center of gravity in the present. But our situation is less precarious than it seems. We shall encounter the same dichotomy of fact and interpretation again in these lectures in other guises—the particular and the general, the empirical and the theoretical, the objective and the subjective. The predicament of the historian is a reflection of the nature of man. Man, except perhaps in earliest infancy and in extreme old age, is not totally involved in his environment and unconditionally subject to it. On the other hand, he is never totally independent of it and its unconditional master. The relation of man to his environment is the relation of the historian to his theme. The historian is neither the humble slave, nor the tyrannical master, of his facts. The relation between the historian and his facts is one of equality, of give-and-take. As any working historian knows, if he stops to reflect what he is doing as he thinks and writes, the historian is engaged on a continuous process of molding his facts to his interpretation and his facts. It is impossible to assign primacy to one over the other.

The historian starts with the provisional selection of facts and a provisional interpretation in the light of which that selection has been made —by others as well as by himself. As he works, both the interpretation and the selection and ordering of facts undergo subtle and perhaps partly unconscious changes through the reciprocal action of one or the other. And this reciprocal action also involves reciprocity between present and past, since the historian is part of the present and the facts belong to the past. The historian and the facts of history are necessary to one another. The historian without his facts is rootless and futile; the facts without their historian are dead and meaningless. My first answer therefore to the question, What is history?, is that it is a continuous process of interaction between the historian and his facts, an unending dialogue between the present and the past.

1961

QUESTIONS

1. *Carr begins with a question but does not answer it until the last sentence. What are the main steps of the discussion leading to his answer? The answer takes the form of a definition: which is the most important of the defining words?*
2. *In his discussion of the facts of history, Carr distinguishes between a "mere fact about the past" and a "fact of history." Into which category should go Bruno Bettelheim's encounter with the infirmary guard (p. 39)?*
3. *If you were commissioned to write a history of the semester or of a particular group during the semester, what would be your most important "facts of history"?*

Frances FitzGerald

REWRITING AMERICAN HISTORY

Those of us who grew up in the fifties believed in the permanence of our American-history textbooks. To us as children, those texts were the truth of things: they were American history. It was not just that we read them before we understood that not everything that is printed is the truth, or the whole truth. It was that they, much more than other books, had the demeanor and trappings of authority. They were weighty volumes. They spoke in measured cadences: imperturbable, humorless, and as distant as Chinese emperors. Our teachers treated them with respect, and we paid them abject homage by memorizing a chapter a week. But now the textbook histories have changed, some of them to such an extent that an adult would find them unrecognizable.

One current junior-high-school American history begins with a story about a Negro cowboy called George McJunkin. It appears that when McJunkin was riding down a lonely trail in New Mexico one cold spring morning in 1925 he discovered a mound containing bones and stone implements, which scientists later proved belonged to an Indian civilization ten thousand years old. The book goes on to say that scientists now believe there were people in the Americas at least twenty thousand years ago. It discusses the Aztec, Mayan, and Incan civilizations and the meaning of the world "culture" before introducing the European explorers.

Another history text—this one for the fifth grade—begins with the story of how Henry B. Gonzalez, who is a member of Congress from Texas, learned about his own nationality. When he was ten years old, his teacher told him he was an American because he was born in the United States. His grandmother, however, said, "The cat was born in the oven. Does that make him bread?" After reporting that Mr. Gonzalez eventually went to college and law school, the book explains that "the melting pot idea hasn't worked out as some thought it would," and that now "some people say that the people of the United States are more like a salad bowl than a melting pot."

Poor Columbus! He is a minor character now, a walk-on in the middle of American history. Even those books that have not replaced his picture with a Mayan temple or an Iroquois mask do not credit him with discovering America—even for the Europeans. The Vikings, they say, preceded him to the New World, and after that the Europeans, having lost or forgotten their maps, simply neglected to cross the ocean again for five hundred years. Columbus is far from being the only personage to have suffered from time and revision. Captain John Smith, Daniel Boone, and Wild Bill Hickok—the great self-promoters of American history—have all but disappeared, taking with them a good deal of the romance of the American frontier. General Custer has given way to Chief Crazy Horse; General Eisenhower no longer liberates Europe single-handed; and, indeed, most generals, even to Washington and Lee, have faded away, as old soldiers do, giving place to social reformers such as William Lloyd Garrison and Jacob Riis. A number of black Americans have risen to prominence: not only George Washington Carver but Frederick Douglass and Martin Luther King, Jr. W. E. B. Du Bois now invariably accompanies Booker T. Washington. In addition, there is a mystery man called Crispus Attucks, a fugitive slave about whom nothing seems to be known for certain except that he was a victim of the Boston Massacre and thus became one of the first casualties of the American Revolution. Thaddeus Stevens has been reconstructed—his character changed, as it were, from black to white, from cruel and vindictive to persistent and sincere. As for Teddy Roosevelt, he now champions the issue of conservation instead of charging up San Juan Hill. No single President really stands out as a hero, but all Presidents—except certain unmentionables in the second half of the nineteenth century—seem to have done as well as could be expected, given difficult circumstances.

Of course, when one thinks about it, it is hardly surprising that modern scholarship and modern perspectives have found their way into children's books. Yet the changes remain shocking. Those who in the sixties complained of the bland optimism, the chauvinism, and the materialism of their old civics text did so in the belief that, for all their protests, the texts would never change. The thought must have had something reassuring about it, for that generation never noticed when its complaints began to take effect and the songs about radioactive rainfall and houses made of ticky-tacky began to appear in the textbooks. But this is what happened.

The history texts now hint at a certain level of unpleasantness in American history. Several books, for instance, tell the story of Ishi, the last "wild" Indian in the continental United States, who, captured in 1911 after the massacre of his tribe, spent the final four and a half years of his life in the University of California's museum of anthropology, in San Francisco. At least three books show the same stunning picture of the breaker boys, the child coal miners of Pennsylvania—ancient children with deformed bodies and blackened faces who stare stupidly out from the entrance to a mine. One book quotes a soldier on the use of torture in the American campaign to pacify the Philippines at the beginning of the century. A number of books say that during the American Revolution the patriots tarred and feathered those who did not support them, and drove many of the loyalists from the country. Almost all the present-day history books note that the United States interned Japanese-Americans in detention camps during the Second World War.

Ideologically speaking, the histories of the fifties were implacable, seamless. Inside their covers, America was perfect: the greatest nation in the world, and the embodiment of democracy, freedom, and technological progress. For them, the country never changed in any important way: its values and its political institutions remained constant from the time of the American Revolution. To my generation—the children of the fifties —these texts appeared permanent just because they were so self-contained. Their orthodoxy, it seemed, left no handholds for attack, no lodging for decay. Who, after all, would dispute the wonders of technology or the superiority of the English colonists over the Spanish? Who would find fault with the pastorale of the West or the Old South? Who would question the anti-Communist crusade? There was, it seemed, no point in comparing these visions with reality, since they were the public truth and were thus quite irrelevant to what existed and to what anyone privately believed. They were—or so it seemed—the permanent expression of mass culture in America.

But now the texts have changed, and with them the country that American children are growing up into. The society that was once uniform is now a patchwork of rich and poor, old and young, men and women, blacks, whites, Hispanics, and Indians. The system that ran so smoothly by means of the Constitution under the guidance of benevolent conductor Presidents is now a rattletrap affair. The past is no highway to the present; it is a collection of issues and events that do not fit together and that lead in no single direction. The word "progress" has been replaced by the word "change": children, the modern texts insist, should learn history so that they can adapt to the rapid changes taking place around them. History is proceeding in spite of us. The present, which was once portrayed in the concluding chapters as a peaceful haven of scientific advances and Presidential inaugurations, is now a tangle of problems: race problems, urban problems, foreign-policy problems, problems of pollution, poverty, energy depletion, youthful rebellion, assassination, and drugs. Some books illustrate these problems dramatically. One, for instance, contains a picture of a doll half buried in a mass of untreated sewage; the caption reads, "Are we in danger of being overwhelmed by the products of our society and wastage created by their production? Would you agree with this photographer's interpretation?" Two books show the same picture of an old black woman sitting in a straight chair in a dingy room, her hands folded in graceful resignation; the surrounding text discusses the problems faced by the urban poor and by the aged who depend on Social Security. Other books present current problems less starkly. One of the texts concludes sagely:

Problems are part of life. Nations face them, just as people face them, and try to solve them. And today's Americans have one great advantage over past generations. Never before have Americans been so well equipped to solve their problems. They have today the means to conquer poverty, disease, and ignorance. The technetronic age has put that power into their hands.

Such passages have a familiar ring. Amid all the problems, the deus ex machina[1] of science still dodders around in the gloaming of pious hope.

Even more surprising than the emergence of problems is the discovery that the great unity of the texts has broken. Whereas in the fifties all texts represented the same political view, current texts follow no pattern of orthodoxy. Some books, for instance, portray civil-rights legislation as a series of actions taken by a wise, paternal government; others convey some suggestion of the social upheaval involved and make mention of such people as Stokely Carmichael and Malcolm X.[2] In some books, the Cold War has ended; in others, it continues, with Communism threatening the free nations of the earth.

The political diversity in the books is matched by a diversity of pedagogical approach. In addition to the traditional narrative histories, with their endless streams of facts, there are so-called "discovery," or "inquiry," texts, which deal with a limited number of specific issues in American history. These tests do not pretend to cover the past; they focus on particular topics, such as "stratification in Colonial society" or "slavery and the American Revolution," and illustrate them with documents from primary and secondary sources. The chapters in these books amount to something like case studies, in that they include testimony from people with different perspectives or conflicting views on a single subject. In addition, the chapters provide background information, explanatory notes, and a series of questions for the student. The questions are the heart of the matter, for when they are carefully selected they force students to think much as historians think: to define the point of view of the speaker, analyze the ideas presented, question the relationship between events, and so on. One text, for example, quotes Washington, Jefferson, and John Adams on the question of foreign alliances and then asks, "What did John Adams assume that the international situation would be after the American Revolution? What did Washington's attitude toward the French alliance seem to be? How do you account for his attitude?" Finally, it asks, "Should a nation adopt a policy toward alliances and cling to it consistently, or should it vary its policies toward other countries as circumstances change?" In these books, history is clearly not a list of agreed-upon facts or a sermon on politics but a babble of voices and a welter of events which must be ordered by the historian.

In matters of pedagogy, as in matters of politics, there are not two

---

1. God from a machine. A reference to early plays in which a god, lowered to the stage by mechanical means, solved the drama's problems; thus, an artificial solution to a difficulty.
2. Radical Black leaders of the 1960s.

sharply differentiated categories of books; rather, there is a spectrum. Politically, the books run from moderate left to moderate right; pedagogically, they run from the traditional history sermons, through a middle ground of narrative texts with inquiry-style questions and of inquiry texts with long stretches of narrative, to the most rigorous of case-study books. What is common to the current texts—and makes all of them different from those of the fifties—is their engagement with the social sciences. In eighth-grade histories, the "concepts" of social sciences make fleeting appearances. But these "concepts" are the very foundation stones of various elementary-school social-studies series. The 1970 Harcourt Brace Jovanovich[3] series, for example, boasts in its preface of "a horizontal base or ordering of conceptual schemes" to match its "vertical arm of behavioral themes." What this means is not entirely clear, but the books do proceed from easy questions to hard ones, such as—in the sixth-grade book—"How was interaction between merchants and citizens different in the Athenian and Spartan social systems?" Virtually all the American-history texts for older children include discussions of "role," "status," and "culture." Some of them stage debates between eminent social scientists in roped-off sections of the text; some include essays on economics or sociology; some contain pictures and short biographies of social scientists of both sexes and of diverse races. Many books seem to accord social scientists a higher status than American Presidents.

Quite as striking as these political and pedagogical alterations is the change in the physical appearance of the texts. The schoolbooks of the fifties showed some effort in the matter of design: they had maps, charts, cartoons, photographs, and an occasional four-color picture to break up the columns of print. But beside the current texts they look as naïve as Soviet fashion magazines. The print in the fifties books is heavy and far too black, the colors muddy. The photographs are conventional news shots—portraits of Presidents in three-quarters profile, posed "action" shots of soldiers. The other illustrations tend to be Socialist-realist-style[4] drawings (there are a lot of hefty farmers with hoes in the Colonial-period chapters) or incredibly vulgar made-for-children paintings of patriotic events. One painting shows Columbus standing in full court dress on a beach in the New World from a perspective that could have belonged only to the Arawaks.[5] By contrast, the current texts are paragons of sophisticated modern design. They look not like *People* or *Family Circle* but, rather, like *Architectural Digest* or *Vogue*. * * * The amount of space given to illustrations is far greater than it was in the fifties; in fact, in certain "slow-learner" books the pictures far outweigh the text in importance. However, the illustrations have a much greater historical value.

3. Major textbook publisher.
4. Socialist realism, which originated in the Soviet Union, is a style of art in which the communal labor of farmers and industrial workers is glorified in works of poster-like crudity.
5. American Indians, then inhabiting the Caribbean area.

Instead of made-up paintings or anachronistic sketches, there are cartoons, photographs, and paintings drawn from the periods being treated. The chapters on the Colonial period will show, for instance, a ship's carved prow, a Revere bowl, a Copley[6] painting—a whole gallery of Early Americana. The nineteenth century is illustrated with nineteenth-century cartoons and photographs—and the photographs are all of high artistic quality. As for the twentieth-century chapters, they are adorned with the contents of a modern-art museum.

The use of all this art and high-quality design contains some irony. The nineteenth-century photographs of child laborers or urban slum apartments are so beautiful that they transcend their subjects. To look at them, or at the Victor Gatto painting of the Triangle shirtwaist-factory fire, is to see not misery or ugliness but an art object. In the modern chapters, the contrast between style and content is just as great: the color photographs of junk yards or polluted rivers look as enticing as Gourmet's photographs of food. The book that is perhaps the most stark in its description of modern problems illustrates the horrors of nuclear testing with a pretty Ben Shahn picture of the Bikini explosion,[7] and the potential for global ecological disaster with a color photograph of the planet swirling its mantle of white clouds. Whereas in the nineteen-fifties the texts were childish in the sense that they were naïve and clumsy, they are now childish in the sense that they are polymorphous-perverse. American history is not dull any longer; it is a sensuous experience.

The surprise that adults feel in seeing the changes in history texts must come from the lingering hope that there is, somewhere out there, an objective truth. The hope is, of course, foolish. All of us children of the twentieth century know, or should know, that there are no absolutes in human affairs, and thus there can be no such thing as perfect objectivity. We know that each historian in some degree creates the world anew and that all history is in some degree contemporary history. But beyond this knowledge there is still a hope for some reliable authority, for some fixed stars in the universe. We may know that journalists cannot be wholly unbiased and that "balance" is an imaginary point between two extremes, and yet we hope that Walter Cronkite will tell us the truth of things. In the same way, we hope that our history will not change—that we learned the truth of things as children. The texts, with their impersonal voices, encourage this hope, and therefore it is particularly disturbing to see how they change, and how fast.

Slippery history! Not every generation but every few years the content of American-history books for children changes appreciably. School-

6. The reference is to John Singleton Copley (1738-1815), greatest of the American old masters; he specialized in portraits and historical paintings.
7. The Bikini atoll, part of the Marshall Is-

lands in the Pacific, was the site of American nuclear-bomb testing from 1946 to 1958. Ben Shahn (1898-1969) was an American painter and graphic artist with strong social and political concerns.

books are not, like trade books,[8] written and left to their fate. To stay in step with the cycles of "adoption"[9] in school districts across the country, the publishers revise most of their old texts or substitute new ones every three or four years. In the process of revision, they not only bring history up to date but make changes—often substantial changes—in the body of the work. History books for children are thus more contemporary than any other form of history. How should it be otherwise? Should students read histories written ten, fifteen, thirty years ago? in theory, the system is reasonable—except that each generation of children reads only one generation of schoolbooks. The transient history is those children's history forever—their particular version of America.

1979

8. Books written for a general audience, as opposed to textbooks.   9. Choice of required textbooks.

QUESTIONS

1. *What sorts of difference does FitzGerald find between the history textbooks of the fifties and those of today? In what ways—according to what she states or implies—have they been improved? Does she see any changes for the worse?*
2. *By "rewriting" does FitzGerald mean changing the facts of history? What is the relationship between the facts of history and history textbooks? Does Thomas S. Kuhn's "The Route to Normal Science" (p. 975) throw any light on this question?*
3. *Why does FitzGerald give the story about George McJunkin (p. 775)? Was his discovery important? In the terms of Edward Hallett Carr, in "The Historian and His Facts" (p. 759), is this a "mere fact about the past" or a "fact of history"?*
4. *On p. 777 FitzGerald says that in the new texts "the word 'progress' has been replaced by the word 'change.'" What is the difference between these two words? What does the replacement imply?*
5. *Is FitzGerald showing that the newer textbooks give a truer account of American history?*

Politics, Economy, Government

George Orwell

SHOOTING AN ELEPHANT

In Moulmein, in Lower Burma, I was hated by large numbers of people —the only time in my life that I have been important enough for this to happen to me. I was sub-divisional police officer of the town, and in an aimless, petty kind of way anti-European feeling was very bitter. No one had the guts to raise a riot, but if a European woman went through the bazaars alone somebody would probably spit betel juice over her dress. As a police officer I was an obvious target and was baited whenever it seemed safe to do so. When a nimble Burman tripped me up on the football field and the referee (another Burman) looked the other way, the crowd yelled with hideous laughter. This happened more than once. In the end the sneering yellow faces of young men that met me everywhere, the insults hooted after me when I was at a safe distance, got badly on my nerves. The young Buddhist priests were the worst of all. There were several thousands of them in the town and none of them seemed to have anything to do except stand on street corners and jeer at Europeans.

All this was perplexing and upsetting. For at that time I had already made up my mind that imperialism was an evil thing and the sooner I chucked up my job and got out of it the better. Theoretically—and secretly, of course—I was all for the Burmese and all against their oppressors, the British. As for the job I was doing, I hated it more bitterly than I can perhaps make clear. In a job like that you see the dirty work of Empire at close quarters. The wretched prisoners huddling in the stinking cages of the lock-ups, the grey, cowed faces of the long-term convicts, the scarred buttocks of the men who had been flogged with bamboos—all these oppressed me with an intolerable sense of guilt. But I could get nothing into perspective. I was young and ill-educated and I had had to think out my problems in the utter silence that is imposed on every Englishman in the East. I did not even know that the British Empire is dying, still less did I know that it is a great deal better than the younger empires that are going to supplant it. All I knew was that I was stuck between my hatred of the empire I served and my rage against the evil-spirited little beasts who tried to make my job impossible. With one part of my mind I thought of the British Raj[1] as an unbreakable tyranny, as something clamped down, in *saecula saeculorum*[2], upon the will of prostrate peoples; with another part I thought that the greatest joy in the world would be to drive a bayonet into a Buddhist priest's guts. Feelings like these are the normal by-products of imperialism; ask any Anglo-Indian official, if you can catch him off duty.

One day something happened which in a roundabout way was enlightening. It was a tiny incident in itself, but it gave me a better glimpse than I had had before of the real nature of imperialism—the real motives for which despotic governments act. Early one morning the sub-inspector at a police station the other end of the town rang me up on the 'phone and said that an elephant was ravaging the bazaar. Would I please come and do something about it? I did not know what I could do, but I wanted to see what was happening and I got on to a pony and started out. I took my rifle, an old .44 Winchester and much too small to kill an elephant, but I thought the noise might be useful *in terrorem*. Various Burmans stopped me on the way and told me about the elephant's doings. It was not, of course, a wild elephant, but a tame one which had gone "must." It had been chained up, as tame elephants always are when their attack of "must" is due, but on the previous night it had broken its chain and escaped. Its mahout, the only person who could manage it when it was in that state, had set out in pursuit, but had taken the wrong direction and was now twelve hours' journey away, and in the morning the elephant had suddenly reappeared in the town. The Burmese population had no weapons and were quite helpless against it. It had already destroyed somebody's bamboo hut, killed a cow and raided some fruit-stalls and devoured the stock; also it had met the municipal rubbish van and, when the driver jumped out and took to his heels, had turned the van over and inflicted violences upon it.

The Burmese sub-inspector and some Indian constables were waiting for me in the quarter where the elephant had been seen. It was a very poor quarter, a labyrinth of squalid bamboo huts, thatched with palm-leaf, winding all over a steep hillside. I remember that it was a cloudy, stuffy morning at the beginning of the rains. We began questioning the people as to where the elephant had gone and, as usual, failed to get any

1. The imperial government of British India and Burma.
2. Forever and ever.

definite information. That is invariably the case in the East; a story
always sounds clear enough at a distance, but the nearer you get to the
scene of events the vaguer it becomes. Some of the people said that the
elephant had gone in one direction, some said that he had gone in
another, some professed not even to have heard of any elephant. I had
almost made up my mind that the whole story was a pack of lies, when we
heard yells a little distance away. There was a loud, scandalized cry of
"Go away, child! Go away this instant!" and an old woman with a switch
in her hand came round the corner of a hut, violently shooing away a
crowd of naked children. Some more women followed, clicking their
tongues and exclaiming; evidently there was something that the children
ought not to have seen. I rounded the hut and saw a man's dead body
sprawling in the mud. He was an Indian, a black Dravidian coolie, almost
naked, and he could not have been dead many minutes. The people said
that the elephant had come suddenly upon him round the corner of the
hut, caught him with its trunk, put its foot on his back and ground him
into the earth. This was the rainy season and the ground was soft, and his
face had scored a trench a foot deep and a couple of yards long. He was
lying on his belly with arms crucified and head sharply twisted to one
side. His face was coated with mud, the eyes wide open, the teeth bared
and grinning with an expression of unendurable agony. (Never tell me,
by the way, that the dead look peaceful. Most of the corpses I have seen
looked devilish.) The friction of the great beast's foot had stripped the
skin from his back as neatly as one skins a rabbit. As soon as I saw the dead
man I sent an orderly to a friend's house nearby to borrow an elephant
rifle. I had already sent back the pony, not wanting it to go mad with
fright and throw me if it smelt the elephant.

The orderly came back in a few minutes with a rifle and five cartridges,
and meanwhile some Burmans had arrived and told us that the elephant
was in the paddy fields below, only a few hundred yards away. As I started
forward practically the whole population of the quarter flocked out of the
houses and followed me. They had seen the rifle and were all shouting
excitedly that I was going to shoot the elephant. They had not shown
much interest in the elephant when he was merely ravaging their homes,
but it was different now that he was going to be shot. It was a bit of fun to
them, as it would be to an English crowd; besides they wanted the meat.
It made me vaguely uneasy. I had no intention of shooting the elephant
—I had merely sent for the rifle to defend myself if necessary—and it is
always unnerving to have a crowd following you. I marched down the
hill, looking and feeling a fool, with the rifle over my shoulder and an
ever-growing army of people jostling at my heels. At the bottom, when
you got away from the huts, there was a metalled road and beyond that a
miry waste of paddy fields a thousand yards across, not yet ploughed but
soggy from the first rains and dotted with coarse grass. The elephant was

standing eight yards from the road, his left side towards us. He took not the slightest notice of the crowd's approach. He was tearing up bunches of grass, beating them against his knees to clean them and stuffing them into his mouth.

I had halted on the road. As soon as I saw the elephant I knew with perfect certainty that I ought not to shoot him. It is a serious matter to shoot a working elephant—it is comparable to destroying a huge and costly piece of machinery—and obviously one ought not to do it if it can possibly be avoided. And at that distance, peacefully eating, the elephant looked no more dangerous than a cow. I thought then and I think now that his attack of "must" was already passing off; in which case he would merely wander harmlessly about until the mahout came back and caught him. Moreover, I did not in the least want to shoot him. I decided that I would watch him for a little while to make sure that he did not turn savage again, and then go home.

But at that moment I glanced round at the crowd that had followed me. It was an immense crowd, two thousand at the least and growing every minute. It blocked the road for a long distance on either side. I looked at the sea of yellow faces above the garish clothes—faces all happy and excited over this bit of fun, all certain that the elephant was going to be shot. They were watching me as they would watch a conjurer about to perform a trick. They did not like me, but with the magical rifle in my hands I was momentarily worth watching. And suddenly I realized that I should have to shoot the elephant after all. The people expected it of me and I had got to do it; I could feel their two thousand wills pressing me forward, irresistibly. And it was at this moment, as I stood there with the rifle in my hands, that I first grasped the hollowness, the futility of the white man's dominion in the East. Here was I, the white man with his gun, standing in front of the unarmed native crowd—seemingly the leading actor of the piece; but in reality I was only an absurd puppet pushed to and fro by the will of those yellow faces behind. I perceived in this moment that when the white man turns tyrant it is his own freedom that he destroys. He becomes a sort of hollow, posing dummy, the conventionalized figure of a sahib. For it is the condition of his rule that he shall spend his life in trying to impress the "natives," and so in every crisis he has got to do what the "natives" expect of him. He wears a mask, and his face grows to fit it. I had got to shoot the elephant. I had committed myself to doing it when I sent for the rifle. A sahib has go to act like a sahib; he has got to appear resolute, to know his own mind and do definite things. To come all that way, rifle in hand, with two thousand people marching at my heels, and then to trail feebly away, having done nothing—no, that was impossible. The crowd would laugh at me. And my whole life, every white man's life in the East, was one long struggle not to be laughed at.

But I did not want to shoot the elephant. I watched him beating his bunch of grass against his knees, with that preoccupied grandmotherly air that elephants have. It seemed to me that it would be murder to shoot him. At that age I was not squeamish about killing animals, but I had never shot an elephant and never wanted to. (Somehow it always seems worse to kill a *large* animal.) Besides, there was the beast's owner to be considered. Alive, the elephant was worth at least a hundred pounds; dead, he would only be worth the value of his tusks, five pounds, possibly. But I had got to act quickly. I turned to some experienced-looking Burmans who had been there when we arrived, and asked them how the elephant had been behaving. They all said the same thing: he took no notice of you if you left him alone, but he might charge if you went too close to him.

It was perfectly clear to me what I ought to do. I ought to walk up to within, say, twenty-five yards of the elephant and test his behavior. If he charged, I could shoot; if he took no notice of me, it would be safe to leave him until the mahout came back. But also I knew that I was going to do no such thing. I was a poor shot with a rifle and the ground was soft mud into which one would sink at every step. If the elephant charged and I missed him, I should have about as much chance as a toad under a steam-roller. But even then I was not thinking particularly of my own skin, only of the watchful yellow faces behind. For at that moment, with the crowd watching me, I was not afraid in the ordinary sense, as I would have been if I had been alone. A white man mustn't be frightened in front of "natives"; and so, in general, he isn't frightened. The sole thought in my mind was that if anything went wrong those two thousand Burmans would see me pursued, caught, trampled on and reduced to a grinning corpse like that Indian up the hill. And if that happened it was quite probable that some of them would laugh. That would never do. There was only one alternative. I shoved the cartridges into the magazine and lay down on the road to get a better aim.

The crowd grew very still, and a deep, low, happy sigh, as of people who see the theatre curtain go up at last, breathed from innumerable throats. They were going to have their bit of fun after all. The rifle was a beautiful German thing with cross-hair sights. I did not then know that in shooting an elephant one would shoot to cut an imaginary bar running from ear-hole to ear-hole. I ought, therefore, as the elephant was sideways on, to have aimed straight at his ear-hole; actually I aimed several inches in front of this, thinking the brain would be further forward.

When I pulled the trigger I did not hear the bang or feel the kick—one never does when a shot goes home—but I heard the devilish roar of glee that went up from the crowd. In that instant, in too short a time, one would have thought, even for the bullet to get there, a mysterious, terrible change had come over the elephant. He neither stirred nor fell, but every line of his body had altered. He looked suddenly stricken, shrunken, immensely old, as though the frightful impact of the bullet had paralysed him without knocking him down. At last, after what seemed a long time—it might have been five seconds, I dare say—he sagged flabbily to his knees. His mouth slobbered. An enormous senility seemed to have settled upon him. One could have imagined him thousands of years old. I fired again into the same spot. At the second shot he did not collapse but climbed with desperate slowness to his feet and stood weakly upright, with legs sagging and head drooping. I fired a third time. That was the shot that did for him. You could see the agony of it jolt his whole body and knock the last remnant of strength from his legs. But in falling he seemed for a moment to rise, for as his hind legs collapsed beneath him he seemed to tower upward like a huge rock toppling, his trunk reaching skywards like a tree. He trumpeted, for the first and only time. And then down he came, his belly towards me, with a crash that seemed to shake the ground even where I lay.

I got up. The Burmans were already racing past me across the mud. It was obvious that the elephant would never rise again, but he was not dead. He was breathing very rhythmically with long rattling gasps, his great mound of a side painfully rising and falling. His mouth was wide open—I could see far down into caverns of pale pink throat. I waited a long time for him to die, but his breathing did not weaken. Finally I fired my two remaining shots into the spot where I thought his heart must be. The thick blood welled out of him like red velvet, but still he did not die. His body did not even jerk when the shots hit him, the tortured breathing continued without a pause. He was dying, very slowly and in great agony, but in some world remote from me where not even a bullet could damage him further. I felt that I had got to put an end to that dreadful noise. It seemed dreadful to see the great beast lying there, powerless to move and yet powerless to die, and not even to be able to finish him. I sent back for my small rifle and pured shot after shot into his heart and down his throat. They seemed to make no impression. The tortured gasps continued as steadily as the ticking of a clock.

In the end I could not stand it any longer and went away. I heard later that it took him half an hour to die. Burmans were bringing dahs[3] and baskets even before I felt, and I was told they had stripped his body almost to the bones by the afternoon.

Afterwards, of course, there were endless discussions about the shooting of the elephant. The owner was furious, but he was only an Indian and could do nothing. Besides, legally I had done the right thing, for a mad elephant has to be killed, like a mad dog, if its owner fails to control it. Among the Europeans opinion was divided. The older men said I was right, the younger men said it was a damn shame to shoot an elephant for

3. Butcher knives.

killing a coolie, because an elephant was worth more than any damn Coringhee coolie. And afterwards I was very glad that the coolie had been killed; it put me legally in the right and it gave me a sufficient pretext for shooting the elephant. I often wondered whether any of the others grasped that I had done it solely to avoid looking a fool.

1936

QUESTIONS

1. *The proportion of this essay devoted to narrative is relatively high. What effect(s) does Orwell aim at? How does he organize his essay? Where does he state his thesis? Would he have done better to argue his thesis directly, rather than mainly by example? Why, or why not?*
2. *What issue does Orwell address and what kind of evidence is proper to it? Does he actually prove anything?*
3. *The following is a sketch from* The Graphic *(London) of January 21, 1888, written by a Major-General H. G. Robley.*

Shooting a Man-Eating Crocodile

It is tedious work waiting for the man-eater to come out of the water, but a fat native child as a lure will make the monster speedily walk out of his aqueous lair. Contracting the loan of a chubby infant, however, is a matter of some negotiation, and it is perhaps not to be wondered at that mammas occasionally object to their offspring being pegged down as food for a great crocodile; but there are always some parents to be found whose confidence the the skill of the British sportsman is unlimited. My sketch [omitted here] gives a view of the collapse of the man-eater, who, after viewing the tempting morsel tethered carefully to a bamboo near the water's edge, makes a rush through the sedges. The sportsman, hidden behind a bed of reeds, then fires, the bullet penetrates the heart, and the monster is dead in a moment. The little bait, whose only alarm has been caused by the report of the rifle, is now taken home by its doting mother for its matutinal banana. The natives wait to get the musky flesh of the animal, and the sportsman secures the scaly skin and the massive head of porous bone as a trophy.

There are probably educational and social similarities between Robley and Orwell and, of course, both were imperial Englishmen in a colonial setting. However, the differences between the two men are far more striking; briefly and basically, what are they? How are these similarities and differences reflected in the essays' style?
4. *Does Robley show any sign that he recognizes what Orwell calls "the futility of the white man's dominion in the East" (p. 785)? Could it be that this dominion was not futile for Robley, or in his day?*
5. *Compare this sketch with Jonathan Swift's "A Modest Proposal" (p. 804). How can you tell that Robley is not ironic and that Swift is? If*

you can't tell, what does your uncertainty suggest about the nature of irony?

Martin Luther King, Jr.

LETTER FROM BIRMINGHAM JAIL[1]

MY DEAR FELLOW CLERGYMEN:

While confined here in the Birmingham city jail, I came across your recent statement calling my present activities "unwise and untimely." Seldom do I pause to answer criticism of my work and ideas. If I sought to answer all the criticisms that cross my desk, my secretaries would have little time for anything other than such correspondence in the course of the day, and I would have no time for constructive work. But since I feel that you are men of genuine good will and that your criticisms are sincerely set forth, I want to try to answer your statement in what I hope will be patient and reasonable terms.

I think I should indicate why I am here in Birmingham, since you have been influenced by the view which argues against "outsiders coming in." I have the honor of serving as president of the Southern Christian Leadership Conference, an organization operating in every southern state, with headquarters in Atlanta, Georgia. We have some eighty-five affiliated organizations across the South, and one of them is the Alabama Christian Movement for Human Rights. Frequently we share staff, educational, and financial resources with our affiliates. Several months ago the affiliate here in Birmingham asked us to be on call to engage in a nonviolent direct-action program if such were deemed necessary. We readily consented, and when the hour came we lived up to our promise. So I, along with several members of my staff, am here because I was invited here. I am here because I have organizational ties here.

But more basically, I am in Birmingham because injustice is here. Just as the prophets of the eighth century B.C. left their villages and carried their "thus saith the Lord" far beyond the boundaries of their home towns, and just as the Apostle Paul left his village of Tarsus and carried

1. This response to a published statement by eight fellow clergymen from Alabama (Bishop C. C. J. Carpenter, Bishop Joseph A. Durick, Rabbi Milton L. Grafman, Bishop Paul Hardin, Bishop Holan B. Harmon, the Reverend George M. Murray, the Reverend Edward V. Ramage and the Reverend Earl Stallings) was composed under somewhat constricting circumstances. Begun on the margins of the newspaper in which the statement appeared while I was in jail, the letter was continued on scraps of writing paper supplied by a friendly Negro trusty, and concluded on a pad my attorneys were eventually permitted to leave me. Although the text remains in substance unaltered, I have indulged in the author's prerogative of polishing it for publication [King's note].

the gospel of Jesus Christ to the far corners of the Greco-Roman world, so am I compelled to carry the gospel of freedom beyond my own home town. Like Paul, I must constantly respond to the Macedonian call for aid.

Moreover, I am cognizant of the interrelatedness of all communities and states. I cannot sit idly by in Atlanta and not be concerned about what happens in Birmingham. Injustice anywhere is a threat to justice everywhere. We are caught in an inescapable network of mutuality, tied in a single garment of destiny. Whatever affects one directly, affects all indirectly. Never again can we afford to live with the narrow, provincial "outside agitator" idea. Anyone who lives inside the United States can never be considered an outsider anywhere within its bounds.

You deplore the demonstrations taking place in Birmingham. But your statement, I am sorry to say, fails to express a similar concern for the conditions that brought about the demonstrations. I am sure that none of you would want to rest content with the superficial kind of social analysis that deals merely with effects and does not grapple with underlying causes. It is unfortunate that demonstrations are taking place in Birmingham, but it is even more unfortunate that the city's white power structure left the Negro community with no alternative.

In any nonviolent campaign there are four basic steps: collection of the facts to determine whether injustices exist; negotiation; self-purification; and direct action. We have gone through all these steps in Birmingham. There can be no gainsaying the fact that racial injustice engulfs this community. Birmingham is probably the most thoroughly segregated city in the United States. Its ugly record of brutality is widely known. Negroes have experienced grossly unjust treatment in the courts. There have been more unsolved bombings of Negro homes and churches in Birmingham than in any other city in the nation. These are the hard, brutal facts of the case. On the basis of these conditions, Negro leaders sought to negotiate with the city fathers. But the latter consistently refused to engage in good-faith negotiation.

Then, last September, came the opportunity to talk with leaders of Birmingham's economic community. In the course of the negotiations, certain promises were made by the merchants—for example, to remove the stores' humiliating racial signs. On the basis of these promises, the Reverend Fred Shuttlesworth and the leaders of the Alabama Christian Movement for Human Rights agreed to a moratorium on all demonstrations. As the weeks and months went by, we realized that we were the victims of a broken promise. A few signs, briefly removed, returned; the others remained.

As in so many past experiences, our hopes had been blasted, and the shadow of deep disappointment settled upon us. We had no alternative except to prepare for direct action, whereby we would present our very bodies as a means of laying our case before the conscience of the local and the national community. Mindful of the difficulties involved, we decided to undertake a process of self-purification. We began a series of work-shops on nonviolence, and we repeatedly asked ourselves: "Are you able to accept blows without retaliating?" "Are you able to endure the ordeal of jail?" We decided to schedule our direct-action program for the Easter season, realizing that except for Christmas, this is the main shopping period of the year. Knowing that a strong economic-withdrawal program would be the by-product of direct action, we felt that this would be the best time to bring pressure to bear on the merchants for the needed change.

Then it occurred to us that Birmingham's mayoral election was com-ing up in March, and we speedily decided to postpone action until after election day. When we discovered that the Commissioner of Public Safety, Eugene "Bull" Connor, had piled up enough votes to be in the run-off, we decided again to postpone action until the day after the run-off so that the demonstrations could not be used to cloud the issues. Like many others, we wanted to see Mr. Connor defeated, and to this end we endured postponement after postponement. Having aided in this com-munity need, we felt that our direct-action program could be delayed no longer.

You may well ask, "Why direct action? Why sit-ins, marches, and so forth? Isn't negotiation a better path?" You are quite right in calling for negotiation. Indeed, this is the very purpose of direct action. Nonviolent direct action seeks to create such a crisis and foster such a tension that a community which has constantly refused to negotiate is forced to con-front the issue. It seeks so to dramatize the issue that it can no longer be ignored. My citing the creation of tension as part of the work of the nonviolent-resister may sound rather shocking. But I must confess that I am not afraid of the word "tension." I have earnestly opposed violent tension, but there is a type of constructive, nonviolent tension which is necessary for growth. Just as Socrates felt that it was necessary to create a tension in the mind so that individuals could rise from the bondage of myths and half-truths to the unfettered realm of creative analysis and objective appraisal, so must we see the need for nonviolent gadflies to create the kind of tension in society that will help men rise from the dark depths of prejudice and racism to the majestic heights of understanding and brotherhood.

The purpose of our direct-action program is to create a situation so crisis-packed that it will inevitably open the door to negotiation. I there-fore concur with you in your call for negotiation. Too long has our beloved Southland been bogged down in a tragic effort to live in mono-logue rather than dialogue.

One of the basic points in your statement is that the action that I and my associates have taken in Birmingham is untimely. Some have asked: "Why didn't you give the new city administration time to act?" The only answer that I can give to this query is that the new Birmingham administration must be prodded about as much as the outgoing one, before it will act. We are sadly mistaken if we feel that the election of Albert Boutwell as mayor will bring the millennium to Birmingham. While Mr. Boutwell is a much more gentle person than Mr. Connor, they are both segregationists, dedicated to maintenance of the status quo. I have hoped that Mr. Boutwell will be reasonable enough to see the futility of massive resistance to desegregation. But he will not see this without pressure from devotees of civil rights. My friends, I must say to you that we have not made a single gain in civil rights without determined legal and nonviolent pressure. Lamentably, it is an historical fact that privileged groups seldom give up their privileges voluntarily. Individuals may see the moral light and voluntarily give up their unjust posture; but, as Reinhold Niebuhr has reminded us, groups tend to be more immoral than individuals.

We know through painful experience that freedom is never voluntarily given by the oppressor; it must be demanded by the oppressed. Frankly, I have yet to engage in a direct-action campaign that was "well timed" in the view of those who have not suffered unduly from the disease of segregation. For years now I have heard the word "Wait!" It rings in the ear of every Negro with piercing familiarity. This "Wait" has almost always meant "Never." We must come to see, with one of our distinguished jurists, that "justice too long delayed is justice denied."

We have waited for more than 340 years for our constitutional and God-given rights. The nations of Asia and Africa are moving with jetlike speed toward gaining political independence, but we still creep at horse-and-buggy pace toward gaining a cup of coffee at a lunch counter. Perhaps it is easy for those who have never felt the stinging darts of segregation to say, "Wait." But when you have seen vicious mobs lynch your mothers and fathers at will and drown your sisters and brothers at whim; when you have seen hate-filled policemen curse, kick, and even kill your black brothers and sisters; when you see the vast majority of your twenty million Negro brothers smothering in an airtight cage of poverty in the midst of an affluent society; when you suddenly find your tongue twisted and your speech stammering as you seek to explain to your six-year-old daughter why she can't go to the public amusement park that has just been advertised on television, and see tears welling up in her eyes when she is told that Funtown is closed to colored children, and see ominous clouds of inferiority beginning to form in her little mental sky, and see her beginning to distort her personality by developing an unconscious bitterness toward white people; when you have to concoct an answer for a five-year-old son who is asking, "Daddy, why do white people treat colored people so mean?"; when you take a cross-country drive and find it necessary to sleep night after night in the uncomfortable corners of your automobile because no motel will accept you; when you are humiliated day in and day out by nagging signs reading "white" and "colored"; when your first name becomes "nigger," your middle name becomes "boy" (however old you are) and your last name becomes "John," and your wife and mother are never given the respected title "Mrs."; when you are harried by day and haunted by night by the fact that you are a Negro, living constantly at tiptoe stance, never quite knowing what to expect next, and are plagued with inner fears and outer resentments; when you are forever fighting a degenerating sense of "nobodiness"—then you will understand why we find it difficult to wait. There comes a time when the cup of endurance runs over, and men are no longer willing to be plunged into the abyss of despair. I hope, sirs, you can understand our legitimate and unavoidable impatience.

You express a great deal of anxiety over our willingness to break laws. This is certainly a legitimate concern. Since we so diligently urge people to obey the Supreme Court's decision of 1954 outlawing segregation in the public schools, at first glance it may seem rather paradoxical for us consciously to break laws. One may well ask: "How can you advocate breaking some laws and obeying others?" The answer lies in the fact that there are two types of laws: just and unjust. I would be the first to advocate obeying just laws. One has not only a legal but a moral responsibility to obey just laws. Conversely, one has a moral responsibility to disobey unjust laws. I would agree with St. Augustine that "an unjust law is no law at all."

Now, what is the difference between the two? How does one determine whether a law is just or unjust? A just law is a man-made code that squares with the moral law or the law of God. An unjust law is a code this is out of harmony with the moral law. To put it in the terms of St. Thomas Aquinas: An unjust law is a human law that is not rooted in eternal law and natural law. Any law that uplifts human personality is just. Any law that degrades human personality is unjust. All segregation statutes are unjust because segregation distorts the soul and damages the personality. It gives the segregator a false sense of superiority and the segregated a false sense of inferiority. Segregation, to use the terminology of the Jewish philosopher Martin Buber, substitutes an "I-it" relationship for an "I-thou" relationship and ends up relegating persons to the status of things. Hence segregation is not only politically, economically, and sociologically unsound, it is morally wrong and sinful. Paul Tillich has said that sin is separation. Is not segregation an existential expression of man's tragic separation, his awful estrangement, his terrible sinfulness? Thus it is that I can urge men to obey the 1954 decision of the Supreme

Court, for it is morally right; and I can urge them to disobey segregation ordinances, for they are morally wrong.

Let us consider a more concrete example of just and unjust laws. An unjust law is a code that a numerical or power majority group compels a minority group to obey but does not make binding on itself. This is *difference* made legal. By the same token, a just law is a code that a majority compels a minority to follow and that it is willing to follow itself. This is *sameness* made legal.

Let me give another explanation. A law is unjust if it is inflicted on a minority that, as a result of being denied the right to vote, had no part in enacting or devising the law. Who can say that the legislature of Alabama which set up that state's segregation laws was democratically elected? Throughout Alabama all sorts of devious methods are used to prevent Negroes from becoming registered voters, and there are some counties in which, even though Negroes constitute a majority of the population, not a single Negro is registered. Can any law enacted under such circumstances be considered democratically structured?

Sometimes a law is just on its face and unjust in its application. For instance, I have been arrested on a charge of parading without a permit. Now, there is nothing wrong in having an ordinance which requires a permit for a parade. But such an ordinance becomes unjust when it is used to maintain segregation and to deny citizens the First-Amendment privilege of peaceful assembly and protest.

I hope you are able to see the distinction I am trying to point out. In no sense do I advocate evading or defying the law, as would the rabid segregationist. That would lead to anarchy. One who breaks an unjust law must do so openly, lovingly, and with a willingness to accept the penalty. I submit that an individual who breaks a law that conscience tells him is unjust, and who willingly accepts the penalty of imprisonment in order to arouse the conscience of the community over its injustice, is in reality expressing the highest respect for law.

Of course, there is nothing new about this kind of civil disobedience. It was evidenced sublimely in the refusal of Shadrach, Meshach, and Abednego to obey the laws of Nebuchadnezzar, on the ground that a higher moral law was at stake. It was practiced superbly by the early Christians, who were willing to face hungry lions and the excruciating pain of chopping blocks rather than submit to certain unjust laws of the Roman Empire. To a degree, academic freedom is a reality today because Socrates practiced civil disobedience.[2] In our own nation, the Boston Tea Party represented a massive act of civil disobedience.

We should never forget that everything Adolf Hitler did in Germany

2. The ancient Greek philosopher Socrates was tried by the Athenians for corrupting their youth through his skeptical, question-ing manner of teaching. He refused to change his ways, and was condemned to death.

was "legal" and everything the Hungarian freedom fighters[3] did in Hungary was "illegal." It was "illegal" to aid and comfort a Jew in Hitler's Germany. Even so, I am sure that, had I lived in Germany at the time, I would have aided and comforted my Jewish brothers. If today I lived in a Communist country where certain principles dear to the Christian faith are suppressed, I would openly advocate disobeying that country's antireligious laws.

I must make two honest confessions to you, my Christian and Jewish brothers. First, I must confess that over the past few years I have been gravely disappointed with the white moderate. I have almost reached the regrettable conclusion that the Negro's great stumbling block in his stride toward freedom is not the White Citizen's Counciler or the Ku Klux Klanner, but the white moderate, who is more devoted to "order" than to justice; who prefers a negative peace which is the absence of tension to a positive peace which is the presence of justice; who constantly says, "I agree with you in the goal you seek, but I cannot agree with your methods of direct action"; who paternalistically believes he can set the timetable for another man's freedom; who lives by a mythical concept of time and who constantly advises the Negro to wait for a "more convenient season." Shallow understanding from people of good will is more frustrating than absolute misunderstanding from people of ill will. Lukewarm acceptance is much more bewildering than outright rejection.

I had hoped that the white moderate would understand that law and order exist for the purpose of establishing justice and that when they fail in this purpose they become the dangerously structured dams that block the flow of social progress. I had hoped that the white moderate would understand that the present tension in the South is a necessary phase of the transition from an obnoxious negative peace, in which the Negro passively accepted his unjust plight, to a substantive and positive peace, in which all men will respect the dignity and worth of human personality. Actually, we who engage in nonviolent direct action are not the creators of tension. We merely bring to the surface the hidden tension that is already alive. We bring it out in the open, where it can be seen and dealt with. Like a boil that can never be cured so long as it is covered up but must be opened with all its ugliness to the natural medicines of air and light, injustice must be exposed, with all the tension its exposure creates, to the light of human conscience and the air of national opinion, before it can be cured.

In your statement you assert that our actions, even though peaceful, must be condemned because they precipitate violence. But is this is logical assertion? Isn't this like condemning a robbed man because his possession of money precipitated the evil act of robbery? Isn't this like

3. In the anti-Communist revolution of 1956, which was quickly put down by the Russian army.

condemning Socrates because his unswerving commitment to truth and his philosophical inquiries precipitated the act by the misguided populace in which they made him drink hemlock? Isn't this like condemning Jesus because his unique God-consciousness and never-ceasing devotion to God's will precipitated the evil act of crucifixion? We must come to see that, as the federal courts have consistently affirmed, it is wrong to urge an individual to cease his efforts to gain his basic constitutional rights because the quest may precipitate violence. Society must protect the robbed and punish the robber.

I had also hoped that the white moderate would reject the myth concerning time in relation to the struggle for freedom. I have just received a letter from a white brother in Texas. He writes: "All Christians know that the colored people will receive equal rights eventually, but it is possible that you are in too great a religious hurry. It has taken Christianity almost two thousand years to accomplish what it has. The teachings of Christ take time to come to earth." Such an attitude stems from a tragic misconception of time, from the strangely irrational notion that there is something in the very flow of time that will inevitably cure all ills. Actually, time itself is neutral; it can be used either destructively or constructively. More and more I feel that the people of ill will have used time much more effectively than have the people of good will. We will have to repent in this generation not merely for the hateful words and actions of the bad people, but for the appalling silence of the good people. Human progress never rolls in on wheels of inevitability; it comes through the tireless efforts of men willing to be co-workers with God, and without this hard work, time itself becomes an ally of the forces of social stagnation. We must use time creatively, in the knowledge that the time is always ripe to do right. Now is the time to make real the promise of democracy and transform our pending national elegy into a creative psalm of brotherhood. Now is the time to lift our national policy from the quicksand of racial injustice to the solid rock of human dignity.

You speak of our activity in Birmingham as extreme. At first I was rather disappointed that fellow clergymen would see my nonviolent efforts as those of an extremist. I began thinking about the fact that I stand in the middle of two opposing forces in the Negro community. One is a force of complacency, made up in part of Negroes who, as a result of long years of oppression, are so drained of self-respect and a sense of "somebodiness" that they have adjusted to segregation; and in part of a few middle-class Negroes who, because of a degree of academic and economic security and because in some ways they profit by segregation, have become insensitive to the problems of the masses. The other force is one of bitterness and hatred, and it comes perilously close to advocating violence. It is expressed in the various black nationalist groups that are springing up across the nation, the largest and best-known being

Elijah Muhammad's Muslim movement. Nourished by the Negro's frustration over the continued existence of racial discrimination, this movement is made up of people who have lost faith in America, who have absolutely repudiated Christianity, and who have concluded that the white man is an incorrigible "devil."

I have tried to stand between these two forces, saying that we need emulate neither the "do-nothingism" of the complacent nor the hatred and despair of the black nationalist. For there is the more excellent way of love and nonviolent protest. I am grateful to God that, through the influence of the Negro church, the way of nonviolence became an integral part of our struggle.

If this philosophy had not emerged, by now many streets of the South would, I am convinced, be flowing with blood. And I am further convinced that if our white brothers dismiss as "rabblerousers" and "outside agitators" those of use who employ nonviolent direct action, and if they refuse to support our nonviolent efforts, millions of Negroes will, out of frustration and despair, seek solace and security in black-nationalist ideologies—a development that would inevitably lead to a frightening racial nightmare.

Oppressed people cannot remain oppressed forever. The yearning for freedom eventually manifests itself, and that is what has happened to the American Negro. Something within has reminded him of his birthright of freedom, and something without has reminded him that it can be gained. Consciously or unconsciously, he has been caught up by the Zeitgeist,[4] and with his black brothers of Africa and his brown and yellow brothers of Asia, South America, and the Caribbean, the United States Negro is moving with a sense of great urgency toward the promised land of racial justice. If one recognizes this vital urge that has engulfed the Negro community, one should readily understand why public demonstrations are taking place. The Negro has many pent-up resentments and latent frustrations, and he must release them. So let him march; let him make prayer pilgrimages to the city hall; let him go on freedom rides —and try to understand why he must do so. If his repressed emotions are not released in nonviolent ways, they will seek expression through violence; this is not a threat but a fact of history. So I have not said to my people, "Get rid of your discontent." Rather, I have tried to say that this normal and healthy discontent can be channeled into the creative outlet of nonviolent direct action. And now this approach is being termed extremist.

But though I was initially disappointed at being categorized as an extremist, as I continued to think about the matter I gradually gained a measure of satisfaction from the label. Was not Jesus an extremist for love: "Love your enemies, bless them that curse you, do good to them

4. The spirit of the times.

that hate you, and pray for them which despitefully use you, and perse-
cute you." Was not Amos an extremist for justice: "Let justice roll down
like waters and righteousness like an ever-flowing stream." Was not Paul
an extremist for the Christian gospel: "I bear in my body the marks of the
Lord Jesus." Was not Martin Luther an extremist: "Here I stand; I
cannot do otherwise, so help me God." And John Bunyan: "I will stay in
jail to the end of my days before I make a butchery of my conscience."
And Abraham Lincoln: "This nation cannot survive half slave and half
free." And Thomas Jefferson: "We hold these truths to be self-evident,
that all men are created equal. . . ." So the question is not whether we will
be extremists, but what kind of extremists we will be. Will we be
extremists for hate or for love? Will we be extremists for the preservation
of injustice or for the extension of justice? In that dramatic scene on
Calvary's hill three men were crucified. We must never forget that all
three were crucified for the same crime—the crime of extremism. Two
were extremists for immorality, and thus fell below their environment.
The other, Jesus Christ, was an extremist for love, truth, and goodness,
and thereby rose above his environment. Perhaps the South, the nation,
and the world are in dire need of creative extremists.

I had hoped that the white moderate would see this need. Perhaps I
was too optimistic; perhaps I expected too much. I suppose I should have
realized that few members of the oppressor race can understand the deep
groans and passionate yearnings of the oppressed race, and still fewer
have the vision to see that injustice must be rooted out by strong,
persistent, and determined action. I am thankful, however, that some of
our white brothers in the South have grasped the meaning of this social
revolution and committed themselves to it. They are still all too few in
quantity, but they are big in quality. Some—such as Ralph McGill,
Lillian Smith, Harry Golden, James McBridge Dabbs, Ann Braden, and
Sarah Patton Boyle—have written about our struggle in eloquent and
prophetic terms. Others have marched with us down nameless streets of
the South. They have languished in filthy, roach-infested jails, suffering
the abuse and brutality of policemen who view them as "dirty nigger-
lovers." Unlike so many of their moderate brothers and sisters, they have
recognized the urgency of the moment and sensed the need for powerful
"action" antidotes to combat the disease of segregation.

Let me take note of my other major disappointment. I have been so
greatly disappointed with the white church and its leadership. Of course,
there are some notable exceptions. I am not unmindful of the fact that
each of you has taken some significant stands on this issue. I commend
you, Reverend Stallings, for your Christian stand on this past Sunday, in
welcoming Negroes to your worship service on a nonsegregated basis. I
commend the Catholic leaders of this state for integrating Spring Hill
College several years ago.

But despite these notable exceptions, I must honestly reiterate that I

have been disappointed with the church. I do not say this as one of those negative critics who can always find something wrong with the church. I say this as a minister of the gospel, who loves the church; who was nurtured in its bosom; who has been sustained by its spiritual blessings and who will remain true to it as long as the cord of life shall lengthen.

When I was suddenly catapulted into the leadership of the bus protest in Montgomery, Alabama, a few years ago, I felt we would be supported by the white church. I felt that the white ministers, priests, and rabbis of the South would be among our strongest allies. Instead, some have been outright opponents, refusing to understand the freedom movement and misrepresenting its leaders; all too many others have been more cautious than courageous and have remained silent behind the anesthetizing security of stainedglass windows.

In spite of my shattered dreams, I came to Birmingham with the hope that the white religious leadership of this community would see the justice of our cause and, with deep moral concern, would serve as the channel through which our just grievances could reach the power structure. I had hoped that each of you would understand. But again I have been disappointed.

I have heard numerous southern religious leaders admonish their worshipers to comply with a desegregation decision because it is the law, but I have longed to hear white ministers declare: "Follow this decree because integration is morally right and because the Negro is your brother." In the midst of blatant injustices inflicted upon the Negro, I have watched white churchmen stand on the sideline and mouth pious irrelevancies and sanctimonious trivialities. In the midst of a mighty struggle to rid our nation of racial and economic injustice, I have heard many ministers say: "Those are social issues, with which the gospel has no real concern." And I have watched many churches commit themselves to a completely otherworldly religion which makes a strange, un-Biblical distinction between body and soul, between the sacred and the secular.

I have traveled the length and breadth of Alabama, Mississippi, and all the other southern states. On sweltering summer days and crisp autumn mornings I have looked at the South's beautiful churches with their lofty spires pointing heavenward. I have beheld the impressive outlines of her massive religious-education buildings. Over and over I have found myself asking: "What kind of people worship here? Who is their God? Where were their voices when the lips of Governor Barnett dripped with words of interposition and nullification? Where were they when Governor Wallace gave a clarion call for defiance and hatred? Where were their voices of support when bruised and weary Negro men and women decided to rise from the dark dungeons of complacency to the bright hills of creative protest?"

Yes, these questions are still in my mind. In deep disappointment I have wept over the laxity of the church. But be assured that my tears have been tears of love. There can be no deep disappointment where there is not deep love. Yes, I love the church. How could I do otherwise? I am in the rather unique position of being the son, the grandson, and the great-grandson of preachers. Yes, I see the church as the body of Christ. But, oh! How we have blemished and scarred that body through social neglect and through fear of being nonconformists.

There was a time when the church was very powerful—in the time when the early Christians rejoiced at being deemed worthy to suffer for what they believed. In those days the church was not merely a thermometer that recorded the ideas and principles of popular opinion; it was a thermostat that transformed the mores of society. Whenever the early Christians entered a town, the people in power became disturbed and immediately sought to convict the Christians for being "disturbers of the peace" and "outside agitators." But the Christians pressed on, in the conviction that they were "a colony of heaven," called to obey God rather than man. Small in number, they were big in commitment. They were too God-intoxicated to be "astronomically intimidated." By their effort and example they brought an end to such ancient evils as infanticide and gladiatorial contests.

Things are different now. So often the contemporary church is a weak, ineffectual voice with an uncertain sound. So often it is an archdefender of the status quo. Far from being disturbed by the presence of the church, the power structure of the average community is consoled by the church's silent—and often even vocal—sanction of things as they are.

But the judgment of God is upon the church as never before. If today's church does not recapture the sacrificial spirit of the early church, it will lose its authenticity, forfeit the loyalty of millions, and be dismissed as an irrelevant social club with no meaning for the twentieth century. Every day I meet young people whose disappointment with the church has turned into outright disgust.

Perhaps I have once again been too optimistic. Is organized religion too inextricably bound to the status quo to save our nation and the world? Perhaps I must turn my faith to the inner spiritual church, the church within the church, as the true *ekklesia*[5] and the hope of the world. But again I am thankful to God that some noble souls from the ranks of organized religion have broken loose from the paralyzing chains of conformity and joined us as active partners in the struggle for freedom. They have left their secure congregations and walked the streets of Albany, Georgia, with us. They have gone down the highways of the South on tortuous rides for freedom. Yes, they have gone to jail with us. Some have been dismissed from their churches, have lost the support of

---

5. The Greek New Testament word for the early Christian church.

their bishops and fellow ministers. But they have acted in the faith that right defeated is stronger than evil triumphant. Their witness has been the spiritual salt that has preserved the true meaning of the gospel in these troubled times. They have carved a tunnel of hope through the dark mountain of disappointment.

I hope the church as a whole will meet the challenge of this decisive hour. But even if the church does not come to the aid of justice, I have no despair about the future. I have no fear about the outcome of our struggle in Birmingham, even if our motives are at present misunderstood. We will reach the goal of freedom in Birmingham and all over the nation, because the goal of America is freedom. Abused and scorned though we may be, our destiny is tied up with America's destiny. Before the pilgrims landed at Plymouth, we were here. Before the pen of Jefferson etched the majestic words of the Declaration of Independence across the pages of history, we were here. For more than two centuries our forebears labored in this country without wages; they made cotton king; they built the homes of their masters while suffering gross injustice and shameful humiliation—and yet out of a bottomless vitality they continued to thrive and develop. If the inexpressible cruelties of slavery could not stop us, the opposition we now face will surely fail. We will win our freedom because the sacred heritage of our nation and the eternal will of God are embodied in our echoing demands.

Before closing I feel impelled to mention one other point in your statement that has troubled me profoundly. You warmly commended the Birmingham police force for keeping "order" and "preventing violence." I doubt that you would have so warmly commended the police force if you had seen its dogs sinking their teenth into unarmed, nonviolent Negroes. I doubt that you would so quickly commend the policemen if you were to observe their ugly and inhumane treatment of Negroes here in the city jail; if you were to watch them push and curse old Negro women and young Negro girls; if you were to see them slap and kick old Negro men and young boys; if you were to observe them, as they did on two occasions, refuse to give us food because we wanted to sing our grace together. I cannot join you in your praise of the Birmingham police department.

It is true that the police have exercised a degree of discipline in handling the demonstrators. In this sense they have conducted themselves rather "nonviolently" in public. But for what purpose? To preserve the evil system of segregation. Over the past few years I have consistently preached that nonviolence demands that the means we use must be as pure as the ends we seek. I have tried to make clear that it is wrong to use immoral means to attain moral ends. But now I must affirm that it is just as wrong, or perhaps even more so, to use moral means to preserve immoral ends. Perhaps Mr. Connor and his policemen have been rather nonviolent in public, as was Chief Pritchett in Albany, Georgia, but they have used the moral means of nonviolence to maintain the immoral end of racial injustice. As T. S. Eliot has said, "The last temptation is the greatest treason: To do the right deed for the wrong reason."

I wish you had commended the Negro sit-inners and demonstrators of Birmingham for their sublime courage, their willingness to suffer, and their amazing discipline in the midst of great provocation. One day the South will recognize its real heroes. They will be the James Merediths,[6] with the noble sense of purpose that enables them to face jeering and hostile mobs, and with the agonizing loneliness that characterizes the life of the pioneer. They will be old, oppressed, battered Negro women, symbolized in a seventy-two-year-old woman in Montgomery, Alabama, who rose up with a sense of dignity and with her people decided not to ride segregated buses, and who responded with ungrammatical profundity to one who inquired about her weariness: "My feets is tired, but my soul is at rest." They will be the young high school and college students, the young ministers of the gospel and a host of their elders, courageously and nonviolently sitting in at lunch counters and willingly going to jail for conscience' sake. One day the South will know that when these disinherited children of God sat down at lunch counters, they were in reality standing up for what is best in the American dream and for the most sacred values in our Judaeo-Christian heritage, thereby bringing our nation back to those great wells of democracy which were dug deep by the founding fathers in their formulation of the Constitution and the Declaration of Independence.

Never before have I written so long a letter. I'm afraid it is much too long to take your precious time. I can assure you that it would have been much shorter if I had been writing from a comfortable desk, but what else can one do when he is alone in a narrow jail cell, other than write long letters, think long thoughts, and pray long prayers?

If I have said anything in this letter that overstates the truth and indicates an unreasonable impatience, I beg you to forgive me. If I have said anything that understates the truth and indicates my having a patience that allows me to settle for anything less than brotherhood, I beg God to forgive me.

I hope this letter finds you strong in the faith. I also hope that circumstances will soon make it possible for me to meet each of you, not as an integrationist or a civil-rights leader but as a fellow clergyman and a Christian brother. Let us all hope that the dark clouds of racial prejudice will soon pass away and the deep fog of misunderstanding will be lifted from our fear-drenched communities, and in some not too distant to-

6. Meredith was the first black to enroll at the University of Mississippi.

morrow the radiant stars of love and brotherhood will shine over our
great nation with all their scintillating beauty.

> Yours for the cause of Peace and Brotherhood,
> MARTIN LUTHER KING, JR.

1963

James Thurber

THE RABBITS WHO CAUSED ALL THE TROUBLE

Within the memory of the youngest child there was a family of rabbits
who lived near a pack of wolves. The wolves announced that they did not
like the way the rabbits were living. (The wolves were crazy about the
way they themselves were living, because it was the only way to live.)
One night several wolves were killed in an earthquake and this was
blamed on the rabbits, for it is well known that rabbits pound on the
ground with their hind legs and cause earthquakes. On another night one
of the wolves was killed by a bolt of lightning and this was also blamed on
the rabbits, for it is well known that lettuce-eaters cause lightning. The
wolves threatened to civilize the rabbits if they didn't behave, and the
rabbits decided to run away to a desert island. But the other animals, who
lived at a great distance, shamed them, saying, "You must stay where you
are and be brave. This is no world for escapists. If the wolves attack you,
we will come to your aid, in all probability." So the rabbits continued to
live near the wolves and one day there was a terrible flood which
drowned a great many wolves. This was blamed on the rabbits, for it is
well known that carrot-nibblers with long ears cause floods. The wolves
descended on the rabbits, for their own good, and imprisoned them in a
dark cave, for their own protection.

When nothing was heard about the rabbits for some weeks, the other
animals demanded to know what had happened to them. The wolves
replied that the rabbits had been eaten and since they had been eaten the
affair was a purely internal matter. But the other animals warned that
they might possibly unite against the wolves unless some reason was
given for the destruction of the rabbits. So the wolves gave them one.
"They were trying to escape," said the wolves, "and, as you know, this is
no world for escapists."

Moral: *Run, don't walk, to the nearest desert island.*

1955

Jonathan Swift

A MODEST PROPOSAL

FOR PREVENTING THE CHILDREN OF POOR PEOPLE IN IRELAND FROM BEING A BURDEN TO THEIR PARENTS OR COUNTRY, AND FOR MAKING THEM BENEFICIAL TO THE PUBLIC

It is a melancholy object to those who walk through this great town[1] or travel in the country, when they see the streets, the roads, and cabin doors, crowded with beggars of the female-sex, followed by three, four, or six children, all in rags and importuning every passenger for an alms. These mothers, instead of being able to work for their honest livelihood, are forced to employ all their time in strolling to beg sustenance for their helpless infants, who, as they grow up, either turn thieves for want of work, or leave their dear native country to fight for the Pretender in Spain, or sell themselves to the Barbadoes.[2]

I think it is agreed by all parties that this prodigious number of children in the arms, or on the backs, or at the heels of their mothers, and frequently of their fathers, is in the present deplorable state of the kingdom a very great additional grievance; and therefore whoever could find out a fair, cheap, and easy method of making these children sound, useful members of the commonwealth would deserve so well of the public as to have his statue set up for a preserver of the nation.

But my intention is very far from being confined to provide only for the children of professed beggars; it is of a much greater extent, and shall take in the whole number of infants at a certain age who are born of parents in effect as little able to support them as those who demand our charity in the streets.

As to my own part, having turned my thoughts for many years upon this important subject, and maturely weighed the several schemes of other projectors,[3] I have always found them grossly mistaken in their computation. It is true, a child just dropped from its dam may be supported by her milk for a solar year, with little other nourishment; at most not above the value of two shillings,[4] which the mother may certainly get, or the value in scraps, by her lawful occupation of begging; and it is

1. Dublin.
2. Many poor Irish sought to escape poverty by emigrating to the Barbadoes and other western English colonies, paying for transport by binding themselves to work for a landowner there for a period of years. The Pretender, claimant to the English throne, was barred from succession after his father, King James II, was deposed in a Protestant revolution; thereafter, many Irish Catholics joined the Pretender in his exile in France and Spain, and in his unsuccessful attempts at counterrevolution.
3. People with projects; schemers.
4. A shilling used to be worth about twenty-five cents.

exactly at one year old that I propose to provide for them in such a manner as instead of being a charge upon their parents or the parish, or wanting food and raiment for the rest of their lives, they shall on the contrary contribute to the feeding, and partly to the clothing, of many thousands.

There is likewise another great advantage in my scheme, that it will prevent those voluntary abortions, and that horrid practice of women murdering their bastard children, alas, too frequent among us, sacrificing the poor innocent babes, I doubt, more to avoid the expense than the shame, which would move tears and pity in the most savage and inhuman breast.

The number of souls in this kingdom being usually reckoned one million and a half, of these I calculate there may be about two hundred thousand couple whose wives are breeders; from which number I subtract thirty thousand couples who are able to maintain their own children, although I apprehend there cannot be so many under the present distresses of the kingdom; but this being granted, there will remain an hundred and seventy thousand breeders. I again subtract fifty thousand for those women who miscarry, or whose children die by accident or disease within the year. There only remain an hundred and twenty thousand children of poor parents annually born. The question therefore is, how this number shall be reared and provided for, which, as I have already said, under the present situation of affairs, is utterly impossible by all the methods hitherto proposed. For we can neither employ them in handicraft or agriculture; we neither build houses (I mean in the country) nor cultivate land. They can very seldom pick up a livelihood by stealing till they arrive at six years old, except where they are of towardly[5] parts; although I confess they learn the rudiments much earlier, during which time they can however be looked upon only as probationers, as I have been informed by a principal gentleman in the county of Cavan, who protested to me that he never knew above one or two instances under the age of six, even in a part of the kingdom so renowned for the quickest proficiency in that art.

I am assured by our merchants that a boy or a girl before twelve years old is no salable commodity; and even when they come to this age they will not yield above three pounds, or three pounds and half a crown[6] at most on the Exchange; which cannot turn to account either to the parents or the kingdom, the charge of nutriment and rags having been at least four times that value.

I shall now therefore humbly propose my own thoughts, which I hope will not be liable to the least objection.

I have been assured by a very knowing American of my acquaintance

5. Obedient.
6. A pound was twenty shillings; a crown, five shillings.

in London, that a young healthy child well nursed is at a year old a most delicious, nourishing, and wholesome food, whether stewed, roasted, baked, or boiled; and I make no doubt that it will equally serve in a fricassee or a ragout.

I do therefore humbly offer it to public consideration that of the hundred and twenty thousand children, already computed, twenty thousand may be reserved for breed, whereof only one fourth part to be males, which is more than we allow to sheep, black cattle, or swine; and my reason is that these children are seldom the fruits of marriage, a circumstance not much regarded by our savages, therefore one male will be sufficient to serve four females. That the remaining hundred thousand may at a year old be offered in sale to the persons of quality and fortune through the kingdom, always advising the mother to let them suck plentifully in the last month, so as to render them plump and fat for a good table. A child will make two dishes at an entertainment for friends; and when the family dines alone, the fore or hind quarter will make a reasonable dish, and seasoned with a little pepper or salt will be very good boiled on the fourth day, especially in winter.

I have reckoned upon a medium that a child just born will weigh twelve pounds, and in a solar year if tolerably nursed increaseth to twenty-eight pounds.

I grant this food will be somewhat dear, and therefore very proper for landlords, who, as they have already devoured most of the parents, seem to have the best title to the children.

Infant's flesh will be in season throughout the year, but more plentiful in March, and a little before and after. For we are told by a grave author, an eminent French physician,[7] that fish being a prolific diet, there are more children born in Roman Catholic countries about nine months after Lent than at any other season; therefore, reckoning a year after Lent, the markets will be more glutted than usual, because the number of popish infants is at least three to one in this kingdom; and therefore it will have one other collateral advantage, by lessening the number of Papists among us.[8]

I have already computed the charge of nursing a beggar's child (in which list I reckon all cottagers, laborers, and four fifths of the farmers) to be about two shillings per annum, rags included; and I believe no gentleman would repine to give ten shillings for the carcass of a good fat child, which, as I have said, will make four dishes of excellent nutritive meat, when he hath only some particular friend or his own family to dine with him. Thus the squire will learn to be a good landlord, and grow popular among the tenants; the mother will have eight shillings net profit, and be fit for work till she produces another child.

7. The sixteenth-century comic writer François Rabelais.
8. The speaker is addressing Protestant An-
glo-Irish, who were the chief landowners and administrators, and his views of Catholicism in Ireland and abroad echo theirs.

Those who are more thrifty (as I must confess the times require) may flay the carcass; the skin of which artificially[9] dressed will make admirable gloves for ladies, and summer boots for fine gentlemen.

As to our city of Dublin, shambles[1] may be appointed for this purpose in the most convenient parts of it, and butchers we may be assured will not be wanting; although I rather recommend buying the children alive, and dressing them hot from the knife as we do roasting pigs.

A very worthy person, a true lover of his country, and whose virtues I highly esteem, was lately pleased in discoursing on this matter to offer a refinement upon my scheme. He said that many gentlemen of this kingdom, having of late destroyed their deer, he conceived that the want of venison might be well supplied by the bodies of young lads and maidens, not exceeding fourteen years of age nor under twelve, so great a number of both sexes in every county being now ready to starve for want of work and service; and these to be disposed of by their parents, if alive, or otherwise by their nearest relations. But with due deference to so excellent a friend and so deserving a patriot, I cannot be altogether in his sentiments; for as to the males, my American acquaintance assured me from frequent experience that their flesh was generally tough and lean, like that of our schoolboys, by continual exercise, and their taste disagreeable; and to fatten them would not answer the charge. Then as to the females, it would, I think with humble submission, be a loss to the public, because they soon would become breeders themselves: and besides, it is not improbable that some scrupulous people might be apt to censure such a practice (although indeed very unjustly) as a little bordering upon cruelty; which, I confess, hath always been with me the strongest objection against any project, how well soever intended.

But in order to justify my friend, he confessed that this expedient was put into his head by the famous Psalmanazar, a native of the island Formosa,[2] who came from thence to London above twenty years ago, and in conversation told my friend that in his country when any young person happened to be put to death, the executioner sold the carcass to persons of quality as a prime dainty; and that in his time the body of a plump girl of fifteen, who was crucified for an attempt to poison the emperor, was sold to his Imperial Majesty's prime minister of state, and other great mandarins of the court, in joints from the gibbet, at four hundred crowns. Neither indeed can I deny that if the same use were made of several plump young girls in this town, who without one single groat[3] to their fortunes cannot stir abroad without a chair,[4] and appear at the playhouse

9. Skillfully.
1. Slaughterhouses.
2. Actually a Frenchman, George Psalmanazar had passed himself off as from Formosa (now Taiwan) and had written a fictitious book about his "homeland," with descriptions of human sacrifice and cannibalism.
3. An English coin worth about four pennies.
4. A sedan chair.

and assemblies in foreign fineries which they never will pay for, the kingdom would not be the worse.

Some persons of a desponding spirit are in great concern about that vast number of poor people who are aged, diseased, or maimed, and I have been desired to employ my thoughts what course may be taken to ease the nation of so grievous an encumbrance. But I am not in the least pain upon that matter, because it is very well known that they are every day dying and rotting by cold and famine, and filth and vermin, as fast as can be reasonably expected. And as to the younger laborers, they are now in almost as hopeful a condition. They cannot get work, and consequently pine away for want of nourishment to a degree that if at any time they are accidentally hired to common labor, they have not strength to perform it; and thus the country and themselves are happily delivered from the evils to come.

I have too long digressed, and therefore shall return to my subject. I think the advantages by the proposal which I have made are obvious and many, as well as of the highest importance.

For first, as I have already observed, it would greatly lessen the number of Papists, with whom we are yearly overrun, being the principal breeders of the nation as well as our most dangerous enemies; and who stay at home on purpose to deliver the kingdom to the Pretender, hoping to take their advantage by the absence of so many good Protestants, who have chosen rather to leave their country than to stay at home and pay tithes against their conscience to an Episcopal curate.

Secondly, the poorer tenants will have something valuable of their own, which by law may be made liable to distress,[5] and help to pay their landlord's rent, their corn and cattle being already seized and money a thing unknown.

Thirdly, whereas the maintenance of an hundred thousand children, from two years old and upwards, cannot be computed at less than ten shillings a piece per annum, the nation's stock will be thereby increased fifty thousand pounds per annum, besides the profit of a new dish introduced to the tables of all gentlemen of fortune in the kingdom who have any refinement in taste. And the money will circulate among ourselves, the goods being entirely of our own growth and manufacture.

Fourthly, the constant breeders, besides the gain of eight shillings sterling per annum by the sale of their children, will be rid of the charge of maintaining them after the first year.

Fifthly, this food would likewise bring great custom to taverns, where the vintners will certainly be so prudent as to procure the best receipts for dressing it to perfection, and consequently have their houses frequented by all the fine gentlemen, who justly value themselves upon

5. Seizure for the payment of debts.

their knowledge in good eating; and a skillful cook, who understands how to oblige his guests, will contrive to make it as expensive as they please.

Sixthly, this would be a great inducement to marriage, which all wise nations have either encouraged by rewards or enforced by laws and penalties. It would increase the care and tenderness of mothers toward their children, when they were sure of a settlement for life to the poor babes, provided in some sort by the public, to their annual profit instead of expense. We should see an honest emulation among the married women, which of them could bring the fattest child to the market. Men would become as found of their wives during the time of their pregnancy as they are now of their mares in foal, their cows in calf, or sows when they are ready to farrow; nor offer to beat or kick them (as is too frequent a practice) for fear of a miscarriage.

Many other advantages might be enumerated. For instance, the addition of some thousand carcasses in our exportation of barreled beef, the propagation of swine's flesh, and improvement in the art of making good bacon, so much wanted among us by the great destruction of pigs, too frequent at our tables, which are no way comparable in taste or magnificence to a well-grown, fat, yearling child, which roasted whole will make a considerable figure at a lord mayor's feast or any other public entertainment. But this and many others I omit, being studious of brevity.

Supposing that one thousand families in this city would be constant customers for infants' flesh, besides others who might have it at merry meetings, particularly weddings and christenings, I compute that Dublin would take off annually about twenty thousand carcasses, and the rest of the kingdom (where probably they will be sold somewhat cheaper) the remaining eighty thousand.

I can think of no one objection that will possibly be raised against this proposal, unless it should be urged that the number of people will be thereby much lessened in the kingdom. This I freely own, and it was indeed one principal design in offering it to the world. I desire the reader will observe, that I calculate my remedy for this one individual kingdom of Ireland and for no other that ever was, is, or I think ever can be upon earth. Therefore let no man talk to me of other expedients: of taxing our absentees at five shillings a pound: of using neither clothes nor household furniture except what is of our own growth and manufacture: of utterly rejecting the materials and instruments that promote foreign luxury: of curing the expensiveness of pride, vanity, idleness, and gaming in our women: of introducing a vein of parsimony, prudence, and temperance: of learning to love our country, in the want of which we differ even from Laplanders and the inhabitants of Topinamboo[6]: of quitting our animosities and factions, nor acting any longer like the Jews, who were murdering one another at the very moment their city was taken: of being a little

6. A district in Brazil.

cautious not to sell our country and conscience for nothing: of teaching landlords to have at least one degree of mercy toward their tenants: lastly, of putting a spirit of honesty, industry, and skill into our shopkeepers; who, if a resolution could now be taken to buy only our native goods, would immediately unite to cheat and exact upon us in the price, the measure, and the goodness, nor could ever yet be brought to make one fair proposal of just dealing, though often and earnestly invited to it.[7]

Therefore I repeat, let no man talk to me of these and the like expedients, till he hath at least some glimpse of hope that there will ever be some hearty and sincere attempt to put them in practice.

But as to myself, having been wearied out for many years with offering vain, idle, visionary thoughts, and at length utterly despairing of success, I fortunately fell upon this proposal, which, as it is wholly new, so it hath something solid and real, of no expense and little trouble, full in our own power, and whereby we can incur no danger in disobliging England. For this kind of commodity will not bear exportation, the flesh being of too tender a consistence to admit a long continuance in salt, although perhaps I could name a country[8] which would be glad to eat up our whole nation without it.

After all, I am not so violently bent upon my own opinion as to reject any offer proposed by wise men, which shall be found equally innocent, cheap, easy, and effectual. But before something of that kind shall be advanced in contradiction to my scheme, and offering a better, I desire the author or authors will be pleased maturely to consider two points. First, as things now stand, how they will be able to find food and raiment for an hundred thousand useless mouths and backs. And secondly, there being a round million of creatures in human figure throughout this kingdom, whose sole subsistence put into a common stock would leave them in debt two millions of pounds sterling, adding those who are beggars by profession to the bulk of farmers, cottagers, and laborers, with their wives and children who are beggars in effect; I desire those politicians who dislike my overture, and may perhaps be so bold to attempt an answer, that they will first ask the parents of these mortals whether they would not at this day think it a great happiness to have been sold for food at a year old in the manner I prescribe, and thereby have avoided such a perpetual scene of misfortunes as they have since gone through by the oppression of landlords, the impossibility of paying rent without money or trade, the want of common sustenance, with neither house nor clothes to cover them from the inclemencies of the weather, and the most inevitable prospect of entailing the like or greater miseries upon their breed forever.

I profess, in the sincerity of my heart, that I have not the least personal

---

7. Swift himself had made these proposals   8. England.
seriously in various previous works.

interest in endeavoring to promote this necessary work, having no other motive than the public good of my country, by advancing our trade, providing for infants, relieving the poor, and giving some pleasure to the rich. I have no children by which I can propose to get a single penny; the youngest being nine years old, and my wife past childbearing.

1729

QUESTIONS

1. *This essay has been called one of the best examples of sustained irony in the English language. Irony is difficult to handle because there is always the danger that the reader will miss the irony and take what is said literally. What does Swift do to try to prevent this? In answering this question, consider such matters as these: Is the first sentence of the essay ironic? At what point do you begin to suspect that Swift is using irony? What further evidence accumulates to make you certain that Swift is being ironic?*
2. *What is the speaker like? How are his views and character different from Swift's? Is the character of the speaker consistent? What is the purpose of the essay's final sentence?*
3. *Why does Swift use such phrases as "just dropt from its dam," "whose wives are breeders," "one fourth part to be males"?*
4. *Does the essay shock you? Was it Swift's purpose to shock you?*
5. *What is the main target of Swift's attack? What subsidiary targets are there? Does Swift offer any serious solutions for the problems and conditions he is describing?*
6. *What devices of argument, apart from the use of irony, does Swift use that could be successfully applied to other subjects?*
7. *In the study questions for George Orwell's "Shooting an Elephant" (p. 782), there is a brief sketch from* The Graphic *of 1888, "Shooting a Man-Eating Crocodile." How can you tell that this sketch is not ironic and that "A Modest Proposal" is? If you can't tell, what does your uncertainty suggest about the nature of irony?*

Niccolò Machiavelli

THE MORALS OF THE PRINCE[1]

On the Reasons Why Men Are Praised or Blamed—Especially Princes

It remains now to be seen what style and principles a prince ought to adopt in dealing with his subjects and friends. I know the subject has been treated frequently before, and I'm afraid people will think me rash for trying to do so again, especially since I intend to differ in this discussion from what others have said. But since I intend to write something useful to an understanding reader, it seemed better to go after the real truth of the matter than to repeat what people have imagined. A great many men have imagined states and princedoms such as nobody ever saw or knew in the real world, for there's such a difference between the way we really live and the way we ought to live that the man who neglects the real to study the ideal will learn how to accomplish his ruin, not his salvation. Any man who tries to be good all the time is bound to come to ruin among the great number who are not good. Hence a prince who wants to keep his post must learn how not to be good, and use that knowledge, or refrain from using it, as necessity requires.

Putting aside, then, all the imaginary things that are said about princes, and getting down to the truth, let me say that whenever men are discussed (and especially princes because they are prominent), there are certain qualities that bring them either praise or blame. Thus some are considered generous, others stingy (I use a Tuscan term, since "greedy" in our speech means a man who wants to take other people's goods. we call a man "stingy" who clings to his own); some are givers, others grabbers; some cruel, others merciful; one man is treacherous, another faithful; one is feeble and effeminate, another fierce and spirited; one humane, another proud; one lustful, another chaste; one straightforward, another sly; one harsh, another gentle; one serious, another playful; one religious, another skeptical, and so on. I know everyone will agree that among these many qualities a prince certainly ought to have all those that are considered good. But since it is impossible to have and exercise them all, because the conditions of human life simply do not allow it, a prince must be shrewd enough to avoid the public disgrace of those vices that would lose him his state. If he possibly can, be should also guard against vices that will not lose him his state; but if he cannot prevent them, he should not be too worried about indulging them. And furthermore, he should not be too worried about incurring blame for any vice without which he would find it hard to save his state. For if you look at matters

1. From *The Prince*, a book on statecraft written for Giuliano de' Medici (1479–1516), a member of one of the most famous and powerful families of Renaissance Italy.

carefully, you will see that something resembling virtue, if you follow it, may be your ruin, while something else resembling vice will lead, if you follow it, to your security and well-being.

On Liberality and Stinginess

Let me begin, then, with the first of the qualities mentioned above, by saying that a reputation for liberality is doubtless very fine; but the generosity that earns you that reputation can do you great harm. For if you exercise your generosity in a really virtuous way, as you should, nobody will know of it, and you cannot escape the odium of the opposite vice. Hence if you wish to be widely known as a generous man, you must seize every opportunity to make a big display of your giving. A prince of this character is bound to use up his entire revenue in works of ostenta-tion. Thus, in the end, if he wants to keep a name for generosity, he will have to load his people with exorbitant taxes and squeeze money out of them in every way he can. This is the first step in making him odious to his subjects; for when he is poor, nobody will respect him. Then, when his generosity has angered many and brought rewards to a few, the slightest difficulty will trouble him, and at the first approach of danger, down he goes. If by chance he foresees this, and tries to change his ways, he will immediately be labeled a miser.

Since a prince cannot use this virtue of liberality in such a way as to become known for it unless he harms his own security, he won't mind, if he judges prudently of things, being known as a miser. In due course he will be thought the more liberal man, when people see that his parsimony enables him to live on his income, to defend himself against his enemies, and to undertake major projects without burdening his people with taxes. Thus he will be acting liberally toward all those people from whom he takes nothing (and there are an immense number of them), and in a stingy way toward those people on whom he bestows nothing (and they are very few). In our times, we have seen great things being accomplished only by men who have had the name of misers; all the others have gone under. Pope Julius II, though he used his reputation as a generous man to gain the papacy, sacrificed it in order to be able to make war; the present king of France has waged many wars without levying a single extra tax on his people, simply because he could take care of the extra expenses out of the savings from his long parsimony. If the present king of Spain had a reputation for generosity, he would never have been able to undertake so many campaigns, or win so many of them.

Hence a prince who prefers not to rob his subjects, who wants to be able to defend himself, who wants to avoid poverty and contempt, and who doesn't want to become a plunderer, should not mind in the least if people consider him a miser; this is simply one of the vices that enable him to reign. Someone may object that Caesar used a reputation for generosity to become emperor, and many other people have also risen in the world, because they were generous or were supposed to be so. Well, I answer, either you are a prince already, or you are in the process of becoming one; in the first case, this reputation for generosity is harmful to you, in the second case it is very necessary. Caesar was one of those who wanted to become ruler in Rome; but after he had reached his goal, if he had lived, and had not cut down on his expenses, he would have ruined the empire itself. Someone may say: there have been plenty of princes, very successful in warfare, who have had a reputation for generosity. But I answer: either the prince is spending his own money and that of his subjects, or he is spending someone else's. In the first case, he ought to be sparing; in the second case, he ought to spend money like water. Any prince at the head of his army, which lives on loot, extortion, and plunder, disposes of other people's property, and is bound to be very generous; otherwise, his soldiers would desert him. You can always be a more generous giver when what you give is not yours or your subjects'; Cyrus, Caesar, and Alexander[2] were generous in this way. Spending what belongs to other people does no harm to your reputation, rather it enhances it; only spending your own substance harms you. And there is nothing that wears out faster than generosity; even as you practice it, you lose the means of practicing it, and you become either poor and contemptible or (in the course of escaping poverty) rapacious and hateful. The thing above all against which a prince must protect himself is being contemptible and hateful; generosity leads to both. Thus, it's much wiser to put up with the reputation of being a miser, which brings you shame without hate, than to be forced—just because you want to appear generous—into a reputation for rapacity, which brings shame on you and hate along with it.

On Cruelty and Clemency: Whether It Is Better to Be Loved or Feared

Continuing now with our list of qualities, let me say that every prince should prefer to be considered merciful rather than cruel, yet he should be careful not to mismanage this clemency of his. People thought Cesare Borgia[3] was cruel, but that cruelty of his reorganized the Romagna, united it, and established it in peace and loyalty. Anyone who views the matter realistically will see that this prince was much more merciful than the people of Florence, who, to avoid the reputation of cruelty, allowed Pistoia to be destroyed.[4] Thus, no prince should mind being called cruel for what he does to keep his subjects united and loyal; he may make

2. Persian, Roman, and Macedonian conquerors and rulers in ancient times.
3. The son of Pope Alexander VI (referred to later) and duke of Romagna, which he subju-

gated in 1499–1502.
4. By unchecked rioting between opposing factions (1502).

examples of a very few, but he will be more merciful in reality than those who, in their tenderheartedness, allow disorders to occur, with their attendant murders and lootings. Such turbulence brings harm to an entire community, while the executions ordered by a prince affect only one individual at a time. A new prince, above all others, cannot possibly avoid a name for cruelty, since new states are always in danger. And Virgil, speaking through the mouth of Dido,[5] says:

> My cruel fate
> And doubts attending an unsettled state
> Force me to guard my coast from foreign foes.

Yet a prince should be slow to believe rumors and to commit himself to action on the basis of them. He should not be afraid of his own thoughts; he ought to proceed cautiously, moderating his conduct with prudence and humanity, allowing neither overconfidence to make him careless, nor overtimidity to make him intolerable.

Here the question arises: is it better to be loved than feared, or vice versa? I don't doubt that every prince would like to be both; but since it is hard to accommodate these qualities, if you have to make a choice, to be feared is much safer than to be loved. For it is a good general rule about men, that they are ungrateful, fickle, liars and deceivers, fearful of danger and greedy for gain. While you serve their welfare, they are all yours, offering their blood, their belongings, their lives, and their children's lives, as we noted above—so long as the danger is remote. But when the danger is close at hand, they turn against you. Then, any prince who has relied on their words and has made no other preparations will come to grief; because friendships that are bought at a price, and not with greatness and nobility of soul, may be paid for but they are not acquired, and they cannot be used in time of need. People are less concerned with offending a man who makes himself loved than one who makes himself feared: the reason is that love is a link of obligation which men, because they are rotten, will break any time they think doing so serves their advantage; but fear involves dread of punishment, from which they can never escape.

Still, a prince should make himself feared in such a way that, even if he gets no love, he gets no hate either; because it is perfectly possible to be feared and not hated, and this will be the result if only the prince will keep his hands off the property of his subjects or citizens, and off their women. When he does have to shed blood, he should be sure to have a strong justification and manifest cause; but above all, he should not confiscate people's property, because men are quicker to forget the death of a father than the loss of a patrimony. Besides, pretexts for confiscation are always plentiful, it never fails that a prince who starts living by

5. Queen of Carthage and tragic heroine of Virgil's epic, *The Aeneid.*

plunder can find reasons to rob someone else. Excuses for proceeding against someone's life are much rarer and more quickly exhausted.

But a prince at the head of his armies and commanding a multitude of soldiers should not care a bit if he is considered cruel; without such a reputation, he could never hold his army together and ready for action. Among the marvelous deeds of Hannibal,[6] this was prime: that, having an immense army, which included men of many different races and nations, and which he led to battle in distant countries, he never allowed them to fight among themselves or to rise against him, whether his fortune was good or bad. The reason for this could only be his inhuman cruelty, which, along with his countless other talents, made him an object of awe and terror to his soldiers; and without the cruelty, his other qualities would never have sufficed. The historians who pass snap judgments on these matters admire his accomplishments and at the same time condemn the cruelty which was their main cause.

When I say, "His other qualities would never have sufficed," we can see that this is true from the example of Scipio,[7] an outstanding man not only among those of his own time, but in all recorded history; yet his armies revolted in Spain, for no other reason than his excessive leniency in allowing his soldiers more freedom than military discipline permits. Fabius Maximus rebuked him in the senate for this failing, calling him the corrupter of the Roman armies. When a lieutenant of Scipio's plundered the Locrians,[8] he took no action in behalf of the people, and did nothing to discipline that insolent lieutenant; again, this was the result of his easygoing nature. Indeed, when someone in the senate wanted to excuse him on this occasion, he said there are many men who knew better how to avoid error themselves than how to correct error in others. Such a soft temper would in time have tarnished the fame and glory of Scipio, had he brought it to the office of emperor; but as he lived under the control of the senate, this harmful quality of his not only remained hidden but was considered creditable.

Returning to the question of being feared or loved, I conclude that since men love at their own inclination but can be made to fear at the inclination of the prince, a shrewd prince will lay his foundations on what is under his own control, not on what is controlled by others. He should simply take pains not to be hated, as I said.

---

6. Carthaginian general who led a massive but unsuccessful invasion of Rome in 218–203 B.C.
7. The Roman general whose successful invasion of Carthage in 203 B.C. caused Hannibal's army to be recalled from Rome. The episode described here occurred in 206 B.C.
8. A people of Sicily, defeated by Scipio in 205 B.C. and placed under Q. Pleminius; *Fabius Maximus:* not only a senator but a high public official and general who had fought against Hannibal in Italy.

The Way Princes Should Keep Their Word

How praiseworthy it is for a prince to keep his word and live with integrity rather than by craftiness, everyone understands; yet we see from recent experience that those princes have accomplished most who paid little heed to keeping their promises, but who knew how craftily to manipulate the minds of men. In the end, they won out over those who tried to act honestly.

You should consider then, that there are two ways of fighting, one with laws and the other with force. The first is properly a human method, the second belongs to beasts. But as the first method does not always suffice, you sometimes have to turn to the second. Thus a prince must know how to make good use of both the beast and the man. Ancient writers made subtle note of this fact when they wrote that Achilles and many other princes of antiquity were sent to be reared by Chiron the centaur,[9] who trained them in his discipline. Having a teacher who is half man and half beast can only mean that a prince must know how to use both these two natures, and that one without the other has no lasting effect.

Since a prince must know how to use the character of beasts, he should pick for imitation the fox and the lion. As the lion cannot protect himself from traps, and the fox cannot defend himself from wolves, you have to be a fox in order to be wary of traps, and a lion to overawe the wolves. Those who try to live by the lion alone are badly mistaken. Thus a prudent prince cannot and should not keep his word when to do so would go against his interest, or when the reasons that made him pledge it no longer apply. Doubtless if all men were good, this rule would be bad; but since they are a sad lot, and keep no faith with you, you in your turn are under no obligation to keep it with them.

Besides, a prince will never lack for legitimate excuses to explain away his breaches of faith. Modern history will furnish innumerable examples of this behavior, showing how many treaties and promises have been made null and void by the faithlessness of princes, and how the man succeeded best who knew best how to play the fox. But it is a necessary part of this nature that you must conceal it carefully; you must be a great liar and hypocrite. Men are so simply of mind, and so much dominated by their immediate needs, that a deceitful man will always find plenty who are ready to be deceived. One of many recent examples calls for mention. Alexander VI[1] never did anything else, never had another thought, except to deceive men, and he always found fresh material to work on. Never was there a man more convincing in his assertions, who sealed his promises with more solemn oaths, and who observed them less. Yet his

9. Half man and half horse, the mythical Chiron was said to have taught the arts of war and peace, including hunting, medicine, music, and prophecy; *Achilles:* foremost among the Greek heroes in the Trojan War.
1. Pope from 1492 to 1503.

deceptions were always successful, because he knew exactly how to manage this sort of business.

In actual fact, a prince may not have all the admirable qualities we listed, but it is very necessary that he should seem to have them. Indeed, I will venture to say that when you have them and exercise them all the time, they are harmful to you; when you just seem to have them, they are useful. It is good to appear merciful, truthful, humane, sincere, and religious; it is good to be so in reality. But you must keep your mind so disposed that, in case of need, you can turn to the exact contrary. This has to be understood: a prince, and especially a new prince, cannot possibly exercise all those virtues for which men are called "good." To preserve the state, he often has to do things against his word, against charity, against humanity, against religion. Thus he has to have a mind ready to shift as the winds of fortune and the varying circumstances of life may dictate. And as I said above, he should not depart from the good if he can hold to it, but he should be ready to enter on evil if he has to.

Hence a prince should take great care never to drop a word that does not seem imbued with the five good qualities noted above; to anyone who sees or hears him, he should appear all compassion, all honor, all human-ity, all integrity, all religion. Nothing is more necessary than to seem to have this last virtue. Men in general judge more by the sense of sight than by the sense of touch, because everyone can see but only a few can test by feeling. Everyone sees what you seem to be, few know what you really are; and those few do not dare take a stand against the general opinion, supported by the majesty of the government. In the actions of all men, and especially of princes who are not subject to a court of appeal, we must always look to the end. Let a prince, therefore, win victories and uphold his state; his methods will always be considered worthy, and everyone will praise them, because the masses are always impressed by the superfi-cial appearance of things, and by the outcome of an enterprise. And the world consists of nothing but the masses; the few who have no influence when the many feel secure. A certain prince of our own time, whom it's just as well not to name,[2] preaches nothing but peace and mutual trust, yet he is the determined enemy of both; and if on several different occasions he had observed either, he would have lost both his reputation and his throne.

                                                                    1513

---

2. Probably Ferdinand of Spain, then allied with the house of Medici.

Theodore Roszak

FORBIDDEN GAMES

Those of us who find ourselves distressed or even horrified at the shape that the technological society is forcing upon our lives find ourselves again and again brought up short by the familiar cliché that technology —in both its mechanical and its organizational aspects—is, after all, a neutral force that can be wielded for man's well-being as well as for his harm. It is a cliché that is bound to leave us unsatisfied as a final verdict on the nature of technological development. For suppose one followed its suggestion and surrendered analysis in favor of a simple-minded act of double-entry tabulation (balancing off "good things" against "bad things"). Surely, sooner or later, any reasonably curious mind would begin to wonder why the technological account finishes with a liability column of such significant size. Or, indeed, those with a utopian bent to their curiosity might wonder why there is a liability column at all. Why haven't *all* of man's inventiveness and organizational skill worked out for the best, as an unmixed blessing?

Unless we insist upon an examination of the human perversity that has again and again cheated us of the full promise of technology, we will have to settle down to the grotesque complacency of the prominent American physicist who found a strange consolation in the fate that would befall mankind in the radioactive environment following World War III. The fall-out would, he concluded, only shorten man's life span by about the same amount that modern medicine had lengthened it in the last sixty years. Science giveth and science taketh away: blessed be the name of science.

In such an attitude may lie the key to technology's indiscriminate scattering of goods and evils. What is it that offends us so much in this easy casting-up of life and death accounts but the technician's implicit denial that technology in all its manifold works has anything to do, *essentially*, with promoting human welfare? Sometimes it does, and sometimes it doesn't: technology produces penicillin *and* the H-bomb . . . and lets the chips fall where they may. It is the same attitude that is reflected in the consoling conclusion of another technician that a thermonuclear disaster, while producing untold devastation to human life and culture, might at the same time lead the way to a renaissance of the arts by clearing away the dead hand of the cultural past.

What the technicians seem to be saying (and they seem very content to be saying it) is that technology is some manner of chance force that has as its main object the unfolding of its own inherent capacities. Its benefits and its destructive features are mere by-products. But, meanwhile, what goes without question is the assertion that the technology *must* be elaborated; it *must* go on "progressing." The technicians leave it to others to put their achievements to good use . . . or to pick up the pieces: a task that becomes increasingly more difficult as technology rapidly proliferates effects beyond anyone's anticipation or full understanding.

But if the technician's exclusive and often compulsive pursuit of progress is taken to have no inherent responsibility for the social results of that progress, then how are we to understand what the technician is about? What is the psychology of his project?

From the humanistic critic's viewpoint, the technician's lack of a clear, moral purpose may make technology seem a monstrosity, a chaos, a blind, erratic force throwing up unaccountable effects without reason or purpose. But what such a characterization overlooks is the fact that the technological project, for all the harm it does, has a very definite structure and discipline to it, an order that ought to be familiar to us all. The scientists, economists, engineers, entrepreneurs, managers, systems analysts, and bureaucrats who contribute to technological excellence are behaving far from blindly and erratically; their lives and careers are not lacking in purpose. They are seeking to do whatever they lay their hands to faster, more economically, and on a larger scale with less friction and with better control over more and more variable factors. And for all of these usually competitive objectives they can produce definitive quantitative measures that are often ingeniously refined and marvelously discriminating. Moreover, each technician is pursuing a career within an established and articulated hierarchy which has a well-developed scale of rewards and honors and some critical public to enforce legal or professional rules and standards. These are, of course, arbitrary—in the sense that the question "why" cannot be sensibly applied to them any more than it can be applied to, say, the standards of dress or the rules of courtship in our society.

We have a name for the sort of human activity that absorbs people in the orderly pursuit of arbitrary—usually competitive—goals according to arbitrary rules. We call it a "game." Why must an economy grow, why must profit be maximized, why must every bureaucracy expand and concentrate control, why must scientific truth and organizational efficiency and industrial productivity be ceaselessly elaborated? As soon as we grasp the fact that the expansion of technology is, for those who participate in the project, a game, these questions have the same logical status as the question: "Why is first base 90 feet from home plate?" or "Why is climbing a difficult mountain better than climbing an easy mountain?" And, of course, there is no answer to such questions other than to reassert the rule.

The elaboration of the technological society is, then, a game played by its own rules and for its own well-established goals. To be sure, because

the players manipulate people and resources, their game is bound to have effects "beyond" itself—in the "real" world outside its perimeters. But whether those effects are good or harmful is as irrelevant to the game as what happens to a baseball once it has been hit outside the ball park: perhaps a father catches it for his son and makes the boy happy; perhaps it hits a bystander in the head and kills him. "Wonderful," we may say, or "too bad" . . . but the game goes on.

One objects, of course: an activity embracing so many people and resources should not be merely a game. Nonetheless, technological progress *is* a game, and those who participate in making the technological society work, and in perfecting its techniques, possess the psychology of people playing games. It is the structure and discipline of game-playing that bound their understanding of themselves and their work. The important questions, then, are: How did technological progress become a game? And how can that game be stopped . . . or, at least, its rules altered?

None of this will sound new to those familiar with the work of the mathematicians Von Neumann and Morgenstern and of the school of game theorists that follows from them. Since the end of World War II their work has made clear that both war and business—the two greatest technological projects—have all the characteristics of games. But the purpose of the game theorists has emphatically *not* been to develop a radical critique of military and economic activity. They do not, for example, ask the question whether such activities ought properly to be games, or how their rules ought to be "moralized." In game theory there is no such category as "forbidden games." Rather, game theory has only reinforced the game structure and practice of war and business by elaborating more elegant strategic principles for their pursuit. Its effect has been to estrange business and war further from their flesh-and-blood implications by imposing a rarefied and intriguingly playful set of mathematical abstractions upon the real world in which men work and live and die.

What we want to know here is not how to play, more cunningly and self-consciously, games that should perhaps not be played at all, but rather how technological progress ever became a game in the first place and so lost its contact with the reality it molds . . . and too often torments.

For answers to these questions, it is not the game theorists we want to turn to, but rather to the work of the Dutch historian Johan Huizinga. In 1938 Huizinga[1] published a book which, although it has since been widely read and cited, has never really been assimilated into the mainstream of contemporary thought. *Homo Ludens* [man-at-play] compares in scope, originality, and profundity with the seminal works of Freud and Marx: a superb effort to create a comprehensive theory of human behavior and social life.

---

1. Johan Huizinga (1872-1945).

In exploring the "play element in culture," Huizinga wished to avoid the conclusion that the need to play is instinctual, recognizing that to call anything an "instinct" is a bad (and dull) way to begin or end a study. And yet, when one tries to summarize Huizinga's theory, there seems no way to avoid the word. Whatever we consider to be an inborn and irreducible animal need—"an absolutely primary category of life," as Huizinga put it —is bound to fall under the classification "instinct." Any one who has ever observed the pointless, just-for-fun antics and romping of a baby or a puppy would grant that playfulness *is* an inherent, spontaneous animal activity—and so qualifies as being one of those mysterious things called "instincts." But what do we gain by adding still another item to the ever lengthening list of instincts psychologists and physiologists have drawn up and squabble over?

It was Huizinga's ingenious thesis that play is a supremely important instinct (or "function" as he preferred to call it) because, in contrast to the other drives—hunger, thirst, sex, etc., which serve to guard, comfort, and propagate the physical being of the species—play is superfluous to survival, safety, physical well-being. Play is what we do just for the fun of it—and, as Huizinga insists, it reaches beyond all moral, biological, and aesthetic considerations. His purpose in *Homo Ludens* was to show how this essential playfulness is elaborated into our repertory of cultural games: ritual, law, art, philosophy, science, war—none of which is simply "game-like," but actually arises from the same mode of human behavior that generates sports and contests.

Homo Ludens is a pioneer effort, and like the work of all intellectual trail-blazers, it is flawed with shortcomings and inconsistencies. There is a great deal more Huizinga might have done with the "gamesmanship" of our social manners, which the humorists Stephen Potter and Jules Feiffer have done so much to popularize. And the grasp contemporary psychiatrists now have of those involuted psychic strategies we call neurosis and psychosis completely eluded him. His interest was in the healthy and productive play of people, not in the secret and diseased games we invent to defend ourselves against the demands of culture. Of business life and technological organization Huizinga says little, beyond recognizing the agonistic drive that underlies capitalist competition. It escaped him wholly that the bureaucracy-building and social engineering of the "organization man"—whether latter-day capitalist or socialist —can have all the game-playing instinct about it that once motivated the robber barons in their drive for monopoly and empire.

But deeper than these lacks is Huizinga's facile identification of "play" and "games." "Play," he decided at the very outset of his study, "demands order absolute and supreme." Play "creates order, *is* order." And because the study rapidly sweeps us along into an analysis of various cultural games that do, indeed, possess a strict orderliness, we tend to accept his statement. Every game must have its rules, its official players, its delimited area, its defined objective. We know this is the case with cocktail parties and presidential conventions, just as it is with golf and bowling.

But, then, think again. "Game" is the word we reserve for this kind of *organized* play. All games draw upon the instinct to play. But it is not always to the regularity and orderliness of a game that play gives itself. Playing is clearly a much more generalized and lawless form of activity. Babies and animals "play" in a perfectly chaotic fashion. In fact, playful babies have very little patience with rules and regulations. They play quite naturally, but they must be taught their *games*.

Playfulness is an animal passion, not a cultural exercise. Indeed, it would not be too much to say that play is antagonistic to order. It satisfies itself in the immediate experience, not in the strategic pursuit of a goal or a score. "Playing around" is what we do when we are clowning, goofing off, being silly, acting spontaneously and randomly, and often so perversely as to subvert all order.

In what is certainly one of the most thorough investigations of the psychology of play in children, *Play, Dreams and Imitation in Childhood*, Jean Piaget clearly recognizes, as we do here, that play at the infantile level—motor-sensory play "purely for functional pleasure"—must be set apart from games with rules. Piaget's classification of play, which he examines entirely from the structural aspects of the child's behavior and not from its content or purpose, is three-fold. At the earliest stage of life, the child indulges in what Piaget calls "practice games," by which he means the reproduction of "behaviors merely for pleasure, accompanied by smiles and even laughter, and without the expectation of results. . . ." This is what I myself would call, simply, "play," as the word is most commonly used in our language. Then, somewhere toward the end of the second year, Piaget discovers that the child's repertory of play broadens to include the manipulation of symbols, a kind of play that increases as the child's mastery of language progresses. At this point, Piaget creates his second category of play: "symbolic games."

The important distinction Piaget's research has discovered is that which divides the young child's free play of body and mind from the older child's interest in games with rules—an interest that develops between the ages of 4 and 7 and that will then usually take over his sense of play for the remainder of his life. Piaget's "games with rules" (which I would simply call "games") are almost the only ones that persist at the adult stage. Somewhere after the first four or five years of life, the free manipulation of body and thought gives way to the pattern of the game with its orientation toward a specific goal and its structured rules.

So, in fact, there would seem to be a profound difference between the orderliness of a game and the chaotic fun of playing. They almost seem to be radically divergent modes of behavior. And yet we also sense that they are essentially related: that our many highly structured social and athletic games somehow absorb the impish spirit of play.

In his study of the "play-element in culture" Huizinga was really investigating the "game-element in culture." Play, being pre-cultural, indeed pre-human in character, escaped his attention. But let us give it our attention now. For if it is the case that technological "progress," with all its attendant, apparently inescapable liabilities of totalitarian politics and ever more efficient methods of genocidal warfare, is a game that strategists, bureaucrats, and social engineers play with the people and resources of the world, then we will want to understand how this compulsively organized game relates to the freedom of play.

The pleasure of infants, Norman Brown reminds us in his study of Freud, *Life Against Death*, "is in the active life of the body." And, he continues, "what is the pattern of activity, free from work, the serious business of life, and the reality-principle, which is adumbrated in the life of children? The answer is that children play." The ground of play, then, lies in that free and all-pervasive eroticism of the infant human being that Freud called "polymorphous perversity." The "*fun* of playing," which Huizinga felt "resists all logical interpretation," yields, I think, to Freud's *psycho*-logical interpretation. Play begins with the child's (and the animal's) sensuous manipulation of his body and all that comes in contact with it, and the *fun* of it all is a very fleshly satisfaction—the satisfaction most of us tend to know in later life only in its abbreviated genital form. But for the infant, stimulation anywhere upon the entire surface of the flesh, the work of the internal organs, the operation of the senses—in and of themselves, without any purpose or goal—is erotically satisfying. There is a simple and immediate joyousness in the functions and capacities of the body simply for what they are: the body's knowledge and enjoyment of itself *is* the act of play.

It is wonderful to imagine that there once glowed in all of us the sensuous satisfaction a painter discovers in the sheer act of seeing, or a musician in the sheer act of hearing, or a dancer in the sheer act of manipulating her muscles. Wonderful, and also tragic, when we realize how little of this sensual capacity survives even in gifted people. For, of course, this erotic tenor of life with all its richness of feeling and imagination is the victim of those life-long denials and repressions "growing-up" demands of us. But it is precisely "the play-element in culture," Norman Brown observes, which "provides a prima facie justification for the psychoanalytical doctrine of sublimation which views 'higher' cultural activities as substitutes for lost infantile pleasures." Games, then, are the hardened, disciplined remnants the forces of repression have left us of infantile play.

Freud arrived at two markedly different explanations of repression in the course of his life's work. In his early writings repression of erotic joy was simply the price reality exacted for survival: survival demands work, and work demands sexual restraint. But in his later writings he modified the dire opposition of culture to sexual joy, and decided, instead, that repression was the product of an internal struggle between Eros, the life principle, and Thanatos, the death principle: man represses himself in attempting to defend his organism against the inevitable advance of death.

Both of these theories have their philosophical charm and both have proved therapeutically useful in one degree or another. But it may not be the psychiatrists who have said the last word on the subject of repression. Just as many of Freud's basic psychic insights arose out of his early training and study as a physician, so the work of A. T. W. Simeons in problems of physical medicine has brought a new approach to repression by calling our attention to the physiology of the brain and the evolutionary development of intelligence.

Since repression is a uniquely human experience, it is only logical to seek its explanation in that faculty which most distinguishes man from other animals: his highly elaborated intelligence. Intelligence, Dr. Simeons reminds us in his book, *Man's Presumptuous Brain*, arose from a very humble origin. It began as a neural complication in the olfactory lobes of man's reptilian ancestors, a kind of loop or hitch in the nervous network that began to behave as a "censor" between incoming stimuli and those more primitive parts of the brain which reacted automatically to such stimuli. The more complicated this neural "trap" became, the more efficiently it could intervene to discriminate among raw experiences and, on the basis of stored-up learning, allow for a choice of responses.

The intervention of this complex "censorial" intelligence between sensory stimuli and the automatic animal reactions to them has placed man in a privileged position among all animals. It has permitted him to make ingenious and novel choices where other animals are bound to the fixed pattern of instinctive behavior. Moreover, in man it has led to the creation of culture, of an artificial and controlled environment within which many of the primordial reactions of rage, fear, sexual excitement, etc., are either unnecessary or disruptive.

But, as Dr. Simeons points out, the advantage of cortical intelligence has had its liabilities. So rapidly have the cerebral hemispheres grown along the course of mammalian evolution that their censorial function has grown significantly out of balance with the primitive brain-stem and its instinctual repertory. He suggests that the development has been "freakish"—a specialization which, like so many successful specializations, has elaborated itself "faster and faster and may even develop of its own accord beyond the limits of usefulness." It is this impaired communication between cortex and diencephalon[2] which Dr. Simeons holds responsible for the phenomenon of psychosomatic disease. Sexual frigidity and impotence, insomnia, arteriosclerosis, the digestive disorders—perhaps even diabetes and lumbago—all may result from the imperfect or even perverse cortical interpretation of organic reactions that have served as beneficial evolutionary responses and that remain locked in the brain-stem below the level of consciousness.

Dr. Simeons' contribution to the study of repression calls special attention to the adverse effects that have followed from the cortical repression, not simply of sex and aggression, but of fear and flight reflexes —extremely useful forms of behavior for the rather timid line of mammals from which we descend but now rendered largely unnecessary by the artificial protection of the cultural environment. In contrast to Freud, who identified the aggressive-destructive aspect of the death instinct as a basic human attribute, Dr. Simeons believes that timidity is the essential attribute of the human animal, and that aggressiveness has actually developed out of a latter-day cortical perversion of man's animal fearfulness. In turn, it is from this aggressive failure to be true to human nature that many of the psychosomatic ailments follow:

". . . when biologically timid man started to arm himself with inorganic armour to which the diencephalon had no functional relationship, he suddenly grew bold. His body and his brain-stem, having spent eons specializing in timidity, could not adjust themselves to the new courage. Their once normal responses became ever more inappropriate as culture and civilization swept onwards. . . . Ferocity was quite contrary to [man's] evolutionary nature, which was pusillanimous and nonviolent. He learned to make up for his lack of natural weapons by impatiently creating an invincible armoury of artificial defenses . . . and to act as if he were the most aggressive creature on earth."

I have spent this much time on Dr. Simeon's work because I want to draw on his observations concerning the structure and evolution of the brain, especially on his conception of repression as being essentially an evolutionary breakdown in communication between complex intelligence and the body it presumes to govern. In choosing the word "intelligence" to summarize the activity of the cortical brain, I realize I am entering into one of the more troubled battlegrounds of professional psychology. But I believe that most of the problems psychologists ever since Binet have had with the "meaning of intelligence" stems from their preoccupation with the task of providing efficient screening tests for various social projects and, in turn, with the historical confusion of this task with the highly prestigious label "intelligence." This has led to what is often for the layman the perplexing but nonetheless professionally utilitarian conclusion that intelligence is what various tests measure.

2. Middle brain.

To approach intelligence as a thing to be measured for immediate social needs may be legitimate enough for some purposes. But it leaves out of consideration the question we are concerned with here, which is the place of intelligence in the total organism. This was the question Henri Bergson raised sixty years ago when he asked in *Creative Evolution* that we reflect on the evolutionary function of intelligent behavior.

Much as we value human intelligence for its capacity to generate a high culture, we are really guilty of the sort of teleological fallacy Bergson himself is often accused of, when we fall into the habit of assuming that intelligence came into existence to create mathematics, philosophy, theoretical physics, etc., and that it is in terms of these highly sophisticated activities that intelligence is best understood. Bergson reminded us that intelligence probed and groped its way into existence long before high culture appeared and that, in its earliest manifestations, it possessed a rather humble character. It was then an instrument of survival, successful enough in its activity to be chosen and strengthened by the process of natural selection. Its orientation was toward "practical action." As a result, the tool remains for the anthropologist the single most concrete evidence of intelligence.

Within the context of evolution Bergson sought to do away with the notion that intelligence is a "thing" or static faculty. He wished, rather, to know what the dynamic relationship was between the intelligent animal and the world in which it had to act and move and survive. As Bergson portrayed intelligence, it was the capacity to rigidify, to quick-freeze, portions of the flow of experience so that these portions could then be acted upon with discretion. This process of solidifying and shaping the ceaseless flow of experience is the way in which intelligence seeks to adjust and orient experience with respect to selected goals: "useful ends," as Bergson called them. Within this provisional field of frozen experience, intelligence seeks constantly to routinize behavior and choice, to eliminate novelty and the unpredictable, to find similarities at the expense of uniqueness so that "a definite end calls forth definite means." In short, intelligence seeks constantly to find dependable rules of behavior that will achieve the same postulated results. From Bergson's point of view, science and technology progress by constantly reformulating or rearranging the field of experience, thus reassessing and generalizing the rules of successful (predictable) action.

Intelligence, then, as Bergson understood it, is that activity of the mind which makes experience "orderly" by isolating fields of attention within which the rules of successful action can be adjusted to selected goals. As he pointed out, intelligent "order" has so usurped our very conception of orderliness that everything which lies outside of it—the whole vast flow of vital experience—is perceived only as "disorder." But "disorder," he contended, is a nonsense concept, for it comes down ultimately to designating a different kind of order that one is unused to or did not expect to discover.

If we can accept Bergson's morphology of intelligence, we recognize at once what it is that intelligence essentially does. The isolation of a field of attention, the postulating of goals, the formation of rules: these are the three essential characteristics of what we call games. Intelligence plays games with reality. Its natural response to experience will always be the same: to define a field, fix a goal, apply rules.

Such is the life of the intelligent animal. He moves from arbitrary field to arbitrary field of activity: business, war, philosophy, politics, law, friendship, courtship, marriage. In each field he adopts the arbitrary goals and arbitrary rules appropriate to that field. And then he "plays the game"—the game being a social projection of the structure of his intelligence. Four hundred years ago Erasmus, perceiving the arbitrariness of man's earthly conduct, could smile good-naturedly at our human follies. But Erasmus was a religious man and could not bring himself to doubt that ultimately man's religious calling transcends the absurdity of his worldly pursuits. In our own time, when even the divine goal of salvation with its cosmic playing field and moral or theological rules has come to seem as arbitrary as any other human activity, nothing but absurdity seems to remain at the foundations of human life. So it is human absurdity that provides the basis for Ionesco's comedy, and for Kierkegaard's spiritual agony, and for the dour heroism of our existentialist philosophers. Indeed, in his *Myth of Sisyphus*, Albert Camus goes so far as to ask if human survival itself is not an arbitrary rule of the human game. Why survival? Why not suicide, he asks; and finishes by simply reasserting the rule . . . in all its naked absurdity. His essay is an excellent example of how impossible it is for the human intellect to get beyond its game-making habits, even when it deals with "ultimate questions."

Now, if we insist once again, with Bergson, that this game-making capacity grows out of an evolutionary background as a tool of survival, we can see what its relationship is to the spirit of play. Play, for all its joyousness, is chaotic and spontaneous. It reaches out toward experience without purpose and without discipline. It moves impractically with the stream of experience, rather than immobilizing and dividing that stream. It gives no power. It manipulates whatever it happens upon not for the sake of controlling, but for the sake of enjoying. Although we have a need to play, play possesses no survival value. Playfulness is, I suggest, what the game-making power of intelligence must discipline—and, in fact, has very effectively disciplined, substituting its own world of goals, symbols, rules, and rigidly defined fields for the fluidity and immediacy of play.

In describing the situation as I have here I have not, of course, identified the social forces, vested professional and economic interests, and historical circumstances that have brought about the apotheosis and dominance of the game-making intelligence. It is not something that has come about automatically or inevitably. Works like Roderick Seidenberg's *Post-historic Man*, which interprets the advance of technical organization as an impersonal and irreversible conquest of "instinct" by "intellect," or Jacques Ellul's *The Technological Society*, which suggests that the progress of *la technique* is a matter of inexorable destiny, contribute a grim urgency to our thinking, but little enlightenment. At least since the time William Blake hurled his visionary verse at England's "Dark Satanic Mills," men have been aware of what technological progress can cost the human spirit. One thinks of the two memorable images Chaplin captured in his film, *Modern Times*. On the one hand, we remember the shabby little operator imprisoned in an automatic feeding machine which was designed to diminish the time and motion required for the lunch hour, a device that batters a scientifically balanced diet into a recalcitrant and therefore probably obsolete human mouth and digestive system. On the other hand, we remember the little operator on roller skates, careening gaily about a department store, symbolically reducing the compulsive orderliness of the modern world to slaphappy chaos. It is a gesture of happy rebellion, of irreverent play, that amounts to more than the vision of a single artist. It is an act of sabotage that an audience of millions has understood, applauded, and, probably in a million secret ways, emulated.

It is at this point that I part company with the technological pessimists. While one would have to be a fool to believe that all is bound to turn out for the best, it may nevertheless be the case that (for better or worse, and usually for the better) the world is really a great deal less organized and under control than its official leadership would have us believe. In his play, *An Angel Comes to Babylon*, Frederick Dürenmatt has dramatized a truth most historians are aware of: there is apt to be an immense difference between the way a society really works and the way in which its domineering élite believes it works and wants it to work.

Once upon a time the reigning monarchs of the world, as a matter of course, kept jesters at their courts to remind them of this discrepancy and of their own presumptuous folly. In our contemporary governments, the commissars and social engineers no longer keep jesters, but they have not necessarily eliminated their own folly along with the jester. In the many back rooms, pool halls, pubs, bedrooms—the secret places that elude discovery and frustrate analysis—a mass life of sarcasm, cynical good sense, and incorrigible resistance to organization continues, mixed with as much superstition and crude incomprehension as ever.

The most critical charge I would level at Jacques Ellul and those other technological pessimists centers on their systematic ignorance of this factor. For them "technique" is that one *efficient* way of doing things which leads, irresistibly and finally, to a single technical solution. Efficiency is thus a purely quantitative and unambiguous measure. But I would call such efficiency by a different name: "idiot efficiency." It is the conception of efficiency that led nineteenth century capitalists to conclude that an army of docile automatons toiling a sixteen-hour work-day at starvation wages and under bestial conditions was the secret of high productivity and industrial wealth. It is the conception of efficiency that led to Stalin's brutal collectivization of Russian agriculture. It is the conception of efficiency that first conceives of the body as a mechanism that must be *made* to run by the brain, and then, in the familiar image of the body politic, conceives of society as a collection of members and organs that must be similarly *made* to function by specialized decision-makers. But the ultimate result of such jealous centralization of "control" is always paralysis and malfunction—to the extent that the whole system collapses as the "head" eventually drives the "members" into intolerable despair or rebellion.

In economics and social engineering, efficiency is a weasel-word which tends to obscure a multitude of human values. When is any social or economic system "efficient"? No doubt the idiot technician will answer: when every factor is organized according to an expert plan and implemented by an omniscient command and control center. But as working men have recognized for generations, "working to rule" is one of the best ways to gum up an economy. When everybody works to rule—no more, no less, and no differently—the system falls apart. So, in the West, we have learned the value of seeking efficiency by way of consensus, by way of encouraging a sense of participation, initiative, and high morale among citizens, as producers, consumers, or voters. To be sure, governing élites, by and large, still seek to engineer consensus and, in a variety of clever ways, to render freedom and initiative illusory. But why bother with the whole intricate hypocrisy of manipulated consensus unless one recognizes that the illusions meet real human needs and that it is actually more "efficient" to cater to those needs than to crush them?

A truly efficient social system—one that is stable, enduring, secure, productive—works *with* the grain of human needs and not against it. Thus, efficiency is not a purely quantitative measure, but a profoundly qualitative one. An efficient technological society, like an efficient machine shop or office, is ultimately one that cares for the quality of life, for the freedom, initiative, and playfulness of the human animal that participates in the enterprise. The fact that idiot efficiency crushes these qualities is undeniable and tragic. But there is also the fact—perhaps the only fact from which one can take consolation and inspiration—that idiot efficiency stagnates and frustrates, subverts and destroys, the systems it creates. Ultimately, those who play forbidden games lose them, and the ruins their loss frequently leaves us with invariably offer an opportunity to rebuild a more natural and livable society.

1966

Abraham Lincoln

SECOND INAUGURAL ADDRESS

At this second appearing to take the oath of the presidential office, there is less occasion for an extended address than there was at the first. Then a statement, somewhat in detail, of a course to be pursued, seemed fitting and proper. Now, at the expiration of four years, during which public declarations have been constantly called forth on every point and phase of the great contest which still absorbs the attention, and engrosses the energies of the nation, little that is new could be presented. The progress of our arms, upon which all else chiefly depends, is as well known to the public as to myself; and it is, I trust, reasonably satisfactory and encouraging to all. With high hope for the future, no prediction in regard to it is ventured.

On the occasion corresponding to this four years ago, all thoughts were anxiously directed to an impending civil war. All dreaded it—all sought to avert it. While the inaugural address was being delivered from this place, devoted altogether to *saving* the Union without war, insurgent agents were in the city seeking to *destroy* it without war—seeking to dissolve the Union, and divide effects, by negotiation. Both parties deprecated war; but one of them would *make* war rather than let the nation survive; and the other would *accept* war rather than let it perish. And the war came.

One-eighth of the whole population were colored slaves, not distributed generally over the Union, but localized in the Southern part of it. These slaves constituted a peculiar and powerful interest. All knew that this interest was, somehow, the cause of the war. To strengthen, perpetuate, and extend this interest was the object for which the insurgents would rend the Union, even by war; while the government claimed no right to do more than to restrict the territorial enlargement of it. Neither party expected for the war, the magnitude, or the duration, which it has already attained. Neither anticipated that the *cause* of the conflict might cease with, or even before, the conflict itself should cease. Each looked for an easier triumph, and a result less fundamental and astounding. Both read the same Bible, and pray to the same God; and each invokes His aid against the other. It may seem strange that any men should dare to ask a just God's assistance in wringing their bread from the sweat of other men's faces; but let us judge not that we be not judged.[1] The prayers of both could not be answered; that of neither has been answered fully. The Almighty has His own purposes. "Woe unto the world because of offenses! for it must needs be that offenses come; but woe to that man by whom the offense cometh!"[2] If we shall suppose that American slavery is one of those offenses which, in the providence of God, must needs come, but which, having continued through His appointed time, He now wills to remove, and that He gives to both North and South, this terrible war, as the woe due to those by whom the offense came, shall we discern therein any departure from those divine attributes which the believers in a Living God always ascribe to Him? Fondly do we hope—fervently do we pray—that this mightly scourge of war may speedily pass away. Yet, if God wills that it continue, until all the wealth piled by the bondman's two hundred and fifty years of unrequited toil shall be sunk, and until every drop of blood drawn with the lash, shall be paid by another drawn with the sword, as was said three thousand years ago, so still it must be said "the judgments of the Lord are true and righteous altogether."[3]

With malice toward none; with charity for all; with firmness in the right, as God gives us to see the right, let us strive on to finish the work we are in; to bind up the nation's wounds; to care for him who shall have borne the battle, and for his widow, and his orphan—to do all which may achieve and cherish a just, and a lasting peace, among ourselves, and with all nations.

1865

1. Lincoln alludes to Jesus' statement in the Sermon on the Mount—"Judge not, that ye be not judged" (Matthew vii.1)—and to God's curse on Adam—"In the sweat of thy face shalt thou eat bread, till thou return unto the ground" (Genesis iii.19).
2. From Jesus' speech to his disciples (Matthew xviii.7).
3. Psalms xix.9.

Thomas Jefferson

ORIGINAL DRAFT OF THE DECLARATION OF INDEPENDENCE

A Declaration of the Representatives of the UNITED STATES OF AMERICA, in General Congress Assembled.

When in the course of human events it becomes necessary for a people to advance from that subordination in which they have hitherto remained, & to assume among the powers of the earth the equal & independant station to which the laws of nature & of nature's god entitle them, a decent respect to the opinions of mankind requires that they should declare the causes which impel them to the change.

We hold these truths to be sacred & undeniable; that all men are created equal & independant, that from that equal creation they derive rights inherent & inalienable, among which are the preservation of life, & liberty, & the spirit of happiness; that to secure these ends, governments are instituted among men, deriving their just powers from the consent of the governed; that whenever any form of government shall become destructive of these ends, it is the right of the people to alter or to abolish it, & to institute new government, laying it's foundation on such principles & organising it's powers in such form, as to them shall seem most likely to effect their safety & happiness. prudence indeed will dictate that governments long established should not be changed for light & transient causes: and accordingly all experience hath shewn that mankind are more disposed to suffer while evils are sufferable, than to right themselves by abolishing the forms to which they are accustomed. but when a long train of abuses & usurpations, begun at a distinguished period, & pursuing invariably the same object, evinces a design to subject them to arbitrary power, it is their right, it is their duty, to throw off such government & to provide new guards for their future security. such has been the patient sufferance of these colonies; & such is now the necessity which constrains them to expunge their former systems of government. the history of his present majesty, is a history of unremitting injuries and usurpations, among which no one fact stands single or solitary to contradict the uniform tenor of the rest, all of which have in direct object the establishment of an absolute tyranny over these states. to prove this, let facts be submitted to a candid world, for the truth of which we pledge a faith yet unsullied by falsehood.

he has refused his assent to laws the most wholesome and necessary for the public good:

he has forbidden his governors to pass laws of immediate & pressing importance, unless suspended in their operation till his assent should be obtained; and when so suspended, he has neglected utterly to attend to them.

he has refused to pass other laws for the accommodation of large districts of people unless those people would relinquish the right of representation, a right inestimable to them, & formidable to tyrants alone:[1]

he has dissolved Representative houses repeatedly & continually, for opposing with manly firmness his invasions on the rights of the people:

he has refused for a long space of time to cause others to be elected, whereby the legislative powers, incapable of annihilation, have returned to the people at large for their exercise, the state remaining in the mean time exposed to all the dangers of invasion from without, &, convulsions within:

he has suffered the administration of justice totally to cease in some of these colonies, refusing his assent to laws for establishing judiciary powers:

he has made our judges dependant on his will alone, for the tenure of their offices, and amount of their salaries:

he has erected a multitude of new offices by a self-assumed power, & sent hither swarms of officers to harrass our people & eat out their substance:

he has kept among us in times of peace standing armies & ships of war:

he has affected[2] to render the military, independent of & superior to the civil power:

he has combined with others to subject us to a jurisdiction foreign to our constitutions and unacknowledged by our laws; giving his assent to their pretended acts of legislation, for quartering large bodies of armed troops among us;

    for protecting them by a mock-trial from punishment for any murders they should commit on the inhabitants of these states;

    for cutting off our trade with all parts of the world;

    for imposing taxes on us without our consent;

    for depriving us of the benefits of trial by jury

he has endeavored to prevent the population of these states; for that purpose obstructing the laws for naturalization of foreigners; refus-

---

1. At this point in the manuscript a strip containing the following clause is inserted: "He called together legislative bodies at places unusual, unco[mfortable, & distant from] the depository of their public records for the sole purpose of fatiguing [them into compliance] with his measures:" Missing parts in the Library of Congress text are supplied from the copy made by Jefferson for George Wythe. This copy is in the New York Public Library. The fact that this passage was omitted from John Adams's transcript suggests that it was not a part of Jefferson's original rough draft.

2. Tried.

ing to pass others to encourage their migrations hither; & raising the conditions of new appropriations of lands;

> for transporting us beyond seas to be tried for pretended offences:
> for taking away our charters & altering fundamentally the forms of our governments;
> for suspending our own legislatures & declaring themselves invested with power to legislate for us in all cases whatsoever:

he has abdicated government here, withdrawing his governors, & declaring us out of his allegiance & protection:

he has plundered our seas, ravaged our coats, burnt our towns & destroyed the lives of our people:

he is at this time transporting large armies of foreign mercenaries to compleat the works of death, desolation & tyranny, already begun with circumstances of cruelty & perfidy unworthy the head of a civilized nation:

he has endeavored to bring on the inhabitants of our frontiers the merciless Indian savages, whose known rule of warfare is an undistinguished destruction of all ages, sexes, & conditions of existence:

he has incited treasonable insurrections of our fellow-citizens, with the allurements of forfeiture & confiscation of our property:

he has waged cruel war against human nature itself, violating it's most sacred rights of life & liberty in the persons of a distant people who never offended him, captivating & carrying them into slavery in another hemisphere, or to incur miserable death in their transportation thither. this piratical warfare, the opprobrium of *infidel* powers, is the warfare of the CHRISTIAN king of Great Britain, determined to keep open a market where MEN should be bought & sold; he has prostituted his negative for suppressing every legislative attempt to prohibit or to restrain this execrable commerce: and that this assemblage of horrors might want no fact of distinguished die, he is now exciting those very people to rise in arms among us, and to purchase that liberty of which *he* has deprived them, by murdering the people upon whom *he* also obtruded them; thus paying off former crimes committed against the *liberties* of one people, with crimes which he urges them to commit against the *lives* of another.

in every stage of these oppressions we have petitioned for redress in the most humble terms; our repeated petitions have been answered by repeated injury. a prince whose character is thus marked by every act which may define a tyrant, is unfit to be the ruler of a people who mean to be free. future ages will scarce believe that the hardiness of one man, adventured within the short compass of twelve years only, on so many acts of tyranny without a mask, over a people fostered & fixed in principles of liberty.

Nor have we been wanting in attentions to our British brethren. we have warned them from time to time of attempts by their legislature to extend a jurisdiction over these our states. we have reminded them of the circumstances of our emigration & settlement here, no one of which could warrant so strange a pretension: that these were effected at the expence of our own blood & treasure, unassisted by the wealth or the strength of Great Britain: that in constituting indeed our several forms of government, we had adopted one common king, thereby laying a foundation for perpetual league & amity with them; but that submission to their [Parliament, was no Part of our Constitution, nor ever in Idea, if History may be]³ credited: and we appealed to their native justice & magnanimity, as to the ties of our common kindred to disavow these usurpations which were likely to interrupt our correspondence & connection. they too have been deaf to the voice of justice & of consanguinity, & when occasions have been given them, by the regular course of their laws, of removing from their councils the disturbers of our harmony, they have by their free election re-established them in power. at this very time too they are permitting their chief magistrate to send over not only soldiers of our common blood, but Scotch & foreign mercenaries to invade & deluge us in blood. these facts have given the last stab to agonizing affection, and manly spirit bids us to renounce for ever these unfeeling brethren. we must endeavor to forget our former love for them, and to hold them as we hold the rest of mankind, enemies in war, in peace friends. we might have been a free & a great people together; but a communication of grandeur & of freedom it seems is below their dignity. be it so, since they will have it: the road to glory & happiness is open to us too; we will climb it in a separate state, and acquiesce in the necessity which pronounces our everlasting Adieu!

We therefore the representatives of the United States of America in General Congress assembled do, in the name & by authority of the good people of these states, reject and renounce all allegiance & subjection to the kings of Great Britain & all others who may hereafter claim by, through, or under them; we utterly dissolve & break off all political connection which may have heretofore subsisted between us & the people or parliament of Great Britain; and finally we do assert and declare these colonies to be free and independant states, and that as free & independant states they shall hereafter have power to levy war, conclude peace, contract alliances, establish commerce, & to do all other acts and things which independant states may of right do. And for the support of this declaration we mutually pledge to each other our lives, our fortunes, & our sacred honour.
1776

---

3. An illegible passage is supplied from John Adams's transcription.

Thomas Jefferson and Others

THE DECLARATION OF INDEPENDENCE

In Congress, July 4, 1776
The unanimous Declaration of the
thirteen united States of America

When in the Course of human events it becomes necessary for one people to dissolve the political bands which have connected them with another, and to assume among the powers of the earth, the separate and equal station to which the Laws of Nature and of Nature's God entitle them, a decent respect to the opinions of mankind requires that they should declare the causes which impel them to the separation.

We hold these truths to be self-evident, that all men are created equal, that they are endowed by their Creator with certain unalienable Rights, that among these are Life, Liberty and the pursuit of Happiness. That to secure these rights, Governments are instituted among Men, deriving their just powers from the consent of the governed. That whenever any Form of Government becomes destructive of these ends, it is the Right of the People to alter or to abolish it, and to institute new Government, laying its foundation on such principles and organizing its powers in such form, as to them shall seem most likely to affect their Safety and Happiness. Prudence, indeed, will dictate that Governments long established should not be changed for light and transient causes; and accordingly all experience hath shewn that mankind are more disposed to suffer, while evils are sufferable, than to right themselves by abolishing the forms to which they are accustomed. But when a long train of abuses and usurpations, pursuing invariably the same Object evinces a design to reduce them under absolute Despotism, it is their right, it is their duty, to throw off such Government, and to provide new Guards for their future security. Such has been the patient sufferance of these Colonies; and such is now the necessity which constrains them to alter their former Systems of Government. The history of the present King of Great Britain is a history of repeated injuries and usurpations, all having in direct object the establishment of an absolute Tyranny over these States. To prove this, let Facts be submitted to a candid world.

He has refused his Assent to Laws, the most wholesome and necessary for the public good.

He has forbidden his Government to pass laws of immediate and pressing importance, unless suspended in their operation till his Assent should be obtained; and when so suspended, he has utterly neglected to attend to them.

He has refused to pass other Laws for the accommodation of large districts of people, unless those people would relinquish the right of Representation in the Legislature, a right inestimable to them and formidable to tyrants only.

He has called together legislative bodies at places unusual, uncomfortable, and distant from the depository of their Public Records, for the sole purpose of fatiguing them into compliance with his measures.

He has dissolved Representative Houses repeatedly, for opposing with manly firmness his invasions on the rights of the people.

He has refused for a long time, after such dissolutions, to cause others to be elected; whereby the Legislative Powers, incapable of Annihilation, have returned to the People at large for their exercise; the State remaining in the mean time exposed to all the dangers of invasion from without, and convulsions within.

He has endeavored to prevent the population of these States; for that purpose obstructing the Laws for Naturalization of Foreigners; refusing to pass others to encourage their migration hither, and raising the conditions of new Appropriations of Lands.

He has obstructed the Administration of Justice, by refusing his Assent to Laws for establishing Judiciary Powers.

He has made Judges dependent on his Will alone, for the tenure of their offices, and the amount and payment of their salaries.

He has erected a multitude of New Offices, and sent hither swarms of Officers to harass our people, and eat out their substance.

He has kept among us, in times of peace, Standing Armies without the Consent of our legislatures.

He has affected to render the Military independent of and superior to the Civil Power.

He has combined with others to subject us to a jurisdiction foreign to our constitution, and unacknowledged by our laws; giving his Assent to their Acts of pretended Legislation: For quartering large bodies of armed troops among us: For protecting them, by a mock Trial, from punishment for any Murders which they should commit on the Inhabitants of these States: For cutting off our Trade with all parts of the world: For imposing Taxes on us without our Consent: For depriving us in many cases, of the benefits of Trial by Jury; For transporting us beyond Seas to be tried for pretended offenses: for abolishing the free System of English Laws in a neighboring Province, establishing therein an Arbitrary government, and enlarging its Boundaries so as to render it at once an example and fit instrument for introducing the same absolute rule into these Colonies: For taking away our Charters, abolishing our most valuable Laws and altering fundamentally the Forms of our Governments: For suspending our own Legislatures, and declaring themselves invested with power to legislate for us in all cases whatsoever.

He has abdicated Government here, by declaring us out of his Protection and waging War against us.

He has plundered our seas, ravaged our Coasts, burnt our towns, and destroyed the lives of our people.

He is at this time transporting large Armies of foreign Mercenaries to complete the works of death, desolation and tyranny, already begun with circumstances of Cruelty & Perfidy scarcely paralleled in the most barbarous ages, and totally unworthy the Head of a civilized nation.

He has constrained our fellow Citizens taken Captive on the high Seas to bear Arms against their Country, to become the executioners of their friends and Brethren, or to fall themselves by their Hands.

He has excited domestic insurrections amongst us, and has endeavored to bring on the inhabitants of our frontiers, the merciless Indian Savages, whose known rule of warfare, is an undistinguished destruction of all ages, sexes, and conditions.

In every stage of these Oppressions We have Petitioned for Redress in the most humble terms: Our repeated Petitions have been answered only by repeated injury. A Prince, whose character is thus marked by every act which may define a Tyrant, is unfit to be the ruler of a free people.

Nor have We been wanting in attention to our British brethren. We have warned them from time to time of attempts by their legislature to extend an unwarrantable jurisdiction over us. We have reminded them of the circumstances of our emigration and settlement here. We have appealed to their native justice and magnanimity, and we have conjured them by the ties of our common kindred to disavow these usurpations, which would inevitably interrupt our connections and correspondence. They too have been deaf to the voice of justice and of consanguinity. We must, therefore, acquiesce in the necessity, which denounces our Separation, and hold them, as we hold the rest of mankind, Enemies in War, in Peace Friends.

We, THEREFORE the Representatives of the UNITED STATES OF AMERICA, in General Congress, Assembled, appealing to the Supreme Judge of the world for the rectitude of our intentions, do, in the Name, and by Authority of the good People of these Colonies, solemnly publish and declare, That these United Colonies are, and of Right ought to be FREE AND INDEPENDENT STATES; that they are Absolved from all Allegiance to the British Crown, and that all political connection between them and the State of Great Britain, is and ought to be totally dissolved; and that as Free and Independent States, they have full Power to levy War, conclude Peace, contract Alliances, establish Commerce, and to do all other Acts and Things which Independent States may of right do. And for the support of this Declaration, with a firm reliance on the protection of Divine Providence, we mutually pledge to each other our Lives, our Fortunes, and our sacred Honor.

1776

QUESTIONS

1. *The Declaration of Independence was addressed to several audiences: the king of Great Britain, the people of Great Britain, the people of America, and the world at large. Show ways in which the final draft was adapted for its several audiences.*
2. *Examine the second paragraph of each version closely. How have the revisions in the final version increased its effectiveness over the first draft?*
3. *The Declaration has often been called a classic example of deductive argument: setting up general statements, relating particular cases to them, and drawing conclusions. Trace this pattern through the document, noting the way each part is developed. Would the document have been as effective if the long middle part had either come first or been left our entirely? Explain.*
4. *Find the key terms and phrases of the Declaration (such as "these truths . . . self-evident," "created equal," "unalienable rights," and so on) and determine how fully they are defined by the contexts in which they occur. Why are no formal definitions given for them?*
5. *The signers of the Declaration appeal both to general principles and to factual evidence in presenting their case. Which of the appeals to principle could still legitimately be made today by a nation eager to achieve independence? In other words, how far does the Declaration reflect unique events of history and how far does it reflect universal aspirations and ideals?*

Carl Becker

DEMOCRACY

Democracy, like liberty or science or progress, is a word with which we are all so familiar that we rarely take the trouble to ask what we mean by it. It is a term, as the devotees of semantics say, which has no "referent" —there is no precise or palpable thing or object which we all think of when the word is pronounced. On the contrary, it is a word which connotes different things to different people, a kind of conceptual Glad-stone bag which, with a little manipulation, can be made to accommodate almost any collection of social facts we may wish to carry about in it. In it we can as easily pack a dictatorship as any other form of government. We have only to stretch the concept to include any form of government supported by a majority of the people, for whatever reasons and by whatever means of expressing assent, and before we know it the empire of Napoleon, the Soviet regime of Stalin, and the Fascist systems of Mussolini and Hitler are all safely in the bag. But if this is what we mean by democracy, then virtually all forms of government are democratic, since virtually all governments, except in times of revolution, rest upon the explicit or implicit consent of the people. In order to discuss democracy intelligently it will be necessary, therefore, to define it, to attach to the word a sufficiently precise meaning to avoid the confusion which is not infrequently the chief result of such discussions.

All human institutions, we are told, have their ideal forms laid away in heaven, and we do not need to be told that the actual institutions conform but indifferently to these ideal counterparts. It would be possible then to define democracy either in terms of the ideal or in terms of the real form—to define it as government of the people, by the people, for the people; or to define it as government of the people, by the politicians, for whatever pressure groups can get their interests taken care of. But as a historian I am naturally disposed to be satisfied with the meaning which, in the history of politics, men have commonly attributed to the word—a meaning, needless to say, which derives partly from the experience and partly from the aspirations of mankind. So regarded, the term democracy refers primarily to a form of government, and it has always meant government by the many as opposed to government by the one—government by the people as opposed to government by a tyrant, a dictator, or an absolute monarch. This is the most general meaning of the word as men have commonly understood it.

In this antithesis there are, however, certain implications, always tacitly understood, which give a more precise meaning to the term. Peisistratus, for example, was supported by a majority of the people, but his government was never regarded as a democracy for all that. Caesar's power derived from a popular mandate, conveyed through established republican forms, but that did not make his government any the less a dictatorship. Napoleon called his government a democratic empire, but no one, least of all Napoleon himself, doubted that he had destroyed the last vestiges of the democratic republic. Since the Greeks first used the term, the essential test of democratic government has always been this: the source of political authority must be and remain in the people and not in the ruler. A democratic government has always meant one in which the citizens, or a sufficient numer of them to represent more or less effectively the common will, freely act from time to time, and according to established forms, to appoint or recall the magistrates and to enact or revoke the laws by which the community is governed. This I take to be the meaning which history has impressed upon the term democracy as a form of government.

1941

E. B. White

DEMOCRACY

We received a letter from the Writers' War Board the other day asking for a statement on "The Meaning of Democracy." It presumably is our duty to comply with such a request, and it is certainly our pleasure.

Surely the Board knows what democracy is. It is the line that forms on the right. It is the don't in don't shove. It is the hole in the stuffed shirt through which the sawdust slowly trickles; it is the dent in the high hat. Democracy is the recurrent suspicion that more than half of the people are right more than half of the time. It is the feeling of privacy in the voting booths, the feeling of communion in the libraries, the feeling of vitality everywhere. Democracy is a letter to the editor. Democracy is the score at the beginning of the ninth. It is an idea which hasn't been disproved yet, a song the words of which have not gone bad. It's the mustard on the hot dog and the cream in the rationed coffee. Democracy is a request from a War Board, in the middle of a morning in the middle of a war, wanting to know what democracy is.

1943

QUESTIONS

1. White's piece is dated July 3, 1943, the middle of World War II. How did the occasion shape what White says about democracy?
2. Look up "democracy" in a standard desk dictionary. Of the several meanings given, which one best applies to White's definition? Does more than one apply?
3. Translate White's definition into non-metaphorical language. (For example, "It is the line that forms on the right" might be translated by "It has no special privileges.") Determine what is lost in the translation, or, in other words, what White has gained by using figurative language.

E. B. White

FOUR LETTERS ON FREEDOM OF EXPRESSION

[*In an editorial published on November 27, 1947, the* Herald Tribune, *though somewhat grudgingly, supported the right of the movie industry to blacklist the "Hollywood Ten" and any others who refused to answer questions before J. Parnell Thomas's House Un-American Activities Committee. The following letter, White's reaction to the editorial, was published in the* Tribune *on December 2.*]

To the New York Herald Tribune

New York, New York
. November 29, 1947

TO THE NEW YORK HERALD TRIBUNE:

I am a member of a party of one, and I live in an age of fear. Nothing lately has unsettled my party and raised my fears so much as your editorial, on Thanksgiving Day, suggesting that employees should be required to state their beliefs in order to hold their jobs. The idea is inconsistent with our Constitutional theory and has been stubbornly opposed by watchful men since the early days of the Republic. It's hard for me to believe that the *Herald Tribune* is backing away from the fight, and I can only assume that your editorial writer, in a hurry to get home for Thanksgiving, tripped over the First Amendment and thought it was the office cat.

The investigation of alleged Communists by the Thomas committee has been a confusing spectacle for all of us. I believe its implications are widely misunderstood and that the outcome is grave beyond exaggerating. The essence of our political theory in this country is that a man's conscience shall be a private, not a public affair, and that only his deeds and words shall be open to survey, censure and to punishment. The idea is a decent one, and it works. It is an idea that cannot safely be compromised with, lest it be utterly destroyed. It cannot be modified even under circumstances where, for security reasons, the temptation to modify it is great.

I think security in critical times takes care of itself if the people and the institutions take care of themselves. First in line is the press. Security, for me, took a tumble not when I read that there were Communists in Hollywood but when I read your editorial in praise of loyalty testing and thought control. If a man is in health, he doesn't need to take anybody else's temperature to know where he is going. If a newspaper or a motion picture company is in health, it can get rid of Communists and spies simply by reading proof and by watching previews.

I hold that it would be improper for any committee or any employer to examine my conscience. They wouldn't know how to get into it, they wouldn't know what to do when they got in there, and I wouldn't let them in anyway. Like other Americans, my acts and my words are open to inspection—not my thoughts or my political affiliation (As I pointed out, I am a member of a party of one.) Your editorialist said he hoped the companies in checking for loyalty would use their powers sparingly and wisely. That is a wistful idea. One need only watch totalitarians at work to see that once men gain power over other men's minds, that power is never used sparingly and wisely, but lavishly and brutally and with unspeakable results. If I must declare today that I am not a Communist, tomorrow I shall have to testify that I am not a Unitarian. And the day after, that I never belonged to a dahlia club.

It is not a crime to believe anything at all in America. To date it has not been declared illegal to belong to the Communist party. Yet ten men have been convicted not of wrongdoing but of wrong believing. That is news in this country, and if I have not misread history, it is bad news.

E. B. WHITE

[On the same page on the same day that White's November 29 letter was published in the Tribune, another editorial appeared entitled "The Party of One." It said that people like Mr. White "have been with us since the dawn of civilization. They have always been highly valuable elements in our civilization and nearly always as destructive as they have been valuable." Members of the party of one were also characterized as "probably the most dangerous single elements in our confused and complicated society."

White's reply to the "Party of One" editorial, appeared on December 9 under the heading "Mr. White Believes Us Needlessly Unkind."]

To the New York Herald Tribune

New York
Dec. 4, 1947

TO THE NEW YORK HERALD TRIBUNE:

The editorial that you wrote about me illustrated what I meant about the loyalty check system and about what would happen if it got going in the industrial world. My letter, expressing a dissenting opinion, was a letter that any conscientious reader might write to his newspaper, and you answered it by saying I belonged to "probably the most dangerous element in our society." Thus a difference of opinion became suddenly a mark of infamy. A man who disagreed with a Tribune editorial used to be called plucky—now he's called dangerous. By your own definition I already belong among the unemployables.

You said that in these times we need "new concepts and new principles" to combat subversion. It seems to me the loyalty check in industry is not a new principle at all. It is like the "new look,"[1] which is really the old, old look, slightly tinkered up. The principle of demanding an expression of political conformity as the price of a job is the principle of hundred percentism. It is not new and it is blood brother of witch burning.

I don't know why I should be bawling out the *Herald Tribune* or why the *Herald Tribune* should be bawling out me. I read those Bert Andrews pieces[2] and got a new breath of fresh air. Then I turned in a dissenting opinion about an editorial and got hit over the head with a stick of wood. These times are too edgy. It is obvious to everyone that the fuss about loyalty arises from fear of war with Russia, and from the natural feeling that we should clear our decks of doubtful characters. Well, I happen to believe that we can achieve reasonably clear decks if we continue to apply our civil rights and duties equally to all citizens, even to citizens of opposite belief. That may be a dangerous and false idea, but my holding it does not necessarily make me a dangerous and false man, and I wish that the *Herald Tribune* next time it sits down to write a piece about me and my party would be good enough to make the distinction. Right now it's a pretty important distinction to make.

E. B. WHITE

[Determined to have the last word, the Tribune printed a parenthetical editorial comment right underneath White's letter. The comment began "Perhaps we were over-emphatic in our disagreement with Mr. White, but since the same editorial which suggested that he belonged to a 'dangerous element' also said that it was a 'highly valuable' element, he can scarcely hold that we were attaching any badge of 'infamy' to him." The editor went on to express the Tribune's regard for White, to deny that its editors were the slightest bit afraid of war with Russia, and to state that they continued to feel that Communism was "exploiting toleration in order to destroy toleration." The comment concluded that "We may be misguided in our attempts to deal with it, but it seems to us that Mr. White fails to deal with it at all."]

* * *

1. A major change in women's fashion introduced in 1947.
2. Bert Andrews, chief of the Washington news bureau of the *New York Herald Tribune*, won a Pulitzer Prize for his reporting on loyalty cases in 1947.

To the Editor of the Ellsworth (Maine) American

[North Brooklin, Me.]
January 1, 1976

To THE EDITOR:

I think it might be useful to stop viewing fences for a moment and take a close look at *Esquire* magazine's new way of doing business. In February, *Esquire* will publish a long article by Harrison E. Salisbury, for which Mr. Salisbury will receive no payment from *Esquire* but will receive $40,000 from the Xerox Corporation—plus another $15,000 for expenses. This, it would seem to me, is not only a new idea in publishing, it charts a clear course for the erosion of the free press in America. Mr. Salisbury is a former associate editor of the *New York Times* and should know better. *Esquire* is a reputable sheet and should know better. But here we go—the Xerox–Salisbury–*Esquire* axis in full cry!

A news story about this amazing event in the December 14th issue of the *Times* begins: "Officials of *Esquire* magazine and of the Xerox Corporation report no adverse reactions, so far, to the announcement that *Esquire* will publish a 23-page article [about travels through America] in February 'sponsored' by Xerox." Herewith I am happy to turn in my adverse reaction even if it's the first one across the line.

Esquire, according to the *Times* story, attempts to justify its new payment system (get the money from a sponsor) by assuring us that Mr. Salisbury will not be tampered with by Xerox; his hand and his pen will be free. If Xerox likes what he writes about America, Xerox will run a "low keyed full-page ad preceding the article" and another ad at the end of it. From this advertising, *Esquire* stands to pick up $115,000, and Mr. Salisbury has already picked up $40,000, traveling, all expenses paid, through this once happy land. . . .

Apparently Mr. Salisbury had a momentary qualm about taking on the Xerox job. The *Times* reports him as saying, "At first I thought, gee whiz, should I do this?" But he quickly conquered his annoying doubts and remembered that big corporations had in the past been known to sponsor "cultural enterprises," such as opera. The emergence of a magazine reporter as a cultural enterprise is as stunning a sight as the emergence of a butterfly from a cocoon. Mr. Salisbury must have felt great, escaping from his confinement.

Well, it doesn't take a giant intellect to detect in all this the shadow of disaster. If magazines decide to farm out their writers to advertisers and accept the advertiser's payment to the writer and to the magazine, then the periodicals of this country will be far down the drain and will become so fuzzy as to be indistinguishable from the controlled press in other parts of the world.

E. B. White

[*Some weeks after his letter on the Xerox–Esquire–Salisbury arrangement was published, White received a letter of inquiry from W. B. Jones,
Director of Communications Operations at Xerox Corporation, outlining
the ground rules of the corporation's sponsorship of the Salisbury piece and
concluding: "With these ground rules, do you still see something sinister in
the sponsorship? The question is put seriously, because if a writer of your
achievement and insight—after considering the terms of the arrangement
—still sees this kind of corporate sponsorship as leading the periodicals of
this country toward the controlled press of other parts of the world, then we
may well reconsider our plans to underwrite similar projects in the future."
White's reply follows.*]

To W. B. Jones

North Brooklin
January 30, 1976

Dear Mr. Jones:

In extending my remarks on sponsorship, published in the Ellsworth
American, I want to limit the discussion to the press—that is, to newspapers and magazines. I'll not speculate about television, as television is
outside my experience and I have no ready opinion about sponsorship in
that medium.

In your recent letter to me, you ask whether, having studied your
ground rules for proper conduct in sponsoring a magazine piece, I still see
something sinister in the sponsorship. Yes, I do. Sinister may not be the
right word, but I see something ominous and unhealthy when a corporation underwrites an article in a magazine of general circulation. This is
not, essentially, the old familiar question of an advertiser trying to
influence editorial content; almost everyone is acquainted with that
common phenomenon. Readers are aware that it is always present but
usually in a rather subdued or non-threatening form. Xerox's sponsoring
of a specific writer on a specific occasion for a specific article is something
quite different. No one, as far as I know, accuses Xerox of trying to
influence editorial opinion. But many people are wondering why a large
corporation placed so much money on a magazine piece, why the writer
of the piece was willing to get paid in so unusual a fashion, and why
Esquire was ready and willing to have an outsider pick up the tab. These
are reasonable questions.

The press in our free country is reliable and useful not because of its
good character but because of its great diversity. As long as there are
many owners, each pursuing his own brand of truth, we the people have
the opportunity to arrive at the truth and to dwell in the light. The
multiplicity of ownership is crucial. It's only when there are a few
owners, or, as in a government-controlled press, one owner, that the truth
becomes elusive and the light fails. For a citizen in our free society, it is

an enormous privilege and a wonderful protection to have access to hundreds of periodicals, each peddling its own belief. There is safety in numbers: the papers expose each other's follies and peccadillos, correct each other's mistakes, and cancel out each other's biases. The reader is free to range around in the whole editorial bouillabaisse and explore it for the one clam that matters—the truth.

When a large corporation or a rich individual underwrites an article in a magazine, the picture changes: the ownership of that magazine has been diminished, the outline of the magazine has been blurred. In the case the Salisbury piece, it was as though *Esquire* had gone on relief, was accepting its first welfare payment, and was not its own man anymore. The editor protests that he accepts full responsibility for the text and that Xerox had nothing to do with the whole business. But the fact remains that, despite his full acceptance of responsibility, he somehow did not get around to paying the bill. This is unsettling and I think unhealthy. Whenever money changes hands, something goes along with it—an intangible something that varies with the circumstances. It would be hard to resist the suspicion that *Esquire* feels indebted to Xerox, that Mr. Salisbury feels indebted to both, and that the ownership, or sovereignty, of *Esquire* has been nibbled all around the edges.

Sponsorship in the press is an invitation to corruption and abuse. The temptations are great, and there is an opportunist behind every bush. A funded article is a tempting morsel for any publication—particularly for one that is having a hard time making ends meet. A funded assignment is a tempting dish for a writer, who may pocket a much larger fee than he is accustomed to getting. And sponsorship is attractive to the sponsor himself, who, for one reason or another, feels an urge to penetrate the editorial columns after being so long pent up in the advertising pages. These temptations are real, and if the barriers were to be let down I believe corruption and abuse would soon follow. Not all corporations would approach subsidy in the immaculate way Xerox did or in the same spirit of benefaction. There are a thousand reasons for someone's wishing to buy his way into print, many of them unpalatable, all of them to some degree self-serving. Buying and selling space in news columns could become a serious disease of the press. If it reached epidemic proportions, it could destroy the press. I don't want IBM or the National Rifle Association providing me with a funded spectacular when I open my paper, I want to read what the editor and the publisher have managed to dig up on their own—and paid for out of the till. . . .

My affection for the free press in a democracy goes back a long way. My love for it was my first and greatest love. If I felt a shock at the news of the Salisbury–Xerox–*Esquire* arrangement, it was because the sponsorship principle seemed to challenge and threaten everything I believe in: that the press must not only be free, it must be fiercely independent—to

survive and to serve. Not all papers are fiercely independent, God knows, but there are always enough of them around to provide a core of integrity and an example that others feel obliged to steer by. The funded article is not in itself evil, but it is the beginning of evil and it is an invitation to evil. I hope the invitation will not again be extended, and, if extended, I hope it will be declined.

About a hundred and fifty years ago, Tocqueville wrote: "The journalists of the United States are generally in a very humble position, with a scanty education and a vulgar turn of mind." Today, we chuckle at this antique characterization. But about fifty years ago, when I was a young journalist, I had the good fortune to encounter an editor who fitted the description quite closely. Harold Ross, who founded the New Yorker, was deficient in education and had—at least to all outward appearances—a vulgar turn of mind. What he did possess, though, was the ferocity of independence. He was having a tough time finding money to keep his foundering little sheet alive, yet he was determined that neither money nor influence would ever corrupt his dream or deflower his text. His boiling point was so low as to be comical. The faintest suggestion of the shadow of advertising in his news and editorial columns would cause him to erupt. He would explode in anger, the building would reverberate with his wrath, and his terrible swift sword would go flashing up and down the corridors. For a young man, it was an impressive sight and a memorable one. Fifty years have not dimmed for me either the spectacle of Ross's ferocity or my own early convictions—which were identical with his. He has come to my mind often while I've been composing this reply to your inquiry.

I hope I've clarified by a little bit my feelings about the autonomy of the press and the dangers of sponsorship of articles. Thanks for giving me the chance to speak my piece.

Sincerely,
E. B. WHITE

[Mr. Jones wrote and thanked White for "telling me what I didn't want to hear." In May another letter arrived from Jones saying that Xerox had decided not to underwrite any more articles in the press and that they were convinced it was "the right decision."]

Walter Lippmann

THE INDISPENSABLE OPPOSITION

Were they pressed hard enough, most men would probably confess
that political freedom—that is to say, the right to speak freely and to act
in opposition—is a noble ideal rather than a practical necessity. As the
case for freedom is generally put today, the argument lends itself to this
feeling. It is made to appear that, whereas each man claims his freedom as
a matter of right, the freedom he accords to other men is a matter of
toleration. Thus, the defense of freedom of opinion tends to rest not on
its substantial, beneficial, and indispensable consequences, but on a
somewhat eccentric, a rather vaguely benevolent, attachment to an
abstraction.

It is all very well to say with Voltaire, "I wholly disapprove of what you
say, but will defend to the death your right to say it," but as a matter of
fact most men will not defend to the death the rights of other men: if they
disapprove sufficiently what other men say, they will somehow suppress
those men if they can.

So, if this is the best that can be said for liberty of opinion, that a man
must tolerate his opponents because everyone has a "right" to say what
he pleases, then we shall find that liberty of opinion is a luxury, safe only
in pleasant times when men can be tolerant because they are not deeply
and vitally concerned.

Yet actually, as a matter of historic fact, there is a much stronger
foundation for the great constitutional right of freedom of speech, and as
a matter of practical human experience there is a much more compelling
reason for cultivating the habits of free men. We take, it seems to me, a
naïvely self-righteous view when we argue as if the right of our opponents to speak were something that we protect because we are magnanimous, noble, and unselfish. The compelling reason why, if liberty of
opinion did not exist, we should have to invent it, why it will eventually
have to be restored in all civilized countries where it is now suppressed, is
that we must protect the right of our opponents to speak because we
must hear what they have to say.

We miss the whole point when we imagine that we tolerate the
freedom of our political opponents as we tolerate a howling baby next
door, as we put up with the blasts from our neighbor's radio because we
are too peaceable to heave a brick through the window. If this were all
there is to freedom of opinion, that we are too goodnatured or too timid
to do anything about our opponents and our critics except to let them
talk, it would be difficult to say whether we are tolerant because we are
magnanimous or because we are lazy, because we have strong principles
or because we lack serious convictions, whether we have the hospitality

of an inquiring mind or the indifference of an empty mind. And so, if we truly wish to understand why freedom is necessary in a civilized society, we must begin by realizing that, because freedom of discussion improves our own opinions, the liberties of other men are our own vital necessity.

We are much closer to the essence of the matter, not when we quote Voltaire, but when we go to the doctor and pay him to ask us the most embarrassing questions and to prescribe the most disagreeable diet. When we pay the doctor to exercise complete freedom of speech about the cause and cure of our stomachache, we do not look upon ourselves as tolerant and magnanimous, and worthy to be admired by ourselves. We have enough common sense to know that if we threaten to put the doctor in jail because we do not like the diagnosis and the prescription it will be unpleasant for the doctor, to be sure, but equally unpleasant for our own stomachache. That is why even the most ferocious dictator would rather be treated by a doctor who was free to think and speak the truth than by his own Minister of Propaganda. For there is a point, the point at which things really matter, where the freedom of others is no longer a question of their right but of our own need.

The point at which we recognize this need is much higher in some men than in others. The totalitarian rulers think they do not need the freedom of an opposition: they exile, imprison, or shoot their opponents. We have concluded on the basis of practical experience, which goes back to Magna Carta and beyond, that we need the opposition. We pay the opposition salaries out of the public treasury.

In so far as the usual apology for freedom of speech ignores this experience, it becomes abstract and eccentric rather than concrete and human. The emphasis is generally put on the right to speak, as if all that mattered were that the doctor should be free to go out into the park and explain to the vacant air why I have a stomachache. Surely that is a miserable caricature of the great civic right which men have bled and died for. What really matters is that the doctor should tell *me* what ails me, that I should listen to him; that if I do not like what he says I should be free to call in another doctor; and that then the first doctor should have to listen to the second doctor; and that out of all the speaking and listening, the give-and-take of opinions, the truth should be arrived at.

This is the creative principle of freedom of speech, not that it is a system for the tolerating of error, but that it is a system for finding the truth. It may not produce the truth, or the whole truth all the time, or often, or in some cases ever. But if the truth can be found, there is no other system which will normally and habitually find so much truth. Until we have thoroughly understood this principle, we shall not know why we must value our liberty, or how we can protect and develop it.

Let us apply this principle to the system of public speech in a totalitarian state. We may, without any serious falsification, picture a condition of affairs in which the mass of the people are being addressed through one broadcasting system by one man and his chosen subordinates. The orators speak. The audience listens but cannot and dare not speak back. It is a system of one-way communication; the opinions of the rulers are broadcast outwardly to the mass of the people. But nothing comes back to the rulers from the people except the cheers; nothing returns in the way of knowledge of forgotten facts, hidden feelings, neglected truths, and practical suggestions.

But even a dictator cannot goven by his own one-way inspiration alone. In practice, therefore, the totalitarian rulers get back the reports of the secret police and of their party henchmen down among the crowd. If these reports are competent, the rulers may manage to remain in touch with public sentiment. Yet that is not enough to know what the audience feels. The rulers have also to make great decisions that have enormous consequences, and here their system provides virtually no help from the give-and-take of opinion in the nation. So they must either rely on their own intuition, which cannot be permanently and continually inspired, or, if they are intelligent despots, encourage their trusted advisers and their technicians to speak and debate freely in their presence.

On the walls of the houses of Italian peasants one may see inscribed in large letters the legend, "Mussolini is always right." But if that legend is taken seriously by Italian ambassadors, by the Italian General Staff, and by the Ministry of Finance, then all one can say is heaven help Mussolini, heaven help Italy, and the new Emperor of Ethiopia.[1]

For at some point, even in a totalitarian state, it is indispensable that there should exist the freedom of opinion which causes opposing opinions to be debated. As time goes on, that is less and less easy under a despotism; critical discussion disappears as the internal opposition is liquidated in favor of men who think and feel alike. That is why the early successes of despots, of Napoleon I and of Napoleon III, have usually been followed by an irreparable mistake. For in listening only to his yes men—the others being in exile or in concentration camps, or terrified —the despot shuts himself off from the truth that no man can dispense with.

We know all this well enough when we contemplate the dictatorships. But when we try to picture our own system, by way of contrast, what picture do we have in our minds? It is, is it not, that anyone may stand up on his own soapbox and say anything he pleases, like the individuals in Kipling's poem[2] who sit each in his separate star and draw the Thing as they see it for the God of Things as they are. Kipling, perhaps, could do this, since he was a poet. But the ordinary mortal isolated on his separate

1. Benito Mussolini was then dictator of Italy, which he led into World War II; after Italy's conquest of Ethiopia in 1936, he had the Italian king, Victor Emanuel III, proclaimed its emperor.
2. "L'Envoi."

star will have an hallucination, and a citizenry declaiming from separate soapboxes will poison the air with hot and nonsensical confusion.

If the democratic alternative to the totalitarian one-way broadcasts is a row of separate soapboxes, than I submit that the alternative is unworkable, is unreasonable, and is humanly unattractive. It is above all a false alternative. It is not true that liberty has developed among civilized men when anyone is free to set up a soapbox, is free to hire a hall where he may expound his opinions to those who are willing to listen. On the contrary, freedom of speech is established to achieve its essential purpose only when different opinions are expounded in the same hall to the same audience.

For, while the right to talk may be the beginning of freedom, the necessity of listening is what makes the right important. Even in Russia and Germany a man may still stand in an open field and speak his mind. What matters is not the utterance of opinions. What matters is the confrontation of opinions in debate. No man can care profoundly that every fool should say what he likes. Nothing has been accomplished if the wisest man proclaims his wisdom in the middle of the Sahara Desert. This is the shadow. We have the substance of liberty when the fool is compelled to listen to the wise man and learn; when the wise man is compelled to take account of the fool, and to instruct him; when the wise man can increase his wisdom by hearing the judgment of his peers.

That is why civilized men must cherish liberty—as a means of promoting the discovery of truth. So we must not fix our whole attention on the right of anyone to hire his own hall, to rent his own broadcasting station, to distribute his own pamphlets. These rights are incidental; and though they must be preserved, they can be preserved only by regarding them as incidental, as auxiliary to the substance of liberty that must be cherished and cultivated.

Freedom of speech is best conceived, therefore, by having in mind the picture of a place like the American Congress, an assembly where opposing views are represented, where ideas are not merely uttered but debated, or the British Parliament, where men who are free to speak are also compelled to answer. We may picture the true condition of freedom as existing in a place like a court of law, where witnesses testify and are cross-examined, where the lawyer argues against the opposing lawyer before the same judge and in the presence of one jury. We may picture freedom as existing in a forum where the speaker must respond to questions; in a gathering of scientists where the data, the hypothesis, and the conclusion are submitted to men competent to judge them; in a reputable newspaper which not only will publish the opinions of those who disagree but will re-examine its own opinion in the light of what they say.

Thus the essence of freedom of opinion is not in mere toleration as such, but in the debate which toleration provides: it is not in the venting of opinion, but in the confrontation of opinion. That this is the practical substance can readily be understood when we remember how differently we feel and act about the censorship and regulation of opinion purveyed by different media of communication. We find then that, in so far as the medium makes difficult the confrontation of opinion in debate, we are driven towards censorship and regulation.

There is, for example, the whispering campaign, the circulation of anonymous rumors by men who cannot be compelled to prove what they say. They put the utmost strain on our tolerance, and there are few who do not rejoice when the anonymous slanderer is caught, exposed, and punished. At a higher level there is the moving picture, a most powerful medium for conveying ideas, but a medium which does not permit debate. A moving picture cannot be answered effectively by another moving picture; in all free countries there is some censorship of the movies, and there would be more if the producers did not recognize their limitations by avoiding political controversy. There is then the radio. Here debate is difficult: it is not easy to make sure that the speaker is being answered in the presence of the same audience. Inevitably, there is some regulation of the radio.

When we reach the newspaper press, the opportunity for debate is so considerable that discontent cannot grow to the point where under normal conditions there is any disposition to regulate the press. But when newspapers abuse their power by injuring people who have no means of replying, a disposition to regulate the press appears. When we arrive at Congress we find that, because the membership of the House is so large, full debate is impracticable. So there are restrictive rules. On the other hand, in the Senate, where the conditions of full debate exist, there is almost absolute freedom of speech.

This shows us that the preservation and development of freedom of opinion are not only a matter of adhering to abstract legal rights, but also, and very urgently, a matter of organizing and arranging sufficient debate. Once we have a firm hold on the central principle, there are many practical conclusions to be drawn. We then realize that the defense of freedom of opinion consists primarily in perfecting the opportunity for an adequate give-and-take of opinion; it consists also in regulating the freedom of those revolutionists who cannot or will not permit or maintain debate when it does not suit their purposes.

We must insist that free oratory is only the beginning of free speech; it is not the end, but a means to an end. The end is to find the truth. The practical justification of civil liberty is not that self-expression is one of the rights of man. It is that the examination of opinion is one of the necessities of man. For experience tells us that it is only when freedom of opinion becomes the compulsion to debate that the seed which our

fathers planted has produced its fruit. When that is understood, freedom will be cherished not be cause it is a vent for our opinions but because it is the surest method of correcting them.

The unexamined life, said Socrates, is unfit to be lived by man. This is the virtue of liberty, and the ground on which we may best justify our belief in it, that it tolerates error in order to serve the truth. When men are brought face to face with their opponents, forced to listen and learn and mend their ideas, they cease to be children and savages and begin to live like civilized men. Then only is freedom a reality, when men may voice their opinions because they must examine their opinions.

The only reason for dwelling on all this is that if we are to preserve democracy we must understand its principles. And the principle which distinguishes it from all other forms of government is that in a democracy the opposition not only is tolerated as constitutional but must be maintained because it is in fact indispensable.

The democratic system cannot be operated without effective opposition. For, in making the great experiment of governing people by consent rather than by coercion, it is not sufficient that the party in power should have a majority. It is just as necessary that the party in power should never outrage the minority. That means that it must listen to the minority and be moved by the criticisms of the minority. That means that its measures must take account of the minority's objections, and that in administering measures it must remember that the minority may become the majority.

The opposition is indispensable. A good statesman, like any other sensible human being, always learns more from his opponents than from his fervent supports. For his supporters will push him to disaster unless his opponents show him where the dangers are. So if he is wise he will often pray to be delivered from his friends, because they will ruin him. But, though it hurts, he ought also to pray never to be left without opponents; for they keep him on the path of reason and good sense.

The national unity of a free people depends upon a sufficiently even balance of political power to make it impracticable for the administration to be arbitrary and for the opposition to be revolutionary and irreconcilable. Where that balance no longer exists, democracy perishes. For unless all the citizens of a state are forced by circumstances to compromise, unless they feel that they can affect policy but that no one can wholly dominate it, unless by habit and necessity they have to give and take, freedom cannot be maintained.

1939

QUESTIONS

1. What is Lippmann's reason for dividing the essay into three parts? What is the purpose of the third part?
2. What is the importance of Lippmann's distinction between "free oratory" and "free speech" (p. 854)?
3. What does Lippmann mean when he says that the point at which we recognize the need for the freedom of others "is much higher in some mean than in others" (p. 851)? Does this assertion in any way weaken his argument?
4. Why has Lippmann discussed motion pictures but not literature (p. 854)? How sound is his view that the motion picture is "a medium which does not permit debate"? Does literature permit debate?
5. What does Lippmann mean by his statement that "the usual apology for freedom of speech . . . becomes abstract and eccentric rather than concrete and human" (p. 851)? Why has he chosen these particular words to contrast the "usual apology" with his own view? Is his argument "concrete and human"?
6. Thurber's rabbits (p. 803) listened to their opposition—that is, "the other animals, who lived at a great distance"—and were annihilated. Does Thurber's fable suggest any necessary qualitication for Lippmann's thesis concerning the value of the opposition? Explain.
7. Lippmann's essay was written before the term "brainwashing" was in common use. If he were writing the essay today, how might he take account of this term?

Kirkpatrick Sale

THE MYTHS OF BIGNESS[1]

In 1979, the Blitz Weinhard Brewing Company of Portland, Oregon, which had served the area for 123 years, was sold to the Pabst Brewing Company of Milwaukee, Wisconsin, for an unspecified sum of several billion dollars. William Wessinger, board chairman of Blitz Weinhard and the grandson of the man who had founded the brewery in 1856, said: "I just hate it. I hate the whole trend of consolidation that the country is in." But, he argued:

> The big guys have more and more leverage with their advertising dollars and big-order techniques. Pabst wanted some of our brands, like Olde English Malt, which is big in New York and Georgia, and there was just one item after

1. The author's notes documenting his discussions of the brewing industry, economies of scale, efficiency, innovation, cheaper prices, and profitability have been deleted.

another that we couldn't match them on—as when they are able to buy beer cans at 26 cents a case under what we pay.

At one time during the nineteenth century there were 121 breweries in New York City. As late as 1915 there were 70 of them, and even after Prohibition had killed off others there were still 23 before World War II. In 1976 there were none. A city that had been making beer since the Red Lion Brewery was established in Nieuw Amsterdam in 1660, and that had known Schaefer, Rheingold, Knickerbocker, Congress, Excelsior, Metropolitan, Eichler, Huppel, Von Hink, Diogenes, Trommers, and those hundred others, now gets its brew from New Jersey and Pennsylvania and Wisconsin, from Holland and Canada and Japan.

In 1935 there were 750 breweries, all regional, in the United States. By 1946 there were only 471, by 1960 there were 200, and by 1980 less than 40, a thirtyfold decrease in just forty-five years. An industry that had always been decentralized because of the limits imposed by batch production and high costs of distribution has succumbed to the processes of monopolization: just five nationwide companies now account for nearly 80 percent of all beer sales. It is assumed that before long there will be no more regional beermakers left in the U.S., the market having been taken over by fewer than a dozen national breweries, most in turn controlled by conglomerates with only a marginal interest in beer-making itself.

There is no pretense by anyone, inside the industry or out, that this development has been beneficial to the consumer or the public at large:

•The quality of the product is not improved when local breweries are taken over by nationals, and indeed the acknowledged idea is to market a beer that is insipid enough to appeal to the lowest common denominator, with blander taste, fewer raw ingredients, and somewhat less alcohol. Most national firms also have switched to "heavy brewing," a process in which a beer concentrate is mixed with water only just before it goes into the bottle, an obvious saving of brewery capacity but accomplished at the expense of texture and taste. Orion P. Burkhardt, an executive of Anheuser-Busch, the leading national brewery, suggested something of the beermaker's concern for quality when he told the New York Times that his firm's only worry is how much beer drinkers "are willing to give up in a taste sense" before they are likely to protest.

•Nor is the product any cheaper when sold by the national firms, in spite of the fact that they are supposed to be able to buy supplies in bulk, use modern technologies, and employ economies of scale in manufacturing and storage. Largely because they have immense advertising and promotion expenses and complex marketing and sales bureaucracies, national breweries actually have to charge more for their beer than local ones do (except when they first come into a region to undersell the local brands); and because customers' loyalties are based actually upon brand image rather than taste and quality, the brewers have to use more and more advertising and more and more gimmicks ("light" beer, eight-ounce bottles, flip-tops) to keep their share of the market. Indeed, because they are mostly beyond the reach of competition, they are actually free to keep raising their prices without fear of being undercut by smaller firms or having bars and supermarkets drop their product.

•To top it all off, the national companies are the ones that created and maintain the system of non-returnable plastic bottles, at an enormous cost to the national ecology, both from the use of petrochemicals when the bottles are made and from the non-biodegradable assault upon the countryside when they are thrown away. Naturally they vigorously oppose returnable bottles—despite the fact that this would save raw materials, improve the environment, lower beer prices, and increase employment—because it is far harder for them to recycle their bottles across the nation than it is for a regional brewer who operates over a much smaller territory.

And the social consequence of this process of consolidation? Well, the people of Portland are in no doubt. The Blitz Weinhard people were always important in the civic affairs of the area. Their main concern was always in making profits, to be sure, but they were rooted enough in their locality to have at least a residual sense of civic responsibility and community concern. Nowadays, it seems, the Pabst people somehow don't share that same attitude: the people brought in from Milwaukee know that there is some value in kicking in to the Community Chest and the like, but they don't know very much about the particular town they're operating in, nor is it very important in the corporate scheme that they should care. Oliver Larson, executive vice president of the Portland Chamber of Commerce, not normally the kind of officer given to criticism of big business, has observed:

> The biggest difference between now and the old days is in the response to community need. Then, some war-horse would call a meeting of the people who decided things and it would get done. Now, they all have to contact corporate headquarters, at somewhere like Gravelswitch, Kansas, and it takes forever to get an answer.

Which is usually unresponsive when it comes.

The process of consolidation is not confined to the beer industry, of course: for many other products—particularly automobiles, soft drinks, and most recently coffee—the story has been similar, and many other industries—supermarkets, motels, restaurants, even bookstores—have been transformed by chain operations. In fact . . . the condition of bigness has stamped itself on the entire American economy, with fewer and fewer firms controlling more and more power with each passing year. It goes by the appropriately ugly name of oligopoly.

Now the usual stance of economists and businesspeople is that all of this bigness is either inevitable or positively beneficial: small firms are often uneconomical, they can't keep up with the new technologies, and eventually they have to lose out to the larger firms, which are more efficient, modern, productive, innovative, and profitable. Such a development, which has been going on for at least a century and seems inherent in modern capitalism, may not have solved all the problems of living, but it is responsible for the cornucopia of labor-saving technologies and the extraordinary high standard of living we now enjoy in the industrialized world. And all of those who have recently jumped on the Schumacher[2] bandwagon with talk of the virtues of small enterprises are most likely leading us back to the Middle Ages and a world of inefficient, wearisome workplaces, and condemning the poor to unabating poverty and everyone else to a life of drudgery and bare subsistence.

Perhaps. But that perspective may be as automatic and as errant as the one that first regards the forest floor as empty and uninteresting—and discovers, only after a few minutes of concentration, that with reoriented vision the dirt is actually teeming with life, ants and earwigs and mites and untold miniature creatures busily going about their lives. A reoriented vision here might perceive that these homilies are, in fact, based on myths. Let us examine in some detail the five most pervasive of them.

Economies of scale. It is an article of faith in the industrial world that bigger plants are more successful than smaller ones because the cost per unit goes down as the total number of units produced goes up. It's called economy of scale, and it is based on the assumption that Giant Widget Corporation, which buys its raw materials at a lower price (because it buys in bulk, a less complicated process for the supplier) and processes them more cheaply (because it has larger machines and plant-space and more specialized workers), will be more successful than Mini-Widget Company because it can either sell its widgets cheaper or make a larger profit at the same price. We are all familiar with industries—book publishing, for example, where price goes down as printing orders increase, and clothes manufacturing, where ready-to-wear is always cheaper than tailor-made—that operate on this principle.

Obviously there is some truth to the idea, and some sizes *are* more efficient than others. But it is *not* true, as all businesspeople and most economists believe, that bigger is continually or progressively better, or that Worldwide Widget Conglomerate will be the most successful of all. For in fact if you plot out costs and quantities you find that there is a clear "U curve": costs will go down for a short time, but quite soon they bottom out as you increase production and then they start to go up again. The reason for this is those "diseconomies" that always creep in after a certain very minimal size: the added costs of supervision and control, of

2. The reference is to E. F. Schumacher's *Small is Beautiful*.

bureaucracy and communication, of transportation and distribution, of warehousing and inventory, of energy use and maintenance, of labor costs for specialized workers, and in the largest and most dehumanizing plants, of absenteeism, strikes, grievances, and alienation. Thus, as economist Barry Stein has convincingly shown, economies of scale are "generally achieved in individual plants of modest size."

That is why, in every industry in every country . . . there are always hundreds of small firms that manage to compete even in areas where the giant firms predominate—so in the U.S., 98.5 percent of all companies (1967 figures) have fewer than 100 employees. That is why every large corporation in no matter what field is broken down into relatively small plants—in the U.S. the number of production workers per unit was only 49.5 in 1947 and declined steadily to 44.9 in 1967 and 43.8 in 1972. And that is why even the largest companies depend upon a whole series of smaller independent firms instead of trying to make a complete product themselves—as auto manufacturers rely on many smaller outside businesses to supply them with glass, tires, brake drums, water pumps, springs, fuses, dynamos, carburetors, ball bearings.

Moreover, there seem to be no clear connections between the economies of scale in a particular plant and the *success* of that company. Even where optimum scales exist, it turns out, there is no way to predict the profitability, durability, efficiency, or overall success of the firm. Barry Stein again has shown that many companies—in fact, in most fields, the majority of companies—operate well *under* the theoretical optimum with no apparent economic penalty. Stein has concluded that "technical economies of scale are not the primary determinant of either competitive ability or true efficiency" and indeed that "there is no strong case to be made for significant economies of firm . . . size."

Finally, economies of scale, even when they are reached, turn out to have relatively little to do with ultimate consumer costs, at least in the complex modern marketplace. Such economies can, at best, affect only the *production* process, and these days that makes up only a rather small part—at the very most a third—of the total cost of a product. Thus a small firm that isn't able to meet absolute economies of scale in its plant can nonetheless offer products more cheaply because it can economize elsewhere along the rest of the pipeline, taking advantage of its size.

Efficiency. Naturally American business has fostered the myth of efficiency with particular fervor, since if bigness can't deliver *this* then most of its other justifications won't mean a whole lot. In typical form it sounds something like the words of engineer-turned-author Samuel Florman who tried to lead an advance against alternative technology in *Harper's* a few years ago by proclaiming that, "like it or not, large organizations with apparently superfluous administrative layers seem to work better than small ones." However you want to measure "work better," that just isn't true.

Just as big corporations have inefficiencies of scale, so they also have other deficiencies of size. They are less efficient in energy use because they have greater areas to heat and cool, typically more energy-intensive machines to operate, larger transportation requirements (particularly in distribution), around-the-clock shifts requiring full-time heating and lighting, and lighting banks geared to whole floors rather than individuals. They are less efficient in the use of raw materials, because there is less control over how the materials are used and hence more wastage per employee, because large production processes can't make corrective adjustments that smaller ones can, and because any error will be on a larger scale and will deplete more before being corrected. They are also less efficient in using the most precious resource of all, the human being, simply because, as countless studies have shown, size and complexity tend to create feelings of anxiety and tension, lack of individuality and self-worth, and other psychological problems that are expressed daily in faulty work, inattention, laziness, delays, and even sabotage.

But the central problem of large corporations seems to be, as we should now expect, the larger bureaucracies they must carry. Coordination is more difficult with large organizations, planning is more intricate, scheduling more rigid, information-gathering more complex, decision-making more attenuated, and assessing consumer reactions more complicated. (Just getting a part from the storeroom can be a chore: I have an IBM "Operating Procedures Guide" for one modest IBM plant in upstate New York, covering 340 pages of tiny six-point type, and Procedure 32, a request for materials from another section, requires no less than forty-one separate steps to be taken among nine separate plant divisions and coordinated with an untold number of forms, slips, files, requests, punch-cards, and printouts, all to be done in triplicate.) Economist Frederick Scherer, after his study of eighty-six companies, said flatly: "The unit cost of management, including the hidden losses due to delayed or faulty decisions and weakened or distorted incentives . . . do tend to rise with organizational size."

It may be even worse than that. As economist Kenneth Boulding has noted: "There is a great deal of evidence that almost all organizational structures tend to produce false images in the decision-maker, and that the larger and more authoritarian the organization, the better the chance that its top decision-makers will be operating in purely imaginary worlds." And if that may be dismissed as an outsider's view, here's one from an insider: not long ago a vice president of Union Carbide, one of America's giant firms, confessed that neither he nor his colleagues "had any idea how to manage a large corporation" and couldn't know enough about all the intricate corporate workings even to solve a clear problem when one was presented to them. Baseline evidence for such statements may be found in the fact that the much-vaunted conglomerate, combining many already large businesses into a single corporation, only very rarely shows higher profitability after its acquisitions than before—and such profitability is usually because it proceeds to *sell off* the acquired firm and thus become smaller. As the House Antitrust Subcommittee once reported, of the twenty-eight conglomerates it studied, only seven showed a profit after acquisitions, three remained unchanged, and "eighteen companies had ratios lower in the years after acquisition [and] it would be reasonable to conclude that these ratios reflect ineffective management."

For those who still may doubt, it may be pertinent to point to the corporate experience of the last decade, hardly one to inspire much optimism about bigness and efficiency. American business in general, dominated as it was by giant companies, went through one of its worst periods, with diminishing productivity rates, recurrent liquidity crises, steady drains on the dollar, and ultimately its own version of the "British Malady"—obsolescent plants, declining markets, uncontrollable wage increases, and unabating price increases. At the same time a remarkable number of the very biggest firms gave a demonstration of their efficiency: a half-dozen railroads, led by the mammoth Penn Central, went bankrupt, as did W. T. Grant, Food Fair, Tishman Realty, and, for 1975, a record-breaking 254,000 others; a number of the largest banks, including Franklin National in New York and U.S. National in San Diego, went under; Lockheed Aircraft was saved from collapse only by a massive government loan, and innumerable other defense companies were propped up with artificial orders and refinancing; real-estate trusts, including the REIT owned by giant Rockefeller-controlled Chase Manhattan Bank, defaulted on millions of dollars; and even on Wall Street more than a third of the investment houses went under, including two of the very biggest, Goodbody and Francis I. DuPont.

Finally, the last word to the U.S. Treasury Department. Its statistics show, unequivocally, that "when efficiency is measured by return on assets, smaller businesses are more efficient than larger businesses in every industry." In fact, the smaller ones are able to increase their output with, on average, one-third less financial backing than big ones—or, in other words, they are three times more efficient.

Innovation. The idea that the inventions of the contemporary world are the result of the innovative genius of big business organizations has always beguiled economists; even the Scotch-cold Galbraith was once inspired to rhapsodize: "A benign Providence . . . has made the modern industry of a few large firms an almost perfect instrument for inducing technical change . . . [providing] strong incentives for undertaking development and for putting it into use."

Were this true, one might be hard-pressed to explain why the U.S., with its many large firms, has declined sharply in innovation over the last decade—the number of patents issued to Americans for inventions between 1971 and 1979 fell by more than 25 percent—and why headlines like "The Crisis in Innovation" have become a staple in business papers and academic seminars. But it is not, not by a long shot. Big organizations are far more resistant to change than small ones, and big corporations have their own particular reasons for resistance: they already have a huge investment in the equipment as it is; they have such highly specialized operations that any little change would mean considerable expense and disruption; they are guided by bureaucracies whose inherent bias is always against taking risks; they operate in general by successful systems of control, and control is inimical to innovation; and they cannot encourage much change within any particular division without risking the cohesion of it all and ending with each component going off its own way. Jane Jacobs gives the telling example of the Minnesota Mining and Manufacturing Company. When it was a small stone-mining company it could easily branch off into making sandpaper, and when it was making sandpaper it could naturally develop certain kinds of adhesives, ultimately creating what the world knows as Scotch tape. But after it became a huge tape company and grew into the giant 3M Corporation, it became increasingly locked into a set production process and fixed market commitment that simply did not encourage change and invention and in fact could not rationally allow very much.

Galbraith notwithstanding, the evidence on this point is considerable. Most businessmen admit it: "Smaller companies are the best innovators," says William Norris, chairman of Control Data Corporation, once small. For Dr. Robert Noyce, chairman of Intel Corporation, creators of the semiconductor revolution, the current "crisis in innovation" is caused by too much "group-think" and work-groups grown too large: "The spirit of the small group is better and the work is much harder." Particularly telling is the testimony of T. K. Quinn, a former board chairman of the General Electric Finance Company:

> Not a single distinctively new electric home appliance has ever been created by one of the giant concerns—not the first washing machine, electric range, dryer, iron or ironer, electric lamp, refrigerator, radio, toaster, fan, heating pad, razor, lawn mower, freezer, air conditioner, vacuum cleaner, dishwasher, or grill. The record of the giants is one of moving in, buying out, and absorbing after the fact.

Several academic studies underscore the point. Economist Jacob Schmookler concludes that "beyond a certain not very large size, the bigger the firm, the less efficient its knowledge-producing activities are likely to be," with the concomitant "decrease per dollar of R & D in (a) the number of patented inventions, (b) the percentage of patented inventions used commercially, and (c) the number of significant inventions." Arnold Cooper in the *Harvard Business Review* has shown that "the average capabilities of technical people are higher in small firms than in large ones" and hence "R & D is more efficient in small companies." And a report done for the U.S. Department of Commerce in 1967 concluded that from one-half to two-thirds of all important inventions in all fields were the product of individuals, public institutions, and small firms rather than big corporations, specifically advocating the encouragement of "independent inventors, inventor-entrepreneurs, and small technically-based businesses."

Most interesting of all is the comprehensive study done by economist John Jewkes and his colleagues a few years ago, in which they drew up a list of the seventy-one major inventions of the twentieth century and then sought to determine where each came from. Twenty-two inventions, they found—including fluorescent light, television, transistors, and Scotch tape—were the product of corporate research laboratories (though some of them, like 3M, may have been relatively small at the time of the invention); ten were of mixed origin or impossible to categorize; and thirty-eight, or 54 percent—including air-conditioning, the ballpoint pen, cellophane, cyclotrons, helicopters, insulin, jets, penicillin, Polaroid, safety razors, Xerox, and the zipper—came from individual inventors working entirely on their own or in institutions where their work was autonomous. The Jewkes team concluded:

> 1. The large research organizations of industrial corporations have not been responsible in the past fifty years for the greater part of the significant inventions.
> 2. These organizations continue to rely heavily upon other sources of original thinking.
> 3. These organizations may themselves be centres of resistance to change.

Cheaper prices. Ralph Borsodi, the genius of American homesteading and one of the rare economic minds of our century, fled New York City in 1920 to establish a small farm in Rockland County, upstate. One day, being shown by his wife a jar of tomatoes she had just finished putting up for the winter, he could not refrain from asking the incurable economist's question: "Does it pay?"

> Mrs. Borsodi had rather unusual equipment for doing the work efficiently. She cooked on an electric range; she used a steam-pressure cooker; she had most of the latest gadgets for reducing the labor to a minimum. I looked around the kitchen, and then at the table covered with shining glass jars filled with tomatoes and tomato juice.
> "It's great," I said, "but does it really pay?"

"Of course it does," was her reply.

Borsodi was skeptical: how could she compete with a firm like Campbell's, which had a skilled management, labor-saving machines, quantity buying, efficient machines, mass-production economies? He sat down to figure it out. He calculated how much the tomatoes had cost to grow, how much time he and Mrs. Borsodi spent in the garden, how much electricity was used in the kitchen, how much the canning jars had cost, and all the other expenses; and then he compared that with what it cost to buy canned tomatoes in the supermarkets near his home. The results astounded him: *"The cost of the home-made product was between 20 percent and 30 percent lower than the price of the factory-made merchandise."*

It was, he felt, as if "the economic activities of mankind for nearly two hundred years had been based upon a theory as false as its maritime activities prior to the discovery of the fact that the world was round."

Eventually, of course. Borsodi figured it out, and it proved to be a devastating indictment of the consequences of bigness. Then, as now, the complications rose not in the plants but far downstream from the lathes and belts and assembly lines. First, distribution. The more goods that are produced, the wider the market area must be, hence the more expensive the costs of distribution (including warehousing and transportation) throughout that area; it is now an accepted standard in the U.S. that, particularly for consumer goods, the unit costs of distribution will be higher than those of production, and they will increase as the price of gasoline goes up. Second, advertising. Mass production naturally necessitates sufficient advertising to create a mass market, and the more extensive it is the more expensive—which is why name-brand items are always more expensive than generics. (The high cost of advertising also tends to keep smaller and cheaper firms out of a market—creating an "entry barrier," in economic terms—thus reducing the competition that might lead to lower consumer prices.) Finally, promotion and packaging. In markets that are saturated, and where Brand A is not especially different from Brand B, it is necessary to find gimmicks that make a product stand out—bigger boxes, added partitions, coupons, toys, contests—and lead to added costs.

There are a few additional wrinkles, though, that Ralph Borsodi did not consider in his time but that also help to explain why big corporations do not provide lower costs. For one thing, the major American firms have discovered that price competition is just plain *uneconomic*—too unstable, too difficult to plan for, too risky. After all, if you've spent tens of millions of dollars and half a dozen years creating a new product—a methane car or yellow toothpaste—you want to be pretty sure of what you'll be able to sell it for, and that takes certain long-range planning and certain boundaries of agreement with your competitors about prices. It is not out-and-out price-fixing in most cases (though the cardboard box people were found guilty of that as recently as 1979), but in every industry there is constant communication among, the largest firms, all of them realizing that it is in their own interests not to fiddle around too much by lowering prices.

In addition, Borsodi could never have foreseen the immense role of the Federal government in the market economy. In some cases the government actually insists on price-fixing and the elimination of competition —as in trucking, where all firms are required to charge pre-fixed prices over pre-determined routes; and in some cases it attempts to limit the number of firms in a particular field or encourage mergers so as to reduce "wasteful" competition (as a Federal Anti-Trust Task Force put it in 1968, "In the regulated sector of the economy, the bias and its enforcement is overwhelmingly against competition"). Moreover, the never-ending billions of dollars from Washington are, in most cases, passed out to the biggest firms, usually without competitive bidding, in "cost-plus" contracts that encourage high prices, with an inevitable effect on consumer prices in all sectors of the market.

It is no accident that during this recent period of the greatest corporate concentration in history—the rise of the multinationals, the wave of mergers and acquisitions, the accelerated growth of the largest firms —the U.S. has undergone its most extreme and prolonged period of inflation—that is, of rising prices. If there were really some connection between big business and low prices it is logical to think that we might have seen some signs of it by now.

Profitability. Finally, what other justification is more important than sheer profitability—as they say, the bottom line? For if a big corporation is not profitable, then what other excuse could there be for its size?

It should be no surprise that, for all of the reasons above—from diseconomies of bureaucracy to higher advertising costs—large firms tend to be simply less profitable than small ones. Nothing new about it —it is a fact that has been documented at least since the Twentieth Century Fund study of corporate profitability in 1919 ("the larger corporations earned less than the average of all corporations ... and the earnings declined almost uninterruptedly, with increasing size"); again by the Temporary National Economic Committee in 1940 ("Those with an investment under $500,000 enjoyed a higher return than those with more than $5,000,000 and twice as high a return as those with more than $50,000,000"); again by California economist H. O. Stekler, examining profits of manufacturing firms in 1949 and 1955-57 ("For the profitable firm, there is a declining relationship between profitability and size"); and yet again by the U.S. Senate Antitrust Subcommittee in 1965 (in twenty-three out of thirty basic industries, profit rates either decreased consistently as firm size increased or else had no connection with in-

creased size). The most graphic demonstration of small firm profitability is probably this table compiled by Stekler:

SIZE AND PROFITABILITY

Assets	Rate of Return
$0–50,000	137
50–100,000	130
100–250,000	120
250–500,000	118
500–1,000,000	119
1–5,000,000	113
5–10,000,000	108
10–50,000,000	105
50–100,000,000	107
100,000,000+	100

As Barry Stein concludes from these figures: "It is clear that, per asset dollar . . . smaller firms are more efficient users of capital." Something to bear in mind when we next hear from Mobil and General Motors.

Myths die hard, of course, particularly when they are fostered by very powerful institutions whose interests they serve. After all, it would be unseemly for this nation to admit the fact that the Boston Tea Party was an act born not of patriotism but of John Hancock's predicament in having a warehouse full of tea that was about to be undersold by the British shipment just then in the harbor—against which he naturally protected himself by hiring a bunch of dockside roustabouts to readjust the competition.

Still, it is always wise to recognize myths for what they are. Repetition may increase their persuasiveness, but it cannot alter the facts. And the facts behind the myths of corporate size are incontrovertible.

1980

QUESTIONS

1. Look at the definitions of "myth" in your desk dictionary. Which seems best to fit the meaning that Sale has in mind?
2. Sale begins his piece with an extended example of what has happened as beer companies have become bigger, swallowing up smaller companies. What advantages might he have seen in using a beer company as example rather than some other kind of company?

3. What assumptions does Sale make about the knowledge and beliefs of his audience? How does he take account of his audience in presenting his argument?
4. At the end of his article, Sale alludes to the Boston Tea Party, suggesting a different account of it than the usual one. How does he tie this in with his major argument?
5. Write an essay in which you explore some "myth" of contemporary life or thought.

Robert L. Heilbroner

DOES CAPITALISM HAVE A FUTURE?

What lies ahead for capitalism? That's a question that makes people nervous. It conjures up visions and specters. It paralyzes thought.

Nevertheless, it is a question that ought to be thought about now, while most of us are concentrating only on the present and the immediate future, worrying about the depression and whether it will get worse. For I believe we are not only in a depression but also in a crisis—a period of change for capitalism. Hence to the question "Does capitalism have a future?" my answer would be, "Yes, but not the future most people expect." Sooner or later, the depression will mend and we will be back to where we were, more or less. But the crisis will not mend in the same way. When it has run its course, we will be on new ground, in unfamiliar territory.

Thinking about long-term change rather than short-term prospects requires that we forget for the moment about tight money and unmanageable deficits and the other well-known reasons for our economic troubles. Instead, we must look back over the history of capitalism's fortunes and misfortunes for the last century or so. Then we can see that capitalism has more than once gone through a period like our own—a period in which a depression or a panic has masked far reaching, but often ill-perceived restructurings. Only later did people realize that they had not only gone through an economic trauma, but a historical one—a period in which familiar institutions were replaced by unfamiliar ones, accustomed ideas by unaccustomed ones. If I am right, that is what we are experiencing today.

What is the nature of our present historic crisis? That question requires that we take a moment to reflect on the nature of capitalism itself. Volumes have been written on what capitalism "is"—a market system, a system of economic and political freedom, a system of wage labor and exploitation. But all these different interpretations have one central area of agreement: It is that the life of capitalism is its incessant and insatiable drive to accumulate wealth. Ask Adam Smith and Karl Marx to name the first necessity of the system they both analyzed, and they would answer from their widely different perspectives that it was *accumulation*—using the capital created by the system to build more capital. Ask any business-man, and his answer will be the same: The first necessity is expansion, growth. Capitalism is a system that cannot stand still.

But what determines the pace of what Smith and Marx called accumu-lation, or what we today call "investment" or "capital formation"? The economist and labor historian David Gordon has developed an original and fruitful way of approaching this question. In "Segmented Work, Divided Workers," written with Richard Edwards and Michael Reich, Gordon stresses the importance of the milieu of institutions and attitudes within which accumulation takes place. That milieu begins at the imme-diate locus of production itself, on the factory floor where the capitalist must equip and organize and discipline his work force. Needless to say, work-floor conditions may be propitious for expansion or not. But the milieu extends beyond the frictions of the workplace to the critical interface between Government and business, and then still further out into the social climate itself. Both of these may or may not be conducive to the process of accumulation. Then, finally, there is the setting, benign or otherwise, of the larger world order within which capitalist nations coexist and compete, and extend their networks of trade and production into noncapitalist regions.

Gordon calls the entire complex set of influences that bears on the pace of investment the "social structure of accumulation." The phrase clarifies the meaning of a crisis period, such as our own, that is larger than just another business downturn. A crisis occurs, Gordon suggests, when an existing social structure of institutions and attitudes loses its capacity to impart momentum to the system, and becomes a drag on its perform-ance. When these junctures arise, the propulsive energy of the system slackens, and business and Government leaders alike engage in a frantic, although usually uncoordinated, search for a new structure that will permit the process of growth to start up once again.

Two periods in American (and European) history within the last century dramatically illustrate this interpretation. The first began in the 1870's, when the capitalist process was becoming seriously imperiled by its inability to cope with the effects of the emerging technology of mass production. As a labor historian, Gordon pays special heed to the difficul-ties of reconciling this technology with the necessary control over labor, still organized in semi-independent craftlike groupings. I would place equal emphasis on the effect of mass production in bringing about business instability, as torrential flows of production forced firms into cutthroat competitive tactics.

Much has been written about this turbulent period, with its robberbaron tactics, its business atmosphere of "panic and pain," its social unrest. But the period has not been much analyzed from Gordon's perspective as a crisis brought on by the failure of an adequate social structure of accumulation. Yet, looking back, we can see that an institutional framework of small business—with a virtual absence of Government regulation, a suspicious view of "monopolists" and a defensive attitude toward foreign trade—could not possibly cope with the massive disruptions of technology. The necessary adaptation came finally from a few bold business leaders who were determined to mitigate the destructive, competitive wars of mass production. Their means was the formation of giant companies or cartels to control production, first by illegal and not very effective voluntary "pools," then by the legal but cumbersome method of "trusts," ultimately by the highly efficacious legal invention of "mergers."

The resulting big businesses were certainly not popular. Trusts and monopolies, as they were called, were the favorite target of cartoonists and politicians, and not least of small businessmen who found themselves undersold or shouldered aside by the giant companies. But there was no stopping the rise of Carnegie's or Rockefeller's or McCormick's enterprises. There was no stopping them because big business succeeded in minimizing its exposure to the vagaries of the market. It did so partly by encompassing more and more phases of production within its own operations, and partly by each huge firm dominating its own industry. Thus, United States Steel mined its own ore, shipped it on its own barges and rail lines, smelted it in its own furnaces, and fabricated the steel in its own plants, out of which finally emerged two-thirds of the nation's entire output of steel. As Alfred Chandler, our foremost business historian, has put it, the rise of big business replaced the invisible hand of the market with the visible hand of management.

Accompanying this radical reorganization of business came a no less far-reaching change in the relation of business to Government. Leaders like Theodore Roosevelt vigorously endorsed the creative powers of what he called the "good" trusts, while simultaneously supporting regulations to modify the behavior of the "bad" trusts. Actually, the regulations themselves, by enforcing minimum standards of performance, also served to mitigate the destructive effects of competition. Meanwhile a complementary change in foreign policy further strengthened the new structure of accumulation by openly adopting a probusiness, imperialist stance. And not least, the suspicious view of monopolists was gradually supplanted by a public attitude of admiration for, even adulation of, the heroic captains of industry.

Thus, the social structure of accumulation—the milieu of institutions and attitudes within which capital formation took place—underwent a sea change between Lincoln's time and the first Roosevelt's, a sea change whose effectiveness is evidenced by the fact that the capitalism of big business industralized the Western world.

Why, then, did it all end in the Great Depression of the 1930's? The answer is that the changes that imparted thrust to capitalism at the end of the 19th century slowly lost their vitality and relevance during the first quarter of the 20th century. The trusts and monopolies, for instance, temporarily lessened but could not eliminate competition, so that as time went on the great giants watched the unruly forces of the market once again invade their precincts. Within the giant firms, a new mode of organizing the work process—semiskilled labor working under the supervision of driving foremen—was also not an unqualified success. It broke the old craft bottlenecks, but laid the basis for the troubles of an incipient industrial union movement.

Meanwhile, the initial euphoria and triumphs of the age of imperialism were followed by political and economic frictions. Even the climate of adulation soured as the captains of industry came to be seen as malefactors of great wealth.

But at the center of the eventual failure of the structure was a problem brought into being by the very emergence of big business itself. This was a new instability introduced into the economic framework—not the instability of markets upset by mass production, but the instability of an entire structure threatened by mass collapse. The downturns of earlier perods were painful enough, but they were not marked by the devastation of huge toppling structures, simply because there were very few such structures in the system. Early 20th-century capitalism was another affair entirely. Interlocked into a grid of national scale, the economic system resembled a vast scaffolding where the displacement of a single beam could destabilize the whole. The shutting down of a steel plant in Pennsylvania could paralyze an entire region; a decline in the order book maintained in Schenectady could throw men out of work in Sacramento; the fortunes of the Ford Motor Company not only reflected but directly affected the fortunes of the national economy.

Thus, the economic structure created by massive enterprise was inherently more dangerous than that of small business. When adversity struck, it was capable of spreading fearful wreckage throughout the system. This is essentially what happened in the 1930's. The Great Crash triggered a self-feeding, self-worsening collapse of the interconnected but unsupported scaffolding. An initial fall of 13 percent in national output from 1929 to 1930 brought a further fall of 17 percent the next year, and that in turn resulted in a 22 percent fall the following year. By 1933, almost half of 1929's production had vanished and a quarter of the nation's work force had lost its jobs. To compound the tragedy, the unemployment appeared in an age when most families had only one, not two, members at work, and when the Government's attitude of enthusiastic support for business did not extend to, and indeed seemed incompatible with, support for the casualties of business failure.

The economy entered a period of free fall—a period that lasted for four seemingly interminable years and that brought the capitalist system to what seemed to many the end of its days. But it was not the end of its days, and the next part of the story has special relevance for the conditions in which we find ourselves today.

Working with no predetermined objective in mind, seeking to do no more than clear away the wreckage, maintain social order and start up the stalled engines of growth, business and Government leaders began to construct a new basis for expansion. Rudimentary floors were laid under the household economy, first as "work relief," then as the initial timid measures of Social Security and the cautious insuring of bank deposits, both violently assailed as unworkable and Communistic. An array of legislative measures sought to restore order to disorganized markets by creating Government marketing agencies in agriculture and by allowing industry for a while to regulate its own competition. Perhaps most important, there gradually emerged the entirely new idea of a *managed* economy, first from the writings of John Maynard Keynes, then from the work of his American disciples.

And so, without the faintest intention of creating a new "social structure of accumulation," the New Deal did create just that. Or rather, it began its creation. The structure was not completed until after World War II, when it received its legitimation from the conservative Governments of Dwight Eisenhower and Konrad Adenauer and Winston Churchill and Charles de Gaulle. Only then did it become widely recognized that a new form of capitalism had come into being—"people's capitalism," Eisenhower liked to call it. The mixed economy or the welfare state (as economists soon named it) openly admitted its reliance on Government support, both as a reserve engine for economic growth and as the main source of personal security against unemployment and the penury of old age. It was widely hailed as the purified descendant of the "bad" capitalism that had led us into the Great Depression, which would never be allowed to happen again.

Fulsome as it was, the praise had a core of truth. The new system did propel capitalism into the most remarkable and extended period of growth it had ever known. The previous burst of growth, under the regime of "bad" capitalism, had industrialized the West. The new burst of growth, under the regime of "good" capitalism, sought to industrialize the world. However, even with the powerful stabilizing influence of a global American hegemony, it did not succeed in that ambition. But it did create an unprecedented degree of widely shared affluence within its own core nations. This was the social structure of accumulation that supported most of us very comfortably until the depression of the 1980's.

Then what happened?

As we come down to the present, we have to disentangle historic trends from current events. Unquestionably, much of our immediate economic distress is the consequence of Government policies combining overoptimism with strategies that work at cross purposes. The ills of tight money and ballooning deficits have not been visited on us by history, but have been put there by the Reagan Administration.

But it would be quite wrong to attribute our woes solely to Government policy. Whether his remedies are effective or not, President Reagan is right when he says that he inherited an economy that was already in trouble. And from our historic perspective it now becomes possible to describe that trouble as the gradual loss of effectiveness of the very institutions that initially gave us our long postwar boom.

In complex ways, the mixed economy and the welfare state, mighty engines of growth in the 1950's, became mighty engines of inflation 20 years later. The American hegemony that assured a stable world in the 1950's lost its efficacy as European nations began to challenge us, and as the underdeveloped world proved unexpectedly resistant to easy industrialization. The social peace that had been achieved by the welfare state ended in a restive and rebellious mood—a taste of social justice had whetted appetites, not satisfied them.

Not least, technology once again posed challenges that exceeded the grasp of existing institutions. The jet plane and the computer—the two great triumphs of the new capitalism—made it possible to transplant high technology around the world in a manner unimaginable in the 1930's. Assembly lines manned by workers barely out of the paddy fields began to mount competitive attacks against the citadels of capitalism itself. Nowhere was this new capacity to raise up an industrial structure of terrific penetrative power more startlingly evidenced than in the conversion of Japan from a maker of Christmas tree ornaments and shoddy textiles into a power capable of leveling the American auto and steel industries, all in a mere 25 years.

This is not, of course, a complete or systematic account of the roots or the extent of our present crisis. I have not mentioned the long steady upward climb in unemployment until it has now surpassed the unemployment rate in 1930. I have not discussed the sagging performance of American productivity, a 10-year source of concern. And then there is the superstructure of shaky credit that looms over the system, all too reminiscent of the rickety scaffolding of the 1930's. Most important of all, I have not drawn attention to the global aspect of our time of troubles.

For virtually the entire capitalist world is experiencing ills similar to ours. There are 30 million without jobs in the Western countries, a virtual nation of the unemployed. In France, Britain, West Germany, even in Japan (which had achieved unsustainably high rates of productivity growth), the pace of productivity has been falling during the last decade—in Japan, by more than half. And the Damoclean sword of a financial debacle hangs over the whole world, not just over America. The international debts of the underdeveloped world are more than a half-trillion dollars. What will happen when they are not paid?

All these deep, persisting and farflung evidences of disarray suggest that we are going through more than a "mere" depression that will cure itself at least partially, as depressions do. In the light of history, it is plausible that the pattern of capitalist development is again at work, and that the institutions and policies that led to expansion in one period have again become ineffective and even detrimental, to expansion in another.

Is President Reagan correct, then, when he says that the mixed economy and the welfare state are the root causes of our difficulties—that what we thought was "good" capitalism is "bad" capitalism, and that we must go back to a simpler way of organizing the economy? I think he is half right. The mixed economy and the welfare state are responsible for many of our problems. Where I think he is completely wrong is in asserting that we should therefore rid ourselves of these encumbrances to the maximum possible extent.

The institutions needed to create a viable system in one period cannot simply be discarded in another, unless we are willing to accept the return of the problems to which those institutions were addressed. The rise of big business assuredly gave us an economy much more vulnerable to cumulative depressions than in the past, but that did not mean that we could therefore get rid of big business. Liberal reformers who have dreamed of doing so have not asked themselves how a reinstated world of small business would control and contain a technology even more destabilizing today than when big business arose to make it manageable. So, too, conservatives who dream of dismantling the welfare state and the mixed economy do not reflect on what will then provide the personal security or the collective underpinning on which we all depend. Indeed, we have already seen from the effects of the Reagan Administration's retrenchments that the answer is—nothing.

So it is futile to think of social evolution as permitting a return to the "simpler" ways of the past. History is a cumulative process that permits no such retreats. If a social structure of accumulation no longer serves its original purpose, it cannot simply be ripped out. Another, better suited

to the times, must be built.

Indeed, just as big business steadily strengthened its strategic place within the American economy *after* the mixed economy and the welfare state were put into place, so I imagine that the welfare state and the mixed economy will steadily strengthen their places within the system after new structures have been added to it. The logical extension of the mixed economy lies in the deliberate encouragement and guidance of investment, the key to economic planning. The natural growth of the welfare state lies in the provision of permanent public employment for those unable to find private employment, in particular for the victims of the robotization that is cutting into factory and office work. Similarly, we can expect more Federal support for our older cities if urban decay is not to become a source of dangerous social infection.

So I do not think the existing structure will shrink, despite the efforts of the present Administration. Rather, I would expect that over the long run these governmental elements of our structure would increase until they reach at least the proportions found in most capitalist countries abroad. Very roughly speaking, a third of our economy is cycled through the Government in the form of welfare payments (including Social Security) and the actual purchases of output from arms to public education. In Europe, that percentage is considerably higher: in West Germany, for example, between 40 and 50 percent of the total.

With all their difficulties and inefficiencies, Government activities will remain and grow because they still provide the necessary underpinning and the essential economic security required for workable capitalism. But their growth will by no means create a new milieu for capitalist expansion, any more than the continued growth of big business after the New Deal constituted the foundation of the new structure within which the postwar boom took place. Something will have to be added to the present, inadequately functioning system, if accumulation is to find a new basis for vitality.

Is it possible to speculate about what such additions might be? With all the risks that such a prognosis entails I shall try.

Let me first deal briefly with two possible directions of evolution, fervently espoused by their supporters, that seem unlikely to lead very far. One I have already mentioned. It is the vision of the Reagan Administration (and to a lesser degree of Mrs. Thatcher's Government in England)—of a born-again capitalism, stripped down to its natural, lean, aggressive fighting weight, once more undertaking its accumulative mission with assurance and pride. Whether this is a realistic vision or a fantasy we should discover fairly soon. My own views must be clear. I only hope that if the Reagan program fails, we do not move on a dangerous course, preaching the gospel of freedom and enterprise, but practicing the economics of military capitalism.

A second vision, entertained much more strongly in Europe than in the United States, sees this period as the forcing ground for a new attempt to create socialism—not the sclerotic socialism of the centrally planned systems, such as the Soviet Union, but a socialism of intensified democratic participation, of widespread workers' management of enterprises and of the gradual elimination of capitalist privileges and waste. Whether this is a fantasy or not may take a little longer to find out. My guess is that the main threat to such democratic socialistic efforts is not the likelihood of clear-cut failure, but of disappointment. High, perhaps even heady, expectations are needed to create socialism. Thus, disappointent can lead easily to disillusion. That is likely to be the greatest challenge that socialism will have to face.

This brings me to the third direction of evolution, to my mind the most probable. It is an effort to restructure things in ways that will once again encourage capital accumulation.

Here I would imagine that the first order of business would be to deal with the chronic ailment of the present structure—inflation. I do not see how this can be done without the introduction of various kinds of ceilings and restraints—price and wage and dividend controls of one kind or another—that will serve as counterparts of the floors and supports that underpin the system today.

It is because of these floors and supports that our present depression, for all its severity, is not likely to repeat the nearly fatal self-feeding contractions of the 1930's. The next structure of accumulation will require ceilings and anti-inflationary controls at least as effective as these floors—not removing the inflationary propensity of the system, but limiting the harm it can do. W. David Slawson, who has perceptively described the upward-ratcheting tendencies of our modern markets, writes in his book *The New Inflation* that we will eventually require an anti-inflationary administrative structure as pervasive in our economic life as that of the Internal Revenue Service. It is a disconcerting image, but I think it is a correct one. Nothing else will match the power of the inflationary process that is now part of the normal workings of the system. And so we will learn to live with ceilings and be grateful to them, as we have learned to live with floors, and have become grateful to them.

Next, I believe there will be a marked lessening in the distinction we now make between the private and public sectors. The idea that growth only originates in the activities of the business world and that the activities of government are essentially inimical to expansion is one that cannot survive the realities of the coming century. To put it boldly, just as the strategic vehicle of accumulation in Adam Smith's day was the pin factory, in Henry Ford's time the national corporation, and in our own day the multinational enterprises, I think tomorrow's vehicle will be the state corporation.

We have already seen the first examples of such a linking of Government's powers of finance and diplomacy with business's capabilities of management in the Japanese system, or in the public-private consortium that builds the European Airbus, or in the Volkswagen company or British Petroleum. These public-private enterprises have considerable advantages over purely private companies in the jockeying that goes on for shares in the global markets. American businessmen who protest the "dumping" and "export subsidies" and "unfair tactics" of these formidable state corporations remind me of nothing so much as the small businessmen of a century ago who railed against the practices of the emerging trusts and monopolies.

To be sure, there is no guarantee that all such state enterprises will succeed. There are plenty of examples of failures in putting together the power of the public treasury and the efforts of private management —Renault, Fiat, not to mention our own Lockheed (on an unacknowledged basis). But that is like saying that the emergence of big business was a failure because most of the trusts eventually lost control over their markets or because some big businesses did not make the grade. The giant enterprise arose to cope with the problems of production on a national scale. The state enterprise will arise to cope with the problems of production on a global scale. And it will arise because business as well as Government will come to see that it is the only possible means of amassing the finance, exerting the political pressure, and supplying the entrepreneurial zeal needed to establish our place in the new arena of global competition.

And so I expect that 20 years from now, General Motors and Boeing and I.B.M. will have Government officials on their boards and access to Government financing; they will no longer clearly know whether they are part of the private or the public undertakings of the economy. They *will* know, however, that they are able to carry on the business of capital accumulation and growth much better than they could in the old-fashioned days of the 1980's.

I have left to the end a wrenching change that I foresee as a precondition for erecting a new structure of accumulation. This is the abandonment of the idea of a unified world market as the global basis for accumulation, and its replacement with a system of regional blocks, each securing a reasonably protected market for its favored producers, and regulating its intercourse with other large blocs.

The reason for this change again lies in the power of modern technology to outflank and bypass established centers of production, as the German tanks in 1940 penetrated the old Maginot line and reduced its great outposts to impotence. The pressures of international competition are largely determined by the technology of transportation and information and communication. As long as these pressures were bearable, a worldwide free market could be held up as the ideal by which the greatest welfare could be achieved for all. In fact, that was not the way the free market worked, so far as the underdeveloped countries were concerned, but unquestionably free trade and the associated free market in currencies served the interests of the industrial countries very well.

Today, though, things have changed. Cities that were Kiplingesque tourist attractions a decade or two ago are now centers of low-wage, high-technology manufacture and assembly. The jobs of German, French, British and American workers are being performed by Taiwanese, South Koreans, Thais—perhaps soon by Chinese. This is all very well for the consumer, but it is not so well for the producer. A successful social structure of accumulation must ultimately support its producers over its consumers, and that includes its working force as well as its capitalists. I believe that the flag of free trade will be hauled down in the coming restructuring of things, as the flag of laissez-faire was hauled down in the last restructuring.

Of course, this is not intended to be an inventory of prospective alterations. I have done no more than sketch the general kinds of changes I think will be needed to set a successful new structure of growth in place. I suppose it can be succinctly described as a movement toward state capitalism or, perhaps more accurately, as a movement toward a capitalism in which the line that divides the economy from the polity is redrawn in favor of the polity. No doubt such a movement will be regarded by many as "socialistic," by others as "fascistic." I think that its political coloration could be as varied—as authoritarian or as liberal—as other forms of capitalism have shown themselves to be.

Two last thoughts seem necessary. First, the period of change will last a long time. The passage from the world of small-scale capitalism to that of big business took more than two decades. The creation of the mixed economy and the welfare state required roughly as long. So it seems altogether possible that the next transformation will also last more than a decade—an extended period during which we can expect all the unease and dissension characteristic of times that have not discovered a consensus, or concluded a social contract, or forged a viable social structure of accumulation.

Second, the change will not necessarily be welcomed. Indeed, it is likely to be greeted as totally incompatible with capitalism, denounced in the names of liberty and freedom, and proclaimed both unworkable and un-American.

But that has been the reception accorded to all major restructurings of the system. Change has come nevertheless, because it has been brought

by the efforts of business and political leaders who were more concerned about finding ways past the obstacles that were blocking capitalism's expansion than about ideological purity. Just as capitalism does not grow by blueprint, so I do not think its adaptation can be easily stymied by sentiment. Capitalism is powered by something stronger than that—the drive for survival. When capitalism can no longer find effective new means for carrying on its task of accumulation, its life energies will have ebbed and its historic career will be finished. For better or worse, I do not think that time is yet at hand.

1982

Jonathan Schell

THE ROOTS OF NUCLEAR PERIL

* * *

If a council were to be empowered by the people of the earth to do whatever was necessary to save humanity from extinction by nuclear arms, it might well decide that a good first step would be to order the destruction of all the nuclear weapons in the world. When the order had been carried out, however, warlike or warring nations might still rebuild their nuclear arsenals—perhaps in a matter of months. A logical second step, accordingly, would be to order the destruction of the factories that make the weapons. But, just as the weapons might be rebuilt, so might the factories, and the world's margin of safety would not have been increased by very much. A third step, then, would be to order the destruction of the factories that make the factories that make the weapons—a measure that might require the destruction of a considerable part of the world's economy. But even then lasting safety would not have been reached, because in some number of years—at most, a few decades —everything could be rebuilt, including the nuclear arsenals, and mankind would again be ready to extinguish itself. A determined council might next decide to try to arrest the world economy in a prenuclear state by throwing the blueprints and technical manuals for reconstruction on the bonfires that had by then consumed everything else, but that recourse, too, would ultimately fail, because the blueprints and manuals could easily be redrawn and rewritten. As long as the world remained acquainted with the basic physical laws that underlie the construction of nuclear weapons—and these laws include the better part of physics as physics is understood in our century—mankind would have failed to put many years between itself and its doom. For the fundamental origin of the peril of human extinction by nuclear arms lies not in any particular social or political circumstances of our time but in the attainment by mankind as a whole, after millennia of scientific progress, of a certain level of knowledge of the physical universe. As long as that knowledge is in our possession, the atoms themselves, each one stocked with its prodigious supply of energy, are, in a manner of speaking, in a perilously advanced state of mobilization for nuclear hostilities, and any conflict anywhere in the world can become a nuclear one. To return to safety through technical measures alone, we would have to disarm matter itself, converting it back into its relatively safe, inert, nonexplosive nineteenth-century Newtonian state—something that not even the physics of our time can teach us how to do. (I mention these farfetched, wholly imaginary programs of demolition and suppression in part because the final destruction of all mankind is so much more farfetched, and therefore seems to give us license to at least consider extreme alternatives, but mainly because their obvious inadequacy serves to demonstrate how deeply the nuclear peril is ingrained in our world.)

It is fundamental to the shape and character of the nuclear predicament that its origins lie in scientific knowledge rather than in social circumstances. Revolutions born in the laboratory are to be sharply distinguished from revolutions born in society. Social revolutions are usually born in the minds of millions, and are led up to by what the Declaration of Independence calls "a long train of abuses," visible to all; indeed, they usually cannot occur unless they are widely understood by and supported by the public. By contrast, scientific revolutions usually take shape quietly in the minds of a few men, under cover of the impenetrability to most laymen of scientific theory, and thus catch the world by surprise. In the case of nuclear weapons, of course, the surprise was greatly increased by the governmental secrecy that surrounded the construction of the first bombs. When the world learned of their existence, Mr. Fukai had already run back into the flames of Hiroshima, and tens of thousands of people in that city had already been killed. Even long after scientific discoveries have been made and their applications have transformed our world, most people are likely to remain ignorant of the underlying principles at work, and this has been particularly true of nuclear weapons, which, decades after their invention, are still surrounded by an aura of mystery, as though they had descended from another planet. (To most people, Einstein's famous formula $E=mc^2$, which defines the energy released in nuclear explosions, stands as a kind of symbol of everything that is esoteric and incomprehensible.)

But more important by far than the world's unpreparedness for scientific revolutions are their universality and their permanence once they have occurred. Social revolutions are restricted to a particular time and place; they arise out of particular circumstances, last for a while, and then pass into history. Scientific revolutions, on the other hand, belong to all places and all times. In the words of Alfred North Whitehead, "Modern science was born in Europe, but its home is the whole world." In fact, of all the products of human hands and minds, scientific knowledge has proved to be the most durable. The physical structures of human life —furniture, buildings, paintings, cities, and so on—are subject to inevitable natural decay, and human institutions have likewise proved to be transient. Hegel, whose philosophy of history was framed in large measure in an attempt to redeem the apparent futility of the efforts of men to found something enduring in their midst, once wrote, "When we see the evil, the vice, the ruin that has befallen the most flourishing kingdoms which the mind of man ever created, we can scarce avoid being filled with sorrow at this universal taint of corruption; and, since this decay is not the work of mere Nature, but of Human Will—a moral embitterment—a revolt of the Good Spirit (if it have a place within us) may well be the result of our reflections." Works of thought and many works of art have a better chance of surviving, since new copies of a book or a symphony can be transcribed from old ones, and so can be preserved indefinitely; yet these works, too, can and do go out of existence, for if every copy is lost, then the work is also lost. The subject matter of these works is man, and they seem to be touched with his mortality. The results of scientific work, on the other hand, are largely immune to decay and disappearance. Even when they are lost, they are likely to be rediscovered, as is shown by the fact that several scientists often make the same discovery independently. (There is no record of several poets' having independently written the same poem, or of several composers' having independently written the same symphony.) For both the subject matter and the method of science are available to all capable minds in a way that the subject matter and the method of the arts are not. The human experiences that art deals with are, once over, lost forever, like the people who undergo them, whereas matter, energy, space, and time, alike everywhere and in all ages, are always available for fresh inspection. The subject matter of science is the physical world, and its findings seem to share in the immortality of the physical world. And artistic vision grows out of the unrepeatable individuality of each artist, whereas the reasoning power of the mind—its ability to add two and two and get four—is the same in all competent persons. The rigorous exactitude of scientific methods does not mean that creativity is any less individual, intuitive, or mysterious in great scientists than in great artists, but it does mean that scientific findings, once arrived at, can be tested and confirmed by shared canons of logic and experimentation. The agreement among scientists thus achieved permits science to be a collective enterprise, in which each generation, building on the accepted findings of the generations before, makes amendments and additions, which in their turn become the starting point for the next generation. (Philosophers, by contrast, are constantly tearing down the work of their predecessors, and circling back to re-ask questions that have been asked and answered countless times before. Kant once wrote in despair, "It seems ridiculous that while every science moves forward ceaselessly, this [metaphysics], claiming to be wisdom itself, whose oracular pronouncements everyone consults, is continually revolving in one spot, without advancing one step.") Scientists, as they erect the steadily growing structure of scientific knowledge, resemble nothing so much as a swarm of bees working harmoniously together to construct a single, many-chambered hive, which grows more elaborate and splendid with every year that passes. Looking at what they have made over the centuries, scientists need feel no "sorrow" or "moral embitterment" at any "taint of corruption" that supposedly undoes all human achievements. When God, alarmed that the builders of the Tower of Babel would reach Heaven with their construction, and so become as God, put an end to their undertaking by making them all speak different languages, He apparently overlooked the scientists, for they, speaking what is often called the "universal language" of their disciplines from country to country and generation to generation, went on to build a new tower—the edifice of scientific knowledge. Their phenomenal success, beginning not with Einstein but with Euclid and Archimedes, has provided the unshakable structure that supports the world's nuclear peril. So durable is the scientific edifice that if we did not know that human beings had constructed it we might suppose that the findings on which our whole technological civilization rests were the pillars and crossbeams of an invulnerable, inhuman order obtruding into our changeable and perishable human realm. It is the crowning irony of this lopsided development of human abilities that the only means in sight for getting rid of the knowledge of how to destroy ourselves would be to do just that—in effect, to remove the knowledge by removing the knower.

Although it is unquestionably the scientists who have led us to the edge of the nuclear abyss, we would be mistaken if we either held them chiefly responsible for our plight or looked to them, particularly, for a solution. Here, again, the difference between scientific revolutions and social revolutions shows itself, for the notion that scientists bear primary responsibility springs from a tendency to confuse scientists with political actors. Political actors, who, of course, include ordinary citizens as well as government officials, act with definite social ends in view, such as the preservation of peace, the establishment of a just society, or, if they are corrupt, their own aggrandizement; and they are accordingly held responsible for the consequences of their actions, even when these are unintended ones, as they so often are. Scientists, on the other hand (and here I refer to the so-called pure scientists, who search for the laws of nature for the sake of knowledge itself, and not to the applied scientists, who make use of already discovered natural laws to solve practical problems), do not aim at social ends, and, in fact, usually do not know what the social results of their findings will be; for that matter, they cannot know what the findings themselves will be, because science is a process of discovery, and it is in the nature of discovery that one cannot know beforehand what one will find. This element of the unexpected is present when a researcher sets out to unravel some small, carefully defined mystery—say, the chemistry of a certain enzyme—but it is most conspicuous in the synthesis of the great laws of science and in the development of science as a whole, which, over decades and centuries, moves toward destinations that no one can predict. Thus, only a few decades ago it might have seemed that physics, which had just placed nuclear energy at man's disposal, was the dangerous branch of science, while biology, which underlay improvements in medicine and also helped us to understand our dependence on the natural environment, was the beneficial branch; but now that biologists have begun to fathom the secrets of genetics, and to tamper with the genetic substance of life directly, we cannot be so sure. The most striking illustration of the utter disparity that may occur between the wishes of the scientist as a social being and the social results of his scientific findings is certainly the career of Einstein. By nature, he was, according to all accounts, the gentlest of men, and by conviction he was a pacifist, yet he made intellectual discoveries that led the way to the invention of weapons with which the species could exterminate itself. Inspired wholly by a love of knowledge for its own sake, and by an awe at the creation which bordered on the religious, he made possible an instrument of destruction with which the terrestrial creation could be disfigured.

A disturbing corollary of the scientists' inability even to foresee the path of science, to say nothing of determining it, is that while science is without doubt the most powerful revolutionary force in our world, no one directs that force. For science is a process of submission, in which the mind does not dictate to nature but seeks out and then bows to nature's laws, letting its conclusions be guided by that which is, independent of our will. From the political point of view, therefore, scientific findings, some lending themselves to evil, some to good, and some to both, simply pour forth from the laboratory in senseless profusion, offering the world now a neutron bomb, now bacteria that devour oil, now a vaccine to prevent polio, now a cloned frog. It is not until the pure scientists, seekers of knowledge for its own sake, turn their findings over to the applied scientists that social intentions begin to guide the results. The applied scientists do indeed set out to make a better vaccine or a bigger bomb, but even they, perhaps, deserve less credit or blame than we are sometimes inclined to give them. For as soon as our intentions enter the picture we are in the realm of politics in the broadest sense, and in politics it is ultimately not technicians but governments and citizens who are in charge. The scientists in the Manhattan Project could not decide to make the first atomic bomb; only President Roosevelt, elected to office by the American people, could do that.

If scientists are unable to predict their discoveries, neither can they cancel them once they have been made. In this respect, they are like the rest of us, who are asked not whether we would like to live in a world in which we can convert matter into energy but only what we want to do about it once we have been told that we do live in such a world. Science is a tide that can only rise. The individual human mind is capable of forgetting things, and mankind has collectively forgotten many things, but we do not know how, as a species, to *deliberately* set out to forget something. A basic scientific finding, therefore, has the character of destiny for the world. Scientific discovery is in this regard like any other form of discovery; once Columbus had discovered America, and had told the world about it, America could not be hidden again.

Scientific progress (which can and certainly will occur) offers little more hope than scientific regression (which probably cannot occur) of giving us relief from the nuclear peril. It does not seem likely that science will bring forth some new invention—some antiballistic missile or laser beam—that will render nuclear weapons harmless (although the unpredictability of science prevents any categorical judgment on this point). In the centuries of the modern scientific revolution, scientific knowledge has steadily increased the destructiveness of warfare, for it is in the very nature of knowledge, apparently, to increase our might rather than to diminish it. One of the most common forms of the hope for deliverance from the nuclear peril by technical advances is the notion that the species will be spared extinction by fleeing in spaceships. The thought seems to be that while the people on earth are destroying themselves communities in space will be able to survive and carry on. This thought does an injustice to our birthplace and habitat, the earth. It assumes that if only we could escape the earth we would find safety—as though it were the earth and its plants and animals that threatened us, rather than the other way around. But the fact is that wherever human beings went there also would go the knowledge of how to build nuclear weapons, and, with it, the peril of extinction. Scientific progress may yet deliver us from many evils, but there are at least two evils that it cannot deliver us from: its own findings and our own destructive and self-destructive bent. This is a combination that we will have to learn to deal with by some other means.

We live, then, in a universe whose fundamental substance contains a supply of energy with which we can extinguish ourselves. We shall never live in any other. We now know that we live in such a universe, and we shall never stop knowing it. Over the millennia, this truth lay in waiting for us, and now we have found it out, irrevocably. If we suppose that it is an integral part of human existence to be curious about the physical world we are born into, then, to speak in the broadest terms, the origin of the nuclear peril lies, on the one hand, in our nature as rational and inquisitive beings and, on the other, in the nature of matter. Because the energy that nuclear weapons release is so great, the whole species is threatened by them, and because the spread of scientific knowledge is unstoppable, the whole species poses the threat: in the last analysis, it is all of mankind that threatens all of mankind. (I do not mean to overlook the fact that at present it is only two nations—the United States and the Soviet Union—that possess nuclear weapons in numbers great enough to possibly destroy the species, and that they thus now bear the chief responsibility for the peril. I only wish to point out that, regarded in its full dimensions, the nuclear peril transcends the rivalry between the present superpowers.)

The fact that the roots of the nuclear peril lie in basic scientific knowledge has broad political implications that cannot be ignored if the world's solution to the predicament is to be built on a solid foundation, and if futile efforts are to be avoided. One such effort would be to rely on secrecy to contain the peril—that is, to "classify" the "secret" of the bomb. The first person to try to suppress knowledge of how nuclear weapons can be made was the physicist Leo Szilard, who in 1939, when he first heard that a nuclear chain reaction was possible, and realized that a nuclear bomb might be possible, called on a number of his colleagues to keep the discovery secret from the Germans. Many of the key scientists refused. His failure foreshadowed a succession of failures, by whole governments, to restrict the knowledge of how the weapons are made. The first, and most notable, such failure was the United States' inability to monopolize nuclear weapons, and prevent the Soviet Union from building them. And we have subsequently witnessed the failure of the entire world to prevent nuclear weapons from spreading. Given the nature of scientific thought and the very poor record of past attempts to suppress it, these failures should not have surprised anyone. (The Catholic Church succeeded in making Galileo recant his view that the earth revolves around the sun, but we do not now believe that the sun revolves around the earth.) Another, closely related futile effort—the one made by our hypothetical council—would be to try to resolve the nuclear predicament through disarmament alone, without accompanying political measures. Like the hope that the knowledge can be classified, this hope loses sight of the fact that the nuclear predicament consists not in the possession of nuclear weapons at a particular moment by certain nations but in the circumstance that mankind as a whole has now gained possession once and for all of the knowledge of how to make them, and that all nations—and even some groups of people which are not nations, including terrorist groups—can potentially build them. Because the nuclear peril, like the scientific knowledge that gave rise to it, is probably global and everlasting, our solution must at least aim at being global and everlasting. And the only kind of solution that holds out this promise is a global political one. In defining the task so broadly, however, I do not mean to argue against short-term palliatives, such as the Strategic Arms Limitation Talks between the United States and the Soviet Union, or nuclear-nonproliferation agreements, on the ground that they are short-term. If a patient's life is in danger, as mankind's now is, no good cause is served by an argument between the nurse who wants to give him an aspirin to bring down his fever and the doctor who wants to perform the surgery that can save his life; there is need for an argument only if the nurse is claiming that the aspirin is all that is necessary. If, given the world's discouraging record of political achievement, a lasting political solution seems almost beyond human powers, it may give us confidence to remember that what challenges us is simply our extraordinary success in another field of activity—the scientific. We have only to learn to live politically in the world in which we already live scientifically.

Since 1947, the *Bulletin of the Atomic Scientists* has included a "doomsday clock" in each issue. The editors place the hands farther away from or closer to midnight as they judge the world to be farther away from or closer to a nuclear holocaust. A companion clock can be imagined whose hands, instead of metaphorically representing a judgment about the likelihood of a holocaust, would represent an estimate of the amount of time that, given the world's technical and political arrangements, the people of the earth can be sure they have left before they are destroyed in a holocaust. At present, the hands would stand at, or a fraction of a second before, midnight, because none of us can be sure that at any second we will not be killed in a nuclear attack. If, by treaty, all nuclear warheads were removed from their launchers and stored somewhere else, and therefore could no longer descend on us at any moment without warning, the clock would show the amount of time that it would take to put them back on. If all the nuclear weapons in the world were destroyed, the clock would show the time that it would take to manufacture them again. If in addition confidence-inspiring political arrangements to prevent rearmament were put in place, the clock would show some estimate of the time that it might take for the arrangements to break down. And if these arrangements were to last for hundreds or thousands of years (as they must if mankind is to survive this long), then some generation far in the future might feel justified in setting the clock at decades, or even centuries, before midnight. But no generation would ever be justified in retiring the clock from use altogether, because, as far as we can tell, there will never again be a time when self-extinction is beyond the reach of our species. An observation that Plutarch made about politics holds true also for the task of survival, which has now become the principal obligation of politics: "They are wrong who think that politics is like an ocean voyage

or a military campaign, something to be done with some end in view, something which levels off as soon as that end is reached. It is not a public chore, to be got over with; it is a way of life."

1982

Science

James C. Rettie

"BUT A WATCH IN THE NIGHT": A SCIENTIFIC FABLE

Out beyond our solar system there is a planet called Copernicus. It came into existence some four or five billion years before the birth of our Earth. In due course of time it became inhabited by a race of intelligent men.

About 750 million years ago the Copernicans had developed the motion picture machine to a point well in advance of the stage that we have reached. Most of the cameras that we now use in motion picture work are geared to take twenty-four pictures per second on a continuous strip of film. When such film is run through a projector, it throws a series of images on the screen and these change with a rapidity that gives the visual impression of normal movement. If a motion is too swift for the human eye to see it in detail, it can be captured and artificially slowed down by means of the slow-motion camera. This one is geared to take many more shots per second—ninety-six or even more than that. When the slow motion film is projected at the normal speed of twenty-four pictures per second, we can see just how the jumping horse goes over a hurdle.

What about motion that is too slow to be seen by the human eye? That problem has been solved by the use of the time-lapse camera. In this one, the shutter is geared to take only one shot per second, or one per minute, or even one per hour—depending upon the kind of movement that is being photographed. When the time-lapse film is projected at the normal speed of twenty-four pictures per second, it is possible to see a bean sprout growing up out of the ground. Time-lapse films are useful in the study of many types of motion too slow to be observed by the unaided, human eye.

The Copernicans, it seems, had time-lapse cameras some 757 million years ago and they also had superpowered telescopes that gave them a clear view of what was happening upon this Earth. They decided to make a film record of the life history of Earth and to make it on the scale of one picture per year. The photography has been in progress during the last 757 million years.

In the near future, a Copernican interstellar expedition will arrive upon our Earth and bring with it a copy of the time-lapse film. Arrangements will be made for showing the entire film in one continuous run. This will begin at midnight of New Year's eve and continue day and night without a single stop until midnight of December 31. The rate of projection will be twenty-four pictures per second. Time on the screen will thus seem to move at the rate of twenty-four years per second; 1440 years per minute; 86,400 years per hour; approximately two million years per day; and sixty-two million years per month. The normal lifespan of individual man will occupy about three seconds. The full period of Earth history that will be unfolded on the screen (some 757 million years) will extend from what the geologists call Pre-Cambrian times[1] up to the present. This will, by no means, cover the full time-span of the Earth's geological history but it will embrace the period since the advent of living organisms.

During the months of January, February, and March the picture will be desolate and dreary. The shape of the land masses and the oceans will bear little or no resemblance to those that we know. The violence of geological erosion will be much in evidence. Rains will pour down on the land and promptly go booming down to the seas. There will be no clear streams anywhere except where the rains fall upon hard rock. Everywhere on the steeper ground the stream channels will be filled with boulders hurled down by rushing waters. Raging torrents and dry stream beds will keep alternating in quick succession. High mountains will seem to melt like so much butter in the sun. The shifting of land into the seas, later to be thrust up as new mountains, will be going on at a grand scale.

Early in April there will be some indication of the presence of single-celled living organisms in some of the warmer and sheltered coastal waters. By the end of the month it will be noticed that some of these organisms have become multicellular. A few of them, including the Trilobites, will be encased in hard shells.

Toward the end of May, the first vertebrates will appear, but they will still be aquatic creatures. In June about 60 per cent of the land area that we know as North America will be under water. One broad channel will occupy the space where the Rocky Mountains now stand. Great deposits of limestone will be forming under some of the shallower seas. Oil and gas deposits will be in process of formation—also under shallow seas. On

1. 500,000,000 years or more before the present.

land there will still be no sign of vegetation. Erosion will be rampant, tearing loose particles and chunks of rock and grinding them into sand and silt to be spewed out by the streams into bays and estuaries.

About the middle of July the first land plants will appear and take up the tremendous job of soil building. Slowly, very slowly, the mat of vegetation will spread, always battling for its life against the power of erosion. Almost foot by foot, the plant life will advance, lacing down with its root structures whatever pulverized rock material it can find. Leaves and stems will be giving added protection against the loss of the soil foothold. The increasing vegetation will pave the way for the land animals that will live upon it.

Early in August the seas will be teeming with fish. This will be what geologists call the Devonian period.[2] Some of the races of these fish will be breathing by means of lung tissue instead of through gill tissues. Before the month is over, some of the lung fish will go ashore and take on a crude lizard-like appearance. Here are the first amphibians.

In early September the insects will put in their appearance. Some will look like huge dragonflies and will have a wing spread of 24 inches. Large portions of the land masses will now be covered with heavy vegetation that will include the primitive spore-propagating trees. Layer upon layer of this plant growth will build up, later to appear as the coal deposits. About the middle of this month, there will be evidence of the first seed-bearing plants and the first reptiles. Heretofore, the land animals will have been amphibians that could reproduce their kind only by depositing a soft egg mass in quiet waters. The reptiles will be shown to be freed from the aquatic bond because they can reproduce by means of a shelled egg in which the embryo and its nurturing liquids are sealed and thus protected from destructive evaporation. Before September is over, the first dinosaurs will be seen—creatures destined to dominate the animal realm for about 140 million years and then to disappear.

In October there will be series of mountain uplifts along what is now the eastern coast of the United States. A creature with feathered limbs —half bird and half reptile in appearance—will take itself into the air. Some small and rather unpretentious animals will be seen to bring forth their young in a form that is a miniature replica of the parents and to feed these young on milk secreted by mammary glands in the female parent. The emergence of this mammalian form of animal life will be recognized as one of the great events in geologic time. October will also witness the high water mark of the dinosaurs—creatures ranging in size from that of the modern goat to monsters like Brontosaurus that weighed some 40 tons. Most of them will be placid vegetarians, but a few will be hideous-looking carnivores, like Allosaurus and Tyrannosaurus. Some of the

2. 405,000,000–345,000,000 years ago.

herbivorous dinosaurs will be clad in bony armor for protection against their flesh-eating comrades.

November will bring pictures of a sea extending from the Gulf of Mexico to the Arctic in space now occupied by the Rocky Mountains. A few of the reptiles will take to the air on bat-like wings. One of these, called Pteranodon, will have a wingspread of 15 feet. There will be a rapid development of the modern flowering plants, modern trees, and modern insects. The dinosaurs will disappear. Toward the end of the month there will be a tremendous land disturbance in which the Rocky Mountains will rise out of the sea to assume a dominating place in the North American landscape.

As the picture runs on into December it will show the mammals in command of the animal life. Seed-bearing trees and grasses will have covered most of the land with a heavy mantle of vegetation. Only the areas newly thrust up from the sea will be barren. Most of the streams will be crystal clear. The turmoil of geologic erosion will be confined to localized areas. About December 25 will begin the cutting of the Grand Canyon of the Colorado River. Grinding down through layer after layer of sedimentary strata, this stream will finally expose deposits laid down in Pre-Cambrian times. Thus in the walls of that canyon will appear geological formations dating from recent times to the period when the Earth had no living organisms upon it.

The picture will run on through the latter days of December and even up to its final day with still no sign of mankind. The spectators will become alarmed in the fear that man has somehow been left out. But not so; sometime about noon on December 31 (one million years ago) will appear a stooped, massive creature of man-like proportions. This will be Pithecanthropus, the Java ape man. For tools and weapons he will have nothing but crude stone and wooden clubs. His children will live a precarious existence threatened on the one side by hostile animals and on the other by tremendous climatic changes. Ice sheets—in places 4000 feet deep—will form in the northern parts of North America and Eurasia. Four times this glacial ice will push southward to cover half the continents. With each advance the plant and animal life will be swept under or pushed southward. With each recession of the ice, life will struggle to reestablish itself in the wake of the retreating glaciers. The woolly mammoth, the musk ox, and the caribou all will fight to maintain themselves near the ice line. Sometimes they will be caught and put into cold storage—skin, flesh, blood, bones and all.

The picture will run on through supper time with still very little evidence of man's presence on the Earth. It will be about 11 o'clock when Neanderthal man appears. Another half hour will go by before the appearance of Cro-Magnon man living in caves and painting crude animal pictures on the walls of his dwelling. Fifteen minutes more will bring Neolithic man, knowing how to chip stone and thus produce sharp cutting edges for spears and tools. In a few minutes more it will appear that man has domesticated the dog, the sheep and, possibly, other animals. He will then begin the use of milk. He will also learn the arts of basket weaving and the making of pottery and dugout canoes.

The dawn of civilization will not come until about five or six minutes before the end of the picture. The story of the Egyptians, the Babylonians, the Greeks, and the Romans will unroll during the fourth, the third and the second minute before the end. At 58 minutes and 43 seconds past 11:00 P.M. (just 1 minute and 17 seconds before the end) will come the beginning of the Christian era. Columbus will discover the new world 20 seconds before the end. The Declaration of Independence will be signed just 7 seconds before the final curtain comes down.

In those few moments of geologic time will be the story of all that has happened since we became a nation. And what a story it will be! A human swarm will sweep across the face of the continent and take it away from the . . . red men. They will change it far more radically than it has ever been changed before in a comparable time. The great virgin forests will be seen going down before ax and fire. The soil, covered for eons by its protective mantle of trees and grasses, will be laid bare to the ravages of water and wind erosion. Streams that had been flowing clear will, once again, take up a load of silt and push it toward the seas. Humus and mineral salts, both vital elements of productive soil, will be seen to vanish at a terrifying rate. The railroads and highways and cities that will spring up may divert attention, but they cannot cover up the blight of man's recent activities. In great sections of Asia, it will be seen that man must utilize cow dung and every scrap of available straw or grass for fuel to cook his food. The forests that once provided wood for this purpose will be gone without a trace. The use of these agricultural wastes for fuel, in place of returning them to the land, will be leading to increasing soil impoverishment. Here and there will be seen a dust storm darkening the landscape over an area a thousand miles across. Man-creatures will be shown counting their wealth in terms of bits of printed paper representing other bits of a scarce but comparatively useless yellow metal that is kept buried in strong vaults. Meanwhile, the soil, the only real wealth that can keep mankind alive on the face of this Earth is savagely being cut loose from its ancient moorings and washed into the seven seas.

We have just arrived upon this Earth. How long will we stay?

1948

Konrad Z. Lorenz

THE TAMING OF THE SHREW

Though Nature, red in tooth and claw,
With ravine, shrieked against his creed.
TENNYSON, *In Memoriam*

All shrews are particularly difficult to keep; this is not because, as we
are led proverbially to believe, they are hard to tame, but because the
metabolism of these smallest of mammals is so very fast that they will die
of hunger within two or three hours if the food supply fails. Since they
feed exclusively on small, living animals, mostly insects, and demand, of
these, considerably more than their own weight every day, they are most
exacting charges. At the time of which I am writing, I had never succeeded in keeping any of the terrestrial shrews alive for any length of
time; most of those that I happened to obtain had probably only been
caught because they were already ill and they died almost at once. I had
never succeeded in procuring a healthy specimen. Now the order Insec-
tivora is very low in the genealogical hierarchy of mammals and is,
therefore, of particular interest to the comparative ethologist. Of the
whole group, there was only one representative with whose behavior I
was tolerably familiar, namely the hedgehog, an extremely interesting
animal of whose ethology Professor Herter of Berlin has made a very
thorough study. Of the behavior of all other members of the family
practically nothing is known. Since they are nocturnal and partly subterranean animals, it is nearly impossible to approach them in field observation, and the difficulty of keeping them in captivity had hitherto
precluded their study in the laboratory. So the Insectivores were officially
placed on my program.

First I tried to keep the common mole. It was easy to procure a healthy
specimen, caught to order in the nursery gardens of my father-in-law, and
I found no difficulty in keeping it alive. Immediately on its arrival, it
devoured an almost incredible quantity of earthworms which, from the
very first moment, it took from my hand. But, as an object of behavior
study, it proved most disappointing. Certainly, it was interesting to
watch its method of disappearing in the space of a few seconds under the
surface of the ground, to study its astoundingly efficient use of its strong,
spadeshaped fore-paws, and to feel their amazing strength when one held
the little beast in one's hand. And again, it was remarkable with what
surprising exactitude it located, by smell, from underground, the earthworms which I put on the surface of the soil in its terrarium. But these
observations were the only benefits I derived from it. It never became any
tamer and it never remained above ground any longer than it took to

devour its prey; after this, it sank into the earth as a submarine sinks into the water. I soon grew tired of procuring the immense quantities of living food it required and, after a few weeks, I set it free in the garden.

It was years afterwards, on an excursion to that extraordinary lake, the Neusiedlersee, which lies on the Hungarian border of Austria, that I again thought of keeping an insectivore. This large stretch of water, though not thirty miles from Vienna, is an example of the peculiar type of lake found in the open steppes of Eastern Europe and Asia. More than thirty miles long and half as broad, its deepest parts are only about five feet deep and it is much shallower on the average. Nearly half its surface is overgrown with reeds which form an ideal habitat for all kinds of water birds. Great colonies of white, purple, and grey heron and spoonbills live among the reeds and, until a short while ago, glossy ibis were still to be found here. Greylag geese breed here in great numbers and, on the eastern, reedless shore, avocets and many other rare waders can regularly be found. On the occasion of which I am speaking, we, a dozen tired zoologists, under the experienced guidance of my friend Otto Koenig, were wending our way, slowly and painfully, through the forest of reeds. We were walking in single file, Koenig first, I second, with a few students in our wake. We literally left a wake, an inky-black one in pale grey water. In the reed forests of Lake Neusiedel, you walk knee deep in slimy, black ooze, wonderfully perfumed by sulphureted-hydrogen-producing bacteria. This mud clings tenaciously and only releases its hold on your foot with a loud, protesting plop at every step.

After a few hours of this kind of wading you discover aching muscles whose very existence you had never suspected. From the knees to the hips you are immersed in the milky, clay-colored water characteristic of the lake, which, among the reeds, is populated by myriads of extremely hungry leeches conforming to the old pharmaceutical recipe, "*Hirudines medicinales maxime affamati.*"[1] The rest of your person inhabits the upper air, which here consists of clouds of tiny mosquitoes whose blood-thirsty attacks are all the more exasperating because you require both your hands to part the dense reeds in front of you and can only slap your face at intervals. The British ornithologist who may perhaps have envied us some of our rare specimens will perceive that bird watching on Lake Neusiedel is not, after all, an entirely enviable occupation.

We were thus wending our painful way through the rushes when suddenly Koenig stopped and pointed mutely towards a pond, free from reeds, that stretched in front of us. At first, I could only see whitish water, dark blue sky and green reeds, the standard colors of Lake Neusiedel. Then, suddenly, like a cork popping up on to the surface, there appeared, in the middle of the pool, a tiny black animal, hardly bigger than a man's

---

1. "In medicine, the hungriest leech is best." Until modern times, patients were bled as a remedy for various ills, and doctors kept live leeches for the purpose.

thumb. And for a moment I was in the rare position of a zoologist who sees a specimen and is not able to classify it, in the literal sense of the word: I did not know to which class of vertebrates the object of my gaze belonged. For the first fraction of a second I took it for the young of some diving bird of a species unknown to me. It appeared to have a beak and it swam on the water like a bird, not in it as a mammal. It swam about in narrow curves and circles, very much like a whirligig beetle, creating an extensive wedge-shaped wake, quite out of proportion to the tiny animal's size. Then a second little beast popped up from below, chased the first one with a shrill, bat-like twitter, then both dived and were gone. The whole episode had not lasted five seconds.

I stood open-mouthed, my mind racing. Koenig turned round with a broad grin, calmly detached a leech that was sticking like a leech to his wrist, wiped away the trickle of blood from the wound, slapped his cheek, thereby killing thirty-five mosquitoes, and asked, in the tone of an examiner, "What was that?" I answered as calmly as I could, "water shrews," thanking, in my heart, the leech and the mosquitoes for the respite they had given me to collect my thoughts. But my mind was racing on: water shrews ate fishes and frogs which were easy to procure in any quantity; water shrews were less subterranean than most other insectivores; they were the very insectivore to keep in captivity. "That's an animal I must catch and keep," I said to my friend. "That is easy," he responded. "There is a nest with young under the floor mat of my tent." I had slept that night in his tent and Koenig had not thought it worth-while to tell me of the shrews; such things are, to him, as much a matter of course as wild little spotted crakes feeding out of his hand, or as any other wonders of his queer kingdom in the reeds.

On our return to the tent that evening, he showed me the nest. It contained eight young which, compared with their mother, who rushed away as we lifted the mat, were of enormous size. They were considerably more than half her length and must each have weighed well between a fourth and a third of their dam: that is to say, the whole litter weighed, at a very modest estimate, twice as much as the old shrew. Yet they were still quite blind and the tips of their teeth were only just visible in their rosy mouths. And two days later when I took them under my care, they were still quite unable to eat even the soft abdomens of grasshoppers, and in spite of evident greed, they chewed interminably on a soft piece of frog's meat without succeeding in detaching a morsel from it. On our journey home, I fed them on the squeezed-out insides of grasshoppers and finely minced frog's meat, a diet on which they obviously throve. Arrived home in Altenberg, I improved on this diet by preparing a food from the squeezed-out insides of mealworm larvae, with some finely chopped small, fresh fishes, worked into a sort of gravy with a little milk. They consumed large quantities of this food, and their little nest-box looked quite small in comparison with the big china bowl whose contents they emptied three times a day. All these observations raise the problem of how the female water shrew succeeds in feeding her gigantic litter. It is absolutely impossible that she should do so on milk alone. Even on a more concentrated diet my young shrews devoured the equivalent of their own weight daily and this meant nearly twice the weight of a grown shrew. Yet, at that time of their lives, young shrews could not possibly engulf a frog or a fish brought whole to them by their mother, as my charges indisputably proved. I can only think that the mother feeds her young by regurgitation of chewed food. Even thus, it is little short of miraculous that the adult female should be able to obtain enough meat to sustain herself and her voracious progeny.

When I brought them home, my young watershrews were still blind. They had not suffered from the journey and were as sleek and fat as one could wish. Their black, glossy coats were reminiscent of moles, but the white color of their underside, as well as the round, streamlined contours of their bodies, reminded me distinctly of penguins, and not, indeed, without justification: both the streamlined form and the light underside are adaptations to a life in the water. Many free-swimming animals, mammals, birds, amphibians and fishes, are silvery-white below in order to be invisible to enemies swimming in the depths. Seen from below, the shining white belly blends perfectly with the reflecting surface film of the water. It is very characteristic of these water animals that the dark dorsal and the white ventral colors do not merge gradually into each other as is the case in "counter-shaded" land animals whose coloring is calculated to make them invisible by eliminating the contrasting shade on their undersides. As in the killer whale, in dolphins, and in penguins, the white underside of the watershrew is divided from the dark upper side by a sharp line which runs, often in very decorative curves, along the animal's flank. Curiously enough, this borderline between black and white showed considerable variations in individuals and even on both sides of one animal's body. I welcomed this, since it enabled me to recognize my shrews personally.

Three days after their arrival in Altenberg my eight shrew babies opened their eyes and began, very cautiously, to explore the precincts of their nest-box. It was now time to remove them to an appropriate container, and on this question I expended much hard thinking. The enormous quantity of food they consumed and, consequently, of excrement they produced, made it impossible to keep them in an ordinary aquarium whose water, within a day, would have become a stinking brew. Adequate sanitation was imperative for particular reasons; in ducks, grebes, and all waterfowl, the plumage must be kept perfectly dry if the animal is to remain in a state of health, and the same premise may reasonably be expected to hold good of the shrew's fur. Now water which has been polluted soon turns strongly alkaline and this I knew to be very bad for the plumage of waterbirds. It causes saponification of the fat to which the feathers owe their waterproof quality, and the bird becomes thoroughly wet and is unable to stay on the water. I hold the record, as far as I know hitherto unbroken by any other birdlover, for having kept dabchicks alive and healthy in captivity for nearly two years, and even then they did not die but escaped, and may still be living. My experience with these birds proved the absolute necessity of keeping the water perfectly clean: whenever it became a little dirty I noticed their feathers beginning to get wet, a danger which they anxiously tried to counteract by constantly preening themselves. I had, therefore, to keep these little grebes in crystal clear water which was changed every day, and I rightly assumed that the same would be necessary for my water shrews.

I took a large aquarium tank, rather over a yard in length and about two feet wide. At each end of this, I placed two little tables, and weighed them down with heavy stones so that they would not float. Then I filled up the tank until the water was level with the tops of the tables. I did not at first push the tables close against the panes of the tank, which was rather narrow, for fear that the shrews might become trapped underwater in the blind alley beneath a table and drown there; this precaution, however, subsequently proved unnecessary. The water shrew which, in its natural state, swims great distances under the ice, is quite able to find its way to the open surface in much more difficult situations. The nest-box, which was placed on one of the tables, was equipped with a sliding shutter, so that I could imprison the shrews whenever the container had to be cleaned. In the morning, at the hour of general cage-cleaning, the shrews were usually at home and asleep, so that the procedure caused them no appreciable disturbance. I will admit that I take great pride in devising, by creative imagination, suitable containers for animals of which nobody, myself included, has had any previous experience, and it was particularly gratifying that the contraption described above proved so satisfactory that I never had to alter even the minutest detail.

When first my baby shrews were liberated in this container they took a very long time to explore the top of the table on which their nest-box was standing. The water's edge seemed to exert a strong attraction; they approached it ever and again, smelled the surface and seemed to feel along it with the long, fine whiskers which surround their pointed snouts like a halo and represent not only their most important organ of touch but the most important of all their sensory organs. Like other aquatic mammals, the water shrew differs from the terrestrial members of its class in that its nose, the guiding organ of the average mammal, is of no use whatsoever in its underwater hunting. The water shrew's whiskers are actively mobile like the antennae of an insect or the fingers of a blind man.

Exactly as mice and many other small rodents would do under similar conditions, the shrews interrupted their careful exploration of their new surroundings every few minutes to dash wildly back into the safe cover of their nest-box. The survival value of this peculiar behavior is evident: the animal makes sure, from time to time that it has not lost its way and that it can, at a moment's notice, retreat to the one place it knows to be safe. It was a queer spectacle to see those podgy black figures slowly and carefully whiskering their way forward and, in the next second, with lightning speed, dash back to the nest-box. Queerly enough, they did not run straight through the little door, as one would have expected, but in their wild dash for safety they jumped, one and all, first onto the roof of the box and only then, whiskering along its edge, found the opening and slipped in with a half somersault, their back turned nearly vertically downward. After many repetitions of this maneuver, they were able to find the opening without feeling for it; they "knew" perfectly its whereabouts yet still persisted in the leap onto the roof. They jumped onto it and immediately vaulted in through the door, but they never, as long as they lived, found out that the leap and vault which had become their habit was really quite unnecessary and that they could have run in directly without this extraordinary detour. We shall hear more about this dominance of path habits in the water shrew presently.

It was only on the third day, when the shrews had become thoroughly acquainted with the geography of their little rectangular island, that the largest and most enterprising of them ventured into the water. As is so often the case with mammals, birds, reptiles, and fishes, it was the largest and most handsomely colored male which played the role of leader. First he sat on the edge of the water and thrust in the fore part of his body, at the same time frantically paddling with his forelegs but still clinging with his hind ones to the board. Then he slid in, but in the next moment took fright, scampered madly across the surface very much after the manner of a frightened duckling, and jumped out onto the board at the opposite end of the tank. There he sat, excitedly grooming his belly with one hind paw, exactly as coypus and beavers do. Soon he quieted down and sat still for a moment. Then he went to the water's edge a second time, hesitated for a moment, and plunged in; diving immediately, he swam ecstatically about underwater, swerving upward and downward again, running quickly along the bottom, and finally jumping out of the water at the same place as he had first entered it.

When I first saw a water shrew swimming I was most struck by a thing which I ought to have expected but did not: at the moment of diving, the little black and white beast appears to be made of silver. Like the plumage of ducks and grebes, but quite unlike the fur of most water mammals, such as seals, otters, beavers or coypus, the fur of the water shrew remains absolutely dry under water, that is to say, it retains a thick layer of air while the animal is below the surface. In the other mammals mentioned above, it is only the short, woolly undercoat that remains dry, the superficial hair tips becoming wet, wherefore the animal looks its natural color when underwater and is superficially wet when it emerges. I was already aware of the peculiar qualities of the waterpfoof fur of the shrew, and, had I given it a thought, I should have known that it would look, under water, exactly like the air-retaining fur on the underside of a water beetle or on the abdomen of a water spider. Nevertheless the wonderful, transparent silver coat of the shrew was, to me, one of those delicious surprises that nature has in store for her admirers.

Another surprising detail which I only noticed when I saw my shrews in the water was that they have a fringe of stiff, erectile hairs on the outer side of their fifth toes and on the underside of their tails. These form collapsible oars and a collapsible rudder. Folded and inconspicuous as long as the animal is on dry land, they unfold the moment it enters the water and broaden the effective surface of the propelling feet and of the steering tail by a considerable area.

Like penguins, the water shrews looked rather awkward and ungainly on dry land but were transformed into objects of elegance and grace on entering the water. As long as they walked, their strongly convex underside made them look pot-bellied and reminiscent of an old, overfed dachshund. But under water, the very same protruding belly balanced harmoniously the curve of their back and gave a beautifully symmetrical streamline which, together with their silver coating and the elegance of their movements, made them a sight of entrancing beauty.

When they had all become familiar with the water, their container was one of the chief attractions that our research station had to offer to any visiting naturalists or animal lovers. Unlike all other mammals of their size, the water shrews were largely diurnal and, except in the early hours of the morning, three or four of them were constantly on the scene. It was exceedingly interesting to watch their movements upon and under the water. Like the whirligig beetle, Gyrinus, they could turn in an extremely small radius without diminishing their speed, a faculty for which the large rudder surface of the tail with its fringe of erectile hairs is evidently essential. They had two different ways of diving, either by taking a little jump as grebes or coots do and working their way down at a steep angle, or by simply lowering their snout under the surface and paddling very fast till they reached "planing speed," thus working their way downward on the principle of the inclined plane—in other words, performing the converse movement of an ascending airplane. The water shrew must expend a large amount of energy in staying down since the air contained in its fur exerts a strong pull upwards. Unless it is paddling straight downwards, a thing it rarely does, it is forced to maintain a constant minimum speed, keeping its body at a slightly downward angle in order not to float to the surface. While swimming under water the shrew seems to flatten, broadening its body in a peculiar fashion, in order to present a better planing surface to the water. I never saw my shrews try to cling by their claws to any underwater objects, as the dipper is alleged to do. When they seemed to be running along the bottom, they were really swimming close above it, but perhaps the smooth gravel on the bottom of the tank was unsuitable for holding on to and it did not occur to me then to offer them a rougher surface. They were very playful when in the water and chased one another loudly twittering on the surface, or silently in the depths. Unlike any other mammal, but just like water birds, they could rest on the surface; this they used to do, rolling partly over and grooming themselves. Once out again, they instantly proceeded to clean their fur—one is almost tempted to say "preen" it, so similar was their behavior to that of ducks which have just left the water after a long swim.

Most interesting of all was their method of hunting under water. They came swimming along with an erratic course, darting a foot or so forward very swiftly in a straight line, then starting to gyrate in looped turns at reduced speed. While swimming straight and swiftly their whiskers were, as far as I could see, laid flat against their head, but while circling they were erect and bristled out in all directions, as they sought contact with some prey. I have no reason to believe that vision plays any part in the water shrew's hunting, except perhaps in the activation of its tactile search. My shrews may have noticed visually the presence of the live tadpoles or little fishes which I put in the tank, but in the actual hunting of its prey the animal is exclusively guided by its sense of touch, located in the wide-spreading whiskers on its snout. Certain small free-swimming species of catfish find their prey by exactly the same method. When these fishes swim fast and straight, the long feelers on their snout are depressed but, like the shrew's whiskers, are stiffly spread out when the fish becomes conscious of the proximity of potential prey; like the shrew, the fish then begins to gyrate blindly in order to establish contact with its prey. It may not even be necessary for the water shrew actually to touch its prey with one of its whiskers. Perhaps, at very close range, the water vibration caused by the movements of a small fish, a tadpole or a water insect is perceptible by those sensitive tactile organs. It is quite impossible to determine this question by mere observation, for the action is much too quick for the human eye. There is a quick turn and a snap and the shrew is already paddling shorewards with a wriggling creature in its maw.

In relation to its size, the water shrew is perhaps the most terrible predator of all vertebrate animals, and it can even vie with the invertebrates, including the murderous Dytiscus larva. It has been reported by A. E. Brehm that water shrews have killed fish more than sixty times heavier than themselves by biting out their eyes and brain. This happened only when the fish were confined in containers with no room for escape. The same story has been told to me by fishermen on Lake Neusiedel, who could not possibly have heard Brehm's report. I once offered to my shrews a large edible frog. I never did it again, nor could I bear to see out to its end the cruel scene that ensued. One of the shrews encountered the frog in the basin and instantly gave chase, repeatedly seizing hold of the creature's legs; although it was kicked off again it did not cease in its attack and finally, the frog, in desperation, jumped out of the water and onto one of the tables, where several shrews raced to the pursuer's assistance and buried their teeth in the legs and hindquarters of the wretched frog. And now, horribly, they began to eat the frog alive, beginning just where each one of them happened to have hold of it; the poor frog croaked heartrendingly, as the jaws of the shrews munched audibly in chorus. I need hardly be blamed for bringing this experiment to an abrupt and agitated end and putting the lacerated frog out of its misery. I never offered the shrews large prey again but only such as would be killed at the first bite or two. Nature can be very cruel indeed; it is not out of pity that most of the larger predatory animals kill their prey quickly. The lion has to finish off a big antelope or a buffalo very quickly indeed in order not to get hurt itself, for a beast of prey which has to hunt daily cannot afford to receive even a harmless scratch in effecting a kill; such scratches would soon add up to such an extent as to put the killer out of action. The same reason has forced the python and other large snakes to evolve a quick and really humane method of killing the well-armed mammals that are their natural prey. But where there is no danger of the victim doing damage to the killer, the latter shows no pity whatsoever. The hedgehog which, by virtue of its armor, is quite immune to the bite of a snake, regularly proceeds to eat it, beginning at the tail or in the middle of its body, and in the same way the water shrew treats its innocuous prey. But man should abstain from judging his innocently-cruel fellow creatures, for even if nature sometimes "shrieks against his creed," what pain does he himself not inflict upon the living creatures that he hunts for pleasure and not for food?

The mental qualities of the water shrew cannot be rated very high. They were quite tame and fearless of me and never tried to bite when I took them in my hand, nor did they ever try to evade it, but, like little tame rodents, they tried to dig their way out if I held them for too long in the hollow of my closed fist. Even when I took them out of their container and put them on a table or on the floor, they were by no means thrown into a panic but were quite ready to take food out of my hand and even tried actively to creep into it if they felt a longing for cover. When, in such an unwonted environment, they were shown their nest-box, they plainly showed that they knew it by sight and instantly made for it, and even pursued it with upraised heads if I moved the box along above them, just out of their reach. All in all, I really may pride myself that I have tamed the shrew, or at least one member of that family.

In their accustomed surroundings, my shrews proved to be very strict creatures of habit. I have already mentioned the remarkable conservatism with which they persevered in their unpractical way of entering their nest-box by climbing onto its roof and then vaulting, with a half turn, in through the door. Something more must be said about the unchanging tenacity with which these animals cling to their habits once they have formed them. In the water shrew, the path habits, in particular, are of a really amazing immutability; I hardly know another instance to which the saying, "As the twig is bent, so the tree is inclined," applies so literally.

In a territory unknown to it, the water shrew will never run fast except under pressure of extreme fear, and than it will run blindly along, bumping into objects and usually getting caught in a blind alley. But, unless the little animal is severely frightened, it moves in strange surroundings, only step by step, whiskering right and left all the time and following a path that is anything but straight. Its course is determined by a hundred fortuitous factors when it walks that way for the first time. But, after a few repetitions, it is evident that the shrew recognizes the locality in which it finds itself and that it repeats, with the utmost exactitude, the movements which it performed the previous time. At the same time, it is noticeable that the animal moves along much faster whenever it is repeating what it has already learned. When placed on a path which it has already traversed a few times, the shrew starts on its way slowly, carefully whiskering. Suddenly it finds known bearings, and now rushes forward a short distance, repeating exactly every step and turn which it executed on the last occasion. Then, when it comes to a spot where it ceases to know the way by heart, it is reduced to whiskering again and to feeling its way step by step. Soon, another burst of speed follows and the same thing is repeated, bursts of speed alternating with very show progress. In the beginning of this process of learning their way, the shrews move along at an extremely slow average rate and the little bursts of speed are few and far between. But gradually the little laps of the course which have been "learned by heart" and which can be covered quickly begin to increase in length as well as in number until they fuse and the whole course can be completed in a fast, unbroken rush.

Often, when such a path habit is almost completely formed, there still remains one particularly difficult place where the shrew always loses its bearings and has to resort to its senses of smell and touch, sniffing and whiskering vigorously to find out where the next reach of its path "joins on." Once the shrew is well settled in its path habits it is as strictly bound to them as a railway engine to its tracks and as unable to deviate from them by even a few centimeters. If it diverges from its path by so much as an inch, it is forced to stop abruptly, and laboriously regain its bearings. The same behavior can be caused experimentally by changing some small detail in the customary path of the animal. Any major alteration in the habitual path threw the shrews into complete confusion. One of their paths ran along the wall adjoining the wooden table opposite to that on which the nest box was situated. This table was weighted with two stones lying close to the panes of the tank, and the shrews, running along the wall, were accustomed to jump on and off the stones which lay right in their path. If I moved the stones out of the runway, placing both together in the middle of the table, the shrews would jump right up into the air in the place where the stone should have been; they came down with a jarring bump, were obviously disconcerted and started whiskering cautiously right and left, just as they behaved in an unknown environ-ment. And then they did a most interesting thing: they went back the way they had come, carefully feeling their way until they had again got their bearings. Then, facing round again, they tried a second time with a rush and jumped and crashed down exactly as they had done a few seconds before. Only then did they seem to realize that the first fall had not been their own fault but was due to a change in the wonted pathway, and now they proceeded to explore the alteration, cautiously sniffing and bewhiskering the place where the stone ought to have been. This method of going back to the start, and trying again always reminded me of a small boy who, in reciting a poem, gets stuck and begins again at an earlier verse.

In rats, as in many small mammals, the process of forming a path habit, for instance in learning a maze, is very similar to that just described; but a rat is far more adaptable in its behavior and would not dream of trying to jump over a stone which was not there. The preponderance of motor habit over present perception is a most remarkable peculiarity of the water shrew. One might say that the animal actually disbelieves its senses if they report a change of environment which necessitates a sudden alteration in its motor habits. In a new environment a water shrew would be perfectly able to see a stone of that size and consequently to avoid it or to run over it in a manner well adapted to the spatial conditions; but once a habit is formed and has become ingrained, it supersedes all better knowledge. I know of no animal that is a slave to its habits in so literal a sense as the water shrew. For this animal the geometric axiom that a straight line is the shortest distance between two points simply does not hold good. To them, the shortest line is always the accustomed path and, to a certain extent, they are justified in adhering to this principle: they run with amazing speed along their pathways and arrive at their destination much sooner than they would if, by whiskering and nosing, they tried to go straight. They will keep to the wonted path, even though it winds in such a way that it crosses and recrosses itself. A rat or mouse would be quick to discover that it was making an unnecessary detour, but the water shrew is no more able to do so than is a toy train to turn off at right angles at a level crossing. In order to change its route, the water shrew must change its whole path habit, and this cannot be done at a moment's notice but gradually, over a long period of time. An unnecessary, loop-shaped detour takes weeks and weeks to become a little shorter, and after months it is not even approximately straight. The biological advantage of such a path habit is obvious: it compensates the shrew for being nearly blind and enables it to run exceedingly fast without wasting a minute on orientation. On the other hand it may, under unusual circumstances, lead the shrew to destruction. It has been reported, quite plausibly, that water shrews have broken their necks by jumping into a pond which had been recently drained. In spite of the possibility of such mishaps, it would be shortsighted if one were simply to stigmatize the water shrew as stupid because it solves the spatial problems of its daily life in quite a different way from man. On the contrary, if one thinks a little more deeply, it is very wonderful that the same result, namely a perfect orientation in space, can be brought about in two so widely divergent ways: by true observation, as we achieve it, or, as the water shrew does, by learning by heart every possible spatial contingency that may arise in a given territory.

Among themselves, my water shrews were surprisingly good-natured. Although, in their play, they would often chase each other, twittering with a great show of excitement, I never saw a serious fight between them until an unfortunate accident occurred: one morning, I forgot to reopen the little door of the nest-box after cleaning out their tank. When at last I remembered, three hours had elapsed—a very long time for the swift metabolism of such small insectivores. Upon the opening of the door, all the shrews rushed out and made a dash for the food tray. In their haste to get out, not only did they soil themselves all over but they apparently discharged, in their excitement, some sort of glandular secretion, for a strong, musk-like odor accompanied their exit from the box. Since they appeared to have incurred no damage by their three hours' fasting, I turned away from the box to occupy myself with other things. However, on nearing the container soon afterwards, I heard an unusually loud, sharp twittering and, on my hurried approach, found my eight shrews locked in deadly battle. Two were even then dying and, though I consigned them at once to separate cages, two more died in the course of the day. The real cause of this sudden and terrible battle is hard to ascertain but I cannot help suspecting that the shrews, owing to the sudden change in the usual odor, had failed to recognize each other and had fallen upon each other as they would have done upon strangers. The four survivors quieted down after a certain time and I was able to reunite them in the original container without fear of further mishap.

I kept those four remaining shrews in good health for nearly seven months and would probably have had them much longer if the assistant whom I had engaged to feed them had not forgotten to do so. I had been obliged to go to Vienna and, on my return in the late afternoon, was met by that usually reliable fellow who turned pale when he saw me, thereupon remembering that he had forgotten to feed the shrews. All four of them were alive but very weak; they ate greedily when we fed them but died nonetheless within a few hours. In other words, they showed exactly the same symptoms as the shrews which I had formerly tried to keep; this confirmed my opinion that the latter were already dying of hunger when they came into my possession.

To any advanced animal keeper who is able to set up a large tank, preferably with running water, and who can obtain a sufficient supply of small fish, tadpoles, and the like, I can recommend the water shrew as one of the most gratifying, charming, and interesting objects of care. Of course it is a somewhat exacting charge. It will eat raw chopped heart (the customary substitute for small live prey) only in the absence of something better and it cannot be fed exclusively on this diet for long periods. Moreover, really clean water is indispensable. But if these clear-cut requirements be fulfilled, the water shrew will not merely remain alive but will really thrive, nor do I exclude the possibility that it might even breed in captivity.

1952

QUESTIONS

1. Lorenz discusses a field trip and some other matters before he reports his laboratory observations. What is the effect of this organization?

2. What features of the shrew's behavior does Lorenz select for special emphasis? What conclusions does he drew about these features?

3. Though this is mainly a report of his observations, Lorenz includes matters which are not necessary to the report of strictly controlled observation of the shrew's habits. Indicate some of the places where his discussion moves beyond strict reporting. Characterize the roles he assumes in these passages. Do these other roles or revelations of personality compromise or support his claim to being a scientist?

Niko Tinbergen

THE BEE-HUNTERS OF HULSHORST[1]

On a sunny day in the summer of 1929 I was walking rather aimlessly over the sands, brooding and a little worried. I had just done my finals, had got a half-time job, and was hoping to start on research for a doctor's thesis. I wanted very much to work on some problem of animal behaviour and had for that reason rejected some suggestions of my well-meaning supervisor. But rejecting sound advice and taking one's own decisions are two very different things, and so far I had been unable to make up my mind.

While walking about, my eye was caught by a bright orange-yellow wasp the size of the ordinary jam-loving *Vespa*. It was busying itself in a strange way on the bare sand. With brisk, jerky movements it was walking slowly backwards, kicking the sand behind it as it proceeded. The sand flew away with every jerk. I was sure that this was a digger wasp. The only kind of that size I knew was *Bembex*, the large fly-killer. But this was no *Bembex*. I stopped to watch it, and soon saw that it was shovelling sand out of a burrow. After ten minutes of this, it turned round, and now, facing away from the entrance, began to rake loose sand over it. In a minute the entrance was completely covered. Then the wasp flew up, circled a few times round the spot, describing wider and wider loops in the air, and finally flew off. Knowing something of the way of digger wasps, I expected it to return with a prey within a reasonable time, and decided to wait.

Sitting down on the sand, I looked round and saw that I had blundered into what seemed to be a veritable wasp town. Within ten yards I saw more than twenty wasps occupied at their burrows. Each burrow had a patch of yellow sand round it the size of a hand, and to judge from the number of these sand patches there must have been hundreds of burrows.

I had not to wait long before I saw a wasp coming home. It descended slowly from the sky, alighting after the manner of a helicopter on a sand patch. Then I saw that it was carrying a load, a dark object about its own size. Without losing hold of it, the wasp made a few raking movements with its front legs, the entrance became visible and, dragging its load after it, the wasp slipped into the hole.

At the next opportunity I robbed a wasp of its prey, by scaring it on its arrival, so that it dropped its burden. Then I saw that the prey was a Honey Bee.

1. Hulshorst is the sparsely populated region in Holland where Tinbergen's observations and experiments were carried out.

I watched these wasps at work all through that afternoon, and soon became absorbed in finding out exactly what was happening in this busy insect town. It seemed that the wasps were spending part of their time working at their burrows. Judging from the amount of sand excavated these must have been quite deep. Now and then a wasp would fly out and, after half an hour or longer, return with a load, which was then dragged in. Every time I examined the prey, it was a Honey Bee. No doubt they captured all these bees on the heath for all to and fro traffic was in the direction of the south-east, where I knew the nearest heath to be. A rough calculation showed that something was going on here that would not please the owners of the bee-hives on the heath; on a sunny day like this several thousand bees fell victims to this large colony of killers.

As I was watching the wasps, I began to realize that here was a wonderful opportunity for doing exactly the kind of field work I would like to do. Here were many hundreds of digger wasps—exactly which species I did not know yet, but that would not be difficult to find out. I had little doubt that each wasp was returning regularly to its own burrow, which showed that they must have excellent powers of homing. How did they manage to find their way back to their own burrow? * * *

Settling down to work, I started spending the wasps' working days (which lasted from about 8 a.m. till 6 p.m. and so did not put too much of a strain on me) on the 'Philanthus plains', as we called this part of the sands as soon as we had found out that *Philanthus triangulum Fabr.* was the official name of this bee-killing digger wasp. Its vernacular name was 'Bee-Wolf'.

An old chair, field glasses, note-books, and food and water for the day were my equipment. The local climate of the open sands was quite amazing, considering that ours is a temperate climate. Surface temperatures of $110°$ F were not rare. * * *

My first job was to find out whether each wasp was really limited to one burrow, as I suspected from the unhesitating way in which the home-coming wasps alighted on the sand patches in front of the burrows. I installed myself in a densely populated quarter of the colony, five yeards or so from a group of about twenty-five nests. Each borrow was marked and mapped. Whenever I saw a wasp at work at a burrow, I caught it and, after a short unequal struggle, adorned its back with one or two colour dots (using quickly drying enamel paint) and released it. Such wasps soon returned to work, and after a few hours I had ten wasps, each marked with a different combination of colours, working right in front of me. It was remarkable how this simple trick of marking my wasps changed my whole attitude to them. From members of the species *Philanthus triangulum* that were transformed into personal acquaintances, whose lives from that very moment became affairs of the most personal interest and concern to me.

While waiting for events to develop, I spent my time having a close look at the wasps. A pair of lenses mounted on a frame that could be worn as spectacles enabled me, by crawling up slowly to a working wasp, to observe it, much enlarged, from a few inches away. When seen under such circumstances most insects reveal a marvellous beauty, totally unexpected as long as you observe them with the unaided eye. Through my lenses I could look at my *Philanthus* right into their huge compound eyes; I saw their enormous, claw-like jaws which they used for crumbling up the sandy crust; I saw their agile black antennae in continuous, restless movement; I watched their yellow, bristled legs rake away the loose sand with such vigour that it flew through the air in rhythmic puffs, landing several inches behind them.

Soon several of my marked wasps stopped working at their burrows, raked loose sand back over the entrance, and flew off. The take-off was often spectacular. Before leaving they circled a little while over the burrow, at first low above the ground, soon higher, describing ever widening loops; then flew away, but returned to cruise once more low over the nest. Finally, they would set out in a bee-line, fifteen to thirty feet above the ground, a rapidly vanishing speck against the sky. All the wasps disappeared towards the south-east. Half a mile away in that direction the bare sands bordered upon an extensive heath area, buzzing with bees. This, as I was to see later, was the wasps' hunting area.

The curious loops my wasps described in the air before leaving their home area had been described by other observers of many other digger wasps. Philip Rau had given them the name of 'locality studies'. Yet so far nobody proved that they deserved that name; that the wasps actually took in the features of the burrow's surroundings while circling above them. To check this if possible was one of my main aims—I thought that it was most probable that the wasps would use landmarks, and that this locality study was what the name implied. First, however, I had to make sure that my marked wasps would return to their own holes. * * *

Before the first day was over, each of them had returned with a bee; some had returned twice or even three times. At the end of that day it was clear that each of them had its own nest, to which it returned regularly.

On subsequent days I extended these observations and found out some more facts about the wasps' daily life. As in other species, the digging of the large burrows and the capturing of prey that served as food for the larvae was exclusively the task of the females. And a formidable task it was. The wasps spent hours digging the long shafts, and throwing the sand out. Often they stayed down for a long time and, waiting for them to reappear, my patience was often put to a hard test. Eventually, however, there would be some almost imperceptible movement in the sand, and a small mound of damp soil was gradually lifted up, little by little, as if a miniature Mole were at work. Soon the wasp emerged, tail first, and all covered with sand. One quick shake, accompanied by a sharp staccato buzz, and the wasp was clean. Then it began to mop up, working as if possessed, shovelling the sand several inches away from the entrance.

I often tried to dig up the burrows to see their inner structure. Usually the sand crumbled and I lost track of the passage before I was ten inches down, but sometimes, by gently probing with a grass shoot first, and then digging down along it, I succeeded in getting down to the cells. These were found opening into the far end of the shaft, which itself was a narrow tube, often more than 2 ft. long. Each cell contained an egg or a larva with a couple of Honey Bees, its food store. A burrow contained from one to five cells. Each larva had its own living room-cum-larder in the house, provided by the hard-working female. From the varying nunber of cells I found in the nests, and the varying ages of the larvae in one burrow, I concluded that the female usually filled each cell with bees before she started to dig a new cell, and I assumed that it was the tunnelling out of a new cell that made her stay down for such long spells.

I did not spend much time digging up the burrows, for I wanted to observe the wasps while they were undisturbed. Now that I was certain that each wasp returned regularly to her own burrow, I was faced with the problem of her orientation. The entire valley was littered with the yellow sand patches; how could a wasp, after a hunting trip of about a mile in all, find exactly her own burrow?

Having seen the wasps make their 'locality studies', I naturally believed that each female actually did what this term implied: take her bearings. A simple test suggested that this was correct. While a wasp was away I brushed over the ground surrounding the nest entrance, moving all possible landmarks such as pebbles, twigs, tufts of grass, Pine cones, etc, so that over an area of 3–4 square metres none of them remained in exactly the same place as before. The burrow itself, however, I left intact. Then I awaited the wasp's return. When she came, slowly descending from the skies, carrying her bee, her behaviour was striking. All went well until she was about 4ft. above the ground. There she suddenly stopped, dashed back and forth as if in panic, hung motionless in the air for a while, then flew back and up in a wide loop, came slowly down again in the same way, and again shied at the same distance from the next. Obviously she was severely disturbed. Since I had left the nest itself, its entrance, and the sand patch in front of it untouched, this showed that the wasp was affected by the change in the surroundings.

Gradually she calmed down, and began to search low over the disturbed area. But she seemed to be unable to find the nest. She alighted now here, now there, and began to dig tentatively at a variety of places at the approximate site of the nest entrance. After a while she dropped her bee and started a thorough trial-and-error search. After twenty-five minutes or so she stumbled on the nest entrance as if by accident, and only then did she take up her bee and drag it in. A few minutes later she came out again, closed the entrance, and set off. And now she had a nice surprise in store for me: upon leaving she made an excessively long 'locality study': for fully two minutes she circled and circled, coming back again and again to fly over the disturbed area before she finally zoomed off.

I waited for another hour and a half, and had the satisfaction of seeing her return once more. And what I had hoped for actually happened: there was scarcely a trace of hesitation this time. Not only had the wasp lost her shyness of the disturbed soil, but she now knew her way home perfectly well.

I repeated this test with a number of wasps, and their reactions to my interference were roughly the same each time. It seemed probable, therefore, that the wasps found their way home by using something like landmarks in the environment, and not by responding to some stimulus (visual or otherwise) sent out by the nest itself. I had now to test more critically whether this was actually the case.

The test I did next was again quite simple. If a wasp used landmarks it should be possible to do more than merely disturb her by throwing her beacons all over the place; I ought to be able to mislead her, to make her go to the wrong place, by moving the whole constellation of her landmarks over a certain distance. I did this at a few nests that were situated on bare sandy soil and that had only a few, but conspicuous, objects nearby, such as twigs, or tufts of grass. After the owner of such a nest was gone, I moved these two or three objects a foot to the southwest, roughly at right angles to the expected line of approach. The result was as I had hoped for and expected, and yet I could not help being surprised as well as delighted: each wasp missed her own nest, and alighted at exactly the spot where the nest 'ought' to be according to the landmarks' new positions! I could vary my tests by very cautiously shooing the wasp away, then moving the beacons a foot in another direction, and allowing the wasp to alight again. In whatever position I put the beacons, the wasp would follow them. At the end of such a series of tests I replaced the landmarks in their original position, and this finally enabled the wasp to return to her home. Thus the tests always had a happy ending—for both of us. This was no pure altruism on my part—I could now use the wasp for another test if I wished.

When engaged in such work, it is always worth observing oneself as well as the animals, and to do it as critically and as detachedly as possible —which, of course, is a tall order. I have often wondered why the outcome of such a test delighted me so much. A rationalist would proba-

bly like to assume that it was the increased predictability resulting from the test. This was a factor of considerable importance, I am sure. But a more important factor still (not only to me, but to many other people I have watched in this situation) is of a less dignified type: people enjoy, they relish the satisfaction of their desire for power. The truth of this was obvious, for instance, in people who enjoyed seeing the wasps being misled without caring much for the intellectual question whether they used landmarks or not. I am further convinced that even the joy of gaining insight was not often very pure either; it was mixed with pride at having had success with the tests.

To return to the wasps: next I tried to make the wasps use landmarks which I provided. This was not only for the purpose of satisfying my lust for power, but also for nobler purposes, as I hope to show later. Since changing the environment while the wasp was away disturbed her upon her return and even might prevent her from finding her nest altogether, I waited until a wasp had gone down into her nest, and then put my own landmarks round the entrance—sixteen Pine cones arranged in a circle of about eight inches diameter.

The first wasp to emerge was a little upset, and made a rather long locality study. On her return home, she hesitated for some time, but eventually alighted at the nest. When next she went out she made a really thorough locality study, and from then on everything went smoothly. Other wasps behaved in much the same way, and next day regular work was going on at five burrows so treated. I now subjected all five wasps, one by one, to a displacement test similar to those already described. The results, however, were not clearcut. Some wasps, upon returning, followed the cones; but others were not fooled, and went straight home, completely ignoring my beacons. Others again seemed to be unable to make up their minds, and oscillated between the real nest and the ring of cones. This half-hearted behaviour did not disturb me, however, for if my idea was correct—that the wasps use landmarks—one would rather expect that my tests put the wasps in a kind of conflict situation: the natural landmarks which they must have been using before I gave them the Pine cones were still in their original position; only the cones had been moved. And while the cones were very conspicuous landmarks, they had been there for no more than one day. I therefore put all the cone-rings back and waited for two more days before testing the wasps again. And sure enough, this time the tests gave a hundred per cent preference for the Pine cones; I had made the wasps train themselves to my landmarks.

The rest of this first summer I spent mainly in consolidating this result in various ways. There was not much time to do this, for the season lasts only two months; by the end of August the wasps became sluggish, and soon after they died, leaving the destiny of their race in the hands of the pupae deep down in the sand, which were to lie there dormant until next July. And even in this short summer season the wasps could not work steadily, but were active on dry sunny days only—and of these a Dutch summer rarely supplies more than about twenty in all.

However, I had time to make sure that the wasps relied for their homing mainly on vision. First, I could cut off their antennae—the bearers of delicate organs of smell, of touch and of other sense organs —without at all disturbing the orientation. Second, when, in other tests, I covered the eyes of intact wasps with black paint, the wasps could not fly at all. Removing the cover of paint restored their eyesight, and with it their normal behaviour. Furthermore, when I trained a wasp to accept a circle of Pine cones together with two small squares of cardboard drenched in Pine oil, which gave off a strong scent, displacement of the cones would mislead the wasps in the usual way, but moving the scented squares had not the slightest effect. Finally, when wasps used to rings of cones were given, instead of cones, a ring of grey pebbles a foot from the nest, they followed these pebbles. This can only have been due to the pebbles being visually similar to the cones.

* * *

We began by investigating the wasp's 'locality study' a little more closely. As I mentioned before, we had already quite suggestive indications that it realy deserved this name, but clear-cut proof was still lacking. The otherwise annoying vagaries of the Atlantic climate provided us with a wonderful opportunity to get this proof. Long spells of cold rainy weather are not uncommon in a Dutch summer—in fact they are more common than periods of sunny weather, which alone could tempt the wasps to 'work'. Rainy weather put a strain on morale in our camp, but the first sign of improvement usually started an outburst of feverish activity, all of us doing our utmost to be ready for the wasps before they could resume their flights.

We had previously noticed that many (though not all) wasps spent cold and wet periods in their burrows. Rain and wind often played havoc with their landmarks and perhaps the wasps also forgot their exact position while sitting indoors. At any rate, with the return of good weather, all the wasps made prolonged 'locality studies' when setting out on their first trip. Could it be that they had to learn anew the lie of the land?

On one such morning, while the ground was still wet but the weather sunny and promising, we were at the colony at 7.30 a.m. Each of us took up a position near a group of nests and watched for the first signs of emerging wasps. We had not to wait long before we saw the sand covering one of the entrances move—a sure sign of a wasp trying to make her way into the open. Quickly we put a circle of pine cones round the burrow. When the wasp came out, she started digging and working at her nest, then raked sand over the entrance and left. In the course of the morning many wasps emerged and each received pine cones round her entrance before she had 'opened the door'. Some of these wasps did not bother to work at the nest, but left at once after coming out. These latter wasps we were going to use for our tests. As expected, they made elaborate locality studies, describing many loops of increasing range and altitude before finally departing. We timed these flights carefully. As soon as one of these wasps had definitely gone, we took the Pine cones away. This was done in order to make absolutely sure that, if the wasp should return unobserved, she could not see cones round her nest. If then, when we saw her return with a bee, a displacement test in which the circle of Pine cones was laid out some distance away from the nest would give positive results (i.e., the wasp would choose these cones), we would have proved that she must have learnt them during her locality study, for at no other time could she have seen them.

Not all such wasps returned on the same day. Their prolonged stay and their fast down in the burrows probably forced them to feed themselves in the Heather first. Some, however, returned with a bee and with these we succeeded in doing some exciting tests. In all we tested 13 wasps. They were observed to choose 93 times between the true nest and a 'sham nest' surrounded by the Pine cones. Seventy-three choices fell on the sham nests, against only 20 on the real nests. In control tests taken after the experiments, when the cones were put back round the real nest, of a total of 39 only 3 choices were now in favour of the sham nests, the other 36 being in favour of the real nests. There was no doubt then that these wasps had learnt the nature and the position of the new landmarks during the locality study.

The most impressive achievement was that of wasp No. 179. She had made one locality study of a mere six seconds and had left without returning, let along alighting. When she was tested upon her return more than an hour later she chose the cones 12 times and never came near the nest. When the original situation was restored she alighted at once on her burrow and slipped in. Nos. 174 and 177 almost equalled this record; both were perfectly trained after uninterrupted locality studies of 13 seconds. All the other wasps either made longer locality studies or interrupted them by alighting on the nest one or more times before leaving again. Such wasps might have learnt during alighting rather than while performing the locality study, so their results were less convincing.

This result, while not at all unexpected, nevertheless impressed us very much. It not only revealed an amazing capacity in these little insects to learn so quickly, but we were struck even more by the fact that a wasp, when not fully oriented, would set out to perform such a locality study, as if it knew what the effect of this specialized type of behaviour would be.

I have already described that a wasp, which has made a number of flights to and from a burrow, makes no, or almost no, locality study, but that it will make an elaborate one after the surroundings have been disturbed. Further tests threw light on the question what exactly made her do this. We studied the effect on locality studies of two types of disturbances. In tests of type A we either added or removed a conspicuous landmark before the wasp returned and then restored the original situation while she was inside. Such wasps, although finding the old, familiar situation upon emerging again, made long locality studies. In tests of type B the wasps were not disturbed at all when entering, but changes similar to those of the A-tests were made just before they left. None of these wasps made locality studies. Wasps used for A-tests always hesitated before alighting. Therefore, disturbances of the familiar surroundings perceived upon returning make the wasps perform a locality study when next departing, while the same disturbances actually present at the time of departure have no influence!

Some further, rather incomplete and preliminary tests pointed to another interesting aspect. Conspicuous new landmarks given before the return of the wasp and left standing until after her departure influenced the form of the locality study as well as its duration: the wasp would repeatedly circle round this particular landmark. If, however, such a landmark was left for some time, so that the wasp passed it several times on her way out and back, and then moved to a new place, the wasp would make a longer locality study than before, yet she would not describe extra loops round the beacon. She obviously recognized the object and had merely to learn its new position. These tests were too few and not fully conclusive, but they did suggest that there is more to this locality study than we had at first suspected. The whole phenomenon is remarkable and certainly deserves further study.

We next turned our attention to the exact nature of the landmarks that were used by the wasps. What exactly did they learn? We spent several seasons examining this and the more striking of our tests are worth describing.

First of all we found that not all objects round the next were of equal value to the wasps. The first indication of this was found when we tried to train them to use sheets of coloured paper about 3 x 4 inches, which we put out near the nests, as a preparation to study colour vision. It proved to be almost impossible to make the wasps use even a set of three of them; even after leaving them out for days on end we rarely succeeded with the same simple displacement tests that worked so well with the Pine cones. Most wasps just ignored them. Yet the bright blue, yellow and red papers were very conspicuous to us. For some reason, the Pine cones were meeting the wasps' requirements for landmarks better than the flat sheets. [We] worked out a method to test this. We provided two types of objects round a nest—for instance, flat discs and Pine cones—arranged in

a circle in alternation. After a day or so, we moved the whole circle and checked whether the wasps used it. If so, we then provided two sham nests at equal distances, one on each side of the real nest, and put all objects of one type round one of these sham nests, all of the other type round the other. If then the wasp had tained herself to one type of landmark rather than to the other, it should prefer one of the two sham nests. Such a preferential choice could not be due to anything but the difference in the wasps' attitude towards the two classes of objects, for all could have been seen by the wasp equally often, their distance to the nest entrance had been the same, they had been offered all round the nest, etc. —in short, they had had absolutely equal chances.

In this way we compared flat objects with solid, dark with light, those contrasting with the colour of the background with those matching it, larger with smaller, nearer with more distant ones, and so on. Each test had, of course, to be done with many wasps and each wasp had to make a number of choices for us to be sure that there was consistency in her preference. This programme kept us busy for a long time, but the results were worth the trouble. The wasps actually showed for landmarks a preference which was different from ours.

When we offered flat circular discs and hemispheres of the same diameter, the wasps always followed the hemispheres (43 against 2 choices). This was not due to the larger surface area of the hemispheres, for when we did similar tests with flat discs of much larger size (of 10 cm. diameter, whereas the hemispheres had a diameter of only 4 cm.), the choices were still 73 in favour of the hemispheres against 19 for the discs.

In other tests we found out that the hemispheres were not preferred because of their shading, nor because they showed contrasts between highlights and deep blacks, nor because they were three—dimensional, but because of the fact that they stood out above the ground. The critical test for this was to offer hollow cones, half of them standing up on top of the soil on their bases, half sunk upside down into the ground. Both were three dimensional, but one extended above the ground while the others formed pits in the ground. The standing cones were almost always chosen (108 against 21).

The preference for objects that projected above the ground was one of the reasons why Pine cones were preferred. Another reason was that Pine cones offered a chequered pattern of light and dark, while yet another reason was the fact that they had a broken instead of a smooth surface —i.e., dented objects were more stimulating than smooth ones. Similar facts had been found about Honey Bees by other students and much of this has probably to do with the organization of the compound eyes of insects.

We further found that large objects were better than small objects; near objects better than the same objects further away from the nest, objects that contrasted in tone with the background better than those matching the background, objects presented during critical periods (such as at the start of digging a new nest or immediately after a rainy period) better than objects offered once a wasp had acquired a knowledge of its surroundings.

It often amazed us, when doing these tests, that the wasps frequently chose a sham nest so readily although the circle offered contained only half the objects to which they had been trained. This would not be so strange if the wasps had just ignored the weaker 'beacons', but this was not the case. If, in our original test with flat discs and hemispheres, we would offer the discs alone, the wasps, confronted with a choice between the discs and the original nest without either discs or hemispheres, often chose the discs. These, therefore, had not been entirely ignored; they were potential beacons, but were less valued than the hemispheres. Once we knew this, we found that with a little perseverance we could train the wasps to our flat coloured papers. But it took time.

The fact that the wasps accepted these circles, with half the number of objects they used to see, suggested that they responded to the circular arrangement as a whole as well as to the properties of the individual beacon. This raised the interesting issue of 'configurational' stimuli and it seemed to offer good opportunities for experiment. This work was taken up by Van Beusekom who, in a number of ingenious tests, showed that the wasps responded to a very complicated stimulus situation indeed.

First of all, he made sure that wasps could recognize beacons such a Pine cones fairly well. He trained wasps to the usual circle of Pine cones and then gave them the choice between these and a similar arrangement of smooth blocks of Pine cone size. The wasps decided predominantly in favour of the Pine cones, which showed that they were responding to details which distinguished the two types of beacons.

He next trained a number of wasps to a circle of 16 Pine cones and subjected them to two types of tests. In Type A the wasp had to choose between two sets of 16 cones, one arranged in a circle, the other in a figure of another shape, such as a square, a triangle, or an ellipse. He found that, unless the figure was very similar to the circle, the wasps could distinguish between the two figures and alighted in the circle. In those tests the individual cones did not count; he could either use the original cones for constructing the circle or use them for the square or triangle. It was the circular figure the wasps chose, not the Pine cones used during training.

In tests of type B, after the usual training to a circle of 16, he offered the 16 cones in a non-circular arrangement against 8 or even fewer cones in a (loose) circle—and found that the wasps chose the circle in spite of the smaller number of cones. He could even go further and offer a circle of quite different elements, such as square blocks (which the wasps could distinguish from cones, as other tests had shown). If such a circle was offered against cones in a noncircular arrangement, it was the circle that won. Thus it was shown in a variety of ways that the wasps responded not only to the individual beacons (as the preference tests * * * had shown), but also to the circle as a whole.

However, all these experiments, while giving us valuable information about the way our wasps perceived their environment, had one limitation in common—they showed us only how the wasps behaved at the last stage of their journey home. We had many indications that the Pine cones were not seen until the wasps were within a few yards from the nest. How did they find their way pevious to this?

Although we were aware of these limitations, it was extremely difficult to extend our tests. However, we did a little about this. More than once we displaced small Pine trees growing at a distance of several yards from nests under observation. In many cases wasps were misled by this and tried to find their nests in the correct position in relation to the displaced tree. The precision of their orientation to such relatively distant marks was truly amazing.

Such large landmarks were used in a slightly different way from the Pine cones. Firstly, they were used even when relatively far from the nest. Secondly, they could be moved over far greater distances than the Pine cones. A circle of Pine cones would fail to draw the wasp with it if it was moved over more than about 7 ft., but a Pine tree, or even a branch of about 4 ft. high, could lure the wasps away even if moved over 8 metres. We further observed in many of our earlier tests that wasps, upon finding the immediate surroundings of the nest disturbed, flew back, circled round a Pine tree or a large sandhill perhaps 70 yards away, and then again approached the nest. This looked very much as though they were taking their bearings upon these larger landmarks.

Van der Linde and others also spent a great deal of time and energy in transporting individual wasps in light-proof cloth over distances up to 1,000 metres in all directions. Since good hunting grounds were to the south and south-east of the colony, whereas in other directions bare sand flats or dense Pine plantations bordered upon the *Philanthus* plains, we could assume that our wasps knew the country to the south and south-east better than in other directions—an assumption which was confirmed by the fact that our wasps always flew out in a south or south-east direction and returned with bees from there. The transported wasps, whose return to their nests was watched, did indeed much better from the south and south-east than from any other direction. From the north-west, for instance, half the wasps never returned as long as our observations lasted. This did indeed suggest that return from unknown country was difficult if not impossible and, therefore, that learning of some kind was essential, but it could not tell us more.

1958

QUESTIONS

1. Which of Tinbergen's activities, as described in this account of his research, are the kind you expect of a scientist? Do any of them surprise you or seem different from what you would expect of science?
2. In the paragraph beginning "When engaged in such work . . ." (p. 910), Tinbergen suggests that it is desirable for the scientific observer to observe himself as well as the object of his study. Why? In his own case, did this attention to himself interfere with his objective study of the facts? What did Tinbergen observe in this particular instance?
3. How did Tinbergen find the question he decided to study?
4. Before Tinbergen started his research, what was known of the "locality studies" made by the wasps? What steps did he go through to find out more about this matter? To what degree and in what ways was his study a matter of observation? What arrangements did he make to change the conditions for observing? Write a description of scientific method as exemplified by Tinbergen's study.
5. Are there resemblances between Tinbergen's account of his research and that of Konrad Z. Lorenz in "The Taming of the Shrew" (p. 893)? If these authors convey to you a sense of excitement about their work, show some of the specific ways in which their writing does this.

Alexander Petrunkevitch

THE SPIDER AND THE WASP

In the feeding and safeguarding of their progeny insects and spiders exhibit some interesting analogies to reasoning and some crass examples of blind instinct. The case I propose to describe here is that of the tarantula spiders and their archenemy, the digger wasps of the genus Pepsis. It is a classic example of what looks like intelligence pitted against instinct—a strange situation in which the victim, though fully able to defend itself, submits unwittingly to its destruction.

Most tarantulas live in the tropics, but several species occur in the temperate zone and a few are common in the southern U.S. Some varieties are large and have powerful fangs with which they can inflict a deep wound. These formidable looking spiders do not, however, attack man; you can hold one in your hand, if you are gentle, without being bitten. Their bite is dangerous only to insects and small mammals such as mice; for man it is no worse than a hornet's sting.

Tarantulas customarily live in deep cylindrical burrows, from which they emerge at dusk and into which they retire at dawn. Mature males wander about after dark in search of females and occasionally stray into houses. After mating, the male dies in a few weeks, but a female lives much longer and can mate several years in succession. In a Paris museum is a tropical specimen which is said to have been living in captivity for 25 years.

A fertilized female tarantula lays from 200 to 400 eggs at a time; thus it is possible for a single tarantula to produce several thousand young. She takes no care of them beyond weaving a cocoon of silk to enclose the eggs. After they hatch, the young walk away, find convenient places in which to dig their burrows and spend the rest of their lives in solitude. The eyesight of tarantulas is poor, being limited to a sensing of change in the intensity of light and to the perception of moving objects. They apparently have little or no sense of hearing, for a hungry tarantula will pay no attention to a loudly chirping cricket placed in its cage unless the insect happens to touch one of its legs.

But all spiders, and especially hairy ones, have an extremely delicate sense of touch. Laboratory experiments prove that tarantulas can distinguish three types of touch: pressure against the body wall, stroking of the body hair, and riffling of certain very fine hairs on the legs called trichobothria. Pressure against the body, by the finger or the end of a pencil, causes the tarantula to move off slowly for a short distance. The touch excites no defensive response unless the approach is from above where the spider can see the motion, in which case it rises on its hind legs, lifts its front legs, opens its fangs and holds this threatening posture as long as the object continues to move.

The entire body of a tarantula, especially its legs, is thickly clothed with hair. Some of it is short and wooly, some long and stiff. Touching this body hair produces one of two distinct reactions. When the spider is hungry, it responds with an immediate and swift attack. At the touch of a cricket's antennae the tarantula seizes the insect so swiftly that a motion picture taken at the rate of 64 frames per second shows only the result and not the process of capture. But when the spider is not hungry, the stimulation of its hairs merely causes it to shake the touched limb. An insect can walk under its hairy belly unharmed.

The trichobothria, very fine hairs growing from dislike[1] membranes on the legs, are sensitive only to air movement. A light breeze makes them vibrate slowly, without disturbing the common hair. When one blows gently on the trichobothria, the tarantula reacts with a quick jerk of its four front legs. If the front and hind legs are stimulated at the same time,

_____
1. Unlike or dissimilar.

the spider makes a sudden jump. This reaction is quite independent of the state of its appetite.

These three tactile responses—to pressure on the body wall, to moving of the common hair, and to flexing of the trichobothria—are so different from one another that there is no possibility of confusing them. They serve the tarantula adequately for most of its needs and enable it to avoid most annoyances and dangers. But they fail the spider completely when it meets its deadly enemy, the digger wasp Pepsis.

These solitary wasps are beautiful and formidable creatures. Most species are either a deep shiny blue all over, or deep blue with rusty wings. The largest have a wing span of about four inches. They live on nectar. When excited, they give off a pungent odor—a warning that they are ready to attack. The sting is much worse than that of a bee or common wasp, and the pain and swelling last longer. In the adult stage the wasp lives only a few months. The female produces but a few eggs, one at a time at intervals of two or three days. For each egg the mother must provide one adult tarantula, alive but paralyzed. The mother wasp attaches the egg to the paralyzed spider's abdomen. Upon hatching from the egg, the larva is many hundreds of times smaller than its living but helpless victim. It eats no other food and drinks no water. By the time it has finished its single Gargantuan meal and become ready for wasphood, nothing remains of the tarantula but its indigestible chitinous skeleton.

The mother wasp goes tarantula-hunting when the egg in her ovary is almost ready to be laid. Flying low over the ground late on a sunny afternoon, the wasp looks for its victim or for the mouth of a tarantula burrow, a round hole edged by a bit of silk. The sex of the spider makes no difference, but the mother is highly discriminating as to species. Each species of Pepsis requires a certain species of tarantula, and the wasp will not attack the wrong species. In a cage with a tarantula which is not its normal prey, the wasp avoids the spider and is usually killed by it in the night.

Yet when a wasp finds the correct species, it is the other way about. To identify the species the wasp apparently must explore the spider with her antennae. The tarantula shows an amazing tolerance to this exploration. The wasp crawls under it and walks over it without evoking any hostile response. The molestation is so great and so persistent that the tarantula often rises on all eight legs, as if it were on stilts. It may stand this way for several minutes. Meanwhile the wasp, having satisfied itself that the victim is of the right species, moves off a few inches to dig the spider's grave. Working vigorously with legs and jaws, it excavates a hole 8 to 10 inches deep with a diameter slightly larger than the spider's girth. Now and again the wasp pops out of the hole to make sure that the spider is still there.

When the grave is finished, the wasp returns to the tarantula to complete her ghastly enterprise. First she feels it all over once more with her antennae. Then her behavior becomes more aggressive. She bends her abdomen, protruding her sting, and searches for the soft membrane at the point where the spider's legs join its body—the only spot where she can penetrate the horny skeleton. From time to time, as the exasperated spider slowly shifts ground, the wasp turns on her back and slides along with the aid of her wings, trying to get under the tarantula for a shot at the vital spot. During all this maneuvering, which can last for several minutes, the tarantula makes no move to save itself. Finally the wasp corners it against some obstruction and grasps one of its legs in her powerful jaws. Now at last the harassed spider tries a desperate but vain defense. The two contestants roll over and over on the ground. It is a terrifying sight and the outcome is always the same. The wasp finally manages to thrust her sting into the soft spot and holds it there for a few seconds while she pumps in the poison. Almost immediately the tarantula falls paralyzed on its back. Its legs stop twitching; its heart stops beating. Yet it is not dead, as is shown by the fact that if taken from the wasp it can be restored to some sensitivity by being kept in a moist chamber for several months.

After paralyzing the tarantula, the wasp cleans herself by dragging her body along the ground and rubbing her feet, sucks the drop of blood oozing from the wound in the spider's abdomen, then grabs a leg of the flabby, helpless animal in her jaws and drags it down to the bottom of the grave. She stays there for many minutes, sometimes for several hours, and what she does all that time in the dark we do not know. Eventually she lays her egg and attaches it to the side of the spider's abdomen with a sticky secretion. Then she emerges, fills the grave with soil carried bit by bit in her jaws, and finally tramples the ground all around to hide any trace of the grave from prowlers. Then she flies away, leaving her descendant safely started in life.

In all this the behavior of the wasp evidently is qualitatively different from that of the spider. The wasp acts like an intelligent animal. This is not to say that instinct plays no part or that she reasons as man does. But her actions are to the point; they are not automatic and can be modified to fit the situation. We do not know for certain how she identifies the tarantula—probably it is by some olfactory or chemo-tactile sense—but she does it purposefully and does not blindly tackle a wrong species.

On the other hand, the tarantula's behavior shows only confusion. Evidently the wasp's pawing gives it no pleasure, for it tries to move away. That the wasp is not simulating sexual stimulation is certain because male and female tarantulas react in the same way to its advances. That the spider is not anesthetized by some odorless secretion is easily shown by blowing lightly at the tarantula and making it jump suddenly. What, then, makes the tarantula behave as stupidly as it does?

No clear, simple answer is available. Possibly the stimulation by the wasp's antennae is masked by a heavier pressure on the spider's body, so that it reacts as when prodded by a pencil. But the explanation may be much more complex. Initiative in attack is not in the nature of tarantulas; most species fight only when cornered so that escape is impossible. Their inherited patterns of behavior apparently prompt them to avoid problems rather than attack them. For example, spiders always weave their webs in three dimensions, and when a spider finds that there is insufficient space to attach certain threads in the third dimension, it leaves the place and seeks another, instead of finishing the web in a single plane. This urge to escape seems to arise under all circumstances, in all phases of life, and to take the place of reasoning. For a spider to change the pattern of its web is as impossible as for an inexperienced man to build a bridge across a chasm obstructing his way.

In a way the instinctive urge to escape is not only easier but often more efficient than reasoning. The tarantula does exactly what is most efficient in all cases except in an encounter with a ruthless and determined attacker dependent for the existence of her own species on killing as many tarantulas as she can lay eggs. Perhaps in this case the spider follows its usual pattern of trying to escape, instead of seizing and killing the wasp, because it is not aware of its danger. In any case, the survival of the tarantula species as a whole is protected by the fact that the spider is much more fertile than the wasp.

1952

QUESTIONS

1. What are the major points of contrast between the spider and the wasp? Why does Petrunkevitch emphasize these particular points and neglect other possible differences?
2. Petrunkevitch says that "insects and spiders exhibit some interesting analogies to reasoning and some crass examples of blind instinct." Why does he use the words "analogies" and "crass"?
3. Why is Petrunkevitch's initial description of the tarantula longer than his initial description of the wasp?
4. Petrunkevitch suggests more than one hypothesis or possible explanation for the behavior of the tarantula, and he says that "no clear, simple answer is available." How does he test the possible explanations? Explain which one you think he prefers.
5. What evidence do you have that Petrunkevitch sees the tarantula and the wasp at least partly in human terms? Explain why you think this is or is not legitimate for a scientist.

Franklin Russell

A MADNESS OF NATURE

Beyond the northern beach, a gray swell rolls in from Greenland and runs softly along the shore. The horizon is lost in a world of gray, and gulls glide, spectral in the livid air. Watching, I am enveloped in the sullen waiting time and feel the silence, drawn out long and thin. I wait for the sea to reveal a part of itself.

A capelin is perhaps the best-hunted creature on earth. It is not more than five inches long, about the size of a young herring, and undistinguished in appearance, except that when it is freshly caught, it is the color of mercury. As the capelin dies, its silvery scales tarnish and the glitter goes out like a light, ending a small allegory about nature, a spectacle of victims, victors, and an imperative of existence. Its death illuminates a dark process of biology in which there are shadows of other, more complex lives.

The capelin are born to be eaten. They transform oceanic plankton into flesh which is then hunted greedily by almost every sea creature that swims or flies. Their only protection is fecundity. One capelin survives to adulthood from every ten thousand eggs laid, and yet a single school may stir square miles of sea.

In mid-June, the capelin gather offshore. They can be seen everywhere and at all times in history, symbols of summer and fertility, of Providence and danger. I see them along the shores of Greenland, Iceland, Norway, and near Spitsbergen. I follow them across the northern coast of Russia. Chill air, gray seas, the northern silence are the capelin's world in Alaska, in the Aleutians, around Hudson Bay, and along the northeastern shores of North America. But the capelin of the Newfoundland coast are the most visible. Here, they spawn on the beaches rather than in deep water offshore, and I have come to see their rush for eternity.

They gather a thousand feet offshore, coalescing into groups of a hundred thousand to break the water's surface with bright chuckling sounds. They gather, and grow. Soon they are in the millions, with other millions swimming up from the offshore deeps. They gather, now in the billions, so densely packed together in places that the sea shimmers silver for miles and flows, serpentine, with the swelling body of a single, composite creature.

The fish do, in fact, possess a common sense of purpose. Nothing can redirect their imperative to breed. I once swam among them and saw them parting reluctantly ahead of me, felt their bodies flicking against my hands. Looking back, I saw them closing in, filling up the space created by

923

my passage. The passive fish tolerated me, in their anticipation of what they were about to do.

At this time of the year they are so engrossed that they barely react when a host of creatures advances to kill them. Beneath and beyond them, codfish pour up out of the deep. They overtake the capelin, eat them, plunge their sleek, dark bodies recklessly into shallow water. Some have swum so rapidly from such depths that their swim bladders are distended by the sudden drop in water pressure. The cod are gigantic by comparison with the capelin. Many weigh one hundred pounds or more, and will not be sated until they have eaten scores of capelin each. The water writhes with movement and foam where cod, headlong in pursuit, drive themselves clear out of the sea and fall back with staccato slaps.

The attack of the codfish is a brutal opening to a ritual, and a contradiction in their character. Normally, they are sedentary feeders on the sea floor. Now, however, they are possessed. Their jaws rip and tear; the water darkens with capelin blood: the shredded pieces of flesh hang suspended or rise to the surface.

Now a group of seabirds, the parrotlike puffins, clumsy in flight, turn over the capelin, their grotesque, axlike beaks probing from side to side as they watch the upper layers of the massacre. They are joined by new formations of birds until several thousand puffins are circling. They are silent, and there is no way of knowing how they were summoned from their nesting burrows on an island that is out of sight. They glide down to the water—stub-winged cargo planes—land awkwardly, taxi with fluttering wings and stamping paddle feet, then dive.

At the same time, the sea view moves with new invasions of seabirds. Each bird pumps forward with an urgency that suggests it has received the same stimulus as the cod. The gulls that breed on cliffs along a southern bay come first, gracefully light of wing, with raucous voice as they cry out their anticipation. Beneath them, flying flat, direct, silent, come murres, black-bodied, short-tailed, close relatives of the puffins. The murres land and dive without ceremony. Well offshore, as though waiting confirmation of the feast, shearwaters from Tristan da Cunha turn long, pointed wings across the troughs of waves and cackle like poultry.

The birds converge, and lose their identity in the mass thickening on the water. Small gulls—the kittiwakes, delicate in flight—screech and drop and rise and screech and drop like snowflakes on the sea. They fall among even smaller birds, lighter than they, which dangle their feet and hover at the water's surface, almost walking on water as they seek tiny pieces of shredded flesh. These are the ocean-flying petrels, the Mother Carey's chickens[1] of mariners' legends, which rarely come within sight of

1. "Mother Carey" is a corruption of *mata cara*,—dear mother. The petrels of the Atlantic Ocean are called Mother Carey's chickens because, in their abundance, they seem to fall, like snow, from heaven.

land. All order is lost in the shrieking tumult of the hundreds of thousands of birds.

Underwater, the hunters meet among their prey. The puffins and
murres dive below the capelin and attack, driving for the surface. The
cod attack at mid-depth. The gulls smother the surface and press the
capelin back among the submarine hunters. The murres and puffins fly
underwater, their beating wings turning them rapidly back and forth.
They meet the cod, flail wings in desperate haste, are caught, crushed,
and swallowed. Now seabirds as well as capelin become the hunted.
Puffin and murre tangle wings. Silver walls of capelin flicker, part, re-
form. Some seabirds surface abruptly, broken wings dangling. Others,
with a leg or legs torn off, fly frantically, crash, skitter in shock across the
water.

I see the capelin hunters spread across the sea, but also remember them
in time. Each year the hunters are different because many of them
depend on a fortuitous meeting with their prey. A group of small whales
collides with the capelin, and in a flurry of movement they eat several
tons of them. Salmon throw themselves among the capelin with the same
abandon as the codfish, and in the melee become easy victims for a score
of seals that kill dozens of them, then turn to the capelin and gorge
themselves nearly stuporous. They rise, well beyond the tumult of the
seabirds, their black heads jutting like rocks from the swell, to lie with
distended bellies and doze away their feast. Capelin boil up around them
for a moment but now the animals ignore them.

The capelin are hosts in a ceremony so ancient that a multitude of
species have adapted to seeking a separate share of the host's bounty.
The riotous collision of cod, seal, whale, and seabird obscures the smaller
guests at the feast. Near the shore wait small brown fish—the cunner
—one of the most voracious species. Soon they will be fighting among
themselves for pieces of flesh as the capelin begin their run for the beach,
or when the survivors of the spawning reel back into deep water, with the
dead and dying falling to the bottom. If the water is calm and the sun
bright, the cunner can be seen in two fathoms, ripping capelin corpses to
pieces and scattering translucent scales like silver leaves in a wind of the
sea.

Closer inshore, at the wave line, the flounder wait. They know the
capelin are coming and their role is also predetermined. They cruise
rapidly under the purling water in uncharacteristic excitement. They are
not interested in capelin flesh. They want capelin eggs, and they will
gorge as soon as spawning starts.

Now, the most voracious of all the hunters appear. Fishing vessels
come up over the horizon. They brought the Portuguese of the fifteenth
century, who anchored offshore, dropped their boats, and rowed ashore
to take the capelin with handnets, on beaches never before walked by

white men. They brought Spaniards and Dutchmen, Englishmen and Irish, from the sixteenth to the twentieth centuries. Americans, Nova Scotians, Gloucestermen, schoonermen, bankermen, longliner captains have participated in the ritual. All of them knew that fresh capelin is the finest bait when it is skillfully used, and can attract a fortune in codfish flesh, hooked on the submarine banks to the south.

But presently, these hunters are Newfoundlanders. They bring their schooners flying inshore like great brown-and-white birds, a hundred, two hundred, three hundred sail. They heel through the screaming seabirds, luff, anchor, and drop their dories with the same precision of movement of the other figures in the ritual. In an hour, three thousand men are at work from the boats. They work as the codfish work, with a frenzy that knots forearms and sends nets spilling over the sterns to encircle the capelin. They lift a thousand tons of capelin out of the sea, yet they do not measurably diminish the number of fish.

Meanwhile, landbound hunters wait for the fish to come within range of their lead-weighted handnets. Women, children, and old people crowd the beach with the able-bodied men. The old people have ancestral memories of capelin bounty. In the seventeenth and eighteenth centuries, when food was often short, only the big capelin harvest stood between them and starvation during the winter.

Many of the shore people are farmers who use the capelin for fertilizer as well as for food. Capelin corpses, spread to rot over thin northern soils, draw obedient crops of potatoes and cabbages out of the ground, and these, mixed with salted capelin flesh, become winter meals.

The children, who remember dried capelin as their candy, share the excitement of waiting. They chase one another up and down the beach and play with their own nets and fishing rods. Some are already asleep because they awoke before dawn to rouse the village, as they do every capelin morning, with the cry: "They've a-come, they've a-come!"

At the top of the beach, old women lie asleep or sit watching the seabirds squabbling and the dorymen rowing. They are Aunt Sadie and Little Nell and Bessie Blue and Mother Taunton, old ladies from several centuries. They know the capelin can save children in hard winters when the inshore cod fishery fails. They get up at two o'clock in the morning when the capelin are running, to walk miles to the nearest capelin beach. They net a barrel of fish, then roll the barrel, which weighs perhaps a hundred pounds, back home. They have finished spreading the fish on their gardens, or salting them, before the first of their grandchildren awakes.

They have clear memories of catching capelin in winter, when the sea freezes close inshore and the tide cracks the ice in places. Then millions of capelin, resting out the winter, rise in the cracks. An old woman with a good net can take tons of passive fish out of the water for as long as her strength lasts and for as far as her net reaches.

A cry rises from the beach: "Here they come!"

The ritual must be played out, according to habit. The dorymen and the seabirds, the rampaging cod and cunner cannot touch or turn the purpose of the capelin. At a moment, its genesis unknown, they start for the shore. From the top of some nearby cliffs I watch and marvel at the precision of their behavior. The capelin cease to be a great, formless mass offshore. They split into groups that the Newfoundlanders call wads —rippling gray lines, five to fifty feet wide—and run for the shore like advancing infantry lines. One by one, they peel away from their surviving comrades and advance, thirty to forty wads at a time.

Each wad has its discipline. The fish prepare to mate. Each male capelin seeks a female, darting from one fish to another. When he finds one, he presses against her side. Another male, perhaps two males, press against her other side. The males urge the female on toward the beach. Some are struck down by diving seabirds but others take their places. Cod dash among them and smash their sexual formations; they re-form immediately. Cunner rise and rip at them; flounder dart beneath them toward the beach.

The first wad runs into beach wavelets, and a hundred nets hit the water together; a silver avalanche of fish spills out on the beach. In each breaking wavelet the capelin maintain their formations, two or three males pressed tightly against their female until they are all flung up on the beach. There, to the whispering sound of tiny fins and tails vibrating, the female convulsively digs into the sand, which is still moving in the wake of the retreating wave. As she goes down, she extrudes up to fifty thousand eggs, and the males expel their milt.

The children shout; their bare feet fly over the spawning fish; the nets soar; sea boots grind down; the fish spill out; gulls run in the shallows under the children's feet; the flounder gorge. A codfish, two feet long, leaps out of the shallows and hits the beach. An old man scoops it up. The wads keep coming. The air is filled with birds. The dorymen shout and laugh.

The flood of eggs becomes visible. The sand glistens, then is greasy with eggs. They pile in driftlines that writhe back and forth in each wave. The female capelin wriggle into masses of eggs. The shallows are permeated with eggs. The capelin breathe eggs. Their mouths fill with eggs. Their stomachs are choked with eggs. The wads keep pouring onward, feeding the disaster on the beach.

Down come the boots and the nets, and the capelin die, mouths open and oozing eggs. The spawning is a fiasco. The tide has turned. Instead of spawning on the shore with the assurance of rising water behind them, each wad strikes ashore in retreating water. Millions are stranded but the wads keep coming.

In the background, diminished by the quantity of fish, other players gasp and pant at their nets. Barrels stack high on the beach. Horses whinny, driven hard up the bank at the back of the beach. Carts laden with barrels weave away. Carts bringing empty barrels bounce and roar down. The wads are still coming. Men use shovels to lift dead and dying fish from driftlines that are now two and three feet high. The easterly wind is freshening. The wavelets become waves. The capelin are flung up on the beach without a chance to spawn. They bounce and twist and the water flees beneath them.

It is twilight, then dark; torches now spot the beach, the offshore dories, and the schooners. The waves grow solidly and pile the capelin higher. The men shovel the heaps into pyramids, then reluctantly leave the beach. Heavy rain blots out beach and sea.

I remain to watch the blow piling up the sea. At the lowest point of the tide, it is driving waves high up on the beach, roiling the sand, digging up the partially buried eggs, and carrying them out to sea. By dawn most of the eggs are gone. The capelin have disappeared. The seabirds, the schooners, the cod, flounder, cunner, seals, whales have gone. Nothing remains except the marks of human feet, the cart tracks on the high part of the beach, the odd pyramid of dead fish. The feast is done.

The empty arena of the beach suggests a riddle. If the capelin were so perfectly adapted to spawn on a rising tide, to master the task of burying eggs in running sand between waves, to know when the tide was rising, why did they continue spawning after the tide turned? Was that, by the ancient rules of the ritual, intentional? If it was, then it indicated a lethal error of adaptation that did not jibe with the great numbers of capelin.

I wonder, then, if the weak died and the strong survived, but dismiss the notion after recalling the indiscriminate nature of all capelin deaths. There was no Darwinian selection for death of the stupid or the inexperienced. Men slaughtered billions, this year and last year and for three hundred years before, but the capelin never felt this pin-pricking on their colossal corporate bodies. Their spawning was a disaster for reasons well beyond the influence of men.

A nineteenth-century observer, after seeing a capelin-spawning, recorded his amazement at "the astonishing *prosperity* of these creatures, cast so wilfully away. . . ." It was in the end, and indeed throughout the entire ritual, the sheer numbers of capelin that scored the memory. The *prosperity* of the capelin preceded the disaster but then, it seemed, created it. Prosperity was not beneficial or an assurance of survival. The meaning of the ritual was slowly growing into sense. Prosperity unhinges the capelin. Prosperity, abundance, success, drive them on. They be-

come transformed and throw themselves forward blindly. . . .
I turn from the beach, warm and secure, and take a blind step forward.

1968

Irenäus Eibl-Eibesfeldt

THE ADVANTAGES OF SOCIABILITY

Some animals live in groups, some are out-and-out loners, but often an animal species is both sociable and aggressive at the same time. As both tendencies have evolved phylogenetically, it makes sense to inquire into the advantages of each in the selection process.

The advantages an animal derives from social combination vary considerably. The Mexican *Leiobunum cactorum* (a species of harvester) cluster together in the dry season in bundles of thousands. In this way they protect themselves against drying out. Animals that become separated from their fellows will quickly seek to rejoin the group. Particular scents attract them to their own kind. The emperor penguins of the Antarctic survive the severe winter storms by huddling close together to reduce their heat loss. In this way they withstand gales of over 60 mph and temperatures of −76° F.

Most fish in the upper ocean live in shoals. Their urge to be with their conspecifics[1] is patently very strong, for individuals that have lost the shoal dart this way and that in a panic in their efforts to rejoin it. Particular signals, for example black markings on the dorsal or caudal fins, ensure that they keep together. These groups are open, and any member of the species can join. They are, moreover, anonymous: the members of a shoal of fish do not generally know one another individually. First and foremost the shoal of fish is a defensive grouping against predators. This may come as a surprise, for at first sight it might seem as if the concentration of so many fish in one place would make it easier for a predatory fish to capture its prey. But this is not the case. Before making its catch, a predatory fish must come right up to its prey and be able to focus on it. Before it can focus on one particular fish in a shoal, however, the latter has generally plunged back among the others and the predator must switch its attention to another. This constant alteration of targets confuses it, and this confusion in turn protects the prey. In the Indian Ocean and off the Galápagos Islands I have observed predatory fish employing special tactics in an attempt to cut off individual fish from the shoal. Once they succeeded in this the predators had no further difficulty in taking the isolated fish out of the clear water.

---

1. Belonging to the same species.

Birds flock for similar reasons; in addition, they will help one another in danger by banding together to mob a bird of prey. Associations of higher vertebrates and insects are also generally defense communities. Jackdaws will attack a dog with a jackdaw in its mouth. Rhesus monkeys and baboons attack anything that seizes a young one. Its cry of help is a signal that releases an attack as a simple reflex action. My marmosets, which are completely tame, attack and threaten me if their young emit a cry of fear. As the little monkeys are very curious to explore me and cry out when they have frightened themselves with their own curiosity, I am the quite innocent target of such attacks. Defense against enemies is an important factor leading to the development of groups of animals. Protection and defense of the young certainly came before true parental care (i.e., feeding and cleansing of the young). In almost all fish and all reptiles which nurture their young, this care is limited to defense against enemies. In the simplest cases one of the adults remains with the offspring; indeed, often both parents remain together for the joint defense of the young—even in the case of fish. This is one of the roots of lasting pair formation, which in extreme cases can be maintained for life. There can, however, be partnerships without brood tending. Butterfly fish, for example, remain together for life, perhaps because in the case of rare fish in the vast spaces of a reef, the chances of finding one another again are too small.

A further advantage of social combination is that it makes possible the division of labor. The male can take over the defense of the young and the female the tasks of feeding, cleaning, and keeping them warm. Wolves that live in packs hunt together, some of them overtaking and cutting off the prey while the rest of the pack pursue and seize the prey. The division of labor attains its most sophisticated form in insect states. In these, different castes arise, each with different tasks. Among the leaf-cutting ants of tropical South America, for example, we find three different worker castes: the largest workers defend the nest as soldiers, the medium-sized workers cut and transport the pieces of leaf, and the minima workers, the smallest, process these leaves into compost for the fungi from which these agricultural ants live. In addition, the minima workers accompany the medium-sized workers and protect them at their work from the attacks of the parasitic flies that try to lay eggs on their necks. When the cut leaves are being transported, the minima themselves ride on the piece of leaf to defend the carrier. Such division of labor permits extreme specialization and thereby increased efficiency. The same is also true of human society.

Life in the group also makes possible the creation of traditions. In various apes and monkeys an individual's inventions are imitated by others and retained for generations by means of tradition. When the macaques[2] of Koshima Island (Japan) were fed with sweet potatoes one female discovered that it was possible to wash off the earth sticking to them. The others imitated her and now this habit is a group-specific character. The monkeys of this region were also fed on corn which was scattered on the shore. In the beginning, they picked up the grains individually until the female that had discovered how to wash potatoes also found out how to scoop up the mixture of sand and grain and wash it in the water. This discovery too was taken over in the course of time by other members of the group. In Kyoto a female learned to warm herself by the open fire, as the guards did. After a short time all the members of the group were doing it. Even among chimpanzees living in the wild there are group-specific habits passed on by tradition. The members of a family or larger group will often help one another to the point of self-sacrifice; short of that they will often do many things not directly in their individual interest. This raises the question of the evolution of altruistic behavior. Can it be explained by the principle of selection?

The answer must be yes. For in the case of social animals we should not so much think of the individual animal as of the group, in which the hereditary tendencies of the individual animal are in any case contained. A group in which individuals will sacrifice themselves, and their lives if need be, for the defense of the group or of their young will transmit its inheritance more successfully than a group that produces no individuals ready to defend it. For the same reason, although individuals that, for example, snatch food away from the others or fight without restraint will have certain immediate advantages within their group, they will weaken the group as a whole and will put it at a disadvantage in competition with other groups. Brutal, antisocial variants may at first prevail within a group, but their genome is less successful. For example, should a mutant occur in a bird population which causes a young bird to push all its siblings out of the nest, then this individual alone will survive and most probably produce offspring. The pushers among the offspring will, in turn, not only push nonpushers out of the nest, but each other as well. Thus, on the average, only one or two birds will survive, a number too low for the species to survive predation and accidents. For this reason these mutants will never prevail within the population.

Groupings of animals can be classified into two major categories according to whether they are open or closed. Open groups are those in which the members will permit others, not previously belonging to the group, to join. The members of an open group do not generally know one another; they are also interchangeable at any time. An example of an open group we have cited is the shoal of fish.

A closed group, on the other hand, is an intolerant entity. Strange conspecifics are not automatically admitted to the group; if they attempt

2. Monkeys of the genus *Macaca*.

to join they are repulsed. This means that the members of the group recognize one another either individually or by means of a distinguishing mark specific to all members of the group. On occasion an intolerant group is simulated, as in the case of the blind *Typhlogobius californiensis*, a species of Goby, in which two fish of different sexes defend a common territory. The male fights every other male of the species and the female equally fights all other females. These fish have nothing against other fish of the opposite sex, however, and one partner can be substituted for another without much ado. The situation is quite different in the case of the authentically conjugal teleost fish, for example the anemone fish (*Amphiprion xanthurus*), where male and female are aggressive toward every conspecific and tolerate only the sexual partner known to them individually.

In many fish, birds, and mammals that live in pairs the young are looked after by both parents. When they become independent they can leave the group. The pair-bond is sometimes broken at the same time, but often the pair remain together as a nuclear family. If the young remain with their parents, extended family groups are created, the members of which frequently know one another individually.

Family groups sometimes grow into lineages in which several generations are combined. Such extended families can still remain individualized groups up to a certain size and in this case will show complicated social hierarchies. But if the group grows beyond a certain size, it generally exceeds the capacity of the individual animal to recognize group members as individuals. In such cases members recognize one another by a common sign. Rats mark one another with urine and thus create a common group scent. If one removes a rat from a group and puts it back again three days later, it will be attacked because it has lost the group scent in the meantime. Conversely a strange rat will be accepted if one smears it with the urine of different members of the group to which it is a stranger. In this case we are dealing with anonymous closed groups. Up to a certain point human beings live both in individualized and in anonymous groups of varying degrees of exclusivity.

A brief survey shows that combination into groups brings various advantages. The evolution of altruistic behavior makes complete sense on Darwinian principles. Even mutual aid to the point of self-sacrifice of the individual is of species-preserving value. Among vertebrates the development of altruistic behavior must be of relatively recent date in the history of the earth. It is true that such behavior can be observed in fish, but only among the group of teleost fish, itself very young in the history of the earth. In amphibians and reptiles altruistic behavior patterns seem to be limited to a few rare cases of defense and carrying of the young. Adults never help one another. There are certainly a few "gregarious" reptiles, but if one observes these animals more closely one sees no

friendly interaction of any kind. The marine iguanas of the Galápagos Islands, for example, often lie in hundreds beside and on top of one another on the rocks, but the only social contact they make with their fellows is limited to an occasional threat: even their courtship consists of modified threatening behavior. They neither groom one another, feed one another, nor help one another in time of danger; there is no individualized bond. In most birds and mammals there is a fundamental difference. They help one another and will look after one another with a whole range of affectionate behavior patterns. With their capacity for cooperation and for altruism the social vertebrates—and by a parallel development the social insects—have achieved a higher degree of organization. It is this step forward that has formed the basis for our own human society.

1971

Stephen Jay Gould

OUR ALLOTTED LIFETIMES

Meeting with Henry Ford in E. L. Doctorow's *Ragtime*, J. P. Morgan praises the assembly line as a faithful translation of nature's wisdom:

> Has it occurred to you that your assembly line is not merely a stroke of industrial genius but a projection of organic truth? After all, the interchangeability of parts is a rule of nature. . . . All mammals reproduce in the same way and share the same designs of self-nourishment, with digestive and circulatory systems that are recognizably the same, and they enjoy the same senses. . . . Shared design is what allows taxonomists to classify mammals as mammals.

An imperious tycoon should not be met with equivocation; nonetheless, I can only reply "yes, and no" to Morgan's pronouncement. Morgan was wrong if he thought that large mammals are geometric replicas of small ones. Elephants have relatively smaller brains and thicker legs than mice, and these differences record a general rule of mammalian design, not the idiosyncracies of particular animals.

Morgan was right in arguing that large animals are essentially similar to small members of their group. The similarity, however, does not lie in a constant shape. The basic laws of geometry dictate that animals must change their shape in order to perform the same function at different sizes. I remind readers of the classical example, first discussed by Galileo in 1638: the strength of an animal's leg is a function of its cross-sectional area (length × length); the weight that the leg must support varies as the animal's volume (length × length × length). If a mammal did not alter the relative thickness of its legs as it got larger, it would soon collapse since body weight would increase much faster than the supporting strength of limbs. Instead, large mammals have relatively thicker leg bones than small mammals. To remain the same in function, animals must change their form.

The study of these changes in form is called "scaling theory." Scaling theory has uncovered a remarkable regularity of changing shape over the 25-millionfold range of mammalian weight from shrew to blue whale. If we plot brain weight versus body weight for all mammals on the so-called mouse-to-elephant (or shrew-to-whale) curve, very few species deviate far from a single line expressing the general rule: brain weight increases only two-thirds as fast as body weight as we move from small to large mammals. (We share with bottle-nosed dolphins the honor of greatest deviance from the curve.)

We can often predict these regularities from the physical behavior of objects. The heart, for example, is a pump. Since all mammalian hearts are similar in function, small hearts will pump considerably faster than large ones (imagine how much faster you could work a finger-sized toy bellows than the giant model that fuels a blacksmith's large forge). On the mouse-to-elephant curve for mammals, the length of a heartbeat increases between one-fourth and one-third as fast as body weight as we move from small to large mammals. The generality of this conclusion has just been affirmed in an interesting study by J. E. Carrel and R. D. Heathcote on the scaling of heart rate in spiders. They used a cool laser beam to illuminate the hearts of resting spiders and drew a crab spider-to-tarantula curve for eighteen species spanning nearly a thousandfold range of body weight. Again, scaling is very regular with heart rate increasing four-tenths as fast as body weight (or .409 times as fast, to be exact).

We may extend this conclusion for hearts to a very general statement about the pace of life in small versus large animals. Small animals tick through life far more rapidly than large ones—their hearts work more quickly, they breathe more frequently, their pulse beats much faster. Most importantly, metabolic rate, the so-called fire of life, scales only three-fourths as fast as body weight in mammals. Large mammals generate much less heat per unit of body weight to keep themselves going. Tiny shrews move frentically, eating nearly all their waking lives to keep their metabolic fire burning at its maximal rate among mammals; blue whales glide majestically, their hearts beating the slowest rhythm among active, warmblooded creatures.

If we consider the scaling of lifetime among mammals, an intriguing synthesis of these disparate data seems to suggest itself. We have all had enough experience with mammalian pets of various sizes to understand that small mammals tend to live for a shorter time than large ones. In fact, the scaling of mammalian lifetime follows a regular curve at about the same rate as heartbeat and breath time—between one-fourth and one-third as fast as body weight as we move from small to large animals. (Again, *Homo sapiens* emerges as a very peculiar animal. We live far longer than a mammal of our body size should. I have argued elsewhere that humans evolved by a process called "neoteny"—the retention of shapes and growth rates that characterize juvenile stages of our primate ancestors. I also believe that neoteny is responsible for our elevated longevity. Compared with other mammals, all stages of human life —from juvenile features to adulthood—arise "too late." We are born as helpless embryos after a long gestation; we mature late after an extended childhood; we die, if fortune be kind, at ages otherwise reached only by the very largest warmblooded creatures.)

Usually, we pity the pet mouse or gerbil that lived its full span of a year or two at most. How brief its life, while we endure for the better part of a century. As the main theme of this column, I want to argue that such pity is misplaced (our personal grief, of course, is quite another matter; with this, science does not deal). J. P. Morgan of *Ragtime* was right—small and large mammals are essentially similar. Their lifetimes are scaled to their life's pace, and all endure for approximately the same amount of biological time. Small mammals tick fast, burn rapidly, and live for a short time; large ones live long at a stately pace. Measured by their own internal clocks, mammals of different sizes tend to live for the same amount of time.

Yet we are prevented from grasping this important and comforting concept by a deeply ingrained habit of Western thought. We are trained from earliest memory to regard absolute Newtonian time as the single valid measuring stick in a rational and objective world. We impose our kitchen clock, ticking equably, upon all things. We marvel at the quickness of a mouse, express boredom at the torpor of a hippopotamus. Yet each is living at the appropriate pace of its own biological clock.

I do not wish to deny the importance of absolute, astronomical time to organisms. Animals must measure it to lead successful lives. Deer must know when to regrow their antlers, birds when to migrate. Animals track the day–night cycle with their circadian rhythms; jet lag is the price we pay for moving much faster than nature intended. Bamboos can somehow count 120 years before flowering again.

But absolute time is not the appropriate measuring stick for all biological phenomena. Consider the song of the humpback whale. These magnificent animals sing with such volume that their sounds travel through water for thousands of miles, perhaps even around the world, as their leading student Roger S. Payne has suggested. E. O. Wilson has described the awesome effect of these vocalizations: "The notes are eerie yet beautiful to the human ear. Deep basso groans and almost inaudibly high soprano squeaks alternate with repetitive squeals that suddenly rise or fall in pitch." We do not know the function of these songs. Perhaps they enable whales to find each other and to stay together during their annual transoceanic migrations.

Each whale has its own characteristic song; the highly complex patterns are repeated over and over again with great faithfulness. No scientific fact that I have learned in the last decade struck me with more force than Payne's report that the length of some songs may extend for more than half an hour. I have never been able to memorize the five-minute first Kyrie of the B-minor Mass[1] (and not for want of trying); how could a whale sing for thirty minutes and then repeat itself accurately? Of what possible use is a thirty-minute repeat cycle—far too long for a human to recognize: we would never grasp it as a single song (without Payne's recording machinery and much study after the fact). But then I remembered the whale's metabolic rate, the enormously slow pace of its life compared with ours. What do we know about a whale's perception of thirty minutes? A humpback may scale the world to its own metabolic rate: its half-hour song may be our minute waltz.[2] From any point of view, the song is spectacular; it is the most elaborate single display so far discovered in any animal. I merely urge the whale's point of view as an appropriate perspective.

We can provide some numerical precision to support the claim that all mammals, on average, live for the same amount of biological time. In a method developed by W. R. Stahl, B. Gunther, and E. Guerra in the late 1950s and early 1960s, we search the mouse-to-elephant equations for biological properties that scale at the same rate against body weight. For example, Gunther and Guerra give the following equations for mammalian breath time and heartbeat time versus body weight.

$$\frac{\text{breath time}\quad = .0000470 \; \text{body}^{0.28}}{\text{heartbeat time} = .0000119 \; \text{body}^{0.28}} = 40$$

(Nonmathematical readers need not be overwhelmed by the formalism. The equations simply mean that both breath time and heartbeat time increase about .28 times as fast as body weight as we move from small to large mammals.) If we divide the two equations, body weight cancels out because it is raised to the same power.

---

1. By Johann Sebastian Bach; the movement is woven together from many independent musical lines.

2. The reference is to the "Minute Waltz," by Frédéric Chopin, which is not only brief but fast-moving.

This says that the ratio of breath time to heartbeat time is 4.0 in mammals of any body size. In other words, all mammals, whatever their size, breathe once for each four heartbeats. Small animals breathe and beat their hearts faster than large animals, but both breath and heart slow up at the same relative rate as mammals get larger.

Lifetime also scales at the same rate to body weight (.28 times as fast as we move from small to large mammals). This means that the ratio of both breath time and heartbeat time to lifetime is also constant over the whole range of mammalian size. When we perform an exercise similar to that above, we find that all mammals, regardless of their size, tend to breathe about 200 million times during their lives (their hearts, therefore, beat about 800 million times). Small mammals breathe fast, but live for a short time. Measured by the sensible internal clocks of their own hearts or the rhythm of their own breathing, all mammals live about the same time. (Astute readers, having counted their breaths, may have calculated that they should have died long ago. But *Homo sapiens* is a markedly deviant mammal in more ways than braininess alone. We live about three times as long as mammals of our body size "should," but we breathe at the "right" rate and thus live to breathe about three times as much as an average mammal of our body size.)

The mayfly lives but a day as an adult. It may, for all I know, experience that day as we live a lifetime. Yet all is not relative in our world, and such a short glimpse of it must invite distortion in interpreting events ticking on longer scales. In a brilliant metaphor, the pre-Darwinian evolutionist Robert Chambers spoke of a mayfly watching the metamorphosis of a tadpole into a frog (from *Vestiges of the Natural History of Creation*, 1844):

> Suppose that an ephemeron [a mayfly], hovering over a pool for its one April day of life, were capable of observing the fry of the frog in the waters below. In its aged afternoon, having seen no change upon them for such a long time, it would be little qualified to conceive that the external branchiae [gills] of these creatures were to decay, and be replaced by internal lungs, that feet were to be developed, the tail erased, and the animal then to become a denizen of the land.

Human consciousness arose but a minute before midnight on the geologic clock. Yet we mayflies, ignorant perhaps of the messages buried in earth's long history, try to bend an ancient world to our purposes. Let us hope that we are still in the morning of our April day.

1977

Paul B. Sears

THE INDIVIDUAL

One may feel, as he looks at a swarm of bees, a haul of sardines, a waving field of wheat, or a rush-hour jam of pedestrians, that the individual living organism is a fairly insignificent thing. Yet the individual is the effective unit of all biological process. Whatever happens in the living world is the resultant of the interactions of individuals with each other and with the physical environment. Upon their ability to survive and function rests the pattern of which we are a part.

The earmark of the individual is form, but to the biologist as to the perceptive artist, form means more than shape. It connotes organization as well. Thanks to brilliant experiment, equally imposing theory and patient observation of life at all levels, we have concepts of the way in which life originated that are considerably better than plausible. Given the states of energy and matter that must have prevailed when our planet was more than a billion years younger than now—conditions which can be simulated in the laboratory—molecules of carbon and nitrogen compounds must have been formed and combined. Such compounds, we recall, contain the energy used in their making, and are the building stones from which proteins are constructed.

Somewhere along the line these primitive systems acquired a still mysterious property called *autocatalysis*. By means of it they could draw upon their surroundings to produce their own substance—duplicating their own chemical structure and in that way growing. But even at this primitive level separation into unit masses must have been necessary to insure effective contact with needed factors of environment. Consider our use of shakers and blenders to get uniform benefit from whatever goes into beverages and dressings.

At this point we must be careful of our language. The ancestral systems of which we speak did not become dispersed into units because they needed to. It was rather that only the dispersed systems survived to become ancestral. From the first, then, there was a selective process, favouring the bits that broke apart over those buried on the inside, out of contact with what they needed. Heaps of poultry, or even human beings piled up in panic, are likely to smother those inside. Separateness of working units was a first step towards the individual.

Abetting this separateness were certain sheer physical properties, notably surface tension such as preserves the form of oil or mercury globules, and enables a needle to float on water. It may seem redundant to say that surfaces so established become the agency of contact between interior contents and the outer world, but this is an important fact. Here

we see in its simplest form a beginning of the division of labour which is so remarkable a characteristic of living organisms. In this instance it would have been due solely to the position or location of particles which in no other respect differed from those inside the surface layer—as in a military camp the same individual does one thing if assigned to outpost duty, another if kept within the interior of the camp.

Eventually the separate units of living matter began to elaborate a variety of chemical substances with distinctive properties. Doubtless some were destructive, others useless, but still others enhanced the process of living in some collaborative fashion. The outcome of this highly selective process of trial and error was the development of those microscopic bodies we call cells, bounded by walls or membranes and structured into organs with definite roles in the economy of living. Among the most remarkable of these organs were the masses of pigment that made possible the production of carbohydrates from water and carbon dioxide with the aid of solar energy, thus initiating the plant kingdom. In the simplest green plants we know today—the blue-green algae—this food-making material is shown by the electron microscope to be arranged in a series of concentric sheaths or layers just under the cell wall, appropriately near the source of light and raw material. On the other hand, the material—and we now know what it is chemically—that transmits the characteristics of old units to the new ones cut off from it, tends to be arranged in the cell interior and thus to be buffered from direct contact with the outer environment.

Increasingly we are coming to regard the cell itself as a kind of ecological system with its components sensitively interrelated, each with its niche and role, the whole maintaining a self-repairing balance that ends only with death. Many substances called enzymes have been identified. These speed up chemical changes, each enzyme its own type, that otherwise would occur at painfully slow rates. Other substances including growth regulators and other hormones appear to control the processes that express themselves in form and organization. And since proteins are inevitably associated with life, it is important to recall a circumstance mentioned earlier, that an infinite number of proteins is possible and that each kind of plant or animal has its own distinctive protein make-up. In contrast the pigments, such as chlorophyll in plants and haemoglobin in animal blood, have generalized functions and are far more uniform throughout. In fact, these two types of pigment, plant and animal, show related chemical structure.

Once cells became established as individual units, slight changes in the material transmitting heredity resulted in a process of variation—a source of trial and error again. Some cells remained solitary, quickly separating into new units, others as they were so formed clung together into colonies of various shapes, the cells meanwhile remaining essentially alike. Judging from examples of this kind that exist today, it is difficult to say which the individual is, the cell or the colony, just as it is a matter of doubt whether to classify many simple forms as plant or animal. Presently, however, as evolution progressed, certain cells within the colony began to take on distinctive forms and compositions and a division of labour within the group was under way. Once this had occurred, there could no longer be any question as to the individual—it was now a self-regulating group of cells, more or less specialized to serve this new kind of biological unit.

Continuing on through the course of two billion years or more, the many-celled individual has become elaborated into the multitude of "higher" species that now inhabit the earth along with subcellular forms such as the viruses, with single-celled organisms and with colonial groups of cells that carry on as did their ancient prototypes.

Yet for elephant or man, bacterium or sponge, moss or oak tree, throughout the entire range of living forms, despite all special powers, needs and limitations, there runs a common thread of characteristics. Simple or complex, the living individual must stay alive, develop and reproduce its own kind. To exist it requires energy and material, which it handles through the various processes known as *metabolism*. It must also adjust to its environment by responding in various ways to stimuli, as by movement and chemical changes. It develops to maturity by growth, and reproduces either with or without sexual process. And finally, if it survives, it has done so by maintaining itself in a balanced working condition by repair and adjustment—a process which, for our own species, Professor Cannon called "the wisdom of the body."

Since none of these processes can proceed in isolation from the environment, they all have a strong ecological component. In fact, the environment, during the long course of evolutionary history, has built itself into the pattern of life. Recall the fact that, in our best judgment, organisms have developed into their present rich variety through environmental selection among variants produced in far greater numbers than can possibly survive. This organic evolution in its majestic sweep of time, space and dynamic change is the grand exemplar of all ecology. Two of its elements, variation and reproduction, we may take for granted. We have abundant evidence with respect to both, largely from specialists not primarily interested in ecology. Concerning the third, natural selection, we are much less well informed, convinced though we are of its operation.

We do know that spineless individuals of cactus sometimes occur, but are greedily eaten by animals and so have no opportunity to hand on this trait, unless protected by a Burbank. We know that a species of moth which produces both light and dark variants is eaten selectively by birds, depending upon the colour of its background and the resulting visibility.

There are species of grasses that vary in the length of summer daylight required to produce flower and fruit. Obviously the long-day strains will perpetuate themselves in the Dakotas, but be handicapped in Texas. In short, convincing proof that natural selection does occur awaits only the attention that has been given to other scientific problems.

So far as variation is concerned, Darwin had to be content with showing that it does occur. To later generations he left much unfinished business in the way of research, inseparably connected with the study of reproduction and inheritance. The issue was long clouded by the fact that some individual differences seem to be inherited, some not. Where a new individual is formed by the separation of a part of the old, characters remain substantially unchanged, as every orchardist who has grafted apple trees well knows. But where two individuals contribute, in sexual reproduction, to the formation of a new one, each contributes only half the necessary complement of determiners, the other half being discarded on a heads-or-tails basis. Thus, as we say, chance enters into the picture twice—once in selecting the contribution of each parent, and again in selecting the contributions that will be combined in any particular case. Sexual reproduction, by making possible new combinations of old characteristics, is a steadily acting means of variation. As reproduction without sex tends to conserve, that with sex tends towards experiment or innovation.

We have mentioned a certain confusion due to the fact that some characters seem not to be inherited. Leaving aside those whose determiners may be present but latent due to the combination or pairing in which they find themselves, we have others clearly caused by response to environment, or experience, if we wish to call it that. It has long been a dogma of biology that acquired characters, e.g., the muscular development of an athlete, cannot be inherited, and by inference, that the environment could not impress itself on the hereditary process. This deserves comment. In the first place, certain individuals and species inherit a capacity to be plastic under environmental stress. There are plants, for example certain buttercups, which will grow either under or above water. If submerged, the leaves are finally dissected. If not, they are entire. What is passed on here is not the leaf form, but the capacity to alter it. Man is perhaps the supreme example of plasticity, not in his capacity to change his bodily structure, but in the physical and psychic equipment that enables him to alter his pattern of behaviour. No one would pretend that he could pass on to his children an innate ability to speak English rather than Chinese. They inherit from him the capacity to do either (or both) depending on environment.

After the remarkable experiments which have enabled us to locate and identify the bodies within the cell that determine inherited capacities, but before we had acquired our present facility with radiant energy and delicate chemical manipulation, these bodies were assumed to be immune from environmental influence. Today, with much of the world's population alarmed over the possible effects of nuclear explosions, we are much less dogmatic. While we know that impacts that can be made on the structure of the material of inheritance are frequently—perhaps generally—harmful, there is a strong school of thought that now credits radiation with a major role in having in the past produced variations with survival value. Even within the very stronghold of the living cell, where the mechanism of inheritance is guarded, it is likely that we must recognize the effect of the external world on ecological relationship. We shall doubtless see many delicate experiments contrived to find out whether environment has been merely the selective agent *after* variation has occurred, or whether it has also played an important role in stimulating, or even determining the nature of, the variations upon which it later turns thumbs up or down.

Once the individual plant or animal is launched, whether by germination of a seed or spore, the hatching of an egg, or birth, its inherited make-up is put to the test. Assuming that it emerges into congenial surroundings so far as temperature, moisture, soil and nutrition are concerned, it is at once subject to the pressure of other individuals both of its own and other species. Science can only deal statistically with these many hazards. The chances are very small, say 1 in 32, 64 or 128, that all conditions will be either highly favourable or quite unfavourable, leaving the greatest likelihood of a mixture of both. Thus it is that the innate qualities of the individual may turn the course of events one way or another for him.

Vigour and timing, for example, may determine the outcome. Every gardener who has grown radishes has noticed that, even if he buys the choicest seed, some of the plants in a row grow larger and faster, developing good roots, than others that may lag behind and produce spindly shoot and root. The runt in a litter of pigs or pups is proverbially handicapped in getting a proper share of nourishment, and the more numerous his brothers and sisters, the worse his plight. The hard truth is that at this stage of the game especially, but later too, the worst potential competition for any organism can come from its own kind, since basic requirements are the same. This does not exclude the possibility of collaboration and mutual aid in nature, but it does make the study of it much more difficult.

The lodge-pole pine of western North America is an instructive organism to study. It comes up very thickly after a fire, since heat is necessary to release its seed from the tight cones and the tree itself thrives in light rather than shade. Consequently one can find even-aged stands of it, say in the Rocky Mountains, and, using a suitable borer, one can obtain pencil-sized cores into the centre of a tree, count the annual growth-layers, and so determine the age of any stand. Selecting stands of various ages, laying out equal areas in each and counting the numbers of individuals, one may find as many as 500 five-year-olds in 100 square feet, 10 to 15 twenty-five-year-olds in an equal area, but only a single specimen of sixty-year-old in a space of 10 by 10 feet. Even in the youngest stand one can select those which, by their slow start or feeble development, are doomed to disappear. Where there is a limit to water, nutrients, light and space the sombre judgment that "to him that hath shall be given" applies.

Among animals there is a similar high mortality, heaviest in early life as a rule. Because animals, unlike young pine trees, can move about, the explanation is more complex. While crowding and starvation certainly operate, predation and disease are probably a more usual source of elimination, not to mention congenital weakness or defect. It has long been known to naturalists that the populations of birds and mammals, while varying from time to time, fluctuate about a fairly level average. Anyone who notes the number of robins, jays, or chickadees nesting in or about his own garden can verify this fact. And if he is a good observer, he has only to count the eggs in their nests and the fledglings that come from them to appreciate the toll levied by such industrious agents as cats, hawks, crows, owls, lice and snakes. Nor are these eaters of the eaten themselves in any way exempt. It is a rare trip along a modern highway that does not show a dead cat or two, and before the invention of automobiles the cat had other survival problems. It is a traditional precaution to protect newborn kittens from their fathers, whose motives are not clear to us.

A single fish may produce thousands of eggs, as any devotee of caviar or shad roe knows. Yet of the many that hatch, only a few are represented by adult survivors. Study of the mackerel, for example, indicates that of 100 hatched only about 25 survive at the end of ten days, and this is just the beginning. Salmon return to spawn in the streams which they left for life in the ocean. Tagging of the young before they leave and checking of the adults that return has shown that only a minute fraction survive to reproduce. Yet the aggregate is so enormous as to support a major industry, now threatened by the construction of great dams to support still other industries.

Clearly enough the high death rate in nature is a harsh process, however we consider it. Yet in the vast economy of nature it serves to maintain a working balance, meanwhile favouring those individuals best adapted to survive. In a more rustic day, the old school arithmetics had a standard problem, based on the village smithy. A farrier agreed to shoe a horse, provided he would receive a penny for the first nail, two for the second, four for the third, and so on. Reckoning on four shoes, each secured by eight nails, the pupil was asked to compute the final bill—a wholesome exercise, revealing that the last nail alone would cost over twenty million dollars! The human population having doubled in the past sixty years and being set to double again in less time than that, it might not be amiss to start present-day pupils gently by asking them to compute what would happen, starting with a single pair of robins that raised four to maturity, if the process continued for thirty-two generations.

We have, of course, greatly interfered with the stern selective process. For our domestic plants and animals we control the rate of reproduction and select breeding stock to fit our wishes. For many forms of wildlife we make survival even more difficult, not only by direct killing, but to a greater degree by destroying their habitats. And for forest trees, notably in New England, we have reversed the process of natural selection of the most vigorous by cutting down the best trees, leaving the inferior individuals to reproduce—a process called "high-grading" by the lumberman.

As to our own species, we have, from the noblest of motives, lowered the death rate and prolonged life expectancy, while the birth rate remains high in most parts of the world. Many individuals whose innate physical vigour would not have been sufficient for survival in an earlier more rugged environment now do survive. Among them are many who have greatly enriched our culture, as well as many who impoverish it in more ways than one. Whether we like it or not, the destiny of the biological world seems to be in our hands, and of that world each individual of us is an inseparable part.

1966

Arthur Koestler

GRAVITY AND THE HOLY GHOST

"If I have been able to see farther than others," said Newton, "it was because I stood on the shoulders of giants." One of the giants was Johannes Kepler (1571–1630) whose three laws of planetary motion provided the foundation on which the Newtonian universe was built. They were the first "natural laws" in the modern sense: precise, verifiable statements expressed in mathematical terms; at the same time, they represent the first attempt at a synthesis of astronomy and physics which, during the preceding two thousand years, had developed on separate lines.

Astronomy before Kepler had been a purely descriptive geometry of the skies. The motion of stars and planets had been represented by the device of epicycles and eccentrics—an imaginary clockwork of circles turning on circles turning on circles. Copernicus, for instance, had used forty-eight wheels to represent the motion of the five known planets around the sun. These wheels were purely fictitious, and meant as such —they enabled astronomers to make more or less precise predictions, but, above all, they satisfied the dogma that all heavenly motion must be uniform and in perfect circles. Though the planets moved neither uniformly nor in perfect circles, the imaginary cogwheels did, and thereby "saved the appearances."

Kepler's discoveries put an end to this state of affairs. He reconciled astronomy with physics, and substituted for the fictitious clockwork a universe of material bodies not unlike the earth, freely floating and turning in space, moved by forces acting on them. His most important book bears the provocative title: A New Astronomy Based on Causation, or Physics of the Sky (1609). It contains the first and second of Kepler's three laws. The first says that the planets move around the sun not in circles but in elliptic orbits; the second says that a planet moves in its orbit not at uniform speed but at a speed that varies according to its position, and is defined by a simple and beautiful law: the line connecting planet and sun sweeps over equal areas in equal times. The third law establishes an equally elegant mathematical correlation between the length of a planet's year and its mean distance from the sun.

Kepler did not start his career as an astronomer, but as a student of theology (at the Lutheran University of Thuebingen); yet already as a student he was attracted by the Copernican idea of a sun-centered universe. Now Canon Copernicus's book, On the Revolutions of the Heavenly Spheres, had been published in the year of his death, 1543; that is, fifty years before Kepler first heard of him; and during that half century it had attracted very little attention. One of the reasons was its supreme unreadability, which made it into an all-time worst-seller: its first edition of a thousand copies was never sold out. Kepler was the first Continental astronomer to embrace the Copernican theory. His Mysterium Cosmographicum, published in 1597 (fifty-four years after Copernicus's death) started the great controversy—Galileo entered the scene fifteen years later.

The reason why the idea of a sun-centered universe appealed to Kepler was repeatedly stated by himself: "I often defended the opinions of Copernicus in the disputations of the candidates and I composed a careful disputation on the first motion which consists in the rotation of the earth; then I was adding to this the motion of the earth around the sun for physical or, if you prefer, metaphysical reasons." I have emphasized the last words because they contain the leitmotif of Kepler's quest, and because he used the same expression in various passages in his works. Now what were those "physical or, if you prefer, metaphysical reasons" which made Kepler prefer to put the sun into the center of the universe instead of the earth?

> My ceaseless search concerned primarily three problems, namely, the num-ber, size, and motion of the planets—why they are just as they are and not otherwise arranged. I was encouraged in my daring inquiry by that beautiful analogy between the stationary objects, namely, the sun, the fixed stars, and the space between them, with God the Father, the Son, and the Holy Ghost. I shall pursue this analogy in my furture cosmographical work.

Twenty-five years later, when he was over fifty, Kepler repeated his credo: "It is by no means permissible to treat this analogy as an empty comparison; it must be considered by its Platonic form and archetypal quality as one of the primary causes."

He believed in this to the end of his life. Yet gradually the analogy underwent a significant change:

> The sun in the middle of the moving stars, himself at rest and yet the source of motion, carries the image of God the Father and Creator. He distributes his motive force through a medium which contains the moving bodies, even as the Father creates through the Holy Ghost.

Thus the "moving bodies"—that is, the planets—are now brought into the analogy. The Holy Ghost no longer merely fills the space between the motionless sun and the motionless fixed stars. It has become an active force, a *vis motrix*, which *drives* the planets. Nobody before Kepler had postulated, or even suspected, the existence of a physical force acting between the sun and the planets. Astronomy was not con-cerned with physical forces, nor with the causes of the heavenly motions, merely with their description. The passages which I have just quoted are the first intimation of the forthcoming marriage between physics and astronomy—the act of betrothal, as it were. By looking at the sky, not through the eyes of the geometrician only, but of the physicist concerned with natural causes, he hit upon a question which nobody had asked before. The question was: "Why do the planets closer to the sun move faster than those which are far away? What is the mathematical relation between a planet's distance from the sun and the length of its year?"

These questions could only occur to one who had conceived the revolutionary hypothesis that the motion of the planet—and therefore its velocity and the duration of its year—was governed by a physical force emanating from the sun. Every astronomer knew, of course, that the greater their distance from the sun the slower the planets moved. But this phenomenon was taken for granted, just as it was taken for granted that boys will be boys and girls will be girls, as an irreducible fact of creation. Nobody asked the cause of it because physical causes were not assumed to enter into the motion of heavenly bodies. The greatness of the philoso-phers of the scientific revolution consisted not so much in finding the

right answers but in asking the right questions; in seeing a problem where nobody saw one before; in substituting a "why" for a "how."

Kepler's answer to the question why the outer planets move slower than the inner ones, and how the speed of their motion is related to their distance from the sun, was as follows:

> There exists only one moving soul in the center of all the orbits that is the sun which drives the planets the more vigorously the closer the planet is, but whose force is quasi-exhausted when acting on the outer planets because of the long distance and the weakening of the force which it entails.

Later on he commented: "If we substitute for the word 'soul' the word 'force,' then we get just the principle which underlies my 'Physics of the Skies.' As I reflected that this cause of motion *diminishes in proportion to distance* just as the light of the sun diminishes in proportion to distance from the sun, I came to the conclusion that this force must be substantial —'substantial' not in the literal sense but . . . in the same manner as we say that light is something substantial, meaning by this an unsubstantial entity emanating from a substantial body."

We notice that Kepler's answer came *before* the question—that it was the answer that begot the question. The answer, the starting point, was the analogy between God the Father and the sun—the former acting through the Holy Ghost, the latter through a physical force. The planets must obey the law of the sun—the law of God—the mathematical law of nature; and the Holy Ghost's action through empty space diminishes, as the light emanating from the sun does, with distance. The degenerate, purely descriptive astronomy which originated in the period of the Greek decline, and continued through the Dark and Middle Ages until Kepler, did not ask for meaning and causes. But Kepler was convinced that physical causes operate between heavenly, just as between earthly, bodies, and more specifically that the sun exerts a physical force on the planets. It was this conviction which enabled him to formulate his laws. Physics became the auxiliary matrix which secured his escape from the blocked situation into which astronomy had maneuvered itself.

The blockage—to cut a very long story short—was due to the fact that Tycho de Brahe[1] had improved the instruments and methods of stargazing, and produced observational data of a hitherto unequaled abundance and precision; and the new data did not fit into the traditional schemes. Kepler, who served his apprenticeship under Tycho, was given the task of working out the orbit of Mars. He spent six years on the task and covered nine thousand foliosheets with calculations in his small handwriting without getting anywhere. When at last he believed he had succeeded he found to his dismay that certain observed positions of Mars differed from those which his theory demanded by magnitudes up to

1. Danish astronomer (1546–1601).

eight minutes arc. Eight minutes arc is approximately one-quarter of the apparent diameter of the moon.

This was a catastrophe. Ptolemy, and even Copernicus, could afford to neglect a difference of eight minutes, because their observations were accurate only within a margin of ten minutes, anyway. "But," Kepler wrote in the *New Astronomy*, "but for us, who by divine kindness were given an accurate observer such as Tycho Brahe, for us it is fitting that we should acknowledge this divine gift and put it to use.... Henceforth I shall lead the way toward that goal according to my ideas. For if I had believed that we could ignore these eight minutes, I would have patched up by hypothesis accordingly. But since it was not permissible to ignore them, those eight minutes point the road to a complete reformation of astronomy...."

Thus a theory, built on years of labor and torment, was instantly thrown away because of a discord of eight miserable minutes arc. Instead of cursing those eight minutes as a stumbling block, he transformed them into the cornerstone of a new science. For those eight minutes arc had at last made him realize that the field of astronomy in its traditional framework was well and truly blocked.

One of the recurrent frustrations and tragedies in the history of thought is caused by the uncertainty whether it is possible to solve a given problem by traditional methods previously applied to problems which seem to be of the same nature. Who can say how many lives were wasted and good minds destroyed in futile attempts to square the circle, or to construct a *perpetuum mobile?*[2] The proof that these problems are *insoluble* was in each case an original discovery in itself (such as Maxwell's second law of thermodynamics);[3] and such proofs could only be found by looking at the problem from a point of view outside its traditional matrix. On the other hand, the mere knowledge that a problem is soluble means that half the game is already won.

The episode of the eight minutes arc had convinced Kepler that his problem—the orbit of Mars—was insoluble so long as he felt bound by the traditional rules of sky-geometry. Implied in those rules was the dogma of "uniform motion in perfect circles." *Uniform* motion he had already discarded before the crisis; now he felt that the even more sacred one of *circular* motion must also go. The impossibility of constructing a circular orbit which would satisfy all existing observations suggested to him that the circle must be replaced by some other curve.

The conclusion is quite simply that the planet's path is not a circle—it curves

---

2. A hypothetical machine which, once set in motion, would continue in motion forever unless stopped by some external force or by its own the wearing out.
3. The second law of thermodynamics, put forward not by James Clerk Maxwell, but by Rudolf Julius Emmanuel Clausius (1822–1888), provides an explanation of why a perpetual-motion machine cannot exist.

inward on both sides and outward again at opposite ends. Such a curve is called an oval. The orbit is not a circle but an oval figure.

This oval orbit was a wild, frightening new departure for him. To be fed up with cycles and epicycles, to mock the slavish imitators of Aristotle was one thing; to assign an entirely new, lopsided, implausible path for the heavenly bodies was quite another. Why indeed an oval? There is something in the perfect symmetry of spheres and circles which has a deep, reassuring appeal to the unconscious mind—otherwise it could not have survived two millennia. The oval lacks that archetypal appeal. It has an arbitrary, distorted form. It destroyed the dream of the "harmony of the spheres," which lay at the origin of the whole quest. At times he felt like a criminal, or worse: a fool. All he had to say in his own defense was: "I have cleared the Augean stables of astronomy of cycles and spirals, and left behind me only a single cartful of dung."

That cartful of dung—nonuniform motion in noncircular orbits —could only be justified and explained by arguments derived not from geometry, but from physics. A phrase kept humming in his ear like a catchy tune, and crops up in his writings over and again: there is a force in the sun which moves the planets, there is a force in the sun. . . . And since there is a force in the sun, there must exist some simple relationship between the planet's distance from the sun, and its speed. A light shines the brighter the nearer one is to its source, and the same must apply to the force of the sun: the closer the planet to it, the quicker it will move. This had been his instinctive conviction; but now he thought that he had found the proof of it. "Ye physicists, prick your ears, for now we are going to invade your territory." The next six chapters in the *Astronomia Nova* are a report on that invasion into celestial physics, which had been out of bounds for astronomy since Plato. He had found the second matrix which would unblock his problem.

That excursion was something of a comedy of errors—which nevertheless ended with finding the truth. Since he had no notion of the principle of inertia, which makes a planet persist in its tangential motion under its own momentum, and had only a vague intuition of gravity, he had to invent a force which, emanating from the sun, sweeps the planet round its path like a broom. In the second place, to account for the eccentricity of the orbits he had to postulate that the planets were "huge round magnets" whose poles pointed always in the same direction so that they would alternately be drawn closer to and be repelled by the sun. But although today the whole thing seems cockeyed, his intuition that there are *two antagonistic forces* acting on the planets, guided him in the right direction. A single force, as previously assumed—the divine Prime Mover and its allied hierarchy of angels—would never produce elliptic orbits and periodic changes of speed. These could only be the result of some dynamic tug of war going on in the sky—as indeed there is. The concept of two antagonistic forces provided rules for a new game in which elliptic orbits and velocities depending on solar distance have their legitimate place.

He made many mistakes during that wild flight of thought; but "as if by miracle"—as he himself remarked—the mistakes canceled out. It looks as if at times his conscious critical faculties had been anesthetized by the creative impulse, by the impatience to get to grips with the physical forces in the solar system. The problem of the planetary orbits had been hopelessly bogged down in its purely geometrical frame of reference, and when he realized that he could not get it unstuck he tore it out of that frame and removed it into the field of physics. That there were inconsistencies and impurities in his method did not matter to him in the heat of the moment, hoping that somehow they would right themselves later on —as they did. This inspired cheating—or, rather, borrowing on credit —is a characteristic and recurrent feature in the history of science. The latest example is subatomic physics, which may be said to live on credit —in the pious hope that one day its inner contradictions and paradoxes will somehow resolve themselves.

Kepler's determination of the orbit of Mars became the unifying link between the two formerly separate realsm of physics and astronomy. His was the first serious attempt at explaining the mechanism of the solar system in terms of physical forces; and once the example was set, physics and cosmology could never again be divorced.

1964

QUESTIONS

1. *What effect is produced by the essay's title, "Gravity and the Holy Ghost"? What relationship between the two terms in the title does the essay explore? Which of the two terms is more familiar to you; which do you think you know more about? Write an account of your understanding of them.*

2. *Why, according to Koestler, was it so difficult for Kepler to discard the notion of circular movement for the heavenly bodies, and why was it difficult to conceive of physical forces acting between the heavenly bodies? Are there any ideas in your own way of thinking that might be similarly difficult to discard or to accept? Perhaps Jacob Bronowski's essays "The Reach of Imagination" (p. 194) and "The Nature of Scientific Reasoning" (p. 951) may help you in thinking or writing about these questions.*

3. *What was the role of Tycho Brahe's observations, fact finding, data gathering, in the formulation of Kepler's thought? Did the facts speak for themselves and make a true conception of the solar system evident at once? Explain the reasons for your answer.*

4. *On p. 948, Koestler says of Kepler, "Instead of cursing those eight minutes as a stumbling block, he transformed them into the cornerstone of a new science." What does this statement mean? Is a differ-*

ence of such small scale between theory and observation necessarily significant in itself? If so, of what? Do you know of similar differences between expectation and actual behavior in your personal relationships? How have you handled such discrepancies?

Jacob Bronowski

THE NATURE OF SCIENTIFIC REASONING

What is the insight in which the scientist tries to see into nature? Can it indeed be called either imaginative or creative? To the literary man the question may seem merely silly. He has been taught that science is a large collection of facts; and if this is true, then the only seeing which scientists need to do is, he supposes, seeing the facts. He pictures them, the colorless professionals of science, going off to work in the morning into the universe in a neutral, unexposed state. They then expose themselves like a photographic plate. And then in the darkroom or laboratory they develop the image, so that suddenly and startlingly it appears, printed in capital letters, as a new formula for atomic energy.

Men who have read Balzac and Zola[1] are not deceived by the claims of these writers that they do no more than record the facts. The readers of Christopher Isherwood[2] do not take him literally when he writes "I am a camera." Yet the same readers solemnly carry with them from their schooldays this foolish picture of the scientist fixing by some mechanical process the facts of nature. I have had of all people a historian tell me that science is a collection of facts, and his voice had not even the ironic rasp of one filing cabinet reproving another.

It seems impossible that this historian had ever studied the beginnings of a scientific discovery. The Scientific Revolution can be held to begin in the year 1543 when there was brought to Copernicus, perhaps on his deathbed, the first printed copy of the book he had finished about a dozen years earlier. The thesis of this book is that the earth moves around the sun. When did Copernicus go out and record this fact with his camera? What appearance in nature prompted his outrageous guess? And in what odd sense is this guess to be called a neutral record of fact?

Less than a hundred years after Copernicus, Kepler published (between 1609 and 1619) the three laws which describe the paths of the planets. The work of Newton and with it most of our mechanics spring from these laws. They have a solid, matter-of-fact sound. For example, Kepler says that if one squares the year of a planet, one gets a number

---

1. Honoré de Balzac and Émile Zola, nine-   2. Modern English novelist and playwright.
teenth-century French novelists.

which is proportional to the cube of its average distance from the sun. Does anyone think that such a law is found by taking enough readings and then squaring and cubing everything in sight? If he does, then, as a scientist, he is doomed to a wasted life; he has as little prospect of making a scientific discovery as an electronic brain has.

It was not this way that Copernicus and Kepler thought, or that scientists think today. Copernicus found that the orbits of the planets would look simpler if they were looked at from the sun and not from the earth. But he did not in the first place find this by routine calculation. His first step was a leap of imagination—to lift himself from the earth, and put himself wildly, speculatively into the sun. "The earth conceives from the sun," he wrote; and "the sun rules the family of stars." We catch in his mind an image, the gesture of the virile man standing in the sun, with arms outstretched, overlooking the planets. Perhaps Copernicus took the picture from the drawings of the youth with outstretched arms which the Renaissance teachers put into their books on the proportions of the body. Perhaps he had seen Leonardo's drawings of his loved pupil Salai. I do not know. To me, the gesture of Copernicus, the shining youth looking outward from the sun, is still vivid in a drawing which William Blake in 1780 based on all these: the drawing which is usually called *Glad Day*.

Kepler's mind, we know, was filled with just such fanciful analogies; and we know what they were. Kepler wanted to relate the speeds of the planets to the musical intervals. He tried to fit the five regular solids into their orbits. None of these likenesses worked, and they have been forgotten; yet they have been and they remain the stepping stones of every creative mind. Kepler felt for his laws by way of metaphors, he searched mystically for likenesses with what he knew in every strange corner of nature. And when among these guesses he hit upon his laws, he did not think of their numbers as the balancing of a cosmic bank account, but as a revelation of the unity in all nature. To us, the analogies by which Kepler listened for the movement of the planets in the music of the spheres are farfetched. Yet are they more so than the wild leap by which Rutherford and Bohr in our own century found a model for the atom in, of all places, the planetary system?

No scientific theory is a collection of facts. It will not even do to call a theory true or false in the simple sense in which every fact is either so or not so. The Epicureans held that matter is made of atoms two thousand years ago and we are now tempted to say that their theory was true. But if we do so we confuse their notion of matter with our own. John Dalton in 1808 first saw the structure of matter as we do today, and what he took from the ancients was not their theory but something richer, their image: the atom. Much of what was in Dalton's mind was as vague as the Greek notion, and quite as mistaken. But he suddenly gave life to the new facts of chemistry and the ancient theory together, by fusing them to give what neither had: a coherent picture of how matter is linked and built up from different kinds of atoms. The act of fusion is the creative act.

All science is the search for unity in hidden likenesses. The search may be on a grand scale, as in the modern theories which try to link the fields of gravitation and electromagnetism. But we do not need to be browbeaten by the scale of science. There are discoveries to be made by snatching a small likeness from the air too, if it is bold enough. In 1935 the Japanese physicist Hideki Yukawa wrote a paper which can still give heart to a young scientist. He took as his starting point the known fact that waves of light can sometimes behave as if they were separate pellets. From this he reasoned that the forces which hold the nucleus of an atom together might sometimes also be observed as if they were solid pellets. A schoolboy can see how thin Yukawa's analogy is, and his teacher would be severe with it. Yet Yukawa without a blush calculated the mass of the pellet he expected to see, and waited. He was right; his meson was found, and a range of other mesons, neither the existence nor the nature of which had been suspected before. The likeness had borne fruit.

The scientist looks for order in the appearances of nature by exploring such likenesses. For order does not display itself of itself; if it can be said to be there at all, it is not there for the mere looking. There is no way of pointing a finger or camera at it; order must be discovered and, in a deep sense, it must be created. What we see, as we seen it, is mere disorder.

This point has been put trenchantly in a fable by Karl Popper. Suppose that someone wished to give his whole life to science. Suppose that he therefore sat down, pencil in hand, and for the next twenty, thirty, forty years recorded in notebook after notebook everything that he could observe. He may be supposed to leave out nothing: today's humidity, the racing results, the level of cosmic radiation and the stockmarket prices and the look of Mars, all would be there. He would have compiled the most careful record of nature that has ever been made; and, dying in the calm certainty of a life well spent, he would of course leave his notebooks to the Royal Society. Would the Royal Society think him for the treasure of a lifetime of observation? It would not. The Royal Society would treat his notebooks exactly as the English bishops have treated Joanna Southcott's box.[3] It would refuse to open them at all, because it would know without looking that the notebooks contain only a jumble of disorderly and meaningless items.

Science finds order and meaning in our experience, and sets about this in quite a different way. It sets about it as Newton did in the story which

3. Joanna Southcott was a nineteenth-century English farm servant who claimed to be a prophetess. She left behind a box which was to be opened in a time of national emergency in the presence of all the English bishops. In 1927, a bishop agreed to officiate; when the box was opened, it was found to contain only some odds and ends.

he himself told in his old age, and of which the schoolbooks give only a caricature. In the year 1665, when Newton was twenty-two, the plague broke out in southern England, and the University of Cambridge was closed. Newton therefore spent the next eighteen months at home, removed from traditional learning, at a time when he was impatient for knowledge and, in his own phrase, "I was in the prime of my age for invention." In this eager, boyish mood, sitting one day in the garden of his widowed mother, he saw an apple fall. So far the books have the story right; we think we even know the kind of apple; tradition has it that it was a Flower of Kent. But now they miss the crux of the story. For what struck the young Newton at the sight was not the thought that the apple must be drawn to the earth by gravity; that conception was older than Newton. What struck him was the conjecture that the same force of gravity, which reaches to the top of the tree, might go on reaching out beyond the earth and its air, endlessly into space. Gravity might reach the moon: this was Newton's new thought; and it might be gravity which holds the moon in her orbit. There and then he calculated what force from the earth (falling off as the square of the distance) would hold the moon, and compared it with the known force of gravity at tree height. The forces agreed; Newton says laconically, "I found them answer pretty nearly." Yet they agreed only nearly: the likeness and the approximation go together, for no likeness is exact. In Newton's science modern sciences is full grown.

It grows from a comparison. It has seized a likeness between two unlike appearances; for the apple in the summer garden and the grave moon overhead are surely as unlike in their movements as two things can be. Newton traced in them two expressions of a single concept, gravitation: and the concept (and the unity) are in that sense his free creation. The progress of science is the discovery at each step of a new order which gives unity to what had long seemed unlike.

* * *

1953, 1965

QUESTIONS

1. In his opening paragraph Bronowski pictures what the "literary man," or perhaps the ordinary non-scientist, thinks of as the nature of science. Is this a fair representation of the layman's view? What features of science or of the presentation of science might contribute to the development of that view? How does the process depicted in that paragraph compare with the actual activity of a scientist, as described in the account of his own work given by Konrad Z. Lorenz in "The Taming of the Shrew" (p. 893), or Niko Tinbergen in "The Bee-Hunters of Hulshorst" (p. 906); or in the account of Kepler given by Arthur Koestler in "Gravity and the Holy Ghost" (p. 944)?

2. In his fourth paragraph Bronowski indicates that an electronic brain has little or no chance of making a scientific discovery. Do you agree? Why, or not?

3. Bronowski recounts the famous story of Newton and the apple. What general principle about science is he exemplifying in this story?

4. On p. 951 Bronowski describes a voice as having "not even the ironic rasp of one filing cabinet reproving another." Is that image more appropriate to the situation? Can you find other such uses of language in the selection?

5. Write an essay comparing Bronowski's description of the process of science with that given by Thomas S. Kuhn in "The Route to Normal Science" (p. 975). In what respects are the views of these authors similar? Do they differ in any important ways? What sorts of language does each of them use to convey his thoughts? How would you account for differences in tone and usage?

6. In "The Reach of Imagination" (p. 194) Bronowski shows the work of imagination in Newton's thinking of the moon as a huge ball, thrown hard, and in Galileo's imaginary experiment with unequal weights. In what particular ways do these examples relate to and supplement Bronowski's remarks on science in "The Nature of Scientific Reasoning"?

Richard S. Westfall

THE CAREER OF ISAAC NEWTON: A SCIENTIFIC LIFE IN THE SEVENTEENTH CENTURY

If anyone has had a good press among the scientific community, surely it is Isaac Newton. He has appeared as the archetype of the modern empirical scientist, the example on which the majority of contemporary scientists would happily model themselves. It is not surprising that Newton should have assumed this role. In his *Principia* he produced the paradigm of the scientific world view. The law of universal gravitation was almost the least of its contents. Its three laws of motion, still presented today at the beginning of any introduction to physics, provided the foundation of a general science of mechanics. The work also presented the ideal of science as exact mathematical description, not confined to ideal situations as mathematical descriptions had been in earlier works such as those of Galileo, but exact descriptions of the extent to which physical reality fails to embody the ideal. In his other great work, *Opticks*, Newton produced one of the earliest exemplars of experimental procedure. Finally, he capped the whole performance with the invention of calculus, the basic instrument of physical science. It was, all in all, an achievement without equal—one indeed without serious rival. More than any other single man, Newton defined what modern science would be.

The case for Newton as the archetype of the empirical scientist extends beyond his achievement in science. Throughout his career he consistently expressed a methodological point of view to which most contemporary scientists would readily subscribe. The first occasion for such utterance came soon after he burst upon the scientific scene, in 1672, with his paper on colors. The paper contained an experimental investigation that established the heterogeneity of light. It was laid before a community convinced by a tradition some two thousand years old, which common sense supported, that primary light—the light of the sun—is homogeneous and that colors appear in certain circumstances, such as rainbows, when media modify primary light. Influenced as well by the mechanical philosophy of nature, the audience who read his paper looked for mechanistic explanations that would explain both the modification light undergoes and the nature of colors.

Not surprisingly, they misunderstood Newton's paper. In reply to their criticism, he took a methodological stand. In science, he insisted, experimental investigations must take precedence over explanatory hypotheses devised to explain phenomena. "For if the possibility of hypotheses is to be the test of the truth and reality of things, I see not how certainty can be obtained in any science; since numerous hypotheses may be devised, which shall seem to overcome new difficulties." "The proper Method for inquiring after the properties of things," he added, in another letter, "is to deduce them from Experiments. And I told you that the Theory wch I propounded was evinced by me, *not by inferring tis thus because not otherwise*, that is not by deducing it onely from the confutation of contrary suppositions, but *by deriving it from Experiments concluding positively & directly*. The way therefore to examin it is by considering whether the experiments wch I propound do prove those parts of the Theory to wch they are applyed, or by prosecuting other experiments wch the Theory may suggest for its examination."

More than forty years later, when he was well past his seventieth year, Newton asserted the same position to distinguish himself from Leibniz. "The Philosophy which Mr. Newton in his *Principles* and *Optiques* has pursued is Experimental," he stated, referring to himself in the third person; "and it is not the Business of Experimental Philosophy to teach the Causes of things any further than they can be proved by Experiments. We are not to fill this Philosophy with Opinions which cannot be proved by Phaenomena. In this Philosophy Hypotheses have no place, unless as Conjectures or Questions proposed to be examined by Experiments. ... And ... one would wonder that Mr. Newton should be reflected upon for not explaining the Causes of Gravity and other Attractions by Hypotheses; as if it were a crime to content himself with Certainties and let Uncertainties alone." In his own age, this was a stance that differed from the prevailing one. It is, in general terms, the one modern science has adopted, and it is small wonder that Newton is seen by contemporary scientists as the archetype of the experimental, empirical scientist.

How familiar he looks, from a distance. Up close and examined in detail, how completely strange Newton's career appears—a career so unlike what we now take for granted that we would hardly recognize it as a career in science were we not convinced a priori that it must have been. "The past is like a foreign country," a character in the movie *The Go-Between* remarked, "they do things differently there." Certainly they pursued science differently in the seventeenth century. Three features of Newton's career—three important features which differ profoundly from the normal career of a twentieth-century scientist who sees Newton as his model—illustrate how foreign the past indeed was.

Physical isolation is the first feature distinguishing past from present. People familiar with Newton's life are apt to object to such a characterization. He was, after all, President of the Royal Society for the final twenty-three years of his life and a fellow of the Society for nearly thirty-two years before that. Newton's relationship to the Royal Society can be misleading if it is not closely inspected. When he assumed its presidency, he had passed well beyond his age of scientific creativity; and during the earlier period when he was a fellow, he lived far away, separated from its activities and its members by sixty miles of impossible roads. With only the smallest exceptions, all of Newton's creative work, all of what we remember him for today, stemmed from his Cambridge years. Physical isolation characterized him in his Cambridge setting; it is necessary to understand him in that context.

Of Newton's isolation, it is hard to distinguish between factors that were purely personal and factors that were general and, therefore, offer some insight into scientific life in his day. Newton was a born recluse if ever one existed. As early as grammar school he found it difficult to get along with fellow students. It did not become any easier at the university, and his isolation only increased when he proceeded to a fellowship in Trinity College. It is striking that only one personal letter from Newton to one of his peers in Trinity exists, and there is some doubt that it was ever mailed. No letters at all from one of them to him is known. He was hardly mentioned by those who reflected on college life during the period when he was a fellow—this despite the fact that he had become the leading intellectual of the land by the time the reflections were set down.

Newton's strange and bizarre habits were the lone characteristics recorded about him. When he set out for dinner in the Hall, he would sometimes take the wrong turn, go out through the gate into the town, and then, when he realized something was wrong, return to his room rather than the Hall. When he did make it to dinner, he was apt to show up disheveled, dressed in the wrong gown, and then to sit there silently, lost in thought, while the meal remained on his plate uneaten. This last habit—about which a number of stories have come down—appeared an excessive peculiarity to the age. Cambridge was at that time going through a disastrous decline. Its dons, who no longer believed in the mission of the university and treated their fellowships as freeholds to be exploited for their personal benefit, happily surrendered to the attractions of the plate and the bottle, becoming, in the splendid phrase of Roger North, wet epicures. They found Newton quite impossible to comprehend. He lived in Trinity College thirty-five years from the time of his admission as an undergraduate. During that time he did not form any close friendships except with his chamber fellow Wickins, and that relationship ended with a breach. After he left, Newton did not exchange a single personal letter with anyone he had known there, and he never returned to Cambridge for any purpose other than electioneering for a university seat in Parliament.

Even though all of the above is true, we can still not ignore the intellectual dimension of Newton's isolation. As an undergraduate he deliberately cut himself off from the established curriculum in order to pursue his own interests: mathematics, as he found it in the writings of Wallis, Viète, and Descartes; and the new natural philosophy, as he found it in Descartes, Galileo, Gassendi, and others. In following this course, Newton very nearly destroyed his prospects. If he wished to remain in the university, where alone he could have pursued the intellectual life from which his achievement sprang, he had to be elected to a scholarship in Trinity College. A scholarship was the necessary preliminary to a fellowship, and since he was a student in Trinity, a Trinity fellowship was the only one to which he could aspire. Even under the best of circumstances, the odds against a sizar (a student who supported himself by performing menial tasks in the college) were enormous. Every year approximately half the scholarships were reserved for a privileged clique of students from Westminster School. The younger sons and clients of powerful men secured most of the rest. The possibilities for Newton, a strange young man without evident connections and from a remote village in Lincolnshire, were hardly great.

Nevertheless, sometime less than a year before the election of 1664, the only one at which he would be eligible, Newton chose to throw over the established curriculum in order to pursue his own line of interests. There is a story, told by Newton in his old age, that he was sent to be examined in mathematics by Isaac Barrow. At this time Newton had mastered Descartes' geometry and was beginning to move beyond it toward his own discoveries. Barrow examined him on Euclid, however,

and formed, as Newton recalled it, a tepid opinion of his knowledge of mathematics. Nevertheless, luck was on Newton's side. He was, in fact, not entirely without connections. Among the most senior fellows in the college was one Humphrey Babington, who not only hailed from Newton's corner of Lincolnshire but was the brother of the woman with whom he had boarded in Grantham. It appears likely that Babington was instrumental in his election. Although his early studies did not finally exclude him from a fellowship, his continuing interest in such things always formed a barrier that separated him from the rest of the college. One of Newton's strange habits, as they were later remembered, was a tendency to draw geometric diagrams in the walks of the fellows' garden. The other fellows were awed as much as they were amused by their strange compatriot, and they carefully walked around the diagrams in order not to disturb them. It is not known if another fellow ever stopped to study them.

Within a year and a half of taking his bachelor's degree, Newton had invented calculus and recorded it in a definitive tract in the notebook that he called his Waste Book. By every indication we have, Newton carried out his education in mathematics and his program of research entirely on his own. At the time, as far as we know, no one at all was aware of his achievement. It was his isolation that set the stage for the destructive conflict with Leibniz half a century later, for initially Newton's accomplishments were not known to anyone, and during the following two decades they were known only within a small circle gathered around John Collins, the London mathematical enthusiast.

By the late 1660s, one man, Isaac Barrow, the Lucasian Professor of Mathematics at Cambridge, had become acquainted with Newton's work. As it happened, Barrow was then preparing to vacate the mathematics chair, and he secured Newton's nomination to succeed him. For his initial lectures, Newton chose the subject of optics, and the lectures served to emphasize his isolation anew. He had discovered a new property of one of the major phenomena of nature: the heterogeneity of light. Not only was the discovery unknown to anyone, but when he presented it in three series of lectures, they were as unknown as the discovery itself. There is no testimony of any kind that a single listener heard and understood what the new Lucasian Professor was presenting.

Optics did bring Newton's complete isolation to an end, however. His theory of colors had led him to the idea of a reflecting telescope to eliminate chromatic aberration, and he was proud enough of the telescope to show it around. Eventually the Royal Society in London heard about it and asked to see it, and ultimately Newton sent them a paper on his theory of colors early in 1672.

The moment Newton ended his isolation, he discovered how much he preferred it. His paper stimulated a modest number of questions and objections which he found it necessary to answer, and he quickly came to resent the intrusion on his time. Thus Newton was no sooner brought into communication with the scientific community, both of Britain and of Europe, than he wanted to sever the connection. He did finally succeed in doing so to a considerable degree and lived mostly in renewed isolation during the decade from the mid-1670s to the mid-1680s. He reinforced his isolation by turning almost entirely away from his studies in mathematics and physics to devote himself to alchemy and theology.

Newton's extraordinary intellectual capacity had become known, however, and letters intermittently intruded upon his isolation. In August 1684, he received a visit from Edmund Halley. We must not overestimate the personal contact that resulted from the visit. Halley put one question to Newton: What would be the shape of the orbit followed by a planet moving in an inverse square force field? That question and all that it implied grasped Newton's attention and refused to let it go. It stimulated the process from which, two and a half years later, the *Principia* emerged. Once more the composition was carried out in isolation. Halley retired to London after he posed his question, made only two brief visits to Cambridge during the following thirty months, and refrained from imposing a burden of correspondence on Newton. The period between his visit and the completion of the manuscript constitutes the largest gap in our knowledge of Newton's adult life, for he had cut himself off from every contact in order to work out the consequences of his ideas alone. The investigation culminated in the book that, by its impact on the scientific world, ended his isolation once and for all. By 1687, however, Newton stood only a few years from the end of his creative intellectual activity, and nearly everything which has made his name immortal had already been accomplished.

Significant personal elements figured in Newton's isolation. He was reclusive by nature. In the early 1670s, after Barrow made Collins aware of Newton's mathematical abilities, Newton consented to Collins's publication of a solution to the annuity problem that he had written only if his, Newton's, name was left off. "It would perhaps increase my acquaintance," he told Collins, "ye thing wch I cheifly study to decline." Nevertheless, the issue stretches far beyond the limits of a personal idiosyncracy. With whom could he have communicated had he not been a recluse? In Britain there were perhaps four men: John Wallis of the previous generation; James Gregory and Christopher Wren of his own; and Edmund Halley of the following. All, for various reasons, would have been less than ideal collaborators. In the rest of Europe, Newton had indeed two scientific peers, Christiaan Huygens and Gottfried Wilhelm Leibniz. Obviously, as such a list implies, we deal here in part with the problem of genius, which is in short supply everywhere always. The short supply of genius does not exhaust the issue, however. The brevity of the list serves to remind us of what we too readily forget, that modern science was created in the seventeenth century by the philosophic rebellion of a tiny handful of men.

By the second half of the seventeenth century, these men were becoming numerous enough to form the first scientific societies. We need to remember how small those societies were. The *Académie Royale des Sciences* in Paris was created in 1666 with sixteen members to cover the entire range of scientific endeavor. The Royal Society in London was a popular organization instead of an exclusive one, and it became for a time a fad in London society, so that its membership swelled to around two hundred. While even two hundred is not an imposing number, it is still misleading as a guide to the size of the English scientific community. It is instructive to listen in briefly on a typical meeting of the Royal Society in the 1690s. John Van de Bembde solemnly informed the society that "cows piss drank to about a pint, will either purge or vomit with great Ease." You may think that he was summarily ejected, whether for indelicacy or irrelevancy. Not at all. The membership seized on the remark as the opportunity for a general discussion of bovine elixir, which was clearly the most stimulating part of the meeting. If we focus, not on the total membership of the Royal Society, but on the number of working scientists in its ranks, we find fewer than the sixteen that made up the Royal Academy. Relative isolation was an unavoidable aspect of the scientific revolution. Newton's reclusive habits only reinforced what would have been his lot in any case.

Physical isolation was of course not equivalent to intellectual isolation. Through the printed page, kindred spirits of more than one locale and more than one age could communicate with one another. Unencumbered as he was with endless committees, colloquia, and consultations, the seventeenth-century scientist had the opportunity to attend carefully to the printed page and to wrestle earnestly with what it presented. It may have been a more effective form of communication than the plethora of immediate contacts in which contemporary scientists of all sorts struggle desperately to preserve some sense of sustained endeavor.

A second distinctive feature of Newton's career was its philosophic breadth. By that phrase I mean to indicate the constant concern in his scientific work more with the total philosophy of nature than with the specific results of immediate investigations. Once again, those familiar with Newton are likely to object. *Opticks*, an experimental investigation of the heterogeneity of light and of the periodicity of some phenomena, especially appears to belie such a characterization. But, in response to the objection, let me call attention first of all to the *Principia*. The *Principia* presented more than the law of universal gravitation, and more than a new science of dynamics which entailed universal gravitation. What it presented, and consciously so, was a new philosophy of nature based on the principle of forces. "I wish we could derive the rest of the phenomena of Nature by the same kind of reasoning from mechanical principles," Newton stated in the preface, with reference to his explanation of the solar system from the concept of gravitational attraction, "for I am induced by many reasons to suspect that they may all depend upon certain forces by which the particles of bodies, by some causes hitherto unknown, are either mutually impelled towards one another, and cohere in regular figures, or are repelled and recede from one another. These forces being unknown, philosophers have hitherto attempted the search of Nature in vain; but I hope the principles here laid down will afford some light either to this or some truer method of philosophy."

During the years that immediately followed the publication of the *Principia*, when Newton first put the *Opticks* together, he treated the work primarily as an exposition of the new philosophy in which he used optical phenomena further to demonstrate the existence of forces in nature. True, in the end, apparently to avoid controversy, he eliminated most of these features, so that the work he eventually published confined such matters mostly, though not entirely, to the Queries at the work's close. Nevertheless, he always saw his scientific work as so many aspects of a new natural philosophy, and the considerable number of followers who wrote popular versions of it in the early eighteenth century all presented it in such terms.

To appreciate this facet of Newton, it is necessary to comprehend his historical situation. When Newton enrolled in Cambridge in 1661, he was educated in a natural philosophy that was more than two thousand years old. The universities of medieval Europe had built themselves in the Aristotelian system. It was still being taught, and not only in Cambridge, when Newton began his university education. In England the Parliamentary statutes that prescribed the curricula of the universities required the study of Aristotle. Newton's first step in natural science was to rebel against the established Aristotelian philosophy and to embrace a new one. The rebellion coincided with his rejection of the standard curriculum, which I mentioned earlier. He was still an undergraduate. Somehow he had found the writings of the men of the previous generation who had offered a radical new approach to nature—among them, Descartes, Gassendi, and Hobbes. Historians call their philosophy (for they agreed on a common core of principles despite their differences on many details) the mechanical philosophy. It provided the intellectual framework of the scientific revolution. Although he did not date his notes, it was apparently in 1664 that Newton embraced the mechanical philosophy and in doing so inaugurated his scientific career.

He did not embrace it for long, however, for he quickly became dissatisfied with aspects of the mechanical philosophy. His dissatisfaction rested partly on religious grounds. Mechanical philosophers proposed, or appeared to propose, the autonomy of the material realm, and Newton decided that such was a program for atheism. In his revulsion, he found in alchemy a concept of nature more in harmony with the demands of religion, and alchemy was one of Newton's major enterprises during the years of silence before the *Principia*.

Alchemy is not a popular topic in many circles. Even to bring it up is to raise doubts in some minds that one is competent to talk about science at all. Newton's alchemical manuscripts are nevertheless authentic. There can be no doubt that he did devote himself to alchemy, and quite extensively. If the goal of history, including the history of science, is to present the past in its own terms to the best of our ability, and not merely to present it as a pale anticipation of the twentieth century, we cannot afford to ignore Newton's immersion in alchemy. We especially cannot afford to ignore its influence on his philosophy of nature, for it appears to have been primarily alchemy that led Newton toward the concept of forces.

The idea of forces was not a single, limited concept; it turned out in the end to involve the entire philosophy of nature. From the beginning, Newton's disenchantment with standard mechanical philosophy had not been solely religious. Mechanical philosophies generated an abundance of talk about the invisible mechanisms by which nature produces phenomena, but their mechanical models proved incapable of yielding exact quantitative results. The great advantage of forces in Newton's eyes was exactly their capacity to generate such results. As he contemplated their import, they promised to revise every corner of natural philosophy. Descartes had argued that nature is a plenum; although atomists rejected the plenum, they nevertheless thought of a universe well filled with matter mixed with dispersed voids. Newton depopulated the universe of matter as he filled it with forces. As he finally conceived of it, nature was an infinite void seasoned with the merest suggestion of solid matter. For example, he paid careful attention to the implications of relative densities. Gold, he argued, cannot be absolutely dense since thin leaves of gold are translucent. He assumed for the moment that gold is made up half of solid matter and half of voids. Gold is nineteen times denser than water; water therefore can contain only one-thirty-eighth part of solid matter. In fact, he continued, water must contain far less solid matter than that, for water readily transmits rays of light in straight lines at every angle. Water in turn cannot be compressed. Newton ended up with a picture of matter in the form of tenuous nets composed of punctiform particles held together by forces, and eighteenth-century Newtonians would argue that all of the solid matter in the universe could fit inside a nutshell.

Method was involved in the change as much as in the system of nature; the statement on method quoted above comes from a passage on his natural philosophy. Most general of all, his position embodied a new ideal of science as the exact mathematical description both of ideal patterns in nature and of the extent to which material embodiments deyiate from the ideal. Even his conception of the relation of God to the physical universe was involved. The dispute with Leibniz over priority in the discovery of calculus, a dispute which reached its climax during the second decade of the eighteenth century, was equally a debate about the philosophy of nature in which all of the above issues were enmeshed.

Moreover, philosophic breadth was not a characteristic unique to Newton. Its greatest interest lies in the fact that it was not. To be sure, Newton may have been of a more contemplative spirit than the average scientist of his time. Despite his reputation as an empirical scientist, he was perhaps the greatest speculator of the age. His meditations on the nature of things, ruminations that extended throughout the length of his career, furnished the warp on which he wove the fabric of his career in science. His concept of forces was only the most fruitful of a long series of speculations. Nevertheless, every member of the scientific community of the age, of necessity, also concerned himself with the philosophy of nature. Virtually without exception, they had been educated like Newton in the Aristotelian philosophy, and like him they had all gone through their own personal rebellions against it. Such was the very meaning of the mechanical philosophy—a new beginning, a determination to reshape natural philosophy according to new principles. In the early eighteenth century, in turn, no one could stand aloof from the controversy that separated Newtonian natural philosophy from the prevailing forms of the mechanical philosophy. It was precisely in this feature that Newton most diverged from the image of the archetype of the modern empirical scientist. It is indeed a distortion of language to call him a scientist at all. In his own eyes, he was a natural philosopher.

A third prominent feature of Newton's career was his theological depth. No one familiar with Newton is likely to protest against this, for Newton's religious concerns are well known. The General Scholium to the *Principia*, to cite only one example, hymns a rhapsody to God. "This most beautiful system of the sun, planets, and comets, could only proceed from the counsel and dominion of an intelligent and powerful Being. . . . This Being governs all things, not as the soul of the world, but as Lord over all; and on account of his dominion He is wont to be called *Lord God, pantokrator*, or *Universal Ruler*. . . . We know him only by his most wise and excellent contrivances of things, and final causes; we admire him for his perfections; but we reverence and adore him on account of his dominion. . . ." "When I wrote my treatise about our Systeme," he wrote to Richard Bentley, "I had an eye upon such Principles as might work wth considering men for the beleife of a Deity. . . ."

These passages and similar ones are well known. They do not, however, constitute Newton's theological depth. They are evidence, rather, of his personal piety. To find the theological depth we must turn to his private papers instead of his published works, to papers fully opened to public scrutiny only within the last decade. They reveal that Newton plunged into serious and sustained theological study in the early 1670s —not in his old age as is usually assumed, but during the full flower of his early manhood, when he was approaching the age of thirty. Together with alchemy, theology constituted the primary substance of his intellectual life from that time until the composition of the *Principia*. The Bible supplied part of his reading; Newton's extensive knowledge of it, which John Locke said was equaled by few whom he knew, undoubtedly derived from the intense study of this period. The Bible was by no means the only object of his attention. He took up the early fathers of the church and read and digested the writings of every father of any significance. He turned to the prophecies and invested immense energy in an interpretation of them. To be sure that he had the correct text of the Book of Revelation, he collated more than twenty versions of the Greek text. Since he regarded the prophecies as the core of the Bible and the key to the rest, he combed the Scriptures for supporting passages; and since he insisted on an exact correlation between prophecy and history, he devoted equal zeal to the history of the early Christian centuries. The prophecies took him into the study of Judaism. As part of that study he became interested in the plan of the Jewish temple. Newton was never interested in things only in a general way. He wanted to know the exact plan of the temple, and for that purpose he reconstructed four chapters of Ezekiel while he drew a detailed plan of the temple to accompany the text.

In such activities one may begin to sense the measure of Newton's theological depth. They do not yet indicate the full depth, however. Behind all his study of theology was a fundamental goal—an anguished reassessment of the whole Christian tradition. The initial stimulus to his theological reading was probably the requirement that bore upon Fellows of Trinity College to be ordained to the Anglican clergy within seven years of taking their M.A. degrees. Almost the first result of Newton's study was an impassable obstacle to ordination, for he quickly convinced himself that the dominant Christian tradition, Trinitarianism, was false. The doctrine of the Trinity, he believed, was more than false; it was a deliberate fraud foisted onto the church in the fourth century by deceitful and evil men pursuing their own selfish interests. Newton adopted the ancient belief of Arianism as his own theological position, a position that denied the full divinity of Christ. Trinitarianism stood at the center of his interpretation of the prophecies. It was the Great Apostacy foretold by God when men would fall away from the true worship into idolatry; the plagues and vials of wrath of the Apocalypse, corresponding to the barbarian invasions of the empire, were God's punishment on a stiff-necked people who had gone whoring after false gods. In a word, Newton was one of the more advanced heretics of his day. His constant concern to conceal opinions which would have led to ostracism, first from the university, and later from the government's service, furnished a basic theme throughout his life. The piety of the General Scholium was sincere. No one should question it. Nevertheless it concealed a reality more complicated than has generally been realized.

This feature of Newton's career was also a general characteristic of the age. The constant references to God and to Christianity in the writings of scientists, like those of Newton, are usually taken as testimonies to the piety of the age. They derived rather from the fact that traditional piety had been called into question. Basil Willey has referred to the seventeenth century's "touch of cold philosophy." It had dissipated the enchanted world of medieval Christianity before the very eyes of scientists like Newton. They were unable to ignore this fact of their existence, as unsettling a piece of reality as one can readily imagine. Not many followed Newton into heterodoxy, but the endless refutations of atheism and proofs of the existence of God with which they filled their books adequately testify that they were aware of the same motives that animated Newton's lifelong inquiry into the true religion. When Robert Boyle died in 1691, after soundly refuting atheism at least fifty times, he left part of his fortune to endow a series of lectures. What were the lectures to do? Refute atheism still more. When during the previous thousand years of Western history had anyone thought that was necessary? Thinkers of the late seventeenth century knew only too well that the ground on which Christianity stood was shifting. In one way or another, most of them took account of the new circumstances. Many things contributed to Willey's touch of cold philosophy, but the birth of modern science was not the least among its sources. No wonder theological depth was a common feature of scientists (or natural philosophers) such as Newton.

Let us now turn the three chief characteristics of Newton's career back on ourselves and use them as a yardstick to measure the contemporary scientific community. No one, I suspect, would suggest that physical isolation is a normal feature of a twentieth-century scientist. Every year throughout the Western and Communist worlds there are meetings, such as those of the AAAS,[1] where thousands of scientists come together; increasingly they are spreading into the third world as well. I teach at Indiana University, a distinguished institution but not, in the opinion of any informed judge, a leading center of contemporary science. Nevertheless, the scientific community at Indiana University is larger than the whole of Europe could have mustered at any time during the seventeenth century. There are several other groups of equal size in the state of

1. American Association for the Advancement of Science.

Indiana and well over fifty centers in the state where scientists can be and are in immediate contact with trained and interested colleagues. This situation is also normal throughout the Western and Communist worlds. When one adds to the scientists the considerable army of technical experts called into being by modern science—an army which had no counterpart in the seventeenth century—the scientific community emerges as a significant portion of the working population. The small handful of natural philosophers who created the scientific revolution has burgeoned into a sociological phenomenon of immense scope.

As for philosophic breadth, it is no longer required. It is true of some contemporary scientists; it is not required of any one—that is, it is no longer necessary for every scientist constantly to consider the fundamental issues of natural philosophy. Although our century has witnessed a profound revision of the conception of nature, virtually no one in the scientific community considers that the system as a whole is in serious question, and it is perfectly proper for scientists to ignore the problems that occupied Newton in order to work at clarifying details of the system. Thus a typical issue of the *Physical Review* contains articles on "Three-body Lippmann-Schwinger Equations," "Influence of Vibrations of Gas Molecules on Neutron Reaction Cross Sections," "Core Coupled States in ^{145}Eu," and "Decays of Mass-separated ^{139}Xe and ^{139}Cs," together with many more in a similar vein. The articles all assume the existence of a coherent philosophy of nature. Without bothering themselves about such questions, their authors devote themselves, without manifest anxiety, to getting on with the work of science.

Theological depth has become for most scientists irrelevant. There are of course a number of scientists as pious as any in the seventeenth century; a like number are equally committed to articulate atheism. For most scientists, however, the issue has ceased to have any meaning. In the three centuries that have passed since Newton published the *Principia*, Christianity and science have exchanged roles, and natural science today occupies the position in Western civilization that Christianity once held. Theologians are now the small handful. Once theology was queen of all the sciences. We have redefined what the word *science* means, and every other intellectual discipline now measures itself against the enterprise that carries the word in its new meaning as its name.

Thus the scientific career of Isaac Newton enables us to appreciate the full extent to which natural science has been the most successful and significant endeavor of the modern world, reshaping first the intellectual structure of the West, then the economic system, and finally society itself. There is no way to avoid the conclusion: the scientists have inherited the earth. The rest of us are waiting breathlessly to see what they will do with it.

1981

QUESTIONS

1. *Westfall states that Isaac Newton's career had three distinguishing characteristics. What are they? What role do they play in the essay's organization?*
2. *How do the three characteristics of Newton's career differ from a typical career in science today, as given in Westfall's concluding paragraphs? Is this difference good or bad, in the view of the author? In your view?*
3. *How did the three distinguishing features of Newton's career contribute to or detract from the work he did in science? What, by the way, does science owe to Newton?*
4. *Does the author succeed in making Newton come alive as a person? If so, by what particular means does he accomplish this? If not, what might he have done to bring out Newton as a person?*
5. *What view of science does the author propose in his closing paragraph? Do you subscribe to that view? Why, or why not?*

Stephen Jay Gould

DARWIN'S MIDDLE ROAD

"We began to sail up the narrow strait lamenting," narrates Odysseus. "For on the one hand lay Scylla, with twelve feet all dangling down; and six necks exceeding long, and on each a hideous head, and therein three rows of teeth set thick and close, full of black death. And on the other mighty Charybdis sucked down the salt sea water. As often as she belched it forth, like a cauldron on a great fire she would seethe up through all her troubled deeps." Odysseus managed to swerve around Charybdis, but Scylla grabbed six of his finest men and devoured them in his sight—"the most pitiful thing mine eyes have seen of all my travail in searching out the paths of the sea."

False lures and dangers often come in pairs in our legends and metaphors—consider the frying pan and the fire, or the devil and the deep blue sea. Prescriptions for avoidance either emphasize a dogged steadiness—the straight and narrow of Christian evangelists—or an averaging between unpleasant alternatives—the golden mean of Aristotle. The idea of steering a course between undesirable extremes emerges as a central prescription for a sensible life.

The nature of scientific creativity is both a perennial topic of discussion and a prime candidate for seeking a golden mean. The two extreme positions have not been directly competing for allegiance of the unwary.

They have, rather, replaced each other sequentially, with one now in the ascendency, the other eclipsed.

The first—inductivism—held that great scientists are primarily great observers and patient accumulators of information. For new and significant theory, the inductivists claimed, can only arise from a firm foundation of facts. In this architectural view, each fact is a brick in a structure built without blueprints. Any talk or thought about theory (the completed building) is fatuous and premature before the bricks are set. Inductivism once commanded great prestige within science, and even represented an "official" position of sorts, for it touted, however falsely, the utter honesty, complete objectivity, and almost automatic nature of scientific progress towards final and incontrovertible truth.

Yet, as its critics so rightly claimed, inductivism also depicted science as a heartless, almost inhuman discipline offering no legitimate place to quirkiness, intuition, and all the other subjective attributes adhering ot our vernacular notion of genius. Great scientists, the critics claimed, are distinguished more by their powers of hunch and synthesis, than their skill in experiment or observation. The criticisms of inductivism are certainly valid and I welcome its dethroning during the past thirty years as a necessary preclude to better understanding. Yet, in attacking it so strongly, some critics have tried to substitute an alternative equally extreme and unproductive in its emphasis on the essential subjectivity of creative thought. In this "eureka" view, creativity is an ineffable something, accessible only to persons of genius. It arises like a bolt of lightning, unanticipated, unpredictable and unanalyzable—but the bolts strike only a few special people. We ordinary mortals must stand in awe and thanks. (The name refers, of course, to the legendary story of Archimedes running naked through the streets of Syracuse shouting eureka [I have discovered it] when water displaced by his bathing body washed the scales abruptly from his eyes and suggested a method for measuring volumes.)

I am equally disenchanted by both these opposing extremes. Inductivism reduces genius to dull, rote operations; eurekaism grants it an inaccessible status more in the domain of intrinsic mystery than in a realm where we might understand and learn from it. Might we not marry the good features of each view, and abandon both the elitism of eurekaism and the pedestrian qualities of inductivism? May we not acknowledge the personal and subjective character of creativity, but still comprehend it as a mode of thinking that emphasizes or exaggerates capacities sufficiently common to all of us that we may at least understand if not hope to imitate?

In the hagiography of science, a few men hold such high positions that all arguments must apply to them if they are to have any validity. Charles Darwin, as the principal saint of evolutionary biology, has therefore been presented both as an inductivist and as a primary example of eurekaism. I will attempt to show that these interpretations are equally inadequate, and that recent scholarship on Darwin's own odyssey towards the theory of natural selection supports an intermediate position.

So great was the prestige of inductivism in his own day, that Darwin himself fell under its sway and, as an old man, falsely depicted his youthful accomplishments in its light. In an autobiography, written as a lesson in morality for his children and not intended for publication, he penned some famous lines that misled historians for nearly a hundred years. Describing his path to the theory of natural selection, he claimed: "I worked on true Baconian principles, and without any theory collected facts on a wholesale scale."[1]

The inductivist interpretation focuses on Darwin's five years aboard the *Beagle* and explains his transition from a student for the ministry to the nemesis of preachers as the result of his keen powers of observation applied to the whole world. Thus, the traditional story goes, Darwin's eyes opened wider and wider as he saw, in sequence, the bones of giant South American fossil mammals, the turtles and finches of the Galapagos, and the marsupial fauna of Australia. The truth of evolution and its mechanism of natural selection crept up gradually upon him as he sifted facts in a sieve of utter objectivity.

The inadequacies of this tale are best illustrated by the falsity of its conventional premier example—the so-called Darwin's finches of the Galapagos. We now know that although these birds share a recent and common ancestry on the South American mainland, they have radiated into an impressive array of species on the outlying Galapagos. Few terrestrial species manage to cross the wide oceanic barrier between South America and the Galapagos. But the fortunate migrants often find a sparsely inhabited world devoid of the competitors that limit their opportunities on the crowded mainland. Hence, the finches evolved into roles normally occupied by other birds and developed their famous set of adaptations for feeding—seed crushing, insect eating, even grasping and manipulating a cactus needle to dislodge insects from plants. Isolation —both of the islands from the mainland and among the islands them-selves—provided an opportunity for separation, independent adapta-tion, and speciation.

According to the traditional view, Darwin discovered these finches, correctly inferred their history, and wrote the famous lines in his notebook: "If there is the slightest foundation for these remarks the zoology of Archipelagoes will be worth examining; for such facts would undermine the stability of Species." But, as with so many heroic tales from Washington's cherry tree to the piety of Crusaders, hope rather

---

1. Francis Bacon (1561–1626), English philosopher, statesman, and essayist, and the first apostle of inductivism.

than truth motivates the common reading. Darwin found the finches to be sure. But he didn't recognize them as variants of a common stock. In fact, he didn't even record the island of discovery for many of them —some of his labels just read "Galapagos Islands." So much for his immediate recognition of the role of isolation in the formation of new species. He reconstructed the evolutionary tale only after his return to London, when a British Museum ornithologist correctly identified all the birds as finches.

The famous quotation from his notebook refers to Galapagos tortoises and to the claim of native inhabitants that they can "at once pronounce from which Island any Tortoise may have been brought" from subtle differences in size and shape of body and scales. This is a statement of different, and much reduced, order from the traditional tale of finches. For the finches are true and separate species—a living example of evolution. The subtle differences among tortoises represent minor geographic variation within a species. It is a jump in reasoning, albeit a valid one as we now know, to argue that such small differences can be amplified to produce a new species. All creationists, after all, acknowledged geographic variation (consider human races), but argued that it could not proceed beyond the rigid limits of a created archetype.

I don't wish to downplay the pivotal influence of the *Beagle* voyage on Darwin's career. It gave him space, freedom and endless time to think in his favored mode of independent self-stimulation. (His ambivalence towards university life, and his middling performance there by conventional standards, reflected his unhappiness with a curriculum of received wisdom.) He writes from South America in 1834: "I have not one clear idea about cleavage, stratification, lines of upheaval. I have no books, which tell me much and what they do I cannot apply to what I see. In consequence I draw my own conclusions, and most gloriously ridiculous ones they are." The rocks and plants and animals that he saw did provoke him to the crucial attitude of doubt—midwife of all creativity. Sydney, Australia—1836. Darwin wonders why a rational God would create so many marsupials on Australia since nothing about its climate or geography suggests any superiority for pouches: "I had been lying on a sunny bank and was reflecting on the strange character of the animals of this country as compared to the rest of the World. An unbeliever in everything beyond his own reason might exclaim, 'Surely two distinct Creators must have been at work.'"

Nonetheless, Darwin returned to London without an evolutionary theory. He suspected the truth of evolution, but had no mechanism to explain it. Natural selection did not arise from any direct reading of the *Beagle's* facts, but from two subsequent years of thought and struggle as reflected in a series of remarkable notebooks that have been unearthed and published during the past twenty years. In these notebooks, we see

Darwin testing and abandoning a number of theories and pursuing a multitude of false leads—so much for his later claim about recording facts with an empty mind. He read philosophers, poets, and economists, always searching for meaning and insight—so much for the notion that natural selection arose inductively from the *Beagle's* facts. Later, he labelled one notebook as "full of metaphysics on morals."

Yet if this tortuous path belies the Scylla of inductivism, it has engendered an equally simplistic myth—the Charybdis of eurekaism. In his maddeningly misleading autobiography, Darwin does record a eureka and suggests that natural selection struck him as a sudden, serendipitous flash after more than a year of groping frustration:

> In October 1838, that is, fifteen months after I had begun my systematic inquiry, I happened to read for amusement Malthus on Population,[2] and being well prepared to appreciate the struggle for existence which everywhere goes on from long-continued observation of the habits of animals and plants, it at once struck me that under these circumstances favorable variations would tend to be preserved, and unfavorable ones to be destroyed. The result of this would be the formation of new species. Here, then, I had at last got a theory by which to work.

Yet, again, the notebooks belie Darwin's later recollections—in this case by their utter failure to record, at the time it happened, any special exultation over his Malthusian insight. He inscribes it as a fairly short and sober entry without a single exclamation point, though he habitually used two or three in moments of excitement. He did not drop everything and reinterpret a confusing world in its light. On the very next day, he wrote an even longer passage on the sexual curiosity of primates.

The theory of natural selection arose neither as a workmanlike induction from nature's facts, nor as a mysterious bolt from Darwin's subconscious, triggered by an accidental reading of Malthus. It emerged instead as the result of a conscious and productive search, proceeding in a ramifying but ordered manner, and utilizing both the facts of natural history and an astonishingly broad range of insights from disparate disciplines far from his own. Darwin trod the middle path between inductivism and eurekaism. His genius is neither pedestrian nor inaccessible.

Darwinian scholarship has exploded since the centennial of the *Origin*[3] in 1959. The publication of Darwin's notebooks and the attention devoted by several scholars to the two crucial years between the *Beagle's* docking and the demoted Malthusian insight has clinched the argument for a "middle path" theory of Darwin's creativity. Two particularly important works focus on the broadest and narrowest scales. Howard E. Gruber's masterful intellectual and psychological biography of this phase in Darwin's life, *Darwin on Man*, traces all the false leads and turning

2. Thomas Malthus, whose work on population was published under several titles be- tween 1798 and 1817.
3. *The Origin of Species* (1859).

points in Darwin's search. Gruber shows that Darwin was continually proposing, testing, and abandoning hypotheses, and that he never simply collected facts in a blind way. He began with a fanciful theory involving the idea that new species arise with a prefixed life span, and worked his way gradually, if fitfully, towards an idea of extinction by competition in a world of struggle. He recorded no exultation upon reading Malthus, because the jigsaw puzzle was only missing a piece or two at the time.

Silvan S. Schweber has reconstructed, in detail as minute as the record will allow, Darwin's activities during the few weeks before Malthus (The Origin of the Origin Revisited, Journal of the History of Biology, 1977). He argues that the final pieces arose not from new facts in natural history, but from Darwin's intellectual wanderings in distant fields. In particular, he read a long review of social scientist and philosopher Auguste Comte's most famous work, the Cours de philosophie positive.[4] He was particularly struck by Comte's insistence that a proper theory be predictive and at least potentially quantitative. He then turned to Dugald Stewart's On the Life and Writing of Adam Smith, and imbibed the basic belief of the Scottish economists that theories of overall social structure must begin by analyzing the unconstrained actions of individuals. (Natural selection is, above all, a theory about the struggle of individual organisms for success in reproduction.) Then, searching for quantification, he read a lengthy analysis of work by the most famous statistician of his time—the Belgian Adolphe Quetelet. In the review of Quetelet, he found, among other things, a forceful statement of Malthus's quantitative claim—that population would grow geometrically and food supplies only arithmetically, thus guaranteeing an intense struggle for existence. In fact, Darwin had read the Malthusian statement several times before; but only now was he prepared to appreciate its significance. Thus, he did not turn to Malthus by accident, and he already knew what it contained. His "amusement," we must assume, consisted only in a desire to read in its original formulation the familiar statement that had so impressed him in Quetelet's secondary account.

In reading Schweber's detailed account of the moments preceding Darwin's formulation of natural selection, I was particularly struck by the absence of deciding influence from his own field of biology. The immediate precipitators were a social scientist, an economist, and a statistician. If genius has any common denominator, I would propose breadth of interest and the ability to construct fruitful analogies between fields.

In fact, I believe that the theory of natural selection should be viewed as an extended analogy—whether conscious or unconscious on Darwin's part I do not know—to the laissez faire economics of Adam Smith. The essence of Smith's argument is a paradox of sorts: if you want an ordered economy providing maximal benefits to all, then let individuals compete

4. Course in Positivist Philosophy (1830-42).

and struggle for their own advantages. The result, after appropriate sorting and elimination of the inefficient, will be a stable and harmonious polity. Apparent order arises naturally from the struggle among individuals, not from predestined principles or higher control. Dugald Stewart epitomized Smith's system in the book Darwin read:

> The most effective plan for advancing a people ... is by allowing every man, as long as he observes the rules of justice, to pursue his own interest in his own way, and to bring both his industry and his capital into the freest competition with those of his fellow citizens. Every system of policy which endeavors ... to draw towards a particular species of industry a greater share of the capital of the society than would naturally go to it ... is, in reality, subversive of the great purpose which it means to promote.

As Schweber states: "The Scottish analysis of society contends that the combined effect of individual actions results in the institutions upon which society is based, and that such a society is a stable and evolving one and functions without a designing and directing mind."

We know that Darwin's uniqueness does not reside in his support for the idea of evolution—scores of scientists had preceded him in this. His special contribution rests upon his documentation and upon the novel character of his theory about how evolution operates. Previous evolutionists had proposed unworkable schemes based on internal perfecting tendencies and inherent directions. Darwin advocated a natural and testable theory based on immediate interaction among individuals (his opponents considered it heartlessly mechanistic). The theory of natural selection is a creative transfer to biology of Adam Smith's basic argument for a rational economy: the balance and order of nature does not arise from a higher, external (divine) control, or from the existence of laws operating directly upon the whole, but from struggle among individuals for their own benefits (in modern terms, for the transmission of their genes to future generations through differential success in reproduction).

Many people are distressed to hear such an argument. Does it not compromise the integrity of science if some of its primary conclusions originate by analogy from contemporary politics and culture rather than from data of the discipline itself? In a famous letter to Engels, Karl Marx identified the similarities between natural selection and the English social scene:

> It is remarkable how Darwin recognizes among beasts and plants his English society with its division of labor, competition, opening up of new markets, 'invention,' and the Malthusian 'struggle for existence.' It is Hobbes' *bellum omnium contra omnes* (the war of all against all).[5]

Yet Marx was a great admirer of Darwin—and in this apparent paradox lies resolution. For reasons involving all the themes I have emphasized

5. From the English philosopher Thomas Hobbes's *Leviathan* (1651).

here—that inductivism is inadequate, that creativity demands breadth, and that analogy is a profound source of insight—great thinkers cannot be divorced from their social background. But the source of an idea is one thing; its truth or fruitfulness is another. The psychology and utility of discovery are very different subjects indeed. Darwin may have cribbed the idea of natural selection from economics, but it may still be right. As the German socialist Karl Kautsky wrote in 1902: "The fact that an idea emanates from a particular class, or accords with their interests, of course proves nothing as to its truth or falsity." In this case, it is ironic that Adam Smith's system of laissez faire does not work in his own domain of economics, for it leads to oligopoly and revolution, rather than to order and harmony. Struggle among individuals does, however, seem to be the law of nature.

Many people use such arguments about social context to ascribe great insights primarily to the indefinable phenomenon of good luck. Thus, Darwin was lucky to be born rich, lucky to be on the *Beagle*, lucky to live amidst the ideas of his age, lucky to trip over Parson Malthus—essentially little more than a man in the right place at the right time. Yet, when we read of his personal struggle to understand, the breadth of his concerns and study, and the directedness of his search for a mechanism of evolution, we understand why Pasteur made his famous quip that fortune favors the prepared mind.[6]

1980

6. Louis Pasteur (1822-95), French chemist.

Thomas S. Kuhn

THE ROUTE TO NORMAL SCIENCE

In this essay, 'normal science' means research firmly based upon one or more past scientific achievements, achievements that some particular scientific community acknowledges for a time as supplying the foundation for its further practice. Today such achievements are recounted, though seldom in their original form, by science textbooks, elementary and advanced. These textbooks expound the body of accepted theory, illustrate many or all of its successful applications, and compare these applications with exemplary observations and experiments. Before such books became popular early in the nineteenth century (and until even more recently in the newly matured sciences), many of the famous classics of science fulfilled a similar function. Aristotle's *Physica*, Ptolemy's *Almagest*, Newton's *Principia* and *Opticks*, Franklin's *Electricity*,

Lavoisier's *Chemistry*, and Lyell's *Geology*—these and many other works served for a time implicitly to define the legitimate problems and methods of a research field for succeeding generations of practitioners. They were able to do so because they shared two essential characteristics. Their achievement was sufficiently unprecedented to attract an enduring group of adherents away from competing modes of scientific activity. Simultaneously, it was sufficiently open-ended to leave all sorts of problems for the redefined group of practitioners to resolve.

Achievements that share these two characteristics I shall henceforth refer to as 'paradigms,' a term that relates closely to 'normal science.' By choosing it, I mean to suggest that some accepted examples of actual scientific practice—examples which include law, theory, application, and instrumentation together—provide models from which spring particular coherent traditions of scientific research. These are the traditions which the historian describes under such rubrics as 'Ptolemaic astronomy' (or 'Copernican'), 'Aristotelian dynamics' (or 'Newtonian'), 'corpuscular optics' (or 'wave optics'), and so on. The study of paradigms, including many that are far more specialized than those named illustratively above, is what mainly prepares the student for membership in the particular scientific community with which he will later practice. Because he there joins men who learned the bases of their field from the same concrete models, his subsequent practice will seldom evoke overt disagreement over fundamentals. Men whose research is based on shared paradigms are committed to the same rules and standards for scientific practice. That commitment and the apparent consensus it produces are prerequisites for normal science, i.e., for the genesis and continuation of a particular research tradition.

Because in this essay the concept of a paradigm will often substitute for a variety of familiar notions, more will need to be said about the reasons for its introduction. Why is the concrete scientific achievement, as a locus of professional commitment, prior to the various concepts, laws, theories, and points of view that may be abstracted from it? In what sense is the shared paradigm a fundamental unit for the student of scientific development, a unit that cannot be fully reduced to logically atomic components which might function in its stead? There can be a sort of scientific research without paradigms, or at least without any so unequivocal and so binding as the ones named above. Acquisition of a paradigm and of the more esoteric type of research it permits is a sign of maturity in the development of any given scientific field.

If the historian traces the scientific knowledge of any selected group of related phenomena backward in time, he is likely to encounter some minor variant of a pattern here illustrated from the history of physical optics. Today's physics textbooks tell the student that light is photons, i.e., quantum-mechanical entities that exhibit some characteristics of waves and some of particles. Research proceeds accordingly, or rather according to the more elaborate and mathematical characterization from which this usual verbalization is derived. That characterization of light is, however, scarcely half a century old. Before it was developed by Planck, Einstein, and others early in this century, physics texts taught that light was transverse wave motion, a conception rooted in a paradigm that derived ultimately from the optical writings of Young and Fresnel in the early nineteenth century. Nor was the wave theory the first to be embraced by almost all practitioners of optical science. During the eighteenth century the paradigm for this field was provided by Newton's *Opticks,* which taught that light was material corpuscles. At that time physicists sought evidence, as the early wave theorists had not, of the pressure exerted by light particles impinging on solid bodies.

These transformations of the paradigms of physical optics are scientific revolutions, and the successive transition from one paradigm to another via revolution is the usual developmental pattern of mature science. It is not, however, the pattern characteristic of the period before Newton's work, and that is the contrast that concerns us here. No period between remote antiquity and the end of the seventeenth century exhibited a single generally accepted view about the nature of light. Instead there were a number of competing schools and sub-schools, most of them espousing one variant or another of Epicurean, Aristotelian, or Platonic theory.[1] One group took light to be particles emanating from material bodies; for another it was a modification of the medium that intervened between the body and the eye; still another explained light in terms of an interaction of the medium with an emanation from the eye; and there were other combinations and modifications besides. Each of the corresponding schools derive strength from its relation to some particular metaphysic, and each emphasized, as paradigmatic observations, the particular cluster of optical phenomena that its own theory could do most to explain. Other observations were dealt with by *ad hoc* elaborations, or they remained as outstanding problems for further research.

At various times all these schools made significant contributions to the body of concepts, phenomena, and techniques from which Newton drew the first nearly uniformly accepted paradigm for physical optics. Any definition of the scientist that excludes at least the more creative members of these various schools will exclude their modern successors as well. Those men were scientists. Yet anyone examining a survey of physical optics before Newton may well conclude that, though the field's practitioners were scientists, the net result of their activity was something less than science. Being able to take no common body of belief for granted, each writer on physical optics felt forced to build his field anew from its foundations. In doing so, his choice of supporting observation and experi-

1. The reference is to the three principal world views of ancient Greek philosophy.

ment was relatively free, for there was no standard set of methods or of phenomena that every optical writer felt forced to employ and explain. Under these circumstances, the dialogue of the resulting books was often directed as much to the members of other schools as it was to nature. That pattern is not unfamiliar in a number of creative fields today, nor is it incompatible with significant discovery and invention. It is not, however, the pattern of development that physical optics acquired after Newton and that other natural sciences make familiar today.

The history of electrical research in the first half of the eighteenth century provides a more concrete and better known example of the way a science develops before it acquires its first universally received paradigm. During that period there were almost as many views about the nature of electricity as there were important electrican experimenters, men like Haukshee, Gray, Desaguliers, Du Fay, Nollett, Watson, Franklin, and others. All their numerous concepts of electricity had something in common—they were partially derived from one or another version of the mechanico-corpuscular philosophy that guided all scientific research of the day. In addition, all were components of real scientific theories, of theories that had been drawn in part from experiment and observation and that partially determined the choice and interpretation of additional problems undertaken in research. Yet though all the experiments were electrical and though most of the experimenters read each other's works, their theories had no more than a family resemblance.

One early group of theories, following seventeenth-century practice, regarded attraction and frictional generation as the fundamental electrical phenomena. This group tended to treat repulsion as a secondary effect due to some sort of mechanical rebounding and also to postpone for as long as possible both discussion and systematic research on Gray's newly discovered effect, electrical conduction. Other "electricians" (the term is their own) took attraction and repulsion to be equally elementary manifestations of electricity and modified their theories and research accordingly. (Actually, this group is remarkably small—even Franklin's theory never quite accounted for the mutual repulsion of two negatively charged bodies.) But they had as much difficulty as the first group in accounting simultaneously for any but the simplest conduction effects. Those effects, however, provided the starting point for still a third group, one which tended to speak of electricity as a "fluid" that could run through conductors rather than as an "effluvium" that emanated from non-conductors. This group, in its turn, had difficulty reconciling its theory with a number of attractive and repulsive effects. Only through the work of Franklin and his immediate successors did a theory arise that could account with something like equal facility for very nearly all these effects and that therefore could and did provide a subsequent generation of "electricians" with a common paradigm for its research.

Excluding those fields, like mathematics and astronomy, in which the first firm paradigms date from prehistory and also those, like biochemistry, that arose by division and recombination of specialties already matured, the situations outlined above are historically typical. Though it involves my continuing to employ the unfortunate simplification that tags an extended historical episode with a single and somewhat arbitrarily chosen name (e.g., Newton or Franklin), I suggest that similar fundamental disagreements characterized, for example, the study of motion before Aristotle and of statics before Archimedes, the study of heat before Black, of chemistry before Boyle and Boerhaave, and of historical geology before Hutton. In parts of biology—the study of heredity, for example—the first universally received paradigms are still more recent; and it remains an open question what parts of social science have yet acquired such paradigms at all. History suggests that the road to a firm research consensus is extraordinarily arduous.

History also suggests, however, some reasons for the difficulties encountered on the road. In the absence of a paradigm or some candidate for paradigm, all of the facts that could possibly pertain to the development of a given science are likely to seem equally relevant. As a result, early fact-gathering is a far more nearly random activity than the one that subsequent scientific development makes familiar. Futhermore, in the absence of a reason for seeking some particular form of more recondite information, early fact-gathering is usually restricted to the wealth of data that lie ready to hand. The resulting pool of facts contains those accessible to casual observation and experiment together with some of the more esoteric data retrievable from established crafts medicine, calendar making, and metallurgy. Because the crafts are one readily accessible source of facts that could not have been casually discovered, technology has often played a vital role in the emergence of new sciences.

But though this sort of fact-collecting has been essential to the origin of many significant sciences, anyone who examines, for example, Pliny's encyclopedic writings or the Baconian natural histories of the seventeenth century will discover that it produces a morass. One somehow hesitates to call the literature that results scientific. The Baconian "histories" of heat, color, wind, mining, and so on, are filled with information, some of it recondite. But they juxtapose facts that will later prove revealing (e.g., heating by mixture) with others (e.g., the warmth of dung heaps) that will for some time remain too complex to be integrated with theory at all. In addition, since any description must be partial, the typical natural history often omits from its immensely circumstantial accounts just those details that later scientists will find sources of important illumination. Almost none of the early "histories" of electricity, for example, mention that chaff, attracted to a rubbed glass rod, bounces off again. That effect seemed mechanical, not electrical. Moreover, since the casual fact-gatherer seldom possesses the time or the tools to be critical, the natural histories often juxtapose descriptions like the above with others, say, heating by antiperistasis (or by cooling), that we are now quite unable to confirm.[2] Only very occasionally, as in the cases of ancient statics, dynamics, and geometrical optics, do facts collected with so little guidance from pre-established theory speak with sufficient clarity to permit the emergence of a first paradigm.

This is the situation that creates the schools characteristic of the early stages of a science's development. No natural history can be interpreted in the absence of at least some implicit body of intertwined theoretical and methodological belief that permits selection, evaluation, and criticism. If that body of belief is not already implicit in the collection of facts —in which case more than "mere facts" are at hand—it must be externally supplied, perhaps by a current metaphysic, by another science, or by personal and historical accident. No wonder, then, that in the early stages of the development of any science different men confronting the same range of phenomena, but not usually all the same particular phenomena, describe and interpret them in different ways. What is surprising, and perhaps also unique in its degree to the fields we call science, is that such initial divergences should ever largely disappear.

For they do disappear to a very considerable extent and then apparently once and for all. Furthermore, their disappearance is usually caused by the triumph of one of the pre-paradigm schools, which, because of its own characteristic beliefs and pre-conceptions, emphasized only some special part of the too sizable and inchoate pool of information. Those electricians who thought electricity a fluid and therefore gave particular emphasis to conduction provide an excellent case in point. Led by this belief, which could scarcely cope with the known multiplicity of attractive and repulsive effects, several of them conceived the idea of bottling the electrical fluid. The immediate fruit of their efforts was the Leyden jar, a device which might never have been discovered by a man exploring nature casually or at random, but which was in fact independently developed by at least two investigators in the early 1740's. Almost from the start of his elctrical researches, Franklin was particularly concerned to explain that strange and, in the event, particularly revealing piece of special apparatus. His success in doing so provided the most effective of the arguments that made his theory a paradigm, though one that was still unable to account for quite all the known cases of electrical repulsion.[3] To be accepted as a paradigm, a theory must seem better than its

2. Bacon [in the *Novum Organum*] says, "Water slightly warm is more easily frozen than quite cold" [Kuhn's note]; *antiperistasis:* an old word meaning a reaction caused by the action of an opposite quality or principle

—here, heating through cooling.
3. The troublesome case was the mutual repulsion of negatively charged bodies [Kuhn's note].

competitors, but it need not, and in fact never does, explain all the facts
with which it can be confronted.

What the fluid theory of electricity did for the subgroup that held it,
the Franklinian paradigm later did for the entire group of electricians. It
suggested which experiments would be worth performing and which,
because directed to secondary or to overly complex manifestations of
electricity, would not. Only the paradigm did the job far more effectively,
partly because the end of interschool debate ended the constant reitera-
tion of fundamentals and partly because the confidence that they were on
the right track encouraged scientists to undertake more precise, esoteric,
and consuming sorts of work.[4] Freed from the concern with any and all
electrical phenomena, the united group of electricians could pursue
selected phenomena in far more detail, designing much special equipment for the task and employing it more stubbornly and systematically
than electricians had ever done before. Both fact collection and theory
articulation became highly directed activities. The effectiveness and
efficiency of electrical research increased accordingly, providing evidence for a societal version of Francis Bacon's acute methodological
dictum: "Truth emerges more readily from error than from confusion."

We shall be examining the nature of this highly directed or paradigm-
based research in the next section, but must first note briefly how the
emergence of a paradigm affects the structure of the group that practices
the field. When, in the development of a natural science, an individual or
group first produces a synthesis able to attract most of the next generation's practitioners, the older schools gradually disappear. In part their
disappearance is caused by their members' conversion to the new paradigm. But there are always some men who cling to one or another of the
older views, and they are simply read out of the profession, which
thereafter ignores their work. The new paradigm implies a new and more
rigid definition of the field. Those unwilling or unable to accommodate
their work to it must proceed in isolation or attach themselves to some
other group.[5] Historically, they have often simply stayed in the depart-

---

4. It should be noted that the acceptance of
Franklin's theory did not end quite all debate. In 1759 Robert Symmer proposed a
two-fluid version of that theory, and for
many years thereafter electricians were divided about whether electricity was a single
fluid or two. But the debates on this subject
only confirm what has been said above about
the manner in which a universally recognized achievement unites the profession.
Electricians, though they continued divided
on this point, rapidly concluded that no experimental tests could distinguish the two
versions of the theory and that they were
therefore equivalent. After that, both
schools could and did exploit all the benefits

that the Franklinian theory provided
[Kuhn's note].
5. The history of electricity provides an excellent example which could be duplicated
from the careers of Priestley, Kelvin, and
others. Franklin reports that Nollet, who at
mid-century was the most influential of the
Continental electricians, "lived to see himself the last of his Sect, except Mr. B.—his
Eleve [pupil] and immediate Disciple." More
interesting, however, is the endurance of
whole schools in increasing isolation from
professional science. Consider, for example,
the case of astrology, which was once an
integral part of astronomy. Or consider the
continuation in the late eighteenth, and

ments of philosophy from which so many of the special sciences have been spawned. As these indications hint, it is sometimes just its reception of a paradigm that transforms a group previously interested merely in the study of nature into a profession or, at least, a discipline. In the sciences (though not in fields like medicine, technology, and law, of which the principal *raison d'être* is an external social need), the formation of specialized journals, the foundation of specialists' societies, and the claim for a special place in the curriculum have usually been associated with a group's first reception of a single paradigm. At least this was the case between the time, a century and a half ago, when the institutional pattern of scientific specialization first developed and the very recent time when the paraphernalia of specialization acquired a prestige of their own.

The more rigid definition of the scientific group has other consequences. When the individual scientist can take a paradigm for granted, he need no longer, in his major works, attempt to build his field anew, starting from first principles and justifying the use of each concept introduced. That can be left to the writer of textbooks. Given a textbook, however, the creative scientist can begin his research where it leaves off and thus concentrate exclusively upon the subtlest and most esoteric aspects of the natural phenomena that concern his group. And as he does this, his research communiqués will begin to change in ways whose evolution has been too little studied but whose modern end products are obvious to all and oppressive to many. No longer will his researches usually be embodied in books addressed, like Franklin's *Experiments . . . on Electricity* or Darwin's *Origin of Species,* to anyone who might be interested in the subject matter of the field. Instead they will usually appear as brief articles addressed only to professional colleagues, the men whose knowledge of a shared paradigm can be assumed and who prove to be the only ones able to read the papers addressed to them.

Today in the sciences, books are usually either texts or retrospective reflections upon one aspect or another of the scientific life. The scientist who writes one is more likely to find his professional reputation impaired than enhanced. Only in the earlier, pre-paradigm, stages of the development of the various sciences did the book ordinarily possess the same relation to professional achievement that it still retains in other creative fields. And only in those fields that still retain the book, with or without the article, as a vehicle for research communication are the lines of professionalization still so loosely drawn that the layman may hope to follow progress by reading the practitioners' original reports. Both in mathematics and astronomy, research reports had ceased already in antiquity to be intelligible to a generally educated audience. In dynamics, research became similarly esoteric in the latter Middle Ages, and it

---

early nineteenth centuries of a previously   [Kuhn's note].
respected tradition of "romantic" chemistry

recaptured general intelligibility only briefly during the early seventeenth century when a new paradigm replaced the one that had guided medieval research. Electrical research began to require translation for the layman before the end of the eighteenth century, and most other fields of physical science ceased to be generally accessible in the nineteenth. During the same two centuries similar transitions can be isolated in the various parts of the biological sciences. In parts of the social sciences they may well be occurring today. Although it has become customary, and is surely proper, to deplore the widening gulf that separates the professional scientist from his collegues in other fields, too little attention is paid to the essential relationship between that gulf and the mechanisms intrinsic to scientific advance.

Ever since prehistoric antiquity one field of study after another has crossed the divide between what the historian might call its prehistory as a science and its history proper. These transitions to maturity have seldom been so sudden or so unequivocal as my necessarily schematic discussion may have implied. But neither have they been historically gradual, coextensive, that is to say, with the entire development of the fields within which they occurred. Writers on electricity during the first four decades of the eighteenth century possessed far more information about electrical phenomena than had their sixteenth-century predecessors. During the half-century after 1740, few new sorts of electrical phenomena were added to their lists. Nevertheless, in important respects, the electrical writings of Cavendish, Coulomb, and Volta in the last third of the eighteenth century seem further removed from those of Gray, Du Fay, and even Franklin than are the writings of these early eighteenth-century electrical discoverers from those of the sixteenth century.[6] Sometime between 1740 and 1780, electricians were for the first time enabled to take the foundations of their field for granted. From that point they pushed on to more concrete and recondite problems, and increasingly they then reported their results in articles addressed to other electricians rather than in books addressed to the learned world at large. As a group they achieved what had been gained by astronomers in antiquity and by students of motion in the Middle Ages, of physical optics in the late seventeenth century, and of historical geology in the early nineteenth. They had, that is, achieved a paradigm that proved able to guide the whole group's research. Except with the advantage of hindsight, it is hard to find another criterion that so clearly proclaims a field a science.

1962

---

6. The post-Franklinian developments include an immense increase in the sensitivity of charge detectors, the first reliable and generally diffused techniques for measuring charge, the evolution of the concept of capacity and its relation to a newly refined notion of electric tension, and the quantification of electrostatic force [Kuhn's note].

QUESTIONS

1. What is Kuhn's thesis? How is the essay organized to develop that thesis?

2. What is the relationship, by Kuhn's account, of the science textbook to the nature and practice of science? Examine a textbook in your course in one of the natural or social sciences. Does it have the character Kuhn ascribes to textbooks? Does regarding the textbook in this light help you in your study of the subject?

3. What does Kuhn mean by a "paradigm" in science, and what advantages for science does he ascribe to it? Can you state the prevailing paradigm in sciences other than those he uses for illustration (for example, chemistry, biology, psychology)? Does the search for or finding of the paradigms help you to understand what these sciences are about?

4. What does Kuhn's essay suggest about the nature of a scientific fact, or the place of fact in science? By and large, does this conclusion accord, or disagree, with Jacob Bronowski's statement of the matter, in "The Reach of Imagination" (p. 194)? Is it not the business of a science to observe and record the facts? Is this not what Niko Tinbergen, for instance, does in "The Bee-Hunters of Hulshorst" (p. 906)? What more should science do?

Literature and the Arts

John Gardner

WHAT WRITERS DO

Everyone knows at least in a general way what writers—that is, writers of fiction—do. They write fiction. But even for writers themselves it's not easy to say just what that means. We listen to the sentence "They write fiction" and nod impatiently, as if the thing were too obvious to need saying, which in a way it is, because we all agree, as speakers of English, on what "they" means, and "write" and "fiction." But maybe we nodded too hastily. What *do* we mean, to start with the easiest question, by "they"—that is, "writers"?

Most of us are snobs and would be inclined to say at once that we need not concern ourselves with the obvious fact that writers are of various sorts ranging from, say, John Jakes (of the Bicentennial series) to Kurt Vonnegut, to Herman Melville. As warthogs, IRS agents, and zebras are all animals, these dissimilar beings—Jakes, Vonnegut, and Melville—are all writers; but though the problem here might amuse a chimpanzee or a positivist, it does not seem, to us snobs, worth attention. The word *writers*, and the pronoun we substitute for it, has various meanings, but the only one we really care about is the one which refers to the class represented by Melville. The trouble with this hasty, respectable judgment lies of course in the fact that every individual writer, even a stern-minded person like Melville, is different people at different times. In one mood, or in one crowd, the serious writer writes fairy tales; in another he writes ponderous novels; in still another, dirty limericks. A great writer is not great because he never writes dirty limericks but because, if he does write one, he tries to write a very good one.

Any writer who's worked in various forms can tell you from experience that it all feels like writing. Some people may feel that they're "really" writing when they work on their novels and just fooling around when they write bedtime stories for their children; but that can mean only one of two things, I think: either that the writer has a talent for writing novels and not much talent for writing children's stories, or else that the writer is a self-important donzel who writes both miserable novels and miserable children's stories. I would say that even in a given work a writer is many different people. Just at the moment when his novel is most serious —most strenuously laboring to capture some profound idea through meticulous analysis of characters in action—the Melvillian heavyweight suddenly notices (as John Jakes would do) that the serving-girl in the corner has lowered her bodice a little, trying to catch the central character's eye. I don't mean that our serious writer's mind has wandered; I mean that another side of him, after vigorous signaling, has gotten his attention. Or to put it another way, wanting to write like Tolstoi at his solemnest, he has suddenly discovered in himself an urge to write like, say, Henry Fielding. If he gives in to the impulse, as he may or may not, and pursues the romance the lowered bodice has invited, he may suddenly, at the height of idealistic love, or the depth of debauchery, find himself feeling a little cynical somehow, or puritanically pious; or he may find himself distracted by the ferns outside the window, which lure him to delicate appositions and fluttering rhythms, lyricism for its own sake.

What's happening here, of course, is not that several writers inside the one writer's head are clubbing each other for control of the typewriter keys. The true writer's mind is not a jungle but a noble democracy, in which all parties have their say, even the crazy ones, even the most violently passionate, because otherwise justice, balance, sanity are impossible. Wanting to write like Tolstoi at his solemnest, the writer finds a part of himself rising to object to a hint of pompous braying, agrarian bigotry, righteousness unredeemed by humor. Swinging toward Fielding, the writer finds a part of himself complaining about the absence of high-mindedness. Scanning possibilities like a chess-playing computer, weighing the votes of his innumerable selves, following now this leading voice, now that, the writer-multitude finds out, page by page and draft by draft, the sane and passionate whole which is his novel.

Every fine writer has within him a John Jakes, a Marquis de Sade, a James Michener, a William Gass, a Melville. If his multitude of selves is rich but anarchic, uncontrollable, so that his work bulges here with pornography, here with dry philosophy, he is likely to be a "serious" writer but not a very good one. If for one reason or another his selection of selves is limited, he is likely to be a lesser writer. Some writers are limited because they are, simply, not very rich personalities: they contain in them no Melville, no Marquis de Sade. Other writers are limited because, though rich in selves, they voluntarily disenfranchise large segments of their inner population to satisfy the whim of some market: they avoid ideas, or sex, or—as in the stock "*New Yorker* story"—unfashion-able emotion.

Writers whose stock of selves is limited by simplicity of personality we dismiss—uncharitably but not unjustly—as stupid. Writers limited by concern about market we dismiss as commercial. How do we distinguish these lesser kinds of writers from the serious, even sublime writer who limits himself by the choice of some relatively simple form—Shakespeare in the sonnets, Hawthorne in his stories for children? And how, we may as well ask in the same breath, does the simplicity of a sonnet or chil-dren's story differ from the simplicity of a porno or mystery thriller?

If you accept my metaphor of the writer as democracy, the answer to both questions seems obvious. The whole community cannot get to-gether on a porno or the usual emotionally simpleminded thriller, at least so long as the porno or thriller remain recognizable themselves, con-scious and intentional distortions of human experience. (Ross Macdonald is the superior mystery writer he is precisely because he refuses to abide by the usual rules of his form, consistently writing, so to speak, better than necessary.) On the other hand, the sonnet and children's story—or the parable, tale, yarn, sketch, and so on—do not of necessity oversim-plify or distort. When the whole community argues about war, pollution, or energy, it argues in one way; when it argues about building swing-sets on playgrounds, it argues in another. I think no part of a writer need be suppressed to write *Charlotte's Web* or the juveniles of Joan Aiken. It is true, of course, that the children's story, like the traditional gothic tale, tends to use a very special language; but it is not a language into which large parts of our common experience cannot be translated.

One might put it this way: important thought is important only insofar as it communicates with those at whom it is aimed; no sensible human being goes on talking when all of his audience has walked away. Great children's literature talks about the complexity of human experience in a way interesting and meaningful to children; bad children's literature talks about what some mistaken person imagines children care about. The bad children's writer writes as he does either because, being of limited personality, he thinks children care about no more than he does, or because, being commercial, he wants to satisfy formulas made up by fools and statisticians.

Great children's writers, like great writers of any other kind, are complex, multitudinous of self. To speak only of living American writers, think of the children's fiction of Nancy Willard, Hilma Wolitzer, or Susan Shreve. All of these writers, as it happens—not by chance—are also respectable writers of adult fiction or poetry. For contrast think of Maxine Kumin or Raoul Dahl, occasionally unsatisfying writers both for children and for adults because, in each case, one side of the writer's personality—the angrily righteous—overwhelms the democratic balance with pious despotism.

So much for the "they" in the truism about writers, "They write fiction." Let me turn to "write."

Writing is an action, a different action from talking. The only conceivable reason for engaging in writing is to make something relatively permanent which one might otherwise forget. That would seem to imply that one thinks there is some value in the thing not to be forgotten —either some value already achieved, as in the case of a good recipe for scalloped potatoes, or some potential value, as in the case of a love poem which stinks at the moment but has the right spirit and might get better under revision. Writers of the Melvillian class, that is, "serious" writers, write only in the second sense: they write works that with luck and devotion may be improved by revision—or, in the end, works that *have* been so improved, so that we may class them with other human treasures, such as good recipes for scalloped potatoes. If one looks at the first drafts of even the greatest writers, like Tolstoi and Dostoevski, one sees that literary art does not come flying like Athena, fully formed, from Zeus' head. Indeed, the first-draft stupidity of great writers is a shocking and comforting thing to see. What one learns from studying successive drafts is that the writer did not know what he meant to say until he said it. A typo of "murder" for "mirror" can change the whole plot of a novel.

To put all this another way, what oral storytellers seem to do is figure out certain parts of the world by telling stories about those parts. The Greeks, as you know, made much of this. Whereas most civilizations feared and hated blindness, the Greeks elevated it, at least as a symbol: the blind man was the man who had to see with his tongue, understanding the world by telling of it. What writers do is somewhat different. They figure out the world by talking about it, then looking at what they've said and changing it. I don't mean, of course, that oral storytellers don't polish and repolish; I only mean to say that there's a great difference between the power and precision of the two instruments—a difference as great as that between, say, a reading glass and a microscope. Think again of Homer. A fair pile of prehomeric poetry survives, all of it fairly good, most of it battle poetry, all the battle pieces relatively short, at least in comparison with the *Iliad*. The standard heroic poem before Homer's time probably ran to about the length of one or two books of the *Iliad*. It may be true, as tradition says, that Homer was a blind oral poet, like Demodokos, his character in the *Odyssey*; but it does not seem likely. Homer appeared at the very moment when writing was reintroduced in ancient Greece, and the complexity of his poems—repeated, cunningly varied references to bows, looms, Odysseus' bed and the great phallic pillar which supports it—images we're forced to describe, finally, as richly and ingeniously symbolic—can only be accounted for in one of two ways: either by a theory that Homer was vastly more intelligent than any other human being who ever lived, or by a theory that Homer wrote things down, studied them patiently and stubbornly, like Beethoven, and, like Beethoven, endlessly, brilliantly revised.

Or think of the sudden, astonishing rise of serious "popular" literature in the late Middle Ages and early Renaissance; I mean the use, in writers like Boccaccio, Chaucer, and Shakespeare, of salacious stories and folktales as the base of psychologically and philosophically serious literature. Before Boccaccio's time, as has recently been pointed out, writers used parchment. To make a Bible you had to kill three hundred cows. Books cost a lot, in money and cattle-blood. One used parchment only for things of the greatest importance—religious writings, cathedral plans, the shopping lists of kings. Then in Boccaccio's time paper was introduced, so that suddenly it was possible for Boccaccio to write down a dirty joke he'd heard, fool around with it a little—change the farmer's daughter to a nun, for instance, or introduce comically disparate high-class symbolism—and produce the *Decameron*. Chaucer did the same only better. We have two drafts—by no means all that once existed—of Chaucer's story borrowed from Boccaccio, *Troilus and Criseyde*. For artists, writing has always meant, in effect, the art of endless revising.

Now let me turn to the third term in the formula "They write fiction." What oral storytellers tell and retell we call legends, a tricky word that, if we derive it from the Latin, means "that which is read," and if we take it (by false etymology, a once common one) from Anglo-Saxon, means—as a result of the softening of g to y—*lying*. Even in the beginning no one knew what to do with that. The primary meaning of *legend* in the Middle Ages was "a saint's life." In any case, *fiction* was from the beginning something else: it can only come from the Latin and means "something shaped, molded, or devised." As everyone knows, the origins of words don't prove much; but it seems true that we still use fiction in the original sense, not to describe some noble old lie which can be told, with no great loss, in a variety of ways, but to describe a specific kind of made-up story, a story we think valuable precisely because of the way it's been shaped. You can tell the legend or fairy tale of *Jack and the Beanstalk* pretty much any way you please, as long as you don't throw out Jack, the giant, the colored beans, or the beanstalk. Jack can make three trips, or two, or one; he can trade in the cow (or something) for the colored beans either on the way in to town or at the fair; and so on. To tell Faulkner's *As I Lay Dying*, Joyce's "The Dead," or William Gass' "In the Heart of the Heart of the Country," one has to use the writer's exact words or all is lost. The essential difference between what we think of as "fiction" and what we think of as "legend" is that, relatively at least, the shaping in fiction counts more heavily.

In the broadest and perhaps most important sense, fiction can go wrong in two ways: it fails as basic legend or it fails in its artifice. Most of the fiction one reads—I mean contemporary fiction, but the same may be said of fiction done in Dickens' day, most of it by now ground to dust by time's selectivity—is trash. It makes no real attempt at original and interesting style, and the story it tells is boring. This is simply to say, of course, that if fiction moves too far from its model, legend, and abandons story, it fails to satisfy our age-old expectations; if it does not move far enough, telling its story without concern for style, it fails to satisfy other, newer expectations. What writers do, if they haven't been misled by false canons of taste or some character defect, is try to make up an interesting story and tell it in an authentically interesting way—that is, some way that, however often we may read it, does not turn out to be boring.

The odds against a writer's achieving a real work of art are astronomical. Most obviously the "they" of our "They write fiction" formula—in other words, the writer's personality—may go wrong. Every good writer is many things—a symbolist, a careful student of character, a person of strong opinions, a lover of pure tale or adventure. In a bad or just ordinary novel, the writer's various selves war with one another. We feel, as we read, not one commanding voice but a series of jarringly different voices, even voices in sharp and confusing disagreement.

The war of the writer's selves can result in great fiction only in the case of an extraordinarily great writer, which is to say, an almost supernaturally wise man—one who has the rare gift of being able to see through his own soul's trickery. Very few people of the kind who make good writers —rather childlike people, as psychologists have often pointed out—are wise in life. They become wise, if they do, by revision—by looking over what they've written down again and again, a hundred times, two hundred, each time in a slightly different mood, with a different model ringing in their ears: one day the writer looks over what he's written just after spending a few hours reading Tolstoi; another day he rereads his own work just after seeing a play by Samuel Beckett, or some simple-minded but good-hearted movie like *The Sound of Music*, or just after returning from his mother's funeral. That process, endless revision and rereading—in different moods, with different models in mind—is the writer's chief hope.

Or anyway it is his chief hope if he has known all along what fiction is and has been trying to write real fiction. I have said that true fiction is, in effect, oral-storytelling written down and fixed, perfected by revision. Let me refine that a little now. What is it that the writer is trying to achieve—or ought to be—as he endlessly fiddles with rough drafts?

A true work of fiction is a wonderfully simple thing—so simple that most so-called serious writers avoid trying it, feeling they ought to do something more important and ingenious, never guessing how incredibly difficult it is. A true work of fiction does all of the following things, and does them elegantly, efficiently: It creates a vivid and continuous dream in the reader's mind; it is implicitly philosophical; it fulfills or at least deals with all of the expectations it sets up; and it strikes us, in the end, not simply as a thing done but as a shining performance.

I will not elaborate that description in much detail. Some of it I've mentioned before, here and there; some of it seems to me to need no elaboration. I've said, first, that fiction creates a vivid and continuous dream in the reader's mind. Any reader knows at a glance that that is true, and that if a given work does not bring a vivid and continuous dream to the reader—almost instantly, after five or six words—the fiction is either bad or, what may be the same thing, a so-called metafiction. One can derive all the principles of effective fiction from the idea that the writer must make his dream vivid and continuous. The dream is not vivid, of course, if too many words are abstract, not concrete, if too many verbs are passive, too many metaphors familiar or dull, and so on; and the dream is not continuous if some element in the writing distracts the reader from the story to thoughts about the stupidity of the writer—his inability to use proper grammar, his excessive loquacity, his deviation into sentimentality, mannerism, or frigidity, and so on. If the student writer can get rid of every one of those common errors which regularly undermine vividness and continuousness, a finite list not difficult to spell out, then that student can consistently avoid writing bad fiction. Whether or not he can write great fiction is of course another matter, one of genius or the lack of it. When the writer is finally writing true fiction, the best he is capable of, he may well discover that he'd better start making some carefully calculated mistakes, disguise his insipidity.

It's the law of the vivid and continuous dream—for it is, I think, something close to an aesthetic law for fiction—that makes writing fiction what I've described as a "wonderfully simple thing." All the writer has to do is see with absolute clarity and vividness, and describe without mistake exactly what he's seen. That was Faulkner's genius—to see very clearly. No one forgets his image of the falling lantern and the fire starting in "Shingles for the Lord," or his image of a Negro shanty's dirt yard, "smooth as an old, worn nickle." What offends in Faulkner, as has often been remarked, is his failure to value that clarity of vision, again and again mucking it up—especially toward the end—with outrageously mannered prose, that is, prose calculated to obscure the vision and call attention to the writer. Joyce did the same. At the end of his life, clear-headedly looking back, he thought "The Dead" the finest thing he'd ever done, and Tolstoi's "How Much Land Does a Man Need?" the finest work of fiction ever written. It had been Joyce himself, of course, who made the claim that the writer should be inconspicuous in his work, like God off in the corner of the universe paring his nails. In *Dubliners* and

Portrait he'd been true to that ideal; from that point on—however great the books in certain ways—Joyce went for mannerism, and the sad truth is he carried most of twentieth-century fiction with him.

To do the wonderfully simple thing real writers do at their best, one needs only to look clearly and levelly at one's character and his situation. If the writer sees his character clearly, and if the character is, as all human beings in fact are, unique in certain respects, that character will inevitably behave in ways no one else would behave in that precise situation. It will prove impossible to write a story which could be equally well played in a film version by Robert Redford, Dustin Hoffman, Alan Arkin, Richard Dreyfus, or Frank Sinatra. If the writer sees each and every one of his characters clearly—even the most minor walk-ons—he can never for a moment slip into cliché. Following actions and reactions second by second through a significant chain of events, keeping a sharp eye out to catch every wince or grin or twitch, always checking his imagination against experience (how do misers really behave in the world), the writer almost cannot help coming up with a dream worth following—not a passive dream, of course, but one the reader struggles with, judges, tries to second-guess, a dream of reality more vivid and powerful than all but the rarest, keenest moments of reality itself.

Of course part of what makes this dream so vivid and powerful is that, like our best nightmares, the dream is thematic, or, as I put it earlier, it is implicitly philosophical. I would say that, at their best, both fiction and philosophy do the same thing, only fiction does it better—though slower. Philosophy is by essence abstract, a sequence of general argument controlled in its profluence by either logic (in old-fashioned systematic philosophy) or emotional coherence (in the intuitive philosophies of, say, Nietzsche and Kierkegaard). We read the argument and it seems to flow along okay, make sense, but what we ask is, "Is this true of my mailman?" or, "Do I really follow the Golden Rule because, unlike Prussian officers, I am a coward? Do I *know* any good Prussian officers?" Fiction comes at questions from the other end. It traces or explores some general argument by examining a particular case in which the universal case seems implied; and in place of logic or emotional coherence—the philosopher's stepping stones—fictional argument is controlled by mimesis: we are persuaded that the characters would indeed do and say exactly what we are told they do and say, whether the characters are lifelike human beings or a congress of insects given human traits. If the mimesis convinces us, then the question we ask is opposite to that we ask of philosophical argument; that is, we ask, "Is this true *in general?*" Convinced by Captain Ahab, we want to know if in some way his story, the story of a madman, applies to all human beings, mad or sane. In great fiction the writer, inching along from particular to particular, builds into his work arrows or vectors pointing us toward the general. He does this, we know, in numerous ways—by relating his particulars to some symbolic system recalling a familiar set of questions of values, by playing his plot off against some old and familiar plot, as Joyce does in *Ulysses*, by old-fashioned allegory, by explicit authorial comment, by arranging that his characters discuss the important issues within the story (the method of Tolstoi and Dostoevski), or by some other means.

What happens in great fiction is that, while we are occupied with the vividness and convincingness of detail—admiring, for instance, the fact that Captain Ahab's personal crew is made up of Chinese never before seen on the ship until now, with the first lowering of the longboats—we are also occupied with the neatness and power of the philosophical argument. When reading great fiction, one never feels that the writer has wandered from the subject. The true writer sets up for us some important question, in dramatic form, and explores it clear-mindedly, relentlessly. We read of Raskolnikov's initial indecision about whether or not he has the right to commit murder, and we instantly recognize the universal significance of the question and lean forward tensely, waiting to see what will happen. We delight in the particulars—the fact that he is very nearly caught on the stairs—and we delight simultaneously in seeing the implied universals. It's in this sense that true fiction is implicitly philosophical.

I need say nothing about the next standard I've mentioned, that fiction at its best satisfies our expectations. At the end of a mystery, we want all the questions answered, red herrings explained away, false clues justified, and so on. In a more serious kind of novel, we want all important issues dealt with, no character left hiding forever behind the tree where the author put him and forgot him. It may be that, finishing the novel, we at first imagine that some thread was left untied—for instance, some symbolic idea. Two different characters may have been subtly identified as Eden serpents, and as we finish the novel we at first can't see how the double identification was resolved. Carefully rereading, we discover that the seeming contradiction was indeed resolved, and the belated satisfaction of our expectation gives pleasure. But whether the satisfaction is immediate or purposely delayed, it must sooner or later come.

Finally, I've said that in the best fiction we get not just a piece of work —efficient energy which moves something—but a "shining performance." We say not just "What a true and good book!" but "What magnificent writing!" To win our applause, it cannot have the fake magnificence of mannerism—flights of purple prose, advance-guard trickery, artifice aimed solely at calling attention to the artificer. It must have the true magnificence of beautiful (some would prefer to say "interesting") technique: adequate and "inspired"—that is, revised, rerevised, polished to near perfection. We recognize this at once, I think, in acting. Some actors do a perfectly good job—we are never distracted to the actor behind the character played—while other actors do a brilliant job: we *do* think of the actor, not as a human being at war with the part being played, but as an artist whose skills come singing through the part, making the character more interesting and "real" than we could have hoped or dreamed from a reading of the script.

What the writers I care most about do is take fiction as the single most important thing in life after life itself—life itself being both their raw material and the object of their celebration. They do it not for ego but simply to make something singularly beautiful. Fiction is their religion and comfort: when they are depressed, they go not to church or psychoanalysis but to Salinger or Joyce, early Malamud, parts of Faulkner, Tolstoi, or the Bible as book. They write, themselves, to make things equally worthy of trust, not stories of creeps and cynics but stories of people capable of a measure of heroism, capable of strong and honest feeling at least some of the time, capable of love and sacrifice—capable of all this, and available as models for imitation. Everything true writers do, I think, from laborious plotting on butcher paper or three-by-five cards to laborious revision, draft after draft, they do to create *characters*—the center and heart of all true fiction—characters who will serve till Messiah comes, characters whose powerful existence in our minds make a real-life messiah unnecessary. Imperfect, even childish human beings, writers raise themselves up by the techniques of fiction to something much better than even the best of writers are in everyday life: ordinary mortals transmuted for the moment into apostles.

1981

Vladimir Nabokov

GOOD READERS AND GOOD WRITERS

"How to be a Good Reader" or "Kindness to Authors"—something of that sort might serve to provide a subtitle for these various discussions of various authors, for my plan is to deal lovingly, in loving and lingering detail, with several European masterpieces. A hundred years ago, Flaubert in a letter to his mistress made the following remark: *Comme l'on serait savant si l'on connaissait bien seulement cinq à six livres:* "What a scholar one might be if one knew well only some half a dozen books."

In reading, one should notice and fondle details. There is nothing wrong about the moonshine of generalization when it comes *after* the sunny trifles of the book have been lovingly collected. If one begins with a ready-made generalization, one begins at the wrong end and travels away from the book before one has started to understand it. Nothing is more boring or more unfair to the author than starting to read, say, *Madame Bovary*, with the preconceived notion that it is a denunciation of the bourgeoisie. We should always remember that the work of art is invariably the creation of a new world, so that the first thing we should do is to study that new world as closely as possible, approaching it as something brand new, having no obvious connection with the worlds we already know. When this new world has been closely studied, then and only then let us examine its links with other worlds, other branches of knowledge.

Another question: Can we expect to glean information about places and times from a novel? Can anybody be so naive as to think he or she can learn anything about the past from those buxom best-sellers that are hawked around by book clubs under the heading of historical novels? But what about the masterpieces? Can we rely on Jane Austen's picture of landowning England with baronets and landscaped grounds when all she knew was a clergyman's parlor? And *Bleak House*, that fantastic romance within a fantastic London, can we call it a study of London a hundred years ago? Certainly not. And the same holds for other such novels in this series. The truth is that great novels are great fairy tales—and the novels in this series are supreme fairy tales.

Time and space, the colors of the seasons, the movements of muscles and minds, all these are for writers of genius (as far as we can guess and I trust we guess right) not traditional notions which may be borrowed from the circulating library of public truths but a series of unique surprises which master artists have learned to express in their own unique way. To minor authors is left the ornamentation of the commonplace: these do not bother about any reinventing of the world; they merely try to squeeze the best they can out of a given order of things, out of traditional patterns of fiction. The various combinations these minor authors are able to produce within these set limits may be quite amusing in a mild ephemeral way because minor readers like to recognize their own ideas in a pleasing disguise. But the real writer, the fellow who sends planets spinning and models a man asleep and eagerly tampers with the sleeper's rib, that kind of author has no given values at his disposal: he must create them himself. The art of writing is a very futile business if it does not imply first of all the art of seeing the world as the potentiality of fiction. The material of this world may be real enough (as far as reality goes) but does not exist at all as an accepted entirety: it is chaos, and to this chaos the author says "go!" allowing the world to flicker and to fuse. It is now recombined in its very atoms, not merely in its visible and superficial parts. The writer is the first man to map it and to name the natural objects it contains. Those berries there are edible. That speckled creature that bolted across my path might be tamed. That lake between those trees will be called Lake Opal or, more artistically, Dishwater Lake. That mist is a mountain—and that mountain must be conquered. Up a trackless slope climbs the master artist, and at the top, on a windy ridge, whom do you think he meets? The panting and happy reader, and there they spontaneously embrace and are linked forever if the book lasts forever.

One evening at a remote provincial college through which I happened to be jogging on a protracted lecture tour, I suggested a little quiz—ten definitions of a reader, and from these ten the students had to choose four definitions that would combine to make a good reader. I have mislaid the list, but as far as I remember the definitions went something like this. Select four answers to the question what should a reader be to be a good reader:

1. The reader should belong to a book club.
2. The reader should identify himself or herself with the hero or heroine.
3. The reader should concentrate on the social-economic angle.
4. The reader should prefer a story with action and dialogue to one with none.
5. The reader should have seen the book in a movie.
6. The reader should be a budding author.
7. The reader should have imagination.
8. The reader should have memory.
9. The reader should have a dictionary.
10. The reader should have some artistic sense.

The students leaned heavily on emotional identification, action, and the social-economic or historical angle. Of course, as you have guessed, the good reader is one who has imagination, memory, a dictionary, and some artistic sense—which sense I propose to develop in myself and in others whenever I have the chance.

Incidentally, I use the word *reader* very loosely. Curiously enough, one cannot *read* a book: one can only reread it. A good reader, a major reader, an active and creative reader is a rereader. And I shall tell you why. When we read a book for the first time the very process of laboriously moving our eyes from left to right, line after line, page after page, this complicated physical work upon the book, the very process of learning in terms of space and time what the book is about, this stands between us and artistic appreciation. When we look at a painting we do not have to move our eyes in a special way even if, as in a book, the picture contains elements of depth and development. The element of time does not really enter in a first contact with a painting. In reading a book, we must have time to acquaint ourselves with it. We have no physical organ (as we have the eye in regard to a painting) that takes in the whole picture and then can enjoy its details. But at a second, or third, or fourth reading we do, in a sense, behave towards a book as we do towards a painting.

However, let us not confuse the physical eye, that monstrous master-piece of evolution, with the mind, an even more monstrous achievement. A book, no matter what it is—a work of fiction or a work of science (the boundary line between the two is not as clear as is generally believed)—a book of fiction appeals first of all to the mind. The mind, the brain, the top of the tingling spine, is, or should be, the only instrument used upon a book.

Now, this being so, we should ponder the question how does the mind work when the sullen reader is confronted by the sunny book. First, the sullen mood melts away, and for better or worse the reader enters into the spirit of the game. The effort to begin a book, especially if it is praised by people whom the young reader secretly deems to be too old-fashioned or too serious, this effort is often difficult to make; but once it is made, rewards are various and abundant. Since the master artist used his imagi-nation in creating his book, it is natural and fair that the consumer of a book should use his imagination too.

There are, however, at least two varieties of imagination in the reader's case. So let us see which one of the two is the right one to use in reading a book. First, there is the comparatively lowly kind which turns for support to the simple emotions and is of a definitely personal nature. (There are various subvarieties here, in this first section of emotional reading.) A situation in a book is intensely felt because it reminds us of something that happened to us or to someone we know or knew. Or, again, a reader treasures a book mainly because it evokes a country, a landscape, a mode of living which he nostalgically recalls as part of his own past. Or, and this is the worst thing a reader can do, he identifies himself with a character in the book. This lowly variety is not the kind of imagination I would like readers to use.

So what is the authentic instrument to be used by the reader? It is impersonal imagination and artistic delight. What should be established, I think, is an artistic harmonious balance between the reader's mind and the author's mind. We ought to remain a little aloof and take pleasure in this aloofness while at the same time we keenly enjoy—passionately enjoy, enjoy with tears and shivers—the inner weave of a given master-piece. To be quite objective in these matters is of course impossible. Everything that is worthwhile is to some extent subjective. For instance, you sitting there may be merely my dream, and I may be your nightmare. But what I mean is that the reader must know when and where to curb his imagination and this he does by trying to get clear the specific world the author places at his disposal. We must see things and hear things, we must visualize the rooms, the clothes, the manners of an author's people. The color of Fanny Price's eyes in *Mansfield Park* and the furnishing of her cold little room are important.

We all have different temperaments, and I can tell you right now that the best temperament for a reader to have, or to develop, is a combination of the artistic and the scientific one. The enthusiastic artist alone is apt to be too subjective in his attitude towards a book, and so a scientific coolness of judgment will temper the intuitive heat. If, however, a would-be reader is utterly devoid of passion and patience—of an artist's passion and a scientist's patience—he will hardly enjoy great literature.

Literature was born not the day when a boy crying wolf, wolf came running out of the Neanderthal valley with a big gray wolf at his heels: literature was born on the day when a boy came crying wolf, wolf and there was no wolf behind him. That the poor little fellow because he lied too often was finally eaten up by a real beast is quite incidental. But here is what is important. Between the wolf in the tall grass and the wolf in the tall story there is a shimmering go-between. That go-between, that prism, is the art of literature.

Literature is invention. Fiction is fiction. To call a story a true story is an insult to both art and truth. Every great writer is a great deceiver, but so is that arch-cheat Nature. Nature always deceives. From the simple deception of propagation to the prodigiously sophisticated illusion of protective colors in butterflies or birds, there is in Nature a marvelous system of spells and wiles. The writer of fiction only follows Nature's lead.

Going back for a moment to our wolf-crying woodland little woolly fellow, we may put it this way: the magic of art was in the shadow of the wolf that he deliberately invented, his dream of the wolf; then the story of his tricks made a good story. When he perished at last, the story told about him acquired a good lesson in the dark around the camp fire. But he was the little magician. He was the inventor.

There are three points of view from which a writer can be considered: he may be considered as a storyteller, as a teacher, and as an enchanter. A major writer combines these three—storyteller, teacher, enchanter—but it is the enchanter in him that predominates and makes him a major writer.

To the storyteller we turn for entertainment, for mental excitement of the simplest kind, for emotional participation, for the pleasure of traveling in some remote region in space or time. A slightly different though not necessarily higher mind looks for the teacher in the writer. Propagandist, moralist, prophet—this is the rising sequence. We may go to the teacher not only for moral education but also for direct knowledge, for simple facts. Alas, I have known people whose purpose in reading the French and Russian novelists was to learn something about life in gay Paree or in sad Russia. Finally, and above all, a great writer is always a great enchanter, and it is here that we come to the really exciting part when we try to grasp the individual magic of his genius and to study the style, the imagery, the pattern of his novels or poems.

The three facets of the great writer—magic, story, lesson—are prone to blend in one impression of unified and unique radiance, since the magic of art may be present in the very bones of the story, in the very marrow of thought. There are masterpieces of dry, limpid, organized thought which provoke in us an artistic quiver quite as strongly as a novel like *Mansfield Park* does or as any rich flow of Dickensian sensual imagery. It seems to me that a good formula to test the quality of a novel is, in the long run, a merging of the precision of poetry and the intuition of science. In order to bask in that magic a wise reader reads the book of genius not with his heart, not so much with his brain, but with his spine. It is there that occurs the telltale tingle even though we must keep a little aloof, a little detached when reading. Then with a pleasure which is both sensual and intellectual we shall watch the artist build his castle of cards and watch the castle of cards become a castle of beautiful steel and glass.
Ca. 1941   1980

Donald Hall

FIRST A WRITER, THEN A SPORTSMAN

Red Smith's final column, called "Writing Less—and Better?" appeared in the sports section of this newspaper [*The New York Times*] last January. The tone was faintly elegiac, as it announced his decision to cut back from four to three columns a week. Alas, the cutback was more severe, for Walter W. Smith, 76, died of heart failure four days later. No longer would he practice the literary form of the sports column—in his hands something like the sonnet. At least we can add to our libraries these two volumes collecting hundreds of Red Smith columns.

Smith himself edited *To Absent Friends*—finishing the book last summer—179 columns of tribute and elegy for men and horses. Dave Anderson edited *The Red Smith Reader* after his friend's death. "If you blindfolded yourself," he says in his introduction, "reached into Red Smith's files and yanked out 130 columns, any 130 columns, you would have a good collection." In the absence of other criteria, Anderson has mostly chosen columns "about big names, big events, big issues"—including pieces from his time with the *St. Louis Star*, the *Philadelphia Record*, *The New York Herald Tribune*, his four years with a syndicate, and ending with his 11 years on *The New York Times*. During some of these years Smith wrote seven columns a week; he figured he had written more than 10,000 columns.

Red Smith was a good reporter, a brilliant phrase-maker, on occasion a fierce moralist—and he was best at telling a story. No writer assembles the brief anecdote with more (necessarily invisible) skill. Often his narrative art is one of omission; the teller gives *just enough* of the tale, so that one word leaps forth to do the work of a hundred. Smith excelled in the anecdotal lead that illustrated character or introduced a theme:

"Society Kid Hogan was hurrying through the Illinois Center pedestrian tunnel under Michigan Avenue on June 9, 1930, when a man in the crowd put a gun to the head of Jake Lingle, a grafting crime reporter, and it went *blooie.*

"The Kid kept right on walking.

"'Why?' the Law asked him later.

"'The last train was leaving for the racetrack,' he said reasonably."

Ah, the art of the adverb! Here's a story from a column about Grantland Rice:

"When Warren Harding was President he asked Granny down to Washington for a round of golf, and Granny invited his friend, Ring Lardner.

"'This is an unexpected pleasure, Mr. Lardner,' Harding said as they hacked around. 'I only knew Granny was coming. How did you happen to make it, too?'

"'I want to be Ambassador to Greece,' Lardner said.

"'Greece?' said the President. 'Why Greece?'

"'Because,' Lardner said, 'my wife doesn't like Great Neck.'"

His friend and model turns up frequently in these pages:

"Grantland Rice, the prince of sportswriters, used to do a weekly radio interview, with some sporting figures. Frequently, in the interest of spontaneity, he would type out questions and answers in advance. One night his guest was Babe Ruth.

"'Well, you know, Granny,' the Babe read in response to a question, 'Duke Ellington said the Battle of Waterloo was won on the playing fields of Elkton.'

"'Babe,' Granny said after the show, 'Duke Ellington for the Duke of Wellington I can understand. But how did you ever read Eton as Elkton? . . .'

"'I married my first wife there,' Babe said."

One could go on quoting; one would never quote enough: The sports reader will need to buy these books.

Or at least one of them. These volumes repeat each other a bit—not so much in the whole columns as in illustrative anecdotes or favorite lines —and *The Red Smith Reader* is the better book because its tone is more varied. *To Absent Friends* ululates a continual elegy, and the obituary note is not always Red Smith's best. A generous and affectionate man, he is given to eulogy (the word "great" uses itself up fast) and sometimes to sentimental distortion; we learn soon enough that the word "guy," as in "class guy," signals disorder among the sincerity neurons. Sometimes we suffer the portentous coda—the sportswriter's devil—as in a column about Red Rolfe, which ends with the brief graph:

"Class was something Red had no trouble recognizing. He saw it every morning when he shaved."

Smith's best columns describe horse playing (he cautions us to avoid "horse racing") and boxing, with baseball a close third; he writes wonderfully about fishing, as a participant—fishing with friends, with sons and grandsons. (The world of his column is old-fashioned in its almost exclusive maleness.) He dislikes basketball, never writes of hockey in these pages and takes potshots at track and field; he repeats once or twice his intuition that, if the Creator had wanted humans to race, he would have given them four legs. Almost every column is funny enough for laughter. Many are also serious.

When he is serious he is never pompous or self-important. "I've always tried to remember," he told Jerome Holtzman in an interview, "that sports isn't Armageddon. These are just little games that little boys can play, and it really isn't important to the future of civilization whether the Athletics or Browns win." Elsewhere he quotes one of his heroes, his old Tribune editor, Stanley Woodward, who warned against "Godding up these ballplayers." I suspect it's useful, if you are as widely praised as Red Smith was, to keep modest sentiments in front of your eyes, like samplers hanging on the wall. We must not God up sportswriters either. But I permit myself to take newspaper sportswriting more seriously than he does—and perhaps more seriously than I take sports.

Within the pastoral of the sporting world, general human concerns become isolated and magnified—success and failure, youth, aging and death—so that if we have moral ideas in our heads, we have a scene to which we can apply them. Thus Smith permits us to enjoy his rare invective as it dissects the vanity of George Steinbrenner (usually "George III"), the hype of Howard Cosell, the hypocrisy of Bowie Kuhn and Avery Brundage. He becomes angriest when sports refuses to look beyond itself—when the NFL refuses to cancel games after Kennedy's assassination, when the Munich Olympics takes the murder of Israeli athletes as a political intrusion on amateurism.

Maybe moral ideas become *most* useful in the ethics of decency in prose style. Smith is a writer before he is a sportsman. ("Writing is easy," he said. "I just open a vein and bleed.") It seems to me that honest sportswriting helps to keep prose alive. For a culture survives not only through its high-art embodiments; we study beauty less from paintings at the Metropolitan than from daily encounters with an honestly designed beer bottle. It is commonplace to observe that the best newspaper writing occurs in the sports pages, that editorials bore, news stories deaden, features inflate, reviews pontificate. But sports pages do remain lively, play with words (when Mr. and Mrs. Zatopek both won gold medals at the 1952 Olympics, Smith called his column "Czech and Double Czech") and seek out figures of speech.

Metaphor is a way of thinking available to everyone, which has nothing to do with elitist education—except that elitist education seems to discourage it. Shakespeare could talk no other way, and the pit had no trouble following him—but modern intellectuals do. It's true that some living cultures encourage metaphorical speech—the Irish, American blacks—but the Department of English is by and large suspicious and hostile: Colorful speech gets confused with language that has designs on us—like the rhetoric of politics and advertising—and intellectuals resist metaphor for fear of being taken in. Textbooks quoting poems for American classrooms footnote metaphors, translating them into the clichés of flat prose.

So the sports column—as Red Smith did it—becomes a wildlife refuge for metaphor and all liveliness, where language lives and breathes. Smith calls the Olympics "this conclave of gristle," providing us synecdoche.[1] Surely hyperbole is his favorite trope: He writes about the place of bicycle racing in French culture: "An army from Mars could invade France, the government could fall, and even the recipe for sauce Béarnaise could be lost, but if it happened during the Tour de France nobody would notice." He loves the bright figure, and continually quotes the bons mots of others: "Lefty Grove was a pitcher who, in the classic words of Bugs Baer, 'could throw a lamb chop past a wolf.'"

I do not mean to say that Red Smith's language is equal to Shakespeare's. I mean to say that because we have taken daily English lessons from our former Secretary of State,[2] we need Red Smith and his progeny.

1982

---

1. A figure of speech that uses a more inclusive term for a less inclusive term or vice versa: for example, *head* for *cattle* or *the law* for a *policeman*.

2. Under President Reagan, Alexander Haig (1924-   ), notorious for his inept manner of expressing himself, (as is suggested by the epithet, Secretary of Haig State).

Northrop Frye

THE MOTIVE FOR METAPHOR

For the past twenty-five years I have been teaching and studying English literature in a university. As in any other job, certain questions stick in one's mind, not because people keep asking them, but because they're the questions inspired by the very fact of being in such a place. What good is the study of literature? Does it help us to think more clearly, or feel more sensitively, or live a better life than we could without it? What is the function of the teacher and scholar, or of the person who calls himself, as I do, a literary critic? What difference does the study of literature make in our social or political or religious attitude? In my early days I thought very little about such questions, not because I had any of the answers, but because I assumed that anybody who asked them was naïve. I think now that the simplest questions are not only the hardest to answer, but the most important to ask, so I'm going to raise them and try to suggest what my present answers are. I say try to suggest, because there are only more or less inadequate answers to such questions—there aren't any right answers. The kind of problem that literature raises is not the kind that you ever "solve." Whether my answers are any good or not, they represent a fair amount of thinking about the questions. As I can't see my audience, I have to choose my rhetorical style in the dark, and I'm taking the classroom style, because an audience of students is the one I feel easiest with.

There are two things in particular that I want to discuss with you. In school, and in university, there's a subject called "English" in English-speaking countries. English means, in the first place, the mother tongue. As that, it's the most practical subject in the world: you can't understand anything or take any part in your society without it. Wherever illiteracy is a problem, it's as fundamental a problem as getting enough to eat or a place to sleep. The native language takes precedence over every other subject of study: nothing else can compare with it in its usefulness. But then you find that every mother tongue, in any developed or civilized society, turns into something called literature. If you keep on studying "English," you find yourself trying to read Shakespeare and Milton. Literature, we're told, is one of the arts, along with painting and music, and, after you've looked up all the hard words and the Classical allusions and learned what words like imagery and diction are supposed to mean, what you use in understanding it, or so you're told, is your imagination. Here you don't seem to be in quite the same practical and useful area: Shakespeare and Milton, whatever their merits, are not the kind of thing you must know to hold any place in society at all. A person who knows nothing about literature may be an ignoramus, but many people don't mind being that. Every child realizes that literature is taking him in a different direction from the immediately useful, and a good many children complain loudly about this. Two questions I want to deal with, then, are, first: what is the relation of English as the mother tongue to English as a literature? Second: What is the social value of the study of literature, and what is the place of the imagination that literature addresses itself to, in the learning process?

Let's start with the different ways there are of dealing with the world we're living in. Suppose you're shipwrecked on an uninhabited island in the South Seas. The first thing you do is to take a long look at the world around you, a world of sky and sea and earth and stars and trees and hills. You see this world as objective, as something set over against you and not yourself or related to you in any way. And you notice two things about this objective world. In the first place, it doesn't have any conversation. It's full of animals and plants and insects going on with their own business, but there's nothing that responds to you: it has no morals and no intelligence, or at least none that you can grasp. It may have a shape and a meaning, but it doesn't seem to be a human shape or a human meaning. Even if there's enough to eat and no dangerous animals, you feel lonely and frightened and unwanted in such a world.

In the second place, you find that looking at the world, as something set over against you, splits your mind in two. You have an intellect that feels curious about it and wants to study it, and you have feelings or emotions that see it as beautiful or austere or terrible. You know that both these attitudes have some reality, at least for you. If the ship you were wrecked in was a Western ship, you'd probably feel that your intellect tells you more about what's really there in the outer world, and that your emotions tell you more about what's going on inside you. If your background were Oriental, you'd be more likely to reverse this and say that the beauty or terror was what was really there, and that your instinct to count and classify and measure and pull to pieces was what was inside your mind. But whether your point of view is Western or Eastern, intellect and emotion never get together in your mind as long as you're simply looking at the world. They alternate, and keep you divided between them.

The language you use on this level of the mind is the language of consciousness or awareness. It's largely a language of nouns and adjectives. You have to have names for things, and you need qualities like "wet" or "green" or "beautiful" to describe how things seem to you. This is the speculative or contemplative position of the mind, the position in which the arts and sciences begin, although they don't stay there very long. The sciences begin by accepting the facts and the evidence about an outside world without trying to alter them. Science proceeds by accurate measurement and description, and follows the demands of the reason rather than the emotions. What it deals with is there, whether we like it or not. The emotions are unreasonable: for them it's what they like and don't like that comes first. We'd be naturally inclined to think that the arts follow the path of emotion, in contrast to the sciences. Up to a point they do, but there's a complicating factor.

That complicating factor is the contrast between "I like this" and "I don't like this." In this Robinson Crusoe life I've assigned you, you may have moods of complete peacefulness and joy, moods when you accept your island and everything around you. You wouldn't have such moods very often, and when you had them, they'd be moods of identification, when you felt that the island was a part of you and you a part of it. That is not the feeling of consciousness or awareness, where you feel split off from everything that's not your perceiving self. Your habitual state of mind is the feeling of separation which goes with being conscious, and the feeling "this is not a part of me" soon becomes "this is not what I want." Notice the word "want": we'll be coming back to it.

So you soon realize that there's a difference between the world you're living in and the world you want to live in. The world you want to live in is a human world, not an objective one: it's not an environment but a home; it's not the world you see but the world you build out of what you see. You go to work to build a shelter or plant a garden, and as soon as you start to work you've moved into a different level of human life. You're not separating only yourself from nature now, but constructing a human world and separating it from the rest of the world. Your intellect and emotions are now both engaged in the same activity, so there's no longer any real distinction between them. As soon as you plant a garden or a crop, you develop the conception of a "weed," the plant you don't want in there. But you can't say that "weed" is either an intellectual or an emotional conception, because it's both at once. Further, you go to work because you feel you have to, and because you want something at the end of the work. That means that the important categories of your life are no longer the subject and the object, the watcher and the things being watched: the important categories are what you have to do and what you want to do—in other words, necessity and freedom.

One person by himself is not a complete human being, so I'll provide you with another shipwrecked refugee of the opposite sex and an eventual family. Now you're a member of a human society. This human society after a while will transform the island into something with a human shape. What that human shape is, is revealed in the shape of the work you do: the buildings, such as they are, the paths through the woods, the planted crops fenced off against whatever animals want to eat them. These things, these rudiments of city, highway, garden, and farm, are the human form of nature, or the form of human nature, whichever you like. This is the area of the applied arts and sciences, and it appears in our society as engineering and agriculture and medicine and architecture. In this area we can never say clearly where the art stops and the science begins, or vice versa.

The language you use on this level is the language of practical sense, a language of verbs or words of action and movement. The practical world, however, is a world where actions speak louder than words. In some way it's a higher level of existence than the speculative level, because it's doing something about the world instead of just looking at it, but in itself it's a much more primitive level. It's the process of adapting to the environment, or rather of transforming the environment in the interests of one species, that goes on among animals and plants as well as human beings. The animals have a good many of our practical skills: some insects make pretty fair architects, and beavers know quite a lot about engineering. In this island, probably, and certainly if you were alone, you'd have about the ranking of a second-rate animal. What makes our practical life really human is a third level of the mind, a level where consciousness and practical skill come together.

This third level is a vision or model in your mind of what you want to construct. There's that word "want" again. The actions of man are prompted by desire, and some of these desires are needs, like food and warmth and shelter. One of these needs is sexual, the desire to reproduce and bring more human beings into existence. But there's also a desire to bring a social human form into existence: the form of cities and gardens and farms that we call civilization. Many animals and insects have this social form too, but man knows that he has it: he can compare what he does with what he can imagine being done. So we begin to see where the imagination belongs in the scheme of human affairs. It's the power of constructing possible models of human experience. In the world of the imagination, anything goes that's imaginatively possible, but nothing really happens. If it did happen, it would move out of the world of imagination into the world of action.

We have three levels of the mind now, and a language for each of them, which in English-speaking societies means an English for each of them. There's the level of consciousness and awareness, where the most important thing is the difference between me and everything else. The English of this level is the English of ordinary conversation, which is mostly monologue, as you'll soon realize if you do a bit of eavesdropping, or listening to yourself. We can call it the language of self-expression. Then there's the level of social participation, the working or technological language of teachers and preachers and politicians and advertisers and lawyers and journalists and scientists. We've already called this the language of practical sense. Then there's the level of imagination, which produces the literary language of poems and plays and novels. They're not really different languages, of course, but three different reasons for using words.

On this basis, perhaps, we can distinguish the arts from the sciences. Science begins with the world we have to live in, accepting its data and trying to explain its laws. From there, it moves towards the imagination: it becomes a mental construct, a model of a possible way of interpreting experience. The further it goes in this direction, the more it tends to speak the language of mathematics, which is really one of the languages of the imagination, along with literature and music. Art, on the other hand, begins with the world we construct, not with the world we see. It starts with the imagination, and then works towards ordinary experience: that is, it tries to make itself as convincing and recognizable as it can. You can see why we tend to think of the sciences as intellectual and the arts as emotional: one starts with the world as it is, the other with the world we want to have. Up to a point it is true that science gives an intellectual view of reality, and that the arts try to make the emotions as precise and disciplined as sciences do the intellect. But of course it's nonsense to think of the scientist as a cold unemotional reasoner and the artist as somebody who's in a perpetual emotional tizzy. You can't distinguish the arts from the sciences by the mental processes the people in them use: they both operate on a mixture of hunch and common sense. A highly developed science and and a highly developed art are very close together, psychologically and otherwise.

Still, the fact that they start from opposite ends, even if they do meet in the middle, makes for one important difference between them. Science learns more and more about the world as it goes on: it evolves and improves. A physicist today knows more physics than Newton did, even if he's not as great a scientist. But literature begins with the possible model of experience, and what it produces is the literary model we call the classic. Literature doesn't evolve or improve or progress. We may have dramatists in the future who will write plays as good as *King Lear*, though they'll be very different ones, but drama as a whole will never get better than *King Lear*. *King Lear* is it, as far as drama is concerned; so is *Oedipus Rex*, written two thousand years earlier than that, and both will be models of dramatic writing as long as the human race endures. Social conditions may improve: most of us would rather live in nineteenth-century United States than in thirteenth-century Italy, and for most of us Whitman's celebration of democracy makes a lot more sense than Dante's Inferno. But it doesn't follow that Whitman is a better poet than Dante: literature won't line up with that kind of improvement.

So we find that everything that does improve, including science, leaves the literary artist out in the cold. Writers don't seem to benefit much by the advance of science, although they thrive on superstitions of all kinds. And you certainly wouldn't turn to contemporary poets for guidance or leadership in the twentieth-century world. You'd hardly go to Ezra Pound, with his fascism and social credit and Confucianism and anti-semitism. Or to Yeats, with his spiritualism and fairies and astrology. Or to D. H. Lawrence, who'll tell you that it's a good thing for servants to be flogged because that restores the precious current of blood-reciprocity between servant and master. Or to T. S. Eliot, who'll tell you that to have a flourishing culture we should educate an élite, keep most people living in the same spot, and never disestablish the Church of England. The novelists seem to be a little closer to the world they're living in, but not much. When Communists talk about the decadence of bourgeois cul-ture, this is the kind of thing they always bring up. Their own writers don't seem to be any better, though; just duller. So the real question is a bigger one. Is it possible that literature, especially poetry, is something that a scientific civilization like ours will eventually outgrow? Man has always wanted to fly, and thousands of years ago he was making sculp-tures of winged bulls and telling stories about people who flew so high on artificial wings that the sun melted them off. In an Indian play fifteen hundred years old, *Sakuntala*, there's a god who flies around in a chariot that to a modern reader sounds very much like a private aeroplane. Interesting that the writer had so much imagination, but do we need such stories now that we have private aeroplanes?

This is not a new question: it was raised a hundred and fifty years ago by Thomas Love Peacock, who was a poet and novelist himself, and a very brilliant one. He wrote an essay called *Four Ages of Poetry,* with his tongue of course in his cheek, in which he said that poetry was the mental rattle that awakened the imagination of mankind in its infancy, but that now, in an age of science and technology, the poet has outlived his social function. "A poet in our times," said Peacock, "is a semi-barbarian in a civilized community. He lives in the days that are past. His ideas, thoughts, feelings, associations, are all with barbarous manners, obsolete customs, and exploded superstitions. The march of his intellect is like that of a crab, backwards." Peacock's essay annoyed his friend Shelley, who wrote another essay called *A Defence of Poetry* to refute it. Shelley's essay is a wonderful piece of writing, but it's not likely to convince anyone who needs convincing. I shall be spending a good deal of my time on this question of the relevance of literature in the world of today, and I can only indicate the general lines my answer will take. There are two points I can make now, one simple, the other more difficult.

The simple point is that literature belongs to the world man con-structs, not to the world he sees; to his home, not his environment. Literature's world is a concrete human world of immediate experience. The poet uses images and objects and sensations much more than he uses abstract ideas; the novelist is concerned with telling stories, not with working out arguments. The world of literature is human in shape, a

world where the sun rises in the east and sets in the west over the edge of
a flat earth in three dimensions, where the primary realities are not atoms
or electrons but bodies, and the primary forces not energy or gravitation
but love and death and passion and joy. It's not surprising if writers are
often rather simple people, not always what we think of as intellectuals,
and certainly not always any freer of silliness or perversity than anyone
else. What concerns us is what they produce, not what they are, and
poetry, according to Milton, who ought to have known, is "more simple,
sensuous and passionate" than philosophy or science.

The more difficult point takes us back to what we said when we were
on that South Sea island. Our emotional reaction to the world varies from
"I like this" to "I don't like this." The first, we said, was a state of identity,
a feeling that everything around us was part of us, and the second is the
ordinary state of consciousness, or separation, where art and science
begin. Art begins as soon as "I don't like this" turns into "this is not the
way I could imagine it." We notice in passing that the creative and the
neurotic minds have a lot in common. They're both dissatisfied with
what they see; they both believe that something else ought to be there,
and they try to pretend it is there or to make it be there. The differences
are more important, but we're not ready for them yet.

At the level of ordinary consciousness the individual man is the centre
of everything, surrounded on all sides by what he isn't. At the level of
practical sense, or civilization, there's a human circumference, a little
cultivated world with a human shape, fenced off from the jungle and
inside the sea and the sky. But in the imagination anything goes that can
be imagined, and the limit of the imagination is a totally human world.
Here we recapture, in full consciousness, that original lost sense of
identity with our surroundings, where there is nothing outside the mind
of man, or something identical with the mind of man. Religions present
us with visions of eternal and infinite heavens or paradises which have
the form of the cities and gardens of human civilization, like the Jerusalem and Eden of the Bible, completely separated from the state of
frustration and misery that bulks so large in ordinary life. We're not
concerned with these visions as religion, but they indicate what the
limits of the imagination are. They indicate too that in the human world
the imagination has no limits, if you follow me. We said that the desire to
fly produced the aeroplane. But people don't get into planes because they
want to fly; they get into planes because they want to get somewhere else
faster. What's produced the aeroplane is not so much a desire to fly as a
rebellion against the tyranny of time and space. And that's a process that
can never stop, no matter how high our Titovs[1] and Glenns[2] may go.

For each of these six talks I've taken a title from some work of litera-

1. Sherman Titov, Russian astronaut and
first man to make a multi-orbital flight (August 1961).

2. John H. Glenn, astronaut and first American to make an orbital flight (February 1962).

ture, and my title for this one is "The Motive for Metaphor," from a poem of Wallace Stevens. Here's the poem:

> You like it under the trees in autumn,
> Because everything is half dead.
> The wind moves like a cripple among the leaves
> And repeats words without meaning.
>
> In the same way, you were happy in spring,
> With the half colors of quarter-things,
> The slightly brighter sky, the melting clouds,
> The single bird, the obscure moon—
>
> The obscure moon lighting an obscure world
> Of things that would never be quite expressed,
> Where you yourself were never quite yourself
> And did not want nor have to be,
>
> Desiring the exhilarations of changes:
> The motive for metaphor, shrinking from
> The weight of primary noon,
> The A B C of being,
>
> The ruddy temper, the hammer
> Of red and blue, the hard sound—
> Steel against intimation—the sharp flash,
> The vital, arrogant, fatal, dominant X.

What Stevens calls the weight of primary noon, the A B C of being, and the dominant X is the objective world, the world set over against us. Outside literature, the main motive for writing is to describe this world. But literature itself uses language in a way which associates our minds with it. As soon as you use associative language, you begin using figures of speech. If you say this talk is dry and dull, you're using figures associating it with bread and breadknives. There are two main kinds of association, analogy and identity, two things that are like each other and two things that are each other. You can say with Burns, "My love's like a red, red rose," or you can say with Shakespeare:

> Thou that art now the world's fresh ornament
> And only herald to the gaudy spring.

One produces the figure of speech called the simile; the other produces the figure called metaphor.

In descriptive writing you have to be careful of associative language. You'll find that analogy, or likeness to something else, is very tricky to handle in description, because the differences are as important as the resemblances. As for metaphor, where you're really saying "this is that," you're turning your back on logic and reason completely, because logically two things can never be the same thing and still remain two things.

The poet, however, uses these two crude, primitive, archaic forms of thought in the most uninhibited way, because his job is not to describe nature, but to show you a world completely absorbed and possessed by the human mind. So he produces what Baudelaire called a "suggestive magic including at the same time object and subject, the world outside the artist and the artist himself." The motive for metaphor, according to Wallace Stevens, is a desire to associate, and finally to identify, the human mind with what goes on outside it, because the only genuine joy you can have is in those rare moments when you feel that although we may know in part, as Paul says, we are also a part of what we know.

                                                                                1964

QUESTIONS

1. At what point in his essay does Frye come to the meaning of his title? What does this essay say the motive for metaphor is? Does it seem to you a satisfactory motive?
2. How far does Frye go in this essay toward responding to the simple, big questions he starts out with? Has he clarified for you or answered any of those questions? Is there indication in the essay that this is a beginning of the discussion, with more to follow?
3. Why does Frye ask his reader to imagine him- or herself a castaway on a South Sea island? Are you ever likely to be in that position, or is it a bit far-fetched? Is it just a colorful way to get his point across? If so, what is his point?
4. Doesn't metaphor distort the truth, mislead us as to the way things really are?
5. What are the three kinds of English Frye talks about in his essay? Do we really need three kinds? Isn't one enough?
6. Why doesn't literature get any better, the way science does? Can literature be much good, seeing that it doesn't improve? Given the fact that it doesn't improve, shouldn't much of it be pretty outdated?
7. Why do you have to take so much English in school when you already know how to use English even before you start school?

Susanne K. Langer

EXPRESSIVENESS

When we talk about "Art" with a capital "A"—that is, about any or all of the arts: painting, sculpture, architecture, the potter's and goldsmith's and other designers' arts, music, dance, poetry, and prose fiction, drama and film—it is a constant temptation to say things about "Art" in this general sense that are true only in one special domain, or to assume that what holds for one art must hold for another. For instance, the fact that music is made for performance, for presentation to the ear, and is simply not the same thing when it is given only to the tonal imagination of a reader silently perusing the score, has made some aestheticians pass straight to the conclusion that literature, too, must be physically heard to be fully experienced, because words are originally spoken, not written; an obvious parallel, but a careless and, I think, invalid one. It is dangerous to set up principles by analogy, and generalize from a single consideration.

But it is natural, and safe enough, to ask analogous questions: "What is the function of sound in music? What is the function of sound in poetry? What is the function of sound in prose composition? What is the function of sound in drama?" The answers may be quite heterogeneous; and that is itself an important fact, a guide to something more than a simple and sweeping theory. Such findings guide us to exact relations and abstract, variously exemplified basic principles.

At present, however, we are dealing with principles that have proven to be the same in all the arts, when each kind of art—plastic, musical, balletic, poetic, and each major mode, such as literary and dramatic writing, or painting, sculpturing, building plastic shapes—has been studied in its own terms. Such candid study is more rewarding than the usual passionate declaration that all the arts are alike, only their materials differ, their principles are all the same, their techniques all analogous, etc. That is not only unsafe, but untrue. It is in pursuing the differences among them that one arrives, finally, at a point where no more differences appears; then one has found, not postulated, their unity. At that deep level there is only one concept exemplified in all the different arts, and that is the concept of Art.

The principles that obtain wholly and fundamentally in every kind of art are few, but decisive; they determine what is art, and what is not. Expressiveness, in one definite and appropriate sense, is the same in all art works of any kind. What is created is not the same in any two distinct arts—this is, in fact, what makes them distinct—but the principle of creation is the same. And "living form" means the same in all of them.

A work of art is an expressive form created for our perception through sense or imagination, and what it expresses is human feeling. The word "feeling" must be taken here in its broadest sense, meaning *everything that can be felt*, from physical sensation, pain and comfort, excitement and repose, to the most complex emotions, intellectual tensions, or the steady feeling-tones of a conscious human life. In stating what a work of art is, I have just used the words "form," "expressive," and "created"; these are key words. One at a time, they will keep us engaged.

Let us consider first what is meant, in this context, by a *form*. The word has many meanings, all equally legitimate for various purposes; even in connection with art it has several. It may, for instance—and often does —denote the familiar, characteristic structures known as the sonnet form, the sestina, or the ballad form in poetry, the sonata form, the madrigal, or the symphony in music, the contredance or the classical ballet in choreography, and so on. This is not what I mean; or rather, it is only a very small part of what I mean. There is another sense in which artists speak of "form" when they say, for instance, "form follows function," or declare that the one quality shared by all good works of art is "significant form," or entitle a book *The Life of Forms in Art*, or *Search for Form*. They are using "form" in a wider sense, which on the one hand is close to the commonest, popular meaning, namely just the *shape* of a thing, and on the other hand to the quite unpopular meaning it has in science and philosophy, where it designates something more abstract; "form" in its most abstract sense means structure, articulation, a whole resulting from the relation of mutually dependent factors, or more precisely, the way that whole is put together.

The abstract sense, which is sometimes called "logical form," is involved in the notion of expression, at least the kind of expression that characterizes art. That is why artists, when they speak of achieving "form," use the word with something of an abstract connotation, even when they are talking about a visible and tangible art object in which that form is embodied.

The more recondite concept of form is derived, of course, from the naive one, that is, material shape. Perhaps the easiest way to grasp the idea of "logical form" is to trace its derivation.

Let us consider the most obvious sort of form, the shape of an object, say a lampshade. In any department store you will find a wide choice of lampshades, mostly monstrosities, and what is monstrous is usually their shape. You select the least offensive one, maybe even a good one, but realize that the color, say violet, will not fit into your room; so you look about for another shade of the same shape but a different color, perhaps green. In recognizing this same shape in another object, possibly of another material as well as another color, you have quite naturally and easily abstracted the concept of this shape from your actual impression of the first lampshade. Presently it may occur to you that this shade is too big for your lamp; you ask whether they have *this same shade* (meaning another one of this shape) in a smaller size. The clerk understands you.

But what is *the same* in the big violet shade and the little green one? Nothing but the interrelations among their respective various dimensions. They are not "the same" even in their spatial properties, for none of their actual measures are alike; but their shapes are congruent. Their respective spatial factors are put together in the same way, so they exemplify the same form.

It is really astounding what complicated abstractions we make in our ordinary dealing with forms—that is to say, through what twists and transformations we recognize the same logical form. Consider the similarity of your two hands. Put one on the table, palm down, superimpose the other, palm down, as you may have superimposed cut-out geometric shapes in school—they are not alike at all. But their shapes are *exact opposites*. Their respective shapes fit the same description, provided that the description is modified by a principle of application whereby the measures are read one way for one hand and the other way for the other —like a timetable in which the list of stations is marked: "Eastbound, read down; Westbound, read up."

As the two hands exemplify the same form with a principle of reversal understood, so the list of stations describes two ways of moving, indicated by the advice to "read down" for one and "read up" for the other. We can all abstract the common element in these two respective trips, which is called the *route*. With a return ticket we may return only by the same route. The same principle relates a mold to the form of the thing that is cast in it, and establishes their formal correspondence, or common logical form.

So far we have considered only objects—lampshades, hands, or regions of the earth—as having forms. These have fixed shapes; their parts remain in fairly stable relations to each other. But there are also substances that have no definite shapes, such as gases, mist, and water, which take the shape of any bounded space that contains them. The interesting thing about such amorphous fluids is that when they are put into violent motion they do exhibit visible forms, not bounded by any container. Think of the momentary efflorescence of a bursting rocket, the mushroom cloud of an atomic bomb, the funnel of water or dust screwing upward in a whirlwind. The instant the motion stops, or even slows beyond a certain degree, those shapes collapse and the apparent "thing" disappears. They are not shapes of things at all, but forms of motions, or dynamic forms.

Some dynamic forms, however, have more permanent manifestations, because the stuff that moves and makes them visible is constantly replenished. A waterfall seems to hang from the cliff, waving streamers of foam.

Actually, of course, nothing stays there in midair; the water is always passing; but there is more and more water taking the same paths, so we have a lasting shape made and maintained by its passage—a permanent dynamic form. A quiet river, too, has dynamic form; if it stopped flowing it would either go dry or become a lake. Some twenty-five hundred years ago, Heracleitos was struck by the fact that you cannot step twice into the same river at the same place—at least, if the river means the water, not its dynamic form, the flow.

When a river ceases to flow because the water is deflected or dried up, there remains the river bed, sometimes cut deeply in solid stone. That bed is shaped by the flow, and records as graven lines the currents that have ceased to exist. Its shape is static, but it expresses the dynamic form of the river. Again, we have two congruent forms, like a cast and its mold, but this time the congruence is more remarkable because it holds between a dynamic form and a static one. That relation is important; we shall be dealing with it again when we come to consider the meaning of "living form" in art.

The congruence of two given perceptible forms is not always evident upon simple inspection. The common logical form they both exhibit may become apparent only when you know the principle whereby to relate them, as you compare the shapes of your hands not by direct correspondence, but by correspondence of opposite parts. Where the two exemplifications of the single logical form are unlike in most other respects one needs a rule for matching up the relevant factors of one with the relevant factors of the other; that is to say, a rule of translation, whereby one instance of the logical form is shown to correspond formally to the other.

The logical form itself is not another thing, but an abstract concept, or better an abstractable concept. We usually don't abstract it deliberately, but only use it, as we use our vocal cords in speech without first learning all about their operation and then applying our knowledge. Most people perceive intuitively the similarity of their two hands without thinking of them as conversely related; they can guess at the shape of the hollow inside a wooden shoe from the shape of a human foot, without any abstract study of topology. But the first time they see a map in the Mercator projection—with parallel lines of longitude, not meeting at the poles—they find it hard to believe that this corresponds logically to the circular map they used in school, where the meridians bulged apart toward the equator and met at both poles. The visible shapes of the continents are different on the two maps, and it takes abstract thinking to match up the two representations of the same earth. If, however, they have grown up with both maps, they will probably see the geographical relationships either way with equal ease, because these relationships are not copied by either map, but expressed, and expressed equally well by both; for the two maps are different projections of the same logical form,

which the spherical earth exhibits in still another—that is, a spherical
—projection.

An expressive form is any perceptible or imaginable whole that exhibits relationships of parts, or points, or even qualities or aspects within the whole, so that it may be taken to represent some other whole whose elements have analogous relations. The reason for using such a form as a symbol is usually that the thing it represents is not perceivable or readily imaginable. We cannot see the earth as an object. We let a map or a little globe express the relationships of places on the earth, and think about the earth by means of it. The understanding of one thing through another seems to be a deeply intuitive process in the human brain; it is so natural that we often have difficulty in distinguishing the symbolic expressive form from what it conveys. The symbol seems to be the thing itself, or contain it, or be contained in it. A child interested in a globe will not say: "This means the earth," but: "Look, this is the earth." A similar identification of symbol and meaning underlies the widespread conception of holy names, of the physical efficacy of rites, and many other primitive but culturally persistent phenomena. It has a bearing on our perception of artistic import; that is why I mention it here.

The most astounding and developed symbolic device humanity has evolved is language. By means of language we can conceive the intangible, incorporeal things we call our *ideas*, and the equally inostensible elements of our perceptual world that we call *facts*. It is by virtue of language that we can think, remember, imagine, and finally conceive a universe of facts. We can describe things and represent their relations, express rules-of their interactions, speculate and predict and carry on a long symbolizing process known as reasoning. And above all, we can communicate, by producing a serried array of audible or visible words, in a pattern commonly known, and readily understood to reflect our multifarious concepts and percepts and their interconnections. This use of language is *discourse*; and the pattern of discourse is known as *discursive* form. It is a highly versatile, amazingly powerful pattern. It has impressed itself on our tacit thinking, so that we call all systematic reflection "discursive thought." It has made, far more than most people know, the very frame of our sensory experience—the frame of objective facts in which we carry on the practical business of life.

Yet even the discursive pattern has its limits of usefulness. An expressive form can express any complex of conceptions that, via some rule of projection, appears congruent with it, that is, appears to be of that form. Whatever there is in experience that will not take the impress—directly or indirectly—of discursive form, is not discursively communicable or, in the strictest sense, logically thinkable. It is unspeakable, ineffable; according to practically all serious philosophical theories today, it is unknowable.

Yet there is a great deal of experience that is knowable, not only as immediate, formless, meaningless impact, but as one aspect of the intricate web of life, yet defies discursive formulation, and therefore verbal expression: that is what we sometimes call the *subjective aspect* of experience, the direct feeling of it—what it is like to be waking and moving, to be drowsy, slowing down, or to be sociable, or to feel self-sufficient but alone; what it feels like to pursue an elusive thought or to have a big idea. All such directly felt experiences usually have no names—they are named, if at all, for the outward conditions that normally accompany their occurrence. Only the most striking ones have names like "anger," "hate," "love," "fear," and are collectively called "emotion." But we feel many things that never develop into any designable emotion. The ways we are moved are as various as the lights in a forest; and they may intersect, sometimes without cancelling each other, take shape and dissolve, conflict, explode into passion, or be transfigured. All these inseparable elements of subjective reality compose what we call the "inward life" of human beings. The usual factoring of that life-stream into mental, emotional, and sensory units is an arbitrary scheme of simplification that makes scientific treatment possible to a considerable extent; but we may already be close to the limit of its usefulness, that is, close to the point where its simplicity becomes an obstacle to further questioning and discovery instead of the revealing, ever-suitable logical projection it was expected to be.

Whatever resists projection into the discursive form of language is, indeed, hard to hold in conception, and perhaps impossible to communicate, in the proper and strict sense of the word "communicate." But fortunately our logical intuition, or form-perception, is really much more powerful than we commonly believe, and our knowledge—genuine knowledge, understanding—is considerably wider than our discourse. Even in the use of language, if we want to name something that is too new to have a name (e.g., a newly invented gadget or a newly discovered creature), or want to express a relationship for which there is no verb or other connective word, we resort to metaphor; we mention it or describe it as something else, something analogous. The principle of metaphor is simply the principle of saying one thing and meaning another, and expecting to be understood to mean the other. A metaphor is not language, it is an idea expressed by language, an idea that in its turn functions as a symbol to express something. It is not discursive and therefore does not really make a statement of the idea it conveys; but it formulates a new conception for our direct imaginative grasp.

Sometimes our comprehension of a total experience is mediated by a metaphorical symbol because the experience is new, and language has words and phrases only for familiar notions. Then an extension of language will gradually follow the wordless insight, and discursive expression will supersede the non-discursive pristine symbol. This is, I think, the normal advance of human thought and language in that whole realm of knowledge where discourse is possible at all.

But the symbolic presentation of subjective reality for contemplation is not only tentatively beyond the reach of language—that is, not merely beyond the words we have; it is impossible in the essential frame of language. That is why those semanticists who recognize only discourse as a symbolic form must regard the whole life of feeling as formless, chaotic, capable only of symptomatic expression, typified in exclamations like "Ah!" "Ouch!" "My sainted aunt!" They usually do believe that art is an expression of feeling, but that "expression" in art is of this sort, indicating that the speaker has an emotion, a pain, or other personal experience, perhaps also giving us a clue to the general kind of experience it is—pleasant or unpleasant, violent or mild—but not setting that piece of inward life objectively before us so we may understand its intricacy, its rhythms and shifts of total appearance. The differences in feeling-tones or other elements of subjective experience are regarded as differences in quality, which must be felt to be appreciated. Furthermore, since we have no intellectual access to pure subjectivity, the only way to study it is to study the symptoms of the person who is having subjective experiences. This leads to physiological psychology—a very important and interesting field. But it tells us nothing about the phenomena of subjective life, and sometimes simplifies the problem by saying they don't exist.

Now, I believe the expression of feeling in a work of art—the function that makes the work an expressive form—is not symptomatic at all. An artist working on a tragedy need not be in personal despair or violent upheaval; nobody, indeed, could work in such a state of mind. His mind would be occupied with the causes of his emotional upset. Self-expression does not require composition and lucidity; a screaming baby gives his feeling far more release than any musician, but we don't go into a concert hall to hear a baby scream; in fact, if that baby is brought in we are likely to go out. We don't want self-expression.

A work of art presents feeling (in the broad sense I mentioned before, as everything that can be felt) for our contemplation, making it visible or audible or in some way perceivable through a symbol, not inferable from a symptom. Artistic form is congruent with the dynamic forms of our direct sensuous, mental, and emotional life; works of art are projections of "felt life," as Henry James called it, into spatial, temporal, and poetic structures. They are images of feeling, that formulate it for our cognition. What is artistically good is whatever articulates and presents feeling to our understanding.

Artistic forms are more complex than any other symbolic forms we know. They are, indeed, not abstractable from the works that exhibit them. We may abstract a shape from an object that has this shape, by disregarding color, weight and texture, even size; but to the total effect that is an artistic form, the color matters, the thickness of lines matters, and the appearance of texture and weight. A given triangle is the same in any position, but to an artistic form its location, balance, and surroundings are not indifferent. Form, in the sense in which artists speak of "significant form" or "expressive form," is not an abstracted structure, but an apparition; and the vital processes of sense and emotion that a good work of art expresses seem to the beholder to be directly contained in it, not symbolized but really presented. The congruence is so striking that symbol and meaning appear as one reality. Actually, as one psychologist who is also a musician has written, "Music sounds as feelings feel." And likewise, in good painting, sculpture, or building, balanced shapes and colors, lines and masses look as emotions, vital tensions and their resolutions feel.

An artist, then, expresses feeling, but not in the way a politician blows off steam or a baby laughs and cries. He formulates that elusive aspect of reality that is commonly taken to be amorphous and chaotic; that is, he objectifies the subjective realm. What he expresses is, therefore, not his own actual feelings, but what he knows about human feeling. Once he is in possession of a rich symbolism, that knowledge may actually exceed his entire personal experience. A work of art expresses a conception of life, emotion, inward reality. But it is neither a confessional nor a frozen tantrum; it is a developed metaphor, a non-discursive symbol that articulates what is verbally ineffable—the logic of consciousness itself.

1957

Carl Gustav Jung

THE POET

Creativeness, like the freedom of the will, contains a secret. The psychologist can describe both these manifestations as processes, but he can find no solution of the philosophical problems they offer. Creative man is a riddle that we may try to answer in various ways, but always in vain, a truth that has not prevented modern psychology from turning now and again to the question of the artist and his art. Freud thought that he had found a key in his procedure of deriving the work of art from the personal experiences of the artist. It is true that certain possibilities lay in this direction, for it was conceivable that a work of art, no less than a neurosis, might be traced back to those knots in psychic life that we call the complexes. It was Freud's great discovery that neuroses have a causal origin in the psychic realm—that they take their rise from emotional states and from real or imagined childhood experiences. Certain of his followers, like Rank and Stekel, have taken up related lines of enquiry and have achieved important results. It is undeniable that the poet's psychic disposition permeates his work root and branch. Nor is there anything new in the statement that personal factors largely influence the poet's choice and use of his materials. Credit, however, must certainly be given to the Freudian school for showing how far-reaching this influence is and in what curious ways it comes to expression.

Freud takes the neurosis as a substitute for a direct means of gratification. He therefore regards it as something inappropriate—a mistake, a dodge, an excuse, a voluntary blindness. To him it is essentially a shortcoming that should never have been. Since a neurosis, to all appearances, is nothing but a disturbance that is all the more irritating because it is without sense or meaning, few people will venture to say a good word for it. And a work of art is brought into questionable proximity with the neurosis when it is taken as something which can be analysed in terms of the poet's repressions. In a sense it finds itself in good company, for religion and philosophy are regarded in the same light by Freudian psychology. No objection can be raised if it is admitted that this approach amounts to nothing more than the elucidation of those personal determinants without which a work of art is unthinkable. But should the claim be made that such an anlaysis accounts for the work of art itself, then a categorical denial is called for. The personal idiosyncrasies that creep into a work of art are not essential; in fact, the more we have to cope with these peculiarities, the less is it a question of art. What is essential in a work of art is that it should rise far above the realm of personal life and speak from the spirit and heart of the poet as man to the spirit and heart of mankind. The personal aspect is a limitation—and even a sin—in the realm of art. When a form of "art" is primarily personal it deserves to be treated as if it were a neurosis. There may be some validity in the idea held by the Freudian school that artists without exception are narcissistic —by which is meant that they are undeveloped persons with infantile and autoerotic traits. The statement is only valid, however, for the artist as a person, and has nothing to do with the man as an artist. In his capacity of artist he is neither auto-erotic, nor hetero-erotic, nor erotic in any sense. He is objective and impersonal—even inhuman—for as an artist he is his work, and not a human being.

Every creative person is a duality or a synthesis of contradictory aptitudes. On the one side he is a human being with a personal life, while on the other side he is an impersonal, creative process. Since as a human being he may be sound or morbid, we must look at his psychic make-up to find the determinants of his personality. But we can only understand him in his capacity of artist by looking at his creative achievement. We should make a sad mistake if we tried to explain the mode of life of an English gentleman, a Prussian officer, or a cardinal in terms of personal factors. The gentleman, the officer and the cleric function as such in an impersonal role, and their psychic make-up is qualified by a peculiar objectivity. We must grant that the artist does not function in an official capacity—the very opposite is nearer the truth. He nevertheless resembles the types I have named in one respect, for the specifically artistic disposition involves an overweight of collective psychic life as against the personal. Art is a kind of innate drive that seizes a human being and makes him its instrument. The artist is not a person endowed with free will who seeks his own ends, but one who allows art to realize its purposes through him. As a human being he may have moods and a will and personal aims, but as an artist he is "man" in a higher sense—he is "collective man"—one who carries and shapes the unconscious, psychic life of mankind. To perform this difficult office it is sometimes necessary for him to sacrifice happiness and everything that makes life worth living for the ordinary human being.

All this being so, it is not strange that the artist is an especially interesting case for the psychologist who uses an analytical method. The artist's life cannot be otherwise than full of conflicts, for two forces are at war within him—on the one hand the common human longing for happiness, satisfaction and security in life, and on the other a ruthless passion for creation which may go so far as to override every personal desire. The lives of artists are as a rule so highly unsatisfactory—not to say tragic—because of their inferiority on the human and personal side, and not because of a sinister dispensation. There are hardly any exceptions to the rule that a person must pay dearly for the divine gift of the creative fire. It is as though each of us were endowed at birth with a certain capital of energy. The strongest force in our make-up will seize and all but monopolize this energy, leaving so little over that nothing of value can come of it. In this way the creative force can drain the human impulses to such a degree that the personal ego must develop all sorts of bad qualities—ruthlessnes, selfishness and vanity (so-called "auto-erotism")—and even every kind of vice, in order to maintain the spark of life and to keep itself from being wholly bereft. The auto-erotism of artists resembles that of illegitimate or neglected children who from their tenderest years must protect themselves from the destructive influence of people who have no love to give them—who develop bad qualities for that very purpose and later maintain an invincible egocentrism by remaining all their lives infantile and helpless or by actively offending against the moral code or the law. How can we doubt that it is his art that explains the artist, and not the insufficiencies and conflicts of his personal life? These are nothing but the regrettable results of the fact that he is an artist—that is to say, a man who from his very birth has been called to a greater task than the ordinary mortal. A special ability means a heavy expenditure of energy in a particular direction, with a consequent drain from some other side of life.

It makes no difference whether the poet knows that his work is begotten, grows and matures with him, or whether he supposes that by taking thought he produces it out of the void. His opinion of the matter does not change the fact that his own work outgrows him as a child its mother. The creative process has feminine quality, and the creative work arises from unconscious depths—we might say, from the realm of the mothers. Whenever the creative force predominates, human life is ruled and moulded by the unconscious as against the active will, and the conscious ego is swept along on a subterranean current, being nothing more than a helpless observer of events. The work in process becomes the poet's fate and determines his psychic development. It is not Goethe who creates *Faust*, but *Faust* which creates Goethe. And what is *Faust* but a symbol? By this I do not mean an allegory that points to something all too familiar, but an expression that stands for something not clearly known and yet profoundly alive. Here it is something that lives in the soul of every German, and that Goethe has helped to bring to birth. Could we conceive of anyone but a German writing *Faust* or *Also sprach Zarathustra?* Both play upon something that reverberates in the German soul—a "primordial image," as Jacob Burckhardt once called it—the figure of a physician or teacher of mankind. The archetypal image of the wise man, the saviour or redeemer, lies buried and dormant in man's unconscious since the dawn of culture; it is awakened whenever the times are out of joint and a human society is committed to a serious error. When people go astray they feel the need of a guide or teacher or even of the physician. These primordial images are numerous, but do not appear in the dreams of individuals or in works of art until they are called into being by the waywardness of the general outlook. When conscious life is characterized by one-sidedness and by a false attitude, then they are activated —one might say, "instinctively"—and come to light in the dreams of individuals and the visions of artists and seers, thus restoring the psychic equilibrium of the epoch.

In this way the work of the poet comes to meet the spiritual need of the society in which he lives, and for this reason his work means more to him than his personal fate, whether he is aware of this or not. Being essentially the instrument for his work, he is subordinate to it, and we have no reason for expecting him to interpret it for us. He has done the best that in him lies in giving it form, and he must leave the interpretation to others and to the future. A great work of art is like a dream; for all its apparent obviousness it does not explain itself and is never unequivocal. A dream never says: "You ought," or: "This is the truth." It presents an image in much the same way as nature allows a plant to grow, and we must draw our own conclusions. If a person has a nightmare, it means either that he is too much given to fear, or else that he is too exempt from it; and if he dreams of the old wise man it may mean that he is too pedagogical, as also that he stands in need of a teacher. In a subtle way both meanings come to the same thing, as we perceive when we are able to let the work of art act upon us as it acted upon the artist. To grasp its meaning, we must allow it to shape us as it once shaped him. Then we understand the nature of his experience. We see that he has drawn upon the healing and redeeming forces of the collective psyche that underlies consciousness with its isolation and its painful errors; that he has penetrated to that matrix of life in which all men are embedded, which imparts a common rhythm to all human existence, and allows the individual to communicate his feeling and his striving to mankind as a whole.

The secret of artistic creation and of the effectiveness of art is to be found in a return to the state of *participation mystique*—to that level of experience at which it is man who lives, and not the individual, and at which the weal or woe of the single human being does not count, but only human existence. This is why every great work of art is objective and impersonal, but none the less profoundly moves us each and all. And this is also why the personal life of the poet cannot be held essential to his art —but at most a help or a hindrance to his creative task. He may go the way of a Philistine, a good citizen, a neurotic, a fool or a criminal. His personal career may be inevitable and interesting, but it does not explain the poet.

1946

QUESTIONS

1. *Jung makes a distinction between the "human being with a personal life" and the "impersonal, creative process." What is the importance of this distinction? How does it help to shape the rest of Jung's argument?*

2. *Jung says that the "personal idiosyncrasies that creep into a work of art are not essential," since art "should rise far above the realm of personal life and speak from the spirit and heart of the poet as man to the spirit and heart of mankind." Is a contradiction involved here? Can a poet speak from his heart without being personal? Are "personal idiosyncrasies" desirable in a work to give it the flavor of a distinctive style?*

3. *Consider the following stanzas (69–72) from Byron's "Childe Harold's*

Pilgrimage." To what extent would Jung feel that psychological considerations were helpful in analyzing these lines?

> To fly from, need not be to hate, mankind:
> All are not fit with them to stir and toil,
> Nor is it discontent to keep the mind
> Deep in its fountain, lest it overboil
> In the hot throng, where we become the spoil
> Of our infection, till too late and long
> We may deplore and struggle with the coil,
> In wretched interchange of wrong for wrong
> Midst a contentious world, striving where none are strong.
>
> There, in a moment we may plunge our years
> In fatal penitence, and in the blight
> Of our own Soul turn all our blood to tears,
> And colour things to come with hues of Night;
> The race of life becomes a hopeless flight
> To those that walk in darkness: on the sea
> The boldest steer but where their ports invite—
> But there are wanderers o'er Eternity
> Whose bark drives on and on, and anchored ne'er shall be.
>
> Is it not better, then, to be alone,
> And love Earth only for its earthly sake?
> By the blue rushing of the arrowy Rhone,
> Or the pure bosom of its nursing Lake,
> Which feeds it as a mother who doth make
> A fair but froward infant her own care,
> Kissing its cries away as these awake;—
> Is it not better thus our lives to wear,
> Than join the crushing crowd, doomed to inflict or bear?
>
> I live not in myself, but I become
> Portion of that around me; and to me
> High mountains are a feeling, but the hum
> Of human cities torture: I can see
> Nothing to loathe in Nature, save to be
> A link reluctant in a fleshly chain,
> Classed among creatures, when the soul can flee,
> And with the sky—the peak—the heaving plain.
> Of ocean, or the stars, mingle—and not in vain.

Robert Frost

EDUCATION BY POETRY: A MEDITATIVE MONOLOGUE[1]

I am going to urge nothing in my talk. I am not an advocate. I am going to consider a matter, and commit a description. And I am going to describe other colleges than Amherst. Or, rather say all that is good can be taken as about Amherst; all that is bad will be about other colleges.

I know whole colleges where all American poetry is barred—whole colleges. I know whole colleges where all contemporary poetry is barred.

I once heard of a minister who turned his daughter—his poetry-writing daughter—out on the street to earn a living, because he said there should be no more books written; God wrote one book, and that was enough. (My friend George Russell, "Æ", has read no literature, he protests, since just before Chaucer.)

That all seems sufficiently safe, and you can say one thing for it. It takes the onus off the poetry of having to be used to teach children anything. It comes pretty hard on poetry, I sometimes think, what it has to bear in the teaching process.

Then I know whole colleges where, though they let in older poetry, they manage to bar all that is poetical in it by treating it as something other than poetry. It is not so hard to do that. Their reason I have often hunted for. It may be that these people act from a kind of modesty. Who are professors that they should attempt to deal with a thing as high and as fine as poetry? Who are *they*? There is a certain manly modesty in that.

That is the best general way of settling the problem; treat all poetry as if it were something else than poetry, as if it were syntax, language, science. Then you can even come down into the American and into the contemporary without any special risk.

There is another reason they have, and that is that they are, first and foremost in life, markers. They have the marking problem to consider. Now, I stand here a teacher of many years' experience and I have never complained of having had to mark. I had rather mark anyone for anything —for his looks, carriage, his ideas, his correctness, his exactness, anything you please—I would rather give him a mark in terms of letters, A, B, C, D, than have to use adjectives on him. We are all being marked by each other all the time, classified, ranked, put in our place, and I see no escape from that. I am no sentimentalist. You have got to mark, and you have got to mark, first of all, for accuracy, for correctness. But if I am going to give a mark, that is the least part of my marking. The hard part is the part beyond that, the part where the adventure begins.

1. An address given at Amherst College in 1930.

One other way to rid the curriculum of the poetry nuisance has been considered. More merciful than the others it would neither abolish nor denature the poetry, but only turn it out to disport itself, with the plays and games—in no wise discredited, though given no credit for. Any one who liked to teach poetically could take his subject, whether English, Latin, Greek or French, out into the nowhere along with the poetry. One side of a sharp line would be left to the rigorous and righteous; the other side would be assigned to the flowery where they would know what could be expected of them. Grade marks were more easily given, of course, in the courses concentrating on correctness and exactness as the only forms of honesty recognized by plain people; a general indefinite mark of X in the courses that scatter brains over taste and opinion. On inquiry I have found no teacher willing to take position on either side of the line, either among the rigors or among the flowers. No one is willing to admit that his discipline is not partly in exactness. No one is willing to admit that his discipline is not partly in taste and enthusiasm.

How shall a man go through college without having been marked for taste and judgment? What will become of him? What will his end be? He will have to take continuation courses for college graduates. He will have to go to night schools. They are having night schools now, you know, for college graduates. Why? Because they have not been educated enough to find their way around in contemporary literature. They don't know what they may safely like in the libraries and galleries. They don't know how to judge an editorial when they see one. They don't know how to judge a political campaign. They don't know when they are being fooled by a metaphor, an analogy, a parable. And metaphor is, of course, what we are talking about. Education by poetry is education by metaphor.

Suppose we stop short of imagination, initiative, enthusiasm, inspiration and originality—dread words. Suppose we don't mark in such things at all. There are still two minimal things, that we have got to take care of, taste and judgment. Americans are supposed to have more judgment than taste, but taste is there to be dealt with. That is what poetry, the only art in the colleges of arts, is there for. I for my part would not be afraid to go in for enthusiasm. There is the enthusiasm like a blinding light, or the enthusiasm of the deafening shout, the crude enthusiasm that you get uneducated by poetry, outside of poetry. It is exemplified in what I might call "sunset raving." You look westward toward the sunset, or if you get up early enough, eastward toward the sunrise, and you rave. It is oh's and ah's with you and no more.

But the enthusiasm I mean is taken through the prism of the intellect and spread on the screen in a color, all the way from hyperbole at one end —or overstatement, at one end—to understatement at the other end. It is a long strip of dark lines and many colors. Such enthusiasm is one object of all teaching in poetry. I heard wonderful things said about Virgil

yesterday, and many of them seemed to me crude enthusiasm, more like a deafening shout, many of them. But one speech had range, something of overstatement, something of statement, and something of understatement. It had all the colors of an enthusiasm passed through an idea.

I would be willing to throw away everything else but that: enthusiasm tamed by metaphor. Let me rest the case there. Enthusiasm tamed to metaphor, tamed to that much of it. I do not think anybody ever knows the discreet use of metaphor, his own and other people's, the discreet handling of metaphor, unless he has been properly educated in poetry.

Poetry begins in trivial metaphors, petty metaphors, "grace" metaphors, and goes on to the profoundest thinking that we have. Poetry provides the one permissible way of saying one thing and meaning another. People say, "Why don't you say what you mean?" We never do that, do we, being all of us too much poets. We like to talk in parables and in hints and in indirections—whether from diffidence or some other instinct.

I have wanted in late years to go further and further in making metaphor the whole of thinking. I find some one now and then to agree with me that all thinking, except mathematical thinking, is metaphorical, or all thinking except scientific thinking. The mathematical might be difficult for me to bring in, but the scientific is easy enough.

Once on a time all the Greeks were busy telling each other what the All was—or was like unto. All was three elements, air, earth, and water (we once thought it was ninety elements; now we think it is only one). All was substance, said another. All was change, said a third. But best and most fruitful was Pythagoras' comparison of the universe with number. Number of what? Number of feet, pounds, and seconds was the answer, and we had science and all that has followed in science. The metaphor has held and held, breaking down only when it came to the spiritual and psychological or the out of the way places of the physical.

The other day we had a visitor here, a noted scientist, whose latest word to the world has been that the more accurately you know where a thing is, the less accurately you are able to state how fast it is moving. You can see why that would be so, without going back to Zeno's problem of the arrow's flight. In carrying numbers into the realm of space and at the same time into the realm of time you are mixing metaphors, that is all, and you are in trouble. They won't mix. The two don't go together.

Let's take two or three more of the metaphors now in use to live by. I have just spoken of one of the new ones, a charming mixed metaphor right in the realm of higher mathematics and higher physics: that the more accurately you state where a thing is, the less accurately you will be able to tell how fast it is moving. And, of course everything is moving. Everything is an event now. Another metaphor. A thing, they say, is an event. Do you believe it is? Not quite. I believe it is almost an event. But I like the comparison of a thing with an event.

I notice another from the same quarter. "In the neighborhood of matter space is something like curved." Isn't that a good one! It seems to me that that is simply and utterly charming—to say that space is something like curved in the neighborhood of matter. "Something like."

Another amusing one is from—what is the book?—I can't say it now; but here is the metaphor. Its aim is to restore you to your ideas of free will. It wants to give you back your freedom of will. All right, here it is on a platter. You know that you can't tell by name what persons in a certain class will be dead ten years after graduation, but you can tell actuarially how many will be dead. Now, just so this scientist says of the particles of matter flying at a screen, striking a screen; you can't tell what individual particles will come, but you can say in general that a certain number will strike in a given time. It shows, you see, that the individual particle can come freely. I asked Bohr about that particularly, and he said, "Yes, it is so. It can come when it wills and as it wills; and the action of the individual particle is unpredictable. But it is not so of the action of the mass. There you can predict." He says, "That gives the individual atom its freedom, but the mass its necessity."

Another metaphor that has interested us in our time and has done all our thinking for us is the metaphor of evolution. Never mind going into the Latin word. The metaphor is simply the metaphor of the growing plant or of the growing thing. And somebody very brilliantly, quite a while ago, said that the whole universe, the whole of everything, was like unto a growing thing. That is all. I know the metaphor will break down at some point, but it has not failed everywhere. It is a very brilliant metaphor, I acknowledge, though I myself get too tired of the kind of essay that talks about the evolution of candy, we will say, or the evolution of elevators—the evolution of this, that, and the other. Everything is evolution. I emancipate myself by simply saying that I didn't get up the metaphor and so am not much interested in it.

What I am pointing out is that unless you are at home in the metaphor, unless you have had your proper poetical education in the metaphor, you are not safe anywhere. Because you are not at ease with figurative values: you don't know the metaphor in its strength and its weakness. You don't know how far you may expect to ride it and when it may break down with you. You are not safe in science; you are not safe in history. In history, for instance—to show that is the same in history as elsewhere—I heard somebody say yesterday that Aeneas was to be likened unto (those words, "likened unto"!) George Washington. He was that type of national hero, the middle-class man, not thinking of being a hero at all, bent on building the future, bent on his children, his descendants. A good metaphor, as far as it goes, and you must know how far. And then he added that Odysseus should be likened unto Theodore Roosevelt. I don't think that is so good. Someone visiting Gibbon at the point of death, said he was the same Gibbon as of old; still at his parallels.

Take the way we have been led into our present position morally, the world over. It is by a sort of metaphorical gradient. There is a kind of thinking—to speak metaphorically—there is a kind of thinking you might say was endemic in the brothel. It is always there. And every now and then in some mysterious way it becomes epidemic in the world. And how does it do so? By using all the good words that virtue has invented to maintain virtue. It uses honesty, first—frankness, sincerity—those words; picks them up, uses them. "In the name of honesty, let us see what we are." You know. And then it picks up the word joy. "Let us in the name of joy, which is the enemy of our ancestors, the Puritans . . . Let us in the name of joy, which is the enemy of the kill-joy Puritan . . ." You see. "Let us," and so on. And then, "In the name of health . . ." Health is another good word. And that is the metaphor Freudianism trades on, mental health. And the first thing we know, it has us all in up to the top knot. I suppose we may blame the artists a good deal, because they are great people to spread by metaphor. The stage too—the stage is always a good intermediary between the two worlds, the under and the upper, if I may say so without personal prejudice to the stage.

In all this, I have only been saying that the devil can quote Scripture, which simply means that the good words you have lying around the devil can use for his purposes as well as anybody else. Never mind about my morality. I am not here to urge anything. I don't care whether the world is good or bad—not on any particular day.

Let me ask you to watch a metaphor breaking down here before you.

Somebody said to me a little while ago, "It is easy enough for me to think of the universe as a machine, as a mechanism."

I said, "You mean the universe is like a machine?"

He said, "No. I think it is one . . . Well, it is like . . ."

"I think you mean the universe is like a machine."

"All right. Let it go at that."

I asked him, "Did you ever see a machine without a pedal for the foot, or a lever for the hand, or a button for the finger?"

He said "No—no."

I said, "All right. Is the universe like that?"

And he said, "No. I mean it is like a machine, only . . ."

". . . it is different from a machine," I said.

He wanted to go just that far with that metaphor and no further. And so do we all. All metaphor breaks down somewhere. That is the beauty of it. It is touch and go with the metaphor, and until you have lived with it long enough you don't know when it is going. You don't know how much you can get out of it and when it will cease to yield. It is a very living thing. It is as life itself.

I have heard this ever since I can remember, and ever since I have taught: the teacher must teach the pupil to think. I saw a teacher once going around in a great school and snapping pupils' heads with thumb and finger and saying, "Think." That was when thinking was becoming the fashion. The fashion hasn't yet quite gone out.

We still ask boys in college to think, as in the nineties, but we seldom tell them what thinking means; we seldom tell them it is just putting this and that together; it is saying one thing in terms of another. To tell them is to set their feet on the first rung of a ladder the top of which sticks through the sky.

Greatest of all attempts to say one thing in terms of another is the philosophical attempt to say matter in terms of spirit, or spirit in terms of matter, to make the final unity. That is the greatest attempt that ever failed. We stop just short there. But it is the height of poetry, the height of all thinking, the height of all poetic thinking, that attempt to say matter in terms of spirit and spirit in terms of matter. It is wrong to call anybody a materialist simply because he tries to say spirit in terms of matter, as if that were a sin. Materialism is not the attempt to say all in terms of matter. The only materialist—be he poet, teacher, scientist, politician, or statesman—is the man who gets lost in his material without a gathering metaphor to throw it into shape and order. He is the lost soul.

We ask people to think, and we don't show them what thinking is. Somebody says we don't need to show them how to think; bye and bye they will think. We will give them the forms of sentences and, if they have any ideas, then they will know how to write them. But that is preposterous. All there is to writing is having ideas. To learn to write is to learn to have ideas.

The first little metaphor . . . Take some of the trivial ones. I would rather have trivial ones of my own to live by than the big ones of other people.

I remember a boy saying, "He is the kind of person that wounds with his shield." That may be a slender one, of course. It goes a good way in character description. It has poetic grace. "He is the kind that wounds with his shield."

The shield reminds me—just to linger a minute—the shield reminds me of the inverted shield spoken of in one of the books of the *Odyssey*, the book that tells about the longest swim on record. I forget how long it lasted—several days, was it?—but at last as Odysseus came near the coast of Phoenicia, he saw it on the horizon "like an inverted shield."

There is a better metaphor in the same book. In the end Odysseus comes ashore and crawls up the beach to spend the night under a double olive tree, and it says, as in a lonely farmhouse where it is hard to get fire

—I am not quoting exactly—where it is hard to start the fire again if it goes out, they cover the seeds of fire with ashes to preserve it for the night, so Odysseus covered himself with the leaves around him and went to sleep. There you have something that gives you character, something of Odysseus himself. "Seeds of fire." So Odysseus covered the seeds of fire in himself. You get the greatness of his nature.

But these are slighter metaphors than the ones we live by. They have their charm, their passing charm. They are as it were the first steps toward the great thoughts, grave thoughts, thoughts lasting to the end.

The metaphor whose manage we are best taught in poetry—that is all there is of thinking. It may not seem far for the mind to go but it is the mind's furthest. The richest accumulation of the ages is the noble metaphors we have rolled up.

I want to add one thing more that the experience of poetry is to anyone who comes close to poetry. There are two ways of coming close to poetry. One is by writing poetry. And some people think I want people to write poetry, but I don't; that is, I don't necessarily. I only want people to write poetry if they want to write poetry. I have never encouraged anybody to write poetry that did not want to write it, and I have not always encouraged those who did want to write it. That ought to be one's own funeral. It is a hard, hard life, as they say.

(I have just been to a city in the West, a city full of poets, a city they have made safe for poets. The whole city is so lovely that you do not have to write it up to make it poetry; it is ready-made for you. But, I don't know —the poetry written in that city might not seem like poetry if read outside of the city. It would be like the jokes made when you were drunk; you have to get drunk again to appreciate them.)

But as I say, there is another way to come close to poetry, fortunately, and that is in the reading of it, not as linguistics, not as history, not as anything but poetry. It is one of the hard things for a teacher to know how close a man has come in reading poetry. How do I know whether a man has come close to Keats in reading Keats? It is hard for me to know. I have lived with some boys a whole year over some of the poets and I have not felt sure whether they have come near what it was all about. One remark sometimes told me. One remark was their mark for the year; had to be —it was all I got that told me what I wanted to know. And that is enough, if it was the right remark, if it came close enough. I think a man might make twenty fool remarks if he made one good one some time in the year. His mark would depend on that good remark.

The closeness—everything depends on the closeness with which you come, and you ought to be marked for the closeness, for nothing else. And that will have to be estimated by chance remarks, not by question and answer. It is only by accident that you know some day how near a person has come.

The person who gets close enough to poetry, he is going to know more about the word *belief* than anybody else knows, even in religion nowadays. There are two or three places where we know belief outside of religion. One of them is at the age of fifteen to twenty, in our self-belief. A young man knows more about himself than he is able to prove to anybody. He has no knowledge that anybody else will accept as knowledge. In his foreknowledge he has something that is going to believe itself into fulfilment, into acceptance.

There is another belief like that, the belief in someone else, a relationship of two that is going to be believed into fulfilment. That is what we are talking about in our novels, the belief of love. And disillusionment that the novels are full of is simply the disillusionment from disappointment in that belief. That belief can fail, of course.

Then there is a literary belief. Every time a poem is written, every time a short story is written, it is written not by cunning, but by belief. The beauty, the something, the little charm of the thing to be, is more felt than known. There is a common jest, one that always annoys me, on the writers, that they write the last end first, and then work up to it; that they lay a train toward one sentence that they think is pretty nice and have all fixed up to set like a trap to close with. No, it should not be that way at all. No one who has ever come close to the arts has failed to see the difference between things written that way, with cunning and device, and the kind that are believed into existence, that begin in something more felt than known. This you can realize quite as well—not quite as well, perhaps, but nearly as well—in reading as you can in writing. I would undertake to separate short stories on that principle; stories that have been believed into existence and stories that have been cunningly devised. And I could separate the poems still more easily.

Now I think—I happen to think—that those three beliefs that I speak of, the self-belief, the love-belief, and the art-belief, are all closely related to the God-belief, that the belief in God is a relationship you enter into with Him to bring about the future.

There is a national belief like that, too. One feels it. I have been where I came near getting up and walking out on the people who thought that they had to talk against nations, against nationalism, in order to curry favor with internationalism. Their metaphors are all mixed up. They think that because a Frenchman and an American and an Englishman can all sit down on the same platform and receive honors together, it must be that there is no such thing as nations. That kind of bad thinking springs from a source we all know. I should want to say to anyone like that: "Look! First I want to be a person. And I want you to be a person, and then we can be as interpersonal as you please. We can pull each other's noses—do all sorts of things. But, first of all, you have got to have the personality. First of all, you have got to have the nations and then they can be as international as they please with each other."

I should like to use another metaphor on them. I want my palette, if I am a painter, I want my palette on my thumb or on my chair, all clean, pure, separate colors. Then I will do the mixing on the canvas. The canvas is where the work of art is, where we make the conquest. But we want the nations all separate, pure, distinct, things as separate as we can make them; and then in our thoughts, in our arts, and so on, we can do what we please about it.

But I go back. There are four beliefs that I know more about from having lived with poetry. One is the personal belief, which is a knowledge that you don't want to tell other people about because you cannot prove that you know. You are saying nothing about it till you see. The love belief, just the same, has that same shyness. It knows it cannot tell; only the outcome can tell. And the national belief we enter into socially with each other, all together, party of the first part, party of the second part, we enter into that to bring the future of the country. We cannot tell some people what it is we believe, partly, because they are too stupid to understand and partly because we are too proudly vague to explain. And anyway it has got to be fulfilled, and we are not talking until we know more, until we have something to show. And then the literary one in every work of art, not of cunning and craft, mind you, but of real art; that believing the thing into existence, saying as you go more than you even hoped you were going to be able to say, and coming with surprise to an end that you foreknew only with some sort of emotion. And then finally the relationship we enter into with God to believe the future in—to believe the hereafter in.

1930

QUESTIONS

1. *In what way does the subtitle describe this essay? Is it rambling? Is it unified?*
2. *How can the "poetry nuisance" be gotten out of the curriculum? Does Frost think it ought to stay in? Why?*
3. *What is meant by "enthusiasm passed through an idea" and "enthusiasm tamed to metaphor" (p. 1027)? What sort of metaphors does Frost use in those phrases, and what do they imply?*
4. *What does Frost mean when he says "unless you have had your proper poetical education in the metaphor, you are not safe anywhere" (p. 1028)? Indicate some of the metaphors Frost examines in this essay. From what fields are they drawn? What does he say about each? Nominate some further metaphors—from politics, science, sociology, or anything else—and analyze them. To what extent are they useful? Do they have a breaking point? How might they mislead beyond the breaking point?*

5. Frost admires a speech that has "range, something of overstatement, something of statement, and something of understatement." Is this spectrum visible in Frost's own speech? Show where and how.

Virginia Woolf

IN SEARCH OF A ROOM OF ONE'S OWN[1]

It was disappointing not to have brought back in the evening some important statement, some authentic fact. Women are poorer than men because—this or that. Perhaps now it would be better to give up seeking for the truth, and receiving on one's head an avalanche of opinion hot as lava, discoloured as dish-water. It would be better to draw the curtains; to shut out distractions; to light the lamp; to narrow the enquiry and to ask the historian, who records not opinions but facts, to describe under what conditions women lived, not throughout the ages, but in England, say in the time of Elizabeth.

For it is a perennial puzzle why no woman wrote a word of that extraordinary literature when every other man, it seemed, was capable of song or sonnet. What were the conditions in which women lived, I asked myself; for fiction, imaginative work that is, is not dropped like a pebble upon the ground, as science may be; fiction is like a spider's web, attached ever so lightly perhaps, but still attached to life at all four corners. Often the attachment is scarcely perceptible; Shakespeare's plays, for instance, seem to hang there complete by themselves. But when the web is pulled askew, hooked up at the edge, torn in the middle, one remembers that these webs are not spun in midair by incorporeal creatures, but are the work of suffering human beings, and are attached to grossly material things, like health and money and the houses we live in.

I went, therefore, to the shelf where the histories stand and took down one of the latest, Professor Trevelyan's *History of England*. Once more I looked up Women, found "position of," and turned to the pages indicated. "Wife-beating," I read, "was a recognised right of man, and was practised without shame by high as well as low.... Similarly," the historian goes on, "the daughter who refused to marry the gentleman of her parents' choice was liable to be locked up, beaten and flung about the

1. This selection is Chapter 3 of Woolf's *A Room of One's Own*, a long essay that began as two lectures on women and fiction given at Newnham College and Girton College, women's colleges at Cambridge University, in 1928. In Chapter 1, Woolf advances the proposition that "a woman must have money and a room of her own if she is to write fiction." In Chapter 2, she describes a day spent at the British Museum (now the British Library) looking for information about the lives of women.

room, without any shock being inflicted on public opinion. Marriage was not an affair of personal affection, but of family avarice, particularly in the 'chivalrous' upper classes. . . . Betrothal often took place while one or both of the parties was in the cradle, and marriage when they were scarcely out of the nurses' charge." That was about 1470, soon after Chaucer's time. The next reference to the position of women is some two hundred years later, in the time of the Stuarts. "It was still the exception for women of the upper and middle class to choose their own husbands, and when the husband had been assigned, he was lord and master, so far at least as law and custom could make him. Yet even so," Professor Trevelyan concludes, "neither Shakespeare's women nor those of authentic seventeenth-century memoirs, like the Verneys and the Hutchinsons, seem wanting in personality and character." Certainly, if we consider it, Cleopatra must have had a way with her; Lady Macbeth, one would suppose, had a will of her own; Rosalind, one might conclude, was an attractive girl. Professor Trevelyan is speaking no more than the truth when he remarks that Shakespeare's women do not seem wanting in personality and character. Not being a historian, one might go even further and say that women have burnt like beacons in all the works of all the poets from the beginning of time—Clytemnestra, Antigone, Cleopatra, Lady Macbeth, Phèdre, Cressida, Rosalind, Desdemona, the Duchess of Malfi, among the dramatists; then among the prose writers: Millamant, Clarissa, Becky Sharp, Anna Karenina, Emma Bovary, Madame de Guermantes—the names flock to mind, nor do they recall women "lacking in personality and character." Indeed, if woman had no existence save in the fiction written by men, one would imagine her a person of the utmost importance; very various; heroic and mean; splendid and sordid; infinitely beautiful and hideous in the extreme; as great as a man, some think even greater.[2] But this is woman in fiction. In fact, as Professor Trevelyan points out, she was locked up, beaten and flung about the room.

A very queer, composite being thus emerges. Imaginatively she is of the highest importance; practically she is completely insignificant. She pervades poetry from cover to cover; she is all but absent from history.

2. "It remains a strange and almost inexplicable fact that in Athena's city, where women were kept in almost Oriental suppression as odalisques or drudges, the stage should yet have produced figures like Clytemnestra and Cassandra, Atossa and Antigone, Phèdre and Medea, and all the other heroines who dominate play after play of the 'misogynist' Euripides. But the paradox of this world where in real life a respectable woman could hardly show her face alone in the street, and yet on the stage woman equals or surpasses man, has never been satisfactorily explained. In modern tragedy the same predominance exists. At all events, a very cursory survey of Shakespeare's work (similarly with Webster, though not with Marlowe or Jonson) suffices to reveal how this dominance, this initiative of women, persists from Rosalind to Lady Macbeth. So too in Racine; six of his tragedies bear their heroines' names; and what male characters of his shall we set against Hermione and Andromaque, Bérénice and Roxane, Phèdre and Athalie? So again with Ibsen; what men shall we match with Solveig and Nora, Hedda and Hilda Wangel and Rebecca West?"—F. L. Lucas, Tragedy, pp. 114–15 [Woolf's note].

She dominates the lives of kings and conquerors in fiction; in fact she was the slave of any boy whose parents forced a ring upon her finger. Some of the most inspired words, some of the most profound thoughts in literature fall from her lips; in real life she could hardly read, could scarcely spell, and was the property of her husband.

It was certainly an odd monster that one made up by reading the historians first and the poets afterwards—a worm winged like an eagle; the spirit of life and beauty in a kitchen chopping up suet. But these monsters, however amusing to the imagination, have no existence in fact. What one must do to bring her to life was to think poetically and prosaically at one and the same moment, thus keeping in touch with fact —that she is Mrs. Martin, aged thirty-six, dressed in blue, wearing a black hat and brown shoes; but not losing sight of fiction either—that she is a vessel in which all sorts of spirits and forces are coursing and flashing perpetually. The moment, however, that one tries this method with the Elizabethan woman, one branch of illumination fails; one is held up by the scarcity of facts. One knows nothing detailed, nothing perfectly true and substantial about her. History scarcely mentions her. And I turned to Professor Trevelyan again to see what history meant to him. I found by looking at his chapter headings that it meant—

"The Manor Court and the Methods of Open-field Agriculture . . . The Cistercians and Sheep-farming . . . The Crusades . . . The University . . . The House of Commons . . . The Hundred Years' War . . . The Wars of the Roses . . . The Renaissance Scholars . . . The Dissolution of the Monasteries . . . Agrarian and Religious Strife . . . The Origin of English Sea-power . . . The Armada . . ." and so on. Occasionally an individual woman is mentioned, an Elizabeth, or a Mary; a queen or a great lady. But by no possible means could middle-class women with nothing but brains and character at their command have taken part in any one of the great movements which, brought together, constitute the historian's view of the past. Nor shall we find her in any collection of anecdotes. Aubrey[3] hardly mentions her. She never writes her own life and scarcely keeps a diary; there are only a handful of her letters in existence. She left no plays or poems by which we can judge her. What one wants, I thought—and why does not some brilliant student at Newnham or Girton supply it?—is a mass of information; at what age did she marry; how many children had she as a rule; what was her house like; had she a room to herself; did she do the cooking; would she be likely to have a servant? All these facts lie somewhere, presumably, in parish registers and account books; the life of the average Elizabethan woman must be scattered about somewhere, could one collect it and make a book of it. It would be ambitious beyond my daring, I thought, looking about the

3. John Aubrey (1626–97), whose biographical writings were published posthumously as *Brief Lives.*

shelves for books that were not there, to suggest to the students of those famous colleges that they should re-write history, though I own that it often seems a little queer as it is, unreal, lop-sided; but why should they not add a supplement to history? calling it, of course, by some inconspicuous name so that women might figure there without impropriety? For one often catches a glimpse of them in the lives of the great, whisking away into the background, concealing, I sometimes think, a wink, a laugh, perhaps a tear. And, after all, we have lives enough of Jane Austen; it scarcely seems necessary to consider again the influence of the tragedies of Joanna Baillie upon the poetry of Edgar Allan Poe; as for myself, I should not mind if the homes and haunts of Mary Russell Mitford were closed to the public for a century at least.[4] But what I find deplorable, I continued, looking about the bookshelves again, is that nothing is known about women before the eighteenth century. I have no model in my mind to turn about this way and that. Here am I asking why women did not write poetry in the Elizabethan age, and I am not sure how they were educated; whether they were taught to write; whether they had sitting-rooms to themselves; how many women had children before they were twenty-one; what, in short, they did from eight in the morning till eight at night. They had no money evidently; according to Professor Trevelyan they were married whether they liked it or not before they were out of the nursery, at fifteen or sixteen very likely. It would have been extremely odd, even upon this showing, had one of them suddenly written the plays of Shakespeare, I concluded, and I thought of that old gentleman, who is dead now, but was a bishop, I think, who declared that it was impossible for any woman, past, present, or to come, to have the genius of Shakespeare. He wrote to the papers about it. He also told a lady who applied to him for information that cats do not as a matter of fact go to heaven, though they have, he added, souls of a sort. How much thinking those old gentlemen used to save one! How the borders of ignorance shrank back at their approach! Cats do not go to heaven. Women cannot write the plays of Shakespeare.

Be that as it may, I could not help thinking, as I looked at the works of Shakespeare on the shelf, that the bishop was right at least in this; it would have been impossible, completely and entirely, for any woman to have written the plays of Shakespeare in the age of Shakespeare. Let me imagine, since facts are so hard to come by, what would have happened had Shakespeare had a wonderfully gifted sister, called Judith, let us say. Shakespeare himself went, very probably—his mother was an heiress —to the grammar school, where he may have learnt Latin—Ovid, Virgil and Horace—and the elements of grammar and logic. He was, it is well

4. Jane Austen (1775–1817), English novelist; Joanna Baillie (1762–1851), Scottish dramatist and poet; Mary Russell Mitford (1787–1855), English novelist and dramatist.

known, a wild boy who poached rabbits, perhaps shot a deer, and had, rather sooner than he should have done, to marry a woman in the neighbourhood, who bore him a child rather quicker than was right. That escapade sent him to seek his fortune in London. He had, it seemed, a taste for the theatre; he began by holding horses at the stage door. Very soon he got work in the theatre, became a successful actor, and lived at the hub of the universe, meeting everybody, knowing everybody, prac- tising his art on the boards, exercising his wits in the streets, and even getting access to the palace of the queen. Meanwhile his extraordinarily gifted sister, let us suppose, remained at home. She was as adventurous, as imaginative, as agog to see the world as he was. But she was not sent to school. She had no chance of learning grammar and logic, let alone of reading Horace and Virgil. She picked up a book now and then, one of her brother's perhaps, and read a few pages. But then her parents came in and told her to mend the stockings or mind the stew and not moon about with books and papers. They would have spoken sharply but kindly, for they were substantial people who knew the conditions of life for a woman and loved their daughter—indeed, more likely than not she was the apple of her father's eye. Perhaps she scribbled some pages up in an apple loft on the sly, but was careful to hide them or set fire to them. Soon, however, before she was out of her teens, she was to be betrothed to the son of a neighbouring wool-stapler. She cried out that marriage was hateful to her, and for that she was severely beaten by her father. Then he ceased to scold her. He begged her instead not to hurt him, not to shame him in this matter of her marriage. He would give her a chain of beads or a fine petticoat, he said; and there were tears in his eyes. How could she disobey him? How could she break his heart? The force of her own gift alone drove her to it. She made up a small parcel of her belongings, let herself down by a rope one summer's night and took the road to London. She was not seventeen. The birds that sang in the hedge were not more musical than she was. She had the quickest fancy, a gift like her brother's, for the tune of words. Like him, she had a taste for the theatre. She stood at the stage door; she wanted to act, she said. Men laughed in her face. The manager—a fat, loose-lipped man—guffawed. He bellowed something about poodles dancing and women acting—no woman, he said, could possibly be an actress.[5] He hinted—you can imagine what. She could get no training in her craft. Could she even seek her dinner in a tavern or roam the streets at midnight? Yet her genius was for fiction and lusted to feed abundantly upon the lives of men and women and the study of their ways. At last—for she was very young, oddly like Shakespeare the poet in her face, with the same grey eyes and rounded brows—at last Nick Greene the actor-manager took pity on her; she found herself with child by that gentleman and so—who shall measure the heat and violence of

5. Boys played women's parts in the Elizabethan theater.

the poet's heart when caught and tangled in a woman's body?—killed herself one winter's night and lies buried at some cross-roads where the omnibuses now stop outside the Elephant and Castle.

That, more or less, is how the story would run, I think, if a woman in Shakespeare's day had had Shakespeare's genius. But for my part, I agree with the deceased bishop, if such he was—it is unthinkable that any woman in Shakespeare's day should have had Shakespeare's genius. For genius like Shakespeare's is not born among labouring, uneducated, servile people. It was not born in England among the Saxons and the Britons. It is not born today among the working classes. How, then, could it have been born among women whose work began, according to Professor Trevelyan, almost before they were out of the nursery, who were forced to it by their parents and held to it by all the power of law and custom? Yet genius of a sort must have existed among women as it must have existed among the working classes. Now and again an Emily Brontë or a Robert Burns blazes out and proves its presence.[6] But certainly it never got itself on to paper. When, however, one reads of a witch being ducked, of a woman possessed by devils, of a wise woman selling herbs, or even of a very remarkable man who had a mother, then I think we are on the track of a lost novelist, a suppressed poet, of some mute and inglorious Jane Austen,[7] some Emily Brontë who dashed her brains out on the moor or mopped and mowed about the highways crazed with the torture that her gift had put her to. Indeed, I would venture to guess that Anon, who wrote so many poems without signing them, was often a woman. It was a woman Edward Fitzgerald,[8] I think, suggested who made the ballads and the folk-songs, crooning them to her children, beguiling her spinning with them, or the length of the winter's night.

This may be true or it may be false—who can say?—but what is true in it, so it seemed to me, reviewing the story of Shakespeare's sister as I had made it, is that any woman born with a great gift in the sixteenth century would certainly have gone crazed, shot herself, or ended her days in some lonely cottage outside the village, half witch, half wizard, feared and mocked at. For it needs little skill in psychology to be sure that a highly gifted girl who had tried to use her gift for poetry would have been so thwarted and hindered by other people, so tortured and pulled asunder by her own contrary instincts, that she must have lost her health and sanity to a certainty. No girl could have walked to London and stood at a stage door and forced her way into the presence of actor-managers without doing herself a violence and suffering an anguish which may have been irrational—for chastity may be a fetish invented by certain societies for unknown reasons—but were none the less inevitable. Chas-

6. Woolf's examples are Emily Brontë (1818–48), the English novelist, and Robert Burns (1759–96), the Scottish poet.
7. Woolf alludes to Thomas Gray's "Elegy Written in a Country Churchyard": "Some mute inglorious Milton here may rest."
8. Edward FitzGerald (1809–83), poet and translator.

tity had then, it has even now, a religious importance in a woman's life, and has so wrapped itself round with nerves and instincts that to cut it free and bring it to the light of day demands courage of the rarest. To have lived a free life in London in the sixteenth century would have meant for a woman who was poet and playwright a nervous stress and dilemma which might well have killed her. Had she survived, whatever she had written would have been twisted and deformed, issuing from a strained and morbid imagination. And undoubtedly, I thought, looking at the shelf where there are no plays by women, her work would have gone unsigned. That refuge she would have sought certainly. It was the relic of the sense of chastity that dictated anonymity to women even so late as the nineteenth century. Currer Bell, George Eliot, George Sand, all the victims of inner strife as their writings prove, sought ineffectively to veil themselves by using the name of a man.[9] Thus they did homage to the convention, which if not implanted by the other sex was liberally encouraged by them (the chief glory of a woman is not to be talked of, said Pericles,[1] himself a much-talked-of man), that publicity in women is detestable. Anonymity runs in their blood. The desire to be veiled still possesses them. They are not even now as concerned about the health of their fame as men are, and, speaking generally, will pass a tombstone or a signpost without feeling an irresistible desire to cut their names on it, as Alf, Bert or Chas. must do in obedience to their instinct, which murmurs if it sees a fine woman go by, or even a dog, Ce chien est à moi.[2] And, of course, it may not be a dog, I thought, remembering Parliament Square, the Sieges Allee and other avenues; it may be a piece of land or a man with curly black hair. It is one of the great advantages of being a woman that one can pass even a very fine negress without wishing to make an Englishwoman of her.

That woman, then, who was born with a gift of poetry in the sixteenth century, was an unhappy woman, a woman at strife against herself. All the conditions of her life, all her own instincts, were hostile to the state of mind which is needed to set free whatever is in the brain. But what is the state of mind that is most propitious to the act of creation, I asked. Can one come by any notion of the state that furthers and makes posible that strange activity? Here I opened the volume containing the Tragedies of Shakespeare. What was Shakespeare's state of mind, for instance, when he wrote Lear and Antony and Cleopatra? It was certainly the state of mind most favourable to poetry that there has ever existed. But Shakespeare himself said nothing about it. We only know casually and by chance that he "never blotted a line."[3] Nothing indeed was ever said by

9. The pseudonyms of Charlotte Brontë (1816–55), English novelist; Mary Ann Evans (1819–80), English novelist; and Amandine Aurore Lucie Dupin, Baronne Dudevant (1804–76), French novelist.

1. Pericles (d. 429 B.C.), Athenian statesman.
2. That dog is mine.
3. As recorded by his contemporary Ben Jonson (Timber: Or Discoveries Made Upon Men and Matter).

the artist himself about his state of mind until the eighteenth century perhaps. Rousseau perhaps began it.[4] At any rate, by the nineteenth century self-consciousness had developed so far that it was the habit for men of letters to describe their minds in confessions and autobiographies. Their lives also were written, and their letters were printed after their deaths. Thus, though we do not know what Shakespeare went through when he wrote *Lear*, we do know what Carlyle went through when he wrote the *French Revolution*; what Flaubert went through when he wrote *Madame Bovary*; what Keats was going through when he tried to write poetry against the coming of death and the indifference of the world.

And one gathers from this enormous modern literature of confession and self-analysis that to write a work of genius is almost always a feat of prodigious difficulty. Everything is against the likelihood that it will come from the writer's mind whole and entire. Generally material circumstances are against it. Dogs will bark; people will interrupt; money must be made; health will break down. Further, accentuating all these difficulties and making them harder to bear is the world's notorious indifference. It does not ask people to write poems and novels and histories; it does not need them. It does not care whether Flaubert finds the right word or whether Carlyle scrupulously verifies this or that fact. Naturally, it will not pay for what it does not want. And so the writer, Keats, Flaubert, Carlyle, suffers, especially in the creative years of youth, every form of distraction and discouragement. A curse, a cry of agony, rises from those books of analysis and confession. "Mighty poets in their misery dead"[5]—that is the burden of their song. If anything comes through in spite of all this, it is a miracle, and probably no book is born entire and uncrippled as it was conceived.

But for women, I thought, looking at the empty shelves, these difficulties were infinitely more formidable. In the first place, to have a room of her own, let alone a quiet room or a sound-proof room, was out of the question, unless her parents were exceptionally rich or very noble, even up to the beginning of the nineteenth century. Since her pin money, which depended on the good will of her father, was only enough to keep her clothed, she was debarred from such alleviations as came even to Keats or Tennyson or Carlyle, all poor men, from a walking tour, a little journey to France, from the separate lodging which, even if it were miserable enough, sheltered them from the claims and tyrannies of their families. Such material difficulties were formidable; but much worse were the immaterial. The indifference of the world which Keats and Flaubert and other men of genius have found so hard to bear was in her

4. Jean-Jacques Rousseau (1712–78), whose *Confessions* were published posthumously.

5. From William Wordsworth's poem "Resolution and Independence."

case not indifference but hostility. The world did not say to her as it said to them, Write if you choose; it makes no difference to me. The world said with a guffaw, Write? What's the good of your writing? Here the psychologists of Newnham and Girton might come to our help, I thought, looking again at the blank spaces on the shelves. For surely it is time that the effect of discouragement upon the mind of the artist should be measured, as I have seen a dairy company measure the effect of ordinary milk and Grade A milk upon the body of the rat. They set two rats in cages side by side, and of the two one was furtive, timid and small, and the other was glossy, bold and big. Now what food do we feed women as artists upon? I asked, remembering, I suppose, that dinner of prunes and custard.[6] To answer that question I had only to open the evening paper and to read that Lord Birkenhead is of opinion—but really I am not going to trouble to copy out Lord Birkenhead's opinion upon the writing of women. What Dean Inge says I will leave in peace. The Harley Street specialist may be allowed to rouse the echoes of Harley Street with his vociferations without raising a hair on my head. I will quote, however, Mr. Oscar Browning, because Mr. Oscar Browning was a great figure in Cambridge at one time, and used to examine the students at Girton and Newnham.[7] Mr. Oscar Browning was wont to declare "that the impression left on his mind, after looking over any set of examination papers, was that, irrespective of the marks he might give, the best woman was intellectually the inferior of the worst man." After saying that Mr. Browning went back to his rooms—and it is this sequel that endears him and makes him a human figure of some bulk and majesty—he went back to his rooms and found a stable-boy lying on the sofa—"a mere skeleton, his cheeks were cavernous and sallow, his teeth were black, and he did not appear to have the full use of his limbs. . . . 'That's Arthur' [said Mr. Browning]. 'He's a dear boy really and most high-minded.'" The two pictures always seem to me to complete each other. And happily in this age of biography the two pictures often do complete each other, so that we are able to interpret the opinions of great men not only by what they say, but by what they do.

But though this is possible now, such opinions coming from the lips of important people must have been formidable enough even fifty years ago. Let us suppose that a father from the highest motives did not wish his daughter to leave home and become writer, painter or scholar. "See what Mr. Oscar Browning says," he would say; and there was not only Mr. Oscar Browning; there was the *Saturday Review*; there was Mr.

6. In Chapter 1, Woolf contrasts the lavish dinner—partridge and wine—she ate as a guest in a men's college at Cambridge University with the plain fare—prunes and custard—served in a women's college.
7. In Chapter 2, Woolf lists the fruits of her day's research on the lives of women, which include Lord Birkenhead's, Dean Inge's, and Mr. Oscar Browning's opinions of women; she does not, however, quote them. Harley Street is where fashionable medical doctors in London have their offices.

Greg[8]—the "essentials of a woman's being," said Mr. Greg emphatically, "are that they are supported by, and they minister to, men"—there was an enormous body of masculine opinion to the effect that nothing could be expected of women intellectually. Even if her father did not read out loud these opinions, any girl could read them for herself; and the reading, even in the nineteenth century, must have lowered her vitality, and told profoundly upon her work. There would always have been that assertion —you cannot do this, you are incapable of doing that—to protest against, to overcome. Probably for a novelist this germ is no longer of much effect; for there have been women novelists of merit. But for painters it must still have some sting in it; and for musicians, I imagine, is even now active and poisonous in the extreme. The woman composer stands where the actress stood in the time of Shakespeare. Nick Greene, I thought, remembering the story I had made about Shakespeare's sister, said that a woman acting put him in mind of a dog dancing. Johnson repeated the phrase two hundred years later of women preaching.[9] And here, I said, opening a book about music, we have the very words used again in this year of grace, 1928, of women who try to write music. "Of Mlle. Germaine Tailleferre one can only repeat Dr. Johnson's dictum concerning a woman preacher, transposed into terms of music. 'Sir, a woman's composing is like a dog's walking on his hind legs. It is not done well, but you are surprised to find it done at all.'"[1] So accurately does history repeat itself.

Thus, I concluded, shutting Mr. Oscar Browning's life and pushing away the rest, it is fairly evident that even in the nineteenth century a woman was not encouraged to be an artist. On the contrary, she was snubbed, slapped, lectured and exhorted. Her mind must have been strained and her vitality lowered by the need of opposing this, of disproving that. For here again we come within range of that very interesting and obscure masculine complex which has had so much influence upon the woman's movement; that deep-seated desire, not so much that she shall be inferior as that he shall be superior, which plants him wherever one looks, not only in front of the arts, but barring the way to politics too, even when the risk to himself seems infinitesimal and the suppliant humble and devoted. Even Lady Bessborough, I remembered, with all her passion for politics, must humbly bow herself and write to Lord Granville Leveson-Gower:[2] ". . . notwithstanding all my violence in politics and talking so much on that subject, I perfectly agree with you that no woman has any business to meddle with that or any other serious

8. Mr. Greg does not appear on Woolf's list (see preceding note).
9. The quotation is from James Boswell's The Life of Samuel Johnson, L.L.D. Woolf, in her tale of Judith Shakespeare, imagines the manager bellowing "something about poodles dancing and women acting."
1. A Survey of Contemporary Music, Cecil Gray, p. 246 [Woolf's note].
2. Henrietta, Countess of Bessborough (1761–1821) and Lord Granville Leveson Gower, first Earl Granville (1773–1846). Their correspondence, edited by Castalia Countess Granville, was published as his Private Correspondence, 1781 to 1821, in 1916.

business, farther than giving her opinion (if she is ask'd)." And so she goes on to spend her enthusiasm where it meets with no obstacle whatsoever upon that immensely important subject, Lord Granville's maiden speech in the House of Commons. The spectacle is certainly a strange one, I thought. The history of men's opposition to women's emancipation is more interesting perhaps than the story of that emancipation itself. An amusing book might be made of it if some young student at Girton or Newnham would collect examples and deduce a theory—but she would need thick gloves on her hands, and bars to protect her of solid gold.

But what is amusing now, I recollected, shutting Lady Bessborough, had to be taken in desperate earnest once. Opinions that one now pastes in a book labelled cock-a-doodle-dum and keeps for reading to select audiences on summer nights once drew tears, I can assure you. Among your grandmothers and great-grandmothers there were many that wept their eyes out. Florence Nightingale[3] shrieked aloud in her agony.[4] Moreover, it is all very well for you, who have got yourselves to college and enjoy sitting-rooms—or is it only bed-sitting-rooms?—of your own to say that genius should disregard such opinions; that genius should be above caring what is said of it. Unfortunately, it is precisely the men or women of genius who mind most what is said of them. Remember Keats. Remember the words he had cut on his tombstone. Think of Tennyson;[5] think—but I need hardly multiply instances of the undeniable, if very unfortunate, fact that it is the nature of the artist to mind excessively what is said about him. Literature is strewn with the wreckage of men who have minded beyond reason the opinions of others.

And this susceptibility of theirs is doubly unfortunate, I thought, returning again to my original enquiry into what state of mind is most propitious for creative work, because the mind of an artist, in order to achieve the prodigious effort of freeing whole and entire the work that is in him, must be incandescent, like Shakespeare's mind, I conjectured, looking at the book which lay open at *Antony and Cleopatra*. There must be no obstacle in it, no foreign matter unconsumed.

For though we say that we know nothing about Shakespeare's state of mind, even as we say that, we are saying something about Shakespeare's state of mind. The reason perhaps why we know so little of Shakespeare —compared with Donne or Ben Jonson or Milton—is that his grudges and spites and antipathies are hidden from us. We are not held up by some "revelation" which reminds us of the writer. All desire to protest, to preach, to proclaim an injury, to pay off a score, to make the world the witness of some hardship or grievance was fired out of him and con-

3. Florence Nightingale (1820–1910), English nurse and philanthropist.
4. See *Cassandra*, by Florence Nightingale, printed in *The Cause*, by R. Strachey [Woolf's note].
5. Keats's epitaph reads "Here lies one whose name was writ in water." Tennyson was notably sensitive to reviews of his poetry.

sumed. Therefore his poetry flows from him free and unimpeded. If ever a human being got his work expressed completely, it was Shakespeare. If ever a mind was incandescent, unimpeded, I thought, turning again to the bookcase, it was Shakespeare's mind.

1929

Christopher Fry

LAUGHTER

A friend once told me that when he was under the influence of ether, he dreamed he was turning over the pages of a great book, in which he knew he would find, on the last page, the meaning of life. The pages of the book were alternately tragic and comic, and he turned page after page, his excitement growing, not only because he was approaching the answer but because he couldn't know, until he arrived, on which side of the book the final page would be. At last it came: the universe opened up to him in a hundred words: and they were uproariously funny. He came back to consciousness crying with laughter, remembering everything. He opened his lips to speak. It was then that the great and comic answer plunged back out of his reach.

If I had to draw a picture of the person of Comedy, it is so I should like to draw it: the tears of laughter running down the face, one hand still lying on the tragic page which so nearly contained the answer, the lips about to frame the great revelation, only to find it had gone as disconcertingly as a chair twitched away when we want to sit down. Comedy is an escape, not from truth but from despair: a narrow escape into faith. It believes in a universal cause for delight, even though knowledge of the cause is always twitched away from under us, which leaves us to rest on our own buoyancy. In tragedy every moment is eternity; in comedy eternity is a moment. In tragedy we suffer pain; in comedy pain is a fool, suffered gladly.

Charles Williams[1] once said to me, indeed it was the last thing he said to me (he died not long after), and it was shouted from the tailboard of a moving bus, over the heads of pedestrians and bicyclists outside the Midland Station, Oxford: "When we're dead we shall have the sensation of having enjoyed life altogether, whatever has happened to us." The distance between us widened, and he leaned out into the space so that his voice should reach me: "Even if we've been murdered, what a pleasure to

1. English writer whose poems, novels, plays, and essays explore the implications of Christian theology and morality for modern life.

have been capable of it!"; and, having spoken the words for comedy, away he went like that revelation which almost came out of the ether.

He was not at all saying that everything is for the best in the best of all possible worlds. He was saying—or so it seems to me—that there is an angle of experience where the dark is distilled into light: either here or hereafter, in or out of time: where our tragic fate finds itself with perfect pitch, and goes straight to the key which creation was composed in. And comedy senses and reaches out to this experience. It says, in effect, that, groaning as we may be, we move in the figure of a dance, and, so moving, we trace the outline of the mystery. Laughter did not come by chance, but how or why it came is beyond comprehension, unless we think of it as a kind of perception. The human animal, beginning to feel his spiritual inches, broke in onto an unfamiliar tension of life, where laughter became inevitable. But how? Could he, in his first unlaughing condition, have contrived a comic view of life and then developed the strange rib-shaking response?

Or is it not more likely that when he was able to grasp the tragic nature of time he was of a stature to sense its comic nature also; and, by the experience of tragedy and the intuition of comedy, to make his difficult way? The difference between tragedy and comedy is the difference between experience and intuition. In the experience we strive against every condition of our animal life: against death, against the frustration of ambition, against the instability of human love. In the intuition we trust the arduous eccentricities we're born to, and see the oddness of a creature who has never got acclimatized to being created. Laughter inclines me to know that man is essential spirit; his body, with its functions and accidents and frustrations, is endlessly quaint and remarkable to him; and though comedy accepts our position in time, it barely accepts our posture in space.

The bridge by which we cross from tragedy to comedy and back again is precarious and narrow. We find ourselves in one or the other by the turn of a thought; a turn such as we make when we turn from speaking to listening. I know that when I set about writing a comedy the idea presents itself to me first of all as tragedy. The characters press on to the theme with all their divisions and perplexities heavy about them; they are already entered for the race to doom, and good and evil are an infernal tangle skinning the fingers that try to unravel them. If the characters were not qualified for tragedy there would be no comedy, and to some extent I have to cross the one before I can light on the other. In a century less flayed and quivering we might reach it more directly; but not now, unless every word we write is going to mock us. A bridge has to be crossed, a thought has to be turned. Somehow the characters have to unmortify themselves: to affirm life and assimilate death and persevere in joy. Their hearts must be as determined as the phoenix; what burns must also light and renew: not by a vulnerable optimism but by a hard-won maturity of delight, by the intuition of comedy, an active patience declaring the solvency of good. The Book of Job is the great reservoir of comedy. "But there is a spirit in man. . . . Fair weather cometh out of the north. . . . The blessing of him that was ready to perish came upon me: and I caused the widow's heart to sing for joy."

I have come, you may think, to the verge of saying that comedy is greater than tragedy. On the verge I stand and go no further. Tragedy's experience hammers against the mystery to make a breach which would admit the whole triumphant answer. Intuition has no such potential. But there are times in the state of man when comedy has a special worth, and the present is one of them: a time when the loudest faith has been faith in a trampling materialism, when literature has been thought unrealistic which did not mark and remark our poverty and doom. Joy (of a kind) has been all on the devil's side, and one of the necessities of our time is to redeem it. If not, we are in poor sort to meet the circumstances, the circumstances being the contention of death with life, which is to say evil with good, which is to say desolation with delight. Laughter may only seem to be like an exhalation of air, but out of that air we came; in the beginning we inhaled it; it is a truth, not a fantasy, a truth voluble of good which comedy stoutly maintains.

1951

E. B. White

SOME REMARKS ON HUMOR

Analysts have had their go at humor, and I have read some of this interpretative literature, but without being greatly instructed. Humor can be dissected, as a frog can, but the thing dies in the process and the innards are discouraging to any but the pure scientific mind.

In a newsreel theatre the other day I saw a picture of a man who had developed the soap bubble to a higher point than it had ever before reached. He had become the ace soap bubble blower of America, had perfected the business of blowing bubbles, refined it, doubled it, squared it, and had even worked himself up into a convenient lather. The effect was not pretty. Some of the bubbles were too big to be beautiful, and the blower was always jumping into them or out of them, or playing some sort of unattractive trick with them. It was, if anything, a rather repulsive sight. Humor is a little like that: it won't stand much blowing up, and it won't stand much poking. It has a certain fragility, an evasiveness, which one had best respect. Essentially, it is a complete mystery. A human frame convulsed with laughter, and the laughter becoming hysterical and uncontrollable, is as far out of balance as one shaken with the hiccoughs or in the throes of a sneezing fit.

One of the things commonly said about humorists is that they are really very sad people—clowns with a breaking heart. There is some truth in it, but it is badly stated. It would be more accurate, I think, to say that there is a deep vein of melancholy running through everyone's life and that the humorist, perhaps more sensible of it than some others, compensates for it actively and positively. Humorists fatten on trouble. They have always made trouble pay. They struggle along with a good will and endure pain cheerfully, knowing how well it will serve them in the sweet by and by. You find them wrestling with foreign languages, fighting folding ironing boards and swollen drainpipes, suffering the terrible discomfort of tight boots (or as Josh Billings[1] wittily called them, "tite" boots). They pour out their sorrows profitably, in a form that is not quite fiction nor quite fact either. Beneath the sparkling surface of these dilemmas flows the strong tide of human woe.

Practically everyone is a manic depressive of sorts, with his up moments and his down moments, and you certainly don't have to be a humorist to taste the sadness of situation and mood. But there is often a rather fine line between laughing and crying, and if a humorous piece of writing brings a person to the point where his emotional responses are untrustworthy and seem likely to break over into the opposite realm, it is because humor, like poetry, has an extra content. It plays close to the big hot fire which is Truth, and sometimes the reader feels the heat.

1954

1. Pseudonym of Henry Wheeler Shaw, nineteenth-century American humorist whose sketches often depended on an exag- gerated imitation of the dialect of rural New England or New York.

QUESTIONS

1. *White uses a number of concrete details (dissected frog, soap bubbles and bubble blower, clowns with a breaking heart, fighting folding ironing boards and swollen drain pipes, suffering the terrible discomfort of tight boots, big hot fire which is Truth). Which of these are metaphors or analogies (comparisons with a different kind of thing) and which are concrete examples of general statements? Why does White use so many metaphors or analogies in his definition?*
2. *Rewrite White's definition in abstract or general language, leaving out the analogies or metaphors and the concrete examples. Then compare the rewritten version with the original. Which is clearer? Which is more interesting to read?*
3. *Compare White's definition of humor with his definition of democracy*

*(p. 842). Is there a recognizable similarity in language or style? In
devices used?*

*4. Compare White's definition of humor with Fry's definition of laugh-
ter. How far do the two definitions agree? Would White agree with
Fry's hint that comedy might even be considered greater than tragedy?*

X. J. Kennedy

WHO KILLED KING KONG?

The ordeal and spectacular death of King Kong, the giant ape, undoubtedly have been witnessed by more Americans than have ever seen
a performance of Hamlet, Iphigenia at Aulis, or even Tobacco Road. Since
RKO-Radio Pictures first released King Kong, a quarter-century has gone
by; yet year after year, from prints that grow more rain-beaten, from
sound tracks that grow more tinny, ticket-buyers by thousands still
pursue Kong's luckless fight against the forces of technology, tabloid
journalism, and the DAR. They see him chloroformed to sleep, see him
whisked from his jungle isle to New York and placed on show, see him
burst his chains to roam the city (lugging a frightened blonde), at last to
plunge from the spire of the Empire State Building, machine-gunned by
model airplanes.

Though Kong may die, one begins to think his legend unkillable. No
clearer proof of his hold upon the popular imagination may be seen than
what emerged one catastrophic week in March 1955, when New York
WOR-TV programmed Kong for seven evenings in a row (a total of
sixteen showings). Many a rival network vice-president must have scowl-
ed when surveys showed that Kong—the 1933 B-picture—had lured
away fat segments of the viewing populace from such powerful competitors as Ed Sullivan, Groucho Marx and Bishop Sheen.

But even television has failed to run King Kong into oblivion. Coffee-
in-the-lobby cinemas still show the old hunk of hokum, with the apology
that in its use of composite shots and animated models the film remains
technically interesting. And no other monster in movie history has won
so devoted a popular audience. None of the plodding mummies, the
stultified draculas, the whitecoated Lugosis[1] with their shiny pinball-
machine laboratories, none of the invisible stranglers, berserk robots, or
menaces from Mars has ever enjoyed so many resurrections.

Why does the American public refuse to let King Kong rest in peace?
It is true, I'll admit, that Kong outdid every monster movie before or since

1. Bela Lugosi, an actor in many horror movies.

in sheer carnage. Producers Cooper and Schoedsack crammed into it dinosaurs, headhunters, riots, aerial battles, bullets, bombs, bloodletting. Heroine Fay Wray, whose function is mainly to scream, shuts her mouth for hardly one uninterrupted minute from first reel to last. It is also true that *Kong* is larded with good healthy sadism, for those whose joy it is to see the frantic girl dangled from cliffs and harried by pterodactyls. But it seems to me that the abiding appeal of the giant ape rests on other foundations.

Kong has, first of all, the attraction of being manlike. His simian nature gives him one huge advantage over giant ants and walking vegetables in that an audience may conceivably identify with him. Kong's appeal has the quality that established the Tarzan series as American myth—for what man doesn't secretly image himself a huge hairy howler against whom no other monster has a chance? If Tarzan recalls the ape in us, then Kong may well appeal to that great-granddaddy primordial brute from whose tribe we have all deteriorated.

Intentionally or not, the producers of *King Kong* encourage this identification by etching the character of Kong with keen sympathy. For the ape is a figure in a tradition familiar to moviegoers: the tradition of the pitiable monster. We think of Lon Chaney in the role of Quasimodo,[2] of Karloff in the original *Frankenstein*. As we watch the Frankenstein monster's fumbling and disastrous attempts to befriend a flower-picking child, our sympathies are enlisted with the monster in his impenetrable loneliness. And so with Kong. As he roars in his chains, while barkers sell tickets to boobs who gape at him, we perhaps feel something more deep than pathos. We begin to sense something of the problem that engaged Eugene O'Neill in *The Hairy Ape*: the dilemma of a displaced animal spirit forced to live in a jungle built by machines.

King Kong, it is true, had special relevance in 1933. Landscapes of the depression are glimpsed early in the film when an impresario, seeking some desperate pretty girl to play the lead in a jungle movie, visits souplines and a Woman's Home Mission. In Fay Wray—who's been caught snitching an apple from a fruitstand—his search is ended. When he gives her a big feed and a movie contract, the girl is magic-carpeted out of the world of the National Recovery Act.[3] And when, in the film's climax, Kong smashes that very Third Avenue landscape in which Fay had wandered hungry, audiences of 1933 may well have felt a personal satisfaction.

What is curious is that audiences of 1960 remain hooked. For in the heart of urban man, one suspects, lurks the impulse to fling a bomb. Though machines speed him to the scene of his daily grind, though IBM comptometers ("freeing the human mind from drudgery") enable him to

---

2. The title character of Victor Hugo's novel *The Hunchback of Notre Dame.*

3. Legislation intended to bring an end to the Great Depression of the 1930s.

drudge more efficiently once he arrives, there comes a moment when he wishes to turn upon his machines and kick hell out of them. He wants to hurl his combination radioalarmclock out the bedroom window and listen to its smash. What subway commuter wouldn't love—just for once —to see the downtown express smack head-on into the uptown local? Such a wish is gratified in that memorable scene in *Kong* that opens with a wideangle shot: interior of a railway car on the Third Avenue El. Straphangers are nodding, the literate refold their newspapers. Unknown to them, Kong has torn away a section of trestle toward which the train now speeds. The motorman spies Kong up ahead, jams on the brakes. Passengers hurtle together like so many peas in a pail. In a window of the car appear Kong's bloodshot eyes. Women shriek. Kong picks up the railway car as if it were a rat, flips it to the street and ties knots in it, or something. To any commuter the scene must appear one of the most satisfactory pieces of celluloid ever exposed.

Yet however violent his acts, Kong remains a gentleman. Remarkable is his sense of chivalry. Whenever a fresh boa constrictor threatens Fay, Kong first sees that the lady is safely parked, then manfully thrashes her attacker. (And she, the ingrate, runs away every time his back is turned.) Atop the Empire State Building, ignoring his pursuers, Kong places Fay on a ledge as tenderly as if she were a dozen eggs. He fondles her, then turns to face the Army Air Force. And Kong is perhaps the most disinterested lover since Cyrano:[4] his attentions to the lady are utterly without hope of reward. After all, between a five-foot blonde and a fifty-foot ape, love can hardly be more than an intellectual flirtation. In his simian way King Kong is the hopelessly yearning lover of Petrarchan convention.[5] His forced exit from his jungle, in chains, results directly from his single-minded pursuit of Fay. He smashes a Broadway theater when the notion enters his dull brain that the flashbulbs of photographers somehow endanger the lady. His perilous shinnying up a skyscraper to pluck Fay from her boudoir is an act of the kindliest of hearts. He's impossible to discourage even though the love of his life can't lay eyes on him without shrieking murder.

The tragedy of King Kong then, is to be the beast who at the end of the fable fails to turn into the handsome prince. This is the conviction that the scriptwriters would leave with us in the film's closing line. As Kong's corpse lies blocking traffic in the street, the enterpreneur who brought Kong to New York turns to the assembled reporters and proclaims: "That's your story, boys—it was Beauty killed the Beast!" But greater forces than those of the screaming Lady have combined to lay Kong low, if you ask me. Kong lives for a time as one of those persecuted near-

---

4. Hero of the romantic drama *Cyrano de Bergerac*, whose extreme sensitivity about his large nose keeps him from professing his love.

5. The attitude of the lover in the sonnets of the fourteenth-century Italian poet Francis Petrarch and his followers.

animal souls bewildered in the middle of an industrial order, whose simple desires are thwarted at every turn. He climbs the Empire State Building because in all New York it's the closest thing he can find to the clifftop of his jungle isle. He dies, a pitiful dolt, and the army brass and publicity-men cackle over him. His death is the only possible outcome to as neat a tragic dilemma as you can ask for. The machine-guns do him in, while the manicured human hero (a nice clean Dartmouth boy) carries away Kong's sweetheart to the altar. O, the misery of it all. There's far more truth about upper-middle-class American life in *King Kong* than in the last seven dozen novels of John P. Marquand.[6]

A Negro friend from Atlanta tells me that in movie houses in colored neighborhoods throughout the South, *Kong* does a constant business. They show the thing in Atlanta at least every year, presumably to the same audiences. Perhaps this popularity may simply be due to the fact that Kong is one of the most watchable movies ever constructed, but I wonder whether Negro audiences may not find some archetypical appeal in this serio-comic tale of a huge black powerful free spirit whom all the hardworking white policemen are out to kill.

Every day in the week on a screen somewhere in the world, King Kong relives his agony. Again and again he expires on the Empire State Building, as audiences of the devout assist his sacrifice. We watch him die, and by extension kill the ape within our bones, but these little deaths of ours occur in prosaic surroundings. We do not die on a tower, New York before our feet, nor do we give our lives to smash a few flying machines. It is not for us to bring to a momentary standstill the civilization in which we move. King Kong does this for us. And so we kill him again and again, in much-spliced celluloid, while the ape in us expires from day to day, obscure, in desperation.

                                                                        1960

---

6. Popular American author of novels of society.

Stanley Kauffmann

THE FILM GENERATION

* * *

There exists a Film Generation: the first generation that has matured in a culture in which the film has been of accepted serious relevance, however that seriousness is defined. Before 1935 films were proportionately more popular than they are now, but for the huge majority of filmgoers they represented a regular weekly or semiweekly bath of escapism. Such an escapist audience still exists in large number, but another audience, most of them born since 1935, exists along with it. This group, this Film Generation, is certainly not exclusively grim, but it is essentially serious. Even its appreciations of sheer entertainment films reflect an overall serious view.

There are a number of reasons, old and new, intrinsic and extrinsic, why this generation has come into being. Here are some of the older, intrinsic reasons.

1. In an age imbued with technological interest, the film art flowers out of technology. Excepting architecture, film is the one art that can capitalize directly and extensively on this century's luxuriance in applied science. Graphic artists have used mechanical and electronic elements, poets and painters have used computers, composers have used electronic tapes. These are matters of choice. The film maker has no choice: he must use complicated electronic and mechanical equipment. This fact helps to create a strong sense of junction with his society, of membership in the present. American artists have often been ashamed of—sometimes have dreaded—a feeling of difference from the busy "real" American world around them. For the film maker the very instruments of his art provide communion with the spirit of his age. I think that the audience shares his feeling of union, sometimes consciously (especially when stereophonic sound, special optical effects, or color processes are used). The scientific skills employed are thus in themselves a link between the artist and the audience, and are a further link between them all and the unseen, unheard but apprehended society bustling outside the film theater.

There is a pleasant paradoxical corollary. In an era that is much concerned with the survival of the human being as such, in an increasingly mechanized age, here a complicated technology is used to celebrate the human being.

2. The world of surfaces and physical details has again become material for art. Just as the naturalistic novel seems to be sputtering to a halt, overdescribed down to the last vest button, the film gives some of its virtues new artistic life. A novelist who employs the slow steam-roller

apparatus of intense naturalism these days is asking for an extra vote of confidence from the reader, because the method and effects are so familiar that the reader can anticipate by pages. Even when there is the interest of an unusual setting, the reader is conscious that different nouns have been slipped into a worn pattern. The "new" French novel of Robbe-Grillet, Duras, Sarraute[1] attempts to counteract this condition by intensifying it, using surfaces as the last realities, the only dependable objective correlatives. Sometimes, for some readers, this works. But both the old and the latter-day naturalisms must strain in order to connect. Rolf Hochhuth, the author of *The Deputy*,[2] has said:

> When I recently saw Ingmar Bergman's *The Silence*, I left that Hamburg movie house with the question, "What is there left for the novelist today?" Think of what Bergman can do with a single shot of his camera, up a street, down a corridor, into a woman's armpit. Of all he can say with this without saying a word.

Despite Hochhuth's understandable thrill-despair, there is plenty left for the novelist to say, even of armpits, but the essence of his remark rightly strips from fiction the primary function of creating material reality. The film has not only taken over this function but exalted it: it manages to make poetry out of doorknobs, breakfasts, furniture. Trivial details, of which everyone's universe is made, can once again be transmuted into metaphor, contributing to imaginative art.

A complementary, powerful fact is that this principle operates whether the film maker is concerned with it or not. In any film except those with fantastic settings, whether the director's aim is naturalistic or romantic or symbolic or anything else, the streets and stairways and cigarette lighters are present, the girl's room is at least as real as the girl —often it bolsters her defective reality. Emphasized or not, invited or not, the physical world through the intensifications of photography never stops insisting on its presence and relevance.

This new life of surfaces gives a discrete verity to many mediocre films and gives great vitality to a film by a good artist. Consciously or not, this vitality reassures the audience, tangentially certifying and commenting on its habitat. Indeed, out of this phenomenon, it can be argued that the film discovered pop art years ago, digested this minor achievement, then continued on its way.

3. The film form seems particularly apt for the treatment of many of the pressing questions of our time: inner states of tension or of doubt or apathy—even doubts about art itself. The film can externalize some psychical matters that, for example, the theater cannot easily deal with; and it can relate them to physical environment in a manner that the

---

1. Alain Robbe-Grillet, Marguerite Duras, and Nathalie Sarraute; Robbe-Grillet and Duras have also worked as screenwriters and directors.

2. Controversial play which accuses Pope Piux XII of tolerating the Nazi persecution of the Jews.

theater cannot contain nor the novel quite duplicate. The film can dramatize post-Freudian man, and his habitat—and the relation between the two. One does not need to believe in the death of the theater or the novel—as I do not—in order to see these special graces in the film.

4. Film is the only art besides music that is available to the whole world at once, exactly as it was first made. With subtitles, it is the only art involving language that can be enjoyed in a language of which one is ignorant. (I except opera, where the language rarely needs to be understood precisely.)

The point is not the spreading of information or amity, as in USIA or UNESCO films, useful though they may be. The point is emotional relationship and debt. If one has been moved by, for instance, Japanese actors in Japanese settings, in actions of Japanese life that have resonated against one's own experience, there is a connection with Japan that is deeper than the benefits of propaganda or travelogue. No one who has been moved by *Ikiru*[3] can think of Japan and the Japanese exactly as he thought before.

Obviously similar experience—emotional and spiritual—is available through other arts, but rarely with the imperial ease of the film. As against foreign literature, foreign films have an advantage besides accessibility in the original language. The Japanese novelist invites us to recreate the scene in imagination. The Japanese film maker provides the scene for us, with a vividness that our minds cannot equal in a foreign setting. Thus our responses can begin at a more advanced point and can more easily (although not more strongly) be stimulated and heightened.

This universality and this relative simultaneity of artistic experience have made us all members of a much larger empathetic community than has been immediately possible before in history.

5. Film has one great benefit by accident: its youth, which means not only vigor but the reach of possibility. The novel, still very much alive, is conscious of having to remain alive. One of its chief handicaps is its history; the novelist is burdened with the achievements of the past. This is also true of poetry. It flourishes certainly; as with fiction, the state of poetry is far better than is often assumed. But poetry, too, is conscious of a struggle for pertinent survival. In painting and sculpture, the desperation is readily apparent; the new fashion in each new season makes it clear. But the film is an infant, only begun. It has already accomplished miracles. Consider that it was only fifty years from Edison's camera to *Citizen Kane*, which is rather as if Stravinsky had written *Petrouchka* fifty years after Guido d'Arezzo[4] developed musical notation. Nevertheless the film continent has only just been discovered, the boundaries are not remotely in sight. It is this freshness that gives the young generation

3. *To Live*, a film, directed by Akira Kurosawa, about the last months in the life of a cancer-stricken Japanese civil servant.
4. In the ballet *Petrouchka*, performed in 1911, the composer Igor Stravinsky experimented with new harmonies and rhythms; Guido d'Arezzo was an Italian Benedictine monk who worked in the first half of the

—what I have called the Film Generation—not only the excitement of its potential but a strong proprietary feeling. The film belongs to them.

These, I think, are some of the reasons for the growth of that new film audience. But they raise a question. As noted, these reasons have been valid to some degree for a long time, yet it is only in about the last twenty years that the Film Generation has emerged. Why didn't this happen sooner? Why have these reasons begun to be strongly operative only since the Second World War?

In that period other elements have risen to galvanize them. Some of these later elements come from outside the film world: the spurt in college education; political and social abrasions and changes; moral, ethical, religious dissolutions and resolutions. All these have made this generation more impatient and more hungry. But, since the Second War, there have also been some important developments within the film world itself. These developments have been in content, not in form. Three elements are especially evident: increased sexuality, an increase in national flavor, and an increased stress on the individual. The latter two are linked.

As for the first, sex has been important currency in the theater since the *Agamemnon*,[5] and with the first films came the first film idols. In fact there are scenes in many silent films that would have censor trouble today. But apart from sexual display or the sex appeal of any actor or actress, there is now—in many foreign films and some American ones—a sexual attitude that can be respected: an attitude closer to the realities of sexual life than the mythology that is preached by clergy of every faith, by mass media, by parents. This relative sexual freedom, long established in fiction and the theater, has been slower to arrive in films because of their wider availability to all ages and mentalities, and the consequent brooding of censors. Now, in a more liberal time, this freedom makes films even more pertinent to this generation. The mythology that still passes for sexual morality is prescriptive, these films are descriptive; but there is more to their merit than verisimilitude. Not by nudity nor bedroom calisthenics nor frank language but by fidelity to the complexities of sexual behavior, these films provide more than recognition. By accepting and exploring complexities, they provide confidence in the fundamental beauty of those complexities, in the desirability of being human, even with all the trouble it involves.

The second element, national flavor, has been described by the English critic Penelope Houston in *The Contemporary Cinema* (1963):

> However partial or distorted an image one gets of a society through its cinema, it is still possible to discern the national face behind the screen. It is

---

eleventh century.

5. Aeschylus's great tragedy, performed in 458 B.C.

individualist, has passed. Mere "coolness" persists; purposeful rebellion fades.

All the national colors described above apply both to popular and serious films. If we concentrate on serious film—film made primarily as personal expression, not as contractual job or money-spinner—then we often find, besides intensified national color, an intensified introspection. This is the third of our elements: a concern with the exploration of the individual as a universe. It is not a novelty in films. No more introspective films have ever been made than Wiene's *The Cabinet of Dr. Caligari* (1919) or Pabst's *Secrets of the Soul* (1926). But merely to mention such names as Bergman, Antonioni, Fellini, Ozu, Torre Nilsson, Olmi, Truffaut[6] is to see that, for many outstanding directors, there has lately been more reliance on inner conflict than on classic confrontation of antagonists. These men and others, including some Americans, have been extending the film into the vast areas of innermost privacy, even of the unconscious, that have been the province of the novel and of metaphysical poetry. Saul Bellow has complained that the modern novelist doesn't tell us what a human being is today. Bellow is a notable exception to his own complaint; but whether we agree or not, we can see that many contemporary film makers have tried to answer that question, with a more consistent application than ever before in the history of the art.

These two elements—national color and the exploration of the individual—are obviously inseparable. Society and the man affect each other, even if it is in the man's withdrawal. These elements are further linked in a curious contradictory motion against our time. In an age when internationalism is promulgated as a solution to political difficulties, national colors have become more evident in films. In an age when social philosophers have begun to question the durability of individualism—which is, after all, a fairly recent concept in history and almost exclusive to the West—the film is tending to cherish the individual. Does this indicate a time lag between the film and the advances of political and social philosophy? On the contrary, I believe it indicates a perverse penetration to truth. The truth of art sometimes runs counter to what seems politically and intellectually desirable; that is always a risk of art. I think the film is showing us that nationalism, in the purely cultural sense, is becoming more necessary to us as jet planes and Telstar[7] threaten to make us one world. I think that just at the time when technological and power structures challenge individualism, our own minds and souls have become more interesting to us. Up to now, technology has outraced self-discovery. Only now—in this postreligious, self-dependent age—are we beginning to appreciate how rich and dangerous each one of us is.

6. Film directors: Ingmar Bergman, Sweden; Michelangelo Antonioni and Federico Fellini, Italy; Yasujiro Ozu, Japan; Leopoldo Torre Nilsson, Argentina; Ermanno Olmi, Italy; and François Truffaut, France.

7. The first commercial communications satellite.

difficult to conceive of a neorealist idealism [in Italy] without the jubilant preface of the liberation of Rome; or to look at Britain's films of the past few years without reference to our redbrick radicalism; or to ignore the effect of the political climate on a French cinema which declares its awareness of strain in the very insistence with which it puts private before public life and creation for creation's sake before either.

It would be easy to add a similar sentence for almost every major film-producing country. Japanese films are concerned with contemporary unrest, directly and indirectly. Many of their costume pictures about samurai swordsmen are set in the 1860s when the feudal system was crumbling and immense social metamorphosis was taking place. The Soviet film has deepened in lethargy as revolutionary fervor wore off, as Stalinist despotism made it nervous, as some subsequent economic and scientific successes made it smug. It has become, with a few exceptions, either war glory or the ideologic equivalent of the petty bourgeois confection. As for America, the poor boy and rich girl story (or rich boy and poor girl) which was the staple of the popular film before the Second War has disappeared. Money as romance, the Gatsby dream, has receded, not because everyone is now rich but because the middle-class image has replaced both the poor image and the rich image. What American would now relish the ancient compliment "poor but honest"? And what is the difference *in appearance* between the clerk's car and the boss'? The much-mooted ascendancy of the middle class has reached the point where it is strong enough to control cultural forms, to magnify its own image in art.

With this ascendancy we have seen the emergence of a new romantic hero, posed against this bourgeois background, since all such heroes must contrast with their societies. The new romantic is the liberated prole, with a motorcyle or a Texas Cadillac, seeking his life by assaulting convention and morality, rather than by striving for success in accepted modes, either with money or with women. This hero scoffs at ideals of excellence and aspiration at the same time that he wants to dominate. There are signs that this hero may have run his course, but in the last twenty years or so he was pre-eminent.

A lesser companion of his still continues: the Frank Sinatra-Dean Martin figure, the smart, cool operator just inside the law, a philanderer righteously resentful of any claims on him by women. His casual *persona* derives in part from the night-club microphone, which was first a necessity, then became a prop, then a source of power and ease for those who had little power and could achieve nothing but ease. The invisible hand-held microphone accompanies the crooner-as-hero wherever he goes. His oblique, slithering solipsism seems likely to persist after the Brando figure, more directly descended from the proletarian rebel and Byronic individualist, has passed. Mere "coolness" persists; purposeful rebellion fades.

All the national colors described above apply both to popular and serious films. If we concentrate on serious film—film made primarily as personal expression, not as contractual job or money-spinner—then we often find, besides intensified national color, an intensified introspection. This is the third of our elements: a concern with the exploration of the individual as a universe. It is not a novelty in films. No more introspective films have ever been made than Wiene's *The Cabinet of Dr. Caligari* (1919) or Pabst's *Secrets of the Soul* (1926). But merely to mention such names as Bergman, Antonioni, Fellini, Ozu, Torre Nilsson, Olmi, Truffaut[6] is to see that, for many outstanding directors, there has lately been more reliance on inner conflict than on classic confrontation of antagonists. These men and others, including some Americans, have been extending the film into the vast areas of innermost privacy, even of the unconscious, that have been the province of the novel and of metaphysical poetry. Saul Bellow has complained that the modern novelist doesn't tell us what a human being *is* today. Bellow is a notable exception to his own complaint; but whether we agree or not, we can see that many contemporary film makers have tried to answer that question, with a more consistent application than ever before in the history of the art.

These two elements—national color and the exploration of the individual—are obviously inseparable. Society and the man affect each other, even if it is in the man's withdrawal. These elements are further linked in a curious contradictory motion against our time. In an age when internationalism is promulgated as a solution to political difficulties, national colors have become more evident in films. In an age when social philosophers have begun to question the durability of individualism—which is, after all, a fairly recent concept in history and almost exclusive to the West—the film is tending to cherish the individual. Does this indicate a time lag between the film and the advances of political and social philosophy? On the contrary, I believe it indicates a perverse penetration to truth. The truth of art sometimes runs counter to what seems politically and intellectually desirable; that is always a risk of art. I think the film is showing us that nationalism, in the purely cultural sense, is becoming more necessary to us as jet planes and Telstar[7] threaten to make us one world. I think that just at the time when technological and power structures challenge individualism, our own minds and souls have become more interesting to us. Up to now, technology has outraced self-discovery. Only now—in this postreligious, self-dependent age—are we beginning to appreciate how rich and dangerous each one of us is.

6. Film directors: Ingmar Bergman, Sweden; Michelangelo Antonioni and Federico Fellini, Italy; Yasujiro Ozu, Japan; Leopoldo Torre Nilsson, Argentina; Ermanno Olmi, Italy; and François Truffaut, France.
7. The first commercial communications satellite.

difficult to conceive of a neorealist idealism [in Italy] without the jubilant preface of the liberation of Rome; or to look at Britain's films of the past few years without reference to our redbrick radicalism; or to ignore the effect of the political climate on a French cinema which declares its awareness of strain in the very insistence with which it puts private before public life and creation for creation's sake before either.

It would be easy to add a similar sentence for almost every major film-producing country. Japanese films are concerned with contemporary unrest, directly and indirectly. Many of their costume pictures about samurai swordsmen are set in the 1860s when the feudal system was crumbling and immense social metamorphosis was taking place. The Soviet film has deepened in lethargy as revolutionary fervor wore off, as Stalinist despotism made it nervous, as some subsequent economic and scientific successes made it smug. It has become, with a few exceptions, either war glory or the ideologic equivalent of the petty bourgeois confection. As for America, the poor boy and rich girl story (or rich boy and poor girl) which was the staple of the popular film before the Second War has disappeared. Money as romance, the Gatsby dream, has receded, not because everyone is now rich but because the middle-class image has replaced both the poor image and the rich image. What American would now relish the ancient compliment "poor but honest"? And what is the difference *in appearance* between the clerk's car and the boss'? The much-mooted ascendancy of the middle class has reached the point where it is strong enough to control cultural forms, to magnify its own image in art.

With this ascendancy we have seen the emergence of a new romantic hero, posed against this bourgeois background, since all such heroes must contrast with their societies. The new romantic is the liberated prole, with a motorcyle or a Texas Cadillac, seeking his life by assaulting convention and morality, rather than by striving for success in accepted modes, either with money or with women. This hero scoffs at ideals of excellence and aspiration at the same time that he wants to dominate. There are signs that this hero may have run his course, but in the last twenty years or so he was pre-eminent.

A lesser companion of his still continues: the Frank Sinatra-Dean Martin figure, the smart, cool operator just inside the law, a philanderer righteously resentful of any claims on him by women. His casual *persona* derives in part from the night-club microphone, which was first a necessity, then became a prop, then a source of power and ease for those who had little power and could achieve nothing but ease. The invisible hand-held microphone accompanies the crooner-as-hero wherever he goes. His oblique, slithering solipsism seems likely to persist after the Brando figure, more directly descended from the proletarian rebel and Byronic

These elements have led, directly and by implication, to the phenomenon we are examining; the historical moment for the rise of the Film Generation, a surge of somewhat nostalgic revolution; a reluctance to lose what seems to be disappearing, accompanied by an impulse to disaffection, an insistence on an amorphous cosmos. ("Stay loose." "Swing.") Doubtless that nostalgia is sentimental, an unwillingness to be banned from an Eden of individualism that in fact never existed. But much of the revolution is clearheaded; not so much an attempt to halt change as to influence it, a natural and valuable impulse to scratch on the chromium fronts of the advancing tanks of factory-society "Kilroy was here."[8]

The divided attitude toward social change leads to another, crucial polarity. This generation has an ambivalent view of cultural tradition. On the one hand there is a great desire for such tradition, admitted or not. Everyone wants to know that he came from somewhere; it's less lonely. But this desire is often accompanied by a mirror attitude that looks on the past as failure and betrayal. It is of course a familiar indictment, the young accusing the old of having made a mess, but now the accusation is more stringent and more general because of the acceleration of change and the diminutions of choice.

This ambivalence toward tradition—this polarity that both wants and rejects it—has created a hunger for art as assurance of origins together with a preference for art forms that are relatively free of the past. Outstanding among these is film. Even though it has been on hand for sixty-five years or so, the film seems much more of the present and future than other forms. It has its roots—of content and method—in older arts: drama, literature, dance, painting; yet it is very much less entailed by the past than these arts. It satisfies this generation's ambivalent need in tradition.

* * *

1966

8. American graffito omnipresent during the Second World War.

QUESTIONS

1. Kauffmann says that film "manages to make poetry out of doorknobs, breakfasts, furniture" by transmuting "trivial details . . . into metaphor" (p. 1054). Choose a film you have seen that illustrates this point and explain what techniques are used to achieve the transmutation and what they contribute to the effectiveness of the film.
2. Kauffmann asserts that "the film form seems particularly apt for the treatment of many of the pressing questions of our time" (p. 1054). Choose a film that concerns one such pressing question and determine how effectively it presents the matter. Compare the treatment in film

to the treatment this subject might have received in an essay or a work of fiction.

3. *According to Kauffmann contemporary films present "an attitude closer to the realities of sexual life than the mythology that is preached by clergy of every faith, by mass media, by parents" (p. 1056). Test this statement by considering the element of sexuality in one or more films that you have recently seen.*

4. *Reread Kauffmann's remarks about the new romantic hero, "the liberated prole," in American films (p. 1057). Then describe the hero in a film you have recently seen, discussing how close to this ideal he comes.*

Aaron Copland

HOW WE LISTEN

We all listen to music according to our separate capacities. But, for the sake of analysis, the whole listening process may become clearer if we break it up into its component parts, so to speak. In a certain sense we all listen to music on three separate planes. For lack of a better terminology, one might name these: (1) the sensuous plane, (2) the expressive plane, (3) the sheerly musical plane. The only advantage to be gained from mechanically splitting up the listening process into these hypothetical planes is the clearer view to be had of the way in which we listen.

The simplest way of listening to music is to listen for the sheer pleasure of the musical sound itself. That is the sensuous plane. It is the plane on which we hear music without thinking, without considering it in any way. One turns on the radio while doing something else and absentmindedly bathes in the sound. A kind of brainless but attractive state of mind is engendered by the mere sound appeal of the music.

You may be sitting in a room reading this book. Imagine one note struck on the piano. Immediately that one note is enough to change the atmosphere of the room—proving that the sound element in music is a powerful and mysterious agent, which it would be foolish to deride or belittle.

The surprising thing is that many people who consider themselves qualified music lovers abuse that plane in listening. They go to concerts in order to lose themselves. They use music as a consolation or an escape. They enter an ideal world where one doesn't have to think of the realities of everyday life. Of course they aren't thinking about the music either. Music allows them to leave it, and they go off to a place to dream, dreaming because of and apropos of the music yet never quite listening to it.

Yes, the sound appeal of music is a potent and primitive force, but you must not allow it to usurp a disproportionate share of your interest. The sensuous plane is an important one in music, a very important one, but it does not constitute the whole story.

There is no need to digress further on the sensuous plane. Its appeal to every normal human being is self-evident. There is, however, such a thing as becoming more sensitive to the different kinds of sound stuff as used by various composers. For all composers do not use that sound stuff in the same way. Don't get the idea that the value of music is commensurate with its sensuous appeal or that the loveliest sounding music is made by the greatest composer. If that were so, Ravel would be a greater creator than Beethoven. The point is that the sound element varies with each composer, that his usage of sound forms an integral part of his style and must be taken into account when listening. The reader can see, therefore, that a more conscious approach is valuable even on this primary plane of music listening.

The second plane on which music exists is what I have called the expressive one. Here, immediately, we tread on controversial ground. Composers have a way of shying away from any discussion of music's expressive side. Did not Stravinsky himself proclaim that his music was an "object," a "thing," with a life of its own, and with no other meaning than its own purely musical existence? This intransigent attitude of Stravinsky's may be due to the fact that so many people have tried to read different meanings into so many pieces. Heaven knows it is difficult enough to say precisely what it is that a piece of music means, to say it definitely, to say it finally so that everyone is satisfied with your explanation. But that should not lead one to the other extreme of denying to music the right to be "expressive."

My own belief is that all music has an expressive power, some more and some less, but that all music has a certain meaning behind the notes and that that meaning behind the note constitutes, after all, what the piece is saying, what the piece is about. This whole problem can be stated quite simply by asking, "Is there a meaning to music?" My answer to that would be. "Yes." And "Can you state in so many words what the meaning is?" My answer to that would be, "No." Therein lies the difficulty.

Simple-minded souls will never be satisfied with the answer to the second of these questions. They always want music to have a meaning, and the more concrete it is the better they like it. The more the music reminds them of a train, a storm, a funeral, or any other familiar conception the more expressive it appears to be to them. This popular idea of music's meaning—stimulated and abetted by the usual run of musical commentator—should be discouraged wherever and whenever it is met. One timid lady once confessed to me that she suspected something seriously lacking in her appreciation of music because of her inability to connect it with anything definite. That is getting the whole thing backward, of course.

Still, the question remains, How close should the intelligent music lover wish to come to pinning a definite meaning to any particular work? No closer than a general concept, I should say. Music expresses, at different moments, serenity or exuberance, regret or triumph, fury or delight. It expresses each of these moods, and many others, in a numberless variety of subtle shadings and differences. It may even express a state of meaning for which there exists no adequate word in any language. In that case, musicians often like to say that it has only a purely musical meaning. They sometimes go farther and say that all music has only a purely musical meaning. What they really mean is that no appropriate word can be found to express the music's meaning and that, even if it could, they do not feel the need of finding it.

But whatever the professional musician may hold, most musical novices still search for specific words with which to pin down their musical reactions. That is why they always find Tchaikovsky easier to "understand" than Beethoven. In the first place, it is easier to pin a meaning-word on a Tchaikovsky piece than on a Beethoven one. Much easier. Moreover, with the Russian composer, every time you come back to a piece of his it almost always says the same thing to you, whereas with Beethoven it is often quite difficult to put your finger right on what he is saying. And any musician will tell you that that is why Beethoven is the greater composer. Because music which always says the same thing to you will necessarily soon become dull music, but music whose meaning is slightly different with each hearing has a greater chance of remaining alive.

Listen, if you can, to the forty-eight fugue themes of Bach's *Well Tempered Clavichord*. Listen to each theme, one after another. You will soon realize that each theme mirrors a different world of feeling. You will also soon realize that the more beautiful a theme seems to you the harder it is to find any word that will describe it to your complete satisfaction. Yes, you will certainly know whether it is a gay theme or a sad one. You will be able, in other words, in your own mind, to draw a frame of emotional feeling around your theme. Now study the sad one a little closer. Try to pin down the exact quality of its sadness. Is it pessimistically sad or resignedly sad; is it fatefully sad or smilingly sad?

Let us suppose that you are fortunate and can describe to your own satisfaction in so many words the exact meaning of your chosen theme. There is still no guarantee that anyone else will be satisfied. Nor need they be. The important thing is that each one feel for himself the specific expressive quality of a theme or, similarly, an entire piece of music. And if it is a great work of art, don't expect it to mean exactly the same thing to you each time you return to it.

Themes or pieces need not express only one emotion, of course. Take such a theme as the first main one of the *Ninth Symphony*, for example. It is clearly made up of different elements. It does not say only one thing. Yet anyone hearing it immediately gets a feeling of strength, a feeling of power. It isn't a power that comes simply because the theme is played loudly. It is a power inherent in the theme itself. The extraordinary strength and vigor of the theme results in the listener's receiving an impression that a forceful statement has been made. But one should never try to boil it down to "the fateful hammer of life," etc. That is where the trouble begins. The musician, in his exasperation, says it means nothing but the notes themselves, whereas the nonprofessional is only too anxious to hang on to any explanation that gives him the illusion of getting closer to the music's meaning.

Now, perhaps, the reader will know better what I mean when I say that music does have an expressive meaning but that we cannot say in so many words what that meaning is.

The third plane on which music exists is the sheerly musical plane. Besides the pleasurable sound of music and the expressive feeling that it gives off, music does exist in terms of the notes themselves and of their manipulation. Most listeners are not sufficiently conscious of this third plane. . . .

Professional musicians, on the other hand, are, if anything, too conscious of the mere notes themselves. They often fall into the error of becoming so engrossed with their arpeggios and staccatos that they forget the deeper aspects of the music they are performing. But from the layman's standpoint, it is not so much a matter of getting over bad habits on the sheerly musical plane as of increasing one's awareness of what is going on, in so far as the notes are concerned.

When the man in the street listens to the "notes themselves" with any degree of concentration, he is most likely to make some mention of the melody. Either he hears a pretty melody or he does not, and he generally lets it go at that. Rhythm is likely to gain his attention next, particularly if it seems exciting. But harmony and tone color are generally taken for granted, if they are thought of consciously at all. As for music's having a definite form of some kind, that idea seems never to have occurred to him.

It is very important for all of us to become more alive to music on its sheerly musical plane. After all, an actual musical material is being used. The intelligent listener must be prepared to increase his awareness of the musical material and what happens to it. He must hear the melodies, the rhythms, the harmonies, the tone colors in a more conscious fashion. But above all he must, in order to follow the line of the composer's thought, know something of the principles of musical form. Listening to all of these elements is listening on the sheerly musical plane.

Let me repeat that I have split up mechanically the three separate planes on which we listen merely for the sake of greater clarity. Actually, we never listen on one or the other of these planes. What we do is to correlate them—listening in all three ways at the same time. It takes no mental effort, for we do it instinctively.

Perhaps an analogy with what happens to us when we visit the theater will make this instinctive correlation clearer. In the theater, you are aware of the actors and actresses, costumes and sets, sounds and movements. All these give one the sense that the theater is a pleasant place to be in. They constitute the sensuous plane in our theatrical reactions.

The expressive plane in the theater would be derived from the feeling that you get from what is happening on the stage. You are moved to pity, excitement, or gayety. It is this general feeling, generated aside from the particular words being spoken, a certain emotional something which exists on the stage, that is analogous to the expressive quality in music.

The plot and plot development is equivalent to our sheerly musical plane. The playwright creates and develops a character in just the same way that a composer creates and develops a theme. According to the degree of your awareness of the way in which the artist in either field handles his material will you become a more intelligent listener.

It is easy enough to see that the theatergoer never is conscious of any of these elements separately. He is aware of them all at the same time. The same is true of music listening. We simultaneously and without thinking listen on all three planes.

In a sense, the ideal listener is both inside and outside the music at the same moment, judging it and enjoying it, wishing it would go one way and watching it go another—almost like the composer at the moment he composes it; because in order to write his music, the composer must also be inside and outside his music, carried away by it and yet coldly critical of it. A subjective and objective attitude is implied in both creating and listening to music.

What the reader should strive for, then, is a more *active* kind of listening. Whether you listen to Mozart or Duke Ellington, you can deepen your understanding of music only by being a more conscious and aware listener—not someone who is just listening, but someone who is listening *for* something.

1957

Edward Rothstein

THE LINKS BETWEEN MATH AND MUSIC

Before setting out to make my way in the music business, I was in training to become a "pure" mathematician. Such esoteric subjects as "Algebraic Topology," "Measure Theory" and "Non-standard Analysis" were my preoccupations. I would stay up nights trying to solve knotty mathematical problems, playing with abstract phrases and structures. But at the same time, I would be lured away from these constructions by another activity. With an enthusiasm that could come only when critical faculties are in happy slumber, I would listen to or play a musical composition again and again, imprinting my ear and mind and hands with its logic and sense. Music and math together satisfied a sort of abstract "appetite," a desire that was partly intellectual, partly esthetic, partly emotional, partly, even, physical.

I offer these autobiographical facts only because they are not extraordinary among those who have been involved with these fields. Not only did I know other people tempted by both worlds, but, in various ways, music and mathematics have been associated throughout history.

Mathematicians and physicists of all epochs have felt such affinities. Galileo speculated on numerical reasons "why some combinations of tones are more pleasing than others." Euclid wondered about those combinations some two thousand years earlier. The eighteenth-century mathematician Leonhard Euler wrote a discourse on the relationship of consonance to whole numbers. Johannes Kepler believed the planets' revolutions literally created a "music of the spheres"—a sonic counterpart to his mathematical laws of planetary motion.

Musicians, on the other hand, have invoked mathematics to describe the orderliness of their art. Chopin said, "The fugue is like pure logic in music." Bach, the fugue's most eminent explorer, also had a predilection for its precise relative, the canon, which he often treated as a puzzle.

In this century, mathematical language has pervaded much musical thinking. Schoenberg's "serial" system for manipulating the scale's twelve tones has exercised enormous influence. Other composers have tried to systematize "duration," "timbre" and "volume." Following suit, contemporary musicologists invoke "set theory," "Markov chains" and other mathematical concepts. Journal articles detail attempts to decompose, perform and compose music using computer programs. Iannis Xenakis applies sophisticated mathematical theories in his compositions. Even John Cage, in his search for *lack* of order, uses computer generated random numbers for composing.

This contemporary use of mathematical concepts in music makes it all the more important that their connections be understood. Why, after all, should math and music be connected? Music is an art, mathematics a science. Music poses no problems, mathematics thrives on them. Music has no practical use, mathematics often does. Music is sensuous, mathematics abstract. Analogies may just be vague metaphor or trivial coincidence.

But fundamental musical elements can be analyzed numerically—as the ancient Greeks knew. Pythagoras, to whom fundamental mathematical discoveries are attributed, believed music to be the expression of number in sound. Aristotle said of the Pythagoreans, "They supposed the whole heaven to be a *harmonia* and a number."

The musical harmony of the Pythagoreans was constructed with the first four integers. Dividing a vibrating string in ratios formed by these numbers, they discovered, generated "pleasing" musical intervals. The ratio 1:2 yields an octave, 3:2 yields the fifth, and 4:3 the fourth.

In later Western music the interval of the fourth fell out of favor and the sixth was added, but the idea remained the same. The rules of counterpoint, which governed combinations of musical lines, restricted intervals to those formed by such simple ratios. The tonal harmonic system, so familiar to us from the music of the eighteenth- and nine-teenth-centuries, is also founded on these ratios, and upon "harmonics" —higher pitched tones created when any note is sounded. Musics of all cultures involve systematic organization of such ratios.

The numerical properties of sound have also been subject to more sophisticated analysis, using techniques developed by an eighteenth-century mathematician, Jean Baptiste Fourier, and, in our century, computer technology. "Digital" recordings, for example, involve exact translations of sound into number. Such precision has also permitted the synthesis and complex organizations of sound found in contemporary electronic music.

But such numerical properties of sound and the musical systems based on them do not say much about the *experience* of music. Few listeners care about integral ratios of string vibrations. Few listeners hear a twelve-tone series played backwards. Few listen to tonal music for the way harmonic "rules" are followed. Music is involved in more than mere combinatorial analysis. And mathematics is more than just a mechanical manipulation of abstract signs. The links between math and music are deeper and more profound.

In fact, if music displays a certain systematic "mathematical" character, there are corresponding "musical" qualities to mathematics, esthetic qualities that have been often described by its practitioners.

The mathematician G. H. Hardy wrote of the "harmonious" character of mathematics: "Beauty is the first test; there is no permanent place in the world for ugly mathematics." The mathematician Henri Poincaré also wrote about "the feeling of mathematical beauty, of the harmony of numbers, of forms, of geometric elegance."

This "harmony" is difficult to explain. But one ancient example of beauty that offers some clues to the esthetics of mathematics is the "golden ratio," considered by the Pythagoreans to be the most beautiful of proportions. The "golden rectangle," with sides in that ratio, has been linked with the proportions of the Parthenon in Athens and exercised fascination on Renaissance artists. In 1509, a book by Luca Pacioli called *De Divina Proportione* was illustrated by Leonardo da Vinci: the painter also used the ratio in his painting. Kepler invoked this "divine proportion" as well. Recently, *The Divine Proportion: A Study in Mathematical Beauty* by H. E. Huntley has attempted a mathematical and esthetic survey of the ratio.

The definition of this ratio is rather simple. A line is divided into a "golden section" when the ratio of its two parts is the same as the ratio between one part and the whole. The ratio, that is, reproduces itself within itself. The diagonals of a pentagon divide each other in this ratio; it appears in other geometrical configurations as well.

As a number, the ratio might seem unattractive (it is equal to $[\sqrt{5} - 1]/2$). But it can be rewritten in a quite remarkable way, as a fraction composed entirely of 1's layered in an infinite series. Seen in that way, the number becomes a sort of arithmetic "image" of the geometric property of the ratio—it is represented endlessly within itself. * * * For example, if a square formed by one side of a golden rectangle is cut off, a golden rectangle remains. If squares are continually removed, there is an infinite spiral of golden rectangles contained within each other.

But dramatically enough, if a curve is drawn based upon the golden rectangle, it is precisely the shape of a chambered nautilus shell. It is a "logarithmic" curve of "continuous growth." Any two segments of the curve are the same shape; they are just different sizes. As a snail grows, it produces shell material in the same formation, only in larger quantities. Similar curves lie in the center of a sunflower, in the shape of a fir cone and in other natural forms that contain the golden ratio.

The golden ratio provides some insight into the ways in which mathematics works in general. Nature might provide the original model for speculation about the ratio. From observation of a pine cone, a snail's shell, a sunflower, certain similarities are noted and an abstraction is made. This abstraction—a proportion, in this case—is itself studied, revealing other properties. Underlying principles are then recognized in different realms—the golden rectangle, the properties of number, the arts; related structures are found at the foundation of seemingly disparate systems. Mathematical thought processes, of course, are vastly more complex, but they are quite similar in essence.

Music also involves this type of analytical thinking. It too begins in the natural world—with physical laws and bodily rhythms. Music, like mathematics, then creates abstract systems, like tonality, for its activities. Within such a system, a musical "element," a theme, may be explored, transformed, revealed in different musical contexts. Its rhythm may be isolated. Its intervallic structure may be considered, its harmonic implications examined. When, for example, at the end of a Bach fugue, the theme enters in a cadence, it carries meanings it did not have when first heard. Like a mathematical object, that theme has been explored in various combinations; it has been inverted, expanded, viewed in differing contexts, dissected. A sort of musical knowledge has been achieved. There is a similar sense in Beethoven's piano sonatas that a concentrated exploration of musical elements is taking place before one's ears; when a theme returns in a recapitulation, it is no longer heard as it was in the beginning. In this manipulation of abstract material, which reveals new relations and structures, math and music may have their common formal ground.

But these processes in math and music also suggest an esthetic that has been central in the West and implicit in the golden ratio. This concept of beauty involves proportion between various elements and a relation between parts and whole—a reproduction of macrocosm in microcosm.

In music, to give an unusual example, Bartok's interest in such ideas was so strong that he literally reproduced the golden ratio in his compositions. In *Bela Bartok: An Analysis of his Music,* the Hungarian musicologist Erno Lendvai demonstrates that in Bartok's music, crucial musical events mark divisions and subdivisions of the work into golden sections. Bartok's unusual harmonic system, Mr. Lendvai argues, is also related to the golden ratio.

But even when parallels are less precise, music often involves a similar esthetic. The classical sonata had an organic character, with musical elements exfoliating into a drama. Heinrich Schenker, this century's most original musicologist, wrote about the "biological nature of form" in tonal music and demonstrated how properties of a single phrase are repeated throughout a work and shape its structure. Many composers of "advanced" serial music have had similar esthetic ambitions, working outside the tonal system.

The ideals of mathematics also, of course, include such coherence and proportion. But there is even an esthetic aspect to the *process* of mathematical activity. It is not simply a search for the "right" answers. There are "styles" of doing mathematics. A proof can have its own form, its own "tempo" in the way it introduces concepts or transforms interpretations or rhythmically follows set rules. Different methods can reveal different —and sometimes surprising—aspects of a problem, pointing out new relations and orders.

That sort of unexpected insight, to give a simple example, was demonstrated by the mathematician Gauss when he was seven years old. He was asked to give the sum of the numbers from 1 to 100. Instead of laboriously adding them he noticed that in grouping 1 and 100, 2 and 99, 3 and 98, 4 and 97, etc., each pair added to 101. The series from 1 to 100 could be ordered to create 50 such combinations. Thus, the sum of the numbers was 50×101. This reordering of the sum is a "beautiful" method—surprising, witty, powerful; it provides a glimpse into the universal properties of a series.

In great mathematics, Hardy wrote, "there is a very high degree of *unexpectedness*, combined with *inevitability* and *economy*."

Those are, of course, also the properties of great music. A more profound counterpart to Gauss's solution, for example, is in Beethoven's Diabelli Variations. Instead of customarily varying the banal waltz, the composer considers it in radically different lights. By focusing on an accent, perhaps, instead of on the melodic line, he reorders the music's priorities, revealing a new way of hearing familiar patterns. He transforms the waltz with surprise, wit and power while revealing general properties of musical structure.

What is *unexpected* about such music, and about similarly deep mathematical work, is its revelation—a new vision of the order of things. What is *inevitable*, is that, somehow, things could not have been any different; such work seems to make an irrefutable statement about the world.

But the unexpectedness and inevitability of such math and music are powerful because they are not merely formal; they ultimately reflect back to the real world. Music has a concrete emotional meaning, with the capacity to change a listener's feelings. Math also has a concrete meaning; the most abstract brain-spun explorations in mathematics have what one physicist called "unreasonable effectiveness" in describing the world. In such a reordered understanding of reality, which seems both surprising and necessary, may lie some qualities of beauty itself.

Stravinsky said that the musician should find in mathematics a study "as useful to him as the learning of another language is to a poet." Such knowledge carries the danger—as in much of the musical theory of the 1950's and 60's—of a false "scientism." But right now there seems to be a return to more fundamental questions in musico-mathematical discussion. Some computer researchers are systematically investigating how music is comprehended. In some strains of today's "avant-garde," mathematics is used in service of a sort of Pythagorean mysticism and applied to very basic properties of music. There have been experiments in vocal overtones, in tuning the piano to create perfect consonances, in extracting elemental characteristics from "natural" folk musics.

Whatever the particular styles of esthetics are, though, music and math are unmistakably linked. When I worked at learning a Beethoven Sonata while also trying to understand the Gödel Incompleteness Theorem, the affinity between these activities was evident. Both mathematics and music create languages that have compelling force in shaping understanding and feeling. Both are attempts to make sense of things, to shape esthetic universes that bear directly upon our own. John William Navin Sullivan—author of both a biography of Newton and a monograph on Beethoven—put it this way: "Mathematics, as much as music or any other art, is one of the means by which we rise to a complete self-consciousness."

Stravinsky, in discussing "the art of combination which is composition" quoted the mathematician Marston Morse: "Mathematics are the result of mysterious powers which no one understands, and in which the unconscious recognition of beauty must play an important part. Out of an infinity of designs a mathematician chooses one pattern for beauty's sake and pulls it down to earth." Morse, Stravinsky says, could as well have been talking about music. It is not only in the clarity of things, but in their beauty and mystery that the two arts join.

1982

Lord Clark

THE BLOT AND THE DIAGRAM

I have been told to "look down from a high place over the whole extensive landscape of modern art." We all know how tempting high places can be, and how dangerous. I usually avoid them myself. But if I must do as I am told, I shall try to find out why modern art has taken its peculiar form, and to guess how long that form will continue.

I shall begin with Leonardo da Vinci, because although all processes are gradual, he does represent one clearly marked turning point in the history of art. Before that time, the painter's intentions were quite simple; they were first of all to tell a story, secondly to make the invisible visible, and thirdly to turn a plain surface into a decorated surface. Those are all very ancient aims, going back to the earliest civilizations, or beyond; and for three hundred years painters had been instructed how to carry them out by means of a workshop tradition. Of course, there had

been breaks in that tradition—in the fourth century, maybe, and towards the end of the seventh century; but broadly speaking, the artist learnt what he could about the technique of art from his master in his workshop, and then set up shop on his own and tried to do better.

As is well known, Leonardo had a different view of art. He thought that it involved both science and the pursuit of some peculiar attribute called beauty or grace. He was, by inclination, a scientist: he wanted to find out how things worked, and he believed that this knowledge could be stated mathematically. He said "Let no one who is not a mathematician read my works," and he tried to relate this belief in measurement to his belief in beauty. This involved him in two rather different lines of thought, one concerned with magic—the magic of numbers—the other with science. Ever since Pythagoras had discovered that the musical scale could be stated mathematically, by means of the length of the strings, etc., and so had thrown a bridge between intellectual analysis and sensory perception, thinkers on art had felt that it should be possible to do the same for painting. I must say that their effort had not been very rewarding; the modulus, or golden section, and the logarithmic spiral[1] of shells are practically the only undisputed results. But Leonardo lived at a time when it was still possible to hope great things from perspective, which should not only define space, but order it harmoniously; and he also inherited a belief that ideal mathematical combinations could be derived from the proportions of the human body. This line of thought may be called the *mystique* of measurement. The other line may be called *the use* of measurement. Leonardo wished to state mathematically various facts related to the act of seeing. How do we see light passing over a sphere? What happens when objects make themselves perceptible on our retina? Both these lines of thought involved him in drawing diagrams and taking measurements, and for this reason were closely related in his mind. No painter except perhaps Piero della Francesca has tried more strenuously to find a mathematical statement of art, nor has had a greater equipment for doing so.

But Leonardo was also a man of powerful and disturbing imagination. In his notebooks, side by side with his attempts to achieve *order* by mathematics, are drawings and descriptions of the most violent scenes of *disorder* which the human mind can conceive—battles, deluges, eruptions. And he included in his treatise on painting advice on how to develop this side of the artistic faculty also. The passages in which he does so have often been quoted, but they are so incredibly foreign to the whole Renaissance idea of art, although related to a remark in Pliny,[2] that

1. A curve that cuts all its radii at the same angle (the mathematical expression of the shape of snail shells); *golden section:* the division of a line such that the ratio of the smaller to the larger part is the same as that of the larger part to the whole; long regarded as a key to artistic proportion.
2. Roman author of the first century A.D., whose comprehensive *Natural History* included a history of painting.

each time I read them, they give me a fresh surprise. I will, therefore, quote them again.

> I shall not refrain from including among these precepts a new and specula-
> tive idea, which although it may seem trivial and almost laughable, is none
> the less of great value in quickening the spirit of invention. It is this: that you
> should look at certain walls stained with damp or at stones of uneven color. If
> you have to invent some setting you will be able to see in these the likeness of
> divine landscapes, adorned with mountains, ruins, rocks, woods, great plains,
> hills and valleys in great variety; and then again you will see there battles and
> strange figures in violent action, expressions of faces and clothes and an
> infinity of things which you will be able to reduce to their complete and
> proper forms. In such walls the same thing happens as in the sound of bells, in
> whose strokes you may find every named word which you can imagine.

Later he repeats this suggestion in slightly different form, advising the painter to study not only marks on walls, but also "the embers of the fire, or clouds or mud, or other similar objects from which you will find most admirable ideas ... because from a confusion of shapes the spirit is quickened to new inventions."

I hardly need to insist on how relevant these passages are to modern painting. Almost every morning I receive cards inviting me to current exhibitions, and on the cards are photographs of the works exhibited. Some of them consist of blots, some of scrawls, some look like clouds, some like embers of the fire, some are like mud—some of them are mud; a great many look like stains on walls, and one of them, I remember, consisted of actual stains on walls, photographed and framed. Leonardo's famous passage has been illustrated in every particular. And yet I doubt if he would have been satisfied with the results, because he believed that we must somehow unite the two opposite poles of our faculties. Art itself was the connection between the diagram and the blot.

Now in order to prevent the impression that I am taking advantage of a metaphor, as writers on art are often bound to do, I should explain how I am going to use these words. By "diagram" I mean a rational statement in a visible form, involving measurements, and usually done with an ulterior motive. The theorem of Pythagoras is proved by a diagram. Leonardo's drawings of light striking a sphere are diagrams; but the works of Mondrian, although made up of straight lines, are not diagrams, because they are not done in order to prove or measure some experience, but to please the eye. That they look like diagrams is due to influences which I will examine later. But diagrams can exist with no motive other than their own perfection, just as mathematical propositions can.

By "blots" I mean marks or areas which are not intended to convey information, but which, for some reason, seem pleasant and memorable to the maker, and can be accepted in the same sense by the spectator. I said that these blots were not intended to convey information, but of

course they do, and that of two kinds. First, they tell us through association, about things we had forgotten; that was the function of Leonardo's
stains on walls, which as he said, quickened the spirit of invention, and it
can be the function of man-made blots as well; and secondly a man-made
blot will tell us about the artist. Unless it is made entirely accidentally, as
by spilling an inkpot, it will be a commitment. It is quite difficult to make
a noncommittal blot. Although the two are connected, I think we can
distinguish between analogy blots and gesture blots.

Now let me try to apply this to modern art. Modern art is not a subject
on which one can hope for a large measure of agreement, but I hope I may
be allowed two assumptions. The first is that the kind of painting and
architecture which we call, with varying inflections of the voice, "modern," is a true and vital expression of our own day; and the second
assumption is that it differs radically from any art which has preceded it.
Both these assumptions have been questioned. It has been said that
modern art is "a racket" engineered by art dealers, who have exploited
the incompetence of artists and the gullibility of patrons, that the whole
thing is a kind of vast and very expensive practical joke. Well, fifty years
is a long time to keep up a hoax of this kind, and during these years
modern art has spread all over the free world and created a complete
international style. I don't think that any honest-minded historian,
whether he liked it or not, could pretend that modern art was the result of
an accident or a conspiracy. The only doubt he could have would be
whether it is, so to say, a long-term or a short-term movement. In the
history of art there are stylistic changes which appear to develop from
purely internal causes, and seem almost accidental in relation to the other
circumstances of life and society. Such, for example, was the state of art in
Italy (outside Venice) from about 1530 to 1600. When all is said about the
religious disturbances of the time, the real cause of the Mannerist style[3]
was the domination of Michelangelo, who had both created an irresistible style and exhausted its possibilities. It needed the almost equally
powerful pictorial imagination of Caravaggio to produce a counter-infec-
tion, which could spread from Rome to Spain and the Netherlands and
prepare the way for Rembrandt. I can see nothing in the history of man's
spirit to account for this episode. It seems to me to be due to an internal
and specifically artistic chain of events which are easily related to one
another, and comprehensible within the general framework of European
art. On the other hand, there are events in the history of art which go far
beyond the interaction of styles and which evidently reflect a change in
the whole condition of the human spirit. Such an event took place
towards the end of the fifth century, when the Hellenistic-Roman style
gradually became what we call Byzantine; and again in the early thir-

3. A late sixteenth-century style characterized by spatial distortion and elongation of the
human figure.

teenth century, when the Gothic cathedrals shot up out of the ground. In each case the historian could produce a series of examples to prove that the change was inevitable. But actually, it was nothing of the sort; it was wholly unpredictable; and was part of a complete spiritual revolution.

Whether we think that modern art represents a transformation of style or a change of spirit depends to some extent on my second assumption, that it differs radically from anything which has preceded it. This too has been questioned; it has been said that Léger is only a logical development of Poussin, or Mondrian of Vermeer.[4] And it is true that the element of design in each has something in common. If we pare a Poussin down to its bare bones, there are combinations of curves and cubes which are the foundations of much classical painting, and Léger had the good sense to make use of them. Similarly, in Vermeer there is a use of rectangles, large areas contrasted with very narrow ones, and a feeling for shallow recessions, which became the preferred theme of Mondrian. But such analogies are trifling compared with the differences. Poussin was a very intelligent man who thought deeply about his art, and if anyone had suggested to him that his pictures were praiseworthy solely on account of their construction, he would have been incredulous and affronted.

So let us agree that the kind of painting and architecture which we find most representative of our times—say, the painting of Jackson Pollock and the architecture of the Lever building[5]—is deeply different from the painting and architecture of the past; and is *not* a mere whim of fashion, but the result of a great change in our ways of thinking and feeling.

How did this great change take place and what does it mean? To begin with, I think it is related to the development upon which all industrial civilization depends, the differentiation of function. Leonardo was exceptional, almost unique in his integration of functions—the scientific and the imaginative. Yet he foreshadowed more than any other artist their disintegration, by noting and treating in isolation the diagrammatic faculty and the blot-making faculty. The average artist took the unity of these faculties for granted. They were united in Leonardo, and in lesser artists, by *interest or pleasure in the thing seen*. The external object was like a magnetic pole which drew the two faculties together. At some point the external object became a negative rather than a positive charge. Instead of drawing together the two faculties, it completely dissociated them; architecture went off in one direction witht he diagram, painting went in the other direction with the blot.

This disintegration was related to a radical change in the philosophy of

4. Léger and Mondrian: French and Dutch modern painters, respectively. Poussin, French, and Vermeer, Dutch, were both seventeenth-century painters.
5. A severely simple office building in New York City, built in the early 1950s, with plain rectangular sides of glass supported by a stainless-steel framework; *Jackson Pollock:* contemporary who in his "action painting" made frequent use of dribbled or spattered pigments.

art. We all know that such changes, however harmless they sound when first enunciated, can have drastic consequences in the world of action. Rulers who wish to maintain the *status quo* are well advised to chop off the heads of all philosophers. What Hilaire Belloc called the "remote and ineffectual don" is more dangerous than the busy columnist with his eye on the day's news. The revolution in our ideas about the nature of painting seems to have been hatched by a don who was considered remote and ineffectual even by Oxford standards—Walter Pater. It was he (inspired, I believe, by Schopenhauer) who first propounded the idea of the aesthetic sensation, intuitively perceived.

> In its primary aspect [Pater said] a great picture has no more difficult message for us than an accidental play of sunlight and shadow for a few moments on the wall or floor; in itself, in truth, a space of such fallen light, caught, as in the colors of an Eastern carpet, but refined upon and dealt with more subtly and exquisitely than by nature itself.

It is true that his comparison with an Eastern carpet admits the possibility of "pleasant sensations" being arranged or organized; and Pater confirms this need for organization a few lines later, when he sets down his famous dictum that "all art constantly aspires towards the condition of music." He does not believe in blots uncontrolled by the conscious mind. But he is very far from the information-giving diagram.

This belief that art has its origin in our intuitive rather than our rational faculties, picturesquely asserted by Pater, was worked out historically and philosophically, in the somewhat wearisome volumes of Benedetto Croce, and owing to his authoritative tone, he is usually considered the originator of a new theory of aesthetics. It was, in fact, the reversion to a very old idea. Long before the Romantics had stressed the importance of intuition and self-expression, men had admitted the Dionysiac nature of art. But philosophers had always assumed that the frenzy of inspiration must be controlled by law and by the intellectual power of putting things into harmonious order. And this general philosophic concept of art as a combination of intuition and intellect had been supported by technical necessities. It was necessary to master certain laws and to use the intellect in order to build the Gothic cathedrals, or set up the stained glass windows of Chartres or cast the bronze doors of the Florence Baptistry. When this bracing element of craftsmanship ceased to dominate the artist's outlook, as happened soon after the time of Leonardo, new scientific disciplines had to be invented to maintain the intellectual element in art. Such were perspective and anatomy. From a purely artistic point of view, they were unnecessary. The Chinese produced some of the finest landscapes ever painted, without any systematic knowledge of perspective. Greek figure sculpture reached its highest point before the study of anatomy had been systematized. But from the Renaissance onwards, painters felt that these two sciences made their art intellectually respectable. They were two ways of connecting the diagram and the blot.

In the nineteenth century, belief in art as a scientific activity declined, for a quantity of reasons. Science and technology withdrew into specialization. Voltaire's efforts to investigate the nature of heat seem to us ludicrous; Goethe's studies of botany and physics a waste of a great poet's time. In spite of their belief in inspiration, the great Romantics were aware of the impoverishment of the imagination which would take place when science had drifted out of reach, and both Shelley and Coleridge spent much time in chemical experiments. Even Turner, whose letters reveal a singular lack of analytic faculty, annotated Goethe's theories of color, and painted two pictures to demonstrate them. No good. The laws which govern the movement of the human spirit are inexorable. The enveloping assumption, within which the artist has to function, was that science was no longer approachable by any but the specialist. And gradually there grew up the idea that all intellectual activities were hostile to art.

I have mentioned the philosophic development of this view of Croce. Let me give one example of its quiet acceptance by the official mind. The British Council sends all over the world, even to Florence and Rome, exhibitions of children's art—the point of these children's pictures being that they have no instruction of any kind, and do not attempt the troublesome task of painting what they see. Well, why not, after all? The results are quite agreeable—sometimes strangely beautiful; and the therapeutic effect on the children is said to be excellent. It is like one of those small harmless heresies which we are shocked to find were the object of persecution by the Mediaeval Church. When, however, we hear admired modern painters saying that they draw their inspiration from the drawings of children and lunatics, as well as from stains on walls, we recognize that we have accomplices in a revolution.

The lawless and intuitive character of modern art is a familiar theme and certain historians have said that it is symptomatic of a decline in Western civilization. This is journalism—one of those statements that sound well to-day and nonsense to-morrow. It is obvious that the development of physical science in the last hundred years has been one of the most colossal efforts the human intellect has ever made. But I think it is also true that human beings can produce, in a given epoch, only a certain amount of creative energy, and that this is directed to different ends and different times—music in the eighteenth century is the obvious example; and I believe that the dazzling achievements of science during the last seventy years have deflected far more of those skills and endowments which go to the making of a work of art than is usually realized. To begin with, there is the sheer energy. In every molding of a Renaissance palace we are conscious of an immense intellectual energy, and it is the absence of this energy in the nineteenth-century copies of Renaissance buildings which makes them seem so dead. To find a form with the same vitality as a window molding of the Palazzo Farnese I must wait till I get back into an aeroplane, and look at the relation of the engine to the wing. That form is alive, not (as used to be said) because it is functional—many functional shapes are entirely uninteresting—but because it is animated by the breath of modern science.

The deflections from art to science are the more serious because these are not, as used to be supposed, two contrary activities, but in fact draw on many of the same capacities of the human mind. In the last resort each depends on the imagination. Artist and scientist alike are both trying to give concrete form to dimly apprehended ideas. Dr. Bronowski has put it very well: "All science is the search for unity in hidden likenesses, and the starting point is an image, because then the unity is before our mind's eye." Even if we no longer have to pretend that a group of stars looks like a plough or a bear, our scientists still depend on humanly comprehensible images, and it is striking that the valid symbols of our time, invented to embody some scientific truth, have taken root in the popular imagination. Do those red and blue balls connected by rods really resemble a type of atomic structure? I am too ignorant to say. I accept the symbol just as an early Christian accepted the Fish or the Lamb, and I find it echoed or even (it would seem) anticipated in the work of modern artists like Kandinsky and Miró.

Finally, there is the question of popular interest and approval. We have grown accustomed to the idea that artists can work in solitude and incomprehension; but that was not the way things happened in the Renaissance or the seventeenth century, still less in ancient Greece. The pictures carried through the streets by cheering crowds, the Te Deum sung on completion of a public building—all this indicates a state of opinion in which men could undertake great works of art with a confidence quite impossible to-day. The research scientist, on the other hand, not only has millions of pounds worth of plant and equipment for the asking, he has principalities and powers waiting for his conclusions. He goes to work, as Titian once did, confident that he will succeed because the strong tide of popular admiration is flowing with him.

But although science has absorbed so many of the functions of art and deflected (I believe) so many potential artists, it obviously cannot be a substitute for art. Its mental process may be similar, but its ends are different. There have been three views about the purpose of art. First that it aims simply at imitation; secondly that it should influence human conduct; and thirdly that it should produce a kind of exalted happiness. The first view, which was developed in ancient Greece, must be reckoned one of the outstanding failures of Greek thought. It is simply contrary to experience, because if the visual arts aimed solely at imitating things they would be of very little importance; whereas the Greeks above all people knew that they were important, and treated them as such. Yet such was the prestige of Greek thought that this theory of art was revived in the Renaissance, in an uncomfortable sort of way, and had a remarkable recrudescence in the nineteenth century. The second view, that art should influence conduct and opinions, is more respectable, and held the field throughout the Middle Ages; indeed the more we learn about the art of the past and motives of those who commissioned it, the more important this particular aim appears to be; it still dominated art theory in the time of Diderot[6]. The third view, that art should produce a kind of exalted happiness, was invented by the Romantics at the beginning of the nineteenth century (well, perhaps *invented* by Plotinus,[7] but given currency by the Romantics), and gradually gained ground until by the end of the century it was believed in by almost all educated people. It has held the field in Western Europe till the present day. Leaving aside the question which of these theories is correct, let me ask which of them is most likely to be a helpful background to art (for that is all that a theory of aesthetics can be) in an age when science has such an overwhelming domination over the human mind. The first aim must be reckoned *by itself* to be pointless, since science has now discovered so many ways of imitating appearances, which are incomparably more accurate and convincing than even the most realistic picture. Painting might defend itself against the daguerreotype, but not against Cinerama.

The popular application of science has also, it seems to me, invalidated the second aim of art, because it is quite obvious that no picture can influence human conduct as effectively as a television advertisement. It is quite true that in totalitarian countries artists are still instructed to influence conduct. But that is either due to technical deficiencies, as in China, where in default of T.V., broadsheets and posters are an important way of communicating with an illiterate population; or, in Russia, to a philosophic time-lag. The fact is that very few countries have had the courage to take Plato's advice and exclude works of art altogether. They have, therefore, had to invent some excuse for keeping them on, and the Russians are still using the pretext that paintings and sculpture can influence people in favor of socialist and national policies, although it must have dawned on them that these results can be obtained far more effectively by the cinema and television.

So it seems to me that of these three possible purposes of art—imitation, persuasion, or exalted pleasure—only the third still holds good in an age of science; and it must be justified very largely by the fact that it is a feeling which is absent from scientific achievements—although mathematicians have told us that it is similar to the feeling aroused by their

6. Near the end of the eighteenth century.
7. Roman philosopher of the third century A.D.

finest calculations. We might say that in the modern world the art of painting is defensible only in so far as it is complementary to science.

We are propelled in the same direction by another achievement of modern science, the study of psychology. That peeling away of the psyche, which was formerly confined to spiritual instructors, or the great novelists, has become a commonplace of conversation. When a good, solid, external word like Duty is turned into a vague, uneasy, internal word like Guilt, one cannot expect artists to take much interest in good, solid, external objects. The artist has always been involved in the painful process of turning himself inside out, but in the past his inner convictions have been of such a kind that they can, so to say, re-form themselves round an object. But, as we have seen, even in Leonardo's time, there were certain obscure needs and patterns of the spirit, which could discover themselves only through less precise analogies—the analogies provided by stains on walls or the embers of a fire. Now, I think that in this inward-looking age, when we have become so much more aware of the vagaries of the spirit, and so respectful of the working of the unconscious, the artist is more likely to find his point of departure in analogies of this kind. They are more exciting because they, so to say, take us by surprise, like forgotten smells; and they seem to be more profound because the memories they awaken have been deeply buried in our minds. Whether Jung is right in believing that this free, undirected, illogical form of mental activity will allow us to pick up, like a magic radio station, some deep memories of our race which can be of universal interest, I do not know. The satisfaction we derive from certain combinations of shape and color does seem to be inexplicable even by the remotest analogies, and may perhaps involve inherited memories. It is not yet time for the art-historian to venture in to that mysterious jungle. I must, however, observe that our respect for the unconscious mind not only gives us an interest in analogy blots, but in what I called "gesture blots" as well. We recognize how free and forceful such a communication can be, and this aspect of art has become more important in the last ten years. An apologist of modern art has said: "What we want to know is not what the world looks like, but what we mean to each other." So the gesture blot becomes a sort of ideogram, like primitive Chinese writing. Students of Zen assure us it is a means of communication more direct and complete than anything which our analytic system can achieve. Almost 2,000 years before Leonardo looked for images in blots, Lao-tzu had written:

> The Tao is something blurred and indistinct.
> How indistinct! How blurred!
> Yet within are images,
> How blurred! How indistinct!
> Yet within are things.

I said that when the split took place between our faculties of measurement and intuition, *architecture* went off with the diagram. Of course architecture had always been involved with measurement and calculation, but we tend to forget how greatly it was also involved with the imitation of external objects. "The question to be determined," said Ruskin, "is whether architecture is a frame for the sculpture, or the sculpture an ornament of the architecture." And he came down on the first alternative. He thought that a building became architecture only in so far as it was a frame for figurative sculpture. I wonder if there is a single person alive who would agree with him. And yet Ruskin had the most sensitive eye and the keenest analytic faculty that has ever been applied to architecture. Many people disagreed with him in his own day; they thought that sculpture should be subordinate to the total design of the building. But that anything claiming to be architecture could dispense with ornament altogether never entered anyone's head till a relatively short time ago.

A purely diagrammatic architecture is only about thirty years older than a purely blottesque painting; yet it has changed the face of the world and produced in every big city a growing uniformity. Perhaps because it is a little older, perhaps because it seems to have a material justification, we have come to accept it without question. People who are still puzzled or affronted by action painting are proud of the great steel and glass boxes which have arisen so miraculously in the last ten years. And yet these two are manifestations of the same state of mind. The same difficulties of function, the same deflection from the external object, and the same triumph of science. Abstract painting and glass box architecture are related in two different ways. There is the direct relationship of style —the kind of relationship which painting and architecture had with one another in the great consistent ages of art like the 13th and 17th centuries. For modern architecture is not simply functional; at its best it has a style which is almost as definite and as arbitrary as Gothic. And this leads me back to my earlier point: that diagrams can be drawn in order to achieve some imagined perfection, similar to that of certain mathematical propositions. Thirty years after Pater's famous dictum, painters in Russia, Holland, and France began to put into practice the theory that "all art constantly aspires to the condition of music"; and curiously enough this Pythagorean mystique of measurements produced a style —the style which reached its purest expression in the Dutch painter, Mondrian. And through the influence of the Bauhaus,[8] this became the leading style of modern architecture.

The other relationship between contemporary architecture and painting appears to be indirect and even accidental. I am thinking of the visual

8. Architectural school founded in Germany in 1919, known for its applications of technology to art.

impact when the whole upper part of a tall glass building mirrors the clouds or the dying embers of a sunset, and so becomes a frame for a marvelous, moving Tachiste[9] picture. I do not think that future historians of art will find this accidental at all, but will see it as the culmination of a long process beginning in the Romantic period, in which, from Wordsworth and De Quincey onwards, poets and philosophers recognized the movement of clouds as the symbol of a newly discovered mental faculty.

Such, then, would be my diagnosis of the present condition of art. I must now, by special request, say what I think will happen to art in the future. I think that the state of affairs which I have called the blot and the diagram will last for a long time. Architecture will continue to be made up of glass boxes and steel grids, without ornament of any kind. Painting will continue to be subjective and arcane, an art of accident rather than rule, of stains on walls rather than of calculation, of inscape rather than of external reality.

This conclusion is rejected by those who believe in a social theory of art. They maintain that a living art must depend on the popular will, and that neither the blot nor the diagram is popular; and, since those who hold a social theory of art are usually Marxists, they point to Soviet Russia as a country where all my conditions obtain—differentiation of function, the domination of science and so forth—and yet what we call modern art has gained no hold. This argument does not impress me. There is of course, nothing at all in the idea that Communist doctrines inevitably produce social realism. Painting in Yugoslavia, in Poland and Hungary is in the same modern idiom as painting in the United States, and shows remarkable vitality. Whereas the official social realism of the U.S.S.R., except for a few illustrators, lacks life or conviction, and shows no evidence of representing the popular will. In fact Russian architecture has already dropped the grandiose official style, and I am told that this is now taking place in painting also. In spite of disapproval amounting to persecution, experimental painters exist and find buyers.

I doubt if the Marxists are even correct in saying that the blot and the diagram are not popular. The power, size, and splendor of, say, the Seagram building in New York makes it as much the object of pride and wonder as great architecture was in the past. And one of the remarkable things about Tachisme is the speed with which it has spread throughout the world, not only in sophisticated centers, but in small local art societies. It has become as much an international style as Gothic in the 14th and Baroque in the 17th centuries. I recently visited the exhibition of a provincial academy in the north of England, a very respectable body then celebrating its hundred and fiftieth anniversary. A few years ago it had

9. A method of nonrepresentational contemporary painting which exploits the quality of freely flowing oil paint for its own sake.

been full of Welsh mountain landscapes, and scenes of streets and harbors, carefully delineated. Now practically every picture was in the Tachiste style, and I found that many of them were painted by the same artists, often quite elderly people, who had previously painted the mountains and streets. As works of art, they seemed to me neither better nor worse. But I could not help thinking that they must have been less trouble to do, and I reflected that the painters must have had a happy time releasing the Dionysiac elements in their natures. However, we must not be too cynical about this. I do not believe that the spread of action painting is due solely to the fact that it is easy to do. Cubism,[1] especially synthetic Cubism, also looks easy to do, and never had this immense diffusion. It remained the style of a small élite of professional painters and specialized art lovers; whereas Tachisme has spread to fabrics, to the decoration of public buildings, to the backgrounds of television programs, to advertising of all kinds. Indeed the closest analogy to action painting is the most popular art of all—the art of jazz. The trumpeter who rises from his seat as one possessed, and squirts out his melody like a scarlet scrawl against a background of plangent dashes and dots, is not as a rule performing for a small body of intellectuals.

Nevertheless, I do not think that the style of the blot and the diagram will last forever. For one thing, I believe that the imitation of external reality is a fundamental human instinct which is bound to reassert itself. In his admirable book on sculpture called *Aratra Pentelici*, Ruskin describes an experience which many of us could confirm. "Having been always desirous," he says,

> that the education of women should begin in learning how to cook, I got leave, one day, for a little girl of eleven years old to exchange, much to her satisfaction, her schoolroom for the kitchen. But as ill fortune would have it, there was some pastry toward, and she was left unadvisedly in command of some delicately rolled paste; whereof she made no pies, but an unlimited quantity of cats and mice. . . .
>
> Now [he continues] you may read the works of the gravest critics of art from end to end; but you will find, at last, they can give you no other true account of the spirit of sculpture than that it is an irresistible human instinct for the making of cats and mice, and other imitable living creatures, in such permanent form that one may play with the images at leisure.

I cannot help feeling that he was right. I am fond of works of art, and I collect them. But I do not want to hang them on the wall simply in order to get an electric shock every time that I pass them. I want to hold them, and turn them round and re-hang them—in short, to play with the images at leisure. And, putting aside what may be no more than a personal prejudice, I rather doubt if an art which depends solely on the first impact

1. School of modern art emphasizing abstract geometric forms rather than realistic representation.

on our emotions is permanently valid. When the shock is exhausted, we have nothing to occupy our minds. And this is particularly troublesome with an art which depends so much on the unconscious, because, as we know from the analysis of dreams, the furniture of our unconscious minds is even more limited, repetitive, and commonplace than that of our conscious minds. The blots and stains of modern painting depend ultimately on the memories of things seen, memories sunk deep in the unconscious, overlaid, transformed, assimilated to a physical condition, but memories none the less. *Ex nihilo nihil fit.*[2] *It is not possible for a painter to lose contact with the visible world.*

At this point the apes have provided valuable evidence. There is no doubt that they are Tachiste painters of considerable accomplishment. I do not myself care for the work of Congo the chimp, but Sophie, the Rotterdam gorilla, is a charming artist, whose delicate traceries remind me of early Paul Klee. As you know, apes take their painting seriously. The patterns they produce are not the result of mere accident, but of intense, if short-lived, concentration, and a lively sense of balance and space-filling. If you compare the painting of a young ape with that of a human child of relatively the same age, you will find that in the first, expressive, pattern-making stage, the ape is superior. Then, automatically and inexorably the child begins to draw *things*—man, house, truck, etc. This the ape never does. Of course his Tachiste paintings are far more attractive than the child's crude conceptual outlines. But they cannot develop. They are monotonous and ultimately rather depressing.

The difference between the child and the ape does not show itself in aesthetic perception, or in physical perception of any kind, but in the child's power to form a concept. Later, as we know, he will spend his time trying to adapt his concept to the evidence of physical sensation; in that struggle lies the whole of style. But the concept—the need to draw a line round his thought—comes first. Now it is a truism that the power to form concepts is what distinguishes man from the animals; although the prophets of modern society, Freud, Jung, D. H. Lawrence, have rightly insisted on the importance of animal perceptions in balanced human personality, the concept-forming faculty has not declined in modern man. On the contrary, it is the basis of that vast scientific achievement which, as I said earlier, seems almost to have put art out of business.

Now, if the desire to represent external reality depended solely on an interest in visual sensation, I would agree that it might disappear from art and never return. But if, as the evidence of children and monkeys indicates, it depends primarily on the formation of concepts, which are then modified by visual sensation, I think it is bound to return. For I consider the human faculty of forming concepts at least as "inalienable" as "life, liberty, and the pursuit of happiness. . . ."

2. "Nothing is made from nothing."

I am not, of course, suggesting that the imitation of external reality will ever again become what it was in European art from the mid-17th to the late 19th centuries. Such a subordination of the concept to the visual sensation was altogether exceptional in the history of art. Much of the territory won by modern painting will, I believe, be held. For example, freedom of association, the immediate passage from one association to another—which is so much a part of Picasso's painting and Henry Moore's sculpture, is something which has existed in music since Wagner and in poetry since Rimbaud and Mallarmé. (I mean existed consciously; of course it underlies all great poetry and music.) It need not be sacrificed in a return to external reality. Nor need the direct communication of intuition, through touch and an instinctive sense of materials. This I consider pure gain. In the words of my original metaphor, both the association blot and the gesture blot can remain. But they must be given more nourishment: they must be related to a fuller knowledge of the forms and structures which impress us most powerfully, and so become part of our concept of natural order. At the end of the passage in which Leonardo tells the painter that he can look for battles, landscapes, and animals in the stains on walls, he adds this caution, "But first be sure that you know all the members of all things you wish to depict, both the members of the animals and the members of landscapes, that is to say of rocks, plants, and so forth." It is because one feels in Henry Moore's sculpture this knowledge of the members of animals and plants, that his work, even at its most abstract, makes an impression on us different from that of his imitators. His figures are not merely pleasing examples of design, but seem to be a part of nature, "rolled round in Earth's diurnal course with rocks and stones and trees."

Those lines of Wordsworth lead me to the last reason why I feel that the intuitive blot and scribble may not dominate painting forever. Our belief in the whole purpose of art may change. I said earlier that we now believe it should aim at producing a kind of exalted happiness: this really means that art becomes an end in itself. Now it is an incontrovertible fact of history that the greatest art has always been *about* something, a means of communicating some truth which is assumed to be more important than the art itself. The truths which art has been able to communicate have been of a kind which could not be put in any other way. They have been ultimate truths, stated symbolically. Science has achieved its triumph precisely by disregarding such truths, by not asking unanswerable questions, but sticking to the question "how." I confess it looks to me as if we shall have to wait a long time before there is some new belief which requires expression through art rather than through statistics or equations. And until this happens, the visual arts will fall short of the greatest epochs, the ages of the Parthenon, the Sistine Ceiling, and Chartres Cathedral.

I am afraid there is nothing we can do about it. No amount of goodwill and no expenditure of money can affect that sort of change. We cannot even dimly foresee when it will happen or what form it will take. We can only be thankful for what we have got—a vigorous, popular, decorative art, complementary to our architecture and our science, somewhat monotonous, somewhat prone to charlatanism, but genuinely expressive of our time.

1963

QUESTIONS

1. *What definition does Clark give of his central metaphor, "the blot and the diagram"? Are "blot" and "diagram" the equivalents of "art" and "science"? Explain.*
2. *What distinction does Clark make between "analogy (or association) blot" and "gesture blot"? What importance does the distinction have for his discussion of modern painting?*
3. *In what ways, according to Clark, is the place of science in the modern world similar to the place occupied by science in the past? What past functions of art has science assumed? To what extent does Clark consider the situation satisfactory? What defects does he mention?*
4. *How does Clark show "blot" painting and "diagram" architecture to be related? Is architecture today an art or a science? How scientific is painting?*
5. *Clark points out that "the closest analogy to action painting is the most popular art of all—the art of jazz" (p. 1082). Is there any jazz analogous to "diagram"? Explain.*
6. *Study closely some examples of advertising layout. To what extent do they appear influenced by "blot"? Is there influence of "diagram" in any? Are any exemplary of "blot" and "diagram" in harmony?*
7. *What extensions into other disciplines can be made of Clark's blot-diagram antithesis? Does it apply in literature? In psychology?*
8. *Why, according to Clark, will man's concept-forming nature eventually bring about a change of style in art?*

Joseph Wood Krutch

MODERN PAINTING

I am, I hope, not insensitive to any of the arts. I have spent happy hours in museums, and I listen with pleasure to Bach, Mozart, and Beethoven. But I have more confidence in my ability to understand what is said in words than I have in my understanding of anything that dispenses with them. Such opinions as I hold concerning modern music or modern painting are as tentative as those I once expressed about modern architecture.

Nevertheless, as I said on that occasion, it is one of the privileges of the essayist to hold forth on subjects he doesn't know much about. Because he does not pretend to any expertness, those who know better than he what he is talking about need be no more than mildly exasperated. His misconceptions may give valuable hints to those who would set him right. If he didn't expose his obtuseness, his would-be mentors wouldn't know so well just what the misconceptions are and how they arose. An honest philistinism is easier to educate than the conscious or unconscious hypocrisy of those who admire whatever they are told that they should.

In the case of modern painting, the very fact that I can take pleasure in some of the works of yesterday's *avant-garde* but little in that of my own day suggests, even to me, that I may be merely the victim of a cultural lag. But there is no use in pretending that I am delighted by what delights me not, and I find that much serious criticism of the most recent painting is no help. Those who write it are talking over my head; they just don't start far enough back.

For instance, I read in the *Nation* that what a certain painter I had never heard of had accomplished during the war might be summarized as "an unstructured painterliness—neither expressionist nor surrealist in character, and therefore out of keeping with available alternatives." Shortly after the war "he followed through with an intimation of the picture facade as its own reason for being, preferring a unitary sensation, by being irregularly blotted out by masses that kept on pushing at, and disappearing past, the perimeters. Executed on a vastness of scale quite unprecedented in easel painting (which he was in any event attacking), these paintings sidestep drawing and the illusion of spatial recession without ever giving the impression of evasiveness. The result was a sense of the picture surface—now extraordinarily flattened—as a kind of wall whereby constricted elements no longer had any exclusive formal relationship with one another."

When I read things like that my first impulse is to exclaim, "If that

young man expresses himself in terms too deep for me . . ."[1] But then I
realize the possibility that the words do say something to those whose
visual perceptions are better trained than mine. I am at best a second
grader, still struggling with the multiplication table, who has wandered
into a seminar at the Institute for Advanced Studies.

When, therefore, I happened to see an advertisement of the Book-of-
the-Month Club explaining that the Metropolitan Museum of Art had
been persuaded to prepare a twelve-part seminar on art, which could be
subscribed to for "only $60," I had the feeling that this might very well be
getting down to my level. The advertisement was adorned by reproduc-
tions of two contrasting pictures: one of the Metropolitan's own "Storm"
(or "Paul and Virginia") by Pierre Cot, and the other of a swirling
abstraction. "Which of these is a good painting?" demanded the head-
line. My immediate answer "Neither." And I was not too much discouraged by the fact that I was pretty sure this was not the right answer.

I think I know at least some of the reasons why "The Storm" is not one
of the great masterpieces—even though some supposedly competent
expert must have once paid a whopping price for it. On the other hand, I
had not the slightest idea why the abstraction was good or even just not
quite as bad as the supposedly horrid example facing it.

I confess that I did not subscribe to the seminars. But I did borrow a set
from an acquaintance who had done so, and I must report that I did
understand what the Metropolitan people were saying as I had not
understood the *Nation* critic. But I was not by any means wholly convinced. Many years ago I read Roger Fry on "Significant Form" and the
terrible-tempered Albert Barnes on *The Art in Painting*. I found nothing
in the Metropolitan seminar that was not this doctrine somewhat up-
dated, and I was no more convinced than I had been by the earlier critics
that what they were talking about was indeed the only thing in painting
worth talking about, or that significant form by itself (if that is possible)
was as good as, if not better than, classical paintings in which equally
significant form had been imposed upon subject matters themselves
interesting or moving in one way or another. In that problem lies the real
crux of the matter. Granted that "composition," "significant form," or
whatever you want to call it is a *sine qua non* of great painting, is it also
the one thing necessary? Is it *the* art in painting or only *an* art in painting?
My mentors from the Metropolitan are by no means fanatical. They
never themselves insist that subject matter, or the communication of an
emotion in connection with it, is irrelevant in judging a picture. But
unless my memory fails me, they never really face the question of the
extent to which the painter who abandons the suggestion of a subject

---

1. " * * * Why, what a most particularly   ingly of himself in Gilbert and Sullivan's *Pa-*
deep young man that deep young man must   *tience.*
be." So the aesthete Bunthorne sings admir-

matter is to that extent lesser than one who at the same time tells a story, reveals a character, or communicates an attitude.

The hopeful student is confronted at the very beginning with what seems to me this unanswered question. He is warned that "Whistler's Mother" was called by the artist "Arrangement in Grey and Black"—and let that be a lesson to you. You may think that your enjoyment of the picture derives from its "appealing likeness of the author's mother and from sentimental associations with old age," but "the *real* [italics in the original] subject is something else . . . We may ask whether the picture would be just as effective if we omitted the subject altogether . . . the abstract school of contemporary painting argues that subject matter is only something that gets in the way. It confuses the issue—the issue being pure expression by means of color, texture, line, and shape existing in their own right and representing nothing at all."

Throughout the course, stress is laid again and again on the comparison between two seemingly very different pictures said to be similar, although I don't think they are ever said to be identical. For instance, Vermeer's "The Artist and His Studio" is compared with Picasso's "The Studio." "Picasso," I am told, "had sacrificed . . . the interest inherent in the objects comprising the picture . . . the fascination and variety of natural textures . . . the harmonies of flowing light, the satisfaction of building solid forms out of light and shape. What has he gained? . . . Complete freedom to manipulate the forms of his picture . . . The abstractionist would argue that the enjoyment of a picture like Picasso's 'The Studio' is more intense because it is purer than the enjoyment we take in Vermeer."

Is "purer" the right adjective? Is it purer or merely thinner? To me the answer is quite plain and the same as that given to the proponents of pure poetry who argued that poetry is essentially only sound so that the most beautiful single line in French literature is Racine's *"La fille de Minos et de Pasiphaé,"*[2] not because the genealogy of Phèdre was interesting but just because the sound of the words is delightful. The sound of "O frabjous day! Callooh! Callay!" is also delightful but I don't think it as good as, for instance, "No spring, nor summer beauty hath such grace,/ As I have seen in one autumnal face."

It is all very well to say that two pictures as different as those by Vermeer and Picasso are somewhat similar in composition and that to this extent they produce a somewhat similar effect. But to say that the total experience of the two is not vastly different is, so it seems to me, pure nonsense and so is the statement that the two experiences are equally rich.

2. "The daughter of Minos and Pasiphaé"—that is, Phèdre, title character of a tragedy by the seventeenth-century French dramatist Jean Racine.

The author of the seminar session just quoted seems himself to think so when he writes: "But we also contend that a painting is a projection of the personality of the man who painted it, and a statement of the philosophy of the age that produced it."

If that is true, then the painter who claims to be "painting nothing but paint" is either a very deficient painter or is, perhaps without knowing it, projecting his personality and making a statement of a philosophy of the age that produced it. He is doing that just as truly and just as inevitably as Whistler was doing more than an arrangement in black and grey. And if that also is true, then the way to understand what is most meaningful and significant in any modern painting is to ask what it is that the painter, consciously or not, is revealing about his personality and about the age that finds his philosophy and his personality congenial.

At least that much seems often to be admitted by admiring critics of certain painters not fully abstract but who seem to be interested primarily in pure form. Take, for instance, the case of Ferdinand Léger and his reduction of the whole visible world, including human beings, to what looks like mechanical drawings. Are they examples of pure form meaning nothing but themselves? Certainly they are not always so considered by admirers. When the painter died in 1955 the distinguished critic André Chastel wrote:

> From 1910 on, his views of cities with smoke-like zinc, his country scenes inspired as if by a woodchopper, his still lifes made as if of metal, clearly showed what always remained his inspiration: the maximum hardening of a world of objects, which he made firmer and more articulate than they are in reality. Sacrifice of color and nuance was total and line was defined with severity and a well-meaning aggressiveness, projecting his violent, cold Norman temperament. This revolution he consecrated himself to seemed rather simple—the exaltation of the machine age, which after 1920 dominated the western world.

To me it seems equally plain that even those who profess to paint nothing but paint are in fact doing a great deal more because they would not find anything of the sort to be the real aim of painting unless they had certain attitudes toward nature, toward society, and toward man. What that attitude is cannot, I think, be very well defined without recourse to two words that I hate to use because they have become so fashionable and are so loosely tossed about. What these painters are expressing is the alienation of the existentialist. They no longer represent anything in the external world because they no longer believe that the world that exists outside of man in any way shares or supports human aspirations and values or has any meaning for him. They are determined, like the existential moralist, to go it alone. They do not believe that in nature there is anything inherently beautiful, just as the existentialist moralizer refuses to believe that there is any suggestion of moral values in the external universe. The great literature and painting of the past have almost invariably been founded upon assumptions the exact opposite of these. They expressed man's attempt to find beauty and meaning in an external world from which he was not alienated because he believed that both his aesthetic and his moral sense corresponded to something outside himself.

Salvador Dali (whom, in general, I do not greatly admire) once made the remark that Picasso's greatness consisted in the fact that he had destroyed one by one all the historical styles of painting. I am not sure that there is not something in that remark, and if there is, then it suggests that in many important respects Picasso is much like the workers in several branches of literature whose aim is to destroy the novel with the antinovel, the theater with the antitheater, and philosophy by philosophies that consist, like logical positivism and linguistic analysis, in a refusal to philosophize. They are all determined, as the surrealist André Breton once said he was, to "wring the neck of literature."

Having now convinced myself of all these things, I will crawl farther out on a limb and confess that I have often wondered if the new styles created by modern painters—pointillism, cubism, surrealism, and the mechanism of Léger (to say nothing of op and pop)—ought not be regarded as gimmicks rather than actual styles. And to my own great astonishment I have discovered that Picasso himself believes, or did once believe, exactly that.

The luxurious French monthly *Jardin des Arts* published (March 1964) a long and laudatory article on Picasso in the course of which it cited "a text of Picasso on himself" which had been reproduced at various times but most recently in a periodical called *Le Spectacle du Monde* (November 1962). I translate as follows:

> When I was young I was possessed by the religion of great art. But, as the years passed, I realized that art as one conceived it up to the end of the 1880's was, from then on, dying, condemned, and finished and that the pretended artistic activity of today, despite all its superabundance, was nothing but a manifestation of its agony . . . Despite appearances our contemporaries have given their heart to the machine, to scientific discovery, to wealth, to the control of natural forces, and of the world . . . From that moment when art became no longer the food of the superior, the artist was able to exteriorize his talent in various sorts of experiments, in new formulae, in all kinds of caprices and fantasies, and in all the varieties of intellectual charlatanism . . .
>
> As for me, from cubism on I have satisfied these gentlemen [rich people who are looking for something extravagant] and the critics also with all the many bizarre notions which have come into my head and the less they understood the more they admired them . . . Today, as you know, I am famous and rich. But when I am alone with my soul, I haven't the courage to consider myself as an artist. In the great and ancient sense of that word, Greco, Titian, Rembrandt, and Goya were great painters. I am only the entertainer of a public which understands its age.

Chirico is another modern painter who has said something very much like this. But enough of quotations. And to me it seems that Picasso said all that I have been trying to say, namely, that a picture somehow involved with the world of reality outside man is more valuable than one that has nothing to say about anything except the painter himself. What he calls painters "in the great and ancient sense of that word" were able to be such only because they were not alienated existentialists.

1967

QUESTIONS

1. Indicate particular details that show what Krutch suggests to be the proper business of an essayist.
2. What is this essay's thesis? What assumptions underlie the thesis?
3. What relationship does Krutch see between modern painting and "the philosophy of the age"? How does he attempt to demonstrate, or illustrate, that relationship? Is this view persuasive? Why, or why not?
4. Does Krutch assume that his audience is disposed at the outset to think of modern painting very much as he does, or very differently? to think as he does in some particulars, and not in others? Show, by specific details of his manner, what attitudes he seems to expect, what responses he anticipates.
5. Why does Krutch quote (p. 1086) a passage he has read about a certain painter? What can be learned from the quotation? Would it help to know the identity of the painter? Why doesn't Krutch name him?
6. What effect does Krutch achieve by referring twice, in two separate connections, to Picasso?

Peter Blake

THE FANTASY OF THE SKYSCRAPER

The skyscraper is, quite obviously, the most visible symbol of the Modern Movement. Without it—and without the technological innovations that have made it possible—most of the new concepts in urban design developed in the first decades of the century would bite the dust. Le Corbusier's[1] vision of the Radiant City—a community of tall buildings spaced far apart in a parklike setting—depended upon a skyscraper technology to make it feasible; and all the subsequent dreams of modern architects and city planners depended, at least to some extent, upon this basic decision: to satisfy the space requirements of a rapidly expanding population, one must go up, into the clouds.

1. Swiss architect, painter, and town planner (1887-1965).

It is impossible to divorce the idea of the vertical city from issues of building technology (swift elevators and strong columns and beams), from issues of transportation technology (horizontal mass transit below ground level, or slightly above it), from the issue of uncontrolled population growth, from issues of land speculation, and from issues of human interaction (do people communicate as well when assembled in vertical tubes as they do when linked by horizontal sidewalks?).

So the skyscraper, that most visible of all modern symbols, involves us in many diverse but interconnected issues. For example, it is quite possible that Le Corbusier's Radiant City is an eminently reasonable —and beautiful—alternative to urban sprawl; but it is also possible that certain critical problems in what is known as "curtain wall" technology made Le Corbusier's vision very questionable for reasons having to do with such mundane problems as high-altitude wind loads and underground water tables.

Let me try to explain. At present, the only way to construct a building 50 or 100 stories high (within very broad budgetary constraints) is to frame it on a skeleton of steel or of reinforced concrete, and to apply a skin of relatively lightweight metal, glass, or plastic to that skeleton. If one were to build a 50- or a 100-story skyscraper of masonry, the walls would have to be at least a couple of dozen feet thick at ground level, which would make our land speculators (who consider the sidewalks of New York, Chicago, London, Tokyo, and Paris to be among their favorite poaching grounds) decidedly unhappy.

So the only way to construct a vertical city, as the modern masters recognized quite clearly, is to frame its buildings the way an Erector set is put together: vertical columns and horizontal beams, with much space in between, and with no wasted floor area at the level of the sidewalk—or at any other level, for that matter. Which, in turn, means that the "walls" must be as thin as possible: skins or curtains of whatever lightweight material seems most suitable in the eyes of the building's designer.

The most suitable material, in the eyes of most modern architects, has always been glass. The reasons can be found in the "purist" orientation of the Modern Movement. To the purists, the load-bearing elements of buildings—the columns and beams—should be strong and vigorously "expressed"; but the nonbearing skin on certain wall should be just as clearly "expressed" for what it is, i.e., a mere film, an ephemeral screen, separating the indoors from the outdoors, but quite obviously without any structural capacity whatsoever.

Glass fulfilled that intention to perfection. (Nothing could be more invisible except a curtain of air, a device used occasionally for doorways into department stores and other public spaces anxious to attract multitudes.) Glass—at least in its unadulterated state, before being subjected to tinting, mirror-coating, and other surface treatments—was, quite

one's neighbor's wall (as I once did while standing on the balcony of an Atlanta hotel room), one cannot conveniently avoid one's neighbor's reflected heat. In Houston, an old downtown hotel successfully sued its new, mirror-faced neighbor because the latter's shiny garb dramatically increased the air-conditioning requirements of the former's guests. Meanwhile, a third party—an entirely new developer of an adjacent parcel of land—announced that he was about to erect still another mirror-faced building, this one presumably angled to incinerate the original offender's tenants.

The prospect of a city made up entirely of mirrored façades, blindly reflecting back and forth into each other and into infinity, is not without its charm, especially if you happen to be the fairest one of all—i.e., the one and only building in a neighborhood that boasts a real facade, and can therefore see itself reflected ad infinitum in all directions. Certain southern and southwestern U.S. cities are rapidly attaining this distinction, as indeed they should, since none of them contain more than one or two buildings worth looking at.

But the prospect of a giant Hall of Mirrors, or Skyline of Mirrors, should chill the blood of anyone who does, in fact, care about the looks of buildings—e.g., an architect. It implies, of course, total abdication. The great Ludwig Mies van der Rohe, the coolest of all the masters of the Modern Movement, sketched an all-glass skyscraper as early as 1919. He built it (and three others) on Lake Shore Drive, in Chicago, some thirty years later, and in one of the four towers he reserved an apartment for himself. "The important thing in a glass tower," Mies had said in 1919, "is the play of reflections." Being an enormously rational man, he realized that "the play of reflections" is best observed not from inside the glass tower, *but from across the street*—which is precisely where his old apartment happened to be located. So he never moved into that apartment set aside for him in his own glass tower; he preferred to contemplate the reflections from his old brick and stone apartment house half a block away.

Mies never would have tolerated the attachment of elaborate exterior blind mechanisms to any of his buildings. Such mechanisms not only conceal whatever goes on behind all that gadgetry (and thus mask not only the skeleton but the skin as well), but they also create one or two further problems—how to clean the exterior gadgetry, how to clean the glass behind it, and, finally, how to keep ice from forming on the exterior blinds in northern climates during the winter months, in order to save innocent passers-by from the terminal effects of falling icicles. (Answer: built-in electric heating systems, to melt the ice on the blinds that are supposed to shade the glass that would admit too much summer heat if it were not shaded—which blinds might thus save the owners of the glass-

clearly, the ideal "skin" if the purpose was to produce maximum invisibility for the wall and maximum visibility for the structural skeleton of the building.

But if the purpose was also to create a tolerable interior environment, then glass left a great deal to be desired. The heat loss (and heat gain) through a wall of one-quarter- or one-half-inch plate glass is absolutely staggering—well in excess of ten times that of a typical masonry cavity wall filled with an insulation board. The flooding of interior spaces behind glass walls with natural light benefits no one but the manufacturers of venetian blinds. And there are problems of interior condensation as well as strange updrafts outside the glass walls that have often defied solution. In 1952, for example, all five thousand windows of the United Nations Secretariat had to be virtually rebuilt when it was found that the pressure differential between the inside and the outside became so great in powerful rainstorms that raindrops were driven up and into the building through so-called weepholes in the double-hung windows. Those weepholes had been routinely installed to permit accumulated consensation to drain out of the building—downward, of course; but because of the curious ways in which winds and pressures affected the 540-foot-high glass wall, it rained *up* rather than *down!* This unplanned paradox has haunted the United Nations ever since.

To counteract the fundamental drawbacks in its material, the glass industry has exerted itself mightily to invent a whole series of ingenious (and expensive) products that are intended to make glass buildings fit for human habitation (and to add profits to the holders of glass company stock).

There are many tinted glasses, designed to reduce the blinding effect of living in a glass tower facing the sun; there are tinted-glass sandwiches —double-glazed panels—designed both to reduce that blinding effect and roughly to double the insulating value of the wall. There are reflective glasses, coated with silver or gold mirror-films, that may reduce glare as well as heat gain (and thus air-conditioning loads) within; and there are innumerable exterior shading devices that may or may not keep the sun's rays from ever touching the glass skin behind all this elaborate scaffolding.

Some of these ingenious inventions and devices border on the ludicrous. For example, the mirror-coated glasses successfully defeat the very objective that attracted the modern pioneers to the glass-skinned building in the first place: because the mirrored glass is utterly opaque in daytime when seen from the outside, it thus effectively conceals the very structural skeleton that the glass-skinned building was supposed to reveal so dramatically! Besides, mirrorfaced buildings—all the rage from Nashville to Dallas to Teheran and beyond—have proved to be somewhat disconcerting to their neighbors. While one can, admittedly, shave in

skinned building some of the cost of their interior consumption of electricity used to air-condition their glass-walled buildings!)

This situation may well be sufficiently grotesque in itself. It becomes even more so when one examines certain technical aspects of those brilliantly innovative glass skins that sheathe office cubage from pole to equator and to that other pole.

The double-glazed insulting sandwiches (with or without mirror-coating, with or without tinting) are clearly in need of some urgent remedial research. Nobody, as of this writing, knows for sure what caused some of the ten thousand mirror-coated and doubleglazed windows to fall out of Boston's stunningly elegant John Hancock Tower—or what caused the rest of them to threaten to follow suit. And nobody may ever know. But now that these ten thousand mirror-coated and double-glazed "lights" have been replaced, it seems possible, in the minds of some experts, that there might have been certain original failings in the material itself that would hardly be tolerated by the aircraft industry, say, or by any other industry concerned with the safety of passengers and bystanders, as the building industry should be.

For example, it turns out that there may occur a certain ultraviolet buildup inside those double-glazed wall sandwiches that can (and often does) play havoc with the strip of sealants that completes the sides and top edges of these sandwiches. This buildup could cause the sealants to "pump out," leaving the sheets of glass relatively free to move out of their metal frames and, ultimately, to pop—and then to slice the craniums of my heedless pedestrians. There may (or may not) be a way of solving this particular problem before half of our urban population has been wiped off the map, but it is clearly a matter of some concern that the building industry continues to market products whose performance it does not understand, products, moreover, that dramatically undercut the very foundations of the architecture the industry pretends to serve.

It may seem that I am picking nits; but it is not inconceivable that certain implacable facts of life—or of building technology—will place in doubt many, if not most, of the fundamental tenets of the Modern Movement.

For instance, not only does the tall, glass-skinned building present problems of a magnitude not even remotely recognized to this day, but the tall, curtain-walled building—glass-skinned or not—presents problems even further removed from current recognition, such as problems of structural analysis and resolution.

Few people outside the professions of architecture and engineering know that the structural design of a skyscraper is not primarily determined by the loads transmitted by its many heavy floors to the ground on which the building stands, *but by the wind loads that a skyscraper must resist in order to keep its balance.* For a tall building acts very much like a huge sail, and it can easily be blown over unless its "keel"—that is, its foundation—is deep and strong. In fact, the shape of the foundation of a tall building is determined not so much by its height as by the acres of exterior wall surface that face the winds.

In a skin-and-bones building, in which the exterior walls are made of a film of glass (or of a similarly fragile material), it becomes necessary to build massive, expensive, diagonal cross-bracing into the skyscraper—for the principal reason that the exterior skin is not rigid enough, or cannot be attached to the columns and beams rigidly enough, to help resist the horizontal pressures that build up during high winds. In other words, the ideal skin-and-bones building could, conceivably, be twisted out of whack unless it were cross-braced between columns and beams much in the way that a radio or TV tower is cross-braced. If the "skin" were more substantial, and made of a material that could be more firmly attached to the bones behind it without impairing the esthetic sensibilities of its designer, there would be much less need for massive and expensive interior cross-bracing—and less need for massive and expensive foundations.

Every New York taxi driver has known for years that the Empire State Building, though largely faced with stone, sways in a storm (or even in a breeze), and that a trip to its top in windy days is likely to induce nausea. But not until very recently have tall or even low buildings been subjected to reliable wind-tunnel tests. The results (recorded on film, while smoke was introduced into the wind tunnels) have been startling: at various altitudes, and under various wind conditions, tall buildings and their walls (or skins) are buffeted in a way that would alarm any experienced sailor.

Tall buildings and their smooth walls are not the only victims of buffeting. Pedestrians who walk past tall, smooth-skinned skyscrapers may be subjected to what someone has called the Mary Poppins syndrome: during high winds, the airstream blocked by the broad side of a tall, flat building will be deflected in two directions—some of it upward, most of it spiraling to the ground, creating a so-called standing vortex (or mini-tornado) at sidewalk level. This amusing encounter may not invariably lift the pedestrian off his or her feet, or induce pirouettes or even nausea, but it will rarely improve the quality of urban life.

The quality of urban life is even less improved if the tall building is set on stilts or, as Le Corbusier called them, "pilotis." It was axiomatic to many of his urban design theories that buildings should be raised off the ground in this fashion. He had pointed out repeatedly, throughout his career, that this device would free the ground floor of the city and leave it open for pedestrians to traverse it, unhampered by buildings that would normally block their paths. It was an important and imaginative notion; unhappily, it is also a diagram almost guaranteed to sweep pedestrians off their feet under certain quite common wind conditions: a down-draft from a tall building on pilotis, or any direct, horizontal wind current, will be greatly accelerated as it becomes compressed and is forced to pass through the restricted opening under a building. The resulting "venturi effect"—a well-known phenomenon in aerodynamics (especially as it relates to buildings and spaces between or under them)—is one of those physical phenomena that the Modern Movement has ignored from its beginning, and continues to ignore. Complexes such as New York's World Trade Center have spacious, semienclosed pedestrian plazas at ground level; but because these plazas are almost certain to have openings between enclosing buildings—at corners, or somewhere in the middle—winds are literally sucked into them and invited to howl through them at greatly accelerated speeds, thus making the plaza a place to be strenuously avoided.

Most of these facts are only just beginning to dawn upon architects of skyscrapers—more than fifty years after the vertical city was proclaimed as the prototype for an anxious and rapidly expanding world. One reason is that *smooth*-skinned skyscrapers, a fairly recent development, generate wind currents very different from those generated by the rough-hewn skyscrapers of the 1920s and 1930s. Another reason is that not until about 1970 have architects and structural engineers been able to use really reliable wind tunnels in which to test tall buildings and their sheer walls. And not until quite recently have architects and structural engineers been able to plot the airstreams generated in cities built on the gridiron plan and frequently interrupted by open pedestrian plazas—designed to generate civic bliss, but more often, in fact, populated by desperate stragglers buffeted by vortices, lurching toward the nearest exit. (Whenever the grand pedestrian plaza is also graced by spectacular fountains, as it frequently is, the desperate stragglers are very likely to be drenched before they clutch the door to that nearest exist, while cursing the designers of that civic bliss.)

There are other unsolved problems that make skyscraper living uncomfortable, to say the least, and occasionally detrimental to one's health. Tall buildings often act much like the flues that draw smoke out of a fireplace—and the taller they are, the more efficient they are in generating spectacular updrafts. Unless expensive (and often unfeasible) air-pressuring systems are installed within the public areas of a tall apartment building, for example, the elevator shafts will act as flues, and elevator doors will close only with great difficulty during high winds. In one such building in which I lived for several years, the hallways could not be adequately pressurized; thus, if a tenant had the temerity to open a window in the apartment, a roar comparable to that of a jet engine would develop, and winds would howl through the apartment and out into the public hallways (through the unclosable crack under one's front door), sweeping everything off tables and shelves located in their path. On one occasion, when I finally succeeded in opening my front door despite the enormous air pressure holding the door in place, a bedroom door *inside* the apartment crashed shut with such force that its steel frame was knocked clean out of the plaster wall. If a small child had happened to be standing in that doorway, it would have been killed.

The trouble with these problems is that they are virtually insoluble, in technological terms, unless some very major and unlikely innovations occur in the control of the external and internal environment. So far, none is in sight. Some astonishing remedial devices have been installed in tall buildings that sway too much in the wind: in the ill-fated, sixty-two-story John Hancock Tower, in Boston, a so-called dual-tuned mass damper system had to be installed on the fifty-eighth floor when it was discovered that the tower might sway rather disconcertingly under certain wind conditions. This "dual-tuned mass damper" consists of something like six hundred tons of lead and steel, and the mass is designed to move in opposition to the direction of strong winds. The system cost three million dollars to install in the John Hancock Tower; in other skyscrapers, the cost has been much higher.

Such grotesque remedies will not alter the facts of life on earth, and natural forces are not very likely to be abolished in the foreseeable future.

Tall buildings, as we have seen, require unusually deep foundations. The reason is that deep foundations will help them resist wind loads, and thus prevent them from toppling. All this is obvious. Less obvious is the fact that deep excavations for deep foundations and deep basements create a serious menace to many older neighbors of the new skyscraper; for when you excavate deeply you must, of course, prop up your neighbor's foundations, but this may not save them if you also have to install pumps to reduce the water pressure on your new basement walls and floor—below the surface of the existing townscape. When you install such pumps, you begin to lower the water table in your immediate neighborhood, and when you do *that*, you may seriously endanger nearby landmarks that, like the palazzi of Venice,[2] were probably constructed on wooden piles.

Wooden piles under palazzi will last for centuries, *if submerged*, but once the water table drops, and the wooden piles are exposed to air, they will start to rot—and the buildings they were built to support may start to crumble. This is especially true in a city like Boston, which is built very largely on man-made landfill. The designers of a skeletal tower next to a Richardsonian church[3] of the nineteenth century may believe that they are creating an exciting and vibrant change of urban scale by erecting their skin-and-bones tower next to some of the architectural heritage

---

2. Old palaces of the Venetian aristocracy.
3. A church designed by the nineteenth-century American architect Henry Hobson Richardson.

they truly respect; but their structural engineers know better—and they know just how unexpectedly vibrant the change may turn out to be!

So we now have this extraordinary chain of circumstance that seriously challenges one of the most unchallengeable precepts of the Modern Movement. The skyscraper, built of steel or concrete bones and draped with a skin of glass, cannot contain an interior environment that humanity can either suffer or afford; moreover, for reasons having to do with structural facts rather than modern technocratic myths, this same sort of structure cannot help but erode or extinguish the older, surrounding urban fabric. So the Modern Movement's ideal—the Radiant City—is revealed, in fact, as the inevitable ravager of our urban heritage. Not the intentional ravager necessarily—though some of the modern pioneers did, quite clearly, act with malice aforethought—but certainly the unwitting ravager of our urban heritage.

All of this is really quite disturbing if you happen to be an architect enamored with the ideals of a dream world, but functioning, willy-nilly, in the real. Your ideals are those of the modern masters, but the moment of truth occurs when the contractors' bids are in, and you find that the real world cannot afford the dream. And you might, in fact, consider it a nightmare—and not in economic terms alone. Admittedly, man or woman does not live by bread alone. But if a great work of art, designed along the precepts established by your masters, turns out to be a disaster in human terms as well, then perhaps the time has come to take stock.

There is no doubt that the vertical city—the Radiant City of Le Corbusier and Hilberseimer and Mies van der Rohe and all the rest—is an eminently rational solution for an irrational planet (unless, of course, the proliferation of the Pill takes care of the problem to which Le Corbusier devoted much of his life). But is the vertical city, in fact, the most desirable human habitat? Is it worth fighting for? Is it even a desirable alternative to low-rise living, or to suburban sprawl?

The answer quite clearly is no. In the vertical city, the sidewalk is replaced by the elevator. The sidewalk, a place of conversation and confrontation, is replaced by a capsule, a mute place enlivened occasionally by piped-in jukebox melodies. In the vertical city, the garden is replaced by a concrete window box labeled "balcony." In the vertical city, your neighbor is your enemy, the person who hammers nails into the other side of your wall. In the vertical city, interior ventilation ducts convey to you the breakup of a marriage in Apartment 27D and the despondency of a French poodle in 30G. In the vertical city, these are likely to be the only human and animal contacts. In the vertical city, alienation is complete.

Much has been written to document these assertions and to explain the reasons. It is not inconceivable that certain kinds of vertical cities could be designed to foster neighborliness and brotherly love, but the facts and figures so far adduced make this seem highly unlikely. (You can only cram so many human beings, per linear foot, onto a "sidewalk in the sky" on the fifth floor, say, of a "linear city," a couple of dozen stories high; but you would have no trouble at all cramming ten times that number onto *real* sidewalks along streets lined with five-story buildings.)

Much has also been written to document the perfectly obvious fact that families with young children are best served by houses with manageable gardens, where the kids can frolic safely by themselves (under remote supervision) until such time as they frolic in groups in equally safe and equally manageable communal gardens.

And a great deal has been said and written to the effect that today's American suburbia—single little houses on single little lots, strung out on boring and expensive streets ad infinitum—does not represent the only alternative to high-rise living; that, in fact, there are perfectly good row-house solutions, and medium-size apartment solutions, and mixed-rise communities with even a skyscraper here and there, which can provide a better life then either the vertical city or horizontal suburbia.

But not much has been said or written to put to rest, once and for all, the Modern Movement's infatuation with Le Corbusier's concept of *La Ville Radieuse*, a concept that dominated much modern urban design from 1922 to the day, in the 1970s, when the first of Pruitt-Igoe's semi-high-rise buildings, in St. Louis, had to be dynamited because there was just no way this depressing project, built in the 1950s, could be made humanly habitable. (Pruitt-Igoe's high-rise buildings, by the way, were also equipped with "sidewalks in the sky." They didn't work.) Pruitt-Igoe's buildings were framed in concrete and faced with a veneer of brick. If they had been substantially taller, the exterior walls would undoubtedly have had to be of a material lighter in weight than masonry, and the façades might well have been handsomer. But it wouldn't have made much difference. "Communities" of exclusively tall buildings, spaced far apart, and sealed off from the outside world physically and philosophically, are inherently doomed, and no architectural cosmetics can save them.

Every modern architect not obsessed with the need to document his manhood in public has known, from the beginning of his time, that the skyscraper is the death of cities. He has known (women architects are rarely as enamored of skyscrapers as men are) that skyscrapers destroy human interaction, that they cause enormous congestion at the ground-floor levels of cities, and that they tend to drive out smaller-scale —human-scale—buildings through economic pressure by raising neighboring land values and real estate taxes, and thus forcing low-rise neighbors to sell out to high-rise developers. Frank Lloyd Wright's[4]

4. American architect (1869–1959).

preposterous scheme for a mile-high tower in the Chicago Loop, advanced in his declining years, was clearly a tongue-in-cheek swipe at his favorite enemy, the high-rise metropolis. He understood, one feels, that the building of his mile-high tower probably would have wiped out the rest of the city, or most of it, which may very well have been his intention. "Decenter and reintegrate" was Wright's most succinct urban axiom. The converse, "centralize and disintegrate," is the principle that shaped his tower. He must have sensed that this was so; and having spent much of his life fighting against land speculation, he must have enjoyed the prospect.

Most of the other modern pioneers were less devious in their advocacies and much more outspoken in their professed beliefs. All of them, at some point in their careers, railed against land speculation and espoused vaguely socialist causes of one sort or another. Yet, when the chips were down, most of them proved entirely willing to supply ethereal motives to prop up their avaricious clients: the land developer was looking for the fastest buck in sight, and the modern pioneer was perfectly willing to sanctify the search by advancing all sorts of idealistic notions that seemed to justify the vertical city in the sight of God. For there is really only one justification for building such atrocities as upper Sixth Avenue in Manhattan—and that is cash.

If you are a land speculator, fully legitimated by the free enterprise system to squeeze every last profitable dollar out of the planet earth, then you will sell your square footage to the next profiteer up the ladder for the highest attainable price; and then the profiteer will sell to the banks, or to some developer, up another rung of that same ladder; and then that bank will propose a skyscraper that will rent at a cost, per square foot, that will wipe out every neighborhood tenant, and every neighborhood store, and drive them into the suburbs or into bankruptcy, or both.

And at that point, there will be an idealistic modern architect who will provide the developer with an idealistic underpinning; and at that point, too, there will be an embattled opportunity—without funds, without hope, but with plenty of guts—and the modern architect, who helped invent the ideal city, will be on the side of the exploiter.

That exploiter shapes the modern skyscraper more decisively than any modern architect in his employ. Skyscraper curtain walls are no longer designed by architects, but by real estate salesmen; today, the rentable square footage in an American office tower is measured from glass skin to glass skin (not from the edge of the interior, carpeted floor to the opposite edge). This means that every skyscraper developer insists upon pushing the glass-line of his building out as far as the laws determining the shape of the "envelope" will permit, with no projections beyond that line. The result is a building package, tightly and smoothly wrapped in glass, that will generate as much rentable interior space as possible. Any building that boasts an irregular exterior wall, with projections and indentations that might cast interesting shadows (and disperse high-velocity up-and down-drafts), may generate as much as 8 to 10 percent less in rentable floor area than a building with a sheer, smooth skin that projects bland-ness and boredom to the outside world (and helps generate fierce mini-tornadoes at sidewalk level).

So the Modern Movement, which grew out of a passionate involve-ment with the human condition, has, via the skyscraper, become the chief apologist for the real estate speculator. Wolf von Eckardt, the *Washington Post* critic who knew Constantinos Doxiades, recently quoted the late architect and city planner as having said, in a colloquium in 1971: "My greatest crime was the construction of high-rise buildings." Then Doxiades enumerated the "crimes" he had confessed earlier:

"One: the most successful cities of the past were those where people and buildings were in a certain balance with nature. But high-rise build-ings work against nature, or, in modern terms, against the environment. They destroy the scale of the landscape and obstruct normal air circula-tion, so causing automotive and industrial discharges to collect in pockets of severe pollution which cannot easily be dispersed.

"Two: high-rise buildings work against man himself, because they isolate him from others, and this isolation is an important factor in the rising crime rate. Children suffer even more because they lose their direct contacts with nature, and with other children. Even when contacts can be maintained, they are subject to parental control. Both children, and parents, suffer as a result.

"Three: high-rise buildings work against society because they prevent the units of social importance—the family . . . the neighborhood, etc. —from functioning as naturally and as normally as before.

"Four: high-rise buildings work against networks of transportation, communication, and of utilities, since they lead to higher densities, to overloaded roads, to [more extensive] water supply systems—and, more importantly, because they form vertical networks which create many additional problems—crime being just one of them.

"Five: high-rise buildings destroy the urban landscape by eliminating all values which existed in the past. Human symbols—such as churches, mosques, temples of all kinds, city halls, which once arose above the city —are now below the skyscrapers. We may not agree that God or govern-ment should rise above man, but are we ready to agree that symbols of capital gain should rise above everything else . . . ?"

Doxiades was not the most profound thinker to have emerged from the Modern Movement, but he was one of the more sensitive. And the questions he posed are not frivolous. "In our fixation with architecture as a sculptural response to an economic equation," Harry Weese, the Chicago architect, has said, "we have neglected the ground, the sky, and most of all, the user."

1977

Prose Forms: Parables

When we read a short story or a novel, we are less interested in the working out of ideas than in the working out of characters and their destinies. In Dickens' Great Expectations, for example, Pip, the hero, undergoes many triumphs and defeats in his pursuit of success, only to learn finally that he has expected the wrong things, or the right things for the wrong reasons; that the great values in life are not always to be found in what the world calls success. In realizing this meaning we entertain, with Dickens, certain concepts or ideas that organize and evaluate the life in the novel, and that ultimately we apply to life generally. Ideas are there not to be exploited discursively, but to be understood as the perspective which shapes the direction of the novel and our view of its relation to life.

When ideas in their own reality are no longer the primary interest in writing, we have obviously moved from expository to other forms of prose. The shift need not be abrupt and complete, however; there is an area where the discursive interest in ideas and the narrative interest in characters and events blend. In allegory, for example, abstract ideas are personified. "Good Will" or "Peace" may be shown as a young woman, strong, confident, and benevolent in her bearing but vulnerable, through her sweet reasonableness, to the single-minded, fierce woman who is "Dissension." Our immediate interest is in their behavior as characters, but our ultimate interest is in the working out, through them, of the ideas they represent. We do not ask that the characters and events be entirely plausible in relation to actual life, as we do for the novel; we are satisfied if they are consistent with the nature of the ideas that define their vitality.

Ideas themselves have vitality, a mobile and dynamic life with a behavior of its own. The title of the familiar Negro spiritual "Sometimes I Feel Like a Motherless Child," to choose a random instance, has several kinds of "motion" as an idea. The qualitative identity of an adult's feelings and those of a child; the whole burgeoning possibility of all that the phrase "motherless child" can mean; the subtle differences in meaning—the power of context—that occur when it is a black who feels this and when it is a white; the speculative possibilities of the title as social commentary or psychological analysis—these suggest something of the *"life" going on in and around the idea.* Definition, analogy, assumption, implication, context, illustration *are some of the familiar terms we use to describe this kind of life.*

There is, of course, another and more obvious kind of vitality which an idea has: its applicability to the affairs of people in everyday life. Both the kind and extent of an idea's relevance are measures of this vitality. When an essayist wishes to exploit both the life in an idea and the life it comprehends, he or she often turns to narration, because there one sees the advantage of lifelike characters and events, and of showing through them the liveliness of ideas in both the senses we have noted. Ideas about life can be illustrated in life. And, besides, people like stories. The writer's care must be to keep the reader's interest focused on the ideas, rather than on the life itself; otherwise, he or she has ceased being essentially the essayist and has become the short-story writer or novelist.

The parable and the moral fable are ideal forms for this purpose. In both, the idea is the heart of the composition; in both the ideas usually assume the form of a lesson about life, some moral truth of general consequence; and in both there are characters and actions. Jesus often depended on parables in his teaching. Simple, economical, pointed, the parables developed a "story," but more importantly, applied a moral truth to experience. Peter asked Jesus how often he must forgive the brother who sins against him, and Jesus answered with the parable of the king and his servants, one of whom asked and got forgiveness of the king for his debts but who would not in turn forgive a fellow servant his debt. The king, on hearing of this harshness, retracted his own benevolence and punished the unfeeling servant. Jesus concluded to Peter, "So likewise shall my heavenly Father do also unto you, if ye from your hearts forgive not every one his brother their trespasses." But before this direct drawing of the parallel, the lesson was clear in the outline of the narrative.

Parables usually have human characters; fables often achieve a special liveliness with animals or insects. Swift, in "The Spider and the Bee," narrates the confrontation of a comically humanized spider and bee who debate the merits of their natures and their usefulness in the world of experience. The exchange between the two creatures is brilliantly and characteristically set out, but by its end, the reader realizes that extraordinary implications about the nature of art, of education, of human psychological and intellectual potential have been the governing idea all along.

The tone and the force of Red Smith's "A Very Pious Story" are fully realized only in the last statement: there is something of the form of a joke operating here. The surprise turn of the concluding statement points up the meaning—the idea, if you will—of the entire narrative in a way the reader had not suspected, but which nevertheless is satisfying as the idea of the piece is, by implication, brought home with comic sur-prise.

The writer will be verging continually on strict prose narrative in writing the parable or fable, but through skill and tact he or she can preserve the essayist's essential commitment to the definition and development of ideas in relation to experience.

Aesop: THE FROGS DESIRING A KING

The frogs always had lived a happy life in the marshes. They had jumped and splashed about with never a care in the world. Yet some of them were not satisfied with their easygoing life. They thought they should have a king to rule over them and to watch over their morals. So they decided to send a petition to Jupiter[1] asking him to appoint a king.

Jupiter was amused by the frogs' plea. Good-naturedly he threw down a log into the lake, which landed with such a splash that it sent all the frogs scampering for safety. But after a while, when one venturesome frog saw that the log lay still, he encouraged his friends to approach the fallen monster. In no time at all the frogs, growing bolder and bolder, swarmed over the log Jupiter had sent and treated it with the greatest contempt.

Dissatisfied with so tame a ruler, they petitioned Jupiter a second time, saying: "We want a real king, a king who will really rule over us." Jupiter, by this time, had lost some of his good nature and was tired of the frogs' complaining.

So he sent them a stork, who proceeded to gobble up the frogs right and left. After a few days the survivors sent Mercury[2] with a private message to Jupiter, beseeching him to take pity on them once more.

"Tell them," said Jupiter coldly, "that this is their own doing. They wanted a king. Now they will have to make the best of what they asked for."

Moral: Let well enough alone!

1. The king of the gods.　　　　　　　2. The messenger of the gods.

Plato: THE ALLEGORY OF THE CAVE

And now, I said, let me show in a figure how far our nature is enlightened or unenlightened: Behold! human beings living in an underground den, which has a mouth open towards the light and reaching all along the den; here they have been from their childhood, and have their legs and necks chained so that they cannot move, and can only see before them, being prevented by the chains from turning round their heads. Above and behind them a fire is blazing at a distance, and between the fire and the prisoners there is a raised way; and you will see, if you look, a low wall built along the way, like the screen which marionette players have in front of them, over which they show the puppets.

I see.

And do you see, I said, men passing along the wall carrying all sorts of vessels, and statues and figures of animals made of wood and stone and various materials, which appear over the wall? Some of them are talking, others silent.

You have shown me a strange image, and they are strange prisoners.

Like ourselves, I replied; and they see only their own shadows, or the shadows of one another, which the fire throws on the opposite wall of the cave?

True, he said; how could they see anything but the shadows if they were never allowed to move their heads?

And of the objects which are being carried in like manner they would only see the shadows?

Yes, he said.

And if they were able to converse with one another, would they not suppose that they were naming what was actually before them?

Very true.

And suppose further that the prison had an echo which came from the other side, would they not be sure to fancy when one of the passers-by spoke that the voice which they heard came from the passing shadow?

No question, he replied.

To them, I said, the truth would be literally nothing but the shadows of the images.

That is certain.

And now look again, and see what will naturally follow if the prisoners are released and disabused of their error. At first, when any of them is liberated and compelled suddenly to stand up and turn his neck round and walk and look towards the light, he will suffer sharp pains; the glare will distress him and he will be unable to see the realities of which in his former state he had seen the shadows; and then conceive some one saying to him, that what he saw before was an illusion, but that now, when he is approaching nearer to being and his eye is turned towards more real existence, he has a clearer vision—what will be his reply? And you may further imagine that his instructor is pointing to the objects as they pass and requiring him to name them—will he not be perplexed? Will he not fancy that the shadows which he formerly saw are truer than the objects which are now shown to him?

Far truer.

And if he is compelled to look straight at the light, will he not have a pain in his eyes which will make him turn away to take refuge in the objects of vision which he can see, and which he will conceive to be in reality clearer than the things which are now being shown to him?

True, he said.

And suppose once more, that he is reluctantly dragged up a steep and rugged ascent, and held fast until he is forced into the presence of the sun himself, is he not likely to be pained and irritated? When he approaches the light his eyes will be dazzled and he will not be able to see anything at all of what are now called realities.

Not all in a moment, he said.

He will require to grow accustomed to the sight of the upper world. And first he will see the shadows best, next the reflections of men and other objects in the water, and then the objects themselves; then he will gaze upon the light of the moon and the stars and the spangled heaven; and he will see the sky and the stars by night better than the sun or the light of the sun by day?

Certainly.

Last of all he will be able to see the sun, and not mere reflections of him in the water, but he will see him in his own proper place, and not in another; and he will contemplate him as he is.

Certainly.

He will then proceed to argue that this is he who gives the season and the years, and is the guardian of all that is in the visible world, and in a certain way the cause of all things which he and his fellows have been accustomed to behold?

Clearly, he said, he would first see the sun and then reason about him.

And when he remembered his old habitation, and the wisdom of the den and his fellow-prisoners, do you not suppose that he would felicitate himself on the change, and pity them?

Certainly, he would.

And if they were in the habit of conferring honors among themselves selves on those who were quickest to observe the passing shadows and to remark which of them went before, and which followed after, and which were together; and who were therefore best able to draw conclusions as to the future, do you think that he would care for such honors and glories, or envy the possessors of them? Would he not say with Homer,

> Better to be the poor servant of a poor master,

and to endure anything, rather than think as they do and live after their manner?

Yes, he said, I think that he would rather suffer anything than entertain these false notions and live in this miserable manner.

Imagine once more, I said, such an one coming suddenly out of the sun to be replaced in his old situation; would he not be certain to have his eyes full of darkness?

To be sure, he said.

And if there were a contest, and he had to compete in measuring the shadows with the prisoners who had never moved out of the den, while his sight was still weak, and before his eyes had become steady (and the time which would be needed to acquire this new habit of sight might be very considerable) would he not be ridiculous? Men would say of him that up he went and down he came without his eyes; and that it was better not even to think of ascending; and if any one tried to loose another and lead him up to the light, let them only catch the offender, and they would put him to death.

No question, he said.

This entire allegory, I said, you may now append, dear Glaucon, to the previous argument, the prison-house is the world of sight, the light of the fire is the sun, and you will not misapprehend me if you interpret the journey upwards to be the ascent of the soul into the intellectual world according to my poor belief, which, at your desire, I have expressed —whether rightly or wrongly God knows. But, whether true or false, my opinion is that in the world of knowledge the idea of good appears last of all, and is seen only with an effort; and, when seen, is also inferred to be the universal author of all things beautiful and right, parent of light and of the lord of light in this visible world, and the immediate source of reason and truth in the intellectual; and that this is the power upon which he who would act rationally either in public or private life must have his eye fixed.

I agree, he said, as far as I am able to understand you.

Moreover, I said, you must not wonder that those who attain to this beatific vision are unwilling to descend to human affairs; for their souls are ever hastening into the upper world where they desire to dwell; which desire of theirs is very natural, if our allegory may be trusted.

Yes, very natural.

And is there anything surprising in one who passes from divine contemplations to the evil state of man, misbehaving himself in a ridiculous manner; if, while his eyes are blinking and before he has become accustomed to the surrounding darkness, he is compelled to fight in courts of law, or in other places, about the images or the shadows of images of justice, and is endeavouring to meet the conceptions of those who have never yet seen absolute justice?

Anything but surprising, he replied.

Any one who has common sense will remember that the bewilderments of the eyes are of two kinds, and arise from two causes, either from coming out of the light or from going into the light, which is true of the mind's eye, quite as much as of the bodily eye; and he who remembers this when he sees any one whose vision is perplexed and weak, will not be too ready to laugh; he will first ask whether that soul of man has come out of the brighter life, and is unable to see because unaccustomed to the dark, or having turned from darkness to the day is dazzled by excess of light. And he will count the one happy in his condition and state of being, and he will pity the other; or, if he have a mind to laugh at the soul which comes from below into the light, there will be more reason in this than in

the laugh which greets him who returns from above out of the light into
the den.

That, he said, is a very just distinction.

4th century B.C.

Jonathan Swift: THE SPIDER AND THE BEE

Things were at this crisis, when a material accident fell out. For, upon
the highest corner of a large window, there dwelt a certain spider,
swollen up to the first magnitude by the destruction of infinite numbers
of flies, whose spoils lay scattered before the gates of his palace, like
human bones before the cave of some giant. The avenues of his castle
were guarded with turnpikes and palisadoes, all after the modern way of
fortification. After you had passed several courts, you came to the center,
wherein you might behold the constable himself in his own lodgings,
which had windows fronting to each avenue, and ports to sally out upon
all occasions of prey or defense. In this mansion he had for some time
dwelt in peace and plenty, without danger to his person by swallows from
above, or to his palace by brooms from below, when it was the pleasure of
fortune to conduct thither a wandering bee, to whose curiosity a broken
pane in the glass had discovered itself, and in he went; where expatiating
a while, he at last happened to alight upon one of the outward walls of the
spider's citadel; which, yielding to the unequal weight, sunk down to the
very foundation. Thrice he endeavored to force his passage, and thrice
the center shook. The spider within, feeling the terrible convulsion,
supposed at first that nature was approaching to her final dissolution; or
else that Beelzebub,[1] with all his legions, was come to revenge the death
of many thousands of his subjects, whom his enemy had slain and devoured. However, he at length valiantly resolved to issue forth, and meet
his fate. Meanwhile the bee had acquitted himself of his toils, and posted
securely at some distance, was employed in cleansing his wings, and
disengaging them from the ragged remnants of the cobweb. By this time
the spider was adventured out, when beholding the chasms, and ruins,
and dilapidations of his fortress, he was very near at his wit's end; he
stormed and swore like a madman, and swelled till he was ready to burst.
At length, casting his eye upon the bee, and wisely gathering causes from
events (for they knew each other by sight), "A plague split you," said he,
"for a giddy son of a whore. Is it you, with a vengeance, that have made
this litter here? Could you not look before you, and be d—nd? Do you
think I have nothing else to do (in the devil's name) but to mend and

1. The Hebrew god of flies.

repair after your arse?" "Good words, friend," said the bee (having pruned himself, and being disposed to droll) "I'll give you my hand and word to come near your kennel no more; I was never in such a confounded pickle since I was born." "Sirrah," replied the spider, "if it were not for breaking an old custom in our family, never to stir abroad against an enemy, I should come and teach you better manners." "I pray have patience," said the bee, "or you will spend your substance, and for aught I see, you may stand in need of it all, towards the repair of your house." "Rogue, rogue," replied the spider, "yet methinks you should have more respect to a person, whom all the world allows to be so much your betters." "By my troth," said the bee, "the comparison will amount to a very good jest, and you will do me a favor to let me know the reasons that all the world is pleased to use in so hopeful a dispute." At this the spider, having swelled himself into the size and posture of a disputant, began his argument in the true spirit of controversy, with a resolution to be heartily scurrilous and angry, to urge on his own reasons, without the least regard to the answers or objections of his opposite, and fully predetermined in his mind against all conviction.

"Not to disparage myself," said he, "by the comparison with such a rascal, what art thou but a vagabond without house or home, without stock or inheritance, born to no possession of your own, but a pair of wings and a drone-pipe? Your livelihood is an universal plunder upon nature; a freebooter over fields and gardens; and for the sake of stealing will rob a nettle as easily as a violet. Whereas I am a domestic animal, furnished with a native stock within myself. This large castle (to show my improvements in the mathematics) is all built with my own hands, and the materials extracted altogether out of my own person."

"I am glad," answered the bee, "to hear you grant at least that I am come honestly by my wings and my voice; for then, it seems, I am obliged to Heaven alone for my flights and my music; and Providence would never have bestowed on me two such gifts, without designing them for the noblest ends. I visit indeed all the flowers and blossoms of the field and the garden; but whatever I collect from thence enriches myself, without the least injury to their beauty, their smell, or their taste. Now, for you and your skill in architecture and other mathematics, I have little to say: in that building of yours there might, for aught I know, have been labor and method enough, but by woful experience for us both, 'tis too plain, the materials are naught, and I hope you will henceforth take warning, and consider duration and matter as well as method and art. You boast, indeed, of being obliged to no other creature, but of drawing and spinning out all from yourself; that is to say, if we may judge of the liquor in the vessel by what issues out, you possess a good plentiful store of dirt and poison in your breast; and, tho' I would by no means lessen or disparage your genuine stock of either, yet I doubt you are somewhat obliged for an increase of both, to a little foreign assistance. Your inherent portion of dirt does not fail of acquisitions, by sweepings exhaled from below; and one insect furnishes you with a share of poison to destroy another. So that in short, the question comes all to this—which is the nobler being of the two, that which by a lazy contemplation of four inches round, by an overweening pride, feeding and engendering on itself, turns all into excrement and venom, produces nothing at last, but flybane and a cobweb; or that which, by an universal range, with long search, much study, true judgment, and distinction of things, brings home honey and wax."

1967   1704

James Thurber: THE GLASS IN THE FIELD

A short time ago some builders, working on a studio in Connecticut, left a huge square of plate glass standing upright in a field one day. A goldfinch flying swiftly across the field struck the glass and was knocked cold. When he came to he hastened to his club, where an attendant bandaged his head and gave him a stiff drink. "What the hell happened?" asked a sea gull. "I was flying across a meadow when all of a sudden the air crystallized on me," said the goldfinch. The sea gull and a hawk and an eagle all laughed heartily. A swallow listened gravely. "For fifteen years, fledgling and bird, I've flown this country," said the eagle, "and I assure you there is no such thing as air crystallizing. Water, yes; air, no." "You were probably struck by a hailstone," the hawk told the goldfinch. "Or he may have had a stroke," said the sea gull. "What do you think, swallow?" "Why, I—I think maybe the air crystallized on him," said the swallow. The large birds laughed so loudly that the goldfinch became annoyed and bet them each a dozen worms that they couldn't follow the course he had flown across the field without encountering the hardened atmosphere. They all took his bet; the swallow went along to watch. The sea gull, the eagle, and the hawk decided to fly together over the route the goldfinch indicated. "You come, too," they said to the swallow. "I—I—well, no," said the swallow. "I don't think I will." So the three large birds took off together and they hit the glass together and they were all knocked cold.

Moral: He who hesitates is sometimes saved.

1955

Jesus: PARABLES OF THE KINGDOM[1]

Then shall the kingdom of heaven be likened unto ten virgins, which took their lamps, and went forth to meet the bridegroom.

And five of them were wise, and five *were* foolish.

They that *were* foolish took their lamps, and took no oil with them:

But the wise took oil in their vessels with their lamps.

While the bridegroom tarried, they all slumbered and slept.

And at midnight there was a cry made, Behold, the bridegroom cometh; go ye out to meet him.

Then all those virgins arose, and trimmed their lamps.

And the foolish said unto the wise, Give us of your oil; for our lamps are gone out.

But the wise answered, saying *Not so*; lest there be not enough for us and you: but go ye rather to them that sell, and buy for yourselves.

And while they went to buy, the bridegroom came; and they that were ready went in with him to the marriage: and the door was shut.

Afterward came also the other virgins, saying, Lord, Lord, open to us.

But he answered and said, Verily I say unto you, I know you not.

Watch therefore, for ye know neither the day nor the hour wherein the Son of man cometh.

For *the kingdom of heaven is* as a man travelling into a far country, *who* called his own servants, and delivered unto them his goods.

And unto one he gave five talents, to another two, and to another one; to every man according to his several ability; and straightway took his journey.

Then he that had received the five talents went and traded with the same, and made *them* other five talents.

And likewise he that *had received* two, he also gained other two.

But he that had received one went and digged in the earth, and hid his lord's money.

After a long time the lord of those servants cometh, and reckoneth with them.

And so he that had received five talents came and brought other five talents, saying, Lord, thou deliveredst unto me five talents: behold, I have gained beside them five talents more.

His lord said unto him, Well done, *thou* good and faithful servant: thou hast been faithful over a few things, I will make thee ruler over many things: enter thou into the joy of thy lord.

He also that had received two talents came and said, Lord, thou deliveredst unto me two talents: behold, I have gained two other talents beside them.

1. From Jesus' sayings to his disciples on the Mount of Olives, as reported in Matthew xxv.

His lord said unto him, Well done, good and faithful servant; thou hast been faithful over a few things, I will make thee ruler over many things: enter thou into the joy of thy lord.

Then he which had received the one talent came and said, Lord, I knew thee that thou art an hard man, reaping where thou hast not sown, and gathering where thou hast not strawed:

And I was afraid, and went and hid thy talent in the earth: lo, *there* thou hast *that is* thine.

His lord answered and said unto him, *Thou* wicked and slothful servant, thou knewest that I reap where I sowed not, and gather where I have not strawed:

Thou oughtest therefore to have put my money to the exchanges, and *then* at my coming I should have received mine own with usury.

Take therefore the talent from him, and give *it* unto him which hath ten talents.

For unto every one that hath shall be given, and he shall have abundance: but from him that hath not shall be taken away even that which he hath.

And cast ye the unprofitable servant into outer darkness: there shall be weeping and gnashing of teeth.

When the Son of man shall come in his glory, and all the holy angels with him, then shall he sit upon the throne of his glory:

And before him shall be gathered all nations: and he shall separate them one from another, as a shepherd divideth *his* sheep from the goats:

And he shall set the sheep on his right hand, but the goats on the left.

Then shall the King say unto them on his right hand, Come, ye blessed of my Father, inherit the kingdom prepared for you from the foundation of the world:

For I was an hungred, and ye gave me meat: I was thirsty, and ye gave me drink: I was a stranger, and ye took me in:

Naked, and ye clothed me: I was sick, and ye visited me: I was in prison, and ye came unto me.

Then shall the righteous answer him, saying, Lord, when saw we thee an hungred, and fed *thee?* or thirsty, and gave *thee* drink?

When saw we thee a stranger, and took *thee* in? or naked, and clothed thee?

Or when saw we thee sick, or in prison, and came unto thee?

And the King shall answer and say unto them, Verily I say unto you, Inasmuch as ye have done *it* unto one of the least of these my brethren, ye have done *it* unto me.

Then shall he say also unto them on the left hand, Depart from me, ye cursed, into everlasting fire, prepared for the devil and his angels:

For I was an hungred, and ye gave me no meat: I was thirsty, and ye gave me no drink.

I was a stranger, and ye took me not in: naked, and ye clothed me not: sick, and in prison, and ye visited me not.

Then shall they also answer him, saying, Lord, when saw we thee an hungred, or athirst, or a stranger, or naked, or sick, or in prison, and did not minister unto thee?

Then shall he answer them, saying, Verily I say unto you, Inasmuch as ye did *it* not to one of the least of these, ye did *it* not to me.

And these shall go away into everlasting punishment: but the righteous into life eternal.

Franz Kafka: PARABLE OF THE LAW

"Before the Law stands a doorkeeper. To this doorkeeper there comes a man from the country who begs for admittance to the Law. But the doorkeeper says that he cannot admit the man at the moment. The man, on reflection, asks if he will be allowed, then, to enter later. 'It is possible,' answers the doorkeeper, 'but not at this moment.' Since the door leading into the Law stands open as usual and the doorkeeper steps to one side, the man bends down to peer through the entrance. When the doorkeeper sees that, he laughs and says: 'If you are so strongly tempted, try to get in without my permission. But note that I am powerful. And I am only the lowest doorkeeper. From hall to hall, keepers stand at every door, one more powerful than the other. And the sight of the third man is already more than even I can stand.' These are difficulties which the man from the country has not expected to meet, the Law, he thinks, should be accessible to every man and at all times, but when he looks more closely at the doorkeeper in his furred robe, with his huge pointed nose and long thin Tartar beard, he decides that he had better wait until he gets permission to enter. The doorkeeper gives him a stool and lets him sit down at the side of the door. There he sits waiting for days and years. He makes many attempts to be allowed in and wearies the doorkeeper with his importunity. The doorkeeper often engages him in brief conversation, asking him about his home and about other matters, but the questions are put quite impersonally, as great men put questions, and always conclude with the statement that the man cannot be allowed to enter yet. The man, who has equipped himself with many things for his journey, parts with all he has, however valuable, in the hope of bribing the doorkeeper. The doorkeeper accepts it all, saying, however, as he takes each gift: 'I take this only to keep you from feeling that you have left something undone.' During all these long years the man watches the doorkeeper almost incessantly. He forgets about the other doorkeepers, and this one seems to him the only barrier between himself and the Law. In the first years he curses his evil fate aloud; later, as he grows old, he only mutters to himself. He grows childish, and since in his prolonged study of the doorkeeper he has learned to know even the fleas in his fur collar, he begs the very fleas to help him and to persuade the doorkeeper to change his mind. Finally his eyes grow dim and he does not know whether the world is really darkening around him or whether his eyes are only deceiving him. But in the darkness he can now perceive a radiance that streams inextinguishably from the door of the Law. Now his life is drawing to a close. Before he dies, all that he has experienced during the whole time of his sojourn condenses in his mind into one question, which he has never yet put to the doorkeeper. He beckons the doorkeeper, since he can no longer raise his stiffening body. The doorkeeper has to bend far down to hear him, for the difference in size between them has increased very much to the man's disadvantage. 'What do you want to know now?' asks the doorkeeper, 'you are insatiable.' 'Everyone strives to attain the Law,' answers the man, 'how does it come about, then, that in all these years no one has come seeking admittance but me?' The doorkeeper perceives that the man is nearing his end and his hearing is failing, so he bellows in his ear: 'No one but you could gain admittance through this door, since this door was intended for you. I am now going to shut it.'"

"So the doorkeeper deceived the man," said K. immediately, strongly attracted by the story. "Don't be too hasty," said the priest, "don't take over someone else's opinion without testing it. I have told you the story in the very words of the scriptures. There's no mention of deception in it." "But it's clear enough," said K., "and your first interpretation of it was quite right. The doorkeeper gave the message of salvation to the man only when it could no longer help him." "He was not asked the question any earlier," said the priest, "and you must consider, too, that he was only a doorkeeper, and as such fulfilled his duty." "What makes you think he fulfilled his duty?" asked K. "He didn't fulfill it. His duty might have been to keep all strangers away, but this man, for whom the door was intended, should have been let in." "You have not enough respect for the written word and you are altering the story," said the priest. "The story contains two important statements made by the doorkeeper about admission to the Law, one at the beginning, the other at the end. The first statement is: that he cannot admit the man at the moment, and the other is: that this door was intended only for the man. If there were a contradiction be-tween the two, you would be right and the doorkeeper would have deceived the man. But there is no contradiction. The first statement, on the contrary, even implies the second. One could almost say that in suggesting to the man the possibility of future admittance the door-keeper is exceeding his duty. At that time his apparent duty is only to refuse admittance and indeed many commentators are surprised that the suggestion should be made at all, since the doorkeeper appears to be a precisian with a stern regard for duty. He does not once leave his post during these many years, and he does not shut the door until the very last minute; he is conscious of the importance of his office, for he says: 'I am powerful'; he is respectful to his superiors, for he says: 'I am only the lowest doorkeeper'; he is not garrulous, for during all these years he puts only what are called 'impersonal questions'; he is not to be bribed, for he says in accepting a gift: 'I take this only to keep you from feeling that you have left something undone'; where his duty is concerned he is to be moved neither by pity nor rage, for we are told that the man 'wearied the doorkeeper with his importunity'; and finally even his external appearance hints at a pedantic character, the large, pointed nose and the long, thin, black, Tartar beard. Could one imagine a more faithful doorkeeper? Yet the doorkeeper has other elements in his character which are likely to advantage anyone seeking admittance and which make it comprehensible enough that he should somewhat exceed his duty in suggesting the possibility of future admittance. For it cannot be denied that he is a little simple-minded and consequently a little conceited. Take the statements he makes about his power and the power of the other doorkeepers and their dreadful aspect which even he cannot bear to see—I hold that these statements may be true enough, but that the way in which he brings them out shows that his perceptions are confused by simpleness of mind and conceit. The commentators note in this connection: 'The right perception of any matter and a misunderstanding of the same matter do not wholly exclude each other.' One must at any rate assume that such simpleness and conceit, however sparingly manifest, are likely to weaken his defense of the door; they are breaches in the character of the doorkeeper. To this must be added the fact that the doorkeeper seems to be a friendly creature by nature, he is by no means always on his official dignity. In the very first moments he allows himself the jest of inviting the man to enter in spite of the strictly maintained veto against entry; then he does not, for instance, send the man away, but gives him, as we are told, a stool and lets him sit down beside the door. The patience with which he endures the man's appeals during so many years, the brief conversations, the acceptance of the gifts, the politeness with which he allows the man to curse loudly in his presence the fate for which he himself is responsible—all this lets us deduce certain feelings of pity. Not every doorkeeper would have acted thus. And finally, in answer to a gesture of the man's he bends down to give him the chance of putting a last question. Nothing but mild impatience—the doorkeeper knows that this is the end of it all—is discernible in the words: 'You are insatiable.' Some push this mode of interpretation even further and hold that these words express a kind of friendly admiration, though not without a hint of condescension. At any rate the figure of the doorkeeper can be said to come out very differently from what you fancied." "You have studied the story more exactly and for a longer time than I have," said K. They were both silent for a little while. Then. K. said: "So you think the man was not deceived?" "Don't misunderstand me," said the priest, "I am only show-ing you the various opinions concerning that point. You must not pay too much attention to them. The scriptures are unalterable and the com-ments often enough merely express the commentators' despair. In this case there even exists an interpretation which claims that the deluded person is really the doorkeeper." "That's a farfetched interpretation," said K. "On what is it based?" "It is based," answered the priest, "on the simple-mindedness of the doorkeeper. The argument is that he does not know the Law from inside, he knows only the way that leads to it, where he patrols up and down. His ideas of the interior are assumed to be childish, and it is supposed that he himself is afraid of the other guardians whom he holds up as bogies before the man. Indeed, he fears them more than the man does, since the man is determined to enter after hearing about the dreadful guardians of the interior, while the doorkeeper has no desire to enter, at least not so far as we are told. Others again say that he must have been in the interior already, since he is after all engaged in the service of the Law and can only have been appointed from inside. This is countered by arguing that he may have been appointed by a voice calling from the interior, and that anyhow he cannot have been far inside, since the aspect of the third doorkeeper is more than he can endure. Moreover, no indication is given that during all these years he ever made any remarks showing a knowledge of the interior, except for the one remark about the doorkeepers. He may have been forbidden to do so, but there is no mention of that either. On these grounds the conclusion is reached that he knows nothing about the aspect and significance of the interior, so that he is in a state of delusion. But he is deceived also about his relation to the man from the country, for he is inferior to the man and does not know it. He treats the man instead as his own subordinate, as can be recognized from many details that must be still fresh in your mind. But, according to this view of the story, it is just as clearly indicated that he is really subordinated to the man. In the first place, a bondman is always subject to a free man. Now the man from the country is really free, he can go where he likes, it is only the Law that is closed to him, and access to the Law is forbidden him only by one individual, the doorkeeper. When he sits down on the stool by the side of the door and stays there for the rest of his life, he does it of his own free will; in the story there is no mention of any compulsion. But the doorkeeper is bound to his post by his very office, he does not dare go out into the country, nor apparently may he go into the interior of the Law, even should he wish to. Besides, although he is in the service of the Law, his service is confined to this one entrance; that is to say, he serves only this man for whom alone the entrance is intended. On that ground too he is inferior to the man. One must assume that for many years, for as long as it takes a man to grow up to the prime of life, his service was in a sense an empty formality, since he had to wait for a man to come, that is to say someone in the prime of life, and so he had to wait a long time before the purpose of his service could be fulfilled, and, moreover, had to wait on the man's pleasure, for the man came of his own free will. But the termination of his service also depends on the man's term of life, so that to the very end he is subject to the man. And it is emphasized throughout that the doorkeeper apparently realizes nothing of all this. That is not in itself remarkable, since according to this interpretation the doorkeeper is deceived in a much more important issue, affecting his very office. At the end, for example, he says regarding the entrance to the Law: 'I am now going to shut it,' but at the beginning of the story we are told that the door leading into the Law always stands open, and if it always stands open, that is to say at all times, without reference to life or death of the man, then the doorkeeper cannot close it. There is some difference of opinion about the motive behind the doorkeeper's statement, whether he said he was going to close the door merly for the sake of giving an answer, or to emphasize his devotion to duty, or to bring the man into a state of grief and regret in his last moments. But there is no lack of agreement that the doorkeeper will not be able to shut the door. Many indeed profess to find that he is subordinate to the man even in knowledge, toward the end, at least, for the man sees the radiance that issues from the door of the Law while the doorkeeper in his official position must stand with his back to the door, nor does he say anything to show that he has perceived the change." "That is well argued," said K., after repeating to himself in a low voice several passages from the priest's exposition. "It is well argued, and I am inclined to agree that the doorkeeper is deceived. But that has not made me abandon my former opinion, since both conclusions are to some extent compatible. Whether the doorkeeper is clear-sighted or deceived does not dispose of the matter. I said the man is deceived. If the doorkeeper is clear-sighted, one might have doubts about that, but if the doorkeeper himself is deceived, then his deception must of necessity be communicated to the man. That makes the doorkeeper not, indeed, a deceiver, but a creature so simple-minded that he ought to be dismissed at once from his office. You mustn't forget that the doorkeeper's deceptions do himself no harm but do infinite harm to the man." "There are objections to that," said the priest. "Many aver that the story confers no right on anyone to pass judgment on the doorkeeper. Whatever he may seem to us, he is yet a servant of the Law; that is, he belongs to the Law and as such is beyond human judgment. In that case one must not believe that the doorkeeper is subordinate to the man. Bound as he is by his service, even only at the door of the Law, he is incomparably greater than anyone at large in the world. The man is only seeking the Law, the doorkeeper is already attached to it. It is the Law that has placed him at his post; to doubt his dignity is to doubt the Law itself." "I don't agree with that point of view," said K., shaking his head, "for if one accepts it, one must accept as true everything the doorkeeper says. But you yourself have sufficiently proved how impossible it is to do that." "No," said the priest, "it is not necessary to accept everything as true, one must only accept it as necessary." "A melancholy conclusion," said K. "It turns lying into a universal principle."

1925

ZEN PARABLES

Muddy Road

Tanzan and Ekido were once traveling together down a muddy road. A heavy rain was still falling.

Coming around a bend, they met a lovely girl in a silk kimono and sash, unable to cross the intersection.

"Come on, girl," said Tanzan at once. Lifting her in his arms, he carried her over the mud.

Ekido did not speak again until that night when they reached a lodging temple. Then he no longer could restrain himself. "We monks don't go near females," he told Tanzan, "especially not young and lovely ones. It is dangerous. Why did you do that?"

"I left the girl there," said Tanzan. "Are you still carrying her?"

A Parable

Buddha told a parable in a sutra:

A man traveling across a field encountered a tiger. He fled, the tiger after him. Coming to a precipice, he caught hold of the root of a wild vine and swung himself down over the edge. The tiger sniffed at him from above. Trembling, the man looked down to where, far below, another tiger was waiting to eat him. Only the vine sustained him.

Two mice, one white and one black, little by little started to gnaw away the vine. The man saw a luscious strawberry near him. Grasping the vine with one hand, he plucked the strawberry with the other. How sweet it tasted!

Learning to Be Silent

The pupils of the Tendai school used to study meditation before Zen entered Japan. Four of them who were intimate friends promised one another to observe seven days of silence.

On the first day all were silent. Their meditation had begun auspiciously, but when night came and the oil lamps were growing dim one of the pupils could not help exclaiming to a servant: "Fix those lamps."

The second pupil was surprised to hear the first one talk. "We are not supposed to say a word," he remarked.

"You two are stupid. Why did you talk?" asked the third.

"I am the only one who has not talked," concluded the fourth pupil.

Maxine Hong Kingston: ON DISCOVERY

Once upon a time, a man, named Tang Ao, looking for the Gold Mountain, crossed an ocean, and came upon the Land of Women. The women immediately captured him, not on guard against ladies. When they asked Tang Ao to come along, he followed; if he had had male companions, he would've winked over his shoulder.

"We have to prepare you to meet the queen," the women said. They locked him in a canopied apartment equipped with pots of makeup, mirrors, and a woman's clothes. "Let us help you off with your armor and boots," said the women. They slipped his coat off his shoulders, pulled it down his arms, and shackled his wrists behind him. The women who kneeled to take off his shoes chained his ankles together.

A door opened, and he expected to meet his match, but it was only two old women with sewing boxes in their hands. "The less you struggle, the less it'll hurt," one said, squinting a bright eye as she threaded her needle. Two captors sat on him while another held his head. He felt an old woman's dry fingers trace his ear; the long nail on her little finger scraped his neck. "What are you doing?" he asked. "Sewing your lips together," she joked, blackening needles in a candle flame. The ones who sat on him bounced with laughter. But the old women did not sew his lips together. They pulled his earlobes taut and jabbed a needle through each of them. They had to poke and probe before puncturing the layers of skin correctly, the hole in the front of the lobe in line with the one in back, the layers of skin sliding about so. They worked the needle through—a last jerk for the needle's wide eye ("needle's nose" in Chinese). They strung his raw flesh with silk threads; he could feel the fibers.

The women who sat on him turned to direct their attention to his feet. They bent his toes so far backward that his arched foot cracked. The old ladies squeezed each foot and broke many tiny bones along the sides. They gathered his toes, toes over and under one another like a knot of ginger root. Tang Ao wept with pain. As they wound the bandages tight and tighter around his feet, the women sang footbinding songs to distract him: "Use aloe for binding feet and not for scholars."

During the months of a season, they fed him on women's food: the tea was thick with white chrysanthemums and stirred the cool female winds inside his body; chicken wings made his hair shine; vinegar soup improved his womb. They drew the loops of thread through the scabs that grew daily over the holes in his earlobes. One day they inserted gold hoops. Every night they unbound his feet, but his veins had shrunk, and the blood pumping through them hurt so much, he begged to have his feet re-wrapped tight. They forced him to wash his used bandages, which were embroidered with flowers and smelled of rot and cheese. He hung the bandages up to dry, streamers that drooped and draped wall to wall. He felt embarrassed; the wrappings were like underwear, and they were his.

One day his attendants changed his gold hoops to jade studs and strapped his feet to shoes that curved like bridges. They plucked out each hair on his face, powdered him white, painted his eyebrows like a moth's wings, painted his cheeks and lips red. He served a meal at the queen's court. His hips swayed and his shoulders swiveled because of his shaped feet. "She's pretty, don't you agree?" the diners said, smacking their lips at his dainty feet as he bent to put dishes before them.

In the Women's Land there are no taxes and no wars. Some scholars say that that country was discovered during the reign of Empress Wu (A.D. 694–705), and some say earlier than that, A.D. 441, and it was in North America.

1980

Milan Kundera: A Fur Cap

* * *

In February 1948, Communist leader Klement Gottwald stepped out on the balcony of a Baroque palace in Prague to address the hundreds of thousands of his fellow citizens packed into Old Town Square. It was a crucial moment in Czech history—a fateful moment of the kind that occurs once or twice in a millennium.

Gottwald was flanked by his comrades, with Clementis standing next to him. There were snow flurries, it was cold, and Gottwald was bareheaded. The solicitous Clementis took off his own fur cap and set it on Gottwald's head.

The Party propaganda section put out hundreds of thousands of copies of a photograph of that balcony with Gottwald, a fur cap on his head and comrades at his side, speaking to the nation. On that balcony the history of Communist Czechoslovakia was born. Every child knew the photograph from posters, schoolbooks, and museums.

Four years later Clementis was charged with treason and hanged. The propaganda section immediately airbrushed him out of history and, obviously, out of all the photographs as well. Ever since, Gottwald has stood on that balcony alone. Where Clementis once stood, there is only bare palace wall. All that remains of Clementis is the cap on Gottwald's head.

* * *

1982

Cynthia Ozick: THE LECTURE, 1

I was invited by a women's group to be guest speaker at a Book-Author Luncheon. The women themselves had not really chosen me: the speaker had been selected by a male leader and imposed on them. The plan was that I would autograph copies of my book, eat a good meal and then lecture. The woman in charge of the programming phoned to ask me what my topic would be. This was a matter of some concern, since they had never had a woman author before, and no one knew how the idea would be received. I offered as my subject "The Contemporary Poem."

When the day came, everything went as scheduled—the autographing, the food, the welcoming addresses. Then it was time to go to the lectern. I aimed at the microphone and began to speak of poetry. A peculiar rustling sound flew up from the audience. All the women were lifting their programs to the light, like hundreds of wings. Confused murmurs ran along the walls. I began to feel very uncomfortable. Then I too took up the program. It read, "Topic: The Contemporary Home."

Moral: Even our ears practice the caste system.

1973

Red Smith: A VERY PIOUS STORY

At the Derby, Walter Haight, a well-fed horse author from Washington, told it this way.

There's this horseplayer and he can't win a bet. He's got patches in his pants from the way even odds-on favorites run up the alley when he's backing them and the slump goes on until he's utterly desperate. He's ready to listen to any advice when a friend tells him: "No wonder you don't have any luck, you don't live right. Nobody could do any good the way you live Why, you don't even go to church. Why don't you get yourself straightened out and try to be a decent citizen and just see then if things don't get a lot better for you?"

Now, the guy has never exactly liked to bother heaven with his troubles. Isn't even sure whether they have horse racing up there and would understand his difficulties. But he's reached a state where steps simply have to be taken. So, the next day being Sunday, he does go to church and sits attentively through the whole service and joins in the hymn-singing and says "Amen" at the proper times and puts his buck on the collection plate.

All that night he lies awake waiting for a sign that things are going to get better; nothing happens. Next day he gets up and goes to the track, but this time he doesn't buy a racing form or scratch sheet or Jack Green's Card[1] or anything. Just gets his program and sits in the stands studying the field for the first race and waiting for a sign. None comes, so he passes up the race. He waits for the second race and concentrates on the names of the horses for that one, and again there's no inspiration. So again he doesn't bet. Then, when he's looking them over for the third, something seems to tell him to bet on a horse named Number 4.

"Lord, I'll do it," he says, and he goes down and puts the last fifty dollars he'll ever be able to borrow on Number 4 to win. Then he goes back to his seat and waits until the horses come onto the track.

Number 4 is a little fractious in the parade, and the guy says, "Lord, please quiet him down. Don't let him get himself hurt." The horse settles down immediately and walks calmly into the starting gate.

"Thank you, Lord," says the guy. "Now please get him off clean. He don't have to break on top, but get him away safe without getting slammed or anything, please." The gate comes open and Number 4 is off well, close up in fifth place and saving ground going to the first turn. There he begins to move up a trifle on the rail and for an instant it looks as though he might be in close quarters.

"Let him through, Lord," the guy says. "Please make them horses open up a little for him." The horse ahead moves out just enough to let Number 4 through safely.

"Thank you, Lord," says the guy, "but let's not have no more trouble like that. Have the boy take him outside." Sure enough, as they go down the backstretch the jockey steers Number 4 outside, where he's lying fourth.

They're going to the far turn when the guy gets agitated. "Don't let that boy use up the horse," he says. "Don't let the kid get panicky, Lord. Tell him to rate[2] the horse awhile." The rider reaches down and takes a couple of wraps[3] on the horse and keeps him running kind, just cooking on the outside around the turn.

Wheeling into the stretch. Number 4 is still lying fourth. "Now, Lord," the guy says. "Now we move. Tell that kid to go to the stick." The boy outs with his bat and, as Ted Atkinson says, he really "scouges" the horse. Number 4 lays his ears back and gets to running.

He's up to third. He closes the gap ahead and now he's lapped[4] on the second horse and now he's at his throat latch[5] and now he's past him. He's moving on the leader and everything behind him is good and cooked. He closes ground stride by stride with the boy working on him for all he's worth and the kid up front putting his horse to a drive.

"Please, Lord," the guy says. "Let him get out in front. Give me one call on the top end, anyway."

---

1. A tipster's predictions (the first of several technical or slang terms from racing).
2. To control the speed of—here, to prevent the horse from using itself up.

3. The jockey wraps the reins around his wrists to restrain the horse.
4. Drawn within a length of.
5. The harness strap at the throat.

Number 4 keeps coming. At the eighth pole[6] he's got the leader collared. He's past him. He's got the lead by two lengths.

"Thank you, Lord," the guy says, "I'll take him from here. Come on, you son of a bitch!"

1948

6. The marker one-eighth of a mile from the finish line.

Philosophy and Religion

James Thurber

THE OWL WHO WAS GOD

Once upon a starless midnight there was on owl who sat on the branch of an oak tree. Two ground moles tried to slip quietly by, unnoticed. "You!" said the owl. "Who?" they quavered, in fear and astonishment, for they could not believe it was possible for anyone to see them in that thick darkness. "You two!" said the owl. The moles hurried away and told the other creatures of the field and forest that the owl was the greatest and wisest of all animals because he could see in the dark and because he could answer any question. "I'll see about that," said a secretary bird, and he called on the owl one night when it was again very dark. "How many claws am I holding up?" said the secretary bird, "Two," said the owl, and that was right. "Can you give me another expression for 'that is to say' or 'namely'?" asked the secretary bird. "To wit," said the owl. "Why does a lover call on his love?" asked the secretary bird. "To woo," said the owl.

The secretary bird hastened back to the other creatures and reported that the owl was indeed the greatest and wisest animal in the world because he could see in the dark and because he could answer any question. "Can he see in the daytime, too?" asked a red fox. "Yes," echoed a dormouse and a French poodle. "Can he see in the daytime, too?" All the other creatures laughed loudly at this silly question, and they set upon the red fox and his friends and drove them out of the region. Then they sent a messenger to the owl and asked him to be their leader.

When the owl appeared among the animals it was high noon and the sun was shining brightly. He walked very slowly, which gave him an appearance of great dignity, and he peered about him with large, staring eyes, which gave him an air of tremendous importance. "He's God!"

screamed a Plymouth Rock hen. And the others took up the cry "He's
God!" So they followed him wherever he went and when he began to
bump into things they began to bump into things, too. Finally he came to
a concrete highway and he started up the middle of it and all the other
creatures followed him. Presently a hawk, who was acting as outrider,
observed a truck coming toward them at fifty miles an hour, and he
reported to the secretary bird and the secretary bird reported to the owl.
"There's danger ahead," said the secretary bird. "To wit?" said the owl.
The secretary bird told him. "Aren't you afraid?" He asked. "Who?" said
the owl calmly, for he could not see the truck. "He's God!" cried all the
creatures again, and they were still crying "He's God!" when the truck
hit them and ran them down. Some of the animals were merely injured,
but most of them, including the owl, were killed.

Moral: *You can fool too many of the people too much of the time.*

1955

Robert Graves

MYTHOLOGY

Mythology is the study of whatever religious or heroic legends are so
foreign to a student's experience that he cannot believe them to be true.
Hence the English adjective "mythical," meaning "incredible"; and
hence the omission from standard European mythologies of all Biblical
narratives even when closely paralleled by myths from Persia, Babylonia,
Egypt, and Greece, and of all hagiological legends. * * *

Myth has two main functions. The first is to answer the sort of awkward questions that children ask, such as: "Who made the world? How
will it end? Who was the first man? Where do souls go after death?" The
answers, necessarily graphic and positive, confer enormous power on the
various deities credited with the creation and care of souls—and incidentally on their priesthoods.

The second function of myth is to justify an existing social system and
account for traditional rites and customs. The Erechtheid clan of Athens,
who used a snake as an amulet, preserved myths of their descent from
King Erichthonius, a man-serpent, son of the Smith-god Hephaestus and
foster-son of the Goddess Athene. The Ioxids of Caria explained their
veneration for rushes and wild asparagus by a story of their ancestress
Perigune, whom Theseus the Erechtheid courted in a thicket of these
plants; thus incidentally claiming cousinship with the Attic royal house.

The real reason may have been that wild asparagus stalks and rushes were woven into sacred baskets, and therefore taboo.

Myths of origin and eventual extinction vary according to the climate. In the cold North, the first human beings were said to have sprung from the licking of frozen stones by a divine cow named Audumla; and the Northern afterworld was a bare, misty, featureless plain where ghosts wandered hungry and shivering. According to a myth from the kinder climate of Greece, a Titan named Prometheus, kneading mud on a flowery riverbank, made human statuettes which Athene—who was once the Libyan Moon-goddess Neith—brought to life, and Greek ghosts went to a sunless, flowerless underground cavern. These afterworlds were destined for serfs or commoners; deserving nobles could count on warm, celestial mead halls in the North, and Elysian Fields in Greece.

Primitive peoples remodel old myths to conform with changes produced by revolutions, or invasions and, as a rule, politely disguise their violence: thus a treacherous usurper will figure as a lost heir to the throne who killed a destructive dragon or other monster and, after marrying the king's daughter, duly succeeded him. Even myths of origin get altered or discarded. Prometheus' creation of men from clay superseded the hatching of all nature from a world-egg laid by the ancient Mediterranean Dove-goddess Eurynome—a myth common also in Polynesia, where the Goddess is called Tangaroa.

A typical case-history of how myths develop as culture spreads: Among the Akan of Ghana, the original social system was a number of queendoms, each containing three or more clans and ruled by a Queen-mother with her council of elder women, descent being reckoned in the female line, and each clan having its own animal deity. The Akan believed that the world was born from the all-powerful Moon-goddess Ngame, who gave human beings souls, as soon as born, by shooting lunar rays into them. At some time or other, perhaps in the early Middle Ages, patriarchal nomads from the Sudan forced the Akans to accept a male Creator, a Sky-god named Odomankoma, but failed to destroy Ngame's dispensation. A compromise myth was agreed upon: Odomankoma created the world with hammer and chisel from inert matter, after which Ngame brought it to life. These Sudanese invaders also worshipped the seven planetary powers ruling the week—a system originating in Babylonia. (It had spread to Northern Euope, bypassing Greece and Rome, which is why the names of pagan deities—Tuisto, Woden, Thor, and Frigg—are still attached to Tuesday, Wednesday, Thursday, and Friday.) This extra cult provided the Akan with seven new deities, and the compromise myth made both them and the clan gods bisexual. Towards the end of the fourteenth century A.D., a social revolution deposed Odomankoma in favor of a Universal Sun-god, and altered the myth accordingly. While Odomankoma ruled, a queendom was still a queendom, the king acting merely as a consort and male representative of the sovereign Queen-mother, and being styled "Son of the Moon": a yearly dying, yearly resurrected, fertility godling. But the gradual welding of small queendoms into city-states, and of city-states into a rich and populous nation, encouraged the High King—the king of the dominant city-state—to borrow a foreign custom. He styled himself "Son of the Sun," as well as "Son of the Moon," and claimed limitless authority. The Sun, which, according to the myth, had hitherto been reborn every morning from Ngame, was now worshipped as an eternal god altogether independent of the Moon's life-giving function. New myths appeared when the Akan accepted the patriarchal principle, which Sun-worship brought in; they began tracing succession through the father, and mothers ceased to be the spiritual heads of households.

This case-history throws light on the complex Egyptian corpus of myth. Egypt, it seems, developed from small matriarchal Moonqueendoms to Pharaonic patriarchal Sun-monarchy. Grotesque animal deities of leading clans in the Delta became city-gods, and the cities were federated under the sovereignty of a High King (once a "Son of the Moon"), who claimed to be the Son of Ra the Sun-god. Opposition by independent-minded city-rulers to the Pharaoh's autocratic sway appears in the undated myth of how Ra grew so old and feeble that he could not even control his spittle; the Moon-goddess Isis plotted against him and Ra retaliated by casting his baleful eye on mankind—they perished in their thousands. Ra nevertheless decided to quit the ungrateful land of Egypt, whereupon Hathor, a loyal Cow-goddess, flew him up to the vault of Heaven. The myth doubtless records a compromise that consigned the High King's absolutist pretensions, supported by his wife, to the vague realm of philosophic theory. He kept the throne, but once more became, for all practical purposes, an incarnation of Osiris, consort of the Moon-goddess Isis—a yearly dying, yearly resurrected fertility godling.

Indian myth is highly complex, and swings from gross physical abandon to rigorous asceticism and fantastic visions of the spirit world. Yet it has much in common with European myth, since Aryan invasions in the second millennium B.C. changed the religious system of both continents. The invaders were nomad herdsmen, and the peoples on whom they imposed themselves as a military aristocracy were peasants. Hesiod, an early Greek poet, preserves a myth of pre-Aryan "Silver Age" heroes: "divinely created eaters of bread, utterly subject to their mothers however long they lived, who never sacrificed to the gods, but at least did not make war against one another." Hesiod but the case well: in primitive agricultural communities, recourse to war is rare, and goddessworship the rule. Herdsmen, on the contrary, tend to make fighting a profession and, perhaps because bulls dominate their herds, as rams do flocks, worship a male Sky-god typified by a bull or a ram. He sends down rain for the pastures, and they take omens from the entrails of the victims sacrificed to him.

When an invading Aryan chieftain, a tribal rainmaker, married the Moon-priestess and Queen of a conquered people, a new myth inevitably celebrated the marriage of the Sky-god and the Moon. But since the Moon-goddess was everywhere worshipped as a triad, in honor of the Moon's three phases—waxing, full, and waning—the god split up into a complementary triad. This accounts for three-bodied Geryon, the first king of Spain; three-headed Cernunnos, the Gallic god; the Irish triad, Brian, Iuchar, and Iucharba, who married the three queenly owners of Ireland; and the invading Greek brothers Zeus, Poseidon, and Hades, who, despite great opposition, married the pre-Greek Moon-goddess in her three aspects, respectively as Queen of Heaven, Queen of the Sea, and Queen of the Underworld.

The Queen-mother's decline in religious power, and the goddesses' continual struggle to preserve their royal prerogatives, appears in the Homeric myth of how Zeus ill-treated and bullied Hera, and how she continually plotted against him. Zeus remained a Thunder-god, because Greek national sentiment forbad his becoming a Sun-god in Oriental style. But his Irish counterpart, a thunder-god named The Dagda, grew senile at last and surrendered the throne to his son Bodb the Red, a war-god—in Ireland, the magic of rainmaking was not so important as in Greece.

One constant rule of mythology is that whatever happens among the gods above reflects events on earth. Thus a father-god named "The Ancient One of the Jade" (Yu-ti) ruled the pre-revolutionary Chinese Heaven: like Prometheus, he had created human beings from clay. His wife was the Queen-mother, and their court an exact replica of the old Imperial Court at Pekin, with precisely the same functionaries: ministers, soldiers, and a numerous family of the gods' sisters, daughters, and nephews. The two annual sacrifices paid by the Emperor to the August One of the Jade—at the winter solstice when the days first lengthen and at the Spring equinox when they become longer than the nights—show him to have once been a solar god. And the theological value to the number 72 suggests that the cult started as a compromise between Moongoddess worship and Sun-god worship. 72 means three-times-three, the Moon's mystical number, multipled by two-times-two-times-two, the Sun's mystical number, and occurs in solar-lunar divine unions throughout Europe, Asia, and Africa. Chinese conservatism, by the way, kept these gods dressed in ancient court-dress, making no concessions to the new fashions which the invading dynasty from Manchuria had introduced.

In West Africa, whenever the Queen-mother, or King, appointed a new functionary at Court, the same thing happened in Heaven, by royal

decree. Presumably this was also the case in China; and if we apply the principle to Greek myth, it seems reasonably certain that the account of Tirynthian Heracles' marriage to Hera's daughter Hebe, and his appointment as Celestial Porter to Zeus, commemorates the appointment of a Tirynthian prince as vizier at the court of the Mycenaean High King, after marriage to a daughter of his Queen, the High Priestess of Argos. Probably the appointment of Ganymede, son of an early Trojan king, as cup-bearer to Zeus, had much the same significance: Zeus, in this context, would be more likely the Hittite king resident at Hattusas.

Myth, then, is a dramatic shorthand record of such matters as invasions, migrations, dynastic changes, admission of foreign cults, and social reforms. When bread was first introduced into Greece—where only beans, poppyseeds, acorns, and asphodel roots had hitherto been known —the myth of Demeter and Triptolemus sanctified its use; the same event in Wales produced a myth of "The Old White One," a Sow-goddess who went around the country with gifts of grain, bees, and her own young; for agriculture, pig breeding and beekeeping were taught to the aborigines by the same wave of neolithic invaders. Other myths sanctified the invention of wine.

A proper study of myth demands a great store of abstruse geographical, historical, and anthropological knowledge, also familiarity with the properties of plants and trees, and the habits of wild birds and beasts. Thus a Central American stone sculpture, a Toad-god sitting beneath a mushroom, means little to mythologists who have not considered the worldwide association of toads with toxic mushrooms or heard of a Mexican Mushroom-god, patron of an oracular cult; for the toxic agent is a drug, similar to that secreted in the sweat glands of frightened toads, which provides magnificent hallucinations of a heavenly kingdom.

Myths are fascinating and easily misread. Readers may smile at the picture of Queen Maya and her prenatal dream of the Buddha descending upon her disguised as a charming white baby elephant—he looks as though he would crush her to pulp—when "at once all nature rejoiced, trees burst into bloom, and musical instruments played of their own accord." In English-speaking countries, "white elephant" denotes something not only useless and unwanted, but expensive to maintain; and the picture could be misread there as indicating the Queen's grave embarrassment at the prospect of bearing a child. In India, however, the elephant symbolizes royalty—the supreme God Indra rides one—and white elephants (which are not albinos, but animals suffering from a vitiliginous skin disease) are sacred to the Sun, as white horses were for the ancient Greeks, and white oxen for the British druids. The elephant, moreover, symbolizes intelligence, and Indian writers traditionally acknowledge the Elephant-god Ganesa as their patron; he is supposed to have dictated the Mahabharata.[1]

Again, in English, a scallop shell is associated either with cookery or with medieval pilgrims returning from a visit to the Holy Sepulcher; but Aphrodite the Greek Love-goddess employed a scallop shell for her voyages across the sea, because its two parts were so tightly hinged together as to provide a symbol of passionate sexual love—the hinge of the scallop being a principal ingredient in ancient love-philters. The lotus-flower sacred to Buddha and Osiris has five petals, which symbolize the four limbs and the head; the five senses; the five digits; and, like the pyramid, the four points of the compass and the zenith. Other esoteric meanings abound, for myths are seldom simple, and never irresponsible.

1959

1. A vast Indian epic of 200,000 lines, written before 500 A.D.

Edward Gibbon

THE PROGRESS OF THE CHRISTIAN RELIGION
* * *

A candid but rational inquiry into the progress and establishment of Christianity may be considered as a very essential part of the history of the Roman empire. While that great body was invaded by open violence, or undermined by slow decay, a pure and humble religion gently insinuated itself into the minds of men, grew up in silence and obscurity, derived new vigour from opposition, and finally erected the triumphant banner of the Cross on the ruins of the Capitol. Nor was the influence of Christianity confined to the period or to the limits of the Roman empire. After a revolution of thirteen or fourteen centuries, that religion is still professed by the nations of Europe, the most distinguished portion of human kind in arts and learning as well as in arms. By the industry and zeal of the Europeans it has been widely diffused to the most distant shores of Asia and Africa; and by the means of their colonies has been firmly established from Canada to Chili, in a world unknown to the ancients.

But this inquiry, however useful or entertaining, is attended with two peculiar difficulties. The scanty and suspicious materials of ecclesiastical history seldom enable us to dispel the dark cloud that hangs over the first age of the church. The great law of impartiality too often obliges us to reveal the imperfections of the uninspired teachers and believers of the Gospel; and, to a careless observer, *their* faults may seem to cast a shade on the faith which they professed. But the scandal of the pious Christian, and the fallacious triumph of the Infidel, should cease as soon as they

recollect not only *by whom*, but likewise *to whom*, the Divine Revelation was given. The theologian may indulge the pleasing task of describing Religion as she descended from Heaven, arrayed in her native purity. A more melancholy duty is imposed on the historian. He must discover the inevitable mixture of error and corruption which she contracted in a long residence upon earth, among a weak and degenerate race of beings.

Our curiosity is naturally prompted to inquire by what means the Christian faith obtained so remarkable a victory over the established religions of the earth. To this inquiry an obvious but unsatisfactory answer may be returned; that it was owing to the convincing evidence of the doctrine itself, and to the ruling providence of its great Author. But as truth and reason seldom find so favourable a reception in the world, and as the wisdom of Providence frequently condescends to use the passions of the human heart and the general circumstances of mankind, as instruments to execute its purpose, we may still be permitted, though with becoming submission, to ask, not indeed what were the first, but what were the secondary causes of the rapid growth of the Christian church? It will, perhaps, appear that it was most effectually favoured and assisted by the five following causes:—I. The inflexible, and, if we may use the expression, the intolerant zeal of the Christians, derived, it is true, from the Jewish religion, but purified from the narrow and unsocial spirit which, instead of inviting, had deterred the Gentiles from embracing the law of Moses. II. The doctrine of a future life, improved by every additional circumstance which could give weight and efficacy to that important truth. III. The miraculous powers ascribed to the primitive church. IV. The pure and austere morals of the Christians. V. The union and discipline of the Christian republic, which gradually formed an independent and increasing state in the heart of the Roman empire.

I. The Jewish religion was admirably fitted for defence, but it was never designed for conquest; and it seems probable that the number of proselytes was never much superior to that of apostates. The obligation of preaching to the Gentiles the faith of Moses had never been inculcated as a precept of the law, nor were the Jews inclined to impose it on themselves as a voluntary duty. Their peculiar distinctions of days, of meats, and a variety of trivial though burdensome observances, were objects of aversion for other nations. The painful and even dangerous rite of circumcision was alone capable of repelling a willing proselyte from the door of the synagogue. Under these circumstances, Christianity offered itself to the world armed with the strength of the Mosaic law and delivered from the weight of its fetters.

II. Since the most sublime efforts of philosophy can extend no farther than feebly to point out the desire, the hope, or at most the probability of a future state, there is nothing except a divine revelation that can ascertain the existence and describe the condition of the invisible country which is destined to receive the souls of men after their separation from the body. When the promise of eternal happiness was proposed to mankind on condition of adopting the faith, and of observing the precepts, of the Gospel, it is no wonder that so advantageous an offer should have been accepted by great numbers of every religion, of every rank, and of every province in the Roman empire. The ancient Christians were animated by a contempt for their present existence, and by a just confidence of immortality, of which the doubtful and imperfect faith of modern ages cannot give us any adequate notion. In the primitive church the influence of truth was very powerfully strengthened by an opinion which, however it may deserve respect for its usefulness and antiquity, has not been found agreeable to experience. It was universally believed that the end of the world, and the kingdom of heaven, were at hand. The near approach of this wonderful event had been predicted by the apostles; the tradition of it was preserved by their earliest disciples, and those who understood in their literal sense the discourses of Christ himself were obliged to expect the second and glorious coming of the Son of Man in the clouds, before that generation was totally extinguished which had beheld his humble condition upon earth, and which might still be witness of the calamities of the Jews under Vespasian or Hadrian.[1] And while the happiness and glory of a temporal reign were promised to the disciples of Christ, the most dreadful calamities were denounced against an unbelieving world.

III. The supernatural gifts, which even in this life were ascribed to the Christians above the rest of mankind, must have conduced to their own comfort, and very frequently to the conviction of infidels. From the first of the fathers to the last of the popes, a succession of bishops, of saints, of martyrs, and of miracles, is continued without interruption, and the progress of superstition was so gradual and almost imperceptible, that we know not in what particular link we should break the chain of tradition. Every age bears testimony to the wonderful events by which it was distinguished, and its testimony appears no less weighty and respectable than that of the preceding generation, till we are insensibly led on to accuse our own inconsistency if, in the eighth or in the twelfth century, we deny to the venerable Bede, or to the holy Bernard, the same degree of confidence which, in the second century, we had so liberally granted to Justin or to Irenæus.

1. The Roman general Vespasian conducted a war against the Jews from A.D. 66–69, when he became emperor and left his son Titus to complete the destruction of Jerusalem. Hadrian (emperor from A.D. 117–38) ruthlessly suppressed the insurrection of the Jews under Bar Kokba (A.D. 132–35).

IV. The primitive Christian demonstrated his faith by his virtue; the desire of perfection became the ruling passion of his soul. A doctrine so extraordinary and so sublime must inevitably command veneration. The Christians acknowledged that governmental institutions might be necessary for the present system of the world, and submitted to the authority of their pagan governors. But while they inculcated the maxims of passive obedience, they refused to take any active part in the civil administration or the military defence of the empire.

V. The primitive Christians were dead to the business and pleasures of the world; but their love of action soon found a new occupation in the government of the church. The public functions of religion were solely intrusted to the established ministers of the church, the *bishops* and the *presbyters*. Provincial synods were soon instituted, and a regular correspondence between them communicated and approved their respective proceedings. Soon the catholic church assumed the form and acquired the strength of a great fœderative republic. The progress of ecclesiastical authority gave birth to the memorable distinction of the laity and of the clergy, which had been unknown to the Greeks and Romans.

* * *

1766-88[2]

2. *The Decline and Fall of the Roman Empire* was published between 1776-88. This excerpt is taken from a condensation by Moses Hadas, published in 1962.

Jonathan Edwards

SINNERS IN THE HANDS OF AN ANGRY GOD[1]

Their foot shall slide in due time.
—DEUT. XXXII, 35[2]

In this verse is threatened the vengeance of God on the wicked unbelieving Israelites, who were God's visible people, and who lived under the means of grace; but who, notwithstanding all God's wonderful works towards them, remained (as ver. 28.)[3] void of counsel, having no

1. Only the first part of the sermon is printed here; the "application" is omitted.
2. The text appears in this context: "[32] For their vine is of the vine of Sodom, and of the fields of Gomorrah: their grapes are grapes of gall, their clusters are bitter: [33] Their wine is the poison of dragons, and the cruel venom of asps. [34] Is not this laid up in store with me, and sealed up among my treasures?

[35] To me belongeth vengeance, and recompence; their foot shall slide in due time: for the day of their calamity is at hand, and the things that shall come upon them make haste." It occurs in the middle of a long denunciatory "song" addressed by Moses to the Israelites.
3. Verse 28: "For they are a nation void of counsel, neither is there any understanding

understanding in them. Under all the cultivations of heaven, they brought forth bitter and poisonous fruit; as in the two verses next preceding the text. The expression I have chosen for my text, *Their foot shall slide in due time*, seems to imply the following things, relating to the punishment and destruction to which these wicked Israelites were exposed.

1. That they were always exposed to *destruction*; as one that stands or walks in slippery places is always exposed to fall. This is implied in the manner of their destruction coming upon them, being represented by their foot sliding. The same is expressed, Psalm lxxiii. 18. "Surely thou didst set them in slippery places; thou castedst them down into destruction."

2. It implies that they were always exposed to sudden unexpected destruction. As he that walks in slippery places is every moment liable to fall, he cannot foresee one moment whether he shall stand or fall the next; and when he does fall, he falls at once without warning: Which is also expressed in Psalm lxxiii. 18, 19. "Surely thou didst set them in slippery places; thou castedst them down into destruction. How are they brought into desolation as an in a moment!"

3. Another thing implied is, that they are liable to fall of *themselves*, without being thrown down by the hand of another; as he that stands or walks on slippery ground needs nothing but his own weight to throw him down.

4. That the reason why they are not fallen already, and do not fall now, is only that God's appointed time is not come. For it is said, that when that due time, or appointed time comes, *their foot shall slide*. Then they shall be left to fall, as they are inclined by their own weight. God will not hold them up in these slippery places any longer, but will let them go; and then, at that very instant, they shall fall into destruction; as he that stands on such slippery declining ground, on the edge of a pit, he cannot stand along, when he is let go he immediately falls and is lost.

The observation from the words that I would now insist upon is this —"There is nothing that keeps wicked men at any one moment out of hell, but the mere pleasure of God"—By the *mere* pleasure of God, I mean his *sovereign* pleasure, his arbitrary will, restrained by no obligation, hindered by no manner of difficulty, any more than if nothing else but God's mere will had in the least degree, or in any respect whatsoever, and hand in the preservation of wicked men one moment. The truth of this observation may appear by the following considerations.

1. There is no want of *power* in God to cast wicked men into hell at any moment. Men's hands cannot be strong when God rises up. The strongest have no power to resist him, nor can any deliver out of his hands. He is not only able to cast wicked men into hell, but he can most easily do it.

---

in them."

Sometimes an earthly prince meets with a great deal of difficulty to subdue a rebel, who has found means to fortify himself, and has made himself strong by the numbers of his followers. But it is not so with God. There is no fortress that is any defense from the power of God. Though hand join in hand, and vast multitudes of God's enemies combine and associate themselves, they are easily broken in pieces. They are as great heaps of light chaff before the whirlwind; or large quantities of dry stubble before devouring flames. We find it easy to tread on and crush a worm that we see crawling on the earth; so it is easy for us to cut or singe a slender thread that any thing hangs by: thus easy is it for God, when he pleases, to cast his enemies down to hell. What are we, that we should think to stand before him, at whose rebuke the earth trembles, and before whom the rocks are thrown down?

2. They *deserve* to be cast into hell; so that divine justice never stands in the way, it makes no objection against God's using his power at any moment to destroy them. Yea, on the contrary, justice calls aloud for an infinite punishment of their sins. Divine justice says of the tree that brings forth such grapes of Sodom, "Cut it down, why cumbereth it the ground?" Luke xiii. 7. The sword of divine justice is every moment brandished over their heads, and it is nothing but the hand of arbitrary mercy, and God's mere will, that holds it back.

3. They are already under a sentence of *condemnation* to hell. They do not only justly deserve to be cast down thither, but the sentence of the law of God, that eternal and immutable rule of righteousness that God has fixed between him and mankind, is gone out against them, and stands against them; so that they are bound over already to hell. John iii. 18. "He that believeth not is condemned already." So that every unconverted man properly belongs to hell; that is his place; from thence he is, John viii. 23. "Ye are from beneath:" And thither he is bound; it is the place that justice, and God's word, and the sentence of his unchangeable law assign to him.

4. They are now the objects of that very same *anger* and wrath of God, that is expressed in the torments of hell. And the reason why they do not go down to hell at each moment, is not because God, in whose power they are, is not then very angry with them; as he is with many miserable creatures now tormented in hell, who there feel and bear the fierceness of his wrath. Yea, God is a great deal more angry with great numbers that are now on earth; yea, doubtless, with many that are now in this congregation, who it may be are at ease, than he is with many of those who are now in the flames of hell.

So that it is not because God is unmindful of their wickedness, and does not resent it, that he does not let loose his hand and cut them off. God is not altogether such an one as themselves, though they may imagine him to be so. The wrath of God burns against them, their damnation does not slumber; the pit is prepared, the fire is made ready, the furnace is now hot, ready to receive them; the flames do now rage and glow. The glittering sword is whet, and held over them, and the pit hath opened its mouth under them.

5. The *devil* stands ready to fall upon them, and seize them as his own, at what moment God shall permit him. They belong to him; he has their souls in his possession, and under his dominion. The scripture represents them as his goods, Luke xi. 12. The devils watch them; they are ever by them at their right hand; they stand waiting for them, like greedy hungry lions that see their prey, and expect to have it, but are for the present kept back. If God should withdraw his hand, by which they are restrained, they would in one moment fly upon their poor souls. The old serpent[4] is gaping for them; hell opens its mouth wide to receive them; and if God should permit it, they would be hastily swallowed up and lost.

6. There are in the souls of wicked men those hellish *principles* reigning, that would presently kindle and flame out into hell fire, if it were not for God's restraints. There is laid in the very nature of carnal men, a foundation for the torments of hell. There are those corrupt principles, in reigning power in them, and in full possession of them, that are seeds of hell fire. These principles are active and powerful, exceeding violent in their nature, and if it were not for the restraining hand of God upon them, they would soon break out, they would flame out after the same manner as the same corruptions, the same enmity does in the hearts of damned souls, and would beget the same torments as they do in them. The souls of the wicked are in scripture compared to the troubled sea, Isa. lvii. 20. For the present, God restrains their wickedness by his mighty power, as he does the raging waves of the troubled sea, saying, "Hitherto shalt thou come, but no further;" but if God should withdraw that restraining power, it would soon carry all before it. Sin is the ruin and misery of the soul; it is destructive in its nature; and if God should leave it without restraint, there would need nothing else to make the soul perfectly miserable. The corruption of the heart of man is immoderate and boundless in its fury; and while wicked men live here, it is like fire pent up by God's restraints, whereas if it were let loose, it would set on fire the course of nature; and as the heart is now a sink of sin, of if sin was not restrained, it would immediately turn the soul into a fiery oven, or a furnace of fire and brimstone.

7. It is no security to wicked men for one moment, that there are no visible means of death at hand. It is no security to a natural man, that he is now in health, and that he does not see which way he should now immediately go out of the world by any accident, and that there is no visible danger in any respect in his circumstances. The manifold and continual experience of the world in all ages, shows this is no evidence,

---

4. Satan, who appeared to Adam and Eve in the form of a serpent.

that a man is not on the very brink of eternity, and that the next step will not be into another world. The unseen, unthought-of ways and means of persons going suddenly out of the world are innumerable and inconceivable. Unconverted men walk over the pit of hell on a rotten covering, and there are innumerable places in this covering so weak that they will not bear their weight, and these places are not seen. The arrows of death fly unseen at noon-day; the sharpest sight cannot discern them. God has so many different unsearchable ways of taking wicked men out of the world and sending them to hell, that there is nothing to make it appear, that God had need to be at the expense of a miracle, or go out of the ordinary course of his province, to destroy any wicked man, at any moment. All the means that there are of sinners going out of the world, are so in God's hands, and so universally and absolutely subject to his power and determination, that it does not depend at all the less on the mere will of God, whether sinners shall at any moment to go hell, than if means were never made use of, or at all concerned in the case.

8. Natural men's prudence and care to preserve their own lives, or the care of others to preserve them, do not secure them a moment. To this, divine providence and universal experience do also bear testimony. There is this clear evidence that men's own wisdom is no security to them from death; that if it were otherwise we should see some difference between the wise and politic men of the world, and others, with regard to their liableness to early and unexpected death: but how is it in fact? Eccles, ii. 16. "How dieth the wise man? even as the fool."

9. All wicked men's pains and *contrivance* which they use to escape hell, while they continue to reject Christ, and so remain wicked men, do not secure them from hell one moment. Almost every natural man that hears of hell, flatters himself that he shall escape it; he depends upon himself for his own security; he flatters himself in what he has done, in what he is now doing, or what he intends to do. Every one lays out matters in his own mind how he shall avoid damnation, and flatters himself that he contrives well for himself, and that his schemes will not fail. They hear indeed that there are but few saved, and that the greater part of men that have died heretofore are gone to hell; but each one imagines that he lays out matters better for his own escape than others have done. He does not intend to come to that place of torment; he says within himself, that he intends to take effectual care, and to order matters so for himself as not to fail.

But the foolish children of men miserably delude themselves in their own schemes, and in confidence in their own strength and wisdom; they trust to nothing but a shadow. The greater part of those who heretofore have lived under the same means of grace, and are now dead, are undoubtedly gone to hell; and it was not because they were not as wise as those who are now alive: it was not because they did not lay out matters as well for themselves to secure their own escape. If we could speak with them, and inquire of them, one by one, whether they expected, when alive, and when they used to hear about hell, ever to be the subjects of that misery: we doubtless, should hear one and another reply, "No, I never intended to come here: I had laid out matters otherwise in my mind; I thought I should contrive well for myself: I thought my scheme good. I intended to take effectual care; but it came upon me unexpected; I did not look for it at that time, and in that manner; it came as a chief: Death outwitted me: God's wrath was too quick for me. Oh, my cursed foolishness! I was flattering myself, and pleasing myself with vain dreams of what I would do hereafter; and when I was saying, Peace and safety, then suddenly destruction came upon me."

10. God has laid himself under *no* obligation, by any promise to keep and natural man out of hell one moment. God certainly has made no promises either of eternal life, or of any deliverance or preservation from eternal death, but what are contained in the covenant of grace, the promises that are given in Christ, in whom all the promises are yea and amen. But surely they have no interest in the promises of the covenant of grace who are not the children of the covenant, who do not believe in any of the promises, and have no interest in the Mediator of the covenant.

So that, whatever some have imagined and pretended about promises made to natural men's earnest seeking and knocking, it is plain and manifest, that whatever pains a natural man takes in religion, whatever prayers he makes, till he believes in Christ, God is under no manner of obligation to keep him a moment from eternal destruction.

So that, thus it is that natural men are held in the hand of God, over the pit of hell; they have deserved the fiery pit, and are already sentenced to it; and God is dreadfully provoked, his anger is as great towards them as to those that are actually suffering the executions of the fierceness of his wrath in hell, and they have done nothing in the least to appease or abate that anger, neither is God in the least bound by any promise to hold them up one moment; the devil is waiting for them, hell is gaping for them, the flames gather and flash about them, and would fain lay hold on them, and swallow them up; the fire pent up in their own hearts is struggling to break out: and they have no interest in any Mediator, there are no means within reach that can be any security to them. In short, they have no refuge, nothing to take hold of; all that preserves them every moment is in the mere arbitrary will, and uncovenanted, unobliged forbearance of an incensed God.

1741

QUESTIONS

1. Trace the steps by which Edwards gets from his text to his various conclusions about man's state. Are they all logical? What assumptions

*does he add to those implied by the text in developing his argument?
(Before answering these questions you will probably want to check the
entire context of the text in Deuteronomy xxxii.)*

2. *What kinds of evidence does Edwards use in supporting his argument?
Are they equally valid?*

3. *How do the concrete details, the imagery, and the metaphors that
Edwards uses contribute to the effectiveness of his argument?*

4. *One might make the assumption that a society's conception of hell
reflects, at least indirectly, some of that society's positive values. What
positive values are reflected in Edwards' picture of hell?*

5. *One of his pupils described Edwards' delivery: "His appearance in the
desk was with a good grace, and his delivery easy, natural and very
solemn. He had not a strong, loud voice, but appeared with such
gravity and solemnity, and spake with such distinctness and precision,
his words were so full of ideas, set in such a plain and striking light, that
few speakers have been so able to demand the attention of an audience
as he. His words often discovered a great degree of inward fervor,
without much noise or external emotion, and fell with great weight on
the minds of his hearers. He made but little motion of his head or hands
in the desk, but spake as to discover the motion of his own heart, which
tended in the most natural and effectual manner to move and affect
others." Would this manner of delivery be effective for the sermon
printed here? Explain.*

John Donne

LET ME WITHER

Let me wither and wear out mine age in a discomfortable, in an
unwholesome, in a penurious prison, and so pay my debts with my bones
and recompense the wastefulness of my youth with the beggary of mine
age. Let me wither in a spital[1] under sharp and foul and infamous
diseases, and so recompense the wantonness of my youth with that
loathsomeness in mine age. Yet if God withdraw not his spiritual blessings, his grace, his patience; if I can call my suffering his doing, my
passion[2] his action; all this that is temporal is but a caterpillar got into one
corner of my garden, but a mildew fallen upon one acre of my corn. The
body of all, the substance of all, is safe as long as the soul is safe.

But when I shall trust to that which we call a good spirit and God shall
deject[3] and impoverish and evacuate[4] that spirit; when I shall rely upon a
moral constancy and God shall shake and enfeeble and enervate, destroy

---

1. Hospital.
2. State of being acted upon.

3. Cast down.
4. Make empty.

and demolish that constancy; when I shall think to refresh myself in the
serenity and sweet air of a good conscience and God shall call up the
damps and vapors of hell itself and spread a cloud of diffidence[5] and an
impenetrable crust of desperation upon my conscience; when health
shall fly from me, and I shall lay hold upon riches to succor me and
comfort me in my sickness, and riches shall fly from me and I shall snatch
after favor and good opinion to comfort me in my poverty; when even
this good opinion shall leave me and calumnies and misinformations shall
prevail against me; when I shall need peace because there is none but
thou, O Lord, that should stand for me, and then shall find that all the
wounds that I have come from thy hand, all the arrows that stick in me
from thy quiver; when I shall see that because I have give myself to my
corrupt nature thou hast changed thine, and because I am all evil towards
thee, therefore thou hast given over being good towards me: when it
comes to this height, that the fever is not in the humors but in the spirits,[6]
that mine enemy is not an imaginary enemy, Fortune, nor a transitory
enemy, Malice in great persons, but a real and an irresistible and an
inexorable and an everlasting enemy, the Lord of Hosts himself, the
Almighty God himself—the Almighty God himself only knows the
weight of this affliction, and except[7] he put in that *pondus gloriae*, that
exceeding weight of an eternal glory, with his own hand into the other
scale, we are weighed down, we are swallowed up irreparably, irrevocably, irrecoverably, irremediably.

1625   1640

5. Distrust.   thought to permeate the blood and organs
6. Not merely in the physical fluids of the   and to serve as a link between body and soul.
body but even in those more refined vapors   7. Unless.

QUESTIONS

   *Donne is perhaps more famous as a poet than as preacher, yet all that
any author writes will in one way or another bear the stamp of his
thought and personality. Read the following poem by Donne, and compare it with the sermon. Does the conception of God suggested in the
poem resemble that in the sermon? Does the poem accomplish any of the
same purposes as the sermon? Is the sermon "poetic" in any way? What
differences arise from the fact that in the sermon Donne is speaking to a
congregation, in the poem he is addressing God?*

> Batter my heart, three person'd God; for, you
> As yet but knocke, breathe, shine, and seeke to mend.
> That I may rise, and stand, o'erthrow mee, and bend
> Your force, to breake, blowe, burn and make me new.
> I, like an usurpt towne, to another due,
> Labour to admit you, but Oh, to no end,
> Reason your viceroy in mee, mee should defend,
> But is captiv'd, and proves weake or untrue.

Yet dearely I love you, and would be loved faine,
But am bethroth'd unto your enemie;
Divorce mee, untie, or breake that knot againe,
Take mee to you, imprison mee, for I
Except you enthrall mee, never shall be free,
Nor ever chast, except you ravish mee.

—JOHN DONNE

C. S. Lewis

THREE SCREWTAPE LETTERS

I

MY DEAR WORMWOOD,[1]

I note what you say about guiding your patient's reading and taking care that he sees a good deal of his materialist friend. But are you not being a trifle naïf? *It sounds as if you supposed that argument* was the way to keep him out of the Enemy's clutches. That might have been so if he had lived a few centuries earlier. At that time the humans still knew pretty well when a thing was proved and when it was not; and if it was proved they really believed it. They still connected thinking with doing and were prepared to alter their way of life as the result of a chain of reasoning. But what with the weekly press and other such weapons we have largely altered that. Your man has been accustomed, ever since he was a boy, to have a dozen incompatible philosophies dancing about together inside his head. He doesn't think of doctrines as primarily "true" or "false", but as "academic" or "practical", "outworn" or "contemporary", "conventional" or "ruthless". Jargon, not argument, is your best ally in keeping him from the Church. Don't waste time trying to make him think that materialism is *true*! Make him think it is strong, or stark, or courageous—that it is the philosophy of the future. That's the sort of thing he cares about.

The trouble about argument is that it moves the whole struggle onto the Enemy's own ground. He can argue too; whereas in really practical propaganda of the kind I am suggesting He has been shown for centuries to be greatly the inferior of Our Father Below. By the very act of arguing, you awake the patient's reason; and once it is awake, who can foresee the result? Even if a particular train of thought can be twisted so as to end in our favour, you will find that you have been strengthening in your patient the fatal habit of attending to universal issues and withdrawing his attention from the stream of immediate sense experiences. Your business

---

1. In these letters from Hell, Screwtape, an experienced devil, is counseling his nephew Wormwood, a neophyte tempter, who has ascended to Earth to begin his work.

is to fix his attention on the stream. Teach him to call it "real life" and don't let him ask what he means by "real".

Remember, he is not, like you, a pure spirit. Never having been a human (Oh that abominable advantage of the Enemy's!) you don't realise how enslaved they are to the pressure of the ordinary. I once had a patient, a sound atheist, who used to read in the British Museum. One day, as he sat reading, I saw a train of thought in his mind beginning to go the wrong way. The Enemy, of course, was at his elbow in a moment. Before I knew where I was I saw my twenty years' work beginning to totter. If I had lost my head and begun to attempt a defence by argument I should have been undone. But I was not such a fool. I struck instantly at the part of the man which I had best under my control and suggested that it was just about time he had some lunch. The Enemy presumably made the countersuggestion (you know how one can never *quite* overhear what He says to them?) that this was more important than lunch. At least I think that must have been His line for when I said "Quite. In fact much *too* important to tackle at the end of a morning", the patient brightened up considerably; and by the time I had added "Much better come back after lunch and go into it with a fresh mind", he was already half way to the door. Once he was in the street the battle was won. I showed him a newsboy shouting the midday paper, and a No. 73 bus going past, and before he reached the bottom of the steps I had got into him an unalterable conviction that, whatever odd ideas might come into a man's head when he was shut up alone with his books, a healthy dose of "real life" (by which he meant the bus and the newsboy) was enough to show him that all "that sort of thing" just couldn't be true. He knew he'd had a narrow escape and in later years was fond of talking about "that inarticulate sense for actuality which is our ultimate safeguard against the aberrations of mere logic". He is now safe in Our Father's house.

You begin to see the point? Thanks to processes which we set at work in them centuries ago, they find it all but impossible to believe in the unfamiliar while the familiar is before their eyes. Keep pressing home on him the *ordinariness* of things. Above all, do not attempt to use science (I mean, the real sciences) as a defence against Christianity. They will positively encourage him to think about realities he can't touch and see. These have been sad cases among the modern physicists. If he must dabble in science, keep him on economics and sociology; don't let him get away from that invaluable "real life". But the best of all is to let him read no science but to give him a grand general idea that he knows it all and that everything he happens to have picked up in casual talk and reading is "the results of modern investigation". Do remember you are there to fuddle him. From the way some of you young fiends talk, anyone would suppose it was our job to *teach*!

Your affectionate uncle
SCREWTAPE

II

My Dear Wormwood,

I note with grave displeasure that your patient has become a Christian. Do not indulge the hope that you will escape the usual penalties: indeed, in your better moments, I trust you would hardly even wish to do so. In the meantime we must make the best of the situation. There is no need to despair; hundreds of these adult converts have been reclaimed after a brief sojourn in the Enemy's camp and are now with us. All the *habits* of the patient, both mental and bodily, are still in our favour.

One of our great allies at present is the Church itself. Do not misunderstand me. I do not mean the Church as we see her spread out through all time and space and rooted in eternity, terrible as an army with banners. That, I confess, is a spectacle which makes our boldest tempters uneasy. But fortunately it is quite invisible to these humans. All your patient sees is the half-finished, sham Gothic erection on the new building estate. When he goes inside, he sees the local grocer with rather an oily expression on his face bustling up to offer him one shiny little book containing a liturgy which neither of them understands, and one shabby little book containing corrupt texts of a number of religious lyrics, mostly bad, and in very small print. When he gets to his pew and looks round him he sees just that selection of his neighbours whom he has hitherto avoided. You want to lean pretty heavily on those neighbours. Make his mind flit to and fro between an expression like "the body of Christ" and the actual faces in the next pew. It matters very little of course, what kind of people that next pew really contains. You may know one of them to be a great warrior on the Enemy's side. No matter. Your patient, thanks to Our Father Below, is a fool. Provided that any of those neighbours sing out of tune, or have boots that squeak, or double chins, or odd clothes, the patient will quite easily believe that their religion must therefore be somehow ridiculous. At his present stage, you see, he has an idea of "Christians" in his mind which he supposes to be spiritual but which, in fact, is largely pictorial. His mind is full of togas and sandals and armour and bare legs and the mere fact that the other people in church wear modern clothes is a real—though of course an unconscious—difficulty to him. Never let it come to the surface; never let him ask what he expected them to look like. Keep everything hazy in his mind now, and you will have all eternity wherein to amuse yourself by producing in him the peculiar kind of clarity which Hell affords.

Work hard, then, on the disappointment or anticlimax which is certainly coming to the patient during his first few weeks as a churchman. The Enemy allows this disappointment to occur on the threshold of every human endeavour. It occurs when the boy who has been enchanted in the nursery by *Stories from the Odyssey* buckles down to really learning Greek. It occurs when lovers have got married and begin the real task of learning to live together. In every department of life it marks the transition from dreaming aspiration to laborious doing. The Enemy takes this risk because He has a curious fantasy of making all these disgusting little human vermin into what He calls His "free" lovers and servants —"sons" is the word He uses, with His inveterate love of degrading the whole spiritual world by unnatural liaisons with the two-legged animals. Desiring their freedom, He therefore refuses to carry them, by their mere affections and habits, to any of the goals which He sets before them: He leaves them to "do it on their own". And there lies our opportunity. But also, remember, there lies our danger. If once they get through this initial dryness successfully, they become much less dependent on emotion and therefore much harder to tempt.

I have been writing hitherto on the assumption that the people in the next pew afford no *rational* ground for disappointment. Of course if they do—if the patient knows that the woman with the absurd hat is a fanatical bridge-player or the man with squeaky boots a miser and an extortioner—then your task is so much the easier. All you then have to do is to keep out of his mind the question "If I, being what I am, can consider that I am in some sense a Christian, why should the different vices of those people in the next pew prove that their religion is mere hypocrisy and convention?" You may ask whether it is possible to keep such an obvious thought from occurring even to a human mind. It is, Wormwood, it is! Handle him properly and it simply won't come into his head. He has not been anything like long enough with the Enemy to have any real humility yet. What he says, even on his knees, about his own sinfulness is all parrot talk. At bottom, he still believes he has run up a very favourable credit-balance in the Enemy's ledger by allowing himself to be converted, and thinks that he is showing great humility and conde-scension in going to church with those "smug", commonplace neighbours at all. Keep him in that state of mind as long as you can.

Your affectionate uncle
SCREWTAPE

III

My Dear Wormwood,

I am very pleased by what you tell me about this man's relations with his mother. But you must press your advantage. The Enemy will be working from the centre outwards, gradually bringing more and more of the patient's conduct under the new standard, and may reach his beha-viour to the old lady at any moment. You want to get in first. Keep in close touch with our colleague Glubose who is in charge of the mother, and build up between you in that house a good settled habit of mutual annoyance; daily pinpricks. The following methods are useful.

1. Keep his mind on the inner life. He thinks his conversion is something *inside* him and his attention is therefore chiefly turned at present to the states of his own mind—or rather to that very expurgated version of them which is all you should allow him to see. Encourage this. Keep his mind off the most elementary duties by directing it to the most advanced and spiritual ones. Aggravate that most useful human characteristic, the horror and neglect of the obvious. You must bring him to a condition in which he can practise self-examination for an hour without discovering any of those facts about himself which are perfectly clear to anyone who has ever lived in the same house with him or worked in the same office.

2. It is, no doubt, impossible to prevent his praying for his mother, but we have means of rendering the prayers innocuous. Make sure that they are always very "spiritual", that he is always concerned with the state of her soul and never with her rheumatism. Two advantages will follow. In the first place, his attention will be kept on what he regards as her sins, by which, with a little guidance from you, he can be induced to mean any of her actions which are inconvenient or irritating to himself. Thus you can keep rubbing the wounds of the day a little sorer even while he is on his knees; the operation is not at all difficult and you will find it very entertaining. In the second place, since his ideas about her soul will be very crude and often erroneous, he will, in some degree, be praying for an imaginary person, and it will be your task to make that imaginary person daily less and less like the real mother—the sharp-tongued old lady at the breakfast table. In time, you may get the cleavage so wide that no thought or feeling from his prayers for the imagined mother will ever flow over into his treatment of the real one. I have had patients of my own so well in hand that they could be turned at a moment's notice from impassioned prayer for a wife's or son's "soul" to beating or insulting the real wife or son without a qualm.

3. When two humans have lived together for many years it usually happens that each has tones of voice and expressions of face which are almost unendurably irritating to the other. Work on that. Bring fully into the consciousness of your patient that particular lift of his mother's eyebrows which he learned to dislike in the nursery, and let him think how much he dislikes it. Let him assume that she knows how annoying it is and does it to annoy—if you know your job he will not notice the immense improbability of the assumption. And, of course, never let him suspect that he has tones and looks which similarly annoy her. As he cannot see or hear himself, this is easily managed.

4. In civilised life domestic hatred usually expresses itself by saying things which would appear quite harmless on paper (the *words* are not offensive) but in such a voice, or at such a moment, that they are not far short of a blow in the face. To keep this game up you and Glubose must

see to it that each of these two fools has a sort of double standard. Your patient must demand that all his own utterances are to be taken at their face value and judged simply on the actual words, while at the same time judging all his mother's utterances with the fullest and most over-sensitive interpretation of the tone and the context and the suspected intention. She must be encouraged to do the same to him. Hence from every quarrel they can both go away convinced, or very nearly convinced, that they are quite innocent. You know the kind of thing: "I simply ask her what time dinner will be and she flies into a temper." Once this habit is well established you have the delightful situation of a human saying things will the express purpose of offending and yet having a grievance when offence is taken.

Finally, tell me something about the old lady's religious position. Is she at all jealous of the new factor in her son's life?—at all piqued that he should have learned from others, and so late, what she considers she gave him such good opportunity of learning in childhood? Does she feel he is making a great deal of "fuss" about it—or that he's getting in on very easy terms? Remember the elder brother in the Enemy's story,[2]

Your affectionate uncle
SCREWTAPE

1942

2. The reference is to Jesus' parable of the prodigal son. The younger brother, having gone out into the world and spent his inheritance, was welcomed back by the father with feasting and celebration; this made the older brother, who had stayed at home and labored diligently for the father, angry and envious.

QUESTIONS

1. *How would you state the serious underlying purpose of the Screwtape letters? Does Lewis derive advantages for that purpose by adopting a humorous manner? Can you show any instances in which that manner places familiar material in a new light?*

2. *What sort of characteristics does Lewis attribute to his devil Screwtape? Are they strange and unfamiliar, or are they human and familiar? What point does Lewis make by portraying his devil as he does?*

3. *Following Lewis, write another letter from Screwtape to Wormwood upon learning that Wormwood's subject has just been reading Robert Graves' "Mythology" (p. 1129), Jonathan Edwards' "Sinners in the Hands of an Angry God" (p. 1137), or Paul Tillich's "The Riddle of Inequality" (p. 1153).*

4. *Try applying Lewis' method of irony to some other topic; write a letter or series of letters from an older student to a freshman on the subject of teachers, for example, or from one parent to another about their college-age children, or from an experienced government official to a newly elected one.*

Sören Kierkegaard

THE KNIGHT OF FAITH

I candidly admit that in my practice I have not found any reliable example of the knight of faith, though I would not therefore deny that every second man may be such an example. I have been trying, however, for several years to get on the track of this, and all in vain. People commonly travel around the world to see rivers and mountains, new stars, birds of rare plumage, queerly deformed fishes, ridiculous breeds of men—they abandon themselves to the bestial stupor which gapes at existence, and they think they have seen something. This does not interest me. But if I knew where there was such a knight of faith, I would make a pilgrimage to him on foot, for this prodigy interests me absolutely. I would not let go of him for an instant, every moment I would watch to see how he managed to make the movements, I would regard myself as secured for life, and would divide my time between looking at him and practicing the exercises myself, and thus would spend all my time admiring him. As was said, I have not found any such person, but I can well think him. Here he is. Acquaintance made, I am introduced to him. The moment I set eyes on him I instantly push him from me, I myself leap backwards, I clasp my hands and say half aloud, "Good Lord, is this the man? Is it really he? Why, he looks like a tax collector!" However, it is the man after all. I draw closer to him, watching his least movements to see whether there might not be visible a little heterogeneous fractional telegraphic message from the infinite, a glance, a look, a gesture, a note of sadness, a smile, which betrayed the infinite in its heterogeneity with the finite. No! I examine his figure from tip to toe to see if there might not be a cranny through which the infinite was peeping. No! He is solid through and through. His tread? It is vigorous, belonging entirely to finiteness; no smartly dressed townsman who walks out to Fresberg on a Sunday afternoon treads the ground more firmly, he belongs entirely to the world, no Philistine more so. One can discover nothing of that aloof and superior nature whereby one recognizes the knight of the infinite. He takes delight in everything, and whenever one sees him taking part in a particular pleasure, he does it with the persistence which is the mark of the earthly man whose soul is absorbed in such things. He tends to his work. So when one looks at him one might suppose that he was a clerk who had lost his soul in an intricate system of bookkeeping, so precise is he. He takes a holiday on Sunday. He goes to church. No heavenly glance or any other token of the incommensurable betrays him; if one did not know him, it would be impossible to distinguish him from the rest of the congregation, for his healthy and vigorous

hymn singing proves at the most that he has a good chest. In the afternoon he walks to the forest. He takes delight in everything he sees, in the
human swarm, in the new omnibuses, in the water of the Sound; when
one meets him on the Beach Road one might suppose he was a shop-
keeper taking his fling, that's just the way he disports himself, for he is not
a poet, and I have sought in vain to detect in him the poetic incommensurability. Toward evening he walks home, his gait is as indefatigable as
that of the postman. On his way he reflects that his wife has surely a
special little warm dish prepared for him, e.g. a calf's head roasted,
garnished with vegetables. If he were to meet a man like-minded, he
could continue as far as East Gate to discourse with him about that dish,
with a passion befitting a hotel chef. As it happens, he hasn't four pence
to his name, and yet he fully and firmly believes that his wife has that
dainty dish for him. If she had it, it would then be an invidious sight for
superior people and an inspiring one for the plain man, to see him eat; for
his appetite is greater than Esau's.[1] His wife hasn't it—strangely enough,
it is quite the same to him. On the way he comes past a building site and
runs across another man. They talk together for a moment. In the
twinkling of an eye he erects a new building, he has at his disposition all
the powers necessary for it. The stranger leaves him with the thought
that he certainly was a capitalist, while my admired knight thinks, "Yes,
if the money were needed, I dare say I could get it." He lounges at an open
window and looks out on the square on which he lives; he is interested in
everything that goes on, in a rat which slips under the curb, in the
children's play, and this with the nonchalance of a girl of sixteen. And yet
he is no genius, for in vain I have sought in him the incommensurability
of genius. In the evening he smokes his pipe; to look at him one would
swear that it was the grocer over the way vegetating in the twilight. He
lives as carefree as a ne'er-do-well, and yet he buys up the acceptable
time at the dearest price, for he does not do the least thing except by
virtue of the absurd. And yet, and yet—actually I could become dubious
over it, for envy if for no other reason—this man has made and every
instant is making the movements of infinity. With infinite resignation he
has drained the cup of life's profound sadness, he knows the bliss of the
infinite, he senses the pain of renouncing everything, the dearest things
he possesses in the world, and yet finiteness tastes to him just as good as to
one who never knew anything higher, for his continuance in the finite did
not bear a trace of the cowed and fearful spirit produced by the process of
training; and yet he has the sense of security in enjoying it, as though the
finite life were the surest thing of all. And yet, and yet the whole earthly
form he exhibits is a new creation by virtue of the absurd. He resigned
everything infinitely, and then he grasped everything again by virtue of
the absurd. He constantly makes the movements of infinity, but he does

1. Esau sold his inheritance to his brother Jacob for a meal (Genesis xxv).

this with such correctness and assurance that he constantly gets the finite out of it, and there is not a second when one has a notion of anything else. It is supposed to be the most difficult task for a dancer to leap into a definite posture in such a way that there is not a second when he is grasping after the posture, but by the leap itself he stands fixed in that posture. Perhaps no dancer can do it—that is what this knight does. Most people live dejectedly in wordly sorrow and joy; they are the ones who sit along the wall and do not join in the dance. The knights of infinity are dancers and possess elevation. They make the movements upward, and fall down again; and this too is no mean pastime, nor ungraceful to behold. But whenever they fall down they are not able at once to assume the posture, they vacillate an instant, and this vacillation shows that after all they are strangers in the world. This is more or less strikingly evident in proportion to the art they possess, but even the most artistic knights cannot altogether conceal this vacillation. One need not look at them when they are up in the air, but only the instant they touch or have touched the ground—then one recognizes them. But to be able to fall down in such a way that the same second it looks as if one were standing and walking, to transform the leap of life into a walk, absolutely to express the sublime in the pedestrian—that only the knight of faith can do—and this is the one and only prodigy.

1941

Paul Tillich

THE RIDDLE OF INEQUALITY

> For to him who has will more be given; and from him
> who has not, even what he has will be taken away.
> —MARK iv. 25

One day a learned colleague called me up and said to me with angry excitement: "There is a saying in the New Testament which I consider to be one of the most immoral and unjust statements ever made!" And then he started quoting our text: "To him who has will more be given," and his anger increased when he continued: "and from him who has not, even what he has will be taken away." We all, I think, feel offended with him. And we cannot easily ignore the offense by suggesting what he suggested —that the words may be due to a misunderstanding of the disciples. It appears at least four times in the gospels with great emphasis. And even more, we can clearly see that the writers of the gospels felt exactly as we do. For them it was a stumbling block, which they tried to interpret in different ways. Probably none of these explanations satisfied them fully, for with this saying of Jesus, we are confronted immediately with the greatest and perhaps most painful riddle of life, that of the inequality of all beings. We certainly cannot hope to solve it when neither the Bible nor any other of the great religions and philosophies was able to do so. But we can do two things: We can show the breadth and the depth of the riddle of inequality and we can try to find a way to live with it, even if it is unsolved.

I

If we hear the words, "to him who has will more be given," we ask ourselves: What *do* we have? And then we may find that much is given to us in terms of external goods, of friends, of intellectual gifts and even of a comparatively high moral level of action. So we can expect that more will be given to us, while we must expect that those who are lacking in all that will lose the little they already have. Even further, according to Jesus' parable, the one talent[1] they have will be given to us who have five or ten talents. We shall be richer because they will be poorer. We may cry out against such an injustice. But we cannot deny that life confirms it abundantly. We cannot deny it, but we can ask the question, do we *really* have what we believe we have so that it cannot be taken from us? It is a question full of anxiety, confirmed by a version of our text rendered by Luke. "From him who has not, even what he *thinks* that he has will be taken away." Perhaps our having of those many things is not the kind of having which is increased. Perhaps the having of few things by the poor ones is the kind of having which makes them grow. In the parable of the talents, Jesus confirms this. Those talents which are used, even with a risk of losing them, are those which we really have; those which we try to preserve without using them for growth are those which we do not really have and which are being taken away from us. They slowly disappear, and suddenly we feel that we have lost these talents, perhaps forever.

Let us apply this to our own life, whether it is long or short. In the memory of all of us many things appear which we had without having them and which were taken away from us. Some of them became lost because of the tragic limitations of life; we had to sacrifice them in order to make other things grow. We all were given childish innocence; but innocence cannot be used and increased. The growth of our lives is possible only because we have sacrificed the original gift of innocence. Nevertheless, sometimes there arises in us a melancholy longing for a purity which has been taken from us. We all were given youthful enthusiasm for many things and aims. But this also cannot be used and increased. Most of the objects of our early enthusiasm must be sacrificed for a few, and the few must be approached with soberness. No maturity is

1. A Middle Eastern coin at the time of Christ.

possible without this sacrifice. Yet often a melancholy longing for the lost possibilities and enthusiasm takes hold of us. Innocence and youthful enthusiasm: we had them and had them not. Life itself demanded that they were taken from us.

But there are other things which we had and which were taken from us, because we let them go through our own guilt. Some of us had a deep sensitivity for the wonder of life as it is revealed in nature. Slowly under the pressure of work and social life and the lure of cheap pleasures, we lose the wonder of our earlier years when we felt intense joy and the presence of the mystery of life through the freshness of the young day or the glory of the dying day, the majesty of the mountains or the infinity of the sea, a flower breaking through the soil or a young animal in the perfection of its movements. Perhaps we try to produce such feelings again, but we are empty and do not succeed. We had it and had it not, and it has been taken from us.

Others had the same experience with music, poetry, the great novels and plays. One wanted to devour all of them, one lived in them and created for oneself a life above the daily life. We had all this and did not have it; we did not let it grow; our love towards it was not strong enough and so it was taken from us.

Many, especially in this group, remember a time in which the desire to learn to solve the riddles of the universe, to find truth has been the driving force in their lives. They came to college and university, not in order to buy their entrance ticket into the upper middle classes or in order to provide for the preconditions of social and economic success, but they came, driven by the desire for knowledge. They had something and more could have been given to them. But in reality they did not have it. They did not make it grow and so it was taken from them and they finished their academic work in terms of expendiency and indifference towards truth. Their love for truth has left them and in some moments they are sick in their hearts because they realize that what they have lost they may never get back.

We all know that any deeper relation to a human being needs watch-fulness and growth, otherwise it is taken away from us. And we cannot get it back. This is a form of having and not having which is the root of innumerable human tragedies. We all know about them. And there is another, the most fundamental kind of having and not having—our having and losing God. Perhaps we were rich towards God in our childhood and beyond it. We may remember the moments in which we felt his ultimate presence. We may remember prayers with an overflow-ing heart, the encounter with the holy in word and music and holy places. We had communication with God; but it was taken from us because we had it and had it not. We did not let it grow, and so it slowly disappeared leaving an empty space. We became unconcerned, cynical, indifferent, not because we doubted about our religious traditions—such doubt belongs to being rich towards God—but because we turned away from that which once concerned us infinitely.

Such thoughts are a first step in approaching the riddle of inequality. Those who have, receive more if they really have it, if they use it and make it grow. And those who have not, lose what they have because they never had it really.

II

But the question of inequality is not yet answered. For one now asks: Why do some receive more than others in the very beginning, before there is even the possibility of using or wasting our talents? Why does the one servant receive five talents and the other two and the third one? Why is the one born in the slums and the other in a well-to-do suburban family? It does not help to answer that of those to whom much is given much is demanded and little of those to whom little is given. For it is just this inequality of original gifts, internal and external, which arouses our question. Why is it given to one human being to gain so much more out of his being human than to another one? Why is so much given to the one that much can be asked of him, while to the other one little is given and little can be asked? If this question is asked, not only about individual men but also about classes, races and nations, the everlasting question of political inequality arises, and with it the many ways appear in which men have tried to abolish inequality. In every revolution and in every war, the will to solve the riddle of inequality is a driving force. But neither war nor revolution can remove it. Even if we imagine that in an indefinite future most social inequalities are conquered, three things remain: the inequality of talents in body and mind, the inequality created by freedom and destiny, and the fact that all generations before the time of such equality would be excluded from its blessings. This would be the greatest possible inequality! No! In face of one of the deepest and most torturing problems of life, it is unpermittably shallow and foolish to escape into a social dreamland. We have to live now; we have to live this our life, and we must face today the riddle of inequality.

Let us not confuse the riddle of inequality with the fact that each of us is a unique incomparable self. Certainly our being individuals belongs to our dignity as men. It is given to us and must be used and intensified and not drowned in the gray waters of conformity which threaten us today. One should defend every individuality and the uniqueness of every human self. But one should not believe that this is a way of solving the riddle of inequality. Unfortunately, there are social and political reactionaries who use this confusion in order to justify social injustice. They are at least as foolish as the dreamers of a future removal of inequality. Whoever has seen hospitals, prisons, sweatshops, battlefields, houses for the insane, starvation, family tragedies, moral aberrations should be cured from any confusion of the gift of individuality with the riddle of inequality. He should be cured from any feelings of easy consolation.

III

And now we must make the third step in our attempt to penetrate the riddle of inequality and ask: Why do some use and increase what was given to them, while others do not, so that it is taken from them? Why does God say to the prophet in our Old Testament lesson that the ears and eyes of a nation are made insensible for the divine message?

Is it enough to answer: Because some use their freedom responsibly and do what they ought to do while others fail through their own guilt? Is this answer, which seems so obvious, sufficient? Now let me first say that it *is* sufficient if we apply it to ourselves. Each of us must consider the increase or the loss of what is given to him as a matter of his own responsibility. Our conscience tells us that we cannot put the blame for our losses on anybody or anything else than ourselves.

But if we look at others, this answer is not sufficient. On the contrary: If we applied the judgment which we *must* apply to anyone else we would be like the Pharisee in Jesus' parable.[2] You cannot tell somebody who comes to you in distress about himself: Use what has been given to you; for he may come to you just because he is unable to do so! And you cannot tell those who are in despair aboutwhat they are: Be something else; for this is just what despair means—the inability of getting rid of oneself. You cannot tell those who did not conquer the destructive influences of their surroundings and were driven into crime and misery that they should have been stronger; for it was just of this strength they had been deprived by heritage or environment. Certainly they all are men, and to all of them freedom is given; but they all are also subject to destiny. It is not up to us to condemn them because they were free, as it is not up to us to excuse them because they were under their destiny. We cannot judge them. And when we judge ourselves, we must be conscious that even this is not the last word, but that we like them are under an ultimate judgment. In it the riddle of inequality is eternally answered. But this answer is not ours. It is our predicament that we must ask. And we ask with an uneasy conscience. Why are they in misery, why not we? Thinking of some who are near to us, we can ask: Are we partly responsible? But even if we are, it does not solve the riddle of inequality. The uneasy conscience asks about the farthest as well as about the nearest: Why they, why not we?

Why has my child, or any of millions and millions of children, died before even having a chance to grow out of infancy? Why is my child, or any child, born feeble-minded or crippled? Why has my friend or relative, or anybody's friend or relative, disintegrated in his mind and lost

---

2. Praying in the temple, the Pharisee said, "God, I thank thee, that I am not as other men are, extortioners, unjust, adulterers . . ." (Luke xviii. 11).

both his freedom and his destiny? Why has my son or daughter, gifted as I belive with many talents, wasted them and been deprived of them? And why does this happen to any parent at all? Why have this boy's or this girl's creative powers been broken by a tyrannical father or by a possessive mother?

In all these questions it is not the question of our own misery which we ask. It is not the question: Why has this happened to *me*?

It is not the question of Job which God answers by humiliating him and then by elevating him into communion with him.[3] It is not the old and urgent question: Where is the divine justice, where is the divine love towards me? But it is almost the opposite question: Why has this *not* happened to me, why has it happened to the other one, to the innumerable other ones to whom not even the power of Job is given to accept the divine answer? Why—and Jesus has asked the same question—are many called and few elected?

He does not answer; he only states that this is the human predicament. Shall we therefore cease to ask and humbly accept the fact of a divine judgment which condemns most human beings away from the community with him into despair and self-destruction? Can we accept the eternal victory of judgment over love? We cannot; and nobody ever could, even if he preached and threatened in these terms. As long as he could not see himself with complete certainty as eternally rejected, his preaching and threatening would be self-deceiving. And who could see himself eternally rejected?

But if this is not the solution of the riddle of inequality at its deepest level, can we trespass the boundaries of the Christian tradition and listen to those who tell us that this life does not decide about our eternal destiny? There will be occasions in other lives, as our present life is determined by previous ones and what we have achieved or wasted in them. It is a serious doctrine and not completely strange to Christianity. But if we don't know and never will know what each of us has been in the previous or future lives, then it is not really *our* destiny which develops from life to life, but in each life it is the destiny of someone else. This answer also does not solve the riddle of inequality.

There is no answer at all if we ask about the temporal and eternal destiny of the single being separated from the destiny of the whole. Only in the unity of all beings in time and eternity can a humanly possible answer to the riddle of inequality be found. *Humanly* possible does not mean an answer which removes the riddle of inequality, but an answer with which we can live.

There is an ultimate unity of all beings, rooted in the divine life from

3. Job, one of God's favored servants, was stricken with afflictions. His question, very briefly, was "Why?" God's answer was to remind Job of how powerless man was in comparison with God, and to refuse to explain His actions. After accepting this pronouncement, Job was elevated again into God's favor.

which they come and to which they go. All beings, nonhuman as well as human, participate in it. And therefore they all participate in each other. We participate in each other's having and we participate in each other's not-having. If we become aware of this unity of all beings, something happens. The fact that others have-not changes in every moment the character of my having: It undercuts its security, it drives me beyond myself, to understand, to give, to share, to help. The fact that others fall into sin, crime and misery changes the character of the grace which is given to me: It makes me realize my own hidden guilt, it shows to me that those who suffer for their sin and crime, suffer also for me; for I am guilty of their guilt—at least in the desire of my heart—and ought to suffer as they do. The awareness that others who *could* have become fully developed human beings and never *have*, changes my state of full humanity. Their early death, their early or late disintegration, makes my life and my health a continuous risk, a dying which is not yet death, a disintegration which is not yet destruction. In every death which we encounter, something of us dies; in every disease which we encounter, something of us tends to disintegrate.

Can we live with this answer? We can to the degree in which we are liberated from the seclusion within ourselves. But nobody can be liberated from himself unless he is grasped by the power of that which is present in everyone and everything—the eternal from which we come and to which we go, which gives us to ourselves and which liberates us *from* ourselves. It is the greatness and the heart of the Christian message that God—as manifest in the Cross of the Christ—participates totally in the dying child, in the condemned criminal, in the disintegrating mind, in the starving one and in him who rejects him. There is no extreme human condition into which the divine presence would not reach. This is what the Cross, the most extreme of all human conditions, tells us. The riddle of inequality cannot be solved on the level of our separation from each other. It is eternally solved in the divine participation in all of us and every being. The certainty of the divine participation gives us the courage to stand the riddle of inequality, though finite minds cannot solve it. Amen.

1963

George Santayana

CLASSIC LIBERTY

When ancient peoples defended what they called their liberty, the word stood for a plain and urgent interest of theirs: that their cities should not be destroyed, their territory pillaged, and they themselves sold into slavery. For the Greeks in particular liberty meant even more than this. Perhaps the deepest assumption of classic philosophy is that nature and the gods on the one hand and man on the other, both have a fixed character; that there is consequently a necessary piety, a true philosophy, a standard happiness, a normal art. The Greeks believed, not without reason, that they had grasped these permanent principles better than other peoples. They had largely dispelled superstition, experimented in government, and turned life into a rational art. Therefore when they defended their liberty what they defended was not merely freedom to live. It was freedom to live well, to live as other nations did not, in the public experimental study of the world and of human nature. This liberty to discover and pursue a natural happiness, this liberty to grow wise and to live in friendship with the gods and with one another, was the liberty vindicated at Thermopylae by martyrdom and at Salamis by victory.[1]

As Greek cities stood for liberty in the world, so philosophers stood for liberty in the Greek cities. In both cases it was the same kind of liberty, not freedom to wander at hazard or to let things slip, but on the contrary freedom to legislate more precisely, at least for oneself, and to discover and codify the means to true happiness. Many of these pioneers in wisdom were audacious radicals and recoiled from no paradox. Some condemned what was most Greek: mythology, athletics, even multiplicity and physical motion. In the heart of those thriving, loquacious, festive little ant-hills, they preached impassibility and abstraction, the unanswerable scepticism of silence. Others practised a musical and priestly refinement of life, filled with metaphysical mysteries, and formed secret societies, not without a tendency to political domination. The cynics railed at the conventions, making themselves as comfortable as possible in the role of beggars and mocking parasites. The conservatives themselves were radical, so intelligent were they, and Plato wrote the charter[2] of the most extreme militarism and communism, for the sake of preserving the free state. It was the swan-song of liberty, a prescription to a diseased old man to become young again and try a second life of superhuman virtue. The old man preferred simply to die.

---

1. The reference is to two famous episodes in the war between the Persians and the Greeks. A small force of Spartans at the narrow pass of Thermopylae fought to the last man to delay the invading Persian army; shortly afterward the Greeks defeated the Persians in the naval battle at Salamis, thus turning back the Persian invasion.
2. The reference is to Plato's *Republic*.

Many laughed then, as we may be tempted to do, at all those absolute physicians of the soul, each with his panacea. Yet beneath their quarrels the wranglers had a common faith. They all believed there was a single solid natural wisdom to be found, that reason could find it, and that mankind, sobered by reason, could put it in practice. Mankind has continued to run wild and like barbarians to place freedom in their very wildness, till we can hardly conceive the classic assumption of Greek philosophers and cities, that true liberty is bound up with an institution, a corporate scientific discipline, necessary to set free the perfect man, or the god, within us.

Upon the dissolution of paganism the Christian church adopted the classic conception of liberty. Of course, the field in which the higher politics had to operate was now conceived differently, and there was a new experience of the sort of happiness appropriate and possible to man; but the assumption remained unchallenged that Providence, as well as the human soul, had a fixed discoverable scope, and that the business of education, law, and religion was to bring them to operate in harmony. The aim of life, salvation, was involved in the nature of the soul itself, and the means of salvation had been ascertained by a positive science which the church was possessed of, partly revealed and partly experimental. Salvation was simply what, on a broad view, we should see to be health, and religion was nothing but a sort of universal hygiene.

The church, therefore, little as it tolerated heretical liberty, the liberty of moral and intellectual dispersion, felt that it had come into the world to set men free, and constantly demanded liberty for itself, that it might fulfil this mission. It was divinely commissioned to teach, guide, and console all nations and all ages by the self-same means, and to promote at all costs what it conceived to be human perfection. There should be saints and as many saints as possible. The church never admitted, any more than did any sect of ancient philosophers, that its teaching might represent only an eccentric view of the world, or that its guidance and consolations might be suitable only at one stage of human development. To waver in the pursuit of the orthodox ideal could only betray frivolity and want of self-knowledge. The truth of things and the happiness of each man could not lie elsewhere than where the church, summing up all human experience and all divine revelation, had placed it once for all and for everybody. The liberty of the church to fulfil its mission was accordingly hostile to any liberty of dispersion, to any radical consecutive independence, in the life of individuals or of nations.

When it came to full fruition this orthodox freedom was far from gay; it was called sanctity. The freedom of pagan philosophers too had turned out to be rather a stiff and severe pose; but in the Christian dispensation this austerity of true happiness was less to be wondered at, since life on earth was reputed to be abnormal from the beginning, and infected with hereditary disease. The full beauty and joy of restored liberty could hardly become evident in this life. Nevertheless a certain beauty and joy did radiate visibly from the saints; and while we may well think their renunciations and penances misguided or excessive, it is certain that, like the Spartans and the philosophers, they got something for their pains. Their bodies and souls were transfigured, as none now found upon earth. If we admire without imitating them we shall perhaps have done their philosophy exact justice. Classic liberty was a sort of forced and artificial liberty, a poor perfection reserved for an ascetic aristocracy in whom heroism and refinement were touched with perversity and slowly starved themselves to death.

Since those days we have discovered how much larger the universe is, and we have lost our way in it. Any day it may come over us again that our modern liberty to drift in the dark is the most terrible negation of freedom. Nothing happens to us as we would. We want peace and make war. We need science and obey the will to believe, we love art and flounder among whimsicalities, we believe in general comfort and equality and we strain every nerve to become millionaires. After all, antiquity must have been right in thinking that reasonable self-direction must rest on having a determinate character and knowing what it is, and that only the truth about God and happiness, if we somehow found it, could make us free. But the truth is not to be found by guessing at it, as religious prophets and men of genius have done, and then damning every one who does not agree. Human nature, for all its substantial fixity, is a living thing with many varieties and variations. All diversity of opinion is therefore not founded on ignorance; it may express a legitimate change of habit or interest. The classic and Christian synthesis from which we have broken loose was certainly premature, even if the only issue of our liberal experiments should be to lead us back to some such equilibrium. Let us hope at least that the new morality, when it comes, may be more broadly based than the old on knowledge of the world, not so absolute, not so meticulous, and not chanted so much in the monotone of an abstracted sage.

1922

E. M. Forster

WHAT I BELIEVE

I do not believe in Belief. But this is an age of faith, and there are so many militant creeds that, in self-defence, one has to formulate a creed of one's own. Tolerance, good temper and sympathy are no longer enough in a world which is rent by religious and racial persecution, in a world where ignorance rules, and science, who ought to have ruled, plays the subservient pimp. Tolerance, good temper and sympathy—they are what matter really, and if the human race is not to collapse they must come to the front before long. But for the moment they are not enough, their action is no stronger than a flower, battered beneath a military jack-boot. They want stiffening, even if the process coarsens them. Faith, to my mind, is a stiffening process, a sort of mental starch, which ought to be applied as sparingly as possible. I dislike the stuff. I do not believe in it, for its own sake, at all. Herein I probably differ from most people, who believe in Belief, and are only sorry they cannot swallow even more than they do. My law-givers are Erasmus and Montaigne, not Moses and St. Paul. My temple stands not upon Mount Moriah[1] but in that Elysian Field[2] where even the immoral are admitted. My motto is: "Lord, I disbelieve—help thou my unbelief."

I have, however, to live in an Age of Faith—the sort of epoch I used to hear praised when I was a boy. It is extremely unpleasant really. It is bloody in every sense of the word. And I have to keep my end up in it. Where do I start?

With personal relationships. Here is something comparatively solid in a world full of violence and cruelty. Not absolutely solid, for Psychology has split and shattered the idea of a "Person," and has shown that there is something incalculable in each of us, which may at any moment rise to the surface and destroy our normal balance. We don't know what we are like. We can't know what other people are like. How, then, can we put any trust in personal relationships, or cling to them in the gathering political storm? In theory we cannot. But in practice we can and do. Though A is not unchangeably A or B unchangeably B, there can still be love and loyalty between the two. For the purpose of living one has to assume that the personality is solid, and the "self" is an entity, and to ignore all contrary evidence. And since to ignore evidence is one of the characteristics of faith, I certainly can proclaim that I believe in personal relationships.

Starting from them, I get a little order into the contemporary chaos.

---

1. Biblical name for a hill in East Jerusalem, the site of Solomon's Temple.   2. In Greek religion, a happy otherworld for heroes favored by the gods.

One must be fond of people and trust them if one is not to make a mess of life, and it is therefore essential that they should not let one down. They often do. The moral of which is that I must, myself, be as reliable as possible, and this I try to be. But reliability is not a matter of contract —that is the main difference between the world of personal relationships and the world of business relationships. It is a matter for the heart, which signs no documents. In other words, reliability is impossible unless there is a natural warmth. Most men possess this warmth, though they often have bad luck and get chilled. Most of them, even when they are politicians, *want* to keep faith. And one can, at all events, show one's own little light here, one's own poor little trembling flame, with the knowledge that it is not the only light that is shining in the darkness, and not the only one which the darkness does not comprehend. Personal relations are despised today. They are regarded as bourgeois luxuries, as products of a time of fair weather which is now past, and we are urged to get rid of them, and to dedicate ourselves to some movement or cause instead. I hate the idea of causes, and if I had to choose between betraying my country and betraying my friend, I hope I should have the guts to betray my country. Such a choice may scandalise the modern reader, and he may stretch out his patriotic hand to the telephone at once and ring up the police. It would not have shocked Dante, though. Dante places Brutus and Cassius in the lowest circle of Hell because they had chosen to betray their friend Julius Caesar rather than their country Rome. Probably one will not be asked to make such an agonising choice. Still, there lies at the back of every creed something terrible and hard for which the worshipper may one day be required to suffer, and there is even a terror and a hardness in this creed of personal relationships, urbane and mild though it sounds. Love and loyalty to an individual can run counter to the claims of the State. When they do—down with the State, say I, which means that the State would down me.

This brings me along to Democracy, "even Love, the Beloved Republic, which feeds upon Freedom and lives." Democracy is not a Beloved Republic really, and never will be. But it is less hateful than other contemporary forms of government, and to that extent it deserves our support. It does start from the assumption that the individual is important, and that all types are needed to make a civilisation. It does not divide its citizens into the bossers and the bossed—as an efficiency-regime tends to do. The people I admire most are those who are sensitive and want to create something or discover something, and do not see life in terms of power, and such people get more of a chance under a democracy than elsewhere. They found religions, great or small, or they produce literature and art, or they do disinterested scientific research, or they may be what is called "ordinary people," who are creative in their private lives, bring up their children decently, for instance, or help their neighbours. All these people need to express themselves; they cannot do so unless society allows them liberty to do so, and the society which allows them most liberty is a democracy.

Democracy has another merit. It allows criticism, and if there is not public criticism there are bound to be hushed-up scandals. That is why I believe in the Press, despite all its lies and vulgarity, and why I believe in Parliament. Parliament is often sneered at because it is a Talking Shop. I believe in it *because* it is a talking shop. I believe in the Private Member who makes himself a nuisance. He gets snubbed and is told that he is cranky or ill-informed, but he does expose abuses which would otherwise never have been mentioned, and very often an abuse gets put right just by being mentioned. Occasionally, too, a well-meaning public official starts losing his head in the cause of efficiency, and thinks himself God Almighty. Such officials are particularly frequent in the Home Office.[3] Well, there will be questions about them in Parliament sooner or later, and then they will have to mind their steps. Whether Parliament is either a representative body or an efficient one is questionable, but I value it because it criticises and talks, and because its chatter gets widely reported.

So Two Cheers for Democracy: one because it admits variety and two because it permits criticism. Two cheers are quite enough: there is no occasion to give three. Only Love the Beloved Republic deserves that.

What about Force, though? While we are trying to be sensitive and advanced and affectionate and tolerant, an unpleasant question pops up: does not all society rest upon force? If a government cannot count upon the police and the army, how can it hope to rule? And if an individual gets knocked on the head or sent to a labour camp, of what significance are his opinions?

This dilemma does not worry me as much as it does some. I realise that all society rests upon force. But all the great creative actions, all the decent human relations, occur during the intervals when force has not managed to come to the front. These intervals are what matter. I want them to be as frequent and as lengthy as possible, and I call them "civilisation." Some people idealise force and pull it into the foreground and worship it, instead of keeping it in the background as long as possible. I think they make a mistake, and I think that their opposites, the mystics, err even more when they declare that force does not exist. I believe that it exists, and that one of our jobs is to prevent it from getting out of its box. It gets out sooner or later, and then it destroys us and all the lovely things which we have made. But it is not out all the time, for the fortunate reason that the strong are so stupid. Consider their conduct for a moment in the Niebelung's Ring.[4] The giants there have the guns, or in other

3. A department of government in Great Britain corresponding to the Department of the Interior in the United States.

4. Four operas by Richard Wagner, based on a Middle High German legend of the thirteenth century.

words the gold; but they do nothing with it, they do not realise that they are all-powerful, with the result that the catastrophe is delayed and the castle of Walhalla, insecure but glorious, fronts the storms. Fafnir, coiled round his hoard, grumbles and grunts; we can hear him under Europe today; the leaves of the wood already tremble, and the Bird calls its warnings uselessly. Fafnir will destroy us, but by a blessed dispensation he is stupid and slow, and creation goes on just outside the poisonous blast of his breath. The Nietzschean would hurry the monster up, the mystic would say he did not exist, but Wotan, wiser than either, hastens to create warriors before doom declares itself. The Valkyries are symbols not only of courage but of intelligence; they represent the human spirit snatching its opportunity while the going is good, and one of them even finds time to love. Brünnhilde's last song hymns the recurrence of love, and since it is the privilege of art to exaggerate, she goes even further, and proclaims the love which is eternally triumphant and feeds upon freedom, and lives.

So that is what I feel about force and violence. It is, alas! the ultimate reality on this earth, but it does not always get to the front. Some people call its absences "decadence"; I call them "civilisation" and find in such interludes the chief justification for the human experiment. I look the other way until fate strikes me. Whether this is due to courage or to cowardice in my own case I cannot be sure. But I know that if men had not looked the other way in the past, nothing of any value would survive. The people I respect most behave as if they were immortal and as if society was eternal. Both assumptions are false: both of them must be accepted as true if we are to go on eating and working and loving, and are to keep open a few breathing holes for the human spirit. No millennium seems likely to descend upon humanity; no better and stronger League of Nations will be instituted; no form of Christianity and no alternative to Christianity will bring peace to the world or integrity to the individual; no "change of heart" will occur. And yet we need not despair, indeed, we cannot despair; the evidence of history shows us that men have always insisted on behaving creatively under the shadow of the sword; that they have done their artistic and scientific and domestic stuff for the sake of doing it, and that we had better follow their example under the shadow of the aeroplanes. Others, with more vision or courage than myself, see the salvation of humanity ahead, and will dismiss my conception of civilisation as paltry, a sort of tip-and-run[5] game. Certainly it is presumptuous to say that we *cannot* improve, and that Man, who has only been in power for a few thousand years, will never learn to make use of his power. All I mean is that, if people continue to kill one another as they do, the world cannot get better than it is, and that since there are more people than

5. A game similar to cricket in which a batsman is required to run each time he touches a bowled ball with his bat.

formerly, and their means for destroying one another superior, the world may well get worse. What is good in people—and consequently in the world—is their insistence on creation, their belief in friendship and loyalty for their own sakes; and though Violence remains and is, indeed, the major partner in this muddled establishment, I believe that creativeness remains too, and will always assume direction when violence sleeps. So, though I am not an optimist, I cannot agree with Sophocles that it were better never to have been born. And although, like Horace, I see no evidence that each batch of births is superior to the last, I leave the field open for the more complacent view. This is such a difficult moment to live in, one cannot help getting gloomy and also a bit rattled, and perhaps short-sighted.

In search of a refuge, we may perhaps turn to hero-worship. But here we shall get no help, in my opinion. Hero-worship is a dangerous vice, and one of the minor merits of a democracy is that it does not encourage it, or produce that unmanageable type of citizen known as the Great Man. It produces instead different kinds of small men—a much finer achievement. But people who cannot get interested in the variety of life, and cannot make up their own minds, get discontented over this, and they long for a hero to bow down before and to follow blindly. It is significant that a hero is an integral part of the authoritarian stock-in-trade today. An efficiency-regime cannot be run without a few heroes stuck about it to carry off the dullness—much as plums have to be put into a bad pudding to make it palatable. One hero at the top and a smaller one each side of him is a favourite arrangement, and the timid and the bored are comforted by the trinity, and, bowing down, feel exalted and strengthened.

No, I distrust Great Men. They produce a desert of uniformity around them and often a pool of blood too, and I always feel a little man's pleasure when they come a cropper. Every now and then one reads in the newspapers some such statement as: "The coup d'état appears to have failed, and Admiral Toma's whereabouts is at present unknown." Admiral Toma had probably every qualification for being a Great Man—an iron will, personal magnetism, dash, flair, sexlessness—but fate was against him, so he retires to unknown whereabouts instead of parading history with his peers. He fails with a completeness which no artist and no lover can experience, because with them the process of creation is itself an achievement, whereas with him the only possible achievement is success.

I believe in aristocracy, though—if that is the right word, and if a democrat may use it. Not an aristocracy of power, based upon rank and influence, but an aristocracy of the sensitive, the considerate and the plucky. Its members are to be found in all nations and classes, and all through the ages, and there is a secret understanding between them when they meet. They represent the true human tradition, the one permanent victory of our queer race over cruelty and chaos. Thousands of them perish in obscurity, a few are great names. They are sensitive for others as well as for themselves, they are considerate without being fussy, their pluck is not swankiness but the power to endure, and they can take a joke. I give no examples—it is risky to do that—but the reader may as well consider whether this is the type of person he would like to meet and to be, and whether (going farther with me) he would prefer that this type should *not* be an ascetic one. I am against asceticism myself. I am with the old Scotsman who wanted less chastity and more delicacy. I do not feel that my aristocrats are a real aristocracy if they thwart their bodies, since bodies are the instruments through which we register and enjoy the world. Still, I do not insist. This is not a major point. It is clearly possible to be sensitive, considerate and plucky and yet be an ascetic too, if anyone possesses the first three qualities, I will let him in! On they go —an invincible army, yet not a victorious one. The aristocrats, the elect, the chosen, the Best People—all the words that describe them are false, and all attempts to organise them fail. Again and again Authority, seeing their value, has tried to net them and to utilise them as the Egyptian Priesthood or the Christian Church or the Chinese Civil Service or the Group Movement, or some other worthy stunt. But they slip through the net and are gone; when the door is shut, they are no longer in the room; their temple, as one of them remarked, is the Holiness of the Heart's Affection, and their kingdom, though they never possess it, is the wide-open world.

With this type of person knocking about, and constantly crossing one's path if one has eyes to see or hands to feel, the experiment of earthly life cannot be dismissed as a failure. But it may well be hailed as a tragedy, the tragedy being that no device has been found by which these private decencies can be transmitted to public affairs. As soon as people have power they go crooked and sometimes dotty as well, because the possession of power lifts them into a region where normal honesty never pays. For instance, the man who is selling newspapers outside the Houses of Parliament can safely leave his papers to go for a drink and his cap beside them: anyone who takes a paper is sure to drop a copper into the cap. But the men who are inside the Houses of Parliament—they cannot trust one another like that, still less can the Government they compose trust other governments. No caps upon the pavement here, but suspicion, treachery and armaments. The more highly public life is organised the lower does its morality sink; the nations of today behave to each other worse than they ever did in the past, they cheat, rob, bully and bluff, make war without notice, and kill as many women and children as possible; whereas primitive tribes were at all events restrained by taboos. It is a humiliating outlook—though the greater the darkness, the brighter shine the little lights, reassuring one another, signalling: "Well, at all events, I'm still here. I don't like it very much, but how are you?" Unquenchable lights of my aristocracy! Signals of the invincible army! "Come along—anyway, let's have a good time while we can." I think they signal that too.

The Saviour of the future—if ever he comes—will not preach a new Gospel. He will merely utilise my aristocracy, he will make effective the good will and the good temper which are already existing. In other words, he will introduce a new technique. In economics, we are told that if there was a new technique of distribution, there need be no poverty, and people would not starve in one place while crops were being ploughed under in another. A similar change is needed in the sphere of morals and politics. The desire for it is by no means new; it was expressed, for example, in theological terms by Jacopone da Todi over six hundred years ago. "Ordina questo amore, O tu che m'ami," he said; "O thou who lovest me—set this love in order." His prayer was not granted, and I do not myself believe that it ever will be, but here, and not through a change of heart, is our probable route. Not by becoming better, but by ordering and distributing his native goodness, will Man shut up Force into its box, and so gain time to explore the universe and to set his mark upon it worthily. At present he only explores it at odd moments, when Force is looking the other way, and his divine creativeness appears as a trivial byproduct, to be scrapped as soon as the drums beat and the bombers hum.

Such a change, claim the orthodox, can only be made by Christianity, and will be made by it in God's good time: man always has failed and always will fail to organise his own goodness, and it is presumptuous of him to try. This claim—solemn as it is—leaves me cold. I cannot believe that Christianity will ever cope with the present world-wide mess, and I think that such influence as it retains in modern society is due to the money behind it, rather than to its spiritual appeal. It was a spiritual force once, but the indwelling spirit will have to be restated if it is to calm the waters again, and probably restated in a non-Christian form. Naturally a lot of people, and people who are not only good but able and intelligent, will disagree here; they will vehemently deny that Christianity has failed, or they will argue that its failure proceeds from the wickedness of men, and really proves its ultimate success. They have Faith, with a large F. My faith has a very small one, and I only intrude it because these are strenuous and serious days, and one likes to say what one thinks while speech is comparatively free: it may not be free much longer.

The above are the reflections of an individualist and a liberal who has found liberalism crumbling beneath him and at first felt ashamed. Then, looking around, he decided there was no special reason for shame, since other people, whatever they felt, were equally insecure. And as for individualism—there seems no way of getting off this, even if one wanted to. The dictator-hero can grind down his citizens till they are all alike, but he cannot melt them into a single man. That is beyond his power. He can order them to merge, he can incite them to mass-antics, but they are obliged to be born separately, and to die separately, and, owing to these unavoidable termini, will always be running off the totalitarian rails. The memory of birth and the expectation of death always lurk within the human being, making him separate from his fellows and consequently capable of intercourse with them. Naked I came into the world, naked I shall go out of it! And a very good thing too, for it reminds me that I am naked under my shirt, whatever its colour.

1939

Gilbert Highet

THE MYSTERY OF ZEN

The mind need never stop growing. Indeed, one of the few experiences which never pall is the experience of watching one's own mind, and observing how it produces new interests, responds to new stimuli, and develops new thoughts, apparently without effort and almost independently of one's own conscious control. I have seen this happen to myself a hundred times; and every time it happens again, I am equally fascinated and astonished.

Some years ago a publisher sent me a little book for review. I read it, and decided it was too remote from my main interests and too highly specialized. It was a brief account of how a young German philosopher living in Japan had learned how to shoot with a bow and arrow, and how this training had made it possible for him to understand the esoteric doctrines of the Zen sect of Buddhism. Really, what could be more alien to my own life, and to that of everyone I knew, than Zen Buddhism and Japanese archery? So I thought, and put the book away.

Yet I did not forget it. It was well written, and translated into good English. It was delightfully short, and implied much more than it said. Although its theme was extremely odd, it was at least highly individual; I had never read anything like it before or since. It remained in my mind. Its name was Zen in the Art of Archery, its author Eugen Herrigel, its publisher Pantheon of New York. One day I took it off the shelf and read it again; this time it seemed even stranger than before and even more unforgettable. Now it began to cohere with other interests of mine. Something I had read of the Japanese art of flower arrangement seemed to connect with it; and then, when I wrote an essay on the peculiar

Japanese poems called *haiku*, other links began to grow. Finally I had to read the book once more with care, and to go through some other works which illuminated the same subject. I am still grappling with the theme; I have not got anywhere near understanding it fully; but I have learned a good deal, and I am grateful to the little book which refused to be forgotten.

The author, a German philosopher, got a job teaching philosophy at the University of Tokyo (apparently between the wars), and he did what Germans in foreign countries do not usually do: he determined to adapt himself and to learn from his hosts. In particular, he had always been interested in mysticism—which, for every earnest philosopher, poses a problem that is all the more inescapable because it is virtually insoluble. Zen Buddhism is not the only mystical doctrine to be found in the East, but it is one of the most highly developed and certainly one of the most difficult to approach. Herrigel knew that there were scarcely any books which did more than skirt the edge of the subject, and that the best of all books on Zen (those by the philosopher D. T. Suzuki) constantly emphasize that Zen can never be learned from books, can never be studied as we can study other disciplines such as logic or mathematics. Therefore he began to look for a Japanese thinker who could teach him directly.

At once he met with embarrassed refusals. His Japanese friends explained that he would gain nothing from trying to discuss Zen as a philosopher, that its theories could not be spread out for analysis by a detached mind, and in fact that the normal relationship of teacher and pupil simply did not exist within the sect, because the Zen masters felt it useless to explain things stage by stage and to argue about the various possible interpretations of their doctrine. Herrigel had read enough to be prepared for this. He replied that he did not want to dissect the teachings of the school, because he knew that would be useless. He wanted to become a Zen mystic himself. (This was highly intelligent of him. No one could really penetrate into Christian mysticism without being a devout Christian; no one could appreciate Hindu mystical doctrine without accepting the Hindu view of the universe.) At this, Herrigel's Japanese friends were more forthcoming. They told him that the best way, indeed the only way, for a European to approach Zen mysticism was to learn one of the arts which exemplified it. He was a fairly good rifle shot, so he determined to learn archery; and his wife co-operated with him by taking lessons in painting and flower arrangement. How any philosopher could investigate a mystical doctrine by learning to shoot with a bow and arrow and watching his wife arrange flowers, Herrigel did not ask. He had good sense.

A Zen master who was a teacher of archery agreed to take him as a pupil. The lessons lasted six years, during which he practiced every single day. There are many difficult courses of instruction in the world:

the Jesuits, violin virtuosi, Talmudic scholars, all have long and hard training, which in one sense never comes to an end; but Herrigel's training in archery equaled them all in intensity. If I were trying to learn archery, I should expect to begin by looking at a target and shooting arrows at it. He was not even allowed to aim at a target for the first four years. He had to begin by learning how to hold the bow and arrow, and then how to release the arrow; this took ages. The Japanese bow is not like our sporting bow, and the stance of the archer in Japan is different from ours. We hold the bow at shoulder level, stretch our left arm out ahead, pull the string and the nocked arrow to a point either below the chin or sometimes past the right ear, and then shoot. The Japanese hold the bow above the head, and then pull the hands apart to left and right until the left hand comes down to eye level and the right hand comes to rest above the right shoulder; then there is a pause, during which the bow is held at full stretch, with the tip of the three-foot arrow projecting only a few inches beyond the bow; after that, the arrow is loosed. When Herrigel tried this, even without aiming, he found it was almost impossible. His hands trembled. His legs stiffened and grew cramped. His breathing became labored. And of course he could not possibly aim. Week after week he practice this, with the Master watching him carefully and correcting his strained attitude; week after week he made no progress whatever. Finally he gave up and told his teacher that he could not learn: it was absolutely impossible for him to draw the bow and loose the arrow.

To his astonishment, the Master agreed. He said, "Certainly you cannot. It is because you are not breathing correctly. You must learn to breathe in a steady rhythm, keeping your lungs full most of the time, and drawing in one rapid inspiration with each stage of the process, as you grasp the bow, fit the arrow, raise the bow, draw, pause, and loose the shot. If you do, you will both grow stronger and be able to relax." To prove this, he himself drew his massive bow and told his pupil to feel the muscles of his arms: they were perfectly relaxed, as though he were doing no work whatever.

Herrigel now started breathing exercises; after some time he combined the new rhythm of breathing with the actions of drawing and shooting; and, much to his astonishment, he found that the whole thing, after this complicated process, had become much easier. Or rather, not easier, but different. At times it became quite unconscious. He says himself that he felt he was not breathing, but being breathed; and in time he felt that the occasional shot was not being dispatched by him, but shooting itself. The bow and arrow were in charge; he had become merely a part of them.

All this time, of course, Herrigel did not even attempt to discuss Zen doctrine with his Master. No doubt he knew that he was approaching it, but he concentrated solely on learning how to shoot. Every stage which

he surmounted appeared to lead to another stage even more difficult. It took him months to learn how to loosen the bowstring. The problem was this. If he gripped the string and arrowhead tightly, either he froze, so that his hands were slowly pulled together and the shot was wasted, or else he jerked, so that the arrow flew up into the air or down into the ground; and if he was relaxed, then the bowstring and arrow simply *leaked* out of his grasp before he could reach full stretch, and the arrow went nowhere. He explained this problem to the Master. The Master understood perfectly well. He replied, "You must hold the drawn bowstring like a child holding a grownup's finger. You know how firmly a child grips; and yet when it lets go, there is not the slightest jerk—because the child does not think of itself, it is not self-conscious, it does not say, 'I will now let go and do something else,' it merely acts instinctively. That is what you must learn to do. Practice, practice, and practice, and then the string will loose itself at the right moment. The shot will come as effortlessly as snow slipping from a leaf." Day after day, week after week, month after month, Herrigel practiced this; and then, after one shot, the Master suddenly bowed and broke off the lesson. He said "Just then it shot. Not you, but *it.*" And gradually thereafter more and more right shots achieved themselves; the young philosopher forgot himself, forgot that he was learning archery for some other purpose, forgot even that he was practicing archery, and became part of that unconsciously active complex, the bow, the string, the arrow, and the man.

Next came the target. After four years, Herrigel was allowed to shoot at the target. But he was strictly forbidden to aim at it. The Master explained that even he himself did not aim; and indeed, when he shot, he was so absorbed in the act, so selfless and unanxious, that his eyes were almost closed. It was difficult, almost impossible, for Herrigel to believe that such shooting could ever be effective; and he risked insulting the Master by suggesting that he ought to be able to hit the target blindfolded. But the Master accepted the challenge. That night, after a cup of tea and long meditation, he went into the archery hall, put on the lights at one end and left the target perfectly dark, with only a thin taper burning in front of it. Then, with habitual grace and precision, and with that strange, almost sleepwalking, selfless confidence that is the heart of Zen, he shot two arrows into the darkness. Herrigel went out to collect them. He found that the first had gone to the heart of the bull's eye, and that the second had actually hit the first arrow and splintered it. The Master showed no pride. He said, "Perhaps, with unconscious memory of the position of the target, *I* shot the first arrow; but the second arrow? *It* shot the second arrow, and *it* brought it to the center of the target."

At last Herrigel began to understand. His progress became faster and faster; easier, too. Perfect shots (perfect because perfectly unconscious) occurred at almost every lesson; and finally, after six years of incessant

training, in a public display he was awarded the diploma. He needed no further instruction: he had himself become a Master. His wife meanwhile had become expert both in painting and in the arrangement of flowers —two of the finest of Japanese arts. (I wish she could be persuaded to write a companion volume, called Zen in the Art of Flower Arrangement; it would have a wider general appeal than her husband's work.) I gather also from a hint or two in his book that she had taken part in the archery lessons. During one of the most difficult periods in Herrigel's training, when his Master had practically refused to continue teaching him—because Herrigel had tried to cheat by consciously opening his hand at the moment of loosing the arrow—his wife had advised him against that solution, and sympathized with him when it was rejected. She in her own way had learned more quickly than he, and reached the final point together with him. All their effort had not been in vain: Herrigel and his wife had really acquired a new and valuable kind of wisdom. Only at this point, when he was about to abandon his lessons forever, did his Master treat him almost as an equal and hint at the innermost doctrines of Zen Buddhism. Only hints he gave; and yet, for the young philosopher who had now become a mystic, they were enough. Herrigel understood the doctrine, not with his logical mind, but with his entire being. He at any rate had solved the mystery of Zen.

Without going through a course of training as absorbing and as complete as Herrigel's, we can probably never penetrate the mystery. The doctrine of Zen cannot be analyzed from without: it must be lived.

But although it cannot be analyzed, it can be hinted at. All the hints that the adherents of this creed give us are interesting. Many are fantastic; some are practically incomprehensible, and yet unforgettable. Put together, they take us toward a way of life which is utterly impossible for westerners living in a western world, and nevertheless has a deep fascination and contains some values which we must respect.

The word Zen means "meditation." (It is the Japanese word, corresponding to the Chinese Ch'an and the Hindu Dhyana.) It is the central idea of a special sect of Buddhism which flourished in China during the Sung period (between a.d. 1000 and 1300) and entered Japan in the twelfth century. Without knowing much about it, we might be certain that the Zen sect was a worthy and noble one, because it produced a quantity of highly distinguished art, specifically painting. And if we knew anything about Buddhism itself, we might say that Zen goes closer than other sects to the heart of Buddha's teaching: because Buddha was trying to found, not a religion with temples and rituals, but a way of life based on meditation. However, there is something eccentric about the Zen life which is hard to trace in Buddha's teaching; there is an active energy which he did not admire, there is a rough grasp on reality which he himself eschewed, there is something like a sense of humor, which he

rarely displayed. The gravity and serenity of the Indian preacher are transformed, in Zen, to the earthy liveliness of Chinese and Japanese sages. The lotus brooding calmly on the water has turned into a knotted tree covered with spring blossoms.

In this sense, "meditation" does not mean what we usually think of when we say a philosopher meditates: analysis of reality, a longsustained effort to solve problems of religion and ethics, the logical dissection of the universe. It means something not divisive, but whole; not schematic, but organic; not long-drawn-out, but immediate. It means something more like our words "intuition" and "realization." It means a way of life in which there is no division between thought and action; none of the painful gulf, so well known to all of us, between the unconscious and the conscious mind; and no absolute distinction between the self and the external world, even between the various parts of the external world and the whole.

When the German philosopher took six years of lessons in archery in order to approach the mystical significance of Zen, he was not given direct philosophical instruction. He was merely shown how to breathe, how to hold and loose the bowstring, and finally how to shoot in such a way that the bow and arrow used him as an instrument. There are many such stories about Zen teachers. The strangest I know is one about a fencing master who undertook to train a young man in the art of the sword. The relationship of teacher and pupil is very important, almost sacred, in the Far East; and the pupil hardly ever thinks of leaving a master or objecting to his methods, however extraordinary they may seem. Therefore this young fellow did not at first object when he was made to act as a servant, drawing water, sweeping floors, gathering wood for the fire, and cooking. But after some time he asked for more direct instruction. The master agreed to give it, but produced no swords. The routine went on just as before, except that every now and then the master would strike the young man with a stick. No matter what he was doing, sweeping the floor or weeding in the garden, a blow would descend on him apparently out of nowhere; he had always to be on the alert, and yet he was constantly receiving unexpected cracks on the head or shoulders. After some months of this, he saw his master stooping over a boiling pot full of vegetables; and he thought he would have his revenge. Silently he lifted a stick and brought it down; but without any effort, without even a glance in his direction, his master parried the blow with the lid of the cooking pot. At last, the pupil began to understand the instinctive alertness, the effortless perception and avoidance of danger, in which his master had been training him. As soon as he had achieved it, it was child's play for him to learn the management of the sword: he could parry every cut and turn every slash without anxiety, until his opponent, exhausted, left an opening for his counterattack. (The same principle was used by the elderly samurai for selecting his comrades in the Japanese motion picture *The Magnificent Seven.*)

These stories show that Zen meditation does not mean sitting and thinking. On the contrary, it means acting with as little thought as possible. The fencing master trained his pupil to guard against every attack with the same immediate, instinctive rapidity with which our eyelid closes over our eye when something threatens it. His work was aimed at breaking down the wall between thought and act, at completely fusing body and senses and mind so that they might all work together rapidly and effortlessly. When a Zen artist draws a picture, he does it in a rhythm almost the exact reverse of that which is followed by a Western artist. We begin by blocking out the design and then filling in the details, usually working more and more slowly as we approach the completion of the picture. The Zen artist sits down very calmly; examines his brush carefully; prepares his own ink; smooths out the paper on which he will work; falls into a profound silent ecstasy of contemplation—during which he does not think anxiously of various details, composition, brushwork, shades of tone, but rather attempts to become the vehicle through which the subject can express itself in painting; and then, very quickly and almost unconsciously, with sure effortless strokes, draws a picture containing the fewest and most effective lines. Most of the paper is left blank; only the essential is depicted, and that not completely. One long curving line will be enough to show a mountainside; seven streaks will become a group of bamboos bending in the wind; and yet, though technically incomplete, such pictures are unforgettably clear. They show the heart of reality.

All this we can sympathize with, because we can see the results. The young swordsman learns how to fence. The intuitional painter produces a fine picture. But the hardest thing for us to appreciate is that the Zen masters refuse to teach philosophy or religion directly, and deny logic. In fact, they despise logic as an artificial distortion of reality. Many philosophical teachers are difficult to understand because they analyze profound problems with subtle intricacy: such is Aristotle in his *Metaphysics*. Many mystical writers are difficult to understand because, as they themselves admit, they are attempting to use words to describe experiences which are too abstruse for words, so that they have to fall back on imagery and analogy, which they themselves recognize to be poor media, far coarser than the realities with which they have been in contact. But the Zen teachers seem to deny the power of language and thought altogether. For example, if you ask a Zen master what is the ultimate reality, he will answer, without the slightest hesitation, "The bamboo grove at the foot of the hill" or "A branch of plum blossom." Apparently he means that these things, which we can see instantly without effort, or imagine in the flash of a second, are real with the ultimate reality; that nothing is more real than these; and that we ought to grasp ultimates as we grasp simple immediates. A Chinese master was once asked the central question, "What is the Buddha?" He said nothing whatever, but held out his index finger. What did he mean? It is hard to explain; but apparently he meant "Here. Now. Look and realize with the effortlessness of seeing. Do not try to use words. Do not think. Make no efforts toward withdrawal from the world. Expect no sublime ecstasies. Live. All *that* is the ultimate reality, and it can be understood from the motion of a finger as well as from the execution of any complex ritual, from any subtle argument, or from the circling of the starry universe."

In making that gesture, the master was copying the Buddha himself, who once delivered a sermon which is famous, but was hardly understood by his pupils at the time. Without saying a word, he held up a flower and showed it to the gathering. One man, one alone, knew what he meant. The gesture became renowned as the Flower Sermon.

In the annals of Zen there are many cryptic answers to the final question, "What is the Buddha?"—which in our terms means "What is the meaning of life? What is truly real?" For example, one master, when asked "What is the Buddha?" replied, "Your name is Yecho." Another said, "Even the finest artist cannot paint him." Another said, "No nonsense here." And another answered, "The mouth is the gate of woe." My favorite story is about the monk who said to a Master, "Has a dog Buddha-nature too?" The Master replied, "Wu"—which is what the dog himself would have said.

Now, some critics might attack Zen by saying that this is the creed of a savage or an animal. The adherents of Zen would deny that—or more probably they would ignore the criticism, or make some cryptic remark which meant that it was pointless. Their position—if they could ever be persuaded to put in into words—would be this. An animal is instinctively in touch with reality, and so far is living rightly, but it has never had a mind and so cannot perceive the Whole, only that part with which it is in touch. The philosopher sees both the Whole and the parts, and enjoys them all. As for the savage, he exists only through the group; he feels himself as part of a war party or a ceremonial dance team or a ploughing-and-sowing group or the Snake clan; he is not truly an individual at all, and therefore is less than fully human. Zen has at its heart an inner solitude; its aim is to teach us to live, as in the last resort we do all have to live, alone.

A more dangerous criticism of Zen would be that it is nihilism, that its purpose is to abolish thought altogether. (This criticism is handled, but not fully met, by the great Zen authority Suzuki in his *Introduction to Zen Buddhism*.) It can hardly be completely confuted, for after all the central doctrine of Buddhism is—Nothingness. And many of the sayings of Zen masters are truly nihilistic. The first patriarch of the sect in China was asked by the emperor what was the ultimate and holiest principle of Buddhism. He replied, "Vast emptiness, and nothing holy in it." Another who was asked the searching question "Where is the abiding-place for the mind?" answered, "Not in this dualism of good and evil, being and non-being, thought and matter." In fact, thought is an activity which divides. It analyzes, it makes distinctions, it criticizes, it judges, it breaks reality into groups and classes and individuals. The aim of Zen is to abolish that kind of thinking, and to substitute—not unconsciousness, which would be death, but a consciousness that does not analyze but experiences life directly. Although it has no prescribed prayers, no sacred scriptures, no ceremonial rites, no personal god, and no interest in the soul's future destination, Zen is a religion rather than a philosophy. Jung points out that its aim is to produce a religious conversion, a "transformation": and he adds, "The transformation process is incommensurable with intellect." Thought is always interesting, but often painful; Zen is calm and painless. Thought is incomplete; Zen enlightenment brings a sense of completeness. Thought is a process; Zen illumination is a state. But it is a state which cannot be defined. In the Buddhist scriptures there is a dialogue between a master and a pupil in which the pupil tries to discover the exact meaning of such a state. The master says to him, 'If a fire were blazing in front of you, would you know that it was blazing?'

"Yes, master."

"And would you know the reason for its blazing?"

"Yes, because it had a supply of grass and sticks."

"And would you know if it were to go out?"

"Yes, master."

"And on its going out, would you know where the fire had gone? To the east, to the west, to the north, or to the south?"

"The question does not apply, master. For the fire blazed because it had a supply of grass and sticks. When it had consumed this and had no other fuel, then it went out."

"In the same way," replies the master, "no question will apply to the meaning of Nirvana, and no statement will explain it."

Such, then, neither happy nor unhappy but beyond all divisive description, is the condition which students of Zen strive to attain. Small wonder that they can scarcely explain it to us, the unilluminated.

1957

QUESTIONS

1. What difficulties does Highest face in discussing Zen? How does he manage to give a definition in spite of his statement that Zen "cannot be analyzed"?
2. Why does Highest describe the training in archery in such detail?

3. *On page 1178 Highet says that "Zen is a religion rather than a philosophy." How has he led up to this conclusion? What definitions of "religion" and "philosophy" does he imply?*
4. *By what means does Highet define "meditation"? Would other means have worked as well? Explain.*
5. *To what extent is Zen "the creed of a savage or an animal"? How does Highet go about refuting this charge?*

Virginia Woolf

THE DEATH OF THE MOTH

Moths that fly by day are not properly to be called moths; they do not excite that pleasant sense of dark autumn nights and ivy-blossom which the commonest yellow-underwing asleep in the shadow of the curtain never fails to rouse in us. They are hybrid creatures, neither gay like butterflies nor sombre like their own species. Nevertheless the present specimen, with his narrow hay-coloured wings, fringed with a tassel of the same colour, seemed to be content with life. It was a pleasant morning, mid-September, mild, benignant, yet with a keener breath than that of the summer months. The plough was already scoring the field opposite the window, and where the share had been, the earth was pressed flat and gleamed with moisture. Such vigour came rolling in from the fields and the down beyond that it was difficult to keep the eyes strictly turned upon the book. The rooks too were keeping one of their annual festivities; soaring round the tree tops until it looked as if a vast net with thousands of black knots in it had been cast up into the air; which, after a few moments sank slowly down upon the trees until every twig seemed to have a knot at the end of it. Then, suddenly, the net would be thrown into the air again in a wider circle this time, with the utmost clamour and vociferation, as though to be thrown into the air and settle slowly down upon the tree tops were a tremendously exciting experience.

The same energy which inspired the rooks, the ploughmen, the horses, and even, it seemed, the lean bare-backed downs, sent the moth fluttering from side to side of his square of the window-pane. One could not help watching him. One was, indeed, conscious of a queer feeling of pity for him. The possibilities of pleasure seemed that morning so enormous and so various that to have only a moth's part in life, and a day moth's at that, appeared a hard fate, and his zest in enjoying his meagre opportunities to the full, pathetic. He flew vigorously to one corner of his compartment, and, after waiting there a second, flew across to the other. What remained for him but to fly to a third corner and then to a fourth? That was all he could do, in spite of the size of the downs, the width of the sky, the far-off smoke of houses, and the romantic voice, now and then, of a steamer out at sea. What he could do he did. Watching him, it seemed as if a fibre, very thin but pure, of the enormous energy of the world had been thrust into his frail and diminutive body. As often as he crossed the pane, I could fancy that a thread of vital light became visible. He was little or nothing but life.

Yet, because he was so small, and so simple a form of the energy that was rolling in at the open window and driving its way through so many narrow and intricate corridors in my own brain and in those of other human beings, there was something marvellous as well as pathetic about him. It was as if someone had taken a tiny bead of pure life and decking it as lightly as possible with down and feathers, had set it dancing and zig-zagging to show us the true nature of life. Thus displayed one could not get over the strangeness of it. One is apt to forget all about life, seeing it humped and bossed and garnished and cumbered so that it has to move with the greatest circumspection and dignity. Again, the thought of all that life might have been had he been born in any other shape caused one to view his simple activities with a kind of pity.

After a time, tired by his dancing apparently, he settled on the window ledge in the sun, and, the queer spectacle being at an end, I forgot about him. Then, looking up, my eye was caught by him. He was trying to resume his dancing, but seemed either so stiff or so awkward that he could only flutter to the bottom of the window-pane; and when he tried to fly across it he failed. Being intent on other matters I watched these futile attempts for a time without thinking, unconsciously waiting for him to resume his flight, as one waits for a machine, that has stopped momentarily, to start again without considering the reason of its failure. After perhaps a seventh attempt he slipped from the wooden ledge and fell, fluttering his wings, on to his back on the window sill. The helplessness of his attitude roused me. It flashed upon me that he was in difficulties; he could no longer raise himself; his legs struggled vainly. But, as I stretched out a pencil, meaning to help him to right himself, it came over me that the failure and awkwardness were the approach of death. I laid the pencil down again.

The legs agitated themselves once more. I looked as if for the enemy against which he struggled. I looked out of doors. What had happened there? Presumably it was midday, and work in the fields had stopped. Stillness and quiet had replaced the previous animation. The birds had taken themselves off to feed in the brooks. The horses stood still. Yet the power was there all the same, massed outside indifferent, impersonal, not attending to anything in particular. Somehow it was opposed to the little hay-coloured moth. It was useless to try to do anything. One could only

watch the extraordinary efforts made by those tiny legs against an oncom-
ing doom which could, had it chosen, have submerged an entire city, not
merely a city, but masses of human beings; nothing, I knew, had any
chance against death. Nevertheless after a pause of exhaustion the legs
fluttered again. It was superb this last protest, and so frantic that he
succeeded at last in righting himself. One's sympathies, of course, were
all on the side of life. Also, when there was nobody to care or to know, this
gigantic effort on the part of an insignificant little moth, against a power
of such magnitude, to retain what no one else valued or desired to keep,
moved one strangely. Again, somehow, one saw life, a pure bead. I lifted
the pencil again, useless though I knew it to be. But even as I did so, the
unmistakable tokens of death showed themselves. The body relaxed, and
instantly grew stiff. The struggle was over. The insignificant little creature now knew death. As I looked at the dead moth, this minute wayside
triumph of so great a force over so mean an antagonist filled me with
wonder. Just as life had been strange a few minutes before, so death was
now as strange. The moth having righted himself now lay most decently
and uncomplainingly composed. O yes, he seemed to say, death is
stronger than I am.

                                                                    1947

QUESTIONS

1. *Explain whether you think another person looking over Virginia
   Woolf's shoulder would have described the moth differently. How
   might Alexander Petrunkevitch (see "The Spider and the Wasp,"
   p. 918) or Henry David Thoreau (see "The Battle of the Ants," p. 719)
   have described it?*
2. *Does Woolf see any resemblances between the moth and human
   beings? How do you know?*
3. *Why does Woolf describe the rooks in some detail, but not the
   ploughmen?*
4. *Observe an insect and describe it from two points of view—one
   objective and one subjective, or one as a scientist might describe it and
   one as a poet or a novelist might describe it.*
5. *Read Robert Frost's poem "To a Moth Seen in Winter" printed
   below. Does Frost feel the same way about his moth that Virginia
   Woolf does about hers? Does one author identify with the moth more
   than the other? Woolf's piece takes place in the fall, Frost's poem in
   winter. What is the significance of the difference in seasons?*

                        To a Moth Seen in Winter
          Here's first a gloveless hand warm from my pocket,
          A perch and resting place 'twixt wood and wood,
          Bright-black-eyed silvery creature, brushed with brown,
          The wings not folded in repose, but spread.
          (Who would you be, I wonder, by those marks

If I had moths to friend as I have flowers?)
And now pray tell what lured you with false hope
To make the venture of eternity
And seek the love of kind in wintertime?
But stay and hear me out. I surely think
You make a labor of flight for one so airy,
Spending yourself too much in self-support.
Nor will you find love either nor love you.
And what I pity in you is something human,
The old incurable untimeliness,
Only begetter of all ills that are.
But go. You are right. My pity cannot help.
Go till you wet your pinions and are quenched.
You must be made more simply wise than I
To know the hand I stretch impulsively
Across the gulf of well nigh everything
May reach to you, but cannot touch your fate.
I cannot touch your life, much less can save,
Who am tasked to save my own a little while.

Annie Dillard

SIGHT INTO INSIGHT

When I was six or seven years old, growing up in Pittsburgh, I used to take a penny of my own and hide it for someone else to find. It was a curious compulsion; sadly, I've never been seized by it since. For some reason I always "hid" the penny along the same stretch of sidewalk up the street. I'd cradle it at the roots of a maple, say, or in a hole left by a chipped-off piece of sidewalk. Then I'd take a piece of chalk and, starting at either end of the block, draw huge arrows leading up to the penny from both directions. After I learned to write I labeled the arrows "SURPRISE AHEAD" or "MONEY THIS WAY." I was greatly excited, during all this arrowdrawing, at the thought of the first lucky passerby who would receive in this way, regardless of merit, a free gift from the universe. But I never lurked about. I'd go straight home and not give the matter another thought, until, some months later, I would be gripped by the impulse to hide another penny.

There are lots of things to see, unwrapped gifts and free surprises. The world is fairly studded and strewn with pennies cast broadside from a generous hand. But—and this is the point—who gets excited by a mere penny? If you follow one arrow, if you crouch motionless on a bank to watch a tremulous ripple thrill on the water, and are rewarded by the sight of a muskrat kit paddling from its den, will you count that sight a chip of copper only, and go your rueful way? It is very dire poverty indeed for a man to be so malnourished and fatigued that he won't stoop to pick up a penny. But if you cultivate a healthy poverty and simplicity, so that finding a penny will make your day, then, since the world is in fact planted in pennies, you have with your poverty bought a lifetime of days. What you see is what you get.

Unfortunately, nature is very much a now-you-see-it, now-you-don't affair. A fish flashes, then dissolves in the water before my eyes like so much salt. Deer apparently ascend bodily into heaven: the brightest oriole fades into leaves. These disappearances stun me into stillness and concentration; they say of nature that it conceals with a grand nonchalance, and they say of vision that it is a deliberate gift, the revelation of a dancer who for my eyes only flings away her seven veils.

For nature does reveal as well as conceal: non-you-don't-see-it, now-you-do. For a week this September migrating red-winged blackbirds were feeding heavily down by Tinker Creek at the back of the house. One day I went out to investigate the racket; I walked up to a tree, an Osage orange, and a hundred birds flew away. They simply materialized out of the tree. I saw a tree, then a whisk of color, then a tree again. I walked closer and another hundred blackbirds took flight. Not a branch, not a twig budged: the birds were apparently weightless as well as invisible. Or, it was as if the leaves of the Osage orange had been freed from a spell in the form of redwinged blackbirds; they flew from the tree, caught my eye in the sky, and vanished. When I looked again at the tree, the leaves had reassembled as if nothing had happened. Finally I walked directly to the trunk of the tree and a final hundred, the real diehards, appeared, spread, and vanished. How could so many hide in the tree without my seeing them? The Osage orange, unruffled, looked just as it had looked from the house, when three hundred red-winged blackbirds cried from its crown. I looked upstream where they flew, and they were gone. Searching, I couldn't spot one. I wandered upstream to force them to play their hand, but they'd crossed the creek and scattered. One show to a customer. These appearances catch at my throat; they are the free gifts, the bright coppers at the roots of trees.

It's all a matter of keeping my eyes open. Nature is like one of those line drawings that are puzzles for children: Can you find hidden in the tree a duck, a house, a boy, a bucket, a giraffe, and a boot? Specialists can find the most incredibly hidden things. A book I read when I was young recommended an easy way to find caterpillars: you simply find some fresh caterpillar droppings, look up, and there's your caterpillar. More recently an author advised me to set my mind at ease about those piles of cut stems on the ground in grassy fields. Field mice make them; they cut the grass down by degrees to reach the seeds at the head. It seems that when the grass is tightly packed, as in a field of ripe grain, the blade won't topple at a single cut through the stem; instead, the cut stem simply drops vertically, held in the crush of grain. The mouse severs the bottom again and again, the stem keeps dropping an inch at a time, and finally the head is low enough for the mouse to reach the seeds. Meanwhile the mouse is positively littering the field with its little piles of cut stems into which, presumably, the author is constantly stumbling.

If I can't see these minutiae, I still try to keep my eyes open. I'm always on the lookout for ant lion traps in sandy soil, monarch pupae near milkweed, skipper larvae in locust leaves. These things are utterly common, and I've not seen one. I bang on hollow trees near water, but so far no flying squirrels have appeared. In flat country I watch every sunset in hopes of seeing the green ray. The green ray is a seldom-seen streak of light that rises from the sun like a spurting fountain at the moment of sunset; it throbs into the sky for two seconds and disappears. One more reason to keep my eyes open. A photography professor at the University of Florida just happened to see a bird die in midflight; it jerked, died, dropped, and smashed on the ground.

I squint at the wind because I read Stewart Edward White: "I have always maintained that if you looked closely enough you could see the wind—the dim, hardly-made-out, fine débris fleeing high in the air." White was an excellent observer, and devoted an entire chapter of *The Mountains* to the subject of seeing deer: "As soon as you can forget the naturally obvious and construct an artificial obvious, then you too will see deer."

But the artificial obvious is hard to see. My eyes account for less than 1 percent of the weight of my head; I'm bony and dense; I see what I expect. I just don't know what the lover knows; I can't see the artificial obvious that those in the know construct. The herpetologist asks the native, "Are there snakes in that ravine?" "No, sir." And the herpetologist comes home with, yessir, three bags full. Are there butterflies on that mountain? Are the bluets in bloom? Are there arrowheads here, or fossil ferns in the shale?

Peeping through my keyhole I see within the range of only about 30 percent of the light that comes from the sun; the rest is infrared and some little ultraviolet, perfectly apparent to many animals, but invisible to me. A nightmare network of ganglia, charged and firing without my knowledge, cuts and splices what I do see, editing it for my brain. Donald E. Carr points out that the sense impressions of one-celled animals are *not* edited for the brain: "This is philosophically interesting in a rather mournful way, since it means that only the simplest animals perceive the universe as it is."

A fog that won't burn away drifts and flows across my field of vision.

When you see fog move against a backdrop of deep pines, you don't see the fog itself, but streaks of clearness floating across the air in dark shreds. So I see only tatters of clearness through a pervading obscurity. I can't distinguish the fog from the overcast sky; I can't be sure if the light is direct or reflected. Everywhere darkness and the presence of the unseen appalls. We estimate now that only one atom dances alone in every cubic meter of intergalactic space. I blink and squint. What planet or power yanks Halley's Comet out of orbit? We haven't seen it yet; it's a question of distance, density, and the pallor of reflected light. We rock, cradled in the swaddling band of darkness. Even the simple darkness of night whispers suggestions to the mind. This summer, in August, I stayed at the creek too late.

Where Tinker Creek flows under the sycamore log bridge to the tear-shaped island, it is slow and shallow, fringed thinly in cattail marsh. At this spot an astonishing bloom of life supports vast breeding populations of insects, fish, reptiles, birds, and mammals. On windless summer evenings I stalk along the creek bank or straddle the sycamore log in absolute stillness, watching for muskrats. The night I stayed too late I was hunched on the log staring spellbound at spreading, reflected stains of lilac on the water. A cloud in the sky suddenly lighted as if turned on by a switch; its reflection just as suddenly materialized on the water upstream, flat and floating, so that I couldn't see the creek bottom, or life in the water under the cloud. Downstream, away from the cloud on the water, water turtles smooth as beans were gliding down with the current in a series of easy, weightless push-offs, as men bound on the moon. I didn't know whether to trace the progress of one turtle I was sure of, risking sticking my face in one of the bridge's spider webs made invisible by the gathering dark, or take a chance on seeing the carp, or scan the mudbank in hope of seeing a muskrat, or follow the last of the swallows who caught at my heart and trailed it after them like streamers as they appeared from directly below, under the log, flying upstream with their tails forked, so fast.

But shadows spread and deepened and stayed. After thousands of years we're still strangers to darkness, fearful aliens in an enemy camp with our arms crossed over our chests. I stirred. A land turtle on the bank, startled, hissed the air from its lungs and withdrew to its shell. An uneasy pink here, an unfathomable blue there, gave great suggestion of lurking beings. Things were going on. I couldn't see whether that rustle I heard was a distant rattle-snake, slit-eyed, or a nearby sparrow kicking in the dry flood debris slung at the foot of a willow. Tremendous action roiled the water everywhere I looked, big action, inexplicable. A tremor welled up beside a gaping muskrat burrow in the bank and I caught my breath, but no muskrat appeared. The ripples continued to fan upstream with a steady, powerful thrust. Night was knitting an eyeless mask over my face, and I still sat transfixed. A distant airplane, a delta wing out of nightmare, made a gliding shadow on the creek's bottom that looked like a stingray cruising upstream. At once a black fin slit the pink cloud on the water, shearing it in two. The two halves merged together and seemed to dissolve before my eyes. Darkness pooled in the cleft of the creek and rose, as water collects in a well. Untamed, dreaming lights flickered over the sky. I saw hints of hulking underwater shadows, two pale splashes out of the water, and round ripples rolling close together from a blackened center.

At last I stared upstream where only the deepest violet remained of the cloud, a cloud so high its underbelly still glowed, its feeble color reflected from a hidden sky lighted in turn by a sun halfway to China. And out of that violet, a sudden enormous black body arced over the water. Head and tail, if there was a head and tail, were both submerged in cloud. I saw only one ebony fling, a headlong dive to darkness; then the waters closed, and the lights went out.

I walked home in a shivering daze, up hill and down. Later I lay openmouthed in bed, my arms flung wide at my sides to steady the whirling darkness. At this latitude I'm spinning 836 miles an hour round the earth's axis; I feel my sweeping fall as a breakneck arc like the dive of dolphins, and the hollow rushing of wind raises the hairs on my neck and the side of my face. In orbit around the sun I'm moving 64,800 miles an hour. The solar system as a whole, like a merry-go-round unhinged, spins, bobs, and blinks at the speed of 43,200 miles an hour along a course set east of Hercules. Someone has piped, and we are dancing a tarantella until the sweat pours. I open my eyes and I see dark, muscled forms curl out of water, with flapping gills and flattened eyes. I close my eyes and I see stars, deep stars giving way to deeper stars, deeper stars bowing to deepest stars at the crown of an infinite cone.

"Still," wrote Van Gogh in a letter, "a great deal of light falls on everything." If we are blinded by darkness, we are also blinded by light. Sometimes here in Virginia at sunset low clouds on the southern or northern horizon are completely invisible in the lighted sky. I only know one is there because I can see its reflection in still water. The first time I discovered this mystery I looked from cloud to no-cloud in bewilderment, checking my bearings over and over, thinking maybe the ark of the covenant was just passing by south of Dead Man Mountain. Only much later did I learn the explanation: polarized light from the sky is very much weakened by reflection, but the light in clouds isn't polarized. So invisible clouds pass among visible clouds, till all slide over the mountains; so a greater light extinguishes a lesser as though it didn't exist.

In the great meteor shower of August, the Perseid, I wail all day for the

that I talk too much. Otherwise, especially in a strange place, I'll never know what's happening. Like a blind man at the ball game, I need a radio.

When I see this way I analyze and pry. I hurl over logs and roll away stones; I study the bank a square foot at a time, probing and tilting my head. Some days when a mist covers the mountains, when the muskrats won't show and the microscope's mirror shatters, I want to climb up the blank blue dome as a man would storm the inside of a circus tent, wildly, dangling, and with a steel knife claw a rent in the top, peep, and, if I must, fall.

But there is another kind of seeing that involves a letting go. When I see this way I sway transfixed and emptied. The difference between the two ways of seeing is the difference between walking with and without a camera. When I walk with a camera I walk from shot to shot, reading the light on a calibrated meter. When I walk without a camera, my own shutter opens, and the moment's light prints on my own silver gut. When I see this second way I am above all an unscrupulous observer.

It was sunny one evening last summer at Tinker Creek; the sun was low in the sky, upstream. I was sitting on the sycamore log bridge with the sunset at my back, watching the shiners the size of minnows who were feeding over the muddy sand in skittery schools. Again and again, one fish, then another, turned for a split second across the current and flash! the sun shot out from its silver side. I couldn't watch for it. It was always just happening somewhere else, and it drew my vision just as it disappeared: flash! like a sudden dazzle of the thinnest blade, a sparking over a dun and olive ground at chance intervals from every direction. Then I noticed white specks, some sort of pale petals, small, floating from under my feet on the creek's surface, very slow and steady. So I blurred my eyes and gazed toward the brim of my hat and saw a new world. I saw the pale white circles roll up, roll up, like the world's turning, mute and perfect, and I saw the linear flashes, gleaming silver, like stars being born at random down a rolling scroll of time. Something broke and something opened. I filled up like a new wineskin. I breathed an air like light; I saw a light like water. I was the lip of a fountain the creek filled forever; I was ether, the leaf in the zephyr; I was flesh-flake, feather, bone.

When I see this way I see truly. As Thoreau says, I return to my senses. I am the man who watches the baseball game in silence in an empty stadium. I see the game purely; I'm abstracted and dazed. When it's all over and the white-suited players lope off the green field to their shadowed dugouts, I leap to my feet, I cheer and cheer.

But I can't go out and try to see this way. I'll fail, I'll go mad. All I can do is try to gag the commentator, to hush the noise of useless interior babble that keeps me from seeing just as surely as a newspaper dangled before my eyes. The effort is really a discipline requiring a lifetime of dedicated struggle; it marks the literature of saints and monks of every order east and west, under every rule and no rule, discalced and shod. The world's spiritual geniuses seem to discover universally that the mind's muddy river, this ceaseless flow of trivia and trash, cannot be dammed, and that trying to dam it is a waste of effort that might lead to madness. Instead you must allow the muddy river to flow unheeded in the dim channels of consciousness; you raise your sights; you look along it, mildly, acknowledging its presence without interest and gazing beyond it into the realm of the real where subjects and objects act and rest purely, without utterance. "Launch into the deep," says Jacques Ellul, "and you shall see."

The secret of seeing, then, is the pearl of great price. If I thought he could teach me to find it and keep it forever I would stagger barefoot across a hundred deserts after any lunatic at all. But although the pearl may be found, it may not be sought. The literature of illumination reveals this above all: although it comes to those who wait for it, it is always, even to the most practiced and adept, a gift and a total surprise. I return from one walk knowing where the killdeer nests in the field by the creek and the hour the laurel blooms. I return from the same walk a day later scarcely knowing my own name. Litanies hum in my ears; my tongue flaps in my mouth, *Alim non*, alleluia! I cannot cause light; the most I can do is try to put myself in the path of its beam. It is possible, in deep space, to sail on solar wind. Light, be it particle or wave, has force: you rig a giant sail and go. The secret of seeing is to sail on solar wind. Hone and spread your spirit till you yourself are a sail, whetted, translucent, broadside to the merest puff.

When her doctor took her bandages off and led her into the garden, the girl who was no longer blind saw "the tree with the lights in it." It was for this tree I searched through the peach orchards of summer, in the forests of fall and down winter and spring for years. Then one day I was walking along Tinker Creek thinking of nothing at all and I saw the tree with the lights in it. I saw the backyard cedar where the mourning doves roost charged and transfigured, each cell buzzing with flame. I stood on the grass with the lights in it, grass that was wholly fire, utterly focused and utterly dreamed. It was less like seeing than like being for the first time seen, knocked breathless by a powerful glance. The flood of fire abated, but I'm still spending the power. Gradually the lights went out in the cedar, the colors died, the cells unflamed and disappeared. I was still ringing. I had been my whole life a bell, and never knew it until at that moment I was lifted and struck. I have since only very rarely seen the tree with the lights in it. The vision comes and goes, mostly goes, but I live for it, for the moment when the mountains open and a new light roars in spate through the crack, and the mountains slam.

1974

QUESTIONS

1. Is the kind of seeing Dillard talks about at the end of her essay the same as that she talks about at the beginning?
2. What accounts for the intensity of her description of staying at the creek too late (pp. 1185–1186)?
3. How does Dillard establish her authority during the course of her argument?
4. Why is verbalization so important to seeing (p. 1190)?

Jean-Paul Sartre

EXISTENTIALISM

Man is nothing else but what he makes of himself. Such is the first principle of existentialism. It is also what is called subjectivity, the name we are labeled with when charges are brought against us. But what do we mean by this, if not that man has a greater dignity than a stone or table? For we mean that man first exists, that is, that man first of all is the being who hurls himself toward a future and who is conscious of imagining himself as being in the future. Man is at the start a plan which is aware of itself, rather than a patch of moss, a piece of garbage, or a cauliflower; nothing exists prior to this plan; there is nothing in heaven; man will be what he will have planned to be. Not what he will want to be. Because by the word "will" we generally mean a conscious decision, which is subsequent to what we have already made of ourselves. I may want to belong to a political party, write a book, get married; but all that is only a manifestation of an earlier, more spontaneous choice that is called "will." But if existence really does precede essence, man is responsible for what he is. Thus, existentialism's first move is to make every man aware of what he is and to make the full responsibility of his existence rest on him. And when we say that a man is responsible for himself, we do not only mean that he is responsible for his own individuality, but that he is responsible for all men.

The word "subjectivism" has two meanings, and our opponents play on the two. Subjectivism means, on the one hand, that an individual chooses and makes himself; and, on the other, that it is impossible for man to transcend human subjectivity. The second of these is the essential meaning of existentialism. When we say that man chooses his own self, we mean that every one of us does likewise; but we also mean by that that in making this choice he also chooses all men. In fact, in creating the man that we want to be, there is not a single one of our acts which does not at the same time create an image of man as we think he ought to be. To choose to be this or that is to affirm at the same time the value of what we choose, because we can never choose evil. We always choose the good, and nothing can be good for us without being good for all.

If, on the other hand, existence precedes essence, and if we grant that we exist and fashion our image at one and the same time, the image is valid for everybody and for our whole age. Thus, our responsibility is much greater than we might have supposed, because it involves all mankind. If I am a workingman and choose to join a Christian trade union rather than be a Communist, and if by being a member, I want to show that the best thing for man is resignation, that the kingdom of man is not of this world, I am not only involving my own case—I want to be resigned for everyone. As a result, my action has involved all humanity. To take a more individual matter, if I want to marry, to have children, even if this marriage depends solely on my own circumstances or passion or wish, I am involving all humanity in monogamy and not merely myself. Therefore, I am responsible for myself and for everyone else. I am creating a certain image of man of my own choosing. In choosing myself, I choose man.

This helps us understand what the actual content is of such rather grandiloquent words as anguish, forlornness, despair. As you will see, it's all quite simple.

First, what is meant by anguish? The existentialists say at once that man is anguish. What that means is this: the man who involves himself and who realizes that he is not only the person he chooses to be, but also a lawmaker who is, at the same time, choosing all mankind as well as himself, cannot help escape the feeling of his total and deep responsibility. Of course, there are many people who are not anxious; but we claim that they are hiding their anxiety, that they are fleeing from it. Certainly, many people believe that when they do something, they themselves are the only ones involved, and when someone says to them, "What if everyone acted that way?" they shrug their shoulders and answer, "Everyone doesn't act that way." But really, one should always ask himself, "What would happen if everybody looked at things that way?" There is no escaping this disturbing thought except by a kind of double-dealing. A man who lies and makes excuses for himself by saying "not everybody does that," is someone with an uneasy conscience, because the act of lying implies that a universal value is conferred upon the lie.

Anguish is evident even when it conceals itself. This is the anguish that Kierkegaard called the anguish of Abraham. You know the story: an angel has ordered Abraham to sacrifice his son; if it really were an angel who has come and said, "You are Abraham, you shall sacrifice your son," everything would be all right. But everyone might first wonder, "Is it really an angel, and am I really Abraham? What proof do I have?"

There was a madwoman who had hallucinations; someone used to speak to her on the telephone and give her orders. Her doctor asked her, "Who is it who talks to you?" She answered, "He says it's God." What proof did she really have that it was God? If an angel comes to me, what proof is there that it's an angel? And if I hear voices, what proof is there that they come from heaven and not from hell, or from the subconscious, or a pathological condition? What proves that they are addressed to me? What proof is there that I have been appointed to impose my choice and my conception of man on humanity? I'll never find any proof or sign to convince me of that. If a voice addresses me, it is always for me to decide that this is the angel's voice; if I consider that such an act is a good one, it is I who will choose to say that it is good rather than bad.

Now, I'm not being singled out as an Abraham, and yet at every moment I'm obliged to perform exemplary acts. For every man, everything happens as if all mankind had its eyes fixed on him and were guiding itself by what he does. And every man ought to say to himself, "Am I really the kind of man who has the right to act in such a way that humanity might guide itself by my actions?" And if he does not say that to himself, he is masking his anguish.

There is no question here of the kind of anguish which would lead to quietism, to inaction. It is a matter of a simple sort of anguish that anybody who has had responsibilities is familiar with. For example, when a military officer takes the responsibility for an attack and sends a certain number of men to death, he chooses to do so, and in the main he alone makes the choice. Doubtless, orders come from above, but they are too broad; he interprets them, and on this interpretation depend the lives of ten or fourteen or twenty men. In making a decision he cannot help having a certain anguish. All leaders know this anguish. That doesn't keep them from acting; on the contrary, it is the very condition of their action. For it implies that they envisage a number of possibilities, and when they choose one, they realize that it has value only because it is chosen. We shall see that this kind of anguish, which is the kind that existentialism describes, is explained, in addition, by a direct responsibility to the other men whom it involves. It is not a curtain separating us from action, but is part of action itself.

When we speak of forlornness, a term Heidegger was fond of, we mean only that God does not exist and that we have to face all the consequences of this. This existentialist is strongly opposed to a certain kind of secular ethics which would like to abolish God with the least possible expense. About 1880, some French teachers tried to set up a secular ethics which went something like this: God is a useless and costly hypothesis; we are discarding it; but, meanwhile, in order for there to be an ethics, a society, a civilization, it is essential that certain values be taken seriously and that they be considered as having an *a priori* exis-

tence. It must be obligatory, a *priori*, to be honest, not to lie, not to beat
your wife, to have children, etc., etc. So we're going to try a little device
which will make it possible to show that values exist all the same,
inscribed in a heaven of ideas, though otherwise God does not exist. In
other words—and this, I believe, is the tendency of everything called
reformism in France—nothing will be changed if God does not exist. We
shall find ourselves with the same norms of honesty, progress, and humanism, and we shall have made of God an outdated hypothesis which
will peacefully die off by itself.

The existentialist, on the contrary, thinks it very distressing that God
does not exist, because all possibility of finding values in a heaven of ideas
disappears along with Him; there can no longer be an *a priori* Good, since
there is no infinite and perfect consciousness to think it. Nowhere is it
written that the Good exists, that we must be honest, that we must not
lie; because the fact is we are on a plane where there are only men.
Dostoievsky said, "If God didn't exist, everything would be possible."
That is the very starting point of existentialism. Indeed, everything is
permissible if God does not exist, and as a result man is forlorn, because
neither within him nor without does he find anything to cling to. He can't
shart making excuses for himself.

If existence really does precede essence, there is no explaining things
away by reference to a fixed and given human nature. In other words,
there is no determinism, man is free, man is freedom. On the other hand,
if God does not exist, we find no values or commands to turn to which
legitimize our conduct. So, in the bright realm of values, we have no
excuse behind us, nor justification before us. We are alone, with no
excuses.

That is the idea I shall try to convey when I say that man is condemned
to be free. Condemned, because he did not create himself, yet, in other
respects is free; because, once thrown into the world, he is responsible for
everything he does. The existentialist does not believe in the power of
passion. He will never agree that a sweeping passion is a ravaging torrent
which fatally leads a man to certain acts and is therefore an excuse. He
thinks that man is responsible for his passion.

The existentialist does not think that man is going to help himself by
finding in the world some omen by which to orient himself. Because he
thinks that man will interpret the omen to suit himself. Therefore, he
thinks that man, with no support and no aid, is condemned every moment to invent man. Ponge, in a very fine article, has said, "Man is the
future of man." That's exactly it. But if it is taken to mean that this future
is recorded in heaven, that God sees it, then it is false, because it would
really no longer be a future. If it is taken to mean that, whatever a man
may be, there is a future to be forged, a virgin future before him, then this

remark is sound. But then we are forlorn.

To give you an example which will enable you to understand forlorn-ness better, I shall cite the case of one of my students who came to see me under the following circumstances: his father was on bad terms with his mother, and, moreover, was inclined to be a collaborationist,[1] his older brother had been killed in the German offensive of 1940, and the young man, with somewhat immature but generous feelings, wanted to avenge him. His mother lived alone with him, very much upset by the half-treason of her husband and the death of her older son; the boy was her only consolation.

The boy was faced with the choice of leaving for England and joining the Free French forces—that is, leaving his mother behind—or remain-ing with his mother and helping her to carry on. He was fully aware that the woman lived only for him and that his going off—and perhaps his death—would plunge her into despair. He was also aware that every act that he did for his mother's sake was a sure thing, in the sense that it was helping her to carry on, whereas every effort he made toward going off and fighting was an uncertain move which might run aground and prove completely useless; for example, on his way to England he might, while passing through Spain, be detained indefinitely in a Spanish camp; he might reach England or Algiers and be stuck in an office at a desk job. As a result, he was faced with two very different kinds of action: one, concrete, immediate, but concerning only one individual; the other concerned an incomparably vaster group, a national collectivity, but for that very reason was dubious, and might be interrupted en route. And, at the same time, he was wavering between two kinds of ethics. On the one hand, an ethics of sympathy, of personal devotion; on the other, a broader ethics, but one whose efficacy was more dubious. He had to choose between the two.

Who could help him choose? Christian doctrine? No. Christian doc-trine says, "Be charitable, love your neighbor, take the more rugged path, etc., etc." But which is the more rugged path? Whom should he love as a brother? The fighting man or his mother? Which does the greater good, the vague act of fighting in a group, or the concrete one of helping a particular human being to go on living? Who can decide a *priori*? No-body. No book of ethics can tell him. The Kantian ethics says, "Never treat any person as a means, but as an end." Very well, if I stay with my mother, I'll treat her as an end and not as a means; but by virtue of this very fact, I'm running the risk of treating the people around me who are fighting, as means; and, conversely, if I go to join those who are fighting, I'll be treating them as an end, and, by doing that, I run the risk of treating my mother as a means.

1. With the occupying German army, or its puppet government in Vichy.

If values are vague, and if they are always too broad for the concrete and specific case that we are considering, the only thing left for us is to trust our instincts. That's what this young man tried to do; and when I saw him, he said, "In the end, feeling is what counts. I ought to choose whichever pushes me in one direction. If I feel that I love my mother enough to sacrifice everything else for her—my desire for vengeance, for action, for adventure—then I'll stay with her. If, on the contrary, I feel that my love for my mother isn't enough, I'll leave."

But how is the value of a feeling determined? What gives his feeling for his mother value? Precisely the fact that he remained with her. I may say that I like so-and-so well enough to sacrifice a certain amount of money for him, but I may say so only if I've done it. I may say "I love my mother well enough to remain with her" if I have remained with her. The only way to determine the value of this affection is, precisely, to perform an act which confirms and defines it. But, since I require this affection to justify my act, I find myself caught in a vicious circle.

On the other hand, Gide has well said that a mock feeling and a true feeling are almost indistinguishable; to decide that I love my mother and will remain with her, or to remain with her by putting on an act, amount somewhat to the same thing. In other words, the feeling is formed by the acts one performs; so, I cannot refer to it in order to act upon it. Which means that I can neither seek within myself the true condition which will impel me to act, nor apply to a system of ethics for concepts which will permit me to act. You will say, "At least, he did go to a teacher for advice." But if you seek advice from a priest, for example, you have chosen this priest; you already knew, more or less, just about what advice he was going to give you. In other words, choosing your adviser is involving yourself. The proof of this is that if you are a Christian, you will say, "Consult a priest." But some priests are collaborating, some are just marking time, some are resisting. Which to choose? If the young man chooses a priest who is resisting or collaborating, he has already decided on the kind of advice he's going to get. Therefore, in coming to see me he knew the answer I was going to give him, and I had only one answer to give: "You're free, choose, that is, invent." No general ethics can show you what is to be done; there are no omens in the world. The Catholics will reply, "But there are." Granted—but, in any case, I myself choose the meaning they have.

When I was a prisoner, I knew a rather remarkable young man who was a Jesuit. He had entered the Jesuit order in the following way: he had had a number of very bad breaks; in childhood, his father died, leaving him in poverty, and he was a scholarship student at a religious institution where he was constantly made to feel that he was being kept out of charity; then, he failed to get any of the honors and distinctions that children like; later on, at about eighteen, he bungled a love affair; finally, at twenty-two, he failed in military training, a childish enough matter, but it was the last straw.

This young fellow might well have felt that he had botched everything. It was a sign of something, but of what? He might have taken refuge in bitterness or despair. But he very wisely looked upon all this as a sign that he was not made for secular triumphs, and that only the triumphs of religion, holiness, and faith were open to him. He saw the hand of God in all this, and so he entered the order. Who can help seeing that he alone decided what the sign meant?

Some other interpretation might have been drawn from this series of setbacks; for exmaple, that he might have done better to turn carpenter or revolutionist. Therefore, he is fully responsible for the interpretation. Forlornness implies that we ourselves choose our being. Forlornness and anguish go together.

As for despair, the term has a very simple meaning. It means that we shall confine ourselves to reckoning only with what depends upon our will, or on the ensemble of probabilities which make our action possible. When we want something, we always have to reckon with probabilities. I may be counting on the arrival of a friend. The friend is coming by rail or streetcar; this supposes that the train will arrive on schedule, or that the streetcar will not jump the track. I am left in the realm of possibility; but possibilities are to be reckoned with only to the point where my action comports with the ensemble of these possibilities, and no further. The moment the possibilities I am considering are not rigorously involved by my action, I ought to disengage myself from them, because no God, no scheme, can adapt the world and its possibilities to my will. When Descartes said, "Conquer yourself rather than the world," he meant essentially the same thing.

The Marxists to whom I have spoken reply, "You can rely on the support of others in your action, which obviously has certain limits because you're not going to live forever. That means: rely on both what others are doing elsewhere to help you, in China, in Russia, and what they will do later on, after your death, to carry on the action and lead it to its fulfillment, which will be the revolution. You even *have* to rely upon that, otherwise you're immoral." I reply at once that I will always rely on fellow-fighters insofar as these comrades are involved with me in a common struggle, in the unity of a party or a group in which I can more or less make my weight felt; that is, one whose ranks I am in as a fighter and whose movements I am aware of at every moment. In such a situation, relying on the unity and will of the party is exactly like counting on the fact that the train will arrive on time or that the car won't jump the track. But, given that man is free and that there is no human nature for me to depend on, I cannot count on men whom I do not know by relying on human goodness or man's concern for the good of society. I don't know what will become of the Russian revolution; I may make an example of it to the extent that at the present time it is apparent that the proletariat plays a part in Russia that it plays in no other nation. But I can't swear that this will inevitably lead to a triumph of the proletariat. I've got to limit myself to what I see.

Given that men are free and that tomorrow they will freely decide what man will be, I cannot be sure that, after my death, fellow-fighters will carry on my work to bring it to its maximum perfection. Tomorrow, after my death, some men may decide to set up Fascism, and the others may be cowardly and muddled enough to let them do it. Fascism will then be the human reality, so much the worse for us.

Actually, things will be as man will have decided they are to be. Does that mean that I should abandon myself to quietism? No. First, I should involve myself; then, act on the old saw, "Nothing ventured, nothing gained." Nor does it mean that I shouldn't belong to a party, but rather that I shall have no illusions and shall do what I can. For example, suppose I ask myself, "Will socialization, as such, ever come about?" I know nothing about it. All I know is that I'm going to do everything in my power to bring it about. Beyond that, I can't count on anything. Quietism is the attitude of people who say, "Let others do what I can't do." The doctrine I am presenting is the very opposite of quietism, since it declares, "There is no reality except in action." Moreover, it goes further, since it adds, "Man is nothing else than his plan; he exists only to the extent that he fulfills himself; he is therefore nothing else than the ensemble of his acts, nothing else than his life."

According to this, we can understand why our doctrine horrifies certain people. Because often the only way they can bear their wretchedness is to think, "Circumstances have been against me. What I've been and done doesn't show my true worth. To be sure, I've had no great love, no great friendship, but that's because I haven't met a man or woman who was worthy. The books I've written haven't been very good because I haven't had the proper leisure. I haven't had children to devote myself to because I didn't find a man with whom I could have spent my life. So there remains within me, unused and quite viable, a host of propensities, inclinations, possibilities, that one wouldn't guess from the mere series of things I've done."

Now, for the existentialist there is really no love other than one which manifests itself in a person's being in love. There is no genius other than one which is expressed in works of art; the genius of Proust is the sum of Proust's works; the genius of Racine is his series of tragedies. Outside of that, there is nothing. Why say that Racine could have written another tragedy, when he didn't write it? A man is involved in life, leaves his impress on it, and outside of that there is nothing. To be sure, this may seem a harsh thought to someone whose life hasn't been a success. But, on the other hand, it prompts people to understand that reality alone is what counts, that dreams, expectations, and hopes warrant no more than to define a man as a disappointed dream, as miscarried hopes, as vain expectations. In other words, to define him negatively and not positively. However, when we say, "You are nothing else than your life," that does not imply that the artist will be judged solely on the basis of his works of art; a thousand other things will contribute toward summing him up. What we mean is that a man is nothing else than a series of undertakings, that he is the sum, the organization, the ensemble of the relationships which make up these undertakings.

When all is said and done, what we are accused of, at bottom, is not our pessimism, but an optimistic toughness. If people throw up to us our works of fiction in which we write about people who are soft, weak, cowardly, and sometimes even downright bad, it's not because these prople are soft, weak, cowardly, or bad; because if we were to say, as Zola did, that they are that way because of heredity, the workings of environment, society, because of biological or psychological determinism, people would be reassured. They would say, "Well, that's what we're like, no one can do anything about it." But when the existentialist writes about a coward, he says that this coward is responsible for his cowardice. He's not like that because he has a cowardly heart or lung or brain; he's not like that on account of his physiological make-up; but he's like that because he has made himself a coward by his acts. There's no such thing as a cowardly constitution; there are nervous constitutions; there is poor blood, as the common people say, or strong constitutions. But the man whose blood is poor is not a coward on that account, for what makes cowardice is the act of renouncing or yielding. A constitution is not an act; the coward is defined on the basis of the acts he performs. People feel, in a vague sort of way, that this coward we're talking about is guilty of being a coward, and the thought frightens them. What people would like is that a coward or a hero be born that way. . . .

From these few reflections it is evident that nothing is more unjust than the objections that have been raised against us. Existentialism is nothing else than an attempt to draw all the consequences of a coherent atheistic position. It isn't trying to plunge man into despair at all. But if one calls every attitude of unbelief despair, like the Christians, then the word is not being used in its original sense. Existentialism isn't so atheistic that it wears itself out showing that God doesn't exist. Rather, it declares that even if God did exist, that would change nothing. There you've got our point of view. Not that we believe that God exists, but we think that the problem of His existence is not the issue. In this sense existentialism is optimistic, a doctrine of action, and it is plain dishonesty for Christians to make no distinction between their own despair and ours and then to call us despairing.

QUESTIONS

1. What are some of the methods or devices Sartre uses to define existentialism? Why does he use more than one method or device? Compare the techniques that Sartre uses with those Highet uses in defining Zen (p. 1170).
2. What is the significance of the words "if existence really does precede essence"? What does this mean? What is the force of "if"? Why does Sartre repeat the words later in the essay?
3. Why does Sartre use three separate terms—anguish, forlornness, despair? What, if any, are the differences among them?
4. Sartre makes a distinction between treating "any person as a means . . . [and] as an end" (p. 1197). What are the implications of this distinction?

Notes on Composition

SAYING SOMETHING THAT MATTERS
*Thesis • Assumptions • Fact and Opinion •
Understanding and Emotions*

THE MEANS OF SAYING IT
DEFINING: *Example • Negation • Comparison and Contrast • Analysis
Cause or Effect • End or Means*
MARSHALING EVIDENCE: *Facts • Authority • "Common Consent"*
DRAWING CONCLUSIONS: *Deduction • Induction • Analogy*

AND THE STYLE
*Diction • Metaphor • Repetition and Variation • Tone
Point of View • Persona • Irony • Audience*

Saying Something That Matters

There is no point in the hard labor of writing unless you expect to *do* something to your readers—perhaps add to their store of information, perhaps get them to change their minds on some issue that you care about. Determining just what that something is, is half the battle; hence the importance of knowing your main point, your central purpose in writing, your **thesis**. It may seem that this step—perhaps in the form of a "thesis sentence" or exact statement of the main point—is inevitably prior to everything else, but in actual practice the case is more compli-cated. Few good writers attain a final grasp of their thesis until they have tried setting down their first halting ideas at some length; to put it another way, you discover more precisely what it is you have to say in the act of trying to say it. Formulating and refining upon a thesis sentence as you work your way through a piece of writing helps you see what needs to be done at each stage; the finished piece, though, instead of announcing its thesis in any one sentence, may simply imply it by the fact of its unity, the determinate way the parts hang together. There is probably no single sentence in E. B. White's "Once More to the Lake" (p. 78) that will serve satisfactorily to represent the entire essay in miniature, yet clearly such a sentence could be formulated: The pleasure of recapturing the past is heavily qualified by an adult awareness of the inevitability of change. But whether you state the main point or leave it to be inferred, you need to decide what your piece is about, what you want to say about it, why, and to whom.

1203

Sometimes a thesis will rest on **assumptions**, related ideas that the writer doesn't mention directly but depends upon the reader to understand and agree to, or—if the real purpose is deception—to overlook and hence fail to reject. Machiavelli (p. 812) appears to assume that it is more important for a prince to stay in power than to be a "good" man. You may feel the question is highly ambiguous, or you may disagree sharply. But even if you decide, finally, that you can live with Machiavelli's assumption, you will have acquired a fuller understanding of what he is saying, and of your own relationship to it, for having scrutinized what is being taken for granted. The habit of scrutiny guards you against the careless or cunning writer whose unstated assumptions may be highly questionable. The same habit, turned on your own mind when you become the writer, can save you from the unthinking use of assumptions that you would be hard pressed to defend.

Some theses lend themselves to verification by laboratory methods or the like; they deal with **questions of fact**. The exact order of composition of Shakespeare's plays could conceivably be settled finally if new evidence turned up. Whether or not the plays are great literature, on the other hand, is a **question of opinion**; agreement (though not hard to reach in this instance) depends on the weighing of arguments rather than on tests or measurements. Not that all theses can be neatly classified as assertions either of fact or of opinion (consider "Shakespeare's influence has been greater than Newton's"); still, the attempt to classify your own effort can help you understand what you really want to do.

Sometimes writers address themselves specifically to their readers' **understanding**, sometimes chiefly to their **emotions**. Although the processes of thinking and feeling are almost always mixed, still it is obvious that a description of a chemical process and a description of a candidate you hope to see elected to office will differ considerably in tone and emphasis. Accordingly you need to give some thought to the kind of result you hope to produce: perhaps simply an addition of information, perhaps a change of attitude, perhaps a commitment of the will to action.

The Means of Saying It

No worthwhile thesis comes without work, and the work of arriving at a thesis is much like the work of writing itself—developing, elaborating, refining upon an idea that is perhaps at first hazy. For convenience the process may be divided into setting bounds, or defining; marshaling evidence; and drawing conclusions.

DEFINING in a broad sense may be thought of as what you do to answer the question "What do you mean?" It sets bounds by doing two things to an idea: grouping it with others like it and showing how it differs from those others. "An island is a tract of land" (like a lot or prairie or peninsula) "completely surrounded by water and too small to be called a continent" (and therefore different from a lot, etc.). This process of classifying and distinguishing may take many forms, depending on the kind of thing you are dealing with and your reason for doing so. (Artifacts, for example, can hardly be defined without reference to purpose; a lock is a device for securing a door; a theodolite is an instrument used to measure horizontal or vertical angles). Some of the standard methods are these: by giving **examples**, pointing to an instance as a short way of indicating class and individual characteristics ("That is a firebreak"; "A liberal is a man like Jefferson"); by **negating**, explaining what your subject is not—i.e., using the process of elimination ("Love vaunteth not itself, is not puffed up"); by **comparing and contrasting**, noting the resemblances and differences between your subject and something else ("A magazine is sometimes as big as a book but differs in binding and layout"); by **analyzing**, breaking down a whole into its constituent parts ("A play may be seen as exposition, rising action, and denouement"); by seeking a **cause** of the thing in question or an **effect** that it has produced ("Scurvy is the result of a dietary deficiency and often leads to anemia"); or by attributing to a thing an **end** or **means**, seeing it as a way of fulfilling purpose or as the fulfillment of a purpose ("Representation is the end of the electoral system and the means to good government").

When we turn to specimens of writing, we see immediately that the various methods of defining may serve not only for one-sentence "dictionary" definitions but also as methods of organizing paragraphs or even whole essays, where unfolding the subject is in a sense "defining" it, showing where its boundaries lie. William G. Perry, Jr. (p. 282) compares two kinds of knowledge as part of his defense of a hapless teaching assistant. William Golding (p. 174) analyzes thought in general into three distinct "grades" as he recounts his own intellectual development as a schoolboy. The choice of method in the above examples, it will be noted, is not random; each author selects according to his purpose in writing, and what suits one purpose exactly might be exactly wrong for another.

MARSHALING EVIDENCE. Once you have said what you mean, the next question is likely to be "How do you know?" Marshaling evidence may be thought of as what you do to answer that question. Where the matter at hand involves questions of fact, **factual evidence** will be most directly appropriate. (A diary, a letter —perhaps a cryptogram hidden in the text—might prove even to die-hard Baconians that Shakespeare himself did in fact write the plays which have been credited to him). Writers on scientific subjects inevitably draw chiefly on facts, often intricately arrayed, to support their conclusions. But it should not be assumed that factual evidence turns up mainly in scientific writing. Dorothy Gies McGuigan's account (p. 733) of what it took for a woman to achieve a doctoral degree in the seventeenth century is obviously based on facts in the form of historical documents. Anthony Burgess (p. 478), adopting a less direct strategy, adduces many familiar facts that seem to point to the imminent breakdown of American society, but then, through a combination of factual and other kinds of evidence, tries to show that such signs are misleading.

Factual evidence is generally thought to carry more weight than any other kind, though the force of a fact is greatly diminished if it is not easily verifiable or attested to by reliable witnesses. Where factual evidence is hard to come by (consider the problems of proving that Bacon did not write Shakespeare's plays), the opinion of **authorities** is often invoked, on the assumption that the people most knowledgeable in a field are most likely to judge truly in a particular case. The testimony of authorities is relevant, of course, not only in questions of fact but also in questions of opinion. Francis Bacon (p. 343), for example, invokes Solomon and Job to support his ideas about revenge. In general, however, the appeal to authority in matters of opinion has lost the rhetorical effectiveness it once had, perhaps because there is less agreement as to who the reliable authorities are.

As changes in the nature of the question draw in a larger and larger number of "authorities," evidence from authority shades into what might be called "the **common consent** of mankind," those generalizations about human experience that large numbers of readers can be counted upon to accept and that often find expression in proverbs or apothegms: "Risk no more than you can afford to lose" and "The first step toward Hell is halfway there." Such generalizations, whether proverbial or not, are a common ground on which writer and reader meet in agreement. Your task as writer is to find and present the ones applicable to your particular thesis and then demonstrate that applicability.

DRAWING CONCLUSIONS. One of the ways of determining the consequences of thought—that is, drawing conclusions—is the process of applying generalizations (**deduction**): "If we should risk no more than we can afford to lose, then we had better not jeopardize the independence of our universities by seeking federal aid." Another way of arriving at conclusions is the process of **induction**, which consists in forming generalizations from a sufficient number of observed instances: "Since universities A, B, and C have been accepting federal aid through research grants for years without loss of independence, it is probably safe for any university to do so." Typically deduction and induction work reciprocally, each helping to supply for the other the materials upon which inference operates. We induce from experience that green apples are sour; we deduce from this generalization that a particular green apple is sour. A third kind of inference, sometimes regarded as only a special kind of deduction or induction, is **analogy**, the process of concluding that two things which resemble each other in one way will resemble each other in another way also: "Federal aid has benefited mental hospitals enormously, and will probably benefit universities just as much." An analogy proves nothing, although it may help the reader see the reasonableness of an idea and is often extremely valuable for purposes of illustration, since it makes an unknown clearer by relating it to a known.

Turning to our essays, we can see something of the variety of ways in which these three kinds of inference manifest themselves: Thomas Jefferson (p. 833) deducing from certain self-evident truths the conclusion that the united colonies are henceforward free and independent states; Wallace Stegner arguing from a series of particular instances to the general conclusion that a community may be judged by what it throws away (p. 6); Stephen Jay Gould turning to the myth of Odysseus for an analogy to scientific creativity (p. 968).

Such a list of examples suggests that in good writing the conclusions we draw, the consequences of thought, are "consequential" in more than one sense: not only do they follow logically from the evidence considered, they are also *significant*; they relate directly or indirectly to aspects of our lives that we care about. To the questions suggested earlier as demands for definition and evidence, then, we must add a third. "What do you mean?" calls for precision yet admits answers vast in scope. "How do you know?" trims the vastness down to what can be substantiated, but may settle for triviality as the price of certainty. The appropriate question to raise finally, then, is simply "So what?" and the conclusions we as writers draw need to be significant enough to yield answers to that question. We have come full circle back to the idea of saying something that matters.

And the Style

One theory of style in writing sees form and content as distinct: style is the way a thing is said, the thing itself an unchanging substance that can be decked out in various ways. Mr. Smith not only *died*, he *ceased to be*, he *passed away*, he *croaked*, he *was promoted to glory*—all mean "the same thing." According to a second theory, however, they are ways of saying different things: variations in **diction** imply variations in reference. To say that Smith *ceased to be* records a privative and secular event; to say that he *was promoted to glory* (a Salvation Army expression) rejoices in an event of a different order altogether. Content and form in this view are inseparable; a change in one is a change in the other.

In **metaphor** we can see that the two theories, instead of contradicting each other, are more like the two sides of a coin; when one idea is expressed in terms of another, it is the same and yet not the same. To view the passage from life to death as if it were a promotion from one military rank to a higher one is to see a common center of reference and widening circles of association at the same time. This seeing as *if* opens up a whole range of expression, since many meanings reside in the relationship between the two parts of a comparison rather than in either part by itself. Charles Lamb (p. 346), ironically extolling borrowers over lenders, exclaims "What a careless, even deportment hath your borrower!" and then adds "what rosy gills!" His metaphor seems to suggest, approximately, that the borrower's healthy contentment depends on a certain fishlike obliviousness, yet no paraphrase captures the humorous aptness of the metaphor itself.

But style is by no means dependent on diction and metaphor alone. Grammatical relationships yield a host of stylistic devices, most of which can be described in terms of **repetition and variation**. Repetition may exist at every level; as commonly understood, its chief application is to the word (including the pronoun as a word-substitute), but the same principle governs the use of parallelism (repetition of a grammatical structure) within and between sentences, even between paragraphs. Failure to observe that principle—that similarity in idea calls for similarity in form—can be detected wherever a change in form implies that a distinction is being made when actually none is relevant to the context: "Their conversation was interrupted by dinner, but they resumed their discussion afterwards"; "She rolled out the dough, placed it over the pie, and pricked holes in it. She also trimmed off the edge." The corollary of the principle of appropriate repetition is the principle of appropriate variation—that difference in idea calls for difference in form. For every failure to repeat when repetition is called for there is a corresponding failure to vary when variation is called for: "Their discussion was interrupted when class discussion of the day's assignment began"; "It had been raining for many days near the river. It has been rising steadily toward the top of the levee." Failures of this sort, which suggest a similarity in idea or parallelism in thought where none exists, often strike the ear as a lack of euphony or appropriate rhythm: "A boxer must learn to react absolutely instantly"; "The slingshot was made of strips of inner tubes of tires of cars." The principle of appropriate variation applies, too, to sentences as wholes: if a separate sentence is used for each detail, or if every sentence includes many details, the reader may be given a false impression of parallelism or equality of emphasis. Here again variation may be a way to avoid misleading grammatical indications of meaning. In a writer like John Henry Newman (p. 348), who works deliberately for a high degree of parallelism, correspondence between repetition and sameness of meaning, or variation and difference of meaning, is perhaps most conveniently illustrated.

All stylistic techniques come together to supply an answer to the question "Who is behind these words?" Words are spoken in a particular tone of voice, but **tone** is not limited to speech; written words convey a tone, too, a tone inferred by the reader from the way something is said and the context in which it occurs. Related to tone is **point of view**, the position from which you approach and deal with your subject: as an insider or an outsider, critic or apologist, and so on.

Tone and point of view contribute, along with other stylistic considerations, to the total impression the reader forms of you as a person. The quality of that impression—your **persona** (which may or may not resemble your actual personality)—obviously has much to do with the reader's willingness to be convinced. Honesty and straightforwardness come first—though the honesty of an ignoramus and the straightforwardness of a fool are unlikely to win assent. Some more sophisticated approaches to the adoption of a persona employ **irony**: you assume a character that the reader can see is at odds with your real intention. Whether direct or ironic, the chosen role must be suited to your **audience**; clearly your sense of who your readers are has a bearing on the kind of role you adopt. And your role must also be suited to your subject and to your own talents; it must be one you can play effectively. You may want to try out several to see what each implies: are you an expert or a humble seeker after truth? a wry humorist or a gadfly deliberately exacerbating hidden guilt? Even writers working in the same general territory—S. J. Perelman (p. 457) and Herb Goldberg (p. 451), for example, both deal with supposed aspects of the American character—may present sharply different personalities to their readers in their characteristic handling of both thought and expression. A self will be revealed in every phrase you set down—even in details of spelling, grammar, and punctuation, which, if ineptly handled, may suggest to your readers a carelessness that destroys their confidence.

Authors

[An * indicates the source of a selection in this anthology. Only a few of each author's works are cited.]

Robert M. Adams (1916–)
American literary critic, scholar (University of California at Los Angeles); author of *After Joyce; Proteus: His Lies, His Truth; *Bad Mouth: Furtive Papers on the Dark Side; The Land and Literature of England.*

Aesop (620?–560? B.C.)
Reputed author of "Aesop's fables"; said to have been a former slave in Greece.

Woody Allen (1935–)
Pseudonym of Heywood Allen Konigsberg; American comedian, writer, actor, film director; author of *Getting Even, *Without Feathers, Play It Again, Sam, Side Effects, The Floating Lightbulb.*

Maya Angelou (1924–)
American actress, journalist, television-scriptwriter, civil-rights worker; author of *I Know Why the Caged Bird Sings, Gather Together in My Name, The Heart of a Woman.*

Hannah Arendt (1906–75)
German-American political analyst (New School for Social Research); author of *The Origins of Totalitarianism, The Human Condition, *Eichmann in Jerusalem, On Revolution, On Violence, Men in Dark Times, Crises of the Republic.*

Michael J. Arlen (1930–)
American journalist and author; television critic for *The New Yorker*; author of *Living Room War, Exiles, An American Verdict, Passage to Ararat, The View from Highway 1, Thirty Seconds, *The Camera Age: Essays on Television.*

Matthew Arnold (1822–1888)
English man of letters, poet, literary critic; author of *Poems, Essays in Criticism, *Culture and Anarchy, Literature and Dogma.*

Roger Ascham (1515–1568)
English scholar, tutor of Queen Elizabeth I; author of *Toxophilus, The Scholemaster.*

Lord Ashby (1904–)
Eric Ashby; English botanist, educator, vice-chancellor (Cambridge University); author of *The Challenge to Education, A Scientist in Russia, Masters and Scholars.*

Isaac Asimov (1920–)
American author, professor of biochemistry (Boston University School of Medicine); author of 200 books, including *The Stars, Like the Dust, Of Time and Space and Other Things, An Easy Introduction to the Slide Rule, *The Left Hand of the Electron, Nightfall and Other Stories, ABC's of the Earth.*

W[ystan] H[ugh] Auden (1907–1973)
English-American poet, playwright, critic; author of *In Time of War, The Sea and the Mirror, Poems, *The Dyer's Hand*; with Christopher Isherwood, of *Ascent of F-6, The Dog Beneath the Skin* (plays); with Louis MacNeice, of *Letters from Iceland.*

Sir Francis Bacon (1561–1626)
English politician, statesman, philosopher; author of *Essays, Advancement of Learning, *New Organon, New Atlantis.*

Russell Baker (1925–)
American journalist, essayist (*The New York Times*); author of *All Things Considered, An American in Washington, Growing Up.*

James Baldwin (1924–   )
American essayist and novelist; Harlem-bred, one-time expatriate in Paris, political activist for civil-rights causes; author of *Go Tell It on the Mountain, Another Country, Tell Me How Long the Train's Been Gone* (novels), *Notes of a Native Son, Nobody Knows My Name, The Fire Next Time, Going to Meet the Man, No Name in the Street*.

Carl Becker (1873–1945)
American historian (Cornell University); author of *Progress and Power, The Beginnings of the American People, *Modern Democracy*.

Jeremy Bernstein (1929–   )
American professor of physics (Stevens Institute of Technology) and staff writer for *The New Yorker*; his books include *Einstein, The Analytical Engine, Science Observed*.

Wendell Berry (1934–   )
American essayist, social critic, poet, farmer; his works include *A Place on Earth, The Long-legged House, Findings, *The Gift of Good Land, There Is Singing Around Me, The Unsettling of America: Culture and Agriculture*.

Bruno Bettelheim (1903–   )
Austrian-American psychologist (University of Chicago); psychoanalyst; author of *Love is Not Enough, *The Informed Heart, The Empty Fortress, Children of the Dream*.

Ambrose Bierce (1842–1914?)
American short-story writer, journalist; author of *Tales of Soldiers and Civilians, The Cynic's Word Book* (retitled *The Devil's Dictionary*).

Caroline Bird (1915–   )
American writer, lecturer, public-relations specialist; author of *The Case Against College; Enterprising Women; Invisible Scar: The Great Depression, and What It Did to American Life, from Then Until Now; The Two Paycheck Marriage*.

Peter [Jost] Blake (1920–   )
American architect, dean (Boston Architectural Center), editor (*Architectural Forum*); author of *The Master Builders, God's Own Junkyard, *Form Follows Fiasco: Why Modern Architecture Hasn't Worked*.

William Blake (1757–1827)
English poet, artist, engraver; author of *Songs of Innocence, Songs of Experience, *The Marriage of Heaven and Hell, The Book of Thel*.

Carol Bly (1930–   )
American short-story writer and poet; her books include *Poetry Northwest, *Home from the Country*.

Giovanni Boccaccio (1313–1375)
Medieval Italian writer; author of the *Decameron*.

Wayne C. Booth (1921–   )
American literary critic, dean (University of Chicago); author of *The Rhetoric of Fiction, The Rhetoric of Irony, Now Don't Try to Reason with Me: Essays and Ironies for a Credulous Age, Modern Dogma and the Rhetoric of Ascent, Critical Understanding: The Powers and Limits of Pluralism*.

Jacob Bronowski (1908–1974)
English critic, statesman, senior fellow and trustee of Salk Institute for Biological Studies; author of *The Poet's Defence, The Common Sense of Science, *Science and Human Values, The Identity of Man, Nature and Knowledge*.

Jerome S. Bruner (1915–   )
American psychologist (Harvard University); author of *The Process of Education, Toward a Theory of Instruction, Processes of Cognitive Growth, Beyond the Information Given, Child's Talk*.

Edward Bunker (1933–   )
American writer, former drug addict and inmate of San Quentin and Folsom state prisons; author of *Straight Time, No Beast So Fierce* (novels).

[John] Anthony Burgess [Wilson] (1917–   )
English novelist; author of *A Clockwork Orange, Re Joyce, The Novel Now, MF, Tremor of Intent, Enderby, Nothing Like the Sun, The Wanting Seed* (novels), *Urgent Copy* (essays).

Herbert Butterfield (1900–   )
British historian; his books include *The Whig Interpretation of History, Christianity and History, History and Human Relations*.

Edward Hallett Carr (1892–1982)
English historian (Cambridge University), journalist, statesman; author of *The Ro-

mantic Exiles; The Bolshevik Revolution, 1917-1923; *What Is History?

[Arthur] Joyce [Lunel] Cary (1888–1957)
Anglo-Irish novelist, poet, political philosopher; author of Aissa Saved, The Horse's Mouth, Mister Johnson, The Captive and the Free (novels), A Case for African Freedom, Power in Men, The Process of Real Freedom.

Lord Chesterfield (1694–1773)
Philip Dormer Stanhope, fourth earl; English statesman, diplomat, well-known letter writer (*Letters to His Son).

Lord Clark (1903–1983)
Kenneth MacKenzie Clark; English art historian, critic; author of Landscape into Art, The Nude, Leonardo da Vinci, Looking at Pictures, Civilisation, *Moments of Vision and Other Essays.

Austin Clarke (1934–   )
Canadian novelist (born in Barbados), short-story writer, literary critic, television scriptwriter, editor; his works include When He Was Free and Young and He Used to Wear Silks: Stories, A Storm of Fortune, A Bigger Light, The Prime Minister, *Growing Up Stupid under the Union Jack.

Samuel Langhorne Clemens (Mark Twain) (1835–1910)
American humorist, itinerant journalist, critic, novelist; author of Roughing It, Tom Sawyer, Life on the Mississippi, Huckleberry Finn, A Connecticut Yankee in King Arthur's Court.

Aaron Copland (1900–   )
American composer for ballet, film, symphony orchestra, vocal and chamber orchestra; musical works include Appalachian Spring and Billy the Kid (for ballet), Of Mice and Men and Our Town (for film), and Fanfare for the Common Man (for symphony orchestra); author of Copland on Music, Music and Imagination, New Music, *What to Listen for in Music.

Malcolm Cowley (1898–   )
American critic, poet, editor, literary historian; his books include Exile's Return, The Literary Situation, Blue Juanita: Collected Poems, *The View from 80.

[William] Robertson Davies (1913–   )
Canadian novelist, playwright, critic, Master of Massey College (University of Toronto); author of Fifth Business, The

Manticore, World of Wonders, The Rebel Angels (novels), more than a dozen plays, three books on the Stratford, Ontario, drama festival, and *One Half of Robertson Davies (essays).

Thomas De Quincey (1785–1859)
English essayist, critic; author of Confessions of an English Opium Eater, *Autobiographic Sketches.

Joan Didion (1934–   )
American writer; author of Play It As It Lays, *Slouching Towards Bethlehem, A Book of Common Prayer, The White Album, Salvador.

Annie Dillard (1945–   )
American writer, editor; author of *Pilgrim at Tinker Creek, Teaching a Stone to Talk: Expeditions and Encounters.

Kildare Dobbs (1923–   )
Canadian writer; author of *Running to Paradise, Reading the Time.

John Donne (1573–1631)
English poet, clergyman, Dean of St. Paul's Cathedral; author of Songs and Sonnets, *Devotions upon Emergent Occasions.

Jonathan Edwards (1703–58)
American Puritan preacher and theologian in Massachusetts Bay Colony.

Irenäus Eibl-Eibesfeldt (1928–   )
Austrian zoologist, science writer, scriptwriter; author of Galapagos, Noah's Ark of the Pacific; The Biology of Peace and War; *Love and Hate: The Natural History of Behavior Patterns.

Loren Eiseley (1907–77)
American anthropologist, historian of science (University of Pennsylvania); author of The Immense Journey, Darwin's Century, The Firmament of Time, The Mind as Nature, Francis Bacon and the Modern Dilemma, The Unexpected Universe, The Invisible Pyramid, *The Night Country, All the Strange Hours.

Ralph Waldo Emerson (1803–82)
American essayist, poet, expositor of the intellectual movement known as Transcendentalism; author of Nature, Representative Men, English Traits, *Journal.

Joseph Epstein (1937–   )
Editor of The American Scholar; author of Divorced in America, Ambition: The Se-

cret *Passion, Familiar Territory: Observations on American Life.*

Erik H. Erikson (1902–)
German-American psychoanalyst (Harvard University); author of *Young Man Luther, Identity and the Life Cycle, *Insight and Responsibility, Identity: Youth and Crisis, Childhood and Society, Gandhi's Truth, The Life Cycle Completed.*

Frances FitzGerald (1940–)
American journalist, writer (*The New Yorker, Atlantic*); author of *Fire in the Lake: The Vietnamese and Americans in Vietnam, America Revised.*

E. M. Forster (1879–1970)
British novelist, critic, essayist; his books include *Passage to India, *Two Cheers for Democracy, Howard's End, Aspects of the Novel.*

Benjamin Franklin (1706–1790)
American statesman, delegate to the Continental Congress and Constitutional Convention, ambassador to France during the American Revolution, inventor, newspaper publisher, practical philosopher; author of *Poor Richard's Almanack, *Autobiography.*

James F. Fries (1938–)
American doctor and medical writer; his books include *Take Care of Yourself, Taking Care of Your Child, Prognosis: A Textbook of Medicine.*

Erich Fromm (1900–1980)
German-American psychoanalyst; author of *Psychoanalysis and Religion, The Sane Society, Sigmund Freud's Mission, The Dogma of Christ and Other Essays on Religion, Psychology and Culture, The Heart of Man.*

Harold Fromm (1933–)
American scholar; writes on literature, literary theory, and environmental affairs; author of *Bernard Shaw and the Theater in the Nineties: A Study of Shaw's Dramatic Criticism.*

Robert Frost (1874–1963)
American poet, lecturer, teacher.

Christopher Fry (1907–)
English playwright, translator; author of *The Boy with a Cart, The Dark Is Light Enough, The Lady's Not for Burning, Venus Observed, A Yard of Sun* (plays).

Northrop Frye (1912–)
Canadian literary critic (University of Toronto); author of *Anatomy of Criticism, Design for Learning, *The Educated Imagination.*

Paul Fussell (1924–)
American professor of English (Rutgers University) and writer; his books include *Samuel Johnson and the Life of Writing, The Great War and Modern Memory, *The Boy Scout Handbook.*

John Kenneth Galbraith (1908–)
Canadian-American economist (Harvard University), broadcaster, writer; author of *The Affluent Society, The New Industrial State, Money, The Age of Uncertainty, A Life in Our Times: Memoirs.*

John Gardner (1933–82)
American writer and educator; his books include *Grendel, The Sunlight Dialogues, Nickel Mountain, October Light.*

Willard Gaylin (1925–)
President of the Institute of Society, Ethics, and the Life Sciences in Hastings, New York; author of *In the Service of Their Country: War Resisters in Prison; Caring, Feelings, The Killing of Bonnie Garland: A Question of Justice.*

Edward Gibbon (1737–94)
English historian and member of Parliament; author of *Decline and Fall of the Roman Empire.*

Herb Goldberg (1937–)
American psychotherapist (California State University, Los Angeles); author of *The Hazards of Being Male.*

William Golding (1911–)
English novelist, poet; winner of the Nobel prize; author of *Lord of the Flies, Pincher Martin.*

Stephen Jay Gould (1941–)
American scientist (Harvard University), writer (*Natural History*); author of *Ever Since Darwin, *The Panda's Thumb, The Mismeasure of Man, Hen's Teeth and Horse's Toes.*

Robert Graves (1895–)
English man of letters; author of *The White Goddess, The Greek Myths, Collected Poems, Love Respelt.*

Donald Hall (1923–)
American poet; his books include *Exiles and Marriages, The Dark Houses, The Yel-*

low Room Love Poems, Kicking the Leaves.

Barbara Grizzuti Harrison (1934–)
American writer; author of *Unlearning the Lie: Sexism in School, Visions of Glory: A History and a Memory of the Witnesses of Jehovah.*

Nathaniel Hawthorne (1804–64)
American novelist, short-story writer, essayist; author of *Twice-told Tales, Mosses from an Old Manse, The Scarlet Letter, The House of the Seven Gables.*

Robert L. Heilbroner (1919–)
American economist and author; his books include *An Inquiry into the Human Prospect, Business Civilization in Decline, Marxism: For and Against, The Worldly Philosophers.*

Carolyn G. Heilbrun (1926–)
American literary critic, mystery writer (as Amanda Cross), and professor of English (Columbia University); author of *Towards a Recognition of Androgyny, Lady Ottoline's Album, The Question of Max, Reinventing Womanhood.*

Lillian Hellman (1905–)
American playwright, writer; author of *The Children's Hour, The Little Foxes* (plays), *An Unfinished Woman, *Pentimento, Scoundrel Time.*

Gilbert Highet (1906–78)
Scottish-American classicist (Columbia University); author of *The Classical Tradition, The Art of Teaching, The Anatomy of Satire, *Talents and Geniuses.*

Edward Hoagland (1932–)
American novelist, writer; author of *Cat Man, *The Courage of Turtles, Red Wolves and Black Bears, African Calliope: A Journey to the Sudan, Walking the Dead Diamond River, The Tugman's Passage.*

John [Caldwell] Holt (1923–)
American educator; author of *How Children Fail, How Children Learn, Underachieving School, What Do I Do Monday?, Never Too Late, Teach Your Own: New and Hopeful Path for Parents and Educators.*

John Houseman (1902–)
Theatrical and motion-picture producer, director, actor, educator (Juilliard School); author of *Front and Center, *Run-Through.*

Ada Louise Huxtable
American architecture critic (*New York Times*), social critic; her books include *Pier Luigi Nervi, Classic New York, Will They Ever Finish Bruckner Boulevard?, Kicked a Building Lately?*

William James (1842–1910)
American philosopher, pioneer psychologist (Harvard University), pragmatist, brother of Henry James; author of *Principles of Psychology, The Varieties of Religious Experience, Pragmatism.*

Thomas Jefferson (1743–1826)
Third president of the United States, first secretary of state, founder of the University of Virginia, drafter of the *Declaration of Independence and the statute of Virginia for religious freedom, founder of the Democratic party; also renowned for his talents as an architect and inventor.

Samuel Johnson (1709–84)
English lexicographer, critic, moralist, journalist (*The Idler, *The Rambler*); author of *A Dictionary of the English Language, Lives of the Poets*; subject of Boswell's *Life.*

Carl Gustav Jung (1875–1961)
Swiss psychiatrist, a founder of analytic psychology; author of *Analytical Psychology, The Undiscovered Self, Man and His Symbols, *Modern Man in Search of a Soul, Psychology and Religion, A Theory of Psychoanalysis.*

Franz Kafka (1883–1924)
Czech novelist and short-story writer; author of *The Trial, The Castle, Amerika.*

Stanley Kauffmann (1916–)
American film and drama critic (*New Republic*); author of *A World on Film, Living Images: Film Comment and Criticism, Albums of Early Life, Before My Eyes: Film Criticism and Comment.*

Garrison Keillor (1942–)
American writer and broadcaster; author of *Happy to Be Here* and host of "A Prairie Home Companion" (radio).

X. J. Kennedy (1929–)
Pseudonym of Joseph C. Kennedy; poet, critic, professor of English (Tufts University); author of *Nude Descending a Staircase, Did Adam Name the Vinegarroon, One Winter Night in August and Other Nonsense Jingles.*

Sören Kierkegaard (1813–1855)
Danish theologian, philosopher; author of *Fear and Trembling, Either/Or, Philosophical Fragments.*

Martin Luther King, Jr. (1929–68)
American Negro clergyman, civil-rights leader, president of Southern Christian Leadership Conference; winner of Nobel Peace Prize; author of *Stride Toward Freedom, Why We Can't Wait.*

Maxine Hong Kingston (1940–   )
American-born author (Chinese descent); her books include *The Woman Warrior: Memoirs of a Girlhood among Ghosts, *China Men.*

Arthur Koestler (1905–83)
Hungarian-English writer; author of *Darkness at Noon* (novel), *The Ghost in the Machine, The Case of the Midwife Toad, Bricks to Babel: Selected Writings with Comments, The God That Failed.*

Joseph Wood Krutch (1893–1970)
American literary and social critic; author of *The Modern Temper, The Measure of Man, Human Nature and the Human Condition.*

Elisabeth Kübler-Ross (1926–   )
Psychologist; author of *On Death and Dying.*

Thomas Kuhn (1922–   )
American historian of science (Princeton University); author of *The Copernican Revolution, Planetary Astronomy in the Development of Western Thought, *The Structure of Scientific Revolutions.*

Milan Kundera (1929–   )
Czechoslovakian-born author, now French citizen; author of *The Joke, Laughable Loves, Life Is Elsewhere, The Farewell Party, *The Book of Laughter and Forgetting, The Unbearable Lightness of Being.*

Charles Lamb (1775–1834)
English essayist, critic; author of *Essays of Elia* and, with his sister Mary, *Tales from Shakespeare.*

Susanne K. Langer (1895–   )
American philosopher (Connecticut College); author of *The Practice of Philosophy, An Introduction to Symbolic Logic, Feeling and Form, *Problems of Art.*

François, duc de la Rochefoucauld (1613–1680)
French moralist; author of *Memoirs, *Reflections or Sentences, Moral Maxims.*

Margaret Laurence (1926–   )
Canadian writer; author of *The Stone Angel, A Jest of God, A Bird in the House, The Diviners* (fiction), *Heart of a Stranger.*

Fran Lebowitz (1951?–   )
American writer; author of *Metropolitan Life.*

Susan Lee (1944–   )
American writer, novelist.

Doris Lessing (1919–   )
British novelist; author of *The Golden Notebook, The Four-Gated City, Briefing for a Descent into Hell, The Summer Before the Dark* (novels), *A Small Personal Voice.*

Michael Levin (1943–   )
American philosopher (City College of New York); author of *Metaphysics and the Mind-Body Problem.*

C[live] S[taples] Lewis (1898–1963)
English novelist, essayist; author of *The Pilgrim's Regress, *The Screwtape Letters, *The Weight of Glory and Other Addresses.*

Abraham Lincoln (1809–1865)
Sixteenth president of the United States, lawyer, congressman, celebrated for his debates with Stephen Douglas on the question of slavery's extension; his voluminous state papers include the Emancipation Proclamation, the Gettysburg Address, the *Second Inaugural Address.*

Walter Lippmann (1889–1974)
American political philosopher, journalist-statesman; author of *Public Opinion, A Preface to Morals, The New Imperative, The Public Philosophy, The Communist World and Ours.*

Konrad Z. Lorenz (1903–   )
Austrian-German scientist, director of Max Planck Institute for Physiology of Behavior; author of *King Solomon's Ring, On Aggression, The Foundation of Ethology.*

John Livingston Lowes (1867–1945)
American literary critic, scholar (Harvard University); author of *Geoffrey Chaucer, The Road to Xanadu.*

Niccolò Machiavelli (1469–1527)
Florentine statesman, political philoso-

pher during the reign of the Medici; author of *The Art of War, History of Florence, Discourses on Livy,* *The Prince.

Norman Mailer (1923–   )
American writer; his books include *The Naked and the Dead, Armies of the Night,* *Miami and the Siege of Chicago, *The Executioner's Song, Ancient Evenings.*

D. Keith Mano (1942–   )
American novelist and nonfiction writer; his books include *The Proselytizer, The Bridge, Take Five.*

William March (1893–1954)
Pseudonym of William Edward March Campbell; American businessman, novelist, short-story writer, fabulist; author of *Company K, The Little Wife and Other Stories, Some Like Them Short,* *99 Fables.

W. Somerset Maugham (1874–1965)
English novelist, dramatist, short-story writer; author of *Of Human Bondage, The Moon and Sixpence* (novels), *The Circle* (play), *The Summing Up *(autobiography).*

Joyce Maynard (1954–   )
Canadian-American writer *(The New York Times)*; author of *Looking Back: A Chronicle of Growing Old in the Sixties, Baby Love.*

Dorothy Gies McGuigan (1914–   )
American historian (University of Michigan); author of *Metternich and the Duchess, The Habsburgs.*

John McPhee (1931–   )
American writer, long associated with *The New Yorker*; his books include *The Curve of Binding Energy, The Survival of the Bark Canoe,* *Coming into the Country, *Basin and Range.*

Margaret Mead (1901–78)
American anthropologist; author of over twenty-five books, including *Coming of Age in Samoa, Male and Female, A Way of Seeing,* *Blackberry Winter: My Early Years.

Stanley Milgram (1933–   )
American social psychologist (Yale University); author of *Obedience to Authority, *The Individual in a Social World.*

Jessica Mitford (1917–   )
American (British-born) writer; author of *Daughters and Rebels,* *The American Way of Death, *The Trial of Dr. Spock.*

N. Scott Momaday (1934–   )
American Indian writer, poet; author of *The Names,* *The Way to Rainy Mountain (nonfiction); *Angle of Geese and Other Poems, The Gourd Dancer* (poetry).

Toni Morrison (1931–   )
American writer; author of *The Bluest Eye, *Song of Solomon, Sula, Tar Baby.*

Vladimir Nabokov (1899–1977)
Russian-born novelist who fled Russia at the time of the Communist Revolution and eventually became a U.S. citizen; also a recognized authority on butterflies; his books include *Laughter in the Dark; Lolita; Pnin; Pale Fire; Ada: Or, Ardor: A Family Chronicle;* *Lectures on Literature: British, French and German Writers.

Helen Nearing (1904–   )
American author and musician; with husband Scott Nearing has been homesteading in Vermont and Maine for over 40 years; author of *Wise Words on the Good Life; with Scott Nearing, of *Living the Good Life, The Maple Sugar Book, Continuing the Good Life.*

John Henry Newman (1801–90)
English Catholic prelate, cardinal; author of *Tracts for the Times,* *The Idea of a University, *Apologia pro Vita Sua.*

George Orwell (1903–50)
Pseudonym of Eric Blair; English novelist, essayist, social commentator, satirist of totalitarianism; author of *Down and Out in Paris and London, Homage to Catalonia, Nineteen Eighty-Four, Animal Farm.*

Cynthia Ozick (1928–   )
American author of fiction, poetry, criticism, reviews, translations; her books include *Trust, The Pagan Rabbi and Other Stories, Bloodshed and Three Novellas, Levitation: Five Fictions, Art and Ardor.*

Walter Pater (1839–94)
English man of letters; author of *Studies in the History of the Renaissance, *Marius the Epicurean, Appreciations.*

Donald Pearce (1917–   )
Canadian professor of English (University of California, Santa Barbara); author of *Journal of a War; Northwest Europe, 1944–1945; In the President's and My Opinion.

Walker Percy (1916–   )
American novelist; his books include *The*

Moviegoer, The Last Gentleman, Love in the Ruins, *The Message in the Bottle, The Second Coming, Lost in the Cosmos.

S[idney] J[oseph] Perelman (1904–79)
American humorist, writer for motion pictures; author of One Touch of Venus, *Vinegar Puss, Eastward Ha!

William G. Perry, Jr. (1913–   )
American educator, director of the Bureau of Study Counsel at Harvard University , author of Forms of Intellectual and Ethical Development in the College Years.

Alexander Petrunkevitch (1875–1964)
Russian-born zoologist and professor (Yale University); his books include Index Catalog of Spiders of North, Central and South America; Choice and Responsibility; Principles of Classification.

Robert Pirsig (1928–   )
American writer, educator; author of *Zen and the Art of Motorcycle Maintenance.

Plato (427?–347 B.C.)
Greek philosopher, pupil and friend of Socrates, teacher of Aristotle, founder of the Academy; author of *The Republic and other dialogues.

Norman Podhoretz (1930–   )
American writer, former editor of Commentary; author of *Doings and Undoings, The Fifties and After in American Writing, Making It.

Ralph A. Raimi (1924–   )
American mathematician (University of Rochester); author of Vested Interests.

James C. Rettie (1904–69)
Economic adviser for the Department of the Interior during Kennedy and Johnson administrations; economist for the National Forest Service Department of Agriculture; author of numerous reports and research papers.

Jean Rhys (1895–1979)
British novelist (born in the West Indies); her books include The Left Bank and Other Stories; After Leaving Mr. MacKenzie; Good Morning Midnight; Wide Sargasso Sea; Sleep It Off, Lady; Voyage in the Dark; *Smile Please: An Unfinished Autobiography.

Adrienne Rich (1929–   )
American poet (Douglass College); author of A Change of World; Snapshots of a Daughter-in-Law; The Will to Change; Diving into the Wreck; Poems: Selected and New; Of Woman Born; *On Lies, Secrets, and Silence, A Wild Patience Has Taken Me This Far.

Betty Rollin (1936–   )
American writer, actress; author of I Thee Wed; First, You Cry.

Theodore Roszak (1933–   )
American author, editor, educator (California State University, Hayward): his books include Making of a Counter-Culture, Where the Wasteland Ends: Politics and Transcendence in Post-Industrial Society, Pontifex: A Revolutionary Entertainment for the Mind's Eye Theater, Unfinished Animal, Person/Planet.

Edward Rothstein (1952–   )
American music critic for the New York Times; also writes on literature, psychology, and the arts for many publications, including Commentary, The American Scholar, Musical Quarterly.

Franklin Russell (1926–   )
New Zealand-born nature writer who came to the United States in 1963; his books include The Secret Islands, The Secret Life of Animals, Watchers at the Pond.

Gilbert Ryle (1900–76)
English philosopher, essayist; author of The Concept of Mind, Dilemmas, Plato's Progress, A Rational Animal, *Essays on Logic and Thinking, Collected Papers.

Carl Sagan (1934–   )
American space scientist (Cornell University), writer; author of *The Dragons of Eden, The Cosmic Connection, Intelligent Life in the Universe (with I. S. Shklovsky), Planetary Exploration, Cosmos.

Kirkpatrick Sale (1937–   )
American writer; his books include *Human Scale, Power Shift.

George Santayana (1863–1952)
American philosopher (Harvard University); author of The Life of Reason, The Realm of Essence, The Realm of Truth, *Soliloquies in England.

May Sarton (1912–   )
American poet, novelist, memoirist; author of Encounter in April, In Time Like Air, A Durable Fire, Collected Poems 1930–1973, Kinds of Love, As We Are Now, *Journal of a Solitude, A Reckoning, I

Knew a Phoenix: Sketches for an Autobiography, Halfway to Silence: New Poems, The House by the Sea, Shadow of a Man.

Jean-Paul Sartre (1905–1980)
French philosopher, playwright, novelist, story writer, social and literary critic, winner of Nobel Prize; author of *Existentialism, Existentialism and Humanism, No Exit, The Wall, Imagination, Of Human Freedom, The Problem of Method, The Words, The Transcendence of the Ego.

Jonathan Schell (1943–)
Writer, (The New Yorker); author of The Village of Ben Suk, The Military Half, The Time of Illusion, *The Fate of the Earth.

Paul B. Sears (1891–)
American ecologist; his books include *The Living Landscape, Lands Beyond the Forest.

Chief Seattle (1790?– ?)
American Indian, chief of the Duwampo tribe in Washington Territory.

John Selden (1584–1654)
English politician, jurist, Oriental scholar, member of Parliament; author of many political tracts and works on law and *Table Talk.

George Bernard Shaw (1856–1950)
Irish playwright, essayist; author of Saint Joan, *Man and Superman, Major Barbara, Caesar and Cleopatra (plays).

Leo Simpson (1934–)
Irish-Canadian novelist, journalist; author of Arkwright (novel).

Walter W. [Red] Smith (1905–82)
American sportswriter; syndicated in over 500 newspapers throughout the world; Pulitzer Prize winner 1976; his works are collected in *The Red Smith Reader, Strawberries in Wintertime, To Absent Friends.

Wallace Stegner (1909–)
American essayist, novelist, professor (Stanford University); author of Remembering Laughter, The Women on the Wall, Beyond the Hundredth Meridian, A Shocking Star, *Wolf Willow, All the Little Live Things, Gathering of Zion: The Story of the Mormon Trail.

John Steinbeck (1902–68)
American novelist, columnist, winner of Nobel Prize; author of In Dubious Battle, Of Mice and Men, The Grapes of Wrath,

East of Eden, *Journal of a Novel: The East of Eden Letters.

Laurence Sterne (1713–1768)
English cleric, novelist, humorist; author of *Tristram Shandy, A Sentimental Journey, Sermons.

James Stevenson (1930–)
American writer and cartoonist (The New Yorker); has written over twenty-five books for children, including The Night After Christmas, We Can't Sleep, Barbara's Birthday; also author of Uptown Local Downtown Express.

Jonathan Swift (1667–1745)
Irish satirist, poet, churchman; author of Gulliver's Travels, A Tale of a Tub, *The Battle of the Books.

[Louis] Studs Terkel (1912–)
American actor, interviewer, writer; author of Hard Times: An Oral History of the Great Depression, Division Street: America, *Working, Talking to Myself.

Theophrastus (371?–287 B.C.)
Greek philosopher, naturalist, successor to Aristotle; author of *Characters, Metaphysics, On Plants.

Dylan Thomas (1914–53)
Welsh poet, story writer, radio scriptwriter, broadcaster; author of Collected Poems (1934–1952), Under Milk Wood (verse drama), Adventures in the Skin Trade and Other Stories, Portrait of the Artist as a Young Dog.

Lewis Thomas (1913–)
American physician, educator, medical administrator; author of *The Lives of a Cell, *The Medusa and the Snail, The Youngest Science: Notes of a Medicine Watcher.

Nicholas S. Thompson (1938–)
American professor of psychology and writer of books and articles on animal behavior and natural history for professional and nonprofessional audiences.

Henry David Thoreau (1817–62)
American philosopher, essayist, naturalist, poet, disciple of Emerson; author of *Walden, "Civil Disobedience," Journals.

James Thurber (1894–1961)
American humorist, cartoonist, social commentator (The New Yorker), playwright; author of *My Life and Hard Times; *Fables for Our Time; *Men, Wo-

men, and Dogs; The Beast in Me and Other Animals.

Paul Tillich (1886–1965)
German-American theologian; author of *The Interpretation of History, The Shaking of the Foundations, Systematic Theology, The Dynamic of Faith, Christianity and the Encounter of the World Religions.*

Niko Tinbergen (1907–   )
British zoologist (Oxford University), winner of Nobel Prize; author of *The Herring Gull's World,* *Curious Naturalists, *The Animal in Its World.*

Calvin Trillin (1935–   )
American essayist (*The New Yorker*); author of *American Fried; *An Education in Georgia; Alice, Let's Eat; Uncivil Liberties.*

John Updike (1932–   )
American novelist, story writer, poet; author of *Rabbit, Run; The Centaur; Couples; Bech; Rabbit Redux; The Coup; Rabbit Is Rich; Bech Is Back* (novels); *Pigeon Feathers; The Music School* (stories).

Naomi Weisstein (1939–   )
American psychologist (Loyola University, Chicago).

Paul West (1930–   )
American novelist (British-born); his books include *Words for a Deaf Daughter, Gala, The Very Rich Hours of Count van Stauffenberg, Out of My Depths.*

Richard S. Westfall (1924–   )
American professor of history and philosophy of science (Indiana University, Bloomington); his books include *Science and Religion in Seventeenth-Century England; Never at Rest, A Biography of Isaac Newton.*

E. B. White (1899–   )
American essayist, poet, journalist (*The New Yorker*); author of *One Man's Meat,* *The Wild Flag, *The Second Tree from the Corner, Points of My Compass.*

Tom Wolfe (1931–   )
American essayist, story writer, social critic; author of *The Kandy-Kolored Tangerine-Flake Streamline Baby, The Pump House Gang, Radical Chic and Mau-Mauing the Flak Catchers, From Bauhaus to Our House, The Right Stuff.*

Virginia Woolf (1882–1941)
English novelist, essayist, critic; author of *Mrs. Dalloway, To the Lighthouse* (novels), *The Common Reader, Granite and Rainbow, The Second Common Reader,* *A Room of One's Own, *The Death of the Moth* (essays).

William Zinsser (1922–   )
American journalist, writer, teacher (Yale University); author of *The City Dwellers, On Writing Well, Pop Goes America.*

Index

ACKNOWLEDGMENTS

Adams: "Dirty Stuff" from *Bad Mouth: Fugitive Papers on the Dark Side* (1977). Copyright ©
by the Regents of the University of California; reprinted by permission of the University of
California Press.
Aesop: "The Frogs Desiring a King" reprinted by permission of Prestige Books Inc.
Allen: Selection from *Without Feathers*, by Woody Allen. Copyright © 1972, 1973, 1974,
1975, by Woody Allen. Reprinted by permission of Random House, Inc.
Angelou: "Graduation" from *I Know Why the Caged Bird Sings* by Maya Angelou. Reprinted
by permission of Random House, Inc.
Arendt: "Denmark and the Jews" from *Eichmann in Jerusalem* by Hannah Arendt. Copyright
© 1963, 1964 by Hannah Arendt. This selection originally appeared in *The New Yorker* in
slightly different form. Reprinted by permission of Viking Penguin Inc.
Arlen: "The Lame Deer" from *The Camera Age* by Michael J. Arlen. Copyright © 1979 by
Michael J. Arlen. Reprinted by permission of Farrar, Straus & Giroux, Inc. This selection
originally appeared in *The New Yorker*.
Ashby: "The University Ideal: A View from Britain" reprinted with permission from *LSA*,
Spring, 1978.
Asimov: "The Eureka Phenomenon" copyright © 1971 by Mercury Press, Inc. from *The Left
Hand of the Electron* by Isaac Asimov. Reprinted by permission of Doubleday & Company,
Inc.
Auden: "Apothegms" plus 3 paragraphs from *The Dyer's Hand*, by W. H. Auden. Copyright
© 1962 by W. H. Auden. Reprinted by permission of Random House, Inc.
Becker: "Democracy" from *Modern Democracy* by Carl L. Becker. Copyright 1941 by Yale
University Press. Reprinted by permission of the Press.
Baldwin: From *Notes of a Native Son* by James Baldwin. Copyright © 1955 by James Baldwin.
Reprinted by permission of Beacon Press.
Becker: "Democracy" from *Modern Democracy* by Carl L. Becker. Reprinted by permission
of the Press.
Bernstein: "Who Was Christy Mathewson?" reprinted by permission; © 1982 Jeremy Bern-
stein. Originally in *The New Yorker*.
Berry: "Home of the Free" from *The Gift of Good Land, Further Essays Cultural and Agricul-
tural,* © 1981 by Wendell Berry. Published by North Point Press.
Bettelheim: "A Victim" reprinted with permission of Macmillan Publishing Company from
The Informed Heart by Bruno Bettelheim. Copyright © 1960 by The Free Press, a
Corporation.
Bird: "College Is a Waste of Time and Money" from *The Case Against College* by Caroline
Bird. Reprinted by permission of the author.
Blake: "The Fantasy of the Skyscraper" from *Form Follows Fiasco: Why Modern Architecture
Hasn't Worked* by Peter Blake. By permission of Little, Brown and Company in association
with the Atlantic Monthly Press.
Bly: "Bruno Bettelheim: Three Ideas to Try in Madison, Minnesota" from *Letters From the
Country* by Carol Bly. Copyright © 1981 by Carol Bly. By permission of Harper & Row,
Publishers, Inc.
Boccaccio: Selection is reprinted from *The Decameron*, by Giovanni Boccaccio, A Norton
Critical Edition, Selected, Translated, and Edited by Mark Musa and Peter E. Bondanella.
With the permission of W. W. Norton & Company, Inc. Copyright © 1977 by W. W.
Norton & Company, Inc.
Booth: "Is There Any Knowledge that a Man Must Have?" from *The Knowledge Most Worth
Having* © by The University of Chicago. Reprinted by permission of the Press. "Boring
from Within: The Art of the Freshman Essay," from an address to the Illinois Council of
College Teachers in 1963. © Wayne C. Booth. Reprinted by permission of the author.
Bronowski: "The Nature of Scientific Reasoning" from *Science and Human Values.* Copyright
© 1956, 1965, by J. Bronowski. Reprinted by permission of Messner Books, a Simon &
Schuster Division of Gulf & Western Corporation. "The Reach of Imagination" from
Proceedings of the American Academy of Arts and Letters and National Institute of Arts and

Huxtable: "Modern-Life Battle: Conquering Clutter" from "Design Notebook" feature, © 1981 by The New York Times Company. Reprinted by permission.

Jung: "The Poet" from *Modern Man in Search of a Soul* by C. G. Jung. Published by Routledge & Kegan Paul Ltd., London, 1933. Reprinted by permission. Also reprinted by permission of Harcourt Brace Jovanovich, Inc.

Kafka: "Parable of the Law" from *The Trial*, Definitive Edition, Revised by Franz Kafka, translated by Willa and Edwin Muir. Copyright 1937, © 1956 and renewed 1965 by Alfred A. Knopf, Inc. Reprinted by permission of the publisher. Also reprinted by permission of Schocken Books Inc. from *Parables and Paradoxes* by Franz Kafka. Copyright 1935 by Schocken Verlag, Berlin. Copyright © 1937 by Alfred A. Knopf, Inc.

Kauffmann: "The Film Generation" from pages 415–423 "The Film Generation: Celebration and Concern" from *A World on Film* by Stanley Kauffmann. Copyright © 1966 by Stanley Kauffmann. By permission of Harper & Row, Publishers, Inc.

Keillor: "Re the Tower Project," in *Happy to Be Here.* Copyright © 1982 by Garrison Keillor. Reprinted with the permission of Atheneum Publishers. "Re the Tower Project" was first published in *The New Yorker*.

Kennedy: "Who Killed King Kong?" from *Dissent*, Spring 1960. Reprinted by permission of *Dissent*.

Kierkegaard: "The Knight of Faith" from *Fear and Trembling*, translated by Walter Lowrie. Copyright 1941 © 1969 by Princeton University Press. Reprinted by permission of Princeton University Press.

King: "Letter from Birmingham Jail"—April 16, 1963—in *Why We Can't Wait* by Martin Luther King, Jr. Copyright © 1963 by Martin Luther King, Jr. By permission of Harper & Row, Publishers, Inc.

Kingston: "On Discovery" from *China Men*, by Maxine Hong Kingston. Copyright © 1977, 1978, 1979, 1980 by Maxine Hong Kingston. Reprinted by permission of Alfred A. Knopf, Inc.

Koestler: "Gravity and the Holy Ghost" from *The Act of Creation* by Arthur Koestler. Reprinted by permission of A. D. Peters & Co., Ltd.

Krutch: "Modern Painting" from *And Even If You Do: Essays on Man, Manners and Machines* by Joseph Wood Krutch. Copyright © 1967 by Joseph Wood Krutch. Reprinted by permission of William Morrow & Company.

Kübler-Ross: "On the Fear of Death" reprinted with permission of Macmillan Publishing Company from *On Death and Dying* by Elisabeth Kübler-Ross. Copyright © 1969 by Elisabeth Kübler-Ross.

Kuhn: "The Route to Normal Science" from *The Structure of Scientific Revolutions* by Thomas S. Kuhn. © 1962, 1970 by the University of Chicago Press.

Kundera: "A Fur Cap" from *The Book of Laughter and Forgetting*, by Milan Kundera, translated by Michael Heim. Copyright © 1980 by Alfred A. Knopf, Inc. Reprinted by permission of the publisher.

Langer: "Expressiveness," in *Problems of Art.* Copyright © 1957 Susanne K. Langer. Reprinted with the permission of Charles Scribner's Sons.

Laurence: "Where the World Began" from *Heart of a Stranger* by Margaret Laurence. Copyright © 1976 by Margaret Laurence. Reprinted by permission of JCA Literary Agency, Inc. Also used by permission of The Canadian Publishers, McClelland and Stewart Limited, Toronto.

Lebowitz: "The Sound of Music: Enough Already" from *Metropolitan Life* by Fran Lebowitz. Copyright © 1974, 1975, 1976, 1977, 1978 by Fran Lebowitz. Reprinted by permission of E. P. Dutton.

Lee: "Friendship, Feminism, and Betrayal" reprinted by permission of the author and *The Village Voice.* Copyright © The Village Voice, Inc., 1975.

Lessing: "My Father" from *A Small Personal Voice* by Doris Lessing. © Doris Lessing 1963. Reprinted by permission of Curtis Brown Group Ltd.

Levin: "The Case for Torture" copyright 1982, by Newsweek, Inc. All Rights Reserved. Reprinted by permission.

Lewis: "The Inner Ring" reprinted with permission of Macmillan Publishing Co., Inc. from *The Weight of Glory and Other Addresses* by C. S. Lewis. Copyright 1949 by Macmillan Publishing Company, renewed 1977 by Arthur Owen Barfield. "Three Screwtape Letters" reprinted with permission of Macmillan Publishing Company from *The Screwtape Letters*

1226